RED SOX

JOURNAL

Year by Year & Day by Day with the Boston Red Sox Since 1901

RED SOX JOURNAL

JOHN SNYDER

emmis
books

Front Cover Photo Credit
© Mike Blake/Reuters/Corbis

Back Cover Photo Credits
Jimmie Foxx, courtesy of Transcendental Graphics/theruckerarchive.com
Roger Clemens, courtesy of Steve Babineau
David Ortiz, courtesy of Steve Babineau

For further information, contact the publisher at:

Emmis Books
1700 Madison Road
Cincinnati, OH 45206

www.emmisbooks.com

Library of Congress Cataloging-in-Publication Data

Snyder, John, 1951-
    Red Sox journal : year by year & day by day with the Boston Red Sox since 1901 / by John Snyder.
        p. cm.
    ISBN-13: 978-1-57860-253-7
    ISBN-10: 1-57860-253-X
    1. Boston Red Sox (Baseball team)--History. I. Title.
      GV875.B62S68 2006
      796.357'640974461--dc22

                    2005034650

Interior designed by Mary Barnes Clark
Edited by Brad Crawford
Cover designed by Steve Sullivan

Distributed by Publishers Group West

About the Author

John Snyder has a master's degree in history from the University of Cincinnati and a passion for baseball. He has authored fifteen books on baseball, soccer, hockey, tennis, football, basketball, and travel and lives in Cincinnati.

Acknowledgments

This book is part of a series that takes a look at Major League Baseball teams. The first was *Redleg Journal: Year by Year & Day by Day with the Cincinnati Reds Since 1866*, the winner of the 2001 Baseball Research Award issued by *The Sporting News* and SABR. That work was followed by *Cubs Journal: Year by Year & Day by Day with the Chicago Cubs Since 1876* and *Cardinals Journal: Year by Year and Day by Day with the St. Louis Cardinals Since 1882*. Each of these books is filled with little-known items that have never been published in book form.

Greg Rhodes was my co-author on *Redleg Journal*, in addition to publishing the book under his company's name, Road West Publishing. While Greg did not actively participate in the books about the Cubs, Cardinals, and Red Sox, he deserves considerable credit for the success of those books because they benefited from many of the creative concepts he initiated in *Redleg Journal*.

The idea for turning *Redleg Journal* into a series of books goes to Richard Hunt, president and publisher of Emmis Books, and editorial director Jack Heffron. Thanks go also to Brad Crawford, Mary Barnes Clark, and Andrea Kupper for their work on *Red Sox Journal*.

I would also like to thank the staff at the Public Library of Cincinnati and Hamilton County. The vast majority of research for this book came from contemporary newspapers and magazines. The library staff was extremely helpful with patience and understanding while retrieving the materials for me, not only for this book but for all of my previous endeavors as well. Dick Miller deserves thanks for providing me with material from his personal collection of baseball books. Dick was a lifelong friend of my father, who passed away in 1999, and instilled in me a love of both history and baseball.

And finally, although they should be the first, thanks to my wife and sons, Derek and Kevin, whose encouragement and support helped me through another book.

Contents

Part One: Boston Red Sox Day by Day

❖ ❖ ❖

Part Two: Boston Red Sox by the Numbers

BOSTON RED SOX

Day by Day

Changing Sox

Red Sox lore begins with the fabrication of a team out of whole cloth in 1901, when the upstart American League lured and kept some of the National League's best players. Guys like Cy Young, Chick Stahl, and Buck Freeman made the jump and soon were inspiring Boston fans' loyalty in a way the Braves had never managed. The Red Sox, then known as the Americans in recognition of the new league, immediately seemed worthy of our attention. Unlike so many other teams, they didn't come from some other city or as a remnant of a defunct league, and no team has played in a ballpark longer.

Though the Sox boast a remarkable tradition, the following pages reveal just how much about the game has changed since 1901—rules, crowds, umpires, uniforms, equipment, and, yes, money. A fan visiting Huntington Grounds, the Sox' original park, at the time would see a very different game from the one we witness today, including lone umpires, startlingly deep fences, a toolshed in center field, and, on occasion, managers brawling. Umpires frequently called games after seven or eight innings because of darkness or travel arrangements. And the changes kept coming, from the new cork-centered ball of the Ruth era to night games and integration. The truth is, it's a dynamic game and team, and browsing through the thousands of entries recorded here reinforces that fact.

Coverage extends beyond the diamond too, with entries on back-room deals, crimes, accidents, and players' marital spats. No matter how well you know the franchise, you're bound to stumble across a player, fact, or anecdote you haven't heard about before, as you uncover the Sox' authentic history, year by year and day by day.

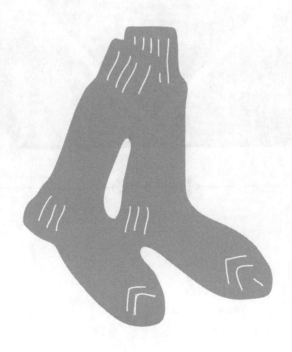

Steve Babineau

2004 World Series at
Fenway Park

THE STATE OF THE RED SOX

The Red Sox had a record of 691–634 during the first decade of the twentieth century, for a winning percentage of .522. It was the fourth-best mark in the eight-team American League during the period, behind the Chicago White Sox, Philadelphia Athletics, and Cleveland Indians and just ahead of the Detroit Tigers. The Red Sox won two American League pennants, in 1903 and 1904. The others were taken by the White Sox (1901 and 1906), Athletics (1902 and 1905), and Tigers (1907, 1908, and 1909). The Red Sox also established themselves as Boston's number one team. When the Red Sox began play in 1901, there was a National League team in Boston that had been around since 1871 and almost always had highly successful teams. The American League Red Sox outdrew the National League Braves every season from 1901 through 1920.

THE BEST TEAM

The 1903 team was 91–47 and coasted to the pennant by a margin of 14 $\frac{1}{2}$ games, then won baseball's first World Series by defeating the Pittsburgh Pirates.

THE WORST TEAM

After winning another pennant in 1904, the Sox went into a freefall and thudded into last place in 1906 with a record of 49–105 as the club seemed to age overnight. The Red Sox recovered by the end of the decade, however, and finished third with an infusion of young talent, including Tris Speaker and Harry Hooper.

THE BEST MOMENT

The first World Series. A best-of-nine affair, the Red Sox lost three of the first four games but recovered to win the final four contests and take the World Championship. Boston won the AL pennant again in 1904, but a chance to repeat didn't take place because the NL champion New York Giants refused to play in the Fall Classic.

THE WORST MOMENT

During spring training in 1907, player-manager Chick Stahl committed suicide.

THE ALL–DECADE TEAM • YEARS WITH BRS

Lou Criger, c	1901–08
Jake Stahl, 1b	1903; 1908–10; 1912–13
Hobe Ferris, 2b	1901–07
Jimmy Collins, 3b	1901–07
Freddie Parent, ss	1901–07
Patsy Dougherty, lf	1902–04
Chick Stahl, cf	1901–06
Buck Freeman, rf	1901–07
Cy Young, p	1901–08
Bill Dinneen, p	1901–07
George Winter, p	1901–08
Jesse Tannehill, p	1904–08

The annual award for the best pitchers in both major leagues is named after Cy Young. The leading winner in baseball history with 511 victories, 192 of them with the Red Sox, he was the best player on the club during this decade. Young was part of a core group that included Jimmy Collins, Freddie Parent, Chick Stahl, and Buck Freeman, who were together on the first Red Sox club in 1901 and helped win the pennants of 1903 and 1904. In addition to playing, Collins was also manager of the Red Sox from 1901 through 1906, and like Young, is in the Hall of Fame. Stahl might have received Hall of Fame consideration if he hadn't committed suicide in 1907.

THE DECADE LEADERS

Batting Avg:	Collins	.296
On-Base Pct:	Stahl	.350
Slugging Pct:	Freeman	.441
Home Runs:	Freeman	48
RBI:	Freeman	504
Runs:	Stahl	464
Stolen Bases:	Parent	109
Wins:	Young	192
Strikeouts:	Young	1,341
ERA:	Young	2.00
Saves:	Young	7

THE HOME FIELD

The Red Sox played their first 11 seasons at Huntington Grounds on Huntington Avenue. (See "Huntington Grounds: The Sox' First Ballpark" on page 33 [next to April 18, 1904] for a description of the ballpark.)

THE GAME YOU WISH YOU HAD SEEN

The best game of the decade was on October 13, 1903, when the Red Sox won baseball's first modern World Series by defeating the Pirates 3–0 at Huntington Grounds.

THE WAY THE GAME WAS PLAYED

In this decade of pitching and defense, the AL set all-time lows in ERA and batting average. In 1908, the AL batting average was .239, and the league earned run average was 2.39. In part, this was the result of a 1903 rule change that counted foul balls as strikes. The merits of the foul-strike rule were hotly debated for years afterward. Offense started a gradual decline that was not reversed until the introduction of the cork-center ball in 1910.

THE MANAGEMENT

The Red Sox were successful in the early years in spite of some instability in ownership. Cleveland businessman Charles Somers was the club's first majority owner. He sold the club to Henry Killilea of Milwaukee in 1903. Under Killilea, the Sox won the World Series in 1903, but he proved to be unpopular because of some underhanded business practices. He sold the club to Bostonian John I. Taylor in 1904. The field manager from 1901 through 1906 was Jimmy Collins, who also played third base. Chick Stahl replaced Collins late in the 1906 season, but Stahl committed suicide during spring training in 1907. Stahl was followed by Cy Young (1907), Bob Unglaub (1907), Deacon McGuire (1907–08), and Fred Lake (1908–09).

THE BEST PLAYER MOVE

There were three brilliant moves in obtaining the services of future Hall of Famers Cy Young, Tris Speaker, and Harry Hooper, and it's nearly impossible to single one out. The Red Sox signed Young away from the St. Louis Cardinals before the start of the 1901 season. He won 192 games in a Red Sox uniform, tied for first all-time with Roger Clemens. In 1907, Speaker was purchased for $800 from a minor league team in Houston. And in 1908, the Red Sox signed Hooper, who had been playing in the minors in Sacramento.

THE WORST PLAYER MOVE

The Red Sox sold Gavvy Cravath to the Senators in August 1908. Cravath went on to have a great career as an outfielder, mostly with the Phillies. He led the National League in home runs six times from 1913 through 1919.

1901   B

Season in a Sentence

The Red Sox overcome a slow start to finish a close second in their first season, and establish themselves as Boston's favorite team by outdrawing the Braves by a nearly 2-to-1 margin.

Finish • Won • Lost • Pct • GB

Second   79   57   .581   4.0

Manager

Jimmy Collins

Stats   Red Sox • AL • Rank

	Red Sox	AL	Rank
Batting Avg:	.278	.277	4
On-Base Pct:	.330	.333	5
Slugging Pct:	381	.371	3
Home Runs:	37		1
Stolen Bases:	157		6
ERA:	3.04	3.66	2
Fielding Pct:	.943	.938	2
Runs Scored:	759		2
Runs Allowed:	608		1

Starting Lineup

Ossee Schreckengost, c
Buck Freeman, 1b
Hobe Ferris, 2b
Jimmy Collins, 3b
Freddie Parent, ss
Tommy Dowd, lf
Chick Stahl, cf
Charlie Hemphill, rf
Lou Criger, c

Pitchers

Cy Young, sp
Ted Lewis, sp
George Winter, sp
Fred Mitchell, sp
Nig Cuppy, sp

Attendance

289,448 (second in AL)

Club Leaders

Batting Avg:	Freeman	.309
On-Base Pct:	Stahl	.377
Slugging Pct:	Freeman	.520
Home Runs:	Freeman	12
RBI:	Freeman	114
Runs:	Stahl	105
Stolen Bases:	Dowd	33
Wins:	Young	33
Strikeouts:	Young	158
ERA:	Young	1.62
Saves:	Lewis	1

JANUARY 3   The American League publicly acknowledges that a franchise would be placed in Boston to compete with the Braves. Buffalo was dropped from the list of teams in the new league.

JANUARY 17   Connie Mack, acting as agent for Charles Somers, signs a lease for Huntington Grounds as the location of the new Red Sox ballpark.

MARCH 2   Jimmy Collins signs with the Red Sox as manager and starting third baseman.

MARCH 12   Groundbreaking for the Red Sox' first ballpark takes place at Huntington Grounds less than two months before the Red Sox home opener.

MARCH 19   Cy Young signs with the Red Sox.

MARCH 28   The Red Sox leave South Station in Boston for their first spring training, held at the University of Virginia in Charlottesville.

APRIL 5   The Red Sox play their first spring training exhibition game, defeating the University of Virginia, 13–0.

APRIL 24   The first regular-season game in Red Sox history, scheduled against the Orioles in Baltimore, is postponed by rain. The contest on April 25 is also postponed.

APRIL 26   The Red Sox finally play their first game and lose 10–6 to the Orioles before a crowd of 10,000 in Baltimore. Larry McLean hit a double as the first pinch hitter in American League history. The starting, and losing, pitcher was Win Kellum. The lineup for the first game featured Tommy Dowd leading off and playing left field, followed by Charlie Hemphill in right, Chick Stahl in center, Jimmy Collins at third, Buck Freeman at first, Freddie Parent at shortstop, Hobe Ferris at second, Lou Criger behind the plate, and Kellum. Prior to the game, a noontime parade of forty carriages containing officials and players from both clubs, along with representatives from the trades unions, manufacturing concerns, and sporting organizations was held, starting at the Eutaw House Hotel (near today's Camden Yards) and ending at Oriole Park. The Red Sox and Orioles players were cheered by thousands along the route, and homes and businesses were decorated for the occasion. At the ballpark, Red Sox were players were presented with a floral scroll bearing the inscription, "Welcome Boston."

McLean and Kellum quickly became footnotes in Red Sox history. Only nineteen years old, McLean was born in Fredericton, New Brunswick, and grew up across the river from Boston in Cambridge. He played only nine games with the Red Sox but had a rollicking thirteen-year major league career, much of it spent battling a severe problem with alcohol. In 1921 he was shot to death by a Boston bartender. Kellum was also a native of Canada. He pitched only six games in Boston, compiling a 2–3 record and a 6.38 earned run average.

APRIL 27   Cy Young makes his debut as a member of the Red Sox, but it's unsuccessful as Boston loses to the Orioles 12–6 in Baltimore. Young allowed ten runs in 5⅓ innings.

Young didn't pitch in the season opener due to illness, and he was still suffering its effects during the April 27 game. He was relieved by Fred Mitchell, who hailed from Cambridge, Massachusetts, and was making his big-league debut in the contest. Mitchell's name was really Fred Yapp, which he changed because in the slang of the day a yap was an ignorant or uncouth person. Mitchell later managed the Cubs in 1918 when they played the Red Sox in the World Series.

The Birth of Red Sox Nation

The creation of the Boston Red Sox and the American League as a major league entity in 1901 was due to the vision, energy, and perseverance of former Cincinnati sportswriter Ban Johnson. The American League had its genesis in November 1893, when a new minor league called the Western League was formed with clubs in Grand Rapids, Sioux City, Minneapolis,

Milwaukee, Kansas City, Toledo, Indianapolis, and Detroit. With the backing of Cincinnati Reds owner John Brush, who had an interest in the Indianapolis franchise, Johnson was asked to head the Western League as president, treasurer, and secretary.

At the time, the National League was baseball's only major league. It had prior competition from the American Association, which existed from 1882 through 1891, the Union Association in 1884, and from the Players League, which lasted only for the 1890 season. From 1892 through 1899, the National League was a twelve-team circuit with clubs in Baltimore, Boston, Brooklyn, Chicago, Cincinnati, Cleveland, Louisville, New York, Philadelphia, Pittsburgh, St. Louis, and Washington. The Boston club had been a charter member of the National League since it was established in 1876.

Like many monopolies, the National League had grown arrogant during the 1890s. Tight controls were placed on the players, including a maximum salary of $2,400. Competitive balance was nonexistent. In 1899, the Cleveland Spiders compiled a record of 20–134 and finished the season 84 games behind the first-place Brooklyn Dodgers. Meanwhile, Johnson's Western League had grown stronger each year as the top circuit in the minor leagues.

The National League reduced its membership from twelve teams to eight in March 1900 by dropping clubs in Baltimore, Cleveland, Louisville, and Washington. This gave Johnson an opening to establish the Western League as a major league outfit to compete with the National League. In 1900, Johnson changed the name of his circuit to the American League. Teams in the smaller cities of Grand Rapids, Sioux City, and Toledo were replaced by new ones in Chicago, Cleveland, and Buffalo. Many players were without jobs because of the elimination of four clubs in the National League, and they cast their lots with the American League. Although his league was still confined to the Midwest, Johnson had plans to expand to the Eastern Seaboard.

Shortly after the end of the 1900 season, Johnson announced plans for his American League to become a second major league to compete with the Nationals. The franchises in Minneapolis, Kansas City, and Indianapolis were eliminated in favor of those in the larger Eastern cities of Baltimore, Philadelphia, and Washington. Johnson wrote a letter in late October 1900 to National League president Nick Young seeking peace and an arrangement in which each league would respect the contracts of the other to eliminate player raids and prevent player salaries from escalating. The National League immedi-

ately rejected the plan. The league owners had vanquished all previous opposition and had no doubt the American League would soon follow into oblivion.

Johnson retaliated by announcing that his new American League would attempt to sign the top players in baseball away from the NL. They certainly found a receptive audience. Players in the National League were not only saddled with a maximum salary of $2,400, but they also had to pay for their own uniforms and other basic amenities.

Bostonians, like others around the world, marked the end of the nineteenth century with parties on December 31, 1900, properly recognizing that the twentieth century began on January 1, 1901. (Twenty-first century revelers celebrated the new millennium a year early in 2000.) Among the items discussed throughout Boston at the New Year's Eve parties in 1900 were rumors that Buffalo's franchise in the American League would be moved to Boston, providing Beantown with two major league teams. The AL publicly acknowledged the fact on January 3.

The new Boston team was headed by Charles Somers, who had made his fortune in Cleveland in coal, lumber, and shipping in the Great Lakes. Somers had financial interests in four American League clubs, including the Cleveland Indians, Philadelphia Athletics, and Chicago White Sox. (A rule passed in 1910 made it illegal for anyone to own stock in more than one club.)

The task of Johnson and Somers to place a team in Boston was daunting. With the opening of the 1901 season fewer than four months away, the new club had no ballpark and owned or leased no land on which to build one. The only player on the Buffalo roster deemed worthy of major league ability was catcher Ossee Schreckengost. In addition, the National League club in Boston was one of the strongest in the older circuit. Boston had won the NL pennant in 1877, 1878, 1883, 1891, 1892, 1893, 1897, and 1898.

Philadelphia Athletics owner Connie Mack, acting as an agent for Somers, signed a five-year lease for Huntington Grounds on January 17 as the location for the new Red Sox ballpark. The site was obtained after negotiations to build at Charles River Park on the Cambridge side of the waterway fell through. The Huntington Avenue property was on the south side of the thoroughfare, just east of Forsyth Street (then known as Rogers Avenue) at the present-day locale of the Cabot Athletic Center on the campus of Northeastern University. The left field fence ran along Huntington, and the third base side was on Rogers. It was easily reached by streetcar from downtown Boston, the Back Bay, Roxbury, and Brookline, a necessity in the days before the automobile was commonplace. The land was owned by the New York, New Haven & Hartford Railroad and leased to the Boston Elevated Railway, which operated most of the streetcars in the city. The Red Sox sublet the property from the streetcar company, which had a line on Huntington. The directors of the Boston Elevated Railway reasoned that a ballpark on the line would increase ridership. Before the Red Sox moved in, Huntington Grounds had been used for carnivals and traveling shows, and it was on the opposite side of the street from a lot where Buffalo Bill's Wild West Show and Barnum and Bailey Circus played in Boston. A deep pond was located on the lot, accompanied by a large water slide. The pond, also used as a skating rink during the winter, had to be filled in. The home field of the National League Boston Braves, called South End Grounds, was located on the other side of the railroad tracks, on the north side of Columbus Avenue, opposite the present-day streets of Cunard, Coventry, and Burke on approximately the same site now occupied by a parking garage near the Ruggles Street MBTA station. The surrounding neighborhood was known as "the Village," a working-class community of Irish immigrants who worked in the nearby factories and on the railroad.

With the ballpark taken care of, Somers turned his attention to finding a manager and players. On March 2, he announced that Jimmy Collins had signed with the Red Sox as the manager and starting third baseman. A future Hall of Famer, the thirty-year-old Collins was lured from the Braves in the first of the defections from the National League. He agreed to a three-year contract calling for about $4,000 per season, nearly double his $2,400 salary with the Braves. (The average American in 1901 earned about $700

per year while working sixty hours a week.) At the time, Collins was the best third baseman in baseball, both offensively and defensively, and was intensely popular with the Boston baseball fans. The signing of Collins gave the Red Sox instant credibility. In explaining the move, Collins told reporters, "I like to play baseball, but this is a business with me, and I can't be governed by sentiment. I am looking out for James J. Collins."

The capture of Collins was only the first step. Within weeks, Collins brought Braves starting outfielders Buck Freeman and Chick Stahl and pitchers Vic Willis, Bill Dinneen, and Ted Lewis to the Red Sox and the American League. He had little trouble luring his former teammates away from the notoriously cheap Braves ownership, headed by Arthur Soden, which had not only alienated the players but fans as well. Dinneen and Willis had second thoughts, however, and returned to the Braves. (Dinneen quickly regretted the U-turn, however, and signed with the Red Sox in 1902.)

The Red Sox added one of the best pitchers in baseball history to their roster on March 19 with the signing of Cy Young. Young had a career record of 286–170 entering the 1901 season, but he was thirty-four years old, the oldest pitcher in either league, and many considered him to be washed up after a 19–19 season with the St. Louis Cardinals in 1900. Young wasted no time in burying that notion with a 33–10 record with Boston in 1901 along with a 1.62 ERA, 38 complete games in 41 starts, five shutouts, 371 innings pitched, and a league-leading 158 strikeouts. He walked only 37 batters. Young followed the great season with a 32–11 record in 1902, 28–9 in 1903, and 26–16 in 1904.

Lou Criger, who was Young's catcher in St. Louis, also inked a contract with the Red Sox. To fill out the roster, the Sox also picked up top minor league talents in Freddie Parent to play shortstop and Hobe Ferris at second base. Parent, from Maine, and Ferris, a native of Rhode Island, had New England connections. They would form the Red Sox double play combination until 1906. New pitchers included rookies George Winter and Fred Mitchell. Charlie Hemphill, who had National League experience with St. Louis and Cleveland in 1899, was added to play right field.

Initially, the arrival of the Red Sox in Boston wasn't well received. Many newspapermen and fans believed that the city wasn't big enough to support two teams. There had been a Boston club in the Union Association in 1884, the Players League in 1890, and another in the American Association in 1891. None could turn a profit, and each lasted only a year despite the fact that the Players League and American Association clubs finished the season in first place in their respective leagues. The Red Sox were dubbed the "Invaders" for taking many of the Braves' top players. Many feared that Boston was left with two mediocre teams instead of one good one and predicted that the Red Sox were doomed to fail. To lure fans, the Red Sox offered bleacher seats for 25¢. The cheapest seats at South End Grounds cost 50¢.

Once the 1901 season started, however, the quality and popularity of the American League brand of baseball was apparent, and the writers and the fans changed their tune. The Red Sox quickly established themselves as Boston's number one team, and the National League Braves resorted to giving away tickets for free to make their crowds look respectable. In 1901, the Red Sox outdrew the Braves 289,448 to 146,502. The Sox were also second in the AL in attendance. Boston's celebrated "Royal Rooters," an organization of noisy and intense fans of Irish ancestry, transferred their allegiance from the National League club to the Red Sox in mid summer. In 1902, the attendance margin between the two teams in Boston stretched to 3–1 as the Red Sox attracted 348,567 to 116,960 for their NL counterparts in a season in which both teams finished the season in third place in their respective leagues. During the 52 seasons that Boston had both an American League and National League team, the Braves outdrew the Red Sox only seven times (1921, 1925–26, and 1930–33). In those seven seasons, the Red Sox fielded awful teams that averaged 97 losses.

APRIL 30   After defeats in the first three games of the season, the Red Sox achieve their first victory, an 8–6 win over the Athletics in Philadelphia. The Athletics jumped ahead 6–1, but the Sox chipped away. Boston tied the game 6–6 on a two-run homer over the right field fence by Buck Freeman in the ninth inning, the first round-tripper in Red Sox history. The Sox scored two tenth-inning runs on a base on balls and three hits in the American League's first-ever extra-inning game. Cy Young was the winning pitcher.

Freeman was Boston's hitting star in 1901 with 12 homers, 114 RBIs, a .339 batting average, .400 on-base percentage, and .520 slugging percentage.

MAY 2   Just a day after losing 14–1 to the Athletics, the Red Sox roll to a 23–12 win in Philadelphia. Boston scored two runs in the first inning, nine in the second, and 10 in the third to take a 21–4 advantage. The starting pitcher for the Athletics was Philadelphia amateur Pete Loos, who was appearing in the only game of his big-league career.

MAY 8   The Red Sox play at home for the first time and defeat the Athletics 12–4 before a crowd of 11,000 at Huntington Grounds. Buck Freeman had three hits, including a homer and a triple. The first ball was thrown out by General "Hi Hi" Dixwell, a Spanish-American War veteran who was considered to be Boston's number one baseball fan. Otherwise, there was no street parade and little pomp and circumstance at the Red Sox opener, unlike the first game at Baltimore two weeks earlier, because Charles Somers vetoed any "circus-like" proceedings. Somers did approve a band to play popular tunes and two carriages bearing famous players from Boston's baseball past that rolled from center field to home plate.

The Boston Braves of the National League played their first home game of the 1901 season on the same day and drew only 2,000. The Braves finished the season in fifth place with a record of 69–69. Despite the loss of Collins, Young, Freeman, and Stahl to the Red Sox, the Braves won three more games than they had in 1900, when they were fourth in the NL with a 66–72 mark.

MAY 15
The Red Sox are the victims of the first shutout in American League history when blanked by Senators rookie Watty Lee in a 4–0 decision at Huntington Grounds.

MAY 25
In a game that begins in a snowstorm, Ted Lewis pitches the first shutout in Red Sox history, defeating the Indians 5–0 at Cleveland.

Ted Lewis had a record of 16–17 for the Red Sox in 1901. Born on Christmas Day in Machynlleth, Wales, in 1872, Lewis later coached college baseball at Harvard, Columbia, and Williams. He served as president of Massachusetts State College in 1926 and 1927 and at the University of New Hampshire from 1927 until his death in 1936.

MAY 30
The Red Sox play a doubleheader for the first time and lose 8–3 and 5–3 to the 1901 American League champion White Sox on Memorial Day in Chicago.

The Red Sox close May with an 11–14 record.

JUNE 1
Buck Freeman becomes the first player in American League history to hit two homers in one game during a 10–5 victory over the White Sox in Chicago.

JUNE 2
The Red Sox tie major league records for most runs scored in the ninth inning with two out and no one on base (nine) and for most consecutive hits (10) during a 13–2 trouncing of the Brewers in Milwaukee. Each of the ten hits came off pitcher Bill Reidy and included four singles, five doubles, and Freddie Parent's first major league home run. Boston accomplished the rally without Jimmy Collins and Buck Freeman, who were ejected by umpire John Haskell in the fourth inning. In 1901, American League rosters had only 14 players. The tossings forced left fielder Tommy Dowd to move to third base for the first time in six years, put pitcher Nig Cuppy in left field, and put another pitcher, Ben Beville, at first base. Beville, whose career in the majors lasted only three games, had both of his big-league hits during the game. The 10 consecutive hits came from Cuppy, Beville, Freddie Parent, Hobe Ferris, Ossee Schreckengost, Cy Young, Tommy Dowd, Charlie Hemphill, Chick Stahl, and Cuppy again.

This was the first game in Red Sox history played on a Sunday. In 1901, American League games were permitted on Sundays only in Milwaukee, Chicago, and Detroit. Sunday games in Boston were prohibited by law until 1929.

The Milwaukee franchise moved to St. Louis in 1902 and was renamed the Browns.

JUNE 8   The Red Sox score eight runs in the fourth inning of a 12–4 victory over Milwaukee at Huntington Grounds.

JUNE 14   The Red Sox break a 7–7 tie with nine runs in the eighth inning and defeat the Detroit Tigers 16–7 at Huntington Grounds.

JUNE 17   The Red Sox take a doubleheader from the White Sox by scores of 11–1 and 10–4 on Bunker Hill Day at Huntington Grounds.

Player-manager Jimmy Collins hit .332 in 1901 with 187 hits, 42 doubles, 16 triples, and 94 RBIs.

JUNE 20   The Red Sox take first place by completing a five-game series sweep of the White Sox. Boston scored two runs in the ninth inning for the 4–3 victory. Buck Freeman drove in the winning run with a single.

The Red Sox and White Sox took turns being in first place between June 20 and July 18, when Chicago took the top spot for good. From June 1 through July 17, the Red Sox won 32 of 41 games. Boston was half a game out of first as late as August 27 but faded in September. Oddly, the Red Sox won all 10 meetings against the White Sox in Boston, and were 12–8 overall against Chicago.

JUNE 22   The Red Sox extend their winning streak to nine games with an 8–1 win over the Cleveland Indians at Huntington Grounds.

JUNE 28   Freddie Parent hits the first grand slam in Red Sox history in dramatic fashion. The Red Sox were trailing the Senators 5–2 in the eighth inning in Washington when Parent hit one out of the park facing pitcher Bill Carrick for a 6–5 victory. Buck Freeman was ejected by the umpires, his third ejection in less than a month. In the American League in 1901, an ejection from a game carried an automatic $5 fine.

Parent hit .306 as a rookie for the Red Sox in 1901.

JULY 3   Cy Young earns his 300th career win with a 9–1 win over Baltimore at Huntington Grounds.

JULY 4   The Red Sox defeat the Orioles 10–2 and 8–3 at Huntington Grounds. In the second game, the Sox scored six runs in the eighth inning to take an 8–3 lead. The first two runs were scored on a home run by Jimmy Collins. Fans celebrated by shooting off firecrackers, firing pistols into the air, and blowing horns. The racket so unnerved Baltimore pitcher Frank Foreman that he gave up four more runs.

JULY 16   Cy Young wins his 12th decision in a row with a 10–8 win over the Indians in Cleveland. Young had to survive a four-run Cleveland rally in the ninth after the Red Sox scored five times in the top of the inning. Angry over his calls, a crowd followed umpire Al Manassau after the game and pelted him with cushions and bottles. Several Cleveland players saved Manassau from the mob.

In 1901, there was only one umpire on the field.

JULY 17   For the second straight day, an umpire has to escape the wrath of Cleveland fans.

Following a 9–3 and 10–2 Red Sox doubleheader sweep of the Indians, umpire Tom Connolly needed a police escort to leave the ballpark.

JULY 18 George Winter hits the first home run by a pitcher in Red Sox history, but he loses 6–5 to the Indians in Cleveland. Despite the homer, Cy Young pinch hit for Winter in the ninth inning.

This was the only home run by Winter during his major league career, which lasted eight years, 226 games, and 589 at-bats. In 1901, Winters was 16–12 with a 2.80 earned run average. He was a teammate of future Hall of Famer Eddie Plank at Gettysburg College.

AUGUST 2 The Red Sox collect 22 hits and thrash the Athletics 16–0 in Philadelphia.

AUGUST 8 Chick Stahl goes 5 for 5, including a double, during the Red Sox' 10–5 win over the Orioles in the first game of a doubleheader in Baltimore. The Red Sox lost the nightcap, 10–4.

Stahl batted .303 with 16 triples for the Red Sox in 1901.

AUGUST 24 Following a 4–2 loss to the Indians at Huntington Grounds, the crowd starts for umpire Joe Cantillion, who made several close calls against the Red Sox during the afternoon. Boston players, led by Chick Stahl and Ted Lewis, kept the angry fans at bay until Cantillion could escape.

AUGUST 27 Cy Young pitches all 15 innings of the Red Sox' 2–1 win over the Tigers at Huntington Grounds and singles in the winning run. In the fourteenth inning, Young worked his way out of a bases-loaded, none-out jam.

SEPTEMBER 3 Ted Lewis allows only two hits but loses 1–0 to the Indians in the first game of a doubleheader in Cleveland. Errors by second baseman Hobe Ferris and catcher Ossee Schreckengost allowed the lone run. The Red Sox were also shut out in the second game, losing 4–0.

Cleveland's Bill Cristall, who was making his major league debut in the second game, pitched the shutout. It was his only major league victory. Cristall finished his major league career with a 1–5 record.

SEPTEMBER 14 Cy Young achieves his 30th victory of the season with a 12–1 decision over the Senators at Huntington Grounds.

SEPTEMBER 19 The Red Sox' game against the Tigers at Huntington Grounds is postponed because of the funeral of President William McKinley, who was shot by Leon Czolgosz during a reception in Buffalo on September 6 and died on September 14. Theodore Roosevelt became the new president.

SEPTEMBER 24 The Red Sox score seven runs in the eighth inning and defeat the White Sox 8–3 at Huntington Grounds.

SEPTEMBER 25 Cy Young wins his 33rd game of the season with a 5–2 decision over the White Sox at Huntington Grounds.

SEPTEMBER 28   The Red Sox end their first season with a doubleheader sweep over Milwaukee 8–3 and 10–9 at Huntington Grounds. In the second game, called after seven innings by darkness, the Red Sox scored seven runs in the fifth inning to wipe out a 6–1 Milwaukee lead.

Jack Slattery, a native of South Boston, made his major league debut as a catcher in the first game, but was removed by an injury in the eighth inning. It was his only game with the Red Sox, although he had a four-year major league playing career. Slattery was a collegiate coach at Harvard, Tufts, and Boston College and served briefly as manager of the Braves in 1928.

B   What's a Red Sox?   **B**

For the purposes of simplicity and consistency, Boston's American League baseball team is called the "Red Sox" throughout this book. A fan of the club prior to 1907 would have been thoroughly confused by the name "Red Sox," however, because it wasn't until that year that the nickname was coined in an announcement by owner John I. Taylor on December 17.

That the nickname began at the insistence of an owner of a team was unusual for the period. Many of the most famous nicknames in baseball, such as Cubs, Reds, Yankees, Dodgers, Giants, Braves, Phillies, Pirates, Cardinals, Indians, Orioles and Tigers, were created not by the clubs themselves but by enterprising sportswriters. The names then caught the imagination of the public and entered everyday speech until they became part of teams' identities. The editors and authors of many baseball histories have attempted retroactively to attach a single nickname to clubs from the nineteenth and early twentieth centuries, when in fact, many of these nicknames were seldom used. Many clubs were most often referred to by the name of their city of origin, such as the "Chicagos," the "New Yorks," the "Pittsburghs," or the "Bostons." Other teams had several nicknames simultaneously.

The present-day Red Sox from 1901 through 1907 were most often called the "Americans" in the newspapers of the day. On occasion, the club was also called the "Pilgrims," the "Puritans," the "Plymouth Rocks," or the "Somersets," this last name a reference to original team owner Charles Somers.

None of those names caught the fancy of the Boston baseball fans. Nicknames like the Pilgrims, Puritans, or Plymouth Rocks had no chance of succeeding because of the social and political climate of the city. The ballparks of both Boston clubs in the American and National Leagues were located in working-class Irish neighborhoods, and the fans of both clubs were predominately Irish. When the Irish began arriving in large numbers in Boston in the mid-nineteenth century, they were subjected to a great deal of prejudice from the "Brahmins," of English descent, who controlled the political and business machinery of the city. Across the Atlantic, Ireland was straining to achieve independence from England in a violent struggle. The Irish were victims of generations of British tyranny, and the names Pilgrims, Puritans, and Plymouth Rocks were too English-sounding and reminded the Irish fans of those who discriminated against them.

The name Boston Americans for the club, a reference to the American League, satisfied nearly everyone but pleased few. It was too generic and failed to identify the club as a Boston institution. Taylor stepped into the breach and called his club the Red Sox.

The name had its origins with the 1869 Cincinnati Red Stockings, baseball's first professional team. The club was managed by Harry Wright, whose brother George was the star player. After the Cincinnati Red Stockings folded after the 1870 season, the Wright brothers moved to

Boston and formed a new club, also called the Red Stockings. It was this team that moved into the newly created National League in 1876.

Boston's National League club wore red stockings as part of the team uniform until 1907. Manager Fred Tenney believed that the red dye on the hosiery could cause infection if one of his players was spiked, and ordered white socks for his athletes.

Taylor took note and made plans to adopt the red stockings and the old name, while shortening it from Red Stockings to Red Sox. Previously, Taylor's teams had been outfitted in uniforms trimmed in pale blue. The new uniforms for 1908 made it abundantly clear that the Boston Americans were now the Red Sox. On the center of the chest was a slanted red stocking symbol with the name Boston in white capital letters inside the stocking. The unique jersey was in use for only one season, but it served its purpose. The nickname Red Sox became firmly entrenched in the minds of fans.

1902   B

Season in a Sentence

Hampered by a leg injury to Jimmy Collins and an overall lack of hitting, the Red Sox finish third.

Finish • Won • Lost • Pct • GB

Third	77	60	.562	6.5

Manager

Jimmy Collins

Stats

Stats	Red Sox	AL	Rank
Batting Avg:	.278	.275	3
On-Base Pct:	.322	.331	7
Slugging Pct:	.383	.369	4
Home Runs:	42		2
Stolen Bases:	3.02	3.57	1
ERA:	132		6
Fielding Pct:	.955	.949	2
Runs Scored:	664		6
Runs Allowed:	600		1

Starting Lineup

Lou Criger, c
Candy LaChance, 1b
Hobe Ferris, 2b
Jimmy Collins, 3b
Freddie Parent, ss
Patsy Dougherty, lf
Chick Stahl, cf
Buck Freeman, rf
Harry Gleason, 3b-cf
John Warner, c

Pitchers

Cy Young, sp
Bill Dinneen, sp
George Winter, sp
Tully Sparks, sp

Attendance

348,567 (second in AL)

Club Leaders

Batting Avg:	Dougherty	.342
On-Base Pct:	Dougherty	.407
Slugging Pct:	Freeman	.502
Home Runs:	Freeman	11
RBI:	Freeman	121
Runs:	Stahl	92
Stolen Bases:	Stahl	24
Wins:	Young	32
Strikeouts:	Young	160
ERA:	Young	2.19
Saves:	Altrock	1

JANUARY 4   Pitcher Bill Dinneen jumps from the National League Boston Braves to the Red Sox. Dinneen won 20 or more games in each of the next three seasons for the Sox.

JANUARY 26   Lulu Ortman, recently jilted by Red Sox outfielder Chick Stahl, is arrested in Fort Wayne, Indiana, after unsuccessfully attempting to shoot him.

Ortman was a twenty-one-year-old stenographer for a lumber company and tipped off a close friend that she intended to shoot Stahl after he ended their relationship. The friend informed the police superintendent of Fort Wayne, who overtook Ortman just as she met Stahl and was drawing her revolver. Stahl not only refused to press charges, but later also resumed his love affair with her.

APRIL 19   The Red Sox open the season at Huntington Grounds on Patriots' Day, rallying with four runs in the ninth to stun the Orioles, 7–6. The entrances of the ballpark proved to be insufficient to handle the unexpectedly large crowd, and the fences collapsed before the wild, surging mob. Several thousand entered the grounds for free, leaving attendance at the game open for speculation. Estimates varied widely.

To take advantage of the holiday, which fell on a Saturday in 1902, the Red Sox and Orioles opened the season four days ahead of the rest of the American League clubs. Some improvements were made to Huntington Grounds, with a new main entrance on Rogers Avenue (present day Forsyth Street) and a bleacher entrance behind third base. A paved walkway was built from the gate around the grandstand, so people wouldn't have to step through the mud. The price of a seat in the third base bleachers was raised from 25 to 50 cents, but a quarter could still fetch a ticket in the right field bleachers.

MAY 1   Umpire Jack Sheridan barely escapes with his life following a 6–4 Red Sox win over the Orioles in Baltimore. In the ninth inning, Orioles player-manager John McGraw was hit by Boston hurler Bill Dinneen, but Sheridan refused to allow McGraw first base, claiming he stepped into the pitch. McGraw was ejected in the ensuing argument. At the conclusion of the game, the crowd surged onto the field and surrounded Sheridan. A cordon of twelve police officers escorted Sheridan to a waiting trolley car. One fan threw a brick, which struck one of the officers in the lip and opened a nasty cut.

MAY 10   The Red Sox defeat the Senators 3–1 at Huntington Grounds in a game that takes only sixty-five minutes to complete.

MAY 30   After losing to the Tigers 10–5 in the first game of a doubleheader at Huntington Grounds, the Red Sox turn the tables and clobber Detroit, 12–0. On the same day, the Red Sox traded Charley "Piano Legs" Hickman to the Indians for Candy LaChance.

Hickman hit .378 in 102 games for the Indians for the remainder of the 1902 season but was horrid defensively. Standing five foot nine and weighing 215 pounds, he lacked speed because he combined spindly legs with an expansive torso, hence the nickname "Piano Legs." The Red Sox had acquired his services during the 1901–02 offseason by signing him away from the New York Giants. Seven clubs tried Piano Legs at every position but catcher during his 12-year big-league career to get his bat into the lineup, but he proved to be incapable of adequately fielding at any of them. Candy LaChance was a light-hitting first baseman who was a regular for three seasons in Boston. He became known as

"Candy" because he preferred peppermints to chewing tobacco. LaChance played every inning of every game for the Red Sox in both 1903 and 1904.

JUNE 5   Cy Young defeats the Indians 3–2 in Cleveland with a fluke home run hit over the head of left fielder Piano Legs Hickman that gets wedged under the scoreboard. By the time Hickman could pry the ball loose, Young had happily made his way around the bases.

JUNE 8   Cy Young wins his 10th consecutive game with a 7–1 win over the Browns in St. Louis to push his season record to 13–1.

JUNE 15   The Red Sox defeat the Indians 5–2 in a Sunday-afternoon game played at Mahaffey Park in Canton, Ohio. There were 6,000 fans, but even that number overwhelmed the small grandstand. Fans were stationed behind ropes in the outfield, and balls hit into the crowd were ground-rule doubles. There were 14 hits in the game, but 11 of them were doubles. Also, Boston second baseman Hobe Ferris hit a home run over the crowd.

With Sunday baseball illegal in Cleveland, the Indians played Sunday "home" games in 1902 and 1903 in Canton, Columbus, and Dayton, Ohio, and in Fort Wayne, Indiana.

JUNE 21   With Cy Young pitching a complete game, the Red Sox triumph 4–1 in 15 innings over the Tigers in Detroit. Patsy Dougherty started the three-run rally in the fifteenth with a single.

Young had a 32–11 record in 1902 with a 2.12 ERA, 160 strikeouts, 41 complete games, and 43 starts and pitched 385 innings. Bill Dinneen performed the rare feat of both winning and losing 20 games in a single season. In 1902, he was 21–21 with 371 innings pitched and a 2.93 ERA.

JUNE 28   With the Red Sox leading 9–4 in the eighth inning against the Orioles in Baltimore, John McGraw is ejected after disputing a call. After McGraw refused to leave the field, umpire Tom Connolly awarded the game to the Red Sox by forfeit. Jimmy Collins went five for five in the game.

American League president Ban Johnson suspended McGraw indefinitely, an act that would have major repercussions. McGraw bolted from the Orioles and the American League and signed to manage the New York Giants on July 9. McGraw convinced most of the Orioles players to sign National League contracts, and by July 17, Baltimore's roster was reduced to five able bodies. At the end of the season, the Baltimore franchise moved to New York, thereby creating the Red Sox' most hated rival—the New York Yankees. McGraw remained bitter toward Johnson and the American League for years and refused to play the Red Sox in the 1904 World Series.

JULY 8   The Red Sox are routed 22–9 by Connie Mack's Philadelphia Athletics, the 1902 American League champions, at Huntington Grounds. The two clubs set an American League record (since tied) for most hits by two teams in a game, 45, 27 of them by Philadelphia. Boston pitcher Merle (Doc) Adkins allowed 12 hits in the sixth inning, a modern major league record. Six of the Athletics' hits were collected by Danny Murphy, who was playing in his first game for the club. He arrived late and didn't enter the contest until the second inning.

Adkins appeared in only six big-league games, four of them with the Red Sox. His career record was 1–1 with a 5.00 ERA.

JULY 12   Red Sox first baseman Candy LaChance wrestles Athletics pitcher Rube Waddell before a game in Philadelphia. The wrestling match took place on the field before the game as curious fans entered the ballpark. Waddell pinned LaChance to the ground and went to the mound to defeat the Red Sox 3–2. LaChance was so exhausted that he asked Jimmy Collins to find someone else to play first base, but Collins insisted that LaChance play. He went hitless in four at-bats.

JULY 25   Jimmy Collins hits a grand slam off Jack Harper in the fourth inning of a 6–3 victory over the Browns at Huntington Grounds.

Collins batted .322 during the 1902 season. The most effective Boston hitter in 1902 was Buck Freeman, who hit .309 with 11 homers, 121 RBIs, 174 hits, 38 doubles, and 19 triples. Patsy Dougherty had a .342 average, and Chick Stahl batted .323.

JULY 28   The Red Sox extend their winning streak to eight with an 8–1 win over the Tigers in Detroit.

AUGUST 23   Tully Sparks pitches the Red Sox to a 1–0, 10-inning victory over the Browns at Huntington Grounds.

Sparks pitched only 17 games for the Red Sox, recording only seven wins and this lone shutout.

AUGUST 26   The Red Sox score eight runs in the second inning en route to a 13–2 win over the Browns in Boston. Buck Freeman hit a ball over the right field fence, a rarity at cavernous Huntington Grounds.

AUGUST 31   The Red Sox win 3–1 in 11 innings over the Indians in Fort Wayne, Indiana, at a ballpark imaginatively named Jailhouse Flats before a crowd of 3,000. Playing in his hometown, Chick Stahl received a gold-headed cane and three floral designs from fans in ceremonies prior to the contest.

The win left the Red Sox with a 62–47 record, only one game behind the first-place Athletics, but Boston gradually sank out of contention in September, losing five times in seven meetings during the season's final month.

SEPTEMBER 1   During an exhausting Labor Day doubleheader, the Red Sox lose 10–0 and 8–0 to the Indians in Cleveland.

SEPTEMBER 6   Cy Young earns his 30th win of the season with a 6–5 decision over the Browns in St. Louis.

SEPTEMBER 15   The Red Sox lose 6–4 and 9–2 in a doubleheader against the Athletics before an overflow crowd at Huntington Grounds. The Sox entered the day trailing the Athletics by three games. The pair of losses effectively ended any chance for

Boston to win the American League pennant.

SEPTEMBER 17 The Red Sox win 13–1 in the first game of a doubleheader against the Orioles at Huntington Grounds before succumbing 5–4 in the second contest.

SEPTEMBER 23 The Red Sox score an easy 14–1 win over the Senators in Washington. It was Cy Young's 32nd win of the season.

SEPTEMBER 27 Bill Dinneen wins his 21st game of the season in a 4–2 decision over the Orioles in the second game of a doubleheader in Baltimore. The Red Sox also won the first game 9–8.

SEPTEMBER 29 The Red Sox close the season with a 9–5 win over the Orioles before 138 fans in Baltimore. Patsy Dougherty collected five hits in five at-bats.

It was the last major league game played in Baltimore until 1954. Before the start of the 1903 season, the Orioles moved to New York, where they were eventually named the Yankees.

1903   B

Season in a Sentence

Spurred by an 11-game winning streak beginning late in May, the Red Sox capture their first American League pennant and baseball's first World Series.

Finish • Won • Lost • Pct • GB

First   91   47   58   +14.5

World Series—The Red Sox
defeat the Pittsburgh Pirates five games to three.

Manager

Jimmy Collins

Stats

Stats	Red Sox	AL	Rank
Batting Avg:	.272	.255	1
On-Base Pct:	.313	.303	2
Slugging Pct:	.392	.344	1
Home Runs:	48		1
Stolen Bases:	141		5
ERA:	2.57	2.96	1
Fielding Pct:	.959	.953	2
Runs Scored:	708		1
Runs Allowed:	504		1

Starting Lineup

Lou Criger, c
Candy LaChance, 1b
Hobe Ferris, 2b
Jimmy Collins, 3b
Freddie Parent, ss
Patsy Dougherty, lf
Chick Stahl, cf
Buck Freeman, rf
Jack O'Brien, cf

Pitchers

Cy Young, sp
Bill Dinneen, sp
Long Tom Hughes, sp
Norwood Gibson, sp
George Winter, sp

Attendance

379,388 (third in AL)

Club Leaders

Batting Avg:	Dougherty	.331
On-Base Pct:	Dougherty	.372
Slugging Pct:	Freeman	.496
Home Runs:	Freeman	13
RBI:	Freeman	104
Runs:	Dougherty	106
Stolen Bases:	Dougherty	35
Wins:	Young	28
Strikeouts:	Young	176
ERA:	Young	2.08
Saves:	Young	2
	Dinneen	2

JANUARY 10   The National and American Leagues agree to peace terms, bringing an end to the player raids that characterized the 1901 and 1902 seasons. It also opened the way for a postseason series between the pennant winners of the two leagues.

One of the attorneys who helped negotiate the agreement was Henry Killilea, a resident of Milwaukee. He soon purchased a controlling interest in the Red Sox from Charles Somers, who had conducted an unsuccessful two-year search to find a resident of Boston to buy the club.

APRIL 20   The Red Sox and Athletics open the season two days ahead of the rest of the American League with a Patriots' Day doubleheader, which was celebrated on April 20 because the nineteenth fell on a Sunday. The Red Sox won the first game 9–4 in the morning contest, but the Athletics won the afternoon affair 10–7. In the second game, the Red Sox blew a 6–0 lead with Cy Young on the mound. There were separate admissions to the pair of games, with 8,276 attending the opener and 19,282 at the second contest.

Duke Farrell, who hailed from Oakdale, Massachusetts, and had been in the majors since 1888, was signed as a catcher by the Red Sox in 1903. Before the first game, fans presented him with a $400 diamond ring. A broken leg limited his season to 17 games, but he hit .404.

Nearly every foul hit at Huntington Grounds during the opening games of the 1903 season drew catcalls from the fans. Prior to 1903 in the American League, a foul ball did not draw a strike. Many skilled batters fouled off pitch after pitch until they received an offering to their liking. [In 1901, the National League adopted the foul-strike rule, in which a batter is charged with a strike if he hit a foul ball unless there were already two strikes called on him.] The AL passed the rule in 1903. The foul-strike rule was a source of great controversy during the early years of the twentieth century, and its merits were a subject of great debate among fans and baseball players and officials.

At the players' request, advertising was removed from the twelve-foot-tall center field fence at Huntington Grounds and painted dark green to improve the background for hitters.

MAY 4   Hobe Ferris hits two inside-the-park homers to lead the Red Sox to a 6–4 victory over the Senators on a wet, wintry day at Huntington Grounds.

In early May, the Red Sox added Jake Stahl to the roster. Many histories report that Jake and Chick Stahl were brothers, but there are no known references in contemporary newspapers or magazines that identify them as siblings.

MAY 7   The Red Sox and Yankees play for the first time, with the Boston club emerging with a 6–2 win at Huntington Grounds.

New York's American League entry was originally known as the "Highlanders" because their home field, called Hilltop Park, was located on the highest point in Manhattan. The club became known as the Yankees around 1910.

JUNE 1   Playing in New York for the first time, the Red Sox defeat the Yankees, 8–2.

JUNE 5 — Hobe Ferris clubs a grand slam homer off Roy Patterson in the fifth inning of a 10–8 win over the White Sox at Huntington Grounds.

JUNE 8 — The Red Sox extend their winning streak to 11 games with a 6–1 victory over the Tigers at Huntington Grounds, in a game terminated by rain in the sixth inning.

On May 26, the Red Sox had a middling 15–15 record, but a long streak set the club on the road to the pennant. The Red Sox were 76–32 over their last 108 games.

JUNE 21 — The Red Sox down the Indians 12–7 in Canton, Ohio, before a Sunday-afternoon crowd of 6,000. Buck Freeman had five hits, including a triple and a homer, in six at-bats.

JUNE 23 — With Cy Young providing shutout pitching, the Red Sox take first place with a 1–0 win over the Tigers in Detroit.

JUNE 28 — The Red Sox defeat the Browns in St. Louis with a pair of shutouts. Cy Young won the opener 1–0, with Long Tom Hughes capturing the nightcap 3–0.

Young and Hughes were two of the Red Sox' three 20-game winners in 1903. Young had a 28–9 record with a 2.08 ERA, 34 complete games, seven shutouts, 342 innings pitched, and 176 strikeouts. During the season, he also posted a stretch of 37 consecutive scoreless innings pitched. Hughes was 20–7 with five shutouts and a 2.57 ERA, while Bill Dinneen was 21–13 with six whitewashings and a 2.26 ERA.

JULY 1 — Cy Young pitches a shutout and drives in the game's lone run with a double in the tenth inning to defeat the White Sox 1–0 in Chicago. It was the third 1–0 win for Young in a span of eight days. He is the only pitcher in major league history to earn 1–0 victories in three consecutive starts. It was also Young's fourth consecutive shutout overall, including a 7–0 win over the Browns on June 13.

The Red Sox hit 112 triples in 1903 to tie an American League record.

JULY 16 — The Red Sox score seven runs in the first inning and beat the Indians 11–4 at Huntington Grounds. The game was called in the eighth inning to allow the Cleveland club to catch a train.

JULY 17 — Norwood Gibson shuts out the Tigers 1–0 in 10 innings at Huntington Grounds. The winning run was scored on a Buck Freeman triple and a throwing error. As Freeman headed for third base, Detroit second baseman Heinie Smith fired the relay throw wildly, and Freeman trotted across the plate.

Gibson was a 1901 graduate of Notre Dame with a degree in chemistry.

JULY 29 — Patsy Dougherty becomes the first Red Sox player in history to hit for the cycle, but Boston commits eight errors, four by shortstop Freddie Parent, and loses 15–14 to the Yankees at Huntington Grounds. A four-run Red Sox rally in the ninth inning fell short. Dougherty also had two singles in addition to his double, triple, and homer for five hits overall. Cy Young allowed all 15 Yankee runs.

When it became apparent by mid-August that the Red Sox and Pirates would win pennants in their respective leagues, Pittsburgh owner Barney Dreyfuss issued a challenge to Henry Killilea to hold a postseason championship series. In early September they met in Pittsburgh and decided on a best-of-nine format. The players, whose contracts expired September 30, would receive two weeks additional pay plus a share of the gate receipts. The Pirates, managed by future Hall of Famer Fred Clarke, compiled a 91–49 record in 1903 to win their third consecutive National League pennant.

AUGUST 10   Cy Young retires the first 21 batters to face him and goes on to defeat the Athletics 7–2 with a three-hitter at Huntington Grounds.

The Red Sox had only a two-game lead over the Athletics on August 4 in the American League pennant race but quickly pulled away. The Sox compiled a 13–6 record against Philadelphia during the season to aid in what eventually became a 14½-game advantage by the end of the season.

SEPTEMBER 5   In a contest played in a steady rain and called by darkness in the eighth inning, Patsy Dougherty collects five hits in five at-bats, including an American League record-tying three triples, during a 12–1 decision over the Athletics at Huntington Grounds.

Dougherty is the only player in Red Sox history to hit three triples in a game. He led the Red Sox in batting average in 1903 with a .331 mark, along with a league-leading 106 runs scored and 195 hits. Buck Freeman led the AL in RBIs (104) and total bases (281), and hit .287 with 39 doubles, 20 triples, and 13 homers. Freddie Parent batted .304, and Jimmy Collins hit .296. Both Collins and Parent collected 17 triples.

SEPTEMBER 15   The Red Sox rout the Yankees 12–3 at Huntington Grounds.

SEPTEMBER 16   The Red Sox clinch their first American League pennant and score in each of their eight turns at bat to stun the Indians 14–7 at Huntington Grounds. Boston got 23 hits during the contest, five from Chick Stahl, who hit three singles, a double, and a triple.

SEPTEMBER 17   The Red Sox score a run in each of the first six innings to defeat the Indians 14–3 at Huntington Grounds in a game called by darkness after eight innings. Combined with all eight innings the previous day and the final three on September 15, the Red Sox set a major league record by plating at least one run in 17 consecutive innings.

SEPTEMBER 18   Freddie Parent hits a two-run, walk-off homer in the ninth inning to defeat the Indians 7–6 at Huntington Grounds. Bill Dinneen was the winning pitcher, earning his 21st victory of the season.

SEPTEMBER 19   The Red Sox continue their terrific batting streak with a 13–3 victory over the White Sox at Huntington Grounds. Cy Young was the winning pitcher, earning his 28th victory of the season.

SEPTEMBER 21   Buck Freeman hits the first extra-inning homer in Red Sox history to defeat the White Sox 4–3 in 12 innings at Huntington Grounds.

OCTOBER 1   In the first game of the first World Series, the Pirates defeat the Red Sox 7–3 before 16,242 at Huntington Grounds as Pittsburgh hurler Deacon Phillippe outduels Cy Young. The Pirates jumped on Young early with four runs in the first inning. In the seventh inning, Pittsburgh's Jimmy Sebring clubbed the first home run in World Series history, which gave the Pirates a 7–0 lead.

Phillippe was forced to start five of the eight Series games because the Pirates' pitching staff was dangerously thin. Ed Doheny was institutionalized at the Danvers Insane Asylum just prior to the Series for violent behavior that included assaulting a doctor, and 25-game winner Sam Leever had a sore shoulder from a rifle's recoil in a trapshooting contest.

OCTOBER 2   Bill Dinneen shuts out the Pirates 3–0 on three hits accompanied by 11 strikeouts before 9,415 at Huntington Grounds to even the Series at one game apiece. Patsy Dougherty led off the first inning with an inside-the-park homer and hit another over the left field fence in the sixth. Only one ball during the regular season had cleared that fence.

Dougherty's homer would prove to be the last in World Series play until 1908. In addition, he hit only 17 regular-season home runs in a 10-year big-league career. Game Two of the 1903 World Series is the only instance in which Dougherty had a multiple–home run game.

OCTOBER 3   On one day's rest, Deacon Phillippe defeats the Red Sox 4–2 in a game attended by 18,801 at Huntington Grounds.

Long Tom Hughes was the starting pitcher for the Red Sox but lasted only two innings. At the time, idle players, even such stars as Cy Young, were expected to help out on the turnstiles and counting the gate receipts. Young wasn't expected to pitch and was in street clothes in the Red Sox offices counting the receipts when he was summoned to replace Hughes on the mound. He pitched the final seven innings.

OCTOBER 6   Following a travel day and a postponement due to rain, Deacon Phillippe defeats the Red Sox for the third time, 5–4, before 7,600 at Exposition Park in Pittsburgh. Most of the game was played in a steady drizzle. Honus Wagner contributed three hits for the Pirates. The Red Sox nearly pulled out a victory with a three-run rally in the ninth inning. With runners on first and second, pinch hitter Jack O'Brien popped out to end the game. The win gave the Pirates a three-games-to-one lead in the Series, with the next three games to be played in Pittsburgh. There seemed to be little chance that the Series would return to Boston, much less result in victory for the Red Sox.

Pittsburgh's Exposition Park was located on the north bank of the Allegheny River opposite downtown Pittsburgh, near the site of present-day PNC Park.

OCTOBER 7   Cy Young and the Red Sox down the Pirates 11–2 in Pittsburgh. Young also drove in three runs on a triple and a single. The game was scoreless until the sixth inning, when the Red Sox broke loose for six runs, aided by two Honus Wagner errors. Boston added four more tallies in the seventh.

OCTOBER 8   The Red Sox win 6–3 in Pittsburgh behind the pitching of Bill Dinneen to even the series with the Pirates at three games apiece.

The First World Series

When the 1901 and 1902 seasons ended, there was no possibility of the champions of the American and National Leagues meeting each other in a postseason series because the two organizations were at war, each actively raiding the other for the rights to players. The peace accord ending two years of viciousness, hostility, broken contracts, lawsuits, and player raids was signed in January 1903, but no provision was made for a postseason series between the pennant winners of the two leagues. There was a precedent for such a meeting. The pennant winners of the National League and American Association played each other from 1884 through 1890. After the American Association folded, the first- and second-place teams in the National League squared off in a postseason series in 1892, 1894–1897, and 1900.

The first modern World Series began with a letter from Pittsburgh Pirates owner Barney Dreyfuss to Red Sox owner Henry Killilea in late July 1903. At the time, the Pirates and Red Sox were both in first place, and Dreyfuss proposed a set of games between the two clubs at the close of the regular season to determine baseball's "world" champion. By mid-August, the Red Sox had established a comfortable lead in the American League pennant race, and Killilea accepted the challenge. It was a chance for the National League to display its perceived superiority and an opportunity for the American League to show it was the equal of the older circuit.

The final agreement was put in writing on September 16. It was to be a best-of-nine affair beginning on October 1, with the first three games in Boston followed by four in Pittsburgh and, if necessary, two more in Boston. Tickets in Boston were $1 for grandstand seats and 50¢ for the bleachers, double the regular-season prices.

Even though the American and National Leagues consisted of sixteen teams in ten cities in seven states, none of them south of Washington or west of St. Louis, the championship was to be called the "World's Series." (The Fall Classic was known as the World's Series until the 1920s. The possessive was dropped gradually and disappeared from use by the 1930s.) Few, except sportswriter William Rankin, noted the irony. "Will [the Boston team] please inform me what foreign team teams they defeated to become the World's Champions?" asked Rankin in *The Sporting News* after the 1903 Series. "Some people have a vague idea of how large the world is, and for the life of them can not see anything beyond the borders of the United States."

The first World Series was nearly stopped before it started, however, because of a contract disagreement between the Boston players and owner Henry Killilea. The Red Sox' contracts expired on September 30, and they needed to negotiate an extension. The players refused to play in the Series on the 50-50 split of gate receipts that Killilea was offering. The players wanted 75 percent. Outraged, Killilea wired Red Sox player-manager Jimmy Collins on September 24 that the Series was off.

The opposing Pirates and fans of both clubs were outraged and disgusted, but the cancellation lasted only one day. American League president Ban Johnson put pressure on Killilea to reach a settlement with the players. Terms were not announced publicly, but it is believed that the players and Killilea agreed to a 60-40 split.

Before the first game in Boston, large sums were wagered on the outcome of the Series. In 1903, there was no rule preventing a player from betting on his own team, as long as he didn't bet on them to lose. As a result, players on both teams laid down money with gamblers and ordinary fans. Even Dreyfuss openly placed bets in the lobby of the Vendome Hotel, where his club was staying in Boston.

The seating capacity at both Huntington Grounds and Exposition Park in Pittsburgh were entirely inadequate to handle the demand for tickets. At the time, there was no such thing as a sellout. Owners kept selling general admission tickets long after every seat had been filled. As a result, fans were placed behind ropes in the outfield at each of the eight games of the 1903 Series. It was agreed beforehand that balls hit into the outfield crowd would be ground-rule triples. This rule was in effect for seven of the eight games. In those seven games, batters were credited with 25 triples but only four doubles. The exception was Game Three in Boston, where the crowd was so close to the infield that balls hit into the multitude were reduced to doubles. In that contest, there were seven doubles and no triples.

It was in Game Three, played on a Saturday afternoon, that a riot nearly ended the contest. The official attendance at Huntington Grounds was announced as 18,801, but it's estimated that as many as 25,000 were inside the enclosure, which had only about 9,000 seats. Many climbed the outfield fences and scrambled into the ballpark for free. Fans were placed behind outfield ropes but began inching forward, first a few people at a time, then in a stampede. The squad of fifty policemen on hand was powerless to keep the fans behind the ropes as hundreds surged onto the field in a party atmosphere. When the crowd made its rush, two women were caught in the crush near third base, and if it hadn't been for the quick work of Red Sox center fielder Chick Stahl and the police, the women might have been trampled to death. The women were escorted under the grandstand.

The fans packed the field, and the police began removing them from the infield. Red Sox business manager Joseph Smart gave the police baseball bats, which they used to try to get the crowd back into the outfield. Their efforts were futile. Just as one group was forced back and an area cleared, another group would rush onto the diamond. At first the crowd was good-natured, but the brute force of the police whacking them with wooden bats roused their ire. It was feared that the game would have to be postponed or, worse, forfeited to the Pirates.

A water hose was brought out to assist in keeping the crowd back, but the angry mob soon hacked it to pieces. A reserve police force was called in and pushed the crowd back, swinging their billy clubs indiscriminately. Pieces of the rubber hose were used as weapons by the police. This action cleared enough of the field to play the game, but the best the police could do was move the crowd about fifty yards behind the diamond, within fifteen feet of home plate, and just three feet from first and third base. Cut off from their benches, the players sat on the grass on either side of the catcher. The Pirates won the game 4–2.

The scene moved to Pittsburgh, where the Pirates took a three-games-to-one lead with a 5–4 decision. The Red Sox fought back, however, by winning four in a row, three of them in Pittsburgh, to take the championship.

The Series turned with the help of a song called "Tessie." About 125 of Boston's band of fanatic Royal Rooters accompanied the Red Sox to Pittsburgh and drove the Pirates players and fans crazy with the song "Tessie." The Royals Rooters were led by Michael McGreevy, who owned a saloon at 940 Columbus Avenue in Roxbury called Third Base, so named because it was often his patron's last stop before heading home. McGreevy was nicknamed "Nuf Ced" because he ended barroom arguments with the phrase, "Enough said." "Tessie" was a popular song of the day, part of a Broadway musical entitled "The Silver Slipper." For reasons unknown, the Royal Rooters began singing the tune. Since it coincided with the comeback by the Red Sox, it was seen as good luck, and "Tessie" became the unofficial anthem of the club. The Royal Rooters played it repeatedly at big games until at least 1916, and it got on the nerves of the 1903 Pittsburgh Pirates, as well as future opponents. Tommy Leach, the Pirates' third baseman in 1903, complained that "Tessie" was still ringing in his ears some sixty years later during an interview with author Lawrence Ritter for his 1966 book, *The Glory of Their Times*.

The Red Sox won the World Series but actually earned less money than the Pirates due to the shortsightedness of Henry Killilea. Despite winning the World Series in his first year as owner, Killilea was vilified in the Boston press for his absentee ownership and skinflint operation. Many accused Killilea of selling the best seats at Huntington Grounds to ticket scalpers in exchange for a portion of the profits. Killilea charged admission to the writers covering the club during the World Series. He even forced Pirates owner Barney Dreyfuss to pay for a ticket. Dreyfuss donated a much larger share of the gate receipts to his athletes than Killilea did, and as a result, the Pirate players earned $1,316 for losing the World Series, while the Red Sox garnered only $1,182 for winning. Killilea sold the Red Sox to the Taylor family six months later, on April 17.

OCTOBER 10   After a postponement due to cold weather on October 9, the Red Sox move within
                one game of the world championship with a 7–3 win over the Pirates before 17,038
                on a Saturday afternoon in Pittsburgh. Boston had five triples in the contest by five
                different players. Most of them would have been easy outs were it not for the over-
                flow crowd ringing the outfield.

OCTOBER 13   Following a travel day and a rain-out, the Red Sox win baseball's first modern World
                Series with a 3–0 win over the Pirates before 7,455 at Huntington Grounds with Bill
                Dinneen providing the shutout pitching. Hobe Ferris drove in all three Boston runs
                with a two-run single in the fourth inning and another single in the sixth. Deacon
                Phillippe, making his fifth start for the Pirates, pitched valiantly but couldn't match
                Dinneen. The Series ended with Dinneen striking out Honus Wagner.

*Bill Dinneen, a pitcher with a career record of 172–176, was the hero of the Series
for Boston with three victories, including two shutouts. His 28 strikeouts remained
a World Series record until it was broken by Bob Gibson in 1964. After his playing
career ended, Dinneen served as an umpire in the American League from 1909
through 1937. As an umpire, Dinneen worked in 45 World Series games.*

1 9 o 4   B

Season in a Sentence

The Red Sox finish first for the
second year in a row following
one of the most exciting pennant
races in history, but they miss out
on a World Series when the
National League champion New
York Giants refuse to play.

Finish • Won • Lost • Pct • GB

First   95   59   .617   +1.5

Manager

Jimmy Collins

Stats   Red Sox • AL • Rank

Stats	Red Sox	AL	Rank
Batting Avg:	.247	.244	4
On-Base Pct:	.301	.295	3
Slugging Pct:	.340	.321	3
Home Runs:	26		4
Stolen Bases:	101		8
ERA:	2.12	2.60	1
Fielding Pct:	.962	.959	2
Runs Scored:	608		2
Runs Allowed:	466		1

Starting Lineup

Lou Criger, c
Candy LaChance, 1b
Hobe Ferris, 2b
Jimmy Collins, 3b
Freddie Parent, ss
Kip Selbach, lf
Chick Stahl, cf
Buck Freeman, rf
Patsy Dougherty, lf
Duke Farrell, c

Pitchers

Cy Young, sp
Bill Dinneen, sp
Jesse Tannehill, sp
Norwood Gibson, sp
George Winter, sp

Attendance

623,295 (first in AL)

Club Leaders

Batting Avg:	Parent	.291
On-Base Pct:	Stahl	.366
Slugging Pct:	Stahl	.416
Home Runs:	Freeman	7
RBI:	Freeman	84
Runs:	Collins	85
	Parent	85
Stolen Bases:	Parent	20
Wins:	Young	26
Strikeouts:	Young	200
ERA:	Young	1.97
Saves:	Young	1

JANUARY 16   A month after Orville and Wilbur Wright's first successful flight, the Red Sox sell George Stone and Jake Stahl to the Senators. The deal was essentially a crash landing. A native of Last Nation, Iowa, Stone had a brief fling as one of the top players in baseball that included a batting title with the Browns in 1906. He was quickly overcome by injuries. Stahl became Washington's starting first baseman but returned to Boston in another deal with the Yankees in 1908.

APRIL 14   In the season opener, the Red Sox lose 8–2 to the Yankees in New York. Buck Freeman hits the first Opening Day homer in Red Sox history.

Prior to the game, players marched shoulder-to-shoulder onto the field accompanied by the Sixty-ninth Regiment band.

APRIL 17   General Charles H. Taylor, publisher of the Boston Globe, purchases the Red Sox from Henry Killilea.

Taylor outbid John Fitzgerald, Boston mayor and grandfather of future President John F. Kennedy, to buy the Sox. Taylor bought the club for his son John I. Taylor, a bon vivant around town who showed no interest in his father's newspaper operation. It was the first time that someone from Boston had owned the Red Sox. John loved sports, and his father figured that running the Red Sox would keep him busy and out of trouble. Taylor's ownership of the Red Sox was often marked by reckless, erratic, and impetuous decisions. He took a pennant-winning team to the American League basement in a short span of two years, and then rebuilt the club into World Champions by 1912.

APRIL 18   In the home opener before 10,685 fans at Huntington Grounds, Jesse Tannehill surrenders only two hits in defeating the Senators 5–0. Prior to the game, both clubs formed in line and marched to the flag pole in center field, where two flags symbolizing the American League pennant and World Championship, were raised by Jimmy Collins. Acquired from the Yankees in an offseason trade for Long Tom Hughes, Tannehill was 21–11 for Boston in 1904 with an ERA of 2.04.

B Huntington Grounds: The Sox' First Ballpark **B**

Today's fans know of the tradition-rich Fenway Park that's so integral to Red Sox lore, but the earliest parks were modest affairs and hardly built for the long haul. That was certainly the case with the Red Sox' first venue, Huntington Grounds, built in 1901, the year the team was born. Plans called for a wood-frame grandstand and bleachers with room for some 9,000 fans. The grandstand was faced with concrete to make it appear more substantial. Prices were set at 50¢ for the 2,600 covered grandstand seats and 25¢ for the open bleachers. Often during the 1901 season, the bleachers were jammed full with bargain hunters while the grandstand was almost empty. The team added bleachers in left field in 1905.

The playing field was far from ideal. Much of the ground consisted of sand, and there were large sandy areas in the outfield where the grass never grew. Center field was so deep that few balls ever reached that far, so the club didn't go to the expense of cutting the hip-high weeds. A toolshed in deep center field was in play, and a steep bank led to the left field fence. Between the 1902 and 1903 seasons, the field sank because of the heavy winter snows and spring thaw and had to be almost completely filled and graded. Players complained that the turf was rocky and uneven, and a year later it was plowed up and leveled.

The diamond was about ninety feet from the stands, giving players plenty of room to snag foul balls. The playing field was approximately 350 feet down the left field line, 440 feet in left-center, a distant 530 feet to straightaway center, and 280 feet in right field. An angle of fencing in right-center was 635 from home plate. Despite the distance of the fences, Huntington Grounds was an excellent home run park, at least compared with the rest of the American League's diamonds. During the Red Sox' 11 seasons at Huntington Grounds (1901–1911), the club hit only 216 homers at home but fared even worse on the road—109. During the same period, the pitching staff allowed 168 home runs at Huntington Grounds and 125 on the road. This was due to an inversion of today's playing style, where cozy parks reinforce robust offenses. In the dead ball era, *larger parks* meant more home runs. The few homers hit out of Huntington Grounds were straight down the left and right field lines. Most of the others were inside the park, splitting the gaps between outfielders and allowing the batter to circle the bases while fielders chased the ball toward distant fences.

Huntington Avenue ran behind the ballpark's left field fence. Fans entered the park through a narrow passageway off Huntington. A sign over the passageway read, "Huntington Avenue American League Base Ball Grounds." The New York, New Haven & Hartford Railroad repair yards bordered the park behind home plate, the stands alongside first base, and beyond the right field fence. The passing trains and locomotives of the period often caused problems. The engines belched ashes and cinders that would drift into the eyes of players and fans. Behind the center field barrier was the Boston YMCA. The huge Boston Storage Warehouse, and later the Boston Opera House (built in 1910), loomed on the other side of Huntington Avenue, opposite the left field bleachers. In 1909, the magnificent Museum of Fine Arts opened just west of Huntington Grounds on Huntington Avenue. Nearby were such venerable Boston institutions as the Christian Science Mother Church (built in 1894), the Massachusetts Historical Society (1899), Symphony Hall (1900), Jordan Hall (1903), and the Isabella Stewart Gardiner Museum (1909).

Huntington Grounds during the Pennant-winning year of 1903.

Courtesy of Transcendental Graphics/theruckerarchive.com

APRIL 19   In a Patriot's Day doubleheader, the Red Sox defeat the Senators, 1–0 and 3–2. In the first game, George Winter pitched the shutout aided by Chick Stahl, who drove in the game's lone run in the fourth inning with a single.

Stahl hit .290 with 19 triples for the Red Sox in 1904. Other leading batters for Boston in 1904 were Freddie Parent (.291), Buck Freeman (.280, 19 triples, 84 RBIs), and Jimmy Collins (.271, 33 doubles).

APRIL 30   Cy Young relieves George Winter in the third inning and holds the Senators hitless the rest of the way for a 4–1 win at Washington.

MAY 2   The Red Sox and Athletics agree to donate 20 percent of the gate receipts at Huntington Grounds to the John L. Sullivan Benefit Fund. The Sox lost, 2–0.

Bostonian John L. Sullivan was a heavyweight boxing champion of the world between 1882 and 1892.

MAY 5   Pitching the first no-hitter in Red Sox history, Cy Young hurls a perfect game to defeat the Athletics 3–0 before 10,267 at Huntington Grounds. Young fanned six and allowed only six balls out of the infield. In the eighth inning, Young retired Lave Cross on a fly ball to right field, easily fielded Socks Seybold's grounder for the second out, and fanned Danny Murphy. During the tense ninth inning, Young struck out Monte Cross and induced Ossee Schreckengost to ground to shortstop. Young completed his perfecto by getting opposing pitcher Rube Waddell out on a high fly ball to Chick Stahl in center field. The game took only one hour and twenty-three minutes to complete.

The perfect game by Young was the first in the majors since 1880 and the first since the four-ball, three-strike count was established in 1889.

MAY 11   Cy Young outduels Ed Killian of the Detroit Tigers to earn a 1–0 victory in 15 innings at Huntington Grounds. The Red Sox bunched three hits to score the winning run, including a single by Duke Farrell, who pinch-hit for Young. Young yielded no hits until the sixth inning, when Sam Crawford singled to break Young's streak of consecutive hitless innings to 23, still a major league record. Young allowed only five hits in 15 innings and collected three hits himself off Waddell.

Young was 26–16 in 1904 with an ERA of 1.97, 10 shutouts, 40 complete games in 41 starts, a club-record 45 consecutive scoreless innings, 200 strikeouts, and only 29 walks in 380 innings pitched.

MAY 21   Red Sox shortstop Bill O'Neill commits six errors, a modern major league record, in a 5–3, thirteen-inning loss to the Browns at Huntington Grounds. The Browns played errorless ball in their victory.

Normally an outfielder, O'Neill was playing his second of two games at shortstop during his big-league career. He was subbing for Freddie Parent, who was ill. Parent missed only two games all year.

JUNE 12   Bill Dinneen goes all the way in completing a 2–1, 16-inning victory over the Browns in St. Louis. Buck Freeman drove in the game winner with a single.

JUNE 18   The Red Sox win a run-filled match against the White Sox 13–10 in 11 innings in Chicago. The White Sox committed eight errors. On the same day, Boston traded Patsy Dougherty to the Yankees for Bob Unglaub.

Dougherty was in a batting slump and was a weak defensive outfielder, but the deal nearly cost the Red Sox the 1904 pennant. Dougherty moved into the Yankees' starting lineup, while Unglaub was a little-used reserve. The swap was cooked up by American League president Ban Johnson, who wanted a strong club in New York to compete with the Giants. On the two previous Sundays, the Giants drew crowds of more than 37,000, then the largest two crowds in major league history. To help compensate for the loss of Dougherty, Johnson arranged for the Red Sox to purchase Kip Selbach from the Senators on July 2 in exchange for Bill O'Neill. Selbach was one of Washington's starting outfielders, while O'Neill was languishing on the Boston bench.

JULY 8   Freddie Parent swats a grand slam off Jack Powell during the second inning of a 12–3 win over the Yankees in New York.

JULY 13   The Red Sox take a 5½-game lead over the Yankees with a 3–2 victory over the Tigers at Huntington Grounds.

The lead soon evaporated. The Red Sox were ousted from first place on August 4 and became embroiled in a three-way tussle for the American League pennant with the Yankees and the White Sox. Also during the month of July, the New York Giants pulled away to a huge lead in the National League and Giants owner John Brush and manager John McGraw stated that he wouldn't play the American League champ in the postseason. Brush and McGraw both held long-standing grudges against American League president Ban Johnson. A particular sore point was the establishment of the Yankees in New York in 1903. There was some consternation in the Boston press over the declaration of Brush and McGraw, but no real panic, because it was more or less assumed that the pair would have a change of heart and compete in baseball's second modern World Series.

JULY 15   Sent into the game as a pinch hitter, pitcher Jesse Tannehill singles in Lou Criger with the winning run in the ninth inning to defeat the Tigers 5–4 at Huntington Grounds.

AUGUST 2   Four Red Sox put out a fire after a 4–1 win over the Indians in Cleveland. Just after arriving at the hotel, Hobe Ferris, Freddie Parent, Bill Dinneen, and Norwood Gibson noticed flames bursting from a room and several employees of the tavern running panic-stricken about the fifth floor. The four dashed out of the elevator, and after the fire had spread from one room to another, managed to put out the blaze by means of a fire hose without calling the fire department.

AUGUST 17 Jesse Tannehill pitches a no-hitter to defeat the White Sox 6–0 in Chicago. He walked one batter and hit another in the first inning before retiring 25 batters in a row while striking out four. With one out in the ninth, Freddie Parent preserved the no-hitter with a fine play at shortstop to beat Danny Green at first base by a split-second. The final out was recorded on a bouncer off the bat of Fielder Jones to second baseman Hobe Ferris. Jesse's younger brother Lee started at third base for the White Sox and went 0 for 3.

The Red Sox entered the contest in third place, two games behind the first-place White Sox. The defeat sent Chicago on a skid that left them out of the pennant race by mid-September.

AUGUST 22   Boston defeats the Browns with a pair of shutouts at Huntington Grounds. Cy Young won the first game 8–0, while Norwood Gibson captured the nightcap 2–0 on a two-hitter.

Amazingly, the Red Sox employed only five pitchers during the 1904 season. Young pitched 380 innings, Bill Dinneen 335 2/3, Jesse Tannehill 281 2/3, Gibson 273, and George Winter 135 2/3. The staff recorded a major league record 148 complete games out of 157 played (including three ties). There wasn't a single contest all year in which Boston used more than two pitchers. The hitters were also durable. Candy LaChance, Chick Stahl, and Buck Freeman played in every game, while Jimmy Collins and Hobe Ferris missed only one game, and Freddie Parent was absent for only two.

AUGUST 23   The Red Sox explode for a 14–1 triumph over the Browns in St. Louis.

AUGUST 29   Bill Dinneen pitches a two-hitter and drives in the game's only run with a ninth-inning single to defeat the Tigers 1–0 at Huntington Grounds. The victory vaulted the Red Sox back into first place.

Dinneen was 23–14 for the Red Sox in 1904 with an ERA of 2.20. He pitched complete games in each of his 37 starts.

AUGUST 30   A seven-run seventh inning paces the Red Sox to a 12–0 win over the Tigers at Huntington Grounds.

The Red Sox pitching staff set a club record with an ERA of 2.12 in 1904.

SEPTEMBER 5   The Red Sox score seven runs in the eighth inning to beat the Senators 12–5 in the first game of a doubleheader at Huntington Grounds. Boston also won the second game, 8–3.

SEPTEMBER 6   The Red Sox defeat the Senators for the 22nd time in a row dating back to 1903 with a 4–1 win in the first game of a doubleheader at Huntington Grounds. Washington ended its losing streak with a 6–3 win in the second game.

SEPTEMBER 10   Cy Young strikes out 12 batters but loses 1–0 to the Athletics in thirteen innings in Philadelphia. In the tenth inning, Young allowed a lead-off triple to Danny Murphy, then struck out Monte Cross, Mike Powers, and opposing pitcher Eddie Plank on nine pitches. Plank, who like Young pitched a complete game, drove in the winning run.

SEPTEMBER 14   Bill Dinneen pitches a two-hitter against the Yankees in the first game of a double-header at Huntington Grounds, but the Red Sox commit seven errors and lose, 3–1. The Red Sox entered the contest with a half-game lead over the Yankees in the pennant race, and the defeat catapulted their New York rivals into first place. The second game was called after five innings by darkness with the score tied, 1–1.

SEPTEMBER 15   The Red Sox move back into first place with a 3–2 win over the Yankees at Huntington

Grounds. The Yankees loaded the bases in the ninth inning, but Jesse Tannehill struck out Wid Conroy to end the game.

SEPTEMBER 16   First place changes hands twice during a doubleheader at Huntington Grounds as the Yankees win the first game 6–4 and the Red Sox take the nightcap, 4–2. A day later, the Sox were back in second place.

SEPTEMBER 20   The Red Sox rout the Athletics 11–1 at Huntington Grounds. The victory was the 400th of Cy Young's career. Despite the win, Boston fell two games behind the Yankees as the New York club won both ends of a doubleheader against the Senators.

SEPTEMBER 21   The Red Sox take a doubleheader from the Athletics 5–1 and 4–3 at Huntington Grounds. Coupled with a Yankee loss, Boston pulled within half a game of first.

SEPTEMBER 26   The Red Sox take a two-game lead over the Yankees in the pennant race with 2–0 and 5–3 wins in a doubleheader against the Tigers in Detroit. In the first game, Tiger pitcher Wild Bill Donovan had a no-hitter going in the sixth inning when he was ejected for disputing the umpire's calls.

SEPTEMBER 27   Chick Stahl breaks up a no-hitter by Bob Rhoades of the Indians with two outs in the ninth, but the Red Sox lose 3–1 in Cleveland. The defeat was the first of three straight in Cleveland, which knocked the Red Sox out of first place again.

OCTOBER 2   The Red Sox leap back into first place with a 2–0 win over the Browns in St. Louis behind Cy Young.

                The 1904 American League pennant came down to a season-ending five-game series against the Yankees. On the original schedule, the series was set for three games in New York on Friday, October 7, Saturday, October 8, and a final contest on Monday, October 10 (with baseball on the Sabbath illegal in New York and Boston in 1904). The Yankees transferred the Saturday game to Boston, however, after they rented out their ballpark for a college football game between Columbia and Williams. Because of early-season postponements for inclement weather and a tie game, the revised schedule called for a single game in New York on the seventh, a doubleheader in Boston on the eighth, and two more games back in New York on the 10th. The Red Sox entered the series with a one-half game lead. The first team to win three games would seize the pennant.

OCTOBER 7   The Yankees take first place with a 3–2 win over the Red Sox in New York. Jack Chesbro was the winning pitcher, earning his 41st victory of the season, a modern major league record.

OCTOBER 8   A crowd of nearly 30,000 shoehorns its way into Huntington Grounds to watch the Red Sox take a doubleheader and regain first place from the Yankees with 13–2 and 1–0 victories. Jack Chesbro, starting for the second day in a row, wasn't up to the challenge and was shelled in the opener. There was no break in between the two games because of concerns about daylight. Yankee left fielder Patsy Dougherty, who made the last out in the first game, was the Yankee leadoff hitter in the nightcap and stayed at the plate while Bill Dinneen walked off the field and Cy Young took the mound. The nightcap was called by darkness after seven innings. The only run of the contest was scored in the fifth on an error by Yankee third baseman Wid

Conroy, one of three he made during the game. It was Young's third consecutive shutout and his 26th win of the season.

The wins meant that the Red Sox had to win only once in their season-ending doubleheader against the Yankees on October 10 to take the AL pennant. After the games, fans carried Sox players off the field on their shoulders, and thousands remained until the players had donned their street clothes and then cheered them on the way to their homes.

OCTOBER 10
The Red Sox clinch the pennant with a 3–2 win before 28,450 in the first game of the doubleheader at Hilltop Park in New York, a ballpark with a seating capacity of about 12,000. The crowd in the outfield stood twelve to fifteen deep. Some 400 fans came from Boston accompanied by a brass band. The Yankees' Jack Chesbro, who pitched 445 innings in 1904 and was making his third start in four days, faced Bill Dinneen, who had pitched a complete game only two days earlier.

The Yankees scored first with two runs in the fifth, the second on a bases-loaded walk, but the Red Sox evened the score with a pair in the seventh on a throwing error by New York second baseman Jimmy Williams. Lou Criger, one of the slowest players of the era, began the ninth inning with an infield single on a slow roller to shortstop Kid Elberfield. Criger advanced to second on Dinneen's sacrifice and to third on Kip Selbach's groundout. Criger scored the deciding tally when Chesbro launched a wild pitch with two out and two strikes on Freddie Parent. The pitch sailed far over the head of Yankee catcher Red Kleinow. Parent singled on the next pitch, but Chesbro got out of the inning with the score 3–2. In the Yankee ninth, Dinneen struck out John Ganzel, walked Wid Conroy, retired Kleinow on a pop-up to second baseman Hobe Ferris, and walked Deacon McGuire, who was pinch hitting for Chesbro. The game ended when Yankee Patsy Dougherty, who started the season as a member of the Red Sox, swung and missed on Dinneen's 2–2 pitch to clinch the American League pennant for Boston. It was Dinneen's 23rd win of the season. The Yankees won the meaningless second contest 1–0 in 10 innings.

There was no World Series, as Giants owner John Brush and manager John McGraw stuck to their guns and refused to play the Red Sox, whom they deemed the champion "in a minor league," conveniently ignoring that the "minor league" champions defeated the Pittsburgh Pirates in the 1903 Series. Red Sox players were not the only ones who were angry over the failure to defend their World Championship on the field. The actions of Brush and McGraw also cost the Giants players a significant wad of cash. The Sporting News declared the Red Sox World Champions by default. McGraw and Brush were roasted in the press for months all across the nation for their refusal to compete in the World Series. To add a bizarre twist to the saga, Brush proposed rules governing future World Series that were passed by the owners of the two leagues in January 1905. Among the stipulations was a $10,000 fine for any club that refused to play in the Series in the future.

1905   B

Season in a Sentence

Saddled with a roster that seemed to age overnight, any chance for a third consecutive American League pennant evaporates when the Red Sox lose the first six games of the season and are never in contention for first place.

Finish • Won • Lost • Pct • GB

Fourth   78   74   .513   16.0

Manager

Jimmy Collins

Stats

Stats	Red Sox	AL	Rank
Batting Avg:	.234	.241	6
On-Base Pct:	.305	.299	3
Slugging Pct:	.311	.314	5
Home Runs:	29		1
Stolen Bases:	131		6
ERA:	2.84	2.65	5
Fielding Pct:	.953	.957	6
Runs Scored:	579		4
Runs Allowed:	564		3

Starting Lineup

Lou Criger, c
Buck Freeman, 1b-rf
Hobe Ferris, 2b
Jimmy Collins, 3b
Freddie Parent, ss
Jesse Burkett, lf
Chick Stahl, cf
Kip Selbach, rf
Moose Grimshaw, 1b

Pitchers

Cy Young, sp
Jesse Tannehill, sp
Bill Dinneen, sp
George Winter, sp
Norwood Gibson, sp

Attendance

468,828 (third in AL)

Club Leaders

Batting Avg:	Collins	.276
On-Base Pct:	Selbach	.355
Slugging Pct:	Collins	.368
Home Runs:	Ferris	6
RBI:	Collins	65
Runs:	Burkett	78
Stolen Bases:	Parent	25
Wins:	Tannehill	22
Strikeouts:	Young	210
ERA:	Young	1.82
Saves:	Dinneen	1

JANUARY 16   The Red Sox are involved in a convoluted deal with the Browns and Senators. After purchasing George Stone from the Senators, the Red Sox traded him to the Browns for Jesse Burkett and Frank Huelsman. The Sox then sold Huelsman to the Senators as payment for Stone.

The thirty-six-year-old Burkett was a future Hall of Famer at the end of a career in which he compiled a .342 batting average and had two seasons in which he hit over .400. He batted just .257 during his only season in Boston.

APRIL 14   In the season opener in Philadelphia, the Red Sox lose 5–2 to the Athletics.

APRIL 18   George Winter pitches a one-hitter but loses 1–0 to the Senators in Washington. The lone hit and RBI for the Senators was a scratch single by second baseman Jim Mullin, a player with a .197 lifetime batting average during a 118-game career.

The Red Sox used only 18 players all season, a major league record low.

APRIL 21   The Red Sox season record drops to 0–6 with a 5–4 defeat in the home opener against the 1905 American League champion Athletics. Entering the eighth inning, Norwood Gibson had a 4–0 lead, a one-hitter, and 11 strikeouts but then allowed five runs and lost the game.

The Red Sox had no regulars under the age of 27 in 1905. Cy Young was 38 years old; Jesse Burkett 36; Jimmy Collins 35; Lou Criger, Kip Selbach, and Buck Freeman 33; and Chick Stahl 32.

MAY 1

Cy Young drives in Lou Criger from third base in the eleventh inning to lift the Red Sox to a 4–3 victory over the Yankees in New York.

MAY 19

A horse-drawn omnibus conveying the Red Sox players to the ballpark in Cleveland is struck by a streetcar at the corner of Euclid and Dunham. The players were badly shaken up, but none was seriously injured. The Indians won the ensuing contest, 11–4.

MAY 30

The Red Sox score three runs in the ninth inning on a two-run double by Kip Selbach and a single by Freddie Parent to defeat the Senators 4–3 in the first game of a doubleheader in Washington. The Sox also won the second game, 2–0. Cy Young was the winning pitcher for both, the first in a relief outing.

JUNE 8

The Red Sox score three runs in the ninth inning with two outs to beat the Browns 4–3 at Huntington Grounds. Buck Freeman missed his first game since 1901, ending a streak of 535 games played, the second longest in Red Sox history.

JUNE 24

The Red Sox collect only two hits but defeat the Yankees 3–0 at Huntington Grounds.

The Red Sox set a club record for fewest hits in a season with 1,177.

JULY 4

The Red Sox lose a 20-inning encounter with the Athletics 4–2 at Huntington Grounds. Cy Young and Rube Waddell both pitched complete games. Waddell recorded 19 consecutive scoreless innings after surrendering two runs in the first. The Athletics tied the score 2–2 in the sixth on a homer by Harry Davis. Young issued no walks but hit John Knight in the head with a pitch in the 20th inning, knocking him unconscious. Monte Cross went to first as Knight's pinch runner. Knight was the only one in either starting lineup who failed to finish the game. The hit batsman, along with an error and two singles, produced the two runs that led to the Boston defeat. The Athletics also won the first game, 5–2. The 29 innings in the two games are the most the Red Sox have ever played in one day.

Young pitched with this kind of hard luck all season long. His ERA of 1.82 was the third best in the American League, but he could muster only an 18–19 record.

JULY 8

The Red Sox and Athletics set an American League record for most doubles hit in a doubleheader at Philadelphia. There were 26 two-baggers hit in all, most of them of the ground-rule variety hit into the overflow crowd of 25,000. The first game was delayed for half an hour to get the spectators under control. Ropes were stretched across the outfield, but the crowd was twenty feet deep behind the outfielders. Others were in foul ground within a few feet of first and third base and ten to fifteen feet from home plate. The Red Sox scored six runs in the fourth inning of the first game, mostly on ground-rule doubles. With the A's at bat in the bottom of the fourth, bleacher fans began throwing cushions at the foul-line spectators, and several fights ensued. This was followed by several arrests, and the crowd surged onto the field. The police were powerless to stop the mob, and play was halted. Calls were sent for more police, and by the time they arrived, a few fans were seated on the pitcher's mound.

After a thirty-minute delay, the crowd was driven back so the game could continue. Many standing in foul territory were injured by foul balls. The Red Sox won the first game 11–8 but lost the second, called after eight innings by darkness, 11–4.

JULY 12   Jesse Tannehill pitches the Red Sox to a 1–0 win over the White Sox in the first game of a doubleheader in Chicago. Boston lost the second game, 4–1.

Tannehill was 22–9 with six shutouts and a 2.48 ERA in 1905.

JULY 23   With Sunday ball illegal in Detroit, the Red Sox and Tigers stage a contest in Columbus, Ohio, won by Boston 6–1 before a crowd of 5,702.

JULY 24   The Red Sox and Tigers stay in Columbus to play again, and once more the Red Sox are victorious, 7–1.

SEPTEMBER 5   Rube Waddell strikes out 17 Red Sox batters and allows only three hits, but Boston wins 3–2 over the Athletics in 13 innings at Huntington Grounds. Jimmy Collins drove in the game winner with a single.

Collins hit .276 with 65 RBIs in 1905.

SEPTEMBER 9   The Red Sox score two runs in the ninth inning and one in the eleventh to beat the Senators 4–3 at Huntington Grounds.

SEPTEMBER 19   The Red Sox win a doubleheader from the Senators in Washington for the second day in a row. Cy Young's two-hitter won the first game 1–0, while a two-run rally in the ninth captured the second, 7–6.

SEPTEMBER 27   Bill Dinneen pitches a no-hitter to defeat the White Sox 2–0 in the first game of a doubleheader at Huntington Grounds. It was Dinneen's first appearance since August 31. He had been sidelined by a sore arm. Dinneen walked two and struck out six. After easily retiring Fielder Jones and Frank Isbell, Dinneen induced George Davis to pop up to Bob Unglaub at third base for the final out. With Cy Young starting the second game, the White Sox took revenge by erupting for nine runs in the first inning and five in the second and won, 15–1. The game ended after six innings due to darkness.

Dinneen is the only individual to both pitch a no-hitter and umpire in one, though not in the same game! During his 29 seasons as an American League umpire, Dinneen officiated in eight no-hitters.

OCTOBER 7   On the final day of the regular season, the Red Sox win a thrilling doubleheader against the Yankees at Huntington Grounds. In the first game, the Yankees scored five runs in the first inning, but Boston rallied to win 7–6 in 10 innings. In the second contest, called after five innings by darkness, the Red Sox won again, 12–9.

OCTOBER 9   The Red Sox and Boston Braves play each other for the first time. In the first contest of a seven-game exhibition series, the Braves won 5–2 at Huntington Grounds. The Red Sox won the final six games of the series.

1906   B

Season in a Sentence

Just two seasons after winning the American League pennant, the Red Sox suffer a total collapse and tumble into last place.

Finish • Won • Lost • Pct • GB

Eighth   49   105   .318   46.5

Managers

Jimmy Collins (35–79)
Chick Stahl (14–26)

Stats   Red Sox • AL • Rank

Stats	Red Sox	AL	Rank
Batting Avg:	.237	.249	7
On-Base Pct:	.284	.303	8
Slugging Pct:	.304	.318	7
Home Runs:	13		5
Stolen Bases:	99		8
ERA:	3.41	2.89	8
Fielding Pct:	.949	.957	8
Runs Scored:	463		8
Runs Allowed:	706		8

Starting Lineup

Charlie Armbruster, c
Moose Grimshaw, 1b
Hobe Ferris, 2b
Red Morgan, 3b
Freddie Parent, ss
Jack Hoey, lf
Chick Stahl, cf
Buck Freeman, rf-1b
Jack Hayden, rf
Kip Selbach, lf
John Godwin, 3b-ss

Pitchers

Cy Young, sp
Joe Harris, sp
Bill Dinneen, sp
Jesse Tannehill, sp
George Winter, sp
Ralph Glaze, sp

Attendance

410,209 (fourth in AL)

Club Leaders

Batting Avg:	Stahl	.286
On-Base Pct:	Stahl	.346
Slugging Pct:	Grimshaw	.383
Home Runs:	Stahl	4
RBI:	Stahl	51
Runs:	Parent	67
Stolen Bases:	Parent	16
Wins:	Tannehill	13
	Young	13
Strikeouts:	Young	140
ERA:	Dinneen	2.92
Saves:	Three tied with	2

APRIL 14   In the season opener, the Red Sox lose 2–1 in 12 innings to the Yankees in New York. Cy Young pitched the complete-game loss.

APRIL 17   The day before the great San Francisco earthquake and fire, the Red Sox lose their home opener 4–3 to the Yankees before 18,000 at Huntington Grounds. The game ended when Moose Grimshaw was thrown out at the plate trying to score from second base on a single.

APRIL 24   The Red Sox collect 20 hits and account for all of their scoring during the first six innings to rout the Senators 19–2 in Washington.

APRIL 28   Trailing 6–3, the Red Sox score one run in the eighth inning and three in the ninth to defeat the Athletics 7–6 in Philadelphia. The final two runs were scored on a two-out double by Moose Grimshaw.

APRIL 30   The Red Sox put together a 23-hit attack and score nine runs in the ninth inning to defeat the Yankees 13–4 in New York.

The win gave the Red Sox a record of 6–7. It would be the club's last victory for nearly a month.

MAY 24   The Red Sox lose a club-record 20th consecutive game with a 7–5 decision against the White Sox, the 1906 World Champions, at Huntington Grounds. Cy Young was the starting pitcher but was removed after allowing four runs in the first inning.

The 20-game losing streak is tied for the second longest in American League history, and the third longest in the majors since 1900. The only longer losing streaks since the dawn of the twentieth century are 23 games by the Phillies in 1961 and 21 by the Orioles in 1988.

MAY 25   The Red Sox end their losing streak with a 3–0 win over the White Sox at Huntington Grounds. Jesse Tannehill pitched a two-hitter, and rookie backup catcher Bob Peterson drove in all three runs. The only Chicago hits were a double by Bill O'Neill and a single by Frank Isbell.

Peterson played in just 43 major league games, in which he accounted for only nine RBIs.

JUNE 1   After losing 4–0 in the first game of a doubleheader against the Senators at Huntington Grounds, the Red Sox explode for nine runs in the first inning of the second contest and win, 12–8.

Ralph Glaze was the winning pitcher in the second game. Before reaching the majors, he was a football star at Dartmouth.

JULY 2   The second game of a doubleheader against the Senators in Washington is stopped after seven innings by mutual consent because of the extreme heat, with the Red Sox losing, 17–3. Boston won the first game, 4–3.

JULY 27   Bill Dinneen pitches a one-hitter to defeat the Browns 1–0 in St. Louis. The lone run in the game crossed the plate on Jack Hoey's single in the ninth. The only Browns hit was a single by Pete O'Brien.

AUGUST 2–6   The Red Sox get shut out in four consecutive games to the Indians in Cleveland. They lose 3–0, 4–0, and 1–0 on August 2, 3, and 4, respectively, and cap the skid with a 4–0 loss on the sixth.

The Red Sox set club records for fewest runs scored in a season (463) and most times shut out (28) in 1906.

AUGUST 8   The Red Sox end their scoreless streak at 40 consecutive innings with a three-run third inning to defeat the Indians 3–1 in the first game of a doubleheader in Cleveland. Boston also won the second game 1–0 behind pitcher Joe Harris.

AUGUST 26   Jimmy Collins is injured while on a carriage ride with friends. A passing automobile frightened the horses, and they bolted. Collins ended up face down on the highway, his face and hands scraped raw.

AUGUST 29   Cy Young retires the first 23 Indians he faces before Elmer Flick singles. Young allowed four more hits but emerged with a 6–2 win at Huntington Grounds. On the same day, Chick Stahl replaced Jimmy Collins as manager of the Red Sox. Collins remained with the Red Sox as a player.

Jimmy Collins battled constantly with owner John I. Taylor during the Red Sox' two-year freefall from American League champions to cellar-dwellers. In June, Collins had put Stahl in charge of the team and taken a week-long vacation at a nearby beach resort without Taylor's permission. Collins and Stahl were the best of friends and had been teammates since 1897, when both played for the Boston Braves. The Red Sox were 14–26 during Stahl's brief tenure as a manager. He was just about the only productive player on the Boston roster in 1906, with a .286 batting average. Once the season ended, Stahl told John I. Taylor that he didn't want to continue as manager, but the Red Sox owner persuaded him to continue.

SEPTEMBER 1   In the longest game in Red Sox history, the second longest in the American League, and the fourth longest in the majors (by time), Boston loses 4–1 to the Athletics before a Saturday-afternoon crowd of 18,000 at Huntington Grounds. Both Jack Coombs of Philadelphia and Joe Harris of the Red Sox pitched complete games in a contest that lasted four hours and forty-seven minutes. Coombs struck out 18, hit a batter, and allowed 14 hits and 6 walks, while Harris fanned 14 and yielded 16 hits and 2 walks. The Athletics scored a run in the third inning on two fielding miscues by Harris, and the Red Sox tied the game 1–1 in the sixth.

The deadlock remained unbroken for 17 innings as neither pitcher allowed a run from the seventh through the twenty-third. During the eighteenth inning, the Red Sox loaded the bases with one out but failed to score when Coombs fanned both Hobe Ferris and Jack Hoey. In the fateful twenty-fourth inning, the Athletics had a runner on first with two out when Harris surrendered a single and then gave up triples to Socks Seybold and Danny Murphy. Harris's 24 innings are a record for most innings pitched in a game in a defeat, a mark that no doubt will stand forever.

Hailing from the Boston suburb of Melrose, Joe Harris had a horrific 2–21 record in 1906, which included a Red Sox record 14 losses in a row. Shortly before the season ended, Harris contracted typhoid fever. During his three-year big-league career, he won only three times while losing 30. Harris worked as a fireman for the Melrose Fire Department during the offseason and continued doing so after his playing days ended until he retired in 1939.

The longest game by innings in major league history is a 1–1 tie between the Dodgers and Braves in 1920 that went 26 innings. The Cardinals and Mets played a 25-inning contest in 1974, which the White Sox and Brewers matched in 1985.

SEPTEMBER 11   Second baseman Hobe Ferris and outfielder Jack Hayden engage in a vicious fight on the field during an 11–3 loss to the Yankees in New York. Ferris accused Hayden of loafing, and Hayden retaliated by punching Ferris. Ferris followed him to the bench, and as Hayden was about to sit down, Ferris kicked him in the mouth. Ferris's spikes sliced open Hayden's face in several places.

Hobe Ferris was suspended by the Red Sox for the remainder of the season. Jack Hayden missed the rest of the year nursing the injuries inflicted by Ferris and never played another game for the Red Sox.

SEPTEMBER 23   Jesse Tannehill earns his 22nd victory of the season with a 7–2 win over the Browns in the first game of doubleheader at Huntington Grounds. The Red Sox also won the second game, 5–0.

SEPTEMBER 30   In his major league debut, Red Sox pitcher Rube Kroh shuts out the Browns on only two hits for a 2–0 win in the second game of a doubleheader in St. Louis. The Red Sox lost the opener, 7–1.

So little was known about the twenty-year-old Kroh that he was referred to as "Crow" in the newspaper accounts of the game. Unfortunately, he won just one of his five decisions with the Red Sox in 1907 and was released. A native of Friendship, New York, Kroh didn't win another major league game until 1909, when he was pitching for the Cubs. His final big-league won-lost record was 14–9.

OCTOBER 2   Reds catcher Larry McLean, who played for the Red Sox in 1901, witnesses an assailant pump five bullets into another man while just outside the Park Street entrance of the Boston subway. McLean chased down the suspect and held him until police arrived. The victim died from the wounds.

OCTOBER 6   In what would be his final major league at-bat, Chick Stahl homers in a 5–4 loss to the Yankees at Huntington Grounds (see March 28, 1907).

1907   B

Season in a Sentence

Beginning with the spring training suicide of Chick Stahl, the Red Sox go through five managers in the space of ten weeks.

Finish • Won • Lost • Pct • GB

Seventh   59   90   .396   43.5

Managers

Chick Stahl (0–0)
Cy Young (3–3)
George Huff (2–6)
Bob Unglaub (9–20)
Deacon McGuire (45–61)

Stats   Red Sox • AL • Rank

Stats	Red Sox	AL	Rank
Batting Avg:	.234	.247	8
On-Base Pct:	.281	.302	8
Slugging Pct:	.292	.309	7
Home Runs:	18		2
Stolen Bases:	125		8
ERA:	2.45	2.54	5
Fielding Pct:	.959	.957	5
Runs Scored:	464		8
Runs Allowed:	558		6

Starting Lineup

Lou Criger, c
Bob Unglaub, 1b
Hobe Ferris, 2b
John Knight, 3b
Heinie Wagner, ss
Jimmy Barrett, lf
Denny Sullivan, cf
Bunk Congalton, rf
Freddie Parent, lf-ss
Al Shaw, c
Moose Grimshaw, rf-1b
Jimmy Collins, 3b

Pitchers

Cy Young, sp
George Winter, sp
Ralph Glaze, sp
Jesse Tannehill, sp
Cy Morgan, sp
Tex Pruett, rp-sp

Attendance

468,828 (third in AL)

Club Leaders

Batting Avg:	Congalton	.286
On-Base Pct:	Congalton	.316
Slugging Pct:	Congalton	.353
Home Runs:	Ferris	4
RBI:	Unglaub	62
Runs:	Sullivan	73
Stolen Bases:	Wagner	20
Wins:	Young	21
Strikeouts:	Young	147
ERA:	Young	1.99
Saves:	Young	2

MARCH 26   Chick Stahl resigns as manager of the Red Sox, citing the strain of the job as adversely affecting his performance.

MARCH 28   Chick Stahl commits suicide by drinking carbolic acid in West Baden, Indiana, where the club had stopped to play an exhibition game.

B   The Suicide of Chick Stahl   B

In an act that came with shocking suddenness, Red Sox player-manager Chick Stahl committed suicide by swallowing three ounces of carbolic acid on the morning of March 28, 1907, at the club's spring training headquarters in West Baden, Indiana. Before dying, Stahl spoke briefly, leaving only the cryptic message: "Boys, I could not help it. It drove me to it." What "it" was perplexed those close to him, as well as baseball historians, for nearly a century.

Charles "Chick" Stahl was born in Indiana in 1873. He reached the major leagues as an outfielder with the Boston Braves in 1897 and became an immediate hit by batting .354. Stahl became close friends with Braves teammate Jimmy Collins, and when Collins moved to the Red Sox as the club's first player-manager in 1901, Stahl signed with the new club in Boston within days.

With Collins as manager and third baseman and Stahl in center field, the Red Sox won the AL pennant in 1903 and 1904, but by 1906, Boston was firmly positioned in last place. On August 29, Red Sox owner John I. Taylor fired Collins and persuaded Stahl, who was the team's most productive player that season, to take the job.

Taylor was a "hands-on" owner who constantly interfered with his manager's decisions, and he and Stahl feuded often during the final days of the 1906 season. The club lost 26 of the 40 games it played under Stahl, and the new manager felt he had no real authority to run the club. Stahl asked for more control over decisions, but Taylor refused. Still, Taylor convinced Stahl to continue as manager for the 1907 season.

Stahl married Julia Harmon, who resided in the Boston neighborhood of Roxbury, on November 14, 1906. It was not a happy union due to Stahl's infidelity. He had been carrying on a liaison with Lulu Ortman in his hometown of Fort Wayne, Indiana, for at least five years. Ortman attempted to shoot him in 1902 when he threatened to end the relationship. In addition, Stahl had impregnated a third woman from Chicago during a casual affair. The mistress blackmailed Stahl, threatening to make the news public, which would have created a major scandal, particularly in light of the mores of the early twentieth century.

Spring training in 1907 called for the Red Sox to work out and play games for a few weeks in Little Rock, Arkansas, then move north through Louisville, Kentucky, the resort town of West Baden, Indiana, and Cincinnati, Ohio, before starting the regular season in Philadelphia, Pennsylvania.

As the training sessions progressed, Red Sox players told newspapermen that Stahl's personality had changed drastically since the previous season, as his normally carefree demeanor had changed to constant brooding over the responsibilities of managing the team. He had little to say and seemed to worry all the time. Working under a man like Taylor certainly didn't help Stahl's mental disposition. Members of the team said that Stahl had been subject to fits of depression at times but that those soon disappeared.

Stahl developed a sore on his foot during the early workouts, and the injury was slow to heal. He was given carbolic acid, which was supposed to be diluted with water to wash the wound, a common remedy at the time.

When the team arrived in Louisville, Stahl was suffering from insomnia, and his depression seemed to go worse. The carbolic acid was taken away from him for a time by a friend when Stahl admitted that he had thoughts of taking his life.

A few days later, a photographer took photos of Stahl. "I guess that will be the last picture taken of me," he said.

Stahl resigned as manager of the Red Sox on March 26. The relief of his burdens as manager seemed to lighten Stahl's frame of mind. The night before his death, Julia Stahl received a message from her husband reading, "Cheer up little girl, and be happy. I am all right now and able to play the game of my life."

Stahl arose early on the morning of March 28 and seemed to be in good health and spirits and remarked to several of his teammates that it seemed to be a fine day for baseball. He had breakfast as usual in the hotel dining room. Just prior to 9:00 AM, Stahl went to the office of Lou Sinclair, owner of the hotel, and talked for some fifteen minutes about bathhouse tickets for members of the team. Sinclair said later he saw nothing out of the ordinary in Stahl's behavior. Stahl went

to his room in the company of Collins to change into his uniform for the morning practice.

Collins had just finished getting into his uniform when Stahl, who had only partly dressed, returned and was staggering. His appearance alarmed Collins, who asked, "What is the matter with you?" Stahl replied, "Nothing," then fell to the floor. Collins ran to him at once, detected the smell of carbolic acid, and telephoned the hotel physician.

Bob Unglaub was passing in the hall at the same time and ran into the room, where Stahl was writhing in agony. He asked him if he had taken the acid, to which Stahl admitted that he had. Stahl then uttered his last words: "It drove me to it."

Two years later, Stahl's widow, Julia, was found dead in a doorway of a house in Boston under mysterious circumstances. A drug addict, she had probably been working as a prostitute.

APRIL 11   On Opening Day, the Red Sox defeat the Athletics 8–4 in a 14-inning game in Philadelphia. Buck Freeman homered during Boston's four-run rally in the fourteenth, the only homer he hit in 1907. Hobe Ferris also hit a home run for the Red Sox.

Cy Young started the season as the Red Sox manager but made it clear to John I. Taylor that he would take the job only on a temporary basis. Originally, Taylor wanted to become the field manager himself following Stahl's suicide, but American League president Ban Johnson refused to allow it and told Taylor to confine his duties to the front office.

APRIL 16   In the home opener, the Red Sox defeat the Senators 4–2 at Huntington Grounds.

APRIL 17   George Huff replaces Cy Young as manager of the Red Sox.

George Huff was thirty-six years old and had been employed as athletic director at the University of Illinois at the time of his appointment as Red Sox manager. A graduate of Dartmouth, Huff coached baseball and football at Illinois and also served as a scout for the Chicago Cubs, a club that had won 116 games in 1906. His professional playing career consisted of four years in the minors.

APRIL 27   The Red Sox collect only two hits but defeat the Athletics 5–2 at Huntington Grounds.

MAY 1   Bob Unglaub replaces George Huff as manager of the Red Sox. On his first day
             as manager, Unglaub hit a bases-loaded triple in the seventh inning to defeat the
             Yankees 4–3 at Huntington Grounds.

             *George Huff managed only eight games with the Red Sox, losing six of them.
             He returned to his job as athletic director at Illinois, a post he held until his
             death in 1936. Only twenty-six years old, Bob Unglaub had just taken over as
             Boston's starting first baseman. He lasted just 29 games as manager, posting a
             9–20 record, although he remained a player with the Red Sox until he was trad-
             ed to the Senators in July 1908. Unglaub died in 1916 at the age of thirty-five
             when the automobile he was driving was struck by a train in the Orangevale
             train yards in Baltimore.*

MAY 19   The Red Sox score four runs in the tenth inning to defeat the White Sox 4–0 in
             Chicago. Cy Young pitched the complete-game shutout.

MAY 20   The Red Sox purchase Bunk Congalton from the Indians.

MAY 30   The Red Sox score five runs in the ninth inning to defeat the Athletics 6–4 in the
             first game of a doubleheader in Philadelphia. Boston lost the first game, 3–1.

JUNE 7   The Red Sox trade Jimmy Collins to the Athletics for John Knight and purchase
             Deacon McGuire from the Yankees. The Red Sox immediately named McGuire to
             replace Bob Unglaub as manager.

             *Jimmy Collins was past his prime but gave the Athletics one solid season before
             retiring after the 1908 season. Knight proved to be an inadequate replacement
             for Collins at third base and was peddled to the Yankees after the 1908 season
             ended. Deacon McGuire had a long major league career as a catcher that lasted
             from 1884 through 1912. He was the first player to appear in 1,500 major
             league games as a catcher, a significant achievement in an era in which catchers
             wore thin gloves with little or no padding and no shinguards. By 1907, McGuire
             was forty-three years old and played five games over two seasons with Boston,
             each as a pinch hitter.*

JUNE 13   The Red Sox stage an exhibition game in Providence, Rhode Island, and donate the
             gate receipts to Chick Stahl's wife.

JUNE 22   The Red Sox rout the Yankees 12–2 at Huntington Grounds. After pinch hitting
             for pitcher Bill Hogg, Yankee manager Clark Griffith took the mound himself and
             gave up eight runs in the eighth inning. On the same day, the Red Sox traded Bill
             Dinneen to the Browns for Beany Jacobson.

             *Bill Dinneen had one more good season playing for the Browns, while Beany
             Jacobson lasted only two games in Boston to close his career with a 23–47 record.*

JUNE 27   Behind the pitching of Jesse Tannehill, the Red Sox defeat the Athletics 1–0 at
             Huntington Grounds. Denny Sullivan drove in the game's lone run with a single.

             *Red Sox owner John I. Taylor was on a campaign to speed up games during the
             summer of 1907. "This year, the games have been dragging a trifle too much in*

both the American and National Leagues, and it is my intention now to get after the players and umpires in our league and make them get a move on," Taylor said. "There is absolutely no reason why the regular nine-inning game should not be finished inside of one hour and forty-five minutes."

JUNE 28 — Jimmy Barrett's twelfth-inning walk-off home run secures a 4–3 Red Sox victory over the Athletics at Huntington Grounds.

The homer was the first that Jimmy Barrett had hit in the majors since 1903, the only one he struck in 1907, and the last of 16 he hit during a 10-year career.

JULY 10 — A two-hitter by George Winter defeats the Indians 5–0 in the first game of a doubleheader in Cleveland. The only Indians hits were singles by Joe Birmingham and Terry Turner. The Red Sox lost the second game, 2–0.

The Red Sox set a club record for lowest slugging percentage in 1907 with a mark of .299.

JULY 15 — The Red Sox beat the Browns 5–2 in 16 innings in St. Louis. The score was 1–1 before Boston scored four runs in the sixteenth. Both Jesse Tannehill of the Red Sox and Barney Peity of the Browns pitched complete games.

JULY 25 — Manager Deacon McGuire inserts himself into the second game of a doubleheader against the 1907 American League champion Detroit Tigers and hits a dramatic walk-off home run. With Detroit leading 2–1 with two out in the ninth inning at Huntington Grounds, McGuire pinch hit for pitcher Tex Pruett. With two strikes on him, McGuire hit a drive that landed on the steep bank in left field. The ball hopped over the left field fence, which, according to 1907 ground rules, was a home run. The Red Sox lost the game 3–2, however, in 11 innings. In the first game, the Sox won, 2–1.

The homer was the first one Deacon McGuire had hit in the majors since 1902. He acted as a pinch hitter four times for the Red Sox in 1907 and collected three hits. McGuire's homer was also the first pinch-hit homer in Red Sox history. There wouldn't be another one until 1916, when Babe Ruth hit a pinch homer.

AUGUST 1 — The Red Sox collect 22 hits and defeat the Indians 14–1 at Huntington Grounds. On the same day, the Red Sox purchased Cy Morgan from the St. Louis Browns.

AUGUST 7 — Cy Young pitches a complete game for the Red Sox in a 2–1, 14-inning victory over the White Sox at Huntington Grounds. A single by Heinie Wagner drove in the game winner.

Cy Young had a comeback season in 1907, compiling a 21–12 record, 33 complete games, 6 shutouts, 343 innings pitched, 147 strikeouts, and a 1.99 ERA.

AUGUST 17 — A shutout by Tex Pruett leads the Red Sox to a 1–0 win over the Browns in St. Louis.

Victories like this won were few and far between for Pruett. His career won-lost record was only 4–18, although three of his victories were shutouts.

AUGUST 18 A shutout by Cy Morgan gives the Red Sox consecutive 1–0 wins over the Browns in the first game of a doubleheader in St. Louis. The Red Sox also won the second game, 2–1.

AUGUST 22 Heinie Wagner hits two inside-the-park homers, but the Red Sox lose 8–7 to the 1907 American League champion Tigers in Detroit.

The homers were the first two of Wagner's career and the only two he hit in 1907. Wagner hit only 10 home runs during his 12-year major league career.

SEPTEMBER 2 On Labor Day, the Red Sox outslug the Yankees 12–1 in New York. The victory was Cy Young's 20th of the season. Originally, there were two games scheduled with separate admissions, but the morning game was rained out. Skies cleared in time for the afternoon contest, but it was played on a water-logged field.

SEPTEMBER 9 Behind the pinpoint pitching of Cy Young and Rube Waddell, the Red Sox and Athletics tie a record for the longest game in big-league history without a walk. The two clubs played to a 0–0 tie in 13 innings at Huntington Grounds.

Young's control was extraordinary throughout his career. He led his league in fewest walks per nine innings over an incredible 14 seasons. He was also second in the category twice, third once, and fourth once.

SEPTEMBER 11 John Knight's ninth-inning walk-off homer leads the Red Sox to a 4–3 win over the Athletics at Huntington Grounds. The homer was an inside-the-parker, hit over the head of Philadelphia center fielder Rube Oldring.

SEPTEMBER 12 Future Hall of Famer Tris Speaker makes his major league debut during a 7–1 loss to the Athletics at Huntington Grounds.

Only nineteen years old, Speaker entered the game as a substitute for Bunk Congalton in right field and was hitless in two at-bats. He was purchased by the Red Sox for $800 from Houston in the Texas League. The Red Sox thought so little of Speaker, however, that the club didn't invite him to spring training in 1908. He paid his own way to Marlin, Texas, and offered his services to the New York Giants, but manager John McGraw turned him away. Speaker asked the Sox for another chance and was allowed to train with the team, but he spent most of the 1908 season in the minors at Little Rock before becoming Boston's starting center fielder in 1909. He played for the Red Sox until a shocking trade sent him to the Indians just prior to the start of the 1916 season.

OCTOBER 3 A month before Oklahoma becomes the 46th state in the Union, the Red Sox end their 16-game losing streak by defeating the Browns 1–0 at Huntington Grounds. Cy Morgan pitched the shutout. The 16-game losing streak actually came in a span of 18 games. Two contests ended in ties.

DECEMBER 17 The Red Sox' team name becomes official in an announcement made by owner John I. Taylor.

1908   B

Season in a Sentence

The Red Sox show marked improvement over 1907 and finish the season four games under .500.

Finish • Won • Lost • Pct • GB

Fifth   75   79   .487   15.5

Managers

Deacon McGuire (53–62)
Fred Lake (22–17)

Stats

Stats	Red Sox	AL	Rank
Batting Avg:	.245	.239	2
On-Base Pct:	.295	.294	5
Slugging Pct:	.312	.304	2
Home Runs:	14		5
Stolen Bases:	167		4
ERA:	2.28	2.39	4
Fielding Pct:	.955	.958	6
Runs Scored:	564		3
Runs Allowed:	513		4

Starting Lineup

Lou Criger, c
Jake Stahl, 1b
Amby McConnell, 2b
Harry Lord, 3b
Heinie Wagner, ss
Jack Thoney, lf
Denny Sullivan, cf
Doc Gessler, rf
Gavvy Cravath, lf
Bob Unglaub, 1b
Bill Carrigan, c

Pitchers

Cy Young, sp
Cy Morgan, sp
Ed Cicotte, sp
Fred Butchell, sp
George Winter, sp
Elmer Steele, sp
Frank Arellanes, sp

Attendance

473,048 (third in AL)

Club Leaders

Batting Avg:	Gessler	.308
On-Base Pct:	Gessler	.394
Slugging Pct:	Gessler	.423
Home Runs:	Gessler	3
RBI:	Gessler	63
Runs:	Wagner	62
Stolen Bases:	McConnell	31
Wins:	Young	21
Strikeouts:	Young	150
ERA:	Young	1.26
Saves:	Three tied with 2	

APRIL 14   Two days after a fire destroys one-fourth of the Boston suburb of Chelsea and kills 19 people, a strong east wind chills the capacity crowd as the Red Sox defeat the Senators 3–1 on Opening Day at Huntington Grounds.

MAY 26   The Red Sox score seven runs in the third inning to take a 13–0 lead and coast to a 16–5 win over the White Sox at Huntington Grounds.

Top hitters for the Red Sox in 1908 were Doc Gessler, with a .308 average, 14 triples, and a league-leading on-base percentage of .394, and Amby McConnell, who batted .279. Gessler was a physician who graduated from Johns Hopkins Medical School.

MAY 30   Cy Young pitches a one-hitter to defeat the Senators 6–0 in the first game of a Memorial Day doubleheader at Huntington Grounds. Ex-Boston player Buck Freeman was the only batter to reach base off Young, connecting with a single. Washington won the second game, 7–4.

JUNE 6   The Red Sox hit into a triple play but defeat the 1908 American League champion Tigers 10–5 in Detroit.

JUNE 7	The Red Sox hit into a triple play but defeat the Tigers 9–5 in Detroit.

> *The 1908 Red Sox are the only team in baseball history to hit into a triple play in consecutive games. The Sox are also the only team to be the victims of two triple plays in a single game (see July 17, 1990).*

JUNE 9	The Indians score 10 runs in the fifth inning and rout the Red Sox 15–6 in Cleveland.
JUNE 10	The Red Sox score five runs in the eleventh inning and defeat the Indians 8–4 in Cleveland.
JUNE 25	Larry Gardner makes his major league debut in a 2–1, 13-inning win over the Senators at Huntington Grounds. As a late-inning substitute for Harry Lord at third base, Gardner had a double in two at-bats.

> *Gardner played for the Red Sox through the 1917 season. He appeared in 1,122 games for Boston and collected 1,106 hits.*

JUNE 30	Cy Young pitches the third no-hitter of his career, and his second with the Red Sox, to beat the Yankees 8–0 in New York. He also drove in four runs by hitting three singles. The only Yankee to reach base was Harry Niles, who walked leading off the first inning on a 3–2 pitch and was caught stealing. In the ninth inning, Young retired Wid Conroy on a leaping catch by Gavvy Cravath in left field, Walter Blair on a pop foul to catcher Lou Criger, and Joe Lake on a grounder to second baseman Amby McConnell. Young struck out only two batters in the no-hitter.

> *At forty-one, Young is the oldest pitcher in major league history to throw a no-hitter other than Nolan Ryan, who threw one at forty-three and another at forty-four. Despite his age, Young had a marvelous year in 1908. He was 21–11 with a 1.26 ERA and 30 complete games.*

Though acquired by the Red Sox at the age of 34, Cy Young gave the team eight good years of service on the mound.

Courtesy of Transcendental Graphics/theruckerarchive.com

JULY 11	The Red Sox trade Frank LaPorte to the New York Yankees for Jake Stahl, Harry Niles, and Harry Rhoades.

> *Stahl immediately became the Red Sox' starting first baseman. In 1912, he was*

named manager of the Red Sox and led the club to a World Championship in his first season.

AUGUST 13   A crowd of 20,000 attends Cy Young Day at Huntington Grounds as the Red Sox defeat a team of All-Stars from the other seven American League teams 3–2 in 11 innings. The Red Sox played in costumes, which included an admiral, a clown, and a cowboy. Manager Deacon McGuire was dressed as Uncle Sam, while Young appeared as a farmer. Political correctness definitely wasn't in vogue in 1908, as others were dressed as a "Chinaman," a "country dude," a "Swedish comedian," and an "Irish comedian," while another was in blackface in the style of the minstrel shows of the period. Young received cash gifts of close to $7,500 plus three silver loving cups, a traveling bag, and two big floral pieces.

AUGUST 24   Two months shy of his nineteenth birthday, Smoky Joe Wood makes his major league debut but allows six runs in only four innings to lose 6–4 to the White Sox at Huntington Grounds. Wood was purchased by the Red Sox for $7,000 from the Kansas City club in the American Association. Deacon McGuire made a pinch-hit appearance during the game. At forty-four years, nine months, and six days, he became the oldest player in Red Sox history.

AUGUST 28   Deacon McGuire resigns as manager of the Red Sox. His resignation came as a surprise, given the improvement of the Red Sox under his leadership, but he wasn't the first, and wouldn't be the last, manager to become disenchanted with the meddlesome, impulsive intrusions posed by owner John I. Taylor. McGuire was replaced by forty-one-year-old Fred Lake.

Lake was born in Nova Scotia and grew up in East Boston. At the time, he was employed as a scout for the Red Sox. McGuire went on to manage the Indians from 1909 through 1911 without bringing the club a winning record.

SEPTEMBER 9   Tris Speaker collects the first double of his major league career during a 5–4 loss to the Senators in Washington.

Speaker finished his career in 1928 with 792 doubles, a major league record. He also batted .345, scored 1,882 runs, drove in another 1,537, hit 222 triples (sixth best all time), stole 434 bases, and collected 3,514 hits. Speaker was as good defensively as he was with the bat and is the all-time leader among outfielders in assists (448) and double plays (139). He played an extremely shallow center field, often just a few steps behind second base after developing a great knack for racing back for a fly ball. His location made him a virtual fifth infielder. On the first Hall of Fame ballot in 1936, Speaker was seventh behind Ty Cobb, Babe Ruth, Honus Wagner, Christy Mathewson, Walter Johnson, and Nap Lajoie and just ahead of Cy Young, who was eighth. Speaker was elected to the Hall in 1937 along with Young.

SEPTEMBER 18   Indians pitcher Bob Rhoades pitches a no-hitter to defeat the Red Sox 2–1 at Cleveland. The Red Sox took a 1–0 lead in the second on a walk to Doc Gessler, followed by a sacrifice, an error, and a wild pitch. Cleveland came back to score single runs in the fourth and eighth.

SEPTEMBER 23   Cy Young wins his 21st game with a 4–1 decision over the Tigers in Detroit.

OCTOBER 3   Smoky Joe Wood earns the first victory of his career with a 5–0 win over the Athletics in Philadelphia in the second game of a doubleheader, shortened to six innings by darkness. The Red Sox lost the first game 8–7.

At 18 years, 11 months, and nine days, Wood is the youngest pitcher in Red Sox history to win a game and to pitch a shutout.

OCTOBER 5   King Brady pitches a shutout in his debut as a member of the Red Sox to defeat the Yankees 4–0 at Huntington Grounds.

The shutout was the only one of Brady's major league career. He pitched only one more game with Red Sox, a 2 2/3-inning relief stint in 1912. Previously, Brady appeared in six games, four of them starts, with the Phillies and Pirates between 1905 and 1907.

DECEMBER 12   Five weeks after the election of William Howard Taft as president, the Red Sox trade Lou Criger to the Browns for Tubby Spencer. Criger was Cy Young's personal catcher for the eight seasons they both played in Boston. The deal foreshadowed the trade of Young two months later (see February 18, 1909). Criger and Young were the only two members of the 1901 Red Sox still playing for the club in 1908.

1909   B

Season in a Sentence

With a transfusion of young talent, including Tris Speaker, Harry Hooper, and Smoky Joe Wood, the Red Sox continue to show improvement and remain in the pennant race until September.

Finish • Won • Lost • Pct • GB

Third   88   63   .583   9.5

Manager

Fred Lake

Stats   Red Sox • AL • Rank

Batting Avg:	.263	.244	2
On-Base Pct:	.321	.303	3
Slugging Pct:	.333	.309	3
Home Runs:	20		2
Stolen Bases:	215		2
ERA:	2.59	2.47	5
Fielding Pct:	.954	.957	7
Runs Scored:	597		3
Runs Allowed:	550		5

Starting Lineup

Bill Carrigan, c
Jake Stahl, 1b
Amby McConnell, 2b
Harry Lord, 3b
Heinie Wagner, ss
Harry Niles, lf-rf
Tris Speaker, cf
Doc Gessler, rf
Harry Hooper, lf
Pat Donahue, c
Charlie French, 2b-ss

Pitchers

Frank Arellanes, sp
Smoky Joe Wood, sp
Eddie Cicotte, sp
Charlie Chech, sp
Elmer Steele, sp-rp
Bill Schlitzer, sp-rp

Attendance

668,965 (second in AL)

Club Leaders

Batting Avg:	Lord	.311
On-Base Pct:	Stahl	.377
Slugging Pct:	Speaker	.443
Home Runs:	Speaker	7
RBI:	Speaker	77
Runs:	Lord	86
Stolen Bases:	Lord	36
Wins:	Arellanes	16
Strikeouts:	Wood	88
ERA:	Cicotte	1.95
Saves:	Arellanes	8

FEBRUARY 18   The Red Sox trade Cy Young to the Indians for Charlie Chech, Jack Ryan, and $12,500. The trade shocked Red Sox fans, who believed that Young would finish his career in Boston. Instead, Young went back to Cleveland, where he had pitched for the National League Spiders from 1890 through 1898. He was 19–15 with the Indians in 1909 before age caught up with him. Young finished his career in Boston, but with the Braves in 1911. Chech and Ryan won only 10 games between them while with the Red Sox.

Among Red Sox pitchers, Young stills ranks tied for first in wins (192), second in games started (297), first in complete games (275), tied for first in shutouts (38), second in innings pitched (2,728⅓), second in earned run average (2.00), and third in strikeouts (1,341).

Young ended his career with an all-time record 511 big-league victories. Walter Johnson is a distant second with 417. Young is also first all time in games started (815), first in complete games (749), first in innings pitched (7,355⅔), and fourth in shutouts (76). He won during a period in which there were constant changes in the game. During his career, the distance from the mound to home plate was increased from fifty feet to sixty feet, six inches. He won during the 1890s when hitters dominated the game, and in the "dead ball era" of the 1900s when pitchers held the advantage.

APRIL 12   In the first ever game at Shibe Park in Philadelphia, the Red Sox lose 8–1 to the Athletics before a capacity crowd of over 30,000.

Shibe Park was baseball's first double-decked ballpark constructed of concrete and steel. The Athletics played there until 1954, when the club moved to Kansas City. Renamed Connie Mack Stadium in 1953, Shibe was also the home of the Philadelphia Phillies from 1939 through 1970.

APRIL 16   Playing left field, future Hall of Famer Harry Hooper makes his major league debut in a 3–2 loss to the Senators in Washington. Hooper was twenty-one years old when he reached the majors.

Before entering professional baseball, Hooper earned a civil engineering degree from St. Mary's College in Oakland, California. He signed with the Red Sox after hitting .344 in 1908 for Sacramento in the California League. The Red Sox offered Hooper $2,500 to sign, but as a California native, he was reluctant to leave the West Coast. Boston owner John I. Taylor sweetened the deal by offering him $2,850 and promised him a job working on the design of the new ballpark that Taylor was planning. Hooper was never asked to contribute to the construction of Fenway Park, however, when it opened in 1912. Hooper did make a significant contribution as a player, remaining in the majors for 17 seasons, 12 of them with the Red Sox. In 1910, he was moved to right field and used his speed and powerful arm to become one of the best defensive outfielders in big-league history. Hooper had a career batting average of .281 and hit a home run an average of just once every 117 at-bats, but he was an effective catalyst at the top of the batting order because of his ability to draw walks. Hooper is also the only Red Sox player to compete in four World Series for the club, playing in 1912, 1915, 1916, and 1918. He finished his career with 2,466 hits and was elected to the Hall of Fame in 1971.

| April 19 | President William Howard Taft and Vice President James Sherman witness an 8–4 Red Sox win over the Senators in Washington. |

APRIL 19   President William Howard Taft and Vice President James Sherman witness an 8–4 Red Sox win over the Senators in Washington.

APRIL 21   In the home opener, the Red Sox pull off a triple steal, with Harry Lord swiping home, and defeat the Athletics, 6–2.

APRIL 26   Charlie Chech pitches a two-hitter to defeat the Yankees 1–0 at Huntington Grounds. Harry Lord's triple in the fifth inning plated the game's lone run. The only New York hits were a double by Red Kleinow and a single by George McConnell.

The shutout was the only one that Chech pitched while a member of the Red Sox.

APRIL 28   Aided by nine Yankee errors, the Red Sox drub the New Yorkers 12–2 at Huntington Grounds.

MAY 4   Cy Morgan throws a two-hitter but loses 1–0 to the Senators at Huntington Grounds. The lone run of the game scored when Morgan committed a balk with Clyde Milan on third base.

MAY 16   A 3–2 win over the Tigers in Detroit ends in a fight. George Moriarty of the Tigers tried to steal home with two outs in the ninth but was tagged out by Boston catcher Bill Carrigan. The two began throwing punches, and during the fracas, Carrigan struck Moriarty as he lay on the ground. Carrigan needed a police escort to leave the premises. Both he and Moriarty were suspended for one game by American League president Ban Johnson.

JUNE 1   The Red Sox and Athletics each post 1–0 wins in Philadelphia. The opener lasted 11 innings, with Jack Ryan pitching for Boston and taking the hard-luck defeat. Eddie Cicotte and Fred Burchell combined to shut out the Athletics in the nightcap. Tris Speaker's single in the eighth inning drove in the only run of the game. Speaker also had an unassisted double play in the game.

In his first full season in the majors, Speaker hit .309, swatted 7 homers, and collected 168 hits. This was the first of a major league record six career unassisted double plays for Speaker, four of which were with the Red Sox. Speaker also pulled off the only unassisted double play in World Series history in 1912. Each of the double plays were accomplished with Speaker, playing his customary shallow position in center field, catching a fly ball and racing in toward the infield to double a runner off second. The only other Red Sox outfielders with unassisted double plays are Tilly Walker in 1916, Dom DiMaggio in 1942, and Leon Culberson in 1945.

JUNE 2   Down 5–0, the Red Sox score two runs in the seventh inning and four in the eighth to defeat the Tigers 6–4 at Huntington Grounds.

JUNE 21   Smoky Joe Wood pitches a two-hitter to defeat the Athletics 4–1 in the second game of a doubleheader at Huntington Grounds. The only Philadelphia hits were singles by Topsy Hartsel and Frank Baker. The Red Sox also won the first game, 6–5.

Harry Lord hit .311 with 86 runs scored, 166 hits, and 36 stolen bases for the Red Sox in 1909.

JUNE 23

The Red Sox collect 21 hits and rout the Yankees 14–5 at Huntington Grounds.

The Red Sox drew a then-record 668,965 into Huntington Grounds in 1909. Despite winning four World Championships between 1912 and 1918 in brand-spanking-new Fenway Park, Boston's 1909 attendance mark stood until 1940.

JUNE 30

Umpire Fred (Bull) Perrine is escorted off the field by the Boston police at the close of a doubleheader in which the Red Sox lose 5–4 and 6–2 to the Athletics at Huntington Grounds. Perrine aroused the hostility with a number of calls the Red Sox crowd thought were unjust.

JULY 6

Red Sox pitcher Larry Pape tosses a four-hit shutout in his major league debut to defeat the Senators 2–0 in the second game of a doubleheader at Huntington Grounds. Boston also won the opener, 3–2.

Pape pitched only one more major league shutout and finished his career with a 13–9 record.

JULY 17

Smoky Joe Wood strikes out 10 batters during a four-inning relief stint, securing a 6–4 win over the Indians in Cleveland.

JULY 19

Indians shortstop Neal Ball pulls off the first unassisted triple play in major league history during a 6–1 Red Sox loss in the first game of a doubleheader in Cleveland. With Heinie Wagner on second base and Jake Stahl on first in the second inning, Amby McConnell hit a vicious liner to Ball. The infielder stepped on second to force out Wagner and tagged out Stahl, who was two strides from second. It was the first officially recognized unassisted triple play in major league history. In the bottom of the second, Ball hit a home run, his first in the majors. He hit only four in 1,609 career at-bats. The Red Sox won the second game, 8–2.

AUGUST 3

An overflow crowd of 29,781 at Huntington Grounds, the largest ever assembled in Boston at the time, watches the Red Sox beat the Tigers 2–1 and 8–7 in a doubleheader. The Sox captured the second game with two runs in the ninth. There were 7 doubles in the first game and 15 in the second due to a ground rule that stipulated any ball hit into the crowd ringing the outfield was a two-base hit.

AUGUST 18

The Red Sox win their 10th and 11th games in a row with a 3–0 and 6–3 sweep of the Yankees in New York.

The wins gave the Red Sox a 67–44 record and put them one game behind the first-place Athletics. The Sox faded, however, and were out of the race by mid-September. The Tigers overtook the Athletics to win the pennant.

SEPTEMBER 9

The Red Sox trade Doc Gessler to the Senators for Charlie Smith.

SEPTEMBER 11

The Red Sox and Athletics trade 1–0 wins in Philadelphia for the second time during the 1909 season. The Athletics won the first game and the Red Sox captured the nightcap. Smoky Joe Wood pitched the Boston shutout, with Jake Stahl providing the RBI with a double in the seventh inning.

Stahl hit .294 with six homers for the Red Sox in 1909.

OCTOBER 2   On the last day of the season, future Hall of Famer Jack Chesbro pitches his last big-league game in his only appearance as a member of the Red Sox, losing 6–5 to the Yankees at Huntington Grounds in the first game of a doubleheader. The Yankees also won the second game, 1–0.

OCTOBER 9   It takes five years, but the Red Sox and New York Giants finally meet in a postseason series. This one was a mere exhibition instead of the World Series, but the Sox took a measure of revenge for the Giants' backing out of the 1904 Fall Classic by winning four of the five games.

NOVEMBER 1   The Red Sox let Fred Lake go as manager. Despite the improvement the club showed under Lake's leadership, John I. Taylor felt that Lake's salary demands for the upcoming 1910 season were too high. Patsy Donovan was hired to replace Lake.

Donovan was born in Queenstown, Ireland, in 1865 and was one of the better outfielders in baseball during a 17-year playing career that began in 1890. He had previously managed the Pirates, Cardinals, Senators, and Dodgers between 1897 and 1908, accumulating a record of 525–732, and failed to finish a season with his club higher in the standings than fourth place. Lake went across town to manage the Braves in 1910 and thudded into last place.

THE STATE OF THE RED SOX

The Red Sox reached the World Series four times between 1910 and 1920 and won all four, defeating the New York Giants in 1912, the Philadelphia Phillies in 1915, the Brooklyn Dodgers in 1916, and the Chicago Cubs in 1918. Overall, Boston had a record of 857–624 during the decade. Their winning percentage of .579 was the best in the American League and the second best in the majors to the Giants, who were 889–597. John McGraw's Giants also played in the World Series four times during the 1910s but failed to win any of them. The other clubs to win the American League pennant in the decade were the Philadelphia Athletics (1910, 1911, 1913, and 1914) and the Chicago White Sox (1917 and 1919).

THE BEST TEAM

The 1912 Red Sox were 105–47, won the AL by 14 games, and beat the Giants in the World Series. Their 105 victories still stand as the club record.

THE WORST TEAM

The only team with a losing record was the 1919 outfit, which was defending world champion. The 1919 Sox were 66–71 and finished sixth. It was their first of 15 consecutive losing seasons.

THE BEST MOMENT

With the help of some errors by the New York Giants defense, the Red Sox scored two runs in the bottom of the tenth to win the final game of the 1912 World Series, 4–3.

THE WORST MOMENT

The Red Sox, conspiring with the Cubs, nearly went on strike during the 1918 World Series.

THE ALL–DECADE TEAM • YEARS WITH BRS

Bill Carrigan, c	1906; 1908–16
Dick Hoblitzel, 1b	1914–17
Steve Yerkes, 2b	1909; 1911–14
Larry Gardner, 3b	1908–17
Heinie Wagner, ss	1906–16; 1918
Duffy Lewis, lf	1910–17
Tris Speaker, cf	1907–15
Harry Hooper, rf	1909–20
Smoky Joe Wood, p	1908–15
Babe Ruth, p	1914–19
Dutch Leonard, p	1913–18
Carl Mays, p	1915–19

Ruth is listed as a pitcher, but by the end of the decade was playing in the outfield and was the best power-hitting threat in the game. Ruth, Speaker, and Hooper are all in the Hall of Fame. Gardner ranked with the top third basemen of the era and had a career comparable to many currently enshrined at Cooperstown. Other outstanding Red Sox during the 1910s were pitchers Ray Collins (1909–15), Ernie Shore (1914–17), Rube Foster (1913–17), and Eddie Cicotte (1908–12), shortstop Everett Scott (1914–21), catcher Wally Schang (1918–20), and first baseman Snuffy McInnis (1918–21).

THE DECADE LEADERS

Batting Avg:	Speaker	.347
On-Base Pct:	Speaker	.425
Slugging Pct:	Speaker	.498
Home Runs:	Ruth	49
RBI:	Lewis	629
Runs:	Hooper	868
Stolen Bases:	Hooper	269
Wins:	Wood	105
Strikeouts:	Wood	887
ERA:	Wood	1.95
Saves:	Mays	12

THE HOME FIELD

The Red Sox began the decade at Huntington Grounds, which had been the club's home since their founding in 1901. In 1912, the Sox moved into Fenway Park. Unlike Huntington Grounds, which was constructed of wood, the main Fenway Park grandstand was built of steel and concrete, but much of the rest of the ballpark was wood, and the interior of the ballpark had a much different appearance than it does today. When it opened, Fenway had wooden bleachers along the left field line, a wooden pavilion in right field, and wooden bleachers in extreme right and center. In addition to the ballpark's irregular contour, adhering to the plot of land on which it was built, there was a ten-foot embankment in front of the left field fence. In time, the incline became known as "Duffy's Cliff" in tribute to Duffy Lewis, who raced up and down the embankment with ease in pursuit of fly balls.

THE GAME YOU WISH YOU HAD SEEN

Playing the Senators on June 23, 1917, starting pitcher Babe Ruth was ejected after he struck the umpire following a walk to the leadoff batter. Ernie Shore picked the runner off first, then retired 26 batters in a row.

THE WAY THE GAME WAS PLAYED

Pitching and defense continued to dominate baseball. Offense spiked after the AL adopted the cork-centered ball in 1910, but by the mid-teens, the league batting average was back around .250. There were more than twice as many triples as home runs, and speedy outfielders were necessary to cover playing fields that were much larger than those common today. AL pitchers completed 56 percent of their starts, still a significant drop from the 79 percent of the previous decade. Between 1910 and 1920, the strategic use of relief pitching, pinch hitters, and platooning became important aspects of the game for the first time.

THE MANAGEMENT

The Red Sox were successful in spite of almost constant change at the top of the organization. John I. Taylor, who bought the Sox in 1904, sold half of his share to Jimmy McAleer and Robert McRoy in 1911. McAleer sold his one-fourth share to Joe Lannin in 1913. Lannin bought out McRoy and Taylor in 1914 and became sole owner. Lannin sold the club to New York theatrical producers Harry Frazee and

Hugh Ward in 1916. The field managers were Patsy Donovan (1910–11), Jake Stahl (1912–13), Bill Carrigan (1913–16), Jack Barry (1917), and Ed Barrow (1918–20). The Sox' four world titles of the decade came under Stahl (1912), Carrigan (1915 and 1916), and Barrow (1918).

THE BEST PLAYER MOVE

The best player move was the purchase of Babe Ruth from the Baltimore Orioles of the International League (see July 9, 1914). The second-best move was the conversion of Ruth from a pitcher into an outfielder in 1918.

THE WORST PLAYER MOVE

The Red Sox traded Tris Speaker to the Indians (see April 8, 1916).

1910   B

Season in a Sentence

After three seasons of steady improvement, the Red Sox take a step backward to finish a disappointing fourth.

Finish • Won • Lost • Pct • GB

Fourth   81   72   .529   22.5

Manager

Patsy Donovan

Stats   Red Sox • AL • Rank

	Red Sox	AL	Rank
Batting Avg:	.259	.243	3
On-Base Pct:	.323	.308	3
Slugging Pct:	.351	.308	2
Home Runs:	43		1
Stolen Bases:	194		4
ERA:	2.45	2.52	3
Fielding Pct:	.954	.956	6
Runs Scored:	638		3
Runs Allowed:	564		4

Starting Lineup

Bill Carrigan, c
Jake Stahl, 1b
Larry Gardner, 2b
Clyde Engle, 3b-2b
Heinie Wagner, ss
Duffy Lewis, lf
Tris Speaker, cf
Harry Hooper, rf
Harry Lord, 3b
Billy Purtell, 3b
Red Kleinow, c

Pitchers

Eddie Cicotte, sp
Ray Collins, sp
Ed Karger, sp
Charlie Smith, sp
Frank Arellanes, sp
Smoky Joe Wood, rp-sp
Sea Lion Hall, rp-sp

Attendance

584,619 (second in AL)

Club Leaders

Batting Avg:	Speaker	.340
On-Base Pct:	Speaker	.404
Slugging Pct:	Speaker	.468
Home Runs:	Stahl	10
RBI:	Stahl	77
Runs:	Speaker	92
Stolen Bases:	Hooper	40
Wins:	Cicotte	15
Strikeouts:	Wood	145
ERA:	Collins	1.62
Saves:	Four tied with 1	

APRIL 14   The Red Sox and Yankees battle to a 14-inning, 4–4 tie on Opening Day in New York. The game was called because of darkness. The assemblage at Hilltop Park was so large that 6,000 fans crowded onto the playing field. The Red Sox led 3–0 in the third inning, but the Yankees battled back to tie the contest in the eighth. Eddie Cicotte, in relief of Smoky Joe Wood, pitched seven innings of scoreless relief.

APRIL 16   Duffy Lewis makes his major league debut, subbing for Harry Hooper in left field during a 4–2 loss to the Yankees in New York.

Hooper soon moved to right field, and Lewis established himself as the starter in left. Hooper, Lewis, and Tris Speaker formed one of the best outfields in baseball history, particularly on defense. The threesome was together from 1910 through 1915. Speaker hit .340 for the Red Sox in 1910, with 183 hits and 92 runs scored. Jake Stahl was Boston's top power hitter with an American League high of 10 home runs to go with 77 runs batted in and 16 triples. Lewis batted .283 and had 29 doubles.

APRIL 19   In the home opener, the Red Sox win both ends of a Patriots' Day doubleheader against the Senators. In the first game, played in the morning before 14,721, the Sox took a 2–1 decision. In the afternoon encounter, Boston scored three runs in the ninth inning on a walk and three singles off Walter Johnson to defeat Washington 5–4 with a crowd of 31,007.

Mayor John F. Fitzgerald, grandfather of future President John F. Kennedy, threw out the first ball.

APRIL 21   Jake Stahl hits a grand slam off Bob Groom in the second inning of a 10–3 win over the Senators at Huntington Grounds. In the eighth inning, catcher Bill Carrigan and pitcher Ed Karger hit back-to-back homers, a rarity in the dead-ball era. It was the only time between 1902 and 1923 that Red Sox batters hit consecutive homers.

APRIL 23   Tris Speaker pulls off an unassisted double play, but the Red Sox lose 5–3 in 11 innings to the Athletics at Huntington Grounds.

APRIL 27   The Red Sox score seven runs in the eighth inning and slaughter the Senators 11–1 in Washington.

MAY 2   The Athletics rally for five runs in the ninth inning to beat the Red Sox 7–6 in Philadelphia.

MAY 28   Duffy Lewis hits a fluke home run during a 9–3 loss to the 1910 World Champion Athletics at Huntington Grounds. In the seventh inning, Duffy's hard grounder hit the shins of Philadelphia third baseman Frank "Home Run" Baker and bounded into in the grandstand.

> *According to the ground rules of the day, any ball that reached the seats after landing in fair territory was considered a home run. Beginning in 1930, hits that bounced into the stands were ground-rule doubles.*

MAY 31   Cy Morgan pitches the Red Sox to a 1–0 win over the Athletics in the first game of a doubleheader at Huntington Grounds. The lone run of the game was scored in the ninth inning on a throwing error by Athletics shortstop Jack Barry. Philadelphia won the second game, 4–2.

JUNE 29   The Red Sox defeat the athletics 6–4 in 15 innings at Shibe Park. The Sox scored three runs in the top of the fifteenth before staving off a Philadelphia rally in the bottom half of the inning. Larry Gardner drove in the first two fifteenth-inning runs with a triple and scored on a single by Duffy Lewis.

JULY 4   The Red Sox defeat the Senators 3–2 in 14 innings in the opener of a twin bill in Washington. Boston completed the sweep with a 6–3 triumph in the nightcap.

JULY 12   The Red Sox hammer the Indians 17–5 at Huntington Grounds.

JULY 14   Ray Collins pitches a shutout to defeat the White Sox 1–0 in the first game of a doubleheader at Huntington Grounds. The Red Sox also won the second game, 6–2.

JULY 19   Ed Karger pitches a 14-inning complete game, a 2–1 victory over the Tigers at Huntington Grounds. The Red Sox earned a sweep with a 6–2 win in the second game.

AUGUST 9   The Red Sox play at Comiskey Park in Chicago for the first time and lose 7–4 to the White Sox. On the same day, the Red Sox traded Harry Lord and Amby McConnell to the White Sox for Frank Smith and Billy Purtell.

AUGUST 23   The Red Sox overcome an 11–6 deficit in the sixth inning to defeat the Browns 13–11 at Huntington Grounds. Smoky Joe Wood hit the first homer of his career with a man on in the seventh inning to tie the score 11–11. Billy Purtell hit a freak homer during the comeback that glanced off the head of Browns third baseman Art Griggs and bounced into the bleachers.

This was the only homer that Purtell hit while playing for the Red Sox, and one of only two he struck during a five-year, 333-game career.

AUGUST 26   Eddie Cicotte pitches a two-hitter to defeat the Indians 3–0 at Huntington Grounds. The only Cleveland hits were a double by Nap Lajoie and a single by Neal Ball.

AUGUST 30   In yet another low-hit performance by a Boston pitcher, Ray Collins throws a one-hitter to beat the White Sox 4–0 at Huntington Grounds. The only Chicago hit was a single by Paul Meloan.

The victory was the eighth in a row for the Red Sox. Boston was in second place at the end of August, though a distant 11 games behind the Athletics. The Sox faded to fourth place by losing 24 of their last 33 games.

1911   B

Season in a Sentence

The Red Sox regress for the second straight season and finish in the second division, only three games above .500.

Finish • Won • Lost • Pct • GB

Fifth   78   75   .510   24.0

Manager

Patsy Donovan

Stats   Red Sox • AL • Rank

Batting Avg:	.275	.273	4
On-Base Pct:	.350	.338	3
Slugging Pct:	.363	.358	4
Home Runs:	35		1
Stolen Bases:	190		7
ERA:	2.74	3.34	1
Fielding Pct:	.949	.953	6
Runs Scored:	680		6
Runs Allowed:	643		3

Starting Lineup

Bill Carrigan, c
Clyde Engle, 1b
Heinie Wagner, 2b-ss
Larry Gardner, 3b-2b
Steve Yerkes, ss
Duffy Lewis, lf
Tris Speaker, cf
Harry Hooper, rf
Rip Williams, 1b-c
Les Nunamaker, c
Joe Riggert, lf-cf

Pitchers

Smoky Joe Wood, sp
Eddie Cicotte, sp
Ray Collins, sp
Larry Pape, sp
Ed Karger, sp
Sea Lion Hall, rp-sp

Attendance

503,961 (third in AL)

Club Leaders

Batting Avg:	Speaker	.334
On-Base Pct:	Speaker	.418
Slugging Pct:	Speaker	.502
Home Runs:	Speaker	8
RBI:	Lewis	86
Runs:	Hooper	93
Stolen Bases:	Hooper	38
Wins:	Wood	23
Strikeouts:	Wood	231
ERA:	Wood	2.02
Saves:	Wood	3

APRIL 12   The Red Sox open the season in Washington, and after taking a 4–0 lead, lose 8–5 to the Senators. President William Howard Taft threw out the first pitch. Also in attendance was Vice President James Sherman, several congressmen, and members of the Cabinet.

Taft began the presidential tradition of throwing out the first pitch on Opening Day in Washington in 1910. A fire had destroyed the Senators' ballpark on March 17. It had been only partially rebuilt, with concrete and steel instead of wood, by the time the season started.

The Red Sox trained at Redondo Beach, a town just south of Los Angeles, during the spring of 1911.

APRIL 18   The Red Sox score seven runs in the seventh inning and six in the ninth to defeat the 1911 Athletics 13–5 in Philadelphia.

APRIL 21   In their home opener, the Red Sox down the Athletics 13–4 at Huntington Grounds.

APRIL 22   Playing through periodic snow flurries, the Red Sox defeat the Athletics 4–3 in 10 innings at Huntington Grounds.

MAY 4   Smoky Joe Wood pitches a two-hitter to defeat the Yankees 2–0 at Hilltop Park. The Yankees hit only two balls as far as the outfield. The only New York hits were singles by Birdie Cree and Ray Caldwell.

At only twenty-one years of age, Wood broke loose in 1911 with a 23–17 record, a 2.02 earned run average, 231 strikeouts, 277 innings pitched, and 5 shutouts.

MAY 5   The Red Sox outplay the Yankees to win 14–6 in New York.

MAY 11   The Red Sox sell Frank Smith to the Reds.

MAY 13   The Red Sox recover from a nine-run deficit to defeat the Tigers 13–11 in 10 innings in Detroit after trailing 10–1 in the fifth inning and 10–4 in the eighth. With an incredible rally, the Sox plated seven runs in the ninth to take an 11–10 lead but allowed the Tigers to tie the game in their half of the inning. Two tallies in the tenth won the game for the Sox. Duffy Lewis keyed the comeback with a grand slam in the ninth off Ed Willett. Ty Cobb also hit a grand slam for the Tigers.

MAY 29   The Red Sox score eight runs in the third inning and beat the Senators 12–0 in the first game of a doubleheader in Washington. The Sox completed the sweep with a 7–6 victory in the second tilt.

JUNE 24   Owner John I. Taylor announces plans to build a new ballpark in the Fenway section of Boston that eventually becomes known as Fenway Park. The plot was owned by the Fenway Realty Company, in which the Taylors were one of the large stockholders. Plans called for a large steel-and-concrete grandstand, wooden bleachers in left field, a right field pavilion, and a large wooden bleacher in extreme right and center field.

Fenway Park was part of a building boom in baseball. Shibe Park in Philadelphia and Forbes Field in Pittsburgh opened in 1909, the first with steel-and-concrete stands. *Those parks were followed by such classics as Comiskey Park in Chicago (1910), the Polo Grounds in New York (1911), Tiger Stadium in Detroit (1912), Crosley Field in Cincinnati (1912), Ebbets Field in Brooklyn (1913), Wrigley Field in Chicago (1914), and Braves Field in Boston (1915). Fenway was also part of a building boom in Boston. As late as 1880, when the city was already 250 years old, the section around present-day Fenway Park was a fetid, swampy saltwater marsh and flooded with sewage that collected from runoff of the Muddy River and Stony Brook. A similar problem plagued the Back Bay, but beginning in 1857, the city began a gigantic landfill project that transformed the area into one of the greatest urban neighborhoods in the country.*

To fix the problem with the Muddy River and Stony Brook, a tidal gate was built to control the sewage problem, and more landfill created the Back Bay Fens and a new residential area called Fenway and Kenmore Square. This created new real estate opportunities, and the Taylor family bought up much of the land and established the Fenway Realty Company. Present-day Fenway Park was a part of the tract purchased and developed by the Taylors. In part, the ballpark was constructed and named Fenway Park to promote this relatively new area of Boston and the Taylor's real estate holdings.

Courtesy of Transcendental Graphics/theruckerarchive.com

Modern, solidly built Fenway Park was a vast improvement over Huntington Grounds, the Red Sox' previous home. The name was no coincidence, as the park anchored new developments around the marshy fens of the Back Bay. The park opened for play in 1912.

JUNE 27   Stuffy McInnis of the Athletics angers the Red Sox by hitting a fluke home run during Philadelphia's 7–3 win at Huntington Grounds. As a timesaving device, American League president Ban Johnson prohibited warm-up pitches between innings. Sox pitcher Ed Karger threw one anyway, and McInnis leaped into the batter's box and stroked the ball into center field. The Red Sox fielders had not yet taken their positions, and none of them pursued the hit by McInnis, who gleefully circled the bases. The umpires upheld the home run despite vigorous protests from Red Sox manager Patsy Donovan.

JULY 3   Trailing 6–1, the Red Sox score one run in the fifth inning, one in the seventh, and five in the eighth to beat the Senators 8–6 at Huntington Grounds.

JULY 7   Smoky Joe Wood carries a no-hitter into the ninth inning against the Browns before Burt Shotton hits a single with one out. Wood struck out 15 batters in the one-hit, 6–1 win in St. Louis.

JULY 29   Smoky Joe Wood pitches a no-hitter to defeat the Browns 5–0 in the first game of a doubleheader at Huntington Grounds. Wood struck out 12, walked 2, and hit a batter. In the ninth inning, Dode Criss grounded out, Burt Shotton flied out to left field, and Jimmy Austin struck out. The Browns won the second game 5–4.

JULY 31   Ray Collins (eight innings) and Smoky Joe Wood (one inning) combine to pitch a two-hitter to defeat the Browns 3–2 in the first game of a doubleheader at Huntington Grounds. The only St. Louis hits, both off Collins, were singles by Willie Hogan and Frank LaPorte. The Browns won the second game by the same 3–2 score.

AUGUST 27   Future Hall of Famer Ed Walsh pitches a no-hitter against the Red Sox to give the White Sox a 5–0 win at Comiskey Park. The only Boston base runner was Clyde Engle, who reached on a walk. The final out was recorded when Joe Riggert lined to Chicago second baseman Amby McConnell.

SEPTEMBER 9   Red Sox pitcher Buck O'Brien pitches a shutout in his major league debut to defeat the Athletics 2–0 in Philadelphia.

SEPTEMBER 14   Jimmy McAleer and Robert B. McRoy purchase a half interest in the Red Sox. The Taylor family no longer wanted to be burdened with sole responsibility for running the Sox, but it still owned the other half of the club's shares.

Before coming to Boston, McAleer spent 11 seasons as a manager with the Indians (1901), Browns (1902–09), and Senators (1910–11). During the 1890s, he was a hustling, brawling, good-field, no-hit outfielder with the National League's Cleveland Spiders. On January 4, 1912, McAleer was elected president of the Red Sox. John I. Taylor was named vice president and Robert McRoy treasurer. New Fenway Park wasn't part of the deal. The Taylors still owned the ballpark and the land. Under the new arrangement, McAleer was in charge of choosing a new manager and of player trades and acquisitions. McRoy handled the business affairs, while the Taylors supervised the construction of Fenway.

SEPTEMBER 16   Behind the pitching of Smoky Joe Wood and Buck O'Brien, the Red Sox shut out the Indians in a doubleheader at Huntington Grounds. Wood won the opener 6–0, while O'Brien struck out 12 batters and captured the nightcap, 3–0.

The shutout was O'Brien's second in two big-league starts. In between, on September 12, he pitched 1$\frac{2}{3}$ innings of relief during a 6–5 win over the Senators in Washington. His streak of 19$\frac{2}{3}$ scoreless innings at the beginning of his career ended in the first inning of a start against the Tigers in Boston on September 21, which he lost 2–1. O'Brien ended the 1911 season with a 5–1 record and a microscopic 0.38 ERA. Already twenty-nine years old when he made his debut, O'Brien wouldn't have long-lasting success. He was 20–13 in 1912 and had a 2.58 earned run average, but arm troubles derailed him, and he was only 4–11 in 1913, his last season in the majors.

SEPTEMBER 23   The Red Sox pound the Browns 14–2 at Huntington Grounds.

Tris Speaker was Boston's top hitter in 1911 with a .334 batting average and eight home runs.

SEPTEMBER 25   Ground is broken for the construction of Fenway Park.

OCTOBER 3   Smoky Joe Wood strikes out 13 batters in a 7–0 win over the Yankees in the second game of a doubleheader in New York that was called on account of darkness after eight innings. It was Wood's 23rd win of the season. The Sox also won the first game, 4–1.

OCTOBER 7   In their final game at Huntington Grounds, the Red Sox defeat the Senators, 8–1.

The Huntington Grounds site is now part of Northeastern University. There is a full-size statue of Cy Young where the pitcher's mound used to be (in the Churchill Hall Mall). About sixty feet away, a plaque in the shape of home plate marks the spot where modern baseball's first World Series took place. Additionally, there is a World Series Exhibit Room in nearby Cabot Physical Education Center with memorabilia from the 1901–11 Red Sox teams, and another plaque attached to the side of the building marks where the left field foul pole stood.

1912   B

Season in a Sentence

The Red Sox easily outdistance their American League foes with a club-record 105 victories and defeat the Giants in one of the most exciting World Series in history.

Finish • Won • Lost • Pct • GB

First   105   49   .691   +14.0

World Series—The Red Sox defeated the New York Giants four games to three with one tie.

Manager

Jake Stahl

Stats   Red Sox • AL • Rank

	Red Sox	AL	Rank
Batting Avg:	.277	.265	2
On-Base Pct:	.355	.333	1
Slugging Pct:	.380	.348	1
Home Runs:	29		1
Stolen Bases:	175		7
ERA:	2.76	3.34	2
Fielding Pct:	.957	.952	2
Runs Scored:	799		1
Runs Allowed:	544		1

Starting Lineup

Bill Carrigan, c
Jake Stahl, 1b
Steve Yerkes, 2b
Larry Gardner, 3b
Heinie Wagner, ss
Duffy Lewis, lf
Tris Speaker, cf
Harry Hooper, rf
Clyde Engle, 1b-2b

Pitchers

Smoky Joe Wood, sp
Buck O'Brien, sp
Hugh Bedient, sp
Ray Collins, sp
Sea Lion Hall, sp

Attendance

597,096 (second in AL)

Club Leaders

Batting Avg:	Speaker	.383
On-Base Pct:	Speaker	.464
Slugging Pct:	Speaker	.567
Home Runs:	Speaker	10
RBI:	Lewis	109
Runs:	Speaker	136
Stolen Bases:	Speaker	52
Wins:	Wood	34
Strikeouts:	Wood	258
ERA:	Wood	1.91
Saves:	Bedient	2

JANUARY 14   Jake Stahl is engaged as player-manager. Stahl sat out the 1911 season to become vice president of the Woodlawn Trust and Savings Bank in Chicago, which his in-laws owned. Previously, Stahl managed the Senators to a pair of seventh-place finishes in 1905 and 1906. He was also given a piece of stock in the new ownership setup.

APRIL 6   Two months after New Mexico is granted statehood, and seven weeks after Arizona becomes the 48th state, the Red Sox play the Reds in the first game ever at Cincinnati's Redland Field. Boston won the exhibition contest, 13–1. Redland Field was renamed Crosley Field in 1934 and served as the home of the Cincinnati club until 1970.

APRIL 9   Amid snow flurries, the Red Sox open Fenway Park to the public for the first time, defeating Harvard University 2–0 in an exhibition game.

> *A unique feature of Fenway Park was a steep ten-foot embankment in left and center fields that was nicknamed "Duffy's Cliff" because of the skill Red Sox left fielder Duffy Lewis displayed in fielding baseballs on the hillside.*

APRIL 11   On Opening Day, the Red Sox score four runs in the ninth inning and defeat the Yankees 5–3 in New York.

APRIL 18   Three days after the sinking of the Titanic, the Red Sox' first regular-season game at Fenway Park, slated against the Yankees, is postponed by rain.

APRIL 19   Fenway's regular-season debut is postponed once again as rain wipes out a Patriots' Day doubleheader against the Yankees.

> *The American League schedule had been purposely set up on a holiday weekend to virtually assure the Red Sox of four sellouts to start the 1912 season. With the rival Yankees as the opposition, the opener on the 18th was to be followed by a two-admission doubleheader on Patriot's Day and another single game on Saturday the twentieth. The rain, combined with the general nationwide gloom, intense newspaper coverage, and distractions surrounding the Titanic disaster, threw those plans into the dumper.*

APRIL 20   With 27,000 attending, the Red Sox finally play a regular-season game at Fenway Park and overcome a 5–1, third-inning deficit to defeat the Yankees 7–6 in 11 innings as a "Sea Lion" defeats a "Hippo." Buck O'Brien started for the Red Sox and put the club in a 5–1 hole in the third inning. The home team rallied with three in the fourth and tied it 5–5 in the sixth. Both teams scored in the eighth. In the eleventh, Steve Yerkes reached second on an error by Yankee third baseman Cozy Dolan and scored on a single by Tris Speaker. Yerkes had five hits, including two doubles, in seven at-bats but also committed three errors at second base. Sea Lion Hall, so nicknamed because of his deep, booming voice, was the winning pitcher. The loser was New York's Hippo Vaughn.

APRIL 26   Red Sox first baseman Hugh Bradley hits the first home run at Fenway Park. The ball sailed over the left field wall during Boston's 7–6 win over the Athletics.

> *This was the second of only two homers that Bradley hit during a five-year career that covered 277 games and 913 at-bats.*

MAY 8   The Red Sox sell a young Jack Fournier to the White Sox.

             *The Red Sox made a miscalculation by dealing Fournier. He spent 15 seasons in
             the majors as a first baseman and batted .313.*

MAY 13   The Red Sox score nine runs in the second inning and beat the Browns 14–9 at
             Fenway Park. Nine different Boston players scored in the inning.

MAY 17   The Red Sox formally dedicate Fenway Park but surrender four runs in the ninth
             inning and lose 5–2 to the White Sox.

             *There were concerns early in the season about the small crowds at Fenway
             Park. "The fact that the park is not as handy to reach and get away from as the
             old park has hurt some," wrote Tim Murnane in the May 16, 1912, edition of
             The Sporting News, "and will until people get accustomed to journeying in the
             new direction." Fans complained that the less-expensive bleacher section was
             farther away from the action at Fenway Park than the stands were at Hunting-
             ton Grounds. "On account of the size of the park, and the entrances being on
             two widely separated ends of the grounds, I find much of the sociability gone,"
             Murnane added. Despite the leap from fifth place in 1911 to first along with the
             attraction of a new ballpark in 1912, attendance increased only 18 percent, from
             503,961 to 597,096.*

MAY 29   The Red Sox and Senators combine to score 52 runs during a doubleheader at Fen-
             way Park. The Sox won both games by scores of 21–8 and 12–11. Boston overcame
             six Washington runs in the first inning to win the second game, which was called
             for darkness after eight innings.

JUNE 5   The Red Sox play at Navin Field in Detroit for the first time and lose 8–6 to the Tigers.

             *The Tigers used the facility until 1999. It was also known as Briggs Stadium
             from 1938 through 1960 and Tiger Stadium after 1961.*

JUNE 9   Tris Speaker hits for the cycle to lead the Red Sox to a 9–2 win over the Browns in
             St. Louis.

             *In one of the greatest offensive seasons in Red Sox history, Speaker hit .383 in
             1912 and led the league in doubles (53) and home runs (10). He also had 136
             runs, 222 hits, and 90 RBIs.*

JUNE 10   The Red Sox jump into first place ahead of the White Sox with a 3–2 triumph over
             the Browns in St. Louis.

             *The Red Sox remained at the top of the American League standings for the rest
             of the season.*

JUNE 13   Eight Red Sox are ejected for protesting the decision of umpire Jack Sheridan dur-
             ing a 3–2 loss to the White Sox in Chicago.

JUNE 20   The Red Sox lambaste the Yankees 15–8 in New York.

JUNE 22	The Red Sox win their eighth and ninth games in a row by scorching the Yankees 13–2 and 10–3 during a doubleheader in New York.
JUNE 24	The Red Sox extend their winning streak to 10 games with a 3–1 decision over the Senators in Washington.
JUNE 29	The Red Sox drub the Yankees 13–5 and 6–0 in a doubleheader at Fenway Park. Smoky Joe Wood pitched a one-hitter in the second game, called after seven innings by darkness.

The Red Sox were 19–3 against the Yankees in 1912, including a stretch of 14 in a row.

JULY 2	Larry Gardner hits two inside-the-park homers, but the Red Sox lose 9–7 to the Yankees at Fenway Park.

Gardner batted .315 and stroked 18 triples for the Red Sox in 1912. Duffy Lewis hit .284 and contributed 109 RBIs and 36 doubles.

JULY 12	The Red Sox sweep the Tigers 4–1 and 1–0 in 11 innings in a doubleheader at Fenway Park. Smoky Joe Wood pitched the extra-inning shutout. Duffy Lewis drove in the game's lone run with a single.
JULY 16	Tris Speaker extends his hitting streak to 30 games during a 7–2 win over the Tigers at Fenway Park.

Ed Walsh of the White Sox stopped Speaker's streak the following day during Boston's 1–0 loss at Fenway.

JULY 22	The Red Sox sell Ed Cicotte to the White Sox.

The Red Sox made a big mistake letting Cicotte go to Chicago. He had a 156–102 record for the White Sox before he was banned from baseball in 1920 for conspiring to fix the 1919 World Series.

JULY 27	A two-run homer by Tris Speaker in the tenth inning beats the White Sox 5–3 in Chicago.
AUGUST 4	Jake Stahl hits a grand slam off Earl Hamilton during the fourth inning of the Red Sox' 9–0 win over the Browns in St. Louis.
AUGUST 14	Tris Speaker extends another long hitting streak to 20 games during the Red Sox' 8–2 and 8–0 sweep of the Browns in a doubleheader at Fenway Park.

The two wins gave the Red Sox a 9½-game lead in the pennant race, virtually assuring Boston of a spot in the World Series.

AUGUST 15	The Red Sox score seven runs in the second inning and hammer out a 13–6 win over the Browns at Fenway Park.
AUGUST 22	Ray Collins pitches a two-hitter to defeat the Indians 9–0 at Fenway Park. The only

Cleveland hits were singles by Buddy Ryan and Bert Adams.

SEPTEMBER 2   Behind Hugh Bedient's two-hitter in the first game and a shutout by Smoky Joe Wood in the second, the Red Sox beat the Yankees 2–1 and 1–0 in a doubleheader played in a drizzling rain in New York. Tris Speaker's sacrifice fly in the first inning drove in the lone run of the nightcap.

Bedient was 20–9 in 1912 with a 2.92 ERA.

SEPTEMBER 6   In one of the most storied pitching matchups in baseball history, Smoky Joe Wood bests Walter Johnson and the Senators 1–0 before 30,000 on a Friday afternoon at Fenway Park. Earlier in the season, Johnson had won 16 consecutive games. Wood entered the contest with a 13-game win streak of his own. In the sixth inning with two out, Tris Speaker hit a ground-rule double into part of the overflow crowd encircling the outfield, and scored on another double by Duffy Lewis that barely eluded the grasp of Washington right fielder Danny Moeller. The Senators loaded the bases in the third inning and had runners on second base in the sixth, eighth, and ninth, but Wood pitched out of the jam on each occasion. The shutout was Wood's third in succession.

SEPTEMBER 10   Smoky Joe Wood wins his 15th consecutive decision by defeating the White Sox 5–4 in Chicago with relief help from Sea Lion Hall.

SEPTEMBER 15   Smoky Joe Wood wins his 16th game in a row, beating the Browns 2–1 in the second game of a doubleheader, called after eight innings by darkness in St. Louis. The Browns won the first game, 5–4.

SEPTEMBER 18   The Red Sox are rained out in Cleveland but clinch the pennant when the Athletics lose 9–1 to the White Sox in Chicago.

SEPTEMBER 19   In an unusual doubleheader between the Red Sox and Indians in Cleveland, neither game lasts the required nine innings. The first contest was called at the end of the fifth inning because of rain with Cleveland leading 9–3. After an hour's wait, the second game began but was called on account of darkness at the end of the sixth inning with the Indians ahead 6–0.

SEPTEMBER 20   Smoky Joe Wood's 16-game winning streak comes to an end with a 6–4 loss to the Tigers in Detroit. The Red Sox led 4–3 before Wood allowed two runs in the fifth inning and one in the eighth. The winning pitcher for the Tigers was Joe Lake, a hurler with a 62–90 lifetime record. Lake was pitching in relief of starter Tex Covington, who was ejected after an argument with umpire Silk O'Loughlin. Lake held the Red Sox hitless over the final four innings.

There have only been 10 single-season winning streaks of 16 games or more since 1900, but three of them occurred in 1912. Besides the 16 in a row by Wood and Walter Johnson, Rube Marquard of the New York Giants won 19 consecutive decisions. The 16-game streaks of Wood and Johnson are still the American League record. It was matched by Lefty Grove of the Athletics in 1931, Schoolboy Rowe for the Tigers in 1934, and Roger Clemens of the Yankees in 2001. The only longer streaks in the National League since 1900 are Marquard's 19 and 17 in a row by Roy Face of the Pirates in 1959. National

Leaguers since 1900 who have strung together 16 wins in a row include Carl Hubbell (1936 Giants), Ewell Blackwell (1947 Reds), and Jack Sanford (1962 Giants).

SEPTEMBER 23   Some 100,000 fans greet the champion Red Sox in Boston following their road trip through the Midwest. Fans lined the streets as the players rode from South Station to the Common. All business stopped, workers thronged to the windows, and trains and streetcars were stalled. At the Common, Mayor John F. Fitzgerald, along with other city officials, welcomed the team and gave them keys to the city.

SEPTEMBER 25   Smoky Joe Wood sets a club record by winning his 34th game of the season in a two-hitter to defeat the Yankees 6–0 at Huntington Grounds. The only New York hits were singles by Harry Wolverton and Jack Lelivelt.

Wood closed out his historic 1912 campaign with a 34–5 record, 35 complete games, 10 shutouts, 344 innings pitched, 258 strikeouts, and a 1.91 earned run average.

SEPTEMBER 26   The Yankees take a 12–3 lead with five runs in the top of the sixth inning, but the Red Sox stage an incredible comeback with four runs in their half of the sixth and eight runs in the eighth, as the sun sets over Fenway Park, to win 15–12. The game was called at the end of eighth by darkness.

OCTOBER 1   Tris Speaker draws five walks and hits a single in six plate appearances during a 12–2 win over the Senators in Washington. Hugh Bedient was the winning pitcher, earning his 20th victory of the season.

OCTOBER 3   Duffy Lewis clubs a grand slam off Boardwalk Brown during the fifth inning of a 17–5 rout of the Athletics in Philadelphia. On the same day, it was announced that Tris Speaker won the American League Most Valuable Player Award by a panel of sportswriters. The award was sponsored by the Chalmers Automobile Company, and Speaker was presented with a bright red car prior to the second game of the World Series. He batted .383 in 1912 with 136 runs scored, 222 hits, 329 total bases, 52 stolen bases, and league-leading figures in home runs (10), doubles (53), and on-base percentage (.464).

OCTOBER 5   The Red Sox win a club-record 105th game with a 5–0 victory over the Athletics in Philadelphia. Third baseman Larry Gardner provided the highlight by making a daring catch of a foul ball. In recording the putout, Gardner jackknifed over the railing in front of the grandstand and landed on his head. Buck O'Brien was the winning pitcher, earning his 20th victory of the season.

With the regular season ended, the Red Sox looked forward to the World Series against the Giants. Managed by John McGraw, the Giants were 103–48 in 1912 and won the National League pennant by 10 games. The series was scheduled to begin on Tuesday, October 8, with the games alternating between New York and Boston. Games One, Three, and Five were scheduled for the Polo Grounds, and the even-numbered contests slated for Fenway Park. If a seventh game was necessary, a coin flip would determine the location.

OCTOBER 8   With Smoky Joe Wood striking out 11 batters, the Red Sox win the first game of the 1912 World Series 4–3 over the Giants before 35,730 at the Polo Grounds in New York City. Boston trailed 2–0 in the sixth before Tris Speaker tripled and scored on a groundout by Duffy Lewis. The Sox took a 4–2 lead in the seventh on a run-scoring double by Harry Hooper and a two-run single by Steve Yerkes. Wood allowed a run in the ninth, and the Giants had runners on second and third with one out, but Smoky Joe fanned Art Fletcher and Doc Crandall to end the game.

OCTOBER 9   The Giants and Red Sox battle to a 6–6 tie in Game Two, called after 11 innings by darkness before 30,148 on a raw, cloudy day at Fenway Park. The Red Sox took a 3–0 lead off Christy Mathewson in the first but let the advantage fritter away. The Giants plated three in the eighth to move ahead 5–4. The Sox tied it 5–5 in their half on a double by Duffy Lewis and one of New York's five errors of the afternoon. The Giants grabbed the lead again 6–5 in the tenth, but Boston rallied again with a drive by Tris Speaker to deep center. Speaker tried to stretch the hit into an inside-the-park homer and appeared to be a dead duck at home plate, but catcher Art Wilson dropped the ball for an error. Giants third baseman Buck Herzog bumped Speaker rounding the bag. After he scored, Speaker was itching for a fight with Herzog, but teammates and the umpires stopped him.

According to the rules agreed upon in advance, if a game was tied, the two clubs would stay over and play off the contest in the same ballpark. As a result, game three was played in Boston.

OCTOBER 10   The Giants even the Series at one win apiece behind the pitching of Rube Marquard in a 2–1 contest witnessed by 34,624 at Fenway Park. The Red Sox rallied in the ninth with their lone run and had runners on second and third when Hick Cady lined out to right fielder Josh Devore, who made a spectacular catch to end the game. Devore pocketed the ball and headed straight for the clubhouse. Many in the crowd believed Devore missed the catch, and went home happily with the notion that the two base runners had scored and the Red Sox had emerged with a dramatic 3–2 win.

OCTOBER 11   The Red Sox take command of the series with a 3–1 win in Game Four in New York. Smoky Joe Wood pitched the complete game with eight strikeouts and no walks.

OCTOBER 12   Hugh Bedient hurls a three-hitter to defeat the Giants 2–1 before 34,683 on Columbus Day at Fenway Park to give the Red Sox a three-games-to-one lead and move within a victory of the World Championship. The Red Sox scored their two runs in the third inning on back-to-back triples by Harry Hooper and Steve Yerkes, and Tris Speaker's groundout.

OCTOBER 14   After a break on Sunday, the Giants stay in the Series by scoring five runs in the first inning off Buck O'Brien and win 5–2 on a dark, cloudy afternoon in New York. On the train back to Boston, O'Brien was punched in the face by Smoky Joe Wood's brother, who had bet $100 on a Red Sox victory. Many Red Sox players, angered over O'Brien's pitching performance, turned their backs and refused to come to his aid.

OCTOBER 15   A Boston starter fails in the first inning for the second game in a row as Smoky Joe Wood is raked for six runs to send the Giants on their way to an 11–4 win over the Red Sox with 32,694 in attendance on a cold, windy day at Fenway Park. The Sox blew one opportunity after another, leaving 12 on base. Play was suspended frequently when dense clouds of dust whirled across the diamond. One of the few Boston highlights was the only unassisted double play by an outfielder in World Series history. Tris Speaker caught Art Fletcher's liner in the ninth inning and raced in to force Buck Herzog at second.

> *The game was delayed for nearly a half an hour because of a ticket snafu. The Royal Rooters had purchased seats in the left field bleachers for the first three games at Fenway and fully expected the Red Sox to hold their seats for Game Seven, the fourth played in Boston. The Red Sox sold their seats to other customers, however. The Royal Rooters marched onto the field before game time only to find their seats occupied. They refused to leave the field, and mounted police were called to herd the group out of the ballpark. Wood's arm stiffened while the field was being cleared, which was a factor in the six runs he surrendered in the first inning. After seven games, the World Series was all even with each team taking three games in addition to the second-game tie. The Red Sox won a coin flip used to determine the host for the unanticipated eighth game, giving them five contests at home in the series. Tickets were hastily put on sale, but after the row with the Royal Rooters and two crushing defeats in Games Six and Seven, only 17,034 were sold.*

OCTOBER 15   In one of the most exciting games in baseball history, the Red Sox win the World Championship with a 3–2 win in 10 innings at Fenway Park. The Giants scored first with a run off Hugh Bedient in the third inning. In the fifth, with a man on and one out, Harry Hooper robbed Larry Doyle of a home run with a spectacular catch by leaping in front of the temporary bleachers in right field and landing on top of the crowd. In the seventh, facing Christy Mathewson, Jake Stahl singled and Heinie Wagner walked. Olaf Henriksen, batting for Bedient, doubled down the left field line to tie the score, 1–1. The Giants opened a 2–1 advantage in the tenth against Smoky Joe Wood on Red Murray's double and a single by Fred Merkle. The Giants were three outs from winning the World Series with Mathewson on the mound. Pinch hitter Clyde Engle began the Boston half of the tenth by lifting an easy fly ball to the outfield, that center fielder Fred Snodgrass dropped, allowing Engle to reach second base. Harry Hooper followed with a low line drive to center, and Snodgrass partially redeemed himself by making a remarkable running catch. Steve Yerkes reached first on a walk. Tris Speaker lofted a pop fly just outside the first base coach's box. First baseman Fred Merkle, catcher Chief Meyers, and Mathewson all made a move for the ball, but in the deafening din of the crowd at Fenway, the three were confused over who would take the catch, and the ball fell harmlessly to earth. With a reprieve, Speaker singled to score Engle and send Yerkes to third. With the score now 2–2, Mathewson intentionally walked Duffy Lewis, and Larry Gardner hit a sacrifice fly to left field, giving the Red Sox the World Championship.

> *Snodgrass's dropped fly ball became known as the "$30,000 muff," the difference between the winner's and loser's share. It haunted him to his grave. When Snodgrass died in 1974, his obituary in the* New York Times *was headlined: "Fred Snodgrass, 86, Dead, Ballplayer Muffed 1912 Fly."*

1913   B

Season in a Sentence

Spring training injuries and a bad start set the stage for a season in which the Red Sox were never in contention for a second straight pennant.

Finish • Won • Lost • Pct • GB

Fourth   79   71   .527   15.5

Managers

Jake Stahl (39–41)
Bill Carrigan (40–30)

Stats

Stats	Red Sox	AL	Rank
Batting Avg:	.269	.256	2
On-Base Pct:	.336	.325	3
Slugging Pct:	.364	.336	2
Home Runs:	17		6
Stolen Bases:	189		7
ERA:	2.94	2.93	4
Fielding Pct:	.961	.959	3
Runs Scored:	631		3
Runs Allowed:	610		4

Starting Lineup

Bill Carrigan, c
Clyde Engle, 1b
Steve Yerkes, 2b
Larry Gardner, 3b
Heinie Wagner, ss
Duffy Lewis, lf
Tris Speaker, cf
Harry Hooper, rf
Hal Janvrin, ss

Pitchers

Ray Collins, sp
Hugh Bedient, sp
Dutch Leonard, sp
Smoky Joe Wood, sp
Earl Moseley, sp
Sea Lion Hall, rp
Buck O'Brien, sp

Attendance

437,194 (fourth in AL)

Club Leaders

Batting Avg:	Speaker	.363
On-Base Pct:	Speaker	.441
Slugging Pct:	Speaker	.533
Home Runs:	Hooper	4
RBI:	Lewis	90
Runs:	Hooper	100
Stolen Bases:	Speaker	46
Wins:	Collins	19
Strikeouts:	Leonard	144
ERA:	Leonard	2.39
Saves:	Wood	2
	Hall	2

APRIL 10   The Red Sox open the season at home and lose 10–9 to the 1913 World Champion Athletics. Philadelphia scored a key run on a bonehead play by the Red Sox. In the Athletics' half of the sixth inning, Jack Lapp was a base runner on third and Jack Coombs was on second when Eddie Murphy hit a grounder to Boston shortstop Heinie Wagner. Lapp made a bluff for home, and Wagner threw to catcher Hick Cady. Lapp made it safely back to third in a rundown, but Coombs also advanced to third on the play. Cady tagged Lapp, who was entitled to the bag, and Coombs retreated toward second, where Murphy was standing. Murphy headed back toward first base. Pitcher Sea Lion Hall made a wild heave past first in trying to retire Murphy, and Lapp scored.

The Sox lost six of their first seven games and weren't over the .500 mark for good until September. The failure of Smoky Joe Wood to match his fantastic 1912 season doomed the club. Wood broke his thumb in spring training and later developed a sore arm, no doubt due in large part to the 366 innings he pitched in 1912 (including the World Series) at the age of twenty-two. He was limited to 144 innings and an 11–5 record in 1913 and was never the same. Wood's pitching days were essentially over in 1915 when he was only twenty-five. The "big three" of Wood, Hugh Bedient, and Buck O'Brien had a combined record of 74–27 in 1912 but were only 35–28 in 1913. Ray Collins picked up some of the slack with a 19–8 record and a 2.63 ERA.

APRIL 22   Seven weeks after his inauguration as president, Woodrow Wilson takes a break from his duties in the White House to watch the Red Sox defeat the Senators 8–3 at Griffith Stadium in Washington.

APRIL 24   Woodrow Wilson is at the game again to watch the Red Sox lose 5–2 to the Senators in Washington.

APRIL 25   With Woodrow Wilson attending for the third time in four days, Buck O'Brien strikes out 12 batters, 6 of them in succession, but the Red Sox lose 5–4 to the Senators.

MAY 11   Trailing 4–1, the Red Sox score three runs in the ninth inning and one in the tenth to beat the Tigers 5–4 in Detroit. Larry Gardner hit a two-run triple to narrow the deficit to 4–3, then scored on a sacrifice fly by Clyde Engle. Harry Hooper's infield hit scored Neal Ball from third base with the winning run. The game ended when Tris Speaker crashed into the fence in left center field to catch a drive by Sam Crawford with runners on second and third.

MAY 15   The Red Sox pummel the Browns 15–4 in St. Louis.

MAY 21   Smoky Joe Wood ends the White Sox' ninth-inning rally to secure a 10–9 Red Sox win at Comiskey Park. Boston entered the ninth inning with a 10–3 lead, but Chicago scored six runs off of Ray Collins and Hugh Bedient to pull within a run. Wood came into the game with the bases loaded and two out and ended the game by picking Babe Borton off first base.

MAY 30   Harry Hooper leads off both games of a doubleheader in Washington with a home run. The Red Sox lost the first game 4–3, but Hooper's homer off Walter Johnson in the nightcap held up for a 1–0 victory. The homers were Hooper's only two hits in seven at-bats during the twin bill. Ray Collins pitched the second-game shutout.

Center fielder Tris Speaker was a key member of the Sox lineup from 1909 through 1915.

Hooper is the only player in major league history to hit two leadoff homers in one day. He hit a total of only four homers in 148 games during the 1913 season.

JUNE 3   The Red Sox raise the American League pennant prior to a 3–2 win over the White Sox at Fenway Park. Tris Speaker extended his hitting streak to 22 games.

Speaker had a .363 batting average in 1913 with 189 hits, 35 doubles, a .441 on-base percentage, and a Red Sox single-season-record 22 triples. His outfield mates were also effective. Harry Hooper hit .288 and scored 100 runs, while Duffy Lewis batted .298 and drove in 90 runs.

JUNE 11   The Indians score four runs in the fifteenth inning, two of them on steals of home, to beat the Red Sox 9–5 at Fenway Park.

JUNE 13   Down 6–2, the Red Sox score two runs in the eighth inning, two in the ninth, and one in the thirteenth to defeat the Browns 7–6 at Fenway Park. A single by Duffy Lewis drove in the game-winner.

Shortstop Heinie Wagner missed playing time in June because of blood poisoning in one of the fingers of his right hand.

JULY 3   The Red Sox tie a major league record for most hits in a shutout loss. Boston collected 15 hits off Walter Johnson but lost 1–0 in 15 innings at Fenway Park. Johnson pitched his way out of one jam after another, including a bases loaded, none out situation in the ninth inning. It took only two hours and thirty-five minutes to play the 15-inning contest. Ray Collins pitched a complete game in the heart-rending loss.

JULY 4   The Red Sox score seven runs in the fourth inning of a 13–6 win over the Athletics in the first game of a two-admission, morning-afternoon doubleheader at Fenway Park. Smoky Joe Wood hit two doubles during the inning. The contest was called after seven innings by mutual agreement because it took two hours and twenty-five minutes to reach that point and the grandstand needed to be cleared for the afternoon encounter. The Athletics won the second game, 5–3.

JULY 9   The Red Sox' baggage fails to reach St. Louis in time, forcing the club to play a game against the Browns in the Browns' road uniforms. Despite the unfamiliar togs, Boston won, 9–0.

JULY 10   Rube Foster carries a no-hitter into the ninth inning and defeats the Browns 6–2 with a two-hitter in St. Louis. The Browns collected both runs on a walk, a triple by Gus Williams, and a single by Jimmy Austin.

JULY 15   The Red Sox replace manager Jake Stahl, who had posted a 39–41 record, with Bill Carrigan. Carrigan took the job after it was turned down by Fielder Jones, who guided the White Sox to a World Championship in 1906.

Stahl battled constantly with club president Jimmy McAleer over the direction of the team throughout the first three months of the 1913 season. Not only was the club losing, but McAleer also wanted Stahl to resume his position at first base. Stahl insisted that his injured foot prevented him from taking the field. He went back to the banking business and never returned to baseball. Stahl died in 1922 at the age of forty-three from tuberculosis. Carrigan was only twenty-nine years old and had been a catcher for the Red Sox since 1906.

AUGUST 5   Dutch Leonard pitches perfect ball through the first six innings and finishes with a two-hitter to defeat the Browns 3–0 in the first game of a doubleheader at Fenway Park. The only St. Louis hits were singles by Burt Shotton and Gus Williams. Duffy Lewis drove in all three Boston runs. The Browns won the second game, 4–2.

AUGUST 15   Earl Moseley (six innings) and Sea Lion Hall (three innings) combine on a two-hitter to beat the Browns 2–1 at Sportsman's Park in St. Louis. Both Browns hits were singles by Burt Shotton, one off each pitcher. The game ended when Tris Speaker reached over the center field fence and took a home run away from Gus Williams.

AUGUST 21   With runners moving on a 3–2 pitch and two out in the third inning, Heinie Wagner hits a three-run single, which accounts for all three Boston runs in a 3–2 win over the Indians in Cleveland. The game was called after seven innings due to rain.

AUGUST 28   The Red Sox stop Walter Johnson's 14-game winning streak, but it takes 11 innings to come out on top 1–0 at Fenway Park. Ray Collins pitched the shutout. Johnson allowed only one hit through the first 10 innings, a single by Steve Yerkes in the second inning. Johnson had retired 26 batters in a row before Yerkes singled again in the eleventh. Yerkes moved to third on a two-base error by Washington center fielder Clyde Milan but was thrown out at the plate on Heinie Wagner's infield grounder. Wagner, however, scored on Bill Carrigan's drive into the left-center field gap.

Johnson had an incredible 36–7 record for the Senators in 1913 with a 1.14 ERA.

SEPTEMBER 3   For the second time in two months, the Red Sox' uniforms are misrouted by the railroad and fail to arrive in time for a game in Philadelphia. The Red Sox played in the Athletics' road jerseys but overcame the inconvenience by sweeping a doubleheader, 8–6 and 5–2.

SEPTEMBER 4   Hugh Bedient pitches seven perfect innings of relief to defeat the Athletics 5–2 in the second game of a doubleheader at Shibe Park in Philadelphia. The Red Sox also won the opener, 8–6.

SEPTEMBER 12 The Red Sox collect 21 hits and clobber the Tigers 18–5 at Fenway Park.

OCTOBER 3   Dutch Leonard throws a two-hitter to beat the Senators 2–0 in the first game of a doubleheader at Griffith Stadium. The only Washington hits were singles by Howard Shanks and George McBride. The Sox lost the nightcap, 11–3. In the second game, right fielder Harry Hooper pitched the sixth and seventh innings and left fielder Duffy Lewis pitched the eighth.

OCTOBER 4   On the final day of the season, the Red Sox lose a farcical 10–9 decision to the Senators in Washington. Hal Janvrin hit two inside-the-park homers for the Sox. Washington used eight pitchers, including infielder Germany Schaefer, catcher Eddie Ainsmith, outfielder Joe Gedeon, and forty-three-year-old manager Clark Griffith. Griffith's catcher was forty-four-year-old coach Jack Ryan, who hadn't donned catcher's gear in a big-league game in 10 years. The makeshift pitchers contributed to a six-run Red Sox rally in the ninth inning. Walter Johnson started the game in center field but was forced to take the mound to stem the rally. The game brought out 3,000 cavalry soldiers from a camp in Winchester, Virginia, for "Army Day."

Janvrin hit only six homers during a 10-year career in which he played in 756 games and accumulated 2,221 at-bats.

DECEMBER 8   Joe Lannin, a real-estate magnate who owned several luxury apartment buildings in the Boston area and hotels in New York City and on Long Island, purchases a one-fourth interest in the Red Sox from Jimmy McAleer. McAleer wanted out because of constant quarrels with part-owner John I. Taylor and American League president Ban Johnson over the direction of the club. McAleer was never again associated with a major league club. Ill with cancer, he died from a self-inflicted gunshot wound in 1931.

DECEMBER 24   Joe Lannin is elected president of the Red Sox. John I. Taylor remained as vice president.

Lannin was born in Quebec, came to Boston at the age of fifteen, and worked his way up in Horatio Alger fashion from bellhop to owner of several hotels.

1914   B

Season in a Sentence

There's a World Series played at Fenway Park, but it's hosted by the Braves, not the Red Sox, as Boston's American League club is unable to keep pace with the front-running Athletics.

Finish • Won • Lost • Pct • GB

Second   91   62   .595   8.5

Manager

Bill Carrigan

Stats   Red Sox • AL • Rank

Stats	Red Sox	AL	Rank
Batting Avg:	.250	.248	3
On-Base Pct:	.320	.319	3
Slugging Pct:	.338	.323	3
Home Runs:	18		4
Stolen Bases:	177		6
ERA:	2.36	2.72	1
Fielding Pct:	.963	.959	3
Runs Scored:	589		3
Runs Allowed:	510		1

Starting Lineup

Bill Carrigan, c
Dick Hoblitzel, 1b
Hal Janvrin, 2b-1b
Larry Gardner, 3b
Everett Scott, ss
Duffy Lewis, lf
Tris Speaker, cf
Harry Hooper, rf
Steve Yerkes, 2b
Hick Cady, c
Wally Rehg, rf-lf

Pitchers

Ray Collins, sp
Dutch Leonard, sp
Rube Foster, sp
Ernie Shore, sp
Smoky Joe Wood, sp
Rankin Johnson, sp
Hugh Bedient, rp-sp

Attendance

481,359 (first in AL)

Club Leaders

Batting Avg:	Speaker	.338
On-Base Pct:	Speaker	.423
Slugging Pct:	Speaker	.503
Home Runs:	Speaker	4
RBI:	Speaker	90
Runs:	Speaker	101
Stolen Bases:	Speaker	42
Wins:	Collins	20
Strikeouts:	Leonard	176
ERA:	Leonard	1.00
Saves:	Leonard	3

APRIL 14   The Red Sox open the season before 24,271 at Fenway Park and lose 3–0 to Walter Johnson and the Senators. The first ball was thrown out by Mayor James M. Curley.

APRIL 18   Hugh Bedient shuts out the Athletics 1–0 at Fenway Park. Duffy Lewis drove in the only run of the game with a third-inning double. During the game, Tris Speaker made a putout at second base. In the sixth inning, Speaker ran in to second from his position in center field to take a throw from first baseman Clyde Engle and tagged Eddie Collins during a rundown.

APRIL 21   Tris Speaker pulls off an unassisted double play in a 1–1 tie against the Athletics at Fenway Park.

APRIL 22   Tris Speaker drives in six runs on a bases-loaded double and two singles in a 9–9 tie against the Athletics at Fenway Park, called after eight innings by mutual agreement to allow both clubs to catch a train.

Speaker's numbers fell somewhat in 1914, but he still batted .338 with 101 runs scored, 18 triples, 42 stolen bases, a .423 on-base percentage, and league-leading totals in hits (193), doubles (46), and total bases (287).

APRIL 23   Red Sox pitcher Rankin Johnson pitches a shutout in his first major league start to defeat Walter Johnson and the Senators 6–0 in Washington's home opener. Woodrow Wilson was scheduled to throw out the first pitch but was unable to attend the game because of an international crisis in Mexico. Two days earlier, the United States had seized the Mexican port of Vera Cruz.

MAY 13   The Red Sox sell Les Nunamaker to the Yankees.

MAY 14   Dutch Leonard pitches a shutout to defeat the Browns 1–0 at Fenway Park. The game's lone run came in the second inning when Larry Gardner tripled and crossed the plate on an infield out.

On the same day, Joe Lannin became the sole owner of the Red Sox by purchasing the Taylor family's stock.

MAY 18   Rube Foster pitches a two-hitter to defeat the Tigers 2–0 at Fenway Park. The only Detroit hits were singles by Ty Cobb and Bobby Veach.

MAY 22   Rube Foster defeats the White Sox 1–0 at Fenway Park. The shutout occurred during a streak of 42 consecutive innings that Foster pitched between May 2 and May 26.

JUNE 1   Rankin Johnson defeats Walter Johnson and the Senators again, by a 1–0 score at Fenway Park. Harry Hooper's single in the fifth inning drove in the only run.

Johnson had a 4–9 record during his only season in Boston but pitched two shutouts, both over Walter Johnson.

JUNE 6   The Red Sox beat the Indians 4–3 in 14 innings in Cleveland. The Red Sox used four right fielders during the game: Harry Hooper, Wally Rehg, Olaf Henriksen, and Clyde Engle. Both Rehg and Henriksen were ejected for disputing the decisions of the umpires.

Henriksen was one of baseball's first pinch-hitting specialists. He played for the Red Sox from 1911 through 1917. Henriksen was nicknamed "Swede," although he was born in Kirkerup, Denmark.

JUNE 9 — The Red Sox parlay a seven-run sixth inning into a 9–6 win over Indians at League Park in Cleveland. Hal Janvrin hit two doubles during the inning.

JUNE 17 — Rankin Johnson and Hick Cady are involved in an elevator accident in St. Louis. The two Boston players were in a department store elevator with four others passengers when it dropped five floors. No one was seriously hurt. Later that day, a shaken Johnson was the starting pitcher in a 4–0 loss to the Browns.

JULY 4 — Six days after the assassination of Archduke Ferdinand of Austria—an event that precipitates the start of World War I in August—Ray Collins shuts out the Senators 1–0 in the first game of a doubleheader in Washington. The Senators won the second game, 3–2.

JULY 9 — The Red Sox purchase nineteen-year-old pitcher Babe Ruth, pitcher Ernie Shore, and catcher Ben Egan from the Baltimore Orioles of the International League.

The price for the three is open to speculation because various sources have reported the exchange to be anywhere from $8,000 to $30,000. At the time of the deal, Red Sox owner Joe Lannin said it was in excess of $25,000. Whatever the price, it was a tremendous bargain. Several other clubs had a chance to purchase Ruth before he was snared by the Red Sox but considered the price to be too steep. Lannin, who had become sole owner of the Red Sox less than two months earlier, was willing to pay up because, in large part, he wished to make a statement to the fans that he would spend what it took to bring Boston another pennant.

JULY 11 — Babe Ruth makes his major league debut, allowing three runs and eight hits in a starting assignment against the Indians at Fenway Park. Ruth was lifted in the seventh inning with the score 3–3 when Duffy Lewis pinch hit for him. Lewis came around to score, and the Red Sox won the game, 4–3. Ruth was the winning pitcher.

Ruth was in Baltimore the previous day and traveled six hundred miles to Boston on the train, arriving in the morning to make his big-league debut. Despite the relatively successful debut, the Red Sox rarely used Ruth in the pitching rotation and sent him back to the minors at Providence in the International League on August 18, although he returned to Boston for the final week of the season. With the Red Sox in 1914, Ruth pitched 23 innings, had a 2–1 record, and posted a 3.91 ERA.

JULY 13 — Ray Collins pitches a two-hitter to defeat the Indians 2–0 at Fenway Park. The only Cleveland hits were a double by Terry Turner and a single by Jack Graney.

JULY 14 — In his first game with the Red Sox, Ernie Shore pitches a two-hitter to defeat the Indians 2–1 at Fenway Park. The only Cleveland hits were a triple by Steve O'Neill and a single by Jack Graney.

JULY 15 — During the course of a 4–0 win over the Indians at Fenway Park, eight Red Sox are ejected by umpire Tom Connolly for making uncomplimentary remarks about the officiating.

JULY 16   The Red Sox purchase Dick Hoblitzel from the Reds.

The recipient of a degree in dentistry, Hoblitzel was Boston's starting first base-man on the 1915 and 1916 World Champions. He was acquired because the Red Sox lost Clyde Engle to the Federal League, an organization formed as a third major league in 1914 before folding after the 1915 season. Steve Yerkes followed Engle to the Federals in August.

JULY 20   The Red Sox need 16 innings to defeat the Tigers 3–2 at Fenway Park. Tris Speaker's single with the bases loaded ended the game. Dutch Leonard pitched eight innings of hitless relief.

JULY 25   Duffy Lewis collects five hits, including a double and a triple, in six at-bats and drives in five runs to lead the Red Sox to an 8–6 win over the Indians in 11 innings in Cleveland. Duffy's bases-loaded triple in the ninth tied the score 6–6.

Lewis batted .279 and clubbed 37 doubles in 1914.

JULY 28   The Red Sox trade Rankin Johnson, Fritz Coumbe, and Ben Egan to the Indians for pitcher Vean Gregg.

Gregg had won 20 or more games during each of the three previous seasons, but by the time he arrived in Boston, his arm was just about spent. Gregg's given name was Sylveanus Augustus.

AUGUST 8   Tris Speaker pulls off an unassisted double play in a 5–2 win over the Tigers in Detroit.

AUGUST 10   The Braves move into Fenway Park because South End Grounds is no longer adequate to handle the crowds flocking to see the club play. The Braves became the talk of the country during the last half of the 1914 season by winning 61 of their final 77 games to leap from last place in July to win the National League pennant by 10½ games. They followed the stunning comeback by sweeping the Athletics in the World Series. The Braves used Fenway as their home park until Braves Field opened on August 18, 1915.

In a column in the August 13, 1914, issue of The Sporting News, *Tim Murnane blamed automobile ownership as the reason for the substandard play of many Red Sox players, including Tris Speaker and Harry Hooper. "To my mind, the great cause of the poor work while at home is the automobile craze that has taken hold of the players," Murnane wrote. The Boston Globe writer noted that Connie Mack refused to allow his Athletics to drive cars during the season. "Several Red Sox players have machines, including manager Carrigan," Murnane said, "and the player-speed merchants can be seen flying over the Greater Boston speedways night and day, a sure handicap to a ball player's effectiveness."*

AUGUST 15   The day after the opening of the Panama Canal, Vean Gregg (eight innings) and Ernie Shore (one inning) combine to shut out the Yankees 1–0 at Fenway Park. Harry Hooper's single in the eighth inning drove in the game's lone run.

AUGUST 20   Ernie Shore pitches a two-hitter to beat the White Sox 3–2 at Comiskey Park. The only Chicago hits were singles by Joe Berger and Wally Mayer.

AUGUST 24   Dutch Leonard defeats the Indians 7–3 at Fenway Park to extend his winning streak to 12 games.

Leonard had a phenomenal ERA of 1.00 in 1914, the lowest in major league history among pitchers who logged at least 200 innings. He had a 19–5 record, 7 shutouts, and 176 strikeouts.

AUGUST 31   Smoky Joe Wood strikes out 14 batters in a 3–3 tie against the Browns in the second game of a doubleheader at Fenway Park, called after 11 innings by darkness. The Red Sox won the first game 4–1.

SEPTEMBER 9   Ray Collins pitches all 11 innings to beat future Hall of Famer Eddie Plank and the 1914 American League champion Athletics 2–0 in Philadelphia. The two runs were scored on bases-loaded walks to Dick Hoblitzel and Larry Gardner.

SEPTEMBER 22   Ray Collins tosses two complete-game victories in one day to defeat the Tigers 5–3 and 5–0 in a doubleheader in Detroit. The second game was called after eight innings by darkness. Collins shut out the Tigers over his last 12 innings on the mound.

SEPTEMBER 27   Ray Collins earns his 20th win of the season with an 8–6 decision over the White Sox in Chicago.

Collins was 20–13 in 1914 with a 2.51 earned run average.

OCTOBER 2   Babe Ruth collects the first of his 2,873 major league hits, a double off King Cole during an 11–5 win over the Yankees at Fenway Park.

OCTOBER 7   Tris Speaker makes the only pitching appearance of his 22-year major league career during an 11–4 loss to the Senators at Fenway Park. Speaker pitched one inning and allowed a run. He also made his first career appearance at first base during the game. Speaker didn't play at first again in the big leagues until 1927.

OCTOBER 17   Babe Ruth marries seventeen-year-old Helen Woodford in the Baltimore suburb of Ellicott City, Maryland.

Ruth met Woodford shortly after he arrived in Boston at the Landers' Coffee Shop, where she worked as a waitress. The newlyweds spent the 1914–15 offseason living with Ruth's father in an apartment above the saloon he owned on Conway Street, which was one block from the site of today's Oriole Park at Camden Yards.

1915 | B

Season in a Sentence

The Red Sox overcome a slow start to take first place in July and ride the wave to the American League pennant and World Championship.

Finish • Won • Lost • Pct • GB

First   101   50   .669 +2.5

World Series—The Red Sox defeated the Philadelphia Phillies four games to one.

Manager

Bill Carrigan

Stats   Red Sox • AL • Rank

Batting Avg:	.260	.248	2
On-Base Pct:	.336	.325	3
Slugging Pct:	.339	.326	3
Home Runs:	14		7
Stolen Bases:	118		8
ERA:	2.39	2.93	2
Fielding Pct:	.964	.959	3
Runs Scored:	669		3
Runs Allowed:	499		2

Starting Lineup

Pinch Thomas, c
Dick Hoblitzel, 1b
Heinie Wagner, 2b
Larry Gardner, 3b
Everett Scott, ss
Duffy Lewis, lf
Tris Speaker, cf
Harry Hooper, rf
Hal Janvrin, ss
Jack Barry, 2b
Hick Cady, c
Del Gainer, 1b

Pitchers

Rube Foster, sp
Ernie Shore, sp
Babe Ruth, sp
Dutch Leonard, sp
Smoky Joe Wood, sp
Carl Mays, rp
Ray Collins, rp-sp

Attendance

539,885 (first in AL)

Club Leaders

Batting Avg:	Speaker	.322
On-Base Pct:	Speaker	.416
Slugging Pct:	Speaker	.411
Home Runs:	Ruth	4
RBI:	Speaker	76
Runs:	Speaker	108
Stolen Bases:	Speaker	29
Wins:	Foster	19
	Shore	19
Strikeouts:	Leonard	116
ERA:	Wood	1.49
Saves:	Mays	7

APRIL 14   On Opening Day in Philadelphia, Herb Pennock of the Athletics comes within one out of pitching a no-hitter against the Red Sox. Harry Hooper collected Boston's only base hit on an infield single with two out in the ninth. The hit bounded over Pennock's head. Second baseman Nap Lajoie made a desperate lunge for it but could only knock the ball down before it reached the outfield. The A's won 2–0 on the bitterly cold day.

Pennock soon had a falling-out with Athletics manager Connie Mack and was sold to the Red Sox just two months later on June 13. Pennock shuffled back and forth between Boston and the minors for several seasons until becoming part of the Red Sox rotation in 1919.

APRIL 22   In the first game of the season at Fenway Park, the Red Sox receive a 7–6 gift-wrapped victory against the Athletics. With Philadelphia leading 6–5 with two out in the ninth and Boston runners on second and third, Heinie Wagner lofted a pop-up in the infield. Third baseman Eddie Murphy dropped the easy play, allowing the two runners to cross the plate for the Red Sox win. Athletics second baseman Nap Lajoie tied a modern major league record by making five errors.

Normally an outfielder, Murphy played only 10 games at third base during his 11-year career.

MAY 5   Ernie Shore shuts out the Senators 1–0 at Fenway Park. Tris Speaker scored the lone run of the game in the ninth inning by hitting a triple and coming home on a wild pitch.

MAY 6   Babe Ruth hits the first home run of his career and pitches a complete game, but the Red Sox lose 4–3 to the Yankees in 13 innings in New York. Ruth's homer landed deep in the stands at the Polo Grounds. The shot came one day before a German submarine sunk the *Lusitania*, resulting in the loss of over 1,200 lives including 124 Americans.

Jack Warhop, near the end of a career in which he posted a 69–93 record, gave up the first of Ruth's 714 career homers. Warhop also surrendered Ruth's second homer on June 2. The Yankees shared the Polo Grounds with the Giants from 1913 through 1922. Duffy Lewis witnessed Ruth's first and last major league homers in addition to Hank Aaron's first home run. Lewis was traveling secretary of the Braves in 1935 when Ruth hit his last homer and was still on the job in 1954 when Hank Aaron hit his first.

MAY 16   The Red Sox defeat the Indians 3–0 in a 14-inning battle in Cleveland. Joe Wood (11 innings) and Carl Mays (three innings) combined for the shutout. Cleveland hurler Guy Morton held the Red Sox hitless for the first 8⅓ innings. Run-scoring doubles by Heinie Wagner and Duffy Lewis settled the issue.

The Red Sox had a 13–14 record on May 24 before catching fire and mounting the run for the pennant.

Babe Ruth dominated as a pitcher before playing primarily in the outfield in 1918.

MAY 31	The Red Sox score seven runs in the seventh inning to break a 2–2 tie in a 9–2 defeat of the Athletics in the first game of a doubleheader in Philadelphia. The Sox also won the first tilt, 2–1.
JUNE 2	Babe Ruth hits second career home run during a 7–1 win over the Yankees. Like his first homer on May 6, it came off Jack Warhop at the Polo Grounds in New York. Late in the game, in a fit of frustration over being intentionally walked twice, Ruth kicked the bench, resulting in a broken toe. The Babe was out of action for two weeks.
JUNE 4	Tris Speaker is replaced twice during a 2–0 loss to the White Sox at Fenway Park. In the first inning, Speaker was hit in the head by a pitch from Jim Scott. Through the courtesy of Chicago manager Pants Rowland, the Red Sox were allowed to use Bill Rodgers as a pinch runner for Speaker and keep him in the game. Speaker resumed his position in center field in the second inning but was forced to come out in the third because of the effects of the beaning. He didn't return to the lineup until June 9.
JUNE 9	The Tigers wallop the Red Sox 15–0 at Fenway Park.
JUNE 17	The Red Sox edge the Browns 11–10 on Bunker Hill Day in the afternoon game of a scheduled two-admission doubleheader at Fenway Park. The morning game had been postponed by rain.
JUNE 24	Harry Hooper scores five runs during a 12–4 win over the Senators in Washington.
JUNE 29	After the Yankees score two runs in the ninth inning and one in the tenth off Babe Ruth to take a 3–2 lead, the Red Sox rally for two runs in their half of the tenth to win 4–3 at Fenway Park. Tris Speaker drove in the winning run with his fifth single of the game.
JUNE 30	The Red Sox cruise to a 10–5 and 10–7 sweep of the Athletics at Fenway Park.
JULY 2	The Red Sox purchase Jack Barry from the Athletics.

Unable to pay the higher salaries brought about by competition from the Federal League, Connie Mack sold his regulars one by one after winning the 1914 American League pennant, and as a result, his Athletics tumbled into last place in 1915. A shortstop on four pennant winners and three World Championship teams with the Athletics, Barry was immediately installed as Boston's starting second baseman and helped the Red Sox win the World Series in both 1915 and 1916. He played collegiate ball at Holy Cross, where he was a teammate of Bill Carrigan.

JULY 3	The Red Sox beat the Athletics 11–0 in the second game of a doubleheader at Fenway Park. Philadelphia won the first game 7–3.
JULY 5	The Red Sox shut out the Senators twice in a separate-admission, morning-afternoon doubleheader at Fenway Park. Rube Foster won the opener 4–0, which was called by rain after six innings. The skies cleared in time for the second game, won by Babe Ruth, 6–0.

Foster had a 19–8 record and 2.11 ERA in 1915.

JULY 7 — Dutch Leonard beats the Senators 1–0 in the second game of a doubleheader against the Senators at Fenway Park. Harry Hooper drove in the only run of the game with a single in the third inning. The Red Sox also won the first game, 9–4.

The Red Sox had an 11–0 record against Washington at Fenway Park in 1915.

JULY 12 — Helped immensely by eight Tiger errors, the Red Sox win 15–12 in 10 innings at Detroit.

JULY 14 — Ray Collins hurls a two-hitter to beat the Indians 7–1 in the second game of a doubleheader in Cleveland. The only Indians hits were a double by Elmer Smith and a single by Billy Southworth. Boston lost the first game, 3–2.

JULY 18 — The Red Sox move past the White Sox into first place with a 6–2 victory at Comiskey Park in Chicago.

The Red Sox would remain in first for the rest of the season but were in a tight race until the final week.

JULY 20 — Ernie Shore pitches a two-hitter to defeat the White Sox 3–0 at Comiskey Park. The only Chicago hits were singles by Buck Weaver and Shano Collins.

JULY 21 — Babe Ruth has a big day in St. Louis with a mammoth home run, two doubles, a single, and a 4–2 complete-game win over the Browns in St. Louis. Ruth's homer cleared the right field bleachers, landed on a sidewalk across Grand Avenue, and shattered the window of an auto dealership. After the game, Ruth proudly posed for pictures in front of the shattered window.

In his first full season, the twenty-year-old Ruth had an 18–8 record and 2.44 earned run average in 1915. His hitting also drew considerable attention. Although his home run total was a modest 4 in 92 at-bats, it was good enough to lead the Red Sox (no one else on the club had more than two) and was exceeded by only eight players in the American League. Braggo Roth led the circuit with seven homers. In addition, Ruth hit .315 and had 10 doubles and a triple. The October 7, 1915, issue of The Sporting News *aptly summarized his early performances: "One of the things that puzzles the admirers of Babe Ruth of the Boston Red Sox is whether the young southpaw is a better pitcher than batter, or a better batter than pitcher."*

JULY 25 — Dutch Leonard (eight innings) and Ray Collins (two innings) combine to produce a two-hitter ending in a 1–1 tie for the second game of a doubleheader. It was called after nine innings by darkness at St. Louis's Sportsman's Park. Leonard struck out 12 batters. The only two Browns hits, both off Leonard, were a double by Tilly Walker and a single by Del Pratt. The Browns won the opener, 9–8.

AUGUST 7 — Smoky Joe Wood fires a one-hitter at the Indians to win 2–0 in the first game of a twin bill in Cleveland. An infield single by Bill Wambsganss was the only hit off Wood. The Red Sox also won the second game, 6–2.

Tris Speaker was once again Boston's most effective hitter in 1915. He had a .322 batting average, 108 runs scored, 176 hits, and a .418 on-base percentage.

AUGUST 16   The Red Sox collect only two hits off Washington's Bert Gallia but win 1–0 at
                 Fenway Park behind the pitching of Smoky Joe Wood. Harry Hooper led off the
                 game with a triple and scored on Everett Scott's sacrifice fly.

                 *Wood recovered well enough from his arm miseries in 1915 to post a 15–5
                 record and a league-leading 1.49 ERA.*

AUGUST 18   Braves Field opens, and 46,500 jam the park to see the Braves defeat the Cardinals,
                 3–1. It was located between Commonwealth Avenue, Babcock Street, Gaffney Street,
                 and the Boston and Albany Railroad, about one-half mile from Fenway Park on the
                 former site of the Allston Golf Club, the scene of several major golf tournaments
                 before 1914. At the time it opened, Braves Field not only had the largest seating
                 capacity in baseball but the largest playing field as well. It was 385 feet to left field, a
                 whopping 580 to center, and five hundred feet down the right field line. The ballpark
                 was the home of the Braves until the club moved to Milwaukee in March 1953.

AUGUST 22   Dutch Leonard strikes out 14 batters during a 5–3 win over the Browns in a second
                 game of a doubleheader in St. Louis. Two of the strikeouts came with the bases
                 loaded. The Red Sox also won the opener, 6–1.

AUGUST 24   The Tigers accuse Ernie Shore of illegally filing baseballs with an emery board hidden
                 somewhere on his person during a 3–1 win over the Tigers in Detroit. Ty Cobb was
                 ejected when umpires George Hildebrand and Silk O'Loughlin refused to act on the
                 allegations. Cobb entered the Boston dugout in search of evidence that Shore violated
                 the rules but was soon surrounded by a dozen Red Sox and forced to his own bench.

AUGUST 25   Ty Cobb stations a young boy behind the plate and instructs him to waive a straw
                 hat in an effort to distract the Red Sox pitchers, but Boston prevails 2–1 in 13
                 innings in Detroit.

AUGUST 29   Dutch Leonard shuts out the Indians 1–0 in Cleveland. With the bases loaded and
                 one out in the ninth inning, Leonard fanned Jack Graney and Jay Kirke.

                 Leonard had a 15–7 record and a 2.36 earned run average in 1915.

SEPTEMBER 8   After losing 1–0 to the Athletics in the first game of a doubleheader at Fenway
                 Park, the Red Sox wallop Connie Mack's crew, 13–2.

SEPTEMBER 9   Ernie Shore pitches a one-hitter to defeat the Athletics 5–0 at Fenway Park. The
                 only Philadelphia hit was a single by Jimmy Walsh.

                 Shore went 9–8 with a 1.64 ERA in 1915.

SEPTEMBER 14   Babe Ruth pitches a two-hitter and breaks a 1–1 tie in the seventh with an RBI dou-
                 ble to lead the Red Sox to a 2–1 victory over the White Sox at Fenway Park. Ruth
                 collected two of Boston's three hits. The only Chicago hits were singles by Shano
                 Collins and Lena Blackburne.

                 *The Red Sox entered a four-game series against the Tigers on September 16
                 with a two-game lead over the Detroit club.*

SEPTEMBER 16   The Tigers move within a game of the Red Sox with a 6–1 win on a raucous day at Fenway Park. In the eighth inning, Carl Mays threw two pitches at Ty Cobb's head. Cobb responded by throwing his bat at Mays. Amazingly, Cobb was allowed to stay in the game, and was promptly hit in the wrist on the next delivery from Mays. After catching a fly ball for the last out, Cobb was surrounded by an angry mob of Red Sox fans and had to be escorted to the clubhouse by teammates brandishing bats and a cordon of police officers.

SEPTEMBER 17   The Red Sox regain their two-game lead with a 7–2 win over the Tigers at Fenway.

SEPTEMBER 18   The Red Sox capture a thrilling 1–0 win over the Tigers in 12 innings before 37,528 on a Saturday afternoon at Fenway Park. Ernie Shore pitched the complete-game shutout. Much of the crowd fringed the outfield, and Tris Speaker and Harry Hooper each made remarkable catches by pushing aside the throng. With the bases loaded and one out in the twelfth, Bill Carrigan inserted himself into the game as a pinch hitter and hit a grounder to Tiger shortstop Donie Bush. Ralph Young dropped Bush's hurried throw to second base to turn the double play and allowed the winning run to cross the plate.

SEPTEMBER 20   The Red Sox beat the Tigers 3–2 at Fenway Park to take a four-game lead. Trailing 2–1, the Sox scored two runs in the sixth inning. Duffy Lewis drove in the tying run with a triple and scored in a close play at the plate after an infield out.

                Among those in the crowd was United States Vice President Thomas Marshall.

SEPTEMBER 30   The idle Red Sox clinch the American League pennant when the Tigers lose 8–2 to the Browns. The Red Sox were boarding a train for Washington when they heard the news that they had wrapped up the pennant.

                The Red Sox met the Philadelphia Phillies in the World Series. Managed by Pat Moran in his first season as a big-league skipper, the Phillies won their first-ever National League pennant with a 90–62 record. This was the second consecutive Philadelphia vs. Boston World Series, following the Athletics-Braves matchup in 1914. It was also the second straight season that a Boston club borrowed their cross-town rivals' ballpark for the World Series. Following the lead of the Braves, who played at Fenway Park in 1914, the Red Sox took advantage of new Braves Field in 1915 because it could accommodate more fans. The Phillies played in a bandbox ballpark called Baker Bowl that held barely 20,000 despite the addition of temporary bleachers. Tickets for the World Series games ranged from $1 to $5.

OCTOBER 8   The Red Sox open the World Series with a 3–1 loss to Grover Cleveland Alexander and the Phillies on a soggy field at Baker Bowl in Philadelphia. The Phillies broke a 1–1 tie by scoring two runs in the eighth inning off Ernie Shore on two walks and two infield singles.

                Babe Ruth made what would be his only appearance in the Series by lining out as a pinch hitter in the ninth. With five solid starters to choose from, manager Bill Carrigan went with a rotation of Shore, Rube Foster, and Dutch Leonard in the Series, benching Ruth and Smoky Joe Wood.

OCTOBER 9   Rube Foster stars in the Red Sox' 2–1 victory over the Phillies at Baker Bowl. He not only pitched a three-hitter with eight strikeouts and no walks but also broke a 1–1 tie in the ninth inning with a single that scored Larry Gardner from second base. The game ended when Tris Speaker reached into the center field bleachers to take a potential home run away from Dode Paskert.

Woodrow Wilson and his fiancée, Edith Bolling Galt, attended the game, thereby making him the first president to attend a World Series contest. A widower since August 1914, Wilson married Mrs. Galt in December 1915. The day was bitterly cold following a morning shower. The field was dried in part by pouring gasoline on the base paths and setting them afire.

OCTOBER 11   The Red Sox again win 2–1 decision with a run in the ninth inning on another three-hitter, this one by Dutch Leonard, before 42,300 at Braves Field. Leonard retired the last 20 batters he faced. The Red Sox tied the score 1–1 in the fourth on a triple by Tris Speaker off Grover Cleveland Alexander and a sacrifice fly by Dick Hoblitzel. In the ninth, Duffy Lewis scored Harry Hooper from third base on a two-out single.

Lewis had eight hits, five RBIs, and a .444 batting average in the 1915 Series.

OCTOBER 12   The Red Sox win over the Phillies for the third straight game by a 2–1 score with 41,096 in attendance on Columbus Day at Braves Field. Ernie Shore pitched the complete game, surrendering seven hits.

OCTOBER 13   The Red Sox use three home runs at tiny Baker Bowl to defeat the Phillies 5–4 and capture the World Championship. Harry Hooper tied the score 2–2 with a solo homer in the third inning. The Phillies took a 4–2 lead in the fourth, but Duffy Lewis clubbed a two-run homer in the eighth to deadlock the contest at 4–4. Hooper won the game with a homer in the ninth off future Hall of Famer Eppa Rixey. All three Red Sox homers landed in the temporary bleachers the Phillies had erected to squeeze a few more patrons into Baker Bowl. Both of Hooper's bounced into bleachers, which, according to the ground rules in effect in 1915, were home runs. Rube Foster pitched a complete game for the Red Sox, ending the series by inducing Bill Killefer to ground out to Everett Scott at short.

During his 17-year career, Hooper had only two regular-season games in which he hit more than one homer. Both were in 1921, when he was a member of the Chicago White Sox.

Just prior to the World Series, promoters lined up a 13-game tour between the Red Sox and Phillies beginning October 24. The two clubs were slated to play one game each in Chicago, Omaha, Denver, and Salt Lake City; seven contests in San Francisco at the Panama-Pacific International Exposition; and two in Los Angeles. Plans fell through, however, when the Phillies backed out at the last minute.

1916   B

Season in a Sentence

The Red Sox lose Tris Speaker in a shocking April trade and Smoky Joe Wood to a season-long salary dispute, but they manage to win the World Series for a second straight year.

Finish • Won • Lost • Pct • GB

First   91   63   .591   +2.0

World Series—The Red Sox defeated the Brooklyn Dodgers four games to one.

Manager

Bill Carrigan

Stats   Red Sox • AL • Rank

Batting Avg:	.248	.248	4
On-Base Pct:	.317	.321	7
Slugging Pct:	.318	.324	5
Home Runs:	14		6
Stolen Bases:	129		8
ERA:	2.48	2.82	2
Fielding Pct:	.972	.965	1
Runs Scored:	550		6
Runs Allowed:	480		1

Starting Lineup

Pinch Thomas, c
Dick Hoblitzel, 1b
Jack Barry, 2b
Larry Gardner, 3b
Everett Scott, ss
Duffy Lewis, lf
Tilly Walker, cf
Harry Hooper, rf
Hal Janvrin, ss-2b
Hick Cady, c

Pitchers

Babe Ruth, sp
Dutch Leonard, sp
Carl Mays, sp
Ernie Shore, sp
Rube Foster, sp

Attendance

496,397 (third in AL)

Club Leaders

Batting Avg:	Gardner	.308
On-Base Pct:	Gardner	.372
Slugging Pct:	Walker	.394
Home Runs:	Walker	3
	Gainer	3
RBI:	Gardner	62
Runs:	Hooper	75
Stolen Bases:	Hooper	27
Wins:	Ruth	23
Strikeouts:	Ruth	170
ERA:	Ruth	1.75
Saves:	Mays	3

APRIL 8   The Red Sox trade Tris Speaker to the Indians for Sad Sam Jones, Fred Thomas, and $55,000.

Clubs in the American and National League made wholesale cuts in salary after the Federal League folded at the end of the 1915 season. The Red Sox wanted to slash Speaker's paycheck in half from $18,000 per year to $9,000, and the center fielder refused to sign his contract. Although the Red Sox would win the World Series in 1916 and 1918 without Speaker, the club definitely came out on the short end of the deal. An angry Speaker hit .386 in 1916 to win the American League batting title. It was the only time from 1907 through 1919 that Ty Cobb failed to lead the league in batting average. Speaker remained one of the top players in the game into the late 1920s. It took Jones until 1918 to win his first game for the Red Sox, although he had a couple of effective seasons in Boston. Thomas contributed nothing to the Red Sox' fortunes.

APRIL 9   The Red Sox purchase Tilly Walker from the Browns to replace Tris Speaker in center field. Tilly spent two unhappy years in Boston and was unimpressive compared with Speaker.

APRIL 12   The Red Sox defeat the Athletics 2–1 on Opening Day on a chilly, rain-soaked day before 5,000 fans at Fenway Park as Babe Ruth outduels Jack Nabors, who would get used to losing. Nabors had a 1–20 record in 1916 and was a woeful 1–25 during his three-year big-league career.

In the Opening Day tradition of the period, players from both teams lined up behind home plate and marched to the center field flag pole for the ceremonial raising of the American flag. Red Sox owner Joe Lannin reduced ticket prices for the 1916 season. Box seat tickets dropped from $1.25 to $1.00, while grandstand seats were decreased from $1.00 to 75¢.

APRIL 14   The game against the Athletics at Fenway Park is postponed by a snowstorm.

MAY 4   Dutch Leonard pitches a two-hitter to best the Yankees 3–0 at Fenway Park. The only New York hits were a double by Roger Peckinpaugh and a single by Les Nunamaker.

MAY 9   Tris Speaker returns to Fenway Park for the first time as a visiting player. Prior to the Red Sox' 5–1 win over the Indians, the Shriners presented Speaker with a fez and a jeweled badge. The Red Sox gave Speaker a massive silver loving cup.

MAY 11   A wind-blown pop-up scores the winning run with two out in the tenth to enable the Red Sox to beat the Indians 6–5 at Fenway Park. Jack Barry hit what appeared to be a high foul to the left of the plate, but the wind carried the ball into fair territory, and Indians catcher Steve O'Neill was unable to make the catch, allowing Dick Hoblitzel to score.

MAY 20   Babe Ruth (5 $\frac{2}{3}$ innings) and Carl Mays (3 $\frac{1}{3}$ innings) combine on a two-hitter to defeat the Browns 3–1 at Fenway Park. Ruth allowed no hits but was sent to the showers because he walked seven batters. The only two hits off Mays were singles by Burt Shotton and Ernie Johnson.

JUNE 1   Babe Ruth beats Walter Johnson and the Senators 1–0 at Fenway Park in a duel between two of the first five players to reach the Hall of Fame. The only run of the game came when hustling Mike McNally scored from second base on a force out in the eighth.

McNally was a utility infielder for 10 seasons in the majors and never appeared in more than 93 games, but he had an amazing affinity for playing on pennant-winning teams. He was on the roster of the American League champion Red Sox in 1915 and 1916, the Yankees in 1921, 1922, and 1923, and the Senators in 1925. McNally missed the 1918 season, when Boston won another pennant, because he was in the military.

Before the game, the Red Sox hoisted the 1915 American League pennant up the flagpole in centerfield. The 1915 World Championship banner wasn't raised until August 16.

JUNE 12   Babe Ruth hits a three-run pinch-hit homer in the seventh inning to tie the score 3–3, but the Red Sox lose 4–3 to the Browns in St. Louis.

"Manager Carrigan has just about decided to make Ruth a regular outfielder on account of his hitting," The Sporting News reported in its June 22, 1916, issue.

"He will do that unless he gets more attack out of the present trio." It was certainly an interesting dilemma. The Red Sox outscored just two teams in the American League in 1916, and only Larry Gardner, with a .308 average, had an outstanding year at the plate. Carrigan had a deep pitching staff at his disposal, but with Ruth as the ace, the Red Sox manager backed off on the gamble of moving the Babe to the outfield. In 1916, Ruth went 23–12 with a 1.75 ERA, 324 innings, 23 complete games, 170 strikeouts, and 9 shutouts, the last figure an American League record for left-handers.

JUNE 20   Everett Scott begins a streak of 1,307 consecutive games played during a 4–1 loss to the Yankees at Fenway Park. During the same game, Tilly Walker hit the only homer by a Red Sox player at Fenway Park in 1916. Walker's homer was hit over the left field wall. Amazingly, the pitching staff also surrendered only one homer at Fenway.

Scott played in a Boston Red Sox record 832 consecutive games before he was traded to the Yankees on December 20, 1921. His total streak ended at 1,307 games on May 6, 1925. The only streaks longer than Scott's in major league history are those of Cal Ripken Jr. (2,632) and Lou Gehrig (2,130). The only other Red Sox player to appear in at least 500 consecutive games is Buck Freeman, who appeared in 535 in a row from 1901 through 1905.

The Red Sox were slow out of the starting gate in 1916 with a 27–27 record after the June 20 loss. By July 30, Boston was in first place and battled the Tigers and White Sox for the pennant during the final two months of the season.

JUNE 21   Rube Foster no-hits the Yankees 2–0 at Fenway Park. He struck out three and walked three during the masterpiece. Foster retired Ray Caldwell, Frank Gilhooley, and Hugh High in order in the ninth. Duffy Lewis drove in both Boston runs.

Joseph Lannin gave Foster a bonus check of $100 for his efforts. Lannin also gave each member of the team an engraved gold-handled pocket knife.

JUNE 22   Babe Ruth shuts out the Yankees 1–0 at Fenway Park. Hal Janvrin hit a double in the third inning to drive in the game's lone run.

JUNE 23   The Red Sox shut out the opposition for the third game in a row as Ernie Shore blanks the Athletics 1–0 at Fenway Park. Tom Sheehan, who had a 1–16 record in 1916, allowed only two hits by the Red Sox. Shore had a record of 17–10 and a 2.63 ERA for the Sox in 1916.

Before the game, Athletics shortstop Whitey Witt was presented with a gold watch, a diamond ring, and a basket of flowers from friends and admirers at the University of Vermont. In the sixth inning, Witt hit a liner into the right field corner that looked to be good for three bases. But Witt tripped and fell between first and second. He apparently reached second base safely for a double but was called out for failing to touch first base.

JUNE 27   Larry Gardner ties a major league record by being caught stealing three times during a 7–2 loss to the Athletics at Fenway Park. Gardner was nabbed repeatedly despite the fact that pitcher Jing Johnson and catcher Doc Carroll were both making their major league debuts.

June 30
Carl Mays two-hits the Senators to win 6–1 at Griffith Stadium. The only Washington hits were singles by Eddie Foster and Clyde Milan.

In the third inning, Mays hit George McBride with a pitch. In an echo of the Ty Cobb incident the previous September, McBride responded by throwing his bat at Mays. Both benches emptied, and in the ensuing brawl, Red Sox catcher Sam Agnew was arrested by the police and hauled off to jail, where he was booked on assault charges for punching Senators manager Clark Griffith in the face. Mays swore out a warrant for McBride's arrest. It wasn't the only bizarre incident of the afternoon. In the seventh inning, Clyde Milan fouled back a pitch that struck umpire Brick Owens in the throat. Owens swallowed the chewing tobacco he had in his cheek, and nearly choked to death. It took fifteen minutes for Owens to regain his faculties and continue the game.

The following day in a Washington courtroom, Agnew was acquitted when Griffith refused to press charges, but Agnew was fined $10 for disorderly conduct. McBride was also exonerated when Mays withdrew his request for a warrant.

July 14
The Red Sox and Browns battle to a 0–0 tie after 17 innings at Fenway Park. Darkness ended the proceedings. Ernie Koob pitched the complete game for St. Louis. Carl Mays (15 innings) and Dutch Leonard (2 innings) combined to whitewash the Browns. Koob should have scored from second in the fifteenth inning on Ward Miller's drive to left field, but he was called out for failing to touch third base.

Throwing with submarine delivery, Mays was 18–13 with a 2.39 ERA in 1916.

July 15
The Red Sox wallop the Browns 17–4 in the second game of a doubleheader at Fenway Park following a 2–1 loss.

July 17
A military exhibition precedes a 3–2 win over the Browns at Fenway Park. The drills were conducted by the Coast Artillery Corps and the First Corps Cadets. Massachusetts Governor Samuel McCall was among those present. Red Sox owner Joe Lannin donated the day's receipts to the Soldiers' Relief Fund.

July 22
Dutch Leonard shuts out the Tigers 1–0 in the second game of a twin bill at Fenway Park. Detroit won the first game, 4–3.

Leonard had an 18–12 record, a 2.36 earned run average, six shutouts, and six saves for the Red Sox in 1916.

July 24
The Red Sox stop off in Toronto to play an exhibition game against the International League Maple Leafs. With Canada battling Germany in World War I, Red Sox players of German ancestry feared for their safety. Dick Hoblitzel elected not to appear in the contest, and Heinie Wagner played under the name Richardson.

July 27
The start of the game between the Red Sox and Indians in Cleveland is delayed for fifteen minutes because umpire Silk O'Loughlin would not signal the start of play until a band had finished playing. The Red Sox won, 7–6.

July 31
Babe Ruth pitches a two-hitter to beat the Tigers 6–0 in Detroit. The only hits off Ruth were a double by George Burns and a single by Ty Cobb.

AUGUST 6   Rube Foster defeats the Browns 1–0 at Sportsman's Park in St. Louis. While batting in the sixth inning for the Browns, Jimmy Austin took exception to remarks from Pinch Thomas and ripped the mask off the Boston catcher and pummeled him. Both were ejected.

AUGUST 15   In a remarkable pitching duel, Babe Ruth beats Walter Johnson 1–0 in a 13-inning encounter at Fenway Park. Larry Gardner's single drove in the only run of the game. Ruth nearly won the game in the twelfth when he launched a long drive, but Washington center fielder Clyde Milan reached into the bleachers to catch it.

AUGUST 16   The Red Sox win another long, hard-fought battle 5–4 in 16 innings over the White Sox in the first game of a doubleheader at Fenway Park. Manager Bill Carrigan used 21 of the 23 players on the Red Sox roster to secure the victory. The Sox set an American League record (since tied) by using four left fielders in the game, including Sad Sam Jones and Rube Foster. It was the only time that either one of them played a position other than pitcher during their major league careers. Boston also won the second game, called after six innings by darkness, 2–1.

AUGUST 21   Jack Barry ties a major league record with four sacrifice hits in four plate appearances during a 4–0 win over the Indians at Fenway Park.

The Red Sox in 1916 became the first team in baseball history to inform fans of scoring decisions by flashing an "H" for a hit or an "E" for an error on the Fenway Park scoreboard.

AUGUST 29   Starting pitcher Dutch Leonard is driven from the mound in the first inning of the first game of a doubleheader against the Browns at Fenway Park, lost by the Red Sox 5–3. Boston also lost the second game, 8–2.

AUGUST 30   A day after failing to survive the first inning, Dutch Leonard pitches a no-hitter against the Browns to win 4–0 at Fenway Park. Leonard struck out 3, walked 2, and set down the first 23 batters he faced. In the ninth, Leonard retired Doc Lavan, walked Grover Hartley, and induced Burt Shotton and Jack Tobin to hit fly balls for the last two outs of the game.

Boston baseball fans entered the month of September with the hopes that the Braves and Red Sox would meet in the World Series. The Braves led the National League as late as September 4 but slipped to third place, four games behind the Brooklyn Dodgers.

SEPTEMBER 16   The Red Sox fall from first place to third after a 6–4 loss to Chicago at Comiskey Park. Boston entered the contest three percentage points ahead of the Tigers and a half-game in front of the White Sox.

SEPTEMBER 17   Babe Ruth wins his 20th game of the season as the Red Sox down the White Sox 6–2 before 40,000 fans in Chicago. The victory boosted the Red Sox into second place.

SEPTEMBER 18   The Red Sox regain first place with a 4–3 win over the White Sox in Chicago.

SEPTEMBER 19   The Red Sox emerge with a 3–1 victory over the Tigers in Detroit.

The Red Sox swept the three-game series in Detroit to increase their lead in the American League pennant race to four games and virtually sew up a place in the World Series.

SEPTEMBER 23   Duffy Lewis collects five hits, including two triples, in five at-bats during a 5–3 win over the Indians in Cleveland.

SEPTEMBER 29   Babe Ruth collects his 23rd victory of the season in a 3–0 win over the Yankees at Fenway Park.

SEPTEMBER 30   Dutch Leonard shuts out the Yankees 1–0 in 10 innings at Fenway Park. Harry Hooper's sacrifice fly drove in the only run of the game. Centerfielder Tilly Walker pulled off an unassisted double play during the game. He raced in on a drive by Walt Alexander and stepped on second base before Tim Hendryx could return.

OCTOBER 1   The idle Red Sox clinch the American League pennant when the White Sox lose 2–0 to the Indians.

The Red Sox met the Brooklyn Dodgers in the World Series. Managed by Wilbert Robinson, the Dodgers had a 94–60 record in 1916. For the second year in a row, the Red Sox played the World Series at Braves Field.

OCTOBER 3   On the final day of the regular season, the Red Sox lose a doubleheader 5–3 and 7–5 to the Athletics at Braves Field. The Sox played the game at the Braves' ballpark to get accustomed to it for the upcoming World Series.

OCTOBER 7   The Red Sox survive a ninth-inning rally and defeat the Dodgers 6–5 in the first game of the World Series before 36,117 at Braves Field. Boston took a 6–1 lead into the ninth before starter Ernie Shore tired. By the time Carl Mays was brought in from the bullpen, the Dodgers had scored three runs and loaded the bases with two out. Mays gave up an infield single that scored one Brooklyn run before shortstop Everett Scott made a great stop deep in the hole on a ground ball and threw to first to retire Jake Daubert by a half a step to end the game. The Red Sox tied a World Series record by turning four double plays in one game.

OCTOBER 9   After an off day on Sunday, Babe Ruth defeats Brooklyn's Sherry Smith 2–1 in 14 innings in one of the best pitching duels in World Series history. A total of 41,373 attended the game at Braves Field. The Dodgers scored in the first on an inside-the-park homer by Hi Myers, and the Red Sox countered with a tally in the third on Everett Scott's triple and a ground-out by Ruth. For the next 10 innings, Ruth and Smith matched zeroes. With darkness rapidly settling over Fenway Park, Dick Hoblitzel led off the fourteenth inning by drawing his fourth walk of the game. He scored on a double by pinch hitter Del Gainer.

The 14-inning encounter is, by innings, the longest game in World Series history.

OCTOBER 10   The Dodgers earn their first win of the Series with a 4–3 decision over the Red Sox in arctic weather at Ebbets Field. Brooklyn took a 4–0 lead in the fifth off Carl Mays. The Red Sox made a gallant comeback but fell short. Larry Gardner hit a seventh-inning homer over the right field wall.

OCTOBER 11   Dutch Leonard puts the Red Sox within one win of the World Championship with a five-hit, 6–2 win over the Dodgers in Brooklyn. Larry Gardner homered for the second straight game, this one an inside-the-parker with two on base in the second inning that gave the Red Sox a 3–2 lead.

Gardner had only three hits in the Series but drove in six runs.

OCTOBER 12   Ernie Shore fires a three-hitter to lead the Red Sox to a World Championship for the second year in a row with a 4–1 triumph over the Dodgers before 42,620 deliriously happy fans on Columbus Day at Braves Field.

Bill Carrigan stepped down as manager at the age of thirty-two following the World Series to go into the banking business in his hometown of Lewiston, Maine.

NOVEMBER 1   Joe Lannin stuns Red Sox fans by selling the ball club to New York theatrical producers Harry Frazee and Hugh Ward. Four years earlier, Frazee had made an unsuccessful bid to purchase the St. Louis Cardinals. Lannin's departure was totally unexpected. He cited heart trouble as the reason for getting out of baseball.

Lannin died in 1928 after falling out of a window (see May 15, 1928). A native of Peoria, Illinois, the thirty-six-year-old Frazee offered half the sale amount of $675,000 in cash and planned to pay the balance off using loans he would cover with profits from the team. The purchase price included Fenway Park. Ward was a silent partner who was rarely heard from. Frazee led the Red Sox to another World Series title in 1918, but he soon dismantled the operation when World War I and a losing club in 1919 cut into his profits about the same time that payment on the loans came due. To help pay his debts, Frazee sold Babe Ruth to the Yankees, an act that sealed his notorious legacy in Boston and baseball history. In addition to producing plays, Frazee owned theaters in New York and Chicago. He also promoted the Jack Johnson–Jess Willard heavyweight boxing title match in Havana in 1915, which many to this day claim was fixed in Willard's favor.

1917   B

Season in a Sentence

The Red Sox win 90 games, but their quest for a third straight World Championship is denied as the stellar pitching staff and defense can't compensate for feeble hitting.

Finish • Won • Lost • Pct • GB

Second   90   62   .592   9.0

Manager

Jack Barry

Stats

Stats	Red Sox	AL	Rank
Batting Avg:	.246	.248	4
On-Base Pct:	.314	.318	5
Slugging Pct:	.319	.320	5
Home Runs:	14		6
Stolen Bases:	105		8
ERA:	2.20	2.66	2
Fielding Pct:	.972	.964	1
Runs Scored:	555		4
Runs Allowed:	454		1

Starting Lineup

Sam Agnew, c
Dick Hoblitzel, 1b
Jack Barry, 2b
Larry Gardner, 3b
Everett Scott, ss
Duffy Lewis, lf
Tilly Walker, cf
Harry Hooper, rf
Pinch Thomas, c
Jimmy Walsh, cf
Del Gainer, 1b
Chick Shorten, cf-lf

Pitchers

Babe Ruth, sp
Carl Mays, sp
Dutch Leonard, sp
Ernie Shore, sp
Rube Foster, sp
Herb Pennock, rp

Attendance

387,856 (fourth in AL)

Club Leaders

Batting Avg:	Lewis	.302
On-Base Pct:	Hooper	.355
Slugging Pct:	Lewis	.392
Home Runs:	Hooper	3
RBI:	Lewis	65
Runs:	Hooper	89
Stolen Bases:	Hooper	21
Wins:	Ruth	24
Strikeouts:	Leonard	144
ERA:	Mays	1.74
Saves:	Ruth	2

JANUARY 6   The Red Sox name twenty-nine-year-old Jack Barry as manager.

Playing for six pennant winners and five World Champions in seven years from 1910 through 1916, Barry certainly knew what it took to win. In taking over a club that had won the World Series the two previous seasons, Barry was in a "no-win" situation in 1917 since it would be nearly impossible to improve upon Bill Carrigan's record as the manager. Barry was largely blamed for the Red Sox' fall to second place.

FEBRUARY 13   Tim Murnane, a first baseman on the Boston Red Stockings in 1876 and later a popular sportswriter in Boston, dies at the age of sixty-four.

FEBRUARY 24   The Red Sox sell Smoky Joe Wood to the Indians. The Indians soon discovered that Wood was through as a pitcher. He was converted to an outfielder in 1918 and had five seasons of middling success as a hitter. From 1923 through 1942, Wood was the baseball coach at Yale University. He died in 1985 at the age of ninety-five.

MARCH 28   The Red Sox wear uniform numbers for a seven-city exhibition tour against the Brooklyn Dodgers beginning in Memphis, Tennessee. The numbers were the idea of Dodgers owner Charles Ebbets so that unfamiliar fans in non-major-league cities would be able to identify the players on the two clubs. The Red Sox wore the numbers on a red-and-white band on the uniform's sleeve. The experiment didn't carry over to the regular season, however. The Red Sox did not begin to wear uniform numbers on a regular basis until 1931.

APRIL 11   Five days after the United States declares war on Germany and enters World War I, the Red Sox defeat the Yankees 10–3 on Opening Day at the Polo Grounds in New York. Dick Hoblitzel homered for the Sox. Tilly Walker collected two triples and a double.

It had snowed six inches in New York City during the previous two days, and the snow had to be cleared from the diamond. Major General Leonard Wood threw out the first pitch and reviewed a military drill conducted by the Yankee players. As a show of patriotism during World War I, major leaguers often performed military drills prior to games in 1917 with bats on their shoulders simulating weapons. American League president Ban Johnson offered a $500 prize to the team with the best drills, which were judged by military experts. The Browns won, with the Red Sox finishing fifth among the eight clubs in the league.

APRIL 21   In the first game of the season at Fenway Park, Babe Ruth hits two doubles and a triple and pitches the Red Sox to a 6–4 win over the Yankees. Prior to the game, the Royal Rooters presented the defending World Champion Red Sox with a floral horseshoe, which the players walked through for good luck.

Ruth had a 24–13 record, a 2.01 ERA, 326 innings pitched, 128 strikeouts, and a league-leading 35 complete games in 38 starts in 1917. As a hitter, the Babe had a .325 average and two homers in 123 at-bats.

APRIL 24   George Mogridge of the Yankees pitches a no-hitter to beat the Red Sox 2–1 at Fenway Park. The Red Sox scored their run in the seventh inning on a walk, an error, a sacrifice bunt, and a sacrifice fly, which tied the score 1–1. The Yankees scored the winning run in the ninth inning.

MAY 7   Babe Ruth pitches a two-hitter and defeats Walter Johnson and the Senators 1–0 at Griffith Stadium. Ruth also drove in the lone run of the contest with a sacrifice fly in the eighth inning. The only Washington hits were singles by George McBride and Eddie Ainsmith.

The victory marked the third time that Ruth had defeated Johnson 1–0 in a span of 11 months.

MAY 10   The game between the Red Sox and the Tigers in Detroit is delayed for half an hour because the Sox missed their train connection in Buffalo. The late-arriving Red Sox won 3–0.

MAY 25   Dutch Leonard's two-hitter beats the Browns 3–0 at Sportsman's Park. The only St. Louis hits were singles by Bob Groom and William Rumler.

MAY 26   An 11–7 win over the Browns in St. Louis is delayed ten minutes when a large group of fans surges out of the right field bleachers toward umpire Brick Owens after a call against the home team. Police stopped the crowd from reaching the infield, and players from both teams armed with bats helped drive them back into the seats.

MAY 29   The Red Sox score seven runs in the fifth inning and beat the Senators 9–0 in the second game of a doubleheader on a chilly, damp day in Washington. The Sox also won the opener 2–1 with a pair of runs in the ninth.

JUNE 5   The Red Sox cut loose with a nine-run second inning in an 11–4 win over the Indians at Fenway Park.

Duffy Lewis was Boston's top hitter in 1917 with a .302 batting average.

JUNE 23   Ernie Shore pitches a "perfect game" against the Senators to win 4–0 in the first game of a doubleheader at Fenway Park. Babe Ruth was the starting pitcher and walked Washington leadoff hitter Ray Morgan on four pitches. Ruth tersely disputed the calls of home plate umpire Brick Owens and was ejected. The Babe responded to the banishment by rushing toward Owens. Catcher Pinch Thomas tried to intercept Ruth but was ineffective, and Ruth succeeded in swatting Owens on the neck. Thomas had a few choice words for Owens and was also ejected. Shore came on in relief, and after Morgan was caught stealing, recorded outs against the only 26 batters he faced. In the ninth, Shore retired Howard Shanks, John Henry (on a running catch by Duffy Lewis in left field), and pinch hitter Mike Menosky (on a pop-up to second baseman Jack Barry). Catcher Sam Agnew, who entered the game with Shore after Thomas was ejected, went three for three. The Red Sox also won the second game 5–0 behind a shutout by Dutch Leonard.

Shore's tremendous pitching effort has long been erroneously listed as a perfect game in many record books. Since Shore was a relief pitcher and there was one Washington base runner, it doesn't fit the criteria of absolute perfection. Ruth was suspended for nine days and fined $100 by league president Ban Johnson because of the incident.

JULY 11   Babe Ruth pitches a one-hitter for a 1–0 win over the Tigers at Navin Field. The only Detroit hit was an infield hit by Donie Bush in the eighth that glanced off Ruth's glove. The run was scored with two out in the ninth inning on triples by Tilly Walker and Chick Shorten.

JULY 18   Carl Mays shuts out the Browns for a 1–0 win in St. Louis.

Mays was 22–9 with a 1.74 ERA in 1917.

JULY 31   A fluke homer by Harry Hooper highlights a 5–2 win over the White Sox at Fenway Park. With two runners on base in the first inning, Hooper hit a line drive down the right field line that struck the glove of Chicago outfielder Shano Collins and caromed into the bleachers.

AUGUST 6   Rube Foster pitches a one-hitter but loses 2–0 to the Indians at Fenway Park. In the first inning, Foster walked two and gave up a double to Joe Harris.

AUGUST 10   The Red Sox score four runs in the ninth inning on a bases-loaded triple by

Dick Hoblitzel and a Harry Hooper single to win 5–4 over the Tigers in the first game of a doubleheader in Detroit. The Red Sox also won the second game, 5–1.

Babe Ruth was the winning pitcher and hit his first homer of the season in the opener but was nearly scratched because of a severe sunburn he received while on an off-day outing at Cape Cod three days earlier. Ruth's homer was the first ever hit into the center field bleachers at Fenway.

AUGUST 18   The Red Sox split a doubleheader against the Indians in Cleveland, losing 2–1 loss and winning 9–1, to fall out of first place behind the White Sox. The Indians won the opener with two ninth-inning runs. With the Red Sox leading 1–0 in the final inning, none out, and the bases loaded, and Dutch Leonard pitching for the Red Sox, umpire Brick Owens called a ball on a 3–2 pitch to Braggo Roth. Owens was suddenly surrounded by a dozen angry Red Sox, who had been objecting to Owens's calls throughout the game. Owens ejected Leonard, Jack Barry, and Dick Hoblitzel. Herb Pennock replaced Leonard and gave up the two winning runs on a single to Jack Graney.

The Red Sox spent 53 days in first place in 1917, but the White Sox won 30 of their last 40 games to run away with the pennant.

AUGUST 21   Del Gainer of the Red Sox and Chick Gandil of the White Sox fight after a 2–0 Boston loss in Chicago. Gandil claimed Gainer tried to spike him on a play at first base in the fourth inning. After the final out, the two traded punches in the White Sox' dugout before players from both clubs separated the combatants.

AUGUST 31   Babe Ruth wins his 20th game of the season with a 5–3 decision over the Athletics in the first game of a doubleheader at Fenway Park. The Red Sox also won the second game, 6–2.

Through his first four seasons in the majors, in which he was strictly a pitcher, Ruth had 361 at-bats, a .299 batting average, nine homers, and a .474 slugging percentage. The American League averages during that period were a batting average of .248 and a slugging percentage of .323. With his big swing, Ruth was also susceptible to the strikeout. He fanned 68 times from 1914 through 1917, or once every 5.3 at-bats. The American League average during the period was one strikeout every 8.6 at-bats.

SEPTEMBER 12   The Red Sox and Senators are deadlocked 1–1 after 16 innings when the contest at Griffith Stadium is called for darkness. Ernie Shore and Washington's Doc Ayers both pitched complete games.

SEPTEMBER 25   Pinch Thomas lives up to his name as he delivers a two-run pinch-hit single in the thirteenth inning to defeat the Indians 4–3 at Fenway Park.

SEPTEMBER 27   The Red Sox stage a benefit game at Fenway Park for the family of sportswriter Tim Murnane, who died on February 13. The Red Sox played a team of All-Stars that included Ty Cobb, Tris Speaker, Joe Jackson, Walter Johnson, and Rabbit Maranville. The Sox defeated the All-Stars 2–0, with Babe Ruth hurling five innings. A total of 17,000 fans attended the contest to raise $14,000.

SEPTEMBER 29   The Red Sox roll in 13–5 and 11–0 wins over the Browns at Fenway Park. The second game victory was Babe Ruth's 24th of the season.

OCTOBER 2   Carl Mays collects his 22nd win of the season with a 2–1 win over the Senators in the second game of a doubleheader at Fenway Park. The contest was called on account of darkness after eight innings. Washington won the opener 9–7.

DECEMBER 14   The Red Sox send Vean Gregg, Merlin Kopp, Pinch Thomas, and $60,000 to the Athletics for Amos Strunk, Joe Bush, and Wally Schang.

Frazee has long been vilified as the man who sold Babe Ruth to the Yankees and liquidated most of the rest of the Red Sox' top players during the early 1920s. During his first two seasons in Boston, however, Frazee was more than willing to open his checkbook in order to build a winning club. The Red Sox received three useful players in this trade, each of whom contributed to Boston's 1918 World Championship team, while giving up next to nothing.

1918   B

Season in a Sentence

Fan interest in 1918 was generally at a low ebb because of World War I, but the Red Sox win their fourth World Series in seven years, and fifth overall.

Finish • Won • Lost • Pct • GB

First   75   51   .595   +2.5

World Series—The Red Sox defeated the Chicago Cubs four games to two.

Manager

Ed Barrow

Stats — Red Sox • AL • Rank

	Red Sox	AL	Rank
Batting Avg:	.249	.254	7
On-Base Pct:	.322	.323	3
Slugging Pct:	.327	.322	3
Home Runs:	15		3
Stolen Bases:	110		6
ERA:	2.31	2.77	2
Fielding Pct:	.971	.964	1
Runs Scored:	474		4
Runs Allowed:	380		1

Starting Lineup

Sam Agnew, c
Stuffy McInnis, 1b
Dave Shean, 2b
Fred Thomas, 3b
Everett Scott, ss
Babe Ruth, lf-p
Amos Strunk, cf
Harry Hooper, rf
George Whiteman, lf
Wally Schang, c

Pitchers

Carl Mays, sp
Joe Bush, sp
Sad Sam Jones, sp
Babe Ruth, sp
Dutch Leonard, sp

Attendance

249,513 (third in AL)

Club Leaders

Batting Avg:	Ruth	.300
On-Base Pct:	Ruth	.410
Slugging Pct:	Ruth	.555
Home Runs:	Ruth	11
RBI:	Ruth	66
Runs:	Hooper	81
Stolen Bases:	Hooper	24
Wins:	Mays	21
Strikeouts:	Bush	125
ERA:	Bush	2.11
Saves:	Bush	2

JANUARY 10 — The Red Sox trade Larry Gardner, Tilly Walker, and Hick Cady to the Athletics for Stuffy McInnis.

> *This was a deal that made little sense, other than the fact that McInnis hailed from nearby Gloucester, Massachusetts. Gardner remained a star third baseman for another four years with the Athletics and Indians. Walker tied Ruth for the American League home run lead with 11 in 1918, and actually outhomered the Babe 37–35 in 1922, Walker's last good season. McInnis had been the Athletics' starting first baseman since 1911, but the Red Sox planned to move him to third base. Those plans were scrapped early in the 1918 season, and Stuffy returned to first. He was one of the best defensive first basemen of his era but was at best an average hitter for his position, and the Red Sox paid too high a price to get him.*

FEBRUARY 11 — With Jack Barry set to miss the 1918 season following his enlistment in the Navy, the Red Sox sign fifty-year-old Ed Barrow as manager. Barrow had previously managed the Tigers in 1903 and 1904 but made his mark prior to 1918 as a minor league executive. At the time of his appointment as manager of the Red Sox, Barrow was the president of the International League. Harry Frazee hired him in part because of his ability to run a club both in the office and on the field. Military service robbed the Red Sox of several players in 1918. In addition to Barry's being out, Duffy Lewis, Hal Janvrin, Del Gainer, Mike McNally, Chick Shorten, Herb Pennock, Jimmy Walsh, Paul Musser, and Jimmy Cooney missed the entire year. Dick Hoblitzel, Dutch Leonard, Fred Thomas, and Wally Mayer were gone before the season ended. With Boston located on the ocean, most of the Red Sox players joined the Navy.

FEBRUARY 13 — The Red Sox sign future Hall of Famer Johnny Evers.

> *The Red Sox acquired Evers to act as a coach and replace Barry at second base. Evers's tightly wound personality infuriated his teammates during spring training, however, and he was released just prior to Opening Day in the interest of team morale. Also, Babe Ruth appeared at first base during spring training for several games against the Brooklyn Dodgers.*

MARCH 17 — Babe Ruth plays right field during an 11–1 exhibition game win over the Dodgers in Hot Springs, Arkansas. Ruth walked and homered twice in three trips to the plate.

MARCH 20 — Harry Hooper, Babe Ruth, Everett Scott, Joe Bush, and Wally Schang narrowly escape death during an automobile ride at spring training in Hot Springs, Arkansas. The five players engaged a cab driver to take them from the racetrack to the team hotel. Halfway to the destination, the cabbie stopped and demanded that he be paid for his services. The players called a policeman, who ordered the driver to take the Sox players where they wanted to go. The driver did so but at a frightening speed. Tearing around the downtown area, he banged into a bus, knocked down a horse, and smashed a wagon before Hooper threatened to beat him up, which allowed the players to escape unharmed.

APRIL 8 — The Dodgers defeat the Red Sox 3–1 in an exhibition game in Birmingham, Alabama, shortened to seven innings by cold weather. The two clubs were so anxious to get off the field and into a warm clubhouse that they played the seven innings in thirty-five minutes. Babe Ruth served as umpire before entering the game as a pinch hitter in the last inning with the bases loaded and two out. Ruth just missed a homer when the ball went foul by a foot, then struck out.

APRIL 15   On Opening Day, the Red Sox defeat the Athletics 7–1 before a crowd of 7,180 at Fenway Park.

APRIL 16   Carl Mays pitches a one-hitter to beat the Athletics 1–0 at Fenway Park. The only hit off Mays was a single by Joe Dugan with one out in the eighth inning. The sole run of the contest came in the ninth inning on a single by Everett Scott.

The Red Sox' pitching staff set a club record with 26 shutouts in 1918.

APRIL 17   The Red Sox score three runs in the ninth inning to defeat the Athletics 5–4 at Fenway Park. The final two runs were driven in on a pinch-single by Wally Schang against his former Philadelphia teammates in his first at-bat as a member of the Red Sox. Among those in attendance was silent film star Mary Pickford.

The Red Sox began the 1918 season with six consecutive victories and had a 12–2 record at the end of April.

APRIL 19   Everett Scott scores from second base on a sacrifice fly off the bat of Babe Ruth during a 9–5 win over the Yankees in the afternoon session of a Patriots' Day doubleheader at Fenway Park. The drive came in the sixth inning and was caught by New York right fielder Frank Gilhooley against the wall. The Red Sox also won the morning game, 2–1.

APRIL 23   The Red Sox win a dramatic 1–0 decision over the Yankees at Fenway Park. New York pitcher Hank Thormahlen held the Red Sox hitless until they had one out in the ninth inning. Boston rallied with two singles by Amos Strunk and Babe Ruth (acting as a pinch hitter) and a sacrifice fly by George Whiteman. Joe Bush pitched the shutout.

As a teenager, Whiteman toured the nation as part of a high-dive act, jumping off a tower and into a barrel of water at carnivals. But when his partner died in an accident in Texas, Whiteman turned to baseball. He was thirty-five years old in 1918. His only prior big-league experience was four games with the Red Sox in 1907 and 11 with the Yankees in 1913.

APRIL 28   Babe Ruth plays first base during an exhibition game against a minor league team in Bridgeport, Connecticut. Ruth made an error and was 0 for 1 at the plate as the Red Sox won 7–0.

MAY 6   Manager Ed Barrow plays Babe Ruth as a position player in a regular-season game for the first time in his career, starting at first base and batting sixth during a 10–3 loss to the Yankees in New York. It was also the first time in his career that Ruth was listed higher than ninth in the batting order. The Babe started the Red Sox on their way to victory by breaking a scoreless tie in the fourth inning with a home run into the upper deck in right field.

The Red Sox had contemplated moving Ruth to first base or the outfield for several years, but turning one of the best pitchers in the game into a hitter was a risk that previous managers Bill Carrigan and Jack Barry had been unable to take. Many had suggested that Ruth remain in the pitching rotation and play in the field between starts, but Carrigan and Barry worried that Ruth would injure his valuable arm, especially on throws from the outfield. On May 6, 1918, Ed Barrow finally pulled the trigger, changing the face of baseball forever. The transition of Ruth from pitcher to hitter at this point was the result of several factors, but it was World War I that tipped the balance. Because of military inductions and enlistments, the club's depth was cut dangerously thin. Duffy Lewis's entering the Navy created a void in left field. First baseman Dick Hoblitze, who was in the throes of a horrible batting slump, was unable to play because of an injured finger, and was soon to join the Army Medical Corps as a dentist. The pitching staff was left relatively unscathed by the service defections. At the time, Ruth was simply the best alternative for the lack of offensive production that Barrow and the Red Sox suffered both in left and at first. Barrow hedged his bets, however, and continued to employ Ruth as a pitcher, though mainly as a spot starter, through the end of the 1919 season.

MAY 7   Babe Ruth bats fourth for the first time and homers off Walter Johnson, but the Red Sox lose 7–2 to the Senators in Washington.

During the 1918 season, Ruth played 47 games in left field, 12 in center, 20 as a pitcher, and 13 at first base. The Babe was essentially a platoon player in 1918, starting almost exclusively against right-handed pitchers.

MAY 9   Pitching and batting in the cleanup spot, Babe Ruth has five hits, including three doubles and a triple, in five at-bats, but the Red Sox lose 4–3 in 10 innings to the Senators at Griffith Stadium.

Ruth is one of only two pitchers since 1900 to collect four extra-base hits in a game. The other was Snake Wiltse for the Athletics in 1901.

MAY 10   Babe Ruth starts in the left field for his first ever appearance in the outfield in the regular season as the Red Sox record a 4–1 win over the Browns at Fenway Park.

Many baseball historians have speculated that Ruth would have reached the Hall of Fame as a pitcher even if he had never quit the mound to become a full-time batter. That scenario is highly unlikely, however. Ruth pitched 868 innings between his twentieth and twenty-third birthdays, including 650 innings in 1916 and 1917, and historically pitchers who have been used that often that young have had short careers. It's probable that at the time Ruth moved to the outfield, a major arm injury was lurking just around the next corner. If so, Ruth would certainly have been converted into a first baseman or an outfielder at the time his arm was unable to withstand the rigors of pitching. In 1918, the Indians were making a similar move with dead-armed, ex-Red Sox star Smoky Joe Wood in the outfield.

MAY 20   The Red Sox hammer the Indians 11–1 at Fenway Park.

MAY 28   Joe Bush pitches a one-hitter and drives in the game's lone run in the fifth inning to beat the White Sox 1–0 at Fenway Park. The only Chicago hit off Bush was a single by Happy Felsch in the first inning.

JUNE 3   Dutch Leonard pitches his second career no-hitter to defeat the Tigers 5–0 in Detroit. The only base runner Leonard allowed was Bobby Veach, who drew a walk with two out in the first inning. From that point forward, Leonard set down 25 batters in a row. In the ninth, Leonard began by retiring Archie Yelle on a grounder to short. Ty Cobb, out of the starting lineup with an injured shoulder, pinch hit and fouled out to third baseman Fred Thomas. Donie Bush ended the game as Leonard's fourth strike-out victim.

Babe Ruth homered in the first inning. It also marked the first time in his big-league career that Ruth played center field and the first occasion in which he batted third in the lineup, eventually his everyday spot.

JUNE 5   Babe Ruth becomes the first player in major league history to hit homers in four consecutive games, but the Red Sox lose 5–4 to the Indians in Cleveland.

Ruth tied for the American League lead in homers in 1918 with 11 in 317 at-bats. He also hit an even .300, had 26 doubles, and drove in 66 runs. As a pitcher, the Babe was 13–7 with an ERA of 2.22. He hit 11 of Boston's 15 home runs in 1918. No other Red Sox player had more than one.

JUNE 6   Sad Sam Jones shuts out the Indians 1–0 in a 10-inning affair in Cleveland. Babe Ruth drove in the only run of the game, scoring Harry Hooper from third base on a force-out.

Nicknamed "Sad Sam" for his downcast demeanor, Jones had a 16–5 record and a 2.25 earned run average in 1918.

JUNE 10   Joe Bush blanks the White Sox 1–0 on a cold day in Chicago. In the fourth inning, Dave Shean tripled and scored on a passed ball.

Bush contributed a 2.11 ERA, 26 complete games, 125 strikeouts, 273 innings pitched, and a record of 15–15 in 1918. Harry Hooper was Boston's top hitter in 1918. He batted .289, scored 81 runs, hit 26 doubles and 13 triples, and had a .391 on-base percentage.

JUNE 21   Carl Mays pitches a one-hitter as the Red Sox rout the Athletics 13–0 at Fenway Park. The Philadelphia hit was an infield single by Jake Munch that rolled down the first base line. Munch had only 8 hits during his entire big-league career.

The shutout by Mays came during a streak in which he hurled 35 consecutive scoreless innings. During the 1918 season, he was 21–13 with 30 complete games, 293 innings pitched, eightshutouts, 114 strikeouts, and a 2.21 ERA.

JUNE 30   Playing center field, Babe Ruth clouts a two-run homer in the tenth inning off of Walter Johnson to defeat the Senators 3–1 at Griffith Stadium in Washington.

JULY 3   Angry after an argument with Ed Barrow during a 3–0 loss to the Senators in Washington the previous day, Babe Ruth leaves the Red Sox and announces his intention to play for the company team of the Chester (Pennsylvania) Shipbuilding Company in the Delaware River Shipbuilding League. Harry Frazee threatened Ruth with an injunction to prevent him from playing for any team except the Red Sox. The Babe rejoined the Red Sox in time for the second game of a July 4 doubleheader against the Athletics.

JULY 4   In a wartime Independence Day doubleheader against the Athletics in Philadelphia, the Red Sox win 11–9 but then lose 2–1 in 11 innings.

JULY 6   The Red Sox push the Indians out of first place with a 5–4 win at Fenway Park. Trailing 4–2 in the sixth, Babe Ruth doubled in two runs and scored on a throwing error.

The Sox remained at the top of the American League standings for the rest of the season.

JULY 8   In the tenth inning, Babe Ruth lifts the Red Sox over the Indians 1–0 in the second game of a doubleheader at Fenway Park with a smash deep into the right field bleachers. Ruth was credited with a triple instead of a home run because of the scoring rules of the day. Amos Strunk was on first base at the time, and the contest was considered to be over as soon as he crossed the plate. The scoring rule was changed in 1920. The Indians won the first game of the day, 4–3.

JULY 9   Joe Bush pitches a complete game 12-inning, 1–0 win over the Indians at Fenway Park. Wally Mayer's single ended the proceedings.

Red Sox pitchers combined for 45 consecutive shutout innings against the Indians and White Sox between July 7 and 12. The contributors were Joe Bush (18 innings), Sad Sam Jones (13), Carl Mays (9), and Lore Bader (5).

JULY 17   The Red Sox sweep the Browns with a pair of shutouts in a doubleheader at Fenway Park. Joe Bush won the first game 7–0, and Babe Ruth pitched the second to win 5–0 in a contest shortened to five innings by rain. In the fourth inning of the second game, Wally Schang of the Red Sox and catcher Hank Severeid of the Browns exchanged blows. Schang claimed that Severeid was too rough in tagging him out.

JULY 22   The Red Sox come up with another doubleheader shutout to defeat the Tigers twice in oppressive 98 degree heat at Fenway Park. In the opener, Joe Bush not only pitched a complete game in the 10-inning 1–0 victory but also scored the only run of the contest. Bush walked, took third on a single, and crossed the plate on an error. In the nightcap, Carl Mays was the winner, 3–0.

JULY 26   Eusebio Gonzalez becomes the Red Sox' first Latin player when he enters as a substitute at shortstop for Everett Scott in a 7–2 loss to the White Sox in Chicago. Gonzalez was from Havana, Cuba.

AUGUST 1   Baseball's governing body, the National Commission, announces that the 1918 season will end on September 2 in order to comply with a draft order requiring all men of draft age to "work or fight." Players participating in the World Series received an extension until September 15.

AUGUST 19   Sad Sam Jones pitches a two-hitter to down the Indians 6–0 at Fenway Park. The only Cleveland hits were singles by Steve O'Neill and Joe Evans.

The victory gave the Red Sox a four-game lead over the White Sox with 14 games left on the schedule.

AUGUST 27   Joe Bush strikes out 13 batters but loses 2–1 to the Tigers at Fenway Park.

AUGUST 30   Carl Mays pitches two complete-game victories over the Athletics at Fenway Park. Mays earned his 20th win of the season in the opener, a 12–0 runaway, and was a 4–1 winner in the nightcap. Mays also starred with the bat, collecting five hits.

Ted Williams was born 3,000 miles away in San Diego, California—while the games were in progress.

AUGUST 31   Behind the pitching of Babe Ruth, the Red Sox clinch the pennant with a 6–1 victory over the Athletics in the first game of a twin bill at Fenway Park. The Athletics won the second game, 1–0.

The Red Sox met the Chicago Cubs in the World Series. Managed by Fred Mitchell, the Cubs had an 84–45 record in 1918 and led the National League by $10^{1}/_{2}$ games. The Cubs used Comiskey Park in the World Series instead of their own playing field at Weeghman Park (now known as Wrigley Field). None of the three games played at Comiskey reached capacity, however. Unlike 1915 and 1916, when the Red Sox played at Braves Field during the Fall Classic, the club stayed home at Fenway Park. With wartime restrictions on travel in effect, the first three games of the Series were scheduled for Chicago, with the rest slated for Boston.

Because of the war-shortened season, the 1918 World Series was played earlier than any other in history. Ironically, if the Series had been played during its normal period in early October, it might have been canceled or postponed by a flu epidemic. From late September through November, a virulent form of flu struck the nation. Public gatherings in many cities, including Boston and Chicago, were banned by health officials. Estimates are that 20 to 25 percent of the nation's population was struck by the flu. The epidemic caused between 400,000 and 500,000 deaths in the United States and 20 million worldwide.

SEPTEMBER 4   The start of the World Series is delayed for a day by rain.

SEPTEMBER 5   In the opening game of the World Series, Babe Ruth pitches the Red Sox to a 1–0 win over the Cubs at Comiskey Park. The Red Sox' run scored in the fourth inning when Hippo Vaughn allowed a walk to Dave Shean and singles to George Whiteman and Stuffy McInnis. The victory came 11 days after Ruth's father died from injuries he suffered in a fight with his brother-in-law in Baltimore.

Combined with the 13 shutout innings he pitched in Game Two of the 1916 World Series, Ruth extended his postseason scoreless streak to 22 consecutive innings. Ruth appeared in only three games in the 1918 World Series: two as a pitcher and one as a substitute in left field in the eighth inning of the final game after George Whiteman was injured. Ruth rarely played in the outfield during the regular season against southpaws, and the Cubs used only Hippo Vaughn and Lefty Tyler as starting pitchers in the Series, who were both left-handed. For some reason, Barrow batted Ruth in the ninth spot in the batting order in the first game. In his fourth game start, Ruth batted sixth.

The 1918 World Champion Red Sox (l–r): (back row) owner and president Harry Frazee, manager Ed Barrow, Walt Kinney, Babe Ruth, George Cochran, Jack Coffey, Carl Mays, secretary Larry Graver, Wally Schang, Harry Hooper, team trainer Martin Lawler; (middle row) Stuffy McInnis, Fred Thomas, George Whiteman, Jean Dubuc, Dave Shean, Wally Mayer, Bill Pertica, Sam Agnew; (front row) Joe Bush, Hack Miller, Sad Sam Jones, Heinie Wagner, unidentified "mascot," Amos Strunk, Everett Scott.

Flyovers of military aircraft are commonplace before outdoor sporting events such as the World Series. The first flyover at a World Series game took place in 1918 during World War I. Prior to the Red Sox-Cubs matchup in Game One, sixty U.S. Army airplanes from nearby Great Lakes Training Center flew over the field in military formation. It had been less than fifteen years after the Wright brothers' first successful flight.

SEPTEMBER 6   The Cubs even the series with a 3–1 win over the Red Sox at Fenway Park. Lefty Tyler pitched a complete game for Chicago and drove in two runs.

Pitchers dominated the series. The Red Sox batted only .186, the lowest ever by a World Series winner, and the Chicago pitching staff had an ERA of 1.04. The combined earned run average for the two clubs over the six games was 1.37.

SEPTEMBER 7   The Red Sox' Carl Mays defeats Hippo Vaughn, who was pitching on one day's rest, 2–1 at Comiskey Park. The Red Sox scored both runs in the fourth inning on a hit batsman and three singles. In the fourth inning the Sox' George Whiteman robbed Dode Paskert of a home run by making a circus catch in left field. The game ended when Charlie Pick of the Cubs was tagged out in a rundown between third and home while trying to score from second base on a passed ball.

Vaughn allowed only three runs in 27 innings of pitching during the 1918 World Series but still had a 1–2 record.

SEPTEMBER 9   The Red Sox move within one game of the World Championship with a 3–2 victory over the Cubs before 22,183 at Fenway Park. Babe Ruth gave the Red Sox a 2–0 lead in the fourth inning by driving in a pair of runs with a triple. The Cubs evened the score with two runs in the eighth, but the Red Sox moved back ahead in their half when Wally Schang hit a pinch-single and made it home on a passed ball, a sacrifice, and an error.

Ruth held the Cubs hitless for the first 7 innings to set a World Series record of 29 consecutive scoreless innings despite being bothered by a cut on one of the fingers on his pitching hand. He had injured it on the train ride from Chicago to Boston when he lost his balance while horsing around with teammate Walt Kinney and shoved his hand through a window.

Ruth's consecutive scoreless inning record was broken by Whitey Ford, who pitched 32 consecutive scoreless innings in 1960 and 1961. During the games in Boston, carrier pigeons were sent at the end of each inning to Camp Devens, thirty miles west of Boston, to appraise soldiers there of the score.

SEPTEMBER 10   The Cubs delay Boston's celebration with a 3–0 win in Game Five with 24,694 at Fenway Park. Hippo Vaughn pitched the shutout.

B   The World Series Strike   B

The 1918 World Series between the Red Sox and the Cubs was an unusual one. It began a month early, on September 5, because of a federal government edict that ended the regular season on Labor Day on account of World War I. Major leaguers either had to enlist or take war-related jobs. The Series almost ended early because players from both teams threatened to strike prior to the fifth game on September 10 at Fenway Park because the winners' and losers' shares of the gate receipts had been drastically reduced.

The players' share was less than one-third of what it had been in previous seasons for a variety of reasons. Preoccupation with the war in Europe reduced attendance at the games. Owners lowered ticket prices to compensate for the lack of interest and also earmarked part of the gate money for wartime charities such as the Red Cross. In addition, the second-, third-, and fourth-place clubs received part of the pot for the first time.

Spirited negotiations delayed Game Five for more than an hour as representatives of the players and the National Commission aired their differences. (The National Commission, baseball's governing body at the time, consisted of Cincinnati Reds president Garry Herrmann, American League president Ban Johnson, and National League president John Heydler.) Red Sox outfielder Harry Hooper was the players' official spokesman. The players asked for a guaranteed $2,000 to players on the winning team and $1,400 to those on the losing club, totals only a little more than half of what players in the 1917 Fall Classic received. The commission rejected the offer, and Hooper, who said the commission members were all intoxicated, was willing to settle for $1,500 and $1,000. The commission also dismissed this proposal, and Boston Mayor John F. Fitzgerald pleaded with both sides for conciliation. The crowd of 24,694 grew restless and repeated cries of "play ball." Extra police were summoned to Fenway because of fears there might be a riot should the contest be called off. Four mounted policemen rode onto the field.

The players backed off their strike threat, however, because they were afraid to appear greedy while the country was fighting a war, particularly given that hundreds of wounded soldiers and sailors were seated in the grandstand. In a backlash against the players, only 15,238 fans showed for Game Six, which the Sox won 2–1 to take the world championship four games to two.

The Red Sox received only $1,103 per player, compared with winning shares of $3,669 in 1917. The Cubs' share was just $671 per player; members of the losing Giants from 1917 had gotten $2,442 apiece. In 1919, the winning and losing shares were $5,207 and $3,254, respectively. The owners also withheld championship pins from the Red Sox in 1918 in retaliation for the threatened strike. (The tradition of granting rings didn't start until the 1920s.) In 1993, the Red Sox bestowed the emblems to the descendants of the 1918 Red Sox in a ceremony at Fenway Park.

SEPTEMBER 11   The Red Sox win their fourth World Series in a span of seven seasons with a 2–1 victory over the Cubs in front of a crowd of only 15,238 at Fenway Park. Both Boston runs were scored in the third inning when Cubs right fielder Max Flack dropped George Whiteman's line drive with runners on second and third and two out. Carl Mays hurled a complete-game three-hitter. George Whiteman cut off a Cubs rally in the eighth with a somersaulting catch in left field. Counting the win by the Braves in 1914, a Boston club won five of the seven World Series played from 1912 through 1918.

At the time the World Series ended, it appeared that the 1919 season might also be in jeopardy because the war's end was not imminent. The military situation in Europe changed quickly, however, and Germany surrendered on November 11. Baseball executives anticipated a poor season at the gate in 1919 and shortened the schedule to 140 games. Red Sox fans would have to wait 17 years, until 1935, before they would even be able to enjoy another winning season, much less a pennant. Boston's next World Series wouldn't come until 1946. They won their first World Championship since the 1918 victory in 2004.

DECEMBER 18   The Red Sox trade Ernie Shore, Duffy Lewis, and Dutch Leonard to the Yankees for Frank Gilhooley, Slim Love, Ray Caldwell, Roxy Walters, and $15,000.

The Red Sox gave up three big names in the deal, but each was past his prime and quickly faded. In exchange, the Red Sox picked up four players who accomplished little in Boston.

1919 B

Season in a Sentence

Babe Ruth stuns the baseball world with 29 homers, but the Red Sox sink into sixth place.

Finish • Won • Lost • Pct • GB

Sixth 66 71 .482 20.5

Manager

Ed Barrow

Stats

Stats	Red Sox •	AL •	Rank
Batting Avg:	.261	.268	6
On-Base Pct:	.336	.333	4
Slugging Pct:	.344	.359	6
Home Runs:	33		3
Stolen Bases:	108		5
ERA:	3.31	3.22	7
Fielding Pct:	975	.965	1
Runs Scored:	564		5
Runs Allowed:	552		4

Starting Lineup

Wally Schang, c
Stuffy McInnis, 1b
Red Shannon, 2b
Ossie Vitt, 3b
Everett Scott, ss
Babe Ruth, lf
Braggo Roth, cf
Harry Hooper, rf
Amos Strunk, cf
Bill Lamar, cf
Roxy Walters, c

Pitchers

Herb Pennock, sp
Sad Sam Jones, sp
Carl Mays, sp
Babe Ruth, sp
Waite Hoyt, sp
Allan Russell, sp-rp
Ray Caldwell, sp-rp

Attendance

417,291 (fifth in AL)

Club Leaders

Batting Avg:	Ruth	.322
On-Base Pct:	Ruth	.456
Slugging Pct:	Ruth	.657
Home Runs:	Ruth	29
RBI:	Ruth	114
Runs:	Ruth	103
Stolen Bases:	Hooper	23
Wins:	Pennock	16
Strikeouts:	Pennock	70
ERA:	Mays	2.47
Saves:	Russell	4

JANUARY 17   The Red Sox trade Hal Janvrin and cash to the Senators for Eddie Ainsmith and George Dumont, then swap Ainsmith, Chick Shorten, and Slim Love to the Tigers for Ossie Vitt.

At the time of the trades, much of Boston's commercial district was covered with molasses. Two days earlier, a fifty-foot-high iron tank full of two million gallons of molasses had exploded in the North End, causing a fifteen-foot tidal wave of the sticky substance that killed twenty-one people.

APRIL 4   Babe Ruth hits a home run estimated to have traveled nearly six hundred feet during an exhibition game against the Giants in Tampa, Florida. Ruth hit the towering homer off George Smith in the second inning of a 5–3 Red Sox win.

Tampa's "ballpark," Plant Field, was laid out in the infield of a horse racing track on the Tampa Fairgrounds. There were no outfield fences. The ball landed over the distant race track railing. Many decades later, a plaque was erected at the site where the blast landed. It is now part of the campus of the University of Tampa.

APRIL 18   Babe Ruth hits four homers in consecutive at-bats during a 12–3 exhibition win over the International League Orioles in Ruth's hometown of Baltimore. Playing left field, Ruth was walked in his other two plate appearances of the game. The following day, Ruth pitched and homered in his first two at-bats, running his streak to six in a row, as the Red Sox swamped the Orioles 16–2.

The home-run barrage set the stage for Ruth to become a truly national phenomenon. He hit a then–major league record 29 homers in 1919, along with a .322 batting average, and league-leading figures in runs batted in (114), runs scored (103), on-base percentage (.456), and slugging percentage (.657).

APRIL 23

The Red Sox clobber the Yankees 10–0 in the season opener in New York. Babe Ruth started the season off on the right foot with an inside-the-park homer in the first inning that bounced over the head of Yankee center fielder Duffy Lewis. Carl Mays pitched the shutout, and Wally Schang collected four hits, including three doubles. Jack Barry had three hits.

Schang hit .306 for the Red Sox in 1919. The Opening Day homer was the only one of Ruth's 29 in 1919 that was inside the park. That year he played 111 games in the outfield, four at first base, and 17 as a pitcher. On the mound he was 9–5 with a 2.97 ERA.

MAY 1

The Red Sox lose the 1919 home opener 7–2 to the Yankees.

MAY 6

The Red Sox collect only two hits but defeat the Senators 2–0 at Fenway Park. Harry Hooper's second-inning single drove in both runs.

MAY 20

In the lineup as a pitcher, Babe Ruth hits a grand slam in the second inning off of Dave Davenport during a 6–4 win over the Browns in St. Louis.

Ruth is one of four Red Sox pitchers with a grand slam. The others are Lefty Grove in 1935, Wes Ferrell in 1936, and Ellis Kinder in 1950.

MAY 30

Carl Mays narrowly escapes arrest during a doubleheader against the Athletics in Philadelphia. Fans were pounding on the roof of the Red Sox' dugout, and Mays fired a ball into the stands, hitting a man in the head. Mays was able to avoid arrest only after Athletics manager Connie Mack convinced the fan not to file charges.

JUNE 25

Sad Sam Jones shuts out the Senators 1–0 in the second game of a doubleheader at Fenway Park. Walter Johnson was the losing pitcher. In what would prove to be his final game with the Red Sox, Amos Strunk drove in the lone run of the game with a single in the first inning. The Red Sox lost the first game, 8–3.

Herb Pennock was Boston's top pitcher in 1919. He was 16–8 with an earned run average of 2.71.

JUNE 26

The Red Sox trade Amos Strunk and Jack Barry to the Athletics for Braggo Roth and Red Shannon.

After his playing career ended, Barry coached for three decades at Holy Cross University, his alma mater.

JUNE 28

Carl Mays pitches two complete games in a doubleheader against the Yankees at Fenway Park. Mays won the first game 2–0 and lost the second, 4–1.

JUNE 30   Babe Ruth hits a grand slam in the sixth inning of the first game of a doubleheader off Bob Shawkey, but the Red Sox lose twice, 7–4 and 4–2, against the Yankees at Fenway Park.

Ruth wasn't helped by Fenway Park during his six seasons with the Red Sox. From 1914 through 1919, he hit 11 homers at home and 38 on the road.

JULY 13   Carl Mays walks off the field after the second inning of a 14–9 loss against the 1919 American League champion White Sox in Chicago, blaming his teammates for lack of support in the field.

The Red Sox suspended Mays because of his actions and tried to trade him to the Yankees. American League president Ban Johnson told owner Harry Frazee not to trade Mays while he was under suspension, but the Red Sox owner defied the order and completed the deal on July 30, receiving Allan Russell, Bob McGraw, and $40,000 in return. Johnson refused to let Mays play for the Yankees, but the New York club obtained a restraining order preventing Johnson from interfering. The case made it to the New York State Supreme Court, though not to the Court of Appeals, the state's highest court.

Mays would have a combined record of 53–20 in 1920 and 1921 for the Yankees and finished his career with 207 wins and 126 losses, but he will always be remembered for one pitch. On August 16, 1920, one of his submarine deliveries struck the Indians' Ray Chapman in the head, resulting in Chapman's death the following day. Mays is the only pitcher who has won 200 major league games with a winning percentage of at least .600 since 1900 who is not in the Hall of Fame, which is a direct result of both his disagreeable disposition and Chapman's death.

JULY 18   Babe Ruth stars with two homers and six RBIs as the Red Sox defeat the Indians 8–7 in Cleveland with five runs in the ninth inning. After Elmer Myers allowed a run and walked the bases loaded, Cleveland manager Lee Fohl brought in Fritz Coumbe, a pitcher who hadn't appeared in a game in two months, to face Ruth. The Babe responded with a grand slam to win the game.

Fohl reacted to the heartbreaking defeat by resigning the following day. He was replaced by Tris Speaker.

JULY 31   In his first game with the Red Sox, nineteen-year–old Waite Hoyt pitches in a complete-game 12-inning, 2–1 victory over the Tigers at Fenway Park. The game ended on a bizarre play. With two out, Mike McNally of the Red Sox was caught in a rundown between third and home. Umpire George Hildebrand ruled that Detroit catcher Eddie Ainsmith interfered with McNally, which gave the Sox the winning run. Detroit players protested and followed Hildebrand to the dressing room.

AUGUST 7   The Red Sox score seven runs in the first inning and hang on for an 8–7 win over the Indians at Fenway Park. The game ended when Tris Speaker was thrown out at home plate on the back end of an attempted double steal.

AUGUST 11 Herb Pennock pitches the Red Sox to a 1–0 win over the Browns at Fenway Park. A bases-loaded walk to Babe Ruth in the seventh inning produced the lone run of the game.

AUGUST 14   The Red Sox collect 20 hits and score 7 times in the third inning, rolling to a 15–6 victory over the White Sox at Comiskey Park.

AUGUST 22   Babe Ruth is ejected by umpire Brick Owens for arguing a third-strike call during a 10–7 loss to the Indians in Cleveland. Ruth threatened to hit Owens but was stopped by players from both clubs.

AUGUST 23   Babe Ruth hits his fourth grand slam of the season, a third-inning shot off Hooks Dauss, but the Red Sox lose 8–4 to the Tigers in Detroit.

The four grand slams by Ruth in 1919 are still the Red Sox season record. Ruth accounted for 29 of Boston's 33 homers in 1919, an unbelievable 88 percent. The only Red Sox players besides Ruth with home runs were Harry Hooper with three and Stuffy McInnis with one. Ruth outhomered 10 of the other 15 major league teams in 1919. The closest individual in the majors to Ruth in 1919 was the Phillies' Gavvy Cravath, who had 12 homers.

SEPTEMBER 5   Babe Ruth collects 5 of Boston's 25 hits during a 15–7 thrashing of the Athletics in Philadelphia. Ruth had three singles, a double, and his 25th homer of the season. Harry Hooper contributed two triples and two doubles.

SEPTEMBER 11   The Red Sox shut out the Browns twice during a doubleheader at Fenway Park. Herb Pennock won the opener 4–0, and Allan Russell took the nightcap 8–0, which was Russell's only shutout as a member of the Red Sox.

The games were played amid civic turmoil in Boston. Some 1,500 members of the Boston police force went on strike on September 9, prompting widespread rioting, looting, and general lawlessness. Massachusetts Governor Calvin Coolidge called in the National Guard to restore order and fired the striking officers.

SEPTEMBER 20   Babe Ruth clubs his 27th homer of the season during the first game of a doubleheader, a 4–3 win against the White Sox before 31,000 on "Babe Ruth Day" at Fenway Park. Ruth started the game as a pitcher and moved to left field in the sixth inning. The Red Sox swept the twin bill with a 5–4 win in the second game.

The home run tied the then-single-season record, set by Ned Williamson with the Cubs in 1884. In between the games, Ruth was feted by the Knights of Columbus. Among the gifts were $600 worth of United States Treasury certificates, cuff links, a fountain pen, a box of cigars, a traveling bag, and a pair of new baseball spikes. No one, except perhaps Harry Frazee, knew that this would be Ruth's last appearance as a member of the Red Sox at Fenway Park. In January 1920, Frazee sold Ruth to the Yankees.

SEPTEMBER 24   In the second game of a doubleheader against the Yankees in New York, Babe Ruth hits his 28th homer of the season, breaking the existing single-season record, although the Red Sox lose 2–1 in 13 innings. The homer sailed over the right field stands and landed in Manhattan Field, which adjoined the Polo Grounds. Ruth's blast tied the score 1–1. Waite Hoyt retired 34 consecutive Yankee batters from the second through the thirteenth innings before taking the loss. The Red Sox won the first game 4–0.

SEPTEMBER 27   Babe Ruth hits his 29th homer of the year during the first game of a doubleheader against the Senators in Washington, but the Red Sox lose twice, 7–5 and 4–1.

From the inception of the American League in 1901 through the 1919 season, the Red Sox had a record of 1,548–1,258 (.551) to rank first during that 19-year period. The White Sox were next at 1,542–1,267 (.549). From 1920 through 1947, the Red Sox were 1,962–2,319. The .458 winning percentage during those 28 seasons was the worst in the American League.

DECEMBER 29   The Red Sox trade Braggo Roth and Red Shannon to the Senators for Mike Menosky, Harry Harper, and Eddie Foster.

THE ALL–DECADE TEAM • YEARS WITH BRS

Phil Todt, 1b	1924–30
Bill Regan, 2b	1926–30
Eddie Foster, 3b	1920–22
Everett Scott, ss	1914–21
Mike Menosky, lf	1920–23
Ira Flagstead, cf	1923–29
Ike Boone, rf	1924–25
Sam Jones, p	1917–21
Howard Ehmke, p	1923–26
Herb Pennock, p	1915–22
Red Ruffing, p	1924–30

Other key contributors to the Red Sox during the 1920s were pitchers Joe Quinn (1922–25), Joe Bush (1918–21), Slim Harriss (1926–28), and Danny Mac-Fayden (1926–32). The Sox usually had a couple of good pitchers at the top of the rotation during the 1920s, but the offense was consistently dreadful. None of the eight position players on the 1920s all-decade team had distinguished careers with the exception of Scott, who was traded after the 1921 season.

THE DECADE LEADERS

Batting Avg:	Harris	.315
On-Base Pct:	Harris	.392
Slugging Pct:	Harris	.475
Home Runs:	Todt	41
RBI:	Todt	347
Runs:	Flagstead	466
Stolen Bases:	Rothrock	56
Wins:	Ruffing	54
Strikeouts:	Ruffing	436
ERA:	Jones	3.57
Saves:	Quinn	14

THE STATE OF THE RED SOX

The Red Sox announced the sale of Babe Ruth to the Yankees on January 5, 1920, and it was all downhill from there. After posting the best record in the American League in the 1910s, the Sox had the worst club of the 1920s with a record of 595–938. The winning percentage of .388 was the second lowest in the majors, trailing only the Philadelphia Phillies, who were 566–962 (.370). In the eight-team American League, Boston was fifth twice, seventh once, and last seven times. The American League champions during the 1920s were the Indians (1920), Yankees (1921, 1922, 1923, 1926, 1927, and 1928), Senators (1924 and 1925), and Athletics (1928 and 1929).

THE BEST TEAM

The Red Sox didn't have a single team with a winning record in the twenties. The best team was in 1921 and had a 75–79 mark.

THE WORST TEAM

The 1926 Red Sox were an abysmal 46–107.

THE BEST MOMENT

There weren't very many, but Howard Ehmke pitched a no-hitter and a one-hitter in back-to-back starts in 1923.

THE WORST MOMENT

The sale of Babe Ruth is arguably the worst moment in Red Sox history.

THE HOME FIELD

Due to underfinanced ownership, Fenway Park deteriorated during the 1920s. In 1926, the wooden bleachers on the third base side were destroyed by fire. They weren't replaced until after Thomas Yawkey purchased the club in 1934.

THE GAME YOU WISH YOU HAD SEEN

Playing the 1927 Yankees, considered by most experts to be the best team of all time, the Red Sox grabbed a thrilling come-from-behind victory in 18 innings, 12–11, on September 5.

THE WAY THE GAME WAS PLAYED

Rule changes in 1920 and the emergence of Babe Ruth as a star transformed baseball from a low-scoring defensive affair to a high-scoring offensive carnival. AL teams went from averaging 3.5 runs a game in 1917 to 5.1 per game in 1921 and 5.4 per game in 1930. Not surprisingly, team ERA jumped by nearly two runs. Pitchers completed fewer than half their starts in the AL in 1923, the first time that had happened, as relief pitching continued to gain importance.

THE MANAGEMENT

When Harry Frazee bought the Red Sox in 1916, he opened his checkbook and spent the money necessary to build a winning team, but a losing season in 1919 left him in a financial bind. Frazee sold or traded the Red Sox' best players, beginning with Babe Ruth in 1920. Frazee sold the club to a group headed by Bob Quinn in 1923, but Quinn's ownership group was even more financially strapped than Frazee and only made a bad team worse. Field managers during the 1920s were Ed Barrow (1918–20), Hugh Duffy (1921–22), Frank Chance (1923), Lee Fohl (1924–26), and Bill Carrigan (1927–29).

THE BEST PLAYER MOVE

The Red Sox purchased journeyman Ira Flagstead from the Tigers in 1923. That Flagstead was Boston's best position player during the 1920s says more about the sorry state of the Red Sox than it does about Flagstead.

THE WORST PLAYER MOVE

The sale of Babe Ruth was one of the worst moves by any team in history, but it didn't stop there. During the 1920s, the Sox traded or sold Waite Hoyt, Harry Hooper, Herb Pennock, Wally Schang, Joe Dugan, Buddy Myer, and Babe Herman for little or nothing in playing talent in return.

1920   B

Season in a Sentence

The Red Sox move up from sixth place in 1919 to fifth in 1920 after stunning the fans by selling Babe Ruth to the Yankees.

Finish • Won • Lost • Pct • GB

Fifth   72   81   .471   25.5

Manager

Ed Barrow

Stats   Red Sox • AL • Rank

Stats	Red Sox	AL	Rank
Batting Avg:	.269	.284	7
On-Base Pct:	.342	.347	6
Slugging Pct:	.350	.387	7
Home Runs:	22		8
Stolen Bases:	98		4
ERA:	3.82	3.79	4
Fielding Pct:	.972	.966	1
Runs Scored:	650		7
Runs Allowed:	698		4

Starting Lineup

Wally Schang, c-cf
Stuffy McInnis, 1b
Mike McNally, 2b
Eddie Foster, 3b
Everett Scott, ss
Mike Menosky, lf
Tim Hendryx, cf
Harry Hooper, rf
Roxy Walters, c
Ossie Vitt, 3b
Cliff Brady, 2b

Pitchers

Sad Sam Jones, sp
Joe Bush, sp
Herb Pennock, sp
Harry Harper, sp
Allan Russell, sp
Waite Hoyt, sp-rp
Elmer Myers, sp
Benn Karr, rp

Attendance

402,445 (fifth in AL)

Club Leaders

Batting Avg:	Hooper	.312
On-Base Pct:	Hooper	.411
Slugging Pct:	Hooper	.470
Home Runs:	Hooper	7
RBI:	Hendryx	73
Runs:	Hooper	91
Stolen Bases:	Menosky	23
Wins:	Pennock	16
Strikeouts:	Bush	88
ERA:	Harper	3.04
Saves:	Pennock	2

JANUARY 5   The Red Sox announce the sale of Babe Ruth to the Yankees. Harry Frazee shipped Ruth to Gotham for $125,000 and a $300,000 loan using Fenway Park as collateral.

B   The Red Sox Lose Ruth   B

Frazee had suffered a financial reversal in the twelve months leading up to Ruth's sale, having lost money on several plays that flopped on Broadway. The shortened baseball schedule in 1918 and a losing club in 1919 caused attendance to drop and also damaged Frazee's financial position. As a result, he was behind on loans he had used to purchase the Red Sox in 1916. At the time, Ruth was entering the second season of a three-year contract in which he was paid $10,000 per annum.

The Babe insisted he wouldn't play for the Red Sox in 1919 unless his contract was torn up and his salary raised to $20,000. Frazee was already upset by much of what he considered to be Ruth's eccentric behavior and believed that the salary demands were outrageous. The Red Sox owner had had his fill of the superstar player and had all but written Ruth off as a stubborn, petulant, self-indulgent, and impulsive man-child. Frazee publicly called Ruth the most selfish and inconsiderate man ever to don a baseball uniform.

Editorial comment regarding Ruth's sale in the eleven newspapers then published in Boston was split about evenly. Those in favor of the deal believed that Ruth had developed a king-sized ego that had become harmful to the team. He was also not very diligent when it came to keeping himself in condition and was considered by many to be an injury risk. Even with the Babe's heroics in 1919, Frazee's club had landed in sixth place and weren't a big draw in Boston. The Red Sox attracted 402,445 fans to Fenway Park during the year, compared with the American League average of 456,780. Obviously, the sale of Ruth was a colossal miscalculation. In 1920 he made that achingly clear by clubbing 54 home runs for the Yankees. His record 29 homers for the Sox the previous year had been only the beginning. By the time his career ended in 1935, Ruth had 714 home runs and a .342 batting average.

For Red Sox fans, things would only grow worse. The $125,000 Frazee received in the sale couldn't pull him out of his financial difficulties. The Red Sox traded one star player after another between 1920 and 1923, most of them following Ruth to New York. Once Ruth left, the Red Sox failed to win a single World Series until 2004. The Yankees, a club that had never appeared in a Fall Classic prior to 1921, have captured 26 World Championships.

Many Sox fans blamed Harry Frazee for the "Curse of the Bambino."

Courtesy of Transcendental Graphics/theruckerarchive.com

JANUARY 20   The Red Sox trade Braggo Roth and Red Shannon to the Senators for Mike Menosky, Harry Harper, and Eddie Foster.

FEBRUARY 9   Three weeks after nationwide Prohibition goes into effect, baseball's rules committee adopts new rules that usher in an era of offense by prohibiting pitchers from using any foreign substances on the ball, such as paraffin, resin, powder, emery boards, files, or saliva. In addition, baseball adopted a livelier ball and agreed to keep a fresh ball in use at all times. The changes were spurred in large part by the owners' recognition of the positive impact of Babe Ruth's home run feats on the game.

APRIL 14   The Red Sox season opener, scheduled against the Senators at Fenway Park, is postponed by cold weather.

APRIL 15   The Red Sox begin the season with a 7–6 win over the Senators at Fenway Park. Boston drove Walter Johnson off the pitcher's mound by taking a 6–1 lead in the third inning.

APRIL 17   The Red Sox overcome the Senators 2–1 in 14 innings at Fenway Park. Harry Hooper drove in the winning run with a single.

APRIL 19   Babe Ruth returns to Fenway Park as a member of the Yankees and collects four hits during a Patriots' Day double-header, including a double. The Red Sox won both ends of the twin bill 4–0 and 8–3. The morning game drew 6,000 fans, while the afternoon tilt attracted 22,000.

APRIL 20   The Red Sox improve their record to 5–0 with a 3–2 victory over the Yankees at Fenway Park, scoring two runs in the ninth inning.

APRIL 22   The Red Sox participate in the first game of the season in Washington and lose 8–5 to the Senators. Woodrow Wilson was unable to carry out the presidential tradition of throwing out the first ball at the Washington opener because of a stroke he suffered in September 1919. Vice President Thomas Marshall threw out the first ball in Wilson's stead.

MAY 10   Harry Harper pitches a two-hitter to defeat the Athletics 7–1 at Shibe Park in Philadelphia. The only Philadelphia hits were singles by George Burns and Frank Welch.

MAY 12   Catcher Wally Schang sets a modern major league record with eight assists, but the Red Sox lose 9–7 to the Indians at Fenway Park.

Schang hit .305 for the Red Sox in 1920.

MAY 25   Harry Hooper's walk-off homer in the eleventh inning defeats the Browns 3–2 at Fenway Park.

During the last of his 12 seasons in Boston, Hooper batted .321 and collected 17 triples for the Red Sox.

MAY 26   The Red Sox move into first place with a 9–5 win over the Browns at Fenway Park.

Boston's 21–9 record on May 26 fooled many into believing that the club was better off without Babe Ruth. The Red Sox' stay atop the American League lasted only two days, however, and the club quickly sank into the second division.

MAY 27   The Red Sox lose 6–1 to the Yankees at Fenway Park, but fans get their money's worth with two Babe Ruth home runs and a fight between a player and an umpire. Yankee pitcher Bob Shawkey was ejected for objecting to the ball and strike calls of umpire George Hildebrand in the fourth inning. Shawkey rushed at the umpire and struck him several times about the head. Hildebrand defended himself with his mask and opened a wound on Shawkey's head. Umpire Billy Evans and Red Sox player Harry Hooper separated the two, and Shawkey was escorted from the field.

JUNE 20   The Red Sox overcome a 6–1, third-inning Indians lead to win 10–9 on a cold and rainy day in Cleveland.

JUNE 25   Harry Hooper and Roger Peckinpaugh of the Yankees both lead off the first inning with homers in a game in New York. The Red Sox won 6–3. Babe Ruth accounted for the Yankees' other two tallies with a pair of homers.

JUNE 29   Stuffy McInnis hits a first-inning grand slam off Ernie Shore, but the Red Sox lose 6–5 to the Yankees in New York.

JULY 1   Walter Johnson pitches a no-hitter against the Red Sox to lead the Senators to a 1–0
                  win at Fenway Park. The only Boston base runner was Harry Hooper, who reached
                  on an error in the seventh inning by second baseman Bucky Harris. Hooper ended
                  the game by grounding out to first baseman Joe Judge.

JULY 2   The Red Sox wipe out a 9–2 Washington advantage in the sixth inning and win 10–9
                  in 10 innings at Fenway Park. Harry Hooper's RBI double ended the contest.

JULY 6   The Red Sox clobber the Athletics 11–0 in the first game of a double-header in
                  Philadelphia before losing, 5–1.

JULY 14   The Red Sox take a 3–1 lead into the ninth inning of the first game of a double-
                  header against the Tigers at Fenway Park, only to allow four runs and fall behind
                  5–3. The Sox rallied, however, with three in the bottom half of the inning to win 6–5,
                  then completed the sweep with a 4–0 victory.

                  *In the 52 seasons that the Red Sox and Braves shared Boston, outfielder Gene
                  Bailey was the only individual to play for both clubs in the same season. In
                  1920, Bailey played in 13 games for the Braves and 46 for the Sox.*

JULY 22   The Red Sox protest the purchase of Pie Traynor by the Pittsburgh Pirates.

                  *Traynor was playing for a minor league club in Portsmouth, Virginia, and the Red
                  Sox claimed they had an agreement guaranteeing them first choice of purchasing
                  any player on the club. Traynor was purchased by the Pirates for $10,000, and
                  the Red Sox lost their claim. Going to Pittsburgh was also a disappointment to
                  Traynor, who was born in Framingham, grew up in Somerville, and was a lifelong
                  Red Sox fan. He went on to a Hall of Fame career as a third baseman.*

AUGUST 21   The Red Sox blank the 1920 World Champion Indians 13–0 and 4–0 in a double-
                  header at Fenway Park. Waite Hoyt and Herb Pennock contributed the shutouts.

AUGUST 25   The day before women are given the right to vote with the passage of the 19th
                  Amendment, the Red Sox score seven runs in the eighth inning and lambaste the
                  Browns 11–1 at Fenway Park.

SEPTEMBER 4   After losing 5–1 in the first game of a double-header against the Yankees before
                  33,027 at Fenway Park, the Red Sox score three times off Carl Mays in the ninth
                  inning of the nightcap to win, 6–5.

                  *Babe Ruth hit his 44th and 45th home runs of the season during the twin bill.
                  He finished the season with 54. The entire Red Sox team combined to hit only
                  22 home runs in 1920.*

SEPTEMBER 13   The Red Sox win 5–4 in 14 innings against the Browns at Sportsman's Park. Harry
                  Hooper drove in the winning run with a sacrifice fly.

SEPTEMBER 17   Red Sox batters draw a major league record 20 walks but lose 14–13 to the Tigers
                  in 12 innings in Detroit. Boston trailed 8–1 and rallied to take a 13–11 lead in the
                  ninth before suffering the defeat. Five Tiger pitchers combined to set the walk
                  record. All five were rookies, two were making their major league debuts, and none

of the five had a big-league career that lasted longer than 13 games.

SEPTEMBER 23   Elmer Myers wins his ninth game in a row and hits a bases-loaded triple during a
9–2 win over the Athletics at Fenway Park.

*After being picked up on waivers from the Indians in June 1920, Myers was
9–1 for the Red Sox over the remainder of the season. He pitched two more
big-league seasons but went only 8–13.*

SEPTEMBER 27   Harry Harper strikes out 13 batters to defeat the Senators 2–0 in the second game
of a double-header at Fenway Park. The Red Sox lost the first game, 2–1.

*This was Harper's only shutout as a member of the Red Sox. He had a 5–14
record during his brief one-season stay in Boston. After his playing career
ended, Harper became a wealthy industrialist in New Jersey.*

OCTOBER 29   Ed Barrow resigns as manager of the Red Sox to take a position as the Yankees'
business manager.

*Barrow remained with the Yankees until 1947 and was successively promoted
to general manager, president, and chairman of the board. While in New York,
he oversaw the construction of Yankee Stadium and the beginning of the great
Yankee dynasty. Barrow was elected to the Hall of Fame in 1953.*

NOVEMBER 5   The Red Sox name Hugh Duffy as manager.

*The hiring of Duffy was a locally popular move. He starred with the Boston
Braves from 1891 through 1900 and recorded a .438 batting average in 1894,
the highest for a single season in major league history. Previously, Duffy had
managed in the majors with the Milwaukee Brewers (1901), Philadelphia
Phillies (1904–06), and Chicago White Sox (1910–11), without finishing higher
than fourth place.*

DECEMBER 15   The Red Sox trade Waite Hoyt, Harry Harper, Wally Schang, and Mike McNally to
the Yankees for Muddy Ruel, Del Pratt, Sammy Vick, and Hank Thormahlen.

*Hoyt, only twenty-one years old with 10 major league wins when he was traded,
was a huge loss. He went on to a career in which he compiled a 238–182 record,
good enough for the Hall of Fame. Pratt had a great season at second base for
the Red Sox in 1921 with a .324 batting average and 100 runs batted in.*

1921   B

Season in a Sentence

The Red Sox allow fewer runs than any team in the league, but a miserable offense results in another fifth-place finish.

Finish • Won • Lost • Pct • GB

Fifth   75   79   .487   23.5

Manager

Hugh Duffy

Stats   Red Sox • AL • Rank

	Red Sox	AL	Rank
Batting Avg:	.277	.292	7
On-Base Pct:	.335	.357	7
Slugging Pct:	.361	.408	8
Home Runs:	17		8
Stolen Bases:	83		6
ERA:	3.98	4.28	4
Fielding Pct:	.975	.965	1
Runs Scored:	668		7
Runs Allowed:	696		1

Starting Lineup

Muddy Ruel, c
Stuffy McInnis, 1b
Del Pratt, 2b
Eddie Foster, 3b
Everett Scott, ss
Mike Menosky, lf
Nemo Leibold, cf
Shano Collins, rf-cf
Ossie Vitt, 3b
Roxy Walters, c
Tim Hendryx, rf

Pitchers

Sad Sam Jones, sp
Joe Bush, sp
Herb Pennock, sp
Elmer Myers, sp
Allan Russell, rp-sp
Benn Karr, rp
Hank Thormahlen, rp

Attendance

279,273 (eighth in AL)

Club Leaders

Batting Avg:	Pratt	.324
On-Base Pct:	Menosky	.388
Slugging Pct:	Pratt	.461
Home Runs:	Collins	4
RBI:	Pratt	100
Runs:	Leibold	88
Stolen Bases:	Collins	15
Wins:	Jones	23
Strikeouts:	Jones	98
ERA:	Jones	3.22
Saves:	Russell	3

MARCH 4   The Red Sox trade Harry Hooper to the White Sox for Shano Collins and Nemo Leibold.

Hooper wanted out of Boston as soon as Harry Frazee sold Babe Ruth to the Yankees. Although Hooper was thirty-three at the time of the trade, he became a fixture in the Chicago outfield for five seasons.

APRIL 13   On Opening Day at Griffith Stadium in Washington, the Red Sox defeat the Senators, 6–3. Sad Sam Jones pitched a complete game and had three hits, including a triple. Mike Menosky also collected three hits. Newly elected President Warren Harding threw out the first pitch and was accompanied by Vice President Calvin Coolidge. General John J. Pershing, commander of the American Expeditionary Forces during World War I, raised the American flag on the pole in center field accompanied by members of both teams.

APRIL 21   In the home opener before 12,000 at Fenway, Sad Sam Jones pitches a two-hitter to defeat the Senators 1–0. Jones also drove in the only run of the game with a single in the second inning that bounced off third base. The only Washington hits were singles by Joe Judge and Patsy Gharrity.

MAY 13   The Red Sox go on a batting rampage and score seven runs in the seventh inning to defeat the White Sox 16–8 in Chicago.

The Red Sox led the American League in fielding average six consecutive seasons from 1916 through 1921.

MAY 15   Del Pratt's homer highlights a four-run tenth inning that lifts the Red Sox to an 11–7 win over the Browns in St. Louis.

JUNE 4   Sad Sam Jones pitches his second two-hitter of 1921 to beat the Indians 6–0 at Fenway Park. The only Cleveland hits were a double by Tris Speaker and a single by Elmer Smith.

> *Jones was 23–16 in 1921 with an earned run average of 3.22, 5 shutouts, and 25 complete games.*

JULY 16   Two days after a jury in suburban Dedham finds Nicola Sacco and Bartolomeo Vanzetti guilty of murder, the Red Sox knock off the White Sox 10–0 at Comiskey Park.

JULY 19   Joe Bush's shutout defeats the White Sox 1–0 in Chicago. The only run of the game was scored in the third inning on a single by Shano Collins.

AUGUST 1   Joe Bush pitches a one-hitter to beat the Browns 2–0 at Sportsman's Park. The only St. Louis hit was a single in the first inning by George Sisler on a grounder past the pitcher's mound.

AUGUST 18   Shano Collins hit a grand slam off Red Oldham during the first inning of a 6–5 win in 11 innings over the Tigers in the first game of a double-header in Detroit. The Red Sox also won the second game, 5–0.

AUGUST 19   The Red Sox score seven runs in the eighth inning to down the Tigers 12–8 in the first game of a double-header at Navin Field in Detroit. In the second game, Ty Cobb collected his 3,000th career hit off Boston's Elmer Myers during a 10–0 Detroit victory.

AUGUST 23   The Red Sox wallop the Browns 15–2 in St. Louis. Joe Bush was the winning pitcher and drove in five runs with a triple, double, and single.

> *Bush was 16–9 with a 3.80 ERA in 1921, and batted .325.*

SEPTEMBER 3   The Red Sox score two runs in the eighth inning to beat the Athletics 11–10 at Fenway Park.

> *Stuffy McInnis made only one error at first base all year. His .999 fielding percentage in still the American League record. He also struck out only 9 times in 584 at-bats. As a team, the Sox fanned only 344 times in 154 games.*

SEPTEMBER 14   Herb Pennock throws a two-hitter to defeat the Tigers 1–0 at Fenway Park. The only Detroit hits were singles by Ralph Young and Lu Blue.

SEPTEMBER 23   Sad Sam Jones wins his 23rd game of the season with a 5–2 decision over the Senators at Fenway Park.

OCTOBER 2   On the final day of the season, Babe Ruth hits his 59th home run of 1921 during a 7–6 Yankees win over the Red Sox in New York. The pitching victim was Curt Fullerton. It was the third straight year that Ruth set the major league home run record. He hit 29 for the Red Sox in 1919, 54 for the Yankees in 1920, and 59 in 1921. He would go on to set another record with 60 in 1927, a mark that stood until Roger Maris struck 61 in 1961.

DECEMBER 20   The Red Sox trade Joe Bush, Sad Sam Jones, and Everett Scott to the Yankees for Roger Peckinpaugh, Jack Quinn, Rip Collins, and Bill Piercy.

Boston traded their two best pitchers and their starting shortstop for almost nothing. Bush and Jones combined were 39–20 in 1922 for the Yankees and 40–23 in 1923. Quinn was thirty-eight years old at the time of the trade and pitched for the Red Sox until 1925. His last major league game was with the Reds on July 7, 1933, two days past his fiftieth birthday. Quinn is the oldest person to appear in a big-league game who was not part of a publicity stunt.

DECEMBER 24   The Red Sox trade Stuffy McInnis to the Indians for George Burns, Joe Harris, and Elmer Smith.

1 9 2 2   B

Season in a Sentence

The Red Sox tumble into last place as Harry Frazee continues to alienate Boston fans by selling off the club's top players for much-needed cash.

Finish • Won • Lost • Pct • GB

Eighth   61   93   .396   33.0

Manager

Hugh Duffy

Stats   Red Sox • AL • Rank

	Red Sox	AL	Rank
Batting Avg:	.263	.285	8
On-Base Pct:	.316	.348	8
Slugging Pct:	.357	.398	8
Home Runs:	45		5 (tie)
Stolen Bases:	64		6
ERA:	4.30	4.03	6
Fielding Pct:	.965	.969	8
Runs Scored:	598		8
Runs Allowed:	769		5

Starting Lineup

Muddy Ruel, c
George Burns, 1b
Del Pratt, 2b
Joe Dugan, 3b
Johnny Mitchell, ss
Mike Menosky, lf
Nemo Leibold, cf
Shano Collins, rf-cf
Joe Harris, lf
Elmer Smith, rf
Frank O'Rourke, ss-3b
Pinky Pittenger, 3b-ss

Pitchers

Rip Collins, sp
Jack Quinn, sp
Alex Ferguson, sp
Herb Pennock, sp
Benn Karr, rp-sp
Allan Russell, rp-sp
Bill Piercy, rp-sp

Attendance

259,184 (eighth in AL)

Club Leaders

Batting Avg:	Burns	.306
On-Base Pct:	Pratt	.361
Slugging Pct:	Burns	.446
Home Runs:	Burns	12
RBI:	Pratt	86
Runs:	Pratt	73
Stolen Bases:	Menosky	9
Wins:	Collins	14
Strikeouts:	Collins	69
ERA:	Quinn	3.48
Saves:	Ferguson	2
	Russell	2

JANUARY 10   The Red Sox trade Roger Peckinpaugh to the Senators for Joe Dugan and Frank O'Rourke.

Peckinpaugh was the Senators' starting shortstop when they won the American League pennant in both 1924 and 1925.

FEBRUARY 24   The Red Sox purchase Alex Ferguson from the Yankees.

APRIL 12   On Opening Day, the Red Sox lose 3–2 to the Athletics at Fenway Park.

APRIL 20   The Red Sox turn the tables and blemish Philadelphia's home opener by thrashing the Athletics 15–4 at Shibe Park.

APRIL 29   The Red Sox score three runs in the fourteenth inning to defeat the 1922 American League champion Yankees 5–2 in New York.

During Boston's game-winning rally, Yankee manager Miller Huggins ordered pitcher Waite Hoyt to intentionally walk Elmer Smith. After the maneuver backfired, Hoyt walked into the dugout and punched Huggins.

MAY 6   Herb Pennock shuts out the Senators 1–0 at Fenway Park. The only run was scored on a balk in the fifth inning by Washington pitcher Tom Zachary.

MAY 13   Pennock holds the White Sox to two hits for a 3–1 win at Fenway Park. The only Chicago hits were a double by Harvey McClellan and a single by Harry Hooper.

MAY 17   The Red Sox score four runs in the ninth inning to defeat the Browns 4–3 at Fenway Park. The runs scored on a two-run single by Joe Dugan and sacrifice flies by George Burns and Eddie Foster.

JUNE 8   Elmer Smith hits a grand slam in the second inning off Elam Vangilder during a 7–5 win over the Browns in St. Louis.

JULY 7   George Burns hits a walk-off homer in the thirteenth inning to defeat the Browns 5–4 in the second game of a double-header at Fenway Park. Boston lost the first game, 1–0.

JULY 21   Down 7–4, the Red Sox score three runs in the ninth inning and one in the eleventh to defeat the White Sox 8–7 at Fenway Park. Shano Collins collected four hits and four RBIs and drove in the winning run with a single.

JULY 23   The Red Sox trade Joe Dugan and Elmer Smith to the Yankees for Chick Fewster, Elmer Miller, Johnny Mitchell, Lefty O'Doul, and $50,000.

Frazee's latest sellout to New York probably won the 1922 American League pennant for the Yankees and dropped Boston's interest in the Red Sox to new lows. The Yankees nosed out the Browns for first place by one game. Dugan was the Yankees' starting third baseman until 1927.

JULY 26   In his first game with the Red Sox following the July 23 trade with the Yankees, Elmer Miller hits two homers during a 3–1 win over the White Sox in Chicago.

AUGUST 8   The Red Sox collect 21 hits and defeat the Indians 15–6 in Cleveland.

AUGUST 11   Red Sox reliever Jack Russell throws just one pitch, which turns into a triple play, although the Red Sox lose 5–4 to the Senators at Fenway Park. Russell came into the game to replace Bill Piercy with none out in the ninth inning and Washington runners Bucky Harris at first base and Sam Rice at second. On Russell's first pitch, Clyde Milan bunted in front of the plate and Boston catcher Muddy Ruel threw to third baseman Pinky Pittenger, forcing Rice. Pittenger relayed to first baseman George Burns to retire Milan. Bucky Harris made a bolt for third and was out, Burns to Pittenger, to complete the triple play.

AUGUST 14   The Red Sox play a team of American All-Stars at Fenway in a benefit for the family of the late Tommy McCarthy. Nearly 6,000 attended the game and raised more than $5,000. The Sox lost 3–2 in 10 innings, even though the "All-Stars" consisted mainly of second stringers from other AL clubs and forty-six-year-old Senators coach Nick Altrock, who pitched the last four innings.

                Lizzie Murphy, a member of the Providence (RI) All-Stars, a semipro team, played one inning at first base against for the AL All-Stars. She became the first woman ever to play against a major league club. Prior to the game, there was a vaudeville show that featured former Boston mayor John F. Fitzgerald singing "Sweet Adeline."

                Tommy McCarthy, who would be elected to the Hall of Fame in 1946, passed away nine days before the event. McCarthy played for the Boston Braves during the 1890s and was a beloved figure in Boston.

AUGUST 15   The Red Sox and White Sox tie a modern major league record for most singles in a game with 36. The White Sox collected 21 of them and won the game 19–11 at Fenway Park. There were 43 hits in the game, 25 of them by the White Sox, including five doubles and two triples. The Red Sox scored seven runs in the sixth inning to take a 10–9 lead before folding.

                The Red Sox sold Eddie Foster to the Browns the same day.

AUGUST 25   Jack Quinn pitches a two-hitter to beat Cleveland 9–0 at Fenway Park. The only Indians hits were singles by Stuffy McInnis and Joe Evans.

AUGUST 30   Del Pratt's homer in the tenth inning defeats the Athletics 6–5 in Philadelphia.

                Pratt batted .301, collected 44 doubles, and had a 23-game hitting streak in 1922.

AUGUST 31   George Burns hits a three-run homer off Slim Harriss that accounts for all three runs in a 3–0 win over the Athletics in Philadelphia. The umpires called the game in the top of the sixth inning because of rain.

SEPTEMBER 2   The Red Sox shut out the Senators twice, 3–0 and 1–0, in a doubleheader in Washington. Alex Ferguson won the opener and Bill Piercy the nightcap in a duel with Walter Johnson. Joe Harris's sacrifice fly in the ninth inning drove in the only run of the second game.

These were the only shutouts that either Ferguson or Piercy pitched while in a Boston uniform. Ferguson had a 31–48 record in four seasons with the Red Sox, while Piercy was 16–33 in three.

SEPTEMBER 6   The Red Sox and the Yankees exchange insults from their respective dugouts during the first three innings of a game in New York. Umpire Billy Evans had enough of the cacophony and banished the extra players on both clubs to the distant bullpens in deep right field at the Polo Grounds. The Yankees won the game, 9–2.

SEPTEMBER 21   The Red Sox swamp the Indians 15–5 in Cleveland.

SEPTEMBER 29   Jack Quinn shuts out the Yankees 1–0 at Fenway Park.

For some strange reason, Boston had New York's number in 1922. The last-place Red Sox had a 13–9 record against the first-place Yankees during the season.

OCTOBER 24   The Red Sox sell Frank O'Rourke to the Tigers.

OCTOBER 30   The Red Sox send Del Pratt and Rip Collins to the Tigers for Carl Holling, Howard Ehmke, Danny Clark, Babe Herman, and $25,000.

The Red Sox didn't know what kind of a hitter they acquired in Herman, who was only nineteen years old at the time of the trade. He never played for the Red Sox and made his major league debut with the Dodgers in 1926. Although he was sub-par defensively, Herman compiled a .324 batting average over a 13-year career. Ehmke was the Red Sox' top pitcher in each of the first three seasons following the trade.

DECEMBER 11   The Red Sox name Frank Chance as manager to replace Hugh Duffy. Chance managed the Chicago Cubs from 1905 through 1912 and won four National League pennants in addition to the club's last two World Championships in 1907 and 1908. He was also Chicago's starting first baseman on the 1906, 1907, and 1908 World Series teams. In 1906, the Cubs won a major league record 116 games. After leaving Chicago, Chance managed the Yankees to two losing seasons in 1913 and 1914. He had been happily retired in California when the Red Sox persuaded him to come to Boston. He was the third consecutive future Hall of Famer to guide the Red Sox, following Ed Barrow and Duffy.

1923   B

Season in a Sentence

Not one to raise false hopes, new manager Frank Chance correctly predicts in spring training that the Red Sox will finish in last place.

Finish • Won • Lost • Pct • GB

Eighth   61   91   .401 37.0

Manager

Frank Chance

Stats   Red Sox • AL • Rank

	Red Sox	AL	Rank
Batting Avg:	.261	.282	8
On-Base Pct:	.318	.351	8
Slugging Pct:	.351	.388	8
Home Runs:	34		7
Stolen Bases:	77		5
ERA:	4.20	3.98	8
Fielding Pct:	.963	.968	8
Runs Scored:	584		8
Runs Allowed:	809		8

Starting Lineup

Val Picinich, c
George Burns, 1b
Chick Fewster, 2b-ss
Howard Shanks, 3b-2b
Johnny Mitchell, ss
Joe Harris, lf
Dick Reichle, cf
Ira Flagstead, rf
Norm McMillan, 3b-2b
Shano Collins, cf-rf
Al Devormer, c
Mike Menosky, lf-cf
Pinky Pittenger, 2b

Pitchers

Howard Ehmke, sp
Jack Quinn, sp
Alex Ferguson, sp
Bill Piercy, sp
George Murray, rp-sp
Curt Fullerton, rp-sp

Attendance

229,688 (eighth in AL)

Club Leaders

Batting Avg:	Harris	.335
On-Base Pct:	Harris	.406
Slugging Pct:	Harris	.520
Home Runs:	Harris	13
RBI:	Burns	82
Runs:	Burns	91
Stolen Bases:	McMillan	13
Wins:	Ehmke	20
Strikeouts:	Ehmke	121
ERA:	Piercy	3.41
Saves:	Quinn	7

JANUARY 3   The Red Sox trade George Pipgras and Harvey Hendrick to the Yankees for Al DeVormer and cash.

It took awhile for Pipgras to develop, but from 1927 through 1932, he was 90–58 as a Yankee. DeVormer spent one year in Boston as a backup catcher.

JANUARY 30   The Red Sox trade Herb Pennock to the Yankees for Camp Skinner, Norm McMillan, George Murray, and $50,000.

The talent pipeline to New York remained wide open with the trade of Pennock for three useless players and cash. Over the next six seasons, Pennock had 115 wins and 57 losses for the Yankees. New York won the World Championship in 1923 with 12 players on their roster who had come from the Red Sox. In addition to Pennock, there was Babe Ruth, Waite Hoyt, Wally Schang, Everett Scott, Mike McNally, Joe Bush, Sad Sam Jones, Joe Dugan, Elmer Smith, George Pipgras, and Harvey Hendrick.

FEBRUARY 10 The Red Sox trade Muddy Ruel and Allan Russell to the Senators for Val Picinich, Howard Shanks, and Ed Goebel.

Both Ruel and Russell helped the Senators win the AL pennant in 1924 and

1925. Picinich, Shanks, and Goebel did little to help the Red Sox escape last place.

APRIL 18   The Red Sox participate in the first game ever played at Yankee Stadium and lose 4–1 before 74,217 fans. Babe Ruth christened the massive new ballpark, dubbed "The House That Ruth Built," with a three-run homer in the third inning off Howard Ehmke. The first batter in Yankee Stadium history was Red Sox shortstop Chick Fewster. Boston's George Burns had the honor of collecting the first hit at Yankee Stadium, a single in the second inning.

APRIL 20   The Red Sox purchase Tigers outfielder Ira Flagstead, a reliable position player and also the best deal the Sox would make in the forgettable 1920s.

APRIL 26   The Red Sox defeat the Yankees 5–4 in the home opener before more than 20,000, the largest first-game crowd at Fenway Park in 10 years. The Sox scored the winning run in the ninth inning on a double by Joe Harris and a single by George Burns.

            Prior to the game, Marines from the Charlestown Navy Yard drilled on the field.

MAY 18   The Red Sox score two runs in the ninth and four in the tenth to defeat the Tigers 6–2 in Detroit. Howard Ehmke hit Ty Cobb with a pitch during the game, and the two nearly came to blows under the grandstand after the contest ended.

            In his first season with the Red Sox, Ehmke had a 20–17 record, 317 innings pitched, 28 complete games, 121 strikeouts, and a 3.78 earned run average. On the other end, Curt Fullerton was 2–15 for the Red Sox in 1923. During his career, all of which was spent with the Sox, Fullerton had an abysmal record of 10–37.

MAY 26   The Red Sox sell Nemo Leibold to the Senators.

JUNE 13   George Burns collects five hits, including a pair of doubles, in six at-bats as the Red Sox down the White Sox 10–9 at Fenway Park. Boston catcher Al DeVormer was ejected in the seventh inning for pushing umpire Pants Rowland in protest over the safe call of Willie Kamm at home plate.

            Burns batted .328 and collected 47 doubles in 1923.

JULY 7   On a day in which the Red Sox set a club record for most runs allowed in a single game, the Indians score in every inning, collect 24 hits, and win 27–3 in Cleveland. The Indians set a major league record in the sixth inning (since tied) by scoring 13 runs with two outs. Lefty O'Doul allowed all 13 runs, a modern big-league mark for most runs allowed by a pitcher in an inning. Manager Frank Chance kept O'Doul on the mound despite the shelling because he was angry that the pitcher had returned to the hotel three hours after the midnight curfew the previous evening. O'Doul would have gotten the third out without a run being scored if center fielder Mike Menosky hadn't dropped a fly ball with the bases loaded. O'Doul gave up two doubles, five singles, and six walks in the inning. In all, O'Doul surrendered 16 runs, 11 hits, and 8 walks in three innings.

            O'Doul pitched in the majors with the Yankees and Red Sox from 1919 through 1923 and appeared on the mound in 34 games, all in relief, with an

ERA of 4.87. After four seasons in the Pacific Coast League, he returned to the big leagues in 1928 as a successful thirty-one-year-old outfielder with the Giants and lasted until 1934. In 970 career games in the majors, O'Doul batted .349. In 1929 with the Phillies he hit .398, missing a .400 batting average by only two hits. After his career ended, O'Doul was a manager in the Pacific Coast League, primarily with San Francisco, for more than two decades. In 1958, he opened a restaurant in downtown San Francisco named O'Doul's that is still open.

JULY 11   Harry Frazee sells the Red Sox to a syndicate of Columbus, Ohio, men headed by J. A. Robert "Bob" Quinn. Previously, Quinn had been the business manager of the St. Louis Browns.

The Red Sox looked at Frazee's sale of the club as the herald of happier days, but the team would be even less successful under Quinn than it had been under Frazee. The Red Sox remained an underfinanced, tail-end outfit until Quinn sold the ball club to Tom Yawkey after the 1932 season.

Frazee produced the enormously successful play No, No, Nannette, which hit Broadway in 1925. The musical opened in Detroit in 1924. It flopped in its early days, which resulted in the replacement of its director, a script revision, and recast leads. Several songs were dumped, and four new numbers were added, including "Tea for Two." Touring companies took the play around the country, and it landed on Broadway in September 1925. It had a New York run of 321 performances, was one of the most successful shows of the 1920s, and came to symbolize the Jazz Age. Frazee made $2.5 million on the play and became a leader in the New York social circuit. He had little time to enjoy the success of the play, however. He died in 1929 of Bright's disease at the age of forty-eight.

The Not-So-Mighty Quinn

The Red Sox had a record of 605–1,081 for a .359 winning percentage from 1922 through 1932, the worst in American League history over 11 consecutive seasons. In an eight-team league, the Red Sox finished last in nine of those 11 campaigns. The only worse record in 11 seasons in the majors since 1900 has been a 584–1,090 (.349) mark by the Philadelphia Phillies from 1933 through 1943. Harry Frazee pushed the Red Sox into the abyss by selling the club's top stars, starting with Babe Ruth, who went to the Yankees.

Frazee sold the Sox in the middle of the 1923 season, however, to a group headed by J. A. Robert "Bob" Quinn. It was Quinn who drove the Red Sox franchise straight into the ground. The worst club under Frazee's regime was the 1922

outfit with a record of 61–93. Most of Quinn's aggregations fell below the standards of Frazee's depleted teams. In the nine full seasons that Quinn ran the Red Sox, seven lost more games than the 1922 club. The best team under Quinn was the first one in 1924, which was 67–87.

Quinn was the baseball brains and a limited partner in a group of Columbus, Ohio, investors headed by Palmer Winslow, a glassworks millionaire. Quinn had been the St. Louis Browns' vice president and business manager since 1917. The Browns were owned by Phil Ball and struggled financially. Still, Quinn managed to put together a Browns team that nearly won the 1922 pennant, finishing one game behind the Yankees. He wanted to see what he could do with a team of his own and grabbed the opportunity to purchase a stake in the Red Sox.

His string of horrendous luck began less than a year after he bought the club when Winslow was struck with a lingering illness. Because of Winslow's precarious health, Quinn couldn't speak to him on baseball matters, let alone ask him for the cash necessary to run the ball club properly. Winslow died in April 1927. Quinn had to go it alone and lost his life fortune trying to revive the Red Sox.

He ran into more problems. In 1926, the third base bleachers at Fenway Park burned to the ground. Quinn was so cash poor that the stands weren't rebuilt for eight years, until Tom Yawkey bought the club, leaving a large void in the park's enclosure along the left field line. Jim Price, the club secretary, committed suicide in 1929 by slashing his throat with a razor in the offices at Fenway Park. In the fall of that year, the stock market crashed, signaling the start of the Great Depression, and most of Quinn's investments became worthless.

Many Red Sox fans were suddenly unemployed as the country's economic woes worsened over the next few years, causing attendance to plummet. In 1932, Ed Morris, one of the club's top pitchers, was stabbed to death at a party held in his honor.

The 1932 season was the worst in Red Sox history. The club lost 111 of its 154 games. The season attendance was only 182,150, less than what the club draws today in a typical six-game homestand. In February 1933, Quinn sold the Red Sox to Tom Yawkey. "I have been carrying a load for many years that would make most men jump out a fourteenth story window," said Quinn in his farewell speech. "I tried and spent plenty of money to build up the Red Sox. I failed and I apologize to the Boston public."

Quinn remained undaunted in his attempts to revive lost causes, however. At the end of the 1935 season, he purchased the Boston Braves. The Braves had just completed a season in which they won only 38 games and lost 115. To change the image of the club, he temporarily changed the nickname of Boston's National League club from the Braves to the Bees. By 1937, the Bees had a winning record, but in the end Quinn didn't have the cash to compete with Yawkey's millions for the allegiance of Boston's baseball fans, and sold the club to a group headed by Lou Perini in 1944.

Quinn's son John became the Braves general manager, however, and brought honor to the family name by leading the club to a National League pennant in 1948. After the Braves moved to Milwaukee in 1953, John Quinn headed two more teams that finished first, in 1957 and 1958. The 1957 Milwaukee Braves won the World Championship by defeating the Yankees. John Quinn's and Bob Quinn's grandson, also named Bob, was the general manager of the 1990 World Champion Cincinnati Reds.

JULY 27   Chick Fewster and Val Picinich fight each other in the Red Sox dugout during a 10–7 loss to the Senators at Fenway Park.

JULY 28   The Red Sox score seven runs in the seventh inning and defeat the Indians 10–5 at Fenway Park.

AUGUST 3   The Red Sox game against the White Sox at Fenway Park is postponed to observe a national day of mourning following the August 2 death of President Warren G. Harding, who died during a trip to San Francisco. The Red Sox game against the Browns on August 10 in Boston was also postponed for Harding's funeral. Former Massachusetts Governor Calvin Coolidge succeeded Harding as president.

AUGUST 11   The Red Sox score three runs in the ninth inning on a two-run, two-out double by Shano Collins and a single by Joe Harris to defeat the Browns 4–3 at Fenway Park.

Harris hit .335 and belted 13 homers for the Red Sox in 1923.

SEPTEMBER 3   The Red Sox plate four runs in the ninth inning to bring down the Senators 5–4 in the first game of a doubleheader at Fenway Park. Howard Shanks drove in the tying and winning run with a two-run single off Walter Johnson. Washington won the second game, 7–2.

SEPTEMBER 7   Howard Ehmke pitches a no-hitter against the Athletics for a 4–0 win in Philadelphia. There was certainly an element of luck involved. With two out in the sixth inning, opposing pitcher Slim Harriss drilled what looked to be a double to left field. Harriss failed to touch first base, however, and was declared out. The hit didn't count. In the eighth, Frank Welch hit a liner that left fielder Mike Menosky muffed. At first, the official scorer ruled it a hit, but within minutes reversed himself and called it an error. In the ninth inning, Ehmke retired Heinie Scheer on a ground-out, Beauty McGowan on a fly ball to center, and Wid Matthews on a grounder. Ehmke walked one and struck out one.

Val Picinich was Ehmke's catcher during the no-hitter. Picinich caught three no-hitters with three different clubs during his career. The other two were Joe Bush's no-hitter with the Athletics in 1916 and Walter Johnson's with the Senators in 1920.

SEPTEMBER 11   In his first start since pitching a no-hitter, Howard Ehmke one-hits the Yankees for a 3–0 victory in New York. The only hit was a single by leadoff batter Whitey Witt in the first inning on a controversial scoring decision. Witt hit a bouncer to third baseman Howard Shanks, who fumbled the ball and threw too late to retire Witt at first base. After Witt's single, Ehmke retired 27 batters in succession. All three Boston runs were scored on a homer by Val Picinich with two on base in the seventh inning. The official scorer who gave Witt a hit on the first play of the game was Fred Lieb, one of the most respected sportswriters ever to cover baseball. The decision robbed Ehmke of back-to-back no-hitters and a perfect game and haunted Lieb until his death in 1980.

Ehmke holds the American League record for fewest hits allowed in two consecutive complete-game starts with one. At the major league level, only Johnny Vander Meer, with his back-to-back no-hitters for the Cincinnati Reds in 1938, has bettered Ehmke's achievement.

SEPTEMBER 14   First baseman George Burns turns an unassisted triple play during a 4–3 win in 12 innings against the Indians at Fenway Park. With Riggs Stephenson on second base and Rube Lutzke on first in the second inning, Burns snared a liner off the bat of Frank Brower. Burns tagged Lutzke and raced to second, sliding into the bag ahead of Stephenson.

SEPTEMBER 19   Howard Ehmke picks up his 20th win of the season with a 2–1 decision over the White Sox at Fenway Park. The Red Sox scored two runs in the ninth for the victory.

SEPTEMBER 21   During a 15–6 loss to the Tigers at Fenway Park, relief pitcher Clarence Blethen is bitten by his own false teeth. Blethen didn't like to pitch with his false teeth, believing that he looked more menacing on the mound without them, and kept them in his back pocket. Blethen slid into second base on a close play, and received a nasty wound when his choppers clamped down on his buttocks.

SEPTEMBER 22   The Red Sox score seven runs in the sixth inning and win 9–7 against the Tigers in the second game of a doubleheader at Fenway Park. The Red Sox almost blew it, however, as the Tigers scored all seven of their runs in the ninth inning. Detroit won the first game, 10–0.

SEPTEMBER 27   The Red Sox announce that Frank Chance will not return as manager in 1924, although he's allowed to finish out the season.

Chance spelled his doom by predicting that the Red Sox would finish last during spring training. The White Sox offered him a job as manager, but Chance declined because of ill health. He died on September 15, 1924, from complications after a bout of influenza.

SEPTEMBER 28   The Yankees collect 30 hits and massacre the Red Sox 24–4 at Fenway Park. Howard Ehmke was the starting pitcher and gave up 17 runs and 21 hits in six innings. In the sixth, Ehmke allowed 11 runs and 11 hits. Clarence Blethen pitched the final three innings.

SEPTEMBER 29   The Red Sox sweep the Yankees at Fenway Park, winning 5–4 in the opener and 3–2 in 16 innings in the nightcap. In the second contest, George Murray pitched a complete game for the Sox. Mike Menosky hit a triple and scored the winning run scored on a sacrifice fly by Shano Collins.

OCTOBER 22   The Red Sox hire Lee Fohl as manager.

Before coming to Boston, Fohl had some success as a manager. In 1918, as skipper of the Indians, he finished only 2 1/2 games behind the Red Sox. At the helm of the Browns in 1922, Fohl missed the American League championship by just one game but was fired midway through the 1923 season with the Browns in third place. In three years in Boston, with next to nothing in the dugout in the way of standout baseball talent, Fohl landed in seventh once and last twice.

1924   B

Season in a Sentence

With a new manager and a revamped lineup, the Red Sox are in first place in mid-June, but quickly sink toward the bottom of the league standings.

Finish • Won • Lost • Pct • GB

Seventh   67   87   .435   25.0

Manager

Lee Fohl

Stats

Stats	Red Sox	AL	Rank
Batting Avg:	.277	.290	8
On-Base Pct:	.356	.358	7
Slugging Pct:	.374	.396	8
Home Runs:	30		7
Stolen Bases:	78		6
ERA:	4.35	4.23	4
Fielding Pct:	.967	.969	6
Runs Scored:	737		7
Runs Allowed:	803		5

Starting Lineup

Steve O'Neill, c
Joe Harris, 1b
Bill Wambsganns, 2b
Danny Clark, 3b
Dud Lee, ss
Bobby Veach, lf
Ira Flagstead, cf
Ike Boone, rf
Homer Ezzell, 3b
Shano Collins, rf-lf
Howard Shanks, ss-3b
Val Picinich, c

Pitchers

Howard Ehmke, sp
Alex Ferguson, sp
Jack Quinn, sp
Curt Fullerton, sp
Bill Piercy, sp
Buster Ross, rp
George Murray, rp
Oscar Fuhr, rp-sp

Attendance

448,566 (eighth in AL)

Club Leaders

Batting Avg:	Boone	.333
On-Base Pct:	Harris	.406
Slugging Pct:	Boone	.492
Home Runs:	Boone	13
RBI:	Veach	99
Runs:	Flagstead	106
Stolen Bases:	Wambsganss	14
Wins:	Ehmke	19
Strikeouts:	Ehmke	119
ERA:	Quinn	3.19
Saves:	Quinn	7

JANUARY 7   The Red Sox trade George Burns, Roxy Walters, and Chick Fewster to the Indians for Steve O'Neill, Bill Wambsganss, Danny Boone, and Joe Connolly.

MARCH 12   The Red Sox purchase Bobby Veach from the Tigers.

APRIL 15   The Yankees defeat the Red Sox 2–1 before 23,856 on Opening Day at Fenway Park. The Red Sox led 1–0 entering the ninth before the Yankees scored two runs off Howard Ehmke, helped by two errors from second baseman Bill Wambsganss, who was playing in his first game for Boston. Waite Hoyt pitched a two-hitter for New York. Prior to the contest, fans presented Babe Ruth with one hundred week-old chicks for his farm in suburban Sudbury.

With a new owner and several new players, there was considerable enthusiasm regarding the Red Sox entering the 1924 season. For the first two months of the season, the optimism would be rewarded.

APRIL 19   The Red Sox score 10 runs in the second inning and wallop the Athletics 12–0 on Patriots' Day before 26,000 in Boston. In a rare scene during the dreadful 1920s, people were clamoring to get inside Fenway Park. A portion of the bleacher gate collapsed under pressure from the crowd, and four people were hospitalized.

APRIL 29   The Red Sox sail past the 1924 World Champion Senators 15–6 in Washington.

            The Red Sox started the season with seven losses in their first 10 games before winning 21 of their next 30 to surge to the top of the standings.

MAY 2   The Red Sox easily handle the Athletics 11–0 at Shibe Park in Philadelphia.

MAY 6   The Red Sox score at will, plating nine runs in the second inning on the way to a 14–4 win over the Senators at Fenway Park.

MAY 14   The Red Sox smother the White Sox 12–0 on a windy day at Fenway Park.

MAY 26   A seven-run Boston fourth inning wipes out a 5–0 Cleveland lead at Fenway Park. The Indians came back to take an 8–7 advantage with three runs in the fifth inning, but the Red Sox rallied to win 10–9.

MAY 28   Jack Quinn pitches a shutout and Ira Flagstead hits a first-inning homer to lead the Red Sox to a 1–0 win over the Athletics in the second game of a doubleheader at Shibe Park. Philadelphia won the opener, 2–1.

MAY 30   In the first game of a doubleheader at Fenway Park, Ike Boone hits a grand slam off Joe Martina during the Red Sox' seven-run fourth inning to win 9–4 over the Senators before 32,000. Washington won the second game 10–5.

            Boone batted .333 and clubbed 13 homers for the Red Sox in 1924.

JUNE 9   The Red Sox take sole possession of first place and improve their record to 25–17 with a 5–1 win over the White Sox in Chicago.

            The Red Sox remained in first place until June 13, but the club quickly disintegrated. By July 2, Boston was in seventh place and fell into the American League cellar in early August. Strange injuries and illnesses led to the collapse. Joe Harris had his tonsils removed, pitcher Bill Piercy suffered a fractured skull when struck by a batted ball, and Oscar Fuhr was hospitalized with jaundice. The Sox finished the year only a half-game ahead of eighth-place Chicago. That slim margin marked the only time in a nine-year stretch from 1922 through 1930 that the Red Sox avoided last place.

JULY 22   The Red Sox end a nine-game losing streak with two runs in the ninth inning and one in the eleventh to beat the Indians 4–3 at Fenway Park. An infield single by Bill Wambsganss with the bases loaded scored the winning run.

JULY 23   The Indians score five runs in the first inning, but the Red Sox rally to win 16–12 at Fenway Park, keyed by a seven-run rally in the fifth inning.

JULY 24   The Red Sox rally to beat the Indians 10–9 in 10 innings at Fenway Park. With two outs, Boston scored two runs in the ninth inning to tie the score 8–8. After Cleveland scored in the top of the tenth, the Red Sox came back with two in their half for the win. A single by Danny Clark drove in both tenth-inning runs.

JULY 28   The Red Sox plate five runs in the tenth inning and down the Browns 10–5 in St. Louis.

AUGUST 13   Howard Ehmke holds the White Sox without a hit until the eighth and pitches the Red Sox to a two-hit, 6–0 win in the first game of a doubleheader at Fenway Park. The only Chicago hits were singles by Harry Hooper and Buck Crouse. The Red Sox completed the sweep with a 4–1 win in the second game.

Ehmke had a 19–17 record with 315 innings pitched, 26 complete games, 4 shutouts, 119 strikeouts, and a 3.46 ERA in 1924.

AUGUST 18   The Red Sox rally with three runs in the ninth to defeat the Browns 3–2 at Fenway Park. Bill Wambsganss drove in the final two runs with a triple.

AUGUST 28   The Red Sox score seven runs in the first inning and hold off the Athletics to win 8–7 in the second game of a doubleheader at Fenway Park. Ike Boone broke the 7–7 tie with a homer in the eighth inning. Boston also won the first game, 6–3.

SEPTEMBER 2   Danny Clark hits a grand slam in the fourth inning off Al Mamaux during the Red Sox' 14–6 win over the Yankees in the first game of a doubleheader in New York. The Red Sox lost the nightcap, 5–2.

SEPTEMBER 10   The Red Sox purchase Ted Wingfield from the Senators.

SEPTEMBER 13   After being shut out by the Browns 6–0 in the first game of a doubleheader in St. Louis, the Red Sox break loose and win the nightcap, 13–11.

SEPTEMBER 14   The Red Sox humble the Browns 10–0 at Sportsman's Park.

SEPTEMBER 18   The game between the Red Sox and White Sox in Chicago is stopped for one minute at 4:30 PM while players and fans stood with bared heads out of respect for Frank Chance, who was buried that day in Los Angeles. Chance died three days earlier. The White Sox won the game, 7–3.

DECEMBER 10   The Red Sox trade Howard Shanks to the Yankees for Mike McNally. The following day, the Sox traded McNally to the Senators for Doc Prothro.

DECEMBER 12   The Red Sox purchase Steve O'Neill from the Indians.

1925 ⬛ B

Season in a Sentence

The Red Sox spend the entire season in last place and lose 105 games.

Finish • Won • Lost • Pct • GB

Eighth   47   105   .309   49.5

Manager

Lee Fohl

Stats	Red Sox	AL	Rank
Batting Avg:	.266	.292	8
On-Base Pct:	.336	.360	8
Slugging Pct:	.364	.407	8
Home Runs:	41		7
Stolen Bases:	42		8
ERA:	4.97	4.40	8
Fielding Pct:	.957	.967	8
Runs Scored:	639		8
Runs Allowed:	922		8

Starting Lineup

Val Picinich, c
Phil Todt, 1b
Bill Wambsganss, 2b
Doc Prothro, 3b
Dud Lee, ss
Roy Carlyle, lf-rf
Ira Flagstead, cf
Ike Boone, rf
Tex Vache, lf
Denny Williams, lf
Homer Ezzell, 3b
Billy Rogell, 2b

Pitchers

Howard Ehmke, sp
Ted Wingfield, sp
Red Ruffing, sp
Ted Zahniser, sp
Oscar Fuhr, rp
Buster Ross, rp

Attendance

267,782 (eighth in AL)

Club Leaders

Batting Avg:	Boone	.330
On-Base Pct:	Boone	.406
Slugging Pct:	Boone	.479
Home Runs:	Todt	11
RBI:	Todt	75
Runs:	Flagstead	84
Stolen Bases:	Prothro	9
	Rogell	9
Wins:	Wingfield	12
Strikeouts:	Ehmke	95
ERA:	Ehmke	3.73
Saves:	Wingfield	2

APRIL 11   The Braves defeat the Red Sox 4–3 in an exhibition game at Braves Field.

From 1925 through 1953, with the lone exception of the 1928 season, the Red Sox and Braves met each other in Boston at the close of the spring training exhibition season in games at both Braves Field and Fenway Park. The series ended when the Braves moved to Milwaukee.

APRIL 14   The Red Sox take a 6–0 lead into the seventh inning on Opening Day but lose 9–8 in 10 innings to the Athletics in Philadelphia. Ira Flagstead had four hits, including a homer. Joe Harris also homered for the Red Sox.

The heart-rending loss sets the stage for a terrible season. The Red Sox finished the year 21 games behind the nearest American League team and 20 games worse than any other club in the majors.

APRIL 22   In the first game of the season in Boston, the Red Sox lose 6–5 to the Athletics in 11 innings. Rookie outfielder Tex Vache hit a three-run homer in his first game at Fenway.

Lee Fohl is the only manager from the American League in 1925 who has not been elected to the Hall of Fame. The other managers that season were Bucky Harris (Senators), Connie Mack (Athletics), George Sisler (Browns), Ty Cobb (Tigers), Eddie Collins (White Sox), Tris Speaker (Indians), and Miller Huggins (Yankees).

APRIL 26   The Red Sox trade Joe Harris to the Senators for Paul Zahniser and Roy Carlyle.

MAY 5   The Red Sox trade Bobby Veach and Alex Ferguson to the Yankees for Ray Francis
                and cash.

MAY 8   Ira Flagstead scores five runs on five walks and a single in the Red Sox' 15–7 victory
                over the Tigers in Detroit. Boston scored seven runs in the eighth inning of the contest.

MAY 17   Buster Ross sets an American League record for pitchers by committing four errors
                during the Red Sox' 11–6 loss to the Browns in St. Louis. Ross also walked eight
                batters in $7\frac{1}{3}$ innings.

JUNE 5   Pinch hitter Ira Flagstead's bases-loaded single scores two runs in the ninth and
                enables the Red Sox to come from behind and defeat the Indians 5–4 at Fenway Park.

                The Red Sox' top hitter in 1925 was Ike Boone, who batted .330.

JUNE 15   The Red Sox' hard hitting gives the club a 13–5 decision over the White Sox at
                Fenway Park.

JUNE 17   On Bunker Hill Day, the Red Sox overcome a five-run White Sox lead to win 7–6 in
                the second game of a doubleheader at Fenway Park. Boston led 6–1 before scoring
                two runs in the sixth inning, two in the eighth, and two in the ninth. Roy Carlyle
                drove in the final two runs on a bases-loaded double, giving him six RBIs in the
                game. Chicago won the first game, 5–3.

JULY 10   The Red Sox sell Jack Quinn to the Athletics.

JULY 11   The Red Sox collect 21 hits to pound the Indians 14–7 in Cleveland.

JULY 13   Carlyle hits a two-run pinch homer in the ninth to beat the Indians 12–11 in Cleve-
                land. The Sox scored five runs in the first inning but fell behind 11–7 in the sixth
                inning before mounting a comeback.

JULY 21   Roy Carlyle hits for the cycle in a 6–3 win over the White Sox in the first game of a
                doubleheader at Comiskey Park. Chicago won the second game 8–3.

AUGUST 11   Three weeks after John Scopes is convicted and fined $100 for teaching evolution in
                the Scopes Monkey Trial in Dayton, Tennessee, Red Ruffing pitches the Red Sox to
                a 1–0 win over the Tigers at Fenway Park. Dud Lee's single in the second inning,
                preceded by a two-out triple from Billy Rogell, scored the only run of the game.
                Two Detroit runners were retired at the plate on throws from left fielder Ken
                Williams and center fielder Ira Flagstead.

AUGUST 22   The Red Sox score eight runs in the first inning and win 10–4 over the Browns in
                St. Louis.

AUGUST 25   The Red Sox lose 14–4 to the Tigers in Detroit but pull off an unusual double play.
                Topper Rigney doubled to deep center with Johnny Bassler on second base and Fred
                Haney on first. Ira Flagstead relayed the ball to shortstop Jack Rothrock, who
                threw to the plate. Haney came down the third base line right on the slow-footed

Bassler's heels, and catcher Al Stokes tagged out both runners on Rothrock's throw.

SEPTEMBER 17   The Red Sox shut out the Browns twice in a doubleheader at Fenway Park. Ted Wingfield won the opener 2–0, and Paul Zahniser took the nightcap, 4–0. Doc Prothro collected six consecutive hits, including a double, during the twin bill, which was played in only two hours and fifty-one minutes.

Prothro drew his nickname from his dental practice. His son Tommy was a successful football coach at UCLA and with the Los Angeles Rams.

DECEMBER 12   The Red Sox sell Bill Wambsganss to the Athletics.

1926   B

Season in a Sentence

As bad as the Red Sox were in 1925, the 1926 campaign is even worse as the club loses 107 games.

Finish • Won • Lost • Pct • GB

Eighth   46   107   .301   44.5

Manager

Lee Fohl

Stats

Stats	Red Sox	AL	Rank
Batting Avg:	.256	.281	8
On-Base Pct:	.321	.351	8
Slugging Pct:	.343	.392	8
Home Runs:	32		6
Stolen Bases:	52		8
ERA:	4.72	4.02	8
Fielding Pct:	.970	.969	4
Runs Scored:	562		8
Runs Allowed:	835		7

Starting Lineup

Alex Gaston, c
Phil Todt, 1b
Bill Regan, 2b
Fred Haney, 3b
Topper Rigney, ss
Si Rosenthal, lf
Ira Flagstead, cf
Baby Doll Jacobson, rf-cf
Mike Herrera, 2b
Jack Tobin, rf
Wally Shaner, lf
Fred Bratschi, lf
Roy Carlyle, rf

Pitchers

Hal Wiltse, sp
Paul Zahniser, sp
Red Ruffing, sp
Fred Heimach, sp
Slim Harriss, sp
Howard Ehmke, sp
Ted Wingfield, rp-sp
Tony Welzer, rp
Jack Russell, rp

Attendance

285,155 (seventh in AL)

Club Leaders

Batting Avg:	Flagstead	.299
On-Base Pct:	Rigney	.395
Slugging Pct:	Flagstead	.429
Home Runs:	Todt	7
RBI:	Todt	69
	Jacobson	69
Runs:	Rigney	71
Stolen Bases:	Haney	13
Wins:	Wingfield	11
Strikeouts:	Wiltse	59
ERA:	Wiltse	4.22
Saves:	Wingfield	3

FEBRUARY 10   The Red Sox sell Val Picinich to the Reds.

APRIL 7   The Red Sox purchase Topper Rigney from the Tigers.

APRIL 13   The Red Sox lose 12–11 to the Yankees on Opening Day before 12,000 on a cold day
                   at Fenway Park. The Yankees led 11–1 in the fifth inning before the Red Sox mounted
                   a futile comeback. Ira Flagstead collected four hits, including two doubles. It was the
                   second year in a row that Flagstead had four hits in the season opener.

                   *The opener was the first Red Sox game ever broadcast over radio. It was carried
                   over WNAC with Gus Rooney at the mike. Regularly scheduled radio broadcasts
                   began in 1927 with Fred Hoey as the announcer. Hoey broadcast games for both
                   the Red Sox and Braves over WNAC radio until 1938.*

APRIL 17   Howard Ehmke pitches a two-hitter to defeat the Athletics 6–1 at Fenway Park.

APRIL 19   Ira Flagstead ties a major league record for outfielders by starting three double plays
                   during a 2–1 victory over the Athletics in the afternoon game of a Patriots' Day dou-
                   bleheader at Fenway Park. Two of Flagstead's throws retired runners at the plate
                   after he made circus catches. Philadelphia won the morning contest, 3–1.

APRIL 22   Phil Todt's second homer of the game breaks a 5–5 tie in the tenth inning and
                   enables the Red Sox to defeat the Yankees 6–5 in New York.

MAY 6   Hal Wiltse shuts out the Indians 1–0 at Fenway Park.

MAY 7   During an 11–2 loss against the Indians, three small fires break out in the refuse and
                   papers strewn beneath the wood-frame bleachers that ran down the left field line from
                   the grandstand to Landsdowne Street. Alert fans extinguished each blaze before any
                   damage was done.

MAY 8   After the crowd clears Fenway Park following a 10–4 loss to the Indians, the ball-
                   park catches fire. Before the fire department could arrive, manager Lee Fohl and a
                   handful of park employees fought the fire with the groundskeeper's hoses, but it was
                   too late. The grass caught fire and spread to a billboard. The wooden third base
                   bleachers, which had been the scene of three fires the day before, were destroyed.
                   Flying embers kept firemen fighting blazes all around the grandstand and properties
                   surrounding Fenway. It took nearly an hour to extinguish the blaze.

                   *The fire department said the fire was accidental, but given that it was the fourth
                   fire in the same place in less than thirty-six hours, the circumstances were suspi-
                   cious. The bleachers weren't replaced until 1934, leaving a huge cinder-strewn
                   expanse in foul territory along the left field line. For eight years, the ground
                   beyond the grandstand was the largest foul territory in the major leagues. Foul
                   balls hit past the stands down the left field line remained in play all the way to
                   the fence paralleling Jersey Street and Brookline Avenue. While chasing after such
                   balls, the left fielder or shortstop sometimes disappeared from sight, sending the
                   base umpire after him and leaving base runners unsure about whether to tag up.*

MAY 10   Howard Ehmke carries a no-hitter into the eighth inning but loses 3–0 to the Indians
                   at Fenway Park.

MAY 21   The Red Sox rally with three runs in the ninth inning to beat the White Sox 8–7 at Fenway Park.

MAY 22   The Red Sox smack the White Sox 14–8 at Fenway Park.

MAY 31   Howard Ehmke pitches a shutout and has a hand in both Red Sox runs in a 2–0 win over the Athletics in the first game of a doubleheader at Fenway Park. In the eighth inning, Ehmke drove in a run with a double off Lefty Grove and scored on a single by Topper Rigney. Philadelphia won the second game, 8–2.

JUNE 15   The Red Sox trade Howard Ehmke and Tom Jenkins to the Athletics for Baby Doll Jacobson, Fred Heimach, and Slim Harriss.

              Baby Doll Jacobson acquired his nickname as a minor leaguer despite being a hefty six feet, three inches and 215 pounds. Shortly after arriving in Boston, Jacobson, an outfielder, set a major league record for playing seven consecutive games without a fielding chance from June 18 through June 25, a span of 64$\frac{1}{3}$ innings. Harriss earned the nickname "Slim" because he carried only 180 pounds on his six-foot-six frame.

JULY 10   Trailing 5–0 in the fifth inning, the Red Sox rally to defeat the Tigers 6–5 in the first game of a doubleheader at Fenway Park. Detroit won the second game 4–2.

JULY 24   The Red Sox belt the Browns 14–9 in the first game of a doubleheader at Fenway Park. The nightcap ended in a 5–5 tie, called after nine innings to allow the Browns to catch a train.

JULY 27   Baby Doll Jacobson collects five hits, including a homer and a double, in five at-bats in a 7–0 win over the Tigers in Detroit.

JULY 31   The Red Sox purchase Jack Tobin from the Senators.

AUGUST 16   The Red Sox tie a major league record with two bases-loaded triples during a 7–1 win in the second game of a doubleheader at Fenway Park, called after seven innings by rain. Red Sox catcher Alex Gaston hit the first one in the second inning off of his brother Milt, who was pitching for St. Louis. Fred Haney's three-base hit with the sacks filled occurred in the third. The Browns won the first game 6-1.

AUGUST 19   Ted Wingfield blanks the White Sox 1–0 at Fenway Park.

              Before reaching the majors, Wingfield fought in World War I and was hospitalized after exposure to mustard gas.

AUGUST 21   Future Hall of Famer Ted Lyons of the White Sox pitches a no-hitter to defeat the Red Sox 6–0 at Fenway Park. Topper Rigney was the last batter of the game and went down on a grounder from first basemen Earl Sheely to Lyons, who was covering first.

              The starting pitcher for Boston was Slim Harriss, who had been the starter for the Athletics on September 7, 1923, when Howard Ehmke hurled a no-hitter for the Red Sox. Slim's given name was William Jennings Bryan

Harriss. The pitcher was born a month after Bryan lost the 1896 presidential election to William McKinley.

AUGUST 28   The Indians use the same starting lineup in two victories over the Red Sox, including Earl Levsen, who pitched a pair of complete games in the 6–1 and 5–1 sweep at Fenway Park.

SEPTEMBER 7   The Red Sox lose their 17th game in a row in a 4–2 decision to the Yankees at Yankee Stadium.

SEPTEMBER 8   The Red Sox check their losing streak with a 5–2 victory over the Yankees in New York.

SEPTEMBER 12 Jack Tobin hits a grand slam homer off Chet Falk in the sixth inning of an 11–2 win over the Browns in the first game of a doubleheader at Sportsman's Park. St. Louis won the nightcap 1–0.

OCTOBER 22   Lee Fohl resigns as manager of the Red Sox.

Fohl ended three seasons in Boston with a record of 160–299. He never managed in the big leagues again and died in 1965 at the age of eighty-five.

NOVEMBER 30   The Red Sox persuade Bill Carrigan to return to baseball as manager of the ball club.

The surprise announcement of Carrigan's return to Boston brought joy to Red Sox fans, who hoped that he would return the club to the glory of its World Championship teams in 1915 and 1916.

1927   B

Season in a Sentence

With little talent, Bill Carrigan is unable to extricate the club from another last-place finish as the club loses more than 100 games for the third year in a row.

Finish • Won • Lost • Pct • GB

Eighth   51   103   .331 59.0

Manager

Bill Carrigan

Stats

Stats	Red Sox	AL	Rank
Batting Avg:	.259	.285	8
On-Base Pct:	.320	.351	8
Slugging Pct:	.357	.399	8
Home Runs:	28		7
Stolen Bases:	81		7
ERA:	4.72	4.14	7
Fielding Pct:	.964	.967	7
Runs Scored:	597		8
Runs Allowed:	856		7

Starting Lineup

Grover Hartley, c
Phil Todt, 1b
Bill Regan, 2b
Billy Rogell, 3b
Buddy Myer, ss
Wally Shaner, lf
Ira Flagstead, cf
Jack Tobin, rf
Jack Rothrock, ss-2b-3b
Cleo Carlyle, rf
Fred Hofmann, c
Red Rollings, 3b
Baby Doll Jacobson, lf

Pitchers

Slim Harriss, sp
Hal Wiltse, sp
Red Ruffing, sp
Tony Welzer, sp-rp
Del Lundgren, sp-rp
Danny MacFayden, rp-sp
Jack Russell, sp-rp

Attendance

305,275 (seventh in AL)

Club Leaders

Batting Avg:	Myer	.288
On-Base Pct:	Flagstead	.374
Slugging Pct:	Regan	.408
Home Runs:	Todt	6
RBI:	Flagstead	69
Runs:	Flagstead	63
Stolen Bases:	Flagstead	12
Wins:	Ruffing	14
Strikeouts:	Ruffing	77
	Harriss	77
ERA:	Harriss	4.18
Saves:	Ruffing	2
	MacFayden	2

APRIL 12   With President Calvin Coolidge opening the festivities by throwing out the first pitch, the Red Sox lose 6–2 to the Senators in Washington on Opening Day. In his first game with Red Sox, shortstop Pee Wee Wanninger collected four hits.

Wanninger played only 18 games with the Red Sox and batted .200.

APRIL 21   Despite a grand slam by Jack Tobin in the sixth inning off George Murray, the Red Sox lose 7–4 to the Senators in the home opener. Prior to the game, fans presented Bill Carrigan with a new automobile.

In two seasons with the Red Sox, Tobin hit only three homers, but two of them were grand slams.

APRIL 30   The Red Sox score three runs in the ninth inning to defeat the Yankees 3–2 at Fenway Park. Jack Rothrock drove the in first two with a pinch-hit double. After Boston loaded the bases again, Fred Haney walked to force in the winning run.

The Red Sox were 4–18 against the 1927 World Champion Yankees, considered by many to be the greatest team in baseball history.

| MAY 2 | The Red Sox trade Topper Rigney to the Senators for Buddy Myer. |

MAY 2   The Red Sox trade Topper Rigney to the Senators for Buddy Myer.

JUNE 12   Three weeks after Charles Lindbergh's solo flight from New York to Paris, the Red Sox sell Baby Doll Jacobson to the Indians.

JUNE 16   The Red Sox edge the Indians 11–10 at League Park in Cleveland.

JUNE 23   Lou Gehrig becomes the first player to hit three homers in a game at Fenway Park during an 11–4 Yankees win over the Red Sox.

> *The first Red Sox player to hit three homers in a game at Fenway was Ted Williams, on July 14, 1946.*

JULY 4   The Red Sox extend their losing streak to 15 games with a 10–2 loss to the Athletics in the first game of a doubleheader at Fenway Park. They broke the streak in the second contest, when they Sox scored six runs in the first inning and won, 11–3.

> *After the first-game loss, the Red Sox' record was only 15–54.*

JULY 5   A throw from Red Sox first baseman Phil Todt breaks the nose of umpire Tommy Connolly in the seventh inning of a game against the Athletics at Fenway. The Red Sox won 6–5 with a run in the ninth inning.

JULY 11   The Red Sox lose 7–6 to the White Sox at Comiskey Park on two errors during a steal attempt. In the ninth inning, Chicago's Bill Barrett took off for second, but Red Sox catcher Fred Hofmann threw the ball past the base. Barrett went to third on the overthrow and scored when Ira Flagstead fumbled the ball in center field.

JULY 12   The Red Sox lose a heartbreaker in the ninth inning for the second day in a row. Playing the Browns in St. Louis, the Sox scored five times in the ninth to take a 5–3 lead but lost 6–5 when George Sisler hit a three-run walk-off homer off Red Ruffing.

JULY 18   The Red Sox score eight runs in the sixth inning and defeat the Indians 14–5 in the first game of a doubleheader in Cleveland but lose the nightcap, 4–0.

JULY 30   The Red Sox score two runs in the ninth and one in the tenth to defeat the Browns 5–4 in the first game of a doubleheader at Fenway Park. Wally Shaner's two-run triple tied the score 4–4, and Jack Rothrock's walk-off single won the contest. St. Louis won the second game, 9–2.

AUGUST 2   Hal Wiltse pitches a two-hitter to defeat the Browns 3–0 in the second game of a doubleheader at Fenway Park. The only St. Louis hits were singles by George Sisler in the seventh inning and Frank O'Rourke in the ninth. The Red Sox lost the opener, 3–2.

AUGUST 29   Two days after the execution of Sacco and Vanzetti, Ira Flagstead scores five runs and Slim Harriss pitches a two-hitter to defeat the Indians 10–3 at League Park. The only Cleveland hits were singles by Charlie Jamieson and George Burns.

SEPTEMBER 4   Phil Todt's two-run homer in the eleventh inning beats the Senators 5–3 in Washington. Todt also homered in the second inning.

The Red Sox had a record of 7–36 against the Senators in 1926 and 1927.

SEPTEMBER 5   The Red Sox earn a sensational 12–11 victory in 18 innings in the first game of a Labor Day doubleheader against the vaunted Yankees before a paid crowd of 34,385 at Fenway Park. About 15,000 more stormed the gates of the ballpark after ticket sales stopped. The game started twenty minutes late because of the difficulty of getting the crowd under control. Hundreds swarmed all over the field, and patrolmen and mounted police were called in to clear the field. The Red Sox led the game 8–6 in the ninth when the Yankees' Earle Combs hit a two-out, two-run double to tie the score. After the Yankees took an 11–8 lead in the seventeenth inning, the Red Sox countered with three in their half. The tying run scored on a pinch-hit double by third-string catcher Billy Moore, who would have only two doubles and four RBIs during his entire 49-game big-league career. The winning run came from doubles by Buddy Myer and Ira Flagstead off Waite Hoyt. Red Ruffing pitched 15 innings for the Red Sox, and Hal Wiltse hurled the final three. Wiltse also started the second game, which was called after five innings by darkness with the Yankees leading, 5–0.

SEPTEMBER 7   The Red Sox score eight runs in the fourth inning to take an 8–1 lead but lose 12–10 to the Yankees at Fenway Park. The Yankee comeback was led by Babe Ruth, who hit two homers and a double.

Ruth hit 60 homers in 1927, which set a major league record that lasted until Roger Maris recorded 61 in 1961. Red Sox pitchers allowed 11 of Ruth's 60, including three each by Slim Harriss and Tony Welzer.

SEPTEMBER 26   Red Sox catcher Bill Moore ties a modern major league record by committing four errors during an 11–1 loss to the Senators in the second game of a doubleheader in Washington. Boston made 10 errors as a team, five of them in the first inning, behind pitcher John Wilson, who was making his first major league start. The Red Sox made no errors and completed a triple play in the first game, but Washington won, 4–2.

DECEMBER 15   The Red Sox purchase Ken Williams from the Browns.

1928   B

Season in a Sentence

Manager Bill Carrigan's second season is little better, as 47 losses in July and August doom the Red Sox to a fourth consecutive last-place finish.

Finish • Won • Lost • Pct • GB

Eighth   57   96   .373   43.5

Manager

Bill Carrigan

Stats   Red Sox • AL • Rank

Batting Avg:	.264	.281	8
On-Base Pct:	.319	.344	8
Slugging Pct:	.361	.397	7
Home Runs:	38		6
Stolen Bases:	99		4
ERA:	4.39	4.04	7
Fielding Pct:	.971	.969	2
Runs Scored:	589		8
Runs Allowed:	770		6

Starting Lineup

Fred Hofmann, c
Phil Todt, 1b
Bill Regan, 2b
Buddy Myer, 3b
Wally Gerber, ss
Ken Williams, lf
Ira Flagstead, cf
Doug Taitt, rf
Jack Rothrock, lf-cf-rf
Billy Rogell, ss
Charlie Berry, c
Johnny Heving, c

Pitchers

Ed Morris, sp-rp
Red Ruffing, sp
Jack Russell, sp
Danny MacFayden, sp
Slim Harriss, sp-rp
Merle Settlemire, rp

Attendance

396,920 (fifth in AL)

Club Leaders

Batting Avg:	Myer	.313
On-Base Pct:	Myer	.379
Slugging Pct:	Taitt	.434
Home Runs:	Todt	12
RBI:	Regan	75
Runs:	Flagstead	84
Stolen Bases:	Myer	30
Wins:	Morris	19
Strikeouts:	Ruffing	118
ERA:	Morris	3.53
Saves:	Morris	5

APRIL 10   On a chilly Opening Day, the Red Sox lose 7–5 to the Senators in Washington. President Calvin Coolidge threw out the first ball, which umpire Brick Owens retrieved with a lunging one-handed catch. Coolidge stayed only through the first inning and then returned to the White House.

APRIL 11   Some 10,000 fans brave cold temperatures to watch the Senators defeat the Red Sox 8–4 in the season opener at Fenway Park. Ken Williams homered in his first home game as a member of the Red Sox.

APRIL 19   Down 6–0, the Red Sox score three runs in the sixth inning and four in the eighth to beat the Yankees 7–6 in the first game of a Patriots' Day doubleheader at Fenway Park. New York won the second game, called after six innings due to rain, 7–2.

APRIL 25   The Red Sox trade Hal Wiltse to the Browns for Wally Gerber.

MAY 12   Red Sox batters go wild with an 11-run third inning on the way to defeating the Browns 15–2 at Fenway Park.

MAY 15   Joe Lannin, who owned the Red Sox from 1914 through 1916, suffers a bizarre death by falling out of a seventh-story window of a hotel he had just purchased in Brooklyn. Lannin had gone to the room to inspect some plaster work, and it was believed that he became dizzy from the fumes, opened the window for some air, and fell.

JUNE 9   Second baseman Bill Regan collects seven hits during a doubleheader against the Tigers in Detroit. Regan was three for five in the first game, won 11–4 by the Red Sox, and four for four in the second tilt, won by the Tigers, 4–1. Regan had four doubles in the two games.

JUNE 15   Danny MacFayden carries a no-hitter into the eighth inning before Harry McCurdy of the White Sox singles. MacFayden wound up with a four-hit, 3–1 win over Chicago at Comiskey Park.

JUNE 16   Bill Regan hits two homers, one inside the park and one over the wall, during Boston's eight-run fourth inning as the Red Sox defeat the White Sox 10–5 in Chicago. Regan's homers were hit off Ted Blankenship and Sarge Connal.

                The only other Red Sox batters to hit two home runs in an inning are Ellis Burks in 1990 and Nomar Garciaparra in 2002.

JUNE 23   Bill Regan hits a grand slam off Waite Hoyt in the seventh inning of an 8–4 victory over the 1928 World Champion Yankees in the first game of a doubleheader in New York. The Red Sox completed the sweep with a 7–1 win in the nightcap.

                Ed Morris, a twenty-eight-year-old rookie, was Boston's top pitcher in 1928. He had a 19–15 record, five saves, and a 3.53 earned run average.

JULY 7   The Tigers score 10 runs in the fifth inning and defeat the Red Sox 20–8 in the first game of a doubleheader at Fenway Park. Detroit also won the nightcap 4–3 in 13 innings.

JULY 21   The Red Sox split a doubleheader against the Indians on Ira Flagstead Day at Fenway Park. Flagstead was presented with $1,000 in cash among his many gifts. The Sox won the first game 5–2 but lost the second, 5–1.

JULY 25   Right fielder Doug Taitt pitches the eighth inning of a 15–5 loss to the Indians in the second game of a doubleheader in Cleveland. Taitt allowed three runs in the inning of work. The Indians also won the first game 10–2 against the beleaguered Boston pitching staff.

AUGUST 30   Appearing as a pinch hitter in the ninth inning, pitcher Red Ruffing doubles in two runs and leads the Red Sox to a 3–2 win over the Athletics in Philadelphia.

                Ruffing was one of the top hitting pitchers in baseball history. He had a .269 batting average and 58 pinch hits during a 22-year career. From 1928 through 1932 with the Red Sox and Yankees, Ruffing had 578 at-bats and hit .324.

SEPTEMBER 3   Jack Rothrock hits a grand slam in the fourth inning off Rosy Ryan during the Red Sox' 8–7 win over the Yankees in the first game of a doubleheader at Yankee Stadium. New York won the second game, 4–3.

SEPTEMBER 24   After starting the game in left field, Jack Rothrock pitches a perfect eighth inning during an 8–0 loss to the Tigers in Detroit. It was his only game as a pitcher in his career.

SEPTEMBER 28   With fewer than 200 fans attending, Jack Russell pitches the Red Sox to a 1–0 win over the Indians in Cleveland. Center fielder George Loepp scored after collecting the first of his two career triples, and his only one with the Red Sox, to produce the game's lone run.

> *After his career ended, Russell was a city commissioner in Clearwater, Florida, from 1951 through 1955. He helped put through a new spring training stadium for the Phillies in Clearwater, which was named in his honor.*

SEPTEMBER 29   Manager Bill Carrigan lists Jack Rothrock as a catcher in the starting lineup against the Indians in Cleveland so he will have appeared at all nine fielding positions in 1928. Rothrock was the catcher only on paper, however, and pitcher Danny MacFayden had a similar status, on the lineup card in left field. In the bottom of the first inning, Rothrock moved to left field, and Johnny Heving went into the game as the catcher. Since Rothrock was listed as the starting catcher on the lineup card, he received credit for an official game at the position even though he didn't don the catcher's gear or take a position behind the plate. The Red Sox won the game 6–5 with three runs in the ninth inning, the final two on Phil Todt's double.

> *During the season, Rothrock played 40 games at shortstop, 36 at second base, 26 in left field, 19 in right, 17 at third base, 16 at first base, 12 in center field, 1 as a catcher, and 1 as a pitcher.*

DECEMBER 15   Six weeks after Herbert Hoover defeats Al Smith in the presidential election, the Red Sox trade Buddy Myer to the Senators for Milt Gaston, Hod Lisenbee, Bobby Reeves, Grant Gillis, and Elliott Bigelow.

> *Even though the Red Sox received five players for Myer, the club made a bad deal. Myer lasted in the majors until 1941, mainly as a second baseman, and compiled a career average of .303.*

1929   B

Season in a Sentence

The Red Sox compile a winning record during August and September, but it's not enough to escape last place.

Finish • Won • Lost • Pct • GB

Eighth   58   96   .377   48.0

Manager

Bill Carrigan

Stats   Red Sox • AL • Rank

Stats	Red Sox	AL	Rank
Batting Avg:	.267	.284	8
On-Base Pct:	.325	.349	8
Slugging Pct:	.365	.407	7
Home Runs:	28		8
Stolen Bases:	85		5
ERA:	4.43	4.24	7
Fielding Pct:	.965	.969	7
Runs Scored:	605		8
Runs Allowed:	803		8

Starting Lineup

Charlie Berry, c
Phil Todt, 1b
Bill Regan, 2b
Bobby Reeves, 3b
Hal Rhyne, ss
Russ Scarritt, lf
Jack Rothrock, cf
Bill Barrett, rf
Bill Narleski, ss-2b
Elliott Bigelow, rf
Johnny Heving, c
Ken Williams, cf

Pitchers

Milt Gaston, sp
Ed Morris, sp
Danny MacFayden, sp
Red Ruffing, sp
Jack Russell, sp
Bill Bayne, rp

Attendance

394,620 (sixth in AL)

Club Leaders

Batting Avg:	Rothrock	.300
On-Base Pct:	Rothrock	.361
Slugging Pct:	Scarritt	.411
Home Runs:	Rothrock	6
RBI:	Scarritt	71
Runs:	Rothrock	70
Stolen Bases:	Rothrock	23
Wins:	Morris	14
Strikeouts:	Ruffing	109
ERA:	MacFayden	3.62
Saves:	Gaston	2

JANUARY 29   The Red Sox' sixty-year-old club secretary, Jim Price, commits suicide by slashing his throat with a razor in his office at Fenway Park. Owner Bob Quinn hired Price in 1924.

FEBRUARY 11   The Braves receive a permit from Boston's city council to open Braves Field for games on Sunday in accordance with a recently passed state law that allowed sports to be played on the Sabbath. The law stipulated that the sporting venue couldn't be within one thousand feet of a church to be used on a Sunday, however, and since that rule applied to Fenway Park, the Red Sox couldn't play on Sunday at home.

FEBRUARY 18   Four days after Chicago's St. Valentine's Day Massacre, officials and businessmen from the Boston suburb of Revere confer with owner Bob Quinn and produce blue prints for a ballpark seating 41,000. The facility was planned on the site of a former amusement tract on Revere Beach Highway. Quinn considered the project but rejected it.

FEBRUARY 19   With Fenway Park unavailable on Sunday, the Red Sox strike a deal with their National League rivals to play 13 Sunday and three holiday games at Braves Field during the 1929 season. Bob Quinn announced that the Red Sox were considering abandoning Fenway altogether to play all home games at Braves Field, although he never carried through with the plan. A revision in the law allowed the Red Sox to begin playing games on Sunday at Fenway in 1932.

While Boston's two major league baseball teams could play on Sunday, the law included a curfew that stipulated that the games must end precisely at 6:30 PM. American League rules passed to adapt to the law specified that if an inning was in progress at 6:30, the results of that inning would be wiped off the records books and the score would revert back to the previous full inning played. Many second games of doubleheaders in Boston were shortened to six, seven, or eight innings because of the law.

APRIL 14   Two weeks after the Bruins win their first Stanley Cup, the first Sunday game in Boston played between two major league teams takes place at Braves Field in an exhibition contest between the Red Sox and the Braves. The Red Sox lost, 4–0.

APRIL 16   Rain and cold weather postpone the Red Sox' first game of the season, scheduled against the Yankees in New York. The April 17 contest was also postponed.

APRIL 18   The Red Sox finally open the 1929 campaign and lose 7–3 to the Yankees in New York. A day after his marriage to Claire Hodgson, Babe Ruth hit an opposite-field home run off Red Ruffing into the left field bleachers.

APRIL 23   Boston's first home game of the season results in a 4–2 Red Sox win over the Yankees before 15,000 at Fenway.

APRIL 28   The Red Sox play a regular-season game on a Sunday in Boston for the first time and lose 7–3 to the 1929 World Champion Athletics with 23,000 fans at Braves Field.

MAY 1   The Athletics collect 29 hits and clobber the Red Sox 24–6 at Fenway Park. The losing pitcher was Milt Gaston, who was making his first start with the Red Sox. His brother Alex was the catcher in the game.

MAY 17   Bill Carrigan uses four shortstops during a 13-inning, 6–3 win over the Yankees in New York. Carrigan pinch hit for starting shortstop Bill Narleski and substitutes Wally Gerber and Hal Rhyne. Bobby Reeves, who started the contest at third base, finished at short.

MAY 19   Tragedy follows a 3–0 Red Sox loss to the Yankees at Yankee Stadium. After the game was called in the sixth inning by rain, a crowd of more than 40,000 surged toward the runways to escape the downpour. Two people were killed in the crush.

MAY 22   The Athletics again rake Red Sox pitching with 12 runs in the fifth inning of a 16–2 rout in Philadelphia.

MAY 25   Red Ruffing ties a major league record for pitchers by hitting three doubles during the second game of a doubleheader against the Yankees at Fenway Park. Ruffing also singled, but the Red Sox lost, 8–3. New York also won the first game, 10–8.

JUNE 5   The Red Sox hammer the White Sox 17–2 at Fenway Park. Nine of Boston's 24 hits came consecutively with two out in the eight-run ninth inning. The nine consecutive hits came from Russ Scarritt, Bill Barrett, Bob Barrett (no relation),

Phil Todt, Grant Gillis, Charlie Berry, Danny MacFayden, Bill Narleski, and Jack Rothrock. The inning ended when Rothrock got thrown out at second base trying to stretch a single into a double. Dan Dugan allowed the first eight hits. Rothrock's hit was surrendered by forty-two-year-old White Sox manager Lena Blackburne, who was so disgusted with the performance that he had taken the mound himself. It was the last of 548 games that Blackburne played during his big-league career, and his only one as a pitcher.

JUNE 9   After the Tigers score three runs in the top of the ninth, the Red Sox produce a spectacular four-run rally in their half of the inning to win 7–6 at Braves Field. A double by Russ Scarritt drove in the winning run.

JULY 11   The Red Sox score 10 runs in the sixth inning and swamp the Tigers 15–8 in Detroit.

JULY 16   A seven-run sixth inning by the Red Sox keys an 11–2 trouncing of the Browns in St. Louis.

After a 31–72 start, the Red Sox won 27 of their final 51 games.

AUGUST 4 Ed Morris pitches a two-hitter to defeat the White Sox 8–0 at Braves Field. The only Chicago hits were singles by Bill Cissell in the fourth inning and Moe Berg in the fifth.

AUGUST 17 Bobby Reeves leads off the game with a homer and Danny MacFayden pitches a shutout to beat the Browns 1–0 in St. Louis.

AUGUST 29 Jack Rothrock hits a grand slam off Jack Quinn to put the Red Sox ahead 6–4 in the fourth inning, but Boston loses 7–6 to the Athletics in Philadelphia.

From 1927 through 1932, the Red Sox had a record of 25–104 against the Athletics.

SEPTEMBER 7   Trailing 3–0, the Red Sox score four times with two out in the ninth inning to defeat the Browns 4–3 at Fenway Park. Jack Rothrock ended the game with a bases-loaded triple.

SEPTEMBER 10 Jack Russell starts and loses both ends of a doubleheader against the Browns in St. Louis. In the opener, Russell was removed after allowing four runs in the first inning of a 6–1 defeat. He was back on the mound at the start of the nightcap and hurled a complete game 1–0 loss on an unearned run in the first.

SEPTEMBER 11 The Red Sox stage a comeback to beat the Tigers 8–7 in 10 innings at Fenway Park. After falling behind 7–2, Boston scored three runs in the eighth inning, two in the ninth, and one in the tenth. Jack Rothrock drove in the game winner with a single.

SEPTEMBER 25 Just before the start of the sixth inning at Fenway Park, the Yankees and Red Sox line up at home plate and the spectators stand in one minute of silent prayer for Yankees manager Miller Huggins, who died at 3:16 PM at St. Vincent's Hospital in New York, just after the start of the game. The Red Sox scored seven runs in the seventh inning to take a 10–7 lead, but the grieving Yankees rebounded to score three in the eighth and one in the tenth to win, 11–10.

Huggins, who entered the Hall of Fame in 1964, died of blood poisoning caused by an infection just under his right eye. He led the Yankees to six AL pennants and three World Championships. All American League games were postponed on September 27 out of respect for Huggins.

SEPTEMBER 29   The Red Sox lambaste the Athletics 10–0 at Braves Field.

Joe Cicero, who played 28 games for the Red Sox in 1929 and 1930, was a cousin of actor Clark Gable.

DECEMBER 20   Bill Carrigan resigns as manager of the Red Sox and retires from baseball.

After three last-place finishes, Carrigan probably wished he had never left the banking business. He jumped out of the frying pan and into the fire by returning to the financial world eight weeks after the stock market crash that started the Great Depression. Carrigan passed away in 1969 at the age of eighty-five.

DECEMBER 21   The Red Sox name Heinie Wagner as manager.

The starting shortstop on the 1912 World Champions, Wagner had been a coach for the Red Sox since 1921.

THE STATE OF THE RED SOX

The early 1930s were a continuation of the miserable 1920s. The teams in 1930 and 1932 each finished in last place. The Red Sox finished eighth in the eight-team American League nine times in 11 seasons from 1922 through 1932. The fortunes of the franchise began to change in February 1933 when wealthy Tom Yawkey purchased the club from financially strapped Bob Quinn. Under Yawkey, the Sox slowly and steadily improved, and in 1938 and 1939 finished in second place. Overall, the Red Sox were 705–815, a winning percentage of .464, which ranked sixth in the AL ahead of the White Sox and Browns. The AL champions during the 1930s were the Athletics (1930 and 1931), Yankees (1932, 1936, 1937, 1938, and 1939), Senators (1933), and Tigers (1934 and 1935).

THE BEST TEAM

The 1938 Red Sox were 88–61 and finished second, 9 1/2 games behind the Yankees.

THE WORST TEAM

The 1932 Red Sox were the worst in club record, thudding into the AL cellar with a record of 43–11, 64 games out of first place.

THE BEST MOMENT

Tom Yawkey bought the Red Sox in February 1933, which instantly turned the Red Sox from one of the poorest teams in baseball to one of the wealthiest.

THE WORST MOMENT

Pitcher Ed Morris was murdered at a party in his honor on March 3, 1932.

THE ALL–DECADE TEAM • YEARS WITH BRS

Rick Ferrell,	1933–37
Jimmie Foxx, 1b	1936–42
Bobby Doerr, 2b	1937–44; 1946–51
Bill Werber, 3b	1933–36
Joe Cronin, ss	1935–45
Roy Johnson, lf	1932–35
Doc Cramer, cf	1936–40
Earl Webb, rf	1930–32
Lefty Grove, p	1935–41
Wes Ferrell, p	1934–37
Fritz Ostermueller, p	1934–40
Jack Wilson, p	1935–41

The all-decade team reflects the positives and negatives of being a Red Sox fan during the 1930s. There are five Hall of Famers, including Grove, Foxx, Doerr, Cronin, and Rick Ferrell. In addition, Ted Williams debuted with a spectacular rookie season in 1939. Wes Ferrell deserves Hall of Fame consideration. But the Red Sox of the 1930s lacked depth, and, despite some of the greatest stars in the history of the game, failed to seriously compete for a pennant.

THE DECADE LEADERS

Batting Avg:	Foxx	.332
On-Base Pct:	Foxx	.439
Slugging Pct:	Foxx	.639
Home Runs:	Foxx	162
RBI:	Foxx	550
Runs:	Cronin	510
Stolen Bases:	Werber	107
Wins:	Grove	191
Strikeouts:	Grove	741
ERA:	Grove	3.15
Saves:	Moore	14
	Wilson	14

THE HOME FIELD

Fenway Park, built in 1912, had badly deteriorated by the early 1930s. The ballpark was almost completely gutted and rebuilt in between the 1933 and 1934 seasons and began to take on much of the look fans know today. Among the improvements were the right field bleachers and the "Green Monster" in left field (see December 13, 1933).

THE GAME YOU WISH YOU HAD SEEN

A total of 46,766 jammed into Fenway Park on August 12, 1934, to see Babe Ruth make his last appearance at the ballpark where he began his major league career.

THE WAY THE GAME WAS PLAYED

The offensive explosion that changed baseball during the 1920s continued throughout the 1930s. Batting averages in the AL floated around .280, with a peak of .289 in 1936, when teams in the circuit averaged 5.7 runs per game. In 1930 there were more home runs than stolen bases in the American League for the first time.

THE MANAGEMENT

Bob Quinn, who bought the Red Sox in 1923, was on the verge of bankruptcy when he sold the club to millionaire Tom Yawkey in the depths of the Great Depression in 1933. Yawkey immediately revived the moribund club. Eddie Collins was hired to run the front office in the role of vice president and general manager. Field managers were Heinie Wagner (1930), Shano Collins (1931–32), Marty McManus (1932–33), Bucky Harris (1934), and Joe Cronin (1935–47).

THE BEST PLAYER MOVE

In the best player move in Red Sox history, the club acquired Ted Williams from San Diego of the Pacific Coast League on December 7, 1937, in exchange for two players and $25,000. The best trade with a major league club occurred on December 10, 1935, when the Sox sent Gordon Rhoades, George Savino, and $150,000 to the Athletics for Jimmie Foxx and Johnny Marcum. Tom Yawkey also opened his wallet to obtain Lefty Grove and Joe Cronin in terrific deals.

THE WORST PLAYER MOVE

The Red Sox sent Red Ruffing to the Yankees on May 6, 1930, for Cedric Durst and $50,000. At the other end of the decade, the Sox sold Pee Wee Reese to the Dodgers in 1939.

1930   B

Season in a Sentence

A feeble offense dooms the Red Sox and new manager Heinie Wagner to a sixth consecutive last-place finish.

Finish • Won • Lost • Pct • GB

Eighth   52   102   .338   50.0

Manager

Heinie Wagner

Stats   Red Sox • AL • Rank

	Red Sox	AL	Rank
Batting Avg:	.264	.288	8
On-Base Pct:	.313	.351	8
Slugging Pct:	.364	.421	8
Home Runs:	47		8
Stolen Bases:	42		8
ERA:	4.68	4.65	3
Fielding Pct:	.968	.968	4
Runs Scored:	612		8
Runs Allowed:	814		3

Starting Lineup

Charlie Berry, c
Phil Todt, 1b
Bill Regan, 2b
Otto Miller, 3b
Hal Rhyne, ss
Russ Scarritt, lf
Tom Oliver, cf
Earl Webb, rf
Cedric Durst, lf-rf
Bobby Reeves, 3b
Bill Sweeney, 1b
Johnny Heving, c
Rabbit Warstler, ss

Pitchers

Milt Gaston, sp
Danny MacFayden, sp
Hod Lisenbee, sp
Jack Russell, sp
Ed Durham, rp-sp

Attendance

444,045 (sixth in AL)

Club Leaders

Batting Avg:	Webb	.323
On-Base Pct:	Webb	.385
Slugging Pct:	Webb	.523
Home Runs:	Webb	16
RBI:	Webb	66
Runs:	Oliver	86
Stolen Bases:	Oliver	6
	Reeves	6
Wins:	Gaston	13
Strikeouts:	Gaston	99
ERA:	Gaston	3.92
Saves:	Gaston	2
	MacFayden	2

JANUARY 29   The Red Sox sell Ken Williams to the Yankees.

APRIL 15   On Opening Day, a crowd of 8,500 at Fenway Park withstands cold and windy conditions to watch the Red Sox lose 6–1 to the Senators.

APRIL 19   The Red Sox go 15 innings to defeat the Yankees 4–3 in the morning game of a Patriots' Day doubleheader. Johnny Heving drove in the winning run with a single. In the afternoon, the Yankees won, 7–2.

APRIL 30   The Red Sox trade Bill Barrett to the Senators for Earl Webb.

At the time of the deal, Webb was a thirty-two-year-old journeyman outfielder who had played in only 166 big-league games, but he gave the Red Sox two great seasons, including 1931, when he set a major league record by collecting 67 doubles. In 1930, Webb batted .323 with 16 homers.

MAY 5   The Red Sox collect 23 hits and score nine runs in the fifth inning to smash the Indians 18–3 at Fenway Park.

MAY 6   The Red Sox trade Red Ruffing to the Yankees for Cedric Durst and $50,000.

Ruffing had only a 39–96 record in seven seasons with the woeful Red Sox and was a few days shy of twenty-six when the trade was completed. He still holds the all-time Red Sox record for losses in a season, when he was 10–25 in 1928, and also posted the second-most defeats in Red Sox history with a 9–22 mark in 1929. With the powerful Yankees, Ruffing thrived, posting 231 wins and 124 losses. He lasted in the majors until 1947 and was elected to the Hall of Fame in 1967.

MAY 7   The Sox lead 7–2 against the Indians at Fenway Park but wind up losing 8–7 after Cleveland scores five runs in the ninth inning and one in the tenth.

MAY 10   Milt Gaston pitches a two-hitter and beats the Browns 2–0 at Fenway Park. The only hits off Gaston were singles by Lu Blue and Heinie Manush.

             Gaston (12–20) and Jack Russell (9–20) were both 20-game losers in 1930. The Red Sox haven't had any pitcher lose more than 18 games in a season since 1930.

MAY 11   A Boston pitcher hurls a two-hitter for the second day in a row as the deliverings of Ed Morris baffle the Browns, resulting in a 2–1 win on a Sunday afternoon at Braves Field. The only St. Louis hits were singles by Frank O'Rourke and Heinie Manush.

JUNE 1   The Red Sox execute a triple play and end a 14-game losing streak with a 7–4 decision over the Yankees in New York.

JUNE 5   The Indians score nine runs in the first inning and collect 25 hits to thrash the Red Sox 17–7 in Cleveland. Starting pitcher Milt Gaston gave up hits to the only six batters he faced. George Smith went the rest of the way and allowed 11 runs and 19 hits in nine innings of pitching.

JULY 2   Pitcher Ed Morris wins his own game with a walk-off double in the ninth inning, which gives the Red Sox a 5–4 win over the Indians at Fenway Park. The Sox scored three runs in the eighth inning to tie the score, 4–4.

JULY 15   The Red Sox wallop the Indians 13–4 at League Park in Cleveland.

JULY 17   Earl Webb has five hits, including a homer and a double, in six at-bats during a 12–2 defeat of the Tigers at Navin Field in Detroit.

JULY 27   The Red Sox blow a 9–2 lead by allowing eight runs to the Browns in the eighth inning and lose 10–9 in the first game of a doubleheader in St. Louis. In the second game, the Browns scored three times in the ninth on a walk-off homer by Alex Metzler to win, 9–6.

             The 1930 Red Sox set a club record for one-run losses in a season with 36. Overall, the Sox record in one-run games was 17–36.

JULY 31   The Red Sox score 13 runs, but that proves to be unlucky as Lou Gehrig drives in eight runs to lead the Yankees to a 14–13 win at Fenway Park. The two teams combined to make 13 errors, six of them by the Red Sox.

AUGUST 11   Earl Webb hits an unusual inside-the-park homer during a 5–1 win over the Tigers at Fenway Park. In the fourth inning, Detroit center fielder Liz Funk badly misjudged a fly ball that should have been an easy out by running in toward second base on a ball hit over his head. Webb circled the bases before Funk could retrieve the ball.

SEPTEMBER 8   A crowd of 30,000 attends an old-timers game at Fenway Park. The team of ex-Red Sox defeated a squad of past stars from other clubs 8–4 in the nine-inning game. Among the future Hall of Famers who played in the game were Frank Baker, Chief Bender, Roger Bresnahan, Frank Clarke, Ty Cobb, Eddie Collins, Jimmy Collins, Hugh Duffy, Johnny Evers, Harry Hooper, Edd Roush, Tris Speaker, Heinie Wagner, Ed Walsh, and Cy Young as well as such former Red Sox stars as Duffy Lewis, Freddie Parent, and Smoky Joe Wood.

SEPTEMBER 21   Four days after the city of Boston celebrates its 300th anniversary, the Red Sox break loose with five runs in the tenth inning to defeat the Indians 9–4 in Cleveland.

SEPTEMBER 28   In the final game of the season, Babe Ruth is the starting pitcher against the Red Sox at Fenway Park. It was Ruth's first game as a pitcher since 1921. He pitched a complete game to lead the Yankees to a 9–3 win over the Red Sox.

SEPTEMBER 29   Manager Heinie Wagner is fired by the Red Sox.

Wagner ended one unhappy season as a manager with a 52–102 record. He never piloted another big-league team.

DECEMBER 1   The Red Sox hire Shano Collins as manager.

The Red Sox flirted with hiring Joe McCarthy as manager but went with the inexperienced Collins instead. A native of Charlestown, Massachusetts, and an outfielder with the Red Sox from 1921 through 1925, Collins had a 73–134 record as the Red Sox manager. McCarthy was hired by the Yankees, where he won eight American League pennants and seven World Championships.

DECEMBER 15   The Red Sox purchase Muddy Ruel from the Senators.

1931   B

Season in a Sentence

The Red Sox lose 90 games and finish sixth, but it's the club's best record in 10 years.

Finish • Won • Lost • Pct • GB

Sixth   62   90   .408   45.0

Manager

Shano Collins

Stats   Red Sox • AL • Rank

	Red Sox	AL	Rank
Batting Avg:	.262	.278	7
On-Base Pct:	.315	.344	8
Slugging Pct:	.349	.396	7
Home Runs:	34		8
Stolen Bases:	42		7
ERA:	4.60	4.38	5
Fielding Pct:	.970	.968	4
Runs Scored:	625		8
Runs Allowed:	800		4

Starting Lineup

Charlie Berry, c
Bill Sweeney, 1b
Rabbit Warstler, 2b
Otto Miller, 3b
Hal Rhyne, ss
Jack Rothrock, lf
Tom Oliver, cf
Earl Webb, rf
Urbane Pickering, 3b
Al Van Camp, lf

Pitchers

Danny MacFayden, sp
Jack Russell, sp
Milt Gaston, sp
Hod Lisenbee, rp-sp
Ed Durham, rp-sp
Ed Morris, rp-sp
Bob Kline, rp-sp
Wilcy Moore, rp

Attendance

350,975 (seventh in AL)

Club Leaders

Batting Avg:	Webb	.333
On-Base Pct:	Webb	.404
Slugging Pct:	Webb	.528
Home Runs:	Webb	14
RBI:	Webb	103
Runs:	Webb	96
Stolen Bases:	Rothrock	13
Wins:	MacFayden	16
Strikeouts:	MacFayden	77
ERA:	Moore	3.88
Saves:	Moore	10

FEBRUARY 3   The Red Sox sell Phil Todt to the Athletics.

APRIL 14   Six weeks after Congress adopts "The Star-Spangled Banner" as the National Anthem, the Red Sox lose the season opener 6–3 to the Yankees before a crowd of 70,000 in New York. Tom Winsett hits a pinch-homer for the Red Sox off Red Ruffing. It was not only Winsett's first major league homer but also his first base hit. He didn't hit another home run in the big leagues until 1936, when he was playing for the Dodgers.

The Red Sox wore uniform numbers for the first time in 1931. The Yankees were the first club in baseball to use them, in 1929, to help fans identify the players. At the start of the 1931 campaign, numbers were issued to:

Bill Sweeney	*1*	*Muddy Ruel*	*10*
Bobby Reeves	*2*	*Ed Connolly*	*11*
Jack Rothrock	*3*	*Russ Scarritt*	*12*
Rabbit Warstler	*4*	*Tom Oliver*	*14*
Otto Miller	*5*	*Earl Webb*	*15*
Hal Rhyne	*6*	*Gene Rye*	*16*
Ollie Marquardt	*7*	*Al Van Camp*	*17*
Pat Creeden	*8*	*Tom Winsett*	*18*
Charlie Berry	*9*	*Howie Storie*	*19*

Milt Gaston	20	Bob Kline	28
Danny MacFayden	21	Walter Murphy	29
Jack Russell	22	Franklin Milliken	30
Ed Morris	23	Wilcy Moore	31
Hod Lisenbee	24	Shano Collins (mgr)	32
Ed Durham	25	Rudy Hulswitt (coach)	33
Wilcy Moore	26	Urbane Pickering	34
Jim Brillheart	27		

APRIL 18   The Red Sox defeat the Yankees 5–4 in a 15-inning affair at Yankee Stadium. Charlie Berry tied the score 4–4 with a homer in the ninth. Earl Webb drove in the winning run with a single, and Wilcy Moore hurled nine innings of shutout relief.

APRIL 20   The Red Sox score seven runs in the seventh inning to break a 2–2 tie and overwhelm the Senators 13–3 in Washington.

APRIL 22   The Yankees win the first game of the season at Fenway Park 7–5 before a crowd of 15,000. The contest was highlighted by a violent collision between Babe Ruth and Red Sox catcher Charlie Berry. Ruth was safe after dislodging the ball from Berry's grasp, but the Babe ended up being taken to the hospital with a strained thigh.

Berry was an All-American end for Lafayette University and led the National Football League in scoring in 1925 while playing for the Pottsville Maroons. He was also a National Football League official from 1941 through 1961 and an American League umpire between 1942 and 1962. In 1958, Berry officiated in both the World Series and the NFL championship game.

MAY 15   Eight White Sox errors help the Red Sox capture a 12–8 win in Chicago.

MAY 27   Earl Webb collects four doubles and a triple in seven at-bats during a doubleheader against the Senators at Fenway Park, but the Red Sox lose twice, 11–3 and 4–3.

MAY 30   The Red Sox topple the Athletics 6–5 with an incredible six-run rally in the ninth inning in the second game of a doubleheader at Fenway Park. Ollie Pickering drove in the final two runs with a double. The Sox failed to score during the first 20 innings of the twin bill. In the first game, the Athletics won 5–0 by breaking open a scoreless duel with five runs in the twelfth inning.

JUNE 23   The Red Sox lose a doubleheader 13–0 and 10–0 to the Indians in Cleveland.

During June, the Short-wave and Television Corporation proposed televising games from Fenway Park, which brought a sarcastic reply from John Quinn. "It has rained every Sunday, our club is in last place, and now you want me to let (the fans) see the games at home," Quinn said. "How do you suppose we are going to pay the players? If you can furnish me with a substitute for money, please let me know immediately." At the time, many in the fledgling industry were predicting the television would become commonplace within five years, but it wasn't until the late 1940s that stations would begin regular programming. The first Major League Baseball telecast occurred in 1939 in a game from Ebbets Field in Brooklyn. Telecasts from Fenway Park began in 1948.

JULY 23   The Red Sox are victims of a triple play but still rout the White Sox 13–4 at Fenway Park. Going from one extreme to the other, Earl Webb hit into the triple play, then clubbed a homer.

JULY 27   The Red Sox score eight runs in the fourth inning and crush the Tigers 13–4 at Fenway Park.

AUGUST 2   With 40,000 attending on a Sunday afternoon at Braves Field, Wilcy Moore blanks the Yankees 1–0 in the second game of a doubleheader. It took only seventy-seven minutes to complete the contest. The Red Sox lost the first game, 4–1.

The Yankees weren't shut out again until August 2, 1933. In between, they established a major league record by scoring a run in 308 consecutive games.

AUGUST 8   Bobby Burke of the Senators no-hits the Red Sox for a 5–0 Washington victory at Griffith Stadium. Earl Webb ended the game by taking a third strike.

Burke is one of the most obscure pitchers in big-league history to throw a no-hitter. He had a 38–46 lifetime record.

AUGUST 15   Danny MacFayden shuts out the White Sox 1–0 in Chicago.

AUGUST 31   The Red Sox trade Muddy Ruel to the Tigers for Marty McManus.

SEPTEMBER 7   The Red Sox are routed 7–5 and 15–1 in a doubleheader against the Senators at Fenway Park. After Washington took a 12–0 lead in the second inning of the second game, infielder Bobby Reeves took the mound and pitched 7 1/3 innings, allowing three runs. It was the only pitching appearances of Reeves's six-year career.

SEPTEMBER 12   Ed Durham pitches a 13-inning complete-game shutout to defeat the Tigers 1–0 at Fenway Park. Tom Oliver drove in the game's lone run with a single.

Oliver played four seasons with the Red Sox (1930–33) and batted 1,931 times without a homer. He holds the all-time modern major league record for most career at-bats without a home run.

SEPTEMBER 17   During a doubleheader against the Indians at Fenway Park, Earl Webb ties the all-time single-season record for most doubles in a season, then breaks it with his 65th two-bagger of 1931 in the nightcap. The previous record of 64 was set by George Burns of the Indians in 1926. Webb finished the season with 67 doubles. In the opener, the Red Sox scored seven runs in the first inning and won 9–2. Cleveland won the second game 2–1.

Webb's single-season doubles record of 67 is one of the strangest statistical flukes in baseball history. He tied and broke the record on his thirty-fourth birthday and prior to 1931 had never hit more than 30 doubles in a season. Webb entered the 1931 campaign with 55 lifetime major league doubles. His season high after 1931 was 28 in 1932, and he finished his career in 1933 with 155 doubles.

DECEMBER 2   The Red Sox trade Milt Gaston to the White Sox for Bob Weiland.

1932   B

Season in a Sentence

With unemployment rampant during the depths of the Great Depression, the Red Sox hit rock bottom with a club-record 111 defeats.

Finish • Won • Lost • Pct • GB

Eighth   43   111   .279   64.0

Managers

Shano Collins (11–44)
Marty McManus (32–67)

Stats

Stats	Red Sox	AL	Rank
Batting Avg:	.251	.277	8
On-Base Pct:	.314	.346	8
Slugging Pct:	.351	.404	8
Home Runs:	57		6
Stolen Bases:	46		7
ERA:	5.02	4.48	8
Fielding Pct:	.963	.969	7
Runs Scored:	566		8
Runs Allowed:	915		8

Starting Lineup

Bennie Tate, c
Dale Alexander, 1b
Marv Olson, 2b
Urbane Pickering, 3b
Rabbit Warstler, ss
Smead Jolley, lf
Tom Oliver, cf
Roy Johnson, rf
Marty McManus, 2b-3b
Cliff Watwood, cf-rf
Ed Connolly, c
Hal Rhyne, ss
Earl Webb, rf
George Stumpf, rf-lf

Pitchers

Bob Weiland, sp-rp
Ed Durham, sp-rp
Ivy Andrews, sp
Gordon Rhoades, sp
Danny MacFayden, sp
Bob Kline, rp-sp
Wilcy Moore, rp
John Michaels, rp

Attendance

182,150 (seventh in AL)

Club Leaders

Batting Avg:	Alexander	.372
On-Base Pct:	Alexander	.454
Slugging Pct:	Alexander	.524
Home Runs:	Jolley	18
RBI:	Jolley	99
Runs:	Johnson	70
Stolen Bases:	Johnson	13
Wins:	Kline	11
Strikeouts:	Weiland	63
ERA:	Durham	3.80
Saves:	Moore	4

MARCH 3   Two days after the kidnapping of the Lindbergh baby, Ed Morris is stabbed to death at a fish fry in Century, Florida, just over the state line from his hometown of Flomaton, Alabama. The event was intended as a farewell to Morris on the eve of his departure for spring training in Savannah, Georgia. The party atmosphere was interrupted by an argument between Morris and Joe White, a gasoline attendant from Brewton, Alabama. White knocked Morris down during the altercation, and as the Red Sox pitcher lay on the ground, White stabbed him. Morris died a few hours later at the hospital.

White was twice put on trial for manslaughter, but he was acquitted both times after pleading self-defense.

APRIL 11   The Red Sox lose 1–0 in 10 innings to the Senators on a bitterly cold day in Washington, wasting a pitching masterpiece by Danny MacFayden. Heinie Manush drove in the game winner with a double. Herbert Hoover upheld presidential tradition by tossing out the first ball of the season, but he heaved it far over the head of umpire George Hildebrand, the president's intended target.

APRIL 12	The Red Sox' home opener against the Senators is postponed by cold weather.
APRIL 13	In the first game of the season at Fenway Park, the Senators score four runs in the ninth inning, the last three on a two-out home run by Heinie Manush off Jack Russell, to beat the Red Sox 7–6. It was the second game in a row in which Manush got a walk-off, game-winning extra-base hit against the Sox.
	Only 5,000 fans attended the game. The Red Sox drew 182,150 in 1932, an all-time club low.
APRIL 21	Behind the pitching of Jack Russell, with the help of a last-out save by Wilcy Moore, the Red Sox defeat the Senators 1–0 in Washington. Marty McManus drove in the only run of the game with a single in the seventh inning.
	The Red Sox finished last in the league in runs scored 10 times in 11 seasons, from 1922 through 1932, and eight in a row beginning in 1925.
APRIL 29	The Red Sox trade Charlie Berry to the White Sox for Smead Jolley, Bernie Tate, and Cliff Watwood.
APRIL 30	The Red Sox sell Jack Rothrock to the White Sox.
MAY 1	The Red Sox trade Wilcy Moore to the Yankees for Gordon Rhodes.
MAY 18	The Red Sox finally win in Boston with a 13–10 decision over the White Sox after dropping their first 17 games of the season at Fenway Park. Smead Jolley led the Red Sox attack with five hits, including a double, in five at-bats.
	Counting the final home game of 1931, the Red Sox lost 18 games in a row at Fenway Park.
MAY 21	Red Sox pitchers combine to walk 15 batters during an 18–6 loss to the Athletics in the first game of a doubleheader in Philadelphia. The bases on balls were issued by John Michaels (three), Bob Weiland (one), Wilcy Moore (three), Regis Leheny (two), and Hod Lisenbee (six).
	The Red Sox set a club record in 1932 for the highest ERA in a season, 5.02.
MAY 28	The governor of Massachusetts signs into law a bill allowing the Red Sox to play at Fenway Park on Sundays.
JUNE 5	The Red Sox trade Danny MacFayden to the Yankees for Ivy Andrews, Hank Johnson, and $50,000.
	Johnson announced that he was retiring rather than pitch for the moribund Red Sox. He returned in 1933, however, and played for three seasons in Boston. MacFayden did little with the Yankees but gave the Boston Braves three solid seasons during the late 1930s.
JUNE 10	The Red Sox trade Jack Russell to the Indians for Pete Jablonowski.

Jablonowski was truly a player to be named later. From 1927 through 1933, he pitched under his given name of Peter William Jablonowski. After two years in the minors, Jablonowski returned to the majors as Pete Appleton in 1936 and lasted in the big leagues until 1945. He pitched 11 games for the Red Sox, all in 1932.

JUNE 12   The Red Sox trade Earl Webb to the Tigers for Dale Alexander and Roy Johnson.

The Red Sox made a great trade in acquiring two players for Webb, whose fifteen minutes of fame had expired. After losing his first-base job in Detroit to Hank Greenberg, Alexander batted .372 in 101 games for the Red Sox in 1932 to win the American League batting title with an overall average of .367. The following season, however, he nearly lost one of his legs when a diathermy treatment was applied incorrectly, resulting in third-degree burns and gangrene. Alexander never played in the majors again. Part Native American, Johnson was a regular with the Red Sox outfield for four seasons. His brother Bob was a star outfielder in the American League during the 1930s and 1940s and played for the Red Sox during World War II.

JUNE 19   With the club buried in last place with a record of 11–44, Shano Collins resigns as manager. He was replaced by Marty McManus. Collins said that he couldn't stand the grief of running a consistent tail-ender any longer and quit in order to preserve his health. He never managed another big-league club.

McManus was thirty-three years old when he was named manager, and he remained a utility infielder for the club.

JUNE 27   Batting in the leadoff slot in the batting order, Roy Johnson hits a grand slam off George Earnshaw in the second inning and drives in seven runs altogether, but the Red Sox lose 15–8 to the Athletics at Shibe Park. Philadelphia also won the second game, 9–4.

The Red Sox ended the month of June with a record of 12–55.

JULY 3   In the first Sunday game ever played at Fenway Park, the Red Sox lose 13–2 to the 1932 World Champion Yankees.

JULY 10   Nine runs in the fourth inning enable the Red Sox to defeat the Tigers in the nightcap of a doubleheader at Fenway Park. Detroit won the first game 7–5. Smead Jolley had seven hits in the twin bill, including a double and a home run, in nine at-bats.

JULY 16   Bob Kline pitches a two-hitter to beat the White Sox 3–0 at Fenway Park. The only Chicago hits were a double by Bob Seeds and a single by Bibb Falk. Marv Olson scored all three Boston runs.

JULY 19   Red Sox left fielder Smead Jolley has some trouble negotiating the small hill known as Duffy's Cliff in front of the left field fence at Fenway Park during a 7–0 loss to the Indians. Jolley ran back and up the embankment to catcher Wes Ferrell's fly ball, which was short of the hill and the wall. Upon realizing this, Jolley tried to backtrack and tumbled back down the hill while Ferrell's fly fell for a hit. The hill was eliminated during Fenway's remodeling between the 1933 and 1934 seasons.

JULY 27   The Red Sox crush the White Sox 15–5 in Chicago.

AUGUST 4   The Red Sox play at Municipal Stadium in Cleveland for the first time and drop a
                 doubleheader to the Indians 8–2 and 8–7, the latter in 11 innings.

                 *The Indians called Municipal Stadium home from July 31, 1932, until the end
                 of the 1993 season, when Jacobs Field replaced it.*

AUGUST 10   The Red Sox extend their losing streak to 11 with a 6–2 loss to the Tigers in Detroit.

AUGUST 18   The Red Sox win a sensational 7–6 decision over the Browns in 15 innings at
                 Fenway Park. The Browns took a 3–2 lead in the eleventh inning, but the Sox tied
                 on a homer by player-manager Marty McManus. When St. Louis added three in
                 the fourteenth, Boston matched the figure. George Stumpf started the Red Sox'
                 half of the fifteenth inning with a triple. After two intentional walks, Stumpf
                 scored on sacrifice fly by Hal Rhyne.

AUGUST 22   A two-run, two-out double by Tom Oliver in the ninth inning defeats the Tigers 6–5
                 at Fenway Park.

AUGUST 27   The Red Sox down the White Sox 13–10 in a hitting festival at Fenway Park.
                 Boston broke a 10–10 tie with three runs in the eighth inning.

AUGUST 28   After losing the opener of a doubleheader at Fenway Park against the Indians 10–1, the
                 Red Sox rally to win the nightcap 4–3 on an eleventh-inning homer by Bernie Tate.

                 *Tate hit only four home runs during a career that spanned 10 seasons, 566
                 games, and 1,560 at-bats. On the original schedule, August 28 was to be the
                 first of four single games in a series against the Indians. But astronomers were
                 calling for a total eclipse of the sun on the afternoon of August 31, and the
                 game was moved up three days to create a doubleheader on the 28th.*

SEPTEMBER 2   The Red Sox lose both ends of a doubleheader to the Athletics 7–3 and 15–0 in
                 Philadelphia.

SEPTEMBER 9   Trailing the White Sox 6–0 in Chicago, the Red Sox score one run in the sixth
                 inning, one in the seventh, three in the eighth, one in the ninth, and three in the tenth
                 to win 9–6. Roy Johnson hit a three-run homer in the eighth during the comeback.

SEPTEMBER 11   Dale Alexander hits a grand slam off Bob Cooney of the Browns in the fifth inning
                 of a 7–1 win over the Browns in the first game of a doubleheader in St. Louis. The
                 Browns won the second game, 8–3.

SEPTEMBER 24   The Red Sox lose their club-record 111th game of the season 8–2 to the Yankees at
                 Fenway Park. The winning pitcher was Charlie Devens, who was making his major
                 league debut. Devens hailed from the Boston suburb of Milton and attended Harvard.

SEPTEMBER 25   On the final day of the season, Dale Alexander collects two hits in four at-bats during
                 an 8–3 win over the Yankees at Fenway to nose out Jimmie Foxx of the Athletics for
                 the batting title, .367 to .364.

Under today's rules Alexander would have needed 477 plate appearances to win the batting title. He fell just short with 453 in 1932, but at the time a player needed only 100 games to qualify. Had Foxx been the 1932 batting champion, he would have won the Triple Crown, an honor he captured in 1933. No one has ever won two Triple Crowns in a row.

DECEMBER 15   Five weeks after Franklin Roosevelt wins the Presidential election over Herbert Hoover, the Red Sox trade Ed Durham and Hal Rhyne to the White Sox for Fats Fothergill, Bob Seeds, Johnny Hodapp, and Greg Mulleavy.

1933   B

Season in a Sentence

Under Tom Yawkey's new and financially solvent ownership, the Red Sox rise to seventh place.

Finish • Won • Lost • Pct • GB

Seventh 63   86   .423 34.5

Manager

Marty McManus

Stats   Red Sox • AL • Rank

Batting Avg:	.271	.273	5
On-Base Pct:	.339	.342	5
Slugging Pct:	.377	.390	5
Home Runs:	50		6
Stolen Bases:	58		5
ERA:	4.35	4.28	4
Fielding Pct:	.966	.972	8
Runs Scored:	700		5
Runs Allowed:	758		4

Starting Lineup

Rick Ferrell, c
Dale Alexander, 1b
Johnny Hodapp, 2b
Marty McManus, 3b
Billy Werber, ss-3b
Smead Jolley, lf
Dusty Cooke, cf-lf-rf
Roy Johnson, rf
Rabbit Warstler, ss
Tom Oliver, cf
Bob Seeds, 1b-lf-rf
Bucky Walters, 3b

Pitchers

Gordon Rhodes, sp
Bob Weiland, sp-rp
Lloyd Brown, sp-rp
Hank Johnson, sp
George Pipgras, sp
Ivy Andrews, sp-rp
Johnny Welch, rp
Bob Kline, rp

Attendance

268,715 (seventh in AL)

Club Leaders

Batting Avg:	Johnson	.313
On-Base Pct:	Johnson	.387
Slugging Pct:	Johnson	.466
Home Runs:	Johnson	10
RBI:	Johnson	95
Runs:	Johnson	88
Stolen Bases:	Werber	15
Wins:	Rhodes	12
Strikeouts:	Weiland	97
ERA:	Weiland	3.87
Saves:	Kline	4

JANUARY 7   The Red Sox purchase Barney Friberg from the Phillies.

FEBRUARY 25   Tom Yawkey purchases the moribund Red Sox franchise from Bob Quinn, who was some $350,000 in debt.

APRIL 2   The Red Sox narrowly escape disaster when the club is involved in a train wreck in Wyoming, Delaware, that kills the train's engineer and fireman. The club was on the way from Norfolk, Virginia, where it played an exhibition game, to New York City. A few players were badly shaken, but no one on the Red Sox was seriously injured. Eight of the twelve cars crashed through an open switch while the train was traveling northbound on a southbound track to pass a slow-moving freight train. Seven passengers were hospitalized.

Tom Yawkey, the new owner of the Red Sox, gets advice from Clark Griffith, the wily owner of the Washington Senators and father-in-law of Joe Cronin, later the Sox' manager and starting shortstop.

Courtesy of Transcendental Graphics/theruckerarchive.com

B   Tom Yawkey Saves the Red Sox   B

The winter of 1932–33 was among the worst in American history. It is estimated that one-third of the labor force was out of work. Fewer than half were working full-time, some for as little as ten cents an hour. Malnutrition was a fact of life all across the country. Many lost their life savings in bank failures, and in February 1933, nearly $1 billion was withdrawn from the nation's banks. The nation's confidence in its future was shaken to the core.

Successful sports teams often provide some relief in hard times, as fans can steal themselves away from their problems for a few hours to root for their favorite teams. But the Red Sox of the early 1930s furnished no such solace. The 1932 Red Sox lost 111 games and won only 43. During the eight seasons from 1925 through 1932, the Red Sox lost an average of 101 games a year. In the midst of this chaos, Tom Yawkey purchased the Red Sox on February 25, 1933.

Thomas Austin Yawkey was originally born Thomas Yawkey Austin on February 21, 1903. His uncle, William Hoover Yawkey, had owned the Detroit Tigers from 1904 until 1907. William Yawkey was fabulously wealthy, with money from interests in mining, logging, and oil. Thomas's father died when he was very young, and his wealthy uncle took in him and his mother. After Tom's mother died in 1917, William Yawkey and his wife formally adopted Tom and changed his named from Thomas Yawkey Austin to Thomas Austin Yawkey.

Hall of Famer Eddie Collins, then coach with the Philadelphia Athletics, suggested in 1933 that Tom Yawkey buy the Red Sox. Yawkey had attended Collins's old prep school, the Irving School in Tarrytown, New York, where he had been runner-up for the institution's prestigious Edward T. Collins Award for best scholar-athlete. Ty Cobb introduced Yawkey and Collins, and the two became fast friends.

Red Sox owner Bob Quinn was in desperate financial straits and needed to sell the club to avoid bankruptcy. Yawkey was just coming into his inheritance, estimated to be about $40 million. He received it on February 21, 1933, on his thirtieth birthday and bought the Red Sox four days later for $1.5 million. Collins, who was sixteen years older than Yawkey, came along as general manager and the new owner's baseball mentor.

Beginning with the sale of Babe Ruth to the Yankees by Harry Frazee in January 1920, the Red Sox had been peddling their star players. With Yawkey, the Red Sox now had an owner with cash to purchase some of the top stars in the game, even when the nation was undergoing a period of economic calamity. When Yawkey bought the club, no one in Boston had ever heard of him. During his first three years as owner of the Sox, he picked up future Hall of Famers Lefty Grove, Jimmie Foxx, Joe Cronin, Heinie Manush, and Rick Ferrell. He also built a highly effective farm system that began to pay dividends by the end of the 1930s and brought players like Ted Williams, Bobby Doerr, Dom DiMaggio, and Johnny Pesky to Boston.

Most important to present-day Red Sox fans, Yawkey rebuilt Fenway Park. Fenway was twenty-one years old when he bought the club, and the ballpark was run down from years of neglect. Yawkey turned it into a cozy landmark. Today, the official address of Fenway Park is 4 Yawkey Way.

Yawkey owned the Red Sox for 44 years, but despite the millions he threw into the ball club, a World Championship eluded him. His teams never lacked superstars or Hall of Fame candidates, but they seldom had the depth or team chemistry necessary to win a pennant. The Sox reached the World Series three times during Yawkey's regime, in 1946, 1967, and 1975, only to lose in the seventh game on each occasion. He also drew considerable criticism for his failure to integrate the Red Sox. Under Yawkey's leadership, the Sox were the last team in baseball to add African-Americans to the roster. Pumpsie Green was the first, in 1959. Despite the problems, Yawkey became a beloved Boston figure because of his benevolence and generosity, even though he was born in Austin, Texas, grew up in Detroit, and lived most of his life on a palatial forty-thousand-acre estate on South Island in South Carolina.

Yawkey died of leukemia on July 9, 1976, at the age of seventy-three. His wife, Jean, served as majority owner and general partner until her death in 1993.

APRIL 12   The scheduled season opener at Yankee Stadium is postponed by rain.

APRIL 13   The Red Sox' first game under Tom Yawkey's ownership results in a 4–3 defeat at the hands of the Yankees in New York.

APRIL 14   Red Sox pitcher Bob Weiland loses 6–2 to the Yankees in New York when he gives up a walk-off grand slam in the ninth inning to opposing pitcher Red Ruffing.

APRIL 21   In the home opener before 18,000 at Fenway, the Red Sox lose 7–3 to the Yankees.

MAY 9   The Red Sox send Merv Shea and cash to the Browns for Rick Ferrell and
                Lloyd Brown.

                *Ferrell spent 5 of his 18 major league seasons in Boston. He caught 1,806
                games during his career, the ninth highest of all time. Although he had little
                power, Ferrell batted .302 as a member of the Red Sox from 1933 through
                1937 and was elected to the Hall of Fame in 1984.*

MAY 12   The Red Sox purchase George Pipgras and Billy Werber from the Yankees for
                $100,000.

                *It was extremely refreshing for fans of the Red Sox to see the club buying players
                from the Yankees instead of selling them. Pipgras was a disappointment, but
                Werber emerged as a star with a tremendous year as a third baseman in 1934.
                Always outspoken, Werber was considered a detriment to team morale, however,
                and was shipped to the Athletics after the 1936 season.*

JUNE 11   The Red Sox play "beat the clock" to defeat the Yankees 11–9 in the second game
                of a doubleheader before 30,000 at Fenway Park. Umpires called the game after six
                innings because of the Massachusetts state law requiring games to end at 6:30 PM on
                Sundays. With time running out, Smead Jolley hit a two-run homer into the center field
                bleachers in the sixth inning to break a 9–9 tie. New York won the first game, 8–7.

JUNE 14   The Red Sox whip the Yankees 13–5 at Fenway Park. Boston broke a 5–5 tie with
                three runs in the seventh inning and five in the eighth.

JUNE 26   The Red Sox wallop the Browns 13–5 in St. Louis. Gordon Rhodes not only
                pitched the Sox to victory but also collected four hits, including two doubles.

JULY 4   The Red Sox explode during an Independence Day doubleheader and trim the
                Athletics 14–4 and 9–1 in Philadelphia.

                *The Red Sox appeared to have righted the ship with a 31–26 record during
                June and July, but a 19–35 mark in August, September, and October sent the
                club into seventh place.*

JULY 6   Rick Ferrell is the starting catcher for the American League in the first All-Star
                Game. Ferrell went hitless in three at-bats as the American League won 4–2 at
                Comiskey Park in Chicago.

JULY 12   Lloyd Brown pitches an 11-inning complete-game shutout of the Tigers at Fenway
                Park. Roy Johnson singled in the winning run for a 1–0 final. Brown worked out of
                bases-loaded jams in the ninth and eleventh innings.

JULY 19   Both Rick Ferrell and his brother Wes, who was pitching for the Indians, homer
                during an 8–7, 13-inning Cleveland win at Fenway Park. Wes Ferrell connected first
                in the top of the fourth off Hank Johnson, with Rick calling the pitch behind the
                plate. In the bottom half, Rick countered with a round-tripper off Wes. Both hits
                traveled over the left field wall.

Wes Ferrell hit 38 homers during his career, the most by any pitcher in baseball history. Rick, on the other hand, hit just 28 lifetime homers in 6,028 at-bats.

AUGUST 7   Before a game against the Athletics at Shibe Park, Red Sox third baseman Bucky Walters receives a silver service from admirers in his hometown of Philadelphia. Walters proceeded to drive in five runs with a homer and a triple in leading the Sox to a 6–5 victory.

AUGUST 11   A sixty-nine-year-old man named John W. Emory from Portsmouth, New Hampshire, dies of a heart attack in his seat at Fenway Park during an 8–4 loss to the Senators.

AUGUST 13   The Red Sox score 11 runs in a first-inning parade around the base paths, keying a 19–10 defeat of the Athletics at Fenway Park.

AUGUST 20   The Indians score 10 runs in the sixth inning to wipe out a 6–4 Red Sox lead and go on to win 14–6 in the first game of a doubleheader in Cleveland. The Indians completed the sweep with a 9–3 victory in the second tilt. In the fifth inning of the nightcap, Red Sox manager Marty McManus took a swing at Cleveland coach Patsy Gharrity during an argument over an umpire's decision.

AUGUST 31   Aided by seven runs in the fourth inning, the Red Sox crush the Yankees 15–2 at Yankee Stadium.

SEPTEMBER 30   Bob Weiland pitches a two-hitter to defeat the Athletics 2–1 in the first game of a doubleheader at Shibe Park. The only Philadelphia hits were a single by Jimmie Foxx and a homer by Eric McNair. The Red Sox also won the second game, 12–1.

The Red Sox had 15 consecutive losing seasons from 1919 through 1933, which is tied for the longest streak in American League history with the Philadelphia/Kansas City Athletics from 1953 through 1967. The only longer streak in major league history is 16 by the Philadelphia Phillies from 1933 through 1948.

OCTOBER 2   Marty McManus is fired as manager of the Red Sox.

McManus was 95–153 as Boston's skipper. He never managed another big-league club.

OCTOBER 8   A National Football League game is played at Fenway Park for the first time as the Boston Redskins defeat the New York Giants 21–20 before a crowd of 15,000. The Redskins used Fenway as their home field until the club moved to Washington in 1937.

The Boston franchise joined the NFL as the Boston Braves in 1932 and played their first season at Braves Field. The club changed its nickname with the move to Fenway in 1933 but kept the Native American theme. The Boston Redskins won the Eastern Division title in 1936, but crowds were so small in Boston during the season that the club moved the NFL championship game against the Green Bay Packers from Fenway to the Polo Grounds in New York.

OCTOBER 12   The Red Sox trade Lloyd Brown to the Indians for Bill Cissell.

OCTOBER 29   The Red Sox hire Bucky Harris as manager.

Harris had 10 seasons of experience as a big-league manager when he was brought aboard to run the Red Sox. He was named player-manager of the Senators in 1924 at the age of twenty-seven and was quickly dubbed the "Boy Manager" while guiding Washington to its first American League pennant and World Championship in 1924 and another AL pennant in 1925. Harris was traded from the Senators to the Tigers in 1929 and headed the Detroit club as manager for five seasons. While with the Senators in 1926, he married the daughter of a U.S. Senator from Virginia. President Calvin Coolidge was among the wedding guests, and while on their European honeymoon, Harris and his bride were entertained by King George V of England.

DECEMBER 12   The Red Sox trade Bob Kline and Rabbit Warstler, along with $160,000, to the Athletics for Lefty Grove, Rube Walberg, and Max Bishop.

After winning the American League pennant for three consecutive seasons between 1929 and 1931, Connie Mack found that he couldn't pay his aging stars in a Depression economy. He was $200,000 in debt, and for the second time in his career, Mack was in the process of dismantling a championship team. With Yawkey's millions behind them, the Red Sox were well positioned. Grove was the best pitcher in baseball in 1933 and, some argue, the best of all time. From 1927 through 1933, he compiled an amazing 172–54 with Philadelphia. His career record against the Red Sox was 35–8. Grove was thirty-four years old when he pitched his first game with the Sox and was no longer in top form, but he still went 105–62 in eight seasons in Boston. He also led the league in ERA for four seasons with the Sox to give him a record nine ERA titles for his career. Grove's first season in New England was not a happy one, however. Plagued from the outset of spring training by a sore arm, Grove was 8–8 with a 6.50 ERA in 1934. Walberg and Bishop were also key members of the Athletics 1929–31 championship teams, but neither was much help to the Red Sox.

DECEMBER 13   The Red Sox send Smead Jolley, Ivy Andrews, and cash to the Browns for Carl Reynolds.

While resurrecting the Red Sox, Yawkey also laid plans during the 1933–34 offseason to rebuild Fenway Park, which had deteriorated into a fire hazard after years of neglect during the Frazee and Quinn regimes. It was nearly a total reconstruction. Yawkey tore down all of the old wooden stands and replaced them with ones built of steel and concrete, leaving little more than the original structural steel supports in the grandstand. The foundations and steel supports were also reinforced to provide for a second deck, which was never built. Right and center fields received new steel-and-concrete bleachers. The seating capacity was increased from 27,642 to 37,500. Crews leveled the ten-foot incline in left field and erected a thirty-seven-foot-high wall in place of the twenty-five-foot-high wooden fence. The lower eighteen feet of the new wall was concrete and topped by a nineteen-foot frame made of railroad ties. Tin covered the concrete and wood. The wall's reinforced steel-and-concrete foundation extended twenty-two feet below the field level. A new scoreboard appeared on the wall. Although remarkably quaint today, it was the first electronically operated scoreboard in baseball with its red, green, and yellow lights to indicate balls, strikes, and outs. The changes, which included pushing home plate toward the outfield, reduced the home run distances at the park. Left field went from 320 feet to 315; center field from 468 to 420; and right field from 358 to 334. One miscalculation, however, was the construction of a pavilion, separate from the main grandstand, that extended from behind first base into the right field corner. The pavilion held 8,900 uncomfortable bench seats and was unpopular with fans. It went largely unoccupied except on days when the grandstand and bleachers were filled to capacity. The team tore down the pavilion between the 1939 and 1940 seasons and replaced it with an extension of the grandstand containing individual seats.

1934   B

Season in a Sentence

In the pennant race into July, Red Sox fans have something to cheer about as the club avoids a losing season for the first time since 1918.

Finish • Won • Lost • Pct • GB

Fourth   76   76   .500   24.0

Manager

Bucky Harris

Stats   Red Sox • AL • Rank

	Red Sox	AL	Rank
Batting Avg:	.274	.279	6
On-Base Pct:	.350	.351	4
Slugging Pct:	.383	.399	5
Home Runs:	51		7
Stolen Bases:	116		2
ERA:	4.32	4.50	4
Fielding Pct:	.969	.970	5
Runs Scored:	820		3
Runs Allowed:	775		4

Starting Lineup

Rick Ferrell, c
Eddie Morgan, 1b
Bill Cissell, 2b
Bill Werber, 3b
Lyn Lary, ss
Roy Johnson, lf
Moose Solters, cf-rf
Carl Reynolds, rf-cf
Dick Porter, rf
Max Bishop, 2b
Dusty Cooke, rf-cf-lf

Pitchers

Wes Ferrell, sp
Gordon Rhodes, sp
Fritz Ostermueller, sp-rp
Johnny Welch, sp-rp
Lefty Grove-sp-rp
Hank Johnson, rp-sp
Rube Walberg, rp-sp

Attendance

610,640 (third in AL)

Club Leaders

Batting Avg:	Werber	.321
On-Base Pct:	Werber	.397
Slugging Pct:	Werber	.472
Home Runs:	Werber	11
RBI:	Johnson	119
Runs:	Werber	129
Stolen Bases:	Werber	40
Wins:	Ferrell	14
Strikeouts:	Welch	91
ERA:	Ostermueller	3.49
Saves:	Ostermueller	3

JANUARY 5   During Tom Yawkey's reconstruction project at Fenway Park, a fire destroys part of the ballpark.

The fire lasted five hours and razed the stands along the left field foul line beyond third base, the left field wall, and the center field bleachers. Two workmen were injured. The fire began when an overturned cement heater ignited tarred canvas used in the remodeling of the ballpark. Seven hundred workmen fled into the outfield as the flames spread rapidly, setting fire to the buildings of two tire companies, three garages, and a furniture warehouse behind the left field fence. Firemen concentrated most of their efforts on the oil tanks of the Neponset Oil Company, which was encircled by flames. The fire turned Yawkey's rebuilding plans into re-rebuilding plans, but with work crews pulling double shifts, the ballpark was ready by Opening Day.

APRIL 14   The Red Sox play their first game at rebuilt Fenway Park and defeat the Braves 8–2 in an exhibition game.

APRIL 16   The scheduled season opener between the Red Sox and Senators at Griffith Stadium in Washington is postponed due to rain.

APRIL 17   The Red Sox play their first regular-season game at rebuilt Fenway Park and lose 6–5 in 11 innings to the Senators. Washington led 5–0 before the Red Sox scored four runs in the sixth inning and one in the eighth. Joe Cronin drove in the winning run with a double. Attendance was 33,336. The home plate umpire was Bill Dinneen, who was the Red Sox' hero in the 1903 World Series. After the first pitch, Dinneen stopped the game to present the ball to Tom Yawkey.

With an improved team and ballpark, the Red Sox drew 145,000 in their first six home games of 1934 and a total of 610,640 over the course of the season, the club's highest figure since 1909 and more than double that of 1933.

APRIL 19   In the morning game of a Patriots' Day doubleheader against the Senators at Fenway Park, Moose Solters hits a walk-off homer in the ninth inning to give the Red Sox a 5–4 win. In the afternoon, with 34,000 attending, Washington won, 7–3.

APRIL 24   With President Franklin Roosevelt throwing out the first ball in the Washington home opener, the Red Sox beat the Senators 5–0 at Griffith Stadium. Johnny Welch pitched the shutout. With an Indian in full traditional regalia at his side and the U.S. Army band and the two ball clubs behind him, Vice President John Garner led the march to center field for the raising of the American flag prior to the game.

MAY 5   Lefty Grove makes his first appearance with the Red Sox, coming out of the bullpen in the fourth inning with Boston leading 9–5 against the Browns at Fenway Park. Grove faced just five batters and allowed a triple, a double, a single, and two walks to tie the score 9–9. The Red Sox fell behind 11–9 in the fifth but rallied to win, 13–12.

Grove had three teeth removed and a tonsillectomy in the belief that the abscessed teeth and inflamed tonsils were causing his arm miseries, but nothing seemed to work and he spent the entire 1934 season nursing his injuries.

MAY 6 — The Red Sox set a major league record with four consecutive triples during a 12-run fourth inning against the 1934 American League champion Tigers at Fenway Park. The triples came from Carl Reynolds, Moose Solters, Rick Ferrell, and Bucky Walters, each of them off Detroit pitcher Firpo Marberry. The Sox won the game 14–4.

> *Werber hit .321 in 1934 with 11 homers, 129 runs scored, and a league-leading 40 stolen bases.*

MAY 13 — Eddie Morgan and Bucky Walters both hit grand slams during a 14–2 trouncing of the White Sox at Fenway Park. Walters hit his slam in the first inning off Milt Gaston. Morgan went deep with the bases loaded in the third against Joe Heving.

MAY 15 — The Red Sox send Freddie Muller and $20,000 to the Yankees for Lyn Lary.

MAY 19 — Lefty Grove wins his first game with the Red Sox by pitching a complete game and hitting a three-run homer in the seventh inning to lead the club to a 4–1 victory over the Browns in St. Louis.

MAY 21 — After the White Sox score six runs in the eighth inning to tie the score 10–10, Eddie Morgan hits a three-run homer in the tenth inning to lift the Red Sox to a 13–10 win in Chicago.

MAY 25 — The Red Sox trade Bob Weiland and Bob Seeds along with $25,000 to the Indians for Wes Ferrell and Dick Porter.

> *Ferrell had four seasons in which he won 20 or more games for the Indians, but the club was convinced that he was washed up and had grown weary of his volcanic temper tantrums. The Red Sox were happy to take a flyer on him, hoping that his older brother Rick would be a steadying influence. Wes rewarded the Sox with a 14–5 record and a 3.63 ERA in 1934. In 1935 and 1936 combined, he won 45 games for Boston.*

JUNE 1 — The Red Sox score nine runs with a shower of base hits in the first inning and wallop the Senators 13–1 in Washington. Boston batters collected 20 hits in the game.

JUNE 2 — The Red Sox score six runs in the twelfth inning and survive a three-run Washington rally to win 10–7 in the second game of a doubleheader at Griffith Stadium. The Senators won the first game, 2–1.

JUNE 6 — The Yankees collect 25 hits and rout the Red Sox 15–3 in the first game of a double-header at Fenway Park. The Sox recovered to win the nightcap, 7–4.

JUNE 8 — Fritz Ostermueller pitches a 12-inning complete game and scores the winning run in a 3–2 victory over the Senators at Fenway Park. Ostermueller started the twelfth with a single, moved to second on a sacrifice, and scored on Eddie Morgan's single.

JUNE 9 — The Senators set an American League record with six doubles in an inning and a major league mark with five consecutive doubles while defeating the Red Sox 8–1 at Fenway Park. The outburst came during an eight-run eighth inning against Lefty Grove. Up to that point, Grove had pitched seven scoreless innings.

JUNE 10   Wes Ferrell wins his first game with the Red Sox by hitting a walk-off sacrifice fly in the ninth inning that beats the Senators 4–3 at Fenway Park.

JUNE 13   The Red Sox score eight runs in the second inning to take an 8–0 lead and survive a six-run Detroit rally in the ninth to win 15–13 at Fenway Park. Carl Reynolds hit two doubles in the big inning. Lefty Grove was the winning pitcher despite allowing eight runs on 13 hits in $4\frac{2}{3}$ innings.

JUNE 14   The Red Sox sell Bucky Walters to the Phillies.

               At the end of the season, the Phillies converted third baseman Walters into a pitcher. In 1938, Walters was traded to the Reds and developed into one of the best hurlers in the game. He won more than 20 games three times and won the National League Most Valuable Player Award in 1939 with a 27–11 record for Cincinnati.

JUNE 18   The Red Sox sweep the Browns 6–5 and 14–9 in a doubleheader against the Browns.

JUNE 20   The Red Sox win 14–9 for the second game in a row, defeating the White Sox in Chicago. Five runs in the seventh inning broke a 9–9 tie.

JUNE 22   The Red Sox continue their terrific hitting with an 11–1 rout of the White Sox at Comiskey Park.

JUNE 23   The Red Sox purchase Flint Rhem from the Cardinals.

JULY 3   Roy Johnson hits a two-run homer in the tenth inning to break an 8–8 tie against the Yankees in New York. The Red Sox won 10–9 after surviving a Yankee rally in the bottom half of the inning.

               Johnson hit .320 and drove in 119 runs for the Red Sox in 1934.

JULY 6   Billy Werber scores five runs during an 18–6 annihilation of the Athletics at Fenway Park. The Red Sox scored nine runs in the sixth inning and collected 20 hits in the game.

JULY 7   Wes Ferrell lines a two-run walk-off pinch double lined off the center field wall to cap a four-run ninth-inning rally that stuns the Athletics 11–10 at Fenway Park.

JULY 8   Max Bishop sets a major league record for most walks drawn in a doubleheader with eight in 10 plate appearances against his former Philadelphia teammates, as the Red Sox win twice, 7–4 and 7–3, at Fenway Park. Bishop walked four times in each game.

               Bishop specialized in drawing walks. He had 1,153 career bases on balls in 5,776 plate appearances during a 12-year career with the Athletics and Red Sox. He later coached at the U.S. Naval Academy for 24 years.

JULY 13   Wes Ferrell hits two homers to lead the Red Sox to a 7–2 victory over the Browns in St. Louis.

Wes holds the all-time major league record for home runs by a pitcher with 37. He also hit one as a pinch hitter for a career total of 38. He hit 19 of his homers with the Red Sox. His seven homers in 1935 are the single-season mark for a Sox hurler. Wes hit more homers than his brother Rick in far fewer at-bats, 38 in 1,176 at-bats vs. Rick's 29 in 6,028 lifetime at-bats. Rick made the Hall of Fame in 1984. In addition to his batting prowess, Wes posted a 193–128 lifetime pitching record on clubs seldom in contention. He has long deserved Hall of Fame honors, but his exploits have been ignored.

JULY 15   The Red Sox defeat the Browns 12–8 in the first game of a doubleheader at Sportsman's Park, only to lose the nightcap, 9–2.

JULY 18   After leading off the game with a double, Bill Cissell clubs a grand slam off Phil Gallivan in his second at-bat in the Red Sox' nine-run first inning against the White Sox in Chicago. Cissell also had another double and drove in seven runs as the Red Sox rolled to a 16–3 victory.

After this win, the Red Sox were in third place, only five games behind the Tigers, before fading to .500 by the end of the season.

AUGUST 8   Two weeks after John Dillinger is killed by FBI agents outside of a Chicago theater, the Red Sox gun down Athletics pitchers with seven runs in the second inning. The Sox took a 10–1 lead in the third and hung on to win 11–9 in Philadelphia. Pitching against his former teammates for the first time, Lefty Grove relieved Wes Ferrell in the third inning and went the rest of the way to emerge as the winning pitcher.

AUGUST 9   The Red Sox-Athletics game at Shibe Park is called by rain after five innings, but Boston finds enough time to clobber the Philadelphia club 15–2. The Sox scored nine runs in the third inning.

AUGUST 12   Before 46,766 at Fenway Park, the Red Sox win 6–4 and lose 7–1 to the Yankees. At least 20,000 were turned away from the ballpark as fans were eager to see what they anticipated was Babe Ruth's last appearance as a Yankee in Boston.

The Yankees sold Ruth to the Boston Braves on February 26, 1935. He played only 28 games with the Braves before announcing his retirement in early June that year.

AUGUST 17   Wes Ferrell limits the Browns to two hits to win 6–0 in the second game of a doubleheader at Fenway Park. The only St. Louis hits were singles by Sammy West in the fourth inning and Bruce Campbell in the fifth. The Browns won the opener, 5–3.

AUGUST 19   A crowd of 46,995 jams Fenway Park, but the Red Sox lose 8–6 and 4–3 to the Tigers. Moose Solters hit a grand slam off General Crowder in the ninth inning of the first game.

Crowds of well over 40,000 were possible at Fenway Park because an area of the outfield was roped off to accommodate fans. Owner Tom Yawkey stopped allowing fans on the playing field in 1937.

AUGUST 22   Pitcher Wes Ferrell hits two homers against the White Sox at Fenway. The first one, hit in the eighth inning, tied the score at 2–2, and the second in the tenth sailed over the center field wall to win the game, 3–2.

Ferrell hit two homers in a game four times while with the Red Sox, two of them in 1934. Other Boston pitchers with two-homer games are Jack Wilson in 1940, Earl Wilson in 1965, and Sonny Siebert in 1971.

AUGUST 31   The Red Sox and Braves play an exhibition game at Braves Field for the benefit of Boston's unemployed. Some 15,000 fans attended the event, won by the Red Sox, 6–4.

SEPTEMBER 12   Rube Walberg records 8 2/3 innings of shutout relief pitching to blank the Tigers 1–0 in Detroit. Walberg relieved Fritz Ostermueller, who was removed from the game by manager Bucky Harris after allowing a single and a one-out walk. Moose Solters drove in the only run of the game on a sacrifice fly.

SEPTEMBER 17   In his first major league start, Red Sox pitcher George Hockette throws a two-hit shutout to defeat the Browns 3–0 at Sportsman's Park. Hockette carried a no-hitter into the eighth inning before Frank Grube singled. Ollie Bejma added another single in the ninth.

The sparkling debut was followed by another shutout in Hockette's third start, but he finished his career with only a 4–4 record and a 4.08 ERA.

SEPTEMBER 18   Bob Newsom of the Browns holds Boston without a hit for nine innings, but the Red Sox emerge with a 2–1, 10-inning win in St. Louis. The Red Sox took a 1–0 lead in the second inning on two walks, an error, and a fielder's choice. The Browns tied the game with a run in the sixth. In the tenth, Max Bishop and Billy Werber walked, and Bishop crossed the plate on Roy Johnson's single. Wes Ferrell was Boston's starting pitcher, but he was ejected while at the plate in the second inning for objecting too strenuously to the calls of home plate umpire Lou Kolls. Rick Ferrell joined in the conversation in defense of his brother and was also tossed. Rube Walberg pitched the final nine innings in relief for the Sox to earn the victory. Both Ferrell brothers were fined $100 for their ejection. Wes was suspended for five days, and Rick for three.

SEPTEMBER 25   Wes Ferrell blanks the Senators 1–0 in the first game of a twin bill at Fenway Park. Rick Ferrell won the game for his brother by driving in the game's lone run with a walk-off single in the ninth inning. The Red Sox also won the second game, 9–3.

OCTOBER 26   The Red Sox send Lyn Lary and $225,000 to the Senators for Joe Cronin, who also became manager of the Red Sox, replacing Bucky Harris. The trade came only a month after Cronin married the adopted daughter and niece of Senators owner Clark Griffith.

If Red Sox fans were still not convinced that Tom Yawkey would spend lavish amounts in pursuit of a pennant, the deal for Cronin certainly persuaded any remaining skeptics. Born in San Francisco in 1906 just six months after the great earthquake and fire struck the city, Cronin was then the top shortstop in base-

ball, and one of the best managers as well. In his first season as manager of the Senators, in 1933 at the age of twenty-seven, he led the club to a World Championship. Cronin spent 25 years in the Red Sox organization as a player (1935–45), a manager (1935–47), and general manager (1947–59). As a player with Boston, he played in 1,134 games and racked up 845 runs, 1,168 hits, 270 doubles, 119 home runs, and 737 RBIs.

Harris managed the Tigers in 1934, then returned to Washington to manage the Senators from 1935 through 1942, and subsequently the Phillies (1943), the Yankees (1947–48), the Senators a third time (1950–54), and the Tigers once more (1955–56). Harris won another World Series with the Yankees in 1947 and was elected to the Hall of Fame in 1975.

1935   B

Season in a Sentence

Despite a combined 45 wins from Wes Ferrell and Lefty Grove, a lack of offense dooms the Red Sox to a fifth-place finish.

Finish • Won • Lost • Pct • GB

Fifth   78   75   .510   16.0

Manager

Joe Cronin

Stats

Stats	Red Sox	AL	Rank
Batting Avg:	.276	.280	6
On-Base Pct:	.353	.351	4
Slugging Pct:	.392	.402	5
Home Runs:	69		7
Stolen Bases:	91		1
ERA:	4.05	4.46	3
Fielding Pct:	.969	.972	7
Runs Scored:	718		6
Runs Allowed:	732		3

Starting Lineup

Rick Ferrell, c
Babe Dahlgren, 1b
Oscar Melillo, 2b
Bill Werber, 3b
Joe Cronin, ss
Roy Johnson, lf
Mel Almada, cf
Dusty Cooke, rf-cf
Dib Williams, 3b-2b-ss
Carl Reynolds, rf

Pitchers

Wes Ferrell, sp
Lefty Grove, sp
Fritz Ostermueller, sp
Gordon Rhodes, sp-rp
Johnny Welch, sp-rp
Rube Walberg, rp

Attendance

558,568 (third in AL)

Club Leaders

Batting Avg:	Johnson	.315
On-Base Pct:	Johnson	.398
Slugging Pct:	Cronin	.460
Home Runs:	Werber	14
RBI:	Cronin	95
Runs:	Almada	85
Stolen Bases:	Werber	29
Wins:	Ferrell	25
Strikeouts:	Grove	121
ERA:	Grove	2.70
Saves:	Walberg	3

APRIL 1	The Red Sox purchase Bing Miller and Dib Williams from the Athletics for $50,000.
APRIL 16	On Opening Day, Joe Cronin makes his Red Sox debut as both player and manager and comes out a winner as Wes Ferrell fires a two-hitter at the Yankees to win 1–0 in New York. The only Yankee hits were singles by George Selkirk in the fourth inning and Lou Gehrig in the seventh. Cronin collected a single in four at-bats. The losing pitcher was future Hall of Famer Lefty Gomez, who entered the game with a career record of 11–0 against the Red Sox. *Ferrell led the American League in victories in 1935, posting a 25–14 record and a 3.52 ERA. He also led the league in complete games (31) and innings pitched (322). Lefty Grove had a comeback year with a 20–12 record, led the league with a 2.70 earned run average, and struck out 121 batters.*
APRIL 17	Down 2–0 to the Yankees in New York, the Red Sox score two runs in the ninth and two in the tenth, then survive a Yankee rally to win, 4–3. Max Bishop tied the score on a two-run homer. The two tenth-inning runs came on a pinch-single from Bing Miller.
APRIL 22	Wes Ferrell collects four hits, including a double and a triple, and pitches a complete game to defeat the Senators 4–2 in Washington.
APRIL 23	In the first game of the season at Fenway Park, the Red Sox pounce on the Yankees 7–4 before 20,500, including Massachusetts Governor James M. Curley. The victory gave the Red Sox a 6–1 record in the young season.
MAY 10	The Red Sox tumble the White Sox 12–2 in Chicago.
MAY 21	The Red Sox send Moose Solters and cash to the Browns for Oscar Melillo. *While playing for the White Sox in 1941, Solters was struck in the temple with a ball during fielding practice. Shortly thereafter, he began to lose his eyesight and within a few years was totally blind.*
MAY 22	The Red Sox spot the Indians a 5–0 lead after four innings before rallying to win with six runs in the fifth inning and six more in the eighth to win 12–5 at Fenway Park.
MAY 29	The Red Sox put together an eight-run seventh inning to wipe out a 6–1 Athletics lead and win 10–9 at Fenway Park.
MAY 30	Wes Ferrell is both a winner and a loser in a doubleheader against the Athletics at Fenway Park. Ferrell pitched a complete game in the opener to win, 7–4. He entered the second contest in relief in the ninth and gave up five runs in the eleventh to lose 13–8.
JUNE 1	Red Sox coach Al Schacht breaks up a fight in a novel way during a 6–0 win over the Yankees in the first game of a doubleheader in New York. In the fifth inning, Boston outfielder Roy Johnson was hit in the head with a pitch from Johnny Allen. Johnson started for the pitcher, but members of both teams came between them. Then Schacht put on a burlesque fight in which he knocked himself out and turned the whole affair into a joke. The Sox also won the nightcap, 4–2. *Schacht was a Red Sox coach in 1934 and 1935. While a respected pitching coach,*

Schacht is best-known for his side-splitting pantomime comedy routines, which he performed at 25 World Series and 18 All-Star Games and which earned him the nickname "The Clown Prince of Baseball."

JUNE 21   Mel Almada makes a remarkable catch during a 3–0 win over the Browns in St. Louis.

Rain stopped the game after six innings. Almada slipped on wet turf while chasing a Harlond Clift fly ball and caught it while sitting in the mud.

JUNE 29   The Red Sox set back the Athletics 6–4 and 13–6 in a doubleheader in Philadelphia.

JULY 3   The Red Sox blast the Senators 14–7 at Fenway Park.

JULY 14   The Red Sox clobber the Indians 14–3 in the first game of a doubleheader at Fenway Park. The nightcap was called after 10 innings with the score 2–2 because of the Sunday curfew law.

JULY 17   Bill Werber ties a major league record with four consecutive doubles during the Red Sox' 13–5 thrashing of the Indians in the first game of a doubleheader. In game two, Moe Berg drove in all of Boston's runs in a 3–1 victory.

B   The Red Sox Catch a Spy   B

Moe Berg played as a catcher for the Red Sox from 1935 through 1939 at the end of a 15-year major league career, and he stayed on as a coach in 1940 and 1941. He may have been the most intelligent man ever to play professional baseball. Berg read and spoke twelve languages, including Sanskrit. He held degrees from Princeton University, Columbia Law School, and the Sorbonne. Berg enthralled newsmen with discourses on ancient Greek history or astronomy. He appeared on the popular radio program *Information Please*, correctly answering questions on Roman mythology, French impressionism, spatial geometry, and the infield fly rule.

Berg was never more than a reserve catcher, but he stayed in the majors because of his intelligence and defensive abilities. He was reportedly the subject of Mike Gonzalez's legendary scouting report: "Good field, no hit." White Sox pitcher Ted Lyons once quipped, "Berg can speak twelve languages and can't hit in any of them."

Few knew that Berg was also working as a spy for the United States government during his playing career. At the end of the 1934 season, just before the Red Sox acquired him from the Indians, Berg was added at the last minute to a team of All-Stars, including Babe Ruth, on a goodwill trip to Japan. Organizers cited his fluent Japanese as the reason for including him on this roster of stars. However, instead of playing, Berg spent much of his time taking photographs. By order of the State Department, Berg was to photograph key Japanese military installations and other potential targets from the roof of a Tokyo hospital. In April 1942, Major General Jimmy Doolittle used these photos in making the first American air attack on Japan during World War II.

Once the war started, Berg quit his job as a coach with the Red Sox and joined the Office of Strategic Services, the forerunner of the CIA. His primary objective was to determine Germany's nuclear potential. Berg undertook several dangerous missions behind enemy lines to keep track of German scientists. Some of these missions were rumored to have involved assassinations. His gift for languages served him well, and he always returned home safely.

JULY 21   With the Red Sox trailing the Tigers 6–4 in the ninth inning at Fenway Park, Wes Ferrell pinch hits for Lefty Grove and hits a three-run, walk-off homer off Tommy Bridges for a 7–6 win.

Grove allowed three runs in the top of the ninth. Joe Cronin ordered him to intentionally walk Hank Greenberg, but two singles followed. Roaring mad, Grove hurled his glove into the grandstand, smashed a bat over the edge of the dugout, and ripped his uniform shirt to shreds.

JULY 22   Wes Ferrell hits a game-winning, walk-off, ninth-inning homer for the second game in a row. He also pitched a complete game to defeat the Browns 2–1 at Fenway Park.

JULY 27   Lefty Grove hits a grand slam in the second inning off George Blaeholder to give the Red Sox a 4–1 lead over the Athletics in the first game of a doubleheader in Philadelphia. On the mound, Grove pitched a 15-inning complete game but lost, 7–6. The Red Sox won the nightcap, 2–0.

Grove is one of four pitchers in Red Sox history to hit grand slams. The others are Babe Ruth in 1919, Wes Ferrell in 1936, and Ellis Kinder in 1950.

JULY 30   Fritz Ostermueller sets a Red Sox club record by walking 12 batters in a game against the Senators in Washington. He also hit a batter but allowed only four hits to win the game, 11–4.

JULY 31   Wes Ferrell hits two homers and drives in four runs to defeat the Senators 6–4 at Griffith Stadium.

AUGUST 5   The Red Sox lose a controversial 10–2 decision to the Yankees at Fenway Park that ends after five innings due to rain. With rain falling and the Yankees leading 8–2 in the top of the fifth, the Red Sox made no attempt to retire the Yankees in the hopes the game would be called before the legal five innings. The Yankees, on the other hand, tried to make outs deliberately to speed the game to a conclusion. In one instance, Red Sox third baseman Billy Werber threw wildly on a grounder by George Selkirk, who loped around the bases for several minutes until someone tagged him out. On another play, Myril Hoag of the Yankees jogged in from third base and crossed the plate with a steal of home without anyone form the Sox making a play on him. The pitcher on Hoag's "steal" of home was Stew Bowers, who was making his major league debut. Joe Cronin and Yankee manager Joe McCarthy were both fined $100 by the American League.

AUGUST 25   The Red Sox sweep the Indians 5–4 and 8–2 as the fans stage a riot in Cleveland. Fans protested the decisions of umpire Brick Owens in the seventh inning of the second game, resulting in a shower of bottles thrown from the stands. About 200 jumped from the bleachers and invaded the field. It took police ten minutes to clear the diamond.

SEPTEMBER 2   Red Sox pitcher Jack Wilson homers into the center field bleachers in the eleventh inning to defeat the Senators 9–8 in the first game of a Labor Day doubleheader at Fenway Park. Boston trailed 7–0 before mounting a comeback, keyed by Joe Cronin's grand slam off Ed Linke during the five-run eighth inning, which tied the score, 8–8. Cronin also doubled and had six RBIs. Washington won the second game 3–2 in 13 innings.

The home run was Wilson's first career base hit. He hit only three major league home runs in 413 at-bats over nine years. Wilson's other two home runs came in 1940 in a single game (see June 16, 1940).

SEPTEMBER 7   Joe Cronin hits into one of the most unusual triple plays in major league history to end a 5–3 loss to the Indians in the first game of a doubleheader at Fenway Park. The Red Sox entered the ninth inning trailing 5–1, then scored two runs and loaded the bases with none out. With Oral Hildebrand on the mound for Cleveland, Cronin hit a vicious line drive that deflected off the glove of third baseman Odell Hale, then struck his forehead with such force that it rebounded to shortstop Billy Knickerbocker, who caught it before it touched the ground. Knickerbocker threw to Roy Hughes at second base to force Billy Werber. Hughes whipped the ball to first baseman Hal Trosky to complete the triple play before Mel Almada could return to the bag. Cleveland also won the second game, 5–4.

SEPTEMBER 13   The Red Sox rout the Browns 13–4 in the first game of a doubleheader at Fenway Park. St. Louis won the second game, 4–2.

SEPTEMBER 18   Acting as a pinch hitter, Wes Ferrell hits a walk-off single with the bases loaded to beat the Tigers 4–3 at Fenway Park.

SEPTEMBER 22   A crowd of 47,627, the largest ever at Fenway Park, watches the Red Sox lose 6–4 and 9–0 to the Yankees.

SEPTEMBER 24   Lefty Grove earns his 20th victory of the season with an 8–2 win over the Athletics in the first game of a doubleheader at Fenway Park. The Sox completed the sweep with a 6–5 win in the nightcap.

SEPTEMBER 25   Wes Ferrell picks up his 25th win of the season with a 7–2 triumph over the Athletics at Fenway Park. Wes was helped by his brother Rick, who drove in four runs.

DECEMBER 10   The Red Sox send Gordon Rhoades, George Saviano, and $150,000 to the Athletics for Jimmie Foxx and Johnny Marcum.

The Red Sox continued to rebuild by purchasing players from Connie Mack's cash-strapped Athletics. One of the best first basemen ever to don a uniform (many baseball historians rank him second only to Lou Gehrig), Foxx was a little past his peak but gave the Red Sox six terrific seasons, particularly in 1938, when he became the only Red Sox player to hit 50 home runs in a season.

DECEMBER 17   The Red Sox trade Carl Reynolds and Roy Johnson to the Senators for Heinie Manush.

Manush was a future Hall of Fame outfielder, but by the time he arrived in Boston, he was just about finished as an effective hitter.

1936   B

Season in a Sentence

With five future Hall of Famers on the roster, the Red Sox seem primed to contend for the pennant but struggle to score runs and finish a disappointing sixth.

Finish • Won • Lost • Pct • GB

Sixth   74   80   .487 28.5

Manager

Joe Cronin

Stats   Red Sox • AL • Rank

Stats	Red Sox	AL	Rank
Batting Avg:	.276	.289	7
On-Base Pct:	.349	.363	7
Slugging Pct:	.400	.421	6
Home Runs:	86		4
Stolen Bases:	55		8
ERA:	4.39	5.04	2
Fielding Pct:	.972	.971	4
Runs Scored:	775		7
Runs Allowed:	764		2

Starting Lineup

Rick Ferrell, c
Jimmie Foxx, 1b
Oscar Melillo, 2b
Bill Werber, 3b
Eric McNair, ss
Heinie Manush, lf
Doc Cramer, cf
Dusty Cooke, rf
Mel Almada, rf
John Kroner, 2b-3b-ss
Joe Cronin, ss

Pitchers

Wes Ferrell, sp
Lefty Grove, sp
Fritz Ostermueller, sp-rp
Johnny Marcum, sp
Jack Wilson. rp
Rube Walberg, rp
Jim Henry, rp

Attendance

626,895 (third in AL)

Club Leaders

Batting Avg:	Foxx	.338
On-Base Pct:	Foxx	.440
Slugging Pct:	Foxx	.631
Home Runs:	Foxx	41
RBI:	Foxx	143
Runs:	Foxx	130
Stolen Bases:	Werber	23
Wins:	Ferrell	20
Strikeouts:	Grove	130
ERA:	Grove	2.81
Saves:	Wilson	3

JANUARY 4   The Red Sox send Hank Johnson, Al Niemiec, and $75,000 to the Athletics for Doc Cramer and Eric McNair. The Red Sox continued to strip the Athletics' roster with the purchase of Cramer, who was Boston's starting center fielder for five seasons.

APRIL 14   In the season opener, the Red Sox win 9–4 over the Athletics before 29,000 at Fenway Park. In his first game as a member of the Red Sox, Jimmie Foxx collects three hits, including a double and a triple, in five at-bats against his former Athletics teammates.

Foxx hit so many balls over the left field wall at Fenway Park during batting practice and games that a twenty-three-foot screen was built on top of the thirty-seven-foot high barrier during the 1936 season to protect parked cars and the windows of the businesses on Landsdowne Street. The screen remained in place until 2003, when it was replaced by seats atop the Green Monster.

APRIL 17   Lefty Grove pitches a two-hitter to blank the 1936 World Champion Yankees 8–0 in the first game of the season at Yankee Stadium. The only New York hits were singles by Lou Gehrig in the fifth and eighth innings.

Grove had a 17–12 record in 1936 and topped the league in earned run average (2.61) and shutouts (six). He fanned 130 batters and completed 22 starts.

APRIL 20   In the morning game on Patriots' Day, the Red Sox score three runs in the ninth to defeat the Senators 6–5 at Fenway Park. Washington won the afternoon tilt 6–2 before a crowd of 44,700.

In his first season in Boston, Jimmie Foxx was the Red Sox' leading hitter with a .338 batting average, a .440 on-base percentage, 41 homers, and 143 RBIs.

APRIL 30   The Red Sox leap out of the starting gate with five runs in the first inning and seven in the second to defeat the White Sox 16–4 at Fenway Park.

MAY 2   Spectators are kept away from the Indians players during a game at Fenway Park. The restrictions were imposed by Boston health authorities because Cleveland outfielder Bruce Campbell was hospitalized with spinal meningitis. The Indians won the game, 7–3.

MAY 3   In a game played in an almost continuous downpour, Wes Ferrell pitches a two-hitter to defeat the Tigers 6–0 at Fenway Park. The only two Detroit hits were singles by Goose Goslin.

Lefty Grove gave the Red Sox five strong seasons in the late 1930s, though he was already thirty-four when he pitched his first game for Boston. He came after the 1933 season in a trade with the Athletics for Bob Kline, Rabbit Warstler, and cash. The Sox sent Rube Walberg and Max Bishop to Philadelphia in the same deal.

Courtesy of Transcendental Graphics/theruckerarchive.com

The Ferrell brothers both had excellent seasons for the Red Sox in 1936. Wes was 22–15 and led the league in innings pitched (301) and complete games (28). Rick batted .312 and hit six home runs.

MAY 5   Lefty Grove has a hand in both runs of a 2–0 win over the Tigers at Fenway Park. In the second inning, Grove doubled in one run and scored on a triple by Dusty Cooke.

On May 18, Grove had a record of 7–0 and an ERA of 0.83 in 65 innings.

MAY 7   Wes Ferrell draws the ire of the Fenway faithful by thumbing his nose toward the spectators during a 9–6 win over the Browns.

The Red Sox were in first place as late as May 9 with a record of 17–7 and were 34–21 on June 11, just 2½ games behind the Yankees before fading to sixth place.

JUNE 2   The Red Sox swamp the Indians 14–6 at Fenway Park.

JUNE 13   The Red Sox trade Joe Cascarella to the Senators for Jack Russell.

JUNE 16   Jimmie Foxx hits a tape-measure homer over the left field roof at Comiskey Park during a 4–2 loss to the White Sox. The other Boston run was scored on another long Foxx homer that landed in the stands in left-center.

JUNE 19   Tom Yawkey and Lefty Grove take an airplane from Chicago to St. Louis so they can reach their hotel rooms in time to listen to the radio broadcast of the Joe Louis-Max Schmeling fight. Schmeling put Louis on the canvas in Round Four and knocked him out in Round Twelve, a victory that Nazis touted as proof of Aryan supremacy. Louis would beat him in a rematch in 1938.

JUNE 21   Wes Ferrell two-hits the Browns to win 3–0 in the first game of a doubleheader at Sportsman's Park. The only St. Louis hits were singles by Tom Carey and Beau Bell. The Browns won the second game 6–3.

JULY 4   Lefty Grove shuts out the Athletics 1–0 in the first game of a doubleheader at Fenway Park. Boston also won the second game, 5–4.

Left-handed pitchers have notoriously had trouble at Fenway Park with the looming Green Monster as a tantalizing target for right-handed batters, but Grove was an exception. He had a 55–17 record at Fenway during his years with the Red Sox, compared with 51–45 on the road. From 1938 through 1941, Grove won 20 consecutive decisions in Boston.

JULY 5   The Red Sox score 11 runs in the second inning and rout the Athletics 16–2 in the first game of a doubleheader at Fenway Park. The Sox completed their second doubleheader sweep of the Athletics in two days with an 8–2 win in the nightcap.

JULY 17   A bases-loaded, walk-off single by Jimmie Foxx in the ninth inning scores two runs to beat the Browns 2–1 at Fenway Park.

JULY 23   The Red Sox stack up seven runs in the fourth inning to take a 9–2 lead and defeat the Indians 9–8 in Cleveland.

JULY 24   Trailing 4–2, the Red Sox score two runs in the ninth inning and three in the tenth to beat the Tigers 7–4 in Detroit.

JULY 25   The Red Sox break loose for 12 runs in the fifth inning to mow down the Tigers 18–3 in Detroit. Boston collected 20 hits in the game.

JULY 26   During a 10–3 win over the Tigers in Detroit, Red Sox outfielder Heinie Manush angrily flings his bat toward the dugout after lining out to center field. In a freak occurrence, the bat bounded into the stands and struck Manush's own daughter. Fortunately, the youngster wasn't injured.

JULY 30   The Red Sox become the first American League team and the second in the majors to travel by airplane. The flight on American Airlines from St. Louis to Chicago took ninety minutes. Five players refused to fly and instead took the train. The next day, the Red Sox defeated the White Sox, 7–3.

               The first major league team to fly was the Cincinnati Reds in 1934. The Reds traveled in three planes, however. The Red Sox were the first big-league club to board a single airplane. Plane travel wasn't common in baseball until the late 1950s, however.

AUGUST 2   The Red Sox lead 10–1 in the fifth and 11–3 in the sixth with ace Wes Ferrell on the mound but lose to the White Sox 12–11 in 12 innings in the second game of a doubleheader at Comiskey Park. Chicago scored one run in the seventh, five in the eighth, two in the ninth, and one in the twelfth. The White Sox also won the first game, 9–1.

AUGUST 12   Wes Ferrell hits two homers and drives in all of the Red Sox' runs in a 6–4 win over the Athletics in the first game of a doubleheader at Fenway Park. Ferrell's hit his homers in the third and fourth innings. He hit the first with his brother on base. The second was a grand slam off Hod Lisenbee. The Red Sox lost the second game, 6–0.

AUGUST 16   Wes Ferrell walks off the mound without warning during a four-run Washington eighth inning that put the Senators ahead 7–3 at Fenway Park. Cronin didn't have a pitcher warming up and was forced to put in Jack Russell cold. The Red Sox went on to lose, 7–6.

AUGUST 21   For the second start in a row, Wes Ferrell storms off the mound in the middle of a game. It happened in the sixth inning of a 4–1 loss to the Yankees in New York after shortstop Eric McNair made a critical error. Joe Cronin responded to the unauthorized departure by fining Ferrell $1,000 and handing him an indefinite suspension. Ferrell threatened to beat Cronin to a pulp. "If he wants to slug me," said Cronin, "I'll be passing through the lobby at six o'clock on my way to dinner." Ferrell never showed.

AUGUST 26   Wes Ferrell returns from his "indefinite suspension" without missing a start and pitches a shutout to defeat the Tigers 7–0 at Fenway Park.

SEPTEMBER 6   The Red Sox drub the Yankees 14–5 in the first game of a doubleheader at Fenway Park. The Red Sox also won the second game, 4–2.

SEPTEMBER 13   A fight between Billy Rogell and Red Sox catcher Rick Ferrell enlivens a 7–4 win over the Tigers in Detroit. Rogell tried to reach home from first in the second inning when Frank Reiber hit a double. Rogell collided with Ferrell and was out at the plate. Ferrell heaved the ball at Rogell as he walked toward the dugout but missed, prompting Rogell to return to the plate. They went into a clinch before anyone could separate them. Both combatants were suspended for three days by the league.

SEPTEMBER 19   Wes Ferrell earns his 20th victory of the season with a 5–1 win over the Athletics in Philadelphia.

DECEMBER 9   A month after Franklin Roosevelt defeats Alf Landon in a landslide in the presidential election, the Red Sox trade Bill Werber to the Athletics for Pinky Higgins.

1937   B

Season in a Sentence

Expecting to challenge the Yankees for the pennant, the Red Sox finish a disappointing fifth.

Finish • Won • Lost • Pct • GB

| Fifth | 80 | 72 | .526 | 21.0 |

Manager

Joe Cronin

Stats   Red Sox • AL • Rank

	Red Sox	AL	Rank
Batting Avg:	.281	.281	3
On-Base Pct:	.357	.355	3
Slugging Pct:	.411	.415	4
Home Runs:	100		4
Stolen Bases:	79		3
ERA:	4.48	4.52	4
Fielding Pct:	.970	.972	7
Runs Scored:	821		3
Runs Allowed:	775		4

Starting Lineup

Gene Desautels, c
Jimmie Foxx, 1b
Eric McNair, 2b
Pinky Higgins, 3b
Joe Cronin, ss
Buster Mills, lf
Doc Cramer, cf
Ben Chapman, rf
Fabian Gaffke, rf-lf
Dom Dallesandro, lf
Bobby Doerr, 2b

Pitchers

Lefty Grove, sp
Bobo Newson, sp
Johnny Marcum, sp
Archie McKain, sp-rp
Jack Wilson, rp-sp
Rube Walberg, rp-sp
Fritz Ostermueller, rp

Attendance

559,659 (fourth in AL)

Club Leaders

Batting Avg:	Chapman	.307
On-Base Pct:	Cronin	.402
Slugging Pct:	Foxx	.538
Home Runs:	Foxx	36
RBI:	Foxx	127
Runs:	Foxx	111
Stolen Bases:	Chapman	27
Wins:	Grove	17
Strikeouts:	Grove	153
ERA:	Grove	3.02
Saves:	Wilson	7

FEBRUARY 17   The Red Sox sell Babe Dahlgren to the Yankees.

Dahlgren gained fame in 1939 when he succeeded Lou Gehrig as the Yankees' first baseman.

APRIL 20   In the first game of the season, the Red Sox overwhelm the Athletics 11–5 in Philadelphia. Batting leadoff and playing second base, nineteen-year-old Bobby Doerr had three hits in five at-bats in his major league debut. Pinky Higgins had a double, two singles, and three RBIs. Joe Cronin had two doubles and a single.

Doerr hit only .224 in 1937 and lost his starting job to Eric McNair. He recovered the second base job in 1938, however, and held it until 1951. He played his entire 15-year career with the Red Sox, appearing in 1,865 games, with 1,094 runs scored, 2,042 hits, 381 doubles, 89 triples, 223 home runs, and 1,247 RBIs. Doerr was elected to the Hall of Fame in 1986. He was the first of five outstanding rookies with the Red Sox in a five-year span, followed by Ted Williams (1939), Dom DiMaggio (1940), Tex Hughson (1941), and Johnny Pesky (1942).

APRIL 23   The Red Sox' scheduled home opener against the Yankees is rained out.

APRIL 24   A crowd of 25,000 watches the Red Sox lose the home opener 6–5 in 10 innings to the 1937 World Champion Yankees. George Selkirk tripled in two runs for the visitors in the top of the tenth. The Red Sox loaded the bases with one out in the home half but scored only one run.

During the 1937 season, Red Sox games were broadcast in Boston on WNAC. Fred Hoey did the play-by-play, a job he had held since 1927. Only home games were broadcast due to an agreement with the Braves. Hoey was also the announcer for the Braves' home games. Red Sox and Braves games were on stations in Worcester, Fall River, New Bedford, Lowell, and Springfield, Massachusetts; Providence, Rhode Island; Waterbury, Bridgeport, New Haven and Hartford, Connecticut; Laconia and Manchester, New Hampshire; Portland, Augusta, and Bangor, Maine; and Waterbury, Vermont.

APRIL 30   Joe Cronin leads the assault on the Athletics with five hits, including a double, in six at-bats during a 15–5 win at Fenway.

MAY 22   Two weeks after the German dirigible *Hindenburg* erupts in flames at Lakehurst, New Jersey, killing fifty-six people, the Red Sox rally from an 8–2 deficit to the Tigers at Fenway Park. Boston scored five runs in the sixth inning and four in the seventh to emerge with an 11–9 victory. Detroit first baseman Hank Greenberg hit a homer off Wes Ferrell that soared over the center field wall to the right of the flagpole and struck the side of a building on Landsdowne Street. The blast was estimated at 450–500 feet.

MAY 26   The Red Sox outlast the Browns 11–9 at Fenway Park.

JUNE 8   Trailing 8–2 in a game that looked hopelessly lost, the Red Sox explode for eight runs in the ninth inning to defeat the Indians 10–8 in Cleveland.

JUNE 10   The Red Sox trade Wes Ferrell, Rick Ferrell, and Mel Almada to the Senators for Bobo Newsom and Ben Chapman. The trade sent two temperamental headaches (the Ferrell brothers) to Washington for two more of them (Newsom and Chapman).

JUNE 16   Bobo Newsom walks 10 batters and allows five hits but defeats the White Sox 3–2 at Fenway Park.

JULY 4   Red Sox players Eric McNair and Oscar Melillo get on the Philadelphia Athletics' train by mistake at South Station in Boston. After discovering their error, the pair left the train in Providence, Rhode Island, and waited for the Red Sox' train to come along.

JULY 5   The Red Sox lose a doubleheader 15–0 and 8–4 to the Yankees before 61,146 at Yankee Stadium.

JULY 9   Down 8–4 as a result of a six-run Philadelphia eighth inning, the Red Sox tie the score with four runs in the ninth and go on to win 12–11 in 12 innings at Shibe Park. Both teams plated three runs in the tenth. Ben Chapman, who stroked a triple, scored the winning run on Joe Cronin's double.

JULY 11   The Red Sox complete a five-game sweep of the Athletics with 9–4 and 8–2 victories in a doubleheader in Philadelphia. The second game was enlivened by Ben Chapman's dispute with umpire John Quinn. Chapman got angry when Quinn called him out on a delayed steal. A few moments later, Chapman fired a ball at Quinn from right field that bounced into the grandstand. When Quinn ordered him out of the game, Chapman rushed him. The Sox outfielder was restrained by teammates and umpire Bill Summers but succeeded in hitting Quinn with a thrown glove.

JULY 14   The Red Sox collect 21 hits in a 15–6 win over the Browns in St. Louis. Fabian Gaffke scored five runs on a triple, a double, two singles, and a walk.

         This was one of the few bright spots in Fabian Sebastian Gaffke's career. He scored a total of just 43 runs during his six-year major league career, in which he batted only .227.

JULY 20   Two days after Amelia Earhart disappears over the Pacific, Ben Chapman fights Tiger catcher Ray Hayworth to a draw in a 10–9, 10-inning loss in Detroit. Chapman went hard into Hayworth in trying to score. As soon as Hayworth tagged him, Chapman bounded to his feet and the two exchanged blows until separated by umpire Steve Basil. Jimmie Foxx hit two homers during the game.

JULY 21   Jimmie Foxx hits two homers for the second game in a row to lead the Red Sox to a 10–3 win over the Tigers in Detroit. Foxx added another homer the following day during a 17–4 loss in Detroit to give him five homers in three games.

JULY 31   The Red Sox smash the Tigers 12–1 at Fenway Park.

AUGUST 3   The Red Sox humble the Indians 13–2 at Fenway.

AUGUST 4   Down 5–0 in the first game of a doubleheader at Fenway, the Red Sox rally to
                defeat the Indians 8–6. In the second game, Joe Cronin hit a two-run, two-out
                double to win the contest, 6–5. The sweep extended the Red Sox' winning streak
                to eight games.

                *Cronin batted .307, hit 18 homers, and drove in 110 runs for the Red Sox in
                1937. He and Jimmie Foxx were Boston's top hitters during the season. Foxx
                had an off season by his standards but still hit 36 homers and drove in 127
                runs. Lefty Grove topped the pitchers with a 17–9 record, 3.02 ERA, 153
                strikeouts, and 21 complete games.*

AUGUST 8   The Red Sox score two runs in the ninth inning to defeat the White Sox 7–6 at
                Fenway Park in the first game of a doubleheader. Jimmie Foxx drove in the first run
                with a triple, then scored on an error. It was the 12th win in a row for Boston. But
                in an attempt to win their 13th game in a row in the second game of the day, the
                Red Sox lost 13–0 at Chicago. The tussle was shortened to eight innings by the Sun-
                day curfew law.

                *The 12-game winning streak gave the Red Sox a 57–37 record and second
                place, though a distant nine games behind the Yankees. The Sox were unable
                to sustain the momentum, however, and lost 35 of their last 57 games. Tom
                Yawkey's purchases of such stars as Joe Cronin, Lefty Grove, and Jimmie
                Foxx earned his club the nicknames "The Millionaires" and "The Gold
                Sox." While 1937 was the first time in 19 years that the Red Sox posted a
                winning season, fans expected more than a fifth-place finish with a team full
                of star players.*

AUGUST 12   In the first game of a doubleheader against the Yankees at Fenway Park, the Red
                Sox fall behind 6–0 in the third inning but rally to win, 16–10. The Sox took a
                13–10 lead with four runs in the sixth inning. In the eighth inning, Jimmie Foxx hit
                a tremendous blast out the ballpark in center field to the right of the flag pole. New
                York won the second tilt, 5–3.

SEPTEMBER 9   The Red Sox overcome a four-run Yankee first inning to win 13–7 in New York.

SEPTEMBER 21   Ben Chapman's grand slam off Detroit pitcher Boots Poffenberger is the feature
                of a 10-run Boston fifth inning during a 12–7 win in the first game of a double-
                header at Fenway. Poffenberger was one strike away from getting out of the big
                inning without a run being scored when he hit Joe Cronin with a pitch. The
                Tigers triumphed in the second game, 4–1. It wasn't a good day for the twenty-
                two-year-old Poffenberger. He also received a letter from Josephine Brown, his
                nineteen-year-old bride of two months, that she wanted a divorce.

SEPTEMBER 23   A three-run, walk-off homer by Ben Chapman lifts the Red Sox to a 4–3 win over
                the Tigers at Fenway Park.

SEPTEMBER 27   Red Sox pitcher Bobo Newsom starts both games of a doubleheader against the
                Athletics at Fenway Park. Newsom pitched a complete game 6–2 win in the opener
                but lasted only until the third inning in the nightcap, a 6–0 loss shortened to six
                innings by darkness.

OCTOBER 2   The Red Sox trade Bobo Newson, Red Kress, and Buster Mills to the Browns for
             Joe Vosmik.

DECEMBER 7   The Red Sox send Dom Dallesandro, Al Niemiec, and $25,000 to the San Diego
             Padres of the Pacific Coast League for nineteen-year-old outfielder Ted Williams.
             The Red Sox outbid the Yankees, Giants, Athletics, and Tigers to obtain
             Williams's services.

             *Williams signed with the minor league Padres at seventeen, shortly after grad-
             uating from San Diego's Hoover High School in 1936. He hit only .271 with
             no homers in his first season but blossomed in 1937 by batting .291 with 23
             home runs. Most scouts considered him to be one of the best prospects in the
             history of the Pacific Coast League but thought he needed at least one more
             season in the minors to be a productive major leaguer.*

1938   B

Season in a Sentence

Tom Yawkey's millions begin to
pay off as the Red Sox finish in
second place, the club's highest
finish in 20 years.

Finish • Won • Lost • Pct • GB

Second   88   6   1.591 9.5

Manager

Joe Cronin

Stats   Red Sox • AL • Rank

Batting Avg:	.299	.281	1
On-Base Pct:	.378	.358	1
Slugging Pct:	.434	.415	2
Home Runs:	98		4 (tie)
Stolen Bases:	55		7
ERA:	4.46	4.79	3
Fielding Pct:	.968	.971	6
Runs Scored:	902		2
Runs Allowed:	751		2

Starting Lineup

Gene Desautels, c
Jimmie Foxx, 1b
Bobby Doerr, 2b
Pinky Higgins, 3b
Joe Cronin, ss
Joe Vosmik, lf
Doc Cramer, cf
Ben Chapman, rf
Johnny Peacock, c
Red Nonnenkamp, of

Pitchers

Jack Wilson, sp
Jim Bagby Jr., sp
Lefty Grove, sp
Fritz Ostermueller, sp-rp
Johnny Marcum, sp
Bill Harris, sp
Joe Heving, sp-rp
Archie McKain, rp
Emerson Dickman, rp-sp

Attendance

646,459 (fourth in AL)

Club Leaders

Batting Avg:	Foxx	.349
On-Base Pct:	Foxx	.462
Slugging Pct:	Foxx	.702
Home Runs:	Foxx	50
RBI:	Foxx	175
Runs:	Foxx	139
Stolen Bases:	Chapman	13
Wins:	Wilson	15
	Bagby Jr.	15
Strikeouts:	Grove	99
ERA:	Grove	3.08
Saves:	McKain	6

MARCH 13   Ted Williams plays his first game in a Red Sox uniform. Playing right field and batting third, Williams went hitless in four at-bats during a 6–2 exhibition loss to the Cincinnati Reds at Sarasota.

The Red Sox sent Williams to their Minneapolis farm club in the American Association on March 21. The Sox didn't need to rush Williams to the majors in 1938 because the team already possessed a strong outfield. Ben Chapman batted .340 and collected 40 doubles; Joe Vosmik had a .324 batting average, scored 121 runs, and led the league with 201 hits; and Doc Cramer was second in the AL in base hits with 198. Williams displayed his vast potential at Minneapolis by batting .366 with 43 home runs and 142 RBIs.

APRIL 18   On Opening Day, the Red Sox defeat the 1938 World Champion Yankees 8–4 at Fenway Park. Joe Cronin unexpectedly selected twenty-one-year-old Jim Bagby Jr. as the starting pitcher. It was Bagby's major league debut. He earned his first big-league win when the Red Sox rallied from a 4–2 deficit with six runs in the sixth inning. Doc Cramer collected three hits, including a double. Threatening weather and a holiday doubleheader against the Yanks the following day held the crowd to 10,500.

Jim Bagby Jr.'s father, Jim Sr., compiled a 127–87 record as a big-league pitcher that included a 31–12 mark with the Indians in 1920. Jim Jr. won 15 games as a rookie with the Sox in 1938, but after two much less successful seasons in Boston, the Sox traded him to the Indians following the 1940 season.

APRIL 19   In the second game of a Patriots' Day doubleheader, Jim Wilson and Fritz Ostermueller combine on a two-hitter to beat the Yankees 6–0 at Fenway Park. The only two New York hits, one off each pitcher, were a double by Joe Gordon and a single by Frankie Crosetti. The Yankees won the first game, 5–3.

APRIL 21   The Red Sox are outhit 13–3 but beat the Yankees 3–2 at Fenway Park.

APRIL 28   The Red Sox end a 6–1 win over the Yankees in New York with a triple play. With George Selkirk on second base and Joe Gordon on first, Joe Glenn hit a liner to first baseman Jimmie Foxx with the runners on the move. Foxx threw to shortstop Joe Cronin to double Selkirk, and Cronin fired the ball back to Foxx to retire Gordon.

MAY 2   The Athletics hammer the Red Sox 13–1 at Fenway Park. All 13 Boston runs were scored with the first three innings: three in the first, five in the second, and five in the third.

MAY 5   Ben Chapman grapples with Tigers catcher Birdie Tebbetts in the fifth inning of a 7–5 loss to the Tigers at Fenway Park. Chapman took a third strike and questioned the judgment of umpire Joe Rue in making the call. Tebbetts taunted Chapman for disputing the decision, and the two players became engaged in a heated argument that escalated into a fistfight. Among those in at the ballpark was Tebbetts's mother, who traveled from Nashua, New Hampshire, to see her son play. Both Chapman and Tebbetts were fined $25 and suspended three days by the league office.

MAY 6   A freak double play halts a Browns rally in the eighth inning of a 7–3 Boston win at Fenway Park. The bases were filled with none out when Beau Bell hit a long fly that left fielder Joe Vosmik trapped against the Green Monster. Red Kress scored from third base, but the other runners, fearing the ball would be caught, held their bases. Vosmik threw to third base, forcing Buster Mills, who had been on second, and the relay to second forced George McQuinn, who had not moved from first base.

MAY 8   Jack Wilson strikes out 12 batters and defeats the Indians 5–0 at Fenway Park.

MAY 9   The Red Sox rout the Indians 15–3 at Fenway.

MAY 13   The Red Sox shut out the Senators 10–0 at Fenway.

MAY 14   Jimmie Foxx hits a walk-off homer into the center field bleachers in the eleventh inning to defeat the Senators 10–9 at Fenway Park. The Red Sox scored three runs in the ninth to tie the score, 9–9.

The win put the Red Sox into first place. Their stay at the top lasted only five days, but the Sox remained in contention for the pennant until late July. On July 25, Boston was only 2 1/2 games behind the Yankees with a record of 48–32, but the Yanks put on the afterburners to pull away from the pack.

MAY 15   The Red Sox run their winning streak to eight games with a 4–3 decision over Washington at Fenway Park.

MAY 20   The Red Sox collect 22 hits and roll to a 16–2 win over the Browns in St. Louis. The Sox scored seven runs in the sixth inning.

Among those in the crowd at Sportsman's Park was FBI chief J. Edgar Hoover.

MAY 30   The Red Sox lose a doubleheader 10–0 and 5–4 to the Yankees before a crowd of 82,990 jammed into Yankee Stadium. The great crowd was thrown into a frenzy of excitement in the first game when Joe Cronin and Yankee outfielder Jake Powell engaged in a fistfight. The trouble started when Powell, who worked as a sheriff's deputy in South Carolina during the offseason, rushed toward Sox pitcher Archie McKain after being hit by a pitch. Before Powell could square off at McKain, the shortstop Cronin took a swing at the Yankee, who retaliated. Cronin and Powell were chased by the umpires but started fighting again under the grandstand. In the second melee, Powell clawed Cronin's face.

MAY 31   Jimmie Foxx hits a sixth-inning grand slam off Joe Beggs to put the Red Sox up 5–3 on the Yankees, but the New York juggernaut rallies to win 12–5 at Yankee Stadium. Lou Gehrig played in his 2,000th consecutive game in a streak that reached 2,130 before it ended eight games into the 1939 season.

JUNE 6   Down 7–2 to the Tigers at Fenway Park, the Red Sox stage a rousing rally with four in the seventh inning, one in the eighth, and one in the ninth to win, 8–7. Bobby Doerr drove in the winning run with a single.

Doerr was born Robert Pershing Doerr in 1918, the last year of World War I. He was named after General John J. Pershing, who was the commander of American Expeditionary Forces during the war.

JUNE 8   Down 5–0 in the fourth inning against the Indians at Fenway Park, the Red Sox rally to win 7–6. Jimmie Foxx paced the comeback with two home runs. After hitting his second homer of the day, an enthusiastic fan rushed out to home plate to offer him a drink from a half-empty liquor bottle. After Foxx spurned the offer, the fan was hustled off the field.

Through the first 43 games of the season, Foxx had 18 home runs and 68 RBIs. He finished the season with 50 home runs and 175 RBIs, both Boston Red Sox club records. Foxx also hit .349, collected 197 hits, and scored 139 runs in 1938. He led the league in batting average and RBIs. He was particularly devastating at Fenway Park, where he hit .405 with 35 homers, 104 RBIs, and an .887 slugging percentage. In most seasons 50 home runs would have been enough to lead the league, but in 1938, Hank Greenberg hit 58 homers for the Tigers.

JUNE 10   On the first pitch of his first major league at-bat, Red Sox pitcher Bill LeFebvre clubs a home run. He hit it off Monty Stratton of the White Sox at Fenway Park. LeFebvre was less than effective on the mound, however, allowing six runs in four innings of a 15–2 loss.

LeFebvre made his major league debut just days after graduating from Holy Cross College, where his baseball coach was former Red Sox manager Jack Barry. He was soon back in the minors, however and didn't appear in another big-league game until the following season. LeFebvre played in 75 big-league games and never hit another homer, but he hit .276 in 87 at-bats. With the Senators in 1944, he had 29 at-bats as a pinch hitter and led the American League with 10 pinch hits. On the mound, LeFebvre ended his career with a 5–5 record and a 5.03 ERA. The only other Red Sox players with homers in their first major league at-bats are Eddie Pellagrini in 1946 and Bob Tillman in 1962. LeFebvre was the only one of the three to do it on the first pitch.

JUNE 14   Lefty Grove, angry over being pulled in favor of reliever Jack Wilson in the seventh inning in St. Louis, throws an iron chair through a clubhouse window. The Sox handle the Browns, 5–3.

JUNE 16   Jimmie Foxx ties a major league record by drawing six walks in six plate appearances during a 12–8 win over the Browns in St. Louis. Foxx swung at only two balls during the afternoon. The Browns pitchers walked a total of eight batters during the game. Foxx drew three walks from Les Tietje, one from Ed Linke, and two from Russ Van Atta. The only other major leaguer with six walks in a nine-inning game is Walt Wilmot of the Chicago Cubs in 1891.

Foxx was suffering from sinus trouble that day, and it affected his vision. Because he couldn't see the pitches clearly, he simply let most sail by. Foxx nearly didn't play, but his potential replacements at first base were also injured.

JUNE 21   Pinky Higgins sets a major league record with hits in 12 consecutive at-bats. Higgins had eight hits in eight at-bats on this day during a doubleheader against the Tigers in Detroit, in which the Red Sox won 8–3 and lost, 5–4.

The streak began on June 19 when Higgins hit a single in his last at-bat during a 3–2 loss to the White Sox in the first game of a doubleheader at Chicago. In the second game, he was three for three in a 6–1 Boston win. The Red Sox were idle on June 20. The streak ended on June 22 when he went hitless in four at-bats facing Vern Kennedy of the Tigers. Higgins's 12 hits included 10 singles and 2 doubles. He also walked twice during the streak to reach base in 14 consecutive plate appearances. The only other major leaguer with hits in 12 consecutive at-bats is Walt Dropo of the Tigers in 1952.

JUNE 30   The Red Sox crush the Senators 11–1 at Fenway Park.

JULY 14   The Red Sox roll over the Tigers 12–1 at Fenway Park.

It was a costly win, as Lefty Grove left the game because of numbness in his pitching hand. The victory was Grove's 14th of the season, but he seldom pitched the remainder of the season and finished with a 14–4 record and a league-leading 3.08 ERA.

JULY 15   Bobby Doerr hits a sixth-inning grand slam off Lefty Mills of the Browns to wipe out a 3–1 deficit and lift the Sox to a 5–3 win at Fenway Park.

JULY 17   The Red Sox batter the Browns 11–5 and 14–4 in a doubleheader at Fenway. Jimmie Foxx had six hits in the twin bill, including four doubles and a homer, in nine at-bats.

JULY 28   The Red Sox score five runs in the tenth inning to beat the White Sox 13–8 in the first game of a doubleheader in Chicago. The Red Sox completed the sweep with an 8–5 win in the second game.

AUGUST 5   Trailing 8–3, the Red Sox score five runs in the ninth inning and one in the tenth to beat the Tigers 9–8 in Detroit. Joe Cronin tied the score 8–8 with a grand slam off Eldon Auker. Back-to-back doubles by Doc Cramer and Joe Vosmik produced the winning run.

Cronin batted .325 in 1938 and led the league in doubles with 51.

AUGUST 6   The Red Sox overcome the Tigers 14–8 in Detroit.

AUGUST 9   In one of the weirdest games in Boston baseball history, the Red Sox scored all of their runs in the final three innings to defeat the Athletics 16–4 in Philadelphia. The Sox scored seven runs in the seventh inning, three in the eighth, and six in the ninth. Not only were the Red Sox held scoreless through the first six innings, but the club had nary a base runner as Athletics starter Nelson Potter retired the first 18 batters to face him. But Potter came apart at the seams in the seventh. Four of the runs scored on a grand slam by Jim Tabor. It was the first homer of Tabor's career, and it came seven days after his big-league debut.

AUGUST 23   The Red Sox down the Indians 13–3 and 14–12 in a doubleheader at Fenway Park. In the second game, the Red Sox trailed 6–0 before mounting a comeback. The thrill-a-minute contest ended with a two-out, walk-off grand slam home run by Jimmie Foxx off Willis Hudlin. Foxx also had a homer in the third inning of the nightcap and later doubled. He had six RBIs in the game.

AUGUST 25   In the first game of a doubleheader at Fenway Park, Jack Wilson shuts out the

White Sox 1–0. Wilson also drove in the game's only run with a single in the seventh inning. Boston won the second game, as well, 9–5.

AUGUST 26   Jimmie Foxx has six hits, including two homers and two doubles, during a doubleheader against the White Sox at Fenway Park. One of the hits was the 2,000th of his career. The Red Sox lost the first game 12–2 and won the second 9–8 in 10 innings.

AUGUST 27   The Red Sox play a doubleheader against the White Sox for the third day in a row and go from one extreme to the other in winning 19–6 and 1–0. The only run of the second game scored when Ben Chapman beat out an infield hit, moved up ninety feet on a sacrifice, and scored all the way from second base on a bunt. Bill Harris pitched the shutout.

The shutout was the only one that Harris pitched with the Red Sox and his first in the majors since 1931. He played seven seasons in the majors, but they were spread out over 15 years. Harris was with the Reds in 1923 and 1924, the Pirates from 1931 through 1934, and the Red Sox in 1938.

AUGUST 30   Center fielder Doc Cramer helps out a beleaguered Red Sox staff by pitching the last four innings of a 9–5 loss to the Browns at Fenway Park. Cramer allowed two runs, three hits, and three walks.

SEPTEMBER 4   Pinky Higgins hits a grand slam off Bud Thomas in the first inning of the second game of a doubleheader in Philadelphia. The Red Sox lost the first game 12–11 and won the second, 12–2.

SEPTEMBER 5   The Red Sox sweep the Senators 14–4 and 8–6 in Washington.

SEPTEMBER 7   Jimmie Foxx drives in eight runs on two three-run homers and a bases-loaded double as the Red Sox smother the Yankees 11–4 at Fenway Park in a game shortened to $5\frac{1}{2}$ innings by rain. It was also Joe Cronin Day at Fenway Park, and he received a $1,250 silver service and an Irish terrier in pre-game services.

SEPTEMBER 20   The Red Sox score seven runs in the ninth inning to defeat the Browns 12–8 in the first game of a doubleheader in St. Louis. The Sox also scored seven runs in the sixth inning of the second game. The big inning accounted for all of the scoring in a 7–0 victory, called by darkness after eight innings.

SEPTEMBER 27   The Red Sox swamp the Athletics 11–1 in a game at Philadelphia stopped by darkness after eight innings.

SEPTEMBER 29   The Red Sox overtake the Senators 13–5 at Fenway Park.

The victory mathematically clinched second place for the Red Sox. It was the first time that either of Boston's two major league teams finished above fourth place since the Red Sox won the American League pennant in 1918.

OCTOBER 1   Jimmie Foxx hits his 49th and 50th home runs of the 1938 season and drives in seven runs during a 9–2 win over the Yankees at Fenway Park. Foxx hit a three-run homer off Bump Hadley in the third inning and a grand slam against Johnny Murphy in the sixth.

OCTOBER 2   Jimmie Foxx sits out the final game of the season, a 6–1 loss to the Yankees at Fenway Park, to protect his lead in the American League batting championship. Foxx won the title with a .349 average, six percentage points ahead of Cleveland's Jeff Heath. It was the only game that Foxx missed all year. Reserve catchers Moe Berg and Johnny Peacock played first base in place of Foxx. It was the only time that either man played at first during their big-league careers.

DECEMBER 15   Six weeks after Orson Welles fools many Americans into believing that Martians are invading New Jersey on his Mercury Theater radio program on Halloween, the Red Sox trade Ben Chapman to the Indians for Denny Galehouse and Tommy Irwin. On the same day, the Sox swapped Pinky Higgins and Archie McKain to the Tigers for Eldon Auker, Jake Wade, and Chet Morgan.

Chapman was dealt to make room in the outfield for Ted Williams. Higgins returned to the Red Sox as a player (1946), manager (1955–62), and general manager (1962–65).

DECEMBER 21   The Red Sox trade Eric McNair to the White Sox for Boze Berger.

1939   B

Season in a Sentence

Despite a phenomenal rookie season by Ted Williams, the Red Sox finish a distant second to the Yankees.

Finish • Won • Lost • Pct • GB

Second   89   62   .589 17.0

Manager

Joe Cronin

Stats   Red Sox • AL • Rank

Batting Avg:	.291	.279	1
On-Base Pct:	.363	.352	2
Slugging Pct:	.436	.407	2
Home Runs:	124		2 (tie)
Stolen Bases:	42		8
ERA:	4.56	4.62	5
Fielding Pct:	.970	.969	3
Runs Scored:	890		2
Runs Allowed:	795		5

Starting Lineup

Johnny Peacock, c
Jimmie Foxx, 1b
Bobby Doerr, 2b
Jim Tabor, 3b
Joe Cronin, ss
Joe Vosmik, lf
Doc Cramer, cf
Ted Williams, rf
Lou Finney, 1b-cf
Gene Desautels, c
Tom Carey, 2b

Pitchers

Lefty Grove, sp
Jack Wilson, sp-rp
Fritz Ostermueller, sp-rp
Eldon Auker, sp
Denny Galehouse, sp-rp
Woody Rich, sp-rp
Jim Bagby Jr., sp-rp
Emerson Dickman, rp
Joe Heving, rp

Attendance

573,070 (fourth in AL)

Club Leaders

Batting Avg:	Foxx	.360
On-Base Pct:	Foxx	.464
Slugging Pct:	Foxx	.694
Home Runs:	Foxx	35
RBI:	Williams	145
Runs:	Williams	131
Stolen Bases:	Tabor	16
Wins:	Grove	15
Strikeouts:	Grove	81
ERA:	Grove	2.54
Saves:	Heving	7

APRIL 1   In a game against the minor league Atlanta Crackers of the Southern Association at Ponce de Leon Park in Atlanta, Ted Williams throws a ball out of the ballpark and missing a short fly in the eighth inning. The throw broke the fourth-story window of a building across the street from the park. Joe Cronin took Williams out of the game after the incident. The Red Sox lost the contest, 10–9.

APRIL 6   The exhibition game between the Red Sox and the Cincinnati Reds in Florence, South Carolina, is called with the score 18–18 in the ninth inning because the clubs ran out of baseballs. The farcical contest that seemed to have been scripted by the Marx brothers was played in a fifty-mile-per-hour gale on a field with no grass in the infield, causing a game-long dust storm. So many balls were blown into the crowd and out of the ballpark that the game ended because the supply of fifty-four baseballs was completely exhausted. Most of the players ended the game capless and with their uniforms covered in dust. Many played in jackets to protect themselves from the inclement conditions. The starting pitcher for the Red Sox was, appropriately, Denny Galehouse.

APRIL 11   The Red Sox lose 11–9 to the Reds in an exhibition game played on historic ground in Petersburg, Virginia. The ball field was located on the Civil War battlefield where General Robert E. Lee and the Confederate Army made their last stand in 1865 before surrendering at Appomattox. Today it is part of the Petersburg National Battlefield.

APRIL 12   The Red Sox and the Reds continue their unusual trip north by playing on a diamond laid out on a football field in Roanoke, Virginia, with the center field fence only 260 feet from home plate. The weather was also more conducive to gridiron activity as the temperatures were in the forties with a freezing wind. The Sox won by the football-like score of 17–14.

APRIL 18   Two days after the Boston Bruins win the Stanley Cup in a five-game series against the Toronto Maple Leafs, the scheduled season opener against the Yankees in New York is postponed by rain.

APRIL 20   The Red Sox open the season with a 2–0 loss to the Yankees in New York. Ted Williams made his major league debut in the game and hit a double off Red Ruffing in four at-bats. In his first at-bat, Williams struck out against Ruffing.

             Williams played right field and batted sixth, behind Doc Cramer, Joe Vosmik, Jimmie Foxx, Joe Cronin, and Jim Tabor, and ahead of Bobby Doerr, Gene Desautels, and Lefty Grove. Williams played right field exclusively in 1939. He didn't play his first game in left field until 1940. The Red Sox had five future Hall of Famers in the lineup on Opening Day in 1939 in Foxx, Cronin, Williams, Doerr, and Grove. There were four Hall of Famers in the Yankee batting order: Joe DiMaggio, Lou Gehrig, Bill Dickey, and Red Ruffing. The April 20, 1939, game was the only one in which both Williams and Gehrig appeared. Gehrig played in only seven more big-league games after the 1939 opener.

             Williams was given uniform number 9. The last player prior to Williams to wear number 9 was Ben Chapman in 1938.

Courtesy of Transcendental Graphics/theruckerarchive.com

Rookie sensation Ted Williams gave the team a new source of power that would last until 1960. He twice won the Triple Crown and nearly did it three times, falling five RBIs short of Joe Dimaggio in 1941 despite hitting .406.

APRIL 21   The Red Sox defeat the Athletics 9–2 before 15,000 in the home opener at Fenway Park. Doc Cramer broke a 2–2 tie with a three-run double in the fifth inning.

> *Frankie Frisch, who starred in the majors with the Giants and Cardinals from 1919 through 1937, was the new radio play-by-play announcer for the Red Sox and the Braves in 1939. He replaced Fred Hoey, who had been broadcasting Red Sox and Braves games since 1927. The games were broadcast on WAAB. Frisch lasted only one year in Boston. In 1940, he took a position managing the Pittsburgh Pirates.*

APRIL 23   Ted Williams hits his first career homer with a first-inning blast against Bud Thomas during a 12–8 loss to the Athletics at Fenway Park. The ball went 420 feet and landed in the right-center field bleachers. Williams also had a double and two singles. He missed a fifth hit when A's left fielder Bob Johnson caught a liner against the wall.

In a remarkable rookie season, Williams hit .327 with 31 homers, 145 RBIs, 185 hits, 131 runs scored, and 44 doubles.

APRIL 25   Jimmie Foxx hits a walk-off homer in the eleventh inning to defeat the Senators 6–5 at Fenway Park. The ball cleared the left field wall and landed on a roof at least 450 feet from home plate.

MAY 4   Ted Williams becomes the first player to hit a ball over the right field roof at Briggs Stadium in Detroit during a 7–6 win over the Tigers. The blow was Williams's second of the game and came on a 3–0 pitch during a five-run fifth inning that put the Sox on top, 7–4. The two-tiered stands in right field were built in 1936. The next player to homer over the right field stands at the ballpark was Mickey Mantle in 1957.

MAY 8   The Red Sox purchase Lou Finney from the Athletics.

MAY 9   Ted Williams hits a three-run homer in the tenth inning to bring the Red Sox a 10–8 win over the Browns in St. Louis. The ball landed on the roof of the right field pavilion at Sportsman's Park.

After the game, the Red Sox boarded an airplane for a trip to Chicago. The cost of the trip on American Airlines for the entire team was $525.

MAY 16   The Red Sox score seven runs in the fourth inning and overwhelm the White Sox 18–4 at Fenway Park.

MAY 19   The Red Sox score seven runs in the third inning and win 15–7 against the Browns at Fenway Park.

Ted Williams was dropped to seventh in the batting order because of a slump attributed to trying too hard to hit home runs. Although he had six homers in 85 at-bats entering the game, Williams was batting only .224.

MAY 25   Ken Keltner of the Indians hits three homers in consecutive at-bats off Boston pitcher Emerson Dickman. Future Hall of Famer Bob Feller pitched a one-hitter for an 11–0 Cleveland win over the Red Sox at Fenway Park.

MAY 27   In the second game of a doubleheader against the Senators at Fenway Park, Joe Vosmik hits a walk-off homer in the ninth inning to lift the Red Sox to a 7–6 win. Ted Williams collected a homer, a triple, and a double. The Sox also won the first game, 11–4.

JUNE 1   The Red Sox wallop the Tigers 14–5 at Detroit.

JUNE 2   Doc Cramer has five hits, including a double, in five at-bats, but the Red Sox lose 8–5 to the Tigers in Detroit.

JUNE 9   The Red Sox pummel the Browns 18–7 in the second game of a doubleheader in St. Louis. Jimmie Foxx scored five runs on a homer, a single, and three walks. Ted Williams drove in six runs with two doubles and a homer. Jack Wilson earned the victory despite walking 10 batters in 7 innings. The Red Sox also won the first game, 4–3.

Foxx hit .360, clubbed a league-leading 35 homers, and scored 130 runs in 1939 despite being hospitalized with sinus trouble in June and the removal of his appendix in September. The sinus trouble led to a unique addition at Fenway Park. In order to protect Foxx from the glare of the sun, a canvas curtain was designed for use in back of the section of grandstand running behind the third base line. The screen was twenty-five feet long and fifteen feet high and hung from a heavy wire.

JUNE 26   Third baseman Jim Tabor is suspended for three days by Joe Cronin "for the good of the team and to discipline him a little." Cronin refused to go into details, merely saying that Tabor "hasn't been acting too well lately."

It was no secret that Tabor was a hard drinker, so there is little doubt that alcohol abuse contributed to the suspension. He also didn't hesitate to speak his mind. Tabor would die of a heart attack in 1953 when he was only thirty-six.

JUNE 27   Ted Williams hits clean-up for the first time in his career as the Red Sox defeat the Senators 8–0 in Washington. Joe Cronin dropped himself from fourth to fifth in the order.

Cronin set a club record for most consecutive games with an RBI with 12 from June 27 through July 9. He drove in 20 runs during the stretch. Williams tied the record by driving in 18 runs in 12 consecutive games from August 31 through September 13, 1942.

JULY 4   Just a week after being suspended for "the good of the team," Jim Tabor stages a holiday hit parade by swatting four homers, including two grand slams, during a doubleheader against the Athletics in Philadelphia. He scored seven runs and had 11 runs batted in. The Red Sox won 17–7 and 18–12 as the two teams combined for 54 runs and 65 hits. In the first game, Tabor had a single, double, and a homer in five at-bats. He drove in two runs and scored two. In the second game, in one of the greatest single-game offensive explosions in Red Sox history, Tabor hit three homers in four at-bats, scored five runs, and drove in nine. Two of the three homers were grand slams, one in the third inning off George Caster and another against Chubby Dean in the sixth.

Tabor is the only player in Red Sox history to hit four home runs during a doubleheader. He was also the first to hit three homers in a game. (Ted Williams was the second in 1946.) Through the 2004 season, there have been 12 major leaguers who have hit two grand slams in a game. Four of them are Red Sox. The three besides Tabor are Rudy York in 1946, Nomar Garciaparra in 1999, and Bill Mueller in 2003.

Tabor was overshadowed by his more glamorous teammates during his seven seasons (1938–44) with the Red Sox. On this day, despite the four homers, his accomplishment was overshadowed on the nation's sports pages by Lou Gehrig Day at Yankee Stadium. Weeks after being diagnosed with ALS (amyotrophic lateral sclerosis), a fatal illness, Gehrig stepped to the microphone and told fans, "[T]oday I consider myself the luckiest man on the face of the earth." Gehrig died in June 1941. Tabor was also pushed somewhat into the background by the son of a Hall of Famer during that afternoon, as Eddie Collins Jr., son of the Red Sox' general manager, made his major league debut playing left field for the Athletics.

JULY 8   The first game of a doubleheader against the Yankees in New York is delayed for a few minutes by a swarm of Japanese beetles that invaded the Yankee dugout. The swarm was so thick that players had trouble seeing the field from the dugout.

JULY 9   The Red Sox complete a shocking five-game series sweep of the Yankees at Yankee Stadium with 4–3 and 5–3 wins in a doubleheader. The Sox won 4–3 on July 7 and 3–1 and 3–2 in a twin bill on July 8. The Yankees entered the series with a won-lost record of 53–17.

The five-game sweep of the Yankees was the highlight for a generation of Red Sox fans that had witnessed a long succession of losing teams since the pennant-winning 1918 season. After a victory in Cleveland on July 13, the Red Sox were $5\frac{1}{2}$ games behind the Yankees, and only two back in the loss column. The Yankees pulled away, however, and finished the season 17 games ahead of the second-place Red Sox.

The Yankees from 1936 through 1939 were one of the greatest teams ever assembled, winning four World Championships in succession. They were 409–201 (.670) during the regular season those four years and 16–3 in the World Series.

JULY 11   Forty-seven former diamond greats take the field again at Fenway Park on Old-Timers Day. The game was staged as Boston's celebration of baseball's centennial. (The origins of the game had been erroneously established as occurring in 1839 as an invention of Abner Doubleday.) A team representing the National League defeated the American League 6–4. A crowd of 5,000 attended the festivities.

Among the Hall of Famers on the field that day were Cy Young, Walter Johnson, Tris Speaker, Grover Alexander, Eddie Collins, Frank "Home Run" Baker, Jimmy Collins, Kid Nichols, Chief Bender, Herb Pennock, Harry Hooper, and George Kelly along with former Red Sox greats Duffy Lewis, Larry Gardner, Smoky Joe Wood, Jack Barry, Howard Ehmke, and Freddie Parent. Wood hit the only home run of the game.

JULY 13   The Red Sox play a regular-season night game for the first time in club history and defeat the Indians 6–5 in 10 innings at Municipal Stadium in Cleveland. The Indians scored five runs in the ninth inning to tie the game before the Sox won it in the tenth on Lou Finney's RBI single.

The first night game in the major leagues took place at Crosley Field in Cincinnati in 1935. The Red Sox played three night games in 1939. The other two were in Chicago and Philadelphia. Night games at Fenway Park didn't take place until 1947.

JULY 16   The Red Sox extend their winning streak to 12 games with a doubleheader sweep over the Tigers in Detroit by scores of 9–2 and 3–0.

All 12 wins came on the road, in Philadelphia, New York, Cleveland, and Detroit.

JULY 17   The Red Sox 12-game winning streak ends with a 13–6 loss to the Tigers in Detroit. It was the second time in three seasons that the Sox allowed 13 runs in an attempt to win their 13th game in a row (see August 8, 1937).

JULY 18   The Red Sox win a 13–10 slugfest against the White Sox in the first game of a doubleheader in Chicago. Boston lost the second game, 8–5.

On the same day, the Red Sox sold Pee Wee Reese to the Dodgers for four minor league players and $75,000. Reese was five days shy of his twenty-first birthday and was playing for the Red Sox' farm club at Louisville in the American Association. Most considered Reese to be the best shortstop prospect in the minors leagues, but Joe Cronin was thirty-two and believed that he had five more years left in him. Cronin told reporters that he didn't think it was fair to keep Reese waiting that long. There were also concerns about Reese's small stature. In 1939, Cronin hit .308 and clubbed 19 homers. He stepped aside as the Red Sox' starting shortstop in 1942 in favor of Johnny Pesky. Reese was the regular shortstop for the Dodgers from 1940 until 1956 and was elected to the Hall of Fame in 1984.

JULY 21   Ted Williams drives in the tying run in the ninth inning with a single and the game-winner in the eleventh with another one-base hit off the glove of Browns first baseman George McQuinn to lift the Red Sox to a 6–5 win in St. Louis.

JULY 23   The Red Sox clobber the Browns 13–5 and 11–3 in a doubleheader in St. Louis. Bobby Doerr had seven hits, including a double and a homer, and scored six runs in ten at-bats.

AUGUST 1   Bobby Doerr leads off the game with a home run off Bob Feller, then hits a grand slam off Feller in the fifth inning. Just prior to the grand slam, Lefty Grove drew a two-out walk that so incensed Indian manager Ossie Vitt that he was thrown out of the game by umpire Cal Hubbard. The Red Sox won the game 7–5 in Cleveland.

Doerr batted .318 with 12 homers in 1939.

AUGUST 3   The Red Sox score nine runs in the eighth inning and defeat the Indians 17–6 in Cleveland. Joe Cronin hit two doubles in the inning.

AUGUST 6   Jimmie Foxx pitches the ninth inning of a 10–1 loss to the Tigers in the first game of a doubleheader in Detroit. Foxx retired all three batters he faced, including a strikeout of Pinky Higgins. The Sox won the second game, 8–5.

AUGUST 8   Ted Williams is removed from a 9–2 win over the Athletics at Fenway Park in the sixth inning for failing to run to first base after hitting a fly ball. Lou Finney replaced Williams in right field.

AUGUST 13   Ted Williams has six hits, including a triple and a homer, in six at-bats during a doubleheader against the Senators at Fenway Park. Williams also drew three walks to reach base in all nine of his plate appearances during the afternoon. The Red Sox won the first game 9–1 but lost the second 6–3 in a contest shortened to eight innings by the Sunday curfew law.

                  Williams had hits in nine consecutive at-bats, including two doubles in his last two at-bats in a 9–5 win over Washington at Fenway on August 12 and a single in his first at bat during a 3–0 loss to the Athletics in Philadelphia on August 15.

AUGUST 19   The Red Sox score five runs in the ninth inning to defeat the Senators 8–6 in the first game of a doubleheader in Washington. Ted Williams put the Red Sox in the lead by hitting a grand slam during the inning off Joe Haynes that soared over the high right field wall at Griffith Stadium. The Senators won the second game 2–1.

AUGUST 29   Ted Williams hits a grand slam off Harry Eisenstat in the fifth inning of a 7–4 win over the Indians in Cleveland.

                  Three days later, Germany invaded Poland, triggering a declaration of war from England and France and the beginning of World War II. The conflict would embroil the United States militarily on December 7, 1941, with the attack by the Japanese on Pearl Harbor.

SEPTEMBER 3   After the Red Sox beat the Yankees 12–11 in the first game of a doubleheader at Fenway Park, the two clubs play "stall ball" during a bizarre second game. The Yankees scored two runs in the top of the eighth inning to take a 7–5 lead. The Sunday curfew of 6:30 PM was fast approaching. If the Red Sox didn't get to bat in the bottom of the eighth, the entire inning would be canceled and the score would revert back to 5–5. In a situation similar to one that took place between the two clubs four years earlier (see August 5, 1935), the Yankees were trying to make outs intentionally, while the Red Sox were trying to extend the contest by taking as much time as possible. Red Sox pitcher Eldon Auker tried to issue an intentional walk to Babe Dahlgren, but the batter swung and missed at three pitches several feet wide of the plate and struck out. Both George Selkirk and Joe Gordon sauntered around the bases until they were tagged out. Many of the 27,000 fans in attendance began to litter the field with a shower of bottles, straw hats, newspapers, and assorted garbage. Finally, umpire Cal Hubbard declared that the field was unplayable and forfeited the game to the Yankees.

                  The Red Sox protested Hubbard's decision to forfeit the game to American League president Will Harridge, who ordered that the contest go into the record books as a 5–5 tie, with a make-up contest scheduled for September 26. Harridge also fined Dahlgren, Selkirk, and Gordon each $100. The rescheduled game was rained out, however, and never played.

SEPTEMBER 11   The Red Sox claim an 11–9 victory over the Athletics in Philadelphia.

SEPTEMBER 13   Lefty Grove shuts out the Tigers 1–0 at Fenway Park. The lone run of the game was driven in on a single by Lou Finney in the fifth inning.

> *Grove was 15–4 in 1939, completed 17 of his 23 starts, and posted a 2.54 ERA to lead the league in a season in which league ERA overall was 4.62. It was the ninth time that Grove had led the AL in earned run average, fourth with the Red Sox (1935, 1936, 1938, and 1939). No one else in major league history has had more than six ERA titles. In 1939, Grove started just one game a week, usually on Sunday, to preserve the strength of his thirty-nine-year-old arm.*

SEPTEMBER 23   The Red Sox score seven runs in the fifth inning to take a 9–0 lead and hold on to defeat the Athletics 10–8 at Fenway Park.

DECEMBER 8   The Red Sox purchase Marv Owen from the White Sox.

THE STATE OF THE RED SOX

The Red Sox had put together a young pennant-contending team in the early 1940s that promised to get much better with players such as Ted Williams, Bobby Doerr, Johnny Pesky, Dom DiMaggio, and Tex Hughson when the United States became involved militarily in World War II. All five went into the service. Williams, Pesky, and DiMaggio missed all of 1943, 1944, and 1945, while Doerr and Hughson missed part of 1944 and all of 1945. When they came back in 1946, the Sox won their first AL pennant since 1918 before losing to the Cardinals in the World Series. Boston lost the pennant in both 1948 and 1949 on the final day of the season. Overall, the club was 854–683 during the 1940s, a winning percentage of .556—second only to the Yankees in the American League. AL pennant winners besides Boston during the decade were the Tigers (1940 and 1945), Yankees (1941, 1942, 1943, 1947, and 1949), Browns (1944), and Indians (1948).

THE BEST TEAM

The 1946 Red Sox started the season with 41 wins in their first 50 games and ran away with the AL pennant with a record of 104–50.

THE WORST TEAM

The Sox were harder hit by the military draft and enlistments during World War II than any other American League club. The 1943 Red Sox were 68–84 and finished in seventh place, a sharp fall from second in 1942.

THE BEST MOMENT

The Red Sox clinched their first pennant since 1918 with a 1–0 win over the Indians on September 13, 1946.

THE WORST MOMENT

This is a tough choice. Was it the Game Seven loss to the Cardinals in the 1946 World Series? Was it the playoff loss to the Indians in 1948? Or the losses to the Yankees in the final two games of 1949 that cost the Sox another pennant? Take your pick.

THE ALL-DECADE TEAM • YEARS WITH BRS

Birdie Tebbetts, c	1947–50
Jimmie Foxx, 1b	1936–42
Bobby Doerr, 2b	1937–44; 1946–51
Jim Tabor, 3b	1938–44
Johnny Pesky, ss	1942; 1946–52
Ted Williams, lf	1939–42; 1946–60
Dom DiMaggio, cf	1940–42; 1946–53
Lou Finney, rf	1939–42; 1944–45
Tex Hughson, p	1941–44; 1946–49
Joe Dobson, p	1941–43; 1946–50
Boo Ferriss, p	1945–50
Mel Parnell, p	1947–56

Other outstanding Red Sox of the 1940s included shortstops Joe Cronin (1935–45) and Vern Stephens (1948–52). Williams, Foxx, Doerr, and Cronin are all in the Hall of Fame. Stephens, Pesky, and DiMaggio are overlooked stars who deserve recognition with a plaque in Cooperstown.

THE DECADE LEADERS

Batting Avg:	Williams	.356
On-Base Pct:	Williams	.496
Slugging Pct:	Williams	.647
Home Runs:	Williams	234
RBI:	Williams	893
Runs:	Williams	951
Stolen Bases:	DiMaggio	75
Wins:	Hughson	96
Strikeouts:	Hughson	693
ERA:	Hughson	2.94
Saves:	Brown	16
	Johnson	16

THE HOME FIELD

There were many changes at Fenway Park during the 1940s. The bullpens in right field were added in 1940, reducing the length of the right field power alley from 402 feet to 382. In addition, the right field stands were rebuilt that year, shortening the distance from home plate to the right field corner by thirty feet, to 302. Skyview seats were added in 1946. The ads were removed from the Green Monster in 1947, and the wall was painted its familiar green. Also that year, night games were staged at Fenway Park for the first time. In 1948, the park got a rooftop press box.

THE GAME YOU WISH YOU HAD SEEN

In the first game of a doubleheader at Fenway Park on July 14, 1946, Indians player-manager Lou Boudreau set an American League record with five extra-base hits, but his club lost 11–10 to the Red Sox because Ted Williams hit three homers. In the second game, Boudreau inaugurated the famous "Boudreau shift" by deploying most of his defensive players to the right of second base.

THE WAY THE GAME WAS PLAYED

The most significant change in the game was integration with the arrival of Jackie Robinson in 1947. The Red Sox did not integrate their roster until 1959, however. League stats and averages in 1949 looked very similar to those of 1940, although offense dipped during the war years and there was a surge in home runs at the end of the decade.

THE MANAGEMENT

Tom Yawkey was in his second decade as owner of the Red Sox. Eddie Collins was the number two man in the front office until 1947, when he retired. Joe Cronin was the field manager from 1935 through 1947. He was promoted to general manager at the end of the 1947 season, replacing Collins. Joe McCarthy took over duties in the dugout following Cronin's promotion and remained with the Sox through June 1950.

THE BEST PLAYER MOVE

The best trade brought Vern Stephens and Jack Kramer from the Browns on November 17, 1947, in exchange for six players and $310,000.

THE WORST PLAYER MOVE

The Red Sox traded Stan Spence and Jack Wilson to the Senators for Ken Chase and Johnny Welaj on December 13, 1941.

1940   B

Season in a Sentence

The Red Sox lead the league for 57 days in April, May, and June, but inconsistent pitching precipitates a slide to fourth place.

Finish • Won • Lost • Pct • GB

Fourth (tie) 82   72   .532   8.0

Manager

Joe Cronin

Stats   Red Sox • AL • Rank

Stats	Red Sox	AL	Rank
Batting Avg:	.286	.271	2
On-Base Pct:	.356	.342	2
Slugging Pct:	.449	.407	1
Home Runs:	145		2
Stolen Bases:	52		7
ERA:	4.89	4.38	6
Fielding Pct:	.972	.970	4
Runs Scored:	872		2
Runs Allowed:	825		6

Starting Lineup

Gene Desautels, c
Jimmie Foxx, 1b-c
Bobby Doerr, 2b
Jim Tabor, 3b
Joe Cronin, ss
Ted Williams, lf
Doc Cramer, cf
Lou Finney, rf-1b
Dom DiMaggio, cf-rf

Pitchers

Jim Bagby, Jr., sp-rp
Lefty Grove, sp
Denny Galehouse, sp
Fritz Ostermueller, sp-rp
Jack Wilson, rp-sp
Herb Hash, rp-sp
Emerson Dickman, rp
Joe Heving, rp

Attendance

716,234 (fourth in AL)

Club Leaders

Batting Avg:	Williams	.344
On-Base Pct:	Williams	.442
Slugging Pct:	Williams	.594
Home Runs:	Foxx	36
RBI:	Foxx	119
Runs:	Williams	134
Stolen Bases:	Tabor	14
Wins:	Wilson	12
	Heving	12
Strikeouts:	Wilson	102
ERA:	Grove	3.99
Saves:	Wilson	5

FEBRUARY 8   The Red Sox sell Eldon Auker to the Browns. They soon regretted making this deal. The Sox thought that Auker was finished after an off year in 1939, but he won 16 games in 1940 for the sixth-place Browns.

> *Auker wasn't the only ex-Red Sox pitcher to star for another team during the season. Bobo Newsom was 21–5 for the 1940 American League champion Tigers, Bucky Walters was 22–10 for the World Champion Reds, and Red Ruffing posted 15 wins for the Yankees. The Red Sox' starting pitching was awful in 1940. Joe Cronin used 16 different starting pitchers during the season, none of whom won more than eight games in a starting role. The leading winner among the starters was Jack Wilson, who was 8–2 in 16 starts and 4–4 with five saves in 25 relief appearances.*

FEBRUARY 12   The Red Sox sell Joe Vosmik to the Dodgers.

APRIL 16   After President Franklin Roosevelt tosses out the first ball of the season at Griffith Stadium in Washington (a wild throw that struck the camera of a Washington Post photographer), forty-year-old Lefty Grove pitches a two-hitter to give the Red Sox a 1–0 win over the Senators. Grove retired the first 21 batters to face him before Ted Williams, playing the first regular-season game of his career in left field, dropped Gee Walker's liner for an error. Williams recovered, however, to throw Walker out at second base. Cecil Travis and Jimmy Bloodworth followed with singles to account for the two Washington hits. The only run of the game was scored in the second inning when Bobby Doerr walked, advanced to second on an infield out, and headed home on a Grove single. Doerr appeared to be an easy out at home, but Senators catcher Rick Ferrell missed the ball for an error. Dom DiMaggio made his major league debut in the game. Batting leadoff and playing right field, DiMaggio was hitless in four at-bats.

The victory gave Grove a career record of 287–128, but it proved to be the last of his 35 career shutouts. Age caught up with Grove in 1940, as he had a record of only 7–6.

APRIL 18   The Red Sox run their record to 2–0 with two shutouts as Jim Bagby Jr. stops the Senators 7–0 in Washington.

APRIL 19   The Red Sox open the home schedule with a Patriots' Day doubleheader and earn a split by defeating the Athletics in the first game 7–6 before losing the second contest, 3–1. Jimmie Foxx hit a homer in the opener.

There were many improvements and changes made at Fenway Park between the 1939 and 1940 seasons. The most significant was the construction of a bullpen area for both teams in front of the bleachers in right field. This was done to help Ted Williams by reducing the distance needed to hit a home run to right. The right-center field power alley at Fenway during Williams's rookie season was 402 feet. The bullpens reduced this to 382. The seating area along the right field line was also changed. The pavilion, built in 1934, was torn out and replaced by an extension of the grandstand with individual seats instead of the uncomfortable benches that the pavilion provided. The grandstand swung around the right field corner and reduced the distance from home plate to the right field foul pole from 332 feet to 302, another move to help Williams reach the seats with his long drives. More box seats were also added in right and left field. The changes met the approval of fans, as the Red Sox drew 716,234 to Fenway in 1940, breaking the old record of 668,965 in 1909, when the club played at Huntington Grounds.

APRIL 28   Jim Tabor hits a twelfth-inning homer to down the Athletics 5–4 in Philadelphia. The Athletics scored three runs in the ninth inning with two outs to tie the score.

Jim Britt became the new radio play-by-play announcer for Boston baseball in 1940, covering the all of home games of the Red Sox and Braves except for those played on Sunday. Britt continued as the announcer of both the Red Sox and the Braves from 1940 through 1942 and again from 1946 through the 1950 season, then did the Braves exclusively in 1951 and 1952. Britt missed three seasons (1943–45) while serving in the military during World War II. During those seasons, the announcer for the Sox and the Braves was George Hartick. In 1940, Red Sox and Braves games were broadcast on a network that included stations in Fall River, Greenfield, Lowell, New Bedford, Pittsfield, and Springfield, Massachusetts; Hartford, New London, and Waterbury, Connecticut; Providence, Rhode Island; Laconia and Manchester, New Hampshire; Rutland, Vermont; and Portland, Augusta, Bangor, and Lewiston, Maine.

MAY 3 — Jim Tabor hits a homer in the ninth that ties the score 8–8 and drives in the winning run in the tenth with a bases-loaded walk-off single to lift the Red Sox to a 9–8 win over the Browns at Fenway Park.

MAY 6 — The Red Sox take first place with an 8–5 win over the Indians at Fenway Park.

The Sox remained in first place for 45 consecutive days from May 6 through June 19.

MAY 11 — Lou Finney hits a grand slam off Marius Russo in the fifth inning that gives the Red Sox a 4–0 lead, but the Yankees rally and force extra innings before the Sox win 9–8 in New York.

MAY 14 — Jimmie Foxx hits a tenth-inning homer to defeat the White Sox 7–6 in Chicago. It was Foxx's second homer of the game.

Foxx hit .297 in 1940 with 36 home runs and 119 RBIs. His 30 homers gave him a major league record 12 consecutive seasons with 30 or more homers. It remained the record until Barry Bonds broke it in 2004.

MAY 20 — Jimmie Foxx hits a grand slam in the fifth inning off Tommy Bridges of the Tigers to put Boston ahead 6–3, but Detroit rallies to win 10–7 at Briggs Stadium. Pinky Higgins hit three homers for the Tigers.

MAY 21 — Jimmie Foxx hits a grand slam for the second game in a row by connecting off Dizzy Trout of the Tigers in the third inning of an 11–8 win at Detroit.

Foxx is the only player in Red Sox history to hit grand slams in consecutive games.

MAY 30 — Two days after the surrender of Holland and Belgium to Germany, Lou Finney collects five hits, including a double, in six at-bats during an 11–4 win over the Yankees The hits came in the second game of a doubleheader before a crowd of 82,437 at Yankee Stadium. The Yankees won the first game 4–0.

After winning their fourth consecutive World Championship in 1939, the Yankees spent much of May 1940 in last place. The Yankees ended the season in third place, but the Red Sox failed to take advantage of the off year and instead finished one slot behind the Bronx Bombers in fourth.

JUNE 2 — Jimmie Foxx hits a walk-off homer with a man on base to defeat the White Sox 10–8 in the second game of a doubleheader at Fenway Park. Chicago won the first game, 6–0.

JUNE 6 — Two days after 350,000 British troops are evacuated at Dunkirk, Jimmie Foxx hits a two-out, two-strike walk-off homer with two men on base to defeat the Browns 3–1 at Fenway Park.

JUNE 8 — On Lefty Grove Day in Boston, the pitcher is honored before a 4–2 loss to the Tigers at Fenway Park, and again at a dinner at the Copley Plaza Hotel for which 500 fans pay $5 to attend. Among his gifts was a sterling silver service, a copy of a

Paul Revere service on display at the Museum of Fine Arts; a sterling silver plaque in the form of a huge open book; a silver bowl; a bronze thermometer; a clock and barometer set; a suede jacket; and an illuminated, embossed scroll bearing the good wishes of Boston fans.

JUNE 16   Pitcher Jack Wilson hits two homers during a 14–5 win over the White Sox in the second game of a doubleheader in Chicago. The Red Sox collected 20 hits in the game, including five homers. In addition to Wilson's two blasts, Joe Cronin hit two home runs, and Jimmie Foxx hit one. In the first game, Ted Williams hit a homer in the twelfth inning to lift the Red Sox to a 4–3 victory.

The sweep gave the Red Sox a 31–16 record on the season and a 2 1/2-game lead in the AL pennant race. The Red Sox lost their next seven games, however, to fall out of first place.

JUNE 23   The day after France surrenders to Germany, Jim Tabor ends the Red Sox' seven-game losing streak by hitting two homers to account for both of the runs in a 2–0 win over the Indians in the second game of a doubleheader in Cleveland. Tabor hit his homers in the second and fifth innings. The Indians won the first game, 4–1.

Tabor hit 21 homers and batted .285 for the Red Sox in 1940.

JULY 2   The Red Sox wallop the Athletics 15–9 in the second game of a doubleheader at Fenway Park. The Athletics won the first game, 4–3.

JULY 3   The Red Sox win 12–11 in a storybook finish against the Athletics at Fenway Park. The Athletics led 8–0 early in the game and were still ahead 10–3 when the Red Sox scored three runs in the eighth inning, mounting the rally after two were out and nobody was on base. Jim Tabor batted in all three of the runs with a homer, but the A's scored a run in the ninth to move ahead 11–6. In the bottom of the inning, the Sox scored six times to win the game. The first five runs were the result of three singles, a walk, and a three-run homer by Ted Williams that tied the score 11–11. Jimmie Foxx won the contest with a walk-off homer.

The Red Sox had a 36–8 record against the Athletics in 1939 and 1940.

JULY 9   Joe Cronin manages the American League to a 4–0 loss in the All-Star Game, played at Sportsman's Park in St. Louis.

Cronin managed the All-Star team in 1940 even though the Red Sox finished second the previous season because Joe McCarthy, who guided the Yankees to their fourth-straight pennant in 1939, said that he had had the honor "often enough."

JULY 11   Bobby Doerr hits a thirteenth-inning, walk-off homer that enables the Red Sox to defeat the White Sox 3–2 at Fenway Park.

The winning pitcher was Emerson Dickman, who had a 22–15 record in five seasons with the Red Sox (1936, 1938–41). Dickman came from a socially prominent family in Buffalo and bore a striking resemblance to actor Robert Taylor.

JULY 14   In the second game of a doubleheader against the Browns at Fenway Park, the Red Sox collect nine hits, one by each player in the lineup, and win 7–3 in a contest shortened to seven innings by Boston's Sunday sports law. The Sox also won the first game 5–4 in 11 innings.

JULY 17   Bobby Doerr hits a first-inning grand slam off Clay Smith of the Tigers to lead the Red Sox to an 8–5 victory in the second game of a doubleheader at Fenway Park. The Red Sox also won the first game, 8–4.

           Doerr hit .291 with 22 home runs and 105 RBIs in 1940.

JULY 21   Ted Williams creates controversy during a conversation with Cleveland writer Harry Grayson. Williams talked about visiting his uncle John Smith, a fireman in Yonkers, during a road trip to New York. It was a quiet day, and everyone was lounging in the sun playing cards. "Hell you can live like this and retire with a pension," Williams told Grayson. "Here I am hitting .340 and everybody's all over me. Maybe I shoulda been a fireman." Williams further added that his $12,500 salary was "chicken feed."

JULY 23   Responding to Ted Williams's regrets about not having been a fireman, White Sox manager Jimmy Dykes supplies his club with bells, sirens, and fire hats during a series against the Red Sox in Chicago and goads the Red Sox outfielder every time he comes to bat.

JULY 26   The Red Sox clobber the Browns 14–7 in St. Louis.

JULY 28   The Red Sox collect 22 hits and defeat the Browns 13–10 in the second game of a doubleheader in St. Louis. The Browns won the first game, 3–1.

JULY 31   Jimmie Foxx becomes the Red Sox' starting catcher in order to get Dom DiMaggio in the lineup.

           Foxx broke into the majors as a catcher in 1925 and had 62 career games behind the plate, but only one of them had come since 1935. Foxx caught 42 games for the Red Sox in 1940. DiMaggio played right field, while Lou Finney went from right to Foxx's old position at first base. The catching position had been a weak spot for the Red Sox since the club traded Rick Ferrell in 1937.

AUGUST 2   Joe Cronin hits for the cycle to lead the Red Sox to a 12–9 win over the Tigers in Detroit.

           Cronin had a .285 batting average, 24 homers, and 111 RBIs in 1940. He also collected his 2,000th career hit in September.

AUGUST 8   Down 5–2, the Red Sox score two runs in the eighth and two in the ninth to beat the Yankees 6–5 at Fenway Park. The game was enlivened by a near-fight in the fifth inning. The Sox' Emerson Dickman hit Joe Gordon with a pitch, and Gordon slung his bat in the direction of the mound as he trotted toward first. The two players started toward each other, but were separated before it came to blows.

AUGUST 15 Ted Williams hits a grand slam during an 11–1 win over the Yankees in New York.

Williams had a .344 batting average, 23 homers, 113 RBIs, 134 runs scored, 43 doubles, and 14 triples in 1940.

AUGUST 16   Jimmie Foxx hits a walk-off home run in the tenth inning to defeat the Senators 7–6 at Fenway Park. It was Foxx's second homer of the game.

Foxx's first homer was the 494th of his career to pass Lou Gehrig for second place on the all-time list. The only man ahead of Foxx in 1940 was Babe Ruth, who ended his career in 1935 with 714 homers. In interviews with reporters after the game, Foxx expressed confidence that he could break Ruth's record. According to a system developed by Bill James to predict the likelihood of play-ers reaching career goals, Foxx had a 40 percent chance at the end of the 1940 season of breaking Ruth's career home run record. Foxx hit the 500th home run of his career on September 24, 1940, at the age of thirty-two years and 337 days. He remains the youngest player ever to hit 500 homers by more than a year. The next youngest are Willie Mays (thirty-four years, 130 days), Sammy Sosa (thirty-four years, 143 days), Hank Aaron (thirty-four years, 159 days), Babe Ruth (thirty-four years, 186 days), and Ken Griffey Jr. (thrity-four years and 212 days). Foxx never came close to breaking Ruth's home run record, however. He slowed consider-ably after the 1940 season and finished his career in 1945 with 535 home runs.

Jimmie Foxx received less attention than Babe Ruth and Lou Gehrig but was every bit their equal as a power hitter.

AUGUST 17   The Red Sox slide past the Senators 12–9 at Fenway Park. Jimmie Foxx homered, which gave him six home runs over a stretch of five games.

                 The Red Sox had a Yank on the team in 1940 in pitcher Yank Terry. His given name was Lancelot Yank Terry. He continued to pitch for the Red Sox until 1945.

AUGUST 19   Jim Tabor hits a grand slam in the fourth inning off Johnny Humphries of the Indians during a 16–7 Red Sox win at Fenway Park.

AUGUST 21   Jim Tabor collapses before a 4–2 loss to the Indians at Fenway Park. Tabor was taken to the hospital, where he underwent an operation for appendicitis.

AUGUST 24   Ted Williams pitches two innings during a 10–1 loss to the Tigers in the first game of a doubleheader at Fenway Park. Williams allowed a run and three hits and struck out one. The Red Sox won the second game 8–7 with two runs in the ninth inning. This was the only game that Williams pitched during his big-league career. His catcher was Joe Glenn, who also caught the last game that Babe Ruth pitched while with the Yankees in 1933.

                 Glenn played only 22 games in a Boston uniform, in which he hit .128.

AUGUST 25   The Red Sox score 11 runs in the sixth inning and pummel the Browns 17–3 in the second game of a doubleheader at Fenway Park, shortened to seven innings by the Sunday curfew. Jimmie Foxx hit a grand slam in the big inning. St. Louis won the first game, 7–2.

AUGUST 30   The Red Sox purchase Charlie Gelbert from the Senators.

SEPTEMBER 2   Lefty Grove pitches 13 innings in the first game of a doubleheader at Griffith Stadium but loses 1–0 to the Senators. Sid Hudson also pitched a complete game for the Senators. It was Grove's first start in three weeks. He had been sidelined by a chipped bone in his foot. The Senators also won the second game, 5–4, shortened to 5½ innings by darkness.

SEPTEMBER 5   The Red Sox take a 6–0 lead in the second inning, fall behind 7–6 when the Athletics score seven runs in the third inning, then rally to win 9–7 at Fenway Park.

                 The win put the Red Sox four games behind the first place Indians in a tight four-way AL pennant race. The Sox were in fourth place, with the Tigers second, one game behind and the Yankees third two games back. The Red Sox lost 12 of their final 22 games, however, and could pull no closer than four games from the top. The Tigers won the pennant by one game over the Indians.

SEPTEMBER 13   Jim Bagby Jr. pitches a two-hitter but loses 1–0 to the Indians at Municipal Stadium. The only Cleveland hits were singles by Jeff Heath and Roy Weatherly in the fourth inning.

SEPTEMBER 24   The Red Sox score seven runs in the sixth inning and rout the Athletics 16–8 in the first game of a doubleheader in Philadelphia. The Sox tied an American League record by collecting seven extra-base hits in the big inning on four homers, a triple, and two doubles. The Sox narrowly missed hitting five homers in a row, which would have been a major league record. Ted Williams, Jimmie Foxx, and Joe Cronin hit successive homers. Next, Bobby Doerr tripled on a drive most observers at the time believed should have been an inside-the-park homer, but Tom Daly, the third base coach, cautiously held Doerr up at third. Jim Tabor followed Doerr with a home run. The Red Sox also won the second game, 4–3.

The homer by Foxx was the 500th of his major league career. Athletics pitcher George Caster allowed a total of six homers in the game, including all four in the sixth inning, tying modern major league records for most homers allowed by a pitcher in a game and in an inning.

SEPTEMBER 27   The Red Sox collect 22 hits to massacre the Senators 24–4 at Fenway Park. The Sox scored 10 runs in the fourth inning to take a 16–2 lead and added seven more in the eighth. Dom DiMaggio scored five runs, reaching base on three singles, a double, and a walk.

DiMaggio played for the Red Sox from 1940 through 1953, with the exception of three seasons (1943–45) during World War II when he was in the Navy. He batted .298 in 1,399 games with the Sox, scored 1,046 runs, and collected 1,690 hits, 308 doubles, 57 triples, and 87 home runs as a center fielder and leadoff hitter. DiMaggio played in seven All-Star Games. He was the third of the three DiMaggio brothers to reach the majors, after Joe and Vince. Overshadowed by his brother Joe, Dom never got the credit he deserved. His unimposing physique contributed to the perception. Because of his glasses and five-foot nine-inch, 168-pound frame, Dom was nicknamed "The Little Professor."

SEPTEMBER 28   The Red Sox wallop the Athletics 16–4 and 8–1 in a doubleheader at Fenway Park. The Sox scored seven runs in the sixth inning of the first game.

SEPTEMBER 29   The Red Sox earn a tie for fourth place in the AL standings with a sweep of the Athletics 9–4 and 4–1 in a doubleheader at Fenway Park. The second game included a triple steal in the sixth inning in which Joe Cronin stole home, Bobby Doerr stole third, and Johnny Peacock took second.

NOVEMBER 20   Two weeks after Franklin Roosevelt defeats Wendell Willkie in the presidential election, the Red Sox sell Denny Galehouse to the Browns.

DECEMBER 12   The Red Sox trade Doc Cramer to the Senators for Gee Walker, then trade Walker, Gene Desautels, and Jim Bagby Jr. to the Indians for Frankie Pytlak, Odell Hale, and Joe Dobson. On the same day, the Red Sox purchased Pete Fox from the Tigers.

Cramer was traded to make room for Dom DiMaggio in center field. Dobson remained in Boston until 1950 and won 106 games in a Red Sox uniform.

1941   B

Season in a Sentence

A nation's eyes turn to Ted Williams as he attempts to finish the season batting better than .400.

Finish • Won • Lost • Pct • GB

Second   84   70   .545   17.0

Manager

Joe Cronin

Stats   Red Sox • AL • Rank

Batting Avg:	.283	.266	1
On-Base Pct:	.366	.341	1
Slugging Pct:	.430	.389	1
Home Runs:	124		2
Stolen Bases:	67		3
ERA:	4.19	4.15	5
Fielding Pct:	.972	.972	4
Runs Scored:	865		1
Runs Allowed:	750		5

Starting Lineup

Frankie Pytlak, c
Jimmie Foxx, 1b
Bobby Doerr, 2b
Jim Tabor, 3b
Joe Cronin, ss
Ted Williams, lf
Dom DiMaggio, cf
Lou Finney, rf
Pete Fox, rf
Johnny Peacock, c
Skeeter Newsome, ss
Stan Spence, lf-rf

Pitchers

Dick Newsome, sp
Charlie Wagner, sp
Mickey Harris, sp-rp
Lefty Grove, sp
Joe Dobson, sp-rp
Earl Johnson, sp
Mike Ryba, rp
Jack Wilson, rp-sp

Attendance

718,497 (third in AL)

Club Leaders

Batting Avg:	Williams	.406
On-Base Pct:	Williams	.551
Slugging Pct:	Williams	.735
Home Runs:	Williams	37
RBI:	Williams	120
Runs:	Williams	135
Stolen Bases:	DiMaggio	13
Wins:	Newsome	19
Strikeouts:	Harris	111
ERA:	Wagner	3.07
Saves:	Ryba	6

FEBRUARY 3   The Red Sox sell Joe Heving to the Indians.

MARCH 17   Lefty Grove cuts the palm of his pitching hand while playing a practical joke on Ted Williams. Grove and some teammates tried to attach a firecracker under the hood of Williams's new Buick. The hood handle broke, and Lefty needed one stitch to close the wound. He pitched only three innings during the spring exhibition games but was ready by Opening Day.

MARCH 27   The Red Sox lose to a team of Cuban All-Stars in Havana, 2–1. During the following three days, the Sox played a three-game series against the Cincinnati Reds in Havana. The Sox won the first game 9–2 but lost the last two 6–3 and 2–1.

APRIL 15   Three days after the Boston Bruins win the Stanley Cup in a three-game sweep of the Detroit Red Wings, the Red Sox score three runs in the ninth inning to defeat the Senators 7–6 in the season opener before 17,500 at Fenway Park. The winning run scored on a bases-loaded walk to Joe Cronin. Cronin and Bobby Doerr both hit homers during the afternoon. Ted Williams had a pinch-hit single during the game-winning rally.

Williams started only one game during the first two weeks of the season because of a chipped bone in his ankle, suffered during a spring training game on March 17.

APRIL 16   The Red Sox score three runs in the ninth inning and one in the twelfth to defeat the Senators 8–7 at Fenway Park. The three ninth-inning runs scored on homers by Bobby Doerr and Jim Tabor. Pete Fox, playing in left field for the injured Ted Williams, drove in the winning run with a single.

Tabor drove in 101 runs in 1941.

APRIL 18   The Red Sox score two runs in the ninth inning to defeat the Athletics 3–2 in Philadelphia. Bobby Doerr accounted for all three Red Sox runs with a solo homer in the seventh inning and a two–run homer in the ninth. Lefty Grove pitched seven innings, and Herb Hash pitched two innings to put together a two-hitter. The only Philadelphia hits, both off of Grove, were a single by Dick Siebert and a home run by Sam Chapman.

Doerr hit four homers in the first three games of the season in 1941. He finished the season with 16 homers and a .282 batting average.

APRIL 20   The Red Sox clobber the Senators 14–8 in Washington.

The Sox started the season with five wins in their first five games but slipped below .500 in May and never seriously contended for the pennant.

APRIL 26   Down 7–0, the Red Sox rally with three runs in the third inning, four in the fifth, and one in the sixth to win 8–7 against the Athletics on a chilly, windswept day at Fenway Park. Bill Fleming pitched 6 1/3 innings of shutout relief and gave up just one hit.

MAY 1   The Red Sox collect 20 hits and maul the Tigers 15–9 in Detroit.

MAY 2   After going hitless in three at-bats during a 7–3 loss to the Indians in Cleveland, Ted Williams's batting average falls to .307. It was his lowest average of the 1941 season.

MAY 7   Ted Williams hits a homer in the eleventh inning to defeat the White Sox 4–3 in Chicago. The ball landed on the roof of the double-decked stands at Comiskey Park and bounced into the parking lot. It was Williams's second homer of the game.

MAY 11   The Red Sox score seven runs in the second inning to take a 9–2 lead and go on to defeat the 1941 World Champion Yankees 13–5 at Fenway Park.

MAY 14   Joe Cronin's grand slam off Pete Appleton highlights a seven-run seventh inning as the Red Sox defeat the White Sox 10–7 in Chicago.

Cronin hit .311 with 16 homers in 1941 but slowed considerably in the field. He frequently pulled himself out of games in the late innings in favor of defensive replacement Skeeter Newsome.

MAY 25   Ted Williams collects four hits in five at-bats during a 10–3 win over the Yankees in New York to push his batting average above .400 for the first time since April 29.

Williams would remain over the .400 mark until July.

MAY 30   After losing the first game of a doubleheader 4-3 in New York, the Red Sox rout the Yankees 13–0 in the second game, which featured a triple steal by the Red Sox. Skeeter Newsome stole home, Frank Pytlak stole third, and Mickey Harris went to second. The stolen base by Harris was the only one of his nine-year major league career.

JUNE 5   The Red Sox drub the Indians 14–1 in Cleveland.

JUNE 6   Ted Williams collects two hits in four at-bats during a 6–3 victory over the White Sox in Chicago to raise his batting average to .438, his highest during the 1941 season.

JUNE 8   Ted Williams extends his hitting streak to 23 games during a 5–4 loss to the White Sox in Chicago.

JUNE 17   The Red Sox score eight runs in the seventh inning and defeat the Tigers 14–6 in the first game of a doubleheader at Fenway Park. Detroit won the first game 8–5.

JUNE 19   The Red Sox sell Odell Hale to the Giants.

JUNE 24   Two days after Germany invades the Soviet Union, the Red Sox thrash the Indians 13–2 at Fenway Park. Jim Tabor hit a grand slam off Mel Harder in the third inning.

JUNE 29   Joe Cronin hits a grand slam in the third inning off Les McCrabb to lead the Red Sox to a 13–1 win over the Athletics in the first game of a doubleheader in Philadelphia. The Sox lost the second game, 3–2.

JUNE 30   The Red Sox purchase Nels Potter from the Athletics.

JULY 2   Joe DiMaggio collects a hit in his 45th consecutive game to break Willie Keeler's record for the longest hitting streak in major league history with a home run in the fifth inning off Dick Newsome of the Red Sox. The Yankees won the game 8–4 in New York.

DiMaggio's record-breaking streak ended at 56 games on July 17.

JULY 3   Lefty Grove wins the 299th game of his career with a 5–2 triumph over the Athletics in Philadelphia, where he played during his first nine years in the majors.

JULY 8   Ted Williams hits a dramatic two-out, three-run, ninth-inning home run in the All-Star Game to lift the American League to a 7–5 win at Briggs Stadium in Detroit. Williams gave the AL a 1–0 advantage in the fourth with an RBI double, but the NL led 5–2 in the eighth. Dom DiMaggio made it 5–3 in the bottom of the eighth by driving in his brother Joe with a single. With one out in the AL ninth, Claude Passeau of the Cubs loaded the bases on two singles and a walk. Joe DiMaggio hit into a force play at second base, which scored one run to make the score 5–4 and left runners on first and third. Williams brought both of them home with his home run, which struck the front of the roof of the double-decked stands in right field. Williams bounded happily around the bases laughing and clapping his hands.

JULY 12   Joe Cronin hits a grand slam off Dizzy Trout in the fourth inning of a 10–2 win over the Tigers in the second game of a doubleheader in Detroit. The Red Sox also won the first game, 7–5.

JULY 19   Ted Williams's batting average drops to .393 after a hitless at-bat as a pinch hitter during a 9–3 loss to the Browns in St. Louis.

JULY 23   At Fenway Park, White Sox manager Jimmy Dykes tries a shift against pull-hitting Ted Williams, deploying the shortstop to the right side of second, moving the third baseman into the vacant hole at short, and swinging the entire outfield around to the right so that the left fielder stood just to the left of center. Williams foiled the strategy by poking a double into left field. The White Sox won, 10–4. Dykes didn't try the shift again, nor did any other AL manager, until Lou Boudreau of the Indians deployed it five years later (see July 14, 1946).

JULY 24   Jim Tabor hits a grand slam off Bill Dietrich in the fifth inning of an 11–1 win over the White Sox at Fenway Park. Tabor also had a two-run double in the eighth to give him six RBIs on the day.

JULY 25   Lefty Grove wins the 300th game of his career with a complete-game 10–6 victory over the Indians at Fenway Park. It was Grove's third attempt to collect number 300. The Red Sox trailed 4–0 after Grove allowed a run in the second inning and two in the third. The Sox tied the score 4–4, only to fall behind again 6–4 when Grove surrendered two runs in the seventh. Boston came back once more with two runs in their half of the seventh on a Jim Tabor home run, then four more in the eighth. Jimmie Foxx broke the 6–6 tie with a two-run triple.

Grove made six more starts but failed to win another game. His final big-league appearance came on September 28, the last day of the season, when he pitched one inning and gave up three runs and four hits against the Athletics in Philadelphia. Grove was released by the Red Sox at the end of the 1941 season, and after failing to hook up with another club, decided to retire. He finished his career with a 300–141 record. His .680 winning percentage is the best of any of the 22 pitchers who have won at least 300 games.

JULY 31   Ted Williams hits a grand slam in the seventh inning off George Caster to give the Red Sox an 11–7 lead, but the Browns rally to win 16–11 in the first game of a doubleheader at Fenway Park. The Sox won the second game, shortened to 6½ innings by darkness, 4–1.

AUGUST 4   Jimmie Foxx hits a walk-off home run in the ninth inning to defeat the Athletics 7–6 at Fenway Park.

Foxx hit 19 homers, batted .300, and drove in 105 runs in 1941. The only players in major league history with 13 consecutive seasons of 100 or more runs batted in are Lou Gehrig (1926–38) and Jimmie Foxx (1929–41).

AUGUST 8   The Red Sox whip the Senators 15–8 at Fenway Park.

Among the new innovations in baseball in 1941 was the introduction of protective headgear for batters, which consisted of one-ounce plastic inserts that fit inside the players' caps. The first member of the Red Sox to wear these "helmets" was infielder Skeeter Newsome, who had been beaned in the head twice earlier in his career.

AUGUST 15   The Red Sox win a forfeit in Washington because the Senators failed to cover the field during a rainstorm. The game was stopped by a rain delay in the eighth inning with the Senators leading, 6–3. For some reason, the grounds crew didn't cover the infield, and the contest was called after forty minutes because the umpires deemed the field to be unplayable. Joe Cronin protested to American League president Will Harridge that the game could have been resumed if the tarp had been spread on the infield. Harridge agreed and forfeited the game to Boston.

AUGUST 19   Ted Williams hits three homers during a doubleheader against the Browns in St. Louis. Williams hit one homer in the first contest, a 3–2 Red Sox loss, and two in the second, won by Boston, 10–7.

AUGUST 20   Ted Williams hits homers in both games of a doubleheader in St. Louis for the second day in a row, but the Red Sox lose twice to the Browns 11–9 and 4–3 in 11 innings.

AUGUST 25   Charlie Wagner pitches a shutout to defeat Bob Feller and the Indians 1–0 in Cleveland. The lone run of the game scored in the seventh inning on a double by Frankie Pytlak.

Wagner was nicknamed "Broadway Charlie" because of his dapper dress and his way with the ladies.

SEPTEMBER 1   The Red Sox crush the Senators 13–9 and 10–2 during a doubleheader at Fenway Park. The Sox scored seven runs in the eighth inning of the first game. Ted Williams hit three homers during the afternoon.

Before the gates opened, Williams fired a revolver from a position behind the Red Sox bench and shot out the red globe that covered the first "out" light on the scoreboard. Shortly after the season ended, Williams came to Boston to sign his contract for 1942. This time, he brought two long-range rifles to Fenway and shot out all of the lights on the scoreboard. Williams also loved to shoot the many pigeons that roosted at Fenway Park, a passion he shared with Tom Yawkey. The activity came to a halt when the Humane Society got wind of the hunting expeditions inside the ballpark.

SEPTEMBER 4   During a 6–3 loss to the Yankees at Fenway Park, fourteen-year-old Billy Kane of South Brewer, Maine, sits on the Boston bench as a guest of Ted Williams.

Kane began hitchhiking from his home to Boston, a distance of 250 miles, three days earlier to see Williams play. He arrived on September 2, an off day for the Sox, and snuck into Fenway Park, where he fell asleep. Park policemen found young Kane while locking up for the night and took him to a station house nearby. The desk sergeant called Williams, who took Kane out for a meal and put him up at a hotel. With Kane on the bench, Williams went one for four with a single.

SEPTEMBER 9   The Red Sox defeat the Tigers 6–0 at Fenway Park. Dom DiMaggio hit a grand slam off Johnny Gorsica in the second inning, in addition to a triple and a double.

DiMaggio batted .283 and scored 117 runs in 1941.

SEPTEMBER 14   Jimmie Foxx hits a first-inning grand slam off Ted Lyons in the first game of a doubleheader at Fenway Park to lead the Red Sox to a 9–2 victory over the White Sox. Boston also won the second game, 5–1.

SEPTEMBER 17   A two-run single in the ninth inning by Dom DiMaggio defeats the Indians 3–2 at Fenway Park. DiMaggio also drove in the first Boston run with a single in the third. The victory was the eighth in a row for the Red Sox.

SEPTEMBER 23   Jimmie Foxx writes the wrong name on the lineup card before a 4–3 loss to the Senators in Washington. In his role as captain, it was Foxx's responsibility to fill out the card and take it to the umpires. Unfortunately, Foxx wrote Dick Newsome as the pitcher instead of intended starter Joe Dobson. According to the rules, Newsome had to pitch to one batter, and he did, retiring George Case before yielding to Dobson.

Newsome was the Red Sox' leading hurler in 1941 with a 19–10 record. He was a thirty-one-year-old rookie who started the season in the minors. The Red Sox purchased him from San Diego in the Pacific Coast League on May 9. He pitched two more seasons with the Red Sox and had a record of 16–23.

SEPTEMBER 24   Dom DiMaggio hits a grand slam off Dutch Leonard in the seventh inning of a 7–2 win over the Senators in Washington. The Sox also won the second game, 5–1.

Ted Williams had only one hit in seven at-bats during the two games to drop his batting average to .401, his lowest mark since July 25. The hit was an infield single on a controversial call by umpire Bill Grieve. Most observers believed the throw beat Williams to the bag. He had three games left to keep his average above .400. After two off days on September 25 and 26, the Red Sox closed the season in Philadelphia with a single game on September 27 and a doubleheader on September 28.

SEPTEMBER 27   The Red Sox defeat the Athletics 5–1 at Shibe Park, but Ted Williams goes one for four to drop his batting average to .39955. Philadelphia's rookie pitcher Roger Wolff threw nothing but knuckleballs to Williams. On one of the four trips to the plate, Williams struck out. He fanned only 27 times in 604 plate appearances in 1941.

Batting averages are rounded off to the nearest thousandth of a decimal point, so Williams's .39955 average went into the books as .400. Joe Cronin gave Williams the option of sitting out the final two games on September 28 to preserve his .400 average, but Williams insisted on playing. To put his average above .400 in the season-ending doubleheader, Williams would need at least three hits in seven at-bats or fewer, or he would need to collect at least four hits in nine at-bats or fewer. During the night of September 27 and early morning of the 28th, Williams walked the Philadelphia streets for hours with Red Sox clubhouse attendant Johnny Orlando to work off his nervous energy.

SEPTEMBER 28   Ted Williams collects six hits in eight at-bats during a doubleheader against the Athletics at Shibe Park to finish the 1941 season with a batting average of .406. Philadelphia manager Connie Mack told his pitchers to do all they could to get Williams out, but to throw strikes. Mack didn't want his pitchers being accused of keeping Williams from reaching the .400 mark by issuing walks. In the first game, won by the Red Sox 12–11, Williams had his first plate appearance in the second inning and hit a single his first time up on a 2–0 pitch against Dick Fowler. That lifted his average to .401. Williams came to bat the second time in the fifth inning. On a 1–0 pitch, Williams drove the ball 440 feet over the right field fence. His average was now .402. In the sixth, Williams singled on a 2–0 pitch facing left-hander Porter Vaughan that all but secured an average of .400 or better on the season. Another single came in the seventh to raise his average to .405 and erase all doubt. In the ninth inning, in his fifth and final at-bat, Williams reached base on an error. In the second contest a 7–1 loss stopped by darkness after eight innings, Williams hit a single and a double. The two-bagger off Fred Caliguri crashed through a loudspeaker on top of the right field wall at Shibe Park over the 460-foot sign.

                Williams finished the season with 185 hits in 456 at-bats. He also had 37 homers, drove in 120 runs, and scored 135. Despite his great season, Williams finished second to Joe DiMaggio in the Most Valuable Player Award voting conducted by the Baseball Writers' Association of America.

DECEMBER 10   Three days after Japan's attack on Pearl Harbor, two days after the United States declares war on Japan, and the day before the declaration of war against Germany and Italy, the Red Sox purchase Mace Brown from the Dodgers.

DECEMBER 13   The Red Sox trade Stan Spence and Jack Wilson to the Senators for Ken Chase and Johnny Welaj.

                This trade worked out badly for the Red Sox, as Spence appeared in four All-Star Games while playing for the Senators.

1942   B

Season in a Sentence

The Red Sox win 93 games, the most by the club since 1915, but still can't compete with the Yankees.

Finish • Won • Lost • Pct • GB

Second   93   59   .612   9.0

Manager

Joe Cronin

Stats

Stats	Red Sox	AL	Rank
Batting Avg:	.276	.257	1
On-Base Pct:	.352	.329	1
Slugging Pct:	.403	.357	1
Home Runs:	103		2
Stolen Bases:	69		5
ERA:	3.44	3.66	3
Fielding Pct:	.974	.971	2
Runs Scored:	761		2
Runs Allowed:	594		3

Starting Lineup

Bill Conroy, c
Tony Lupien, 1b
Bobby Doerr, 2b
Jim Tabor, 3b
Johnny Pesky, ss
Ted Williams, lf
Dom DiMaggio, cf
Lou Finney, rf
Johnny Peacock, c
Pete Fox, rf

Pitchers

Tex Hughson, sp
Charlie Wagner, sp
Joe Dobson, sp
Dick Newsome, sp
Oscar Judd, sp-rp
Yank Terry, sp-rp
Ken Chase, sp
Bill Butland, rp-sp

Attendance

730,340 (second in AL)

Club Leaders

Batting Avg:	Williams	.356
On-Base Pct:	Williams	.499
Slugging Pct:	Williams	.648
Home Runs:	Williams	36
RBI:	Williams	137
Runs:	Williams	141
Stolen Bases:	DiMaggio	16
Wins:	Hughson	22
Strikeouts:	Hughson	113
ERA:	Hughson	2.59
Saves:	Brown	6

JANUARY 15   President Franklin Roosevelt gives baseball commissioner Kenesaw Mountain Landis the go-ahead to play ball despite the nation's involvement in World War II, precipitated by Japan's attack on Pearl Harbor five weeks earlier. In his statement, Roosevelt said he believed that the continuation of the sport would be beneficial to the country's morale.

> *There were five members of the 1941 Red Sox in military uniforms by the start of the 1942 season. They were pitchers Mickey Harris, Emerson Dickman, and Earl Johnson, catcher Frankie Pytlak, and first baseman Al Flair. Johnson enlisted right after the attack on Pearl Harbor and was a highly decorated veteran of World War II. He returned to the Red Sox in 1946 with a Silver Star, Bronze Star, and a cluster for heroism earned during the Battle of the Bulge after braving enemy fire to save a jeep that carried needed electronic equipment.*

FEBRUARY 27   President Franklin Roosevelt rules on the draft status of Ted Williams. Williams had been reclassified in early January from 3-A, a designation he received as the sole financial support of his mother, to 1-A, making him eligible for the draft. The decision was made by Williams's draft board in Princeton, Minnesota, where he spent his winters. Roosevelt changed Williams's draft status back to 3-A. In instructions to General Lewis Hershey, head of the Selective Service Board, the president said that being eligible for the draft would place "undue hardship" on Williams.

Williams bore considerable criticism from fans for the change because many believed he was receiving preferential treatment. A week later, he said that he would enlist as soon as the baseball season was over. He enlisted as a Navy aviation cadet on May 22 and entered the service in November 1942.

APRIL 14   In the season opener, Ted Williams hits a three-run homer in his first at-bat and later adds two singles in an 8–3 win over the Athletics before 9,901 at Fenway Park.

The game was played five days after the fall of Bataan, one of the many shocking military defeats suffered at the hands of Japan early in 1942. Four days after the opener, Major General James Doolittle staged a daring air raid on Tokyo.

APRIL 16   The Red Sox collect 21 hits and wallop the Athletics 19–4 at Fenway Park to complete a sweep in the opening three-game series of the season.

APRIL 22   The Red Sox swamp the Senators 13–4 in Washington.

MAY 2   The Red Sox stage a three-run rally in the ninth inning to defeat the Browns 11–10 at Fenway Park. Ted Williams tied the score 10–10 with a two-run homer that soared 450 feet into the right-center field bleachers. Bobby Doerr doubled in the game winner.

Williams won the Triple Crown in 1942 by leading the American League in batting average (.356), home runs (36), and runs batted in (137). He also led the AL in runs scored, with 141, and collected 186 hits. Despite his great season, Williams was robbed of the Most Valuable Player Award by finishing second in the balloting to Yankee second baseman Joe Gordon.

MAY 5   The Red Sox bombard the Indians 13–3 at Fenway Park.

MAY 6   At Fenway Park against the White Sox, Bobby Doerr ties the score 1–1 with a homer in the eighth inning and wins the game 3–1 with a two-run, walk-off homer in the eleventh. Both came off future Hall of Fame pitcher Ted Lyons.

In 1942, Doerr batted .290, hit 15 homers, and drove in 102 runs.

MAY 23   Prior to a 4–3 loss to the Athletics at Fenway Park, two service teams meet in a five-inning game. A squad from the Newport, Rhode Island, Naval Training Station, which featured Bob Feller, played a team from Fort Devens, Massachusetts, led by pitcher Hugh Mulcahy of the Phillies, who was the first major leaguer drafted by the military in 1941. Fort Devens won, 5–0. All of the gate receipts and concession sales went to the Army-Navy Relief fund. The crowd of 12,216 contributed $13,221.

MAY 24   Just before the Sunday curfew, the Red Sox score four runs in the eighth inning to defeat the Athletics 6–5 in the second game of a doubleheader at Fenway Park. The Sox lost the first game by the same 6–5 score.

MAY 25   While pitching batting practice before a game at Yankee Stadium, Jimmie Foxx suffers a broken rib when struck by a line drive off the bat of Tony Lupien.

The rib injury followed a beaning Foxx suffered during the 1941–42 offseason when he was struck by a pitch from Negro Leagues hurler Chet Brewer during an exhibition game. In spring training and the early weeks of the 1942 season, Foxx and Lupien battled for the starting first base job. Although Lupien's aim was unintentional, it was certainly an effective way to earn a spot in the lineup. Six days after the injury, Foxx was sold to the Cubs. Lupien, whose given name was Ulysses John, was born in Chelmsford, Massachusetts, and had a degree from Harvard University.

MAY 29   The Red Sox romp to a 14–2 win over the Athletics in Philadelphia. Ted Williams drove in seven runs on a two-run homer, a single, and a grand-slam homer off Dick Fowler in the eighth inning.

MAY 30   Dom DiMaggio collects seven hits, including two doubles, in 10 at-bats during a doubleheader against the Athletics in Philadelphia. The Red Sox won the first game 10–6 but lost the second, 5–4.

MAY 31   The Red Sox sweep the Senators 11–1 and 4–3 at Fenway Park. The second game ended after $7\frac{1}{2}$ innings because of the Sunday curfew.

JUNE 1   The Red Sox sell Jimmie Foxx to the Cubs.

The Sox correctly presumed that Foxx, at 34, was finished as an everyday player. He concluded his career in Boston with a .320 batting average, 222 home runs, 788 RBIs, and 720 runs scored. After he left the Red Sox, Foxx had 449 more at-bats in the majors through 1945 and hit just .229 with 10 homers. He even tried pitching, hurling nine games for the Phillies in 1945. Foxx had serious financial problems after he left baseball and died at age fifty-nine while choking on a piece of meat on a visit with his brother in Miami.

JUNE 6   The only four hits the Red Sox get off Orval Grove of the White Sox are a single, double, triple, and homer in a 3–1 loss at Fenway Park. Dom DiMaggio led off the first inning with a homer. Later in the contest, Bill Conroy tripled, Jim Tabor doubled, and Johnny Pesky singled.

JUNE 7   The day after America's victory over Japan in the Battle of Midway, the Red Sox win an exciting doubleheader over the White Sox, both by 3–2 scores, at Fenway Park. In the first game, Bobby Doerr and Jim Tabor both hit homers in the ninth inning to erase a 2–1 Chicago lead. The Red Sox scored a run in the eighth inning of the second tilt to take a 3–2 advantage. Because of the Sunday sports law, the game had to end at precisely 6:30 PM. With that time approaching, White Sox manager Jimmy Dykes tried to prolong the contest as long as possible. If the eighth didn't end before six thirty, the entire inning would be wiped out and the game would have gone into the books as a seven-inning 2–2 tie. With the crowd in an uproar, Dykes changed pitchers three times and was prevented from making a fourth change only because the umpires threatened a forfeit.

Dykes was fined $250 by American League president Will Harridge for the stalling tactics.

JUNE 11   The Red Sox spot the Browns a 5–0 lead at Fenway Park but battle back to win, 8–7.

JUNE 13   Pesky collects five hits, including a double, in five at-bats leading the Red Sox to a
               6–5 win over the Tigers at Fenway Park.

               *Pesky was born on September 27, 1919, the date that Babe Ruth played his last
               game with the Red Sox.*

The great double-play combination of Bobby Doerr, and Johnny Pesky turns two against the Yankees.

JUNE 19   The Red Sox defeat the White Sox 1–0 at Comiskey Park on a freak inside-the-park
               homer by Dom DiMaggio. In the fifth inning, DiMaggio hit a ball into right field
               that rolled under the bench in the Boston bullpen. By the time Chicago right fielder
               Wally Moses retrieved the ball, DiMaggio had circled the bases. Charlie Wagner
               pitched the shutout.

               DiMaggio hit .286 with 110 runs scored and 36 doubles in 1942.

JUNE 24   Ted Williams hits a seventh-inning homer to defeat the Tigers 1–0 in Detroit.
               Charlie Wagner pitched the shutout, his second 1–0 victory in as many starts.

JULY 1   The Red Sox drop the Yankees' lead in the pennant race to three games by sweeping
               the Senators 3–2 and 7–1 in a doubleheader at Fenway Park. Ted Williams was pulled

from the second game in the fifth inning for what Joe Cronin termed "a rest." The fans were riding Williams throughout the afternoon. Cronin yanked him from the contest when he drilled a double into right field and loafed getting to second base.

By the end of July, the Red Sox were 12 games behind the Yankees. The Sox won 34 of their last 44 games but could get no closer than 7½ games of the Yanks.

JULY 3   The Red Sox–Yankees game begins at 6:00 PM, the first twilight home contest ever at Fenway Park. The 1942 American League champion Yankees won, 5–3.

JULY 15   The Red Sox score seven runs in the eighth inning and defeat the White Sox 10–1 in the first game of a doubleheader at Fenway Park. Chicago won the second game 11–6.

JULY 19   Pitcher Mike Ryba catches in both ends of a doubleheader loss to the Indians at Fenway Park. The Sox lost the first game 10–7 and the second 4–0 when it was stopped after seven innings by the Boston Sunday sports law.

Ryba is one of the few individuals in major league history to play as both a pitcher and a catcher. He played for the Browns from 1935 through 1938 and the Red Sox from 1941 through 1946. Ryba appeared in 240 games as a pitcher and 10 as a catcher.

JULY 25   The Red Sox collect 20 hits and defeat the Browns 9–8 in St. Louis. Tony Lupien had five hits, including a triple and two doubles, in six at-bats.

AUGUST 15   A two-run triple in the ninth inning by Lou Finney beats the Senators 7–6 in the second game of a doubleheader at Fenway Park. The Red Sox also won the first game, 2–1.

During a stretch in August and September, the Red Sox won 22 of 25 games.

AUGUST 22   The Red Sox pound the Athletics 11–3 and 11–5 in a doubleheader in Philadelphia.

AUGUST 23   Behind the pitching of Tex Hughson and Joe Dobson, the Red Sox shut out the Athletics in both ends of a twin bill in Philadelphia, 2–0 and 7–0. In the second game, fans in the left field stands at Shibe Park showered Ted Williams with garbage. Police were called in to quell the disturbance. Williams left the contest in the ninth inning for his own protection. The gate receipts were donated to the Army-Navy Relief Fund. The crowd of 26,014 witnessed a display of America's military might between games, staged by mechanized Troop A of the United States Cavalry stationed in Philadelphia. It included a display of armored scout cars, two-way radios, jeeps, and motorcycles.

Dobson was the youngest of 14 children of a Durrant, Texas, family. At the age of nine, he lost his left thumb and forefinger playing with a dynamite cap.

AUGUST 26   The Red Sox win their ninth game in a row by beating the Indians 4–1 at Fenway Park.

Johnny Pesky, whose given name was John Paveskovitch, took over at shortstop for Joe Cronin in 1942 and had a sensational rookie season. Pesky batted .331, collected 205 hits, and scored 105 runs. He was part of an overall youth movement. The Red Sox finished second to the Yankees in 1942 for the fourth time in five years, but the club was almost completely made over from the second-place

*team of 1938. The only player who was a regular on both the 1938 and 1942
clubs was Bobby Doerr. The 1942 team included such young stars as Ted
Williams (age 23), Pesky (22), Doerr (24), Dom DiMaggio (25), Tony Lupien
(25), Jim Tabor (25), Joe Dobson (25), and Tex Hughson (26). World War II
prevented Boston from enjoying what might have been a baseball dynasty, as
most of them spent time in military service. Williams, DiMaggio, and Pesky each
missed the 1943, 1944, and 1945 seasons; Dobson 1944 and 1945; and Doerr
and Hughson part of 1944 and all of 1945.*

SEPTEMBER 11   The Red Sox have a field day in downing the Indians 15–3 in Cleveland.

*Tom Carey spent the entire season on the Red Sox roster in 1942 but played in
only one game. His lone appearance was in July as a late-inning defensive replacement at second. He singled in his only at-bat to finish the season with a 1.000
batting average. Carey spent the next three seasons in the service and didn't play
in another major league game until 1946.*

SEPTEMBER 17   Tex Hughson earns his 20th victory of the season by defeating the Browns 5–1 in
St. Louis.

*Playing in his first full season in the majors, Hughson had a 22–6 record in 1942
with a 2.59 ERA. He led the league in wins, complete games (22), innings pitched
(281), and strikeouts (113).*

SEPTEMBER 27   On the final day of the season, a Fenway Park crowd of 26,166, including 4,293
youngsters who gained free admission by bringing 29,000 pounds of scrap metal for
the war effort, watches the Red Sox beat the Yankees, 7–6. It was Ted Williams's
last appearance in a major league game until 1946.

NOVEMBER 28   Before an overflow football crowd of 42,000 at Fenway Park, Holy Cross pulls off
a shocking upset by defeating previously unbeaten Boston College 55–12.

*Many of those who attended the game at Fenway went directly to the Coconut
Grove, a popular night club in Boston. That night, a fire broke out at the
Coconut Grove that resulted in the deaths of 487 people.*

DECEMBER 28   The Red Sox announce that spring training in 1943 will be conducted at Tufts College
in Medford, Massachusetts. Teams had been ordered by Commissioner Kenesaw
Mountain Landis to train north of the Ohio River and east of the Mississippi River
to save on travel expenses.

*A new training camp wasn't the only contingency plan the Red Sox had to
come up with in 1943 due to World War II. The club had to find a whole new
starting outfield, as Ted Williams and Dom DiMaggio went into the service and
Lou Finney retired to tend to his farm in Buffalo, Alabama (Finney returned to
the Sox in 1944). Shortstop Johnny Pesky also went into the service, along with
Mickey Harris, Charlie Wagner, Bill Butland, Paul Campbell, Tom Carey, and
Andy Gilbert. No team in baseball was hit harder by World War II than the
Red Sox. After a 93-win season in 1942, the Sox won only 68 in 1943, 77 in
1944, and 71 in 1945. After the players returned from the service in 1946,
Boston posted 104 victories and won the AL pennant.*

1943   B

Season in a Sentence

With Ted Williams, Dom DiMaggio, and Johnny Pesky wearing military uniforms instead of baseball uniforms, the Red Sox fall to seventh place.

Finish • Won • Lost • Pct • GB

Seventh   68   84   .447 29.0

Manager

Joe Cronin

Stats   Red Sox • AL • Rank

Stats	Red Sox	AL	Rank
Batting Avg:	.244	.249	7
On-Base Pct:	.308	.322	7
Slugging Pct:	.332	.341	6
Home Runs:	57		4
Stolen Bases:	86		3
ERA:	3.45	3.30	7
Fielding Pct:	.976	.973	1
Runs Scored:	563		7
Runs Allowed:	607		7

Starting Lineup

Roy Partee, c
Tony Lupien, 1b
Bobby Doerr, 2b
Jim Tabor, 3b
Skeeter Newsome, ss
Johnny Lazor, lf
Leon Culberson, cf
Pete Fox, rf
Catfish Metkovich, cf-rf
Eddie Lake, ss

Pitchers

Tex Hughson, sp
Yank Terry, sp
Dick Newsome, sp
Joe Dobson, sp
Oscar Judd, sp
Pinky Woods, sp-rp
Mike Ryba, rp
Mace Brown, rp

Attendance

358,275 (sixth in AL)

Club Leaders

Batting Avg:	Fox	.288
On-Base Pct:	Doerr	.339
Slugging Pct:	Doerr	.412
Home Runs:	Doerr	16
RBI:	Tabor	85
Runs:	Doerr	78
Stolen Bases:	Fox	22
Wins:	Hughson	12
Strikeouts:	Hughson	114
ERA:	Hughson	2.64
Saves:	Brown	9

APRIL 21   Three months after Franklin Roosevelt and Winston Churchill begin meetings in Casablanca, Morocco, to formulate strategy for the war in Europe, the scheduled season opener between the Red Sox and Athletics in Philadelphia is postponed by inclement weather.

APRIL 22   There are only five hits in the season opener as the Red Sox defeat the Athletics 1–0 in Philadelphia. Tex Hughson pitched a three-hit shutout. Still, the Sox collected only two hits off of Jesse Flores. Pete Fox came around to score the lone run of the game after hitting a double in the fourth inning.

The Red Sox didn't put the uniforms numbers of their top players into mothballs when they left for the service during World War II. Lou Finney, Hal Wagner, and Johnny Peacock wore Ted Williams's number 9. Ty LaForest was given Bobby Doerr's number 1 in 1945. Eddie Lake took Dom DiMaggio's number 7.

APRIL 27   In the first game of the season at Fenway Park, the Red Sox beat the Yankees 5–1 before a crowd of 6,895.

Tom Yawkey closed the parking lot adjacent to Fenway Park "in the interest of the national gasoline rationing program." Gasoline was rationed to civilians during World War II to preserve oil for use by the military.

MAY 5   The Red Sox score two runs to tie the Yankees 3–3 in the top of the ninth in New York, then lose 4–3 when rookie pitcher Andy Karl commits a bases-loaded balk in the bottom half. Future Hall of Famer Al Simmons tied the score with a home run in the top of the ninth.

The home run would be Simmons's last of his career, number 307. At the age of forty-one, Simmons provided little help to the Red Sox with a .203 batting average in 40 games.

MAY 27   Two weeks after Germany surrenders North Africa, Bobby Doerr drives in both Red Sox runs with a single in the fifth inning of a 2–0 win over the Indians in the first game of a doubleheader at Fenway Park. Tex Hughson pitched the shutout. The Sox completed the sweep with a 4–3 victory in the second tilt.

MAY 31   The Red Sox win both ends of a doubleheader in extra innings against the Browns at Fenway. Boston won the first game 2–1 in 13 innings and the second 7–6 with two runs in the tenth after St. Louis scored a run in their half.

The Red Sox played a club-record 31 extra-inning games in 1943.

JUNE 2   After their June 1 game is postponed by rain, the Red Sox and Browns play another doubleheader at Fenway Park in which both games are decided in extra innings. St. Louis won the first game 7–4 in 12 innings, and Boston took the second 3–2 in 10.

JUNE 6   The Red Sox score three runs in the ninth to beat the White Sox 4–3 in the first game of a doubleheader at Fenway Park. Boston completed the sweep with a 3–2 triumph in the nightcap.

JUNE 13   Ken Chase walks 11 batters during a four-inning relief stint as the Red Sox lose 16–5 to the Senators in the first game of a doubleheader at Fenway Park. The Sox won the second contest, 7–0.

The Sox traded Chase to the Giants the following day.

JUNE 17   Player-manager Joe Cronin hits a three-run pinch-hit home run in each game of a doubleheader on Bunker Hill Day against the Athletics at Fenway Park. In the first game, Cronin inserted himself into the game batting for Lou Lucier with the Sox trailing 4–1 and two runners on in the seventh inning. He tied the score with a homer off Russ Christopher, and the Red Sox went on to win 5–4 with a run in the ninth. In the second tilt, Cronin pinch hit for Mike Ryba and hit another homer with two on base in the eighth, facing Don Black. Boston lost, 8–7.

Cronin had hit another three-run, pinch-hit homer against the Athletics two days earlier. He had five pinch-hit homers during the 1943 season, which still stands as the American League record. They were also the only five pinch-hit homers of Cronin's 20-year playing career. Overall, he was 18 for 42 as a pinch hitter in 1943, a batting average of .429.

JUNE 23   Leon Culberson hits a fourth-inning homer off Don Black of the Athletics for a 1–0 Red Sox win in Philadelphia. Oscar Judd (8 2/3 innings) and Mace Brown (one-third of an inning) combined on the shutout.

During the evening, there was a mandatory blackout in Philadelphia as part of the Civilian Defense program. In the sixth inning, the lights were turned off at Shibe Park, which stopped the game for sixty-five minutes.

JULY 3   Leon Culberson hits for the cycle and draws a walk during a 12–4 win over the Indians in Cleveland. The Red Sox scored seven runs in the ninth inning.

JULY 12   Ted Williams plays on a service all-star team in an exhibition game against the Braves at Fenway Park. Williams's teammates included Joe DiMaggio and forty-eight-year-old Babe Ruth. The Babe appeared as a pinch hitter in the eighth inning and flied out. Williams hit a home run to lead his team to a 9–8 victory.

JULY 13   Bobby Doerr hits a three-run homer in the second inning to lead the American League to a 5–3 victory in the All-Star Game at Shibe Park in Philadelphia.

Doerr hit .270 with 16 homers and played in every inning of every game in 1943.

JULY 23   Trailing 7–1, the Red Sox score one in the fifth inning, two in the eighth, three in the ninth, and one in the tenth to win 8–7 against the White Sox in the first game of a doubleheader at Fenway Park. Chicago won the second game, 5–1.

AUGUST 11 The Red Sox score seven runs in the eighth inning and defeat the White Sox 10–0 in Chicago.

AUGUST 24 Dick Newsome pitches a two-hitter in a 7–0 win over the Indians in the second game of a doubleheader in Cleveland. The only two hits off Newsome were singles by Roy Cullenbine and Hank Edwards. Cleveland won the first game, 5–2.

SEPTEMBER 19   Two weeks after the beginning of the Allied invasion of the Italian mainland, the Red Sox go from one extreme to the other during a doubleheader against the Athletics in Philadelphia, winning the first game 14–0 and losing the second 6–1. Rookie outfielder Ford Garrison collected seven hits, including a double and a triple, in nine at-bats.

SEPTEMBER 23   The Red Sox divide a doubleheader against the Indians at Fenway Park, winning 13–7 and losing 6–4. Ford Garrison had another great doubleheader with six hits, including a double and a homer, in 10 at-bats.

SEPTEMBER 24   The Red Sox beat the Indians 1–0 in 10 innings at Fenway Park. Tony Lupien drove in the winning run with a single. Joe Dobson pitched a two-hitter for Boston. The only Cleveland hits were singles by Lou Boudreau and Otis Hockett.

SEPTEMBER 26   Jim Tabor hits a walk-off homer in the tenth inning to beat the Tigers 3–2 in the first game of a doubleheader at Fenway Park. The Sox completed the sweep with a 6–2 win in the second tilt.

SEPTEMBER 27   Only 714 fans attend a 6–3 loss to the Tigers at Fenway Park.

DECEMBER 4   The Red Sox purchase Bob Johnson from the Senators.

> *Johnson was thirty-seven years old when the Red Sox acquired him, but he provided the club with much-needed batting punch in the outfield in 1944 with a .324 batting average, 17 homers, 40 doubles, 106 RBIs, and 106 runs. Because he was part Cherokee, Johnson was nicknamed "Indian Bob." His brother Roy played for the Red Sox from 1932 through 1935.*

1944   B

Season in a Sentence

The best offense in the league is balanced by the worst pitching staff and results in a .500 record.

Finish • Won • Lost • Pct • GB

Fourth   77   77   .500 12.0

Manager

Joe Cronin

Stats

Stats	Red Sox	AL	Rank
Batting Avg:	.270	.260	1
On-Base Pct:	.336	.325	1
Slugging Pct:	.380	.353	2
Home Runs:	69		4
Stolen Bases:	60		5
ERA:	3.82	3.43	8
Fielding Pct:	.972	.971	3
Runs Scored:	739		1
Runs Allowed:	676		7

Starting Lineup

Roy Partee, c
Lou Finney, 1b
Bobby Doerr, 2b
Jim Tabor, 3b
Skeeter Newsome, ss
Bob Johnson, lf
Catfish Metkovich, cf
Pete Fox, rf
Leon Culberson, cf
Jim Bucher, 3b-2b
Hal Wagner, c
Tom McBride, lf-rf-cf
Joe Cronin, 1b

Pitchers

Ted Hughson, sp
Joe Bowman, sp
Emmett O'Neill, sp
Pinky Woods, sp-rp
Yank Terry, sp
Mike Ryba, rp
Frank Barrett, rp
Clem Hausmann, rp-sp

Attendance

506,975 (sixth in AL)

Club Leaders

Batting Avg:	Doerr	.325
On-Base Pct:	Johnson	.431
Slugging Pct:	Johnson	.528
Home Runs:	Johnson	17
RBI:	Johnson	106
Runs:	Johnson	106
Stolen Bases:	Metkovich	13
Wins:	Hughson	18
Strikeouts:	Hughson	112
ERA:	Hughson	2.26
Saves:	Barrett	8

APRIL 18   In the season opener, the Red Sox lose 3–0 to the Yankees in New York before 8,520 at Fenway Park. Hank Borowy pitched the shutout.

Members of the 1943 Red Sox who were in the military by the start of the 1944 season included pitchers Bill Donovan, Ray Martin, and Lou Tost; infielder Johnny McCarthy; and outfielder Sam Gentile. None of those players was a regular, but before the 1944 campaign was over, the Sox lost starters Bobby Doerr, Jim Tabor, and Hal Wagner plus pitching ace Tex Hughson to the military.

APRIL 25   The Red Sox whip the Senators in a 5–4, 14-inning battle in Washington. The winning run was driven in on a single by pinch hitter Joe Bowman that scored Bobby Doerr.

Bowman was a pitcher but hit well enough to accumulate 109 pinch-hit at-bats during an 11-year major league career.

MAY 1   George Myatt of the Senators collects six hits in six at-bats during an 11–4 win over the Red Sox at Fenway Park.

MAY 3   The Red Sox beat the Senators 11–10 in a slugfest at Fenway Park.

MAY 7   The Red Sox trade Ford Garrison to the Athletics for Hal Wagner.

MAY 17   Bobby Doerr hits for the cycle, although the Red Sox lose 12–8 to the Browns in the second game of a doubleheader at Fenway Park. Boston pitchers combined for 14 walks in the defeat. The Sox won the first game, 5–1.

Doerr left for the Army in September after hitting .325 with 15 homers and 95 runs scored in 1944. Pete Fox hit .315 with 38 doubles for the Sox that season, and Jim Tabor batted .285 and swatted 13 homers.

MAY 18   The Red Sox trounce the Browns 12–1 at Fenway Park.

MAY 19   A walk-off single by relief pitcher Mike Ryba with the bases loaded in the twelfth inning beats the White Sox 3–2 at Fenway Park.

MAY 20   The Red Sox score a run on a triple play during an 8–1 win over the White Sox at Fenway Park. With the bases loaded in the first inning, Leon Culberson scored from third on Bob Johnson's grounder to shortstop Jimmy Webb, which was relayed to second baseman Roy Schalk and first baseman Hal Trosky for two outs. Catfish Metkovich, who was at second base at the start of the play, tried to score and was out on a throw from Trosky to catcher Tom Turner.

MAY 26   Nels Potter of the Browns retires the first 23 Boston batters he faces, but the Red Sox come back from a 2–0 deficit to score a run in the eighth inning, another in the ninth, and two more in the eleventh to win 4–2 in St. Louis.

JUNE 1   Catfish Metkovich hits a two-out, three-run homer in the ninth inning to beat the Indians 7–6 in Cleveland.

Metkovich had a 25-game hitting streak in 1944, the longest by a Red Sox player between Tris Speaker's 30-game streak in 1912 and one of 26 games by Johnny Pesky in 1947.

JUNE 3   Two days before Allied troops enter Rome, infielder Jim Bucher drives in six runs during an 11–1 win over the Tigers in Detroit. Bucher drove in two on a bases-loaded single in the second inning, and four on a grand slam off Chief Hogsett in the ninth.

Due to a shortage of pitching talent, the Red Sox used shortstop Eddie Lake as a reliever in six games in 1944. Lake had a 0–0 record and a 4.19 ERA in $19\frac{1}{3}$ innings. In an exhibition game on August 24, Lake pitched a complete game against an all-star team of soldiers at Fort Monmouth, New Jersey, winning, 9–7.

JUNE 6   All major league games are postponed in observance of the D-Day landing in France. President Franklin Roosevelt urged Americans to spend the day in prayer at home or in church.

JUNE 15   The Red Sox win their ninth game in a row with an 8–1 decision over the Athletics at Fenway Park.

On June 18, the Red Sox were 31–25 and in second place, only one-half game behind the Browns in a tightly bunched American League pennant race. Boston's pennant express was slowed by six losses in the next seven games.

JUNE 30   The Red Sox pound out an 11–0 win over the White Sox at Fenway Park.

JULY 2   The Red Sox win 1–0 and 4–3 in 11 innings for a doubleheader sweep of the Browns at Fenway Park. Tex Hughson pitched the shutout in the opener.

JULY 6   Bob Johnson hits for the cycle as the Red Sox rout the Tigers 13–3 at Fenway Park. Johnson was taken out of the game in the seventh inning by manager Joe Cronin to give him a rest. The Sox collected 20 hits.

JULY 8   After the Indians score four runs in the top of the first, the Red Sox counter with five tallies in their half of the inning and six more in the second, then coast to an 11–7 triumph at Fenway Park.

JULY 23   The Red Sox score seven runs in the second inning and overpower the Browns 12–1 in the first game of a doubleheader against the Browns at Sportsman's Park. St. Louis won the second game, 9–3.

JULY 28   The Red Sox roll to a 15–5 win over the Tigers in Detroit.

JULY 30   Red Sox pitcher Pinky Woods walks 10 batters, hits another, throws a wild pitch, and loses a 3–2 decision to the Indians in Cleveland when he allows a run in the ninth inning.

JULY 31   The Red Sox collect only two hits but beat the Indians 1–0 in Cleveland. Pete Fox drove in the lone run of the game with a single in the ninth inning. Mike Ryba (eight innings) and Frank Barrett (one inning) combined on the shutout.

AUGUST 4   Emmett O'Neill pitches a two-hitter to beat the Senators 4–0 in the second game of a doubleheader at Fenway Park. The only Washington hits were singles by Gil Torres and Joe Kuhel.

AUGUST 9   Tex Hughson pitches his last game for the duration of World War II and defeats the White Sox 9–1 at Fenway Park.

                 Hughson volunteered for duty in the Navy. He had a terrific season in 1944, with a record of 18–5 and an ERA of 2.26.

AUGUST 12   On a 101 degree day in Boston, the Red Sox defeat the White Sox 5–4 at Fenway Park.

AUGUST 13   Red Sox pitcher Rex Cecil makes a successful major league debut as the winning pitcher in a 13-inning, 7–6 decision over the Browns in the first game of a doubleheader at Fenway Park. St. Louis won the second game 6–1.

                 Cecil came from the San Diego Padres of the Pacific Coast League. He barely made it to Fenway in time for the Sunday-afternoon game following a hectic coast-to-coast trip. On Friday, Cecil was tossed off a plane in Tucson, Arizona, because of military priorities. After several hours walking the streets in search of lodging, he finally got a flight Saturday afternoon and arrived in Boston on Sunday. The secretary of general manager Eddie Collins met Cecil at the Boston airport and hustled him into a taxicab. When he arrived at Fenway, it was the first time he had ever been in a major league ballpark. With almost no sleep during the previous forty-eight hours, Cecil made his big-league debut, entering the contest in the tenth inning with the score 6–6 and the temperature reading 100 degrees. He pitched four shutout innings for the win. Cecil had little more success in the majors, however. He finished his career with a 6–10 record and a 5.18 ERA.

SEPTEMBER 2   Eight days after Allied troops liberate Paris, Roy Partee's walk-off, bases-loaded single in the ninth inning scores two runs to beat the Athletics 6–5 at Fenway Park.

                 The win put the Red Sox $1\frac{1}{2}$ games behind the first-place Browns in a four-way race for the AL flag. The Sox were in fourth place. The Tigers and Yankees were tied for second one game back from the Browns.

SEPTEMBER 18   The Red Sox score eight runs in the eighth inning of an 11–5 win over the Senators in Washington.

                 Three games out of first place with two weeks left on the schedule, the Red Sox still had pennant aspirations, but the bubble burst with a 10-game losing streak that began on September 19.

SEPTEMBER 26   A National Football League team called the Boston Yanks plays its first game at Fenway Park and loses 28–7 to the Philadelphia Eagles before 19,851 on a Tuesday night.

                 The NFL franchise was owned by Ted Collins. It lasted five seasons in Boston, posting a record of 14–38–3. Meager crowds at Fenway forced Collins to move the club to New York after the 1948 season. Through many relocations and name changes, the former Boston Yanks franchise is now the Indianapolis Colts. Before reaching Indiana in 1984, the club was the New York Bulldogs in 1949, the New York Yanks in 1950 and 1951, the Dallas Texans in 1952, and the Baltimore Colts from 1953 through 1983.

SEPTEMBER 28 Catfish Metkovich scores five runs during an 11–2 win over the White Sox at Fenway Park.

NOVEMBER 4 Franklin Roosevelt gives his final campaign speech at Fenway Park. Facing Thomas Dewey, Roosevelt was seeking his fourth term as president. Three days later, Roosevelt won the election.

DECEMBER 25 Tom Yawkey marries Jean Hiller in a simple ceremony before a judge and two witnesses in Georgetown, South Carolina. Yawkey divorced his first wife, Elise, in November in Reno, Nevada. Elise married wealthy businessman Harry Dorsey Watts on December 2.

1945   B

Season in a Sentence

In the final year of World War II, the Red Sox lose their first eight games, rebound to move into pennant contention by July, then collapse down the stretch.

Finish • Won • Lost • Pct • GB

Seventh 71 83 .461 17.5

Manager

Joe Cronin

Stats

Stats	Red Sox	AL	Rank
Batting Avg:	.260	.255	4
On-Base Pct:	.330	.325	3
Slugging Pct:	.346	.346	4
Home Runs:	50		5
Stolen Bases:	72		3
ERA:	3.80	3.36	8
Fielding Pct:	.973	.973	4
Runs Scored:	599		4
Runs Allowed:	674		8

Starting Lineup

Bob Garbark, c
Catfish Metkovich, 1b-cf
Skeeter Newsome, 2b
Johnny Tobin, 3b
Eddie Lake, ss
Bob Johnson, lf
Leon Culberson, cf
Johnny Lazor, rf
Tom McBride, lf-rf-cf
Ben Steiner, 2b
Pete Fox, rf
Ty LaForest, c
Dolph Camilli, 1b

Pitchers

Boo Ferriss, sp
Emmett O'Neill, sp
Jim Wilson, sp
Randy Heflin, sp
Pinky Woods, sp-rp
Otie Clark, sp
Frank Barrett, rp
Mike Ryba, rp
Clem Hausmann, rp-sp
Vic Johnson, rp-sp

Attendance

603,794 (fifth in AL)

Club Leaders

Batting Avg:	Johnson	.280
On-Base Pct:	Lake	.412
Slugging Pct:	Johnson	.425
Home Runs:	Johnson	12
RBI:	Johnson	74
Runs:	Lake	81
Stolen Bases:	Metkovich	19
Wins:	Ferriss	21
Strikeouts:	Ferriss	94
ERA:	Ferriss	2.96
Saves:	Barrett	3

APRIL 16   Four days after Franklin Roosevelt dies of a cerebral hemorrhage, elevating Harry Truman to the presidency, the Red Sox offer a tryout to African-American players Jackie Robinson, Sam Jethroe, and Marvin Williams, each of whom was a star in the Negro Leagues.

The Red Sox were under pressure from many directions to employ African-Americans, including civil rights groups, BOSTON DAILY RECORD sportswriter Dave Egan, an advocate of integration, and Boston City Council member Isadore Muchnick. Muchnick threatened to revoke the permit that allowed the Red Sox to play Sunday games at Fenway Park. The tryout was a charade, as the Red Sox had no intention of breaking baseball's color line, which had been in existence since the 1880s. Following the workout, the Sox' front office made no attempt to contact Robinson, Jethroe, or Williams. The color line was finally broken when Robinson was signed by the Brooklyn Dodgers on October 23, 1945. He played one season for Montreal in the International League before making his major league debut with the Dodgers in 1947. Jethroe played for the Boston Braves from 1950 through 1952. Williams never played in the majors. It would be 1959 before an African American played in a regular-season game for the Red Sox.

APRIL 17   In the season opener, the Red Sox lead 4–1 before the Yankees score seven runs in the seventh inning to win 8–4 in New York. Red Sox first baseman Catfish Metkovich made three errors in the fateful seventh.

Members of the Red Sox who entered military service during the 1944–45 off-season included catchers Roy Partee and Bill Conroy. Partee participated in the invasion of the Philippines.

APRIL 19   Joe Cronin fractures his right leg during a 4–3 loss to the Yankees in New York when he catches his spikes at second base in the seventh inning. The game ended when Mike Ryba hit Johnny Lindell with a pitch with the bases loaded.

Cronin was away from the club for 12 days while he was recuperating. Coach Del Baker guided the club in Cronin's place. Cronin never played another big-league game.

APRIL 20   In the home opener, the Red Sox' record falls to 0–4 with a 5–3 loss to the Athletics before a chilled and skimpy crowd of 3,489.

The war in Europe was winding to a close, but the end of the conflict with Japan was nowhere in sight. The country was well into its fourth year of war, and everyone in the Fenway Park stands could claim a loved one, friend, or neighbor who had been or currently was involved in fighting somewhere in the world. While the 1945 opener was taking place, U.S. forces were involved in a deadly struggle to capture Okinawa. The brother of Red Sox pitcher Clem Dreisewerd was among those who were killed in action at Okinawa.

APRIL 27   The Red Sox fall to 0–8 on the season with a 5–3 loss to the Athletics at Philadelphia.

The eight losses at the start of a season is a club record.

APRIL 28   The Red Sox finally win their first game of the 1945 season with an 8–4 triumph over the Athletics in Philadelphia.

APRIL 29   Boo Ferriss pitches a five-hit shutout in his major league debut, defeating the Athletics 2–0 in the first game of a doubleheader in Philadelphia. Ferriss started the game by walking the first two hitters on eight pitches, then ran the count to 2–0 on the third batter and loaded the bases on walks in the first inning before settling down. Ferriss also collected three hits of his own. In the second game, the Red Sox tied the score 3–3 with two runs in the ninth, then won it 6–3 with three in the thirteenth.

Dave (Boo) Ferriss was the talk of baseball early in the 1945 season. Attendance increased by thousands every time he pitched. Ferriss's only previous professional experience was a 7–7 record with Greensboro in the Piedmont League in 1942 before entering the service. Pitching was relatively new to him. At Mississippi State University, Ferriss was a left-handed outfielder until his arm went bad. Fortunately, Ferriss was ambidextrous, which allowed him to make a remarkable conversion to become a right-handed pitcher. Ferriss was given his discharge from the Army Air Corps in February 1945 because of asthma but wasn't expected to provide much help to the Sox. The team had more players than lockers in the clubhouse at Fenway Park, and Ferriss had to hang his clothes from a rusty nail on the wall and on pipes protruding from the wall.

Joe Cronin turned to him after the club lost their first eight games, however, and Ferriss responded by winning his first eight major league starts, each of them complete games. Four were shutouts, and Ferriss allowed just eight runs in his first 72 innings. In late July, Ferriss had a record of 17–3 and was on a pace to win 30 games on the season, but asthma trouble in August and September reduced his effectiveness. He was allergic to grass and dust, which is not a good combination for a baseball player. Still, Ferriss finished the season with a record of 21–10 with 26 complete games in 31 starts, 265 innings pitched, and an ERA of 2.95. No other Red Sox pitcher had more than eight victories in 1945.

MAY 6   The day before Germany's surrender closes the European phase of World War II, Boo Ferriss pitches his second shutout in his second major league game, defeating the Yankees 5–0 in the first game of a doubleheader at Fenway Park. New York won the second game, 2–0.

MAY 13   In his third major league game, Boo Ferriss defeats the Tigers 8–2 in the first game of a doubleheader in Detroit. Ferriss held the Tigers scoreless through the first four innings to set an American League records for most consecutive scoreless innings at the start of a career with 22. Detroit won the second tilt, 2–0.

MAY 18   Boo Ferriss pitches his third shutout in his fourth big-league game, shutting down the White Sox 2–0 in Chicago.

MAY 25   Center fielder Leon Culberson pulls off an unassisted double play, but the Red Sox lose 5–0 to the Browns at Fenway Park.

MAY 27   The Red Sox allow the White Sox only three hits in a doubleheader at Comiskey Park. In the opener, Boo Ferriss pitched a one-hitter for a 7–0 win. The only Chicago hit was a single by Tony Cuccinello in the second inning. It was Ferriss's sixth win, and fourth shutout, in six big-league games. He allowed only three runs in his first

54 innings in the majors. In the nightcap, Emmett O'Neill hurled a two-hitter for a 2–1 victory. The only Chicago hits in that game were singles by Guy Curtright and Roy Schalk.

MAY 30

Down 6–1, the Red Sox score six runs in the eighth inning to beat the Indians 7–6 in the second game of a doubleheader at Fenway Park. Cleveland won the first game 4–3 with three runs in the ninth.

JUNE 6

Boo Ferriss runs his record to 8–0 with his eighth complete game in his eighth major league game by defeating the Athletics 5–2 in the first game of a doubleheader at Fenway Park. The Red Sox completed the sweep with a 3–2 win in the second tilt.

JUNE 10

Boo Ferriss's eight-game winning streak comes to an end with a 3–2 loss to the Yankees in New York.

JUNE 11

The Red Sox beat the Yankees 7–6 in an exhibition game at Camp Upton on Long Island before 5,000 convalescing soldiers.

JUNE 14

The Red Sox defeat the Athletics 1–0 in Philadelphia. A triple by Leon Culberson in the ninth inning drove in the lone run of the game. Clem Hausmann pitched the shutout.

JUNE 15

The Red Sox win 6–5 in 14 innings in the first game of a twinight doubleheader against the Senators at Griffith Stadium. Johnny Lazor's single drove in the lone run of the game. Boo Ferriss pitched all 14 innings. He had a record of 9–1 and victories over all seven AL opponents. The second game ended in a 4–4 tie after 14 innings because of an American League rule that stipulated that no inning could start after 12:50 AM.

JUNE 19

Clem Hausmann pitches his second straight 1–0 victory, defeating the Yankees at Fenway Park. Johnny Lazor drove in the lone run of the game with a single in the first inning.

The two 1–0 shutouts on June 14 and 19, 1945, were the only two of Hausmann's career. He finished his stay in the majors with a 9–14 record and a 4.21 ERA.

JUNE 21

On the day Japan surrenders Okinawa to U.S. forces, the dam bursts on the Red Sox as the Yankees break a 1–1 tie with 13 runs in the fifth inning at Fenway Park. The Boston pitchers in the big inning were Boo Ferriss, Frank Barrett, and Randy Heflin. New York won the game, 14–4.

JUNE 27

The day after the signing of the United Nations charter, the Red Sox score three runs in the ninth inning to beat the White Sox 11–0 in Chicago. Eddie Lake broke the 9–9 tie with a two-run single, his fourth hit of the game.

Lake hit .279 along with a league-leading .412 on-base percentage in 1945.

JUNE 29

Boo Ferriss breaks a 1–1 tie in the ninth inning with a two-run homer and goes on to defeat the White Sox 4–2 in Chicago.

The homer was the only one that Ferriss hit in 372 big-league at-bats, but he was a good hitter for a pitcher. Ferriss had a career batting average of .250 and was 10 for 41 as a pinch hitter.

JULY 10   The Red Sox play the Braves in an exhibition game at Fenway Park before 22,809 with the proceeds going to the War Service Relief Fund. The Sox won, 8–1.

Originally, the All-Star Game was scheduled for this date at Fenway Park, but the game was canceled due to wartime travel restrictions. The All-Star Game was played at Fenway in 1946.

JULY 14   In a strange pitching performance, Emmett O'Neill allows only one run and three hits, but walks 10, in a 7–1 victory over the Tigers at Fenway Park.

On July 15, the Red Sox had a record of 41–35 and were in fourth place, 2½ games behind the first-place Tigers. The Red Sox never drew any closer to the top, however, and had a record of 30–48 the rest of the way.

JULY 27   The Red Sox sell Lou Finney to the Browns.

JULY 29   Bob Johnson collects his 2,000th career hit with a fifth-inning single during an 8–4 win over the Senators at Fenway Park. Johnson was four for four on the day.

Playing left field, Johnson hit .280 with 12 homers in 1945 in his last season in the majors. He was thirty-nine years old on Opening Day in 1946, however, and with Ted Williams returning from the war, Johnson was released.

AUGUST 4   The Red Sox score 12 runs in the fourth inning to break a 2–2 tie and go on to defeat the Senators 15–4 in the second game of a doubleheader at Griffith Stadium. Tom McBride tied an American League record by driving in six runs in the inning. He cleared the bases twice with a double and a triple. The only other Red Sox batter with six RBIs in an inning is Carlos Quintana in 1991. Washington won the first game, 4–0.

Bert Shepard pitched the final 5⅓ innings for the Senators, allowing one run and three hits. Shepard pitched on a wooden leg after losing the lower part of his right leg in aerial combat over Germany. It was his only major league appearance. Washington pitcher Joe Cleary also made his only major league appearance in the contest and gave up seven runs in one-third of an inning to finish his career with an ERA of 189.00.

AUGUST 8   Two days after an atom bomb is dropped on Hiroshima, Red Sox rookie pitcher Jim Wilson suffers a fractured skull when hit by a line drive off the bat off Hank Greenberg during a 12-inning, 7–4 win over the Tigers in Detroit. The drive hit Wilson such force that it lifted him off the ground, spun him around, then dropped him on his face. He was knocked unconscious and later underwent two hours of surgery. He recovered from the injury and pitched 12 seasons in the majors and won 86 games.

AUGUST 10   The Red Sox score seven runs in the sixth inning to break a scoreless tie and move on to defeat the Tigers 9–0 in Detroit.

AUGUST 18   Four days after Japan's surrender ends World War II, the White Sox pummel the
                 Red Sox 16–1 in Chicago.

AUGUST 26   Boo Ferriss wins his 20th game of the season by driving in the winning run in the
                 tenth inning with a walk-off double that beats the Athletics 4–3 in the first game of
                 a doubleheader at Fenway Park. The Sox also won the second tilt 4–3 in the con-
                 ventional nine innings.

AUGUST 29   Vic Johnson pitches the Red Sox to a 1–0 win over the Yankees in New York. It
                 was his first major league complete game. Bob Johnson drove in the lone run with
                 a single in the fourth inning.

                 *The shutout was the only one that Johnson pitched as a big leaguer. He was
                 6–7 with a 4.55 ERA during a three-year career in the majors.*

SEPTEMBER 19   The Red Sox score four runs in the eighth inning to defeat the Athletics 11–10 in
                 the first game of a doubleheader at Fenway Park. The Sox completed the sweep
                 with a 3–0 victory in the nightcap.

                 *There was trouble with some Fenway Park pigeons during the afternoon. In the
                 third inning, Red Sox outfielder Tom McBride took a bead on what he felt sure
                 was a long fly off the bat of Sam Chapman but discovered too late that he was
                 following the flight of a pigeon. The ball was hit behind him and clanged off
                 the left field wall for a double. In the bottom of the same inning, Boston's
                 Skeeter Newsome hit a drive to left field for what appeared to be a sure double.
                 Philadelphia outfielder Hal Peck picked up the ball and fired it toward the
                 infield. It struck a pigeon in mid-flight and deflected to the second baseman,
                 who tagged Newsome out.*

SEPTEMBER 23   Eddie Lake's walk-off double in the fourteenth inning beats the Yankees 6–5 in the
                 first game of a doubleheader at Fenway Park. The second game went only five
                 innings, with the Yankees winning 2–1, because of the Boston Sunday sports law.

                 *It was Boo Ferriss Day at Fenway Park. The star pitcher was presented with a
                 new Lincoln Zephyr that was originally built for Mrs. Edsel Ford.*

DECEMBER 12   The Red Sox send Vic Johnson and cash to the Indians for Jim Bagby Jr. and sell
                 Skeeter Newsome to the Phillies.

1946   B

Season in a Sentence

The Red Sox win 41 of their first 50 games and cruise to their first AL pennant in 28 years before suffering a crushing seventh-game loss to the Cardinals in the World Series.

Finish • Won • Lost • Pct • GB

First   104   50   .675   +12.0

World Series—The Red Sox lost to the St. Louis Cardinals four games to three.

Manager

Joe Cronin

Stats   Red Sox • AL • Rank

Stats	Red Sox	AL	Rank
Batting Avg:	.271	.256	1
On-Base Pct:	.356	.328	1
Slugging Pct:	.402	.364	1
Home Runs:	109		2
Stolen Bases:	45		6
ERA:	3.38	3.50	4
Fielding Pct:	.977	.973	1
Runs Scored:	792		1
Runs Allowed:	594		3

Starting Lineup

Hal Wagner, c
Rudy York, 1b
Bobby Doerr, 2b
Rip Russell, 3b
Johnny Pesky, ss
Ted Williams, lf
Dom DiMaggio, cf
Catfish Metkovich, rf
Pinky Higgins, 3b
Leon Culberson, rf-cf
Wally Moses, rf
Tom McBride, rf

Pitchers

Boo Ferriss, sp
Tex Hughson, sp
Mickey Harris, sp
Joe Dobson, sp
Jim Bagby, Jr., sp-rp
Earl Johnson, rp

Attendance

1,416,944 (third in AL)

Club Leaders

Batting Avg:	Williams	.342
On-Base Pct:	Williams	.497
Slugging Pct:	Williams	.667
Home Runs:	Williams	38
RBI:	Williams	123
Runs:	Williams	142
Stolen Bases:	DiMaggio	10
Wins:	Ferriss	25
Strikeouts:	Hughson	172
ERA:	Hughson	2.75
Saves:	Klinger	9

JANUARY 3   The Red Sox trade Eddie Lake to the Tigers for Rudy York.

This was a classic example of a trade that helped both teams. York hit .276 with 17 homers and 119 runs batted in for the Red Sox in 1946.

JANUARY 22   The Red Sox sell Jim Tabor to the Phillies.

FEBRUARY 26   Back from his tour with the Navy, Ted Williams hits the first spring training pitch he sees for a home run.

The 1946 major league camps were unique as returning veterans competed with wartime fill-ins for spots on the roster. The Red Sox' spring training roster included 28 players who spent the entire 1945 season in the military. Many of them, such as Ted Williams, Johnny Pesky, Bobby Doerr, Dom DiMaggio, Tex Hughson, Mickey Harris, Hal Wagner, and Joe Dobson, reclaimed their old positions. Wartime players such as Bob Johnson, Bob Garbark, Johnny Tobin, Ben Steiner, Pete Fox, Dolph Camilli, Ty LaForest, Pinky Woods, and Otie Clark were released. Of the 35 players who appeared in a game for the Red Sox in 1945, only 11 played for the club in 1946.

The 1946 training camp was also conducted in Sarasota, Florida, where the club held pre-season drills from 1933 through 1942. Because of wartime travel restrictions, the Red Sox held spring training at Tufts College in Medford, Massachusetts, in 1943, both Medford and Baltimore in 1944, and Pleasantville, New Jersey, located near Atlantic City, in 1945.

MARCH 10   The Red Sox play the Washington Senators in an exhibition game in Havana, Cuba, and win 7–3. The Red Sox and Senators played in Havana again on March 16, with the Senators winning, 10–9.

APRIL 16   President Harry Truman throws out the first ball prior to the Red Sox' 6–5 victory over the Senators on Opening Day in Washington. In his first game since 1942, Ted Williams hit a 430-foot homer. Tex Hughson, another returning war veteran, pitched a complete game.

APRIL 17   The Red Sox thrash the Senators 13–6 in Washington.

APRIL 20   In the home opener, the Red Sox defeat the Athletics 2–1 before 30,466 at Fenway Park. Johnny Pesky broke a 1–1 tie with a homer in the eighth inning. It was one of only two hits off Philadelphia pitcher Dick Fowler.

APRIL 21   In the first game of a doubleheader against the Athletics at Fenway Park, the Red Sox fall behind 7–0 in the third inning and still trail 11–5 heading into the bottom of half of the ninth. They then explode for an incredible six-run rally to tie the contest 11–11 and send it into extra innings. The last three runs came on a two-out homer by Catfish Metkovich. Ted Williams's bases-loaded, walk-off single in the tenth lifted Boston to a 12–11 victory. In the second game, Red Sox starting pitcher Jim Bagby Jr. walked the first four batters he faced before being lifted for a reliever. Philadelphia won 3–0 in a contest stopped after five innings by the Sunday sports law.

Williams won the AL Most Valuable Player Award in 1946 by hitting .342 with 37 doubles, 38 homers, and 123 RBIs. He led the league in runs (142), walks (156), on-base percentage (.497), and slugging percentage (.667).

APRIL 22   Eddie Pellagrini hits a homer in his first major league plate appearance. His homer broke a 4–4 tie in the seventh inning and gave the Red Sox a 5–4 victory over the Senators at Fenway Park. Pellagrini entered the game in the fifth inning at shortstop when Johnny Pesky left the game after he was hit in the head with a pitch.

Pellagrini, who grew up in the Boston neighborhood of Dorchester, was twenty-eight years old when he made his big-league debut. He played two seasons with the Red Sox at the start of a big-league career that ended in 1954. Pellagrini hit 20 homers with a .226 batting average in the majors while playing for five teams. He was extremely superstitious about the number 13 and wore it while playing with the Phillies, Reds, and Pirates. Eddie was born on March 13 and married a woman born on the thirteenth. He went so far as to sign his contract every year on the thirteenth of the month. Pellagrini finished his career with 13 triples and 13 stolen bases and was hit by pitches 13 times.

APRIL 25   Eddie Pellagrini collects a homer, a triple, and a double during a 12–5 win over the Yankees at Fenway Park.

APRIL 28   The Braves play a doubleheader at Fenway Park against the Phillies while Braves Field is being repainted.

More than 5,000 fans left the Braves home opener on April 16 with green paint on their clothing because the new paint on all of the seats had not yet dried. The Braves had to pay more than $6,000 for the dry cleaning bills of irate fans, and had to repaint the seats.

MAY 1   The Red Sox rout the Tigers 13–1 at Fenway Park.

MAY 2   Ted Williams drives a tenth-inning homer into the right field bleachers at Fenway Park to give the Red Sox a 5–4 win over the Tigers at Fenway Park.

On the same day, the Red Sox announced that lights would be added to Fenway Park before the start of the 1947 season. During the 1946 season, the Red Sox, Tigers, and Cubs were the only clubs that didn't play home games at night. The Tigers began hosting night games in 1948. The Cubs held out until 1988 before installing lights at Wrigley Field. (See June 13, 1947.)

MAY 6   Johnny Pesky collects four hits in his first four at-bats during a 7–5 win over the Browns at Fenway Park. The hits extended Pesky's streak of hits in consecutive at-bats to 11, one short of the major league record. He had hits in his last three at-bats on May 3 in a 9–4 win over the Indians at Fenway Park and hits in all four at-bats on May 4, a 6–2 victory over Cleveland in Boston. Pesky's streak was stopped by Al Milnar on a ground-out.

Pesky hit .335, scored 115 runs, and led the league in hits with 208. Bobby Doerr batted .271 with 18 homers and 116 runs batted in, and Dom DiMaggio batted .316.

MAY 7   Leon Culberson's walk-off grand slam off Tex Shirley of the Browns in the fourteenth inning lifts the Red Sox to a 10–6 triumph at Fenway Park. The Sox trailed 6–2 before scoring two in the seventh inning and two more in the eighth. It was Boston's 12th straight win.

MAY 8   Johnny Pesky sets an American League record (since tied) by scoring six runs during a 14–10 win over the White Sox at Fenway Park. It was the Sox' 13th consecutive victory.

MAY 10   The Red Sox extend their winning streak to 15 games with a 5–4 win over the Yankees before 64,183 on a Friday afternoon in New York. The win gave the Sox a record of 21–3. The 15-game winning streak is a club record.

MAY 11   The Red Sox 15-game winning streak is snapped with a 2–0 defeat at the hands of the Yankees in New York. Tiny Bonham pitched the shutout.

MAY 18   The Red Sox wallop the Browns 18–8 in St. Louis. Ted Williams hit a grand slam off Ellis Kinder in the fifth inning. In his other four plate appearances, Williams walked four times, three of them intentionally.

MAY 19   The Red Sox purchase Pinky Higgins from the Tigers.

MAY 22 — Ted Williams breaks a 4–4 tie with a two-run homer in the twelfth inning, then the Red Sox add one more run to beat the Indians 7–4 in Cleveland. Sox outfielder Johnny Lazor sent the game into extra innings with a homer in the ninth. It was Lazor's only homer in 1946 and the last of the six he hit during his big-league career.

MAY 26 — Tex Hughson pitches the Red Sox to a 1–0 win over the Yankees in the first game of a doubleheader at Fenway Park. Ted Williams drove in the lone run of the game with a single in the seventh inning. New York won the second game, called after seven innings by darkness.

JUNE 6 — After being ejected by the umpires, Browns pitcher Jack Kramer heaves a ball over the Fenway Park grandstand. The Red Sox won the game, 5–4.

JUNE 8 — The Red Sox take a 12–0 lead after three innings and trounce the Tigers 15–4 at Fenway Park.

The Red Sox had a record of 60–17 at Fenway in 1946.

JUNE 9 — The Red Sox extend their winning streak to 10 games with a 7–1 and 11–6 sweep of the Tigers in a doubleheader at Fenway Park. Boo Ferriss was the winning pitcher in the second game, which gave him a record of 10–0 on the season. Ted Williams hit one of the longest homers ever hit at Fenway Park in the first inning of the second game. It landed in row 33 of the bleachers and struck construction worker Joe Boucher on the head, knocking a hole in his straw hat.

That home run is still marked today by a single red seat amidst the green.

JUNE 11 — The Red Sox win their 12th game in a row with a 10–5 decision over the Indians at Fenway Park. The winning streak is tied for the third longest in Red Sox history, and it came a month after the longest winning streak in club history. The June 11 win gave the Red Sox a 41–9 record on the season.

With the war over and a fast start, the Red Sox shattered all previous home attendance records. The Sox drew 1,416,944 into Fenway Park in 1946, breaking the old mark of 730,340 set in 1942.

JUNE 21 — Tex Hughson bests Bob Feller and the Indians in a 1–0 mound duel in Cleveland. The lone run of the game was scored in the second inning on a triple by Bobby Doerr and a sacrifice fly by Rudy York.

JUNE 23 — In his first start with the Red Sox, Bill Zuber shuts out the Indians 6–0 in the second game of a doubleheader in Cleveland. The Sox also won the opener, 5–1.

A native of Middle Amana, Iowa, Zuber was acquired on waivers from the Yankees on June 18. The shutout was his first since 1944, his only one as a member of the Red Sox, and the last of three he pitched during his career.

JUNE 25 — Tex Hughson pitches the Red Sox to a 1–0 win over the Tigers in Detroit. It was his second straight 1–0 victory. The lone run of the game was scored in the eighth inning when Tiger pitcher Fred Hutchinson walked four batters in a row, the last one Bobby Doerr, after two were out. Ted Williams was walked intentionally with runners on first and second.

JUNE 26   The Tigers take a 15–0 lead after only two innings and cruise to a 16–2 win over the Red Sox in the first game of a doubleheader in Detroit. Boston rebounded in the second tilt with seven runs in the eighth inning to win, 9–3.

The Red Sox played 27 doubleheaders in 1946 and were never swept. The Sox won both games in 14 of the twin bills and split the two games in the other 13.

JUNE 28   The Red Sox vanquish the Senators 12–1 at Fenway Park.

JUNE 29   The Red Sox score seven runs in the third inning to overcome a 4–0 deficit and outlast the Senators 12–8 at Fenway Park.

JUNE 30   The Red Sox continue to strafe Washington pitching with eight runs in the first inning of a 15–8 victory in the first game of a doubleheader at Fenway Park. Boston bats were cooled in the nightcap as the Senators won, 9–2.

JULY 7   The Red Sox hammer the Senators 11–4 and 9–4 in a doubleheader in Washington.

JULY 9   The American League wallops the National League 12–0 in the All-Star Game at Fenway Park. Ted Williams was the star of the game with two homers, two singles, and a walk in five plate appearances. He also drove in five runs. One of his homers was one of the most memorable in All-Star history. In the eighth inning, Pirate pitcher Rip Sewell threw an arching blooper pitch that Williams smacked into the right field bleachers. Charlie Keller of the Yankees homered in the first. Bob Feller, Hal Newhouser, and Jack Kramer each pitched three innings for the shutout and allowed only three hits combined.

Future Hall of Famers on the roster of the two teams included Luke Appling, Bill Dickey, Joe DiMaggio, Bobby Doerr, Bob Feller, Johnny Mize, Stan Musial, Hal Newhouser, Pee Wee Reese, Red Schoendienst, Enos Slaughter, and Ted Williams.

JULY 14   Ted Williams hits three homers and collects eight RBIs to lead the Red Sox an 11–10 win over the Indians in the first game of a doubleheader at Fenway Park. One of the homers was a grand slam off Steve Gromek. Williams also hit a single and scored four times. Cleveland player-manager Lou Boudreau tied a major league record with extra-base hits in the contest by collecting four doubles and a homer. The Red Sox completed the sweep with a 6–4 victory in the nightcap.

Boudreau had a career game but still wound up on the losing end of the score. In the second game, he deployed the famous "Boudreau shift" by moving his fielders to the right side of the diamond with only the left fielder on the left side, and he was positioned in left-center field. The maneuver was an attempt to frustrate Williams. The Boudreau shift was soon copied by other AL clubs and used for several years. Williams refused to change his batting style by slicing hits to the opposite field, but the shifts failed to slow him down.

Williams led the American League in batting average in 1947 and 1948, and missed a third consecutive crown in 1949 by one base hit.

Courtesy of Transcendental Graphics/theruckerarchive.com

Stan Musial slides into second base for a double in the sixth inning of Game One of the 1946 World Series. Johnny Pesky takes the throw from the outfield. Musial's hit knocked in the Cardinals' first run, tying the score at 1–1, but Rudy York's home run in the tenth inning would win the game for the Sox, 3–2.

JULY 19   Umpire Red Jones ejects 14 White Sox players during a 9–2 Red Sox win at Fenway Park.

JULY 21   Ted Williams collects seven consecutive hits during a doubleheader against the Browns at Fenway Park. In the opener, won by the Red Sox 5–0, Williams had a double and two singles in four at-bats. In the second tilt, Williams hit for the cycle in five at-bats in leading Boston to a 7–4 victory. He homered in the second inning, tripled in the third, singled in the fifth, and doubled in the sixth. It was the only time he hit for the cycle during his illustrious career.

JULY 23   The Red Sox purchase Wally Moses from the Athletics.

JULY 26   Rudy York drives in four runs during an 8–5 win over the Browns in St. Louis.

JULY 27   Rudy York drives in 10 runs, eight of them on a pair of grand slams, leading the Red Sox to 13–6 win over the Browns in St. Louis. In the first inning, York doubled in two runs off Bob Muncrief after Ted Williams drew an intentional walk. In the second, Williams walked to load the bases, and York followed with a homer off Tex Shirley. In the fifth, Williams was again given an intentional walk to load the bases, and facing Shirley again, York hit his second grand slam of the game. Rudy also came to bat with runners in the seventh and ninth inning. He struck out with one runner on base and hit into a double play with two on.

On July 30, the Red Sox had a record of 70–28.

AUGUST 13   Boo Ferriss wins his 20th game of the season with a 7–5 decision over the Athletics in Philadelphia.

Ferriss had a record of 13–0 at Fenway Park in 1946.

AUGUST 15   Sam Chapman hits three homers for the Athletics in a 5–3 win over the Red Sox in Philadelphia. All three were hit off Joe Dobson.

AUGUST 21   The Red Sox score seven runs in the second inning to take an 11–1 lead, then hold on to defeat the Browns 12–9 at Fenway Park.

AUGUST 25   The Red Sox beat the Indians 2–1 and 13–6 in a twin bill at Fenway Park.

Between games of the doubleheader, manager Joe Cronin and all of the players and coaches were presented with chairs by a delegation from Gardner, Massachusetts. In addition, tricycles and doll carriages were given to those on the club with small children. Ted Williams was presented with a bat as tall as himself, a baseball of proportionate size, and a huge chair some twenty-five feet tall.

AUGUST 26   At Fenway Park, as Ted Williams prepares to bat against the Boudreau shift, three-foot-tall Marco Songini runs out of the stands and onto the field and occupies the empty third base position. The umpires chased him off the field, the game resumed, and the Red Sox won 5–1 over the Indians.

SEPTEMBER 1   Athletics pitcher Bob Savage, a native of Manchester, New Hampshire, and a World War II veteran who was wounded three times in battle, is given a car by his fellow townspeople before a game at Fenway Park. Savage took a 3–2 lead into the bottom of the tenth inning before giving up two runs to lose, 4–3.

SEPTEMBER 2   Boo Ferriss wins his 12th consecutive game and runs his season record to 24–4 with a 5–2 decision over the Yankees in the first game of a doubleheader in New York. The Sox completed the sweep with a 3–1 win in the second contest.

Ferriss finished the season with a 25–6 record and a 3.25 ERA. He pitched 274 innings, completed 26 of his 35 starts, and tossed six shutouts. At the end of the 1946 season, Ferriss was twenty-four years old and had a career record of 46–16, but he was brutally overworked with 542⅓ innings and 52 complete games in just two seasons, which ruined a promising career. After 1946, Ferriss won only 19 more big-league games. Tex Hughson was 20–11 with a 2.75 ERA, 21 complete games, 172 strikeouts, 278 innings, and six shutouts in 1946. Mickey Harris, who missed four full seasons while in the service, had a record of 17–9.

SEPTEMBER 5   Jim Bagby Jr. pitches the Red Sox to a 1–0 win over the Senators in Washington. A single by Rip Russell in the second inning drove in the lone run of the game.

SEPTEMBER 13   The Red Sox break a six-game losing streak and clinch their first AL pennant since 1918 with a 1–0 win over the Indians at League Park in Cleveland. The sole run in the game scored on the only inside-the-park homer of Ted Williams's career. Picking on a 3–1 pitch in the first inning, Williams foiled the Boudreau shift by hitting an opposite-field fly ball into empty left field and circled the bases before left fielder Pat Seerey could retrieve the ball, which rolled into a gutter along the distant left field wall about four hundred feet from home plate. Seerey had been stationed twenty feet behind the skinned portion of the infield. If Seerey had been playing in a conventional defense, he probably would have caught the ball for an out. Williams's homer was one of only two hits off Cleveland pitcher Red Embree. Tex Hughson pitched the shutout for the Red Sox.

SEPTEMBER 27   Tex Hughson wins his 20th game of the season with a 5–4 decision over the Senators at Fenway Park.

> *The regular season ended on September 29 with the World Series scheduled to begin on October 2. The National League pennant race ended in a tie, however, between the Cardinals and the Dodgers. The two clubs met in a best-two-of-three playoff to determine the league champion beginning on October 1, which pushed back the start of the Fall Classic to October 6. The Cardinals won the series two games to none to reach the Series against the Red Sox. To keep his team fresh during the layoff, Joe Cronin arranged for the Sox to play three exhibitions games against a team of American League all-stars that included Joe DiMaggio, Hank Greenberg, and Luke Appling. In the game on October 1, Ted Williams was squarely hit on the elbow by a pitch from Mickey Haefner of the Senators. The blow sent Williams to the hospital in excruciating pain for x-rays, which turned out negative. The elbow swelled to three times its normal size and hampered Ted's swing throughout the Series. After the injury, the last two games against the All-Stars were canceled. The Red Sox entered the Series as 3–1 favorites.*

OCTOBER 6   The World Series opens with a 3–2 Red Sox win over the Cardinals as Rudy York hits a tenth-inning homer on a 2–0 count off Howie Pollet at Sportsman's Park in St. Louis. The ball landed in a refreshment stand atop the left field bleachers. Earl Johnson, in relief of Tex Hughson, was the winning pitcher. The Sox tied the game in the ninth when Pinky Higgins's easy grounder took a freak bounce and went through shortstop Marty Marion's legs. Rip Russell and Tom McBride followed with singles to score Higgins.

> *McBride made the first out of the Series as the leadoff batter in Game One and the last out in Game Seven.*

OCTOBER 7   Cardinals pitcher Harry Brecheen allows only four hits in shutting out the Red Sox 3–0 in St. Louis. Brecheen also drove in the first run of the game.

> *The 1946 World Series was the last one that wasn't televised. The first World Series on TV was in 1947 between the Yankees and Dodgers, although it was available only to stations in New York, Philadelphia,*

Washington, and Schenectady, New York. The first World Series shown in Boston was in 1948 between the Braves and the Indians.

OCTOBER 9   Boo Ferriss shuts out the Cardinals 4–0 before 34,500 at Fenway Park to give the Sox a two-games-to-one lead. The Red Sox took command of the game on Rudy York's three-run homer in the first.

Tickets prices for the World Series at Fenway Park were $7.20 for box seats, $6.00 for the reserved grandstand section, $3.60 for general admission, and $1.20 for the bleachers.

OCTOBER 10   The Series evens at two games apiece as the Cardinals collect 20 hits off six pitchers and rout the Red Sox 12–3 before 35,645 at Fenway Park. Enos Slaughter, Whitey Kurowski, and Joe Garagiola each had four hits for the Cardinals. Wally Moses picked up four hits and Bobby Doerr homered in the losing effort.

Doerr didn't play in Game Five because of migraine headaches.

OCTOBER 11   The Red Sox move within one game of the World Championship with a 6–3 win over the Cardinals before 35,982 at Fenway Park. The score was 3–3 when the Red Sox scored three runs in the seventh. Pinky Higgins broke the 3–3 tie with an RBI double. Joe Dobson struck out eight in pitching a four-hit complete game. Leon Culberson homered and Johnny Pesky collected three hits.

The Red Sox had three different starting right fielders in the Series. Tom McBride started the first and second games, Wally Moses the third fourth and seventh, and Culberson the fifth and sixth.

OCTOBER 13   With their backs to the wall, the Cardinals defeat the Red Sox 4–1 in St. Louis in Game Six. Harry Brecheen was the winning pitcher with a complete game.

Both Stan Musial and Ted Williams struggled throughout the Series. Musial was six for 27, and Williams had five singles in 25 at-bats and only one RBI.

OCTOBER 14   Enos Slaughter sprints all the way from first base and slides into home plate with the winning run in the eighth inning on Harry Walker's two-out double off Bob Klinger, as the Cardinals edge the Red Sox 4–3, giving St. Louis the World Series four games to three. Center fielder Leon Culberson fielded the ball and threw to shortstop Johnny Pesky. When Pesky received the relay from Culberson, Slaughter had just rounded third base. Pesky was surprised to see Slaughter dashing for home and held the ball for a split second. The Sox shortstop pulled the ball down slightly and needed an additional second to get into position to make a quick throw, which had little on it. Slaughter scored easily.

The Cardinals headed into the eighth with a 3–1 lead, but Dom DiMaggio tied the score in the top of the inning with a two-run double off the right-center field wall after Rip Russell and Catfish Metkovich connected for pinch hits. But DiMaggio sprained his ankle rounding first on his double and was replaced by Culberson, setting up the dramatics in the bottom of the inning. Joe Cronin also made a controversial pitching choice in the fateful eighth. Joe Dobson was lifted for a pinch hitter in the top of the inning, and Cronin went with reliever Bob Klinger, who hadn't pitched in three weeks after being away from the club because of sickness in the family. He had been released unconditionally by the Pirates earlier in the year. In the ninth inning, the Sox had runners on first and second after Rudy York and Bobby Doerr singled. Cardinal hurler Harry Brecheen, who entered the game in the eighth as a reliever a day after pitching a complete game, earned his third victory of the Series by retiring Pinky Higgins, Roy Partee, and Tom McBride.

Johnny Pesky immediately took the responsibility for the loss. "I'm the goat," he said in the locker room after the game. "I never expected he'd try to score. I couldn't hear anybody hollering at me above the noise of the crowd. I gave Slaughter at least six strides with the delay. I know I could have nailed him if I had suspected he would try for the plate. I'm the 'goat.' No mistake about that."

1947 B

Season in a Sentence

A run of injuries to the club's top pitchers prevents the Red Sox from repeating as American League champions.

Finish • Won • Lost • Pct • GB

Third 83 71 .539 14.0

Manager

Joe Cronin

Stats   Red Sox • AL • Rank

Batting Avg:	.265	.256	2
On-Base Pct:	.349	.333	3
Slugging Pct:	.382	.364	3
Home Runs:	103		3 (tie)
Stolen Bases:	41		5
ERA:	3.81	3.71	6
Fielding Pct:	.977	.977	4
Runs Scored:	720		2
Runs Allowed:	669		6

Starting Lineup

Birdie Tebbetts, c
Jake Jones, 1b
Bobby Doerr, 2b
Eddie Pellagrini, 3b-ss
Johnny Pesky, ss
Ted Williams, lf
Dom DiMaggio, cf
Sam Mele, rf
Wally Moses, rf
Sam Dente, 3b
Rudy York, 1b
Roy Partee, c

Pitchers

Joe Dobson, sp
Boo Ferriss, sp
Tex Hughson, sp
Denny Galehouse, sp
Earl Johnson, rp-sp
Harry Dorish, rp

Attendance

1,427,315 (third in AL)

Club Leaders

Batting Avg:	Williams	.343
On-Base Pct:	Williams	.499
Slugging Pct:	Williams	.634
Home Runs:	Williams	32
RBI:	Williams	114
Runs:	Williams	125
Stolen Bases:	Pesky	12
Wins:	Dobson	18
Strikeouts:	Hughson	119
ERA:	Dobson	2.95
Saves:	Johnson	8

FEBRUARY 10   The Red Sox sell Jim Bagby Jr. to the Pirates.

APRIL 2   The Red Sox sell Catfish Metkovich to the Indians.

                   *On the same day, the Dallas Rebels of the Texas League employed an unusual
                   shift on Ted Williams during an exhibition game in Dallas. When Williams
                   batted in the first inning, the entire Dallas team, excluding the pitcher and
                   catcher, made a mad dash for the right field bleachers, climbed the waist-
                   high wooden fence, and lined up in a defensive position along the first row
                   of seats.*

APRIL 15   In the season opener, the Red Sox win 7–6 over the Senators before 30,822 at
                   Fenway Park. Tex Hughson retired the first 15 batters he faced before faltering.
                   Washington tied the score 6–6 with four runs in the top of the eighth. The Red
                   Sox won the game in the bottom of the inning on a bases-loaded sacrifice fly by
                   Bobby Doerr. Eddie Pellagrini hit a homer earlier in the contest, and Dom DiMaggio
                   collected three hits, including a double.

                   The Red Sox won their first four games in 1947.

APRIL 24   Tex Hughson pitches a two-hitter to beat the Yankees 1–0 at Yankee Stadium. The
                   only two New York hits were a check-swing double by Joe DiMaggio in the sixth
                   inning and a single by Aaron Robinson in the eighth. The lone run of the game
                   came in on a sacrifice fly by Sam Mele in the fifth.

                   As a twenty-four-year-old rookie in 1947, Mele hit .302 with 12 homers.

APRIL 26   Rudy York causes a hotel fire after falling asleep while smoking in bed. He was
                   dragged to safety by the hotel night engineer, who found smoke billowing from
                   beneath the door of York's second floor room, and unable to arouse the Red
                   Sox first baseman by knocking, entered with a passkey. The whole room was
                   blazing. As a result of York's negligence, 450 guests at the Miles Standish Hotel
                   in Boston were forced to evacuate. York suffered only slight burns and smoke
                   inhalation.

                   *York holds the all-time major league record for "most hotel fires started in a
                   season" with two. After he was traded to the White Sox, York started a fire at
                   the Stevens Hotel in Chicago on August 23 by leaving his room with a lit ciga-
                   rette on a window sill. The drapes and window sash were destroyed before the
                   fire was extinguished. Ironically, one of York's post-playing career jobs was as a
                   fire prevention officer with the Georgia State Forestry Commission.*

MAY 6   Ted Williams smashes two clutch homers against the Browns at Sportsman's Park.
                   The first tied the score in the ninth, and the second accounted for three runs in the
                   eleventh. Williams's second homer gave Boston a 6–3 lead, and the Sox withstood a
                   St. Louis rally in the bottom of the inning to win, 6–5.

                   *Home games of the Red Sox and Braves in 1947 were carried on radio on WHDH
                   with Jim Britt and Tom Hussey reporting. No road games of either team were car-
                   ried, and as yet, no Boston television station was equipped to telecast games.*

MAY 13   Ted Williams hits two homers over the left field wall, and Bobby Doerr hits for the cycle as the Red Sox overwhelm the White Sox 19–6 at Fenway Park. The Red Sox broke a 5–5 tie with five runs in the seventh inning and added nine more tallies in the eighth.

> *The Green Monster was devoid of advertising for the first time in 1947. In 1946, there were ads for Lifebuoy Soap, Gem Razor Blades, and Calvert Whiskey on the big wall, as well as the home schedule of the Boston Yanks football team. In another change, the Sox placed foam-rubber padding on the right field wall to help protect the outfielders from injury.*

MAY 16   Ted Williams hits a grand slam in the fifth inning off Walter Brown of the Browns during a 12–7 win at Fenway Park.

MAY 17   A game between the Red Sox and Browns at Fenway Park is stopped briefly when a seagull drops a three-inch long smelt on the pitcher's mound just behind St. Louis hurler Ellis Kinder with Bobby Doerr at the plate. Umpire Bill Summers walked to the mound to remove the dead fish. The Red Sox won the contest, 4–2.

MAY 19   Ted Williams hits a two-run walk-off homer in the ninth inning on a 3–0 pitch off Virgil Trucks that beats the Tigers 5–4 at Fenway Park.

MAY 20   In a trade of starting catchers, the Red Sox swap Hal Wagner to the Tigers for Birdie Tebbetts.

MAY 29   The Red Sox score seven runs in the fifth inning and defeat the Athletics 9–2 at Fenway Park.

JUNE 13   The Red Sox play a night game at Fenway Park for the first time and win 5–3 over the White Sox before 34,510.

> *Night games proved to be an enormous success, as the Red Sox drew 463,822 in 14 nocturnal tilts, an average of 33,130. The Red Sox drew 1,427,315 at home in 1947, breaking the record of 1,416,944 set in 1946.*

JUNE 14   In a trade of starting first basemen, the Red Sox swap Rudy York to the White Sox for Jake Jones.

JUNE 15   In his first two games with the Red Sox, Jake Jones hits homers in both ends of a doubleheader at Fenway Park against the White Sox, the club that traded him the day before. In the first game, Jones homered in the seventh inning of a 7–3 Boston win. He saved the best for last. In the nightcap, Jones hit a walk-off grand slam in the ninth off of Orval Grove to give the Red Sox an 8–4 victory.

JUNE 18   The Red Sox edge the Browns 6–5 in a 15-inning struggle at Fenway Park.

> *St. Louis scored one run in the thirteenth and two in the fourteenth, but the Sox rallied to tie the game both times. A walk-off single by Johnny Pesky drove in the winning run.*

JUNE 20   Indians catcher Jim Hegan is given an automobile by fans from his hometown of

Lynn, Massachusetts, in pre-game ceremonies at Fenway Park, then drives in all three Cleveland runs with a homer and a single to beat the Red Sox, 3–2.

On the same day, the Red Sox purchased Denny Galehouse from the Browns.

JUNE 21   Bobby Doerr hits a grand slam in the first inning off Bob Feller, leading the Red Sox to a 9–1 win over the Indians at Fenway Park.

On June 26, the Red Sox were 34–26 in second place, 2 1/2 games behind the Yankees, but were soon out of the pennant race when their New York rivals embarked on a 19-game winning streak. Injuries to Boo Ferriss, Tex Hughson, and Mickey Harris led to Boston's winning only 83 games in 1947, compared with 104 the previous season. In 1946, the three had a combined record of 62–26. In 1947, the trio was 29–26. None of the three was ever effective again. After 1947, Ferriss and Hughson each won only seven more big-league games with ERAs over 5.00, and Harris was 18–42.

JULY 8   Ted Williams and Bobby Doerr contribute to a 2–1 American League victory in the All-Star Game, played at Wrigley Field in Chicago. Williams had a double and a single, and Doerr scored the winning run in the seventh inning. Joe Cronin managed the American League squad.

JULY 17   Trailing 3–1, the Red Sox score two runs in the ninth inning on Bobby Doerr's homer, then add three more in the eleventh to beat the White Sox 6–3 in the second game of a doubleheader in Chicago. The Red Sox also won the first game, 4–1.

JULY 18   Ted Williams collects five hits, including two homers, in five at-bats and drives in five runs, but the Red Sox lose 9–8 in St. Louis.

While the Red Sox were on the road trip, a tryout camp was held at Fenway Park. A fifteen-year-old from the Boston neighborhood of Roxbury named John Kennedy showed up, but he wasn't allowed to play because he was too young. Kennedy went to sit in the dugout, where he was hit in the face with a baseball and tragically lost his right eye.

JULY 20   Two African Americans play as teammates for the first time in major league history. The two were Willard Brown and Hank Thompson playing for the Browns against the Red Sox in a doubleheader in St. Louis. Brown and Thompson were also the first African Americans to play in a regular-season game against the Sox. Boston won both games, 4–3 and 7–6.

Brown and Thompson were the third and fourth African-American players in big-league history. They were preceded by Jackie Robinson with the Dodgers and Larry Doby of the Indians earlier in 1947. Brown also became the first African American to play in an American League game at Fenway Park, on July 25.

JULY 23   A bases-loaded bunt by Don Gutteridge in the fourteenth inning beats the White Sox 8–7 at Fenway Park.

JULY 26   The Red Sox trounce the Browns 12–1 at Fenway Park.

In a span of six at-bats on July 24, 25, and 26, Ted Williams had four homers and two singles. Williams won baseball's batting Triple Crown in 1947 by leading the league in batting average (.343), home runs (32), and RBIs (114). He also led the league in runs (125), total bases (335), walks (162), on-base percentage (.499), and slugging percentage (.634) and was second in doubles (40) and third in hits (181). Despite the numbers, Williams finished second to Joe DiMaggio in the MVP voting in a controversial decision by the writers panel. DiMaggio received 202 points to 201 for Williams. One writer inexplicably left Williams off his ballot, believing that he was not among the 10 most valuable players in the league. If he had placed Williams in any of the 10 places available, Williams would have been the MVP.

JULY 27   Jake Jones hits a freak sixty-foot triple during a 4–3 win over the Browns at Fenway Park. In the sixth inning, Jones hit a ball down the third-base line that rolled foul.

St. Louis pitcher Fred Sanford threw his glove at the ball, and according to the rules, if a fielder attempts to "stop or catch a batted ball or thrown ball with his cap, glove or any part of his uniform while detached from its proper place on his person, the runner or runners shall be entitled to three bases." In 1954, the rule was changed to apply only to fair balls.

AUGUST 2   The Red Sox beat the Tigers 2–1 on Bobby Doerr Night. In pre-game ceremonies, Doerr was presented with a Cadillac sedan, a power unit for his ranch, an outboard motor, a Chevrolet truck, and a deed to 12 lots on the Los Angeles shoreline. Mrs. Doerr received a mink stole.

During the 1947 season, Doerr batted .258 with 17 homers and 95 RBIs.

AUGUST 11   Earl Johnson pitches the Red Sox to a 1–0 win over the Senators at Fenway Park. The only run of the game scored on a third-inning homer by Sam Mele off Mickey Haefner. The game was delayed for several minutes in the eighth inning after fans threw seat covers, bottles, and beer cans onto the field after umpire Joe Rue called Bobby Doerr out on a stolen base attempt.

AUGUST 19   Dom DiMaggio cracks a grand slam off Glen Moulder in the fifth inning of a 9–5 victory over the Browns in St. Louis.

SEPTEMBER 5   Ferris Fain of the Athletics fights Eddie Pellagrini during a 9–7 Red Sox loss at Fenway Park. In the seventh inning, Fain charged toward Pellagrini, claiming that the Boston third baseman tried to clip him as he rounded third base. Fain threw several punches before being pulled away.

SEPTEMBER 11   In his first two major league starts, Red Sox catcher Matt Batts has five hits, including a homer, in seven at-bats during a doubleheader against the Indians at Fenway Park. Batts made his big-league debut a day earlier as a pinch hitter. Cleveland won the first game 10–8, and the Red Sox countered with an 8–3 victory in the second tilt, shortened to 5½ innings by darkness. The game was called by darkness despite the presence of lights at Fenway Park because American

League rules at the time stipulated that lights could not be turned on to finish day games. The rule was changed in 1951.

The Red Sox installed lights at Fenway for the first time in 1947. They were the 14th of 16 major league teams to add lights.

SEPTEMBER 15   At Fenway Park, the Red Sox and White Sox combined to tie an American League record by turning 12 double plays in a doubleheader. The Red Sox turned seven of the dozen twin killings. Chicago won the first game 6–3, and the Red Sox took the second tilt, 7–5.

SEPTEMBER 17   Joe Dobson pitches a one-hitter to defeat the Browns 4–0 in the second game of a doubleheader at Fenway Park. The only hit off Dobson was a broken-bat double by Wally Judnich in the seventh inning. St. Louis won the first game, 9–4.

Dobson had an 18–8 record and a 2.95 ERA in 1947.

SEPTEMBER 26   Johnny Pesky extends his batting streak to 26 games with hits in both games of a doubleheader against the Senators at Fenway Park. The Red Sox lost the first game 6–3 and won the second, 7–2.

Pesky hit .324 with 106 runs and a league-leading 207 hits in 1947. He had at least 200 hits and led the AL in the category in each of his first three seasons in the majors. Pesky had 205 hits as a rookie in 1942 and, after three years in the service, collected 208 more in 1946.

SEPTEMBER 29   Joe McCarthy is named manager of the Red Sox. Joe Cronin moved into the front office as general manager, replacing Eddie Collins, who retired due to health reasons.

Although he never played a single game in the majors as a player, McCarthy is one of the most successful managers in big-league history. He guided the Cubs from 1926 through 1930. After taking an eighth-place team to fourth in his first season, McCarthy won the National League pennant in 1929 before losing the World Series to the Athletics. He was fired by impatient Cubs owner William Wrigley Jr. late in the 1930 season and was hired by the Yankees. At New York from 1931 through 1946, McCarthy guided the Yankees to eight AL pennants and seven World Championships, the latter a record he shares with Casey Stengel. Mercurial Larry MacPhail purchased the Yankees in 1945, however, and he and McCarthy clashed often. McCarthy resigned in May 1946 pleading ill health. McCarthy managed the Red Sox for two full seasons, and each time lost the pennant on the final day with some questionable pitching decisions. He resigned in June 1950. Cronin was the Red Sox' general manager until 1959, when he became president of the American League.

NOVEMBER 17   The Red Sox send Roy Partee, Jim Wilson, Al Widmar, Eddie Pellagrini, Pete Layden, Joe Ostrowski, and $310,000 to the Browns for Vern Stephens and Jack Kramer. The two clubs weren't done dealing. A day later, the Red Sox sent Sam Dente, Clem Dreisewerd, Bill Sommers, and $65,000 to St. Louis for Ellis Kinder and Billy Hitchcock.

Tom Yawkey opened his wallet in attempt to overtake the Yankees by making the trades with the Browns, who were near bankruptcy. It was an excellent transaction, as the Red Sox gave up nine players who couldn't make the starting lineup for one of the best shortstops of the period and two excellent pitchers. Arguably the most underrated player of his generation, Stephens became Boston's starting shortstop, while Johnny Pesky moved to third base. Displaying rare power for a man of his position, Stephens hit .285 with 98 homers and 440 RBIs in 459 games in his first three seasons with the Red Sox. Kramer won 18 games for the Red Sox in 1948, and Kinder won 23 in 1949.

DECEMBER 10   The Red Sox trade Leon Culberson and Al Kozar to the Senators for Stan Spence.

1948   B

Season in a Sentence

Eleven games out of first place in May, the Red Sox rally to take a 3½-game lead in September, only to lose a one-game playoff to the Indians to decide the AL champion.

Finish • Won • Lost • Pct • GB

Second   96   59   .619   1.0

Manager

Joe McCarthy

Stats   Red Sox • AL • Rank

Batting Avg:	.274	.266	3
On-Base Pct:	.374	.349	1
Slugging Pct:	.409	.382	3
Home Runs:	121		3
Stolen Bases:	38		6
ERA:	4.26	4.29	4
Fielding Pct:	.981	.977	3
Runs Scored:	907		1
Runs Allowed:	720		3

Starting Lineup

Birdie Tebbetts, c
Billy Goodman, 1b
Bobby Doerr, 2b
Johnny Pesky, 3b
Vern Stephens, ss
Ted Williams, lf
Dom DiMaggio, cf
Stan Spence, rf
Wally Moses, rf
Sam Mele, rf

Pitchers

Joe Dobson, sp
Jack Kramer, sp
Mel Parnell, sp
Ellis Kinder, sp
Mickey Harris, sp
Denny Galehouse, sp
Earl Johnson, rp
Boo Ferriss, rp

Attendance

1,558,798 (fourth in AL)

Club Leaders

Batting Avg:	Williams	.369
On-Base Pct:	Williams	.497
Slugging Pct:	Williams	.615
Home Runs:	Stephens	29
RBI:	Stephens	137
Runs:	DiMaggio	127
Stolen Bases:	DiMaggio	10
Wins:	Kramer	18
Strikeouts:	Dobson	116
ERA:	Parnell	3.15
Saves:	Johnson	5

MARCH 26   The Red Sox sell Don Gutteridge to the Pirates.

APRIL 16   Billy Hitchcock of the Red Sox and Earl Torgeson of the Braves engage in a vicious fist fight during a 19–6 Sox exhibition game win at Braves Field. The battle started when the two became entangled in a tag play at first base.

APRIL 19   The Red Sox open the season with a Patriots' Day doubleheader against the Athletics at Fenway Park and lose twice—5–4 in 11 innings and later, 4–2. The games were separate-admission affairs, with 22,409 attending the morning game and 33,875 in the afternoon. Governor Robert Bradford threw out the first ball in the opener. In the second inning of the first game, Stan Spence, Vern Stephens, and Bobby Doerr hit consecutive homers off Phil Marchildon. It was Stephens's first at-bat as a member of the Red Sox, and Spence's first since being reacquired in a trade with the Senators. Marchildon, who was in the Canadian Air Force during World War II and spent nearly a year as a German prisoner of war, settled down and pitched all 11 innings for the win. In the afternoon contest, Lew Brissie went the distance for the Athletics for his first major league victory. Like Marchildon, Brissie had to survive combat during the war. Fighting in Northern Italy in 1944, he was the only survivor of his 12-man infantry unit. However, an exploding shell shredded his left leg, and it took 23 operations to save it. In the sixth inning, Ted Williams lined a pitch off Brissie's injured leg. A stretcher was brought onto the field, but Brissie, who had been through much worse, stayed in the game.

Among the additions at Fenway Park in 1948 was a rooftop press box.

APRIL 22   With two Athletics on base, two out in the ninth, and the Red Sox leading 4–3 at Fenway Park, right fielder Sam Mele loses an easy fly ball in the sun and allows both runners to score for a 5–4 Philadelphia win.

MAY 5   Eleven days after the start of the Berlin airlift, a walk-off homer by Vern Stephens in the eleventh inning beats the Tigers 4–3 at Fenway Park. The Sox tied the score 3–3 with two runs in the ninth.

In his first season with the Red Sox, Stephens hit 29 homers, drove in 137 runs, scored 114, and hit .269. He played in every inning of every game in 1948.

MAY 6   A fistfight between Birdie Tebbetts and George Vico highlights an 8–3 win over the Tigers at Fenway Park. The rhubarb grew out of an unsuccessful squeeze play in the fourth inning after Hal White missed a bunt with Vico on third. Tebbetts chased Vico back toward the base and tagged him. Tebbetts stumbled over Vico, who popped up and took a swing at the Red Sox catcher. After both were banished by the umpires, the pair scuffled again in the grandstand tunnel leading to the dressing rooms. Vico suffered a cut under his left eye, and Tebbetts got a scratch on his nose.

MAY 12   After the White Sox score two runs in the tenth inning at Fenway Park, the Red Sox roar back with three in their half and win 6–5 on Bobby Doerr's walk-off, three–run homer.

Doerr hit .285 with 27 homers and 111 RBIs in 1948.

MAY 16   The Red Sox wallop the Senators 14–5 at Fenway Park.

Red Sox catcher Matt Batts refused to fly and took the train whenever the club traveled by air. His fear of flying stemmed from an incident during World War II. Batts was on a transport plane when he opened a window because it was hot. As a practical joke, the pilot went into a dive and the change in air pressure sent Batts to the roof of the plane and nearly sucked him out of the window.

MAY 20   Mickey Harris and Mickey McDermott combine to walk 18 batters to tie a major league record by a team in a nine-inning game during a 12–4 loss to the Indians in Cleveland. Harris walked seven batters in $1\frac{1}{3}$ innings, and McDermott 11 in $6\frac{2}{3}$. Three of the walks were with the bases loaded.

At the end of May, the Red Sox had a record of 14–23 and were in seventh place, $11\frac{1}{2}$ games behind the first-place Athletics, which caused many fans to circulate petitions calling for the ouster of new manager Joe McCarthy. But the Red Sox maintained a torrid pace for over three months. The club was in first place by late July. From June 3 through September 9, the Red Sox had a record of 69–24.

JUNE 3   The Red Sox are on Boston television for the first time and win 3–2 over the Browns at Fenway Park. The game was telecast over WBZ-TV. The first baseball game telecast by the station took place between the Braves and the Cardinals from Braves Field on May 21.

The June 3 game was the first Red Sox contest that reached the homes and businesses of Boston-area television owners. Television cameras made their first appearance at Fenway Park during the May 12, 1948, game, but it was only to test equipment and the telecast wasn't carried outside the ballpark.

JUNE 6   The Red Sox win both ends of a doubleheader against the Tigers 5–4 and 12–4 at Fenway Park. In the opener, Vern Stephens hit a homer in the eighth inning to tie the score 4–4, then drove in the winning run in the ninth on a bases-loaded single. In the second tilt, Ted Williams, Stan Spence, and Stephens hit back-to-back-to-back homers in the sixth inning off Fred Hutchinson.

Williams led the league in batting average (.369), on-base percentage (.497), slugging percentage (.615), and doubles (44) in 1948. He also hit 25 homers, drove in 127 runs, and scored 124.

JUNE 7   The Red Sox lose 2–0 to the Indians at Fenway Park on a disputed two-run homer by Lou Boudreau. The drive landed about six rows into the stands in the right field corner, and nearly everyone in the ballpark thought it was foul except for first umpire Charlie Berry, who signaled home run.

JUNE 10   The Red Sox score eight runs in the third inning off Bob Feller and roll to a 15–7 win over the Indians at Fenway Park.

JUNE 11   Ted Williams drives in seven runs on two doubles, a single, and a bases-loaded walk to lead the Red Sox to a 12–4 victory over the White Sox at Fenway Park.

JUNE 27   Joe Dobson pitches a two-hitter to beat the Browns 2–0 in the first game of a doubleheader at Sportsman's Park. The only St. Louis hits were singles by Paul Lehner and Chuck Stevens. The Sox completed the sweep with a 6–3 win in the second tilt, which was stopped by rain at the end of the seventh inning.

Dobson had a record of 16–10 and a 3.56 ERA in 1948.

JULY 4   The Red Sox explode for 14 runs in the seventh inning, breaking a 5–5 tie, and swamp the Athletics 20–8 at Fenway Park. In the 14-run seventh, Ted Williams was the first man up in the inning and walked with rookie pitcher Charlie Harris on the mound. Stan Spence beat out a bunt. Vern Stephens walked to load the bases. Bobby Doerr walked, and Williams scored, putting the Red Sox ahead 6–5. Billy Goodman singled, scoring Spence and Stephens (8–5). The bases were reloaded when Harris threw late to third on Matt Batt's sacrifice bunt. Ellis Kinder singled scoring Doerr and Goodman (10–5). Dom DiMaggio doubled, scoring Batts and moving Kinder to third (11–5). Johnny Pesky singled, scoring Kinder and DiMaggio (13–5). Williams walked. Spence flied to outfielder Ray Coleman for the first out. Stephens singled scoring Pesky (14–5). Doerr walked, loading the bases.
Philadelphia manager Connie Mack, who drew criticism for leaving Harris in the game to absorb the beating, brought Bill McCahan as a reliever. Goodman

was thrown out at first for the second out, Williams scoring (15–5). Batts doubled, scoring Stephens and Doerr (17–5). Kinder singled, Batts holding third. DiMaggio walked, loading the bases. Pesky singled, and Kinder and DiMaggio scored the 13th and 14th runs of the inning (19–5). Up for the third time, Williams grounded out to end the inning.

JULY 15   The Red Sox defeat the Tigers 13–5 and 3–1 in a day-night doubleheader at Fenway Park. The Sox scored seven runs in the seventh inning in the first game.

Ted Williams missed 13 games in July with a rib injury caused by a punch he received from Sam Mele when the two were playfully sparring on a train from Boston to Philadelphia.

JULY 19   A grand slam by Bobby Doerr in the first inning off Fred Sanford accounts for all of the Red Sox' runs in a 4–1 win over the Browns at Fenway Park.

JULY 21   The Red Sox score three runs in the ninth inning to beat the White Sox 10–9 in the second inning of a doubleheader at Fenway Park. A sacrifice fly by Matt Batts broke the 9–9 tie. Chicago took a 6–0 lead in the third inning, but the Red Sox rallied to tie the score 6–6 before falling behind again. The Red Sox also won the first game, 3–1.

JULY 23   The Red Sox rout the White Sox 13–1 at Fenway Park. It was Boston's ninth win in a row.

JULY 25   The Red Sox win their 12th game in a row and move into first place with a 3–0 victory over the Indians at Fenway Park. Joe Dobson pitched the shutout.

JULY 27   The Red Sox win their 13th game in a row, the second-longest winning streak in club history, with an 8–0 win over the Tigers in Detroit.

JULY 28   The Red Sox' 13-game winning streak comes to an end with a 13–0 loss to the Tigers in Detroit.

JULY 29   Billy Goodman hits a grand slam in the seventh inning of Virgil Trucks during an 8–1 win over the Tigers in Detroit. It was Goodman's first major league homer.

AUGUST 1   During a 12–2 loss to the Indians in the first game of a doubleheader in Cleveland, Lou Boudreau steals home on a close play at the plate. Joe McCarthy came out to argue the call, but he was just as angry at catcher Matt Batts for allowing Boudreau to score as he was at the umpire. McCarthy kicked Batts in the rear end but later denied doing so despite thousands of witnesses. McCarthy's disposition didn't improve when the Sox dropped the second game, 6–1.

The 1948 pennant race was so tight that the Red Sox dropped from first to fourth with the doubleheader loss. The Indians, Yankees, Athletics, and Red Sox were separated by only one game after play ended on August 1. The Athletics, led by eighty-five-year-old Connie Mack in his 48th year as manager, dropped out of the race by Labor Day, but the Sox, Indians, and Yankees battled each other until the final weekend of the season.

AUGUST 3   Jack Kramer earns his 11th win in a row with a 15–8 decision over the Browns in St. Louis.

                In his first season with the Red Sox, Kramer was 18–5 with an ERA of 4.35.

AUGUST 4   In St. Louis, the Red Sox score six runs in the first inning, but the Browns counter with seven in their half. After the Sox scored a run in the second and another in the sixth to take the lead, the Browns plated two in the ninth for a 9–8 win.

AUGUST 16   Babe Ruth dies of cancer at the age of fifty-three.

AUGUST 20   The Red Sox win a thrilling 10-inning, 5–4 decision over the Senators in the first game of a doubleheader at Fenway Park. A three-run homer by Vern Stephens in the ninth tied the score. Stan Spence's walk-off homer won the game. In the second contest, Dom DiMaggio belted a grand slam during a seven-run second inning as the Sox won, 10–4.

                DiMaggio scored 127 runs and hit .285 in 1948.

AUGUST 21   Vern Stephens hits two homers, one of them a grand slam off Dick Welteroth in the fourth inning of a 10–6 win over the Senators at Fenway Park.

AUGUST 24   The Red Sox recapture first place in the hot pennant race with three runs in the ninth, the last two on a walk-off homer by Vern Stephens, to beat the Indians 9–8 at Fenway Park.

AUGUST 29   The Red Sox score seven times in the first inning, four of them on a grand slam by Birdie Tebbetts off Bryan Stephens, and go on to beat the Browns 10–2 in the first of two at Fenway Park. St. Louis won the second game, 12–4.

SEPTEMBER 6   The Red Sox score nine runs in the fifth inning and roll to a 14–6 win over the Senators in the first game of a Labor Day doubleheader in Washington. The Sox completed the sweep with a 2–1 triumph in the nightcap.

SEPTEMBER 9   The Red Sox score eight runs in the third inning and coast to a 9–4 win over the Yankees at Fenway Park. The win gave the Red Sox a 3½-game lead over the second-place Yankees in the AL pennant race. The Indians were third, 4½ games back. The Sox had a record of 84–48 and had 22 games left to play.

SEPTEMBER 15   The White Sox score 10 runs in the seventh inning and rout the Red Sox 17–10 in Chicago. Red Sox outfielder Tom Wright made his major league debut as a pinch hitter in the ninth inning and hit a triple on the first pitch.

SEPTEMBER 22   The Indians tie the Red Sox for first place with a 5–2 win in Cleveland. The Yankees were one game behind. There were eight games left on the schedule.

SEPTEMBER 24   The Red Sox lose 9–6 to the Yankees in New York, creating a three-way tie for first place. Boston, Cleveland, and New York each had 91–56 records.

SEPTEMBER 26   The Boston Braves clinch their first National League pennant since 1914, creating the possibility of an all-Boston World Series.

SEPTEMBER 28   The Senators defeat the Red Sox 4–2 at Fenway Park. The loss put the Red Sox two games back of the Indians in a second-place tie with the Yankees.

SEPTEMBER 29   The Red Sox retain a slim hope of winning the pennant with a 5–1 win over the Senators at Fenway Park. The Sox were still two games behind the Indians with three contests remaining.

SEPTEMBER 30   The Red Sox continue to keep their pennant hopes alive with a 7–3 victory over the Senators at Fenway Park before a slim crowd of 4,998. Heading into the final two games of the season, the Red Sox and Yankees were tied for second, one game behind the Indians.

OCTOBER 2   The Red Sox beat the Yankees 5–1 before 32,118 at Fenway Park. Ted Williams hit a two-run homer in the first inning, and Jack Kramer pitched a complete game. The Indians, behind Gene Bearden, beat the Tigers 8–0 in Cleveland. At the end of day, the Sox were one game back of the Indians, and the Yankees were eliminated from pennant consideration.

OCTOBER 3   On the final day of the regular season, the Red Sox beat the Yankees 10–5 before 31,204 at Fenway Park, while the Indians lose 7–1 to the Tigers in Cleveland in a duel between future Hall of Fame pitchers Hal Newhouser and Bob Feller. In Boston, the Yankees led 2–0 when the Sox scored five runs in the third. The Yankees battled back to narrow the gap to 5–4 before Boston scored four runs in sixth, paced by home runs from Dom DiMaggio and Vern Stephens.

The Boston win and Cleveland loss left the two clubs tied after 154 games with records of 96–58. The AL pennant would be decided with a one-game playoff game at Fenway Park on October 4.

OCTOBER 4   The Indians defeat the Red Sox 8–3 in a one-game playoff to decide the AL champion before 33,957 at Fenway Park. Indians player-manager Lou Boudreau sent rookie Gene Bearden, pitching on one day of rest, to the mound against Denny Galehouse of the Red Sox. Bearden, supported by two homers and two singles from Boudreau, pitched a complete game and allowed only one earned run. Galehouse was removed with none out in the fourth inning after allowing a three-run homer to Ken Keltner, which broke a 1–1 tie. Reliever Ellis Kinder couldn't hold the Indians either, allowing four runs and eight hits in six innings. The Indians moved on to win the World Series in six games against the Boston Braves.

McCarthy's choice of Galehouse to start the crucial playoff has long been a sore point with Red Sox fans. Boston's starting rotation during the final week of the season consisted of Ellis Kinder, Mel Parnell, Jack Kramer, and Joe Dobson. Heading into the playoff, Kinder had four days of rest and Parnell three. Kinder was riding a five-game winning streak. Yet McCarthy chose the thirty-six-year-old Galehouse, who hadn't started a game since September 18, when he allowed four runs and six hits in 3⅔ innings to the lowly Browns. Galehouse's only other appearance between September 18 and October 4 was a three-inning relief stint against the Yankees on September 26 in which he gave up two runs and seven hits. In his previous start against the Indians, on August 25 in Boston, Galehouse allowed four runs and seven hits before being relieved in the second inning. Galehouse also warmed up several times in the bullpen in the October 3 game against the Yankees.

McCarthy said that he wanted a veteran on the mound against the Indians, but Kinder was thirty-three years old, had a slightly better year than Galehouse, and was well rested. Heading into the pennant-deciding game against the Indians, Kinder was 10–7 with an ERA of 3.66, while Galehouse was 8–6 with an earned run average of 3.82. Parnell was only in his second season in the majors but was the Red Sox' best pitcher in 1948 with a 15–8 record and a 3.14 ERA, surrendered only one run in his previous start, and beat the Indians three times during the season. McCarthy was influenced heavily by a game in Cleveland on July 30 in which Parnell gave up six runs in $\frac{1}{3}$ of an inning, while Galehouse stopped the Indians on one run and two hits in $8\frac{2}{3}$ innings of relief. The Red Sox rallied to win 8–7. The October 4 playoff loss was Galehouse's last major league start. He pitched only two more games, both in relief in 1949.

1949   B

Season in a Sentence

In a near repeat of 1948, the Red Sox fall 12 games behind in July, surge into first place in September, and lose the pennant in the final game of the season.

Finish • Won • Lost • Pct • GB

Second   96   58   .623   1.0

Manager

Joe McCarthy

Stats

Stats	Red Sox	AL	Rank
Batting Avg:	.282	.263	1
On-Base Pct:	.381	.353	1
Slugging Pct:	.420	.379	1
Home Runs:	131		1
Stolen Bases:	43		5
ERA:	3.97	4.20	4
Fielding Pct:	.980	.977	2
Runs Scored:	896		1
Runs Allowed:	667		4

Starting Lineup

Birdie Tebbetts, c
Billy Goodman, 1b
Bobby Doerr, 2b
Johnny Pesky, 3b
Vern Stephens, ss
Ted Williams, lf
Dom DiMaggio, cf
Al Zarilla, rf
Matt Batts, c

Pitchers

Mel Parnell, sp
Ellis Kinder, sp-rp
Joe Dobson, sp
Chuck Stobbs, sp
Jack Kramer, sp
Mickey McDermott, sp

Attendance

1,596,650 (fourth in AL)

Club Leaders

Batting Avg:	Williams	.343
On-Base Pct:	Williams	.490
Slugging Pct:	Williams	.650
Home Runs:	Williams	43
RBI:	Williams	159
	Stephens	159
Runs:	Williams	150
Stolen Bases:	DiMaggio	9
Wins:	Parnell	25
Strikeouts:	Kinder	138
ERA:	Parnell	2.77
Saves:	Kinder	4
	Hughson	4

APRIL 19   In the season opener, the Red Sox lose 3–2 to the Athletics in Philadelphia.

APRIL 22   In the first game of the season at Fenway Park, the Red Sox lose 5–3 to the Yankees before a crowd of 33,955.

Leo Egan joined Jim Britt and Tom Hussey in the Red Sox radio booth in 1949. Red Sox road games were on the radio for the first time, but only on days in which the Braves were not playing at home. The road contests were studio recreations as the announcers received pitch-by-pitch descriptions of the games via teletype. All home games of both the Red Sox and Braves were on television on WBZ-TV and WNAC-TV. The announcers were Britt, Hussey, and Bump Hadley. Hadley was an ex–major league pitcher from Lynn, Massachusetts.

APRIL 23   Vern Stephens hits a triple and two homers, one a grand slam, during an 11–8 win over the Yankees at Fenway Park. Stephens's slam occurred in the fourth inning off Fred Sanford and put the Sox ahead 7–6.

MAY 1   Ted Williams hits a grand slam in the sixth inning off Spec Shea during an 11–2 win over the Yankees in New York. The game was stopped after eight innings by rain.

Vern Stephens and Ted Williams were a devastating batting duo in 1949 as both drove in 159 runs to share the league lead. Williams also led the AL in home runs (43), on-base percentage (.490), slugging percentage (.650), runs (150), doubles (39), total bases (368), and walks (162). He narrowly missed winning the Triple Crown, finishing second in batting average by a razor-thin .0002 margin to George Kell. Kell's batting average was .3429, and Williams's was .3427. Williams did win the Most Valuable Player Award, however. Stephens hit 39 homers, scored 113 runs, and hit .290.

MAY 3   The Red Sox and the Tigers battle to a 13-inning 14–14 tie in Detroit. The game was called due to darkness. The Sox were down 10–4 after three innings, surged ahead 14–11, then allowed the Tigers to tie the game with three tallies in the ninth.

MAY 8   The Red Sox send Stan Spence and cash to the Browns for Al Zarilla.

MAY 9   Red Sox minor leaguer Chuck Koney, who was playing for Louisville in the American Association, loses his right leg after a water heater explosion at his home in Chicago. The blast of water and metal burned and nearly tore off his leg, necessitating amputation. Koney was recovering from another injury when he left the Louisville club and traveled to Chicago to see his wife and two-year-old son. Two days after the accident, Tom Yawkey gave Koney a five-year contract as a scout. Koney was employed as a scout by the Red Sox for more than forty years.

MAY 11   In a rare defensive lapse, Bobby Doerr makes three errors in an inning during a 12–8 loss to the White Sox at Comiskey Park. The White Sox scored in all eight turns at bat.

Doerr hit .309 with 18 homers and 109 runs batted in during the 1949 season.

MAY 12   A home run by Vern Stephens in the eleventh inning is the deciding blow in a 2–1 victory over the White Sox in Chicago.

MAY 13   With President Harry Truman in attendance, the Red Sox lose 5–4 to the Senators in Washington.

MAY 22   Mel Parnell pitches a 12-inning complete game and hits a walk-off single to beat the Tigers 3–2 at Fenway Park.

              A left-hander best known for his wicked breaking balls, Parnell had a 25–7 record and a 2.77 ERA in 295$\frac{1}{3}$ innings. He completed 27 of his 33 starts. On the negative side, Parnell set a club record for walks in a season with 134.

MAY 24   After the Tigers score in the top of the tenth inning at Fenway Park, the Red Sox come back with two in their half on Bobby Doerr's walk-off homer to win, 8–7.

              Before the game, Ted Williams was presented with the second Atlantic salmon of the season caught in the Penobscot River. Harry Truman received the first. During the game, Williams threw his bat thirty feet into the air in disgust after striking out.

MAY 30   Al Zarilla's grand slam off Phil Marchildon in the sixth inning highlights a 10–2 win over the Athletics in the first game of a doubleheader at Fenway Park. The Sox completed the sweep with a 4–3 win in the second tilt.

              The Red Sox had a record of 61–16 at Fenway Park in 1949, including an 11–0 mark against the Athletics. The Sox were 35–42 on the road.

JUNE 12   The Red Sox sweep the White Sox 15–3 and 7–5 in Chicago.

              Johnny Pesky scored 111 runs and hit .306 in 1949.

JUNE 13   The Red Sox trade Sam Mele and Mickey Harris to the Senators for pitcher Walt Masterson.

JUNE 14   The Red Sox allow the Indians to use a "courtesy runner" in the first inning of a 10–5 loss at Fenway Park. Lou Boudreau was hit on the elbow by a pitch and was taken to the dressing room for treatment. The man who went in to run for Boudreau was Ken Keltner, who was already in the game and had scored earlier in the inning. While serving as a runner for Boudreau, Keltner scored again. Keltner was credited with two runs scored in the inning. Boudreau returned to the game in the second inning.

JUNE 24   Ted Williams drives in seven runs on two homers and a single as the Red Sox rout the Browns 21–2 at Fenway Park. Boston collected 25 hits in the contest. Billy Goodman had five of them, including a double, in seven at-bats.

              Goodman often had to play through a painful fungus growth on his hands that itched, developed into blisters, and caused his skin to crack. The disease reoccurred at unpredictable moments. He contracted the ailment while in the Navy during World War II fighting in the Pacific Islands.

JUNE 25   The Red Sox continue their heavy bombardment of Browns pitching with a 13–2 win at Fenway Park. Boston scored seven runs in the third inning.

JUNE 28   After missing the first 65 games of the season because of a heel ailment, Joe DiMaggio plays for the first time in 1949 and collects a homer and a single to lead the Yankees to a 5–4 win over the Red Sox at Fenway Park.

               In a three-game series against the Red Sox from June 28 through June 30, DiMaggio hit four homers and drove in nine runs. The Yankees won all three games.

JULY 4   The Red Sox lose their seventh and eighth games in a row, dropping a doubleheader to the Yankees in New York by scores of 3–2 and 6–4. The second game was called after 7½ innings by rain. A misjudgment by Johnny Pesky contributed to the first-game loss. In the ninth inning with the bases loaded, Pesky tagged up at third believing a drive by Al Zarilla to right field would be caught. The ball landed in front of Yankee right fielder Cliff Mapes, and Pesky was out at home on a force play.

               After the twin defeats, the Red Sox appeared to be hopelessly out of the pennant race. The club had a record of 35–36 and was in fourth place, 12 games out of first. "That's it," declared Yankee manager Casey Stengel. "The Red Sox won't bother us." The Sox won 61 of their next 81 games, however, and moved into first place in late September.

JULY 7   The Red Sox draw 13 walks from Senators pitchers in an 8-3 win at Washington in a contest called after six innings to permit the Sox to catch a train.

JULY 10   The Red Sox sweep the Athletics 8–5 and 11–10 in a doubleheader at Fenway Park. The Red Sox scored seven runs in the first inning of the second game, which was called after 7½ innings by darkness.

               The Red Sox set a single-season attendance record for the fourth straight year in 1949, drawing 1,596,650 into Fenway Park. It would be 1967 before the Sox drew that many fans again.

JULY 12   During an 11–7 American League victory in the All-Star Game at Ebbets Field in Brooklyn, Dom DiMaggio collects a double and a single, scores twice, and drives in a run. Birdie Tebbetts had a double, a single, and an RBI in two at-bats.

               DiMaggio scored 126 runs and hit .307 in 1949.

JULY 14   The Red Sox notch their eighth win in a row, defeating the Tigers 5–2 in Detroit.

JULY 26   The Red Sox uncork a 10-run outburst in the eighth inning to defeat the White Sox 11–2 at Fenway Park. Vern Stephens collected a homer and a double in the inning.

AUGUST 3   Ellis Kinder fans 14 batters during a 9–3 win over the Browns at Fenway Park. Dom DiMaggio tied Tris Speaker's record for the longest hitting streak in club history by collecting a hit in his 30th consecutive game.

Heading into the 1949 season, Kinder was thirty-four years old and had a life-time record of 21–25. During his breakout year in '49, he posted a record of 23–6 and had an ERA of 3.36. The son of an Arkansas sharecropper, Kinder didn't make his professional debut until he was twenty-four years old and didn't reach the majors with the Browns until 1946 when he was thirty-one, earning him the nickname "Old Folks." Ellis pitched for the Red Sox until 1955 and was forty-two when he pitched his last big-league game in 1957.

AUGUST 4   During a 12–2 trouncing of the Browns at Fenway Park, Dom DiMaggio breaks Tris Speaker's club consecutive-game hit record by collecting a hit in his 31st straight game.

AUGUST 7   Dom DiMaggio runs his hit streak to 34 games during a 6–4 loss to the Tigers at Fenway Park. The streak was halted on August 9 by Vic Raschi during a 6–3 win over the Yankees in Boston. Hitless in his first four at-bats, Dom hit a sinking line drive in the eighth that his brother Joe caught off of the tops of his shoes.

The 34-game hitting streak by DiMaggio is still the club record, although he was 22 shy of his brother Joe's major league record of 56, set in 1941. Dom owns two of the three longest major league hitting streaks in the DiMaggio family, however. Dom had another hitting streak of 27 games in 1951. Joe's second-longest streak was 23 games in 1940.

AUGUST 12   The Red Sox sweep the Senators 15–7 and 13–11 in a day-night doubleheader at Fenway Park. In the first game, the Red Sox scored seven runs in the sixth inning. In the nightcap, Boston plated eight runs in the third to take a 9–4 lead but allowed Washington to come back and tie the contest 11–11, before the Sox scored twice in the eighth for the win.

AUGUST 13   Vern Stephens hits a walk-off grand slam off Joe Haynes in the twelfth inning to defeat the Senators 5–1 at Fenway Park.

AUGUST 14   The Red Sox sweep the Senators 9–3 and 13–4 at Fenway Park.

AUGUST 15   The Red Sox sign African-American second baseman Piper Davis of the Birmingham Black Barons in the Negro Leagues.

Davis was the first African-American player in the Red Sox' minor league system. He was purchased from the Barons for $7,500. While scouting Davis, the Red Sox also looked at Barons outfielder Willie Mays but failed to sign him because the club's scouts didn't believe that Mays was major league material. Davis claimed to be twenty-nine years old but was really thirty-two. He was sent to the Red Sox' Scranton club in the Eastern League in 1950 and hit .333 with three homers in 15 games before he was released on May 13 for "financial reasons"— two days before the other half of his $7,500 purchase price was due to the Barons. Following his release, Davis played for several seasons in the Pacific Coast League and never reached the majors.

AUGUST 17   Red Sox pitcher Chuck Stobbs walks 10 batters but pitches a 10-inning complete game to beat the Athletics 5–1 in Philadelphia.

AUGUST 26   The Red Sox sweep the White Sox 11–4 and 10–7 in a doubleheader in Chicago. Mel Parnell won his 20th game in the opener.

SEPTEMBER 5   The Red Sox sweep the Senators 5–2 and 12–2 at Fenway Park.

SEPTEMBER 14   Ted Williams hits a homer in the sixth inning off Hal Newhouser that beats the Tigers 1–0 at Fenway Park. Ellis Kinder pitched the shutout for his 20th win of the season.

From July 1 through September 28, Ted Williams reached base in 84 consecutive games, a major league record. Williams holds three of the top four streaks of reaching base in major league history. He did it in 69 consecutive games in 1946 and in 65 games in 1948. Joe DiMaggio is second on the list, with 74 in 1941.

SEPTEMBER 18   Ted Williams drives in six runs on two homers, leading the Red Sox to an 11–5 win over the White Sox at Fenway Park.

SEPTEMBER 20   The Red Sox defeat the Indians 5–2 at Fenway Park, but the first-place Yankees also win, leaving Boston three games behind with 11 games left on the schedule.

SEPTEMBER 24   The day after President Harry Truman announces that the Soviet Union has developed and tested an atomic bomb, the Red Sox win their eighth game in a row and move within one game of the first-place Yankees with a 3–0 win over the Bronx Bombers at Fenway Park. Ellis Kinder pitched the shutout. It was his 23rd win of the season and his 13th in a row.

SEPTEMBER 25   The Red Sox climb into a tie for first place by whipping the Yankees 4–1 at Fenway Park. It was Mel Parnell's 25th win of the season and the ninth in a row for the Sox. It was also the first time that the Red Sox had even a share of first place all year.

After the game, the two clubs traveled to New York to make up a contest postponed earlier in the season.

SEPTEMBER 26   The Red Sox take a one-game lead in the AL pennant race by winning a thrilling 7–6 decision over the Yankees before 67,434 on a Monday afternoon in New York. The Sox trailed 6–3 before exploding for four runs in the eighth inning. The winning run was scored when Bobby Doerr executed a squeeze bunt that brought in Johnny Pesky. The throw from first baseman Tommy Henrich to catcher Ralph Houk beat Pesky by several yards, but umpire Bill Grieve called Pesky safe. Casey Stengel and Houk argued long and loud that Pesky was out, to no avail. After the game, Yankee outfielder Cliff Mapes asked Grieve how much he had bet on the game and had to be restrained from punching the umpire. Stengel, Houk, and Mapes were all fined by AL president Will Harridge. It was Boston's 10th win in a row. It was also the first time that the Yankees had been out of first place all season.

SEPTEMBER 27   The Red Sox register their 11th win in a row and retain their one-game lead over the Yankees with a 6–4 decision over the Senators in Washington.

SEPTEMBER 28   The Red Sox drop back into a tie with the Yankees for first place after losing 2–1 to the Senators in Washington. The Sox had a 1–0 lead before the Senators scored two runs in the ninth inning. The game ended on a bases-loaded wild pitch by Mel Parnell.

SEPTEMBER 30   The Red Sox eke out an 11–9 win over the Senators at Griffith Stadium and take first place after the Yankees lose 4–1 to the Athletics in Philadelphia. Boston collected only five hits, winning with the help of 14 Washington walks and three errors. The game ended on a bases-loaded double play.

> *There were two games left on the schedule, both against the Yankees in New York. All the Red Sox needed was one victory in the two games to reach the World Series.*

OCTOBER 1   The Yankees defeat the Red Sox 5–4 at Yankee Stadium. The win put the Yankees back into a tie for first place with the Red Sox with one game remaining. The Red Sox led 4–0 with a run in the first inning and three more in the third, but the Yankees scored two runs in fourth and two in the fifth to tie the contest, 4–4. Johnny Lindell broke the deadlock with a two-out, eighth-inning homer off Boston hurler Joe Dobson. Joe Page pitched $6\frac{2}{3}$ innings of shutout relief for the Yankees, allowing only one hit. Joe DiMaggio, who had missed the previous two weeks with viral pneumonia, provided inspiration with a double and a single.

OCTOBER 2   The Red Sox lose the pennant on the final day of the season with a 5–3 defeat at the hands of the Yankees in New York. The Yankees picked up a run in the first inning, before the two clubs matched goose eggs for the next six frames. Still trailing 1–0 in the eighth, Boston manager Joe McCarthy made the controversial decision to lift starting pitcher Ellis Kinder for pinch hitter Tom Wright, a rookie outfielder with only six career at-bats in the majors. Wright walked but was erased when Dom DiMaggio hit into a double play. Mel Parnell, who started the game the previous day, took the mound in the last half of the inning and yielded a homer to Tommy Henrich and a single to Yogi Berra. Parnell was relieved by Tex Hughson, who gave up three more runs on a two-out, bases-loaded double to Jerry Coleman for a 5–0 Yankee advantage. Right fielder Al Zarilla, who many believe was playing two deep, just missed a shoestring catch on Coleman's drive. The Red Sox rallied desperately in the ninth for three runs before Yankee pitcher Vic Raschi could retire the side. The Yankees moved on to win the World Series in five games against the Brooklyn Dodgers.

> *The Red Sox of 1948 and 1949 are the only clubs in baseball history to finish one game out of first place two seasons in a row. It is part of Joe McCarthy's curious legacy that he never won a close pennant race. He won nine league titles—one with the Cubs and eight with the Yankees—and the smallest margin over the second-place club in those nine seasons was nine games. Yet he lost five pennants by margins of three games or less. Those five were with the Cubs in 1930 (two games), Yankees in 1935 (three games), Yankees in 1940 (two games), Red Sox in 1948 (one game), and Red Sox in 1949 (one game).*

OCTOBER 8   The Red Sox trade Billy Hitchcock to the Athletics for Buddy Rosar.

Courtesy of Transcendental Graphics/theruckerarchive.com

The DiMaggio brothers, Joe and Dom, flank Ted Williams. All lost three seasons to World War II but played in the majors together for nine years.

THE STATE OF THE RED SOX

The Red Sox began the decade after losing the AL pennant on the final day of the season in both 1948 and 1949. The club was in contention for most of the 1950 and 1951 seasons but fell short. Between 1952 and 1959, the Red Sox hovered between third place and sixth place in an eight-team league. Overall, they were 814–725 during the 1950s, a winning percentage of .529, fourth-best in the AL behind the Yankees, Indians, and White Sox. The Yankees won eight of the 10 pennants during the fifties, missing only in 1954, when the Indians won, and in 1959, when the White Sox reached the World Series.

THE BEST TEAM

The 1950 Red Sox had a record of 94–60 and finished in third place, four games behind the Yankees.

THE WORST TEAM

The 1954 Red Sox had the worst record of the decade at 69–85 and finished 42 games behind Cleveland, but they ended the season in fourth place. The 1952 Sox were 76–78, but finished in sixth, the lowest position in the standing of any club during the 1950s.

THE BEST MOMENT

Considered washed-up near the end of an excellent career, Mel Parnell pitched a no-hitter against the White Sox at Fenway Park on July 14, 1956.

THE WORST MOMENT

The promising career of first baseman Harry Agganis came to a tragic end when he died suddenly at the age of twenty-five while recuperating from a battle with pneumonia on June 27, 1955.

THE ALL–DECADE TEAM • YEARS WITH BRS

Sammy White, c	1951–59
Dick Gernert, 1b	1952–59
Billy Goodman, 2b	1947–57
Frank Malzone, 3b	1955–65
Don Buddin, ss	1956, 1958–61
Ted Williams, lf	1939–42, 1946–60
Jimmy Piersall, cf	1950, 1952–58
Jackie Jensen, rf	1954–59, 1961
Mel Parnell, p	1947–56
Ellis Kinder, p	1948–55
Frank Sullivan, p	1953–60
Tom Brewer, p	1954–61

Other prominent Red Sox players during the 1950s included pitchers Ike Delock (1953–63), Mickey McDermott (1948–53), and Willard Nixon (1950–58), outfielder Dom DiMaggio (1940–42, 1946–53), and second baseman–first baseman Pete Runnels (1958–62).

THE DECADE LEADERS

Batting Avg:	Williams	.336
On-Base Pct:	Williams	.476
Slugging Pct:	Williams	.622
Home Runs:	Williams	227
RBI:	Williams	729
Runs:	Williams	661
Stolen Bases:	Jensen	86
Wins:	Parnell	81
Strikeouts:	Sullivan	723
ERA:	Kinder	3.13
Saves:	Kinder	87

THE HOME FIELD

There were few notable changes to Fenway Park during the 1950s, although there would have been a major alteration if the city government had cooperated. Tom Yawkey wanted to close Lansdowne Street and move back the left field wall, but officials blocked the plan. Season attendance ranged from a high of 1,344,080 in 1950 to a low of 931,127 in 1954. The number of night games at Fenway Park increased from 14 in 1956 to 21 in 1957 and 24 in 1959.

THE GAME YOU WISH YOU HAD SEEN

The Red Sox set a modern major league record for most runs scored in a game in a 29–4 thrashing of the Browns on June 8, 1950. In another explosion, the Sox set a modern mark for most runs in an inning with 17 in a 23–3 trouncing of the Tigers on June 18, 1953, in Boston.

THE WAY THE GAME WAS PLAYED

The number of home runs continued to rise during the 1950s, with AL teams averaging 120 homers per season, compared with 85 per year during the 1930s. The number of complete games continued to decline, from 63 per team in 1950 to 46 in 1959. Relievers were making more appearances, and the relief specialist emerged, including such Red Sox as Ellis Kinder, Ike Delock, and Mike Fornieles. The increased use of relievers to close out victories led to a new statistic called the "save," although it wasn't officially recognized by Major League Baseball until 1969. Games were also taking longer to play. The average length of a game rose from two hours and twenty-three minutes to two hours and thirty-eight minutes. In addition, the first franchise shifts in fifty years took place. In the NL, the Boston Braves moved to Milwaukee in 1953, making the Red Sox the only team in New England. In the AL, the St. Louis Browns moved to Baltimore in 1954, where they were renamed the Orioles, and the Athletics transferred from Philadelphia to Kansas City. In 1958, Major League Baseball was played west of the Rocky Mountains for the first time when the Dodgers and Giants moved from New York to California.

THE MANAGEMENT

Tom Yawkey began his third decade as owner of the Red Sox. Joe Cronin ran the front office as general manager until he became president of the American League in 1959. Bucky Harris succeeded Cronin as the general manager. Field managers were Joe McCarthy (1948–50), Steve O'Neill (1950–51), Lou Boudreau (1952–54), Pinky Higgins (1955–59), and Billy Jurges (1959–60).

THE BEST PLAYER MOVE

The best player move was the signing of Carl Yastrzemski out of the University of Notre Dame in December 1958. After two years in the minors, Yaz reached the Red Sox in 1961. The best trade brought Jackie Jensen from Washington in December 1953 for Mickey McDermott and Tom Umphlett.

THE WORST PLAYER MOVE

The worst move was the refusal of the Red Sox to promote an African-American player to the parent club until 1959. The Sox were the last team in the majors to integrate, and became a symbol of racism in baseball that the franchise hasn't completely shaken to this day. The worst transaction with another major league club was the sale of Charlie Maxwell to the Orioles in November 1954.

1950   B

Season in a Sentence

The Red Sox score 1,027 runs, post a team batting average of .302, and contend for the pennant in late September, but an inconsistent pitching staff dooms them to third place.

Finish • Won • Lost • Pct • GB

Third   94   60   .610   4.0

Managers

Joe McCarthy (31–28)
Steve O'Neill (63–32)

Stats   Red Sox • AL • Rank

	Red Sox	AL	Rank
Batting Avg:	.302	.271	1
On-Base Pct:	.385	.356	1
Slugging Pct:	.464	.402	1
Home Runs:	161		2
Stolen Bases:	32		6
ERA:	4.88	4.58	6
Fielding Pct:	.981	.976	1
Runs Scored:	1,027		1
Runs Allowed:	804		5

Starting Lineup

Birdie Tebbetts, c
Walt Dropo, 1b
Bobby Doerr, 2b
Johnny Pesky, 3b
Vern Stephens, ss
Ted Williams, lf
Dom DiMaggio, cf
Al Zarilla, rf
Billy Goodman, lf-3b-1b
Matt Batts, c
Clyde Vollmer, lf-cf-rf

Pitchers

Mel Parnell, sp
Joe Dobson, sp-rp
Chuck Stobbs, sp
Willard Nixon, sp
Ellis Kinder, rp-sp
Mickey McDermott, rp-sp
Walt Masterson, rp-sp

Attendance

1,344,080 (fourth in AL)

Club Leaders

Batting Avg:	DiMaggio	.328
On-Base Pct:	Pesky	.437
Slugging Pct:	Dropo	.583
Home Runs:	Dropo	34
RBI:	Dropo	144
	Stephens	144
Runs:	DiMaggio	131
Stolen Bases:	DiMaggio	15
Wins:	Parnell	18
Strikeouts:	McDermott	96
ERA:	Parnell	3.61
Saves:	Kinder	9

FEBRUARY 7   Three weeks after the infamous Brink's armored car robbery in Boston, Ted Williams becomes the highest paid player of all time when the Red Sox give him a new $125,000 contract.

MARCH 26   The Red Sox sell Jack Kramer to the Giants.

APRIL 14   The Red Sox sign Ken Keltner following his release by the Indians.

APRIL 18   On Opening Day, before 31,822 at Fenway Park, the Red Sox blow a nine-run lead and lose 15–10 to the Yankees. The matchup had been anticipated for months after the Yankees won the final two games of the 1949 season to steal the AL pennant from Boston. The Sox led 9–0 after five innings with Mel Parnell on the mound. The *Boston American* hit the streets with the headline "Sox Romp." But the Yankees broke loose with four runs in the sixth. The Red Sox scored again in the seventh to pull ahead 10–4 before the Yankees exploded for eight runs in the eighth off five pitchers, then added two more in the ninth. In his major league debut, Billy Martin had two hits in the eight-run eighth. Billy Goodman homered for the Red Sox. It was only his second major league homer, and his first since 1948. Vern Stephens had three hits, including a double. Bobby Doerr collected three hits, and Ted Williams scored three runs.

On the same day, Sam Jethroe became the first African-American player on a Boston major league team when he debuted with the Braves. The Red Sox remained an all-white team until 1959, but there was a billboard underneath the stands at Fenway Park in 1950 urging fans to "fight for racial and religious understanding." The billboard depicted a white youth holding a bat, standing next to a black youngster, and addressing another white boy. The slogan on the sign was, "What's his race or religion got to do with it—he can pitch." The sign was sponsored by the Massachusetts Committee of Catholics, Protestants, and Jews, and by the Red Sox.

APRIL 19   A total of 58,285 pay to see a Patriots' Day doubleheader against the Yankees in Fenway Park. In the morning, 25,425 attended a 6–3 Red Sox win. In the afternoon, 32,860 watched the Yankees pummel the Sox 16–7 in a game called after eight innings by darkness.

APRIL 21   A grand slam by Vern Stephens in the ninth inning off Harry Byrd caps an 8–2 win over the Athletics in Philadelphia.

Stephens had another great season in 1950 with 30 homers, 144 RBIs, 125 runs scored, and a .295 batting average.

APRIL 23   The Red Sox pound the Athletics 12–2 in the second game of a doubleheader at Shibe Park in a contest stopped after six innings by darkness. Philadelphia won the first game, 9–4.

The Red Sox ganged up on the Browns and the Athletics in 1950, with a 19–3 record against both clubs.

APRIL 24   Al Zarilla collects all three Red Sox hits off Ray Scarborough in a 3–0 loss to the Senators in Washington.

Zarilla hit .325 with nine homers in 1950.

APRIL 30   The Red Sox massacre the Athletics 19–0 in the first game of a doubleheader at Fenway Park. The Sox struck early with four runs in the first inning, three in the second, and 11 in the fourth to take an 18–0 lead. Ted Williams hit a pair of three-run homers. Dom DiMaggio scored five runs. Boston completed the sweep with a 6–5 victory in the second tilt.

First baseman Billy Goodman suffered a chipped bone fracture in his left ankle when he jammed his foot beating out a bunt in the second game. The Red Sox called up Walt Dropo from their farm club in Louisville to play first while Goodman was out of action. Dropo was twenty-seven years old and had a previous trial with the Red Sox in 1949 but hit only .146 in 11 games the first time around. Dropo made the most of his second chance. In his first 73 games after being recalled, through July 19, Dropo hit .355 with 23 homers and 93 RBIs. He was elected the starting first baseman in the 1950 All-Star Game in a vote of the fans. Dropo finished the season with 144

RBIs to tie Vern Stephens for the league lead. He also hit .322 and clubbed 34 homers. A three-sport star at the University of Connecticut, the six-foot-five Dropo was drafted by the Providence Steamrollers in the first round of the 1947 NBA draft and in the ninth round of the NFL draft by the Chicago Bears in 1948. He played with the Red Sox until 1952 and in the majors until 1961, but he never again came close to the numbers he compiled in his sensational rookie season.

MAY 6   The Red Sox hit six homers and rout the White Sox 11–1 at Fenway Park. Birdie Tebbetts hit two of the home runs, and Ted Williams, Bobby Doerr, Dom DiMaggio, and Vern Stephens added one each.

          DiMaggio led the AL in runs scored in 1950 with 131 and hit .328. He also led the AL in stolen bases with 15, the lowest ever recorded by a league leader in the category.

MAY 8   The Red Sox trade Tommy O'Brien and Merrill Combs to the Senators for Clyde Vollmer.

MAY 11   Ted Williams hits a grand slam in the eighth inning off Fred Hutchinson, but the Red Sox fall to the Tigers 13–4 at Fenway Park. Detroit also won the second game, 5–3.

          Williams made two errors during the twin bill, one with the bases loaded when a grounder went past him that led to the winning runs in the nightcap. Never one to throttle his emotions, he was enraged by the boos that cascaded from the Fenway crowd of 27,758 following his first-game error and flipped the multitude an obscene gesture. After the second-game miscue, Williams raised two middle fingers skyward three times to three different sections of the ballpark. Then, while in the on-deck circle, he made a bad situation worse by spitting toward the grandstand. The following day, he apologized for his actions.

MAY 18   The Red Sox eke out a 13–12 win over the Tigers in Detroit. The Sox took an 11–1 lead after scoring seven runs in the fourth inning but were forced to stave off a Tiger rally to win.

MAY 25   The Red Sox pull out a 15–12 win over the Browns at Sportsman's Park.

          St. Louis led 11–7 when the Sox scored six eighth-inning runs, four of them on a grand slam by Walt Dropo off Stubby Overmire, to take the lead.

JUNE 2   The Red Sox score six runs in the first inning and defeat the Indians 11–5 at Fenway Park.

JUNE 3   The Red Sox score six runs in the first inning for the second day in a row and beat the Indians 11–9 at Fenway Park.

JUNE 4   The Red Sox collect 21 hits to overpower the White Sox 17–7 at Fenway Park.

JUNE 5   The Red Sox rout the White Sox 12–0 at Fenway Park. It was the fourth game in a row that the club reached double digits in runs.

JUNE 7   The Red Sox unload on the Browns 20–4 with 23 hits at Fenway Park. The Sox scored seven runs in the third inning to break a 3–3 tie and hit five home runs in the game. Clyde Vollmer and Vern Stephens each struck two homers, and Walt Dropo hit one.

The Red Sox scored 216 runs in 22 games against the Browns in 1950. The 20-run output on June 7 was only a prelude to the explosion the following day.

JUNE 8   The Red Sox set a modern major league record (since tied) for most runs in a game with a 29–4 trouncing of the Browns at Fenway Park. The 25-run winning margin is also a modern record. Boston scored eight runs in the second inning, five in the third, seven in the fourth, two in the fifth, two in the seventh, and five in the eighth. The 28-hit attack included nine doubles, one triple, and seven homers. The Browns pitchers were Cliff Fannin (eight runs in two innings), Cuddles Marshall (nine runs in $1\frac{2}{3}$ innings), Sid Schacht (12 runs in $3\frac{2}{3}$ innings) and Tom Feerick (no runs in two-thirds of an inning).

Bobby Doerr hit three home runs, and Ted Williams and Walt Dropo each added two. Boston also set major league records for most total bases in a game (60) and most extra-base hits (17). Counting the 20–4 rout the previous day, the Sox set a major league record for most runs in consecutive games, with 49. Other modern records they set included most hits in consecutive games (51), most RBIs in a game (29), most players scoring four or more runs (four), most players scoring at least three runs (seven), and an American League record for most players with four or more hits (four). Al Zarilla tied a major league record with four doubles and also hit a single. Zarilla, Johnny Pesky, and Clyde Vollmer tied a modern record for most at-bats in a nine-inning game, with seven. Vollmer tied a modern record for most plate appearances in a nine-inning game, with eight. Chuck Stobbs tied a record for most base on balls by a pitcher with four. He also had two hits. Doerr drove in eight runs. Dropo scored five runs and drove in seven. Pesky had five hits, including two doubles. The only other major league club since 1900 with as many as 29 runs in a game was the White Sox against the Athletics in 1955.

From June 2 through June 10, the Red Sox scored 119 runs in nine games. During the month of June, the club scored 245 runs in 29 games, but posted a mediocre 16–13 record because the pitching staff had trouble stopping anyone. On the season, the Sox scored 1,027 runs and had a batting average of .302. Both are the highest of any major league club from 1936 to the present. The worst batting average among the regulars was Bobby Doerr, who hit .294. Playing their home games in the small confines of Fenway Park helped the Red Sox amass the high batting numbers. The Red Sox scored 625 runs at Fenway and only 402 on the road. The Yankees (474), Tigers (432), and Indians (420) all scored more runs in road games in 1950 than the Red Sox.

JUNE 13   Chuck Stobbs pitches a two-hitter to stop the Indians 8–1 at Municipal Stadium. The only Cleveland hits were a homer by Bob Kennedy in the first inning and a single by Lou Boudreau in the fourth.

JUNE 23   In their first game under new manager Steve O'Neill, the Red Sox win 12–9 against the Browns in St. Louis.

Joe McCarthy resigned earlier in the day, citing health reasons. He had been suffering with the flu and pleurisy and had been drinking heavily. McCarthy was ordered by his doctor to take some time off. "I'm simply disgusted after three years of beating my brains out," McCarthy said. "I've had enough of baseball, and I don't want to go on anymore." The Red Sox had lost 11 of the previous 13 games and had a disappointing record of 31–28. The Sox entered the season as consensus favorites to win the AL pennant and were determined to make up for their two near-misses in 1948 and 1949. McCarthy had invested well, which allowed him to live a comfortable retirement. He never managed another team, finishing his career with a record of 2,133-1,333, for a winning percentage of .615. McCarthy was elected to the Hall of Fame in 1957 and died in 1978 at the age of ninety.

Steve O'Neill was fifty-eight years old and a Red Sox coach when he was hired to manage the club. He was one of four brothers who played in the majors, and a catcher in the big leagues from 1911 through 1928. He previously had managed the Indians 1935–1937 and the Tigers 1943–1949, including a World Championship in 1945. O'Neill joined a long line of Irish managers with the Red Sox stretching back a half-century: Jimmy Collins, Deacon McGuire, Patsy Donovan, Bill Carrigan, Jack Barry, Hugh Duffy, Shano Collins, Marty McManus, Joe Cronin, and Joe McCarthy.

JUNE 24   Billy Goodman hits a grand slam off Cliff Fannin in the second inning of a 12–3 win over the Browns in St. Louis.

JUNE 25   The Red Sox execute nine double plays during an 11–5 and 8–2 sweep of the Browns in St. Louis.

On the same day, North Korean military forces attacked South Korea. The United States quickly entered the conflict on the side of South Korea. Ted Williams returned to duty with the Marine Air Corps, saw action as a pilot in Korea, and missed most of the 1952 and 1953 seasons. Other Red Sox players who served in the military during the Korean War before it ended in 1953 included Karl Olson, Norm Zauchin, Leo Kiely, Dick Brodowski, and Faye Throneberry.

JUNE 29   The Red Sox outslug the Athletics 22–14 in Philadelphia in the highest-scoring game in American League history. There were 36 hits in the game and 21 walks, but just one home run. Ted Williams drove in six of the runs. In the first inning, the Red Sox scored six runs and the Athletics scored four. In the second, Boston added nine runs, and Philadelphia countered with three to make the score 14–7. The score was 15–7 at the end of the fourth, 16–8 after five, 18–9 after six, 20–12 after seven and 20–14 after eight before the Sox scored twice in the ninth.

JULY 1   Walt Dropo drives in seven runs during a 13–4 win over the Yankees at Fenway Park. He hit a grand slam off Tommy Byrne in the first inning. Whitey Ford made his major league debut in the game and gave up five runs in 4⅔ innings.

JULY 11   Ted Williams breaks his elbow during the All-Star Game, won 4–3 by the National League in 14 innings at Comiskey Park. The injury happened in the first inning when Williams made a spectacular catch off a drive by Ralph Kiner, then put out his gloved hand to brace himself for the collision with the wall. The bones of the lower and upper arm took the force of the blow, smashing into each other, breaking seven bone chips from the elbow. Despite the continuous pain, Williams played until the ninth inning, even driving in a run with a single in the eighth, but x-rays taken the following day revealed the fracture. On July 13, surgeons removed the bone chips in a 75-minute operation.

Williams didn't play again until September 15. Billy Goodman took over for Williams in left field and played well enough to win the batting title with an average of .354. Goodman also hit in Williams's third slot in the Red Sox line-up. During the season, the versatile Goodman played 45 games in left field, 27 at third base, 21 at first base, five at second base, and one at shortstop.

Francis Miller/Time & Life Pictures/Getty Images

A consistent hitter throughout his years in Boston, Billy Goodman enjoyed a career year in 1950.

JULY 14   The Red Sox produce 11 runs in the third inning and defeat the White Sox 13–1 at Fenway Park.

JULY 16   Walt Dropo drives in seven runs during a doubleheader as the Red Sox win 13–10 and lose 8–4 against the Indians at Fenway Park.

JULY 18   The Red Sox outlast the Tigers 12–9 at Fenway Park.

On July 19, the Red Sox had a record of 39–39 and were in fourth place, 9 ½ games behind the first-place Tigers. The Sox won 47 of their next 59 games, however, to surge back into the race. It was the third straight year the Sox appeared to be out of the race in midsummer before staging an amazing run after the All-Star break.

JULY 20   After spotting the Tigers a 5–0 lead, the Red Sox rally to win 6–5 in 11 innings at Fenway Park. Dom DiMaggio drove in the winning run with a double.

JULY 28   Red Sox pitcher Dick Littlefield gives up consecutive homers to Larry Doby, Al Rosen, and Luke Easter in the eighth inning of a 13–1 loss to the Indians in Cleveland.

AUGUST 2   The Red Sox score three runs in the ninth with two out to beat the Browns 9–8 in St. Louis. Vern Stephens tied the score with a two-run double and scored the winning run on Walt Dropo's single.

AUGUST 5   The Red Sox wipe out a 6–2 Chicago lead with seven runs in the seventh inning and go on to win 12–7 on the road.

AUGUST 6   Ellis Kinder hits a grand slam and drives in a total of six runs during a 9–2 win over the White Sox in the first game of a doubleheader in Chicago. The slam was hit off Billy Pierce in the fifth inning following an intentional walk to Birdie Tebbetts. The Red Sox completed the sweep with a 4–3 win in the second tilt after plating two runs in the ninth.

The homer was the only one that Kinder hit as a major leaguer over 444 at-bats and 12 seasons.

AUGUST 16 During his 50th and final season as manager of the Athletics, Massachusetts native Connie Mack is honored between games of a doubleheader at Fenway Park. The Red Sox beat the A's 8–3 and 9–4. In the first game, Walt Dropo was hit in the head by a pitch from Philadelphia pitcher Hank Wyse, and Birdie Tebbetts was ejected after he rushed the mound and punched Wyse.

AUGUST 18 Bobby Doerr hits a walk-off homer in the tenth inning that beats the Senators 7–6 at Fenway Park.

Doerr hit 27 homers with 120 RBIs and a .294 batting average in 1950.

AUGUST 19 Buddy Rosar's two-out, two-run, walk-off single off the left field wall in the ninth inning beats the Senators 5–4 at Fenway Park. Rosar entered the game as a catcher after Matt Batts was lifted for a pinch hitter in the eighth inning.

AUGUST 24   A walk-off grand slam by Vern Stephens off Ned Garver caps a five-run ninth-inning rally that beats the Browns 6–2 at Fenway Park. It was the Red Sox' 10th win in a row.

AUGUST 25   The Red Sox capture their 11th win in a row, beating the Tigers 6–2 at Fenway Park.

AUGUST 27   Down 7–0 in the third inning and 9–5 after six, the Red Sox score seven runs in the seventh inning to beat the Indians 11–9 at Fenway Park. Clyde Vollmer's pinch-hit grand slam off Al Benton put the Sox ahead.

AUGUST 28   One day after coming from seven runs behind, the Red Sox rally from an 11-run deficit for an amazing 15–14 win over the Indians at Fenway Park. Cleveland led 12–1 when Boston scored eight runs in the fourth inning. The Indians were still ahead 15–13 when the Red Sox scored four runs in the eighth.

The 11 runs was the largest deficit ever overcome by the Red Sox to win a game.

AUGUST 29   The Red Sox defeat the White Sox 13–6 at Fenway Park.

SEPTEMBER 10   The Red Sox defeat the Athletics for the 22nd time in a row at Fenway Park with a 6–2 victory. Chuck Stobbs allowed only two hits in eight innings but walked 10 batters.

The Sox were 11–0 against the Athletics in Boston in both 1949 and 1950.

SEPTEMBER 12   The Red Sox win for the 24th time in a stretch of 27 games by defeating the White Sox 2–1 in Chicago. The victory left the Red Sox only one game behind the first-place Tigers and half a game back of the second-place Yankees in the tight three-way AL pennant race.

SEPTEMBER 15   Ted Williams returns to the lineup for the first time since breaking his elbow and collects a homer and three singles in six at-bats during a 12–9 win over the Browns in St. Louis.

To make room for Williams, Billy Goodman moved from left field to third base, benching Johnny Pesky, who hit .312 in 127 games in 1950. Williams ended the season with a .317 batting average, 28 homers, and 97 RBIs in 89 games.

SEPTEMBER 18   The Red Sox score two runs in the ninth inning to beat the Tigers 3–2 in Detroit. The victory put the Red Sox in second place ahead of the Tigers and one game behind the first place Yankees.

On September 19, the Yankees lost and the Tigers won while the Red Sox were idle. This put the Tigers and the Red Sox into a second-place tie, one-half game back of the Yankees with 12 days left in the season.

SEPTEMBER 20   The Red Sox' pennant hopes receive two severe jolts with a 6–3 and a 7–1 double-header loss to the Indians in Cleveland.

The Red Sox lost seven of their last 11 games and finished in third place, four games out. The Yankees won the pennant, ending the season three games ahead of Detroit. It was another tough season for Red Sox fans after missing a pennant by one game in both 1948 and 1949. The Sox of 1948–50 had a team of stars who seemed to be able to do everything except win the pennant. With a few breaks, the Red Sox of 1946–50 could have won four American League pennants and created a dynasty, and the careers of such players as Ted Williams, Bobby Doerr, Johnny Pesky, Dom DiMaggio, Vern Stephens, Mel Parnell, and Ellis Kinder would have been viewed much more favorably. The only other club in baseball history to finish a season within four games of first place three seasons in row without winning a pennant is the San Francisco Giants from 1964–1966. The Giants of the 1960s were similar to the Red Sox of 1946–1950. San Francisco lost Game Seven of the World Series in 1962 by one run, like the Sox of 1946, and had top-flight stars such as Willie Mays, Willie McCovey, Orlando Cepeda, Juan Marichal, and Gaylord Perry.

SEPTEMBER 25   The Red Sox break a four-game losing streak with an 8–0 and 3–0 doubleheader sweep of the Athletics at Shibe Park. Mel Parnell pitched the first-game shutout, and Harry Taylor, in his first game as a member of the Red Sox, tossed a two-hitter in the second tilt. The only Philadelphia hits were singles by Paul Lehner in the first inning and Eddie Joost in the fourth.

Parnell was the Red Sox' top pitcher in 1950, with an 18–10 record and a 3.61 ERA. Taylor was purchased from the Dodgers in September for $75,000. Despite the two-hit shutout in his first game with the Red Sox, he proved to be a poor investment. Taylor never pitched another major league shutout and was 7–9 with a 4.65 ERA for the Red Sox over three seasons.

NOVEMBER 27   The Red Sox sign Lou Boudreau as a player. Boudreau had long been a nemesis of the Sox. He originated the Boudreau shift against Ted Williams in 1946 and almost single-handedly kept the Red Sox from winning the 1948 AL pennant by collecting four hits, including two homers, in the one-game playoff to decide the title.

Boudreau had been fired as manager of the Indians on November 22. He had been a shortstop for the Indians since 1938 and player-manager since 1941. Boudreau had been the American League's MVP as recently as 1948. He was thirty-three years old when the Sox acquired him. He was Boston's starting shortstop at the start of the 1951 season, with Vern Stephens moving to third base. Boudreau was bothered by injuries, however, and hit .267 with five homers in 82 games. He became manager of the Red Sox in October 1951 and held the job through the end of the 1954 season.

DECEMBER 10   The Red Sox trade Joe Dobson, Al Zarilla, and Dick Littlefield to the White Sox for Ray Scarborough and Bill Wight.

DECEMBER 13   The Red Sox sell Birdie Tebbetts to the Indians.

Tebbetts sealed his fate at the end of the 1950 season when newspapers picked up his quote calling the Red Sox players "moronic malcontents and juvenile delinquents."

1951

B

Season in a Sentence

For the fourth year in a row, the Red Sox are within sight of a pennant in late September but fall short.

Finish • Won • Lost • Pct • GB

Third   87   67   .565   11.0

Manager

Steve O'Neill

Stats

Stats	Red Sox	AL	Rank
Batting Avg:	.266	.262	3
On-Base Pct:	.358	.342	1
Slugging Pct:	.392	.381	2
Home Runs:	127		3
Stolen Bases:	20		8
ERA:	4.14	4.12	4
Fielding Pct:	.977	.975	3
Runs Scored:	804		1
Runs Allowed:	725		4

Starting Lineup

Les Moss, c
Billy Goodman, 1b-2b-rf
Bobby Doerr, 2b
Vern Stephens, 3b
Johnny Pesky, ss
Ted Williams, lf
Dom DiMaggio, cf
Clyde Vollmer, rf
Walt Dropo, 1b
Lou Boudreau, ss
Buddy Rosar, c
Fred Hatfield, 3b

Pitchers

Mel Parnell, sp
Ray Scarborough, sp
Chuck Stobbs, sp
Mickey McDermott, sp
Bill Wight, sp-rp
Leo Kiely, sp
Ellis Kinder, rp-sp
Willard Nixon, rp-sp
Harry Taylor, rp

Attendance

1,312,282 (fourth in AL)

Club Leaders

Batting Avg:	Williams	.318
On-Base Pct:	Williams	.464
Slugging Pct:	Williams	.556
Home Runs:	Williams	30
RBI:	Williams	126
Runs:	DiMaggio	113
Stolen Bases:	Goodman	7
Wins:	Parnell	18
Strikeouts:	McDermott	127
ERA:	Parnell	3.26
Saves:	Kinder	14

MARCH 10   Prior to the first spring-training game of the season, actress Dorothy Lamour throws out the first ball. The Reds defeated the Red Sox 4–0 in Sarasota, Florida. Best known for her roles in the Bob Hope–Bing Crosby road pictures, Lamour was in town for the location filming of *The Greatest Show on Earth*, which won the 1952 Oscar for best picture.

MARCH 18   Ted Williams reacts badly to striking out twice in one inning during a 15–12 loss to the Reds in Tampa, Florida. Williams waved his bat over his head as though he were going to toss it into the crowded stands, then spit several times in the direction of the stands.

APRIL 17   Six days after President Harry Truman relieves General Douglas MacArthur of his command in Korea, the Red Sox lose the season opener 5–0 to the Yankees in New York. Vic Raschi pitched the shutout. Mickey Mantle made his major league debut in the game. He collected his first hit, a single, off Bill Wight.

All Red Sox road games were on radio for the first time in 1951. Previously, road games had been broadcast only when the Braves were not playing at home on the same day, due to an arrangement between the two clubs. In 1951, the

Braves wanted to break the agreement, which allowed the Red Sox to air games on the road. Curt Gowdy and Robert DeLancey joined Tom Hussey in the Red Sox booth beginning in 1951. As in 1949 and 1950, all home games were telecast, but none on the road. Gowdy, DeLancey, and Hussey did the televised games, which were sponsored by the Narragansett Brewing Company and the Atlantic Refining Company. Jim Britt and Bump Hadley, who had previously broadcast both the Red Sox and Braves games, were announcers for the Braves exclusively in 1951. With competition from the Red Sox on radio, home attendance for Braves games continued to plummet. In 1953, the Braves relocated to Milwaukee.

APRIL 20   In the first game of the season at Fenway Park, the Red Sox lose 6–5 to the Athletics before a chilled crowd of 11,461. It was the first loss by the Sox to the A's in Boston since 1948, breaking a 22-game winning streak against the Philadelphia club. Lou Boudreau homered in his first game as a member of the Red Sox at Fenway Park.

APRIL 26   The Red Sox outscore the Yankees 13–7 at Fenway Park.

APRIL 29   The Red Sox score four runs in the thirteenth inning, capped by a two-run homer from Ted Williams, to beat the Athletics 12–8 in Philadelphia. It was the third extra-inning homer of the game for the Sox. Tom Wright homered in the eleventh and Dom DiMaggio in the twelfth, but the A's rallied to tie the contest each time. Bobby Doerr hit two home runs during the first nine innings.

Williams recovered from the elbow injury he suffered in the 1950 All-Star Game to hit .316 with 30 homers, 126 RBIs, 109 runs scored, and 169 hits. He led the AL in walks (144), on-base percentage (.464), and slugging percentage (.556). Williams had the widest home-road split of his career in 1951. He hit .403 with 18 homers and a .709 slugging percentage at Fenway. Outside of Boston, he had a batting average of .235 and a slugging percentage of .399.

MAY 6   Ted Williams hits a homer in the tenth inning to defeat the Browns 5–4 in the first game of a doubleheader at Sportsman's Park. St. Louis won the second game, 8–3.

MAY 7   Willard Nixon pitches a two-hitter and hits his first major league homer to beat the Browns 2–0 in St. Louis. The home run came off Ned Garver. The only St. Louis hits were singles by Bobby Young in the fourth inning and Johnny Berardino in the seventh.

Nixon hit only two homers in 459 big-league at-bats. The other one was in 1954.

MAY 15   The Red Sox celebrate their 50th anniversary with festivities before an 11-inning, 9–7 loss to the White Sox at Fenway Park. A parade was staged between the State House and Fenway Park that included 29 players and managers who were in the American League in 1901. They rode in vehicles from the turn of the twentieth century.

Included in the celebration were Hall of Famers Cy Young, Connie Mack, Clark Griffith, and Hugh Duffy. The old-timers were amused by a bit of strategy employed by Chicago manager Paul Richards. In the ninth inning, Richards moved pitcher Harry Dorish to third base and brought in Billy Pierce to pitch to Ted Williams. After Williams popped up, Dorish went back to the mound. In the seventh inning, Williams collected his 300th career home run. The pitcher was Howie Judson.

MAY 17   The Red Sox send Matt Batts, Jim Suchecki, Jim McDonald, and $100,000 to the Browns for Les Moss.

MAY 22   Catcher Les Moss hits a grand slam in the seventh inning off Ted Gray that breaks a 2–2 tie in a 6–3 win over the Tigers at Fenway Park.

Despite hitting a grand slam only five days after being acquired by the Red Sox, Moss was a colossal failure in Boston. At a cost of three players and $100,000, he hit only .198 with three homers in 202 at-bats. Moss was dealt back to the Browns after the season was over.

MAY 23   Ted Williams draws five walks in six plate appearances during a 12–0 win over the Browns at Fenway Park. Mel Parnell starred with his arm and his bat by pitching the shutout and collecting four hits and a walk.

Parnell was 18–11 with a 3.26 ERA in 1951.

MAY 25   The Red Sox trounce the Senators 14–2 at Fenway Park.

Left-handers started 106 of the Red Sox' 154 games in 1951. The southpaws were Mel Parnell (29 games), Chuck Stobbs (25), Mickey McDermott (19), Bill Wight (17), and Leo Kiely (16).

MAY 26   The Red Sox wallop the Senators for the second day in a row at Fenway Park with an 11–1 victory.

MAY 30   The Red Sox run their winning streak to 10 games by knocking off the Yankees 11–10 in 15 innings and 9–4 in a Memorial Day twin bill at Fenway Park. A walk-off homer by Vern Stephens won the opener. It was his second homer of the game, and he had five hits in all.

JUNE 4   Billy Goodman collects seven hits, including a double, in nine at-bats, but the Red Sox lose a doubleheader 6–5 and 2–0 to the White Sox in Chicago. The Red Sox turned a double play in each game to set a major league record (since tied) for most consecutive games with a double play, with 25. The Sox completed 38 double plays in the 25 contests.

JUNE 7   Dom DiMaggio hits safely in his 27th consecutive game, helping the Red Sox to a 5–3 win over the Tigers in Detroit.

DiMaggio hit .296 and scored 113 runs in 1951.

JUNE 10   Dom DiMaggio collects five hits, including two doubles, in five at-bats to lead the Red Sox to a 9–6 win over the Indians in the first game of a doubleheader in Cleveland. The Red Sox also won the second game, 8–2.

JUNE 20   Indians second baseman Bobby Avila hits three homers in a 14–8 win over the Red
               Sox at Fenway Park.

               *Johnny Pesky started the 1951 season as a utility infielder but won back his
               starting shortstop job and hit .313.*

JUNE 25   The Red Sox send Walt Dropo to the minors.

               *After a 1950 rookie season in which he hit 34 homers, drove in 144 runs, and
               hit .322, Dropo suffered a hairline fracture of his right wrist during spring
               training and was hampered by the injury during the early months of the 1951
               season, causing a batting slump. Dropo was in the minors for five weeks and
               finished 1951 with 11 homers, 57 RBIs, and a .239 batting average.*

JULY 1   Bobby Doerr collects his 2,000th career hit during an 8–2 loss to the Yankees in
               New York. The milestone hit was a single off Eddie Lopat.

JULY 7   Sparked by a first-inning grand slam from Clyde Vollmer off Allie Reynolds, the
               Red Sox beat the Yankees 10–4 at Fenway Park.

               *Clyde Vollmer had a surreal month of July in 1951. At the start of the month,
               he was on the bench, with Charlie Maxwell as the regular in right field, but
               Vollmer started both games of the July 4 doubleheader and immediately
               embarked on a batting tear that included several game-winning hits. During
               July he had 13 homers, drove in 40 runs, and batted .298.*

JULY 12   The Red Sox take first place by sweeping the White Sox 3–2 and 5–4 in a 26-inning
               doubleheader at Comiskey Park. The two wins ran the Red Sox' winning streak to
               eight games and gave the club a 49–29 record on the season. The second game was
               a 17-inning marathon. Clyde Vollmer drove in the winning run with a sacrifice fly.
               Ellis Kinder pitched the last 10 innings without allowing a run. Saul Rogovin
               pitched all 17 innings for Chicago.

               The Red Sox' stay in first place lasted 10 days.

JULY 13   The day after playing a 26-inning, twilight doubleheader, including a 17-inning
               nightcap, the Red Sox and White Sox play 19 innings before a crowd of 52,592 at
               Comiskey Park, with Chicago emerging with a 5–4 victory. The score was 2–2 after
               five innings before the two clubs combined for 13 consecutive scoreless frames. The
               Red Sox seemed to have the game in hand when they scored two runs in the top of
               the nineteenth, but the White Sox came back with three in their half off Harry Tay-
               lor and Ray Scarborough for the victory. Mickey McDermott pitched the first 17
               innings for the Red Sox.

JULY 14   Clyde Vollmer's two-run single in the ninth inning beats the White Sox 3–2 in Chicago.

JULY 20   Police in Maine capture nineteen-year-old escaped reformatory inmate Darryll
               Roos, who had been missing for seven weeks. Roos eluded authorities by hiding
               out in the woods in a pup tent. Upon surrendering, Roos asked, "How are the
               Red Sox doing?"

JULY 22   The Red Sox beat the Tigers 10–9 in 10 innings at Fenway Park, but drop out of first place when the Yankees sweep the Browns in New York.

At the end of the day, the Yankees were in first place, two percentage points ahead of the Red Sox and Indians. The White Sox were fourth, 2½ games back. The Red Sox never returned to first place in 1951 but remained in contention until the third week of September.

JULY 26   Clyde Vollmer raps three homers and drives in six runs during a 13–10 win over the White Sox at Fenway Park. His first homer, off Luis Aloma, broke a 3–3 tie in the first inning. Vollmer's second homer, hit off Randy Gumpert, broke a 7–7 tie in the fifth. Vollmer hit his third tie-breaking homer in the seventh inning, again off Gumpert, snapping a 10–10 deadlock. Dom DiMaggio collected five hits in five at-bats.

JULY 28   Clyde Vollmer is again the hero, driving in five runs in extra innings during a 16-inning, 8–4 victory over the Indians at Fenway Park. Vollmer tied the score 3–3 with an RBI single in the fifteenth. After Cleveland scored in the sixteenth, the Red Sox countered with five runs in their half, the last four on Vollmer's walk-off grand slam off Bob Feller. Mickey McDermott pitched all 16 innings and fanned 15 batters.

Vollmer turned back into a pumpkin at the end of July. Over the remainder of the 1951 season, he hit .218 with four homers in 206 at-bats. Vollmer finished a relatively undistinguished career in 1954 with a .251 batting average and 69 homers in 685 games.

AUGUST 2   The Red Sox overwhelm the Browns 12–1 and 11–6 in a doubleheader at Fenway Park. Charlie Maxwell hit a pinch-hit grand slam off Satchel Paige in the seventh inning of the second game.

Maxwell hit his first three career homers in 1951, and all three came in a pinch-hit role off future Hall of Famers Paige, Bob Lemon, and Bob Feller.

AUGUST 6   The Red Sox purchase Aaron Robinson from the Tigers.

AUGUST 17   Fred Hatfield hits his first major league home run during a three-run twelfth inning as the Red Sox defeat the Senators 7–4 in Washington.

AUGUST 22   The Red Sox leave 22 men on base but beat the Browns 3–1 in 13 innings at Sportsman's Park. St. Louis pitcher Tommy Byrne walked 16 batters in 12⅓ innings.

SEPTEMBER 7 Bobby Doerr plays his last major league game as the Red Sox beat the Athletics 8–5 in Philadelphia.

Doerr was only thirty-three and was still a productive player, with a .289 batting average and 13 homers in 106 games in 1951, but he had to retire because of back trouble. He was elected to the Hall of Fame in 1986. Two years later, the Red Sox retired his uniform number 1.

SEPTEMBER 14 Bob Nieman of the Browns homers in his first two major league at-bats, both off Mickey McDermott at Fenway Park, during a 9–6 Red Sox win.

Ellis Kinder pitched 29 consecutive scoreless innings of relief from August 17 through September 21. He had an 11–2 record with 14 saves and a 2.55 ERA in 1951. Mel Parnell was the top starter with an 18–11 record and a 3.26 ERA.

SEPTEMBER 17   The Red Sox advance to within 2½ games of the league lead with a 12–5 win over the White Sox at Fenway Park. The Sox were in third place. The Yankees were in first, three percentage points ahead of the Indians. The Red Sox dropped out of contention quickly, however, losing 12 of their last 13 games, including the final nine. The Yankees ended the season five games ahead of Cleveland.

SEPTEMBER 28   Allie Reynolds of the Yankees pitches a no-hitter to beat the Red Sox 8–0 in New York. With two out in the ninth, Ted Williams lifted a towering pop-up into foul territory that Yankee catcher Yogi Berra dropped for an error. On the next pitch, Williams hit another foul pop, which Berra held on to for the final out.

OCTOBER 22   Lou Boudreau replaces Steve O'Neill as manager of the Red Sox.

O'Neill was fired despite leading the Red Sox to a record of 150–99 from June 1950 through the end of the 1951 season, a winning percentage of .602. Boudreau lasted three seasons as manager of the Sox. O'Neill managed the Phillies from 1952 through 1954.

NOVEMBER 4   The Celtics become the second major sports team in Boston to integrate when African-American Chuck Cooper makes his debut with the club. The first club in the city to integrate was the Boston Braves in 1950.

NOVEMBER 13   The Red Sox trade Mel Hoderlein and Chuck Stobbs to the White Sox for Randy Gumpert and Don Lenhardt.

NOVEMBER 28   The Red Sox trade Les Moss and Tom Wright to the Browns for Ken Wood and Gus Niarhos.

1952   B

Season in a Sentence

Despite a massive roster turnover and the loss of Ted Williams to the Marines, the Red Sox are in pennant contention until late August, but a September collapse results in a losing season.

Finish • Won • Lost • Pct • GB

Sixth   76   78   .494 19.0

Manager

Lou Boudreau

Stats   Red Sox • AL • Rank

Stats	Red Sox	AL	Rank
Batting Avg:	.255	.253	3
On-Base Pct:	.329	.330	4
Slugging Pct:	.377	.365	3
Home Runs:	113		3
Stolen Bases:	59		2
ERA:	3.80	3.67	5
Fielding Pct:	.976	.977	5
Runs Scored:	668		3
Runs Allowed:	658		5

Starting Lineup

Sammy White, c
Dick Gernert, 1b
Billy Goodman, 2b
George Kell, 3b
Johnny Lipon, ss
Hoot Evers, lf
Dom DiMaggio, cf
Faye Throneberry, rf
Vern Stephens, ss-3b
Ted Lepcio, 2b-3b
Clyde Vollmer, lf-rf
Jimmy Piersall, ss-rf

Pitchers

Mel Parnell, sp
Mickey McDermott, sp-rp
Dizzy Trout, sp-rp
Sid Hudson, sp
Willard Nixon, sp-rp
Dick Brodowski, sp-rp
Bill Henry, sp
Ike Delock, rp
Ray Scarborough, rp
Ellis Kinder, rp

Attendance

1,115,750 (fourth in AL)

Club Leaders

Batting Avg:	Goodman	.306
On-Base Pct:	DiMaggio	.371
Slugging Pct:	DiMaggio	.429
Home Runs:	Gernert	19
RBI:	Gernert	67
Runs:	DiMaggio	81
Stolen Bases:	Throneberry	16
Wins:	Parnell	12
Strikeouts:	McDermott	117
ERA:	Parnell	3.62
Saves:	Benton	6

JANUARY 9   Ted Williams is recalled to duty by the Marines with the rank of captain. He was ordered to report to the Willow Grove Naval Reserve Base near Philadelphia on May 2, pending a physical. Williams served three years during World War II but saw no combat. He was a flying instructor at Chapel Hill, North Carolina, Pensacola, Florida, and Pearl Harbor. Williams started the 1952 season with the Red Sox and played his last game on April 30. In Korea, he participated in 39 missions as a pilot and didn't return to baseball until August 1953.

Williams and Bob Kennedy are the only players to have their major league careers interrupted by both World War II and Korea. Jerry Coleman also served in both wars, although he didn't reach the majors until after World War II was over. Kennedy and Coleman, like Williams, were Marine pilots.

JANUARY 20   The Red Sox school for rookies opens in Sarasota, Florida, with outfield prospect Jimmy Piersall moved to shortstop, a position he had never played. Manager Lou Boudreau predicted, "Piersall will be the Red Sox shortstop for the next eight to ten years." Piersall opened the season at shortstop, but the pressure proved to be too much for the high-strung rookie, and he was moved back to the outfield during the first week of June.

The switch from the outfield, to short and back to the outfield would have an adverse effect on Piersall's mental stability. He believed that the Red Sox were trying to get rid of him, and the inner turmoil resulted in paranoid-schizophrenic tendencies (see June 11, 1952). It's true that the move to short-stop made no sense. The Red Sox needed help in the infield following the retirement of Bobby Doerr (and in light of age and injuries reducing the effectiveness of Johnny Pesky and Vern Stephens), but Piersall was already a major league–caliber outfielder defensively. He led the American Association in 1949 and 1950 and the Southern Association in 1951 in putouts per game and was among the league leaders in assists. But the Red Sox had doubts that Piersall would hit well enough to become a regular outfielder, leading them to consider a move to the infield.

APRIL 15   With President Harry Truman on hand to throw out the first ball, the Red Sox beat the Senators 3–0 on Opening Day in Washington. Mel Parnell pitched a three-hit shutout and hit seventh in the batting order, ahead of second baseman Ted Lepcio and catcher Gus Niarhos. Jimmy Piersall was the starter at shortstop.

Red Sox rookies Jimmy Piersall, Sammy White, Dick Gernert, Ted Lepcio, Faye Throneberry, Bill Henry, Dick Brodowski, and Ike Delock saw extensive action in 1952 as the club embarked on a youth movement.

APRIL 17   Faye Throneberry hits a grand slam off Don Johnson in the sixth inning of a 9–2 win over the Senators in Washington. It was Throneberry's first big-league homer, and he hit it in his third game in the majors.

APRIL 18   In the first game of the season at Fenway Park, the Red Sox win 5–4 over the Athletics in 10 innings before 12,338. The Sox scored three runs in the ninth inning to tie the score, 4–4. Clyde Vollmer drove in the game winner with a single.

APRIL 19   The Red Sox score seven runs in the fourth inning and defeat the Athletics 11–2 in the first game of a doubleheader at Fenway Park. Don Lenhardt hit a grand slam in the big inning off Dick Fowler. The Sox completed the sweep with a 6–1 win in the second tilt.

The Red Sox had a record of 10–2 in April.

APRIL 30   Ted Williams wallops a homer in his last game before leaving for duty with the Marines. The Red Sox won 5–3 over the Tigers at Fenway Park. It was his first start since Opening Day. Williams was out of the lineup with a calf injury, although he appeared in four games as a pinch hitter.

In farewell ceremonies held before the game, Williams was presented with a new Cadillac. Among those making speeches were Massachusetts Governor Paul Dever and Boston Mayor John Hynes.

MAY 2   Walt Dropo wallops a grand slam off Ned Garver during a nine-run sixth inning as the Red Sox pummel the Browns 13–6 at Fenway Park. The slam followed an intentional walk to Vern Stephens.

MAY 3   The Red Sox' 5–2 win over the Browns at Fenway Park is interrupted twice by fans running onto the field. In the second inning, two college fraternity brothers jumped out of the right field stands as part of an initiation prank and started playing with a rubber ball before they were ejected. In the third inning, a one-legged man on crutches came out of the left field stands and reached the mound, where he brandished a crutch at Browns pitcher Earl Harrist. The fan was angry because Harrist plunked Walt Dropo and Ted Lepcio with pitches.

MAY 4   Faye Throneberry hits a grand slam in the third inning off Early Wynn, but the Red Sox lose 9–6 to the Indians at Fenway Park. Throneberry's first two major league homers were grand slams.

MAY 6   Clyde Vollmer drives in six runs on two homers, a double, and a single during an 11–2 win over the White Sox at Fenway Park.

MAY 10   The Yankees score 11 runs in the seventh inning and wallop the Red Sox 18–3 in New York.

MAY 15   Ray Scarborough pitches the Red Sox to a 1–0 win over the White Sox in Chicago. Ted Lepcio drove in the lone run of the game with a single in the fourth inning.

MAY 24   Jimmy Piersall and Yankee Billy Martin engage in a vicious fight before a 5–2 Red Sox win over the Yankees at Fenway Park. Piersall and Martin had been riding each other all spring. Before the May 24 games, Martin was warming up on the sideline while Piersall took fielding practice at shortstop when they began exchanging insults. Martin invited Piersall to meet him under the stands, where he dropped Piersall with two punches. Ellis Kinder and coaches Oscar Melillo of the Red Sox and Bill Dickey of the Yankees were hit in the head trying to break up the battle. Piersall went into the clubhouse and became involved in another fight with teammate Mickey McDermott.

MAY 29   Mickey McDermott pitches a one-hitter to beat the Senators 1–0 at Fenway Park. The only Washington base runners were Eddie Yost on a first-inning walk and Mel Hoderlein on a single in the fourth. Both were erased on double plays, and McDermott faced the minimum 27 batters. The lone run of the game was driven in on a triple by Fred Hatfield in the sixth inning.

JUNE 1   Ellis Kinder wins his 18th game in a row against the White Sox, dating back to 1948, with 2⅔ innings of relief in a 3–2 decision at Fenway Park.

JUNE 2   Don Lenhardt hits a walk-off grand slam off of Ken Holcombe that caps a five-run tenth inning to lift the Red Sox to a 6–2 win over the White Sox at Fenway Park. The win put the Red Sox into first place, four percentage points ahead of the Indians.

The following day, Lenhardt was traded. In a nine-player swap, the Red Sox sent Johnny Pesky, Walt Dropo, Bill Wight, Fred Hatfield, and Lenhardt to the Tigers for George Kell, Dizzy Trout, Hoot Evers, and Johnny Lipon. When the 1952 season started, few people considered the Red Sox to be pennant contenders, but the club was surprisingly in first place on June 2. With a pennant in sight, the youth movement was temporarily abandoned as the Sox acquired four veterans past their peak. Kell, a future Hall of Fame third baseman, was the only one of the quartet of any real value, however, and then only for the short term. The five players the Red Sox surrendered in the deal were not a great loss. Pesky's days as a regular were over, and Dropo never recaptured the magic he possessed in 1950.

JUNE 4   George Kell hits a homer in his first game with the Red Sox, helping his new club beat the Indians 13–11 at Fenway Park. Kell's two-run homer broke a 9–9 tie in the fifth inning. Billy Goodman collected five hits in five at-bats. Larry Doby hit for the cycle for Cleveland.

JUNE 7   The Red Sox chalk up an 11–9 win over the Tigers at Fenway Park.

The Red Sox in 1952 were first in the AL in runs scored at home (406) and last in runs scored on the road (262). From 1946 through 1952, the Red Sox were nearly unbeatable at home with a record of 381–158, a .707 winning percentage. Road games were another story. During those seven seasons, the Sox were 255–284, a winning percentage of .473. A club built for the cozy confines of Fenway Park, the Red Sox led the AL in home winning percentage in 1946, 1948, 1949, 1950, 1952, and 1958 but won a pennant in only one of those seasons.

JUNE 9   Six days after being traded from Boston to Detroit, Walt Dropo and Don Lenhardt homer for the Tigers against the Red Sox at Fenway Park. Lenhardt's homer was a grand slam, but the Red Sox prevailed, 9–8.

JUNE 10   The Red Sox trade Randy Gumpert and Walt Masterson to the Senators for Sid Hudson.

The Red Sox used 48 players in 1952, 26 of whom played for the club for the first time.

JUNE 11   Sammy White's walk-off grand slam off of Satchel Paige climaxes a six-run ninth inning that brings the Red Sox from behind to beat the Browns 11–9 at Fenway Park. White crawled the last 10 feet of his sojourn around the bases and kissed home plate.

Paige entered the game with a streak of 26 consecutive scoreless innings, but was unnerved by the antics of Jimmy Piersall. Piersall led off the inning and told Paige he was going to bunt, then pushed a bunt toward first base on the first pitch and beat it out. Once on base, Piersall went into gyrations, bouncing up and down like a jumping jack, snorting like a pig, flapping his arms like a chicken, whistling, and imitating Paige going through his pitching motions.

JUNE 14   The Red Sox are knocked out of first place with a 4–3 loss to the White Sox in Chicago.

The Sox never returned to first place in 1952, but they remained in contention for the pennant until late August.

JUNE 15   In the first game of a doubleheader against the White Sox in Chicago, Jimmy Piersall gestures as if thumbing a ride from the auto that brought relief pitchers from the bullpen to the mound, performs a hula dance, and flexes his arms like a bodybuilder while in the outfield. Lou Boudreau benched Piersall in the second game, claiming the rookie "wasn't hitting" even though he had tallied 14 hits in his last 37 at-bats. The Red Sox lost the first game 7–2, then won the second, 3–2.

JUNE 23   Twelve Red Sox batters reach base consecutively during an 11-run fourth inning as the Red Sox crush the Tigers 12–6 in Detroit. The 12 reached on seven singles, a double, three walks, and a fielder's choice.

JUNE 27   Jimmy Piersall continues to spin out of control during a 5–3 loss against the Senators at Fenway Park. While standing in the batter's box against Connie Marrero, he mocked the pitcher's motion and struck out without swinging.

JUNE 28   The Red Sox demote Jimmy Piersall to Birmingham in the Southern Association even though he was hitting a respectable .267. In justifying the move, Lou Boudreau explained that "Piersall's attitude was detrimental to the club" (see July 19, 1952).

JULY 4   Billy Goodman collects seven hits and Vern Stephens drives in seven runs in a doubleheader, but the Red Sox can only split, winning 10–5 and losing 4–3 against the Athletics in Philadelphia.

            Goodman hit .306 in 1952.

JULY 5   President Harry Truman attends a 4–3 Red Sox loss to the Senators in Washington.

JULY 11   The Red Sox sweep the Tigers 16–6 and 5–3 against the Tigers at Fenway Park. Hoot Evers hit a grand slam in the first game off Ted Gray.

JULY 13   A three-run, walk-off homer by Sammy White beats the Browns 8–5 at Fenway Park. The Sox completed the sweep with a 4–0 victory in the nightcap behind Mickey McDermott's two-hitter. The only St. Louis hits were singles by Bob Nieman in the first innings and Ned Garver in the third.

JULY 19   After being tossed out of four games in three weeks at Birmingham, Jimmy Piersall is sent to a sanitarium.

            The demotion to the minors had only worsened Piersall's problems. During his brief stay in Birmingham, his self-destructive behavior continued as he cleaned home plate with a water pistol, got down on all fours to chase a ground ball, performed calisthenics in the outfield, and led cheers for himself. He spent six weeks in the violent room at Westborough State Hospital in Massachusetts and received shock therapy. Piersall has no memory of the period between January and September 1952. Jimmy later wrote a book called Fear Strikes Out, *co-authored with Boston sportswriter Al Hirshberg, about his battle with mental illness. The book was published in 1955 (see August 18, 1955).*

            Piersall recovered and played 151 games for the Red Sox in 1953. Even though the opposition and many fans rode him unmercilessly, he hit .272. Although Piersall continued to battle manic depression and some of his bizarre behavior occasionally resurfaced, his big-league career lasted until 1967. Since then, he has been active in baseball as a coach, broadcaster, and talk show host.

JULY 22   Dick Gernert drives in all four Red Sox runs in a 13-inning, 4–2 win over the White
                   Sox in Chicago. Gernert hit a single in the ninth inning that tied the score 1–1 and
                   hit a three-run homer in the thirteenth.

JULY 23   The Red Sox explode for seven runs in the ninth inning to beat the White Sox 10–4
                   in Chicago.

AUGUST 2   Dom DiMaggio hits a grand slam off Hal Newhouser in the first inning of a 10–5
                   victory over the Tigers in Detroit.

AUGUST 9   Dick Gernert and Dom DiMaggio each hit home runs during the tenth inning of a
                   3–1 win over the Yankees in New York.

AUGUST 19   In his first major league game at third base, Ted Lepcio starts three double plays
                   during a 6–5 win over the Indians at Fenway Park.

AUGUST 20   The Indians score 10 runs in the third inning and beat the Red Sox 18–8 at Fenway
                   Park.

AUGUST 22   The Red Sox sell Ray Scarborough to the Yankees.

AUGUST 24   The Red Sox score eight runs in the fifth inning and wallop the Browns 12–1 in the
                   second game of a doubleheader at Fenway Park. The Sox also won the opener, 2–1
                   in 10 innings.

AUGUST 27   The Red Sox defeat the Tigers 5–0 at Fenway Park. The win put the Sox in third
                   place behind the Yankees and Indians, 3½ games out of first.

                   *The Sox' pennant bubble burst quickly as the club lost 24 of its last 32 games
                   and sank to sixth place.*

AUGUST 28   Catcher Sammy White fights with Billy Hitchcock of the Athletics during a 6–4
                   loss at Philadelphia. White was ejected for questioning umpire Bill McGowan's judg-
                   ment on balls and strikes. Hitchcock was in the on-deck circle and laughed at White's
                   predicament. The Red Sox catcher tore into Hitchcock and both went into a tangle of
                   arms and legs. During the ensuing bench-clearing melee, twenty-four-year-old Sox
                   pitcher Willard Nixon fought with forty-nine-year-old Athletics coach Tom Oliver.

AUGUST 31   The Red Sox pound the Athletics 11–1 in the first game of a doubleheader in
                   Philadelphia before losing 2–0 in the nightcap. On the same day, the Red Sox
                   purchased Al Zarilla from the Browns.

SEPTEMBER 7   The Red Sox score seven runs in the eighth inning to break a 5–5 tie and beat the
                   Athletics 12–5 at Fenway Park.

SEPTEMBER 13   Ted Lepcio hits a homer in the tenth inning off Bob Lemon to beat the Indians 4–3
                   in Cleveland.

SEPTEMBER 17   Red Sox outfielder George Schmees makes his debut as a starting pitcher and gives
                   up four hits and two runs in two innings before being removed. The Red Sox lost
                   10–4 to the Browns in St. Louis.

Schmees played 76 major league games but hit only .168 with no homers. He had a strong throwing arm, however, and the Sox decided to try him out as a pitcher. Schmees lasted only two games as a big-league hurler.

SEPTEMBER 20   Mel Parnell's 17-game winning streak against the Senators dating back to 1948 ends with a 10–6 loss to the Senators in Washington.

SEPTEMBER 21   The Braves close out their home schedule with an 8–2 loss to the Dodgers at Braves Field.

Although no one knew it at the time, this would be the last Major League Baseball game played at Braves Field. Before the start of the 1953 season, the Braves moved to Milwaukee (see March 17, 1953). Braves Field, which opened in 1915, was situated in a horrible location—on a single streetcar line on Commonwealth Avenue hemmed in by railroad tracks and the Charles River. Parking was hopelessly inadequate. The main entrance was on a dead-end street crowded with trucks opposite a busy armory. Unlike most pre–World War I ballparks, there was little intimacy, as most seats were located too far from the field.

1953   B

Season in a Sentence

Backed by a strong pitching staff and an infusion of young talent, the Red Sox rise to fourth place.

Finish • Won • Lost • Pct • GB

Fourth   84   69   .549 16.0

Manager

Lou Boudreau

Stats

Stats	Red Sox	• AL •	Rank
Batting Avg:	.264	.262	4
On-Base Pct:	.332	.337	6
Slugging Pct:	.384	.383	4
Home Runs:	101		6
Stolen Bases:	33		6 (tie)
ERA:	3.58		3
Fielding Pct:	.975	.978	7
Runs Scored:	656		6
Runs Allowed:	632		5

Starting Lineup

Sammy White, c
Dick Gernert, 1b
Billy Goodman, 2b
George Kell, 3b
Milt Bolling, ss
Hoot Evers, lf
Tom Umphlett, cf
Jimmy Piersall, rf
Gene Stephens, lf
Floyd Baker, 3b-2b
Ted Lepcio, 2b-ss
Johnny Lipon, ss

Pitchers

Mel Parnell, sp
Mickey McDermott, sp
Hal Brown, sp
Sid Hudson, sp-rp
Willard Nixon, sp-rp
Bill Henry, sp-rp
Ellis Kinder, rp
Ben Flowers, rp

Attendance

1,026,133 (fourth in AL)

Club Leaders

Batting Avg:	Goodman	.313
On-Base Pct:	Goodman	.384
Slugging Pct:	Kell	.483
Home Runs:	Gernert	21
RBI:	Kell	73
Runs:	Piersall	76
Stolen Bases:	Piersall	11
Wins:	Parnell	21
Strikeouts:	Parnell	136
ERA:	McDermott	3.01
Saves:	Kinder	27

FEBRUARY 9   Two weeks after Dwight Eisenhower is inaugurated as president following his victory over Adlai Stevenson, the Red Sox trade Vern Stephens to the White Sox for Hal Brown, Marv Grissom, and Bill Kennedy.

FEBRUARY 19   In a close call during a combat mission over Korea, Ted Williams escapes without injury when his F-9 Panther jet is hit by enemy fire. Flying with the 33rd Marine Air Group, Williams was one of two hundred pilots in a huge mission aimed at Kyomipo, a troop and supply center fifteen miles south of the North Korean capital of Pyongyang. North Korean soldiers hit Williams's plane with small-arms fire, causing it to catch fire and knocking out the landing gear. He turned his crippled jet toward the nearest American air base and crash-landed it on its belly with the flaming aircraft traveling at about 225 miles per hour. The plane skidded for more than a mile before coming to a stop and exploded shortly after Williams exited.

MARCH 17   The Red Sox become the only big-league baseball team in New England after the Braves move to Milwaukee. It was the first franchise shift in the majors since 1903.

Attendance at Braves Field peaked at 1,455,439 in 1948, when the club won the National League pennant, but dropped to 944,381 in 1951, 487,475 in 1951, and 281,278 in 1952. Following the 1952 season, Braves owner Lou Perini considered moving his club to Milwaukee, where he owned a minor league club in the American Association, but he decided to give it a go in Boston for at least one more season. But Browns owner Bill Veeck wanted out of St. Louis and had also set his sights on Milwaukee. Perini had the rights to the territory and blocked Veeck's move. This made Perini a villain in the Wisconsin city because he was denying fans there a major league team. Backed into a corner, he moved the Braves less than a month before the start of the 1953 season. The Braves were an immediate success in Milwaukee, drawing 1,826,397 fans in 1953 and more than two million in 1954. The Braves were also an athletic success in their new home and became an immediate contender. Milwaukee won the NL pennant in both 1957 and 1958 with such future Hall of Famers as Hank Aaron, Eddie Mathews, Warren Spahn, and Red Schoendienst. Veeck sold the Browns in September 1953 to a group from Baltimore, where the club moved and was renamed the Orioles.

Perini sold Braves Field to Boston University in July 1953. The sale included everything except the scoreboard and eight transformers. (The scoreboard was relocated to Municipal Stadium in Kansas City in 1955.) Most of Braves Field was torn down in 1957 and rebuilt as Nickerson Field, where Boston University's football and soccer teams play today. It was also used by the Patriots from 1960 through 1962 and the Boston Breakers of the USFL in 1983. The virtually unchanged Gaffney Street ticket office that was located down the right field line is now used a child-care center and a security office for the university. Directly behind the ticket office building is a grandstand that made up the right field bleachers at Braves Field. A plaque near the ticket office building commemorates the historical significance of the site. In addition, a crumbling, peeling portion of the original right field wall still stands.

APRIL 10   The Red Sox play the Braves in Milwaukee. The game was rained out after two innings with the Sox leading, 3–0.

The contest was originally scheduled for Braves Field in Boston before the Braves moved to the Midwest. The Red Sox and Braves had been meeting each other at the end of the spring training exhibition season since 1925. The Red Sox and Braves played occasional exhibition games against each other after 1953, but without the intracity rivalry, it wasn't the same.

APRIL 12   The Red Sox lose to the Braves 4–1 at Fenway Park in the final contest of their three-game series, which closes the exhibition season and officially brings an end to Boston's distinction as a two-team city for baseball.

Lolly Hopkins, one of the Boston Braves' most loyal fans, was struck in the mouth by a foul ball off the bat of Gus Niarhos of the Red Sox. She had to be taken from the ballpark for treatment.

APRIL 14   The scheduled season opener between the Red Sox and Senators at Fenway Park is postponed by snow. The April 15 contest between the same two clubs was also called off due to wintry weather.

APRIL 16   The Red Sox finally get under way and win 11–6 against the Athletics in Philadelphia in the first game of the season. George Kell had four hits, including a double, and drove in four runs. The Sox trailed 4–2 before scoring five runs in the fifth inning.

APRIL 17   Sammy White is ejected after fighting with Allie Clark of the Athletics during a 5–0 loss in Philadelphia. White tagged Clark in a close play at the plate, and Clark came up swinging. Umpire Charlie Berry was knocked to the ground trying to separate them. Both battlers were ejected.

APRIL 19   The Red Sox play at Fenway Park for the first time in 1953 and defeat the Senators 4–2 and 11–4 in a separate admission Patriots' Day doubleheader at Fenway Park. The first game drew 5,385, while the second attracted 7,534. During the two games, Dick Gernert hit three homers and a bases-loaded double.

APRIL 22   The Red Sox sell Clyde Vollmer to the Senators.

MAY 8   Billy Goodman's dramatic walk-off homer in the eleventh inning beats the Yankees 2–1 at Fenway Park, snapping a 13-game losing streak against the Yanks dating back to the previous season.

Goodman hit .313 with two homers in 1953.

MAY 10   Billy Goodman suffers a rib injury in a freak accident during the fifth inning of a 7–4 loss to the Yankees at Fenway Park. Goodman made a rush for umpire Jim Duffy after disagreeing with a call, and Jimmy Piersall grabbed Goodman and lugged him from the field. As he struggled to break free of Piersall's grasp, Goodman bruised his ribs, which put him out of action for three weeks.

MAY 12   Dom DiMaggio announces his retirement, effective immediately.

DiMaggio was the Red Sox starting center fielder from 1940 through 1952, with the exception of the three years (1943–45) when he was in the service. In spring training he lost his job to Tom Umphlett, and DiMaggio had had but three at-bats in the first four weeks of the 1953 season. Umphlett was twenty-three years old and part of the Red Sox' massive youth movement. Other young players on the 1953 roster included Billy Consolo (18), Gene Stephens (20), DickBrodowski (20), Faye Throneberry (22), Milt Bolling (22), Karl Olson (22), Leo Kiely (23), Norm Zauchin (23), Jimmy Piersall (23), Ike Delock (23), Frank Sullivan (23), Mickey McDermott (24), Dick Gernert (24), Bill Henry (25), Willard Nixon (25), and Sammy White (25). The contingent was nicknamed "Boudreau's Babes." More youthful talent arrived in 1954 or 1955: Frank Malzone, Tom Brewer, Harry Agganis, Russ Kemmerer, Tex Clevenger, Pete Daley, and Frank Baumann. Many predicted that this group would form a dynasty in Boston, but none of them came close to playing on a pennant winner with the Red Sox.

MAY 16   Mickey McDermott pitches a two-hitter to beat the Indians 1–0 at Fenway Park. George Kell's homer in the sixth inning off Bob Lemon accounted for the lone run of the game. The only Cleveland hits were singles by Al Rosen in the fourth inning and Bobby Avila in the fifth.

Kell hit .307 with 12 homers for Boston in 1953.

MAY 20   Del Wilber's walk-off, pinch-hit home run in the fourteenth inning beats the Browns 3–2 at Fenway Park.

Wilber hit four pinch homers for the Red Sox in 1953, three of them in May.

MAY 23   Smashing a total of 20 hits, the Red Sox outslug the Yankees 14–10 in New York. Mickey McDermott collected four hits in four at-bats, including a double, but allowed seven runs in $5\frac{1}{3}$ innings.

JUNE 3   The Red Sox score three runs in the ninth inning off Early Wynn to beat the Indians 4–3 in Cleveland. A two-run single by Sammy White drove in the tying and winning runs.

The Red Sox had a record of 35–16 record in one-run games in 1953.

JUNE 6   The Red Sox win a doubleheader 6–2 and 1–0 over the Tigers in Detroit. Mel Parnell pitched the second-game shutout. The lone run of the contest scored in the sixth inning on a triple by George Kell and a single by Floyd Baker.

JUNE 10   Jimmy Piersall collects six hits, including a double, in six at-bats during the first game of a doubleheader against the Browns in St. Louis. The Sox won 11–2. Piersall went hitless in five at-bats in the second contest, but Boston won again, 3–2.

Piersall was dusted by Satchel Paige in the second tilt in retaliation for Piersall's antics a year earlier (see June 11, 1952). Fearing further problems, Jimmy didn't play against the Browns the following day. Instead, he was sent to Chicago, where the Red Sox were slated to play on June 12. It was one of only two games that Piersall missed all season.

JUNE 17   The Red Sox score seven runs in the fourth inning and breeze to a 17–1 triumph over the Tigers at Fenway Park. The Sox collected 20 hits in the contest.

JUNE 18   The Red Sox set a modern major league record for most runs in an inning by scoring 17 runs in the seventh inning of a 23–3 victory over the Tigers at Fenway Park. The Sox sent 23 batters to the plate in 47 minutes against Detroit pitchers Steve Gromek,

How Do You Score 17 Runs in an Inning?

The Red Sox set a modern major league record for most runs in an inning by scoring 17 in a 23–3 trouncing of the Tigers at Fenway Park on June 18, 1953. The bottom half of the seventh inning took 47 minutes to complete. The only club in the big leagues to score more in a single inning was the Chicago Cubs, who plated 18 on September 6, 1883. When the inning began, the Red Sox led the Tigers 5–3 with Steve Gromek pitching for Detroit. Here's how they scored:

BATTER	RESULT
Sammy White	Single to short right
Gene Stephens	Single to right; White to third; Stephens stole second
Tom Umphlett	Single to left; White and Stephens score (7–3 Red Sox).
Johnny Lipon	Strike out; **first out**
George Kell	Double off left-field wall; Umphlett to third
Billy Goodman	Intentional walk; bases loaded
Jimmy Piersall	Single to right; Umphlett and Kell score; Goodman to second (9–3)
Dick Gernert	Home run into left-field screen; Goodman and Piersall score ahead of Gernert (12–3)
Ellis Kinder	Single to right
White	Walk; Kinder goes to second, and Dick Weik replaces Gromek as the Detroit pitcher; Weik throws a wild pitch, and Kinder and White advance to second and third
Stephens	Double to short right; Kinder and White score (14–3)
Umphlett	Walk
Lipon	Single to right; Stephens scores (15–3)
Kell	Fly to Don Lund in right field for **second out**
Goodman	Single to short center; Umphlett scores (16–3); Ted Lepcio pinch-runs for Goodman, and Earl Harrist replaces Weik as the Detroit pitcher
Al Zarilla	Walk as pinch hitter for Piersall; bases loaded
Gernert	Walk; Lipon scores (17–3)
Kinder	Single; Lepcio and Zarilla score (19–3)
White	Single; Gernert scores (20–3)
Stephens	Single; Kinder scores (21–3)
Umphlett	Single; White scores (22–3)
Lipon	Walk; bases loaded
Kell	Fly to Lund in right field for **third out**

Dick Weik, and Earl Harrist. Boston banged out 14 hits to set an American League mark for a single inning and had 27 hits in the game, 23 singles, two doubles and two homers. Gene Stephens had three hits (two singles and a double), and Sammy White scored three runs in the big inning to set records of their own. Tom Umphlett, Johnny Lipon, and George Kell also batted three times in the inning. In the two games of June 17 and 18, the Red Sox outscored the Tigers, 40–4.

There was considerable ill will between the two teams, as Jimmy Piersall exchanged insults with Matt Batts and Fred Hatfield of the Tigers throughout the series. Piersall was taken out of the game by Lou Boudreau in the third inning. Stephens had his three-hit inning during a season in which he hit only .204 in 221 at-bats. The only other major leaguer since 1883 to collect three hits in an inning is Johnny Damon of the Red Sox in 2003.

JUNE 30   A two-out, two-run, walk-off homer in the ninth inning by Sammy White off Allie Reynolds beats the Yankees 5–4 at Fenway Park.

JULY 1   The Red Sox sell Marv Grissom to the Giants.

            Grissom gave the Red Sox little reason to hang on to him. He was thirty-five years old and had a 2–6 record and a 4.70 ERA in Boston, although he gave the Giants six excellent seasons as a reliever.

JULY 8   The Red Sox score eight runs in the first inning and beat the Athletics 10–2 in Philadelphia.

JULY 10   After smashing a home run in the ninth inning to tie the score 2–2, Jimmy Piersall draws a bases-loaded walk in the twelfth to defeat the Athletics 3–2 at Fenway Park.

JULY 12   Angered by heckling from the Athletics, Jimmy Piersall fires a warm-up ball into the visitors bullpen at Fenway Park that strikes Philadelphia catcher Neal Watlington on the hand. A police officer sat in the bullpen for the rest of the day. The Red Sox split the doubleheader, a 9–5 win and a 4–1 loss.

JULY 14   Shortly after his discharge from the Marines, Ted Williams throws out the first pitch at the All-Star Game, won by the National League 5–1 at Crosley Field in Cincinnati.

            Williams signed a contract to play the balance of the season on July 29 and played in his first game on August 6.

JULY 19   Mickey McDermott allows only one hit but walks eight in eight innings in the first game of a doubleheader against the Indians in Cleveland. McDermott also homered off Early Wynn in the eighth inning. Ellis Kinder added a hitless ninth to close out a 2–0 Boston win. The only Cleveland hit was a single by Al Smith in the fourth inning. The Sox completed the sweep with a 7–5 win in the second tilt.

            At the age of thirty-eight, Kinder was sensational in relief in 1953 with a 10–6 record, 27 saves, and a 1.65 ERA in 69 games. Prior to 1953, the only Red Sox pitchers to reach double digits in saves in a season were Wilcy Moore with 10 in 1931 and Kinder with 14 in 1951.

JULY 24   The Red Sox shut out the Browns twice, 8–0 and 6–0, in a doubleheader in St. Louis. The shutouts were thrown by Bill Henry and Mickey McDermott.

JULY 25   The Red Sox score two runs in the seventh inning to beat the Browns 7–6 in St. Louis. The winning run came on a squeeze bunt by Johnny Lipon that trickled down the first base line and struck the bag, enabling Tom Umphlett to score from third. Lipon was hitless in his previous 26 at-bats.

JULY 30   Three days after the signing of the armistice ending the Korean War, the White Sox crush the Red Sox 17–1 at Fenway Park.

Reversing their normal trend, the Red Sox were 38–38 at Fenway Park in 1953 and 46–31 on the road.

AUGUST 1   During a 4–3 loss to the Tigers at Fenway Park, Red Sox hurler Ben Flowers becomes the first American Leaguer and the second in the majors to pitch in relief eight games in a row.

AUGUST 5   Ben Flowers makes his first major league start, a shutout of the Browns 5–0 in St. Louis.

              This would be Flowers's only victory in a Red Sox uniform. He finished his big-league career in 1956 with 76 pitching appearances, 13 starts, and a 3–7 record with a 4.49 ERA. The August 5, 1953, contest not only was Flowers's only major league shutout but his only complete game as well.

AUGUST 6   Ted Williams plays in his first game since April 30, 1952, and pops out as a pinch hitter in the ninth inning of a ten-inning, 8–7 loss to the Browns at Fenway Park.

              Williams shook off the rust in a hurry. Although he turned thirty-five on August 30, Williams had a .407 batting average with 13 homers and 34 RBIs in just 91 at-bats in 1953.

AUGUST 16   In his first start since returning from Korea, Ted Williams hits a double and a single in three at-bats, but the Red Sox lose 7–4 to the Senators in the second game of a doubleheader at Fenway Park. The Sox won the opener, 4–1.

AUGUST 28   Jimmy Piersall touches off a near riot in the third inning of a 4–3 win over the White Sox at Comiskey Park. In the third inning, Piersall upset Chicago shortstop Chico Carrasquel with a slide trying to break up a double play. Carrasquel rose from the tangle as if ready to throw at Piersall, and as players from both clubs swarmed onto the field, Gus Niarhos of the Red Sox started swinging and was ejected from the game. Piersall remained in the game and helped break a 2–2 tie in the seventh by scoring a run after hitting a triple.

SEPTEMBER 8   The Red Sox sell Johnny Lipon to the Browns.

SEPTEMBER 10 The Red Sox overwhelm the Indians 14–4 at Fenway Park.

SEPTEMBER 19 Mel Parnell wins his 20th game of the season with a 3–0 win over the Yankees at Fenway Park.

              Parnell had a record of 21–8 in 1953. He had an ERA of 3.06 and pitched five shutouts, four of them against the Yankees. At the end of the 1953 season, Parnell was twenty-nine years old and had a lifetime record of 111–59. It was his last good season, however, as a run of injuries including a broken arm, enlarged kneecap, sprained ankle, and strained elbow hampered Parnell's effectiveness. He was 12–16 for the remainder of his career, which ended in 1956. Parnell ranks third all time among Red Sox victories in wins (123), fourth in innings pitched (1,752⅔), fourth in games started (232), sixth in complete games (113), sixth in shutouts (20), seventh in games (289), and ninth in winning percentage (.621).

SEPTEMBER 30   At Yankee Stadium, Cy Young throws out the ceremonial first pitch prior to Game
One of the World Series, played between the Yankees and the Brooklyn Dodgers.

> *Six surviving members of the 1903 World Series, the first one in modern histo-
> ry, threw out the first pitch prior to the six contests of the 1953 Series to cele-
> brate the anniversary of the event. In addition to Young, first pitches were
> thrown by Bill Dinneen and Freddie Parent of the Red Sox and Fred Clarke,
> Tommy Leach, and Otto Kruger of the Pirates. Parent lived longer than any
> player who participated in the 1903 Fall Classic. He died on November 2,
> 1972, at the age of ninety-six.*

From 1948 through 1953, the underrated Mel Parnell gave the Sox a reliable winner on the mound.

DECEMBER 9   The Red Sox trade Mickey McDermott and Tommy Umphlett to the Senators for Jackie Jensen.

Red Sox fans howled in anger when this trade was made, but it proved to be one of the best in club history. McDermott was 18–10 with a 3.01 ERA in 1953 and was only twenty-five years old. Cocky and good-natured, he was extremely popular with Red Sox fans and sang in several Boston night spots and Grossinger's in the Catskills with Eddie Fisher. McDermott drove club management crazy, however, because of his drinking and late-night carousing. He fizzled after leaving Boston and had a record of 21–35 over the remainder of his career. Jensen was twenty-six when the Sox acquired him. He was a football star at the University of California, where he scored on a 67-yard touchdown run in the 1949 Rose Bowl. His wife was Zoe Ann Olsen, who won silver and bronze medals in the Olympics as a springboard diver. Both were athletic and good-looking and were called the "world's most famous sweethearts." There were one thousand guests at their 1949 wedding reception.

In seven seasons as an outfielder with Boston, Jensen hit .282 with 170 homers and 733 RBIs. He drove in more than 100 runs in a season five times, including three in which he led the AL, and was the league MVP in 1958. Jensen's career ended prematurely, however, because he had a pathological fear of flying. He tried all sorts of remedies, including psychoanalysis and hypnosis, to overcome his panic attacks when stepping onto a plane. One analyst theorized that Jensen's fear originated when he went on a 30-day trip through Asia in 1954 with a group of major league players. His plane nearly collided with another aircraft during a landing in Fukuoka, Japan. A hypnotist claimed that the phobia was "...merely a subterfuge. Jackie needed the fear as an excuse to get home and patch up his marriage. Subconsciously, it developed as a good reason to leave the Red Sox and go home." Jensen had an unstable childhood, which added to his guilt over leaving his family for long periods during the baseball season. His parents divorced when he was five, and his mother, a warehouse worker, moved the family "every time the rent came due." Jensen took long train trips alone and sometimes missed games because he failed to arrive on time. Jensen retired at the end of the 1959 season (see January 25, 1960) but came back in 1961 before quitting for good.

1954
B

Season in a Sentence

The Red Sox youth movement takes a wrong turn as most of the "can't-miss" prospects develop into mediocrities.

Finish • Won • Lost • Pct • GB

Fourth 69 85 .448 42.0

Manager

Lou Boudreau

Stats   Red Sox • AL • Rank

	Red Sox	AL	Rank
Batting Avg:	.266	.257	3
On-Base Pct:	.348	.334	3
Slugging Pct:	.395	.373	3
Home Runs:	123		3
Stolen Bases:	51		2
ERA:	4.01	3.72	7
Fielding Pct:	.972	.977	7
Runs Scored:	700		4
Runs Allowed:	728		7

Starting Lineup

Sammy White, c
Harry Agganis, 1b
Billy Goodman, 2b
Grady Hatton, 3b
Milt Bolling, ss
Ted Williams, lf
Jackie Jensen, cf
Jimmy Piersall, rf
Ted Lepcio, 2b
Billy Consolo, ss
Karl Olson, cf-lf-rf

Pitchers

Frank Sullivan, sp
Willard Nixon, sp
Tom Brewer, sp-rp
Leo Kiely, sp-rp
Mel Parnell, sp
Bill Henry, sp-rp
Ellis Kinder, rp
Hal Brown, rp

Attendance

931,127 (sixth in AL)

Club Leaders

Batting Avg:	Williams	.345
On-Base Pct:	Williams	.513
Slugging Pct:	Williams	.635
Home Runs:	Williams	29
RBI:	Jensen	117
Runs:	Williams	93
Stolen Bases:	Jensen	22
Wins:	Sullivan	15
Strikeouts:	Sullivan	124
ERA:	Sullivan	3.14
Saves:	Kinder	15

MARCH 1 Ted Williams escapes combat in Korea without a scratch only to be injured almost immediately at Sarasota, Florida's Payne Park on his return from the service. Only 15 minutes into his first workout on the first day of spring training, Williams took a tumble in the outfield and broke his left collarbone. Williams went after a low liner hit by Hoot Evers. Realizing he couldn't get to it, Williams started to slow up. Suddenly he tripped and fell forward and landed heavily on his left shoulder. The fracture was at the junction of the middle third and outer clavicle. Physicians said that Williams's muscles were so strong they pulled the collarbone apart. He didn't play again until May 15.

APRIL 13 The Red Sox lose 6–4 to the Athletics in Philadelphia on Opening Day. Sammy White and Jackie Jensen each hit homers for Boston. It was Jensen's first game with the Sox.

Bob Murphy replaced Bob DeLancey in the Red Sox' radio and television booth where he joined Curt Gowdy and Tom Hussey. It was Hussey's last year as the club's broadcaster. Also, road games were televised for the first time in 1954, with 18 in all, and the number of home games was scaled back from all 77 to 59.

APRIL 15 The Red Sox win 6–1 over the Senators in the Fenway Park opener before 17,272. Bill Henry pitched a complete-game three-hitter, and Sammy White homered.

The Red Sox added padding to the outfield walls at Fenway Park in 1954.

APRIL 18   On Easter Sunday, Jackie Jensen hits a walk-off homer in the thirteenth inning to beat the Athletics 4–3 in the second game of a doubleheader at Fenway Park. Philadelphia won the first game, 6–4.

The Red Sox ran into some foul weather early in the season. Eleven of the first 20 scheduled home games were postponed by rain or cold.

MAY 13   The Red Sox play a regular-season game in Baltimore for the first since 1902 and defeat the Orioles, 9–1.

MAY 15   Ted Williams plays his first game in 1954. Williams entered the contest in the seventh inning as a pinch hitter, then went to left field. He was hitless in two at-bats in a 2–1 loss to the Orioles in Baltimore.

MAY 16   In his first two starts of 1954, Ted Williams collects eight hits, including two homers and a double, in nine at-bats during a doubleheader against the Tigers in Detroit. Grimacing in his pain on every swing, Williams was three for four in the opener and five for five in the second contest. He also drove in eight runs in the twin bill, six of them in the nightcap. The Tigers won both games, however, 7–6 and 9–8, the second in 14 innings.

Williams hit .345 with 29 homers in 117 games and 386 at-bats in 1954. Under the rules then in force, a player needed 400 at-bats to qualify for the league lead in batting average. Bobby Avila of the Indians was awarded the crown with a .341 mark. There was some controversy over the 1954 AL batting championship because Williams failed to accumulate the required number of official at-bats in large part because he drew 136 walks. A change was made in 1957 in which plate appearances were the basis for qualifying for the batting title. A player needed 3.1 plate appearances per scheduled game. Williams had more than enough plate appearances to qualify in 1954, but the rule change wasn't retroactive, and Avila still holds the 1954 AL batting title.

MAY 18   The day after the Supreme Court rules that segregation of schools is illegal in *Brown v. Board of Education of Topeka*, the Red Sox sell Hoot Evers to the Orioles.

MAY 23   The Red Sox send George Kell and $100,000 to the White Sox for Grady Hatton.

MAY 25   Sammy White grounds into three double plays in his first three at-bats, then smashes a homer in the ninth inning in his fourth trip to the plate to beat the Athletics 3–2 in Philadelphia.

White hit .282 with 14 homers in 1954.

MAY 28   A grand slam by Jackie Jensen in the third inning off Allie Reynolds gives the Red Sox a 5–0 lead over the Yankees at Fenway Park, but New York rallies to win 10–9.

In his first season with the Red Sox, Jensen hit .276 with 25 homers, 117 RBIs, and 22 stolen bases to become the first Red Sox player with at least 20 homers and 20 steals in a season. In a statistical oddity, Jensen led the AL in steals and most times grounding into a double play (32).

MAY 31   The Red Sox trounce the Athletics 20–10 and 9–0 in a doubleheader at Fenway Park. The Sox scored seven runs in the fourth inning of the opener.

JUNE 8   Prior to a 7–4 loss against the Orioles at Fenway Park, Dick Gernert suffers a broken nose in batting practice when he fouls off a bunt attempt that caroms into his face. Trainer Jack Fadden set the fracture, and Gernert remained in uniform. He was called upon as a pinch hitter in the ninth inning with the bases loaded but grounded out.

              Ted Williams was out of action from June 6 until June 23 with pneumonia.

JUNE 23   The Red Sox pull off a triple play in the first inning and score four runs in the ninth inning to tie the score 7–7, but wind up losing 8–7 in a 17-inning marathon against the Orioles in Baltimore. The Red Sox left 21 runners on base, and the Orioles stranded 17.

JUNE 30   Tom Morgan of the Yankees hits three Red Sox batters in the third inning of a 6–1 Boston victory at Fenway Park. Morgan plunked Billy Goodman, Ted Lepcio, and Milt Bolling.

JULY 5   The Red Sox rout the Senators 14–0 in the first game of a doubleheader in Washington, then lose 7–1 in the nightcap. Ted Lepcio hit a grand slam off Camilo Pascual during an eight-run sixth inning in the opener.

              The Red Sox had a record of 28–48 and were in last place on July 8.

JULY 11   The Red Sox overwhelm the Athletics 18–0 and 11–1 in a doubleheader in Philadelphia. Boston whacked 40 hits in the two games.

JULY 18   In his first major league start, Russ Kemmerer pitches a one-hitter to beat the Orioles 4–0 in the first game of a doubleheader at Fenway Park. Kemmerer had made five previous relief appearances. The only Baltimore hit was a single by Sam Mele. The Orioles won the second game, 4–1.

              Kemmerer pitched only one more shutout as a major league player. The second one wasn't achieved until 1960, when Russ pitched for the White Sox. Kemmerer was 6–4 in three seasons with the Red Sox and 45–59 with a 4.46 ERA during a 12-year big league career.

JULY 19   A walk-off grand slam by Mickey Owen climaxes a six-run Red Sox rally in the ninth inning to beat the Orioles 9–7 in the first game of a doubleheader at Fenway Park. In the second tilt, the Red Sox used five home runs to win, 8–5. Jackie Jensen hit two of the homers, and Milt Bolling, Jimmy Piersall, and Ted Williams each added one.

              The dramatic homer by Owen was the first one he had hit in the majors since 1950, the only one he hit as a member of the Red Sox, and the last one he struck in his big-league career. Owen hit only 14 home runs in 3,649 at-bats over 13 seasons as a major leaguer.

JULY 20   The Red Sox and Indians play 16 innings to a 5–5 tie at Fenway Park. The game was called at 12:57 AM because of an American League rule stipulating that no inning could start after 12:50 AM.

JULY 21   The Red Sox and Indians play a tie game for the second day in a row. The contest ended in a 7–7 deadlock when rain brought play to a halt at the end of the eighth inning.

JULY 29   The Red Sox purchase Sam Mele from the Orioles.

AUGUST 6   Ted Williams hits a two-run homer in the tenth inning that defeats the Orioles 3–1 in Baltimore.

AUGUST 15   Harry Agganis hits a grand slam in the sixth inning off Bob Grim, but the Red Sox lose 14–9 to the Yankees in New York.

AUGUST 16   In a contest of throwing accuracy between Jimmy Piersall and Willie Mays before a Red Sox–Giants charity exhibition game in New York, Piersall hurts his arm. He didn't play again for two weeks, and for the remainder of his career, he never threw quite as well as he had before the injury.

AUGUST 19   Red Sox coach Paul Schreiber suffers a broken rib aboard an airplane during a turbulent flight from Washington to Boston.

AUGUST 21   After the Yankees score in the top of the twelfth inning, the Red Sox rally to win 10–9 when Don Lenhardt hits a two-run, bases-loaded single with two out in the bottom of the inning to end a thrilling contest at Fenway Park. The Sox had scored a run in the ninth inning to tie the game 6–6, and following a two-run Yankee rally in the tenth, Boston tied the contest again. Lenhardt entered the game in the tenth in left field after Ted Williams was lifted for a pinch runner.

AUGUST 26   Batting leadoff, Sam Mele hits the first pitch of the first inning for a homer, then closes the contest with a walk-off single in the eleventh to beat the Orioles 3–2 at Fenway Park.

The Red Sox lost all 11 games they played against the Indians at Fenway Park in 1954. Overall, the Sox were 2–20 against Cleveland, a club that had a record of 111–43 during the season.

AUGUST 31   Hurricane Carol postpones the game between the Red Sox and the White Sox at Fenway Park.

SEPTEMBER 3   The Red Sox overwhelm the Athletics 12–1 in Philadelphia. Ted Williams hit a long home run off Arnie Portocarrero. The ball sailed 40 feet over the fence at the 375-foot sign in right and hit the chimney of a home across North 20th Street.

SEPTEMBER 6   Trailing 7–0, the Red Sox score one run in the sixth inning, five in the seventh, and two in the eighth to defeat the Yankees 8–7 in the second game of a doubleheader at Yankee Stadium. The two eighth-inning runs were scored on a homer by Jimmy Piersall. New York won the first game 6–5 with two runs in the ninth.

SEPTEMBER 25   The Red Sox score three runs in the ninth inning to beat the Senators 7–6 at Fenway Park. Billy Consolo drove in the winning run with a single.

SEPTEMBER 26   In what he says will be the final game of his career, Ted Williams hits a home run in an 11–2 win over the Senators at Fenway Park.

Williams stated that 1954 would be his last season, but few really believed that he was serious. The Red Sox kept him on the active roster. He sat out spring training in 1955 and the first few weeks of the season before returning in May (see May 13, 1955).

OCTOBER 11   Pinky Higgins replaces Lou Boudreau as manager of the Red Sox.

The 85 defeats suffered by the Red Sox in 1954, the most by the club since 1933, greased the skids for Boudreau's departure. He later managed the Athletics from 1955 through 1957 and the Cubs in 1960, and he had a long career as the Cubs radio and television announcer. Higgins previously played for the Red Sox as a third baseman in 1937 and 1938 and again on the 1946 AL pennant winners. He managed in the Red Sox minor league system from 1947 through 1954.

NOVEMBER 24   The Red Sox sell Charlie Maxwell to the Orioles.

The Orioles passed Maxwell onto the Tigers in May 1955. Maxwell became a home run threat in Detroit, belting 120 of them in five seasons from 1956 through 1960.

1955   B

Season in a Sentence

A midseason surge in which the Red Sox win 44 of 60 games stirs pennant hopes before the club wilts in September.

Finish • Won • Lost • Pct • GB

Fourth   84   70   .545   12.0

Manager

Pinky Higgins

Stats   Red Sox • AL • Rank

Stat	Red Sox	AL	Rank
Batting Avg:	.264	.258	3
On-Base Pct:	.354	.339	1
Slugging Pct:	.402	.381	2
Home Runs:	137		3
Stolen Bases:	43		3
ERA:	3.72	3.96	4
Fielding Pct:	.977	.977	4
Runs Scored:	755		3
Runs Allowed:	652		4

Starting Lineup

Sammy White, c
Norm Zauchin, 1b
Billy Goodman, 2b
Grady Hatton, 3b
Billy Klaus, ss
Ted Williams, lf
Jimmy Piersall, cf
Jackie Jensen, rf
Gene Stephens, lf

Pitchers

Frank Sullivan, sp
Willard Nixon, sp
Tom Brewer, sp
George Susce, sp-rp
Ike Delock, sp-rp
Ellis Kinder, rp
Tom Hurd, rp
Leo Kiely, rp

Attendance

1,203,200 (fifth in AL)

Club Leaders

Batting Avg:	Williams	.356
On-Base Pct:	Williams	.496
Slugging Pct:	Williams	.703
Home Runs:	Williams	28
RBI:	Jensen	116
Runs:	Goodman	100
Stolen Bases:	Jensen	16
Wins:	Sullivan	18
Strikeouts:	Sullivan	129
ERA:	Sullivan	2.91
Saves:	Kinder	18

APRIL 12	In the first game of the season, Ted Lepcio hits two homers during a 7–1 win over the Orioles in Baltimore. Frank Sullivan pitched the complete-game victory.

Standing six-foot-six, Sullivan had an 18–13 record and an ERA of 2.91 in 1955. There were no 20-game winners in the AL during the season, and Sullivan's 18 victories were enough to lead the league. He also topped the AL in innings pitched (260) and games started (35).

APRIL 14	The Red Sox win the Fenway Park opener 8–4 against the Yankees before 22,246. Jimmy Piersall and Sammy White homered for the Sox.

APRIL 17	On a cold and drizzly day at Fenway Park, the Red Sox pound out two wins, 14–5 and 12–9, against the Orioles.

APRIL 20	Willard Nixon pitches the Red Sox to a 1–0 win over the Senators in Washington. Norm Zauchin drove in the lone run of the game with a single in the fourth inning.

Zauchin met his wife in unusual fashion. While playing in the minors for Birmingham in 1950, he chased a foul pop into the stands and landed in the lap of an attractive woman named Janet Mooney. He got her name from an usher and asked her out on a date. They were married two years later.

APRIL 24	Willard Nixon wins 1–0 again, this time with a two-hitter to beat the Yankees at Yankee Stadium. The only New York hits were singles by Bill Skowron in the second inning and opposing pitcher Ed Lopat in the eighth.

APRIL 26	The Red Sox play in Kansas City during the regular season for the first time and lose 8–7 in 11 innings to the Athletics.

The Athletics moved from Philadelphia to Kansas City after the 1954 season.

MAY 13	Ted Williams ends his retirement by signing a contract for 1955.

Williams and his wife, Doris, filed for divorce in December 1954, and the divorce became final in a Miami, Florida, court on May 9. Two days later, he reached a financial settlement with her. The ink was barely dry on the settlement when Williams "unretired" and returned to the Red Sox. The timing of Williams's retirement and eventual return strongly suggests that his "retirement" was designed to exclude his new contract from the divorce settlement. Williams played his first game on May 28 and finished the 1955 season with a .356 batting average and 28 homers in 98 games.

MAY 14	Jackie Jensen hits a two-run, walk-off homer in the thirteenth inning to beat the Athletics 3–1 at Fenway Park. Jensen also accounted for the first Boston run of the game with a solo homer in the fifth, which tied the score, 1–1.

Jensen led the AL in RBIs in 1955 with 116. He also hit 26 homers and batted .275.

MAY 18	The Indians score 11 runs in the fifth inning and wallop the Red Sox 19–0 at Fenway Park. It was, and still is, the worst shutout loss in Red Sox history.

MAY 21   In a game marked by a fistfight between Jackie Jensen and former Red Sox pitcher Mickey McDermott, the Senators defeat the Red Sox 1–0 in 12 innings in Washington. The scrap followed a play at first base in which Jensen knocked the ball out of McDermott's glove.

MAY 27   In a completely unexpected performance, Red Sox rookie first baseman Norm Zauchin explodes for three homers and 10 RBIs during a 16–0 thrashing of the Senators at Fenway Park. Zauchin hit a two-run homer off Bob Porterfield in the first inning, a grand slam off Dean Stone in the second, a one-run double facing Ted Abernathy in the fourth, and a three-run homer off Abernathy in the fifth. Zauchin struck out against Pedro Ramos in the seventh.

> *Entering the game, Zauchin had only 98 big-league at-bats with one homer, five RBIs, and a .208 batting average. He finished the 1955 season with 27 homers and 93 RBIs, but hit just .239 and led the league in strikeouts. Zauchin sat on the bench for most of the remainder of his career, which ended in 1959.*

> *On June 4, the Red Sox had a record of 19–30, then won 44 of their next 60 games to surge into the pennant race.*

JUNE 9   Ellis Kinder almost meets with disaster before entering the ninth inning of a 4–2 win against the Indians in Cleveland. Called to the mound to relieve Frank Sullivan, Kinder was riding in the red convertible used to transport hurlers from the bullpen to the mound when the vehicle rammed the left field stands. Neither Kinder nor the driver was injured, however, and Kinder snuffed out an Indians rally to earn a save.

JUNE 14   The Red Sox score eight runs in the third inning and rap the Athletics 12–4 at Fenway Park.

> *Mel Parnell failed to show up for the afternoon contest because he thought it was a night game.*

JUNE 16   A two-run, walk-off homer by Billy Klaus in the ninth inning beats the Athletics 7–6 at Fenway Park.

> *Klaus came out of nowhere to hit .283 with seven homers as the Red Sox shortstop in 1955. At the start of the season, he was twenty-six years old and had played in only nine major league games. Before turning to Klaus the first week of June, the Red Sox tried Milt Bolling, Eddie Joost, and Owen Friend at short. Klaus was never able to sustain the success of his rookie season, however.*

JUNE 23   Frank Sullivan pitches a two-hitter and Jackie Jensen hits a grand slam in the fourth inning off Duke Maas to highlight a 7–0 win over the Tigers at Fenway Park. The only Detroit hits were doubles by Bill Tuttle in the fourth inning and Ferris Fain in the eighth.

> *On the same day, the Red Sox sell Sam Mele to the Reds.*

JUNE 27   Red Sox first baseman Harry Agganis dies suddenly at the age of twenty-five at Sancta Maria Hospital in Cambridge, Massachusetts, of a massive pulmonary embolism caused by a blood clot in his leg that shot into his lung. Agganis had been in the hospital since May 16 with pneumonia and seemed to be recovering. His death came without warning.

Known as the Golden Greek, Agganis was a native of Lynn, Massachusetts. He had a brilliant sports career at Boston University, where he starred in both football and baseball. Agganis was the number-one draft choice of the Cleveland Browns with the idea that he would succeed Otto Graham as quarterback. Agganis passed up football to sign with the Red Sox in 1952. He reached the majors in 1954 and hit .251 with 11 homers as a rookie. In 1955, he hit .313 in 25 games and seemed to be on the verge of greatness before succumbing to illness.

JUNE 28   The Red Sox score eight runs in the ninth inning to beat the Senators 8–2 in the second game of a doubleheader in Washington. The Sox also won the opener, 4–0.

JULY 4   Jackie Jensen hits a third-inning grand slam off the Yankees' Tom Morgan in the second game of a doubleheader in New York. They won, 10–5. The Sox also won the opener, 4–2.

JULY 12   Frank Sullivan gives up a walk-off homer to Stan Musial in the twelfth inning of the All-Star Game at County Stadium in Milwaukee, giving the National League a 6–5 victory.

JULY 20   Red Sox rookie George Susce pitches a one-hitter to beat the Athletics 6–0 in Kansas City. His father, also named George, was the pitching coach for the Athletics and watched the game with mixed emotions from the home bullpen. The only Kansas City hit was a single by Vic Power to lead off the first inning.

George Susce never pitched another shutout as a major leaguer. He finished his career in 1959 with a record of 22–17.

JULY 31   Ted Williams hits a grand slam in the fourth inning off Ned Garver during an 8–3 win over the Tigers in the first game of a doubleheader at Fenway Park. In the second tilt, Jimmy Piersall hit a walk-off homer in the ninth inning for a 3–2 victory.

Tigers shortstop Harvey Kuenn created a controversy in the first game by walking back and forth behind second base in an attempt to distract Williams during his fifth- and seventh-inning at-bats. Kuenn stopped his strolling after umpire Ed Rommel threatened to eject him from the game if he continued.

AUGUST 7   The Red Sox outlast the Athletics 16–12 at Fenway Park.

The Red Sox were in fourth place on August 7, but were only 1 1/2 games out of first place with a tight pennant race. The White Sox were first, the Yankees second, and the Indians third. The Tigers were in fifth place, only 5 1/2 games behind the White Sox.

AUGUST 11   Ted Williams collects his 2,000th career hit in a 5–3 loss to the Yankees in New York. The landmark hit was a single off Bob Turley.

AUGUST 13   Jim Pagliaroni becomes the youngest player in Red Sox history when he makes his major league debut at the age of 17 years, 248 days during an 18–9 loss to the Senators at Fenway Park. He entered the game as a substitute catcher for Sammy White after the game was hopelessly lost and hit a sacrifice fly in his only plate appearance.

Pagliaroni was on the team because of a rule passed in 1955 stipulating that any amateur player who signed a contract with a bonus of at least $4,000 would have to remain on the roster for two years. The rule was rescinded in 1958. The Red Sox gave him $70,000 to sign just after graduating from high school. Pagliaroni didn't play in another major league game until 1960. He went into the Army after the 1955 season ended, and after his discharge, spent three seasons in the minors. Pagliaroni was the Red Sox' starting catcher in 1961 and 1962 before being traded to the Pirates.

AUGUST 15   Paced by a 450-foot grand slam from Ted Williams in the second inning off Ted Abernathy, the Red Sox defeat the Senators 8–4 at Fenway Park.

Fenway Park continued to skew the Red Sox' batting and pitching statistics in 1955. The Red Sox led the league in runs scored at home with 470 in 77 games at Fenway. The Sox scored only 285 runs in away games, however, which ranked dead last in the AL. The pitching staff surrendered 395 runs at home, the seventh-most in an eight-team league, but led the AL in fewest runs allowed on the road with 257.

AUGUST 18   A 60-minute dramatic television adaptation of Jimmy Piersall's book, *Fear Strikes Out*, which was co-authored by Boston sportswriter Al Hirshberg and detailed Piersall's fight against mental illness, appears on the CBS anthology series *Climax!* Tab Hunter played Piersall.

Less than two weeks later, Paramount Pictures bought the movie rights to Fear Strikes Out *for $50,000 (see July 12, 1956). It was released in theaters around the country in March 1957 with Anthony Perkins portraying Piersall. Perkins received strong reviews for his dramatic portrayal of Piersall, but the actor's lack of athletic ability in baseball scenes strained the credibility of the film. Piersall himself hated the movie, particularly with regard to the depiction of his father, played by Karl Malden. He believed that the film was entirely too harsh on his father, who was depicted as the source for his mental illness. Subsequent medical research over the past 50 years has revealed that Piersall's problems were likely inherited. His mother spent much of her adult life in and out of mental hospitals.*

AUGUST 27   Only one out away from a 3–0 defeat, the Red Sox win 4–3 when Ted Williams hits a dramatic grand slam off Al Aber to beat the Tigers in Detroit. Boston pitchers Frank Baumann (six innings), Tom Hurd (two innings), and Ellis Kinder (one inning) combined on a two-hitter. The only Tiger hits were a single by Bubba Phillips in the first inning and a homer by Bill Tuttle in the fourth.

AUGUST 28   Grady Hatton hits a grand slam in the first inning off Vic Raschi during a 14–2 win over the Athletics in Kansas City.

SEPTEMBER 2   Ellis Kinder pitches 4⅔ innings of shutout relief and hits a run-scoring single in the twelfth inning to beat the Orioles 2–1 in Baltimore.

SEPTEMBER 7   The Red Sox win their sixth game in a row with a 7–4 decision over the Tigers at Fenway Park.

On September 7, the Red Sox were in fourth place but were only three games out of first place in a tight four-team race with the Yankees, Indians, and White Sox. The Sox lost 14 of their last 18 games, however, and ended the season 12 games behind the pennant-winning Yankees.

SEPTEMBER 20   In his first two major league starts, Frank Malzone collects six hits, including a double, in 10 at-bats during a doubleheader against the Orioles in Baltimore. The six hits came in consecutive at-bats, four of them in the first game. The Sox lost both games, 3–2 in 10 innings in the first contest and 7–4 in the second.

Malzone began the 1956 season as the Red Sox third baseman but was sent back to the minors after batting only .165 in 103 at-bats. The death of his fourteen-month-old daughter during the previous offseason was a contributing cause to the slump. Malzone reclaimed the Sox' third base job in 1957, however, and held it until 1965.

NOVEMBER 8   The Red Sox trade Tex Clevenger, Neil Chrisley, Karl Olson, Dick Brodowski, and Al Curtis to the Senators for Mickey Vernon, Tom Umphlett, Bob Porterfield, and Johnny Schmitz. The Red Sox traded five players twenty-five years old or younger for thirty-seven-year-old Vernon, thirty-five-year-old Schmitz, and thirty-two-year-old Porterfield as the club abandoned its youth movement for a shot at the pennant.

Vernon gave the Sox one good year, hitting .310 with 15 homers in 119 games in 1956, before age caught up with him. Umphlett, Porterfield, and Schmitz were no help at all. Porterfield was a 22-game winner as recently as 1953 but was only 3–12 with a 5.14 ERA for Boston in 1956. Fortunately, none of the five athletes that were sent to the Senators developed into quality big-league players.

DECEMBER 4   The Red Sox sell Ellis Kinder to the Cardinals.

DECEMBER 18   Joe Cronin squashes rumors that the Red Sox were moving to San Francisco, terming them "silly." The rumors had been circulating for several months after the Red Sox purchased the San Francisco Seals of the Pacific Coast League as a farm club. San Francisco was Cronin's hometown. The New York Giants moved to San Francisco in 1958.

1956   B

Season in a Sentence

Touted as pennant contenders when the season began, the Red Sox are never in the race and finish in fourth place for the fourth year in a row.

Finish • Won • Lost • Pct • GB

Fourth   84   70   .545   13.0

Manager

Pinky Higgins

Stats   Red Sox • AL • Rank

	Red Sox	AL	Rank
Batting Avg:	.275	.260	2
On-Base Pct:	.365	.344	1
Slugging Pct:	.419	.394	3
Home Runs:	139		4
Stolen Bases:	28		8
ERA:	4.17	4.16	5
Fielding Pct:	.972	.975	7
Runs Scored:	780		3
Runs Allowed:	751		6

Starting Lineup

Sammy White, c
Mickey Vernon, 1b
Billy Goodman, 2b
Billy Klaus, 3b
Don Buddin, ss
Ted Williams, lf
Jimmy Piersall, cf
Jackie Jensen, rf
Dick Gernert, lf-1b
Ted Lepcio, 2b
Pete Daley, c
Gene Stephens, lf

Pitchers

Tom Brewer, sp
Frank Sullivan, sp
Willard Nixon, sp
Mel Parnell, sp
Bob Porterfield, sp
Ike Delock, rp
Tom Hurd, rp
Dave Sisler, rp-sp

Attendance

1,137,158 (second in AL)

Club Leaders

Batting Avg:	Williams	.345
On-Base Pct:	Williams	.479
Slugging Pct:	Williams	.605
Home Runs:	Williams	24
RBI:	Jensen	97
Runs:	Klaus	91
	Piersall	91
Stolen Bases:	Jensen	11
Wins:	Brewer	19
Strikeouts:	Brewer	127
ERA:	Sullivan	3.42
Saves:	Delock	9

APRIL 17   On Opening Day, Ted Williams collects two doubles and a single during an 8–1 win over the Orioles at Fenway Park. It was his first opener since 1952. He missed 1953 when he was in the service, 1954 with a broken collarbone, and 1955 with his temporary retirement. Both doubles were hit to left field and crossed up the defensive shift, placing three infielders on the right side of the diamond. Jimmy Piersall also contributed three hits and two sensational catches in center field. Frank Sullivan pitched a complete game.

APRIL 19   Tom Brewer pitches a two-hitter to beat the Orioles 4–2 on Patriots' Day at Fenway Park. The only Baltimore hits were a double by Dave Philley in the first inning and a single by Wayne Causey in the fourth.

Following the game, Ted Williams slipped in the shower while removing a pair of wooden shower slippers and suffered a badly bruised right instep. The injury kept him out of the starting lineup for five weeks. Williams didn't hit his first home run of 1956 until June 22, in his 99th at-bat, but finished the season with 24 homers and a .345 batting average in 400 at-bats.

APRIL 21   Trailing 8–0 after four innings in New York, the Red Sox rally to take a 10–9 lead in the top of the eighth, only to lose 14–10 when the Yankees score five runs in their half of the eighth.

MAY 11   The Red Sox sell Grady Hatton to the Cardinals.

MAY 14   The Red Sox sell Johnny Schmitz to the Orioles.

MAY 16   Northeastern University dedicates a plaque commemorating the first World Series in 1903. The plaque, marking the site of Huntington Grounds, home field of the Red Sox from 1901 through 1911, was unveiled by eighty-year-old Freddy Parent, who played shortstop for the Red Sox from 1901 through 1907. Baseball commissioner Ford Frick was the principal speaker at the ceremonies. Northeastern now occupies the former site of Huntington Grounds. The plaque is situated on the outside wall of the athletic building bordering Huntington Avenue, where the old left field fence bordered the street.

MAY 20   Red Sox catcher Pete Daley hits a grand slam in the fifth inning off Dick Donovan during a 12–5 win over the White Sox in the first game of a doubleheader in Chicago. Boston completed the sweep with a 2–1 win in the nightcap.

MAY 27   Trailing 6–1, the Red Sox score seven runs in the third inning and outlast the Senators 9–7 in the first game of a doubleheader at Fenway Park. Washington won the second contest 11–10 in 10 innings.

JUNE 17   The Red Sox smash the Tigers 12–2 in Detroit.

JULY 8   Ted Williams hits his 399th career homer and drives in his 1,500th run during a 9–0 win in the first game of a doubleheader against the Orioles at Fenway Park. The Sox also won the second game, 8–4.

JULY 10   Ted Williams hits a two-run homer off Warren Spahn in the sixth inning of the All-Star Game. The American League lost 7–3 at Griffith Stadium in Washington.

JULY 12   A crew from Paramount Pictures arrives at Fenway Park to film sequences for *Fear Strikes Out*, the movie based on the life of Jimmy Piersall. Piersall rose to the occasion by making two brilliant catches in center field, then put a Hollywood ending on the evening by hitting a two-run, walk-off homer to beat the White Sox, 3–1. *Fear Strikes Out* was released in theaters in March 1957.

JULY 14   Mel Parnell pitches a no-hitter to beat the White Sox 4–0 before 14,542 at Fenway Park. It was the first Red Sox no-hitter since 1923. In the ninth inning, Parnell walked Sammy Esposito on a 3–2 pitch. Luis Aparicio followed with a grounder up the middle, which Billy Goodman stopped with a diving grab and flipped to short-stop Don Buddin for the force. Had there been no runner on first, Aparicio likely would have beat the ball to first for a single. Bubba Phillips also hit into a force for the second out. The game ended when Walt Dropo tapped the ball to the right of the mound, where Parnell fielded it and raced all the way to first for the unassisted out. Parnell walked two and struck out four.

          Parnell was considered washed up after he followed his 21–8 season in 1953 with a 3–7 record in 1954 and 2–3 showing in 1955. He was 2–2 at the time of his no-hitter. Parnell won only four more big-league games after the no-hitter, finishing the 1956 season with a 7–6 record. He retired early in the 1957 season because of an elbow injury.

JULY 15   Dave Sisler (eight innings) and Ike Delock (one inning) combine on a two-hitter to beat the Indians 3–1 in the second game of a doubleheader at Fenway Park. The only Cleveland hits were a single by Al Smith in the first inning and a double by Al Rosen in the seventh. The Indians won the first game, 10–7.

JULY 17   Ted Williams hits his 400th career home run to account for the only run in a 1–0 victory over the Athletics in the second game of a doubleheader at Fenway Park. The homer came in the sixth inning off Tom Gorman. Williams was only the fifth player in big-league history behind Babe Ruth, Jimmie Foxx, Mel Ott, and Lou Gehrig to hit 400 homers. Bob Porterfield pitched the shutout. The Sox also won the first game 10–0 behind a shutout performance by Tom Brewer.

When Williams crossed the plate after he hit the milestone homer, he showed his contempt for the Boston writers by looking up at the press box and pursing his lips as if to spit, then sneered for an instant before disappearing into the dugout. Williams said afterward that he intended to spit, but held back because he was afraid he would hit teammate Mickey Vernon in the on-deck circle.

JULY 20   On Joe Cronin Night at Fenway Park, Ted Williams spits toward the press box after hitting a homer in the seventh inning of a 9–6 loss to the Tigers.

In pregame ceremonies, Cronin was given a new Cadillac. Three days later, he was inducted into the Hall of Fame at Cooperstown.

JULY 26   Ted Williams homers in the tenth inning to beat the Athletics 5–3 in Kansas City.

JULY 28   The Red Sox wallop the White Sox 13–1 in Chicago.

AUGUST 2   Jackie Jensen drives in nine runs during an 18–3 trouncing of the Tigers in Detroit. Jensen hit a homer with two on base in the first inning, lofted a sacrifice fly in the fifth, tripled with the bases loaded in the sixth, and singled in two runs in the seventh. Jensen batted with the bases loaded in the eighth but grounded out. During practice, Ted Williams flung his bat in frustration and almost coldcocked writer Bob Holbrook in the dugout.

Jensen hit .315 with 20 homers in 1956.

AUGUST 7   Willard Nixon pitches an 11-inning shutout to beat the Yankees 1–0 before 36,350 at Fenway Park, but Ted Williams gets all the headlines. In the top of the eleventh, Williams dropped an easy fly ball from Mickey Mantle and was booed by the fans. After Williams made a leaping catch off a drive by Yogi Berra to end the inning, the crowd cheered. Williams became enraged at the fickle nature of the fans and before entering the dugout, he spat toward the crowd behind first base, then turned and did so toward third base. In the bottom of the inning, with the bases loaded, Williams spat twice more as he walked to the plate, once in the direction of the Yankee bench. Facing Tommy Byrne, Williams walked, driving in the winning run, and tossed the bat 40 feet into the air. The Red Sox responded by fining Williams $5,000. Many claim, however, that the Red Sox never assessed Williams the fine and that it was only a publicity ploy to stem public opinion.

Williams wasn't the only Red Sox outfielder in trouble during the afternoon.

Before the game, Jackie Jensen had to be restrained by Mel Parnell and coach Paul Schreiber from going after a heckling fan in the right field stands.

AUGUST 8   The day after his third spitting incident in three weeks, Ted Williams hits a homer in the sixth inning to break a 2–2 tie against the Orioles at Fenway Park. Williams drew laughs from the crowd by slapping his hands over his mouth as he entered the dugout. The Red Sox won the game, 7–3.

AUGUST 16   Willard Nixon pitches a two-hitter to beat the Yankees 2–1 in New York. Nixon held the Yankees hitless until Yogi Berra singled in the eighth. The Red Sox hurler entered the ninth with a one-hitter and a 2–0 lead before loading the bases with none out on a walk, a single by Mickey McDermott, and an error. Nixon pitched his way out of the jam, allowing only one run to preserve the win.

AUGUST 22   Down 6–1 against the White Sox in the second game of a doubleheader at Fenway Park, the Red Sox rally to win 7–6 with one run in the sixth inning, two in the seventh, two in the eighth, and one in the ninth. Billy Consolo drove in the winning run with a bases-loaded single. Chicago won the first game, 6–3.

AUGUST 28   A boneheaded play by catcher Sammy White and his Boston teammates contributes to a 6–3 loss to the Tigers at Fenway Park. With the Tigers leading 4–0 in the sixth inning and Detroit's Bill Tuttle on second base, Red Wilson poked a grounder through the middle of the infield. Red Sox shortstop Milt Bolling fielded the ball behind second base and was surprised to see Tuttle heading for the plate. Bolling threw home, and umpire Frank Umont ruled that Tuttle was safe. White vehemently protested the decision and threw the ball into center field. While the Red Sox continued to argue, they failed to notice Wilson running around the bases. As he reached home, Wilson had to brush against Umont, who was sweeping off the plate. Since the Red Sox failed to call time, the umpires had to choice but to award the Tigers a run.

SEPTEMBER 2 The Red Sox take an 8–0 lead with four runs in the first inning and four in the second, but lose 11–10 to the Orioles at Fenway Park.

SEPTEMBER 3 Jimmy Piersall drives in eight runs during a doubleheader as the Red Sox roll to 7–5 and 16–0 wins over the Senators in Washington. Piersall had a homer, a double, four singles, and a sacrifice fly. The Sox collected 20 hits in the second game.

SEPTEMBER 8 Tom Brewer wins his 19th game of a season with a 6–1 decision over the Orioles in Baltimore.

             Brewer started three more games in 1956 but failed to win number 20. He finished the season with a 19–9 record and a 3.50 ERA.

SEPTEMBER 14 Dave Sisler pitches a two-hitter to beat the Indians 4–3 in the second game of a doubleheader at Municipal Stadium. Both Cleveland hits and all three runs came in the eighth inning on a walk, a single by Joe Caffie, a triple by Jim Hegan, and an error. The rally gave the Indians a 3–1 lead, but the Red Sox countered with three runs in the ninth on a two-run pinch double by Ted Williams and a single by Sammy White. Cleveland won the first game, 10–2.

A graduate of Princeton University with an engineering degree, Sisler had a 38–44 lifetime record in the majors. He was the youngest son of Hall of Fame first baseman George Sisler, who played in the majors from 1915 through 1930, and the brother of major leaguer Dick Sisler.

SEPTEMBER 21 The Yankees strand 20 runners, a major league record for a nine-inning game, during a 13–7 loss to the Red Sox at Fenway Park. Mickey Mantle hit a home run estimated at 480 feet. The drive struck only inches from the top of the center field wall above the bleachers.

SEPTEMBER 25 The Massachusetts State House of Representatives approves a bill calling for a fifty-dollar fine for using profanity at sporting events. The bill stemmed from fans heckling Ted Williams at Fenway Park. The statute failed to become law, however, when the Massachusetts Senate voted against it.

1957   B

Season in a Sentence

After turning thirty-nine in August, Ted Williams defies Father Time by hitting .388 with 38 homers.

Finish • Won • Lost • Pct • GB

Third   82   72   .532   16.0

Manager

Pinky Higgins

Stats

Stats	Red Sox	AL	Rank
Batting Avg:	.262	.255	2
On-Base Pct:	.343	.329	2
Slugging Pct:	.405	.382	2
Home Runs:	153		2
Stolen Bases:	29		7
ERA:	3.88	3.79	5
Fielding Pct:	.976	.979	7
Runs Scored:	721		2
Runs Allowed:	668		5

Starting Lineup

Sammy White, c
Dick Gernert, 1b
Ted Lepcio, 2b
Frank Malzone, 3b
Billy Klaus, ss
Ted Williams, lf
Jimmy Piersall, cf
Jackie Jensen, rf
Mickey Vernon, 1b
Gene Mauch, 2b
Billy Consolo, ss
Pete Daley, c
Gene Stephens, lf

Pitchers

Tom Brewer, sp
Frank Sullivan, sp
Willard Nixon, sp
Dave Sisler, sp
Mike Fornieles, sp
Ike Delock, rp
Bob Porterfield, rp
George Susce, rp

Attendance

1,181,087 (third in AL)

Club Leaders

Batting Avg:	Williams	.388
On-Base Pct:	Williams	.526
Slugging Pct:	Williams	.731
Home Runs:	Williams	38
RBI:	Jensen	103
	Malzone	103
Runs:	Piersall	103
Stolen Bases:	Piersall	14
Wins:	Brewer	16
Strikeouts:	Brewer	128
ERA:	Sullivan	2.73
Saves:	Delock	11

APRIL 13   The day the Celtics win their first NBA championship in a seven-game series against the St. Louis Hawks, the Red Sox purchase Russ Meyer from the Reds.

APRIL 16   The Red Sox open the season with a 4–2 victory over the Orioles in Baltimore. All four Boston runs were scored in the fourth inning.

                  The Red Sox had eight different starting shortstops on Opening Day from 1950 through 1957. They were Vern Stephens (1950), Lou Boudreau (1951), Jimmy Piersall (1952), Ted Lepcio (1953), Milt Bolling (1954), Eddie Joost (1955), Don Buddin (1956), and Bill Klaus (1957).

APRIL 18   The Red Sox lose 3–2 to the Yankees in the Fenway Park opener before 30,468. Dick Gernert homered for the Sox.

APRIL 20   Bill Skowron of the Yankees hits a homer over the center field wall at Fenway Park near the center field corner of the bleachers during a 12-inning, 10–7 Red Sox loss.

APRIL 21   The Red Sox score four runs in the eighth inning to beat the Yankees 5–4 at Fenway Park. The winning run was scored on a windblown pop-up by Sammy White that landed near the mound. The ball carried away from catcher Yogi Berra, who made a futile chase while the other Yankees stood by and failed to cover the plate, allowing Gene Mauch to score all the way from second.

APRIL 29   The Red Sox trade Milt Bolling, Russ Kemmerer, and Faye Throneberry to the Senators for Dean Stone and Bob Chakales.

MAY 8   Ted Williams hits three homers to drive in all four Boston runs in a 4–1 win over the White Sox at Comiskey Park. All three were struck at the expense of Chicago pitcher Bob Keegan. Williams struck solo homers in the first and third innings and a two-run shot in the eighth. He missed a chance for a fourth homer when the White Sox intentionally walked him in the ninth.

                  Williams would turn thirty-nine on August 30, but he defied those who believed he was in his declining years by hitting a league-leading .388 in 1957. It was the second-highest batting average of his career over a full season, exceeded only by his .406 mark in 1941. In addition, Williams belted 38 homers, which was also the second-highest figure of his career, topped only by the 43 he hit in 1949.

MAY 12   Tom Brewer pitches a two-hitter to beat the Senators 10–0 in the first game of a doubleheader at Fenway Park. The only Washington hits were singles by Pete Runnels in the first inning and Whitey Herzog in the fifth.

MAY 22   The Red Sox connect for four homers in the sixth inning of an 11–0 win over the Indians at Fenway Park. All four were struck off Cal McLish. Gene Mauch and Ted Williams hit the first two, and after a walk to Jackie Jensen, Dick Gernert and Frank Malzone joined in the homer parade.

                  In his first full season in the majors, Malzone hit .292 with 15 homers and 103 RBIs. Jensen also drove in 103 runs, posted a .281 average, and hit 23 home runs.

MAY 30 — Jackie Jensen hits a walk-off homer in the tenth inning to beat the Orioles 7–6 in the first game of a doubleheader at Fenway Park. The Sox completed the sweep with a 10–5 victory in the second tilt.

JUNE 10 — Dick Gernert drives in six runs on two homers and a double during an 11–4 win over the Athletics in Kansas City.

JUNE 13 — Ted Williams hits three homers in a game for the second time in 1957 to lead the Red Sox to a 9–3 win over the Indians in Cleveland. Williams hit two homers off Early Wynn and another against Bob Lemon to rack up five RBIs.

JUNE 14 — The Red Sox trade Billy Goodman to the Orioles for Mike Fornieles.

Goodman was traded after spending 11 seasons with the Red Sox. He hit only 14 homers in 1,177 games with the Sox but compiled a .306 batting average. Fornieles gave the Red Sox seven up-and-down seasons. In 1960, he was 10–5 with 14 saves and a 2.64 ERA in 70 games as a reliever.

JUNE 23 — The Red Sox pound out 10–6 and 10–1 wins over the Athletics at Fenway Park.

JUNE 29 — Frank Malzone drives in six runs on a grand slam and two singles during a 12–4 win over the Tigers at Fenway Park. The slam was hit off Frank Lary in the first inning.

JUNE 30 — Jackie Jensen tags Paul Foytack for a grand slam in the fourth inning of a 10–3 triumph over the Tigers at Fenway Park.

JULY 4 — A two-run pinch homer by Mickey Vernon in the ninth inning beats the Yankees 3–2 in the first game of a doubleheader in New York. The Yankees won the first game, 4–1.

JULY 23 — Frank Sullivan pitches the Red Sox to a 1–0 win over the Athletics at Fenway Park. Billy Consolo drove in the winning run with a single in the fourth inning.

Sullivan had a 14–11 record and a 2.73 ERA in 1957.

JULY 26 — Tom Yawkey's plantation home on South Island, South Carolina, is destroyed by fire, along with many prized possessions, including baseball trophies. The home was accessible only by ferry across an inland waterway.

JULY 29 — Down 6–1 against the Indians at Fenway Park, the Red Sox score four runs in the seventh inning. After Cleveland plates two in the eighth, Boston comes back with four in its half to win, 9–8. Dick Gernert drove in the tying run with a double, then scored on Ted Lepcio's single.

AUGUST 26 — The Red Sox hit four homers in an inning for the second time in 1957 during a 16–0 trouncing of the Athletics in Kansas City. The Sox exploded with the home run barrage during the seventh inning when they piled up 10 runs, with Frank Malzone, Norm Zauchin, Ted Lepcio, and Jimmy Piersall hitting for the circuit. Malzone had previously homered in the third inning and Gene Stephens added another one in the ninth.

Piersall hit .261 with 19 homers and 103 runs scored in 1957.

AUGUST 28   Frank Sullivan pitches the Red Sox to a 1–0 win over the Tigers in Detroit. Tiger pitcher Jim Bunning allowed only two hits, but one of them was a homer by Ted Williams in the seventh inning.

SEPTEMBER 4   Pete Daley drives in two runs in the ninth with a pinch-hit single to put the Red Sox ahead 5–3 against the Yankees in New York, and after the Yanks tie the score with two tallies in their half of the inning, Daley hits a two-run homer in the eleventh to lift Boston to a 7–5 victory.

SEPTEMBER 10   A two-run homer by Dick Gernert in the seventh inning off Billy O'Dell beats the Orioles 2–0 at Fenway Park.

SEPTEMBER 14   The Red Sox outslug the Indians 13–10 at Fenway Park. Cleveland and Boston both scored four runs in each of the first two innings to make the score 8–8, then both scored once in the third to knot the contest at 9–9. The Sox overcame a 10–9 deficit with three runs in the sixth.

SEPTEMBER 17   In his first appearance since September 1 after missing action with a heavy cold, Ted Williams hits a pinch-hit homer in the eighth to tie the score 8–8, and the Sox add another tally later in the inning to win 9–8 against the Athletics at Fenway Park.

SEPTEMBER 18   Jimmy Piersall leads off the first inning with a homer off Tom Gorman on the first pitch, but the Red Sox fail to score again and lose 2–1 to the Athletics at Fenway Park.

SEPTEMBER 20   Ted Williams hits a pinch-hit homer during a 7–4 loss to the Yankees in New York.

SEPTEMBER 21   In his first start since August 31, Ted Williams hits a grand slam in the second inning off Bob Turley to lead the Red Sox to an 8–3 win over the Yankees in New York. Williams also walked three times before being removed for a pinch runner in the sixth inning.

SEPTEMBER 22   Ted Williams connects for a home run in his fourth consecutive official at-bat and ties a major league record during a 5–1 loss to the Yankees in New York. Williams also hit a single and drew two walks to extend his streak of reaching base in consecutive plate appearances to 11.

Williams tied the record for most consecutive at-bats with a home run with homers on September 17, 18, 20, and 22.

SEPTEMBER 23   With Vice President Richard Nixon attending, Ted Williams sets a major league record for most consecutive plate appearances reaching base with 16 over five games during a 9–4 win over the Senators in Washington. Williams singled, walked three times, and was hit by a pitch.

Williams set the record with four homers, nine walks, two singles, and being hit by a pitch over six games from September 17 through 23. The streak is all the more remarkable when one considers that Williams was thirty-nine years old and had just recovered from a bout with pneumonia.

SEPTEMBER 24   Ted Williams's streak of reaching base in consecutive plate appearances is stopped at 16 when he grounds out on a 3–2 pitch in the first inning facing Hal Griggs of the Senators. Williams homered in the fourth, however, and the Red Sox won 2–1 in Washington.

Stopping Williams's streak was a career highlight for Griggs, who pitched in the majors from 1956 through 1959 and had a lifetime record of 6–26 and an ERA of 5.50.

SEPTEMBER 25   The day after President Dwight Eisenhower sends federal troops to Little Rock, Arkansas, to integrate Central High School, and nine days before the Soviet Union launches the earth satellite Sputnik, Frank Malzone hits a homer in the eleventh inning to beat the Senators 7–6 in Washington. It was his second homer of the game.

1958   B

Season in a Sentence

Once again, the Red Sox enter a season with high hopes that are dashed quickly with a 4–12 April.

Finish • Won • Lost • Pct • GB

Third	79	75	.513	13.0

Manager

Pinky Higgins

Stats

Stats	Red Sox	AL	Rank
Batting Avg:	.256	.254	5
On-Base Pct:	.340	.325	1
Slugging Pct:	.400	.383	3
Home Runs:	155		3
Stolen Bases:	29		6
ERA:	3.92	3.77	6
Fielding Pct:	.976	.979	7
Runs Scored:	697		2
Runs Allowed:	691		6

Starting Lineup

Sammy White, c
Dick Gernert, 1b
Pete Runnels, 2b
Frank Malzone, 3b
Don Buddin, ss
Ted Williams, lf
Jimmy Piersall, cf
Jackie Jensen, rf
Gene Stephens, lf
Lou Berberet, c

Pitchers

Tom Brewer, sp
Frank Sullivan, sp
Dave Sisler, sp
Ike Delock, sp-rp
Leo Kiely, rp
Murray Wall, rp
Mike Fornieles, rp

Attendance

1,077,047 (third in AL)

Club Leaders

Batting Avg:	Williams	.328
On-Base Pct:	Williams	.458
Slugging Pct:	Williams	.584
Home Runs:	Jensen	35
RBI:	Jensen	122
Runs:	Runnels	103
Stolen Bases:	Piersall	12
Wins:	Delock	14
Strikeouts:	Brewer	124
ERA:	Sullivan	3.57
Saves:	Kiely	12

JANUARY 17   The Boston Bruins sign Willie O'Ree, the first African American in the history of the National Hockey League, to a contract. The Bruins became the third major sports team in Boston to integrate, following the Braves and the Celtics in 1950. The Red Sox had no African Americans on their 40-man roster during spring training in 1958.

JANUARY 23   The Red Sox trade Albie Pearson and Norm Zauchin to the Senators for Pete Runnels.

Joe Cronin was the son-in-law of Clark Griffith, who owned the Senators until his death in 1955, and the brother-in-law of Calvin Griffith, who inherited the club after his father's passing. Considering the number of times the Red Sox robbed the Senators in trades, it's amazing that the Washington club answered the phone when Cronin called, much less invited him to family functions. The Runnels trade was a prime example. In five seasons with the Red Sox as a second baseman and first baseman, Runnels hit .320 and won two batting titles, in 1960 and 1962. In 1958, he batted .322 and finished second in the league to Ted Williams.

The Sox front office never fully appreciated the contributions of Runnels, however, which goes a long way toward explaining why the club failed to contend for a pennant. The Sox management complained that Runnels was inadequate at second base, but he led the league in total chances per game in both 1958 and 1959 and in fielding percentage in 1960. He was moved to first base, but the Sox liked their first basemen to be right-handed power hitters and Runnels was a left-handed singles hitter. Despite winning the batting title in 1960, he was on the bench at the start of the 1961 season behind rookie second baseman Chuck Schilling and aging Vic Wertz at first. Runnels nonetheless worked his way into the lineup, hit .317 in 360 at-bats, and won another batting title in 1962 as a first baseman. After that season, he was traded to make room for Dick Stuart, the kind of home run–hitting first baseman the Sox coveted. Although the trade that brought Runnels to Boston was a positive one for the Red Sox, it wasn't without cost. A five-foot-five center fielder, Pearson was the AL Rookie of the Year in 1958 and had several solid seasons with the Angels during the early 1960s.

JANUARY 29   The Red Sox sell Mickey Vernon to the Indians.

APRIL 14   President Dwight Eisenhower throws out the first ball before the Red Sox lose 5–2 on Opening Day against the Senators in Washington. The Sox took a 2–0 lead in the third inning on Jackie Jensen's homer, but Frank Sullivan couldn't hold the lead.

Ted Williams didn't start in a single exhibition game, as Pinky Higgins gave him permission to set his own conditioning pace. Williams batted five times as a pinch hitter and had two homers, two singles, and a walk. He missed the season opener with food poisoning, however, after eating some tainted shrimp on the train from Richmond, where the Sox played an exhibition game on April 13.

APRIL 15   In the home opener, the Red Sox lose 3–0 to the Yankees before 35,223 at Fenway Park. Don Larsen pitched the complete-game shutout.

Among those in the crowd were Massachusetts Governor Foster Furcolo, Boston Mayor John Hynes, and comedian Bob Hope. At the time, Hope was a minor stockholder in the Cleveland Indians, his hometown team. Tom Yawkey wasn't at the game, however, preferring to remain at his Georgetown, South Carolina, estate.

APRIL 21   Billy Sullivan, former publicity director of the Boston Braves, announces plans to build a 65,000-seat stadium in Norwood, Massachusetts, 14 miles north of Boston. Sullivan hoped that the stadium would house the Red Sox and attract a pro football team to the Boston area. Sullivan was the head of a local oil company.

Sullivan never got his Norwood stadium built, but in November 1959 became one of the founding members of the American Football League as the majority owner of the Boston Patriots. One of Sullivan's original partners was ex–Red Sox star Dom DiMaggio. The AFL began play in 1960. The Patriots played at Boston University's Nickerson Field (the site of old Braves Field) from 1960 through 1962, Fenway Park from 1963 through 1968, Boston College's Alumni Field in 1969, and Harvard Stadium in 1970. Sullivan finally built a stadium of his own in 1971, Foxboro's Schaefer Stadium, which was later known as Sullivan Stadium and Foxboro Stadium. In conjunction with the move to Foxboro, the Boston Patriots were renamed the New England Patriots.

MAY 7   The Red Sox sell Bob Porterfield to the Pirates.

MAY 9   The Red Sox clobber the Orioles 13–5 at Fenway Park.

Bill Crowley joined Curt Gowdy and Bob Murphy in the Red Sox television and radio booth in 1958.

MAY 13   Jackie Jensen hits a grand slam off Pedro Ramos in the first inning of a 9–6 win over the Senators in Washington.

MAY 22   Ted Williams hits a grand slam in the fourth inning off Jack Urban to lead the Red Sox to an 8–5 win over the Athletics in Kansas City.

Williams was off to a slow start in 1958 and entered the game with a .255 batting average in 89 at-bats.

MAY 30   Frank Sullivan pitches a two-hitter to beat the Orioles 2–0 in the first game of a doubleheader at Memorial Stadium. Al Pilarcik accounted for both Baltimore hits with singles in the first and fourth innings. Both Boston runs were scored on a home run by Frank Malzone in the fourth inning. The Orioles also won the second game, 2–0.

JUNE 6   Ozzie Virgil makes his debut with the Tigers, making the Red Sox the only team in Major League Baseball without an African-American player on its roster.

JUNE 16   The Red Sox play an exhibition game at Metropolitan Stadium in Bloomington, Minnesota. The Sox lost 14–10 to the Minneapolis Millers, Boston's Class AAA farm club in the American Association. Ted Williams, who played for Minneapolis in 1938, hit a home run.

Metropolitan Stadium was built in 1956 in order to attract a major league team to Minnesota. It was the home of the Twins from 1961 through 1981.

JUNE 17   Ted Williams appears in his 2,000th major league game, but the Red Sox lose 4–0 to the White Sox in Chicago.

JUNE 18   The Red Sox slug five homers in a 13–9 victory over the White Sox in Chicago. The homers were struck by Marty Keough, Don Buddin, Jackie Jensen, Frank Malzone, and Ted Williams. The home run by Keough was the first of his big-league career.

Malzone batted .295 with 15 homers in 1958.

During the mid 1950s, the Sox relied on a powerful outfield of Ted Williams, Jimmy Piersall, and Jackie Jensen, shown here during a moment of laughter.

Carl Iwasaki/Time & Life Pictures/Getty Images

JUNE 22   A tornado passes within sight of Municipal Stadium in Kansas City just south of the ballpark only minutes before the start of a 2–1 Red Sox loss to the Athletics.

JUNE 26   In his first start of the season after 12 relief appearances, Ike Delock strikes out 12 batters and wins 2–1 over the Indians in Cleveland. It was Delock's first win as a starter since July 14, 1956.

JULY 2   The Red Sox announce the move of their spring training base from Sarasota, Florida, to Scottsdale, Arizona, beginning with the 1959 season.

The Sox had trained at Sarasota since 1933, except for the 1943–45 seasons during World War II. The club trained at Scottsdale until 1965 before returning to Florida.

JULY 5   The Red Sox misses out on a chance to beat the Yankees in New York because of the American League's Saturday-night curfew rule, which stipulates that no game can continue past 11:59 PM. The Red Sox scored two runs in the eleventh inning to take a 5–3 lead when the clock struck 11:59 PM. According to the rule, the score then reverted back to the end of the previous full inning, and the contest went into the books as a 10-inning 3–3 tie.

Joe Cronin and Tom Yawkey were livid, and convinced their fellow owners to eliminate the rule in a meeting during the All-Star break four days later. In the future, games similar to the one on July 5 in which the visiting team had a lead when a curfew prohibited completion, the contest would be suspended and continued at a later date.

JULY 8   Frank Malzone contributes to a 4–3 American League victory in the All-Star Game, played at Memorial Stadium in Baltimore. With the score tied 3–3 in the sixth inning, Malzone hit a single and came around to score the winning run.

JULY 10   Jackie Jensen hits a grand slam in the fourth inning off Bob Keegan during an 11–2 win over the White Sox at Fenway Park.

           In the first 84 games of the 1958 season, Jensen hit 27 homers and drove in 81 runs. He hit 14 homers during the month of June, a club record for most home runs in a month. Jensen cooled off in the second half but led the league with 122 RBIs and had 35 homers and a .286 batting average to win the AL MVP award.

JULY 18   A grand slam by Frank Malzone in the seventh inning off Bill Fischer sews up an 11–9 win over the Tigers at Fenway Park. Malzone's homer broke a 3–3 tie. Pete Runnels contributed five hits, including three doubles, in six at-bats.

JULY 19   After Detroit takes a 6–5 lead in the top of the twelfth, Ted Williams turns jeers into cheers with a two-run, walk-off homer in the bottom of the inning to beat the Tigers, 7–6. Williams earlier had drawn boos from the Fenway Park crowd with a misplay in left field in the eighth inning and for grounding out with a runner on third in the ninth. The Sox tied the game 5–5 in the ninth on a two-run homer by Sammy White.

JULY 20   Tigers pitcher Jim Bunning pitches a no-hitter to beat the Red Sox 3–0 in the first game of a doubleheader at Fenway Park. Ted Williams ended the game by flying out to Al Kaline in right field. In the second tilt, Ike Delock ran his season record to 10–0 with a 5–3 victory.

           Delock won 13 games in a row, including his last three decisions in 1957. He finished the 1958 season with a 14–8 record.

JULY 23   Ted Williams spits at Kansas City fans during a 3–1 Red Sox loss to the Athletics. Williams jogged two-thirds of the way down the first base line after grounding to first baseman Harry Simpson, which drew boos from the crowd at Municipal Stadium. Reacting to the catcalls, Williams wheeled around and spit toward the stands. He was fined $250 by AL president Will Harridge.

JULY 29   Ted Williams drives in seven runs on a grand slam off Jim Bunning in the third inning and a three-run homer off Bill Fischer in the eleventh to beat the Tigers 11–8 in Detroit.

           Williams finished his career with 17 career grand slams. The only players with more are Lou Gehrig (23), Eddie Murray (19), and Willie McCovey (18).

AUGUST 3   Ted Williams hits a two-run homer in the ninth inning to beat the Indians 3–2 in the first game of a doubleheader in Cleveland. The Red Sox completed the sweep with a 4–2 triumph in the second tilt.

Although known for his outbursts against fans and writers, Williams rarely argued with umpires. He said he believed that objecting to calls broke the umpire's concentration and that it was up to the hitter to adjust to each arbiter's strike zone.

AUGUST 24   On State of Maine Day at Fenway Park, the Red Sox beat the Athletics 14–3 in the first game of a doubleheader and 3–2 in 11 innings in the second tilt. Maine residents came bearing gifts. Dick Gernert was given a bear cub named Homer, which he later donated to the Birmingham, Alabama, zoo. Jackie Jensen was presented with a barrel of lobsters, had them cooked during the second game, and then provided them to teammates after he drove in the winning run with a single.

On the same day, the Red Sox disclosed plans to enlarge Fenway Park. The Sox wanted the city to close Lansdowne Street behind the left field wall, tear down the businesses on the other side of the street, extend the left field line to 330 to 350 feet, and build additional stands. With the construction of the Massachusetts Turnpike just north of Fenway, Tom Yawkey wanted a special road directly from the turnpike to the ballpark. The baseball club also wanted to pave some nearby park land to create parking space for 4,000 cars. The city of Boston and the state of Massachusetts failed to approve the changes, however, and the Green Monster remained in place.

SEPTEMBER 21   The Red Sox beat the Senators 2–0 for the third straight game. Tom Brewer pitched the shutout on September 19, Frank Sullivan on the 20th, and Ike Delock on the 21st.

Ted Williams's fiery temper boiled up again during the September 21 game when he threw his bat 75 feet and struck sixty-year-old Gladys Heffernan, who was the housekeeper of general manager Joe Cronin. Distressed after looking at a called third strike on a pitch from Bill Fischer, Williams flipped the bat in the air. Heffernan was seated in the first row and was hit by the knob end of the bat an inch above her left eye. Fighting back tears, Williams went over to console her. She suffered a contusion on the left side of her forehead and was hospitalized overnight as a precaution. Williams was fined fifty dollars by AL president Will Harridge. The relatively low fine was in part due to Williams's obvious remorse over the incident.

SEPTEMBER 26   At the conclusion of a 6–4 and 3–1 sweep of the Senators in Washington, Ted Williams and Pete Runnels are in a tie for first place in the AL batting race. Williams was two for three in the first game, but sat out the second contest. Runnels had two hits in nine at-bats during the twin bill. Carrying the percentages all the way to the tenth decimal point, Williams and Runnels both had batting averages of .3225806452. There were two games left in the season.

SEPTEMBER 27   Ted Williams goes three for four and Pete Runnels three for six during a 9–5 win over the Senators in Washington. Williams took the lead in the batting race, .327 to .324.

SEPTEMBER 28   In the last game of the season, Ted Williams collects two hits in four trips to the plate while teammate Pete Runnels is hitless in four at-bats. Williams won the batting title with a .328 average. He had 14 hits in his last 28 at-bats, and seven in his final 11. Runnels finished at .322.

Williams became the oldest player in history to win a batting title. He turned forty on August 30. Williams held the record until Barry Bonds led the NL in

*batting average in 2004 a little more than two months after celebrating his for-
tieth birthday. The 1958 title was Williams's sixth during his major league
career. He also won in 1941, 1942, 1947, 1948, and 1957.*

NOVEMBER 28 The Red Sox sign Notre Dame sophomore Carl Yastrzemski for a contract calling
for $108,000.

DECEMBER 2 The Red Sox trade Jimmy Piersall to the Indians for Vic Wertz and Gary Geiger.

*Piersall had an off season in 1958, and Geiger provided a younger alternative in
center field. Wertz was yet another right-handed power hitter acquired to take
advantage of the close proximity of the Green Monster to home plate.*

DECEMBER 15 The Red Sox trade Billy Klaus for Jim Busby.

1959   B

Season in a Sentence

Ted Williams suffers through
the worst season of his career,
but the team finally integrates
with black utility infielder
Pumpsie Green.

Finish • Won • Lost • Pct • GB

Fifth   75   79   .487   19.0

Managers

Pinky Higgins (31–42)
Rudy York (0–1)
Billy Jurges (44–36)

Stats

Stats	Red Sox	AL	Rank
Batting Avg:	.256	.253	5
On-Base Pct:	.338	.326	1
Slugging Pct:	.385	.384	5
Home Runs:	125		5
Stolen Bases:	68		2
ERA:	4.17	3.86	6
Fielding Pct:	.978	.977	5
Runs Scored:	726		2
Runs Allowed:	696		5

Starting Lineup

Sammy White, c
Dick Gernert, 1b
Pete Runnels, 2b-1b
Frank Malzone, 3b
Don Buddin, ss
Ted Williams, lf
Gary Geiger, cf-lf
Jackie Jensen, rf
Gene Stephens, lf
Marty Keough, cf
Vic Wertz, 1b
Pumpsie Green, 2b
Pete Daley, c

Pitchers

Jerry Casale, sp
Tom Brewer, sp
Ike Delock, sp
Frank Sullivan, sp
Bill Monbouquette, sp
Mike Fornieles, rp
Leo Kiely, rp
Frank Baumann, rp

Attendance

984,102 (fifth in AL)

Club Leaders

Batting Avg:	Runnels	.314
On-Base Pct:	Runnels	.415
Slugging Pct:	Jensen	.492
Home Runs:	Jensen	28
RBI:	Jensen	112
Runs:	Jensen	101
Stolen Bases:	Jensen	20
Wins:	Casale	13
Strikeouts:	Brewer	121
ERA:	Brewer	3.76
Saves:	Fornieles	11

JANUARY 14   Two weeks after Alaska becomes the 49th state, Joe Cronin is named American League president, succeeding Will Harridge, who retired. Cronin officially took office on January 31.

JANUARY 15   Bucky Harris succeeds Joe Cronin as general manager of the Red Sox. Harris previously managed the Red Sox from the dugout in 1934, after which Cronin replaced him. Harris was a special assistant in Boston's front office when he was promoted to general manager.

FEBRUARY 21   The first black player on the 40-man roster, Pumpsie Green is denied accommodations at the Red Sox' spring training headquarters, located at the Safari Hotel in Scottsdale, Arizona. Segregation wasn't unusual during spring training in 1959. Most black players lived apart from their white teammates because of Jim Crow policies in both Arizona and Florida. Many black players in the towns where the clubs trained were housed either at hotels that catered exclusively to African Americans or in private residences. The Red Sox, however, could find no place in Scottsdale that would allow him to stay overnight. The club had to put Green up at a hotel in Phoenix, 17 miles away, that the San Francisco Giants used for their black players, and they provided Green with a driver to take him back and forth from Phoenix to Scottsdale.

APRIL 10   The day after the Celtics win the NBA championship in a four-game sweep of the Minneapolis Lakers, the Red Sox' scheduled season opener against the Yankees in New York is rained out. The April 11 contest was also postponed.

APRIL 11   The Red Sox create a controversy by sending Pumpsie Green back to the minors after he had a sensational spring, including a .400 batting average. Green was assigned to the Red Sox Class AAA farm club in Minneapolis in the American Association. The Red Sox claimed that Green needed more experience. He waged a battle against Don Buddin for the starting shortstop job during spring training. On Opening Day, the Red Sox were the only team in the majors without a black player.

              The NAACP charged the Red Sox with discrimination and initiated an investigation into the team's practices by the Massachusetts Commission Against Discrimination. The commission absolved the Sox of charges of racial bias after extracting a promise, in writing, that the club would make "every effort to end segregation." The Sox had seven black players in their minor league system, but that was the fewest number of any club in the big leagues. The Giants had nine black players on their major league roster alone in 1959. The Pirates, Dodgers, Reds, and Cardinals each had seven. There were 67 African Americans in the majors during the 1959 season. Of those, 50 were in the National League (see July 21, 1959).

APRIL 12   The Red Sox open the season with a 3–2 loss to the Yankees in New York. The Yanks broke a 2–2 tie with a run in the eighth on a home run by Norm Siebern. Tom Brewer pitched a complete game for Boston.

              Ted Williams missed the season opener with a pinched nerve in his neck that bothered him all season. Williams hit only .254 with 10 homers in 103 games. It was the ninth time that Williams didn't play on Opening Day due to military service, injuries, or illness. When he did play on Opening Day, Williams had 22 hits in 49 at-bats, for a .449 average. He had two homers, one in 1942 and the other in 1960, and drove in 14 runs.

APRIL 14   In the Fenway Park opener, the Red Sox win 7–3 over the Senators before 16,467. Dick Gernert hit a home run.

APRIL 15   In his first major league start, Jerry Casale is not only the winning pitcher, but also hits a 450-foot home run over the left field wall at Fenway Park in a 7–3 decision over the Senators. It was Casale's first big-league homer. The ball landed on the roof of a building across Lansdowne Street.

            Casale had a 13–8 record as a rookie in 1959 but was only 4–16 with a 5.90 ERA over the remainder of his career.

APRIL 17   Tom Brewer pitches a two-hitter to beat the Yankees 4–0 at Fenway Park. The only New York hits were singles by Mickey Mantle in the fourth inning and Andy Carey in the fifth.

APRIL 19   Frank Malzone hits a walk-off homer in the twelfth inning to beat the Yankees 5–4 at Fenway Park.

MAY 2   The Red Sox trade Dave Sisler and Ted Lepcio to the Tigers for Billy Hoeft.

MAY 6   The Red Sox hit six homers and overpower the Tigers 17–6 in Detroit. All 17 Boston runs were scored between the fifth and eighth innings. Gary Geiger hit two homers, and Frank Malzone, Marty Keough, Dick Gernert, and Jackie Jensen added one each.

            Malzone hit .280 with 19 homers in 1959.

MAY 10   Don Buddin hits a homer in the tenth inning to beat the Orioles 3–2 in the first game of a doubleheader at Fenway Park. The Sox completed the sweep with a 5–1 victory in the nightcap.

MAY 12   In his first game of the season after being sidelined with neck trouble, Ted Williams is hitless in five at-bats in a 12-inning, 4–3 loss to the White Sox at Fenway Park.

MAY 21   The Red Sox purchase Bobby Avila from the Orioles.

            Avila was the American League batting champion as recently as 1954. He lasted only two months with the Red Sox and was sold to the Braves on July 21.

MAY 28   Frank Sullivan pitches a two-hitter to beat the Senators 3–1 at Griffith Stadium. The only Washington hits were singles by Faye Throneberry in the third inning and Hal Naragon in the seventh.

MAY 29   With President Dwight Eisenhower in the stands, the Red Sox lose 7–6 to the Senators in Washington.

JUNE 2   Ted Williams collects his 2,500th career hit during a 5–3 loss to the Athletics in Kansas City. The milestone hit was a double in the second inning off Ray Herbert.

Williams was benched for nine days beginning on June 15 because of a batting slump. He was hitting .208 with three homers in 106 at-bats.

JUNE 11   The Red Sox trade Billy Consolo and Murray Wall to the Senators for Dick Hyde and Herb Plews.

Hyde reported to the Red Sox with a sore arm, and three days layer, he was returned to Washington and Wall to Boston. Wall pitched one game for the Senators before coming back to the Sox under the unusual circumstances of playing for a club that had traded him away.

JUNE 15   The Red Sox trade Billy Hoeft to the Orioles for Jack Harshman.

JUNE 25   The Tigers beat the Red Sox 10–5 in Detroit in the last major league game between two clubs with all-Caucasian rosters.

The Red Sox didn't integrate until Pumpsie Green made his debut on July 21, 1959. The Tigers had an all-white team from May 13, 1959, when they sold Larry Doby to the White Sox, until the following September, when William Proctor was called up from the minors. The Kansas City Athletics had no black players from May 26, 1959, when Hector Lopez was dealt to the Yankees, through the 1960 season. The 1960 A's were the last all-white team in major league history.

JUNE 26   Jackie Jensen hits a grand slam in the third inning off Cal McLish, but the Red Sox lose 11–5 to the Indians in Cleveland.

JUNE 30   Vice President Richard Nixon attends a 6–1 Red Sox loss to the Senators in Washington.

JULY 3   The Red Sox relieve Pinky Higgins as manager and replace him with Billy Jurges. Rudy York was the interim manager for one game until Jurges arrived. The Red Sox had a record of 31–42 when the change was made.

Jurges was a shortstop in the majors with the Cubs and Giants from 1931 through 1947. He was a coach with the Senators when he was appointed as manager by the Sox. Over the remainder of the 1959 season, the Sox were 44–36 under Jurges. Higgins was made a scout and later a special assistant in the front office. He would also return for another stint as a manager in Boston (see June 12, 1960).

JULY 11   Don Buddin hits a walk-off grand slam off Bob Turley in the tenth inning to defeat the Yankees 8–4 at Fenway Park. Earlier in the inning, catcher Yogi Berra and pitcher Ryne Duren were ejected by umpire Bill Summers for arguing ball and strike calls.

JULY 13   The Red Sox complete a five-game sweep of the Yankees with a 13–3 victory at Fenway Park. The Sox score nine runs in the sixth inning, four of them on a grand slam by Gene Stephens off Jim Bronstad.

JULY 21   Pumpsie Green becomes the first African American to play in a regular-season game for the Red Sox when he serves as a pinch runner for Vic Wertz in the eighth inning of a 2–1 loss to the White Sox in Chicago. Green remained in the game and played an inning at shortstop.

> *Green was promoted after hitting .320 at Minneapolis. He was never more than a utility infielder, however. In four seasons with the Red Sox he hit .244 with 12 homers in 327 games. The Sox didn't have a black player make the All-Star team until George Scott in 1966.*

JULY 28   Earl Wilson becomes the first black pitcher in Red Sox history with a scoreless inning in a 5–3 loss to the Indians in the first game of a doubleheader in Cleveland. The Sox won the second game, 8–4.

JULY 30   The Red Sox sell Jack Harshman to the Indians.

JULY 31   Red Sox pitchers issue 15 walks, but the club wins 6–5 in Detroit. In his first major league start, Earl Wilson pitched 3⅔ hitless innings but walked nine batters. Before being taken out of the game, Wilson delivered an RBI single. Relievers Leo Kiely walked one, Ike Delock four, and Mike Fornieles one.

AUGUST 3   Frank Malzone hits a homer in the second inning off Don Drysdale during a 5–3 American League win in the All-Star Game, played in Memorial Coliseum in Los Angeles.

> *The game in Los Angeles was the second All-Star Game played in 1959. There were two All-Star games each season from 1959 through 1962.*

AUGUST 4   Pumpsie Green plays his first game at Fenway Park. Batting leadoff, Green tripled in his first at-bat, helping the Red Sox to a 4–1 win over the Athletics in the first game of a doubleheader. Kansas City won the second tilt, 8–6.

AUGUST 5   The Red Sox wallop the Athletics 17–6 at Fenway Park. Gary Geiger drove in six runs with a homer, a triple, and a double.

AUGUST 8   Gary Geiger hits a walk-off homer in the tenth inning to beat the Tigers 4–3 at Fenway Park.

AUGUST 14   Trailing 6–2, the Red Sox score nine runs in the eighth inning to beat the Yankees 11–6 in New York. Vic Wertz hit a pinch-hit grand slam off Ryne Duren.

AUGUST 20   Bob Cerv hits three homers for the Athletics against the Red Sox in Kansas City, but Boston overcomes the slugging outburst to win, 11–10. The Sox trailed 6–2 before mounting the comeback.

AUGUST 27   Five days after Hawaii becomes the 50th state, Dick Gernert hits a two-run, walk-off homer in the tenth inning to beat the Orioles 6–4 at Fenway Park. Gernert entered the game as a pinch hitter in the eighth, tied the score 4–4 with a sacrifice fly, and remained in the contest in left field.

SEPTEMBER 5   The Senators score 10 runs in the third inning during a 14–2 win over the Red Sox in Washington. Jim Lemon drove in six of the 10 runs with two homers off Bill Monbouquette and Earl Wilson.

SEPTEMBER 7   Don Buddin, Jerry Casale, and Pumpsie Green, the number eight, nine, and one hit-
               ters in the lineup, hit consecutive homers in the second inning of a 12–4 win over
               the Yankees at Fenway Park.

               *Green's younger brother Cornell played defensive back for the Dallas Cowboys
               from 1962 through 1974.*

SEPTEMBER 15   Tom Brewer pitches the Red Sox to a 1–0 win over the Indians at Fenway Park. Frank
               Malzone ended the game with a walk-off homer in the ninth inning off Mudcat Grant.

               *Pete Runnels led the Red Sox in batting average with a .314 mark in 1959. He
               hit six homers and scored 95 runs.*

SEPTEMBER 26   Jackie Jensen hits a walk-off homer in the eleventh inning that beats the Senators 5–4
               at Fenway Park. In the ninth, Jensen tied the score 4–4 with a two-run double.

               *The three RBIs put Jensen into a tie for the league lead in the category with
               Rocky Colavito. Jensen bypassed a chance to win the RBI title when he missed
               the final game of the season, with club approval, to return to his home in Lake
               Tahoe, Nevada. Jensen finished the season with 28 homers, 112 RBIs, and a
               .277 batting average. Although he was only thrity-two years old, Jensen hinted
               that he might retire after the 1959 season. He made it official four months later
               (see January 26, 1960).*

NOVEMBER 21   The Red Sox trade Dick Gernert to the Cubs for Dave Hillman and Jim Marshall.

DECEMBER 1   The Red Sox trade Al Schroll to the Cubs for Bobby Thomson.

THE STATE OF THE RED SOX

The Red Sox suffered through their eighth consecutive losing season in 1966, finishing in ninth place with a record of 72–90. Everything changed in 1967, when Dick Williams arrived as manager and the Sox stunned the baseball world by winning the AL pennant. It was a watershed year for the franchise. The 1967 season was the first of 16 consecutive winning seasons. The 1966 season was the last in which Boston lost as many as 90 games in a season. Overall, the Red Sox were 764–845 during the 1960s. Among the eight teams in the league during all 10 seasons, the Sox' winning percentage of .475 was the seventh best, ahead of only the Athletics. The Yankees won the AL pennant five seasons in a row from 1960 through 1964. The Orioles won in 1966 and 1969, the Twins in 1965, and the Tigers in 1968.

THE BEST TEAM

Several books have been written about the "Impossible Dream" season of 1967, when the Red Sox won a pennant on the last day of the season with a record of 92–70 before losing the World Series to the Cardinals.

THE WORST TEAM

The 1965 team was 62–100. It is the only Red Sox club since 1932 to have lost at least 100 games.

THE BEST MOMENT

In the final at-bat of his major league career on September 28, 1960, Ted Williams hit a home run.

THE WORST MOMENT

Tony Conigliaro was struck in the face by a pitch from Jack Hamilton of the Angels on August 18, 1967, all but ending a promising career.

THE ALL–DECADE TEAM • YEARS WITH BRS

Bob Tillman, c	1962–67
Pete Runnels, 1b	1958–62
Mike Andrews, 2b	1966–70
Frank Malzone, 3b	1955–65
Rico Petrocelli, ss	1963, 1965–76
Carl Yastrzemski, lf	1961–83
Reggie Smith, cf	1966–73
Tony Conigliaro, rf	1964–67, 1969–70, 1975
Bill Monbouquette, p	1958–65
Dick Radatz, p	1962–66
Earl Wilson, p	1959–66
Jim Lonborg, p	1965–71

Yastrzemski is the only Hall of Famer on the 1960s All-Decade Team. Smith put up Hall of Fame numbers during his career but never received the credit he deserved. Other Red Sox players with significant contributions during the decade were shortstop Eddie Bressoud (1962–65), first baseman George Scott (1966–71, 1977–79), third baseman Joe Foy (1966–68), and center fielder Gary Geiger (1959–65).

THE DECADE LEADERS

Batting Avg:	Yastrzemski	.293
On-Base Pct:	Yastrzemski	.383
Slugging Pct:	Conigliaro	.492
Home Runs:	Yastrzemski	202
RBI:	Yastrzemski	767
Runs:	Yastrzemski	795
Stolen Bases:	Yastrzemski	80
Wins:	Monbouquette	86
Strikeouts:	Monbouquette	852
ERA:	Monbouquette	3.65
Saves:	Radatz	104

THE HOME FIELD

There were no significant changes to Fenway Park during the 1960s. In fact, the ballpark went essentially unchanged from 1940 through the mid-1970s. Tom Yawkey refused to invest money in improvements to the ballpark because he wanted a new stadium (see October 11, 1963). The Red Sox in 1965 lost 100 games and drew only 652,201 fans, seventh in the AL in attendance and 15th in the majors. With a pennant in 1967, the Sox attracted 1,727,832 to finish first in the AL in attendance and second in the majors. Despite a ballpark that held only 34,000, the Sox were first or second in attendance in the American League every year from 1967 through 1978, topping the league seven times.

THE GAME YOU WISH YOU HAD SEEN

The Red Sox concluded their "Impossible Dream" season in 1967 with a 5–3 win over the Twins on October 1, the final day of the season, to clinch the American League crown.

THE WAY THE GAME WAS PLAYED

Baseball was played in several new cities and ballparks during the 1960s. Expansion and franchise shifts brought American League baseball to Minnesota, Southern California, Oakland, and Seattle for the first time. The expansion of the strike zone in 1963 brought a decline in offense in the 1960s until the owners lowered the mound for the 1969 season. The league ERA dipped to 2.98 in 1968, the only time it has been below 3.00 since 1918.

THE MANAGEMENT

Tom Yawkey was in his fourth decade of ownership. Bucky Harris ran the front office at the start of the decade. He was fired at the end of the 1960 season and was replaced by Pinky Higgins, who was unable to shake the Red Sox out of their second-division doldrums. Dick O'Connell became general manager after Higgins was fired at the end of the 1965 season. O'Connell almost immediately transformed the franchise into a consistent winner. Field managers were Billy Jurges (1959–60), Del Baker (1960), Higgins (1960–62), Johnny Pesky (1963–64), Billy Herman (1964–66), Pete Runnels (1966), Dick Williams (1967–69), and Eddie Popowski (1969).

THE BEST PLAYER MOVE

The best player moves were the drafting of Carlton Fisk in the first round in 1967 and Dwight Evans in the fifth round in 1969. The best trade brought Ed Bressoud from Houston for Don Buddin in November 1961.

THE WORST PLAYER MOVE

The worst player move was the loss of Jim Fregosi in the expansion draft in December 1960. He was selected by the Angels and became a star at shortstop. The Red Sox also let Amos Otis and Wilbur Wood get away from the organization without receiving any playing talent in return. The worst trade sent Earl Wilson and Joe Christopher to the Tigers for Don Demeter and Julio Navarro in June 1966.

1960   B

Season in a Sentence

In Ted Williams's final season, the Red Sox drop to seventh place and suffer through their worst season since 1933.

Finish • Won • Lost • Pct • GB

Seventh 65   89   .422 32.0

Managers

Billy Jurges (15–27)
Del Baker (2–5)
Pinky Higgins (48–57)

Stats   Red Sox • AL • Rank

Batting Avg:	.261	.255	4
On-Base Pct:	.336	.331	2
Slugging Pct:	.389	.388	3
Home Runs:	124		5
Stolen Bases:	34		7
ERA:	4.62	3.87	8
Fielding Pct:	.976	.978	7
Runs Scored:	658		6
Runs Allowed:	775		8

Starting Lineup

Russ Nixon, c
Vic Wertz, 1b
Pete Runnels, 2b-1b
Frank Malzone, 3b
Don Buddin, ss
Ted Williams, lf
Willie Tasby, cf
Lu Clinton, rf
Pumpsie Green, 2b-ss
Gary Geiger, rf

Pitchers

Bill Monbouquette, sp
Tom Brewer, sp
Ike Delock, sp
Frank Sullivan, sp-rp
Billy Muffett, sp-rp
Mike Fornieles, rp
Tom Sturdivant, rp
Jerry Casale, sp-rp

Attendance

1,129,849 (fifth in AL)

Club Leaders

Batting Avg:	Runnels	.320
On-Base Pct:	Williams	.451
Slugging Pct:	Williams	.645
Home Runs:	Williams	29
RBI:	Wertz	103
Runs:	Buddin	82
Stolen Bases:	Runnels	5
Wins:	Monbouquette	14
Strikeouts:	Monbouquette	134
ERA:	Monbouquette	3.64
Saves:	Fornieles	14

JANUARY 8   The Red Sox trade Leo Kiely to the Indians for Ray Webster.

JANUARY 26   Jackie Jensen announces his retirement.

> Jensen was only thirty-two but had grown weary of the travel connected with baseball. He hated the long separations from his family, who lived in Nevada, and had a pathological fear of flying. "I have only one life to live," said Jensen, "and I'll be happier when I can spend it with my family. Being away from home for seven months a year doesn't represent the kind of life my wife and children want." The retirement of Jensen left the Red Sox with a huge hole in their outfield and batting order. Over the previous six seasons, Jensen drove in 667 runs, the most of any player in the majors during that period. After sitting out the 1960 campaign, Jensen returned for one more season (see February 7, 1961).

MARCH 10   Red Sox players Marty Keough and Dave Hillman are involved in an auto accident in Scottsdale, Arizona, at 1:15 AM, fifteen minutes after the club's spring training curfew. Keough was fined twenty dollars in court for speeding at seventy miles per hour. He suffered a mild back injury. Hillman had several stitches placed in his scalp and sustained lingering shoulder and hand injuries, which bothered him all season.

MARCH 16   The Red Sox trade Sammy White and Jim Marshall to the Indians for Russ Nixon.

The trade with the Indians was canceled on March 25 when White announced that he was retiring.

MARCH 29   The Red Sox trade Jim Marshall to the Giants for Al Worthington.

APRIL 18   Nine days after the Celtics capture their second consecutive NBA championship by winning a seven-game series against the St. Louis Hawks, the Red Sox open the season with a 10–1 loss to the Senators in Washington. President Dwight Eisenhower and Vice President Richard Nixon were among those present. Camilo Pascaul pitched a three-hitter for the Senators and struck out 15 batters. The only Boston run scored on a 450-foot home run to center field by Ted Williams in the second inning. It was Williams's first plate appearance of the season. In the opener, he hit fifth in the lineup with Gene Stephens batting in the cleanup spot.

Art Gleeson replaced Bob Murphy in the Red Sox radio and TV booth in 1960, joining Curt Gowdy and Bob Crowley. Murphy, who had been with the Red Sox since 1954, moved to broadcast games for the Orioles in 1960 and the Mets in 1962. He remained with the Mets into the twenty-first century.

APRIL 19   In the home opener, the Red Sox lose 8–4 to the Yankees before 35,162. In his first game as a Yankee, Roger Maris hit two homers, a double, and a single. Ted Williams hit his 494th homer in the game to pass Lou Gehrig for fourth place on the all-time list. The only players ahead of Williams in 1960 were Babe Ruth (714), Jimmie Foxx (534), and Mel Ott (512). Williams pulled a thigh muscle running the bases, however, and didn't play again for nearly a month.

In his final season, in which he turned forty-two in August, Williams hit .316 and hit 29 homers and drove in 72 runs in 310 at-bats.

APRIL 22   Vic Wertz hits a home run in the eleventh inning to beat the Senators 5–4 in Washington.

Wertz hit 19 homers and drove in 103 runs in 1960, but he scored only 45 runs. Of his 19 homers, he hit 16 at Fenway Park.

APRIL 24   The Red Sox collect 20 hits but lose 11–10 in Washington.

MAY 6   The Red Sox score three runs in the ninth inning off Jim Bunning to beat the Tigers 3–2 at Fenway Park. Frank Malzone drove in the game winner with a single.

On the same day, the Red Sox traded Nels Chittum to the Dodgers for Rip Repulski.

MAY 7   Bill Monbouquette pitches a one-hitter to defeat the Tigers 5–0 at Fenway Park. The lone Detroit hit was a double by Neil Chrisley in the first inning.

MAY 10   Grand slams by Vic Wertz and Rip Repulski power the Red Sox to a 9–7 win over the White Sox at Fenway Park. The slam by Repulski came in his first at-bat in a Red Sox uniform. Wertz delivered his bases-loaded wallop in the first inning off

Early Wynn. In the eighth, with the score 5–5, Ted Williams was walked intentionally to load the bases. Gary Geiger was sent up to pinch hit, and White Sox manager Al Lopez replaced pitcher Don Ferrarese with Turk Lown. Sox skipper Billy Jurges countered by substituting Repulski for Geiger. The move worked perfectly as Repulski cleared the bases.

MAY 12   Tom Brewer pitches the Red Sox to a 1–0 win over the White Sox at Fenway Park. A walk-off, bases-loaded single in the ninth inning by Pete Runnels drove in the lone run of the game.

MAY 17   The Red Sox trade Ron Jackson to the Braves for Ray Boone.

MAY 24   The Red Sox lose their 10th game in a row, dropping a 6–2 decision to the Athletics in Kansas City.

> *The Red Sox engaged in a promotional tie-in with a Boston grocery chain in 1960. One ticket to a Red Sox game was given for every fifty dollars worth of groceries purchased at First National stores. It was estimated that the deal increased the turnstile count at Fenway Park by 350,000, which accounts for the attendance bump in 1960. The Sox drew 984,102 in 1959 for a club that won 75 games, 1,129,866 for a 65-win team in 1960, and 850,859 in 1961 when the Sox won 76 times.*

MAY 27   Camilo Pascual throws a pitch at Pete Runnels's head, which prompts a brawl in the fifth inning of a 4–3 win over the Senators in Washington. Runnels charged Pascaul, and the benches emptied.

JUNE 7   Billy Jurges starts Bobby Thomson at first base with disastrous results. Thomson was thirty-six and had never before played first in a major league game. He wore a fielder's glove instead of a first baseman's glove and made two critical errors in a 12–3 loss to the Indians at Fenway Park.

JUNE 8   In Del Baker's debut as manager, the Red Sox sweep the Indians 8–7 and 5–2 in a doubleheader at Fenway Park. Pumpsie Green hit a grand slam in the fourth inning of the opener off Jim Perry.

> *Billy Jurges was replaced as manager on an interim basis by Baker, a sixty-eight-year-old coach, for "an indefinite period." The Red Sox had a record of 18–31 when Jurges was relieved of his duties. Ill health was cited as the reason. Dr. Richard Wright, a Boston internal medicine specialist, examined Jurges and said the Sox skipper was "completely exhausted from a fruitless task." The fruitless task was trying to turn an untalented Red Sox team into a winner. Jurges went to his home in Silver Springs, Maryland, and composed a letter to Tom Yawkey, stating the conditions under which he would return as manager. The letter was sent by airmail special delivery. After receiving the letter on June 10, Yawkey sent Jurges a letter by airmail special delivery letter informing Jurges that he had been fired (see June 12, 1960).*

JUNE 9   The Red Sox trade Gene Stephens to the Orioles for Willie Tasby.

> *Tasby was the first African American acquired by the Red Sox in a trade with another big-league club.*

JUNE 12   Pinky Higgins returns as manager of the Red Sox, replacing Billy Jurges, who had replaced Higgins as manager on July 3, 1959. Higgins's second term as manager of the Red Sox lasted through the end of the 1962 season.

JUNE 13   The Red Sox trade Marty Keough and Ted Bowsfield to the Indians for Russ Nixon and Carroll Hardy.

JUNE 16   Ted Williams hits the 499th home run of his career to tie the game 5–5, but the Red Sox lose 6–5 to the Tigers in Detroit in 10 innings.

Williams hit 55 homers in Detroit during his career, more than in any other opponent's ballpark.

JUNE 17   Playing against the Indians in Cleveland, Ted Williams hits the 500th home run of his career. The milestone homer came off of Wynn Hawkins, a rookie who was three years old when Williams made his major league debut. Williams hit the homer with a man on base in the third inning and broke a 1–1 tie in a 3–1 Red Sox victory. Frank Sullivan struck out 12 batters in the game.

During a stretch in June and July, Williams hit 12 homers in a span of 80 at-bats, the best sustained streak of his career.

JUNE 26   The Red Sox lose the second game of a doubleheader against the White Sox at Comiskey Park 21–7. Chicago scored 11 runs in the fourth inning to take an 18–1 lead. Boston also lost the first game, 4–3.

The Red Sox lost all 11 games they played at Comiskey Park in 1960.

JUNE 28   Ike Delock is suspended for three days by AL president Joe Cronin for giving Fenway Park fans an "improper gesture" during a 10–1 loss to the Tigers. Delock was angry at the boos he received after being taken out of the game in the second inning.

JULY 3   The Red Sox score eight runs in the seventh inning and trounce the Athletics 13–2 at Fenway Park. Willie Tasby collected his first homer as a member of the Red Sox with a grand slam off Ray Blemker in the seventh inning. It was the only game of Blemker's major league career.

JULY 10   Willie Tasby collects five hits, including a double, in five at-bats during a 9–5 win over the Yankees at Fenway Park. Vic Wertz hit a grand slam off Whitey Ford in the second inning.

JULY 11   Bill Monbouquette is the starting pitcher in the first of two All-Star Games played in 1960. Monbouquette surrendered four runs and five hits in two innings and was the losing pitcher. The NL won 5–3 at Municipal Stadium in Kansas City.

JULY 16   Ike Delock pitches the Red Sox to a 1–0 win against the Athletics in Kansas City. Willie Tasby drove in the lone run of the game with a double in the eighth inning.

JULY 23   Playing center field for the Indians, Jimmy Piersall is ejected by umpire Ed Hurley for dashing back and forth in the outfield while Ted Williams is batting during the sixth and eighth innings. Piersall rushed in to confront Hurley and argued with the umpire for 10 minutes before leaving the field. The Red Sox lost the game, 4–2.

JULY 24   Willie Tasby is hitless in five at-bats during a doubleheader against the Indians at Fenway Park, but scores five runs after drawing four walks and being hit by a pitch. The Red Sox won both games, 10–6 and 7–6.

Organ music was played at Fenway Park for the first time during the twin bill. The instrument was played by John Kiley, who also supplied the organ music at Boston Garden.

JULY 28   Gary Geiger is hospitalized after suffering a collapsed lung and misses the remainder of the 1960 season.

Geiger was twenty-three and had a .302 batting average and nine homers in 77 games and seemed to be on the verge of stardom. He returned in 1961 and remained in the majors until 1970, but he was never again the same player.

JULY 29   Bill Monbouquette pitches the Red Sox to a 1–0 win over the Tigers at Fenway Park. Ted Williams drove in the lone run of the game with a single in the third inning.

AUGUST 6   Down 6–1 after two innings, the Red Sox rally to defeat the Tigers 11–9 in Detroit. Frank Malzone hit a homer, triple, and double.

AUGUST 7   Billy Muffett pitches the Red Sox to a 1–0 win over the Tigers in the second game of a doubleheader in Detroit. Muffett not only pitched the shutout but also collected three hits in three at-bats and scored the winning run in the eighth inning on a double by Pete Runnels.

AUGUST 9   Red Sox right fielder Lu Clinton kicks a fly ball hit by the Indians Vic Power over the fence for a home run, leading to a 6–3 loss in Cleveland. The game was tied 3–3 in the bottom of the fifth inning with a Cleveland runner on base when Power hit a drive over Clinton's head. The ball hit the top of the wire fence and bounced toward Clinton, who was running with his back to the infield. The carom fell in front of Clinton and hit his foot while he was racing full speed, causing him to accidentally kick it over the fence. Since the ball never touched the ground, umpire Al Smith ruled it a home run.

AUGUST 10   In Cleveland, Ted Williams moves from fourth place to third on the all-time home run list by hitting his 512th and 513th homers to pass Mel Ott. The Red Sox beat the Indians, 6–1.

AUGUST 16   The Red Sox introduce a jeep-like vehicle to haul pitchers from the bullpen to the mound at Fenway Park. It was also used to tote the batting cage in and out and drag the mat used to smooth the infield. Yankee manager Casey Stengel instructed his relief pitchers to refuse the ride, however, during their 11–7 win over the Red Sox.

AUGUST 20   Ted Williams draws the 2,000th walk of his career and hits his 514th and 515th homers during an 8–6 win over the Orioles in the first game of a doubleheader at Memorial Stadium. Baltimore won the second game, 6–0.

AUGUST 25   Vic Wertz hits a pinch-hit grand slam in the fourth inning off Don Newcombe during a 10–7 win over the Indians at Fenway Park.

AUGUST 30   Pete Runnels ties a major league record with nine hits in a doubleheader against the Tigers at Fenway Park. In the first game, Runnels collected six hits in seven at-bats. His sixth hit was a walk-off double in the fifteenth inning that gave the Red Sox a 5–4 victory. In the second tilt, Runnels was three for four in a 3–2 Boston win.

After finishing second in 1958 and third in 1959, Runnels won the batting title in 1960 with a .320 average. During the last month of the season, Runnels battled painful ulcers and was on a strict diet.

SEPTEMBER 2   Ted Williams hits a home run off Don Lee of the Senators during a 5–1 loss in the first game of a doubleheader at Fenway Park. Williams also homered off Don's father, Thornton Lee, in 1939. Washington completed the sweep with a 3–2 win in the nightcap.

SEPTEMBER 11   On the day the Patriots defeat the Boncos 13–10 in the first game ever in the American Football League, at Nickerson Field in Boston, Hurricane Donna destroys the two-story, two-bedroom home of Ted Williams in Islamorada, Florida.

SEPTEMBER 20   Carroll Hardy pinch hits for Ted Williams, who is forced to leave the game after fouling a ball off his ankle in the first inning. Hardy hit into a double play against Hal Brown of the Orioles. The Red Sox lost 4–3 in Baltimore.

Although a .225 batter in 433 big-league games, Hardy was a pinch hitter for the stars. In 1958, while playing for the Indians, he hit for Roger Maris and hit a three-run homer. In 1961, Hardy pinch hit for Carl Yastrzemski.

SEPTEMBER 25   Tom Yawkey announces that Ted Williams will retire at the end of the 1960 season. The Red Sox had six games left on the schedule: three games against the Orioles in Boston on September 26, 27, and 28, and three in New York against the Yankees on September 29, 30, and October 1.

SEPTEMBER 27   Bucky Harris is dismissed as general manager and replaced by Pinky Higgins. Higgins retained his duties as field manager as well.

SEPTEMBER 28   In his final major league plate appearance, Ted Williams picks out a 1–1 pitch from Jack Fisher of the Orioles in the eighth inning and drives it into the right center-field bleachers before a crowd of 10,454 at Fenway Park. It was Williams's 521st career homer. The homer gave the Red Sox a 5–4 victory. Williams took his defensive position in left field at the start of the ninth and was replaced immediately by Carroll Hardy. Williams left the field to a standing ovation.

After the game, he made the surprise announcement that he had just played his last game, bypassing the upcoming three-game series against the Yankees in New York. Williams was honored in ceremonies prior to the September 28 contest. "Baseball has been the most wonderful thing that ever happened to me," Williams said, "and if I could do it all over again, I would want to play for the best owner in the business, Tom Yawkey, and the greatest fans in America."

In addition to the 521 homers, Williams finished his career with a .344 batting average, 1,798 runs, 2,654 hits, 525 doubles, 1,839 RBIs, and 2,019 walks. How his final career stats would have looked if he hadn't missed three full seasons and most of two others in military service is open to speculation. One formula is to add his statistics for the 1940, 1941, 1942, 1946, 1947, and 1948 seasons and divide by two to replicate the 1943, 1944 and 1945 seasons. Then add his statistics for 1950, 1951, 1954, and 1955 and divide by two to replicate the time he lost in 1952 and 1953. This would give Williams 2,958 games, 10,037 at-bats, 2,379 runs, 3,469 hits, 688 doubles, 95 triples, 658 homers, 2,404 RBIs, and 2,661 walks, a .346 batting average, and a .630 slugging percentage. If these figures are accurate, at the end of the 2005 season, Williams would have ranked first in runs, first in RBIs, first in walks, second in total bases, second in extra-base hits, third in slugging percentage, fifth in home runs, fifth in doubles, sixth in hits, seventh in batting average, and eleventh in games played. No one in baseball history ranks in the top 11 in all 12 of those categories. Hank Aaron is the next best with nine but doesn't rank in walks and batting average.

OCTOBER 26   The American League announces plans to expand to 10 teams for the 1961 season. The Washington Senators moved to Minnesota, where they were renamed the Twins. A new expansion team was created in Washington, also named the Senators. Another expansion outfit was installed in Los Angeles and named the Angels.

DECEMBER 14   Six weeks after Massachusetts Senator John Kennedy wins the presidential election over the Richard Nixon, the Red Sox lose Jim Fregosi, Jerry Casale, Fred Newman, and Ed Sadowski to the Angels and Tom Sturdivant, Jim Mahoney, and Willie Tasby to the Senators in the expansion draft.

Fregosi was a huge loss for the Red Sox. He was eighteen years old and only six months out of high school when drafted by the Angels. Fregosi reached the majors in 1961 and had a stellar career that included six All-Star Game appearances, although he was severely underrated because he played on mostly losing teams with the Angels in pitcher's ballparks and was on the wrong end of a 1971 trade to the Mets for Nolan Ryan. In 2001 Bill James ranked Fregosi as the 15th best shortstop in baseball history. A right-handed hitter with good power, Fregosi might have put up Hall of Fame numbers playing half of his games at Fenway Park. Newman was a Boston native who had a couple of good seasons in the Angels. None of the other five lost in the expansion draft were effective players after 1960. Sadowski was the last player, prior to Carl Yastrzemski, to wear uniform number 8. Casale gave up Yastrzemski's first major league home run on May 9, 1961.

DECEMBER 16   In a trade of tall pitchers, the Red Sox swap Frank Sullivan to the Phillies for Gene Conley.

The six-foot-six Sullivan was traded for the six-foot-eight Conley. A two-sport player, Conley was already familiar to Boston's sports fans. He played briefly for the Boston Braves in 1952, with the Celtics in the 1952–53 season, and again in a Celtics uniform from 1958 through 1961. In his second term with the Celts, Conley played on three NBA champions as a backup center to Bill Russell and for the Red Sox from 1960 through 1963.

1961   B

Season in a Sentence

Despite the addition of a strong brigade of rookies led by Carl Yastrzemski, Don Schwall, Chuck Schilling, and Jim Pagliaroni, the Red Sox continue to flounder.

Finish • Won • Lost • Pct • GB

Sixth   76   86   .469   33.0

Manager

Pinky Higgins

Stats   Red Sox • AL • Rank

Stats	Red Sox	AL	Rank
Batting Avg:	.254	.256	5
On-Base Pct:	.336	.332	3
Slugging Pct:	.374	.395	8
Home Runs:	112		9
Stolen Bases:	56		5
ERA:	4.29	4.02	8
Fielding Pct:	.977	.976	5
Runs Scored:	729		6
Runs Allowed:	792		9

Starting Lineup

Jim Pagliaroni, c
Pete Runnels, 1b
Chuck Schilling, 2b
Frank Malzone, 3b
Don Buddin, ss
Carl Yastrzemski, lf
Gary Geiger, cf
Jackie Jensen, rf
Vic Wertz, 1b
Carroll Hardy, cf-rf-lf
Russ Nixon, c
Pumpsie Green, ss

Pitchers

Bill Monbouquette, sp
Don Schwall, sp
Gene Conley, sp
Ike Delock, sp
Mike Fornieles, rp
Tracy Stallard, rp-sp
Billy Muffett, rp

Attendance

850,849 (sixth in AL)

Club Leaders

Batting Avg:	Malzone	.266
	Yastrzemski	.266
On-Base Pct:	Geiger	.349
Slugging Pct:	Geiger	.407
Home Runs:	Geiger	18
RBI:	Malzone	87
Runs:	Schilling	87
Stolen Bases:	Geiger	16
Wins:	Schwall	15
Strikeouts:	Monbouquette	161
ERA:	Schwall	3.22
Saves:	Fornieles	15

FEBRUARY 7   After sitting out the 1960 season, Jackie Jensen signs a contract for 1961.

It wasn't a smooth return to baseball for Jensen, as the year away from the sport diminished his skills. He hit .263 with 13 homers and 66 RBIs, left the club for eight days in April, and missed several games because of his fear of flying. Jensen retired from baseball for good at the end of the 1961 season.

APRIL 11   In the season opener, the Red Sox lose 5–2 to the Athletics before only 10,277 on a windy, cold, drizzly day at Fenway Park. Carl Yastrzemski made his major league debut and had a single in five at-bats. The hit was off Ray Herbert. Yastrzemski played left field and hit fifth in the batting order. Later that evening at Boston Garden, the Celtics won their third consecutive NBA championship in a five-game series against the St. Louis Hawks.

Ned Martin replaced Bill Crowley in the Red Sox' radio and TV booth in 1961. Crowley moved into the front office as director of public relations. Martin remained as one of the Red Sox' broadcasters until 1992.

APRIL 15   Carl Yastrzemski collects his first major league RBI during a 3–0 win over the Angels at Fenway Park. He singled home a run in the first for his first career RBI and tripled in the third. It was also the first time that the Red Sox played the Angels.

The Angels were born in 1961 as the Los Angeles Angels. The club changed its name to the California Angels in September 1965 and moved from Los Angeles to Anaheim in 1966. They were renamed the Anaheim Angels in 1997 and the Los Angeles Angels of Anaheim in 2005.

APRIL 22   Six days after the launching of the unsuccessful Bay of Pigs invasion of Cuba, Pumpsie Green hits a homer in the eleventh inning to defeat the White Sox 7–6 in Chicago. The Red Sox scored five runs in the top of the ninth to take a 6–4 lead, the last two on a homer by Gary Geiger, but allowed the White Sox to tie the score with two runs in the bottom of the inning. The victory broke a 13-game losing streak by the Red Sox at Comiskey Park dating back to 1959.

APRIL 25   In his Red Sox debut, Gene Conley beats the Senators 6–1 at Fenway Park.

It was just two weeks after Conley played for the Celtics in the NBA Championship Series. It was also the Sox' first game against the expansion Senators, a franchise known today as the Texas Rangers. The Senators moved to Texas at the end of the 1971 season.

APRIL 30   Jackie Jensen leaves the Red Sox before a doubleheader against the Indians without informing manager Pinky Higgins. Jensen said he felt he was taking money under false pretenses. He had only six hits, all singles, in 46 at-bats for a batting average of .130. Jensen returned to the Red Sox on May 8.

MAY 3   The Red Sox trail 8–0 before scoring two runs in the seventh inning and six in a ninth-inning explosion to forge an 8–8 tie, only to lose 9–8 to the Athletics in Kansas City.

MAY 5   On the day Alan Shepard becomes the first American in space, the Red Sox play a regular-season game in Minnesota for the first time and lose 5–1 to the Twins at Metropolitan Stadium.

MAY 7   Chuck Schilling drives in six runs with a grand slam and a two-run double in an 11–9 win over the Twins in Minnesota. The slam was hit off Camilo Pascaul in the fourth inning.

MAY 8   The Red Sox play a regular-season game in Los Angeles for the first time and lose 6–5 to the Angels. In his first game since returning to the Red Sox after an eight-day absence, Jackie Jensen hit a home run.

The Angels played at Wrigley Field in Los Angeles in 1961. It was used by the L.A.'s Pacific Coast League club, also named the Angels, from 1925 through 1957. The ballpark was built by the Wrigley family, which owned the Chicago Cubs from 1919 through 1981. The Los Angeles version of Wrigley Field can still be seen occasionally on ESPN Classic in reruns of the 1959 TV series Home Run Derby *and as a backdrop for many Hollywood movies. It was torn down in 1965.*

MAY 9   Carl Yastrzemski hits the first home run of his career during an 8–7 loss to the Angels in Los Angeles. The pitcher was Jerry Casale, whom the Sox had lost to the Angels in the offseason's expansion draft.

As a twenty-one-year-old rookie, Yastrzemski played in 148 games and hit .266 with 11 home runs.

MAY 12   Bill Monbouquette strikes out 17 batters in a 2–1 win over the Senators in Washington. The Sox won the game despite collecting only two hits.

Monbouquette was the first Red Sox pitcher to strike out more than 15 batters in a game. The only other Sox pitcher with as many as 15 strikeouts in a game prior to 1961 was Smoky Joe Wood in 1911.

The man who would come to be known simply as "Yaz" and who would replace Ted Williams as the team's signature player began his career in 1961 as part of a youth movement that included several other stellar rookies.

National Baseball Hall of Fame Library/Major League Baseball/Getty Images

MAY 18   Gene Conley pitches the Red Sox to a 1–0 win over the Tigers at Fenway Park. The only run of the game was driven by Don Buddin on a double in the fifth inning.

MAY 30   The Yankees hit seven home runs in a 12–3 win over the Red Sox at Fenway Park. Mickey Mantle, Roger Maris, and Bill Skowron each hit two homers, and Yogi Berra one.

JUNE 8   A base-running blunder by Gary Geiger costs the Red Sox a win against the Angels in the second game of a doubleheader at Fenway Park. With the score 4–3 in favor of the Angels in the bottom of the eleventh, Geiger drove in Chuck Schilling with a triple to tie the score. Unfortunately, Geiger thought the drive won the game, and trotted jubilantly off third. Before he realized his mistake, Geiger was tagged out. Carl Yastrzemski followed with a fly ball that would have scored the winning run with a sacrifice fly if Geiger had remained on third. The game ended in a 4–4 tie at the end of the eleventh when a thunderstorm ended the contest. The Sox managed to win the first game, 6–5.

JUNE 9   Ryne Duren of the Angels strikes out seven Boston batters in a row and is the winning pitcher in a 3–1 decision over the Red Sox in the second game of a doubleheader at Fenway Park. The Sox won the first game, 5–3.

JUNE 12   Unable to make train connections or overcome his fear of flying, Jackie Jensen drives from Boston to Detroit for a series against the Tigers.

JUNE 15   Vic Wertz hits a grand slam in the fifth inning off Jim Bunning during a 10–1 win over the Tigers in Detroit.

On the same day, the Red Sox sold Sammy White to the Braves. White had

informed the Red Sox on June 2 that he wanted to come off of the voluntarily retired list. The Sox didn't want him back but contacted other clubs about a possible trade. White played two more seasons in the majors.

JUNE 16   The Red Sox score eight runs in the fourth inning and outslug the Senators 14–9 at Fenway Park. The Sox trailed 6–0 in the third before mounting the comeback. There were 26 walks issued in the game, 15 of them by Washington pitchers.

JUNE 17   Jim Pagliaroni hits a two-run pinch homer in the sixth inning to provide the tying and winning runs in a 6–5 win over the Senators at Fenway Park.

JUNE 18   In an incredible ninth-inning rally, the Red Sox score eight runs with two outs to beat the Senators 13–12 in the first game of a doubleheader at Fenway Park. Washington scored five runs in the top of the ninth, four on a grand slam by ex–Red Sox Willie Tasby, to take what appeared to be an insurmountable 12–5 lead. With two out in the bottom of the inning, the score was still 12–5, and Don Buddin was on first base. Chuck Schilling and Carroll Hardy singled to bring Buddin across the plate. Gary Geiger walked to load the bases, and Dave Sisler came in as the new Senators pitcher to replace Carl Mathias. Sisler immediately walked Jackie Jensen and Frank Malzone to force home two runs and narrow the gap to 12–8. Jim Pagliaroni stepped to the plate with the bases still jammed and delivered a grand slam to tie the game, 12–12. Vic Wertz got aboard with a walk and scored the winning run with help from two singles by Buddin and Russ Nixon, the latter as a pinch hitter. In the second game, Jim Pagliaroni clubbed his third dramatic home run in two days by hitting a pitch out of the park in the thirteenth inning to lift the Sox to a 6–5 victory.

JUNE 22   Mike Fornieles pitches five hitless innings of relief in a 3–2 win over the Angels in Los Angeles.

JULY 30   Down 7–0 to the White Sox in the second game of a doubleheader at Fenway Park, the Red Sox rally to win 9–8 in 10 innings. Vic Wertz tied the game with a homer in the ninth inning. A single by Jackie Jensen drove in the winning run. Chicago won the first game, 4–2.

The Red Sox were once again a schizophrenic team in 1961 with a record of 50–31 at home and 26–51 on the road.

JULY 31   The second All-Star Game of 1961 is played at Fenway Park and results in a 1–1 tie. The game was called at the end of the ninth inning when heavy rain stopped play. Despite playing in one of the best hitter's parks in baseball, pitchers dominated the game. The AL scored first on a first-inning homer by Rocky Colavito over the Green Monster off Warren Spahn, who began his major league career in Boston with the Braves. The National League tied the score in the sixth on a two-run double by Bill White off Red Sox rookie pitcher Don Schwall. Jim Bunning and Camilo Pascual each pitched three hitless innings for the American League. Bunning hurled the first three innings, and Pascual threw the last three. Ted Williams threw out the ceremonial first pitch.

Future Hall of Famers on the two teams included Hank Aaron, Luis Aparicio, Ernie Banks, Yogi Berra, Jim Bunning, Roberto Clemente, Don Drysdale,

Whitey Ford, Nellie Fox, Al Kaline, Harmon Killebrew, Sandy Koufax, Mickey Mantle, Eddie Mathews, Willie Mays, Stan Musial, Brooks Robinson, Frank Robinson, Warren Spahn, and Hoyt Wilhelm.

Don Schwall looked like he might be headed for the Hall of Fame with a spectacular start as a rookie in 1961. A six-foot-six former University of Oklahoma basketball player, Schwall started the season with the Red Sox farm club in Seattle in the Pacific Coast League. Although he didn't appear in his first major league game until May 21, he pitched well enough to make the All-Star team. On August 7, Schwall had a record of 13–2 before missing two weeks with a kidney ailment. He finished the season at 15–7 with an ERA of 3.22 and won the American League Rookie of the Year Award over teammate Carl Yastrzemski. It was Schwall's last run of success in the majors, however. In 1962, he had a 9–15 record and was traded to the Pirates at the end of the season. Schwall's big-league career ended in 1967 with 49 wins and 48 losses.

AUGUST 2   A walk-off homer by Chuck Schilling in the ninth inning beats the Angels 8–7 in the second game of a doubleheader at Fenway Park. The Sox also won the first game, 7–2.

Schilling looked like a future star when he hit .259, scored 87 runs, and was exceptional defensively as a twenty-year-year-old rookie in 1961. Like Don Schwall, Schilling proved to be a major disappointment after a fine rookie campaign, and his big-league career lasted only five years.

AUGUST 8   Gary Geiger hits a grand slam in the third inning off Camilo Pascaul, but the Red Sox lose 6–5 to the Twins at Fenway Park.

AUGUST 15   Frank Malzone collects five hits, including two homers, in five at-bats during an 8–0 win over the Indians in Cleveland.

AUGUST 24   Jackie Jensen hits a walk-off homer in the tenth inning to beat the Senators 5–4 at Fenway Park. Jensen also hit a two-run homer in the sixth to tie the score, 4–4.

Jensen was given permission to miss a three-game series against the Angels in Los Angeles August 25–27 because of his fear of flying. He met the club in Kansas City on August 28 after taking a train from Boston to Kansas City. Jensen also missed the September 2 game in Minnesota because he refused to step on an airplane. He retired from playing baseball for good at the end of the 1961 season. Later, Jensen said, "It was silly retiring. I was at the height of my career." After leaving baseball, Jensen drifted from one business venture from another, most of which failed. He left the game in part to save his marriage, but his wife divorced him in 1963. They remarried in 1965, then divorced again in 1968. For a time, Jensen was the baseball coach at the University of Nevada and at the University of California at Berkeley, his alma mater. He owned a Christmas tree farm and ran a baseball camp for youngsters in Charlottesville, Virginia, when he died of a heart attack at the age of fifty-five in 1982.

AUGUST 25   The day before his wife gives birth to a daughter, Carroll Hardy hits a grand slam in the second inning off John James during a 12–6 win over the Angels in Los Angeles.

Hardy played in the NFL in 1955 with the San Francisco 49ers as a halfback and caught four touchdown passes from Y. A. Tittle. After his baseball career ended, Hardy was an assistant general manager with the Denver Broncos.

AUGUST 29   The Red Sox score six runs with two outs in the ninth and defeat the Athletics 8–4 in Kansas City.

SEPTEMBER 8   In an unusual pitching performance, Tracy Stallard allows only one hit in $4\frac{2}{3}$ innings but walks 10. Mike Fornieles allowed just one hit in $4\frac{1}{3}$ innings of relief, and the Red Sox beat the Tigers 9–2 at Fenway Park.

On the same day, the Red Sox sold Vic Wertz to the Tigers. The Sox planned to honor the slugging first baseman with "Vic Wertz Day" at Fenway Park on September 23, but the Tigers deal put an end to the festivities.

SEPTEMBER 15   A walk-off homer by Carl Yastrzemski beats the Orioles 3–2 at Fenway Park.

SEPTEMBER 17   Bill Monbouquette pitches the Red Sox to a 1–0 win over the Orioles at Fenway Park. Jim Pagliaroni drove in the lone run of the game with a double in the fourth inning.

OCTOBER 1   On the final game of the season, the Red Sox play a supporting role in baseball history as Roger Maris breaks Babe Ruth's single-season home run record with his 61st of 1961 for the only run of a 1–0 Yankee win over Boston in New York. The homer was struck in the fourth inning off Tracy Stallard. Maris was one for four in the game. Stallard induced Maris to fly to Carl Yastrzemski in left in the second inning, and struck out Maris on a 3–2 pitch in the sixth. In the eighth against Chet Nichols, Maris popped to second baseman Chuck Schilling.

Stallard had a 30–57 lifetime record and was on the wrong end of history again on June 21, 1964. While pitching for the Mets against the Phillies, Stallard was the losing pitcher when Jim Bunning pitched a perfect game.

NOVEMBER 26   The Red Sox trade Don Buddin to Houston for Ed Bressoud.

Buddin played for the Red Sox from 1956 through 1961 as the club slowly deteriorated, and he was a constant target of fans' boos at Fenway for his erratic play, especially on defense. The trade was an excellent one for the Red Sox. Buddin played only two more seasons in the majors and hit only .196 with two homers in that time. Bressoud was nearly thirty when he opened the 1962 season as the Red Sox' starting shortstop and had yet to prove he could handle the load of being an everyday player. He had a .239 lifetime batting average and was coming off a season in which he had hit only .211. In his first three seasons with the Sox, Bressoud more than proved his worth by batting .277 with 49 home runs.

1962   B

Season in a Sentence

Season two of the post–Ted Williams era is no better than season one.

Finish • Won • Lost • Pct • GB

Eighth   76   84.4   75   19.0

Manager

Pinky Higgins

Stats

Stats	Red Sox	AL	Rank
Batting Avg:	.258	.255	4
On-Base Pct:	.326	.328	7
Slugging Pct:	.403	.394	4
Home Runs:	146		6
Stolen Bases:	39		8
ERA:	4.22	3.97	9
Fielding Pct:	.979	.978	5
Runs Scored:	707		6 (tie)
Runs Allowed:	798		9

Starting Lineup

Jim Pagliaroni, c
Pete Runnels, 1b
Chuck Schilling, 2b
Frank Malzone, 3b
Ed Bressoud, ss
Carl Yastrzemski, lf
Gary Geiger, cf
Carroll Hardy, rf-cf
Lu Clinton, rf
Bob Tillman, c
Billy Gardner, 2b

Pitchers

Gene Conley, sp
Bill Monbouquette, sp
Earl Wilson, sp
Don Schwall, sp
Ike Delock, sp
Dick Radatz, rp
Mike Fornieles, rp

Attendance

733,080 (seventh in AL)

Club Leaders

Batting Avg:	Runnels	.326
On-Base Pct:	Runnels	.408
Slugging Pct:	Yastrzemski	.496
Home Runs:	Malzone	21
RBI:	Malzone	95
Runs:	Yastrzemski	99
Stolen Bases:	Geiger	18
Wins:	Conley	15
	Monbouquette	15
Strikeouts:	Monbouquette	153
ERA:	Monbouquette	3.33
Saves:	Radatz	24

JANUARY 22   Jackie Jensen announces his retirement from baseball, this time for good.

MARCH 24   A month after John Glenn circles the globe as the first American to orbit the earth, the Red Sox trade Tom Borland to Houston for Dave Philley.

During the Korean War, Glenn served in the same jet fighter squadron as Ted Williams.

MARCH 25   A fire breaks out on the roof of Fenway Park and destroys the press room, which was used to entertain members of the press and visiting dignitaries. The fire was discovered by a woman living nearby.

APRIL 10   In the season opener, the Red Sox lose 4–0 to the Indians before 14,736 at Fenway Park. Dick Donovan pitched the shutout. Don Schwall was the losing pitcher.

The scoreboard at Fenway Park posted the lineups of the two teams for the first time in 1962. The number and position of each player was listed on the electronic board. It was taken down in 1976 when a new electronic was built on top of the bleachers.

APRIL 11   Carroll Hardy hits a walk-off grand slam homer in the twelfth inning that accounts for all the runs in a 4–0 win over the Indians at Fenway Park. Hardy's homer broke up a brilliant pitching duel between Bill Monbouquette and Ron Taylor, each of whom pitched a complete game. Monbouquette allowed only one hit through the first nine innings and just four in all. In the Boston twelfth, Carl Yastrzemski led off with a triple. Intentional walks were issued to Frank Malzone and Russ Nixon before Hardy homered. The game was Taylor's major league debut. He pitched until 1972, mostly as a reliever, and never pitched a shutout.

The four runs on Hardy's homer were the only runs the Red Sox scored in the first three games of the 1962 season.

APRIL 19   The day after the Celtics win Game Seven of the NBA Championship Series in overtime against the Los Angeles Lakers at Boston Garden, Lu Clinton hits a grand slam off Jerry Casale during a 9–5 win over the Tigers at Fenway Park.

Chuck Schilling started the season hitless in his first 31 at-bats.

APRIL 21   The Red Sox celebrate the 50th anniversary of the opening of Fenway Park prior to a 4–3 win over the Tigers. Nine members of the World Champion 1912 club were on hand, including Bill Carrigan, Hugh Bedient, Smoky Joe Wood, Larry Gardner, Duffy Lewis, Olaf Henriksen, Ray Collins, Steve Yerkes, and Harry Hooper.

MAY 1   The Red Sox play at D.C. Stadium in Washington for the first time and lose 2–1 to the Senators.

The ballpark was renamed Robert F. Kennedy Stadium in 1968. It was the home of the Senators from 1962 until 1971, when the club moved to Texas, and the Nationals beginning in 2005.

MAY 4   Trailing 4–0, the Red Sox explode for 12 runs in the fifth inning and defeat the White Sox 13–6 at Fenway Park. The 12 runs were scored on six singles, two doubles, and five walks. Russ Nixon had two hits as a pinch hitter. He singled while batting for Mike Fornieles, came up again, and single once more.

MAY 9   Bill Monbouquette holds the Yankees hitless until there's one out in the seventh, then gives up four runs to lose 4–1 in New York.

MAY 12   Red Sox pitchers Gene Conley and Dick Radatz each drive in two runs during a 5–1 win over the Tigers in Detroit.

Radatz created a sensation as a twenty-five-year-old rookie relief pitcher in 1962. At six-foot-six and 235 pounds, Radatz possessed a devastating fastball, earned the nickname "The Monster," and was a terrifying sight to American League batters. In 1962, he had a 9–5 record, a league-leading 24 saves, a 2.24 ERA, and 144 strikeouts in 62 games and 124 2/3 innings.

MAY 15   The Red Sox score nine runs in the sixth inning and overwhelm the Yankees 14–4 at Fenway Park.

MAY 19   Catcher Bob Tillman hits a home run in his first official at-bat in the majors facing Ted Bowsfield in the fourth inning of a 6–5 loss to the Angels in 10 innings at Fenway Park. Tillman walked in his first big-league plate appearance in the second inning.

MAY 25   Baltimore first baseman Jim Gentile hits a homer estimated at 500 feet into the center field bleachers at Fenway Park during a 9–5 Orioles win over the Red Sox.

MAY 30   The Red Sox play at Dodger Stadium for the first time and lose twice to the Angels, 10–5 and 4–0.

           The Angels shared Dodger Stadium with the Dodgers from 1962 through 1965.

JUNE 6   Frank Malzone hits a walk-off homer in the ninth inning that beats the Tigers 2–1 in the first game of a doubleheader at Fenway Park. Detroit won the second tilt 3–2 in 11 innings.

JUNE 10   Bob Tillman hits a walk-off homer in the eleventh inning to defeat the Indians 4–3 in the first game of a doubleheader at Fenway Park. Cleveland won the nightcap, 9–3.

JUNE 13   Don Schwall pitches a two-hitter to beat the Orioles 4–0 on a cold, windy, drizzly night at Fenway Park. The only Baltimore hits were a double by Jackie Brandt and a single by Whitey Herzog in the seventh.

JUNE 26   Earl Wilson pitches a no-hitter to defeat the Angels 2–0 before 14,002 at Fenway Park. Wilson also hit a homer in the third inning off Bo Belinsky to give the Sox a 1–0 lead. Belinsky pitched a no-hitter of his own six weeks earlier. It was also Wilson's first major league shutout. He struck out five, walked four, and retired the last 11 batters in order. In the ninth, Billy Moran led off for the Angels and hit a blooper into short left that shortstop Ed Bressoud caught one-handed. Leon Wagner followed with a weak fly ball to Carl Yastrzemski in left. The final out was recorded on a liner to center that was caught by Gary Geiger 400 feet from home plate.

JUNE 29   Lu Clinton drives in six runs in a 9–3 win over the Athletics at Fenway Park. Clinton hit a grand slam in the sixth inning off Diego Segui and a two-run double in the eighth.

           When Clinton stepped to the plate with the bases loaded in the sixth, he had only six hits on the season in 62 at-bats for a batting average of .097. He was playing only because of an illness to Carroll Hardy. From June 29 through July 13, Clinton had one of the most spectacular batting streaks in Red Sox history. In 13 consecutive games, he had 30 hits in 54 at-bats, a batting average of .556. His 30 hits included seven homers, two triples, and four doubles. He also scored 20 runs and drove in 26.

JULY 4   Lu Clinton collects seven hits, including two homers and two doubles, in eight at-bats during a doubleheader against the Twins at Fenway Park. The seven hits came in consecutive at-bats. The Red Sox lost the first game 8–4 and won the second, 9–5.

JULY 12   The Red Sox erupt for five runs in the eleventh inning to win 9–4 over the Athletics in the second game of a doubleheader at Municipal Stadium. Kansas City won the first game, 5–4.

JULY 13   Lu Clinton hits for the cycle, including two singles, in seven at-bats during an 11–10 win over the Athletics in 15 innings in Kansas City. Clinton's fifth hit of the contest was a single that drove in the winning run. The A's led 9–2 at the end of the third inning before the Sox mounted their comeback. A Boston run in the ninth tied the score 10–10. Dick Radatz pitched seven innings of shutout relief.

JULY 22   White Sox outfielder Floyd Robinson collects six hits in six at-bats during a 7–3 Chicago win over the Red Sox at Fenway Park.

JULY 26   Following a 13–3 loss to the Yankees in New York in which Gene Conley gives up eight runs in $2\frac{2}{3}$ innings, Conley and Pumpsie Green mysteriously disappear. The pair left the team bus in traffic to use a restroom and failed to return. Conley decided he wanted to fly to Israel and went to the airport, but he was refused a ticket because he didn't have a visa.

Green returned to the Sox on July 28 and Conley on July 30. Conley said he bolted the club because he was "tired" and was fined $2,000.

B   A Little Side Trip   B

Gene Conley and Pumpsie Green participated in the most bizarre disappearance in the history of baseball on July 26, 1962. It all began in a bus that took the Red Sox from Yankee Stadium to the Newark Airport after the Sox were thrashed, 13–3. Conley was the starting pitcher and allowed eight runs in $2\frac{2}{3}$ innings. During the last six innings of the game, he sat in the clubhouse drinking one beer after another.

Little in Conley's life seemed to be going right. He had been playing both professional basketball and baseball for four years, and he was worn out both physically and mentally. His shoulder ached constantly, which not only diminished the effectiveness of his pitches, but also of his trademark hook shot, which helped him score more than 2,000 points during his NBA career. At the age of thirty-one, it looked as though his athletic career was nearing an end.

Leaving Yankee Stadium at 5:20 PM, the air conditioning on the Sox' bus broke and the vehicle became ensnarled in a massive traffic jam. Around 175th Street and Wadsworth Avenue, the bus was stalled for about 20 minutes. It was hot, and Conley was getting irritable and had to use the men's room. There wasn't one on the bus. He told manager Pinky Higgins that he was going to a washroom in a garage on Wadsworth. Green went with him.

The traffic began to move, and the team bus took off without Conley and Green. Higgins said he was sure the two players would get to Washington in time for the twinight doubleheader at 6 PM the next day.

When the Sox' bus in Washington left the hotel for the ballpark at 3:30 PM on July 27, Conley's and Green's bags were still in the lobby. Their room keys were still at the mail desk.

Instead of going to Washington, Conley and Green went to a bar, where more alcohol failed to improve Conley's mood, then to downtown Manhattan and checked into the Hotel Commodore. On the afternoon of July 27, Conley had an inspiration. Maybe if he got closer to God, his problems would be solved. "Do you want to go to Jerusalem, or do you want to go to Washington?" Conley asked Green. Green was named after a prophet—Elijah is his real name—but he failed to see how a trip to the Holy Land would help his career. Green decided on Washington and rejoined the Red Sox about 27 hours after walking off the bus.

Conley called the Israeli Airlines to make a reservation for Tel Aviv that evening. He cashed a check for $1,000 at the hotel and headed for Idlewild Airport (present-day JFK airport) to pick up his reservation for Israel. When he got to the airline ticket desk, he couldn't purchase a ticket because he didn't have a passport. Conley went back to the Hotel Commodore for a day, where he was met by his wife and children. Conley then traveled with his family to his home in Foxboro before returning to the Sox on July 30.

Conley refused to divulge the reasons for leaving the club other than to say he was "tired." The club fined Conley $1,500 and Green $1,000. Conley pitched well over the remainder of the 1962 season, but in the process of pitching 241 $2/3$ innings, the only time in his career he topped the 200-inning mark, his arm was all but ruined. In September, the Boston Celtics traded him to the New York Knicks, and during the 1962–63 NBA season, he played a career-high 1,544 minutes.

Conley reported to the Red Sox 1963 training camp with a bad shoulder and two injured hands sustained during the previous basketball season. He was only 3–4 with a 6.64 ERA before going on the disabled list.

By the spring of 1964, Conley's athletic career was over. He remained in the Boston area and became owner of the Foxboro Paper Company before retiring to Florida.

JULY 30   Pete Runnels hits a home run in the second All-Star Game of 1962, won by the American League 9–4 at Wrigley Field in Chicago.

Runnels won his second American League batting title in 1962 by hitting .326. During the regular season, he hit 10 homers.

AUGUST 1   Bill Monbouquette no-hits the White Sox for a 1–0 win at Comiskey Park. It was the second Red Sox no-hitter in five weeks, following the one by Earl Wilson on July 26. The lone Chicago base runner was Al Smith, who walked on a 3–2 pitch with two outs in the second inning. Monbouquette retired the next 22 batters in a row. In the ninth inning, he struck out Sherm Lollar for the first out, retired Nellie Fox on a grounder to third baseman Frank Malzone, and fanned Luis Aparicio. Monbouquette struck out seven batters. Lu Clinton drove in Jim Pagliaroni with a single in the eighth inning with the game's only run, off Early Wynn.

In his previous four starts prior to the no-hitter, Monbouquette allowed 17 runs in 10 $2/3$ innings.

AUGUST 8   In his second start since leaving the club on the team bus in New York, Gene Conley shuts out the Indians 5–0 at Fenway Park.

AUGUST 9   Bill Monbouquette shuts out the Indians 4–0 at Fenway Park.

AUGUST 11   In the third straight shutout by a Red Sox pitcher, Ike Delock defeats the Orioles 5–0 in the first game of a doubleheader at Fenway Park. It was Delock's first appearance since July 2. He missed 40 days because of an injured knee. In the second game, Don Schwall extended the Red Sox' shutout streak to 32 innings before allowing three runs in the sixth inning, but he emerged with a 7–3 victory.

AUGUST 12   Lu Clinton hits a two-run homer in the ninth inning to beat the Angels 2–1 in the first game of a doubleheader in Los Angeles. In the second game, the Sox scored nine runs in the first two innings and won, 9–5.

Carl Yastrzemski followed up his rookie season with a .294 average, 19 homers, 191 hits, 99 runs, 94 RBIs, and 43 doubles in 1962.

SEPTEMBER 5   The Red Sox score seven runs in the third inning and beat the Athletics 12–4 at Fenway Park.

Galen Cisco, who pitched for the Red Sox in 1961, 1962, and 1967, played fullback and linebacker on Ohio State's 1957 National Championship football team. With the Red Sox, Cisco had a 6–12 record and a 6.28 ERA.

SEPTEMBER 9   After winning the first game of a doubleheader against the Yankees in New York 9–3, the Red Sox take the nightcap 5–4 in a 16-inning marathon. Bob Tillman scored the winning run by doubling, going to third on a wild pitch, and coming home on Billy Gardner's bunt single. Dick Radatz pitched nine innings of relief and allowed only one run.

SEPTEMBER 30   In the final game of the season, Don Gile hits a two-run, walk-off homer that beats the Senators 3–1 in the second game of a doubleheader at Fenway Park. Washington won the first game, 3–1.

Gile went into the doubleheader hitless in 34 at-bats on the season. He was two for seven in the two games to finish the season with an .049 average. The walk-off homer proved to be Gile's final major league at-bat. He ended his four-year career with 18 hits, three homers, and a .150 batting average.

OCTOBER 6   Johnny Pesky replaces Pinky Higgins as manager.

Higgins stayed with the club as general manager. After Pesky's major league playing career ended in 1954, he spent seven seasons managing in the Red Sox' minor league system, the last two for the Class AAA affiliate in Seattle.

NOVEMBER 20   The Red Sox trade Jim Pagliaroni and Don Schwall to the Pirates for Dick Stuart and Jack Lamabe.

Cocky and with a penchant for controversy, Stuart both thrilled and exasperated fans in two seasons with the Red Sox with his big bat, big mouth, and iron glove. He hit 75 homers and drove in 232 runs, but he earned the nickname "Dr. Strangeglove" with his atrocious fielding and cared little about anyone but himself. "I'm not going to get famous hitting singles or fielding ground balls," Stuart said. He was wrong. His fielding, or lack of it, was the stuff of legend. In two seasons with the Sox, Stuart made 53 errors, more than any other two AL first basemen put together. He led the league in errors seven straight years beginning in 1958. Despite his vanity, Stuart could be personally likable when the mood struck him, and his outrageous behavior made him popular with fans. He even had his own television program on WBZ, called Stuart on Sports, which was on every Sunday night after the news. He signed for the show before he had played so much as a single game for the Sox. But he was not a team player, and Stuart's selfishness undermined manager Johnny Pesky's efforts to change the team's attitude. The arrogant and boorish Stuart constantly criticized and berated Pesky, mostly over trivial matters. After two years, the Red Sox had had enough and shipped Stuart to the Phillies.

NOVEMBER 26   The Red Sox trade Pete Runnels to Houston for Roman Mejias.

The acquisition of Stuart made Runnels expendable, even though he won the AL batting title in 1960 and 1962. A native Texan, Runnels was a big disappointment in Houston, hitting only .246 with two homers over the final two seasons of his career. Runnels returned to the Red Sox as a coach in 1965 and 1966 and was also the interim manager for 16 games in 1966. Mejias had a breakout season in 1962, clubbing 24 homers, but proved to be a one-year wonder. He hit only .229 with 13 homers in two seasons in Boston.

DECEMBER 10   The Red Sox trade Carroll Hardy to Houston for Dick Williams. The trade of two bench warmers gained little notice in Boston when it was announced, but it would become pivotal four years later when Williams was named manager of the Red Sox and awoke a slumbering franchise.

DECEMBER 11   The Red Sox trade Tracy Stallard, Pumpsie Green, and Al Moran to the Mets for Felix Mantilla.

Mantilla was twenty-seven years old and wasn't expected to be anything more than a utility infielder. His .287 average and 54 homers over three seasons were a pleasant surprise.

1963   B

Season in a Sentence

Dick Stuart, Dick Radatz, and a hot start keeps the fans interested until June, when the club's losing ways surface again.

Finish • Won • Lost • Pct • GB

Seventh   76   85   .472 28.0

Manager

Johnny Pesky

Stats

Stats	Red Sox	AL	Rank
Batting Avg:	.252	.247	4
On-Base Pct:	.313	.315	6
Slugging Pct:	.400	.380	3
Home Runs:	171		3
Stolen Bases:	27		10
ERA:	3.97	3.63	9
Fielding Pct:	.978	.978	6
Runs Scored:	666		5
Runs Allowed:	704		8(tie)

Starting Lineup

Bob Tillman, c
Dick Stuart, 1b
Chuck Schilling, 2b
Frank Malzone, 3b
Ed Bressoud, ss
Carl Yastrzemski, lf
Gary Geiger, cf
Lu Clinton, rf
Roman Mejias, cf
Russ Nixon, c
Felix Mantilla, ss

Pitchers

Bill Monbouquette, sp
Earl Wilson, sp
Dave Morehead, sp
Bob Heffner, sp
Dick Radatz, rp
Jack Lamabe, rp
Arnold Earley, rp

Attendance

942,642 (fourth in AL)

Club Leaders

Batting Avg: Yastrzemski	.321
On-Base Pct: Yastrzemski	.419
Slugging Pct: Stuart	.521
Home Runs: Stuart	42
RBI: Stuart	118
Runs: Yastrzemski	91
Stolen Bases: Geiger	9
Wins: Monbouquette	20
Strikeouts: Monbouquette	174
ERA: Wilson	3.76
Saves: Radatz	25

MARCH 15   Roman Mejias is reunited with his family after a separation of 14 months. With the help of the Red Sox front office, Mejias's family, including his wife, daughter, son, and two sisters, were able to leave Fidel Castro's Cuba for the United States.

APRIL 9   In the season opener, the Red Sox lose 4–1 in Los Angeles. Carl Yastrzemski scored the only Boston run scored on a homer.

             Yastrzemski won the first of his three career batting titles in 1963 with an average of .321. He also led the league in hits (183), walks (95), on-base percentage (.418), and doubles (40), along with 91 runs, 14 homers, and 68 RBIs.

APRIL 11   Senators catcher Don Leppert hits three homers against the Red Sox during an 8–0 Washington win at D.C. Stadium.

APRIL 13   Dave Morehead pitches a shutout in his major league debut to beat the Senators 3–0 in Washington. He struck out 10 batters.

             Morehead was only twenty years old when he reached the majors. In his first four starts, he had a 3–0 record and a 1.13 ERA in 32 innings. Despite the excellent beginning, he went only 10–13 as a rookie and 40–64 during his career, which included a no-hitter in 1965.

APRIL 16   In the home opener, the Red Sox win 6–1 before 26,161. In his first game with the Sox at Fenway Park, Dick Stuart hit a homer and drove in four runs.

             Stuart hit 42 homers and led the AL in RBIs with 118 in 1963.

APRIL 19   Ike Delock pitches a two-hitter to defeat the Tigers 5–1 in the second game of a Patriots' Day doubleheader at Fenway Park. The only Detroit hits were a homer by Al Kaline in the first inning and a single by Rocky Colavito in the seventh. The Sox also won the first game, 3–1.

APRIL 20   After the Tigers score two runs in the top of the fifteenth, the Red Sox roar back with three in their half to win 4–3 at Fenway Park. The game-winning rally started with two out. Frank Malzone, pinch hitter Billy Gardner, and Chuck Schilling each singled to score one run, and Roman Mejias smacked a two-run double.

APRIL 21   Dick Stuart launches his weekly television program *Stuart on Sports* on WBZ.

MAY 1   Seven days after the Celtics win their fifth consecutive NBA Championship in a six-game series against the Los Angeles Lakers, the Red Sox maul the Twins 14–5 in Minnesota.

MAY 12   In just his fourth major league game, Dave Morehead pitches a one-hitter to beat the Senators 4–1 in the second game of a doubleheader at Fenway Park. The only Washington hit was a homer by Chuck Hinton with two out in the first inning. The Senators won the opener 3–2 in 14 innings.

MAY 13   Bob Tillman hits a titanic homer at Fenway Park that strikes the center field wall over the bleachers, about three feet from the top, during an 8–5 win over the Senators.

MAY 15	Dick Stuart drives in seven runs during a doubleheader against the Angels at Fenway Park won by the Red Sox 9–3 and 7–3. Stuart hit a grand slam off Bo Belinsky in the third inning of the opener.
MAY 16	Earl Wilson pitches a two-hitter to defeat the Angels 3–0 at Fenway Park. The only Los Angeles hits were singles by Lee Thomas in the second inning and Bob Rodgers in the fifth.

The win put the Red Sox in first place with an 18–11 record. The stay on the top of the AL standings lasted four days.

MAY 19	Frank Malzone collects four hits, including two homers, in four at-bats along with five RBIs during a 7–3 triumph over the Athletics in the first game of a doubleheader at Fenway Park. Kansas City won the second tilt, 9–7.

Malzone hit .291 with 15 homers in 1963.

MAY 24	Bill Monbouquette strikes out 12 batters during a 5–2 win over the Tigers in Detroit.
JUNE 2	The Red Sox thump the White Sox 11–9 in the first game of a doubleheader at Comiskey Park. The White Sox won the second contest, 10–0.
JUNE 9	Chuck Schilling drives in the tying and winning runs during a 14-inning, 3–2 win over the Orioles in Baltimore. Schilling tied the score 2–2 with a single in the ninth and drove in the winner with another single in the fourteenth.
JUNE 11	Frank Malzone and Dick Stuart smash homers in the fifteenth inning to beat the Tigers 7–3 in Detroit. Dick Radatz pitched 8⅔ innings of shutout relief, striking out 11.

Radatz pitched 33 consecutive scoreless innings in May and June. He had another sensational season in 1963. Radatz had a 15–6 record and 25 saves. His ERA was 1.97 and he struck out 162 batters in 132⅓ innings over 66 games.

JUNE 14	Dick Stuart hits a home run estimated at 500 feet into the center field bleachers at Fenway Park, the highlight of a 5–1 win over the Orioles. On the same day, the Red Sox sold Mike Fornieles to the Twins.

Stuart hit homers in five consecutive games from June 11 through 16.

JUNE 16	Carl Yastrzemski scores five times during a 12–5 win over the Orioles in the second game of a doubleheader at Fenway Park. The Sox also won the first game, 8–1.
JUNE 21	The Red Sox defeat the Yankees 7–4 at Fenway Park to pull to within two games of first place.

The win gave them a record of 35–26 on the season and caused a mild case of pennant fever in New England. The Yankees provided the cure by winning the last three games of the four-game series. The Red Sox played .500 ball for about a month before losing 43 of their last 68 games. The Sox won 76 games in 1963. It would be the third straight season that the club won exactly 76 contests.

JUNE 23	Defensively challenged Dick Stuart ties a major league record with three assists in an inning, although the Red Sox lose 8–0 to the Yankees at Fenway Park. Pitcher Bob Heffner made all three putouts.
JUNE 24	A two-run, two-out, walk-off homer by Gary Geiger beats the Indians 7–5 at Fenway Park.
JUNE 27	Indians right fielder Al Luplow makes a spectacular catch to help defeat the Red Sox 6–4 in the second game of a doubleheader at Fenway Park. With Cleveland leading 6–3 in the eighth inning and two Boston runners on base, Dick Williams hit a drive to right. Running at full speed, Luplow headed toward the five-foot-high barrier that fronted the bullpen. He reached over the fence and backhanded the ball just as his knees hit the wall. Luplow flipped over the fence head-first and hung on for the out. The Red Sox won the first game, 6–5.
JULY 2	Dave Morehead pitches a two-hitter for a 6–1 win over the Indians at Municipal Stadium. The only Cleveland hits were a single by Fred Whitfield in the seventh inning and a homer by John Romano in the ninth.
JULY 10	Dick Stuart hits a three-run homer in the tenth that beats the Twins 7–4 in Minnesota. It was Stuart's second homer of the game.
JULY 14	Lu Clinton hits a grand slam in the third inning off Paul Foytack, but the Red Sox lose 14–8 to the Angels in the first game of a doubleheader in Los Angeles. The Red Sox won the second contest, 5–0.
JULY 21	Bob Tillman homers in the tenth inning to beat the White Sox 3–2 in Chicago. Dick Stuart hit a two-run single in the ninth to tie the game.
JULY 23	The Red Sox sign Bob Turley after his release by the Angels.
AUGUST 2	Earl Wilson pitches a shutout and hits a three-run homer to defeat the Senators 5–0 in Washington.
AUGUST 14	Dick Stuart collects six hits and drives in six runs as the Sox claim both ends of a doubleheader, 14–7 and 5–4, over the Yankees at Fenway Park. The Sox scored seven runs in the fifth inning of the first game.
AUGUST 19	Dick Stuart hits a freak inside-the-park homer in the second inning of an 8–3 loss to the Indians at Fenway Park. The drive hit a ledge on the scoreboard in left-center field and bounced crazily into the left field corner. In the ninth, Stuart hit a ball over the screen atop the Green Monster.
AUGUST 22	Ed Bressoud hits a grand slam in the seventh inning off Taylor Phillips during an 11–2 win over the White Sox at Fenway Park.

Bressoud hit .260 with 20 homers for the Red Sox in 1963.

AUGUST 25	Bob Heffner strikes out 12 batters in 11 innings, but the Red Sox lose 2–1 in 15 innings to the Indians in the second game of a doubleheader in Cleveland. Boston pitchers fanned 27 batters in the two games. Bill Monbouquette recorded 11

strikeouts in the opener, won by the Sox 8–3, and Dick Radatz struck out four in relief of Heffner.

SEPTEMBER 14   Two weeks after Martin Luther King Jr.'s "I Have a Dream" speech in Washington, Bill Monbouquette picks up his 20th victory of the season with a 6–4 decision over the Athletics in Kansas City.

Monbouquette had a 20–10 record and a 3.81 ERA in 1963.

SEPTEMBER 21   Roman Mejias drives in seven runs on two homers and a single during an 11–2 win over the Twins in the second game of a doubleheader at Fenway Park. Harmon Killebrew hit four homers during the twin bill, three of them in a 13–4 Minnesota victory in the opener. Rico Petrocelli made his major league debut in the first game and had a double in four at-bats.

Louis Requena/Major League Baseball/Getty Images

Appearing in just one game in '63 and not appearing again until '65, shortstop Rico Petrocelli would become a Sox mainstay for more than ten years, bringing surprising power to the middle infield.

SEPTEMBER 23   Only 674 fans attend a 5–1 win over the Athletics at Fenway Park.

OCTOBER 11   The Patriots play at Fenway Park for the first time and defeat the Oakland Raiders
                20–14 before 26,494 on a Friday night.

                *Patriots owner Bill Sullivan chaired a stadium commission in 1963 that drew
                interest from the Red Sox. Sullivan wanted to build a 60,000-seat multipurpose
                stadium with a retractable roof in the South Station area. The plan also included
                a hotel and a garage. The fanciful design coincided with the "New Boston" eco-
                nomic development scheme proposed by the city, which was trying to shake itself
                out of economic doldrums through a series of redevelopment plans such as the
                Prudential Center and the Government Center complex surrounding the new City
                Hall. Many other cities had replaced, or were in the process of replacing, old, inti-
                mate ballparks with multipurpose stadiums.*

                *Tom Yawkey believed that Fenway Park was too small, too old, too expen-
                sive to maintain, too difficult to reach by car, and had insufficient parking.
                Yawkey wanted the Red Sox to play in a stadium similar to those built in
                Atlanta, St. Louis, Cincinnati, Pittsburgh, and Philadelphia, with a capacity of
                50,000–60,000 and artificial turf. Like other owners of big-league teams,
                Yawkey wanted the government to foot the bill for any new stadium project.
                City, county, and state officials had other priorities, however, and the stadium
                proposal became mired in Boston and Massachusetts politics. In June 1967,
                Yawkey warned that the Red Sox might leave Boston if a stadium wasn't built.
                "While other cities build stadiums, Boston talks," Yawkey said. "I do not know
                how long I can continue to take the losses which I think are inescapable so long
                as the Red Sox must play in Fenway Park. If this city is to remain a major
                sports center, a new stadium must be built somewhere in the Boston vicinity.
                Otherwise it appears inevitable the city will lose both the Red Sox and the
                Patriots." Yawkey added that in five years he doubted the club would still be
                playing in Fenway.*

                *The stadium proposal had the backing of Governor John Volpe, and funding
                was approved in the Massachusetts House of Representatives, but in July 1968
                the Massachusetts Senate killed two stadium bills, putting an end to hopes for a
                new stadium in Greater Boston. By that time, crowds were flocking to Fenway
                Park as the Sox were winning again, and Yawkey put the notion of building a
                new ballpark behind him. He began to realize that the attendance problems the
                Red Sox experienced during the early 1960s were due to an inadequate ball
                club, not an inadequate facility.*

DECEMBER 2   Ten days after the assassination of President John Kennedy in Dallas, the Red Sox
                draft Reggie Smith from the Twins organization.

                *At the time, Smith was an eighteen-year-old shortstop who had one year of pro-
                fessional experience at the rookie classification in the Appalachian League,
                where he hit .257 and made 41 errors in 65 games. Smith was converted to the
                outfield by the Red Sox and reached the majors in 1966.*

1964   B

Season in a Sentence

The arrival of Tony Conigliaro gives some hope to fans after a power-laden, lead-footed club (186 homers, 18 stolen bases) that can't pitch (4.50 ERA) or win on the road (27–54) finishes in eight place.

Finish • Won • Lost • Pct • GB

Eighth   72   90   .444   27.0

Managers

Johnny Pesky (70–90)
Billy Herman (2–0)

Stats

Stats	Red Sox	AL	Rank
Batting Avg:	.258	.247	1
On-Base Pct:	.324	.317	2
Slugging Pct:	.416	.382	2
Home Runs:	186		2
Stolen Bases:	18		10
ERA:	4.50	3.83	9
Fielding Pct:	.977	.980	8
Runs Scored:	688		5
Runs Allowed:	793		9

Starting Lineup

Bob Tillman, c
Dick Stuart, 1b
Felix Mantilla, 2b-lf
Frank Malzone, 3b
Ed Bressoud, ss
Tony Conigliaro, lf
Carl Yastrzemski, cf
Lee Thomas, rf
Dalton Jones, 2b
Chuck Schilling, 2b
Russ Nixon, c

Pitchers

Bill Monbouquette, sp
Earl Wilson, sp
Dave Morehead, sp
Jack Lamabe, sp-rp
Dick Radatz, rp
Bob Heffner, rp

Attendance

883,278 (fifth in AL)

Club Leaders

Batting Avg:	Bressoud	.293
On-Base Pct:	Yastrzemski	.374
Slugging Pct:	Mantilla	.553
Home Runs:	Stuart	3
RBI:	Stuart	114
Runs:	Bressoud	86
Stolen Bases:	Jones	6
	Yastrzemski	6
Wins:	Radatz	16
Strikeouts:	Radatz	181
ERA:	Radatz	2.29
Saves:	Radatz	29

APRIL 14   The scheduled season opener between the Red Sox and Yankees in New York is rained out. The April 15 contest was also postponed, although the Red Sox scheduled a workout after the weather cleared. Tony Conigliaro, who had yet to play in his first regular-season game, overslept and arrived at Yankee Stadium 45 minutes late. Johnny Pesky fined him $100.

APRIL 16   In the midst of Beatlemania, with the Fab Four holding the top five spots on the Billboard singles chart, the Red Sox defeat the Yankees 4–3 in 11 innings in New York. The winning run was scored on a triple by Bob Tillman, his fourth hit of the game, and a wild pitch by Whitey Ford. Dick Radatz was the winning pitcher in $3\frac{2}{3}$ innings of relief. Tony Conigliaro made his major league debut and singled in five at-bats. In his first plate appearance, he nearly grounded into an around-the-horn triple play, narrowly beating the throw to first base. Conigliaro impetuously accused Ford of throwing a spitter.

APRIL 17   In the first game of the season at Fenway Park, the Red Sox defeat the White Sox 4–1 before 20,213. On the first pitch of his first at-bat at Fenway, Tony Conigliaro hit a home run onto Lansdowne Street. He was just three months past his 19th birthday with one year of experience in the minors at the Class A level. Frank Malzone also clubbed a homer for the Sox. Jack Lamabe pitched a complete game, his first as a major leaguer.

The proceeds of the game went to the presidential library fund in the memory of John Kennedy, who was murdered in Dallas on November 22 the previous year. His brother Robert, then attorney general, threw out the first pitch. Others in attendance included Senator Edward Kennedy, sisters Jean Smith and Patricia Lawford, Massachusetts Governor Endicott Peabody, Mayor John Collins, Stan Musial, then the head of the national physical fitness program, actor Fredric March, stage star Carol Channing, TV comedian Frank Fontaine, and former boxing champions Jack Dempsey and Gene Tunney. The gate receipts totaled $36,818. The library opened in 1979 on Columbia Point after plans to build it in Cambridge failed to materialize.

APRIL 28   Two days after the Celtics win their sixth NBA title in a row in a five-game series against the San Francisco Warriors, Dick Stuart hits a walk-off grand slam in the twelfth inning off Dick Hall to beat the Orioles 6–4 at Fenway Park. The Sox scored two runs in the ninth, one on a Stuart double off Robin Roberts, to tie the score, 2–2. Baltimore took a 4–2 lead with two tallies in the top of the twelfth.

Stuart hit 33 homers and drove in 114 runs in 1964 and hit .279.

MAY 3   Carl Yastrzemski drives in six runs, four on a grand slam, during an 11–7 win over the Tigers at Fenway Park. Yastrzemski's slam came in a six-run fifth inning and broke a 7–7 tie. The pitcher was Julio Navarro.

Yastrzemski hit .289 with 15 homers in 1964.

MAY 8   The Red Sox score seven runs in the seventh inning and defeat the Senators 9–3 in Washington.

MAY 9   Ed Bressoud extends his hitting streak to 20 games, but the Red Sox lose 5–4 in 10 innings to the Senators in Washington.

Bressoud hit .293 with 15 homers and 41 doubles in 1964.

MAY 12   Gary Geiger retires at the age of twenty-seven. He had an operation for bleeding ulcers on February 17, and recovery was slow. Geiger returned in 1965, but his days as a regular were over, and he was never again more than a pinch hitter and spare outfielder.

MAY 16   Dick Radatz hits a walk-off single in the tenth inning to beat the Twins 6–5 at Fenway Park.

Radatz had his third sensational year in a row as a reliever in 1964. He had a 16–9 record, 29 saves, and a 2.29 ERA. Radatz struck out 181 batters over 157 innings over 79 games. From 1962 through 1964, Radatz made 207 relief appearances, hurled 414 innings, struck out 487 batters, and had an ERA of 2.17. The workload took a toll, however, and Radatz was never again effective after 1964. Over the remainder of his career, which ended in 1969, Radatz had an ERA of 4.54.

MAY 19   Shut out for eight innings, the Red Sox suddenly explode for four runs in the ninth inning and defeat the Angels 4–3 at Fenway Park. All four runs were scored with two out. Roman Mejias was hit by a pitch with the bases loaded to score the first run, and pinch hitter Dalton Jones cleared the bases with a three-run double.

MAY 23   A two-run, walk-off homer by Felix Mantilla in the ninth inning beats the Athletics 5–4 at Fenway Park.

Mantilla didn't have a starting job when the season started, but he ended with 30 homers and a .289 batting average. He played 45 games at second base, 36 in left field, eight in right, seven at third, six at shortstop, and five in center field.

MAY 24   Dick Stuart hits a grand slam off Moe Drabowsky during a 6–2 win over the Athletics in the first game of a doubleheader at Fenway Park. Stuart's slam was struck following an intentional walk to Carl Yastrzemski that loaded the bases during a five-run eighth inning and broke a 2–2 tie. In the second tilt, Dick Radatz struck out the last five batters he faced to save a 3–1 victory.

Stuart hit seven homers in nine games from May 24 through June 1.

JUNE 3   Tony Conigliaro hits a grand slam off Dan Osinski in the fifth inning, but the Red Sox lose 9–8 to the Angels in the second game of a doubleheader in Los Angeles. The Angels also won the first game, 2–0.

At the age of 19 years and 148 days, Conigliaro became the youngest major leaguer ever to hit a grand slam. The talented, enduring Conigliaro immediately became a fan favorite in Boston. In addition, he was a local product who grew up in East Boston and the towns of Revere, Lynn, and Swampscott just north of the city. As a rookie, Conigliaro was limited to 111 games because of injury but hit 24 homers and batted .290. The 24 homers are the most ever by a player before his 20th birthday. The second-highest number of home runs struck by a teenager is 19, by Mel Ott, who hit one as an eighteen-year-old in 1927 and 18 more as a nineteen-year-old in 1928.

JUNE 4   The Red Sox trade Lu Clinton to the Angels for Lee Thomas.

JUNE 5   Dick Stuart hits his third grand slam of the season during a nine-run second inning to spark a 14–7 win over the Athletics in Kansas City. Stuart hit the slam off Aurelio Monteagudo following an intentional walk to Carl Yastrzemski. It was the second time in two weeks that Athletics manager Ed Lopat issued a free pass to Yastrzemski to load the bases only to have Stuart hit a home run. Lee Thomas made his debut with the Sox during the game and hit a home run.

In his first three games with the Sox, Thomas had eight hits, including two homers, in 11 at-bats.

JUNE 10   Homers by Tony Conigliaro and Dick Williams in the tenth inning beat the Yankees 7–6 in the first game of a doubleheader at Fenway Park. The Yankees scored once in the top of the inning to take a 6–5 lead. Williams entered the game at first base in the eighth inning after Dick Stuart was removed for a pinch runner. In the second game, a boneheaded play by Sox catcher Russ Nixon contributed to a 10–6 loss.

With the Yanks leading 7–6 in the seventh and two outs, New York pitcher Pete Mikkelsen swung and missed for a third strike on a pitch in the dirt. Nixon flipped the ball to Mikkelsen and headed for the dugout followed by his teammates. The ball was in play, however, since Nixon didn't catch the third strike cleanly. After prodding by teammates, Mikkelsen dropped the ball and ran toward first base, where he hesitated briefly before heading for second. He reached second safely before the Red Sox realized their error. Mikkelsen scored on a single by Tony Kubek.

JUNE 12   Dave Morehead strikes out 12 batters during a 7–3 win over the Orioles at Fenway Park.

JUNE 26   A two-run, two-out, pinch-hit, walk-off homer by Russ Nixon off Tommy John beats the Indians 3–2 at Fenway Park.

             The homer was Nixon's only one in 1964. He didn't hit another until he played for the Twins in 1967.

JULY 4   Two days after the passage of the Civil Rights Act, prohibiting racial discrimination in employment and places of public accommodation, the Red Sox score nine runs in the first inning and crush the Angels 13–5 at Fenway Park. A month after being traded to the Angels by the Red Sox, Lee Thomas hit a grand slam off Ken McBride.

JULY 7   Dick Radatz allows four runs in the ninth, the last three a two-out, walk-off homer to Johnny Callison of the Phillies, which gives the National League a 7–4 victory in the All-Star Game at Shea Stadium in New York. Radatz entered the game in the seventh inning and retired the National League in order in the seventh and eighth, four on strikeouts, before folding in the ninth.

JULY 10   A two-run, pinch-hit homer by Dalton Jones in the ninth inning beats the Tigers 7–6 in the first game of a doubleheader in Detroit. The Tigers won the second game, 8–3.

JULY 15   Dick Stuart drives in six runs on a pair of three-run homers during an 11–2 win over the White Sox at Fenway Park.

JULY 18   Bob Tillman drives in six runs with two homers, one of them with the bases loaded in the sixth inning off Steve Ridzik during a 12–6 win over the Senators at Fenway Park.

             After batting .225 in 1963, Tillman had a breakout year in 1964 with 17 homers and a .278 average at the age of twenty-seven. In 1965, Tillman hit only .215 and lost his job as a starting catcher.

JULY 19   Pitching in relief in both ends of a doubleheader against the Senators at Fenway Park, Dick Lamabe is both the winning and losing pitcher. The Red Sox won the first game 11–10 and lost the second 5–4 in 10 innings.

JULY 26   Tony Conigliaro breaks his arm after being hit by a pitch from Pedro Ramos of the Indians in the fifth inning of the second game of a doubleheader in Cleveland, won by the Red Sox, 3–1. In the first game of the twin bill, Tony hit his 20th homer of the season during a 6–1 Sox victory. When he arrived at the park, he learned he was being fined $250 by Johnny Pesky for missing the midnight curfew.

Conigliaro liked to take his stance as close to the plate as the rules permitted. He suffered two broken bones in 1964 as a result of being hit by pitches. In May 1964, Conigliaro was hit by Moe Drabowsky and suffered a hairline fracture of the hand and was out 10 days. After being plunked by Ramos, Conigliaro missed six weeks of action. Newspapers at the time reported that Conigliaro also suffered a broken thumb in April 1963 when hit by a pitch thrown by his uncle Vinnie Martelli. In fact, Conigliaro broke the thumb in a fight. The day before he was to leave on his first minor league assignment, he was talking to a girl who was dating the captain of the football team. The other teen began swearing at him, and Conigliaro punched him in the face and broke his thumb in the process. His father concocted the story that the injury happened during batting practice, and Uncle Vinnie took the rap. The ruse was cruelly ironic, however, because in 39 months between May 1964 and August 1967, Conigliaro suffered five broken bones from being hit by pitches. The fifth one nearly killed him (see August 18, 1967).

AUGUST 21   Bob Tillman hits a grand slam in the eighth off Stan Williams during a 7–0 win over the Yankees at Fenway Park.

The Red Sox ended July with a record of 52–52, then lost 38 of their last 58 games.

SEPTEMBER 6   Bill Monbouquette pitches a one-hitter but loses 2–1 to the Twins in Minnesota. In the sixth inning, with the Red Sox leading 1–0, Rich Rollins reached on an error and scored on a Zoilo Versailles homer.

SEPTEMBER 7   Dave Morehead, Jay Ritchie, and Dick Radatz combine on an unusual two-hitter as the Red Sox lose 4–1 to the Angels in the first game of a doubleheader in Los Angeles. Morehead didn't allow a hit in 2⅔ innings but walked seven batters and gave up two runs. Ritchie followed with 4⅓ hitless innings of relief. Radatz gave up two runs and two hits in the eighth. Combined with the contest against the Twins the previous day, Sox pitchers allowed only three hits in consecutive games and lost both. The Angels also won the nightcap of the twin bill, 4–3 in 11 innings.

SEPTEMBER 9   Carl Yastrzemski hits a two-run homer in the tenth inning to beat the Indians 6–5 in Cleveland.

SEPTEMBER 15   Red Sox rookie pitcher Ed Connolly strikes out 12 batters and pitches a two-hitter to beat the Athletics 8–0 at Fenway Park. The only Kansas City hits were a double by Bert Campaneris in the sixth inning and a single by Tommie Reynolds in the seventh.

Connolly entered the game with a record of 2–10. He finished his career with four wins and 11 losses. The September 15, 1964, contest was Connolly's only major league shutout and complete game.

SEPTEMBER 21   The Red Sox score three runs in the ninth inning to beat the Senators 3–0 in Washington.

OCTOBER 1   Four days after the release of the Warren Commission, which declared that Lee Harvey Oswald acted alone in the assassination of John Kennedy, the smallest crowd in the history of Fenway Park, 306, watches the Red Sox defeat the Indians, 4–2.

OCTOBER 2   With two games left in the season, fifty-five-year-old Billy Herman replaces Johnny Pesky as manager of the Red Sox.

Herman had a Hall of Fame career as a second baseman, mostly with the Cubs and Dodgers, from 1931 through 1947. He previously managed the Pirates in 1947 to a 61–92 record. Herman came to the Red Sox as a coach in 1960 under Billy Jurges, his double-play partner with the Cubs during the 1930s. Herman vowed he would restore discipline to the Red Sox, but Boston lost 100 games in 1965. The Sox fired him late in the 1966 campaign. Pesky went to the Pirates as a coach in 1965. He was a broadcaster with the Red Sox from 1969 through 1974 and a coach from 1975 through 1984. Pesky never managed another big-league club.

OCTOBER 3   In Billy Herman's first game as manager of the Red Sox, Bill Monbouquette shuts out the Senators for the fourth time in 1964, winning 7–0 at Fenway Park. Dick Stuart collected five hits, including a double, in five at-bats.

OCTOBER 4   In the final game of the season, the Red Sox score seven runs in the first inning and win 14–8 over the Senators at Fenway Park.

NOVEMBER 29 Four weeks after Lyndon Johnson wins the presidential election against Barry Goldwater, the Red Sox trade Dick Stuart to the Phillies for Dennis Bennett.

Trading the self-centered Stuart was one of the first steps in changing the team's attitude. With an excellent young first baseman in Tony Horton, plus Lee Thomas on the big-league squad, the Red Sox had no qualms about trading Stuart even though he had hit 75 homers over the previous two seasons. The total was the highest by any Red Sox player over a two-year period between Jimmie Foxx (85 in 1938–39) and Carl Yastrzemski (80 in 1969–70).

Bennett had only 30 big-league wins when he was acquired by the Red Sox. Handicapped by a bad shoulder, Bennett was just 12–13 for Boston over three seasons from 1965 through 1967, lived in an apartment over the Playboy Club, and frightened teammates by carrying around a suitcase full of handguns. During spring training at Scottsdale in 1965, Bennett fired half a dozen rounds from two pistols at the door of the team's hotel. On another occasion, roommate Lee Thomas asked him to turn out the lights. Bennett did so by shooting the light bulb with a gun. Later, he shot six rounds over the head of Boston sportswriter Will McDonough with a .38 after objecting to one of McDonough's stories. Bennett's daredevil activities also hampered his growth as a pitcher. He participated in bareback bronco events on the rodeo circuit and was a forest firefighter in California. Fortunately, Stuart wasn't much better for the Phillies and had only one more year as a regular after leaving Boston. He hit 28 homers in Philadelphia in 1965 but batted only .234.

1965   B

Season in a Sentence

The Red Sox lose 100 games for the only time since 1932 and draw fewer fans than any season since 1945.

Finish • Won • Lost • Pct • GB

Ninth   62   100   .383   40.0

Manager

Billy Herman

Stats   Red Sox • AL • Rank

Stats	Red Sox	AL	Rank
Batting Avg:	.251	.242	2
On-Base Pct:	.329	.314	1
Slugging Pct:	.400	.369	1
Home Runs:	165		1
Stolen Bases:	47		8
ERA:	4.24	3.46	10
Fielding Pct:	.974	.978	9
Runs Scored:	669		3
Runs Allowed:	791		10

Starting Lineup

Bill Tillman, c
Lee Thomas, 1b
Felix Mantilla, 2b
Frank Malzone, 3b
Rico Petrocelli, ss
Carl Yastrzemski, lf
Lenny Green, cf
Tony Conigliaro, rf
Dalton Jones, 3b
Jim Gosger, cf
Ed Bressoud, ss
Chuck Schilling, 2b
Tony Horton, 1b

Pitchers

Earl Wilson, sp
Bill Monbouquette, sp
Dave Morehead, sp
Jim Lonborg, sp
Dennis Bennett, sp-rp
Dick Radatz, rp
Arnold Earley, rp
Jay Ritchie, rp

Attendance

652,201 (seventh in AL)

Club Leaders

Batting Avg:	Yastrzemski	.312
On-Base Pct:	Yastrzemski	.395
Slugging Pct:	Yastrzemski	.536
Home Runs:	Conigliaro	32
RBI:	Mantilla	92
Runs:	Conigliaro	82
Stolen Bases:	Green	8
	Jones	8
Wins:	Wilson	13
Strikeouts:	Wilson	164
ERA:	Monbouquette	3.70
Saves:	Radatz	22

FEBRUARY 15   With ambitions of moonlighting as a rock 'n' roll singer, Tony Conigliaro signs a recording contract with RCA Victor. In 1964, Conigliaro recorded an independently produced single that sold 15,000 copies in New England.

APRIL 12   Five weeks after the first US official combat troops arrive in Vietnam, the Red Sox beat the Senators 7–2 in Washington in the season opener with Lyndon Johnson on hand to throw out the ceremonial first pitch. The Sox hit five homers. Lenny Green hit two homers in his first game as a member of the Red Sox. Lee Thomas, Felix Mantilla, and Tony Conigliaro added one each. Bill Monbouquette pitched a complete game.

Mel Parnell joined the Red Sox radio and TV team in 1965, broadcasting alongside Curt Gowdy and Ned Martin. Parnell replaced Art Gleeson.

APRIL 17   The Red Sox overcome five Oriole homers to win 12–9 in the first game of the season at Fenway Park before 19,018. The Sox were down 6–2 in the third inning before mounting the comeback, breaking an 8–8 tie with four runs in the eighth. Carl Yastrzemski hit a home run.

Yastrzemski led the league in doubles in 1965 with 45, batted .312, and hit 20 homers.

APRIL 20   Felix Mantilla drives in all five Boston runs in a 5–2 win over the Senators at Fenway Park. He hit a grand slam in the first inning off Buster Narum in the first inning and a run-scoring single in the third.

Mantilla batted .275 with 18 home runs and 92 RBIs in 1965.

APRIL 24   Lee Thomas hits a three-run homer in the twelfth inning to break a 4–4 tie, providing the winning run in a 7–5 victory over the Orioles in Baltimore.

Thomas hit .271 with 22 homers in 1965.

MAY 1   Six days after the Celtics win their seventh consecutive NBA title in a five-game series against the Lakers, Chuck Schilling hits a pinch-homer for the second game in a row, although the Red Sox still lose 9–8 against the Tigers in Detroit. The previous day, Schilling hit a pinch-homer against the Tigers in a 4–1 defeat.

MAY 2   In just his second major league game, Mike Ryan hits two homers as the Red Sox defeat the Tigers 10–3 in the second game of a doubleheader in Detroit. The Sox also won the first game, 2–1.

Ryan made his major league debut on October 3, 1964. He lasted four seasons with the Red Sox and 11 in the majors because of his excellent defensive skills. He batted only .193 and hit 28 homers in 1,920 big-league at-bats.

MAY 8   The Red Sox outslug the Indians 15–8 at Fenway Park.

MAY 14   Carl Yastrzemski hits for the cycle, including two homers, accounting for 14 total bases and five RBIs, but the Red Sox lose 12–8 to the Tigers at Fenway Park.

MAY 25   At the age of 18 years and 289 days, Gerry Moses becomes the youngest player in Red Sox history to hit a home run. It came off Mudcat Grant during a 17–5 loss to the Twins, and was also Moses's first major league hit. A catcher, Moses didn't collect his second hit and second homer until 1968. He finished his big-league career in 1975 with 25 homers.

On May 30, the Red Sox had a record of 21–20. Over the remainder of the 1965 season, the Sox were 41–80, including a stretch of 39 losses in 51 games from May 31 through July 23.

JUNE 5   Dick Radatz hits a two-run homer in the eleventh inning to beat the Athletics 5–3 in Kansas City. He also pitched five shutout innings, striking out eight batters.

The homer was the only one of Radatz's major league career in 145 at-bats.

JUNE 8   In the first amateur free-agent draft in baseball history, the Red Sox select Tony Conigliaro's younger brother Billy, an outfielder who had just graduated from Swampscott High School in Swampscott, Massachusetts, just north of Boston.

Billy played for the Red Sox from 1969 through 1971 and had a five-year big-league career in which he batted .256 with 40 homers. Other players drafted and signed by the Red Sox in 1965 included Ken Poulsen (third round), Amos Otis (fifth round), and Ray Jarvis (18th round). Otis was by far the best of the bunch, but in a huge blunder the Red Sox failed to place him on the 40-man roster at the end of the 1966 season, and the Mets drafted him. He played 17 years in the majors, mostly with the Royals, and collected 2,020 hits and 193 homers.

JUNE 15   Tiger relievers combine to strike out 18 Red Sox batters in a 6–5 Detroit win at Tiger Stadium. Denny McLain took over for starter Dave Wickersham with one out in the first and struck out 14 batters in $6\frac{2}{3}$ innings, an American League record for a reliever in a nine-inning game. McLain fanned the first seven Red Sox he faced. Fred Gladding succeeded McLain and struck out four Sox hitters in two innings.

JUNE 20   Lenny Green's two homers account for the only two Red Sox runs in a 2–1 victory over the White Sox in Chicago. Green homered in the third and eighth innings. His eighth-inning homer, off Hoyt Wilhelm, broke a 1–1 tie.

JUNE 25   The Red Sox score seven runs in the fifth inning and beat the Senators 8–6 at Fenway Park.

A new addition to the Kenmore Square area in 1965 was the now-famous Citgo sign. The 60-foot double-sided sign, with its two miles of blinking red, white, and blue neon tubing, is visible over the left field wall at Fenway Park. An immediate pop-art hit, the sign inspired one filmmaker to create a short film called "Go Go Citgo" in which the sign did its off-and-on routine to music by the Monkees and Ravi Shankar. The sign was turned off during the energy crisis of the 1970s and came close to being torn down in 1982. It was saved by its fans, led by Arthur Krim, who was a Cambridge resident, college professor, and member of the Society for Commercial Archeology, which works to preserve urban and roadside Americana such as neon signs, diners, and gas stations. Eventually, the Oklahoma-based Citgo Corporation agreed to keep Kenmore Square's illuminated icon plugged in and maintained.

JULY 6   Dalton Jones collects five hits, including a double, in six at-bats during a 10–1 win over the Senators in the second game of a doubleheader at D.C. Stadium. Washington won the first game, 2–1.

JULY 27   Tony Conigliaro hits a grand slam in the third inning off Catfish Hunter, but the Red Sox lose 10–8 to the Athletics in the first game of a doubleheader at Municipal Stadium. Kansas City also won the first game, 7–3.

JULY 28   Tony Conigliaro gets hit on the hand by a pitch from Wes Stock of the Athletics during a 6–0 win at Fenway Park. Conigliaro suffered a hairline fracture, the third time in 14 months that he broke a hand or an arm as a result of being hit by a pitch. He was out of action for three weeks.

Despite missing 24 games, Conigliaro hit 32 homers in 1965 to lead the American League. At twenty, he is the youngest home-run champion in major league history.

JULY 30   A free-for-all erupts over a beanball battle in the eighth inning of a 9–2 loss to the Angels in Los Angeles. In the sixth, Red Sox hurler Dave Morehead hit Jose Cardenal, and in turn, the pitcher was plunked by Angels hurler Dean Chance. In the eighth, Morehead hit Jim Fregosi by a pitch and was relieved by Arnold Earley, who struck Bob Rodgers with his first delivery to the plate. Rodgers rushed the mound and grabbed Earley around the neck and pummeled him with short rights. Both benches emptied, and fights broke out all over the field. Many players suffered painful bruises, scrapes, and spike wounds.

AUGUST 10 The Red Sox explode for 12 runs in the fifth inning of the first game of a doubleheader against the Orioles. The Sox entered the big inning at Fenway Park trailing 4–2 and scored the dozen tallies on eight hits, four walks, two errors, and a wild pitch. The final score was 15–5. Baltimore won the second game, 12–4.

Before the twin bill, Bill Herman was stricken with appendicitis and rushed to the hospital for surgery. The Sox manager was away from the club for 11 days. Pete Runnels managed the club in Herman's absence.

AUGUST 21 The Red Sox outlast the Tigers 13–10 at Fenway Park.

AUGUST 24 Tony Conigliaro hits a grand slam in the first inning off Buster Narum to spark a 9–3 win over the Senators in the first game of a doubleheader at Fenway Park. It was the second time in 1965 that Narum gave up a grand slam to a Boston batter. Washington won the second game, 8–5.

AUGUST 25 The Red Sox hit five homers and Earl Wilson strikes out 13 batters during an 8–3 win over the Senators at Fenway Park. The five homers were struck by Carl Yastrzemski, Tony Conigliaro, Rico Petrocelli, Felix Mantilla, and Bob Tillman.

AUGUST 31 A three-run homer by Tony Horton in the tenth inning beats the Senators 8–5 in the second game of a doubleheader in Washington. Horton entered the game as a pinch hitter in the eighth inning. Russ Nixon tied a major league record by hitting three sacrifice flies. The Red Sox also won the opener, 4–0.

SEPTEMBER 4 Dave Morehead pitches the Red Sox to a 1–0 win over the Yankees in the first game of a doubleheader against the Yankees in New York. The lone run of the game was scored on a single by Rico Petrocelli in the eighth inning. The Sox completed the sweep with a 7–2 win in the nightcap.

SEPTEMBER 8 A two-run homer by Tony Horton in the tenth inning beats the Indians 5–3 in Cleveland.

SEPTEMBER 14 A walk-off homer by Carl Yastrzemski in the thirteenth inning defeats the Indians 5–4 at Fenway Park. Tony Horton's homer in the ninth tied the game, 4–4.

SEPTEMBER 16 Dave Morehead pitches a no-hitter to defeat the Indians 2–0 at Fenway Park. The only Cleveland base runner was Rocky Colavito, who walked leading off the second inning on a 3–2 pitch that was 12 inches outside the plate. Morehead struck out eight. He faced three pinch hitters in the ninth. Larry Brown was the first and belted a liner toward left field, but Sox shortstop Ed Bressoud leaped and speared it. Lu Clinton followed by lining hard to Jim Gosger in center field. With two out, Vic Davalillo swung at an 0–2 and hit a hopper toward the mound. Morehead tried to field the ball over his head, but it got away and landed about four feet behind him. He retrieved the ball, took a couple of steps toward first, stumbled momentarily, and then threw toward Lee Thomas at first base. The throw was aimed and too soft, but Thomas scooped it out of the dirt to retire Davalillo by a step. Paid attendance was only 1,247. Morehead was just 11 days past his 23rd birthday when he threw his no-hitter, but he had little additional success in the majors, with a record of 12–20 over the remainder of his career. He didn't pitch another complete game until 1967.

Just 45 minutes after the game, the Red Sox made the stunning announcement that Pinky Higgins had been fired as general manager. He was replaced by fifty-two-year-old Dick O'Connell. The Red Sox had stagnated under Higgins, who hadn't made a bold trade since acquiring Dick Stuart in November 1962. Higgins chose not to do anything rather than risk being wrong. He also resisted the racial integration of baseball, and in his position of authority in Boston, his obstinate, racist policies left the Red Sox at an incredible disadvantage. The only black or Latin players on the 1965 Red Sox were Earl Wilson, Lenny Green, and Felix Mantilla. On February 17, 1968, an intoxicated Higgins ran over and killed a black Louisiana state highway worker in Ruston, Louisiana, and injured three others. He was found guilty of negligent homicide and sentenced to four years of hard labor, but he was paroled after serving two months. He died of a heart attack in 1969, two days after being released from jail.

O'Connell had gone to work for Tom Yawkey in 1946 as business manager of the Lynn Red Sox of the old New England League. He worked his way up the ladder in the Red Sox front office as secretary, director of park operations, and business manager. Haywood Sullivan was hired to help O'Connell with player development. The Sox were a dissension-ridden team that drew only 652,201 fans in 1965 and lost 100 games amid rumors that the club might leave Boston. O'Connell set out immediately to completely overhaul the team, and in 1967, the Sox won the American League pennant and attracted 1,727,832 into Fenway Park.

SEPTEMBER 22   The Red Sox play the Angels at Dodger Stadium for the last time and lose 10–1 and 2–0 in a doubleheader.

The Angels moved to Anaheim in 1966. In anticipation of the move, the name of the club was changed from the Los Angeles Angels to California Angels on September 3, 1965.

SEPTEMBER 25   In a publicity stunt concocted by Athletics owner Charlie Finley, Satchel Paige pitches against the Red Sox in Kansas City. Paige was fifty-nine years old and hadn't appeared in a big-league game since 1953. He pitched three innings, allowing no runs and one hit, a double by Carl Yastrzemski in the first inning. The Red Sox won the game, 5–2.

SEPTEMBER 29   A day after drawing only 461 fans for a game against the Angels, the Red Sox attract 409 for another contest against the California club. The Sox won, 2–1.

OCTOBER 3   The Red Sox close the season by taking their 100th loss of 1965, dropping an 11–5 decision to the Yankees at Fenway Park.

OCTOBER 4   The Red Sox trade Bill Monbouquette to the Tigers for George Smith and George Thomas.

OCTOBER 15   The Red Sox purchase Jose Santiago from the Athletics.

Santiago was 12–4 for the pennant-winning Red Sox in 1967, including an 8–0 mark after the All-Star break, and he was 9–4 in 1968 before blowing out his arm.

NOVEMBER 24 After 11 seasons with the club, the Red Sox release Frank Malzone. Six days later, he signed a contract with the Angels.

NOVEMBER 28 The Red Sox name Haywood Sullivan as director of player personnel.

Sullivan was a Red Sox player from 1955 through 1960. He rose quickly through the Red Sox ranks, and by 1978 he was one of the three principal owners.

NOVEMBER 30 The Red Sox trade Ed Bressoud to the Mets for Joe Christopher.

DECEMBER 15 The Red Sox trade Lee Thomas, Arnold Earley, and Jay Ritchie to the Braves for Bob Sadowski and Dan Osinski.

1966   B

Season in a Sentence

The Red Sox finish in ninth place, their eighth losing season in a row, but an infusion of young talent gives fans hope for the future.

Finish • Won • Lost • Pct • GB

Ninth   72   90   .444   26.0

Managers

Billy Herman (64–82)
Pete Runnels (8–8)

Stats

Stats	Red Sox	AL	Rank
Batting Avg:	.240	.240	4
On-Base Pct:	.312	.308	4
Slugging Pct:	.376	.369	4
Home Runs:	145		5
Stolen Bases:	35		10
ERA:	3.92	3.44	10
Fielding Pct:	.975	.978	10
Runs Scored:	655		4
Runs Allowed:	73		110

Starting Lineup

Mike Ryan, c
George Scott, 1b
George Smith, 2b
Joe Foy, 3b
Rico Petrocelli, ss
Carl Yastrzemski, lf
Don Demeter, cf
Tony Conigliaro, rf
Dalton Jones, 2b
Bob Tillman, c
Jose Tartabull, cf
George Thomas, cf

Pitchers

Jose Santiago, sp
Jim Lonborg, sp-rp
Lee Stange, sp-rp
Earl Wilson, sp
John Wyatt, rp
Darrell Brandon, rp-sp
Don McMahon, rp
Dan Osinski, rp

Attendance

811,172 (eighth in AL)

Club Leaders

Batting Avg:	Yastrzemski	.278
On-Base Pct:	Yastrzemski	.368
Slugging Pct:	Conigliaro	.487
Home Runs:	Conigliaro	28
RBI:	Conigliaro	93
Runs:	Foy	97
Stolen Bases:	Tartabull	11
Wins:	Santiago	12
Strikeouts:	Lonborg	131
ERA:	Santiago	3.66
Saves:	Wyatt	8

FEBRUARY 26   Black pitcher Earl Wilson is refused service at two bars in Winter Haven, Florida, where the Red Sox trained for the first time in 1966 after eight seasons in Scottsdale, Arizona. Wilson went to one establishment with teammates Dave Morehead and Dennis Bennett, both white, and a friend of Bennett's. The four sat at the bar and Wilson was turned away. The four went to another bar and were stopped at the door. The Red Sox front office wanted to keep the incident out of the newspapers but the story broke, embarrassing the ball club. The Sox publicly expressed outrage and barred players from entering the two business that refused to serve Wilson.

APRIL 3   The Red Sox trade Felix Mantilla to the Astros for Eddie Kasko.

APRIL 6   The Red Sox trade Russ Nixon and Chuck Schilling to the Twins for Dick Stigman and Jose Calero.

APRIL 12   In the season opener, the Red Sox lose 5–4 to the Orioles in 13 innings before 12,386 at Fenway Park. The winning run scored on a balk by Jim Lonborg with the bases loaded. The Orioles tied the score 4–4 with a run in the ninth. Mike Ryan collected three hits, including a double.

The Red Sox lost their first five games in 1966.

APRIL 30   Two days after the Celtics win their eighth NBA championship in a row with a Game Seven win over the Lakers, the Angels overcome a 9–3 Red Sox lead at Fenway Park by exploding for 12 runs in the eighth inning. Rick Reichardt hit two home runs in the inning. The final score was 16–9.

Ken Coleman replaced Curt Gowdy in the Red Sox radio and TV booth. Gowdy went to NBC-TV to do the Game of the Week *on Saturday afternoons. Coleman, a Boston native, broadcast Indians and Browns games in Cleveland for 14 years.*

MAY 1   At Fenway Park, the Red Sox and Angels tie an American League record for most double plays in a doubleheader with 12. The Angels turned eight of them and won the first game 6–1 before the Sox took the nightcap, 9–1.

MAY 4   George Scott hits two homers and drives in five runs during a 7–0 win over the Tigers in Detroit.

MAY 6   George Scott hits two homers for the second game in a row, although the Red Sox lose 5–4 to the Twins in Minnesota.

Scott added another homer on May 7 during a 6–4 loss to the Twins, giving him five home runs in three consecutive games. A rookie first baseman in 1966, Scott had 10 homers in his first 79 big-league at-bats. He finished the season with 27 homers, 90 RBIs, and a .245 batting average. Scott was a third baseman in the minors and moved to first to make room for Joe Foy, another rookie, in 1966. Scott was six-foot-two and weighed between 210 and 250 pounds depending on the stage of his latest diet. Despite his bulk, he was nimble defensively and won eight Gold Gloves during his career.

MAY 8   The Red Sox break a 17-game losing streak against the Twins dating back to May 27, 1965, by sweeping a doubleheader 8–1 and 3–1 at Metropolitan Stadium. The Sox also broke a 17-game losing streak in Minnesota going back to May 3, 1964. Rico Petrocelli hit a grand slam in the seventh inning of the first game off Paul Cimino.

From July 13, 1963, through May 26, 1968, the Red Sox were 6–40 at Metropolitan Stadium.

MAY 13   The Red Sox play at Anaheim Stadium in Anaheim for the first time and lose 4–1 to the Angels.

With Pinky Higgins and his status quo policies from the front office, the Red Sox underwent a massive roster turnover for the first time as 25 players made their debut with the club.

MAY 17   Rico Petrocelli hits a grand slam in the fourth inning off Gene Brabender during an 8–6 loss to the Orioles in Baltimore.

MAY 18   Earl Wilson stars with his arm and his bat by pitching a 10-inning complete game and hits a tenth-inning homer to beat the Orioles 2–1 in Baltimore.

Wilson hit 35 homers during his career, 17 of them as a member of the Red Sox. Wilson holds the all-time Red Sox record for home runs by a pitcher. Wes Ferrell also hit 17 while playing for the club from 1934 through 1937, but one of them was as a pinch hitter. Babe Ruth hit 15 homers for the Sox in games in which he appeared as a pitcher.

MAY 20   Jose Santiago pitches a two-hitter to defeat the Athletics 3–0 at Fenway Park. The only Kansas City hits were singles by Dick Green in the third inning and Larry Stahl in the fourth. It was Santiago's first complete game and shutout.

MAY 29   Senators pitcher Phil Ortega fans seven Red Sox batters in a row during a 3–2 Washington win at D.C. Stadium.

MAY 31   Tony Conigliaro hits a homer off Joe Horlen in the second inning to beat the White Sox 1–0 in Chicago. Dick Stigman pitched the shutout.

The shutout was the only one that Stigman pitched as a member of the Red Sox. It was also his only complete game for the club. Stigman played for the Sox in the last of his seven years in the majors and had a record of 2–1 with a 5.44 ERA.

JUNE 2   The Red Sox trade Dick Radatz to the Indians for Don McMahon and Lee Stange.

JUNE 4   Jim Gosger's walk-off homer in the sixteenth inning beats the Yankees 6–3 at Fenway Park. He hit the homer at 11:53 PM to beat the curfew by six minutes. Boston city ordinances prohibited play from continuing past 11:59 PM on Saturday nights. Sox relievers Don McMahon, Dan Osinski, Jerry Stephenson, Lee Stange, Dick Stigman, and Ken Sanders combined to allow no runs and only one hit in 10 innings.

In June, Billy Herman was hit in the face by a thrown ball during batting practice. The Red Sox installed a screen in front of the Fenway Park dugouts to prevent similar accidents.

JUNE 7   With the fourth overall pick in the amateur draft, the Red Sox select left-handed pitcher Ken Brett of El Segundo High School in El Segundo, California.

                  Brett is best known as the older brother of George, but he had a fine 14-season career in his own right. Ken reached the majors in 1967 as a nineteen-year-old and appeared in the World Series that season, becoming the youngest pitcher ever in the history of the Fall Classic. He played four years with the Red Sox, the first of his 10 major league teams. After he retired, Ken did a Miller Lite commercial in which he couldn't remember what town he was in. Others drafted and signed by the Red Sox in 1966 who reached the majors were Mike Nagy, Ed Phillips, Dick Mills, Dick Baney, and Mark Schaeffer. Like Brett, each of them was a pitcher. Nagy was 12–2 as a twenty-one-year-old rookie in 1969 before fading. He won only seven games after his rookie campaign. None of the other four had much more than a cup of coffee in the big leagues.

JUNE 11   The Red Sox score seven runs in the seventh inning with two outs and defeat the Orioles 8–2 in Baltimore.

JUNE 13   The Red Sox trade Jim Gosger, Ken Sanders, and Guido Grilli to the Athletics for John Wyatt, Rollie Sheldon, and Jose Tartabull.

                  Wyatt was the closer during the "Impossible Dream" season of 1967 with a 10–7 record, 20 saves, and a 2.60 ERA.

JUNE 14   The Red Sox trade Earl Wilson and Joe Christopher to the Tigers for Don Demeter and Julio Navarro.

                  Wilson's days were numbered as soon as he talked to the media about the discrimination he faced in Florida during spring training (see February 26, 1966). It was a horrible trade. Wilson was 13–6 over the remainder of the 1966 season, won 22 games for the Tigers in 1967, and pitched in the World Series in 1968. Navarro never pitched a game for Boston, and Wilson hit more homers for the Tigers as a pitcher (17) than Demeter did for the Sox as an outfielder (10). Despite the Wilson trade, the Red Sox had a strong African-American and Latin presence for the first time in 1966. There were 10 minority players on the team that season. In 1965, the Celtics had more African Americans in their starting lineup (four) than the Red Sox had on the entire team (three).

JUNE 26   The Red Sox score seven fifth-inning runs in the first game of a doubleheader, a 13–7 win against the Senators at Fenway Park. The Red Sox lost the second game, 9–3.

                  The Red Sox entered the game with a 24–46 record in 1966 and were 65–126 since May 31, 1965. The Sox were 48–44 over the remainder of 1966.

JULY 1   The Major League Baseball Players Association hires Marvin Miller to be the new executive director. Under Miller's leadership, the association would lead a revolution in player-owner relations, including free agency beginning in the 1970s.

JULY 4   Lee Stange pitches the Red Sox to a 1–0 win over the Senators in the second game of a doubleheader at Fenway Park. George Scott drove in the lone run of the game with a single in the first inning. Washington won the first game, 6–4.

JULY 10   A walk-off grand slam by George Smith off Juan Pizarro in the tenth inning beats
                 the White Sox 10–6 in the second inning of a doubleheader at Fenway Park. The
                 slam followed an intentional walk to Joe Foy. The Sox also won the first game, 8–4.

JULY 16   Jose Santiago pitches a two-hitter to beat the Angels 7–1 in Anaheim. The only Cal-
                 ifornia hits were a single by Rick Reichardt in the seventh inning and a homer by
                 Norm Siebern with two outs in the ninth.

JULY 17   An inside-the-park homer by Joe Foy in the tenth inning beats the Athletics 3–2 in
                 the second game of a doubleheader in Kansas City. It was an exact reversal of the
                 first game, won by the Athletics, 3–2.

JULY 20   Darrell Brandon pitches a two-hitter to beat the Angels 6–1 in the first game of a dou-
                 bleheader at Fenway Park. The only hits off Brandon were a single by Frank Malzone
                 in the second inning and a triple by Norm Siebern in the seventh. California won the
                 second game 1–0 in 10 innings.

JULY 25   Ted Williams is formally inducted into the Hall of Fame in ceremonies at Cooper-
                 stown.

                 *Williams used part of his induction speech to deliver a message: "I hope that
                 someday, Satchel Paige and Josh Gibson will be voted into the Hall of Fame
                 as symbols of the great Negro players who are not here only because they
                 weren't given the chance." Paige was elected to the Hall of Fame in 1971
                 and Gibson in 1972.*

AUGUST 3   On the first pitch thrown to him following the birth of his daughter Jill, Dom Demeter
                 hits a home run, although the Red Sox lose 7–2 to the Twins in Minnesota. Baby Jill
                 was born in Newton-Wellesley Hospital near Boston.

AUGUST 7   Joe Foy hits a homer in the tenth inning to beat the Tigers 7–6 in the second inning
                 of a doubleheader in Detroit. Carl Yastrzemski tied the game in the ninth inning
                 with a two-run pinch-homer. The Tigers won the first game, 9–2.

                 As a rookie in 1966, Foy hit .262 with 15 homers and 97 runs scored.

AUGUST 8   Fog interrupts play at Fenway Park six times, but the Red Sox and Indians manage
                 to play nine innings. The Sox won, 3–1.

AUGUST 10   George Scott stuns the Fenway Park crowd with a long homer during a 2–0 win
                 over the Indians. The ball landed high in the center field bleachers, almost clearing
                 the wall 30 feet to the right of the flagpole.

AUGUST 11   The Red Sox trounce the Indians 13–3 at Fenway Park.

AUGUST 12   Scoring 13 runs for the second game in a row, the Red Sox outslug the Tigers 13–9
                 at Fenway Park.

AUGUST 15   Boog Powell hits three homers at Fenway Park, the last a two-run shot in the
                 eleventh inning that lifts the Orioles over the Red Sox, 4–3.

AUGUST 25   Joe Foy hits a two-run, walk-off home run in the ninth inning to beat the Athletics 8–6 in the first game of a doubleheader at Fenway Park. The Sox completed the sweep with a 4–1 win in the second tilt.

AUGUST 29   A two-run, pinch-single by Jose Tartabull in the ninth inning defeats the Angels 4–3 in Anaheim.

SEPTEMBER 3 Jim Lonborg pitches a two-hitter to defeat the Athletics 7–0 at Municipal Stadium. Bert Campaneris accounted for both Kansas City hits with a triple in the third inning and a single in the sixth.

Before signing with the Red Sox in 1964, Lonborg earned a degree in biology from Stanford University.

SEPTEMBER 8 Billy Herman is fired as Red Sox manager and is replaced, on an interim basis, by Pete Runnels, who finishes out the 1966 season.

The firing came without warning. When the press conference was called by the Red Sox, most in the media believed it would be an announcement that Herman would return in 1967. The Sox had won 40 of their last 76 games.

SEPTEMBER 16 After hitting a homer in the eighth inning to pull the Sox within a run, Carl Yastrzemski hits a two-run, two-out, walk-off homer in the ninth to beat the Angels 5–4 at Fenway Park.

SEPTEMBER 18 Reggie Smith makes his major league debut during a 5–3 loss to the Angels at Fenway Park. Playing center field, Smith hit in leadoff position and was hitless in five at-bats.

Tony Conigliaro finished the 1966 season with 28 homers, 93 RBIs, and a .265 batting average.

SEPTEMBER 23 Lee Stange pitches a two-hitter to beat the Yankees 2–1 at Yankee Stadium. Tony Conigliaro drove in both runs with a homer off Mel Stottlemyre in the first inning. The only New York hits were singles by Horace Clarke in the first inning and Bobby Murcer in the third.

Both the Red Sox and the Senators finished the 1966 season on September 27, five days ahead of the rest of the American League. The unusual scheduling was done to prepare D.C. Stadium in Washington and Fenway Park for football. The Sox ended the season in ninth place in a 10-team league, one-half game ahead of the last-place Yankees.

SEPTEMBER 28 The Red Sox hire thirty-seven-year-old Dick Williams as manager.

In contrast to his predecessors, Williams was a strict taskmaster, and his tough, brusque demeanor proved to be just what the lethargic, jaded, and selfish Red Sox needed. In his first season as manager, he took the club from ninth place to the American League pennant. As a player, Williams spent 14 seasons in the majors for five different clubs from 1951 through 1964, mostly in a utility role with a reputation as an individual who would give up his last drop of blood to win. He began his career in the Dodgers organization when the club won pennant after pennant with "The Boys of Summer." Williams ended his playing career with the Red Sox in 1963 and 1964. In 1965 and 1966, he managed the Red Sox' Class AA farm club in Toronto in the International League. When he was elevated to the parent club, Williams made it clear from day one that he had assumed total command. On the very first day, he announced that Carl Yastrzemski was being stripped of his captaincy. "There's only one chief," Williams said. With his crew cut and sharp tongue, he had the air of a Marine drill sergeant. Williams used any means necessary to motivate his players, including benchings and public ridicule.

1967   B

Season in a Sentence

In a season forever known as the "Impossible Dream," the Red Sox shock everyone by leaping from ninth place to first against 100–1 odds in one of the most thrilling pennant races in baseball history.

Finish • Won • Lost • Pct • GB

First   92   70   .568   +1.0

World Series The Red Sox lost to the St. Louis Cardinals four games to three.

Manager

Dick Williams

Stats   Red Sox • AL • Rank

Stats	Red Sox	AL	Rank
Batting Avg:	.255	.236	1
On-Base Pct:	.323	.305	1
Slugging Pct:	.395	.351	1
Home Runs:	158		1
Stolen Bases:	68		3
ERA:	3.36	3.23	8
Fielding Pct:	.977	.979	8
Runs Scored:	722		1
Runs Allowed:	614		7

Starting Lineup

Mike Ryan, c
George Scott, 1b
Mike Andrews, 2b
Joe Foy, 3b
Rico Petrocelli, ss
Carl Yastrzemski, lf
Reggie Smith, cf
Tony Conigliaro, rf
Jerry Adair, 3b-ss-2b
Jose Tartabull, rf
Dalton Jones, 3b

Pitchers

Jim Lonborg, sp
Gary Bell, sp
Lee Stange, sp-rp
John Wyatt, rp
Jose Santiago, rp
Darrell Brandon, rp

Attendance

1,727,832 (first in AL)

Club Leaders

Batting Avg:	Yastrzemski	.326
On-Base Pct:	Yastrzemski	.418
Slugging Pct:	Yastrzemski	.622
Home Runs:	Yastrzemski	44
RBI:	Yastrzemski	121
Runs:	Yastrzemski	112
Stolen Bases:	Smith	16
Wins:	Lonborg	22
Strikeouts:	Lonborg	246
ERA:	Stange	2.77
Saves:	Wyatt	20

JANUARY 28   Two weeks after the Green Bay Packers defeat the Kansas City Chiefs in the first Super Bowl, the Red Sox select Carlton Fisk in the first round of the free agent draft.

At the time, a draft was held each year in January for players who had been drafted previously but didn't sign with their original club. Fisk was drafted by the Orioles in 1965 in the 48th round but elected to attend the University of New Hampshire instead of becoming a professional.

MARCH 16   In a bizarre spring training exhibition game, the Red Sox score 10 runs in the top of the ninth and defeat the Mets 23–18 in St. Petersburg.

MARCH 18   Tony Conigliaro suffers a hairline fracture of the shoulder when hit by a pitch from John Wyatt before a game against the Tigers in Lakeland, Florida. It was the fifth broken bone Conigliaro had suffered since April 1963—four from being struck by pitches and one from punching a guy in an argument over a girl. He fractured a hand three times and a forearm once prior to the broken shoulder. Conigliaro was ready to play by Opening Day but would be hit by a pitch again later in the season that all but ended his career (see August 18, 1967).

MARCH 23   Playing right field, George Scott runs full speed into a cement wall chasing a fly ball during a 7–4 win against the Dodgers in Winter Haven. Scott's head and arm struck the wall. He fell unconscious but wasn't seriously injured. The Sox had been experimenting with playing Scott in the outfield to make room for Tony Horton at first base. The experiment ended the moment Scott crashed into the wall.

MARCH 31   The Red Sox and the Yankees play the first-ever major league game in the Virgin Islands. The Sox won the exhibition contest 3–1 before 4,000 fans in St. Croix. The following day, the Sox defeated the Yankees again 13–4 on the 50th anniversary of the US purchase of the islands.

Odds maker Jimmy the Greek put the chances of a Red Sox American League pennant at 100–1. Dick Williams said, "We'll win more than we lose," something the Red Sox hadn't accomplished since 1958. The 1967 Sox were an extremely young club with Billy Rohr (age 21 on Opening Day), Tony Conigliaro (22), Reggie Smith (22), Tony Horton (22), Billy Rohr (22), George Scott (23), Mike Andrews (23), Dalton Jones (23), Jerry Stephenson (23), Rico Petrocelli (23), Joe Foy (24), Dave Morehead (24), Jim Lonborg (24), and Mike Ryan (25).

APRIL 11   The Red Sox' scheduled season opener against the White Sox at Fenway Park is postponed. Temperatures were in the high thirties with 40-mile-per-hour winds. The same day, the Celtics' streak of eight consecutive NBA championships came to an end after losing the fifth game of a best-of-seven series against the Philadelphia 76ers.

APRIL 12   The Red Sox open the historic 1967 season with a 5–4 win over the White Sox before 8,234 at Fenway Park in 40-degree weather. Jim Lonborg was the winning pitcher. Rico Petrocelli hit a homer and two singles in three at-bats and drove in four runs. Johnny Mathis sang the national anthem.

Lonborg was four days shy of his 25th birthday on Opening Day and had a career record of only 19–27. He turned things around in 1967 with a 22–9 mark and a 3.16 ERA, earning him the Cy Young Award. Lonborg led the league in games started (39), strike-outs (246), and hit batsmen (19) and was second in innings pitched (273 1/3).

The surprise ace of the Impossible Dream Team, Jim Lonborg became a Red Sox immortal with his Cy Young performance in 1967.

APRIL 14 In one of the most sensational debuts in major league history, twenty-one-year-old Red Sox pitcher Billy Rohr comes within one strike of a no-hitter for a 3–0 victory over Whitey Ford and the Yankees in the first game of the season at Yankee Stadium. With none out in the ninth, Carl Yastrzemski made a spectacular diving catch in left to snag a drive hit over his head by Tom Tresh. Yaz landed on his knee and did a complete somersault. Joe Pepitone lifted a lazy fly to right fielder Tony Conigliaro for the second out. Rohr took Elston Howard to a 3–2 count, only to have Howard line a single to right-center field for the Yankees' only hit. The normally partisan New York crowd booed Howard before Rohr retired Charley Smith for the final out. Rohr walked five batters and struck out two.

The Red Sox' catcher was Russ Gibson, who hailed from Fall River, Massachusetts, and like Rohr, was making his major league debut. Gibson was three weeks shy of the 28th birthday and spent 10 years in the minors. Among those in the crowd of 14,375 was Jackie Kennedy and her six-year-old son, John Jr. After the game, Rohr signed a ball for John Jr. Two days later, Rohr took a bow on The Ed Sullivan Show.

Reggie Smith led off the game with a home run off Whitey Ford. Because of injuries to Mike Andrews and George Smith, Reggie began the season as the starting second baseman, but after six games, he went back to center field.

APRIL 16 The Red Sox lose 7–6 to the Yankees in an 18-inning marathon in New York. The winning run scored on a two-out single by Joe Pepitone off Lee Stange. The Red

Sox left 20 runners on base. Tony Conigliaro collected five hits, including a double, in seven at-bats. Carl Yastrzemski had five hits, including two triples, in eight at-bats. Russ Gibson, who caught Billy Rohr's one-hitter in his first major league game, caught 18 innings in his second big-league contest.

APRIL 21   In his second major league start, Billy Rohr pitches a complete game and beats the Yankees 6–1 at Fenway Park. The lone run off Rohr was driven in on a single in the eighth inning by Elston Howard, who broke up Rohr's no-hit bid seven days earlier.

Rohr never won another game for the Red Sox and was back in the minors in June. He pitched 17 games for the Indians in 1968 but won only one game. In his first two big-league starts, Rohr was 2–0 with an ERA of 0.50. Over the rest of his brief big-league career, he had a record of 1–3 and an earned run average of 7.80.

APRIL 28   Jim Lonborg strikes outs 13 batters and defeats the Athletics 3–0 at Fenway Park.

APRIL 29   After the Athletics take a 10–9 lead in the top of the fifteenth inning on Rick Monday's first major league homer, the Red Sox come back with two runs in their half to win 11–10 at Fenway Park. A two-run, walk-off single by Jose Tartabull drove in the tying and winning runs.

MAY 1   Dennis Bennett hits a three-run homer and pitches a shutout to defeat the Angels 4–0 in Anaheim.

MAY 9   Facing a doubleheader loss to the Athletics in Kansas City after dropping the opener 4–3, the Sox score five runs in the ninth to beat the A's 5–2 in the nightcap. Carl Yastrzemski broke a 2–2 tie with a bases-loaded double.

MAY 12   A throwing blunder by catcher Bob Tillman leads to a 5–4 loss to the Tigers at Fenway Park. With Detroit leading 4–2 in the eighth inning, Al Kaline attempted to steal second. Tillman fired the ball toward the bag and struck pitcher John Wyatt on the side of the head. The ball bounced all the way to the on-deck circle on the first base side. Kaline went to third on the error and scored on a sacrifice fly by Willie Horton.

MAY 14   The Red Sox sweep the Tigers 8–5 and 13–9 in a doubleheader at Fenway Park. The two clubs combined for 28 extra-base hits, 16 of them by the Red Sox, to set an American League record for most extra hits in a twin bill. There were 12 homers (six by each team), a triple, and 15 doubles.

The Red Sox started the day with a record of 11–14 and were in a three-way tie for last place, 6 1/2 games out of first.

MAY 17   In a slugfest marked by 10 homers from nine different players—seven of them Orioles—the Red Sox lose 12–8 at windy Fenway Park. The Orioles hit four homers in a nine-run seventh, which wiped out a 6–2 Boston lead. Sox homers came from Andy Etchebarren and Sam Bowens, off Baltimore hurlers Galen Cisco and Boog Powell, and from Dave Johnson against Bill Landis.

MAY 24   Dalton Jones hits a homer in the second inning off Denny McLain to beat the Tigers 1–0 in Detroit. Jim Lonborg pitched the shutout, striking out 11 batters.

JUNE 2   On the first day of a two-day riot in the largely African-American Boston neighbor-
          hood of Roxbury, Jim Lonborg carries a no-hitter into the eighth inning before giving
          up a one-out double to Duke Sims. Lonborg settled for a three-hit 2–1 victory over
          the Indians at Fenway Park.

JUNE 3   The Red Sox trade Don McMahon and Bob Snow to the White Sox for Jerry Adair.

          *Adair provided the Red Sox with invaluable veteran leadership during the 1967
          pennant drive. Backing up the young infielders, Adair hit .291 in 316 at-bats
          for Boston over the remainder of the '67 season.*

JUNE 4   The Red Sox trade Tony Horton and Don Demeter to the Indians for Gary Bell.

          *A thirty-year-old veteran pitcher, Bell was 12–8 with a 3.16 ERA for the Red
          Sox in 1967.*

JUNE 6   With the third overall pick in the first round of the amateur draft, the Red Sox draft
          right-handed pitcher Mike Garman from Caldwell High School in Caldwell, Idaho.

          *Garman advanced quickly and made his major league debut in 1969 just six
          days after his 20th birthday, but he compiled a so-so 22–27 record and a 3.63
          ERA in nine big-league seasons. He was 2–2 with an earned run average of 4.95
          in four seasons with the Red Sox. It was an unproductive draft, as Garman was
          the only player selected and signed by the Red Sox who reached the majors.*

JUNE 8   Carl Yastrzemski collects six hits, including a homer and a double, in nine at-bats
          and makes three great catches in left field during a doubleheader against the White
          Sox in Chicago. The Red Sox lost the first game 5–2 but won the second, 7–3.

          *Two days earlier, White Sox manager Eddie Stanky angered Yastrzemski and Red
          Sox fans by saying that Yaz was "an All-Star, but only from the neck down."
          Responding to an off year in 1966, Yastrzemski became one of the first players in
          baseball to undergo a rigorous offseason training regimen. In 1967, Yaz had one
          of the best seasons in Red Sox history by winning the Triple Crown when he led
          the AL in batting average (.326), home runs (44), and RBIs (121). No one in the
          majors since Yastrzemski in 1967 has won the Triple Crown. He also topped the
          league in runs (112), hits (189), total bases (360), on-base percentage (.418), and
          slugging percentage (.622) in addition to collecting 31 doubles and 91 walks. The
          big difference was in the home run department. Prior to 1967, Yastrzemski never
          hit more than 20 homers in a season and had 95 in six seasons. His 44 homers in
          1967 were the most by a Red Sox hitter between 1938 and 1978.*

JUNE 9   Joe Foy hits a two-run pinch-homer in the fifth inning with the Red Sox trailing 6–2,
          stays in the game at third, and hits another homer in the eighth to help the Sox to
          an 8–7 win over the Senators at Fenway Park. Carl Yastrzemski also hit two
          homers, and Reggie Smith added another.

          *Foy hit .251 with 16 homers in 1967. He was part of a terrific young infield that
          looked as though it would be together for years. George Scott batted .303 with
          19 homers. Rico Petrocelli had a .259 average and 17 home runs. Rookie Mike
          Andrews hit .263. When the season ended, Foy, Petrocelli, and Andrews were*

each twenty-four years old, and Scott was twenty-three. But the young infield never quite developed as well as the Red Sox had hoped. By 1971, only Petrocelli remained with the club.

JUNE 15   After the White Sox score in the top of the eleventh inning to take a 1–0 lead, the Red Sox come back to win 2–1 in the bottom half when Joe Foy hits a two-out single and Tony Conigliaro strikes a two-run, walk-off homer.

Fans were all over White Sox manager Eddie Stanky during the three-game series on June 14 and 15 because of his comments a little more than a week earlier about Carl Yastrzemski. Stanky was bombarded with boos and everything from cups of beer to batteries. After leaving town, Stanky threatened to sue the Red Sox for $3 million for failing to protect him.

JUNE 16   The phrase "Impossible Dream" appears in a Boston newspaper for the first time in connection with the Red Sox in a headline in the *Boston Globe*. It was the name of a hit song by Jack Jones from the musical *Man of La Mancha*.

JUNE 18   After the Red Sox experience a rough flight from Washington to New York in which the plane drops 1,500 feet, Joe Foy arrives in New York to find his family home on fire. Foy lived on the second floor of a three-family house in the East Bronx, 13 blocks from Yankee Stadium. When he arrived, his parents were inside, confused by the smoke, and Foy led them to safety. The blaze destroyed the house, and Foy lost all of his clothes, trophies, and scrapbooks.

JUNE 20   Just two days after saving his parents from a burning building, Joe Foy hits a grand slam in the fifth inning off Mel Stottlemyre to lead the Red Sox to 7–1 win over the Yankees in New York.

JUNE 21   A fight breaks out during the second inning of an 8–1 win over the Yankees in New York. In the second inning, Yankee hurler Thad Tillotson hit Joe Foy in the head with a pitch. In the bottom half, Jim Lonborg retaliated by plunking Tillotson in the shoulder, and after words were exchanged, both benches emptied. Rico Petrocelli and Joe Pepitone, both Brooklyn natives, exchanged several punches, and Reggie Smith body slammed Tillotson to the turf. It took 12 members of the Yankee Stadium security detail (including Petrocelli's brother Dave) to break up the melee. In the third inning, Tillotson hit Lonborg with a pitch, and the benches cleared again. This time, there was little more than rudimentary pushing and shoving, but the two clubs continued to throw beanballs for the remainder of the game.

JULY 8   With a 2–0 loss to the Tigers in Detroit, the Red Sox fall seven games out of first place. The Sox had a record of 40–38 and were in fifth place.

JULY 11   Carl Yastrzemski collects three hits, including a double, in four at-bats in the All-Star Game, but the American League loses 2–1 in 15 innings in Anaheim.

JULY 16   The Red Sox purchase Norm Siebern from the Giants.

JULY 20   Pennant fever takes a firm grip on New England as the Red Sox win their sixth in a row with a 6–4 decision over the Orioles in Baltimore. The victory put the Sox only 1½ games out of first place.

JULY 22   The Red Sox pull within half a game of the first-place White Sox with a 4–0 victory over the Indians in Cleveland. It was Boston's eighth win in a row.

JULY 23   On the first day of rioting in Detroit that leaves 43 dead, the Red Sox run their winning streak to 10 games by sweeping the Indians 8–5 and 5–1 in Cleveland. The streak gave the Sox a 52–40 record and convinced fans the club was for real. The Red Sox flew back to Boston after the sweep and were greeted by a riotous scene at Logan Airport as thousands turned out to welcome them back. The plane had to pull into a very remote part of the airport, but fans surged toward the aircraft, spilling over onto the runway in the path of another jet that was taxiing for takeoff.

Tony Conigliaro hit home runs in both games of a doubleheader to give him 101 for his career. At 22 years and 197 days, Conigliaro is the second-youngest player ever to hit 100 homers. Mel Ott was two months younger (22 years 132 days) when he hit number 100 in 1931. The only other player to hit 100 homers before his 23rd birthday was Eddie Mathews, from 1952 to 1954.

JULY 27   The Red Sox score three runs in the ninth inning on a two-run homer by Joe Foy and a solo shot by Tony Conigliaro to tie the score 5–5, then win 6–5 in the tenth against the Angels at Fenway Park. The winning run scored on a triple by Reggie Smith and an error.

JULY 31   Lee Stange defeats the Twins 4–0 with a three-hitter at Fenway Park. Stange retired the first 20 batters to face him before Harmon Killebrew singled.

AUGUST 3   The Red Sox trade Ron Klimkowski and Pete Magrini to the Yankees for Elston Howard, who was infamous in Boston for breaking up Billy Rohr's no-hitter on April 14 and for his 13-year association with the hated Yankees.

Catching was a weakness all season, and the thirty-eight-year-old Howard was acquired to solve the problem. He hit only .147 with one homer in 42 games in 1967 but is credited with providing a steady hand over the pitching staff.

AUGUST 6   Dean Chance of the Twins retires all 15 batters he faces in a rain-shortened perfect game at Fenway Park. The contest was called in the top of the sixth inning with Minnesota leading, 2–0.

AUGUST 9   The Red Sox play the Athletics in Kansas City for the last time and win, 5–1.

The Athletics moved to Oakland in 1968. Kansas City was granted an expansion franchise named the Royals, which began play in 1969.

AUGUST 18   In one of the worst tragedies in baseball history, Tony Conigliaro is beaned by Jack Hamilton of the Angels in the fourth inning of a 3–2 Red Sox win at Fenway Park. Conigliaro was hit in the face, which knocked him unconscious, caused a severe hemorrhage of his nose, broke his cheekbone, and sent bone fragments into his left eye. He was carried off the field on a stretcher before being taken to Sancta Maria Hospital.

The day after the injury, doctors predicted that Conigliaro would be playing again in two weeks. But within days it became apparent that the damage caused by the beaning was much more serious when his eyesight failed to return to normal.

Conigliaro missed the rest of the 1967 season and all of 1968. He returned in 1969 but had problems with his eyesight for the remainder of his career.

AUGUST 19   Still reeling from the injury to Tony Conigliaro, the Red Sox outlast the Angels 12–11 at Fenway Park.

AUGUST 20   The Red Sox sweep the Angels 12–2 and 9–8, the second in an incredible comeback, in a doubleheader at Fenway Park. In the first game, Reggie Smith become the first player in the Red Sox history to hit homers from both sides of the plate in a single game. In the nightcap, the Angels led 8–0 before the Red Sox stormed back with one run in the fourth inning, three in the fifth, four in the sixth and one in the eighth. Smith started the comeback with his third homer of the day. Jerry Adair finished it with a homer into the net above the Green Monster. In the ninth inning, the Angels had runners on second and third with none out, but Jose Santiago pitched out of the jam.

AUGUST 23   The Red Sox sign Jim Landis following his release by the Tigers.

Landis was a veteran of 1,341 major league games when acquired by the Sox as an outfielder, but lasted only five days with the club. He was released when the Red Sox signed Ken Harrelson. Landis's only hit in seven at-bats with the Red Sox was a home run.

AUGUST 26   The Red Sox move into first place, one-half game ahead of the Twins, with a 6–2 win over the White Sox in Chicago. It was the first time that the Red Sox had been in first place in either August or September since 1949.

AUGUST 27   The Red Sox' stay in first lasts only one day after splitting a doubleheader with the White Sox at Fenway Park. The Sox won the first game 4–3, then lost the second 1–0 in 11 innings. Despite dropping out of first, it was a memorable day in the "Impossible Dream" season because of the play that ended the first game. With two outs in Chicago's half of the ninth and Ken Berry on third base, Duane Josephson hit a drive to Jose Tartabull in right field. Tartabull caught the ball and fired it to home. The throw was high, and Elston Howard made a leaping, one-handed catch. He landed with his foot one inch on the third base side of home, which deflected Berry away from the plate. With a swooping motion, Howard tagged Berry to end the game.

AUGUST 28   Ken Harrelson signs a free agent contract with the Red Sox following his release by the Athletics.

Athletics owner Charlie Finley released Harrelson after Harrelson called Finley "a menace to baseball." Finley and his players had battled for more than two weeks after he fined and suspended pitcher Lew Krausse for allegedly harassing a flight attendant. Harrelson was a productive front-line player, and the unconditional release made him a free agent. Teams lined up for his services. With Tony Conigliaro out for the season, the Red Sox needed a right-handed power hitter who could play right field, and Harrelson fit the bill on both counts. The Red Sox won the bidding war by offering Harrelson a bonus of $75,000 at a time when only a small handful of superstars earned as much as $100,000 in a season. Nicknamed "The Hawk" because of his prominent nose, Harrelson didn't help much in 1967 with a .200 batting average and *three homers in 23 games. He became an immensely popular figure in Boston in 1968, however, with a great offensive season, an eccentric personality, Southern charm, long hair (one of the first athletes to do so), and wildly colored "mod" outfits. Harrelson was a particular favorite of young fans in a city full of college students at the height of antiestablishment rebellion against authority. Fitting right in with the changing times of the "psychedelic sixties," Harrelson drove to the ballpark in a lavender dune buggy with flowers on the roof. He even had a one-hour variety show on WHDH-TV entitled* The Hawk.

AUGUST 29   The Red Sox and Yankees play 29 innings in a doubleheader in New York. It tied the record for the longest doubleheader in American League history, set by the Red Sox and Athletics in 1905. The Red Sox won the first game 2–1 and lost the second 4–3 in a 20-inning marathon. Ken Harrelson made his Red Sox debut in the second game and hit a homer in his first at-bat to give the Sox a 2–0 lead. The score was 2–2 after nine innings. Both teams scored in the eleventh. In the twentieth inning, Horace Clarke singled in the winning run off Jose Santiago. Despite the split, the Red Sox moved back into sole possession of first place by one-half game.

In a five-day span from August 25 through 29, the Red Sox played eight games and 85 innings. From August 15 through September 5, the Sox played 28 games in 22 days and won 19 of them.

AUGUST 30   Breaking out of an 0-for-18 slump, Carl Yastrzemski hits a homer in the eleventh inning to beat the Yankees 2–1 in New York. Dick Williams sat Yastrzemski out at the start of the game for a rest. He entered the contest in the eighth.

SEPTEMBER 1   Ken Harrelson drives in four runs with a homer, triple, and double during a 10–2 win over the White Sox at Fenway Park.

SEPTEMBER 2   The Red Sox fall back out of first place with a 4–1 loss to the White Sox at Fenway Park.

SEPTEMBER 12   Jim Lonborg wins his 20th game of the season with a 3–1 decision over the Athletics at Fenway Park. He also hit a triple in the eighth inning and scored on a sacrifice fly by Mike Andrews that broke a 1–1 tie. The win moved the Red Sox into a tie for first place.

SEPTEMBER 18   Carl Yastrzemski hits a homer in the ninth to tie the score 5–5, and Dalton Jones adds another in the tenth to beat the Tigers 6–5 in Detroit. At the end of the day, the Red Sox, Tigers, and Twins were tied for first with records of 85–66. The fourth-place White Sox were only one-half game back at 85–67.

Yastrzemski carried the Red Sox over the last two weeks of the season. In the last 12 regular-season games, he had 23 hits in 44 at-bats, for an average of .523, and drove in 16 runs. Among his hits were five homers and four doubles. In the final two games on September 30 and October 1, which decided the AL pennant, Yaz went seven for eight and drove in six of Boston's 11 runs. He continued his hot streak in the World Series with 10 hits, including three homers, in 25 at-bats.

SEPTEMBER 19   The Red Sox score three runs in the ninth inning off Mickey Lolich and Earl Wilson to defeat the Tigers 4–2 in Detroit. The tie-breaking run scored on a wild pitch by Wilson. In the heated AL pennant race, the Tigers dropped from a tie for first place to fourth in one day. The Red Sox and Twins were in a two-way tie for first.

SEPTEMBER 20   The Red Sox score the winning run in their final at-bat for the third game in a row. With the score tied 4–4 in the ninth, Reggie Smith singled in Carl Yastrzemski for the winning tally in a 5–4 decision over the Indians in Cleveland.

The Red Sox drew 1,727,832 fans in 1967, breaking the record of 1,596,650 set in 1949. In 1966, the Sox drew 811,172, and in 1965, a post–World War II low of 652,201. The 1967 figure led the AL in attendance and was second in the majors to the Cardinals. It was the first time that Boston led the American League in attendance since 1915.

SEPTEMBER 22   The Red Sox split a doubleheader against the Orioles in Baltimore and drop out of first place. The Sox lost the first game 10–0 and won the second, 10–3. At the end of the day, Boston was half a game behind the Twins in the emotionally exhausting pennant race.

SEPTEMBER 23   The Red Sox rally from a 4–0 deficit to beat the Orioles 7–5 in Baltimore.

SEPTEMBER 27   A 6–0 loss to the Indians before 18,415 on a Wednesday afternoon at Fenway Park leaves the Red Sox one game in back of the Twins. Dick Williams started Jim Lonborg on two days' rest, but the gamble failed. On the same day, the White Sox lost a crushing doubleheader to the last-place Athletics in Kansas City to all but eliminate Chicago from the pennant race.

The Red Sox had days off on both September 28 and 29. There were two remaining games, both against the Twins at Fenway Park, on September 30 and October 1. In order to win the pennant, the Red Sox had to win both games. Heading into the September 30 contest, the Twins were in first place with a record of 91–69. The Tigers were in second at 89–69, and the Red Sox third at 90–70. The White Sox, at 89–71, were eliminated with a September 29 loss to the Senators. The Tigers had four games left, playing doubleheaders on September 30 and October 1 against the Angels in Detroit. The Red Sox hadn't been playing particularly well of late and headed into the final weekend with seven losses in their previous 13 games. In addition, the Red Sox were 5–11 against the Twins in 1967 and 20–61 against them since July 13, 1963.

SEPTEMBER 30   The Red Sox defeat the Twins 6–4 to move into a tie for first place. With 32,909 in attendance at Fenway, including vice president and Twins fan Hubert Humphrey, Minnesota scored first with a run off Jose Santiago in the first. The Sox caught a break in the third when Twins starter Jim Kaat pulled a tendon in his elbow and had to leave the game. Boston took a 2–1 lead in the fifth, both runs scoring with two outs, but the Twins tied it 2–2 in the sixth. In the bottom half of the inning, George Scott homered off Ron Kline into the center field bleachers to break the deadlock and lift the Sox to a 3–2 advantage. In the seventh, Carl Yastrzemski hit a three-run homer into the bullpen against Jim Merritt to put the game away. The Sox survived a two-run Minnesota rally in the ninth for the victory. The Tigers won the first game of their doubleheader 5–0 against the Angels to take temporary possession of first place by one percentage point but lost the second contest, 8–6. The Tigers led 6–2 before allowing California to score six runs in the eighth inning.

At the end of the day, the Red Sox and Twins were tied at the top of the league at 91–70. The Tigers were 90–70. With one day remaining, the loser of the Red Sox-Twins game on October 1 would be eliminated from the pennant race. The winner would be assured of at least a tie for first. The Tigers could force a tie with the Red Sox–Twins victor by sweeping the Angels in a doubleheader.

OCTOBER 1   On the final day of the season, the Red Sox complete the "Impossible Dream" by defeating the Twins 5–3 before 35,770 delirious Fenway Park fans to capture the AL pennant. Among those in the crowd were movie stars Cliff Robertson and Lee Remick, along with Joseph P. Kennedy and sons Bobby and Ted. Jim Lonborg started for the Red Sox and Dean Chance for the Twins. Lonborg had a career record of 0–6 against the Twins. Chance was 16–8 against the Sox, including four wins in 1967. After 5½ innings, Chance and the Twins led 2–0. The Sox exploded for five runs in the sixth. Lonborg led off the inning and reached first base with a perfect bunt single down the first base line. Jerry Adair and Dalton Jones followed with singles to load the bases with none out. Carl Yastrzemski was once again the hero with a two-run single to tie the score, 2–2. Ken Harrelson followed with a grounder to shortstop Zoilo Versailles, who threw home. Jones scored easily to put the Sox up, 3–2. Two more runs made it 5–2. The Twins scored once in the eighth in a rally cut short by a brilliant defensive play by Yastrzemski. It was 5–3 heading into the ninth. Lonborg retired the Twins on an infield single, a double play, and a pop-up by former Red Sox Russ Nixon to Rico Petrocelli at short. Fans swarmed onto the field like a tidal wave and lifted Lonborg. He was carried all the way into right field. The crowd clawed, patted, and pounded on him, ripped the buttons off his uniform shirt, tore his sweatshirt off completely, and took his cap and shoelaces. Several policemen fought their way into the crowd to rescue Lonborg and formed a wedge to allow him to reach the clubhouse safely.

The pennant race still wasn't completely over, however, when the game ended. The Tigers won the first game of their doubleheader against the Angels, 6–4. If Detroit won the second game, the Red Sox would have to play the Tigers in a one-game playoff the following day to decide the AL champion. The Red Sox listened to the game on the radio in the clubhouse. The Tigers lost 8–5, with the final out coming at 7:43 PM. The Sox were in the World Series for the first time since 1946. And just like 1946, the Red Sox' opponent would be the St. Louis Cardinals, a club managed by Red Schoendienst that posted a 101–60 record in 1967.

OCTOBER 4   In the first game of the World Series, Bob Gibson six-hits the Red Sox and fans 10 for a 2–1 Cardinals victory before 34,796 at Fenway Park. Sox pitcher Jose Santiago homered in the third inning in his first World Series at-bat but took the loss. Lou Brock had four hits in four at-bats and stole two bases. He also scored the winning run in the seventh when he singled and crossed the plate on a stolen base and two infield outs.

Santiago is the only pitcher in Series history to hit a home run and lose the game. During his career, he hit only one regular-season homer in 162 at-bats.

OCTOBER 5   In Game Two, Jim Lonborg evens the Series with a one-hit gem to defeat the Cardinals 5–0 before 35,186 at Fenway Park. He retired the first 19 batters he faced before walking Curt Flood. The only St. Louis hit was a two-out double by Julian Javier in the eighth inning. Carl Yastrzemski hit two homers and a single and drove in four runs.

The only two Red Sox players with World Series experience prior to 1967 were Elston Howard and Norm Siebern. Manager Dick Williams had played for the Dodgers in the 1953 Series.

OCTOBER 7   The Cardinals win Game Three 5–2 at Busch Stadium in St. Louis. Nelson Briles pitched a complete game for the Cards. Reggie Smith hit a home run for the Sox.

OCTOBER 8   The Cardinals take a three-games-to-one lead in the World Series with a 6–0 victory in St. Louis. Bob Gibson pitched a five-hit shutout. The Cardinals put the game away with four runs in the first inning and two in the second. Starting pitcher Jose Santiago retired only two batters.

Focus on Sport/Getty Images

On his way to winning the triple crown, Carl Yastrzemski carried the Red Sox to the pennant with outstanding hitting, fielding, and leadership.

Ken Brett became the youngest pitcher to appear in a World Series by hurling a scoreless eighth. He was less than a month past his 19th birthday. Brett's prior major league experience consisted of only one game, a two-inning relief appearance on September 27. He also pitched one-third of an inning in Game Seven of the '67 World Series.

OCTOBER 9   In Game Five in St. Louis, Jim Lonborg keeps the Red Sox in the World Series by outpitching Steve Carlton for a 3–1 victory. Lonborg went the distance and allowed only three hits to set a record for fewest hits allowed in consecutive complete-game World Series starts with four. He lost the shutout when Roger Maris hit a homer with two outs in the ninth.

OCTOBER 11   Back at Fenway Park, the revived Red Sox even the Series with an 8–4 win in Game Six. The Sox hit four homers, three of them consecutively in the fourth inning by Carl Yastrzemski, Reggie Smith, and Rico Petrocelli off Cardinals hurler Dick Hughes. Rico also homered in the second. The four homers produced only four runs, however, and the Sox needed four more runs in the seventh to break a 4–4 tie. Joe Foy's double broke the deadlock. The winning pitcher was John Wyatt in relief of surprise starter Gary Waslewski, who went $5\frac{1}{3}$ innings. Waslewski was in his first major league season, had started only eight games in his career, and possessed just two big-league victories.

OCTOBER 12   On Columbus Day, the "Impossible Dream" season comes to a close as the Red Sox lose Game Seven 7–2 at Fenway Park in a matchup of aces Bob Gibson and Jim Lonborg, each of whom entered the game with two victories in the Series. Gibson pitched a three-hitter and struck out 10 to give the Cardinals the World Championship. He also hit a homer. Pitching on just two days' rest, Lonborg had nothing left and went six innings, giving up seven runs, six of them earned, and 10 hits.

NOVEMBER 30   The Red Sox send Bill Schlesinger and cash to the Cubs for Ray Culp.

DECEMBER 15   The Red Sox send Mike Ryan and cash to the Phillies for Dick Ellsworth and Gene Oliver.

The acquisitions of Culp and Ellsworth saved the Red Sox from a losing season in 1968. Both filled the breech after Jim Lonborg and Jose Santiago were shelved with injuries. Culp and Ellsworth tied for the team lead in victories in 1968 with 16. No other Sox pitcher won more than 11. The Red Sox gave up little to obtain the two pitchers. Culp was only 8–11 in 1967, but he had a 16–6 record and a 2.91 ERA in 1968 and won 17 games for the Sox in both 1969 and 1970. Ellsworth was a 22-game winner for the Cubs in 1963 but was 14–29 combined in 1966 and 1967. He gave the Red Sox one good season, posting a 16–7 record in 1968.

DECEMBER 24   Jim Lonborg suffers an injury to his left knee while skiing at the Heavenly Ski Resort in California near Lake Tahoe.

Lonborg tore ligaments and completely underestimated the severity of the injury. It wasn't until 1972, after he left the Red Sox, that Lonborg was again a consistently effective pitcher.

1968

B

Season in a Sentence

Injuries to key players such as Tony Conigliaro and Jim Lonborg keep the Red Sox from repeating the magic of 1967.

Finish • Won • Lost • Pct • GB

Fourth   86   76   .531   17.0

Manager

Dick Williams

Stats   Red Sox • AL • Rank

	Red Sox	AL	Rank
Batting Avg:	.236	.230	3
On-Base Pct:	.316	.300	1
Slugging Pct:	.352	.339	2
Home Runs:	125		3
Stolen Bases:	76		7
ERA:	3.33	2.98	8
Fielding Pct:	.979	.978	3
Runs Scored:	614		2
Runs Allowed:	611		8

Starting Lineup

Russ Gibson, c
George Scott, 1b
Mike Andrews, 2b
Joe Foy, 3b
Rico Petrocelli, ss
Carl Yastrzemski, lf
Reggie Smith, cf
Ken Harrelson, rf
Dalton Jones, 1b-2b
Jerry Adair, ss
Elston Howard, c

Pitchers

Ray Culp, sp
Dick Ellsworth, sp
Gary Bell, sp
Jose Santiago, sp
Jim Lonborg, sp
Juan Pizarro, sp-rp
Lee Stange, rp
Sparky Lyle, rp
Gary Waslewski, rp-sp

Attendance

1,940,266 (second in AL)

Club Leaders

Batting Avg:	Yastrzemski	.301
On-Base Pct:	Yastrzemski	.426
Slugging Pct:	Harrelson	.518
Home Runs:	Harrelson	35
RBI:	Harrelson	109
Runs:	Yastrzemski	90
Stolen Bases:	Foy	26
Wins:	Culp	16
	Ellsworth	16
Strikeouts:	Culp	190
ERA:	Culp	2.91
Saves:	Stange	12

APRIL 9   The season opener against the Tigers in Detroit is postponed to avoid conflict with the funeral of Martin Luther King Jr. Dr. King was murdered in Memphis on April 4.

Just before the regular season started, the Red Sox announced that Tony Conigliaro wouldn't play in 1968 because of deteriorating vision in his left eye, damaged by the beaning on August 18, 1967. Conigliaro played in spring training games in 1968 and appeared to be making progress before suffering a setback.

APRIL 10   Carl Yastrzemski hits two homers, one inside the park in the seventh inning and one over the wall in the ninth, in the season opener, a 7–3 victory over the Tigers in Detroit. Rico Petrocelli drove in three runs. Dick Ellsworth made his debut with the Red Sox and pitched a complete game.

APRIL 16   In the home opener, the Red Sox lose 9–2 to the Tigers before 32,949 at Fenway Park. Detroit scored eight runs in the fourth inning. Mike Andrews hit a homer for the Sox.

Andrews hit .271 with seven homers in 1968.

APRIL 18   Jose Santiago pitches a two-hitter to beat the White Sox 3–0 at Fenway Park. The only Chicago hits were singles by Wayne Causey in the sixth inning and Russ Snyder in the seventh.

APRIL 27   Tom Phoebus of the Orioles beats the Red Sox 6–0 with a no-hitter in Baltimore. The final out was a strikeout of Joe Foy.

MAY 3   The day after the Celtics win the NBA title in a six-game series against the Lakers, Red Sox pitcher Jerry Stephenson loses his contact lens, then loses the game 7–2 to the Oakland Athletics at Fenway Park. In a hilarious scene, Stephenson spent several minutes crawling around on the ground looking for the lens.

MAY 16   The Red Sox overcome a 10–5 deficit with six runs in the eighth inning to beat the Yankees 11–10 at Fenway Park. A squeeze bunt by Jerry Adair drove in the winning run.

MAY 18   The Red Sox sell John Wyatt to the Yankees.

MAY 27   The Red Sox play the Athletics in Oakland for the first time and win, 3–2.

MAY 28   In conjunction with expansion to 12 teams, the American League owners vote to split the league into two divisions along with a postseason playoff to determine the champion beginning with the 1969 season. The Red Sox were placed in the Eastern Division with the Yankees, Tigers, Orioles, Indians, and Senators.

JUNE 2   Fewer than six innings of a scheduled doubleheader against the Orioles are played because of deplorable conditions at Fenway Park, which resembled nearby Muddy River. With a crowd of 34,053 on hand, the Red Sox didn't want to postpone the game and insisted that the umpires start play. The scheduled first game started in a driving rain. Players slipped and slid all over the field, and two batters fell in the mud of the batter's box when they tried to run to first base. The contest was called in the sixth inning with the Orioles leading, 4–3. Fans were irate when they learned their rain checks were no good. To defray criticism over the decision to start the game, Tom Yawkey announced that he donated $62,000, an amount equal to the gate receipts, to charity.

JUNE 4   Although held to two hits by Mickey Lolich, the Red Sox defeat the Tigers 2–0 in the first game of a doubleheader at Fenway Park. Both runs scored on a double by George Scott in the sixth inning. Detroit turned the tables by winning the second game, 2–0.

JUNE 6   In the first round of the amateur draft, the Red Sox select outfielder-catcher John Maggard from John Glenn High School in Norwalk, California.

Maggard never reached the majors. He died in 1974 from an insect bite. Despite the tragedy involving Maggard, the Red Sox had an excellent draft in 1968. The club picked Lynn McGlothlen in the third round, Cecil Cooper in the sixth, Ben Oglivie in the 11th, Bill Lee in the 23rd, and John Curtis in the first round of the secondary phase, which consisted of previously drafted players who didn't sign a contract. McGlothlen, Cooper, Oglivie, and Lee all pitched in All-Star games during their careers, but unfortunately only Lee did so with the Sox. The other three were traded before developing into star players.

JUNE 9   The game between the Red Sox and White Sox at Fenway Park is postponed so as not to conflict with the funeral of Robert Kennedy, who was shot in Los Angeles on June 5 and died 25 hours later.

JUNE 14   Ken Harrelson hits three consecutive homers and drives in all seven Red Sox runs in a 7–2 win over the Indians in Cleveland. Harrelson hit a two-run homer off Luis Tiant in the fifth inning, a three-run homer off Tiant in the sixth, and a two-run shot off Eddie Fisher in the eighth. Harrelson was the first Red Sox player since Ted Williams in 1957 to hit three homers in a game, and the first Red Sox batter ever to hit three in consecutive at-bats in a single game. Over five games from June 14 through June 19, Harrelson hit five homers and drove in 17 runs.

              At the start of the season, Harrelson played only against left-handed pitchers in a platoon situation in right field with rookie Joe Lahoud. Harrelson quickly established himself as an everyday player. He led the American League with 109 RBIs in 1968 and also contributed 35 homers and a .275 batting average.

JUNE 27   The Red Sox purchase Juan Pizarro from the Pirates.

              The Red Sox ended June with a 34–38 record, and unlike 1967, were never serious contenders for the pennant. The failure of Tony Conigliaro to play was a major reason, in addition to injuries to Jim Lonborg and Jose Santiago. George Scott experienced a miserable season-long slump, epitomizing the failures of the 1968 Red Sox to repeat as champions. Trying to pull every pitch over the left field wall, he hit only .171 with three homers in 350 at-bats. No amount of batting instruction could convince Scott to change his approach at the plate. "Talking to Scott," Dick Williams said, "is like talking to cement."

JULY 7   The Red Sox run their winning streak to eight games with a sweep of the Twins at Fenway Park by scores of 4–3 and 6–3.

JULY 9   Dick Williams manages the American League to a 1–0 loss in the All-Star Game, played at the Astrodome in Houston.

JULY 17   In his first at-bat since being recalled from Pittsfield in the Eastern League, Russ Nixon hits a three-run pinch-double to break a 3–3 tie and enable the Red Sox to beat the Twins 6–5 in Minnesota.

JULY 26   A spectacular catch by Reggie Smith in center field saves a 2–1 win over the Senators in Washington. With two outs in the ninth inning and two Senators on base, Hank Allen hit a drive toward center. Smith braced himself against the fence with one hand and leaped high above the fence with the other to stab Allen's drive and wipe out a potential game-winning three-run homer.

              Smith hit .265 with 15 homers in 1968.

JULY 29   Mike Andrews hits a walk-off homer in the tenth inning to beat the Orioles 3–2 in the first game of a doubleheader at Fenway Park. Ray Culp pitched the complete game and struck out 12. The Sox also won the second tilt, 8–3.

JULY 31   The Red Sox purchase Floyd Robinson from the Athletics.

AUGUST 4   A walk-off grand slam by Ken Harrelson in the ninth inning off Andy Messersmith beats the Angels 5–1 at Fenway Park. The contest began on June 13 but was suspended in the sixth inning with the score 1–1 to allow the Angels sufficient time to make a flight connection to California. The Angels won the regularly scheduled game, 12–6.

AUGUST 8   The Red Sox defeat the White Sox 1–0 at County Stadium in Milwaukee. Ray Culp pitched the shutout and also drove in the lone run of the game with a single in the second inning.

               The White Sox played nine home games in Milwaukee in 1968 and 11 more in 1969.

AUGUST 9   Joe Foy hits a grand slam in the eighth inning off John Wyatt to provide the winning runs in a 5–3 victory over the Tigers in Detroit. The Sox trailed 2–1 when Foy cleared the bases.

AUGUST 11   Reggie Smith hits homers from both sides of the plate, but the Red Sox lose 6–5 in the second game of a doubleheader in Detroit when the Tigers score four runs in the ninth. The Tigers also won the first game, 5–4 in 14 innings.

AUGUST 17   The Red Sox score seven runs in the sixth inning to tie the game 8–8 but lose 10–9 to the Tigers in 11 innings at Fenway Park.

AUGUST 23   Carl Yastrzemski plays first base for the first time in his career during a 4–3 win over the Orioles in Baltimore.

AUGUST 25   The Red Sox lose an 18-inning struggle 3–2 to the Orioles in Baltimore. Brooks Robinson drove in the winning run with a two-out single off Jerry Stephenson.

AUGUST 29   On the fourth day of the Democratic National Convention in Chicago, marred by violent confrontations between antiwar demonstrators and police, Reggie Smith hits a grand slam in the fourth inning off Jack Aker during an 11–2 win over the Athletics at Fenway Park.

AUGUST 31   Joe Foy hits a grand slam off Frank Bertainia in the fifth inning of a 6–4 win over the Senators at Fenway Park. The Sox trailed 4–2 when Foy cleared the bases.

               Pitchers dominated in 1968. The league-wide earned run average in the AL was 2.98, and the league batting average was only .230. On September 8, Carl Yastrzemski led the American League in hitting with an average of .289. A late-season surge gave Yaz his third batting title with a mark of .301. Danny Cater of the Athletics was second at .290. Yastrzemski also led the league in walks (119) and on-base percentage (.426) and posted 90 runs, 162 hits, 32 doubles, and 23 homers.

SEPTEMBER 9   Both Ken Harrelson and Reggie Smith smash homers in the tenth inning to power the Red Sox to a 6–4 win over the Athletics in Oakland.

               After his playing career ended, Harrelson entered into a long career in broadcasting. He did the Red Sox games from 1975 through 1981 and can still be heard on White Sox telecasts on WGN-TV over New England cable systems.

SEPTEMBER 13   Ray Culp beats the Twins 3–0 at Fenway Park.

SEPTEMBER 17   Ray Culp strikes out 12 batters and defeats the Orioles 2–0 at Fenway Park.

SEPTEMBER 18   Through six innings, the Red Sox are held hitless and are victims of 13 strikeouts by Roger Nelson of the Orioles, but Boston scores three times in the seventh inning and beats Baltimore 4–0 at Fenway Park.

SEPTEMBER 21   Posting his third straight shutout, Ray Culp pitches a one-hitter to beat the Yankees 2–0 in New York. The only New York hit was a single by Roy White with two outs in the seventh inning.

SEPTEMBER 25   Ray Culp pitches his fourth straight shutout, beating the Senators 1–0 in Washington. A single by Carl Yastrzemski drove in the lone run of the game.

In five consecutive starts from September 7 through September 25, Culp allowed just one run and 23 hits in 45 innings and struck out 47 batters. His streak of 39 consecutive scoreless innings was snapped in his final start of 1968, a 4–3 loss to the Yankees at Fenway Park on September 29.

SEPTEMBER 27   The Red Sox splatter the Yankees 12–2 at Fenway Park.

The Red Sox were never in serious contention for the pennant in 1968 but drew 1,940,788 fans, breaking the previous record of 1,727,832 set in 1967. The 1968 mark stood until the Red Sox drew more than two million for the first time in 1977.

OCTOBER 15   In the expansion draft, the Red Sox lose Gary Bell, Darrell Brandon, and Dick Baney to the Seattle Pilots and Joe Foy, Jerry Adair, and Dave Morehead to the Kansas City Royals.

The failure to protect Foy, who had been the starting third baseman for three seasons, was a shock, but Foy hit only .225 in 1968 and would play only three more years. None of the six selected in the expansion draft was a big loss to the Red Sox.

DECEMBER 2   Four weeks after Richard Nixon defeats Hubert Humphrey in the presidential election, the Red Sox trade Gary Waslewski to the Cardinals for Dick Schofield.

1969   B

Season in a Sentence

Just two years after shocking the world by guiding the Red Sox to the pennant, Dick Williams is fired after a distant third-place finish.

Finish • Won • Lost • Pct • GB

Third   87   75   .537   22.0

Managers

Dick Williams (82–71)
Eddie Popowski (5–4)

Stats   Red Sox • AL • Rank

Stats	Red Sox	AL	Rank
Batting Avg:	.251	.246	3
On-Base Pct:	.335	.324	3
Slugging Pct:	.415	.369	1
Home Runs:	197		1
Stolen Bases:	41		11
ERA:	3.92	3.62	9
Fielding Pct:	.975	.978	10
Runs Scored:	743		3
Runs Allowed:	736		11

Starting Lineup

Russ Gibson, c
Dalton Jones, 1b
Mike Andrews, 2b
George Scott, 3b-1b
Rico Petrocelli, ss
Carl Yastrzemski, lf
Reggie Smith, cf
Tony Conigliaro, rf
Syd O'Brien, 3b
Dick Schofield, 2b
Joe Lahoud, rf-lf

Pitchers

Ray Culp, sp
Sonny Siebert, sp-rp
Mike Nagy, sp
Jim Lonborg, sp
Sparky Lyle, rp
Vicente Romo, rp
Bill Landis, rp
Lee Stange, rp-sp
Ray Jarvis, rp-sp

Attendance

1,833,246 (first in AL)

Club Leaders

Batting Avg:	Smith	.309
On-Base Pct:	Petrocelli	.403
Slugging Pct:	Petrocelli	.589
Home Runs:	Petrocelli	40
	Yastrzemski	40
RBI:	Yastrzemski	111
Runs:	Yastrzemski	98
Stolen Bases:	Yastrzemski	15
Wins:	Culp	17
Strikeouts:	Culp	172
ERA:	Nagy	3.11
Saves:	Lyle	17

APRIL 8   The Red Sox open the 1969 season with a 5–4 win over the Orioles in 12 innings in Baltimore. Tony Conigliaro played in his first game since his August 18, 1967, beaning and hit a home run in the tenth inning to give the Red Sox a 4–2 lead. The Orioles rallied to tie the score 4–4 in their half before the Sox pulled out a win with a sacrifice fly by Dalton Jones in the twelfth. Bill Landis was the winning pitcher.

Four games into the season, the Red Sox had a record of 3–1, and Landis was the winning pitcher in all three victories. He finished the season with a record of 5–5.

APRIL 10   The Red Sox lose 2–1 to the Orioles in 13 innings in Baltimore.

Johnny Pesky joined Ken Coleman and Ned Martin in the Red Sox' radio and TV booth in 1969. Pesky replaced Mel Parnell.

APRIL 11   Playing in the third consecutive extra-inning game to open the season, the Red Sox defeat the Indians 2–1 in 16 innings in Cleveland. Billy Conigliaro made his major league debut as a pinch runner.

In his first eight big-league plate appearances, Billy Conigliaro had three homers and struck out five times.

APRIL 14   In the first game of the season at Fenway Park, the Red Sox score one run in each of the first five innings and defeat the Orioles 5–3 before 33,899.

APRIL 18   The Red Sox smash five homers in windblown Fenway Park and beat the Indians 10–7. Ken Harrelson hit two homers and Tony Conigliaro, Carl Yastrzemski, and Rico Petrocelli added one each.

Petrocelli had a breakout year in 1969, with 40 homers, 97 RBIs, and a .297 average.

APRIL 19   The Red Sox trade Ken Harrelson, Dick Ellsworth, and Juan Pizarro to the Indians for Sonny Siebert, Joe Azcue, and Vincente Romo.

In an attempt to nullify the trade, Harrelson immediately announced his retirement. He explained he couldn't leave Boston because of outside business interests that earned him considerably more than his $50,000 annual salary from the Red Sox. According to his agent Bob Wolff, the move from New England would cost Harrelson $750,000. The trade was held up for three days before Harrelson was placated when the Indians convinced him that business opportunities in Cleveland were equal to those in Boston and agreed to double his salary. Red Sox fans were outraged at the trade of Harrelson, but with the return of Tony Conigliaro, the club was set in the outfield and at first base. Pickets consisting of Harrelson's cult following of young fans marched in the streets protesting the trade. Although he was only twenty-seven at the time of the trade, Harrelson played only 218 more big-league games and hit only .220 with 33 homers in 719 at-bats. It was a positive trade, as Siebert had a 45–28 record in his first three years in Boston and Romo gave the Red Sox one effective season as a reliever.

APRIL 20   Gerry Moses hits a grand slam in the second inning off Steve Hargan during a 9–4 win over the Indians at Fenway Park. Ray Jarvis relieved Ken Brett with one out in the first inning and pitched $8\frac{2}{3}$ innings, allowing only one run and two hits. On the negative side, Jarvis batted five times and struck out all five to tie a major league record for most strikeouts in a nine-inning game.

APRIL 23   On the 30th anniversary of his first major league home run, Ted Williams returns to Fenway Park as manager of the Senators and beats the Red Sox, 9–3.

APRIL 26   Carl Yastrzemski hits two homers, one with the bases loaded, during a 7–4 triumph over the Tigers in Detroit. The slam was struck in the second inning off Joe Sparma.

MAY 2   Carl Yastrzemski drives in all three Red Sox runs with two homers and a double for a 3–2 win over the Tigers at Fenway Park.

Yastrzemski hit 40 homers in 1969, along with 96 runs and 111 RBIs, but his batting average dipped to .255.

MAY 4   Rico Petrocelli hits a two-run, walk-off homer in the eleventh inning to beat the Tigers 4–2 at Fenway Park.

MAY 5   On the day the Celtics win their 11th NBA title in 13 years with a Game Seven win over the Lakers, the Red Sox trade Rudy Schlesinger to the Phillies for Don Lock.

MAY 6

The Red Sox play the Pilots in Seattle for the first time and win 12–2 at Sicks Stadium.

The Pilots were one of two expansion franchises that debuted in the American League in 1969. The other was the Kansas City Royals. The Pilots lasted only one season in Seattle. In 1970, the franchise moved to Milwaukee and was renamed the Brewers.

MAY 9

The Red Sox break a 2–2 tie with five runs in the ninth inning, three of them on a bases-loaded triple by Mike Andrews, to beat the Angels 7–2 in Anaheim.

Andrews hit .293 with 15 homers in 1969.

MAY 10

A bases-loaded triple by Tony Conigliaro in the tenth inning defeats the Angels 6–3 in Anaheim.

The twenty-four-year-old Conigliaro dated thirty-six-year-old actress Mamie Van Doren in 1969. Previously, Van Doren had dated big-league pitcher Bo Belinsky and married minor league hurler Lee Meyers. In his first season back from his eye injury, Conigliaro hit .255 with 20 homers.

MAY 11

The Red Sox win their eighth game in a row, defeating the Angels 7–3 in Anaheim.

The eight-game streak gave the Red Sox a 19–10 record, but the Sox were unable to keep up with an Orioles club that won 109 games.

MAY 16

The Pilots play the Red Sox at Fenway Park for the first time, and the two clubs combine for 11 runs in the eleventh inning of a game won 10–9 by Seattle. The Pilots scored six runs in the top of the eleventh before the Red Sox countered with five in their half in a futile rally.

MAY 18

Carl Yastrzemski hits a grand slam in the ninth inning off Mike Marshall, but the Red Sox lose 9–6 to Seattle at Fenway Park.

After batters complained that fans' light-colored clothing in the center field bleachers made it difficult to follow the ball to the plate, the Red Sox posted signs asking those fans to move to another section of the bleachers. Fans who didn't take the hint were often ordered by the ushers to move.

MAY 25

George Scott homers in the fifth inning off Tommy John to beat the White Sox 1–0 in Chicago. The Sox collected only two hits in the game. Jim Lonborg (seven innings) and Vicente Romo (two innings) combined on the shutout.

MAY 27

The Red Sox play the Royals in Kansas City for the first time and lose 5–4 at Municipal Stadium.

JUNE 5

George Scott ties the score 2–2 with a homer in the tenth inning, then Dalton Jones wins it with a two-run, walk-off home run in the eleventh to beat the Royals 4–2 at Fenway Park. It was the first time that the Royals played in Boston.

On the same day, the Red Sox selected outfielder Noel Jenke from the University of Minnesota in the first round of the amateur draft. An all-around athlete,

Jenke played football and hockey in college and was also selected in the NFL and NHL drafts. After three years in the Red Sox' minor league system, Jenke gave up on baseball and turned to the gridiron. From 1971 through 1974, he played linebacker for the Vikings, Falcons, and Packers. Even though Jenke never reached the majors, it was an excellent draft for the Sox because of the selection of Rick Miller in the second round and Dwight Evans in the fifth. Others drafted and signed by the Red Sox in 1969 who made it to the majors were Buddy Hunter (third round), Jim Wright (fourth), and Steve Barr (seventh).

JUNE 11   Joe Lahoud puts together a surprising display of power by stroking three homers in a 13–5 win over the Twins in Minnesota. His major league record entering the game consisted of a .151 batting average with one homer and seven RBIs in 126 at-bats. Lahoud hit a two-run homer off Dave Boswell in the second inning and solo shots against Dick Woodson in the fifth and Bob Miller in the eighth.

JUNE 14   Reggie Jackson drives in 10 runs against the Red Sox, powering the Athletics to a 21–7 win at Fenway Park.

JUNE 15   The Red Sox trade Joe Azcue to the Angels for Tom Satriano.

JUNE 19   Ray Culp pitches a two-hitter for a 3–0 win over the Indians at Municipal Stadium. The only Cleveland hits were singles by Lou Klimchock in the third inning and Lee Maye in the fifth.

Culp had a 17–8 record for the Red Sox in 1969. From July 1, 1968, through August 31, 1969, he was 29–10.

JUNE 21   After the Yankees score three runs in the top of the eleventh, the Red Sox rally for four in their half for a thrilling 6–5 victory in the first game of a doubleheader at Fenway Park. Joe Lahoud drove in two runs with a bases-loaded double, and George Thomas hit a two-run single. New York won the second game, 6–3.

JULY 5   The Red Sox score eight runs in the sixth inning and defeat the Senators 11–4 in the second game of a doubleheader at Fenway Park. Washington won the first game, 6–2.

On the same day, the Red Sox purchased Ron Kline from the Giants.

JULY 11   Reggie Smith collects seven hits, including two doubles, in a doubleheader against the Orioles in Baltimore. In the second tilt, Mike Andrews had five hits, including a double, in five at-bats. The Red Sox won both contests, 7–4 and 12–3. Boston batters collected 22 hits in the second tilt.

After two mediocre seasons, Reggie Smith broke out in 1969 to lead the team in batting, establishing himself as a productive hitter in the lineup for years to come.

Louis Requena/Major League Baseball/Getty Images

JULY 15 | Reggie Smith collects five hits, including two doubles, during a 7–6 win in the first game of a doubleheader against the Yankees at Yankee Stadium. New York won the second game, 4–1.

In five consecutive games from July 11 through July 15, Smith had 14 hits in 21 at-bats. He finished the season batting .309 with 25 homers.

JULY 25 | Five days after Neil Armstrong becomes the first man to walk on the moon, Tony Conigliaro strains his back while hitting a home run during a 7–6 win over the Pilots in Seattle. He had to walk slowly around the bases and didn't play again for a week.

JULY 27 | The Red Sox defeat the Pilots 5–3 in a 20-inning marathon in Seattle. The score was 1–1 after 18 innings. Both teams scored in the nineteenth. Joe Lahoud broke a 2–2 tie with a homer in the twentieth. The Red Sox added an insurance run before the Pilots scored in their half.

AUGUST 1 | Carl Yastrzemski is benched by Dick Williams for failing to hustle in the second inning of a 4–3 loss to the Athletics on Oakland. Williams was angry because Yastrzemski failed to score from third base on a grounder to the third baseman. Yaz was thrown out at the plate.

Williams fined Yastrzemski $500 for "dogging it" and made it clear that he believed that the Sox outfielder had been loafing for weeks. Tom Yawkey took Yastrzemski's side in the dispute, and the showdown between Yaz and Williams would lead to Williams's dismissal (see September 23, 1969).

AUGUST 7 | The Red Sox score three runs in the ninth inning, the last two on Reggie Smith's bases-loaded, walk-off single, to beat Seattle 5–4 at Fenway Park.

AUGUST 17 | On the final day of the Woodstock Music Festival in Bethel, New York, Vicente Romo ($7\frac{2}{3}$ innings), Sparky Lyle (one inning), and Sonny Siebert (one-third of an inning) combine to shut out the Royals 1–0 in Kansas City. The lone run of the game scored on Reggie Smith's single in the sixth inning.

AUGUST 19 | Carl Yastrzemski hits a grand slam off Jim Perry in the third inning to tie the score 4–4, keying an 8–6 win over the Twins at Fenway Park. It was Yastrzemski's third grand slam of the year.

SEPTEMBER 1 | Rico Petrocelli hits a grand slam in the first inning off Joe Dobson to lead the Red Sox to a 6–2 win over the Athletics at Fenway Park.

SEPTEMBER 5 | The Red Sox rally from a 7–0 deficit in the fifth inning to win 9–8 over the Senators at Fenway Park. Darold Knowles walked Rico Petrocelli with the bases loaded in the ninth for the winning run.

Jim Lonborg's season ended two weeks early when he slipped getting out of a car on a rainy Boston night and suffered a deep gash on his foot. Later, he was hospitalized with an infection.

SEPTEMBER 18 | In his major league debut, Carlton Fisk is hitless in four at-bats in a 6–4 loss to the Orioles in the first game of a doubleheader in Baltimore. The Red Sox won the second game, 5–0.

Fisk wore number 40 in his debut. After spending the entire 1970 season in the minors, he switched to number 27 in 1971.

SEPTEMBER 23   Dick Williams is fired as manager. Coach Eddie Popowski was named interim manager for the remainder of the season.

The controversial Williams was fired with one year remaining on his three-year contract. The Red Sox couldn't repeat the magic of 1967 in either 1968 or 1969, and the mean and sarcastic side of Williams surfaced. He was extremely bitter over being fired and remained popular with fans, who fired off angry letters to the Red Sox front office and to newspapers. Carl Yastrzemski, who was viewed as the orchestrator of the dismissal, was booed every time he stepped to the plate at Fenway Park for the remainder of the season. Yastrzemski wasn't the only player who had problems with Williams, however. Others complained that Williams was too tough on them, and he was often brutal when commenting on their play in public statements to the press.

He later managed the Athletics (1971–73), Angels (1974–76), Expos (1977–81), Padres (1982–85), and Mariners (1986–88). Williams guided the A's to the World Championship in both 1972 and 1973 and the Padres to an NL pennant in 1984. Each of the five stops followed the familiar self-destructive pattern he established in Boston. Williams remained outspoken, forceful, and opinionated, and after some initial success, he alienated both players and management alike with his constant harping and "my way or the highway" attitude and was soon in search of another job.

SEPTEMBER 24   The Red Sox defeat the Yankees 1–0 in a long 14-inning encounter at Fenway Park. A double by Mike Andrews drove in the winning run.

OCTOBER 2   The Red Sox name thirty-eight-year-old Eddie Kasko as manager to succeed Dick Williams.

Kasko was soft-spoken and unflappable, a direct contrast to Dick Williams. Kasko was an infielder in the majors from 1957 through 1966 with four clubs, including the 1961 National League Champion Reds, and managed the Red Sox' Class AAA team in Louisville in the American Association from 1967 through 1969. He lasted four seasons as skipper of the Red Sox.

DECEMBER 13   The Red Sox trade Syd O'Brien, Gerry Janeski, and Billy Farmer to the White Sox for Gary Peters and Don Pavletich.

The American League Rookie of the Year in 1963, Peters won 16 games for the Red Sox in 1970 and 14 more in 1971.

THE STATE OF THE RED SOX

The Red Sox had a record of 895–714, a winning percentage of .556 that was the second in the American League only to the Orioles'. The Sox reached the World Series in 1975, and none of the seventies teams had a losing record. Yet it was largely a decade of disappointment. The Sox lost the seventh game of the 1975 Fall Classic to the Reds and blew large Eastern Division leads in both 1974 and 1978. The 1978 season concluded with an excruciating playoff loss to the Yankees. American League champions outside of Boston during the 1970s were the Orioles (1970, 1971, and 1979), Athletics (1972, 1973, and 1974) and Yankees (1976, 1977, and 1978). Eastern Division champs were the Orioles (1970, 1971, 1973, 1974, and 1979), Tigers (1972), and Yankees (1976, 1977, and 1978).

THE BEST TEAM

In terms of winning percentage, the 1978 club was the best with a record of 99–64, but it will be remembered only for losing to the Yankees. The 1975 team, 95–65 during the regular season, was the only one to win a pennant.

THE WORST TEAM

The 1976 club never got on track in the season after the Sox played in the World Series and finished with a record of 83–79.

THE BEST MOMENT

The flight of Carlton Fisk's home run to win Game Six of the 1975 World Series.

THE WORST MOMENT

The flight of Bucky Dent's home run, which beat the Red Sox in the 1978 playoff game against the Yankees.

THE ALL–DECADE TEAM • YEARS WITH BRS

Carlton Fisk, c	1969, 1971–80
Carl Yastrzemski, 1b	1961–83
Doug Griffin, 2b	1971–77
Rico Petrocelli, 3b	1963, 1965–76
Rick Burleson, ss	1974–80
Jim Rice, lf	1974–89
Fred Lynn, cf	1974–80
Dwight Evans, rf	1972–90
Luis Tiant, p	1971–78
Bill Lee, p	1969–78
Ray Culp, p	1968–73
Sonny Siebert, p	1969–73

Carl Yastrzemski and Carlton Fisk are in the Hall of Fame. Jim Rice is eligible on the Baseball Writers Association of America ballot until 2009 and has a chance to be elected in that time frame. Tiant and Evans both deserve Hall of Fame consideration. Yastrzemski and Rico Petrocelli were both on the All-Decade Team of the 1960s at different positions. Yaz was in left field and Petrocelli was at shortstop. Other outstanding Red Sox during the 1970s were center fielder Reggie Smith (1966–73), first baseman George Scott (1966–71, 1977–79), outfielder Tommy Harper (1972–74), and Hall of Fame pitcher Dennis Eckersley (1978–84, 1998). Every member of the 1970s All-Decade Team played in at least one All-Star Game during their career with the exception of Doug Griffin.

THE DECADE LEADERS

Batting Avg:	Rice	.310
On-Base Pct:	Yastrzemski	.384
Slugging Pct:	Rice	.552
Home Runs:	Yastrzemski	202
RBI:	Yastrzemski	846
Runs:	Yastrzemski	845
Stolen Bases:	Harper	107
Wins:	Tiant	122
Strikeouts:	Tiant	1,075
ERA:	Eckersley	2.99
Saves:	Campbell	44

THE HOME FIELD

An electronic scoreboard was installed above the bleachers in right-center field in 1976. It was the first significant addition to Fenway Park since 1940. While there were few physical changes to the ballpark, there was a dramatic shift in the perception of Fenway Park between the beginning of the 1960s and the end of the 1970s. The early 1960s was a period of urban renewal across America in which planners tried to solve the problems and declining populations of the city, particularly in the Northeast and Midwest, with a bulldozer. Old neighborhoods were leveled in favor of large-scale projects. This was best exemplified in Boston by the construction of Government Center and the Prudential Center. In the West End, 56 acres of homes and businesses were swept away to build Government Center, including a new City Hall as the centerpiece. The Prudential Center replaced largely abandoned railroad yards. If Tom Yawkey and many city politicians had their way, Fenway Park would have been among the facilities to be torn down.

Cities like Washington, New York, Oakland, San Diego, Atlanta, St. Louis, Cincinnati, Pittsburgh, and Philadelphia built large multipurpose stadiums during this period to accommodate both baseball and football. Yawkey wanted a similar structure in Boston, at taxpayer expense, but was unable to convince either the city or state government to foot the bill. Meanwhile, the Red Sox turned from chronic losers to winners, beginning with the 1967 pennant, and fans came to Fenway in record numbers. By the 1970s, politicians and private citizens began to see the value in the city's old buildings. Quincy Market and the surrounding Faneuil Hall Marketplace was the focal point of the effort to save the past. The market was spared demolition, and after a period of restoration, became Boston's top tourist attraction. Fenway Park, too, was no longer viewed as an aging relic in need of replacement, but a valuable reminder of the past and of the history of baseball. By the 1990s, most of the cities that had built multipurpose stadiums during the 1960s and 1970s were tearing them down in favor of baseball-only ballparks that tried to replicate the vibrancy that Fenway has held all along.

THE GAME YOU WISH YOU HAD SEEN

Game Six of the 1975 World Series against the Reds on October 22 had all of the drama and excitement one could hope for in a baseball game.

THE WAY THE GAME WAS PLAYED

Speed and defense were more prominent in the 1970s that in any decade since the lively ball was introduced in 1920. Stolen bases per team in the American League rose from 72 in 1970 to 107 in 1979, while home runs per team declined from 146 in 1970 to 94 in 1976 before surging upward again by the end of the decade. The Red Sox, however, playing at Fenway Park, were more rooted in the past. Boston was below the league average in stolen bases eight of the 10 seasons during the 1970s, and above the league average in home runs in nine of the 10. The designated hitter rule was introduced in the AL in 1973.

THE MANAGEMENT

Tom Yawkey died on July 9, 1976, after owning the Red Sox for 43 years. Ownership passed to his widow, Jean, who assumed the club presidency. Dick O'Connell, who had been general manager since 1965, was fired at the end of the 1977 season and replaced by Haywood Sullivan. Field managers were Eddie Kasko (1970–73), Darrell Johnson (1974–76), and Don Zimmer (1976–80).

THE BEST PLAYER MOVE

The best move was drafting Wade Boggs in the seventh round of the 1976 free-agent draft, closely followed by picking Jim Rice in the first round in 1971. The best deal with another club was the waiver purchase of Luis Tiant from the Braves in May 1971. The best trade brought Dennis Eckersley from the Indians in March 1978 with Fred Kendall in exchange for Rick Wise, Bo Diaz, Ted Cox, and Mike Paxton.

THE WORST PLAYER MOVE

The Red Sox sent Sparky Lyle to the Yankees for Danny Cater in March 1972. The trades of Ben Oglivie to the Tigers in October 1973 and Cecil Cooper to the Brewers in December 1976 were also ill-conceived.

1970   B

Season in a Sentence

Under new manager Eddie Kasko, the Red Sox hit 203 home runs but are unable to overcome a slow start, lack of speed, and bad defense.

Finish • Won • Lost • Pct • GB

Third   87   75   .537   21.0

Manager

Eddie Kasko

Stats

Stats	Red Sox	AL	Rank
Batting Avg:	.262	.250	2
On-Base Pct:	.338	.325	2
Slugging Pct:	.428	.379	1
Home Runs:	203		1
Stolen Bases:	50		10
ERA:	3.87	3.71	8
Fielding Pct:	.974	.978	12
Runs Scored:	786		2
Runs Allowed:	722		9

Starting Lineup

Jerry Moses, c
Carl Yastrzemski, 1b-lf
Mike Andrews, 2b
George Scott, 3b-1b
Rico Petrocelli, ss
Billy Conigliaro, lf
Reggie Smith, cf
Tony Conigliaro, rf
Luis Alvarado, 3b-ss
Tom Satriano, c

Pitchers

Ray Culp, sp
Gary Peters, sp
Sonny Siebert, sp
Mike Nagy, sp
Sparky Lyle, rp
Vincente Romo, rp
Ken Brett, rp-sp

Attendance

1,595,278 (first in AL)

Club Leaders

Batting Avg:	Yastrzemski	.329
On-Base Pct:	Yastrzemski	.452
Slugging Pct:	Yastrzemski	.592
Home Runs:	Yastrzemski	40
RBI:	Conigliaro	116
Runs:	Yastrzemski	125
Stolen Bases:	Yastrzemski	23
Wins:	Culp	17
Strikeouts:	Culp	197
ERA:	Culp	3.04
Saves:	Lyle	20

APRIL 7   The Red Sox win the season opener 4–3 against the Yankees in New York. In his debut with the Sox, Gary Peters was the starting pitcher and had a 4–0 lead before allowing three runs in the sixth. Bill Lee earned a save with $3\frac{2}{3}$ innings of scoreless relief.

APRIL 14   In the first game of the season at Fenway Park, the Red Sox defeat the Yankees 8–3 before 34,002. George Scott, Tony Conigliaro, and Reggie Smith all hit homers.

             Smith scored 109 runs and hit .303 with 22 homers in 1970. Scott batted .296 and hit 16 home runs.

APRIL 29   A beanball battle results in a fight during a 5–3 win against the Athletics at Fenway Park. The brawl broke out in the sixth inning when Sonny Siebert hit Reggie Jackson with a pitch. Earlier, Siebert nearly hit Oakland pitcher Pat Dobson in the head with a pitch, and Dobson retaliated by plunking Siebert. Jackson and Blue Moon of the A's and Siebert and George Thomas of the Sox were ejected by the umpires.

             In 1970, the old flagpole, which stood in play in center field, was removed and repositioned atop the center field wall.

MAY 5   The day after Ohio National Guardsmen shoot and kill four students at Kent State University, the Red Sox play the Brewers for the first time in Milwaukee and win, 6–0.

MAY 11   Ray Culp strikes out the first six batters he faces against the Angels in Anaheim. Culp struck out a total of eight batters in 7⅓ innings, but the Red Sox lost 2–1 in 16 innings.

Culp had a record of 17–14 with a .304 ERA in 1970.

MAY 16   Carl Yastrzemski hits a tremendous homer over Fenway Park's center field wall to the right of the flag pole during a 6–2 win over the Indians.

Yastrzemski had one of the best seasons of his career in 1970, with a .329 batting average, 40 homers, 102 RBIs, 125 runs, 186 hits, and 128 walks. He even stole 23 bases. Yaz led the league in on-base percentage (.452) and slugging percentage (.592). He was one of three Red Sox batters with at least 100 RBIs in 1970. Tony Conigliaro hit 36 homers and drove in 116 runs. Rico Petrocelli had 29 homers and 103 RBIs. Despite the terrific year, fans cast about for a scapegoat and focused on Yastrzemski, who was booed often at Fenway Park. He was viewed as the instigator of the firing of popular manager Dick Williams at the end of the 1969 season. Fans were also growing increasingly resentful over the Red Sox' failure to repeat the "Impossible Dream" season of 1967 and targeted Yaz as the object of their wrath. Many expected Yastrzemski to duplicate his once-in-a-lifetime season of 1967 and came down hard when he failed to deliver the nearly impossible.

MAY 29   Down 3–0, the Red Sox score one run in the eighth inning and three in the ninth to beat the White Sox 4–3 at Fenway Park. Jerry Moses broke the 3–3 tie with a walk-off single.

MAY 30   Vincente Romo pitches four innings of shutout relief and hits a two-run homer in the sixth to break a 5–5 tie, enabling the Red Sox to defeat the White Sox 7–5 at Fenway Park.

The homer was the only one that Romo hit in 121 major league at-bats.

MAY 31   The Red Sox lose 22–13 to the White Sox in the second-highest-scoring game in American League history. The record was set on June 29, 1950, when the Red Sox defeated the Athletics 22–14 in Philadelphia. There were 40 hits in the game, including 11 doubles, two triples, and three homers. Red Sox starter Gary Peters gave up six runs in the first inning.

The Red Sox ended the month of June with a record of 20–25.

JUNE 4   The Red Sox select shortstop Jimmy Hacker from Temple High School in Temple, Texas, in the first round of the amateur draft.

Hacker didn't sign with the Red Sox, opting for college instead. He never reached the majors. Three players who were drafted and signed by the Sox in 1970 made it to the big leagues. Rick Burleson was picked in the first round of the January draft. In June, Tim Blackwell was selected in the 13th round and John LaRose in the first round of the secondary phase.

JUNE 7   Rico Petrocelli hits a grand slam in the eighth inning off Alan Fitzmorris to give the Red Sox a 5–2 win over the Royals in the second game of a doubleheader at Fenway Park. The Sox also won the first game, 7–4.

JUNE 10   Trailing 5–0 after three innings, the Red Sox rally to defeat the White Sox 7–6 in 14 innings in Chicago. The rally started on a freak grand slam by Rico Petrocelli in the fourth inning off Joe Horlen. A long fly by Petrocelli bounced off the glove of right fielder Tommy McCraw and into the bullpen. A two-run home run by Tony Conigliaro in the ninth tied the score. The winning run crossed the plate on an error by Chicago third baseman Bill Melton.

JUNE 16   A grand slam by Mike Andrews off Bob Johnson in the ninth inning caps a five-run rally that gives the Red Sox a 7–2 lead over the Royals in Kansas City. The Sox survived a three-run rally in the bottom of the ninth to win, 7–5. Reggie Smith saved the game with a leaping catch of Lou Piniella's drive against the left center field wall with two outs in the ninth.

JUNE 19   In an odd pitching performance, Sonny Siebert holds the Yankees hitless for eight innings at Fenway Park, then gives up four runs and four hits in the ninth before retiring a batter. Sparky Lyle recorded the final three outs for a 7–4 victory.

JUNE 29   The Red Sox sell Lee Stange to the White Sox.

JULY 4   Sonny Siebert pitches a two-hitter to beat the Indians 5–1 at Fenway Park. The only Cleveland hits were a homer by Ray Fosse in the seventh inning and a single by Lou Klimchock in the eighth. Billy and Tony Conigliaro both hit homers. Billy homered off Steve Dunning in the fourth, and Tony hit his against Fred Lasher in the seventh.

JULY 5   In his first at-bat with the Red Sox, John Kennedy hits a pinch-hit, inside-the-park homer to spark the Red Sox to an 8–4 win over the Indians at Fenway Park. Kennedy's hit in the fifth got past Cleveland right fielder Roy Foster, who missed a diving catch.

John Kennedy also hit a home run in his first major league at-bat on September 5, 1962, while playing for the Washington Senators at a time when another John Kennedy resided in the White House. Kennedy the ballplayer and Kennedy the president were both born on May 29.

JULY 14   Carl Yastrzemski earns the All-Star Game Most Valuable Player Award, although the American League loses 5–4 in 12 innings at Riverfront Stadium in Cincinnati. Yastrzemski collected four hits, including a double, in six at-bats.

President Richard Nixon attended the game, and Yastrzemski told White House staff members that he would like to give Nixon the MVP trophy as a gift. The president accepted, and Yastrzemski went to the White House in April 1971 to present the trophy to Nixon. In exchange, he received souvenirs for his four children, a golf ball with the presidential seal, and an autographed picture of the president.

JULY 21   In his major league debut, Carmen Fanzone is hit by a pitch in his first at-bat and makes two errors at third base, as the Red Sox lose 10–6 to the Angels at Fenway Park.

Fanzone appeared in only 10 games for the Red Sox. He later played four seasons for the Cubs. After his playing career ended, Fanzone played trumpet in Johnny Carson's Tonight Show *Band.*

JULY 29   Ray Culp strikes out 12 batters to beat the Athletics 4–1 in Oakland.

JULY 31   Sonny Siebert pitches a one-hitter to defeat the Angels 2–0 in Anaheim. The only California hit was a single by Jay Johnstone in the third inning.

AUGUST 10   The Red Sox hold an 11–3 lead after eight innings, then survive a seven-run Tiger rally in the ninth to win 11–10 at Fenway Park.

AUGUST 13   In his first major league game, John Curtis gives up a grand slam to Ed Kirkpatrick of the Royals in an 11–3 Red Sox loss at Fenway Park.

AUGUST 19   The White Sox score 11 runs in the ninth inning off five pitchers to wipe out a 5–2 Red Sox lead and win 13–5 at Fenway Park.

AUGUST 25   A 1–0 win over the Twins at Metropolitan Stadium in Bloomington, Minnesota, is interrupted for 43 minutes by a bomb scare. In the fourth inning, the crowd of 17,697 had to evacuate. A caller informed police that the bomb would explode at 9:30 PM. At 9:15 PM, the crowd was told to file calmly out of the ballpark. After a search found nothing, play resumed at 9:58 PM. The lone run of the contest scored in the eighth on a home run by Tony Conigliaro off Tom Hall. Vincente Romo (four innings), Ken Brett (four innings), and Gary Wagner (one inning) combined on the shutout.

AUGUST 30   For the second time in 1970, the Red Sox and White Sox play a game at Fenway Park in which more than 30 runs are scored. The White Sox won the first, on May 31, 22–13. This time Boston collected 22 hits and won 21–11 in the first game of a doubleheader at Fenway. The Red Sox scored eight runs in the second inning and led 13–10 at the end of the fourth. A more conventional 4–1 victory in the second tilt completed the sweep of Chicago.

SEPTEMBER 1   A grand slam by Tony Conigliaro in the second inning off John Hiller helps the Red Sox to an 8–1 lead, but the Tigers rally to win 10–9 at Fenway Park.

For the second game in a row, bomb threats were phoned in to Fenway Park. Unlike in Minnesota a week earlier, the game wasn't stopped, and only a portion of the ballpark was evacuated. The caller stated that the bomb was planted in the bleachers, and fans in that section were ordered to move into the right field stands to allow the Boston police bomb squad to conduct a search, which fortunately found no bomb.

SEPTEMBER 4   Tony Conigliaro hits a grand slam in the first inning off Mike Cuellar, but the Red Sox lose 8–6 to the Orioles at Fenway Park.

SEPTEMBER 6   Down 6–0 in the fourth inning, the Red Sox rally to beat the Orioles 9–8 in 11 innings at Fenway Park. A wild pitch by Pete Richert scored Tony Conigliaro from third base with the winning run.

SEPTEMBER 10   The Red Sox trounce the Tigers 14–0 at Fenway Park.

On the same day, the Red Sox purchased Bob Bolin from the Brewers.

SEPTEMBER 19   The Conigliaro brothers both homer in an 11–3 win in the second game of a double-header versus the Senators at Fenway Park. Billy smacked a three-run homer off Jim Hannan in the fourth inning, and Tony hit one against Joe Grzenda in the seventh. The Sox also won the first game, 7–3.

SEPTEMBER 24   Tony Conigliaro drives in all four Red Sox runs with a pair of two-run homers in a 4–3 win over the Senators in Washington. Conigliaro homered in the first and third innings.

SEPTEMBER 25   Ray Culp retires the first 18 batters to face him, then settles for a four-hitter to win 5–1 over the Senators in Washington.

SEPTEMBER 30   In his quest for his fourth career batting title, Carl Yastrzemski collects one hit in four at-bats during a 4–3 loss to the Yankees at Fenway Park. Yastrzemski had to beat out Alex Johnson of the Angels to claim the title Yaz had already won in 1963, 1967, and 1968. Later that evening, Johnson went one for three in a 5–1 California win over the White Sox in Anaheim.

At the end of the day, Yastrzemski had an average of .3286, with 12 hits in his last 20 at-bats. Johnson's average was .3273. The September 30 game was the last of the season for the Red Sox. The Angels had one contest left on the schedule.

OCTOBER 1   After grounding out in his first at-bat, Alex Johnson collects two hits to pull ahead of Carl Yastrzemski in the batting race during a 13-inning, 5–4 Angels win over the White Sox in Anaheim. Johnson's average was .3289 to .3286 for Yastrzemski. With the batting title assured, Johnson left the game after picking up his second hit.

OCTOBER 11   In a shocking trade, the Red Sox swap Tony Conigliaro, Ray Jarvis, and Jerry Moses to the Angels for Doug Griffin, Ken Tatum, and Jarvis Tatum.

The trade was announced at 11:00 PM on a Sunday night, and New Englanders, many of whom first learned of it over their Monday morning coffee, reacted in disbelief. Conigliaro was coming off the best season of his career and was a Boston hero with his local ties, home run bat, and stirring comeback from a near-fatal injury. He was angry over leaving the city, especially since his brother Billy was a teammate and Tom Yawkey promised him he wouldn't be traded, but he figured Southern California was the next best place to go. Conigliaro had designs on a singing and acting career and rented a home in the Hollywood Hills. Ken Tatum was acquired to help alleviate the Red Sox' bullpen problem. The Sox lost four games in 1970 in which they had a lead of at least six runs. In 1969 and 1970, Tatum's first two seasons in the majors, he had a 14–6 record with 39 saves and a 2.16 ERA.

It wasn't a good trade for either club. Conigliaro's eye troubles intensified, and he hit only .222 with four homers in 266 at-bats for the Angels in 1971 before announcing his retirement in July at the age of twenty-six. Moses never developed into anything more than a second-string catcher, and Ray Jarvis never played another major league game. Ken Tatum had troubles with injuries and adjusting to Fenway Park's cozy dimensions, and failed to become the closer the Sox envisioned. Jarvis Tatum never played a game for the Sox. Griffin became the starting second baseman in Boston out of dire necessity. In seven seasons with the Red Sox, he hit only .248 and seven homers in 2,081 at-bats.

DECEMBER 1   The Red Sox trade Mike Andrews and Luis Alvarado to the White Sox for Luis Aparicio.

In the second major deal of the 1970–71 offseason, the Red Sox acquired a future Hall of Famer in shortstop Luis Aparicio. With Aparicio installed at shortstop, Rico Petrocelli was moved to third base. Trading Andrews and moving Petrocelli in favor of the new Doug Griffin/Aparicio double-play combination was designed to strengthen the defense. The loss of firepower in the offense, however, couldn't make up for the improvement defensively. Aparicio was thirty-six when he came to Boston, but he had the best offensive season of his career in 1970, batting .313. In three seasons with the Red Sox, the last three of his career, Aparicio hit .253 with seven homers. Andrews also played only three more years and ended his playing career when he was only twenty-nine. He's best known for making two errors in one game for the Athletics in the 1973 World Series. Athletics owner Charlie Finley tried to maneuver Andrews onto the disabled list, but Commissioner Bowie Kuhn ordered that Andrews be reinstated. Alvarado was nothing more than a light-hitting utility infielder.

1971   B

Season in a Sentence

The Red Sox win 29 of their first 44 games, but clubhouse cliques, feuds, and petty quarrels ruin a promising season.

Finish • Won • Lost • Pct • GB

Fourth   85   77   .525   18.0

Manager

Eddie Kasko

Stats

Stats	Red Sox	AL	Rank
Batting Avg:	.252	.247	5
On-Base Pct:	.325	.320	6
Slugging Pct:	.397	.364	3
Home Runs:	161		2
Stolen Bases:	51		11
ERA:	3.80	3.46	10
Fielding Pct:	.981	.980	4
Runs Scored:	691		3
Runs Allowed:	667		10

Starting Lineup

Duane Josephson, c
George Scott, 1b
Doug Griffin, 2b
Rico Petrocelli, 3b
Luis Aparicio, ss
Carl Yastrzemski, lf
Billy Conigliaro, cf
Reggie Smith, rf-cf
John Kennedy, 3b-ss
Joe Lahoud, rf
Bob Montgomery, c

Pitchers

Sonny Siebert, sp
Ray Culp, sp
Gary Peters, sp
Jim Lonborg, sp
Sparky Lyle, rp
Bob Bolin, rp
Bill Lee, rp

Attendance

1,678,792 (first in AL)

Club Leaders

Batting Avg:	Smith	.283
On-Base Pct:	Yastrzemski	.381
Slugging Pct:	Yastrzemski	.489
Home Runs:	Smith	30
RBI:	Smith	96
Runs:	Smith	85
Stolen Bases:	Smith	11
	Griffin	11
Wins:	Siebert	16
Strikeouts:	Culp	151
ERA:	Siebert	2.91
Saves:	Lyle	16

MARCH 11   Rico Petrocelli and the Red Sox are named as defendants in a one-million-dollar dam-
                age suit charging Petrocelli with assault and battery. The suit was filed on behalf of
                Susanne Mondlin of Roosevelt, New Jersey, who was a flight attendant with United
                Air Lines. Mondlin accused Petrocelli of assaulting her on a flight from Boston to
                Detroit on April 19, 1970. She claimed that he grabbed her "indecently" while she
                was serving coffee and later scratched and kicked her. The case was settled out of
                court.

MARCH 31   The Red Sox trade Vincente Romo and Tony Muser to the White Sox for Duane
                Josephson and Danny Murphy.

                *Josephson was the Red Sox' starting catcher for a year before he yielded to injuries
                and the development of Carlton Fisk. In July 1972, Josephson was placed on the
                disabled list because of an inflammation of the heart. The ailment ended his career
                at the age of thirty and claimed his life in 1997, when he was fifty-four.*

APRIL 6   The Red Sox win the season opener 3–1 over the Yankees before 34,517 at Fen-
                way Park. Ray Culp pitched the complete-game victory. Duane Josephson collected
                three hits in his first game with the Sox. Reggie Smith also picked up three hits
                and made a game-saving defensive play in the eighth inning by throwing out Jim
                Lyttle at the plate. Carl Yastrzemski also made a miracle catch off a drive by
                Horace Clarke.

                Snow fell in Boston in the morning. The game concluded in thirty-nine-degree weather.

APRIL 10   Luis Aparicio drives in six runs on a grand slam and a two-run double, but the Red
                Sox lose 11–10 to the Indians in Cleveland. The slam was struck in the second
                inning off Steve Hargan.

APRIL 18   Carl Yastrzemski homers in the fourth inning off Dean Chance to give the Red Sox
                a 1–0 win over the Tigers in Detroit. Sonny Siebert pitched the shutout.

                *Yastrzemski suffered a horrible season in 1971. He hit only .254 with 15 homers.
                The slump lasted two years. In 1972, he didn't hit a homer until July 22, his 58th
                game of the season. Yaz finished that year with 12 home runs and a .264 average.
                To make matters worse, Yastrzemski signed a three-year deal just before the start
                of the 1971 season for $500,000, which at the time made him the highest-paid
                player in baseball history. Throughout the two-year ordeal, the underperforming
                Yastrzemski was booed relentlessly at Fenway.*

MAY 1   Luis Aparicio and Reggie Smith lead off the first inning with back-to-back homers
                off Jim Perry, but the Red Sox lose 7–3 to the Twins at Fenway Park.

                *Smith hit 30 homers, drove in 96 runs, collected a league-leading 33 doubles,
                and hit .283 in 1971.*

MAY 2   Ray Culp pitches a two-hitter to defeat the Twins 1–0 in the first game of a double-
                header at Fenway Park. The only Minnesota hits were a single by Cesar Tovar in
                the first inning and a double by Leo Cardenas in the sixth. The Sox also won the
                second tilt, 9–8, with two runs in the ninth. George Scott tripled in the first run and
                scored on a pinch single by George Thomas.

MAY 17   Following his release by the Braves, the Red Sox sign Luis Tiant. It was the second time in five weeks that Tiant had been released. The Twins let him go at the end of spring training. The Sox assigned Tiant to their Louisville farm club in the American Association. He spent three weeks in the minors before being called up to Boston.

This proved to be one of the best moves ever made by the Red Sox. Tiant won 122 games with the Sox, a figure exceeded only by Cy Young (192), Roger Clemens (192), and Mel Parnell (123). Among Red Sox pitchers, Tiant is also third in innings (1,774⅔), fourth in shutouts (26), fifth in strikeouts (1,075), and sixth in complete games (113). Tiant had a lifetime record of 82–67 when acquired by the Red Sox that included a 1968 season in which he was 21–9 with a 1.60 ERA. But he was at least thirty years old when he came to Boston (his exact age is open to speculation) and was considered to be washed up by nearly every club in the majors. He was overweight and was recovering from a broken clavicle that doctors concluded would heal only with rest.

The acquisition didn't look like much at the start. After 53 innings with the Sox, Tiant had an ERA of 6.23 and lost his first seven decisions. In June 1972, he had been in Boston for more than a year, and his record with the Red Sox was a dismal 1–9. Suddenly, in midseason in 1972, Tiant regained his touch and became one of the best pitchers in baseball. He liked to celebrate victories with a postgame cigar in the shower or in the whirlpool, and he did so often. With his trademark whirling-dervish motion to the plate, in which he made a 180-degree turn and began his windup with his back to the batter, Tiant was 15–6 in 1972, 20–13 in 1973, 22–13 in 1974, 18–14 in 1975, and 22–12 in 1976. He could deliver almost any pitch from any angle and was a delight to watch. In the process, the Cuban-born Tiant became one of the most popular players ever to play for the Sox.

MAY 23   Pitcher Ken Tatum fractures his cheekbone in three places when struck in the face by a ball hit by coach Dolph Camilli during a pregame workout. Tatum spent four weeks on the disabled list.

MAY 25   Carl Yastrzemski draws five consecutive walks, but the Red Sox lose 6–5 in 11 innings to the Senators at Fenway Park.

Yastrzemski led AL outfielders in assists seven times during his career (1962, 1963, 1964, 1966, 1969, 1971, and 1977) and won seven Gold Gloves.

MAY 28   Sonny Siebert runs his season record to 9–0 to defeat the Athletics and previously unbeaten Vida Blue 4–3 at Fenway Park. Blue entered the game with a record of 10–0. The matchup of two unbeaten pitchers with a combined record of 18–0 drew 35,714, the largest crowd at Fenway in three years. Siebert not only had a 9–0 record but also a 1.76 earned run average. He had won 11 games in a row over two seasons. Siebert cooled off, however, and finished the season at 16–10 with a 2.91 ERA.

May 28 was the high point of the 1971 season. The club was 29–15 and had a four-game lead over the second-place Orioles.

JUNE 2   The Red Sox drop out of first place with a 6–1 loss to the Yankees in New York.

The Sox never regained the top spot but remained within striking distance of the first-place Orioles until August.

JUNE 8   In the first round of the amateur draft, the Red Sox select outfielder Jim Rice from Hannah High School in Anderson, South Carolina.

One of the best selections ever made by the Red Sox in the June draft, Rice arrived in the majors in 1974 for the start of 16 seasons in Boston. The Sox selected no one else of consequence, however. The only other players drafted and signed by the club in 1971 to reach the majors were Bill Moran (ninth round), Mark Bomback (25th), Jack Baker (26th), and Jim Burton, who was taken in the first round of the secondary phase of previously drafted players.

JUNE 11   In his debut with the Red Sox, Luis Tiant gives up five runs, all earned, in one inning of a 6–3 loss to the Royals in Kansas City.

JUNE 14   The Red Sox defeat the Angels 4–3 in 15 innings in Anaheim. Doug Griffin drove in the game winner with a single.

In May and June, Luis Aparicio suffered through a streak in which he went hitless in 44 consecutive at-bats. He received a letter of encouragement from President Richard Nixon. "In my own career," Nixon wrote, "I have experienced long periods when I couldn't get a hit no matter how hard I tried, but in the end, I was able to hit a home run." Aparicio was elected as the starting shortstop in the All-Star Game by the fans, even though he was hitting as low as .150 in early June and .206 at the All-Star break.

JUNE 28   The Red Sox score seven runs in the eighth inning and defeat the Senators 10–4 at Fenway Park.

JULY 1   Rico Petrocelli hits a three-run homer in the ninth inning to defeat the Tigers 8–7 in Detroit.

The victory gave the Red Sox a 44–31 record and put them just one-half game behind the Orioles. The Sox were only 2½ games out as late as July 25 before Baltimore pulled away to win its third straight Eastern Division title.

JULY 7   Ray Culp pitches a two-hitter to defeat the Indians 4–0 in the first game of a doubleheader at Municipal Stadium. The only Cleveland hits were singles by Graig Nettles in the sixth inning and Eddie Leon in the eighth.

JULY 11   At a 5:15 AM press conference, Tony Conigliaro announces his retirement. Examinations by Angels' opthamologists showed the sight in Conigliaro's left eye, injured in the 1967 beaning, had deteriorated markedly over the previous 13 months and hampered his depth perception, along with causing severe headaches.

On the same day, Billy Conigilaro became involved in a controversy with fellow outfielders Carl Yastrzemski and Reggie Smith. Billy bore a grudge against the club for trading his brother and said that Tony was sent to California because Yastrzemski went to Tom Yawkey and demanded that Tony be traded. Billy also said that Yaz wanted to get rid of managers Johnny Pesky, Billy Herman, and Dick Williams, that his appeals to Yawkey led to their firings, and that Yaz had insisted Ken Harrelson be traded. In addition, the younger Conigliaro accused Yaz of going to the front office and demanding that Billy's playing time be reduced. Billy was at the time in a platoon situation in right field with Joe Lahoud. He even accused equipment manager Don Fitzpatrick of conspiring against the Conigliaro family.

Smith said that Billy's comments were calculating and malicious and that he no longer wanted to play with Billy. "With his brother Tony, it is baseball first, other things second," Smith said. "Not so with Billy. It's the other way around." Three days later, there was a bizarre scene in the office of a Boston attorney who represented both Yastrzemski and Conigliaro to smooth over their differences. Within a week, all of the parties involved had made conciliatory statements, but no one really believed that the hatchet had been buried.

JULY 15   A three-run, walk-off homer by Rico Petrocelli in the thirteenth inning provides all three runs in a 3–0 win over the Twins at Fenway Park. Luis Tiant (10 innings) and Bill Lee (three innings) combined on the shutout.

Petrocelli hit 28 homers and drove in 89 runs in 1971.

JULY 17   The Red Sox defeat the Brewers 13–11 and 5–3 in a doubleheader at Fenway Park. The second game was called after six innings by rain.

AUGUST 2   After Luis Tiant gives up four runs in the first inning, Bill Lee allows no runs and just two hits over 8⅔ innings of relief to beat the Orioles 8–4 in Baltimore.

Despite the performance, the Red Sox did not see Lee as a starting pitcher. From his big-league debut in 1969 through 1972, Lee pitched in 125 games, but only nine of them were starting assignments. At the conclusion of the 1972 season, Lee had a career record of 19–11 and an ERA of 3.47. He moved into the starting rotation shortly after the start of the 1973 season.

AUGUST 9   A walk-off pinch-single by Rico Petrocelli in the ninth inning gives the Red Sox a 12–11 win over the Tigers at Fenway Park. Detroit led 7–2 after three innings, but the Red Sox scored eight runs in the fourth to take a 10–7 lead. Bob Montgomery hit a grand slam off Les Cain in the big inning and had six RBIs in the game. The Sox let the Tigers come back and tie the game 11–11, however, setting up Petrocelli's heroics. Bill Freehan hit three homers in the game for Detroit.

AUGUST 16 Billy Conigliaro hits a three-run, walk-off homer in the ninth inning to beat the Angels 6–5 at Fenway Park. The victory snapped a seven-game losing streak.

AUGUST 20 In a duel between Gary Peters and Vida Blue, the Red Sox win 1–0 over the Athletics in Oakland.

AUGUST 22 Gary Peters hits a pinch-homer in the eighth inning against the Athletics in the first game of a doubleheader in Oakland, but the Red Sox lose, 9–3. The Sox also lost the second tilt, 2–1.

Peters had 66 at-bats as a pinch hitter during his big-league career and had 16 hits, for an average of .252. He was five for 18 (.278) in a pinch-hit role in 1971. Overall, Peters had a .222 lifetime batting average and clubbed 19 homers in 807 at-bats.

AUGUST 26   After losing their first 11 games of the season against the Royals, the Red Sox finally win the last meeting of the year between the two clubs by a 7–0 score in Kansas City.

AUGUST 31   After losing his first seven decisions as a member of the Red Sox, Luis Tiant finally wins with $2\frac{2}{3}$ innings of hitless relief in a 4–3 win over the Orioles at Fenway Park.

SEPTEMBER 2   Sonny Siebert drives in all three Red Sox runs with two homers and pitches a shutout to defeat the Orioles 3–0 at Fenway Park. Siebert hit a solo homer in the third inning and a two-run shot in the fifth, both off Pat Dobson.

   Siebert is the last American League pitcher to hit two homers in a game. The designated hitter rule was adopted in 1973. Siebert hit six homers in 1971 and batted .266 in 79 at-bats. Other Red Sox pitchers with five or more homers in a season are Wes Ferrell (seven in 1935 and five in 1936) and Earl Wilson (five in 1964 and six in 1965).

SEPTEMBER 4   Rico Petrocelli publicly states that manager Eddie Kasko is responsible for the Red Sox' failure to win the pennant in 1971. Petrocelli said that Kasko showed favoritism, did nothing to promote team unity, and caused the club to break into factions.

SEPTEMBER 5   The Red Sox announce that Kasko would be back as manager in 1972 for the first year of a two-year contract. On the same day, Red Sox shortstop Juan Beniquez collected three hits in his first major league start. The Red Sox won 8–1 against the Indians at Fenway Park.

SEPTEMBER 6   Eddie Kasko employs 18 different players in the starting lineup during a double-header against the Yankees in New York. In the first game, the lineup was:
   John Kennedy, 2b
   Luis Aparicio, ss
   Carl Yastrzemski, lf
   Reggie Smith, cf
   Billy Conigliaro, rf
   Mike Fiore, 1b
   Phil Gagliano, 3b
   Bob Montgomery, c
   Ray Culp, p

   In the second tilt, the starters were:
   Dour Griffin, 2b
   Rick Miller, cf
   Joe Lahoud, rf
   Rico Petrocelli, 3b
   George Scott, 1b
   Ben Oglivie, lf
   Juan Beniquez, ss
   Carlton Fisk, c
   John Curtis, p

   The lineup shuffling did no good, as the Sox lost both games, the first 3–2 in 10 innings, and the second, 5–3.

SEPTEMBER 9   The Red Sox score seven runs in the eighth inning to win 12–6 in Detroit.

SEPTEMBER 12   Carlton Fisk hits his first major league homer, although the Red Sox lose 3–2 to the Tigers in Detroit. The pitcher was Les Cain.

SEPTEMBER 19   The Red Sox play in Washington for the last time and win 4–3 over the Senators.

At the end of the season, the Senators moved to Dallas–Fort Worth, where they were renamed the Texas Rangers.

OCTOBER 11   In a 10-player deal, the Red Sox trade George Scott, Jim Lonborg, Ken Brett, Joe Lahoud, Don Pavletich, and Billy Conigliaro to the Brewers for Tommy Harper, Marty Pattin, Lew Krausse, and Pat Skrable.

It was the second straight year that the Red Sox made a blockbuster trade late at night on October 11. This one was announced just after midnight. Off-the-field influences had as large an impact on the deal with the Brewers as what took place on the diamond. By getting rid of Conigliaro and Lahoud, both of whom criticized teammates and management, plus perpetual disappointments Scott and Lonborg, the team hoped that chemistry would improve. The trade wasn't a great deal, however. Away from the pressures of trying to duplicate his 1967 season and attempting to pull every pitch over the Green Monster, Scott regained his power stroke during five seasons in Milwaukee. He hit a career-high 36 homers in 1975 and twice drove in more than 100 runs, something he failed to do in Boston.

Lonborg also struggled with the Red Sox after winning 22 games in 1967. He never fully recovered from the serious knee injury he suffered on Christmas Eve at Lake Tahoe and was a constant reminder of what might have been. From 1968 through 1971, Lonborg was 27–29 with an ERA of 4.22. He never pitched more than 167 2/3 innings in a season and spent parts of the 1970 and 1971 seasons in the minors. Like Scott, Lonborg regained his effectiveness in Milwaukee, posting a 14–12 record for a losing club with an earned run average of 2.83. The Brewers traded him to the Phillies, where he won 17 games in 1974 and 18 in 1976. After his playing career ended, Lonborg attended Tufts Dental School and became a dentist in the Boston area.

Brett was an above-average pitcher for several more seasons in the mid-1970s. Conigliaro, Lahoud, and Pavletich weren't missed. Two of the four players acquired from the Brewers gave the Red Sox a few good seasons and helped offset the loss of Scott, Lonborg, and Brett. Harper provided the Red Sox with an element of speed that the club hadn't enjoyed in more than half a century. In three seasons in Boston he stole 107 bases, the most over a three-year period of any Red Sox player since Tris Speaker from 1913 through 1915. Harper also hit 36 home runs. Pattin started the 1972 season poorly. He had a 2–8 record and a 5.67 ERA on June 20 but finished at 17–13 with an earned run average of 3.24. He won 15 games in 1973 before being dealt to the Royals. The Sox hoped the big trade would pull them out of a rut. The club won 86 games in 1968, 87 in 1969, 87 in 1970, and 85 in 1971. It didn't work. The Sox won 85 in 1972, 89 in 1973, and 84 in 1974.

1972   B

Season in a Sentence

The Red Sox are seven games under .500 in late June but put on a rush to take first place in September only to lose the pennant in the final series of the season.

Finish • Won • Lost • Pct • GB

Second   85   70   .548   0.5

Manager

Eddie Kasko

Stats   Red Sox • AL • Rank

Stats	Red Sox	AL	Rank
Batting Avg:	.248	.239	3
On-Base Pct:	.320	.308	2
Slugging Pct:	.376	.343	1
Home Runs:	124		2
Stolen Bases:	66		7
ERA:	3.47	3.06	11
Fielding Pct:	.978	.979	8
Runs Scored:	640		1
Runs Allowed:	620		11

Starting Lineup

Carlton Fisk, c
Danny Cater, 1b
Doug Griffin, 2b
Rico Petrocelli, 3b
Luis Aparicio, ss
Carl Yastrzemski, lf-1b
Tommy Harper, cf
Reggie Smith, rf
Ben Oglivie, rf-lf
John Kennedy, 2b-ss

Pitchers

Marty Pattin, sp
Sonny Siebert, sp
John Curtis, sp
Lynn McGlothlen, sp
Ray Culp, sp
Luis Tiant, rp-sp
Bill Lee, rp

Attendance

1,441,718 (second in AL)

Club Leaders

Batting Avg:	Fisk	.293
On-Base Pct:	Fisk	.370
Slugging Pct:	Fisk	.538
Home Runs:	Fisk	22
RBI:	Petrocelli	75
Runs:	Harper	92
Stolen Bases:	Harper	25
Wins:	Pattin	17
Strikeouts:	Pattin	168
ERA:	Tiant	1.91
Saves:	Lee	5

MARCH 22   The Red Sox trade Sparky Lyle to the Yankees for Danny Cater.

This turned out to be one of the worst trades in Red Sox history. After trading George Scott just after the 1971 season, the Red Sox spent all winter looking for a right-handed, power-hitting first baseman to replace him. Failing in that, they settled on Cater, who was right-handed and played first base but was a thirty-two year-old singles hitter—four years older than Scott. It didn't take long for the Red Sox to realize that trading Scott was a colossal blunder that cost them the 1972 pennant. He began the season as the Red Sox' starting first baseman but lost his job and hit only .237. Lyle, on the other hand, had a 9–5 record, saved 35 games, and posted a 1.92 ERA. He finished third in the MVP balloting. Cater lasted only three years in Boston, the last two as a seldom-used spare part. Lyle was twenty-seven when the Red Sox traded him and had pitched effectively as the club's closer. In 331 $\frac{1}{3}$ innings with Boston over 260 games and five season in Boston, Lyle had a 2.85 ERA, an excellent perform-ance for a pitcher playing half of his games at Fenway Park. He was even better with the hated Yankees, where he pitched in three World Series and was named to three All-Star teams. From 1972 through 1977, he had a record of 48–37 with 132 saves and a 2.23 ERA. In 1977, Lyle won the Cy Young Award. While he was starring in New York, the Red Sox went through an assortment *of mediocre closers, including Bob Bolin, Bob Veale, Diego Segui, Dick Drago, Tom Murphy, and Jim Willoughby.*

APRIL 6   The Red Sox' scheduled season opener against the Tigers at Fenway Park is canceled by baseball's first players' strike. Boston's first seven games were eliminated by the labor action, which began on April 1 and ended on April 13.

The seven games lost by the Red Sox had a profound impact on the American League Eastern Division pennant race. The Tigers had six games wiped out and finished the season with a record of 86–70, one-half game ahead of the 85–70 Red Sox.

APRIL 15   With the strike settled, the Red Sox open the season in Detroit and lose 3–2 to the Tigers. The Sox lost a run when Luis Aparicio tripped over third base on a hit by Carl Yastrzemski, a base-running mishap that would prove to be prophetic (see October 2, 1972). Marty Pattin was the losing pitcher in his Red Sox debut.

At the start of the 1972 season, only Carl Yastrzemski, Reggie Smith, and Rico Petrocelli remained from the 1967 pennant-winning club.

APRIL 17   In the home opener, the Red Sox lose 4–0 to the Indians before 24,989 at Fenway Park. Milt Wilcox pitched a two-hitter for Cleveland. Duane Josephson collected both Boston hits.

Josephson started the first three games of the season at catcher but was shelved by a pulled muscle. Bob Montgomery started the fourth game, but the Indians stole four bases on him. Eddie Kasko then turned to rookie Carlton Fisk. "Fisk may be inexperienced," Kasko said, "but at least he can throw." The Red Sox considered Fisk to be more of a defensive weapon than an offensive threat. In 592 at-bats at Class AAA, he hit 22 homers but batted only .247. Fisk was an immediate sensation in the majors however, and by midseason he had performed well enough to make the American League All-Star team. By the end of the season, he had a .293 average and a league-leading nine triples, 28 doubles, 22 homers, and a .538 slugging percentage. The 22 homers were a record for Red Sox catchers. The previous high was 17, by Bob Tillman in 1964. Fisk won the Rookie of the Year Award by a unanimous vote, was fourth in the MVP balloting, and earned a Gold Glove. By the time his career was over in 1993, Fisk had caught more games than anyone in history, hit one of the most dramatic homers in World Series annals, and hit more career homers than any other catcher before Mike Piazza surpassed him in 2004. Fisk was elected to the Hall of Fame in 2000 in his second year on the ballot.

APRIL 28   The Red Sox play a regular-season game in Texas for the first time and defeat the Rangers 9–6 at Arlington Stadium.

The Washington Senators moved to Texas after the 1971 season and were renamed the Rangers. The Rangers moved from the Eastern Division to the West, and the Milwaukee Brewers transferred to the East with the Red Sox.

APRIL 30   The Red Sox score three runs in the tenth inning to beat the Rangers 3–0 in Texas. Tommy Harper drove in two of the runs with a double and scored on another double by Luis Aparicio. Lew Krausse (nine innings) and Bill Lee (one inning) combined on a two-hitter. Lenny Randle collected both Texas hits with singles in the first and ninth innings.

The Red Sox didn't hit a home run until the 12th game of the 1972 season and started the campaign with a record of 4–10.

MAY 12

The day after the Bruins win the Stanley Cup in a six-game series against the New York Rangers, Tommy Harper hits a homer in the twelfth inning, his second of the game, to beat the Athletics 7–6 in Oakland.

Harper finished the season with 92 runs scored, 29 doubles, 25 stolen bases, and a .254 average.

MAY 14

The Red Sox suffer a weird 6–5 loss to the Athletics in Oakland. The Red Sox' Duane Josephson hit a two-run homer in the eighth to tie the score, 5–5. In the Boston ninth, with Bob Burda on second base with one out, A's center fielder Angel Mangual caught a fly ball. Believing it was the third out, Mangual trotted toward the dugout. Burda tried to score from second, and Mangual, at the urging of his teammates, finally realized his mistake and fired home. Burda was out at the plate on a controversial call. The A's won the game in the ninth on a throwing error by Josephson, who spent most of his career behind the plate but was making a rare appearance as a first baseman.

The Red Sox split their radio and TV teams in 1972. Ken Coleman and Johnny Pesky handled the telecasts while Ned Martin and newcomer Dave Martin formed the radio team.

MAY 16

A run-scoring single by Danny Cater and a three-run homer by Rick Miller in the tenth inning beat the Brewers 5–1 in Milwaukee.

Bob Gallagher, a native of Newton, Massachusetts, who played seven games for the Red Sox in 1972, was the grandson of Shano Collins, who played for the Sox from 1921 through 1925 and managed the team in 1931 and 1932.

JUNE 6

In the first round of the amateur draft, the Red Sox select shortstop Joel Bishop from McClatchy High School in Sacramento, California.

Bishop was a complete disaster and never advanced beyond Class A ball. The Red Sox drafted and signed four future major leaguers: Steve Dillard (second round), Don Aase (sixth), Andy Merchant (10th), and Ernie Whitt (15th). None had a significant impact in Boston.

JUNE 19

Two days after the break-in to Democratic Party National Committee headquarters at the Watergate complex in Washington, the Red Sox whip the Rangers 12–0 at Fenway Park.

Several Red Sox players, including Reggie Smith, Doug Griffin, Luis Tiant, and Luis Aparicio, grew mustaches during the 1972 season. They were the first Sox players with facial hair since Candy LcChance, who played for the club from 1902 through 1905.

JUNE 21   Rich Petrocelli drives in six runs on only one hit to lead the Red Sox to an 11-inning, 10–9 win over the Rangers at Fenway Park. Petrocelli hit a grand slam off Bill Gogolewski in the fifth inning and contributed the other two RBIs on sacrifice flies. Carl Yastrzemski collected five hits, including two doubles, in six at-bats. Neither Petrocelli nor Yastrzemski figured in the winning run in the eleventh, which scored on Doug Griffin's RBI single.

JUNE 27   On Eddie Kasko's 41st birthday, the Red Sox score seven runs in the fourth inning and defeat the Indians 9–2 in Cleveland.

JUNE 29   The Tigers score eight runs in the ninth inning and defeat the Red Sox 8–4 at Fenway Park.

The defeat looked like the end of the season for the Sox. The club was 27–34 and eight games behind the first-place Tigers. By August 2, Boston had improved to 48–48 but still trailed Detroit by 6½ games.

JULY 2   The Red Sox romp to a 15–4 win over the Brewers in the first game of a double-header at Fenway Park. Rico Petrocelli hit a grand slam in the first inning off Skip Lockwood, and Reggie Smith homered from both sides of the plate. The Sox completed the sweep in the second game with a 3–2 win in 11 innings. Ben Oglivie drove the winning run with a single, his sixth hit of the twin bill.

JULY 4   Lynn McGlothlen earns his first career victory with a complete-game shutout, defeating the Twins 2–0 at Fenway Park.

McGlothlen was the Louisiana high school tennis champion for three years.

JULY 7   Ben Oglivie, a last-minute replacement in right field for the injured Reggie Smith, hits a two-run homer in the tenth inning to beat the Angels 5–3 in Anaheim. With the Red Sox leading 3–2 in the ninth, Ben Oglivie was called safe by umpire Hank Morganweck on a close play at the plate while sidestepping Angels catcher Jeff Torborg. The Angels claimed that Oglivie was out of the base line. Morganweck huddled with second-base umpire John Rice and reversed his decision, calling Oglivie out. Kasko exploded from the dugout. When words failed him, Kasko keeled over backward on the grass as if he had fainted from disbelief over the call. The umpires weren't amused by Kasko's pantomime act and threw him out. Kasko followed as much of the game as he could from a tunnel behind the dugout. He blew his stack over a tenth-inning umpiring decision, ran onto the field, and was ejected again.

JULY 9   Nolan Ryan strikes out 16 Red Sox batters and pitches a one-hitter in a 3–0 Angels win at Anaheim. He retired the last 26 batters to face him. From the first inning through the third, Ryan set an American League record (since tied) for most consecutive strikeouts with eight. The eight victims were Reggie Smith, Rico Petrocelli, Carlton Fisk, Bob Burda, Juan Beniquez, Sonny Siebert, Tommy Harper, and Doug Griffin. In the second, Fisk, Burda, and Beniquez struck out on nine total pitches.

JULY 11   Only two outs from a no-hitter, Marty Pattin gives up a single to Reggie Jackson and settles for a one-hitter and a 4–0 win over the Athletics in Oakland.

JULY 13   Rookie Juan Beniquez makes three errors at shortstop during a 10–0 loss to the Twins in Minnesota.

JULY 14   Juan Beniquez makes three errors at shortstop for the second game in a row during a 7–6 loss to the Twins at Metropolitan Stadium. One bobble was in the ninth inning when Minnesota scored three runs for the victory.

> *The Red Sox soon gave up on the idea of Beniquez playing shortstop. He moved to the outfield and had a 17-year major league career during which he played for an AL-record eight clubs. In addition to the Sox, Beniquez appeared in games with the Rangers, Yankees, Mariners, Angels, Orioles, Royals, and Blue Jays.*

JULY 21   The Red Sox edge the Athletics in 14 innings at Fenway Park. Doug Griffin scored the winning run from first base on an error by second baseman Sal Bando when the ball glanced off his glove and into right-center field. Normally a third baseman, Bando moved to second in extra innings because A's manager Dick Williams ran out of infielders.

JULY 28   The Red Sox rally for four runs in the ninth inning, the last three on Bob Montgomery's homer, to beat the Yankees 6–5 in the first game of a doubleheader in New York. The Yanks won the second game, 3–1.

AUGUST 4   Marty Pattin pitches a two-hitter to defeat the Orioles 2–0 at Fenway Park. The only Baltimore hits were a double by Terry Crowley in the fourth inning and a single by Bobby Grich in the sixth.

AUGUST 5   Rico Petrocelli drives in all six Red Sox runs with a two-run double in the first inning and a grand slam in the third, both off Dave McNally, to lead Boston to a 6–3 win over the Orioles at Fenway Park.

AUGUST 7   At an autograph session in Springfield, Massachusetts, Carlton Fisk criticizes Carl Yastrzemski and Reggie Smith for a lack of leadership.

AUGUST 12 Luis Tiant no-hits the Orioles for six innings, then settles for a three-hit, 5–3 win in the first game of a doubleheader at Memorial Stadium. Baltimore won the first game, 3–2.

> *For the first half of the season, Tiant was a seldom-used mop-up reliever, but injuries to the rotation forced him into a starting role in late July. For the rest of the season, he was phenomenal. From August 1 through the end of the season, Tiant was 11–2. He finished the season with a 15–6 record, a league-leading 1.91 ERA and six shutouts, four in them in consecutive starts.*

AUGUST 15 Reggie Smith hits two homers to drive in all three Boston runs in a 3–0 win over the Rangers in Arlington. Smith hit a solo homer in the fifth inning and a two-run blast in the eighth.

AUGUST 16 Reggie Smith's grand slam in the fifth inning off Rich Hand is wasted in a 10-inning, 9–8 loss to the Rangers in Arlington.

AUGUST 17   Reggie Smith is the star for the third straight game at Arlington Stadium with a three-run homer in the eighth inning to wipe out a two-run Rangers lead and lift the Red Sox to a 4–3 victory.

Smith hit .270 with 21 homers in 1972.

AUGUST 19   Luis Tiant pitches a two-hitter to defeat the White Sox 3–0 at Comiskey Park. Tiant held Chicago hitless until Carlos May doubled with two out in the seventh. Tony Muser added a single in the ninth. It was Tiant's first shutout since April 26, 1970, when he pitched for the Twins. Over the next 32 days, he would pitch five more shutouts.

AUGUST 25   Luis Tiant pitches his second straight shutout, defeating the Rangers 4–0 at Fenway Park.

AUGUST 26   The Red Sox stun the Rangers with five runs in the ninth inning to win 7–6 at Fenway Park. The Sox collected only two hits in the first eight innings. The first three runs in the ninth scored on two walks, a double, and two singles. Phil Gagliano drove in the tying and winning runs on a pinch-double.

AUGUST 29   Luis Tiant pitches his third straight shutout, defeating the White Sox 3–0 at Fenway Park. Reggie Smith had a hand in all three runs, scoring one and driving in two on a pair of doubles.

SEPTEMBER 1   Marty Pattin pitches the Red Sox to a 1–0 win over the Royals at Fenway Park. Rico Petrocelli drove in the lone run of the game with a single in the fourth inning.

SEPTEMBER 2   The Red Sox purchase Bob Veale from the Pirates.

At the end of play on September 3, the Orioles were in first place, and the Red Sox, Tigers, and Yankees were in a virtual tie for second, half a game back.

SEPTEMBER 4   Luis Tiant pitches his fourth consecutive shutout with a 2–0 win over the Brewers in the first game of a doubleheader at County Stadium. Both runs scored on a two-run homer in the third inning by Carl Yastrzemski off Jim Lonborg. Milwaukee won the second game, 6–2.

Tiant had a streak of 40 consecutive scoreless innings from August 19 through September 8. He pitched six shutouts from August 19 through September 20.

SEPTEMBER 6   A two-run homer by Reggie Smith in the fifth inning off Mel Stottlemyre beats the Yankees 2–0 at Fenway Park.

SEPTEMBER 7   The Red Sox take over first place with a 10–4 win over the Yankees in New York.

SEPTEMBER 10   Triggered by a home run from Carlton Fisk, the Red Sox score four runs in the twelfth inning to beat the Indians 5–1 in the first game of a doubleheader in Cleveland. The Sox completed the sweep with a 2–0 win in the nightcap.

SEPTEMBER 16   The Red Sox clobber the Indians 10–0 at Fenway Park. Dwight Evans made his major league debut, subbing for Reggie Smith in right field when the game was in the bag. Evans was hitless in his lone at-bat.

> *Evans wore number 40 in his big-league debut. He switched to number 24 in 1973.*

SEPTEMBER 20   The Red Sox score seven runs in the fourth inning and defeat the Orioles 9–1 in the first game of a doubleheader at Fenway Park. The Sox completed the sweep with a 4–0 win in the second tilt, in which Dwight Evans hit his first major league home run and Luis Tiant pitched his sixth shutout in less than five weeks.

SEPTEMBER 24   The Red Sox defeat the Tigers 7–2 at Fenway Park in the fourth game of a crucial four-game series, in which the Red Sox won two of the contests to maintain a one-game lead.

SEPTEMBER 26   The Red Sox lose a critical 5–4 decision to the Brewers at Fenway Park. The Sox led early 4–0 on two-run homers by Carl Yastrzemski and Marty Pattin. The Brewers cut the lead to 4–2, then scored three runs in the eighth, the final two on a homer into the center field bleachers by ex–Red Sox George Scott.

SEPTEMBER 29   Carl Yastrzemski's two-run homer in the tenth inning beats the Orioles 4–2 in Baltimore.

> *The win gave the Red Sox a 1½-game lead over the Tigers. Each club had five games left on the schedule. The final three games were head-to-head pennant showdowns between the Sox and the Tigers in Detroit on October 2, 3, and 4. The 1972 Tigers were managed by Billy Martin.*

SEPTEMBER 30   The Red Sox maintain their 1½-game lead over the Tigers by defeating the Orioles 3–1 in Baltimore. Bob Veale entered the game in relief of Marty Pattin with no outs in the ninth and runners on first and second and retired the Orioles on a strikeout and a double play.

OCTOBER 1   The Red Sox lose 2–1 to the Orioles in Baltimore, which chops Boston's lead over Detroit in the AL East to half a game.

> *The pennant would be decided in the final three-game series against the Tigers in Detroit. Whichever club won two games would clinch the pennant.*

OCTOBER 2   The Tigers defeat the Red Sox 4–1 in the first game of the showdown series in Detroit. Mickey Lolich struck out 15 batters. A base-running mishap proved costly to the Red Sox. With the score 1–0 Tigers in the Red Sox' half of the third inning, the Sox had Tommy Harper on third base and Luis Aparicio on first. When Yastrzemski hit a drive off the top of the center field wall, Harper crossed the plate with the tying run. Aparicio was headed for the go-ahead tally when he stumbled as he neared third, regained his balance, slipped on the bag, and stumbled awkwardly into foul territory and fell down. Aparicio scrambled back to third. Yastrzemski had designs on a triple and, running with his head down, didn't see Aparicio fall. Yaz arrived at third only to find Aparicio on the bag. Aparicio tried to head for home, but slipped and fell again on the wet grass and had to scramble back to third again. In the process, he cut his knee with his own spikes. Yaz tried to retreat to second but was tagged out. Reggie Smith struck out to end the rally. Aurelio Rodriguez drove in the final three runs for the Tigers, including a solo homer in the fifth that broke a 1–1 tie.

The loss dropped the Red Sox into second place, one-half game in back of the Tigers. The Sox needed to win both of the remaining two games of the series to win the pennant.

OCTOBER 3   The Tigers clinch the AL East with a 3–1 win over the Red Sox at Tiger Stadium. The Tigers broke a 1–1 tie with two runs in the seventh inning off Luis Tiant, the first on a single by Al Kaline.

OCTOBER 4   The Red Sox conclude the season with a meaningless 4–1 win over the Tigers at Detroit to finish half a game out of first. The Tigers moved on to lose the American League Championship Series three games to two to the Oakland Athletics.

DECEMBER 10   Five weeks after Richard Nixon earns a second term as president with an election victory over George McGovern, the American League votes to adopt the designated hitter rule on a three-year experimental basis. Under the new rule, the designated hitter replaced the pitcher in the batting order unless otherwise noted before the start of the game. The rule was adopted permanently by the AL in 1975, but to this day the NL has declined to go along with the change.

Carlton Fisk began his tenure as full-time catcher in 1972 and would be one of the team's most productive and popular players throughout the '70s.

Steve Babineau

1973   B

Season in a Sentence

The Red Sox are in first place in July and win 89 games but are unable to keep pace with the Orioles.

Finish • Won • Lost • Pct • GB

Second   89   73   .549   8.0

Manager

Eddie Kasko

Stats   Red Sox • AL • Rank

	Red Sox	AL	Rank
Batting Avg:	267	.259	2
On-Base Pct:	.340	.331	4
Slugging Pct:	.401	.381	3
Home Runs:	147		3 (tie)
Stolen Bases:	114		3
ERA:	3.65	3.82	5
Fielding Pct:	.979	.977	3
Runs Scored:	738		4
Runs Allowed:	647		4

Starting Lineup

Carlton Fisk, c
Carl Yastrzemski, 1b
Doug Griffin, 2b
Rico Petrocelli, 3b
Luis Aparicio, ss
Tommy Harper, lf
Reggie Smith, cf-rf
Rick Miller, rf-cf
Orlando Cepeda, dh
Dwight Evans, rf
Mario Guerrero, ss-2b
Danny Cater, 1b-3b
John Kennedy, 2b-3b

Pitchers

Luis Tiant, sp
Bill Lee, sp
Marty Pattin, sp
John Curtis, sp
Roger Moret, sp-rp
Bobby Bolin, rp
Bob Veale, rp

Attendance

1,481,002 (second in AL)

Club Leaders

Batting Avg:	Yastrzemski	.296
On-Base Pct:	Yastrzemski	.407
Slugging Pct:	Yastrzemski	.463
Home Runs:	Fisk	26
RBI:	Yastrzemski	95
Runs:	Harper	92
Stolen Bases:	Harper	54
Wins:	Tiant	20
Strikeouts:	Tiant	208
ERA:	Lee	2.75
Saves:	Bolin	15

JANUARY 18   The Red Sox sign Orlando Cepeda, who was released by the Athletics on December 18, 1973.

Cepeda was the first player acquired by a club with the new designated-hitter rule in mind. The DH was used for the first time during the 1973 season. From his rookie season in 1958 through 1970, Cepeda was one of the best first baseman in baseball with the Giants, Cardinals, and Braves. Two surgically repaired knees made it impossible for him to play defense on a regular basis, however, and Cepeda appeared in only 31 games in 1972 with the Braves and Athletics. He was thirty-five years old, and many believed his career was over when the Sox acquired him, but he had 358 career homers and hit right-handed. The club hoped his knee could stand the strain if Cepeda was called upon only to hit. The gamble worked, as he batted .289 with 20 homers in 1973 and became a fan favorite at Fenway Park.

JANUARY 24   The Red Sox trade Mike Nagy to the Cardinals for Lance Clemons.

The Red Sox' uniforms in 1973 underwent their first radical change since the 1930s. The new double-knit jerseys featured a pullover shirt and built-in sash belt. The new home and road jerseys featured red-navy-red striping on the V-neck collar.

The cap's crown was changed in 1975 to solid red with a navy visor, and the traditional Old English "B" reverted to navy with a white outline. The team also introduced red shoes.

APRIL 6   With the help of a thirty-mile-per-hour wind, Carlton Fisk hits two homers, including his first major league grand slam, in a 15–5 trouncing of the Yankees on Opening Day before 32,867 at Fenway Park. The slam came in the fourth inning off Lindy McDaniel. Fisk also hit a double and scored four runs. The Sox collected 20 hits. Doug Griffin had four hits, and Rico Petrocelli and Tommy Harper had three each. Carl Yastrzemski hit a homer. Orlando Cepeda, as the first designated hitter in Red Sox history, was 0 for 6. The game was the first to be played in the American League that season. Ron Blomberg was the Yankees' DH and hit before Cepeda came up for the Red Sox, thus becoming the first designated hitter in baseball history.

Fisk hit five homers in his first seven games in 1973. By the end of the season he had a .246 average and 26 home runs.

APRIL 8   After going hitless in his first 11 at-bats with the Red Sox, Orlando Cepeda hits a walk-off homer to beat the Yankees 4–3 at Fenway Park.

The Red Sox started the season with wins in their first four games but dropped to 21–25 by June 3.

APRIL 11   The Red Sox' game against the Brewers in Milwaukee is postponed by snow.

APRIL 16   Reggie Smith homers from both sides of the plate during a 9–7 loss to the Tigers on Patriots' Day at Fenway Park. Smith hit the homers off Mickey Lolich and Lerrin LaGrow.

Smith hit .303 with 21 homers in 1973 but became the target of disgruntled fans at Fenway Park. By June, Smith resorted to wearing a batting helmet in center field because many fans were pelting him with objects thrown from the bleachers, in addition to shouting racial epithets. "There are a lot of sick people up there, and I'm getting pretty fed up with it," Smith said. The racial climate in Boston was strained at the time because of a controversial bussing plan in the city's schools.

MAY 3   Orlando Cepeda hits a grand slam off Pete Broberg in the third inning of a 6–2 win over the Rangers at Fenway Park.

MAY 4   The Red Sox sell Sonny Siebert to the Rangers.

MAY 13   Tommy Harper hits a grand slam off Steve Mingori in the sixth inning of an 8–3 win over the Indians at Fenway Park.

MAY 14   Breaking up a scoreless duel, Orlando Cepeda drives in the winning run with a walk-off single in the eleventh inning to beat the Orioles at Fenway Park. Bill Lee (nine innings) and Bob Bolin (two innings) combined on the shutout.

Lee was twenty-six years old and in his fifth season in the majors in 1973. He was used primarily as a reliever throughout his first four seasons with the Sox but was converted to a starting role early in the 1973 campaign. It was an excellent decision. He had a 12–3 record at the All-Star break and finished the season with 17 wins and 11 losses with a 2.85 ERA in 284⅔ innings. It was the first of three consecutive 17-win seasons for Lee. Outrageous, irreverent, and fascinating, Lee seemed like a work of fiction. He earned the nickname "Space Man" because he was never at a loss for words and had some unusual but entertaining and often hilarious ideas. For instance, Lee said that the Red Sox should hire beautiful women as first- and third-base coaches. "That way the players would pay attention," Lee said, and would never miss a sign. His acid tongue and frequent criticisms of team managers, whom Lee believed were his intellectual inferiors, divided the Red Sox Nation into pro-Lee and anti-Lee factions. Few were ambivalent. He became a cult hero to young fans with his personal explorations into Eastern religions, pacifism, drugs, and rock 'n' roll and unnerved the baseball establishment. Despite his flaky, paradoxical, and iconoclastic persona, Lee was one of the most competitive players in the game. He wasn't averse to throwing at hitters or getting into the center of a brawl.

MAY 24   A brawl erupts during a 10–1 win over the Brewers at Fenway Park. Bill Lee hit Milwaukee's Ellie Rodriguez with a pitch in the third inning. Rodriguez went to the mound with bat in hand but was restrained before any damage was done. Before the day was finished, Lee fought Reggie Smith in the clubhouse.

Lee had been waiting for three years to get even with Rodriguez. In 1970, while pitching in the Puerto Rican Winter League, Lee hit Rodriguez with a pitch. The following day, Rodriguez, backed by two friends, jumped Lee from behind and threw him against a wall. Lee lost four teeth in the fight in the collision with the wall.

MAY 27   The Red Sox play at Royals Stadium in Kansas City for the first time and split a doubleheader. The Royals won the first game 13–3, and the Sox won the second, 7–2.

MAY 30   Rico Petrocelli and Jeff Torborg of the Angels trade punches in the fifth inning of a 2–1 Red Sox victory at Fenway Park.

It all started when Alan Gallagher of the Angels was caught in a rundown between third and home. Gallagher crashed into Carlton Fisk as he was tagged out. When Gallagher came to bat in the seventh, Luis Tiant knocked him down with a close pitch high and inside. After Gallagher grounded out, he bumped Fisk as he was returning to the California dugout. Both benches emptied, and Petrocelli and Torborg landed a few blows before order was restored.

JUNE 5   In the first round of the amateur draft, the Red Sox select shortstop Ted Cox from Midwest City High School in Midwest City, Oklahoma.

Cox arrived in the majors in 1977 and played only 13 games with the Red Sox before a trade to the Indians. He had a five-year career as a utility player. The club hit the jackpot in the second round by picking outfielder Fred Lynn from the University of Southern California. In 1975, Lynn won both the Rookie of the Year Award and the MVP balloting in helping the Sox reach the World Series. Others drafted and signed by the Red Sox in 1973 who later reached the majors were Rick Jones (fourth round) and Butch Hobson (eighth).

JUNE 6 — Bob Montgomery hits a walk-off homer, his second dinger of the game, in the tenth inning to beat the Royals 5–4 at Fenway Park.

JUNE 9 — During a 12–1 trouncing of the Rangers in Arlington, Carl Yastrzemski collects the 2,000th hit of his major league career.

JUNE 20 — Rick Miller and Reggie Smith lead off the first inning with back-to-back homers against Bill Parsons to spark a 3–2 win over the Brewers in Milwaukee.

JUNE 24 — Orlando Cepeda's homer in the second inning off Doyle Alexander beats the Orioles 1–0 at Fenway Park. John Curtis pitched the shutout.

> *Curtis's great-uncle laid the original sod at Fenway Park, and his uncle was Tom Yawkey's roommate at Yale.*

JUNE 28 — After losing the opener of a doubleheader 4–2 to the Indians at Fenway Park, the Red Sox explode for a 16–7 victory in the nightcap.

JULY 1 — Luis Aparicio steals the 500th base of his career during a 9–5 loss to the Brewers at Fenway Park.

JULY 2 — Dwight Evans hits a homer in the fifth inning off Fritz Peterson to beat the Yankees 1–0 in New York. It was one of only two Boston hits off Peterson. John Curtis pitched the shutout, his second 1–0 win in a span of three starts.

> *Evans was in his first full season in the majors in 1973. He played 19 years with the Red Sox and ranks among the all-time club leaders in nearly every category, with 2,505 games, 1,435 runs, 2,373 hits, 474 doubles, 79 triples, 379 homers, 1,346 RBIs, and 1,337 walks. His Red Sox batting average was .272 to go with an on-base percentage of .369 and a slugging percentage of .473. Evans also won eight Gold Gloves for his work in right field. Strangely, he had his best offensive seasons late in his career. All four years in which he drove in more than 100 runs came after he turned thirty, and so did the four years in which he scored 100 or more runs and the three years he hit 30 or more home runs. The only year Evans hit higher than .300 was in 1987, when he was thirty-five.*

JULY 4 — The Red Sox defeat the Yankees 1–0 again, this time in the second game of a doubleheader in New York. Roger Moret pitched the shutout. Carl Yastrzemski drove in the winning run with a single in the fifth inning. The Sox also won the first game, 2–1, with two runs in the ninth.

> *Yastrzemski rebounded from off years in both 1971 and 1972 to bat .296 with 19 home runs in 1973.*

JULY 5 — The Red Sox score seven runs in the fourth inning and beat the Yankees 9–4 in New York.

JULY 8 — After scoring just three runs in the first 18 innings of a doubleheader at Comiskey Park, the Red Sox erupt for nine runs in the tenth inning of the second game to beat the White Sox, 11–2. Bob Montgomery hit a grand slam off Steve Kealey. Chicago won the first game, 6–1.

JULY 10 — Luis Tiant pitches a two-hitter to beat the Twins 2–1 at Metropolitan Stadium. The only Minnesota hits were a double by Joe Lis in the second inning and a single by Rod Carew in the ninth.

The win put the Red Sox into first place with a record of 45–38. The club's stay in first place lasted only one day, but the Sox remained within striking distance of first place until late August.

JULY 16 — Reggie Smith hits a homer in the eleventh inning, his second of the game, to beat the White Sox 9–8 at Fenway Park.

AUGUST 1 — The Red Sox defeat the Yankees 3–2 at Fenway Park with a run in the ninth in a contest highlighted by a brawl between Carlton Fisk and Thurman Munson. In the ninth inning, Yankee batter Gene Michael attempted a bunt with Munson on third. Michael missed but tried to get in Fisk's way as he stepped forward to tag Munson coming down the line. Fisk brushed Michael aside with one swipe of his arm, and Munson barreled into Fisk. Fisk held onto the ball for the out, with Munson landing on top of him. Fisk flipped Munson, who came up swinging. Fisticuffs followed, with Michael leaping over Munson to get in a few swings at Fisk. Fisk managed to pin Michael's neck to the ground. Yankee manager Ralph Houk had to crawl through the pile to pull Fisk's elbow off Michael's throat and allow him to breathe. Both catchers were ejected, but Michael was allowed to remain in the game, prompting a long argument from Eddie Kasko. Fisk emerged with a scratch on his face and a bruised eye. Bob Montgomery, Fisk's replacement, started the game-winning rally with a single.

AUGUST 2 — The Red Sox smash the Yankees 10–0 at Fenway Park.

AUGUST 8 — Orlando Cepeda ties a major league record with four doubles in addition to collecting six RBIs during a 9–4 win over the Royals in Kansas City.

AUGUST 10 — Booed at Fenway Park for failing to run out a ground ball and for letting a fly ball fall in front of him, Reggie Smith walks off the field in the second inning without permission from Eddie Kasko. Smith then showered, dressed, and went home. The Red Sox lost 5–3 to the Angels. Smith was fined $750 by the club.

Smith was playing with torn ligaments in his knee. Club management told him he was ready to play, but Smith objected, producing medical testimony that he had not yet fully recovered. Accusations of malingering were leveled by the club, which helped lead to the reaction of the fans.

AUGUST 12 — Orlando Cepeda collects five hits, including a homer and a double, in five at-bats during a 14–8 triumph over the Angels at Fenway Park.

AUGUST 20 — A two-run homer by Carlton Fisk in the ninth inning beats the Rangers 5–4 in Arlington. It was Fisk's second homer of the game.

AUGUST 21 — The Red Sox outslug the Rangers 15–9 in Arlington.

AUGUST 22 — The Red Sox lead 9–0 before allowing the Rangers to score eight runs in the eighth inning and escape with a 9–8 victory in Arlington.

AUGUST 24	Smith takes a shot at the city of Boston in an interview with a reporter in Anaheim: "I feel I have to move away from Boston for the benefit of my family," he said. "It's no secret things are difficult in Boston. I found out in the black community why they don't come out to our games. It's difficult for them to get good tickets. The Red Sox were the last team to get black players. I think Boston is a racist city again, in some ways, and I'm not sure they want a black star."
AUGUST 25	The Red Sox win their eighth game in a row with a 4–0 decision over the Angels in Anaheim.

The win gave the Red Sox a record of 70–57 and kept them four games back of the first-place Orioles. On the same day, the Orioles won their 12th consecutive game in a winning streak that eventually reached 14. The Sox were unable to keep pace with the streaking Orioles and finished eight back.

SEPTEMBER 3	Down 8–2, the Red Sox storm back for seven runs in the eighth inning to stun the Orioles 9–8 in the second game of a doubleheader at Fenway Park. Baltimore won the first game, 13–8.

Tommy Harper stole 54 bases in 1973 to break the club record of 52 set by Tris Speaker in 1912.

SEPTEMBER 4	Ben Oglivie hits a walk-off homer in the twelfth inning off Jim Palmer to defeat the Orioles 2–1 at Fenway Park. Prior to Oglivie's homer, Palmer retired 16 batters in a row. Palmer and Luis Tiant both pitched complete games.

Carl Yastrzemski played 31 games at third base in 1973, but the experiment ended when he made 12 errors.

SEPTEMBER 12	Roger Moret runs his record to 11–0 with a 7–1 win over the Yankees in New York.

A pencil-thin left-hander, Moret ended the 1973 season with a 13–2 record and a 3.17 ERA. He pitched for the Red Sox from 1970 through 1975 and had a 41–18 won-lost ledger in Boston.

SEPTEMBER 24	Tommy Harper hits a grand slam in the sixth inning off Ed Farmer during a 14–0 win over the Tigers in Detroit.
SEPTEMBER 28	Luis Tiant wins his 20th game of the season with an 11–2 decision over the Brewers in the first game of a doubleheader in Milwaukee. Carl Yastrzemski hit a grand slam in the first inning off Eduardo Rodriguez. The Red Sox completed the sweep with a 5–3 win in the second tilt.

Tiant had a 20–13 record and a 3.34 earned run average in 1973.

SEPTEMBER 29	Bobby Mitchell of the Brewers hits a long home run over the center field wall at Fenway Park to the right of the flagpole during a 9–4 Red Sox win.
SEPTEMBER 30	The Red Sox fire Eddie Kasko as manager and hire Darrell Johnson.

Kasko was fired after a season in which the Red Sox posted their second-highest winning percentage since 1951. He lasted four years as manager of the Sox and had a record of 345–295 but couldn't win a pennant. Under Kasko's laissez-faire tenure, the Red Sox were wracked with dissension and the team broke into factions. General manager Dick O'Connell was forced into disadvantageous trades to get rid of disgruntled players and improve team chemistry. Kasko remained with the organization as an "executive scout" and never managed another big-league club.

Johnson was forty-five when he started as manager of the Red Sox. He had a six-year playing career as a backup catcher and played in the 1961 World Series with the Reds as a teammate of Kasko. Johnson was the Red Sox' pitching coach in 1968 and 1969 and managed the club's top farm clubs in Louisville and Pawtucket from 1971 through 1973. He lasted three seasons as manager of the Red Sox and led the club to the World Series in 1975.

OCTOBER 23   Two weeks after Vice President Spiro Agnew resigns due to financial improprieties, the Red Sox trade Ben Oglivie to the Tigers for Dick McAuliffe.

The Red Sox gave up on Oglivie much too soon. In three seasons with the Sox, he hit .235 with 10 homers in 438 at-bats, but he was only twenty-four years old when they sent him to Detroit. The Tigers considered Oglivie no more than a platoon outfielder and traded him to the Brewers in 1978. In Milwaukee, Oglivie blossomed. He twice drove in more than 100 runs and hit 41 homers in 1980. McAuliffe was thirty-four at the time of the trade and batted only .206 in 107 games with the Sox.

OCTOBER 24   The Red Sox trade Marty Pattin to the Royals for Dick Drago.

OCTOBER 26   The Red Sox trade Reggie Smith and Ken Tatum to the Cardinals for Rick Wise and Bernie Carbo.

Smith's comments about racism in Boston (see August 24, 1973) made it inevitable that the Red Sox would trade him. After leaving the team, Smith continued to perform at a high level. He played nine more seasons in the majors with three teams and hit .294 with 165 homers in 3,253 at-bats. One of the last three remaining members of the 1967 Red Sox (along with Carl Yastrzemski and Rico Petrocelli), Smith played in two more World Series after leaving Boston (with the Dodgers in 1977 and 1978) and five All-Star Games (1974, 1975, 1977, 1978, and 1981).

The Red Sox gave up a star and received little in return. After an injury-filled 1974, Wise won 19 games for the Red Sox in 1975 in addition to winning the dramatic Game Six of the World Series when Carlton Fisk homered, but he couldn't duplicate that season. Carbo was little more than a platoon outfielder or designated hitter, although his offbeat sense of humor, Italian ancestry, and two pinch-hit homers in the 1975 World Series made him a popular figure among Boston fans. He frustrated Sox management with periods in which he hit like Ted Williams followed by deep slumps in which he hit like Esther Williams, and with his constant criticism about the way the club was run. In the offseason Carbo worked as a hairdresser.

DECEMBER 7   The Red Sox trade Lynn McGlothlen, John Curtis, and Mike Garman to the Cardinals for Reggie Cleveland, Diego Segui, and Terry Hughes.

The Red Sox made two trades with the Cardinals in six weeks involving front-line players. In both cases, the Sox gave up more talent than they received.

DECEMBER 8   The Red Sox purchase Juan Marichal from the Giants.

A future Hall of Famer, Marichal had a career record of 238–141 when acquired by the Red Sox, but he was thirty-six years old and near the end of the line. Hampered by a herniated disc, he pitched only 11 games for the Sox and was 5–1 with a 4.87 ERA.

1974   B

Season in a Sentence

In Darrell Johnson's first season as manager, the Red Sox turn a seven-game lead on August 23 into a seven-game deficit during a late-season collapse.

Finish • Won • Lost • Pct • GB

Third   84   78   .519   7.0

Manager

Darrell Johnson

Stats   Red Sox • AL • Rank

Stats	Red Sox	AL	Rank
Batting Avg:	.264	.256	4
On-Base Pct:	.336	.326	3
Slugging Pct:	.377	.371	3
Home Runs:	109		8
Stolen Bases:	104		7
ERA:	3.72	3.62	7
Fielding Pct:	.977	.977	7
Runs Scored:	696		1
Runs Allowed:	661		7

Starting Lineup

Bob Montgomery, c
Carl Yastrzemski, 1b-lf
Doug Griffin, 2b
Rico Petrocelli, 3b
Rick Burleson, ss-2b
Bernie Carbo, lf-rf
Juan Beniquez, cf
Dwight Evans, rf
Tommy Harper, dh-lf
Cecil Cooper, 1b-dh
Rick Miller, cf
Mario Guerrero, ss
Dick McAuliffe, 2b-3b
Carlton Fisk, c

Pitchers

Luis Tiant, sp
Bill Lee, sp
Reggie Cleveland, sp-rp
Roger Moret, sp-rp
Dick Drago, sp-rp
Diego Segui, rp

Attendance

1,556,411 (first in AL)

Club Leaders

Batting Avg:	Yastrzemski	.301
On-Base Pct:	Yastrzemski	.414
Slugging Pct:	Yastrzemski	.445
Home Runs:	Yastrzemski	15
	Petrocelli	15
RBI:	Yastrzemski	79
Runs:	Yastrzemski	93
Stolen Bases:	Harper	28
Wins:	Tiant	22
Strikeouts:	Tiant	176
ERA:	Tiant	2.92
Saves:	Segui	10

MARCH 26   Seven weeks after the kidnapping of Patty Hearst, the Red Sox release thirty-six-year-old Orlando Cepeda and thirty-nine-year-old Luis Aparicio.

In a single day, the Red Sox released two future Hall of Famers. In the process, new manager Darrell Johnson made it clear that it was his team and that he wanted to emphasize youth and speed. Aparicio, coming off of a 1973 season in which he played 132 games and hit .271, nine points above his career average, never played in another big-league game. Cepeda hooked up with the Royals and batted .215 in 33 games in 1974, his last season in the majors.

APRIL 5   The Red Sox defeat the Brewers 9–8 in Milwaukee on Opening Day. Carl Yastrzemski hit a two-run homer in the seventh inning with the Sox trailing 8–7 to provide the winning run. Bob Montgomery hit a homer and drove in three runs. Doug Griffin also had three RBIs.

Jim Woods replaced Dave Martin in the Red Sox radio booth beginning in 1974, joining Ned Martin. Ken Coleman and Johnny Pesky continued on TV.

APRIL 9   The first scheduled game of the season at Fenway Park, against the Orioles, is postponed by rain. The April 10 contest between the Sox and Baltimore was called off because of snow.

APRIL 11   After two days of delay because of bad weather, the Red Sox open their home season before 23,196 at Fenway Park but lose to the Orioles 7–6 in 11 innings. Both teams scored in the tenth, the Red Sox tallying on a homer by Juan Beniquez. The winning run crossed the plate on a throwing error by second baseman Doug Griffin.

APRIL 12   Bernie Carbo hits a grand slam in the first inning off Lerrin LaGrow during a 6–3 win over the Tigers at Fenway Park.

Carbo took a stuffed gorilla dressed in a Cardinals uniform and nicknamed "Mighty Joe Young" everywhere he went. The gorilla usually had a seat on the Red Sox bench. It was given to Carbo in 1973 by Cardinals teammate Scipio Spinks.

APRIL 13   In a nationally televised game played at Fenway Park, Rick Wise wins his debut with the Red Sox 8–1 against the Tigers. NBC-TV insisted on playing the game despite rain, sleet, and temperatures in the mid-thirties. The Tigers built a fire in the bullpen, and Detroit left fielder Willie Horton twice fell in the mud chasing fly balls.

Pitching a nine-inning complete game in the abominable conditions ruined Wise's season. He soon developed shoulder trouble and pitched in only nine games in 1974 with a 3–4 record.

APRIL 16   The Red Sox play at Shea Stadium for the first time and lose 2–1 to the Yankees.

The Yankees played at Shea Stadium in 1974 and 1975 while Yankee Stadium was remodeled.

APRIL 21   The Red Sox win a thrilling 6–5 decision in 10 innings over the Indians at Fenway Park. Down 5–1 heading into the ninth, the Sox scored four runs to tie it up, 5–5. In the tenth, the Indians brought in Milt Wilcox to face Cecil Copper with Dick

McAuliffe on second and Bob Montgomery on first. Before delivering a pitch to the plate, Wilcox tried to pick McAuliffe off the base and threw the ball into center field. McAuliffe scored all the way from second for the winning run.

APRIL 30   Doug Griffin is beaned by Nolan Ryan during a 16–6 loss to the Angels at Fenway Park. Griffin was struck above the left ear and spent two days in intensive care at Boston's Hahnemann Hospital. He didn't play again until July 1.

MAY 2   Darrell Johnson is attacked in a robbery attempt while entering his room at the Kenmore Square Hotel. "I had one hand on the key and the other reaching for the light when this guy belted me," the Red Sox manager said. "I grappled with him, but he got up and ran down the stairs."

MAY 4   In his first major league game at shortstop, Rick Burleson makes three errors during a 1–0 loss to the Rangers at Fenway Park.

The Red Sox lost 15 of their first 25 games in 1974 before turning things around. From the second game of a doubleheader on May 5 through August 23, the Sox had a record of 60–39. The club spent 98 days in first place during the 1974 season.

MAY 21   Nine days after the Celtics win the NBA title with a Game Seven win over the Milwaukee Bucks, the Red Sox take a 10–0 lead into the third inning and roll to a 14-6 victory over the Yankees at Fenway Park.

From August 2, 1972, through July 29, 1974, the Red Sox had a 20–1 record against the Yankees in Boston.

MAY 26   The Red Sox move into first place with a 4–1 win over the Brewers at Fenway Park.

The Red Sox jumped from last place on May 8 to first in just 18 days.

MAY 27   Bernie Carbo drives in all three runs in a 10-inning, 3–2 win over the Twins at Fenway Park. Carbo hit a two-run homer in the fourth inning and a walk-off single in the tenth.

JUNE 5   The Red Sox draft shortstop Eddie Ford from the University of South Carolina in the first round of the amateur draft.

Eddie was the son of Hall of Fame pitcher Whitey Ford, but the younger Ford never reached the majors. It was a terrible draft for the Red Sox. The only players drafted in June and later signed to a contract were Sam Bowen in the seventh round and Joel Finch in the ninth. The two combined to play 23 games in the majors. The previous January the Red Sox did much better, selecting Bob Stanley, who played 13 seasons with the club beginning in 1977, along with future big-leaguers Chuck Rainey and Steven Burke.

JUNE 7   An 8–6 Red Sox loss to the White Sox in Chicago is delayed for more than an hour by a fire. The blaze started when a bundle of paper bags fell into a gas burner used for popping corn at a concession stand. Fans were evacuated onto the playing field, and 11 were treated for smoke inhalation. The fire caused $100,000 in damage.

JUNE 14   Nolan Ryan strikes out 19 Red Sox and walks 10 in 13 innings in Anaheim. Barry Raziano struck out one more Boston batter in a two-inning relief stint and was the winning pitcher in a 15-inning, 4–3 Angels victory. Luis Tiant pitched all 15 innings for the Sox. Cecil Cooper was hitless in eight at-bats and tied a major league record by striking out six times. Carl Yastrzemski sent the game into extra innings with a homer in the ninth.

               Yastrzemski led the AL in runs in 1974 with 93. He hit .301 with 15 homers and 104 walks.

JUNE 16   The Red Sox stage a six-run rally in the ninth inning to beat the Angels 7–4 in Anaheim.

JUNE 22   The Red Sox face the Perry brothers in a doubleheader against the Indians at Fenway Park. In the first game, the Sox lost to Gaylord Perry, 11–0. In the second contest, the Sox defeated Jim Perry, 8–3.

JUNE 24   Rico Petrocelli hits a grand slam off Jim Colborn in the sixth inning of a 9–0 win over the Brewers at Fenway Park.

JUNE 28   Carlton Fisk tears up his knee in a home plate collision during a 2–1 loss to the Indians in Cleveland. Fisk was hit by Leron Lee. The injury put Fisk out for the year.

               It was Fisk's third major injury in a span of eight months. He didn't play for the first three weeks of the 1974 season because he was hit in the groin by a foul tip during a spring-training game on St. Patrick's Day. In October 1973, Fisk chopped off the tip of a finger in his garage door.

JUNE 29   Juan Beniquez hits two homers, including a grand slam, during a 12–2 trouncing of the Indians in Cleveland. The slam came in the second inning off Fritz Peterson.

               The day didn't start well. Beniquez showed up late for batting practice and became engaged in a heated argument with coach Eddie Popowski. Manager Darrell Johnson took Beniquez aside for a "fatherly chat."

JULY 7   Rick Miller collects five hits, including a grand slam, in five at-bats, but the Red Sox lose 11–9 in 10 innings in the first game of a doubleheader against the Royals at Fenway Park. Miller hit his slam in the sixth inning off Gene Garber. The Sox rebounded to win the second tilt, 5–3.

               During the 1973–74 offseason, Miller married Carlton Fisk's sister.

JULY 25   Carl Yastrzemski collects the 300th home run of his career during a 12–4 win over the Tigers in Detroit. The milestone homer was struck off Mickey Lolich.

JULY 26   Reggie Cleveland holds the Tigers hitless for $7\frac{2}{3}$ innings but winds up losing a three-hitter 1–0 in 11 innings at Detroit. Joe Coleman pitched a complete-game shutout for the Tigers.

AUGUST 7   Roger Moret pitches no-hit ball for $7\frac{2}{3}$ innings against the Brewers in Milwaukee before Pedro Garcia singles. Moret was taken out of the game following Garcia's hit. Dick Drago and Bob Veale each pitched two-thirds of an inning for a 1–0 Red Sox win.

AUGUST 12   Four days after Richard Nixon resigns as president in the wake of the Watergate scandal, Nolan Ryan strikes out 19 Boston batters for the second time in 1974 to give the Angels a 4–2 win in Anaheim.

AUGUST 19   Jim Rice makes his major league debut during a 6–1 win over the White Sox at Fenway Park. Rice was 0 for 2 as a DH and drove in a run with a sacrifice fly.

AUGUST 21   Roger Moret pitches a one-hitter and strikes out 12 batters in a 4–0 win over the White Sox at Fenway Park. The only Chicago hit was an infield single by Richie Allen in the seventh inning. Allen rapped a grounder that trickled off Moret's glove and deflected to second baseman Doug Griffin, whose throw failed to beat Allen to the bag.

AUGUST 23   Luis Tiant picks up his 20th win of the season with a 3–0 decision over the Athletics in Oakland.

         Tiant started the season with a 2–5 record before winning 18 of his next 21 decisions. He lost five of his last seven to finish at 22–13. Tiant completed 25 of his 38 starts, pitched 311$\frac{1}{3}$ innings, collected a league-leading seven shutouts, and posted a 2.92 ERA.

          At the conclusion of the August 23 victory, the Red Sox were in first place with a 70–54 record, seven games ahead of the Yankees and Orioles, who were tied for second. From August 24 through September 20, the Sox went 7–19 to blow the big lead. The Orioles, who won 28 of their last 34 games, won the AL East, finishing two games in front of the Yankees and seven games ahead of the third-place Red Sox.

AUGUST 24   Bill Lee becomes a father for the second time shortly after a 4–1 loss to the Athletics at Fenway Park.

         The circumstances of the birth were fitting for Lee's unique lifestyle. He started the game facing Catfish Hunter, and his wife, Mary Lou, sat in back of the screen, as she always did when Lee was pitching. As he came off the mound at the end of each inning, Mary Lou indicated the length of her contractions. They were down to three minutes apart when Lee had to leave the game in the eighth with a blister on one of his fingers and the score 1–1. He got her to the hospital just in time. She gave birth to a son named Andrew Lee.

SEPTEMBER 1   The Red Sox purchase Tim McCarver from the Cardinals.

SEPTEMBER 2   The Red Sox suffer a devastating pair of 1–0 losses to the Orioles in a doubleheader in Baltimore. In the first game, Ross Grimsley beat Luis Tiant. In the second tilt, Mike Cuellar outdueled Bill Lee. The Sox collected only five hits in the two games.

         With the doubleheader loss, the Red Sox became the only team in American League history to lose two 1–0 games in one day.

SEPTEMBER 5   Just 13 days after taking a seven-game lead in the AL East, the Red Sox are knocked out of first after a 4–3 loss to the Brewers at Fenway Park. The Sox carried a 3–2 lead into the ninth before Gorman Thomas hit a game-winning two-run homer off Diego Segui. Fred Lynn made his major league debut and was retired in a pinch-hitting appearance.

SEPTEMBER 6   The Red Sox suffer their eighth loss in a row with a 2–0 defeat at the hands of the Brewers at Fenway Park. The defeat was the Red Sox' fourth shutout loss in five games.

SEPTEMBER 7   The Red Sox purchase Deron Johnson from the Brewers.

A thirty-six-year-old first baseman and designated hitter, Johnson was acquired for batting help during the stretch drive, but he got only three hits in 25 at-bats. The Red Sox released him shortly after the season ended, and Johnson signed with the White Sox. The Red Sox picked him up again in a trade on September 22, 1975, for another stretch run at a pennant. This time, Johnson delivered six hits in 10 at-bats. He played 15 games for Boston in 1976 before drawing another release, which ended his big-league career. In his three seasons with the Red Sox, Johnson hit .120, .600, and .132.

SEPTEMBER 8   The Red Sox jump back into a first-place tie with the Yankees by overcoming a 4–0 deficit to defeat the Brewers 8–6 at Fenway Park. The Orioles were in third place, one game back.

SEPTEMBER 9   The Red Sox drop out of first with a 6–3 loss to the Yankees at Fenway Park.

The Sox were unable to recapture the top spot in the AL East the rest of the season.

SEPTEMBER 12   Alex Johnson, in his first game with the Yankees after being acquired from the Rangers, hits a twelfth-inning homer off Diego Segui to defeat the Red Sox 2–1 at Fenway Park.

There was almost a riot at Fenway during the game. With one out, Chris Chambliss hit a ball into the right field corner to score pinch runner Larry Murray from first base and tie the score, 1–1. The drive jumped over the low wall, where a spectator dropped it back onto the field. No umpire saw the play clearly, and the decision was spectator interference. It should have been called a ground-rule double, in which case the run would have been nullified and Murray would have been awarded third base. The Red Sox argued the play for 25 minutes, during which Chambliss was hit by a steel-tipped dart. The Sox were threatened with forfeit because fans were pelting the New York dugout.

SEPTEMBER 15   In his first major league start, Fred Lynn hits a home run, but the Red Sox lose 9–5 to the Brewers in Milwaukee.

SEPTEMBER 21   The Red Sox rally for four runs in the ninth inning and one in the tenth to defeat the Orioles 6–5 at Fenway Park. A three-run homer by Dwight Evans in the ninth tied the score, 5–5. Three rain delays halted play for three and a half hours. Bill Lee pitched a complete game in a contest that started at 2:19 PM. and ended at 8:48 PM. He had to warm up four times and relieved boredom during one of the rain delays by helping the grounds crew with the tarp.

Lee finished the season with a 17–15 record and a 3.51 ERA in 282 innings.

SEPTEMBER 25   The Red Sox waste an excellent pitching performance by Bill Lee and lose 1–0 to the Yankees in 10 innings in New York. The loss left the Red Sox 4½ games behind the Orioles with eight games left and all but extinguished hopes for a 1974 pennant in Boston.

SEPTEMBER 26 Bob Montgomery hits a two-run homer in the ninth inning to tie the Tigers 3–3 in Detroit, then drives in two more with a bases-loaded single in the tenth to lift the Red Sox to a 5–3 victory. Montgomery entered the game in the seventh inning when starting catcher Tim Blackwell was lifted for a pinch-hitter.

OCTOBER 1 Jim Rice's first major league homer breaks a 4–4 tie in the fourth inning of a 7–4 victory over the Indians at Fenway Park. The pitcher was Steve Kline.

DECEMBER 2 The Red Sox trade Tommy Harper to the Angels for Bob Heise.

After three seasons as a starting outfielder in Boston, the thirty-four-year-old Harper was traded to make room for emerging youngsters Jim Rice, Fred Lynn, and Dwight Evans. Despite the late-season collapse in 1974, the Red Sox seemed to have a bright future. In addition to Rice, Lynn, and Evans, the club had Rick Burleson, Juan Beniquez, Cecil Cooper, and Roger Moret, all of whom were twenty-five or younger on Opening Day in 1975. Carlton Fisk was twenty-seven and hadn't yet reached his peak.

1975

Season in a Sentence

Buoyed by rookies Fred Lynn and Jim Rice, the Red Sox win their first American League pennant since the 1967 miracle but blow a three-run, sixth-inning lead to the Reds in Game Seven of the World Series.

Finish • Won • Lost • Pct • GB

First   95   65   .594 + 4.5

AL Championship Series—

The Red Sox defeated the Oakland Athletics three games to none.

World Series—

The Red Sox lost to the Cincinnati Reds four games to three.

Manager

Darrell Johnson

Stats

Stats	Red Sox	AL	Rank
Batting Avg:	.275	.258	1
On-Base Pct:	.347	.331	1
Slugging Pct:	.417	.379	1
Home Runs:	134		4 (tie)
Stolen Bases:	66		10
ERA:	3.98	3.78	9
Fielding Pct:	.977	.975	5
Runs Scored:	796		1
Runs Allowed:	709		7

Starting Lineup

Carlton Fisk, c
Carl Yastrzemski, 1b
Denny Doyle, 2b
Rico Petrocelli, 3b
Rick Burleson, ss
Jim Rice, lf-dh
Fred Lynn, cf
Dwight Evans, rf
Cecil Cooper, dh-1b
Bernie Carbo, lf-rf
Doug Griffin, 2b
Juan Beniquez, lf-dh
Bob Montgomery, c

Pitchers

Rick Wise, sp
Luis Tiant, sp
Bill Lee, sp
Reggie Cleveland, sp-rp
Dick Pole, sp-rp
Dick Drago, rp
Roger Moret, rp-sp

Attendance

1,748,587 (first in AL)

Club Leaders

Batting Avg:	Lynn	.331
On-Base Pct:	Lynn	.401
Slugging Pct:	Lynn	.566
Home Runs:	Rice	22
RBI:	Lynn	105
Runs:	Lynn	103
Stolen Bases:	Lynn	10
	Rice	10
Wins:	Wise	19
Strikeouts:	Tiant	142
ERA:	Wise	3.95
	Lee	3.95
Saves:	Drago	15

MARCH 5   Tony Conigliaro signs a minor league contract for the 1975 season.

               Conigliaro was thirty years old and hadn't played since retiring in July 1971 because of vision problems that adversely affected his depth perception. His eye problems seemed to clear up, which spurred Conigliaro to try another come-back. After a fine spring, he won the starting job as a club's designated hitter by the beginning of the regular season. Conigliaro's vision failed again, however, and he hit a measly .123 with two home runs in 57 at-bats. The Red Sox sent him to their farm club in Pawtucket in the International League on June 14. Conigliaro played 37 games there and hit just .203 with three homers before retiring on August 21, this time for good. He then went into television and did the sports news for a station in Providence for a year before moving to KGO-TV in San Francisco in 1976.

MARCH 12   The injury jinx continues to haunt Carlton Fisk as he breaks his right forearm getting hit by a pitch from Fred Holdsworth of the Tigers during a spring training game.

               Between the knee injury in 1974 and the arm injury in 1975, Fisk didn't play a reg-ular-season game between June 28, 1974, and June 23, 1975. Combining his stats for 1974 and 1975, Fisk accumulated 450 at-bats, hit 21 homers, and batted .318.

MARCH 29   The Red Sox trade Danny Cater to the Cardinals for Danny Godby.

APRIL 8   The Red Sox defeat the Brewers 5–2 on Opening Day before 34,019 at Fenway Park. The game had a World Series atmosphere because Tony Conigliaro was playing in his first game since 1971, and Henry Aaron appeared in his first American League contest. Both were designated hitters. Batting fourth in the lineup, Conigliaro singled in his first at-bat and received four standing ovations. He went one for four. Aaron was hitless in three at-bats. Luis Tiant was the winning pitcher with a complete game.

               The new Red Sox television team in 1975 was Dick Stockton and Ken Harrelson, who replaced Ken Coleman and Johnny Pesky. Pesky became a coach for the club. The telecasts moved to independent station WSBK-TV, which doubled the number of road games broadcast to more than 60.

APRIL 11   Carl Yastrzemski's homer in the twelfth inning propels the Red Sox to a 6–5 win over the Orioles in Baltimore. Tony Conigliaro homered in the fifth inning, his first since his comeback.

               The Red Sox opened the season with only eight pitchers on the 25-man roster.

APRIL 25   Luis Tiant holds the Tigers to two hits, but one is a homer to Dan Meyer in the fifth inning that hands Tiant the 1–0 loss in Detroit.

               Tiant had an 18–14 record and a 4.02 ERA in 1975.

MAY 3   The Red Sox score six runs in the first inning to launch a 12–2 win over the Tigers at Fenway Park.

MAY 17   The Red Sox lose their fifth game in a row by dropping a 5–3 decision to the Roy-als at Fenway Park.

The loss put the Sox below the .500 mark at 14–15. Over the remainder of the season, Boston was 81–50.

MAY 18   Bernie Carbo drives in all four runs in a 4–2 win over the Royals at Fenway Park. Carbo hit a three-run homer in the third inning and a solo shot in the fifth.

MAY 20   Bill Lee throws a two-hit shutout on only 78 pitches to defeat the Athletics 7–0 at Fenway Park. The only Oakland hits were a double by Sal Bando in the fifth inning and a single to Angel Mangual with none out in the ninth.

Lee added a high, slow, arching curve, popularly known as a "blooper pitch," to his arsenal in 1975. He finished the season with a 17–9 record and a 3.95 earned run average.

MAY 21   Carl Yastrzemski hits a grand slam off Ken Holtzmann in the seventh inning of a 7–3 win over the Athletics at Fenway Park.

MAY 24   The Angels take batting practice in the lobby of the Sheraton Hotel in Boston before losing to Bill Lee and the Red Sox 6–0 at Fenway Park in a contest televised nationally on NBC.

Known for his outspoken and sometimes outrageous behavior as much as for his brilliant pitching, Bill "Spaceman" Lee posted 17 wins three years in a row, 1973–75.

Focus on Sport/Getty Images

A couple of days earlier, Lee had told reporters that the weak-hitting Angels "could take batting practice in a hotel lobby without breaking a chandelier." Angels manager Dick Williams decided to go along with the gag. He told his players to report to the lobby at noon instead of the ballpark. With plastic bats and Nerf balls, Williams pitched to Winston Llenas before hotel security officers ordered an end to the hijinks. Lee pitched the complete-game shutout, allowing just four hits.

MAY 31   After trailing 7–3 at the end of the fourth inning, the Red Sox pound their way to a 12–8 win over the Twins in Minnesota.

JUNE 1   The Red Sox race to a 9–0 lead after three innings and outslug the Twins 11–9 in Minnesota.

JUNE 4   The Red Sox rally for four runs in the ninth inning and beat the White Sox 7–6 at Fenway Park. Pinch hitters Bernie Carbo, Tim McCarver, and Cecil Cooper each delivered hits during the rally. Rick Burleson drove in the winning run with a single.

On the same day, the Red Sox selected first baseman Otis Foster of High Point High School in High Point, North Carolina, in the first round of the amateur draft. Foster never reached the majors and peaked at Class AAA before calling it quits in 1980. The Red Sox drafted and signed five future major leaguers, including Dave Schmidt (second round), Ed Jurak (third), Dave Stapleton (10th), Mike O'Berry (22nd), and Mike Paxton (23rd). Stapleton was the only one of the five to develop into a regular and had a great rookie season, but he was little more than a stopgap at both first and second base.

JUNE 6   Dwight Evans hits two homers, including a grand slam, and drives in six runs during a 13–10 win over the Twins at Fenway Park. The slam was hit off Joe Decker in the first inning. The Sox collected their 13 runs on only 9 hits.

JUNE 8   The Red Sox lose an unusual 7–5 decision to the Twins at Fenway Park. The score was 1–1 after eight innings before Minnesota scored six runs in the ninth and the Sox countered with four.

JUNE 9   Bernie Carbo hits a grand slam in the sixth inning off Jackie Brown, but the Red Sox lose 12–4 to the Rangers at Fenway Park.

JUNE 11 Carl Yastrzemski hits a two-run homer in the fourteenth inning that beats the White Sox 9–7 in Chicago.

JUNE 14 The Red Sox purchase Denny Doyle from the Angels. On the same day, the Sox sent Tony Conigliaro to the minors in Pawtucket.

Doyle proved to be a tremendous short-term solution to the Red Sox' lack of production at second base. At the time he came to Boston, Doyle was thirty-one years old with a .244 lifetime batting average. Yet over the remainder of the 1975 season, he hit .310 and four home runs in 89 games. Doyle was the starter at second in both 1976 and 1977, but he reverted back to his previous level and hit .245 with only two homers in 254 games over those two seasons.

JUNE 15 Fred Lynn runs his hitting streak to 20 games in an 8–7 win over the Royals in Kansas City.

JUNE 18 In a devastating display of power, Fred Lynn drives in 10 runs with three homers, a triple, and a single in a 15–1 romp over the Tigers in Detroit. Lynn had seven RBIs after only three innings. He hit a two-run homer in the first inning off Joe Coleman, a three-run homer off Coleman in the second, and a two-run triple off Lerrin LaGrow in the third that hit the outfield fence about three feet from the top.

After beating out an infield single in the eighth, Lynn capped the evening with a three-run homer off Tom Walker in the ninth. The 10 RBIs tied a club record set by Rudy York in 1946 and tied by Norm Zauchin in 1955. Lynn's 16 total bases in the game tied an American League record.

By season's end, Lynn was not only the American League Rookie of the Year but the MVP as well. A member of three NCAA championship teams at the University of Southern California, he hit .331 with 21 homers and 105 RBIs in 1975, led the league in runs (103) and doubles (47), and drew favorable comparisons to Stan Musial, all at the age of twenty-three. With the exception of 1979, however, Lynn never reached those numbers again in a career that ended after 1,969 games in 1990 with a .283 lifetime batting average and 306 home runs. As a result of his aggressive play and propensity for running into walls, he suffered nagging injuries for most of his career and the burden of unrealistic expectations brought on by a stellar rookie campaign. Lynn played a career-high 150 games in 1978, and he appeared in 140 or more only four times.

JUNE 20   The Red Sox win 4–3 in 12 innings with a comeback against the Orioles at Memorial Stadium. Down 2–0, the Sox rallied for three runs in the ninth. After Baltimore tied the scored in their half, the Sox won it in the twelfth on a sacrifice fly by Rick Burleson.

In May and June, Juan Beniquez hit safely in 28 consecutive games in which he started. The streak was interrupted by two contests in which he entered as a substitute.

JUNE 28   Following an 8–6 loss to the Yankees at Fenway Park, Doug Griffin and Dwight Evans push Boston Globe writer Bob Ryan out of the clubhouse. The incident stemmed from a critical column Ryan had written. American League president Lee MacPhail fined both Griffin and Evans.

JUNE 29   The Red Sox take first place with a 3–2 victory over the Yankees at Fenway Park. The Sox remained at the top of the AL East for the rest of the season.

On his way to the game, Reggie Cleveland was involved in an auto accident. The Red Sox pitcher hit some water traveling through a tunnel on Boston's notoriously dangerous Storrow Drive, and his vehicle flipped over. Cleveland was pinned beneath the car and knocked unconscious. He had 15 stitches around his right ear and eight in his mouth.

JUNE 30   Red Sox pitcher Dick Pole is hit by a Tony Muser line drive in the ninth inning of a 5–2 win over the Orioles at Fenway Park. The ball smashed into Pole's cheekbone, causing a fracture near the right eye. He didn't pitch again until September.

JULY 2   Rick Wise pitches a two-hitter to beat the Brewers 6–3 in the first game of a doubleheader at County Stadium. Wise was only one out away from a no-hitter when he walked Bob Sharp on four pitches with two outs in the ninth. George Scott and Bobby Darwin followed with back-to-back homers. The Brewers won the second game, 4–3.

Wise previously pitched a no-hitter with the Phillies in 1971. He was 19–12 with a 3.95 ERA in 1975.

JULY 8   Sidelined with a jammed wrist, Fred Lynn comes off the bench and delivers a walk-off pinch-single with two outs in the ninth to beat the Twins 6–5 at Fenway Park.

JULY 9   After trailing 7–1 in the third inning and 8–7 entering the ninth, the Red Sox rally for two runs to defeat the Twins 9–8 at Fenway Park. Doug Griffin drove in the tying run on a pinch-single and scored on Jim Rice's double.

Rice, along with Fred Lynn, was a part of Boston's spectacular one-two rookie punch in 1975. Only twenty-two years old, Rice hit .309 with 22 homers and 102 RBIs. Although Lynn had the better rookie campaign, Rice had the better career. Rice played 16 seasons with the Red Sox and ranks third all time among Boston hitters in home runs (382), RBIs (1,451), hits (2,452), and total bases (4,129), fourth in runs (1,249), and sixth in doubles (373), triples (79), and slugging percentage (.502). Rice's career batting average was .298. He will remain on the writers' Hall of Fame ballot until 2009 and has a chance to make it. Rice needs 75 percent of the vote for induction. He was added to the ballot in 1995 and passed the 50 percent mark in 2000. His vote totals have been rising gradually each year. Rice might already have a plaque in Cooperstown if he had had a better relationship with the press. His quiet nature was too often misunderstood by the media and the fans as moodiness and surliness.

JULY 10   For the third straight game, the Red Sox win with a walk-off hit with two outs in the ninth as Cecil Cooper's single beats the Rangers 8–7 at Fenway Park.

JULY 13   Carl Yastrzemski collects five hits, including two doubles, in five at-bats during a 7–5 win over the Rangers at Fenway Park.

JULY 15   Pinch hitting in the sixth inning of the All-Star Game at County Stadium in Milwaukee, Carl Yastrzemski lines Tom Seaver's first pitch for a homer. The American League lost, 6–3.

JULY 17   Cecil Cooper collects a homer, a triple, and a double during an 8–3 win over the Royals in Kansas City.

JULY 18   Jim Rice hits a home run over Fenway Park's center field wall to the right of the flagpole during a 9–3 victory over the Royals. The drive was estimated to have traveled 500 feet.

JULY 19   The Red Sox breeze to their 10th win in a row with an 8–0 decision over the Rangers in Texas.

JULY 27   The Red Sox shut out the Yankees twice during a doubleheader in New York. Bill Lee won the first game, 1–0. The only Boston run scored in the ninth inning came when Fred Lynn reached on an error with two out, stole second, and scored on Rick Miller's single. Lynn saved the game with a diving, tumbling catch of a Graig Nettles drive in deep center in the bottom of the inning. Roger Moret defeated the Yankees 6–0 in the second tilt.

JULY 28   Carlton Fisk collects four hits and drives in five runs, the last on a walk-off single in the ninth, to beat the Brewers 7–6 at Fenway Park.

AUGUST 2 With the official temperature in Boston reaching 102 degrees, the Red Sox defeat the Tigers 7–2 on a steamy Saturday afternoon at Fenway Park.

AUGUST 3 The Red Sox defeat the Tigers 6–4 at Fenway Park to take a 9½-game lead in the AL East.

AUGUST 4 Denny Doyle runs his hitting streak to 22 games, but the Red Sox lose 12–8 to the Orioles at Fenway Park.

AUGUST 5 Roger Moret suffers lacerations about the head in an auto accident. Moret drove his car into a parked tractor-trailer. He was fined heavily by the club for the accident, which occurred at 4:36 AM in North Stonington, Connecticut, a two-hour drive from Boston. Moret was scheduled to start against the Orioles the following evening.

AUGUST 9 Coach Johnny Pesky's electric blanket develops a short and catches fire at the Edgewater Hotel in Oakland and brings a contingent from the Alameda County Fire Department. Pesky wasn't injured and there was no major damage to the room.

AUGUST 16 Roger Moret (seven innings) and Jim Willoughby (two innings) combine on a two-hitter to beat the White Sox 5–0 at Comiskey Park. The only Chicago hits were singles by Bill Stein in the third inning and Bucky Dent in the seventh.

AUGUST 21 Tony Conigliaro's playing career comes to an end when he retires.

AUGUST 22 Luis Tiant reunites with his parents. He hadn't seen his father since 1961 or his mother since 1968 because both were trapped in Cuba and unable to leave. Nor was Tiant allowed back in his native country. Fidel Castro allowed Tiant's parents to leave for a visit after responding to a request from Massachusetts Senator Edward Brooke on Tiant's behalf. That winter, both of Tiant's parents died within three months of each other.

SEPTEMBER 3 Cecil Cooper hits a homer in the tenth inning off Jim Palmer to beat the Orioles 3–2 in Baltimore.

SEPTEMBER 6 The Red Sox collect 24 hits and overwhelm the Brewers 20–6 in Milwaukee. The big inning was the second, when the Sox scored seven runs. Dwight Evans collected five hits, including a double, in six at-bats.

SEPTEMBER 11 Luis Tiant carries a no-hitter for 7⅔ innings before settling on a three-hit, 3–1 win over the Tigers at Fenway Park. The first Detroit hit was a single by Aurelio Rodriguez with two out in the eighth.

SEPTEMBER 16 Luis Tiant outduels Jim Palmer 2–0 at Fenway Park to give the Red Sox a 5½-game lead over the Orioles in the AL East race with 10 games left on the schedule. Home runs by Carlton Fisk in the third inning and Rico Petrocelli in the fifth provided the two runs. The official attendance was 34,724, but club treasurer John Harrington later admitted that the Red Sox allowed 47,000 into the ballpark in violation of fire laws.

Before the crucial series against the Red Sox, Johnny Walker, a disc jockey for WFBR in Baltimore, flew to Nairobi to ask a witch doctor to place a hex on *the Red Sox. Walker claimed the voodoo man was a sports specialist, Kenya's top practitioner of spells on soccer teams. Walker paid the witch doctor $200 and two cases of beer to put a curse on the Red Sox by wrapping an autographed baseball in human hairs and placing it in a monkey's paw.*

SEPTEMBER 21   The Red Sox retain a 3½-game lead over the Orioles in the AL East race by scoring two runs in the ninth inning to defeat the Tigers 6–5 in Detroit. Both runs were driven in on a bases-loaded double by Denny Doyle.

The win was a costly one, however. Jim Rice broke his hand when hit by a pitch from Vern Ruhle. The injury put Rice out for the rest of the season. Carl Yastrzemski moved from first base to left field to cover for Rice's absence, and Cecil Cooper took over at first base.

SEPTEMBER 22   The Red Sox trade Chuck Erickson to the White Sox for Deron Johnson.

SEPTEMBER 26   The Red Sox shut out the Indians twice in a doubleheader at Fenway Park, both by 4–0 scores. Luis Tiant pitched the first game and Reggie Cleveland the second.

In September, Boston radio station WMEX signed a five-year contract to broadcast Red Sox games, beginning with the 1975 postseason. The contract ended the club's association with WHDH, which had broadcast Sox games for 30 years.

SEPTEMBER 27   Although defeated by the Indians 5–2 at Fenway Park, the Red Sox clinch the pennant when the Orioles lose twice to the Yankees in New York, 3–2 in ten innings and again, 7–3.

The AL East pennant put the Red Sox in the postseason for the first time since 1967. Their opponent in the American League Championship Series, then a best-of-five affair, was the Oakland Athletics. The Athletics, managed by Al Dark, were gunning for their fourth consecutive World Championship. The A's defeated the Reds in the World Series in 1972, the Mets in 1973, and the Dodgers in 1974. The 1975 Athletics had a record of 98–64 and were heavy favorites to beat the Red Sox in the ALCS on the strength of a better regular-season record and championship experience.

OCTOBER 4   In Game One of the American League Championship Series, Luis Tiant pitches a three-hitter to defeat the Athletics 7–1 before 35,878 at Fenway Park. Tiant struck out eight and allowed three walks. The Sox took a 2–0 lead in the first inning off Ken Holtzman on three Oakland errors, then broke the game open with five runs in the seventh.

OCTOBER 5   The Red Sox go up two games to none in the ALCS and move within one victory of a World Series appearance with a 6–3 win over the Athletics before 35,878 at Fenway Park. Reggie Cleveland got the win with relief help from Dick Drago. The A's opened the scoring on a two-run homer by Reggie Jackson in the first inning and took a 3–0 lead in the fourth. The Sox tied the score in their half of the fourth on Carl Yastrzemski's two-run homer, Carlton Fisk's double, Fred Lynn's single, and a double-play grounder. The go-ahead run scored in the sixth when Yastrzemski doubled and Fisk drove him home with a single. Rico Petrocelli homered in the seventh off Rollie Fingers.

OCTOBER 7   The Red Sox complete a sweep of the Athletics in the ALCS with a 5–3 win in Oakland. Rick Wise picked up the victory with a save from Dick Drago. The A's sent Ken Holtzman to the mound on only two days' rest, and the Sox scored four runs off of him in 4⅔ innings to take a 4–0 lead.

The Red Sox reached the World Series against the Cincinnati Reds, who were managed by Sparky Anderson. With a lineup of future Hall of Famers including Johnny Bench, Joe Morgan, and Tony Perez, plus Pete Rose, who would be in the Hall if weren't for his gambling issues, the Reds were 108–54 in 1975 and swept the Pirates in the playoffs. The Reds won 102 regular-season games in 1970, and after slumping to 79 victories in 1971, won 95 in 1972, 99 in 1973, and 98 in 1974. Despite the run of regular-season success, the Reds had been unable to win a World Series. Cincinnati's last World Championship was in 1940. Red Sox fans knew the frustration well, as Boston hadn't celebrated a title in the Fall Classic since 1918.

OCTOBER 11   The Red Sox win the first game of the World Series 6–0 on a gray, drizzly day before 35,205 at Fenway Park. Luis Tiant pitched a five-hit shutout. The game was a scoreless battle between Tiant and Don Gullett until the seventh inning, when the Sox scored six runs. Tiant started the rally by leading off the inning with a single. Because of the designated-hitter rule, it was the first time that Tiant had been on the bases since 1972. The six runs in the seventh were driven in by five different players, starting with Carl Yastrzemski, who hit a bases-loaded single to break the 0–0 deadlock. Rick Burleson was three for three in his first World Series game.

OCTOBER 12   The Reds even the Series with a 3–2 win over the Red Sox on another miserable day at Fenway Park before a crowd of 35,205 that included Henry Kissinger. *Sports Illustrated* reporter Ron Fimrite wrote that the game was "played in conditions better suited to a staging of *The Hound of the Baskervilles*." The score was 1–1 in the sixth when Rico Petrocelli drove in a run with a single. The Sox still led 2–1 entering the ninth inning with Bill Lee, who was making his first start since straining an elbow ligament in August, working on a four-hitter. After Johnny Bench led off with a double, Dick Drago came in from the bullpen. Drago retired the first two batters he faced. Only one out from going to Cincinnati with a two-games-to-none lead, Dave Concepcion drove in Bench with a single and scored on a double by Ken Griffey.

OCTOBER 14   The Reds win a controversial Game Three by beating the Red Sox 6–5 in 10 innings at Riverfront Stadium in Cincinnati. The Reds had a 5–1 lead after five innings, but the Red Sox battled back to tie the score 5–5 with a run in the sixth, another in the seventh, and two more in the ninth. Cesar Geronimo led off the Cincinnati tenth with a single to center field. Pinch hitter Ed Armbrister then bunted in front of the plate and bumped into Carlton Fisk as the Red Sox catcher fielded the ball. Fisk threw the ball into center field in an attempt to retire Geronimo at second base. Geronimo moved on to third base and Armbrister to second on the play. Home plate umpire Larry Barnett ruled there was no interference on Armbrister's part, despite furious protests from the Red Sox. After Pete Rose was walked intentionally, Joe Morgan hit a fly ball over Fred Lynn's head to score Geronimo with the winning run. After two games at Fenway Park in which no one hit a home run, there were six homers in Game Three, three by each club. Fisk, Bernie Carbo (in a pinch-hit role), and Dwight Evans (a two-run shot that tied the score in the ninth) homered for Boston. Geronimo, Johnny Bench, and Dave Concepcion went deep for the Reds.

OCTOBER 15   The Red Sox even the Series in Game Four with a 5–4 win in Cincinnati behind the complete-game pitching of Luis Tiant. Tiant was constantly in trouble, allowing nine hits and four walks, but he hung on for the win despite throwing 163 pitches. The Red Sox scored five runs in the fourth inning to take a 5–2 lead. Dwight Evans drove in the first two runs with a triple and scored the go-ahead run on Rick Burleson's double.

The Red Sox won all three games started by Luis Tiant in the 1975 World Series and lost the other four. Bill Lee was the starter in two games, and Rick Wise and Reggie Cleveland one each.

OCTOBER 16   The Reds move within one game of a World Championship with a 6–2 win over the Red Sox in Cincinnati in Game Five.

Rico Petrocelli (#6), Cecil Cooper (#17), and Fred Lynn (#19) congratulate Bernie Carbo on his three-run pinch-homer in the eighth inning of Game Six of the 1975 World Series. Lynn had already homered in the first to put the Sox up 3–0. Carbo's shot tied the game 6–6. At far left, the Reds' Johnny Bench looks on.

Focus On Sport/Getty Images

OCTOBER 18   Game Six is postponed by a rain storm that sweeps down the New England coast.

The two teams were also unable to play on October 19 and 20. The Red Sox and Reds each played only eight games in a 22-day span from September 29 through October 20.

OCTOBER 21   The sixth game of the 1975 World Series is worth the three-day wait as the Red Sox win a 7–6 thriller in 12 innings before 35,205 at Fenway Park. The contest is considered by many to be the most exciting in World Series history. Duffy Lewis, who was eighty-seven years old and played on the 1912, 1915, and 1916 World Champions for the Red Sox, threw out the first ball. The Sox struck first on a three-run, first-inning homer by Fred Lynn off Gary Nolan. Luis Tiant held the Reds scoreless until the fifth, when Ken Griffey hit a triple off the center field wall to score two runs. The Reds took a 5–3 lead in the seventh on George Foster's two-run double. Cesar Geronimo's eighth-inning homer made it 6–3, and the Red Sox were six outs from elimination.

But in the Boston eighth, Bernie Carbo hit a two-out, three-run, pinch-homer into the center field bleachers off Rawly Eastwick to tie the score, 6–6. The Sox loaded the bases in the ninth with no outs when Reds left fielder George Foster started a dramatic double play by catching Fred Lynn's fly ball in shallow left and threw to the plate to nail Denny Doyle. In the eleventh, Dwight Evans made a leaping catch in right field to rob Joe Morgan of a home run, then fired the ball back to the infield to complete an inning-ending double play. At 12:34 AM, Carlton Fisk led off the bottom of the twelfth by hitting a Pat Darcy pitch off the left field foul pole to win the game 7–6 and tie the Series three games apiece. As Fisk rounded the bases, Fenway Park organist John Kiley boomed the opening notes of Handel's "Hallelujah Chorus."

One of the most enduring television images in World Series history took place when Fisk ended Game Six with his home run. He stopped to watch the flight of the ball a few feet down the first-base line and waved his arms in an attempt to "steer" the ball into fair territory. After the ball struck the foul pole for a homer, Fisk leaped into the air and circled the bases amid jubilant fans who stormed the field. Television cameras might not have caught Fisk's gyrations if it hadn't been for a large rat inside the Fenway Park scoreboard. Cameraman Lou Gerard was stationed inside the scoreboard with his lens poked through a hole, and his instructions were to follow the flight of the ball. When Fisk made contact with Darcy's pitch, Gerard was distracted by the rat four feet away from him, and the sight of the rodent froze him long enough to allow him to stay with Fisk and get the famous reaction shot. Since then, reaction shots have been a staple of sports television coverage.

OCTOBER 22   The Red Sox blow a 3–0 lead and lose Game Seven 4–3 before 35,205 at Fenway Park on a Reds run in the ninth. Bill Lee was the starting pitcher for the Sox. The "Space Man" was angry over the fact that he was bypassed in Game Six in favor of Luis Tiant, but Lee hadn't won a game since August 24. The Sox scored all three of their runs in the third inning off Don Gullett, the first on a single by Carl Yastrzemski and the last two on bases-loaded walks to Rico Petrocelli and Dwight Evans. The Cincinnati comeback started in the sixth. With Johnny Bench on second and two out, Tony Perez hit a Lee "blooper pitch" over the left field wall to make the score 3–2. In the seventh, Ken Griffey walked and stole second. Roger Moret replaced Lee and recorded two outs. The Red Sox were just seven outs from a World Championship when Moret issued a walk to pinch-hitter Ed Armbrister and a single to Pete Rose to tie the score, 3–3. In the ninth, with rookie reliever Jim Burton on the mound for the Sox, Griffey walked again and went to second on a sacrifice. With two outs and the count 1–2, Joe Morgan's shallow single to center scored Griffey to give the Reds the lead, 4–3. Will McEnaney retired the Sox in order in the ninth, retiring Yastrzemski on a fly ball to center field for the final out. Burton, whose big-league career consisted of only 29 regular-season games prior to the 1975 postseason, pitched only one more game in the majors after taking the Game Seven loss. Moret, who gave up the tying run in the seventh, never pitched again for the Red Sox.

> *The 1975 World Series has often been called the most exciting in history. There were five one-run games, five come-from-behind victories, and another in which the Red Sox wiped out a four-run deficit to tie the Reds before losing. Two contests went into extra innings, four were decided in the final inning, and there were several spectacular defensive plays. The Red Sox had the lead in all four Cincinnati victories.*

NOVEMBER 17   The Red Sox trade Juan Beniquez, Steve Barr, and Craig Skok to the Rangers for Ferguson Jenkins.

> *Jenkins came to the Red Sox following a 1975 season with the Rangers in which he posted a 17–18 record. He was 25–12 in 1974, however, and had a 191–138 lifetime won-lost mark during his career at the time of the trade, including seven seasons of 20 wins or more, six of them in succession with the Cubs, beginning in 1967. Jenkins never played on a pennant-winner, though, and he hoped that situation would change coming to the defending American League Champion Red Sox. It didn't happen. Jenkins spent two unhappy years with the Sox, had 22 wins and 21 losses, and was traded back to the Rangers after the 1977 season.*

DECEMBER 12   The Red Sox trade Roger Moret to the Braves for Tom House.

1976   B

Season in a Sentence

Less than nine months after taking the Red Sox to the brink of a World Championship, Darrell Johnson is fired after the club gets off to a slow start.

Finish • Won • Lost • Pct • GB

Third   83   79   .512   15.5

Managers

Darrell Johnson (41–45)
Don Zimmer (42–34)

Stats   Red Sox • AL • Rank

Batting Avg:	.263	.256	5
On-Base Pct:	.327	.323	5
Slugging Pct:	.402	.361	1
Home Runs:	134		1
Stolen Bases:	95		9
ERA:	3.52	3.52	8
Fielding Pct:	.978	.977	6
Runs Scored:	716		3
Runs Allowed:	660		9

Starting Lineup

Carlton Fisk, c
Carl Yastrzemski, 1b-lf
Denny Doyle, 2b
Butch Hobson, 3b
Rick Burleson, ss
Jim Rice, lf-dh
Fred Lynn, cf
Dwight Evans, rf
Cecil Cooper, dh-1b
Rick Miller, cf-rf-lf
Rico Petrocelli, 3b
Steve Dillard, 3b-2b-ss

Pitchers

Luis Tiant, sp
Rick Wise, sp
Ferguson Jenkins, sp
Rick Jones, sp-rp
Bill Lee, sp-rp
Jim Willoughby, rp
Reggie Cleveland, rp-sp
Tom Murphy, rp
Dick Pole, rp-sp

Attendance

1,895,846 (second in AL)

Club Leaders

Batting Avg:	Lynn	.314
On-Base Pct:	Lynn	.367
Slugging Pct:	Rice	.482
Home Runs:	Rice	25
RBI:	Yastrzemski	102
Runs:	Lynn	76
	Fisk	76
Stolen Bases:	Lynn	14
	Burleson	14
Wins:	Tiant	21
Strikeouts:	Jenkins	142
ERA:	Tiant	3.06
Saves:	Willoughby	10

MARCH 3   The Red Sox trade Dick Drago to the Angels for John Balaz, Dick Sharon, and Dave Machemer.

APRIL 9   In the season opener, the Red Sox lose 1–0 to the Orioles in Baltimore. Ferguson Jenkins, in his first game with the Sox, allowed only three hits in a complete game. The lone run of the game was unearned and scored in the fourth inning on two Boston errors. Jim Palmer and Dyar Miller combined on the shutout.

APRIL 13   In the home opener, the Red Sox defeat the Indians before 32,127. The Sox broke a 4–4 tie with a run in the fifth inning, driven in on a double by Denny Doyle and a single by Fred Lynn. Carlton Fisk hit a home run. Reggie Cleveland pitched 5 1/3 innings of shutout relief.

A new addition at Fenway Park in 1976 was an electronic scoreboard with video replay capability above the center field bleachers. A sheet metal addition was added to the wall above the bleachers to support advertising panels. They were the first commercial advertisements in the ballpark since 1946. The left field wall was also rebuilt. Before 1976, the wall was composed of wooden railroad ties covered with tin and set atop a concrete base. The old tin panels were replaced by a Formica-type covering that yielded more consistent caroms and less noise. Padding was also added to the wall to protect outfielders. The National League portion of the scoreboard was removed, and the remaining portion of the board was recentered by shifting it to the right. The tin panels were cut into small squares and sold, the proceeds going to the Jimmy Fund.

APRIL 20   The Red Sox score seven runs in the third inning and trounce the Twins 12–3 at Fenway Park.

APRIL 28   The Red Sox are rained out for their fourth consecutive game. Foul weather prevented the Sox from playing the White Sox in Chicago on April 24 and 25, and the Royals in Kansas City on April 27 and 28.

MAY 11   The Red Sox lose their 10th game in a row, dropping a 4–3 decision to the Indians in Cleveland. The defeat dropped the Red Sox record to 6–15.

              Due to postponements and scheduled days off, the 10-game losing streak lasted 19 days.

MAY 12   The 10-game losing streak ends with a 12-inning, 6–4 win against the Indians in Cleveland. The Sox trailed 4–1 before scoring single runs in the fourth, fifth, and sixth innings. Carl Yastrzemski's sacrifice fly broke a 4–4 tie.

              In an attempt to end the 10-game losing streak, a Boston television station sent Laurie Cabot, an instructor in witchcraft at Salem State College, to Cleveland to cast a favorable spell on the club. "Having her around didn't hurt," reliever Tom House said. "Maybe she took our minds off the streak."

MAY 13   In response to the Red Sox' use of a witch, the Indians dress a woman in a fairy godmother costume to cast a favorable spell on the Cleveland club before a game at Municipal Stadium. It didn't work. The Red Sox won, 7–5.

MAY 15   The Red Sox explode for eight runs in the seventh inning and beat the Brewers 9–4 at Fenway Park.

MAY 19   Carl Yastrzemski smashes three homers and a single in a 9–2 win over the Tigers in Detroit. Yaz clubbed a two-run homer in the fourth and a solo shot in the fifth off Dave Roberts and a solo homer in the ninth off John Hiller.

              In the next game, an 8–2 victory over the Yankees in New York, Yastrzemski hit two more homers. His five home runs in consecutive games tied a major league record. The only other Red Sox batter with five homers in consecutive games is Nomar Garciaparra in 2002.

MAY 20   Bill Lee is injured in a vicious brawl during an 8–2 win over the Yankees in the Red Sox' first game at remodeled Yankee Stadium.

              The fight started in the sixth inning when Lou Piniella crashed into Carlton Fisk in a play at the plate. Fisk held onto the ball for the out, then jumped on Piniella, who was still stretched out at the plate. The dugouts emptied, and fights broke out everywhere. Lee came in from the mound firing punches, and

Mickey Rivers sucker-punched Lee in the back of the head. Lee ended up under one pile, and after he got up, was grabbed by Graig Nettles. The two began throwing punches at one another. Nettles lifted Lee off the ground and slammed him shoulder-first into the ground. Lee chased Nettles around the field shouting obscenities, and Nettles dropped him with another punch to the eye. Lee suffered torn ligaments in his pitching shoulder. In a press conference the following day, Lee called Yankee manager Billy Martin a "Nazi" and referred to the Yankees as "Steinbrenner's Brown Shirts." Lee didn't pitch again until July and was rarely effective, finishing the season with a record of 5–7 and a 5.63 ERA.

MAY 24   Rick Wise pitches a two-hitter to beat the Tigers 3–0 at Fenway Park. The only Detroit hits were singles by Alex Johnson in the first inning and Ron LeFlore in the third.

MAY 25   Carl Yastrzemski's two-run homer in the fourth inning off Mark Fidrych provides the only runs in a 2–0 win over the Tigers at Fenway Park. Luis Tiant pitched the shutout.

MAY 31   The umpires threaten the Red Sox with a forfeit when a cherry bomb explodes in front of Yankee center fielder Mickey Rivers in the eighth inning of an 8–3 loss at Fenway Park. It was the first meeting between the Sox and Yanks since the May 20 brawl, and fans threw cherry bombs, golf balls, and other objects onto the field.

JUNE 3   The Red Sox trade Bernie Carbo to the Brewers for Tom Murphy and Bobby Darwin.

JUNE 8   Two days after the Celtics win the NBA Championship in a six-game series against the Phoenix Suns, the Red Sox choose left-handed pitcher Bruce Hurst from Dixie High School in St. George, Utah, in the first round of the amateur draft.

Overall, 1976 was the best draft year in Red Sox history. Hurst arrived in the majors in 1980 and pitched nine seasons for the Red Sox, posting a record of 88–73. He won 145 big-league games. The best pick in the 1976 draft was in the seventh round when the Sox picked up an infielder from Plant High School in Tampa named Wade Boggs. The previous January, the club had drafted John Tudor. Other future major leaguers drafted and signed by the Red Sox in '76 were Glenn Hoffman (second round), Mike Smithson (fifth), Gary Allenson (ninth), Reid Nichols (12th), and Chico Walker (22nd).

JUNE 11   Carlton Fisk and Darrell Johnson argue in the dugout during a 10–4 loss to the Twins in Minnesota. Fisk fired a batting helmet in Johnson's direction during the heated discussion.

JUNE 14   Rick Wise pitches a one-hitter to defeat the Twins 5–0 at Metropolitan Stadium. The only infield hit was an infield single by Jerry Terrell in the third inning.

JUNE 15   The Red Sox purchase Rollie Fingers and Joe Rudi from the Athletics for two million dollars. On the same day, the Yankees bought Vida Blue from the A's for $1.5 million.

Almost immediately, baseball commissioner Bowie Kuhn questioned the big-money deals and indicated that he might void the sales. Kuhn dictated that the three players remain on the Oakland active roster until he reached a decision, but the three could not participate in any games. Before Kuhn issued the edict,

Rudi and Fingers were in Red Sox uniforms for a game against the Tigers in Detroit, won by the Red Sox 6–2 in 12 innings. Fingers threw in the bullpen late in the game. Rudi was available for pinch-hit duty, but Darrell Johnson kept him on the bench.

On June 17, Kuhn called for a hearing. Invited to attend were officials from the Red Sox and Yankees as well as Athletics owner Charlie Finley and Marvin Miller, head of the Players' Association. On June 18, Kuhn canceled the transactions "in the best interests of baseball." Kuhn feared that the sale of players for such large amounts of cash would adversely effect "the public's confidence in baseball" by upsetting the game's "competitive balance." The Red Sox were outraged by Kuhn's edict. "Who do we check with now if we want to buy a player?" general manager Dick O'Connell asked. "Who determines if his batting average is low enough, or if the price is low enough?" Rudi and Fingers became free agents at the end of the 1976 season. Rudi signed with the Angels, and Fingers with the Padres. Rudi later played for the Sox in 1981. Blue remained in Oakland until March 1978, when he was traded to the Giants.

JUNE 22   Bobby Darwin hits a grand slam in the first inning off Rudy May, but the Red Sox have to battle 15 innings to defeat the Orioles 6–5 in Baltimore. Darwin also drove in the winning run with an infield grounder that scored Fred Lynn from third base.

               Lynn's numbers declined from his rookie season, but he still hit .314 with 10 homers.

JUNE 26   Rico Petrocelli drives in both runs, including a walk-off single in the ninth inning, in a 2–1 win over the Tigers at Fenway.

JUNE 28   Butch Hobson hits a homer in his first major league game. Hobson's homer was inside the park with a man on base and broke an 8–8 tie in the sixth inning of a 12–8 win over the Orioles in Baltimore. With Hobson playing third base, Rico Petrocelli started the game at second, the first time in his professional baseball career that Rico played the position. The experiment lasted only five games.

               Hobson played quarterback under Bear Bryant at the University of Alabama and carried his gridiron mentality onto the baseball diamond. Hobson's all-out play led to numerous injuries and helped shorten his career to seven seasons. His given name was Clell Lavern.

JUNE 29   Rick Wise pitches his second one-hitter in two weeks, beating the Orioles 2–0 at Fenway Park. The only Baltimore hit was a single by Paul Blair in the sixth inning.

JULY 9   Tom Yawkey dies of leukemia at the age of seventy-three.

               Ownership of the Red Sox passed to a trust controlled by Yawkey's widow, Jean; James Curran, an old friend and business associate; and executor Joseph LaCour. It was a convoluted and unsatisfactory arrangement, as various factions struggled for control of the club and left a muddle that took decades to properly resolve (see May 23, 1978).

JULY 13   Fred Lynn homers off Tom Seaver in the fourth inning of the All-Star Game, played at Veterans Stadium in Philadelphia. The homer accounted for the only American League run in a 7–1 loss. Darrell Johnson managed the AL squad.

JULY 19   Darrell Johnson is fired as manager of the Red Sox and is replaced by Don Zimmer.

Less than nine months after the end of the 1975 World Series, Johnson had clearly lost control of a clubhouse full of strong personalities. The Red Sox had a 41–45 record at the time of his firing. Johnson later managed the Seattle Mariners from 1977 through 1980 and the Rangers in 1982, where he oddly enough replaced Zimmer as manager. Zimmer had been the Sox third-base coach under Johnson since 1974. He previously managed a dismal Padres club in 1972 and 1973 to a record of 114–190. Zimmer had a playing career as an infielder, mostly with the Dodgers, from 1954 through 1965. He managed the Red Sox until 1980 with much more success than he had in San Diego. Zimmer was the first manager to guide the Red Sox to three consecutive seasons of 90 wins or more since Bill Carrigan from 1914 through 1916, but Zimmer will be remembered most in Boston for allowing the Yankees to overcome a 14-game deficit to overtake the Sox in 1978, and for Bill Lee categorizing him as a "gerbil." The match between the crew cut, conservative, no-nonsense Zimmer and the city of Boston seemed to fit together like mustard and clam chowder. Disparaged by fans and players alike, he was constantly booed at Fenway Park and received almost no credit for the 411 victories the club recorded while he was the manager, but he did receive the bulk of the blame for the 304 defeats. Despite Zimmer's unpopularity, the Red Sox drew more than two million fans for the first time in 1977 and 2.3 million in 1979.

JULY 25   Entering the game with a 5–3 lead with two out in the bottom of the ninth and two Yankees on base, Tom House throws only one pitch which results in a three-run homer by Chris Chambliss and a 6–5 Red Sox defeat in New York.

JULY 27   Ferguson Jenkins earns his 200th career victory with an 8–7 victory over the Indians at Fenway Park. Jenkins allowed seven runs and 14 hits in seven innings.

AUGUST 1   The Red Sox rally for three runs in the ninth inning on a two-run double by Rick Burleson and a sacrifice fly by Carl Yastrzemski to beat the Yankees 5–4 at Fenway Park.

Burleson hit .291 with seven homers in 1976.

AUGUST 8   Rookie pitcher Rick Jones misses a flight to Anaheim. The following morning, Jones was spotted by one club official walking around Kenmore Square, but when he arrived in Anaheim later that night, Jones told Don Zimmer that he had gone to Florida to visit his sick father. At the time, Jones was twenty-one and showed some promise with a 4–1 record and a 2.84 ERA, but because of the missed flight, several missed curfews, and his general immaturity, the Sox sent him back to Pawtucket. He came back to the club in September, pitched ineffectively, and went to the Mariners in the expansion draft. Jones's big-league career ended in 1978 when he was only twenty-three. Three of his high school buddies were members of the rock band Lynyrd Skynyrd, named after Leonard Skinner, their football coach at Forrest High School in Jacksonville, Florida, who had suspended Jones and the band members from the athletic program because they refused to cut their hair.

AUGUST 20   Mrs. Jean Yawkey is named team president by the trust that owns the Red Sox.

In August, Boston City Council voted to change the name of Jersey Street, located on the west (third-base) side of Fenway Park, to Yawkey Way.

AUGUST 29   The Red Sox score seven runs in the first inning and five in the second to take a 12–0 lead and go on to rout the Royals 15–6 at Fenway Park.

SEPTEMBER 9   Rick Wise pitches a two-hitter to defeat the Tigers 5–0 at Fenway Park. Wise retired the first 19 batters he faced before allowing consecutive singles to Phil Mankowski and Ben Oglivie.

During the 1976 season, Wise pitched two one-hitters and a pair of two-hitters. He finished the year with a 14–11 record and a 3.54 ERA.

SEPTEMBER 16   Butch Hobson hits a two-run homer in the ninth inning to beat the Brewers 4–3 in Milwaukee.

SEPTEMBER 20   The Red Sox score seven runs in the fourth inning to take a 10–4 lead and outmuscle the Tigers 12–6 in Detroit.

SEPTEMBER 21   Luis Tiant wins his 20th game of 1976 and strikes out 12 batters in a 7–1 decision over the Brewers in the first game of a doubleheader at Fenway Park. Tiant held the Brewers hitless for 6⅓ innings before George Scott tripled. Luis settled for a three-hitter. Milwaukee won the second tilt, 3–1.

SEPTEMBER 25   Luis Tiant pitches a two-hitter to beat the Orioles 1–0 at Memorial Stadium. Dwight Evans accounted for the lone run of the game with a homer in the fifth inning off Ross Grimsley. The only Baltimore hits were singles by Reggie Jackson in the fourth inning and Dave Duncan in the fifth.

Tiant finished the season with a 21–12 record and a 3.06 ERA in 279 innings.

OCTOBER 2   Reggie Cleveland (eight innings), Tom House (one-third of an inning) and Jim Willoughby (two-thirds of an inning) combine on a shutout to defeat the Orioles 1–0 in Baltimore. Jim Rice drove in the lone run of the game with a triple in the first inning.

Rice finished the season with a .282 batting average and 25 homers.

OCTOBER 3   In the last game of the season, the Red Sox win 3–2 in 15 innings against the Orioles at Fenway Park. Butch Hobson tied the score 2–2 with a run-scoring single in the eleventh and crossed the plate with the winning run in the fifteenth on a two-out single by Rick Burleson.

The Red Sox won 15 of the last 18 games to finish the season four games over .500.

NOVEMBER 5   Three days after Jimmy Carter defeats Gerald Ford in the presidential election, the Red Sox lose Rick Jones, Steve Burke, Dick Pole, and Luis Delgado to the Mariners and Ernie Whitt to the Blue Jays in the expansion draft.

NOVEMBER 6   The Red Sox sign Bill Campbell, most recently with the Twins, as a free agent.

Campbell was the first free agent to sign with any major league club after the system went into effect at the end of the 1976 season. He was the losing pitcher in the first two games of the 1977 season but finished the year with a 13–9 record, 31 saves, and a 2.96 ERA. With the starters struggling for consistency,

Campbell's 13 wins led the club. He pitched 140 innings of relief in 1977 after throwing an average of 136 innings in his last three years in Minnesota. An elbow injury in 1978, which was probably the result of overwork, ended Campbell's days as a closer, although he remained in the majors until 1987. He pitched for the Sox until 1982, when he was traded to the Cubs.

DECEMBER 6   The Red Sox trade Cecil Cooper to the Brewers for George Scott and Bernie Carbo.

The trade brought George Scott back to Boston after five years in Milwaukee. Scott hit 33 homers for the Sox in 1977 before his age and weight problems caught up with him and reduced him to a reserve role. Ironically, the Sox traded Scott to the Brewers in October 1971 because they believed that Cooper was ready to take over at first base. When Cooper failed to develop to the satisfaction of Red Sox management, the club dealt him to Milwaukee to get Scott back. It was a huge mistake. While Scott had one good season in his return to New England, Cooper had seven great seasons with the Brewers. From 1977 through 1983, Cooper hit .300 or better each season and .316 overall, along with an average of 22 homers and 95 RBIs per season.

1977   B

Season in a Sentence

The Red Sox hit 213 homers, including 33 in a stretch of 10 June games, and win a total of 97 games, but it's not enough to reach the postseason.

Finish • Won • Lost • Pct • GB

Second (tie) 97   64   .602   2.5

Manager

Don Zimmer

Stats   Red Sox • AL • Rank

Stats	Red Sox	AL	Rank
Batting Avg:	.281	.266	2
On-Base Pct:	.349	.333	2
Slugging Pct:	.465	.405	1
Home Runs:	213		1
Stolen Bases:	66		12
ERA:	4.11	4.05	8
Fielding Pct:	.978	.977	5
Runs Scored:	867		1
Runs Allowed:	712		6

Starting Lineup

Carlton Fisk, c
George Scott, 1b
Denny Doyle, 2b
Butch Hobson, 3b
Rick Burleson, ss
Carl Yastrzemski, lf
Fred Lynn, cf
Rick Miller, rf-cf
Jim Rice, dh
Dwight Evans, rf
Bernie Carbo, rf

Pitchers

Luis Tiant, sp
Ferguson Jenkins, sp
Reggie Cleveland, sp-rp
Rick Wise, sp
Bill Lee, sp-rp
Don Aase, sp
Bill Campbell, rp
Bob Stanley, rp-sp
Mike Paxton, rp-sp

Attendance

2,074,549 (second in AL)

Club Leaders

Batting Avg:	Fisk	.315
On-Base Pct:	Fisk	.402
Slugging Pct:	Rice	.593
Home Runs:	Rice	39
RBI:	Rice	114
Runs:	Fisk	106
Stolen Bases:	Burleson	13
Wins:	Campbell	13
Strikeouts:	Tiant	124
ERA:	Jenkins	3.68
Saves:	Campbell	31

MARCH 26   After 13 seasons with the club, the Red Sox release Rico Petrocelli.

Petrocelli played 1,553 games with the Red Sox, scoring 653 runs with 1,352 hits, 237 doubles, 210 homers, and 773 RBIs.

APRIL 7   The Red Sox lose 5–4 in 11 innings to the Indians on Opening Day before 34,790 at Fenway Park. In his first appearance with the Sox, Bill Campbell took over for Ferguson Jenkins in the eighth inning with a 4–2 lead and allowed two runs in the ninth on Buddy Bell's homer and one in the eleventh. Bernie Carbo hit a homer, a double, and a single. Dwight Evans also homered. Carl Yastrzemski began the season as the starting right fielder in an experiment that lasted only a few games.

In his 17th big-league season, Yastrzemski batted .296, hit 28 homers, and drove in 102 runs.

APRIL 10   The Red Sox and Indians combine for 19 runs in the eighth inning at Fenway Park in a game won by Cleveland, 19–9. The 19 runs by two clubs in one inning is a major league record. The game was routine through seven innings with the score 3–3 when the Indians erupted for 13 runs off Bill Campbell, Jim Willoughby, Tom House, and Tom Murphy. The Red Sox countered with six runs in their half of the eighth before the Indians added three runs in the ninth. Bill Campbell was the losing pitcher, giving him an 0–2 record just two games into the 1977 season.

APRIL 13   The Red Sox drop to 0–4 on the season with a 7–3 loss to the White Sox in Chicago.

APRIL 21   Club president Jean Yawkey announces that the Red Sox are for sale (see September 29, 1977).

APRIL 24   The Red Sox play a regular-season game in Toronto for the first time and defeat the Blue Jays 9–0 at Exhibition Stadium. Ferguson Jenkins, who was born in nearby Chatham, Ontario, pitched the complete-game shutout.

MAY 3   The Seattle Mariners play at Fenway Park for the first time and beat the Red Sox 10–8 after plating five runs in the first inning.

MAY 13   Fred Lynn, making his first appearance of the season after suffering a foot injury in spring training, hits a homer in each of his first two at-bats in a 7–5 win over the Mariners in Seattle. It was the first time that the Red Sox played a game at the Kingdome.

MAY 21   The Red Sox score four runs in the ninth inning to defeat the Brewers 10–9 at Fenway Park. The rally started with a long homer by Jim Rice that struck the center field wall behind the bleachers. An RBI double by George Scott pulled the Red Sox within a run. After a walk to Carlton Fisk, Dwight Evans hit a single that scored Scott to tie it and sent Fisk to third. Butch Hobson grounded to Don Money at second base for a forceout, but Evans's takeout slide prevented the Brewers from completing a double play and allowed Fisk to score the winning run.

Fisk had a rare injury-free season and played in 152 games, batting .315 with 26 homers, 102 RBIs, and 106 runs.

MAY 22	Down 10–7, the Red Sox score seven runs in the eighth inning to beat the Brewers 14–10 in the first game of a doubleheader at Fenway Park. George Scott broke the 10–10 tie with a grand slam off Rick Folkers. The game produced 11 homers in all, six by the Red Sox. In addition's to Scott's home run, Fred Lynn hit a pair, and Carl Yastrzemski, Butch Hobson, and Dwight Evans added one each. Evans's homer cleared the center field wall about 20 feet to the right of the flagpole. Don Money hit two for the Brewers, and Sixto Lezcano, Mike Hegan, and Von Joshua hit one apiece. The Red Sox' bats were silent in the second game as Milwaukee won, 6–0.
MAY 28	Trailing 10–4, the Red Sox score seven runs in the fifth inning to take an 11–10 lead and outslug the Royals 17–12 at Fenway Park. There were six Boston homers in the contest. Jim Rice hit two, and Carl Yastrzemski, Carlton Fisk, Dwight Evans, and George Scott added one each.

Rice led the AL in 1977 in homers (39), total bases (382), and slugging percentage (.593). He also hit .320, drove in 114 runs, scored 104, collected 206 hits, and hit 15 triples.

JUNE 1	Down 5–0, the Red Sox score two runs in the fourth inning, four in the sixth, and one in the seventh to beat the Rangers 7–5 in Arlington.
JUNE 4	Fred Lynn makes a spectacular catch on a nationally televised Saturday afternoon game to help the Red Sox to a 5–2 win over the Twins in Minnesota. Lynn robbed Dan Ford of a home run by leaping above the wooden right-center field fence 430 feet from home plate.
JUNE 6	Carl Yastrzemski accounts for the only run of a 1–0 win over the Royals in Kansas City with a homer off Dennis Leonard in the seventh inning. Luis Tiant (seven innings) and Bill Campbell (two innings) combined on the shutout.
JUNE 7	The Red Sox select six-foot-seven-inch pitcher Andrew Madden from New Hartford High School in New Hartford, New York, in the first round of the amateur draft.

Madden developed arm problems early and never made it past Class A. The Sox drafted and signed five players who reached the majors, including Bobby Sprowl (second round), Roger LaFrancois (eighth), Steve Shields (10th), Pete Ladd (25th), and Lee Graham (26th), but none made a significant contribution in Boston. The Sox did sign Rich Gedman out of St. Peter's High School in Worcester, Massachusetts, as an undrafted free agent in August.

JUNE 8	The Red Sox erupt for 11 runs in the second inning and add three more in the third to wallop the Orioles 14–5 at Fenway Park.
JUNE 9	Carl Yastrzemski collects the 500th double of his career in a 7–3 win over the Orioles at Fenway Park. The milestone two-bagger came off Jim Palmer in the first inning.
JUNE 13	The Red Sox take over first place from the Yankees in the AL East with a 10-inning, 5–4 win over the White Sox at Fenway Park. Carlton Fisk's walk-off single with the bases loaded drove in the winning run.

JUNE 17
The Red Sox tag Catfish Hunter for four home runs in the first inning to set the stage for a 9–4 win over the Yankees at Fenway Park. Rick Burleson and Fred Lynn, the first hitters in the lineup, led off the inning with back-to-back homers. After Hunter retired the next two hitters, Carlton Fisk and George Scott homered. Fisk and Carl Yastrzemski homered off Dick Tidrow in the seventh.

JUNE 18
The Red Sox collect five homers during a 10–4 triumph over the Yankees at Fenway Park. Carl Yastrzemski and Bernie Carbo each hit two homers, and George Scott hit one.

JUNE 19
The Red Sox club five more homers in an 11–1 thrashing of the Yankees at Fenway Park. The homers were struck by Denny Doyle, Bernie Carbo, Jim Rice, Carl Yastrzemski, and George Scott. It was the fifth consecutive game that Scott hit a home run. He had six homers over the five games, played from June 14 through 19. Yastrzemski's homer, in the eighth inning off Dick Tidrow, is the longest known home run to the right of the bleachers. It reached approximately 460 feet before striking the facing of the right field roof about 20 feet to the right of where the retired number 42 now appears. It is the only ball ever to reach the right field roof facade.

The 16 homers in the three games against the Yankees set a major league record for the most hit by a club in three consecutive games.

JUNE 20
Rick Wise pitches a two-hitter for a 4–0 win over the Orioles at Memorial Stadium. The only Baltimore hits were doubles by Mark Belanger in the third inning and Lee May in the seventh.

JUNE 21
Luis Tiant pitches a two-hitter to beat the Orioles 7–0 at Memorial Stadium. It was the second game in a row that a Boston pitcher recorded a two-hitter against the Orioles. The only Baltimore hits were a single by Lee May in the fourth inning and a double by Pat Kelly in the ninth. In the top of the ninth, Orioles pitcher Dennis Martinez plunked George Scott with a high pitch. Scott rushed toward the mound, and the slender, 160-pound Martinez wanted no part of the hefty Scott. Martinez turned and ran off the mound into the outfield, and Scott slipped and fell down in the infield grass chasing him.

On the same day, the Red Sox signed Tommy Helms, most recently with the Pirates, as a free agent.

JUNE 22
Carlton Fisk and Butch Hobson each hit two-run homers off Jim Palmer in the ninth inning to beat the Orioles 7–4 at Memorial Stadium. Fisk's homer was his second of the game and put the Sox ahead, 5–4. The drive glanced off the glove of Baltimore left fielder Pat Kelly and deflected over the fence. Earlier, George Scott and Jim Rice went deep for the Sox.

Hobson hit .265 with 30 homers and 112 RBIs in 1977.

JUNE 23
The Red Sox take a five-game lead over the Yankees in the AL East with a 7–3 victory over the Orioles in Baltimore.

From June 14 through June 24, the Red Sox set a major league record for most home runs in 10 consecutive games with 33. The 33 homers were struck by

George Scott (nine), Carl Yastrzemski (five), Bernie Carbo (four), Carlton Fisk (four), Butch Hobson (four), Jim Rice (four), Rick Burleson (one), Denny Doyle (one), and Fred Lynn (one). The Sox scored 90 runs in the 10 games and won eight of them.

JULY 3

George Scott is robbed of three potential home runs in a 12–8 loss to the Orioles at Fenway Park. All three were caught over the low bullpen wall by center fielder Al Bumbry and right fielder Ken Singleton. Each of the three drives advanced Carlton Fisk from first base to second. The loss was the ninth in a row for the Red Sox and knocked the club out of first place.

JULY 4

The Red Sox set a club record for most homers in a game with eight during a 9–6 win over the Blue Jays at Fenway Park. The eight homers were struck in a span of four innings. George Scott got things started with a two-run homer in the fifth. The rest were all solo home runs. Fred Lynn hit one in the sixth, and Bernie Carbo and Butch Hobson connected for the circuit in the seventh. There were four homers in the eighth, which tied a club mark for most homers in an inning. Lynn, Jim Rice, and Carl Yastrzemski hit back-to-back-to-back homers, and after Carlton Fisk was retired, Scott hit his second homer of the game. It was the first time that the Blue Jays played a game at Fenway Park.

The Red Sox hit 83 homers in a 44-game span from May 19 through July 4. The 83 homers were hit by George Scott (16), Jim Rice (14), Carl Yastrzemski (14), Butch Hobson (11), Carlton Fisk (nine), Fred Lynn (seven), Bernie Carbo (six), Dwight Evans (four), Rick Burleson (one) and Denny Doyle (one). The Sox set a club record for homers with 213, breaking the old mark of 203 set in 1970. The 1977 Red Sox held the mark until the 2003 club struck 238 home runs. A total of 124 of the 213 Boston home runs in 1977 were hit at Fenway Park.

JULY 10

The Red Sox leave 20 men on base but beat the Brewers 8–5 in 11 innings in the first game of a doubleheader in Milwaukee. The Sox completed the sweep with a 7–3 win in the nightcap.

JULY 13

A two-run homer by Butch Hobson in the tenth inning beats the Indians 9–7 in Cleveland.

JULY 14

Carl Yastrzemski collects his 2,655th career hit to break the club record set by Ted Williams. Yaz passed Williams with a single in the fifth inning off Alan Fitzmorris during a 7–4 win over the Indians in Cleveland.

JULY 19

George Scott hits a two-run homer off Goose Gossage in the ninth inning of the All-Star Game, but the American League loses 7–5 at Yankee Stadium.

JULY 21

Trailing 3–2, the Red Sox score nine runs in the seventh inning and beat the Indians 11–4 in the first game of a doubleheader at Fenway Park. Luis Tiant recorded his 2,000th career strikeout in the game by fanning Rico Carty in the fourth inning. Cleveland won the second tilt, 8–2.

JULY 26

In his major league debut, twenty-two-year-old Don Aase strikes out 11 batters, pitching a complete-game 4–3 victory over the Brewers at Fenway Park (see July 31, 1977).

JULY 27   The Red Sox sell Tom Murphy to the Blue Jays.

JULY 28   The Red Sox romp to a 12–0 win over the Brewers at Fenway Park.

JULY 29   Bernie Carbo's homer in the tenth inning beats the Angels 6–5 in Anaheim.

JULY 31   In his second major league game, Don Aase beats the Angels 1–0 at Anaheim Stadium. Aase was born a few miles away in Orange, California, and went to high school in Anaheim. The lone run of the game was scored on a single by Carlton Fisk in the ninth inning. The victory put the Red Sox back in first place, ahead of the Orioles.

              In his first three major league games, Aase had a 3–0 record allowing four runs in 25 innings. He finished his rookie season with a 6–2 record and a 3.13 ERA but was traded to the Angels on December 8, 1977, for Jerry Remy.

AUGUST 3   Bernie Carbo hits a grand slam in the sixth inning off Mike Kekich during a 12–4 win over the Mariners in Seattle. Jim Rice hit two homers in the game, and Butch Hobson and George Scott added one each.

AUGUST 5   Luis Tiant pitches the Red Sox to a 1–0 win over the Athletics in Oakland. The lone run of the game scored in the sixth inning on a double by Carlton Fisk and a single by Rick Miller. It was the Red Sox' eighth win in a row.

AUGUST 7   The Red Sox break a 1–1 tie with four runs in the ninth inning and beat the Athletics 5–2 in Oakland.

              The victory was the 10th in a row for the Red Sox and completed a 9–0 West Coast road trip in which the Sox won three games each against the Mariners in Seattle, the Angels in Anaheim, and the Athletics in Oakland.

AUGUST 10   The Red Sox run their winning streak to 11 with an 11–10 victory over the Angels at Fenway Park. Trailing 10–5, the Sox scored three runs in the seventh inning and three in the eighth. Bernie Carbo tied the score 10–10 with a two-run homer. Carl Yastrzemski drove in the winning run with a single.

AUGUST 11   The Red Sox 11-game winning streak comes to an end with a 7–3 defeat at the hands of the Angels at Fenway Park. Prior to the game, there was a contest between the Bristol Red Sox, Boston's farm club in the Eastern League, and the Eastern League All-Stars. Bristol lost, 5–3.

AUGUST 13   George Scott, Butch Hobson, and Dwight Evans smash consecutive homers in the sixth inning of a 13–6 win over the Mariners at Fenway Park. The Red Sox scored seven runs in the seventh inning to overcome a 7–2 Seattle lead.

AUGUST 14   The Red Sox rout the Mariners 11–1 at Fenway Park.

AUGUST 16   The Red Sox pick up their 16th win in a stretch of 17 games with a 5–2 triumph over the Royals at Fenway Park.

AUGUST 18   The Red Sox take a 3½ game lead in the AL East with an 8–4 win over the Brewers in Milwaukee. It was a costly win, however. Dwight Evans and Rick Miller collided in the outfield, and Evans was placed on the disabled list for nearly a month because of injuries sustained in the mishap.

AUGUST 23   The Red Sox are knocked out of first place with a 7–0 loss to the Twins in Minnesota. It was the Sox' fifth loss in a row.

The Red Sox never regained first place for the remainder of the season. Overall, the Sox were in first for 48 days during the season.

AUGUST 24   The Red Sox' losing streak reaches seven with a 3–0 and 6–3 sweep at the hands of the Rangers in a twinight doubleheader at Fenway Park. Due to rain delays, the twin bill ended at 2:20 AM.

AUGUST 29   Jim Rice hits three homers to drive in four runs, but the Red Sox lose 8–7 to the Athletics at Fenway Park. Rice hit a homer into the center field bleachers in the second inning and another over the left field screen in the third, both off Joe Coleman. His third came off Pablo Torrealba in the sixth inning with a man on base.

SEPTEMBER 5   The Red Sox sweep the Blue Jays in Toronto with a pair of complete-game shutouts. Don Aase won the first game 8–0 and Reggie Cleveland the second 6–0.

SEPTEMBER 6   Carlton Fisk drives in seven runs with a grand slam in the first inning off Mike Darr and a three-run homer off Pete Vuckovich in the eighth to lead the Red Sox to an 11–2 win at Toronto. It was Darr's only appearance in a major league game.

SEPTEMBER 11   Jim Rice hits a grand slam in the eleventh inning off John Hiller during a 6–2 win over the Tigers in Fenway Park.

George Scott missed two games in September after Don Zimmer dropped him to seventh in the batting order. Scott refused to take the field, stating that he wasn't "mentally prepared to play."

SEPTEMBER 17   The Red Sox send Frank Newcomer and cash to the Reds for Bob Bailey.

SEPTEMBER 18   In his major league debut, twenty-two-year-old Ted Cox collects four hits, including a double, in four at-bats during a 10–4 win over the Orioles in Baltimore. Cox is the only player in Red Sox history to collect four hits in his first major league game.

During the game, Dom Zimmer called coach Walt Hriniak in the bullpen to have Ferguson Jenkins warm up. Hriniak couldn't find Jenkins, and Zimmer had to go to another pitcher. Jenkins was later found asleep in a TV truck, where he had gone to watch a football game. Jenkins never pitched another game for the Sox.

SEPTEMBER 19   In his second big-league game, Ted Cox collects two singles in his first two at-bats during a 6–3 win over the Yankees at Fenway Park.

Cox is the only player in major league history to collect six hits in his first six major league at-bats. He played 13 games for the Red Sox in 1977 and hit .362. The Sox traded Cox to the Indians before the beginning of the 1978 season. Despite the fast start to his major league career, Cox lasted only five years in the majors and finished his career with a .245 batting average and 10 home runs in 272 games.

SEPTEMBER 20   A 3–2 win over the Yankees in New York cuts the Yankees' lead over the Red Sox in the AL East to 2 ½ games.

SEPTEMBER 28   The Red Sox top two million in home attendance for the first time in club history when 20,362 at Fenway watch the Sox lose 3–2 to the Blue Jays.

SEPTEMBER 29   Executors of Tom Yawkey's estate pick a 13-member group to buy the Red Sox. The group was headed by Tom's widow, Jean (who was in effect both seller and buyer), team vice president Haywood Sullivan, and former trainer Buddy LeRoux. Sullivan was a former catcher with the Red Sox who had worked for the Sox for the previous 12 years in scouting and player development. LeRoux was the club's trainer from 1966 through 1974 and made his wealth through various businesses and real estate holdings in Florida. The sale price was sixteen million dollars, pending the approval of American League owners. A-T-O Inc., the parent firm of Rawlings Sporting Goods, offered $18,375,000 for the club, but it was rejected by the executors of the Yawkey estate, leading to charges that the open bidding for the club was a charade. A-T-O went to court to block the sale of the Sox to the Sullivan-LeRoux group, but it lost the case (see December 8, 1977).

SEPTEMBER 30   The Red Sox outslug the Orioles 11–10 at Fenway Park and keep alive Boston's slim hope of winning an AL East title thanks to a 5–2 Yankee loss to the Tigers in New York. With two days left in the season, the Yankees had a record of 99–61, while the Red Sox were 97–63. In order to win the pennant, the Sox needed to win their last two games while the Yankees lost two, then beat the Yanks in a one-game playoff.

OCTOBER 1   The Red Sox are eliminated from the pennant race with an 8–7 loss to the Orioles at Fenway Park.

                The Red Sox were 26–12 over their last 38 games in 1977 but couldn't close the gap on the Yankees. The Sox finished the season in a second-place tie with the Orioles, 2 ½ games behind the Yankees.

OCTOBER 24   The Red Sox fire Dick O'Connell as general manager.

                O'Connell had been the general manager since September 1965. He guided the club to pennants in 1967 and 1975, and the Sox had recorded winning seasons in each of his last 11 years at the helm. Haywood Sullivan took over as the general manager.

NOVEMBER 23   The Red Sox sign Mike Torrez, most recently with the Yankees, as a free agent.

                Torrez came to the Red Sox a little over a month after pitching a complete-game victory in the sixth and final game of the 1977 World Series to clinch a World Championship for the Yankees. He will be long-remembered in Boston for the home run pitch he threw to the Yankees' Bucky Dent in the 1978 playoff game, but overall was an effective pitcher for the Red Sox. He was 16–13 in both 1978 and 1979. During his career, Torrez won at least 10 games in a season for seven different clubs. The others were the Cardinals, Expos, Orioles, Athletics, Yankees, and Mets.

DECEMBER 8   The American League rejects the sale of the Red Sox to a group headed by Jean Yawkey, Haywood Sullivan, and Buddy LeRoux. The AL was concerned about the shaky financial foundation of the arrangement. Sullivan and LeRoux were to be general partners, even though they contributed only $200,000 between them to the sixteen-million-dollar purchase price. In addition, the group took out eight million dollars in loans that required $800,000 annually in interest charges, and the State Street Bank and Trust, which financed the deal, placed restrictions on the Red Sox' ability to invest in players' salaries and development, which were in violation of the Basic Agreement between the players and owners (see May 23, 1978).

On the same day, the Red Sox traded Don Aase to the Angels for Jerry Remy. A native of Fall River, Massachusetts, Remy was the Sox' starting second baseman from 1978 through 1983 when he wasn't sidelined by frequent injuries. Inconsistent as a starter, Aase was converted exclusively to relief in 1981 and lasted in the majors until 1990. He had a 66–60 career record with 82 saves, mostly with the Angels and Orioles.

DECEMBER 14   The Red Sox trade Ferguson Jenkins to the Rangers for John Poloni and cash.

Jenkins won at least 14 games in every season but two between 1967 and 1979. Those two seasons were the two he spent in Boston, where he had a combined record of 22–21. To make matters worse, Jenkins aligned himself with a group of players dissatisfied with the managerial abilities of Don Zimmer. The outspoken and free-spirited group constantly belittled and ridiculed Zimmer and called themselves "The Loyal Order of the Buffalo." The name came from Jenkins's nickname for Zimmer, which was "Buffalohead" because the buffalo was "the dumbest animal alive." The other members were Bill Lee, Bernie Carbo, Rick Wise, Reggie Cleveland, and Jim Willoughby. All were traded or sold by the beginning of the 1979 season. The Red Sox could have used Jenkins in 1978 when he posted an 18–8 record with a 3.04 ERA with the Rangers and in 1979 when he was 16–14. He finished his Hall of Fame career in 1983 with 284 wins.

DECEMBER 21   Rick Miller signs a free-agent contract with the Angels.

Miller spent seven frustrating seasons with the Red Sox, unable to break into an outfield with Carl Yastrzemski, Reggie Smith, Tommy Harper, Fred Lynn, Jim Rice, and Dwight Evans ahead of him on the depth chart. Miller played three seasons in California before returning to play for the Sox again from 1981 through 1985.

1978   B

Season in a Sentence

The Red Sox take a 14-game lead over the Yankees on July 19, but fritter it away and lose a one-game playoff to the Yanks for the AL East crown on Bucky Dent's go-ahead home run.

Finish • Won • Lost • Pct • GB

Second   99   64   .607   1.0

Manager

Don Zimmer

Stats

Stats	Red Sox	AL	Rank
Batting Avg:	.267	.261	4
On-Base Pct:	.339	.329	3
Slugging Pct:	.424	.385	2
Home Runs:	172		2
Stolen Bases:	74		12
ERA:	3.54	3.75	4
Fielding Pct:	.977	.978	9
Runs Scored:	796		2
Runs Allowed:	657		7

Starting Lineup

Carlton Fisk, c
George Scott, 1b
Jerry Remy, 2b
Butch Hobson, 3b
Rick Burleson, ss
Carl Yastrzemski, lf-1b
Fred Lynn, cf
Dwight Evans, rf
Jim Rice, lf-dh
Jack Brohamer, 3b-dh-2b

Pitchers

Dennis Eckersley, sp
Mike Torrez, sp
Bill Lee, sp
Luis Tiant, sp
Bob Stanley, rp
Dick Drago, rp
Tom Burgmeier, rp
Bill Campbell, rp

Attendance

2,320,643 (first in AL)

Club Leaders

Batting Avg:	Rice	.315
On-Base Pct:	Lynn	.380
Slugging Pct:	Rice	.600
Home Runs:	Rice	46
RBI:	Rice	139
Runs:	Rice	121
Stolen Bases:	Remy	30
Wins:	Eckersley	20
Strikeouts:	Eckersley	162
ERA:	Eckersley	2.99
Saves:	Stanley	10

FEBRUARY 17   Four weeks after a blizzard drops twenty-three inches of snow on Boston in one day, the Red Sox sign Tom Burgmeier, most recently with the Twins, as a free agent.

MARCH 20   The Red Sox trade Rick Wise, Mike Paxton, Bo Diaz, and Ted Cox to the Indians for Dennis Eckersley and Fred Kendall.

Eckersley was only twenty-three when acquired by the Red Sox and paid immediate dividends with a 20–8 record and a 2.99 ERA 268⅓ innings in 1978. He was off to a 16–5 start in 1979 before arm troubles surfaced. He finished that season 17–10 and was 47–52 with a 4.47 ERA from 1980 through 1984 when Eckersley was traded to the Cubs. While in Boston, "Eck" endeared himself to fans with a vocabulary all his own. A homer was a "bridgepiece," a game-winning homer was a "walk-off piece," a fastball was "cheese," a fastball up and in was "cheese in your kitchen," a curve was called a "yakker," and a big game was a "Bogart."

MARCH 22   Many of the Red Sox watch world-famous tightrope-artist Karl Wallenda fall to his death in San Juan, Puerto Rico. The Sox were in San Juan for a two-game series of exhibitions against the Pirates. Wallenda, who was seventy-three years old, attempted to walk a 200-foot tightrope, 150 feet above the ground, at the Condaldo Holiday Inn.

Wallenda lost his balance and fell to the street. He landed on a spot just 15 feet from where Dom Zimmer was standing.

MARCH 25   Red Sox rookie pitcher Bobby Sprowl is shot in the right arm as he and his wife are asleep in their Winter Haven apartment. Sprowl's arm was grazed by a .22-caliber bullet and was treated at a Winter Haven hospital. The bullet was fired through the wall of an adjacent apartment by a person who thought he heard a prowler.

APRIL 7   In the season opener, the White Sox score two runs in the ninth inning off Dick Drago to beat the Red Sox 6–5 in Chicago.

APRIL 14   In the first game of the season at Fenway Park, the Red Sox win 5–4 over the Rangers in 10 innings before 34,747. The winning

Dennis Eckersley's mix of pitches and panache wowed Sox fans in '78 and '79, but then arm problems plagued his career until he found success in the mid-'80s with Oakland as a closer.

run scored on a 395-foot single by Jim Rice that clanged off the left field wall to score Butch Hobson from third base. Earlier in the game, Hobson and Fred Lynn both hit homers.

Rice was the AL MVP in 1978 with a season in which he led the league in home runs (46), RBIs (139), hits (213), triples (15), slugging percentage (.600), and total bases (406). Rice is the only major leaguer between Hank Aaron in 1959 and Larry Walker in 1997 to collect at least 400 total bases in a season. No one else in the American League in 1978 had more than 300 total bases. Rice also hit .315 and scored 121 runs.

APRIL 18   Playing second base, Jack Brohamer collects four hits in his first start with the Red Sox and plays a key role in the two-run rally in the ninth inning to beat the Brewers 7–6 at Fenway Park. Brohamer singled in the tying run, and after Frank Duffy pinch-ran for him, Carlton Fisk delivered a game-winning double.

On the same day, the Red Sox sell Reggie Cleveland to the Rangers.

APRIL 21   The Red Sox win their eighth game in a row with a 9–7 decision over the Indians at Fenway Park.

APRIL 23   Butch Hobson drives in five runs in a doubleheader against the Indians at Fenway Park to extend his streak of consecutive games with at least one run batted in to 10. The Red Sox won the first game 6–3 but lost the second 10–7 in 11 innings.

The doubleheader drew 36,388 to Fenway Park, the largest crowd since 1934. The crowd prompted a flurry of complaints from fans in the reserved seats, who said they were being jostled by those in the standing room area. In June, the City of Boston clamped down on overcrowding at the ballpark. Building Commissioner Francis Gems declared the maximum capacity at Fenway to be 36,005, which allowed the club to sell 2,500 standing-room tickets. There were also numerous complaints about rowdiness at the ballpark that brought a new alcohol policy. Beer could be sold only in containers no larger than 12 ounces, and only one per customer. No beer was sold more than 45 minutes before the start of the game, and no later than the end of the sixth inning. Sales of beer in the bleachers were restricted to the concession stands.

MAY 3   The Red Sox outslug the Twins 11–9 at Fenway Park.

MAY 6   Jim Wright pitches a shutout in his first major league start, defeating the White Sox 3–0 in the second game of a doubleheader at Fenway Park. The Red Sox also won the opener 6–4 on a two-run, walk-off homer by Dwight Evans in the tenth inning.

Wright got his chance to start when Mike Torrez couldn't answer the call because of a back injury. Previously, Wright made three relief appearances and gave up five runs in five innings. He lasted only two years in the majors, in which he posted a 9–4 record and a 3.82 ERA.

MAY 23   The American League owners approve the sale of the club by the Yawkey estate to a group headed by Jean Yawkey, Haywood Sullivan, and Buddy LeRoux. The owners previously disallowed a sale of the club to the three on December 8, 1977, but reconsidered after a new financing deal. Yawkey remained as club president, with LeRoux serving as vice president of administration and Sullivan as vice president and general manager. The three were also named general partners. There were nine limited partners, each of whom put up a substantial amount of cash. Yawkey owned 22 percent of the team, with LeRoux and Sullivan holding 10 percent each. The limited partners, who held 58 percent of the club, included individuals from Kentucky, Maine, and New Hampshire.
From the start, Sullivan and LeRoux squabbled. The new ownership pinched pennies and was indecisive, which crippled the club's ability to compete for a pennant. Yawkey was supposed to be a silent partner. Her cash was needed to obtain approval of the sale to the AL owners, and as the widow of the beloved Tom Yawkey, her inclusion was good public relations. Yawkey insisted on giving her two cents' worth on major decisions, however, and when Sullivan and LeRoux disagreed over the direction of the club, she aligned herself with Sullivan. As a result, LeRoux was left out of the loop, which led continuing frustration and his attempt to take control of the team (see June 6, 1983). After LeRoux sold his shares in 1987, John Harrington became club president and soon became the power behind the throne as Sullivan fell out of Yawkey's favor. Harrington and Yawkey consistently outflanked and outvoted Sullivan, who had a contractual right of first refusal if Yawkey ever decided to sell the team. Sullivan stayed on despite having little real power and refused to be bought out. Lines of authority

were constantly blurred, and employees were caught between the two warring factions and were afraid of making decisions for fear of alienating one of the three principal owners.

MAY 27 Jim Rice's homer in the sixth off Jack Morris beats the Tigers 1–0 at Fenway Park. Luis Tiant pitched the shutout.

Rice's tremendous power extended to golf. According to professional golfer Lou Graham, who played with Rice in a pro-am tournament during the 1977–78 offseason, Rice was "longer off the tee than anyone on the tour right now." Several of Rice's Red Sox teammates who accompanied him on the links claimed he bent golf clubs on his downswing.

MAY 30 The Red Sox win their eighth game in a row with a 4–0 decision over the Blue Jays at Fenway Park. It was Boston's second eight-game winning streak of 1978 and gave the club a record of 34–15.

JUNE 3 An earthquake shakes the stands during a 5–4 Red Sox win over the Angels at Anaheim Stadium. Fred Lynn, a Southern California native, broke the 4–4 tie with a homer in the ninth.

Lynn hit .298 with 22 homers in 1978.

JUNE 6 Butch Hobson makes three errors at third base during a 7–1 loss to the Athletics in Oakland.

Hobson made 43 errors in 1978 for a fielding percentage of .899. He was the first major league regular since 1916 to post a fielding percentage below .900.

JUNE 8 In the worst amateur draft in club history, the only future major leaguer selected and signed by the Red Sox plays in only one major league game. John Lickert, who was chosen in the 13th round, made his only big-league appearance as a catcher in 1981. The draft was the first under the direction of new general manager Haywood Sullivan. The Red Sox lost their picks in the first three rounds of the draft as compensation to other teams for signing free agents.

JUNE 10 The Red Sox score eight runs in the fourth inning and coast to a 13–1 win over the Mariners in Seattle.

Carlton Fisk played in 157 games in 1978, 154 of them as a catcher. He hit .284 and had 20 homers and 39 doubles.

JUNE 13 Jim Wright pitches a two-hitter to beat the Angels 5–0 at Fenway Park. The only California hits were singles by Joe Rudi in the second inning and Lyman Bostock in the sixth.

JUNE 15 The Red Sox sell Bernie Carbo to the Indians.

Bill Lee walked out on the club for 24 hours in protest over the trade of his close friend Carbo.

JUNE 17   The Red Sox score two runs in the ninth inning to beat the Mariners 5–4 at Fenway Park. It was Boston's ninth win in a row. Carl Yastrzemski singled home Rick Burleson for the winning run.

JUNE 18   The Mariners, carrying a 10-game losing streak into the contest, end the Red Sox' nine-game winning streak with a 3–2 win at Fenway Park.

JUNE 26   The rampaging Red Sox are 9½ games in front of the second-place Yankees after a 4–1 win in New York. The victory gave the Sox a record of 51–21.

From July 4, 1977, through June 29, 1978, the Red Sox had a record of 108–54.

JULY 6   A homer by Fred Lynn in the tenth inning beats the White Sox 7–6 in Chicago.

JULY 8   The Red Sox take a 10-game lead over the second-place Brewers with a double-header sweep of the Indians in Cleveland by scores of 12–5 and 3–2. The Yankees were third, 11½ games behind.

JULY 19   The Red Sox beat the Brewers 8–2 in Milwaukee. The victory gave the Sox a record of 62–28 and lead of 9½ games over the Brewers. The Orioles were third, 12½ games behind, and the Yankees fourth, 14 games out. With his Yankee team in turmoil, George Steinbrenner fired manager Billy Martin on July 24 and replaced him with Bob Lemon.

JULY 27   Outfielder Sam Bowen hits his first major league homer in a 3–1 loss to the Rangers in Arlington.

Bowen was sent to the minors the next day. He never hit another big-league homer and ended his career in 1980 with only 22 at-bats and a .136 batting average.

JULY 29   Jim Wright pitches the Red Sox to a 1–0 win over the Royals at Fenway Park. Fred Lynn drove in the lone run of the game with a single in the fourth inning.

The Red Sox lost 10 games in 12 tries from July 20 through July 30. The skid reduced Boston's lead in the AL East to 4½ games over the Brewers. The Yankees and Orioles were tied for third, 7½ back.

AUGUST 2   The game between the Yankees and Red Sox in New York is suspended by curfew with the score 5–5 at the end of the fourteenth inning. The Yanks led 5–0 before the Sox scored two in the fourth, two in the sixth, and one in the eighth.

AUGUST 3   The suspended game of August 2 is completed, with the Red Sox winning 7–5 in 17 innings. In the seventeenth, Dwight Evans, Butch Hobson, Rick Burleson, and Jim Rice all hit singles to produce the two runs. The Sox also won the regularly scheduled game 8–1, which was stopped after 6½ innings by rain.

Bob Stanley was the winning pitcher in the 17-inning contest. He was 15–2 in 1978. Stanley's .882 winning streak during the year is the best of any Red Sox pitcher in a season of at least 15 victories. He also had 10 saves and a 2.60 ERA in 1978. Stanley pitched 13 seasons with the Red Sox in a variety of roles, moving from the starting rotation to long relief, setup roles, and closing. His 637 games pitched are the most of any Red Sox pitcher in history. Stanley also ranks first in saves (132), fifth in innings (1,707), and seventh in wins (115).

AUGUST 10   The Red Sox score twice in the thirteenth inning to defeat the Indians 6–5 at Fenway Park. Cleveland scored in the top of the thirteenth on first baseman Andre Thornton's homer to take a 5–4 lead. Butch Hobson led off the bottom of the thirteenth with a high pop-up, which Thornton dropped 90 feet from home plate. The hustling Hobson kept running, and was rounding second when the ball kicked away from Thornton. Catcher Bo Diaz retrieved the ball and threw wildly past third to attempt to retire Hobson, who crossed the plate on a pop-up and two errors. The winning run scored on a double by George Scott and a single by Rick Burleson.

AUGUST 16   Luis Tiant records his 200th career victory with a 4–2 decision over the Angels in Anaheim.

AUGUST 20   The Red Sox' lead in the AL East seems secure again after a 4–2 win over the Athletics in Oakland. The Sox were 8 1/2 games ahead of both the Brewers and Yankees with 39 games left to play.

AUGUST 27   Butch Hobson's walk-off single caps a two-run, twelfth-inning rally which beats the Angels 4–3 at Fenway Park.

AUGUST 28   The Red Sox score three runs in the ninth inning to defeat the Mariners 10–9 at Fenway Park. The last two runs scored on Butch Hobson's walk-off double off the left field wall. It was Hobson's second walk-off hit in consecutive games, and the second game in a row in which the Sox won after trailing heading into their last at-bat. Fred Lynn collected five hits, including a double, and scored four runs.

AUGUST 29   George Scott hits a grand slam off Glenn Abbott in the fifth inning of a 10–5 win over the Mariners at Fenway Park.

The win maintained the Red Sox' 7 1/2-game lead in the AL East with 32 games left to play.

SEPTEMBER 6   A two-run homer by Carl Yastrzemski in the seventh inning off Dennis Martinez gives the Red Sox a 2–0 win over the Orioles at Memorial Stadium. Luis Tiant pitched a two-hitter. The only Baltimore hits were singles by Rich Dauer in the third inning and Terry Crowley in the seventh.

The win maintained the Red Sox' four-game lead over the Yankees in the AL East heading into a four-game series against the Yankees in Boston from September 7 through 10.

SEPTEMBER 7   Drawing first blood in the crucial four-game series, the Yankees unleash a 21-hit attack to stomp the Red Sox 15–3 and move within three games of first.

SEPTEMBER 8   The Red Sox commit seven errors and suffer a 13–2 loss at the hands of the Yankees to narrow the gap to two games.

SEPTEMBER 9   The Yankees score seven runs in the seventh inning and trounce the Red Sox 7–0 at Fenway Park. The seven-run inning was sparked by a pop fly that landed amidst five Boston players.

SEPTEMBER 10   The Yankees complete the four-game sweep of the Red Sox and move into a tie for first place with a 7–4 win over the Red Sox at Fenway Park. Don Zimmer made a controversial choice in his starting pitcher in the key game by going with twenty-two-year-old rookie Bobby Sprowl, who was appearing in only his second big-league game. Sprowl didn't make it out of the first inning. He only pitched one more game with the Red Sox before being traded to the Astros. Sprowl pitched four years in the majors and never won a single game, finishing his career with an 0–3 record and a 5.44 ERA.

Forever known as the "Boston Massacre," the Yankees outscored the Red Sox 42–9 in the four games. The Sox gave up 67 hits, collected only 21, and made 12 errors. Both teams had 20 games left to play.

SEPTEMBER 11   The Red Sox move into first place one-half game ahead of the idle Yankees with a 5–4 win over the Orioles at Fenway Park.

SEPTEMBER 13   The Red Sox drop out of first place with a 2–1 loss to the Indians at Fenway Park. The Yankees took over the top spot with a 7–3 victory over the Tigers at Detroit.

SEPTEMBER 16   The Red Sox lose 3–2 to the Yankees in New York to fall 3½ games back with 14 games left on the schedule.

From August 30 through September 16, the Red Sox lost 14 of 17.

SEPTEMBER 17   After losing the first two games of a three-game series at Yankee Stadium, the Red Sox beat the Yanks 7–3 to close the gap in the pennant race to 2½ games.

SEPTEMBER 23   The Red Sox pull back within a game of the Yankees with a 3–1 win over the Blue Jays in Toronto. Both the Sox and the Yankees had seven games left to play.

SEPTEMBER 24   The Sox win a 14-inning marathon 7–6 over the Blue Jays at Exhibition Stadium. The Sox scored two runs in the ninth to tie the score, 6–6. The winning run scored on singles by Jim Rice and Fred Lynn and an error by Toronto third baseman Roy Howell.

SEPTEMBER 28   Jim Rice hits a home run off Kip Young in the fourth inning to beat the Tigers 1–0 at Fenway Park. Mike Torrez pitched the shutout.

The win over the Tigers completed a three-game sweep, but the Sox were unable to gain any ground in the pennant race because the Yankees won three in a row from the Blue Jays in New York. Heading into the final three games of the season, the Sox still trailed the Yankees by one game.

SEPTEMBER 29   The Red Sox crush the Blue Jays 11–0 at Fenway Park. The Yankees stayed a game ahead of the Sox with a 3–1 victory over the Indians in New York.

On the same day, Pope John I died. Charles Lazquidra of WBCN teased the upcoming newscast with "Pope Dies. Sox Still Alive."

SEPTEMBER 30   The Red Sox keep their pennant hopes alive with a 5–1 win over the Blue Jays at Fenway Park. It was Dennis Eckersley's 20th win of the season. The Yankees defeated the Indians 7–0 at Yankee Stadium. The Sox' only hope for a pennant was a win in the last game of season along with a Yankee loss, followed by a victory over the Yanks in a one-game playoff.

OCTOBER 1   The Red Sox finish the regular season in a tie with the Yankees with a 5–0 win over the Blue Jays at Fenway Park. The Yankees lost a chance to clinch the pennant by losing 9–2 to the Indians in New York. Luis Tiant pitched a two-hitter to defeat the Blue Jays. The only Toronto hits were singles by Roy Howell in the fourth inning and John Mayberry in the seventh. It was the Red Sox' eighth win in a row and their 12th in their last 14 games. Boston pitchers allowed only three runs in six games from September 26 through October 1.

                The game proved to be Tiant's last in a Red Sox uniform.

OCTOBER 2   A three-run homer by Bucky Dent in the seventh inning pushes the Yankees to a 5–4 win over the Red Sox at Fenway Park in a one-game playoff to determine the AL East champion. The Sox led 2–0 at the end of the sixth inning, scoring twice against Ron Guidry, who entered the game with a 24–3 record. Carl Yastrzemski homered in the second inning just inside the right field foul pole to put the Sox ahead, 1–0. In the sixth, a double by Rick Burleson and a single by Jim Rice scored another run. Mike Torrez cruised along with six shutout innings until the fateful seventh. Chris Chambliss and Roy White led off the inning with singles. After retir-

Battery mates Carlton Fisk and Luis Tiant rush off the field at the end of the division-tying win over the Blue Jays that earned the Sox an ill-fated playoff game with the Yankees for the division championship.

ing the next two hitters, Torrez faced Dent. The Sox pitcher had an 0–2 count when Dent fouled a pitch off his foot, causing a delay as the Yankee trainer examined the Yankee shortstop. Dent also cracked his bat on the pitch and had to retrieve a new one. Torrez stood on the mound growing cold instead a tossing a few warm-up pitches. On Torrez's first pitch after play resumed, Dent hit a fly ball to left. In most major league ballparks, it would have been a warning-track fly ball, at worst. At Fenway, with the nearby Green Monster, it was a three-run homer into the net above the wall. It was only Dent's fifth homer of 1978 in 123 games. The Yankees added another run in the seventh and one more in the eighth, on Reggie Jackson's homer off Bob Stanley, to take a 5–2 lead. The Red Sox scored twice in their half of the eighth off Goose Gossage, who relieved Guidry in the seventh, to narrow the gap to 5–4 on a double by Jerry Remy and singles by Yastrzemski, Carlton Fisk, and Fred Lynn. Boston threatened in the ninth when Burleson drew a one-out walk and advanced to second on a single by Remy, which right fielder Lou Piniella lost in the sun but recovered with amazing quickness to hold Burleson at second. Gossage retired Rice on a fly ball to right field for the second out. Had Burleson been able to reach third on Remy's single, he would have scored easily on Rice's fly. Yastrzemski made the final out on a pop foul to Graig Nettles at third to end Boston's dreams of a pennant. The Yankees moved on to defeat the Royals in the ALCS and the Dodgers in the World Series.

OCTOBER 27   The Red Sox purchase Mike Easler from the Pirates.

On March 15, 1979, the Red Sox sent Easler back to the Pirates for George Hill, Martin Rivas, and cash. Easler would eventually play for the Sox in 1984 and 1985.

NOVEMBER 13   Luis Tiant sings a free-agent contract with the Yankees.

As if losing the 1978 pennant race to the Yankees weren't enough of a shock to the fans, the Red Sox let their most popular player leave for New York. Tiant was 13–8 for the Yanks in 1979 before his indeterminate age caught up with him.

DECEMBER 7   The Red Sox trade Bill Lee to the Expos for Stan Papi.

Lee was the last member of "The Loyal Order of the Buffalo" to remain with the Red Sox. The group, which also included Ferguson Jenkins, Bernie Carbo, Rick Wise, Jim Willoughby, and Reggie Cleveland, made life miserable for Don Zimmer, and most were practically given away by the Red Sox front office to get them out of Boston. Lee was no exception. He had one good season left and was 16–10 with a 3.04 ERA for Montreal in 1979. Papi was a weak-hitting infielder who had knee surgery before he played a game for the Sox. He played only 51 games in Boston and had a .188 batting average with one home run.
    The loss of Tiant and Lee, two pitchers who combined for 216 career wins for the Red Sox, changed the dynamic of the team. Both were popular with team-mates and the fans. Under Tom Yawkey, the Sox always had colorful players who kept the fans entertained. His widow, Jean, and co-owner Haywood Sullivan got rid of anyone who strayed from the neutral path. From 1979 through 1985, the Red Sox were seldom in contention and attendance declined with a roster consist-ing mostly of relatively colorless and dull players assembled by a front office with a corporate mentality.

1979   B

Season in a Sentence

Still reeling from the late-season collapse in 1978, the Red Sox are in contention for the pennant until August, when crippling injuries end the dreams.

Finish • Won • Lost • Pct • GB

Third   91   69   .569   11.5

Manager

Don Zimmer

Stats   Red Sox • AL • Rank

Stats	Red Sox	AL	Rank
Batting Avg:	.283	.270	1
On-Base Pct:	.347	.338	3
Slugging Pct:	.456	.406	1
Home Runs:	194		1
Stolen Bases:	60		14
ERA:	4.03	4.22	4
Fielding Pct:	.977	.978	10
Runs Scored:	841		3
Runs Allowed:	711		4

Starting Lineup

Gary Allenson, c
Bob Watson, 1b
Jerry Remy, 2b
Butch Hobson, 3b
Rick Burleson, ss
Jim Rice, lf
Fred Lynn, cf
Dwight Evans, rf
Carl Yastrzemski, dh-1b-lf
Carlton Fisk, dh-c
Jack Brohamer, 3b-2b
George Scott, 1b

Pitchers

Dennis Eckersley, sp
Mike Torrez, sp
Bob Stanley, sp
Steve Renko, sp
Chuck Rainey, sp
Dick Drago, rp
Tom Burgmeier, rp
Bill Campbell, rp

Attendance

2,353,114 (third in AL)

Club Leaders

Batting Avg:	Lynn	.333
On-Base Pct:	Lynn	.423
Slugging Pct:	Lynn	.637
Home Runs:	Lynn	39
	Rice	39
RBI:	Rice	130
Runs:	Rice	117
Stolen Bases:	Remy	14
Wins:	Eckersley	17
Strikeouts:	Eckersley	150
ERA:	Eckersley	2.99
Saves:	Drago	13

JANUARY 20   Steve Renko, most recently with the Athletics, signs a free-agent contract with the Red Sox.

MARCH 15   Jim Dwyer signs a free-agent contract with the Giants.

APRIL 5   Five days after the nuclear disaster at Three Mile Island, the Red Sox win the season opener 7–1 over the Indians before 34,433 at Fenway Park. Dennis Eckersley went seven innings and allowed no runs and two hits. Jim Rice hit a three-run homer in the third inning to start the scoring. Dwight Evans and Fred Lynn also homered.

Ken Coleman returned to the Red Sox as the club's radio announcer. He had previously been in the Sox' broadcasting booth from 1966 through 1974, then spent four seasons in Cincinnati announcing Reds games. Coleman was joined in 1979 by former player Rico Petrocelli. Rico lasted only one season, however, before he was dismissed for too many critical comments about the team to suit club management.

APRIL 12   The Red Sox score two runs in the ninth inning to outlast the Brewers 12–10 in Milwaukee. Earlier in the game, Carl Yastrzemski hit a grand slam in the seventh inning off Bob Galasso. Yastrzemski also had two doubles and a single in the contest and scored four runs in addition to the four RBIs.

The Red Sox sported new/old uniforms in 1979. In 1973, the club went to double-knit pullover jerseys, and in 1975 changed the cap color from blue to red. In 1979, the Sox went back to knit versions of the more traditional flannel uniforms worn from the late-1930s through the early-1970s, with button-up shirts and blue caps.

Jim Rice's .325 batting average in 1979 was a career high, but he gave the Sox many productive seasons during his 16-year career, all of which he spent in Boston.

Steve Babineau

APRIL 15   The Red Sox bombard the Indians 14–4 at Fenway Park.

APRIL 16   A two-run, walk-off homer by Fred Lynn in the ninth inning beats the Brewers 6–5 at Fenway Park.

Fenway Park's 7,400 bleacher seats were reduced by one dollar for six games in 1979 under an agreement that penalized the Red Sox for an improper price hike in 1978. State Attorney Francis Bellotti ruled that the Sox would have to donate the proceeds from the sale of 10,000 reserved bleacher seats, worth three dollars apiece, to charity. In the out-of-court settlement, the Boston club in effect agreed with the court's allegation that the team occasionally violated its stated 1978 ticket policy, boosting unreserved bleachers seats from two to three dollars.

APRIL 25   Butch Hobson is robbed of a home run when his long drive clangs off a speaker at the Kingdome in Seattle during a 4–1 win over the Mariners. The speaker, which was suspended from the ceiling 275 feet from home plate and 110 feet above the floor, was in play according to the ground rules. Hobson had to settle for a triple.

APRIL 26   A two-run single by Rick Burleson in the third inning drives in both runs in a 2–0 win over the Mariners in Seattle. Bob Stanley pitched the shutout.

The win gave the Red Sox a 12–4 record and a 2½-game lead in the AL East.

MAY 9 · A two-run, walk-off homer by Carl Yastrzemski in the ninth inning gives the Red Sox a 9–8 victory over the Angels at Fenway Park. California took an 8–7 lead in the top of the ninth with two runs.

MAY 11 · The Red Sox score eight runs in the fourth inning to beat the Athletics 11–2 at Fenway Park.

MAY 12 · Jerry Remy collects five hits, including a double, in five at-bats during an 8–2 win over the Athletics at Fenway Park.

MAY 16 · Rick Burleson bumps umpire Jim Pratt during a 10–6 loss to the Orioles at Fenway Park after Pratt rules him out on a called third strike. Burleson received a three-day suspension from the American League.

MAY 22 · The Red Sox explode for seven runs in the second inning to take a 7–0 lead and hang on to beat the Orioles 7–5 at Baltimore.

MAY 27 · Playing in his first game with the Red Sox, Stan Papi drives in the winning run in the third inning with a single that holds up for a 1–0 win over the Blue Jays in Toronto. Chuck Rainey pitched the shutout.

> *Papi had to undergo a trying ordeal in the minors with Tulsa in 1974 to reach the big leagues. He developed symptoms of a nervous breakdown and was confined to a mental hospital for months, where he underwent drug therapy and electric shock treatments. For a time, Papi contemplated suicide. Later, blood tests revealed that he suffered from a severe blood disorder called hypoglycemia and that his problems were physical, not mental.*

JUNE 4 · The Red Sox score eight runs in the fifth inning and defeat the Rangers at Fenway Park. Rick Burleson hit a grand slam in the big inning off David Rajsich.

JUNE 5 · The Red Sox draft second baseman Marty Barrett from Arizona State University in the first round of the secondary phase of the amateur draft.

> *Barrett was Boston's starting second baseman for five years beginning in 1984. The only other future major leaguers drafted and signed by the Sox in 1979 were Marc Sullivan (second round) and Tom McCarthy (seventh).*

JUNE 11 · The Red Sox score four runs in the tenth inning on only one hit and beat the Royals 4–0 in Kansas City. A double by Dwight Evans, three walks, and an error scored the four runs. Bob Stanley pitched the complete-game shutout.

JUNE 13 · Gary Allenson hits a grand slam off Steve Mingori in the ninth inning of an 11–3 win over the Royals in Kansas City.

> *On the same day, the Red Sox sent Bobby Sprowl, Pete Ladd, and cash to the Astros for Bob Watson. The Sox also dealt George Scott to the Royals for Tom Poquette. The Watson acquisition proved to be a tremendous short-term addition. Over the remainder of the 1979 season, he hit .337 with 13 homers in 84 games. After the season, Watson declared himself a free agent and signed with the Yankees. In 1993, he became the general manager of the Astros, the first African American in major league history to hold the position.*

JUNE 16   Carl Yastrzemski collects his 1,000th career extra-base hit with a double during an 11–5 win over the White Sox in Chicago.

JUNE 20   The Red Sox crash six homers and trim the Tigers 13–3 at Fenway Park. The homers were struck by Fred Lynn, Carl Yastrzemski, Bob Watson, Dwight Evans, Butch Hobson and Jim Dwyer.

Lynn had a year in 1979 that was even better than the one he put together in 1975 when he was the MVP. He led the league in batting average with a .333 mark in addition to topping the circuit in on-base percentage (.423) and slugging percentage (.637). He also scored 116 runs, drove in 122, and collected 39 homers and 42 doubles.

JUNE 23   A walk-off homer by Bob Watson on the first pitch of the eleventh inning beats the Blue Jays 4–3 at Fenway Park.

JUNE 30   Carl Yastrzemski hits a homer in the ninth inning to beat the Yankees 3–2 in New York. It was the 399th home run of Carl's career.

JULY 1   Jerry Remy tears up his knee sliding into home plate during a 6–5 loss to the Yankees in New York. Remy played in only seven games the rest of the season.

JULY 3   The Red Sox swamp the Royals 10–0 at Fenway Park.

JULY 4   A two-run, walk-off homer by Dwight Evans off Al Hrabosky beats the Royals 6–4 at Fenway Park.

JULY 13   Steve Renko carries a no-hitter into the ninth inning before surrendering a one-out single to Rickey Henderson in Oakland. After walking Mitchell Page with two out, Renko was removed in favor of Bill Campbell, who saved the Red Sox a 2–0 win.

JULY 14   After blowing a 4–0, fourth-inning lead, the Sox need three runs in the ninth to beat the Athletics 8–7 in Oakland. Following a double, three singles, and an intentional walk, Carlton Fisk drove in the winning run with a sacrifice fly.

Fisk was limited to 91 games, only 39 of those as a catcher, in 1979 because of a sore arm. He hit .272 in 320 at-bats.

JULY 15   The Red Sox win for the second game in a row after trailing at the end of eight innings by scoring two in the ninth to defeat the Athletics 3–2 in Oakland.

JULY 17   Fred Lynn hits a two-run homer off Steve Carlton in the first inning of the All-Star Game, but the American League loses 7–6 at the Kingdome in Seattle.

JULY 19   The Red Sox defeat the Mariners 7–1 at Fenway Park to pull within 3½ games of the first-place Orioles.

JULY 22   The Red Sox rally for three runs in the ninth inning and one in the tenth to defeat the Angels 6–5 at Fenway Park. All of the ninth-inning runs scored on a homer by Dwight Evans. Bob Watson drove in the game winner with a single.

JULY 24   Carl Yastrzemski cracks his 400th career homer during a 7–3 win over the Athletics at Fenway Park. The milestone homer was struck in the seventh inning off Mike Morgan.

JULY 25   The Red Sox rout the Athletics 16–4 at Fenway Park.

JULY 28   Dennis Eckersley shuts out the Rangers 1–0 in Arlington. The lone run of the game scored on doubles by Butch Hobson and Jim Dwyer in the third inning. The Red Sox completed their third triple play of 1979 during the game to tie a major league record. Only eight big-league clubs in major league history have completed three triple plays in a season, including the 1924 Red Sox. The triple killing happened in the first inning with Johnny Grubb on third base and Buddy Bell on first. Sox second baseman Jack Brohamer made a diving catch of Al Oliver's pop-up with both runners taking off. Brohamer threw to Carl Yastrzemski at first, and Yaz fired the ball across the diamond to Butch Hobson at third. Yastrzemski was the third Boston first baseman to participate in a triple play in 1979. The other two were George Scott and Bob Watson.

Eckersley had a record of 17–10 and an earned run average of 2.99 in 1979. Eckersley and Mike Torrez (16–13) were often the only two effective starters on the club. In 1948, the Boston Braves were in a similar situation with Warren Spahn and Johnny Sain at the top of the rotation, and the refrain during that pennant-winning season was "Spahn and Sain and pray for rain." In Boston in 1979, the call was "Torrez and Eck and pray like heck."

AUGUST 3   Win Remmerswaal makes his major league debut and pitches the last three innings of a 5–3 loss to the Brewers in Milwaukee.

Remmerswaal was born in the Netherlands. He was the first player born and trained in Europe to reach the majors. He pitched two seasons in the big leagues and was 3–1 with a 5.50 ERA.

AUGUST 5   The Red Sox clobber the Brewers 7–2 and 19–5 in a doubleheader at County Stadium. The Sox shelled Milwaukee, pitching for 27 hits and scoring in every inning but the fourth.

AUGUST 13   The Twins score five runs in the first inning at Fenway Park, but the Red Sox bounce back with one run in the fourth inning, four in the seventh, and one in the eighth to win, 6–5. Boston took the lead on a homer by Butch Hobson.

AUGUST 14   Fred Lynn drives in six runs on two homers and a double during a 12–1 thrashing of the Twins at Fenway Park.

During August, a Boston newspaper sent television chef Julia Child to critique the food served at Fenway Park. She didn't like the taste of the famous Fenway Frank. "I do love a good hot dog, but I was disappointed" she said. "A most ordinary frank, rather thin and pale, and a squashy bun with no butter, no relish, just the squirt of ballpark mustard." The french fries were "not bad if you like 'em limp. McDonald's still holds its own there for good french fries." Mrs. Child handed out good marks for the popcorn which was "good, fresh and crisp." The beer "was very good indeed."

AUGUST 15   The Red Sox defeat the Twins at Fenway Park for the 13th consecutive time over three seasons with a 9–5 victory. The Sox didn't lose to Minnesota in Boston between August 16, 1977, and May 12, 1980.

AUGUST 17   The Red Sox send Mike O'Berry and cash to the Cubs for Ted Sizemore.

AUGUST 18   In his first game with the Red Sox, Ted Sizemore collects three hits, including a double, in three at-bats during an 8–2 win over the White Sox at Fenway Park in a contest called after 5½ innings by rain.

The victory put the Red Sox four games behind the first-place Orioles with a record of 75–45. The Sox were 16–24 over the remainder of the season, however, and finished in third place, 11½ games back of Baltimore. From September 18, 1976, through August 18, 1979, the Red Sox had a record of 286–176, a winning of percentage of .619, which translates to 100 wins over a 162-game schedule. Despite the run of success, the Red Sox failed to win a division title during the stretch.

AUGUST 22   On his 40th birthday, Carl Yastrzemski is honored by Minnesota fans before a 9–4 Red Sox win at Metropolitan Stadium. Yaz was two for four in the contest, which was called after eight innings by rain. Yastrzemski played a full season in Minneapolis in 1960 when it was the Red Sox' top farm club in the American Association.

In August, James G. Odom was arrested by Boston police after he impersonated Jim Rice and New England Patriots defensive back Mike Haynes for nearly a year. Odom used the names of both athletes in signing checks totaling thousands of dollars. "I'd like to have a few minutes alone with him in a room," Rice said. "I guarantee the real Jim Rice would walk out." Rice had another terrific season in 1979, with a .325 batting average, 201 hits, 39 homers, 117 runs scored, 130 RBIs, and a .596 slugging percentage.

SEPTEMBER 9   Carl Yastrzemski collects the 2,999th hit of his major league career during a 16–4 loss to the Orioles at Fenway Park.

SEPTEMBER 12   Carl Yastrzemski gets his 3,000th hit in the eighth inning of a 9–2 win over the Yankees before 34,337 at Fenway Park. Facing Jim Beattie, Yaz reached the milestone with a single just past the outstretched glove of second baseman Willie Randolph. A mob of Red Sox teammates rushed the field to congratulate Yastrzemski. Reggie Jackson fielded the ball in right field and ran in to first base to hand the ball to Yaz. Microphones were brought onto the field, and he was honored in a 15-minute ceremony at first base. He was presented with a trophy as his father, Carl Sr., and his son Mike stood nearby. Yastrzemski then left the game, as Jim Dwyer pinch-ran for him. Yaz had gone hitless in 12 plate appearances (including two walks) between hits number 2,999 and 3,000. The hit also put Yastrzemski in exclusive company. The only players in major league history with at least 3,000 hits and 400 homers are Hank Aaron, Willie Mays, Eddie Murray, Stan Musial, Cal Ripken Jr., and Dave Winfield.

Earlier in the day, 50,000 jammed into Faneuil Hall Marketplace for "Carl Yastrzemski Day," which was proclaimed by Boston mayor Kevin White. Not to be outdone, Massachusetts governor Ed King proclaimed September 12

"Carl Yastrzemski Forever Day." The following day, Yaz went to Washington and had lunch with Speaker of the House Tip O'Neill in O'Neill's office on Capitol Hill.

SEPTEMBER 15   Bob Watson hits for the cycle during a 10–2 win over the Orioles in Baltimore. Watson reached the cycle by collecting the hits in ascending order. He singled in the second inning and doubled in the fourth off Dennis Martinez, tripled in the eighth against Tippy Martinez, and homered in the ninth facing Tim Stoddard.

SEPTEMBER 27   Carlton Fisk hits a walk-off homer in the ninth inning to beat the Blue Jays 6–5 at Fenway Park.

The Red Sox drew a club-record 2,353,114 fans in 1979, breaking the old mark of 2,320,643 set in 1978. The 1979 figure would stand as the Fenway Park record until 1988.

OCTOBER 5   Carl Yastrzemski meets President Jimmy Carter in the White House. Carter invited Yaz to Washington to congratulate him on collecting his 3,000th career hit. The next day, Yastrzemski met Pope John Paul II at the White House.

NOVEMBER 8   Four days after 63 Americans are taken hostage by militant followers of the Ayatollah Khomeini at the American embassy in Iran, Bob Watson signs a free-agent contract with the Yankees.

NOVEMBER 20   Tony Perez, most recently with the Expos, signs a free-agent contract with the Red Sox.

While playing for the Reds, Perez hit two key home runs, including one in Game Seven against the Red Sox in the 1975 World Series. He turned thirty-eight shortly after Opening Day in 1980 but gave the Red Sox one great season with 25 homers and 105 RBIs.

NOVEMBER 27   Skip Lockwood, most recently with the Mets, signs a free-agent contract with the Red Sox.

Lockwood gave the Red Sox 24 games and a 5.32 ERA before being shelved by a pulled muscle he suffered after he tripped over a garden hose.

THE STATE OF THE RED SOX

The Red Sox were 821–742 during the 1980s for a winning percentage of .525, which was the fourth best of the 14 teams in the American League, trailing the Yankees, Tigers, and Royals. The Sox won AL East titles in 1986 and 1988 and reached the World Series in 1986, suffering an excruciating loss to the Mets that will never be forgotten in Boston. Seven of the 10 Red Sox teams during the decade had winning records, one finished at .500, and two lost more than they won. It was a very competitive decade, as eight different AL franchises (and seven in the National League) reached the World Series. Besides the Red Sox, the AL pennant winners were the Royals (1980 and 1985), Yankees (1981), Brewers (1982), Orioles (1983), Tigers (1984), Twins (1987), and Athletics (1988 and 1989). Every AL East franchise except the Indians won the division at least once. Besides the two captured by the Sox, the Yankees won in 1980 and 1981, the Brewers in 1982, the Orioles in 1983, the Tigers in 1984 and 1987, and the Blue Jays in 1985 and 1989.

THE BEST TEAM

The Red Sox won the AL pennant in 1986 with a 95–66 record and a thrilling comeback win over the Angels in the ALCS before losing to the Mets in the Fall Classic after twice coming within one strike of the World Championship.

THE WORST TEAM

Both the 1983 and 1987 Red Sox were 78–84 and finished 20 games out of first place. The 1983 club finished sixth in the seven-team AL East. The 1987 club landed one spot higher, in fifth place, but was a greater disappointment following the Sox' trip to the World Series.

THE BEST MOMENT

After losing three of the first four games in the 1986 ALCS against the Angels in Anaheim, the Red Sox rally from a 5–2 ninth-inning deficit to win Game Five 7–6 in 11 innings.

THE WORST MOMENT

Bill Buckner lets a ground ball slip through his legs to allow the winning run to score in Game Six of the 1986 World Series against the Mets.

THE ALL–DECADE TEAM • YEARS WITH BRS

Rich Gedman, c	1980–90
Bill Buckner, 1b	1984–87
Marty Barrett, 2b	1982–90
Wade Boggs, 3b	1982–92
Glenn Hoffman, ss	1980–87
Jim Rice, lf	1974–89
Ellis Burks, cf	1987–92, 2004
Dwight Evans, rf	1972–90
Carl Yastrzemski, dh	1961–83
Roger Clemens, p	1984–96
Bob Stanley, p	1977–89
Bruce Hurst, p	1980–88
Oil Can Boyd, p	1982–89

Yastrzemski and Boggs are in the Hall Fame. Clemens is a lock to be elected in his first year on the ballot and Rice might join them someday. Yastrzemski is on three All-Decade teams. He was the left fielder in the 1960s and the first baseman in the 1970s. The inclusion of Hoffman reflects the Red Sox' decade-long quest to find an adequate shortstop. Every one of the 13 members of the 1980s All-Decade team was a product of the Red Sox farm system with the exception of Buckner. Second baseman Jerry Remy (1978–84) also starred for the Sox during the 1980s.

THE DECADE LEADERS

Batting Avg:	Boggs	.352
On-Base Pct:	Boggs	.443
Slugging Pct:	Evans	.497
Home Runs:	Evans	256
RBI:	Evans	900
Runs:	Evans	956
Stolen Bases:	Burks	73
Wins:	Clemens	95
Strikeouts:	Clemens	1,215
ERA:	Clemens	3.06
Saves:	Stanley	118

THE HOME FIELD

A total of 44 luxury boxes were added to the roof during the 1980s, and the 600 Club (later renamed the .406 club) behind home plate opened in 1989.

THE GAME YOU WISH YOU HAD SEEN

Roger Clemens set a major league record by striking out 20 batters on April 29, 1986, against the Mariners at Fenway Park.

THE WAY THE GAME WAS PLAYED

The 1980s had a little something for everybody. Trends that surfaced in the 1970s continued, with teams still emphasizing speed. In 1987, offense spiked in a year that combined the speed of the dead-ball era with the power of the 1950s. AL teams averaged 124 stolen bases and 188 home runs.

THE MANAGEMENT

Jean Yawkey continued to head the organization throughout the 1980s, but the front office was not a tranquil place. When the decade began, Yawkey, Haywood Sullivan, and Buddy LeRoux served as the general partners. In 1983, LeRoux called a new conference to announce that he and two limited partners were taking control of the club. Sullivan called a news conference to say that LeRoux would do no such thing. The LeRoux group failed in its takeover attempt, and after a year-long battle in the courts, was forced to relinquish its shares in the club to Yawkey and Sullivan. In the spring of 1984, Sullivan gave up his position as general manager to Lou Gorman. Field managers were Don Zimmer (1976–80), Johnny Pesky (1980), Ralph Houk (1981–84), John McNamara (1985–88), and Joe Morgan (1988–91).

THE BEST PLAYER MOVE

The best player move was the drafting of Roger Clemens off the campus of the University of Texas in the 1983 draft. There were no outstanding trades. The best deal brought Lee Smith from the Cubs for Al Nipper and Calvin Schiraldi in December 1987.

THE WORST PLAYER MOVE

The worst player move was the loss of Carlton Fisk to free agency in 1981. The worst trade sent Curt Schilling and Brady Anderson to the Orioles in July 1988 for Mike Boddicker.

1980   B

Season in a Sentence

After struggling all year with injuries and pitching problems, the Red Sox collapse in September and fire Don Zimmer.

Finish • Won • Lost • Pct • GB

Fourth   83   77   .519   19.0

Managers

Don Zimmer (82–73)
Johnny Pesky (1–4)

Stats   Red Sox • AL • Rank

Stats	Red Sox	AL	Rank
Batting Avg:	.283	.269	3
On-Base Pct:	.343	.335	6
Slugging Pct:	.436	.399	2
Home Runs:	162		3
Stolen Bases:	79		10
ERA:	4.38	4.03	11
Fielding Pct:	.977	.978	12
Runs Scored:	757		5
Runs Allowed:	767		11

Starting Lineup

Carlton Fisk, c
Tony Perez, 1b
Dave Stapleton, 2b
Butch Hobson, 3b-dh
Rick Burleson, ss
Jim Rice, lf
Fred Lynn, cf
Dwight Evans, rf
Carl Yastrzemski, dh-lf
Glenn Hoffman, 3b
Jim Dwyer, cf
Jerry Remy, 2b

Pitchers

Dennis Eckersley, sp
Mike Torrez, sp
Steve Renko, sp
John Tudor, sp
Chuck Rainey, sp
Tom Burgmeier, rp
Bob Stanley, rp
Dick Drago, rp

Attendance

1,956,092 (fourth in AL)

Club Leaders

Batting Avg:	Stapleton	.321
On-Base Pct:	Lynn	.383
Slugging Pct:	Rice	.504
Home Runs:	Perez	25
RBI:	Perez	105
Runs:	Rice	81
Stolen Bases:	Remy	14
Wins:	Eckersley	12
Strikeouts:	Eckersley	121
ERA:	Renko	4.19
Saves:	Stanley	24

MARCH 12   Tom Yawkey is elected to the Hall of Fame. Yawkey was the first club owner elected to the Hall of Fame who was not also a player, manager, or general manager.

MARCH 30   The Red Sox send Stan Papi and cash to the Phillies for Dave Rader.

APRIL 10   The Red Sox lose the season opener 9–5 to the Brewers in Milwaukee on a walk-off grand slam by Sixto Lezcano in the ninth inning off Dick Drago. The Sox tied the score 5–5 in the top of the ninth on homers by Carl Yastrzemski and Butch Hobson. Yaz also had a pair of singles in the game.

APRIL 12   In the second game of the season, the Brewers belt two grand slams in the second inning and wallop the Red Sox 18–1 in Milwaukee. Cecil Cooper hit the first grand slam off Mike Torrez. After the Brewers loaded the bases again, Don Money homered off Chuck Rainey.

                 Jon Miller replaced Rico Petrocelli on the Red Sox radio broadcasts. Miller worked alongside Ken Coleman.

APRIL 14   In the home opener, the Red Sox defeat the Tigers 3–1 before 33,512.

Mike Eruzione, captain of the 1980 gold medal-winning Olympic hockey team, threw out one of the two ceremonial first pitches. The other was tossed by eighty-two-year-old Joe Dugan, who played for the Athletics, Red Sox, and Yankees during the 1910s and 1920s.

APRIL 16   Tony Perez collects four hits in four at-bats and drives in four runs during a 10–9 win over the Tigers at Fenway Park.

APRIL 17   Carlton Fisk hits a walk-off homer on the first pitch of the eleventh inning to beat the Tigers 5–4 at Fenway Park.

On the same day, the Colonial Provision Company, manufacturer of the Fenway Frank, was declared a "chronic problem" plant by the Department of Agriculture because of sanitation and other problems. Dr. Donald Houston, head of the Compliance Division of Food Safety and Quality Service said, "We're not saying the products aren't fit to eat. Colonial is a company which operates in a marginal manner. Our policy is to let the public know when plants have trouble meeting our requirements."

APRIL 29   The Red Sox rout the White Sox 11–1 in Chicago.

MAY 3   Heading into the game hitless in his first 13 major league at-bats, Red Sox rookie third baseman Glenn Hoffman collects four hits, including a double and a triple, during a 7–0 win over the Royals in Kansas City.

After picking up his first four major league hits in a single game, Hoffman went 0 for 7 before picking up his fifth hit in a 7–2 loss to the Indians at Fenway Park on May 24. Hoffman went three for three in that game. He finished his rookie season with a .285 average in 114 games. Shifted to shortstop in 1981, Hoffman hit only .238 over the rest of his career, which ended in 1989.

MAY 12   The Red Sox purchase Jack Billingham from the Tigers.

Billingham pitched $24\frac{1}{3}$ innings for the Red Sox and had an ERA of 11.10 before drawing his release.

MAY 13   Fred Lynn hits for the cycle in a 10–5 win over the Twins at Fenway Park. Lynn doubled in the first inning off Al Williams, hit a two-run homer in the fourth facing John Verhoeven, singled in the sixth against Mike Marshall, and tripled in the eighth off Marshall.

In five games between May 7 and 13, Lynn had 13 hits, including four doubles, a triple, and three homers, in 20 at-bats.

MAY 21   Three days after the volcanic eruption of Mt. St. Helens, Jim Dwyer and Tony Perez each hit two homers and Jim Rice adds another during an 11–2 win over the Blue Jays in Toronto.

MAY 27   A two-run homer by Carl Yastrzemski beats the Blue Jays 5–4 at Fenway Park.

Yastrzemski's son Mike played in the 1980 College World Series as a freshman with Florida State. Mike Yastrzemski won the Most Outstanding Player Award in the South Regional with two homers and seven RBIs in three games. The Most Outstanding Player in the College World Series in 1980 was future Red Sox manager Terry Francona, who led the University of Arizona to the NCAA Championship.

MAY 31   The Red Sox smash six homers, including four in one inning, but can't match the batting of the Brewers and lose 19–8 at Fenway Park. With the Red Sox trailing 8–1 in the fourth, Dave Stapleton hit his first major league homer. After Jim Rice was retired, Carlton Fisk, Tony Perez, and Butch Hobson hit consecutive home runs. All four circuit blasts were hit off Mike Caldwell. Rice previously homered in the first inning, and Stapleton added another one in the ninth.

The power display by Stapleton came in only his second major league game. He looked like a coming star by hitting .321 with seven homers in 106 games as a twenty-six-year-old rookie but batted only .257 over the remainder of his career, which ended in 1986.

JUNE 3   With their first selection in the amateur draft, the Red Sox choose pitcher Mike Brown from Clemson University. Brown was drafted in the second round. The Sox lost their first-round pick as compensation for signing other teams' free agents.

Brown put up tremendous minor league numbers but was only 12–18 over a seven-year major league career. Other future major leaguers drafted and signed by the Red Sox in 1980 were Pat Dodson (sixth round), Al Nipper (eighth), Oil Can Boyd (16th), and Tim Bolton (20th).

JUNE 6   The Red Sox score seven runs in the fifth inning and defeat the Athletics 14–8 in Oakland. Tony Perez hit a grand slam in the big inning off Ernie Camacho. The double-play team of Rick Burleson and Jerry Remy, who also batted one-two in the batting order, collected nine hits between them. Burleson was five for six, including a double, and Remy four for four with four runs batted in.

JUNE 10   Fred Lynn hits a homer in the eleventh inning to beat the Mariners 5–4 in Seattle. Jim Rice tied the score 4–4 with a home run in the ninth.

JUNE 11   The Red Sox score seven runs in the second inning to take a 7–0 lead and hang on to beat the Mariners 7–5 in Seattle.

JUNE 12   The Red Sox rout the Angels 13–2 in Anaheim.

JUNE 14   Jerry Remy steals four bases during a 7–3 win over the Angels in Anaheim.

JUNE 20   Diminutive Angels shortstop Freddie Patek hits three homers and a double and drives in seven runs during a 20–2 drubbing of the Red Sox at Fenway Park. Patek, who stood five-foot-five, hit only five home runs all year in 1980. The Angels collected 26 hits in the game and led 20–0 before the Sox scored two runs in the ninth.

JUNE 29   During a long rain delay at Fenway Park that eventually forces a postponement of the game, Orioles catcher Rick Dempsey entertains the crowd by slipping and sliding across the wet tarp to the accompaniment of the Fenway organist. Wearing an overstuffed uniform, Dempsey imitated Babe Ruth hitting a home run and Carlton

Fisk's "stay fair" body English when he hit the famous twelfth-inning home run to win the sixth game of the 1975 World Series.

Fisk recovered from his 1979 sore elbow to hit .289 with 18 homers in 1980 in what would be his last year with the Red Sox.

JULY 5   The Red Sox edge the Orioles 1–0 in Baltimore. Dave Stapleton drove in the lone run of the game with a sacrifice fly in the second inning to score Carl Yastrzemski. John Tudor (six innings), Bob Stanley (1 1/3 innings), and Tom Burgmeier (1 2/3 innings) combined on the shutout.

JULY 8   Fred Lynn hits a two-run homer in the All-Star Game to provide the only two American League tallies in a 4–2 loss at Dodger Stadium. Lynn's homer came in the fifth inning off Bob Welch.

Lynn hit four homers in All-Star Games, three of them with the Red Sox. He also homered in 1976, 1979, and 1983, the last year while playing for the Angels. Other Red Sox players with All-Star home runs are Ted Williams (one in 1941, two in 1946, and one in 1956), Bobby Doerr (1943), Frank Malzone (1959), Pete Runnels (1962), Carl Yastrzemski (1975), George Scott (1977), Jim Rice (1983), Wade Boggs (1989), Manny Ramirez (2004), and David Ortiz (2004).

JULY 17   The Red Sox score seven runs in the fifth inning and thrash the Royals 12–4 at Fenway Park.

JULY 19   Dave Stapleton hits a walk-off homer in the tenth inning off Roger Erickson to beat the Twins 1–0 at Fenway Park. Mike Torrez pitched the complete-game shutout.

JULY 20   Butch Hobson has to be restrained from going after Minnesota pitcher Doug Corbett during a 5–4 loss to the Twins at Fenway Park. Hobson tried to knock the ball out of Corbett's glove during a tag play at first base, and Corbett made a few unkind remarks about Butch's behavior. The incident occurred about 15 hours after Hobson's wife, Allen, gave birth to the couple's third daughter.

JULY 30   The Red Sox score six runs in the ninth inning to break a 1–1 tie and beat the Royals 7–1 in Kansas City. Dwight Evans, Dave Rader, Gary Hancock, Rick Burleson, Dave Stapleton, and Fred Lynn lashed out six consecutive singles with one out.

Evans was hitting .198 at the All-Star break when he changed his batting style at the behest of batting coach Walt Hriniak. Instead of trying to pull the ball, Evans concentrated on hitting the ball up the middle and had a career turnaround at the age of twenty-eight. Batters normally peak when they turn twenty-seven, which in Dwight's case was 1979. Instead, he had his best years after twenty-seven. Not only did his batting average improve with the change in his approach at the plate, but his power numbers went up as well. During the 1970s, Evans played in 916 games, batted .261, and slugged .443. In the 1980s, he appeared in 1,466 contests with a batting average of .280 and a slugging percentage of .497.

AUGUST 2   Bob Ojeda records his first major league win with a 1–0 decision over the Rangers in Texas. Ojeda went six innings, and Bob Stanley pitched the final three. The lone run of the game scored on a double by Jim Rice and a single by Jim Dwyer.

AUGUST 3   Pitcher Tom Burgmeier plays left field during a 6–4 win over the Rangers in Arlington. Skip Lockwood was brought in from the bullpen by Don Zimmer to pitch to right-handed batter Dave Roberts with two outs in the ninth. Zimmer wanted Burgmeier to face left-handed hitter Mickey Rivers, should Roberts have reached base, and put Burgmeier in left. Lockwood retired Roberts for the final out.

AUGUST 20   Dennis Eckersley pitches a two-hitter but loses 2–1 to the Athletics in Oakland. Eckersley held the A's hitless until Mitchell Page singled in the seventh and scored on a stolen base, error, and sacrifice fly. Ex–Red Sox infielder Mario Guerrero broke a 1–1 tie with a homer in the eighth.

AUGUST 22   The Red Sox score an unearned run in the ninth inning to beat the Mariners 1–0 in Seattle. Steve Renko (eight innings) and Bob Stanley (one inning) combined on the shutout.

Renko played quarterback on a 1964 Kansas University football team that featured Gayle Sayers.

AUGUST 30   Down 6–2, the Red Sox stage a thrilling ninth-inning rally by scoring four runs to tie the score 6–6, then add one more in the tenth to beat the Athletics 7–6 at Fenway Park. Glenn Hoffman tied the game with a two-run triple, and Jim Rice won it with a walk-off homer.

Playing in his 20th season eight days after his 41st birthday, Carl Yastrzemski fractured a rib when he crashed into the scoreboard in the seventh inning. He played two more innings before the pain became too much to handle. Yaz didn't play again for the rest of the season.

SEPTEMBEr 2   The Red Sox win their ninth game in a row with a 10–2 decision over the Angels at Fenway Park.

The win put the Red Sox 6½ games behind the Yankees with a 72–56 record and a slim chance of a pennant. The Sox were 11–21 the rest of the way, however.

SEPTEMBER 7   Red Sox rookie Chico Walker's first major league hit is a home run struck in a 12–6 loss to the Mariners in Seattle.

It took Walker 11 years to hit his next two big-league homers. He hit his second home run with the Cubs in 1986 and his third with the Cubs in 1991. Walker finished his career in 1993 with 17 home runs.

SEPTEMBER 16   Dave Stapleton collects five hits, including two doubles, in five at-bats during a 9–5 win over the Indians at Fenway Park.

SEPTEMBER 26   Dennis Eckersley pitches a one-hitter to beat the Blue Jays 3–1 at Exhibition Stadium. The only Toronto hit was a home run by John Mayberry in the fifth inning. Jim Rice extended his hitting streak to 21 games.

The Red Sox received a scare on a flight from Baltimore to Toronto the previous day. The pilot landed in London, Ontario, because a cockpit light indicated a fire. The team waited two hours for buses that took them to Toronto, two hours away.

OCTOBER 1   The Red Sox fire Don Zimmer as manager. According to general manager Haywood Sullivan, the club made the change "because of economics, fan reaction, public relations, and change for change's sake." Attendance at Fenway Park dropped by 350,000 between 1979 and 1980. Johnny Pesky was named interim manager for the rest of the season.

Zimmer hasn't been out of work since he was fired the Red Sox. He managed the Rangers in 1981 and 1982 and the Cubs from 1988 through 1991 and has also served as a coach with the Yankees (1983, 1996–2003), Cubs (1984–86), Giants (1987), Red Sox (1992), Rockies (1993–95), and Devil Rays (2004–05). Zimmer never managed a club in the World Series despite 906 wins during the regular season as a big-league skipper, but he was Joe Torre's bench coach with the Yankees in six Fall Classics.

OCTOBER 4   Dwight Evans collects five hits, including three doubles and a homer, but the Red Sox lose 7–6 in 17 innings against the Blue Jays in the first game of a doubleheader at Fenway Park. Evans's four extra-base hits tied a club record. Toronto won the second game, 3–1.

OCTOBER 27   The Red Sox hire sixty-one-year-old Ralph Houk as manager.

Houk had been retired for two years when the Red Sox contacted him and he returned because he said he missed the "fun and excitement of baseball." His playing career consisted of only 91 games during the 1950s as a backup catcher to Yogi Berra with the Yankees, but he had served as a major during World War II and was known for his leadership abilities. Houk was named manager of the Yankees in 1961, won a World Championship in his first season, and followed that with AL pennants in 1962 and 1963. He earned a promotion to general manager and headed the front office until George Steinbrenner bought the club in 1973. Houk managed the Tigers from 1974 through 1978 before retiring. His stint with the Red Sox lasted four seasons until he retired again, this time for good.

DECEMBER 10 Five weeks after Ronald Reagan wins the presidential election against Jimmy Carter, and two days after John Lennon is shot by a crazed fan, the Red Sox trade Rick Burleson and Butch Hobson to the Angels for Carney Lansford, Rick Miller, and Mark Clear.

An unsung star, Lansford played two seasons with the Red Sox. In 1981, he won the AL batting title with an average of .336 and followed it with a .301 mark in 1982, when he was traded to the Athletics following Wade Boggs's arrival. Miller returned to the Red Sox, where he played from 1971 through 1977. He replaced Fred Lynn as Boston's starting center fielder.

DECEMBER 22 The Red Sox mail contracts for the 1981 season to Fred Lynn and Carlton Fisk.

According to a clause in the Basic Agreement between the players and owners, a player must be tendered a contract by December 20. If a club failed to do so, a player could declare himself a free agent. Since the envelopes containing their contracts were dated December 22, both Lynn and Fisk were eligible to become free agents. Both exercised the option to be free agents, and through a monumental error by the front office, the Red Sox lost two perennial All-Stars by mailing their contracts two days after the deadline. Both players filed a grievance to be heard by an arbitrator to establish their rights to free agency. The Sox had been trying to trade Lynn since the previous October and nearly had a deal worked out with the Dodgers. Lynn wanted to play in Southern California and waived his right to free agency when the Sox worked out a deal to send him to the Angels moments before his case was to he heard by the arbitrator assigned to the case (see January 23, 1981) . On February 12, 1981, arbitrator Raymond Goetz ruled that Fisk was entitled to become a free agent (see March 9, 1981).

DECEMBER 23   Jim Dwyer signs a free-agent contract with the Giants.

1981   B

Season in a Sentence

The Red Sox' 15th consecutive winning season isn't enough to compensate for the loss of Carlton Fisk and Fred Lynn due to a paperwork snafu, and the loss of one-third of the season to a strike by the players.

Finish • Won • Lost • Pct • GB

| * | 59 | 49 | .546 | * |

* Because of the players' strike, the season was split in two. The Red Sox finished in fifth place with a 30–26 record in the first half and tied for second with a 29–23 record in the second half.

Manager

Ralph Houk

Stats

Stats	Red Sox	AL	Rank
Batting Avg:	.275	.256	1
On-Base Pct:	.343	.324	1
Slugging Pct:	.399	.373	1
Home Runs:	90		5
Stolen Bases:	32		14
ERA:	3.81	3.66	9
Fielding Pct:	.979	.980	10
Runs Scored:	519		1
Runs Allowed:	481		12

Starting Lineup

Rich Gedman, c
Tony Perez, 1b
Jerry Remy, 2b
Carney Lansford, 3b
Glenn Hoffman, ss
Jim Rice, lf
Rick Miller, cf
Dwight Evans, rf
Carl Yastrzemski, dh-1b
Dave Stapleton, ss-3b-2b
Gary Allenson, c
Joe Rudi, dh

Pitchers

Mike Torrez, sp
Dennis Eckersley, sp
Frank Tanana, sp
Bobby Ojeda, sp
John Tudor, sp
Steve Crawford, sp
Mark Clear, rp
Bob Stanley, rp
Tom Burgmeier, rp
Bill Campbell, rp

Attendance

1,060,379 (sixth in AL)

Club Leaders

Batting Avg:	Lansford	.336
On-Base Pct:	Evans	.415
Slugging Pct:	Evans	.522
Home Runs:	Evans	22
RBI:	Evans	71
Runs:	Evans	84
Stolen Bases:	Lansford	15
Wins:	Torrez	10
Strikeouts:	Eckersley	79
ERA:	Torrez	3.68
Saves:	Clear	9

JANUARY 23   Three days after Ronald Reagan is inaugurated as president and the American hostages in Iran are released from captivity, the Red Sox trade Fred Lynn and Steve Renko to the Angels for Frank Tanana, Joe Rudi, and Jim Dorsey.

Lynn played until 1990 and appeared in three more All-Star Games, but he was beset by numerous injuries and played in more than 130 games in a season only twice after 1981. He reached a high of 142 games played in 1984. After the trade to the Angels, Lynn played in 1,141 more big-league games and had a batting average of .263 (compared with .308 while with the Sox) and a slugging percentage of .457 (compared with .520 in Boston). The Sox received two players well past their peak in exchange for Lynn. Tanana was 4–10 in his only season with Boston, and Rudi hit .180 in 49 games.

MARCH 9   Carlton Fisk signs a free-agent contract with the White Sox.

Even after arbitrator Raymond Goetz declared that Fisk was entitled to free agency, the Red Sox offered the catcher a hefty contract and thought that the money, Carlton's New England ties, and 11 years with the club would be enough to keep him in Boston. Fisk signed a contract with Chicago. He played 13 seasons with the White Sox and retired after the 1993 season when he was forty-five years old (see April 10, 1981).

APRIL 8   Nine days after Ronald Reagan is wounded by John Hinckley in an assassination attempt, the Red Sox trade Dick Drago to the Mariners for Manny Sarmiento.

APRIL 10   Carlton Fisk hits a three-run homer in the eighth inning in his first game with the White Sox to spark his new club to a 5–3 win over his former Red Sox teammates on Opening Day before 35,124 at Fenway Park. Before Fisk homered, the Red Sox led, 2–0. Dennis Eckersley pitched seven shutout innings before putting two on base in the eighth. Eckersley yielded to Bob Stanley, who gave up Fisk's storybook homer. Dwight Evans and Gary Allenson hit homers for the Red Sox.

Carl Yastrzemski, playing in his 21st season with the Red Sox, failed to play in the season opener for the first time. After playing every Opening Day from 1961 through 1980, he missed the 1981 game because of back spasms.

APRIL 12   On the day of the launch of Columbia, the first space shuttle, the Red Sox overcome a 3–0 deficit by scoring five runs in the eighth inning to beat the White Sox 5–3 at Fenway Park. The rally was capped by Jim Rice's grand slam off Ed Farmer.

APRIL 14   Frank Tanana suffers chin lacerations that require 10 stitches when the car he is driving is involved in a head-on collision in suburban Boston. A car driven by Thomas King of Watertown, Massachusetts, swerved and struck Tanana's vehicle.

APRIL 18   The Red Sox farm club in Pawtucket in the International League plays 32 innings against Rochester before the contest is suspended with the score 2–2 at 4:07 AM, after eight hours and seven minutes of play. It was the longest game in the history of organized baseball.

The game was completed on June 23, the next time that Rochester played in Pawtucket. The game drew considerable interest, not only because of the historic significance of being the longest game ever in organized baseball, but also because the major league players were on strike at the time. Several Red Sox players motored down to Pawtucket to watch the conclusion. Pawtucket won the game 3–2 in the 33rd inning. Marty Barrett scored the winning run, and Bob Ojeda was the winning pitcher. Among the others who played in the game were future Hall of Famers Wade Boggs for Pawtucket and Cal Ripken Jr. for Rochester. Both Boggs and Ripken played third base in the game.

MAY 5   Dwight Evans reaches base seven times in seven plate appearances on four walks and three singles during a 12-inning, 8–7 win over the Royals in Kansas City. The game took two days to play. It started on May 4 but was stopped with the score 5–5 at the end of the tenth inning because of the American League rule stipulating that no inning could start after 1:00 AM. When play resumed on May 5, the Red Sox scored three runs in the twelfth before the Royals countered with two. The victory broke Boston's eight-game losing streak. Kansas City won the regularly scheduled game, 2–1.

Evans led the AL in home runs with 22 during the 108-game, strike-shortened season. He also topped the league in total bases with 215, drove in 71 runs, scored 84, batted .296, and had a slugging percentage of .522.

Rich Pilling/Major League Baseball/Getty Images

Though never a star, Dwight Evans played 19 seasons for the Sox, supplying steady production through the team's many ups and downs.

MAY 11   Rick Miller ties a major league record with four doubles during a 7–6 win over the Blue Jays in Toronto. Miller also singled to give him five hits in five at-bats. Gary Allenson drove in the game winner in the ninth, his fifth RBI of the contest.

MAY 14   On the day the Celtics win the NBA Championship in a six-game series against the Houston Rockets, Red Sox rookie catcher Dave Schmidt leads off the eleventh inning with his first major league homer to break a 7–7 tie against the Twins in Minnesota. The Red Sox added an insurance run to win, 9–7. It was the last time that the Red Sox played at Metropolitan Stadium in Bloomington, Minnesota. The Twins opened the Metrodome in 1982. Metropolitan Stadium is now the site of the massive Mall of America.

               Schmidt played in only 15 big-league games and hit two home runs.

MAY 17   Carney Lansford collects five hits in five at-bats, but the Red Sox lose 5–4 to the Royals at Fenway Park.

MAY 21   A three-run, walk-off homer by Jim Rice off Brian Kingman in the ninth inning beats the Athletics 3–0 at Fenway Park. Dennis Eckersley pitched a two-hitter. The only Oakland hits were a single by Brian Doyle in the third inning and a double by Tony Armas in the fourth.

               Rice hit .284 with 17 homers in 1981.

MAY 25   Carl Yastrzemski plays in his 3,000th career game and contributes to an 8–7 win over the Indians at Fenway Park. Yastrzemski scored the winning run in the ninth inning after drawing a walk, crossing the plate on a double by Jim Rice and a single by Carney Lansford. Yaz also drove in two runs.

               Yastrzemski finished his career having played in 3,308 games, the second-highest figure in major league history. The only player to appear in more games than Yastrzemski is Pete Rose, who holds the all-time record with 3,562. Others with 3,000 or more major league games are Hank Aaron (3,298), Rickey Henderson (3,081), Ty Cobb (3,033), Eddie Murray (3,026), Stan Musial (3,026), and Cal Ripken Jr. (3,001).

MAY 30   The Red Sox stage an incredible comeback victory by overcoming a 6–1 deficit with five runs in the ninth inning and one in the tenth to defeat the Brewers 7–6 at Fenway Park. A three-run homer by Dwight Evans tied the score, 6–6. In the tenth, Dave Stapleton drove in the winning run with a single.

JUNE 8   The Red Sox select shortstop Steve Lyons from Oregon State University in the first round of the amateur draft.

               Lyons played with the Red Sox as a utility player in 1985 and 1986 and after a stint with the White Sox returned to Boston from 1991 through 1993. He was nicknamed "Psycho" because of his reckless hustle and his offbeat behavior and became a fan favorite. Lyons hosted a radio call-in show while still a player and has served as a network television analyst on FOX Sports since his playing days ended. Other future major leaguers drafted and signed by the Red Sox in 1981 were Rob Woodward (third round), Todd Benzinger (fourth), and

Steve Ellsworth, the son of former Red Sox pitcher Dick Ellsworth (first round of the secondary phase).

JUNE 11   In the last game before the strike, the Red Sox lose 7–2 to the Angels in Anaheim.

JUNE 12   Major League Baseball players begin a strike that lasts 50 days and wipes out nearly two months of the 1981 season. The strike reduced the Red Sox' schedule to 108 games.

JULY 31   Two days after Prince Charles marries Lady Diana Spencer in London, the players and owners hammer out an agreement that ends the strike.

AUGUST 6   The owners vote to split the 1981 pennant race with the winners of the two halves of the season and compete in an extra round of playoffs for the division title. The Red Sox ended the first half of the season in fifth place with a record of 30–26.

AUGUST 10   In the first game since the end of the strike, the Red Sox lose 7–1 to the White Sox at Fenway Park before 20,228.

AUGUST 12   The Red Sox belt six homers during an 8–1 win over the White Sox at Fenway Park. Joe Rudi hit two homers, and Dwight Evans, Gary Allenson, Dave Stapleton, and Jim Rice each added one.

SEPTEMBER 3   The game between the Red Sox and Mariners at Fenway Park is suspended at the end of the nineteenth inning with the score 7–7 because of the American League's 1:00 AM curfew. The Sox trailed 7–3 before scoring a run in the eighth inning and three in the ninth. The score was tied on a two-run single by Joe Rudi and another single by Rich Gedman. The two clubs combined for 10 consecutive scoreless innings before play was halted. The contest resumed the following evening.

SEPTEMBER 4   The suspended game of September 3 reaches a conclusion with the Mariners winning 8–7 with a run in the twentieth inning. The winning tally crossed the plate on a triple by Joe Simpson off Bob Stanley. Jerry Remy tied a club record for most hits in a game with six, all of which were singles, in 10 at-bats. The 20-inning affair is the longest game in Fenway Park history and is tied for the second longest in club history. The Sox played a 24-inning game against the Athletics at Huntington Grounds in 1906, a 20-inning contest against the Athletics at Huntington Grounds in 1905, and another 20-inning game against the Seattle Pilots in Seattle in 1969.

Remy hit .307 in 1981.

SEPTEMBER 12 Bob Ojeda carries a no-hitter into the ninth inning before allowing two hits and needing relief from Mark Clear to defeat the Yankees 2–1 in New York. Rick Cerone broke up the no-hitter by leading off the ninth with a double and scored on another double by Dave Winfield. Clear then replaced Ojeda and retired three batters to earn the save.

SEPTEMBER 19 Trailing the Yankees 5–1 at Fenway Park, the Red Sox score seven runs in the eighth inning to win, 8–5. It was the first win over the Yankees at Fenway Park since 1979. A three-run homer by Rick Miller on a 3–0 pitch broke the 5–5 tie.

SEPTEMBER 23   The Red Sox score eight runs in the seventh inning and beat the Brewers 11–5 at Fenway Park. Gary Allenson hit a grand slam in the big inning off Reggie Cleveland.

SEPTEMBER 25   The Red Sox pull into a tie for first place with the Tigers in the second-half AL East race after downing the Indians 5–4 at Fenway Park. The Brewers were in third place, one game back.

SEPTEMBER 30   The Red Sox lose 10–5 to the Brewers in Milwaukee to virtually eliminate Boston from the 1981 postseason. After losing twice to the Indians at Fenway Park on September 26 and 27, the Sox lost two of three in a showdown series at County Stadium on September 28, 29, and 30. Boston finished the second half in a tie for second with the Tigers, 1½ games behind the Brewers.

DECEMBER 4   Joe Rudi signs a free-agent contract with the Athletics.

DECEMBER 8   Bill Campbell signs a free-agent contract with the Cubs.

1982   B

Season in a Sentence

With an outstanding bullpen and little else, the Red Sox hold a five-game lead in late June and are still in first at the start of August, but they fade to third place.

Finish • Won • Lost • Pct • GB

Third   89   73   .549   6.0

Manager

Ralph Houk

Stats

Stats	Red Sox	AL	Rank
Batting Avg:	.274	.264	4
On-Base Pct:	.342	.331	4
Slugging Pct:	.407	.402	7
Home Runs:	136		8 (tie)
Stolen Bases:	42		13
ERA:	4.03	4.07	9
Fielding Pct:	.981	.980	6
Runs Scored:	753		6
Runs Allowed:	713		7

Starting Lineup

Gary Allenson, c
Dave Stapleton, 1b
Jerry Remy, 2b
Carney Lansford, 3b
Glenn Hoffman, ss
Jim Rice, lf
Rick Miller, cf
Dwight Evans, rf
Carl Yastrzemski, dh
Wade Boggs, 1b-3b
Rich Gedman, c
Reid Nichols, of
Tony Perez, dh

Pitchers

Dennis Eckersley, sp
John Tudor, sp
Mike Torrez, sp
Chuck Rainey, sp
Bruce Hurst, sp
Bob Stanley, rp
Mark Clear, rp
Tom Burgmeier, rp
Luis Aponte, rp

Attendance

1,950,124 (fifth in AL)

Club Leaders

Batting Avg:	Rice	.309
On-Base Pct:	Evans	.402
Slugging Pct:	Evans	.534
Home Runs:	Evans	32
RBI:	Evans	98
Runs:	Evans	122
Stolen Bases:	Remy	16
Wins:	Eckersley	13
	Tudor	13
Strikeouts:	Tudor	146
ERA:	Stanley	3.10
Saves:	Clear	14
	Stanley	14

JANUARY 6   Frank Tanana signs a free-agent contract with the Rangers.

JANUARY 9   Tragedy continues to haunt Tony Conigliaro as he suffers a massive heart attack at
               the age of thirty-seven.

*Conigliaro had just auditioned for a job as the color man on the Red Sox tele-
casts. He was being driven to the airport by his brother Billy when he was
stricken by the heart attack while traveling through the Callahan Tunnel. Tony
was in a coma for four months. He needed round-the-clock care from nurses for
the last eight years of his life, which placed an enormous financial burden on
the family. Conigliaro was not fully aware of his surroundings and stayed either
with his mother or his brother Billy. Further complications required the removal
of a part of Tony's right lung in May 1983 because of breathing problems. He
died of kidney failure on February 24, 1990, when he was only forty-five.*

FEBRUARY 25   The Red Sox sign Mark Fidrych to a minor league contract.

*A native of Northborough, Massachusetts, about 50 miles from Boston, Fidrych
became a national sensational as a twenty-two-year-old rookie pitcher with the
Tigers in 1976. Nicknamed "The Bird," for his resemblance to Big Bird, Fidrych
filled ballparks around the country for his unrestrained joy on the mound, which
included shaking hands with infielders after good plays and talking to the ball. He
could also pitch. Fidrych was 19–9 that season with a league-leading 2.34 ERA.
He soon developed arm problems, however, and won only 10 more big-league
games, earning his release from the Tigers. Fidrych spent two years in the Red Sox
minor league system and was still a drawing card at Pawtucket and other International League cities, but he was never promoted to the majors. Fidrych was
released in 1983 after posting a 2–5 record and a 9.68 ERA at Pawtucket.*

APRIL 6   The Red Sox' scheduled season opener against the White Sox in Chicago is post-
               poned by snow. With no hope for a break in the wintry weather, the remainder
               of the series at Comiskey Park was postponed, and the Red Sox returned to their
               spring training base in the aptly named Winter Haven, Florida, for two days of
               workouts on April 7 and 8. The Sox flew to Baltimore for a game against the
               Orioles on April 9, but that contest was also postponed by rain and cold.

APRIL 10   The Red Sox finally get started on the 1982 season by playing a doubleheader
               against the Orioles in Baltimore. The Red Sox won the first game 2–0 before drop-
               ping the nightcap, 5–3. Dennis Eckersley pitched a complete-game shutout in the
               opener, scattering six hits. Both Boston runs scored on a two-out, two-run single by
               Jim Rice in the third inning. Wade Boggs made his major league debut in the second
               tilt. Playing first base and batting ninth, Boggs was hitless in four at-bats.

*Bob Montgomery replaced Ken Harrelson on the Red Sox television broadcasts.
Harrelson moved to Chicago, where he was a part of the White Sox telecasts.*

APRIL 12   The Red Sox lose the home opener 3–2 to the White Sox before 32,555 at Fenway
               Park.

APRIL 26   Wade Boggs collects his first major league hit during a 3–2 win over the White Sox
               in Chicago. With the score 2–2 in the eighth inning, Boggs singled, went to second

on a sacrifice, third on a grounder, and home on a single by Jim Rice. The Red Sox also won the second game, 5–0.

APRIL 27   The Red Sox win their eighth game in a row with a 7–5 decision over the Royals at Fenway Park.

MAY 1   The Red Sox stage an old-timers game at Fenway Park for the first time in decades. Ted Williams, at the age of sixty-three, was the main attraction. He flied out to right field in his only at-bat and made a shoestring catch in left field.

MAY 9   The Red Sox edge the Rangers 1–0 at Arlington. Tony Perez drove in the lone run of the game with a double in the sixth inning. John Tudor ($4\frac{1}{3}$ innings), Bob Stanley ($3\frac{2}{3}$ innings), and Mark Clear (one inning) combined on the shutout.

MAY 10   The Red Sox play at the Metrodome in Minneapolis for the first time and win 9–5 against the Twins.

MAY 23   The Red Sox defeat the Athletics 6–0 in a contest at Fenway Park, called after $5\frac{1}{2}$ innings by rain.

The victory gave the Sox a record of 28–13 and a two-game lead over the second-place Tigers. The Red Sox opened a five-game lead by June 23, when the club was 42–24. The Sox were in first as late as August 2 but had faded to third, six games behind the pennant-winning Brewers, by the end of the season.

MAY 31   Rick Miller hits a grand slam off Bo McLaughlin in the fourth inning of a 5–2 win over the Athletics in Oakland.

JUNE 4   The Red Sox erupt for seven runs in the eleventh inning and beat the Angels 11–4 in Anaheim. Carney Lansford contributed a three-run homer.

Lansford hit .301 with 11 homers in 128 games in 1982. Dwight Evans scored 122 runs, hit 32 homers, drove in 98 runs, drew 112 walks, hit .298, and led the league with an on-base percentage of .402. Jim Rice batted .309 with 24 homers and 97 RBIs.

JUNE 5   The Red Sox score all of their runs in a seven-run sixth inning and beat the Angels 7–2 in Anaheim.

JUNE 7   The Red Sox select first baseman Sam Horn from Morse High School in Dallas, Texas, in the first round of the amateur draft.

Horn spent eight seasons in the majors, three of them with the Red Sox, beginning in 1987. He could hit for power but could do little else, and he was used only as a pinch hitter and substitute first baseman. Horn collected 16 homers and a .223 batting average in 273 big-league at-bats. Other players drafted and signed by the Red Sox in 1982 were Mike Rochford (first round of the January draft), Charlie Mitchell (fourth round of the January draft), Kevin Romine (second round in June), Mike Greenwell (third round in June), and Jeff Sellers (eighth round in June). Among the 1982 draftees, only Greenwell became a major league regular.

JUNE 22 — Wade Boggs hits a walk-off homer in the eleventh inning that beats the Tigers 5–4 at Fenway Park. It was his first major league home run. Boggs entered the game as a pinch hitter and stayed in the contest as a first baseman. Dwight Evans tied the contest with a homer in the ninth inning.

JUNE 23 — Carney Lansford severely sprains his ankle on a play at the plate while trying for an inside-the-park homer during a 10–4 win over the Tigers at Fenway Park.

> *The injury changed the history of the Red Sox because it gave Wade Boggs a chance to play regularly while Lansford was recuperating. When the season began, Boggs was a twenty-three-year-old rookie. He had hit over .300 in each of the previous five seasons in the minors, including a batting title at Pawtucket in 1981 with a .335 average, but the Red Sox didn't consider him to be a solid major league prospect. The club hierarchy believed that he lacked the power to play first base, and failed to possess the defensive skills to handle third. During the first 65 games of the 1982 season, Boggs was one of the last options off the Red Sox bench. He appeared in just 14 games and had only 29 at-bats with 7 hits for an average of .241. Boggs immediately proved his worth by hitting .349 over the season in 104 games, although as late as August, Ralph Houk still wasn't convinced that he could play effectively on a daily basis. "I feel he can best help the club as a left-handed pinch hitter," Houk said. "He has proven himself, but we're a better team with Lansford at third and (Dave) Stapleton at first." Fortunately, Houk came to his senses a few weeks later and put Boggs at first ahead of Stapleton.*
>
> *During the following offseason, Lansford was traded and Boggs moved back to third. Guided by an unparalleled work ethic and a series of rituals such as eating chicken before every game, Boggs played 11 seasons with the Red Sox and hit .338 in 1,625 games with the club. He collected 2,098 hits and had 1,067 runs, 422 doubles, 1,004 walks, and 85 home runs. Boggs ended his big-league career in 1999 with 3,098 hits and a .328 career average. No one who has played at least 1,000 career games at third base has a batting average higher than .320. Boggs's extreme dedication to his craft also applied to defense. During his career, he went from being one of the worst defensive third basemen in the game to one of the best. He was never fully embraced by many Sox fans, however, who viewed him as selfish and arrogant. Boggs was elected to the Hall of Fame his first time on the ballot in 2005.*

JUNE 25 — In his first start following Lansford's injury, Wade Boggs commits errors on the first two balls hit to him, both in the first inning, of a 9–3 loss to the Brewers at Fenway Park. When Boggs finally fielded a ball cleanly, the crowd gave him a standing ovation.

JULY 2 — Tony Perez collects his 2,500th career hit during a 14–5 loss to the Brewers in Milwaukee. The milestone hit was a single off Bob McClure.

JULY 13 — Dennis Eckersley is the American League starting pitcher in the All-Star Game, but allows three runs in three innings and is charged with the loss in a 4–1 NL victory at Olympic Stadium in Montreal.

JULY 19 — Down 5–0, the Red Sox score four runs in the seventh inning and five in the eighth in a 9–5 win over the Rangers at Fenway Park.

JULY 21   Mike Torrez (eight innings) and Bob Stanley (one inning) combine on a two-hitter to beat the Rangers 6–1 in the second game of a doubleheader at Fenway Park. The only Texas hits were doubles by Mike Richardt and Don Werner in the third inning. The Rangers won the first game, 6–3.

AUGUST 3   The Red Sox drop out of first place behind the Brewers after splitting a doubleheader against the Orioles at Memorial Stadium.

             The Sox never regained first place but remained in contention until September. The bullpen kept the club within striking distance of a pennant. Mark Clear was 14–9 with 14 saves and a 3.00 ERA. Bob Stanley pitched 168 1/3 innings of relief, an American League record, and was 12–7 with 14 saves and a 3.10 earned run average. Tom Burgmeier was 7–0 and had an ERA of 2.29.

AUGUST 15   The Red Sox put all of their eggs in one basket by using an eight-run seventh inning to defeat the Orioles 8–0 at Fenway Park.

AUGUST 21   Bobby Ojeda is placed on the disabled list after spraining his shoulder in a fall in a hotel bathtub in Oakland.

AUGUST 24   Reid Nichols homered in the twelfth inning, his second in the game, to beat the Mariners 5–4 in Seattle. It became his only multihomer game of his big-league career.

AUGUST 28   Down 5–0 to the Angels at Fenway Park, the Red Sox score five runs in the seventh inning to tie the game, then win 7–6 with a run in the seventh inning. A bunt single by Gary Allenson with the bases loaded drove in the winning run.

SEPTEMBER 5 The Red Sox score three runs in the ninth inning and one in the tenth to beat the Mariners 6–5 at Fenway Park. Dave Stapleton tied the score with a two-out, two-run single in the ninth inning. Carl Yastrzemski drove in the game winner with a grounder to second baseman Julio Cruz with the bases loaded. Cruz threw home too late to get Jerry Remy at the plate.

SEPTEMBER 12 The Red Sox defeat the Tigers 10–7 at Fenway Park to remain in the pennant race.

             With three weeks to play, the Sox were in third place four games in back of the Brewers, but could get no closer, losing 11 of their next 17 games.

SEPTEMBER 19 Carney Lansford hits a grand slam off Dave Tobik in the eighth inning of a 6–4 win over the Tigers in Detroit.

             It was Boston's 82nd win of the season, ensuring a winning record for the 16th consecutive season. The only longer streaks are 39 by the Yankees from 1926 through 1964, 18 by the Orioles (1968–85), and 17 by the White Sox (1951–67).

SEPTEMBER 28 Carl Yastrzemski signs a contract for 1983, stating that it will be his final season.

             The 1983 season was Yastrzemski's 23rd with the Red Sox. The only player to play for one club in as many as 23 seasons is Brooks Robinson, who was with the Orioles from 1955 through 1977. Those with one club for 22 seasons are Cap Anson (Cubs, 1876–97), Ty Cobb (Tigers, 1905–26), Mel Ott (Giants,

1926–47), Stan Musial (Cardinals, 1941–44, 1946–63), and Al Kaline (Tigers, 1953–74). Yastrzemski played in 3,308 games for the Sox, an all-time record with one club. Musial is second with 3,026 games for the Cardinals.

OCTOBER 3   On the last day of the season, Roger LaFrancois, making his first major league start, collects two hits in five at-bats during an 11-inning, 5–3 win over the Yankees in New York.

LaFrancois never played in another major league game. He spent the entire 1982 season on the Red Sox' active roster, but he played in only eight games. LaFrancois ended his career with a batting average of .400 with four hits in 10 at-bats.

NOVEMBER 1   The Red Sox release Tony Perez.

NOVEMBER 15   Tom Burgmeier signs a free-agent contract with the Athletics.

DECEMBER 6   The Red Sox trade Carney Lansford, Gary Hancock, and Jerry King to the Athletics for Tony Armas and Jeff Newman.

DECEMBER 10   The Red Sox trade Chuck Rainey to the Cubs for Doug Bird.

1983   B

Season in a Sentence

The Red Sox stumble to their first losing season since 1966.

Finish • Won • Lost • Pct • GB

| Sixth | 78 | 84 | .481 | 20.0 |

Manager

Ralph Houk

Stats

Stats	Red Sox	AL	Rank
Batting Avg:	.270	.266	5
On-Base Pct:	.337	.331	6
Slugging Pct:	.409	.401	7
Home Runs:	142		7
Stolen Bases:	30		14
ERA:	4.34	4.06	11
Fielding Pct:	.979	.979	9
Runs Scored:	724		7
Runs Allowed:	775		10

Starting Lineup

Gary Allenson, c
Dave Stapleton, 1b
Jerry Remy, 2b
Wade Boggs, 3b
Glenn Hoffman, ss
Jim Rice, lf
Tony Armas, cf
Dwight Evans, rf
Carl Yastrzemski, dh
Reid Nichols, of
Rick Miller, of
Rich Gedman, c
Ed Jurak, ss-1b

Pitchers

John Tudor, sp
Bruce Hurst, sp
Bobby Ojeda, sp
Dennis Eckersley, sp
Mike Brown, sp
Oil Can Boyd, sp
Bob Stanley, rp
Mike Clear, rp

Attendance

1,782,285 (ninth in AL)

Club Leaders

Batting Avg:	Boggs	.361
On-Base Pct:	Boggs	.444
Slugging Pct:	Rice	.550
Home Runs:	Rice	39
RBI:	Rice	126
Runs:	Boggs	100
Stolen Bases:	Remy	11
Wins:	Tudor	15
Strikeouts:	Tudor	136
ERA:	Tudor	4.09
	Hurst	4.09
Saves:	Stanley	33

JANUARY 14   The Red Sox trade Mike Torrez to the Mets for Mike Davis.

Red Sox fans never forgave Torrez for giving up the Bucky Dent home run in the 1978 playoff game, and a segment of the Fenway faithful booed him every time he pitched during his last four seasons with the club. Davis never played a major league game, but the Sox didn't miss Torrez, who was clearly at the end of the line. He was 9–9 with a 5.23 ERA with Boston in 1982 and had an 11–23 record in two seasons with the Mets.

APRIL 5   The Red Sox open the season with a 7–1 loss to the Blue Jays before 33,842 at Fenway Park. Dennis Eckersley gave up seven runs in four innings. Dave Stapleton hit a homer for the only Boston run.

There were new luxury boxes added to Fenway Park down the left field line along with a rebuilt roof, an entire new lighting system, and a renovated visiting clubhouse.

APRIL 13   Glenn Hoffman collects five hits, including a double, in six at-bats to lead a 21-hit attack that downs the Royals 18–4 in Kansas City.

Joe Castiglione replaced Jon Miller on the radio broadcasts, joining Ken Coleman. Miller left Boston to become the lead announcer with the Orioles and drew a national audience in 1990 when he was assigned to the ESPN Sunday-night telecasts with Joe Morgan.

APRIL 20   The Red Sox score three runs in the ninth inning to defeat the Brewers 5–4 at Fenway Park. Jim Rice tied the game 4–4 with a two-run homer. After the bases were loaded, Jamie Easterly walked in Tony Armas, the winning run, on a 3–2 pitch with two outs.

Rice and Armas, along with Wade Boggs, paced the Red Sox' batting attack in 1983. Rice led the AL in home runs with 39 and drove in 126 runs while batting .305. In his first season with the Red Sox, Armas made an immediate impact by hitting 36 home runs with 107 RBIs. Ralph Houk claimed that Armas was as tough a player as he had ever managed. Rice and Armas finished 1–2 in the AL in home runs, the first pair of teammates to top a league since Willie Mays and Willie McCovey with the 1965 Giants. Armas did little in 1983 except hit home runs, however. He hit only .218, the lowest batting average in history by a player with at least 100 RBIs. Armas drew just 29 walks while striking out 131 times. His on-base percentage was an abysmal .254, he failed to steal a base, and he grounded into a league-leading 31 double plays. Boggs led the American League in batting by posting an average of .361. He also collected 210 hits and scored 100 runs.

APRIL 21   Jim Rice hits a two-run, ninth-inning homer for the second game in a row. The home run broke a 1–1 tie and gave the Red Sox a 3–1 win over the Athletics in Oakland.

APRIL 23   A benefit concert is held at Symphony Hall in Boston to help defray the medical costs of Tony Conigliaro, who was slowly recovering from the heart attack he suffered on January 9, 1982. Highlights of the concert included performances by Frank

Sinatra, Dionne Warwick, and Marvin Hamlisch. Ted Williams, Willie Mays, and Joe DiMaggio also made appearances on stage. The event raised $200,000.

MAY 1   After trailing 6–0 at the end of the third inning and 9–4 at the end of the fifth, the Red Sox battle back to win 10–9 over the Angels in Anaheim. Jerry Remy's single in the ninth inning broke a 9–9 tie.

MAY 6   Red Sox infielder Julio Valdez is arrested on statutory rape charges in the Fenway Park dugout during the seventh inning of a 6–4 win over the Mariners.

The charges were filed by the parents of a fourteen-year-old female runaway from Berkeley, Massachusetts, who was returned to the family after police found her outside of Fenway Park on April 20. She revealed that she had had sexual relations with Valdez. The girl told Valdez she was seventeen. The age of consent in Massachusetts was sixteen. The Red Sox took Valdez off the roster and placed him on the restricted list until his trial was concluded. Valdez was cleared of the charges in July, but the Red Sox sent him to the minors. Valdez never played in another major league game.

MAY 7   Tony Armas hits a grand slam off Bill Caudill in the seventh inning of an 8–0 win over the Mariners at Fenway Park.

At the end of the game, the Red Sox had a 15–9 record and were in first place, half a game ahead of the Orioles. The Sox were 28–21 on June 4 and still had a tenuous hold on first place, but a seven-game losing streak that started on June 5 put to rest any illusions of a division pennant flying over Fenway Park.

MAY 11   John Tudor allows only three Angels base runners in 8 ⅓ innings of pitching, but all three score to beat the Red Sox 3–1 at Fenway Park. Bobby Clark hit a solo homer for California, and Ellis Valentine connected for a two-run shot.

MAY 14   Ex–Red Sox outfielder Ben Oglivie hits three homers for the Brewers in a 10-inning, 8–7 win over Boston in Milwaukee.

MAY 25   Reid Nichols hits a two-run single with the bases loaded in the ninth inning to provide the only runs in a 2–0 win over the White Sox in Chicago. Bruce Hurst pitched the shutout, his first as a major leaguer.

Through his first three seasons in the majors from 1980 through 1982, Hurst had a 7–9 record and a 6.17 ERA in 170⅔ innings. Thereafter, he flirted with greatness and posted an overall 88–73 record in nine seasons with Boston and 145–113 in his big-league career. Oddly, Hurst posted a 56–33 record at Fenway Park even though he was left-handed and playing in a ballpark built for right-handed power hitters. He was 32–40 in road contests while with the Sox. A devout Mormon from the tiny town of St. George, Utah, Hurst's religious beliefs made him somewhat of a loner in the often profane and raucous atmosphere of a major league ball club. "I'm not a big clubhouse guy," Hurst said. "I just don't feel comfortable in there. My life is not going to be consumed by the game."

MAY 27   John Tudor pitches a one-hitter to defeat the Blue Jays 2–0 at Exhibition Stadium. The only Toronto hit was a single by Dave Collins in the fourth inning.

Bob Stanley had an outstanding season with 33 saves and a 2.85 ERA, but he didn't have much support from the rest of the staff. Mark Clear and Dennis Eckersley were particular disappointments. Clear had a 6.28 ERA in 96 relief innings. Eckersley was 9–13 with an earned run average of 5.81. Doug Bird, acquired in a trade with the Cubs for Chuck Rainey, was 1–4 with a 6.65 ERA. Rainey won 14 games for the Cubs. On the offensive side, Dwight Evans slumped to a .238 average.

JUNE 6   On an eventful day in Boston, the Red Sox stage "Tony Conigliaro Night" at Fenway Park. Twenty-two teammates from the 1967 Red Sox made an appearance on the field prior to the game. The net proceeds of the contest were earmarked to help defray Conigliaro's staggering medical costs. A crowd of 23,961 watched the Sox lose 11–6 to the Tigers. On the same day, the Sox selected University of Texas pitcher Roger Clemens in the first round of the amateur draft. Clemens reached the majors in less than a year and went on to become one of the greatest pitchers in major league history. It was a tremendous draft year for Boston. In January, the Sox picked Ellis Burks. Others selected in the June draft who reached the majors included Mike Brumley (second round) and John Mitchell (seventh).

The biggest news on June 6, 1983, wasn't "Tony Conigliaro Night" or the drafting of Roger Clemens, but the attempted takeover of the team by majority partner Buddy LeRoux. In a master stroke of awful timing, when the spotlight should have been focused on the stricken Conigliaro, LeRoux rocked the organization by calling a press conference at 4:30 PM to announce that his partnership with Jean Yawkey and Haywood Sullivan had been reorganized. After feuding with Yawkey and Sullivan for several months over the direction of the club, LeRoux said he had teamed with the minority partners and that he was in charge. LeRoux claimed that Yawkey and Sullivan had been trying to force him to sell his share of the club at below market value. In addition, LeRoux announced that Sullivan was out as general manager, and Dick O'Connell, who had been fired by the Red Sox in 1977, was coming back.

When LeRoux's conference ended, Sullivan started one of his own. He claimed that LeRoux's coup was illegal and that he was in charge. LeRoux's takeover attempt was tawdry and crass and desecrated what should have been a celebratory evening. In effect, the Sox had two owners and two general managers. Employees were in a quandary because LeRoux said that they should take orders from him and ignore Sullivan. Sullivan gave orders that countermanded those from LeRoux. Sullivan and Yawkey went into court seeking a temporary restraining order to prevent LeRoux's action, and following two days of testimony, it was granted by Judge Andrew W. Linscott. The action also prevented the hiring of O'Connell. In July, Chief Justice James P. Lynch Jr. of the Massachusetts Superior Court ruled that the LeRoux takeover was illegal and barred him and his co-conspirators, limited partners Rogers Badgett and Albert Curran, from further attempts to gain control of the Red Sox (see May 30, 1984).

JUNE 22   Starting pitcher Bobby Ojeda lasts only one-third of an inning after allowing five runs in a game against the Indians at Fenway Park, lost by the Red Sox, 9–4. Ojeda said that he was stung by a bee during the National Anthem that caused him to lose his concentration.

JUNE 29   Jim Rice hits two homers and a double and drives in five runs during an 11–10 win over the Indians in the second game of a doubleheader at Municipal Stadium. Cleveland won the first game, 5–3.

JULY 4   Dave Righetti of the Yankees beats the Red Sox 4–0 with a no-hitter in New York. Righetti recorded the final out by fanning Wade Boggs.

JULY 6   In the final season of his career, Carl Yastrzemski plays in his 14th All-Star Game and strikes out as a pinch-hitter. The American League won the game 13–3 at Comiskey Park in Chicago.

JULY 21   The Red Sox outlast the Mariners 14–13 in 10 innings at the Kingdome. The Sox scored seven runs in the sixth inning to take a 13–4 lead, but squandered it away when Seattle scored three runs in their half of the sixth, five in the seventh, and one in the ninth to tie the contest, 13–13. An error by Mariners left fielder Steve Henderson with two out in the ninth on a drive by Tony Armas allowed Marty Barrett to score the winning run from third base.

JULY 22   The Red Sox score three runs in the ninth inning to defeat the Mariners 5–4 in Seattle. Wade Boggs drove in the last two runs with a bases-loaded single.

AUGUST 10   The Citgo sign is turned on during the seventh inning of a 4–2 win over the Rangers at Fenway Park.

               The sign had been turned off for several years, first because of the energy crisis of the 1970s, then because the Oklahoma-based Citgo corporation threatened to tear it down. It was saved by a group of Boston area citizens and plugged back in after renovation.

AUGUST 13   The Red Sox score eight runs in the second inning to break a 2–2 tie and move on to defeat the Royals 12–3 in the second game of a doubleheader at Fenway Park. Kansas City won the opener, 5–4.

AUGUST 17   Swarms of flying insects invade County Stadium, harassing fans and Red Sox and Brewers players during a 4–3 Milwaukee win in 10 innings in the first game of a doubleheader. The swarm arrived in the seventh inning. The insects disappeared by the start of the second tilt, won 5–1 by the Brewers.

AUGUST 20   Jim Rice hits a grand slam off Dave Steib in the third inning of a 5–2 win over the Blue Jays at Fenway Park.

AUGUST 26   Jim Rice hits two homers to account for all three runs during a 3–1 win over the White Sox in Chicago.

AUGUST 29   Jim Rice collects three homers and drives in six runs during an 8–7 win over the Blue Jays in the second game of a doubleheader at Exhibition Stadium. Rice hit a two-run homer off Jim Acker in the second inning, another two-run shot off Acker in the sixth, and with the Sox trailing 7–6 in the ninth, he connected for his third two-run homer of the game facing Randy Moffitt. Toronto won the first game, 5–1.

SEPTEMBER 10   Carl Yastrzemski hits the last home run of his career during an 8–6 loss to the Indians in Cleveland.

Yastrzemski finished his career with 452 home runs. He also homered on September 12 in the fourth inning off the Orioles' Jim Palmer at Fenway Park, but the contest was rained out before it became an official game.

SEPTEMBER 24   Tony Armas hits a homer over the wall in the first inning and one inside the park in the eighth during a 5–3 win over the Tigers in Detroit.

SEPTEMBER 30   The Red Sox rout the Indians 10–0 at Fenway Park.

OCTOBER 1   In celebration of his 23-year major league career, Carl Yastrzemski is honored in pregame festivities at Fenway Park. When he walked out of the dugout to second base, where the microphones were placed, he received a six-minute standing ovation. During the 58-minute ceremony, a letter from President Ronald Reagan was read. Among the dignitaries on hand were Senator Edward Kennedy and Governor Michael Dukakis. Kennedy presented Yastrzemski with a plaque from Congress. The ceremony ended with Yastrzemski taking a dramatic and emotional trot around the perimeter of the playing field, during which he shook hands with as many fans as possible and waved to the crowd of 33,491. Yaz was hitless in four at-bats, including the final out, in a 3–1 Red Sox loss to the Indians. After the game, he repeated his lap around the field, shaking more hands.

OCTOBER 2   Carl Yastrzemski plays in the final game of his career. Facing the Indians at Fenway Park, Yastrzemski played at his old spot in left field, a position he hadn't played all season. Yaz collected a single in three at-bats before leaving the game in the seventh inning to a standing ovation when replaced by Chico Walker. He also fielded a drive off the Green Monster and held Toby Harrah to a single. Jim Rice drove in all three Boston runs with a three-run homer for a 3–1 victory. Al Nipper earned his first major league win with a complete game. After the game, Yastrzemski circled the field to shake hands as he had the previous day, then spent an hour signing autographs outside of the ballpark.

Yastrzemski finished his career as the all-time Red Sox record holder in games played (3,308), at-bats (11,988), runs (1,816), hits (3,419), doubles (646), RBIs (1,844), extra-base hits (1,157), and total bases (5,539). He ranks second in home runs (452) and walks (1,845). Among major leaguers at the end of the 2005 season, Yastrzemski is second in games, third in at-bats, fourth in times reached base (on a hit, walk, or hit batsman), sixth in walks, seventh in hits, eighth in doubles, eighth in total bases, ninth in extra-base hits, 11th in RBIs, and 13th in runs.

DECEMBER 6   Six weeks after a bomb rips through a Marine compound in Beirut, Lebanon, killing 241, the Red Sox trade John Tudor to the Pirates for Mike Easler.

Easler gave the Red Sox one great season as a designated hitter, but it wasn't worth the loss of Tudor, who had a record of 78–40 with an ERA of 2.66 over the remainder of his career after departing Boston. In 1985 with the Cardinals, Tudor was 21–8 with an earned run average of 1.93.

1984   B

Season in a Sentence

A strong finish with young players such as Roger Clemens, Wade Boggs, Marty Barrett, Rich Gedman, Bobby Ojeda, Bruce Hurst, Al Nipper, and Oil Can Boyd provides some hope for the future.

Finish • Won • Lost • Pct • GB

Fourth   86   78   .531 18.0

Manager

Ralph Houk

Stats

Stats	Red Sox	AL	Rank
Batting Avg:	.283	.264	1
On-Base Pct:	.343	.329	2
Slugging Pct:	.441	.398	1
Home Runs:	181		2
Stolen Bases:	38		14
ERA:	4.18	3.99	11
Fielding Pct:	.977	.979	12
Runs Scored:	810		2
Runs Allowed:	764		11

Starting Lineup

Rich Gedman, c
Bill Buckner, 1b
Marty Barrett, 2b
Wade Boggs, 3b
Jackie Gutierrez, ss
Jim Rice, lf
Tony Armas, cf
Dwight Evans, rf
Mike Easler, dh

Pitchers

Bruce Hurst, sp
Bobby Ojeda, sp
Oil Can Boyd, sp
Al Nipper, sp
Roger Clemens, sp
Bob Stanley, rp
Mark Clear, rp

Attendance

1,661,618 (eighth in AL)

Club Leaders

Batting Avg:	Boggs	.325
On-Base Pct:	Boggs	.407
Slugging Pct:	Evans	.532
Home Runs:	Armas	43
RBI:	Armas	123
Runs:	Evans	121
Stolen Bases:	Gutierrez	12
Wins:	Three tied w/	12
Strikeouts:	Ojeda	137
ERA:	Nipper	3.89
Saves:	Stanley	22

FEBRUARY 1   The Red Sox hire fifty-four-year-old Lou Gorman as general manager to replace Haywood Sullivan. Sullivan continued to direct the business affairs of the club as one of the three general partners along with Jean Yawkey and Buddy LeRoux.

The Red Sox hired Gorman away from the Mets where he was in charge of the farm system, scouting, player development, and negotiating player contracts. Gorman is given much of the credit for putting together both the Mets' and Red Sox' teams that met in the 1986 World Series. Prior to his employment by the Mets and Red Sox, Gorman worked in the front offices of the Orioles, Royals, and Mariners.

APRIL 2   In the season opener, the Red Sox lose 2–1 to the Angels in Anaheim on two ninth-inning runs. The Angels loaded the bases in the ninth inning with two out when Bob Boone hit a grounder to rookie shortstop Jackie Gutierrez for what appeared to be the final out. Gutierrez threw the ball past first base, however, and allowed two men to score. Bruce Hurst pitched eight shutout innings before the fateful ninth.

Gutierrez hailed from Cartagena, Colombia. His father competed in track in the 1936 Olympics, and his brother followed in the 1964 games.

APRIL 4	Mike Easler hits a two-run homer in the ninth inning to defeat the Angels 2–1 in Anaheim.

The Red Sox opened the 1984 season with a three-city West Coast road trip through Anaheim, Oakland, and Seattle. The Sox were 3–5 on the trip.

APRIL 13	In the first game of the season at Fenway Park, the Tigers defeat the Red Sox 13–9 before 35,177. There were 13 runs scored in a wild first inning. The Tigers scored eight runs, and the Red Sox five. Starting pitcher Bruce Hurst gave up seven runs after allowing no earned runs in $17\frac{1}{3}$ innings in his first two starts of 1984. Rich Gedman and Dwight Evans hit home runs. In his first game with the Red Sox at Fenway, Mike Easler collected four hits, including a double, in five at-bats.

The Red Sox appeared on local cable television for the first time in 1984 over the New England Sports Network. There were 86 games broadcast on cable, and the number of over-the-air telecasts was reduced from about 100 to 69. The cable announcers were Kent Derdananis and Mike Andrews. The pair lasted only a year, however. In 1985, Ned Martin and Bob Montgomery covered the telecasts on both cable and over-the-air television.

APRIL 22	The Red Sox outlast the Athletics 12–8 at Fenway Park.
APRIL 24	In the fourth inning of an 8–7 loss to the Angels at Fenway Park, Oil Can Boyd surrenders consecutive homers to Reggie Jackson, Brian Downing, and Bobby Grich.
APRIL 28	Down 6–0 at the end of the sixth inning, the Red Sox score three runs in the seventh inning, three in the eighth, and two in the ninth to defeat the White Sox 8–7 in Chicago. Boston entered the ninth trailing 7–6. Ed Jurak tripled in the tying run and scored the winning run on an error. It was Jurak's only triple of the 1984 season and the last of the five he hit during his six-year major league career. Earlier in the contest, Tony Armas hit a home run into the center field bleachers at Comiskey Park, which was built in 1910. Armas was only the sixth player to reach those seats, a drive estimated at 500 feet.

The 1984 Red Sox were the first club since the 1929 Cubs with three outfielders who drove in at least 100 runs. Tony Armas led the league in both home runs (43) and RBIs (123). He also scored 107 runs and batted .268. Dwight Evans clubbed 32 homers, drove in 104 runs, batted .295, hit 37 doubles, and drew 96 walks in addition to leading the league in runs with 121. Jim Rice collected 122 RBIs, good enough for second in the league to Armas, along with 28 homers and a .280 average. The 1984 Sox were also the first club with four players with at least 300 total bases. Armas led the league with 339 total bases, and Evans was second with 335. Designated hitter Mike Easler had 310, and Jim Rice had 307. Easler had 27 homers, drove in 91 runs, and hit .313. But the offensive firepower wasn't limited to those four. Rich Gedman had 24 homers and hit .269. Wade Boggs batted .325, collected 203 hits, and scored 109 runs. Marty Barrett batted .303

MAY 1	In an unusual play during an 11–2 loss to the Tigers in Detroit, second baseman Jerry Remy is called for a balk.

In the bottom of the fourth inning with Detroit leading 4–2, Marty Castillo of the Tigers grounded past third base for a double. The Red Sox claimed that Castillo missed first base. Preparing for the appeal, Remy went into foul territory to back up the throw from pitcher Bruce Hurst. After the appeal was denied by first-base umpire Rocky Roe, Tigers manager Sparky Anderson claimed that Remy had played in foul territory, a violation of the rules. After agreeing with him, home plate umpire Ken Kaiser called a balk on Remy and waved Castillo to third. Rule 4.03 stated that all players except the catcher must be in fair territory when the ball was in play. The penalty was a balk call.

MAY 3   Dwight Evans hits a home run off Jack Morris in the eighth inning to defeat the Tigers 1–0 in Detroit. Bobby Ojeda pitched the shutout.

MAY 6   Bruce Hurst pitches a two-hitter to beat the White Sox 3–1 at Fenway Park. Hurst was six outs away from a no-hitter when Vance Law opened the eighth inning with a homer. Later in the inning, Scott Fletcher hit a single.

MAY 13   Jerry Remy is involved in another strange play during a 6–1 loss to the Royals in Kansas City. Remy was called out after he hit a chopper down the first-base line and struck him on the bill of the helmet while he was in fair territory.

Remy played seven seasons with the Red Sox, from 1978 through 1984, and failed to hit a single home run at Fenway Park. Overall, he had 2,809 at-bats with the Red Sox and hit only two homers. Both were hit in 1978 on the road. During his last six seasons in the big leagues, Remy batted 2,226 times without a homer. He was only thirty-one when he played his last big-league game. He retired following his sixth operation on his left knee. Remy returned to the Sox in 1988 as a television commentator.

MAY 15   Roger Clemens makes his major league debut at the age of twenty-one. He allowed five runs, four of them earned, and 11 hits in $5\frac{2}{3}$ innings of a 7–5 loss to the Indians in Cleveland.

Clemens took uniform number 21, which he also wore at the University of Texas. The last player to wear number 21 for the Red Sox was Mike Torrez.

MAY 17   The Red Sox outslug the Indians 11–10 in 10 innings in Cleveland. The Sox led 10–3 before allowing the Indians back in the game with three runs in the eighth inning and four in the ninth.

MAY 20   Roger Clemens picks up his first major league win with a 5–4 decision over the Twins in Minnesota. He went seven innings, allowing four runs and seven hits. Bob Stanley went the final two innings for the save.

MAY 25   The Red Sox trade Dennis Eckersley and Mike Brumley to the Cubs for Bill Buckner.

The Red Sox were desperate for a first baseman who could hit after trying to make do with Dave Stapleton at the position since 1980. Buckner was thirty-four years old when acquired by the Sox. He wasn't much of a power hitter, with 119 career homers in 6,683 at-bats when he arrived in Boston, but he had a .295 lifetime batting average. From 1976 through 1983, Buckner batted .301. In four seasons with the Red Sox, he batted .279 with 48 homers in 526 games.

Eckersley hadn't pitched well for years and looked washed up at the age of twenty-nine. In 1983 and 1984, he pitched 241 innings for the Sox and was 13–17 with an ERA of 5.45. Eckersley pitched well in spots for the Cubs before they traded him to the Athletics in 1986. There, he was converted from a starter to a reliever and became one of the most dominant closers in the history of the game. From 1988 through 1992, Eckersley saved 220 games and had an ERA of 1.93 in 354 innings. He played for the Red Sox again in 1998, the 24th and last season of his career. Eckersley was elected to the Hall of Fame in 2004, the first year he appeared on the ballot.

MAY 27   Bill Buckner's first hit as a member of the Red Sox is a two-run homer, struck during a 6–0 win over the Royals at Fenway Park.

MAY 29   The Red Sox officially retire uniform numbers for the first time. The two numerals retired were number 9 for Ted Williams and number four for Joe Cronin. The ceremonies took place before a scheduled game against the Twins, but the contest was called by a Boston rain storm.

Williams's number 9 had been unofficially retired since his playing days ended in 1960. Cronin wore number 4 as a player and manager in 1935 and again from 1937 through 1947. Cronin sported number 6 in 1936. From 1948 through 1983, number 4 was worn by several players, including Sam Mele, Ken Keltner, Lou Boudreau, Jackie Jensen, Lu Clinton, Roman Mejias, Jim Gosger, Rudy Schlesinger, Don Demeter, Norm Siebern, Billy Conigliaro, Tom Satriano, Ben Oglivie, Tommy Harper, Butch Hobson, and Carney Lansford. The honor was bestowed on Cronin just in time. He died on September 7, 1984, at the age of seventy-seven.

MAY 30   Jim Rice drives in both runs in a 2–0 win over the Twins at Fenway Park. Rice had a sacrifice fly in the third inning and a homer in the sixth.

On the same day, Buddy LeRoux lost the last round of his legal battle to take control of the Red Sox. The Massachusetts Appeals Court agreed with a Superior Court judge who ruled in August 1983 that LeRoux's attempted takeover, which took place on June 6, 1983, was illegal. Judge John M. Greaney ordered that LeRoux and limited partners Rogers Badgett and Albert Curran must sell their shares to Jean Yawkey and Haywood Sullivan. The court said the actions of LeRoux, Badgett, and Curran in staging the attempted coup "went substantially beyond acceptable behavior." LeRoux took a parting swipe at Yawkey. "We brought her in as window dressing, and she's been pulling the shade up and down ever since." LeRoux sold his shares to Yawkey and Sullivan for seven million dollars in 1987.

JUNE 4   In the first round of the amateur draft, the Red Sox select catcher John Marzano from Temple University.

Marzano was never more than a backup catcher in the majors. He hit .232 in 301 major league games over 10 seasons, six of them with the Red Sox beginning in 1987. Other future major leaguers drafted and signed by the Red Sox in the June 1984 draft were Steve Curry (seventh round), Jody Reed (eighth round), and Zachary Crouch (13th round). The Sox drafted Jack McDowell out of high school in the 20th round, but he opted to attend Stanford University instead. In 1987, McDowell was a first-round pick of the White Sox.

JUNE 5   Haywood Sullivan is named chief executive officer and chief operating officer of the Red Sox. His previous title had been executive vice president.

JUNE 9   The Red Sox rout the Brewers 15–6 at Fenway Park.

Reliever Mark Clear had control problems throughout his career, walking 554 batters in 804$\frac{1}{3}$ innings between 1979 and 1990. With the Red Sox in 1984, he walked 70 batters in just 67 innings but was reasonably effective. He struck out 76 hitters and allowed only 47 hits in posting an 8–3 record and a 4.03 ERA.

JUNE 11   The day before the Celtics win the NBA Championship with a Game Seven victory over the Lakers at Boston Garden, the Red Sox stage a thrilling six-run rally in the ninth inning to beat the Yankees 9–6 at Fenway Park. The first was driven in on a single by Jim Rice. Bill Buckner tied the contest 6–6 with a two-run single, and Reid Nichols followed with a three-run, walk-off homer.

JUNE 24   Down 3–0 heading into the bottom of the ninth inning against the Blue Jays at Fenway Park, the Red Sox win 5–3 with three runs in the ninth and two in the tenth. In the ninth, Reid Nichols drove in three runs with a bases-loaded double as a pinch hitter. Dwight Evans won the game with a walk-off homer.

JUNE 27   Bill Buckner collects the 2,000th hit of his major league career during a 3–1 loss to the Orioles in Baltimore. The milestone hit was a single off Scott McGregor.

JUNE 28   Dwight Evans hits for the cycle, completing it with a three-run, walk-off homer in the eleventh inning to defeat the Mariners 9–6 at Fenway Park. The homer was struck off the first pitch from Seattle reliever Edwin Nunez. The Sox scored a run in the ninth to tie the game, 4–4. After the Mariners scored two in the tenth, the Sox deadlocked the contest again with two in their half.

JULY 4   Jim Rice hits a walk-off grand slam off Gorman Heimueller in the tenth inning to beat the Athletics 13–9 at Fenway Park. It was Rice's fifth hit of the game and gave him six RBIs in the contest.

JULY 5   Dwight Evans drives in six runs, including a grand slam in the fifth inning off Bruce Kison, during a 12–7 win over the Angels at Fenway Park.

JULY 21   Bill Buckner hits a grand slam off Curt Kaufman in the sixth inning of a 16–4 win over the Angels in Anaheim. The Red Sox collected 20 hits in the contest.

JULY 25   Mike Easler leads off the twelfth inning with a walk-off homer to defeat the White Sox 3–2 at Fenway Park.

JULY 26   Roger Clemens pitches his first major league shutout, defeating the White Sox 7–0 at Fenway Park.

It was a career-turning victory for Clemens. Heading into the game, he had pitched 71$\frac{2}{3}$ major league innings in which he allowed 99 hits, had 57 strikeouts, *and posted a 5.78 ERA and 3–4 won-lost record. From July 26 through the end of the season, he was 6–0 in 61 ²/₃ innings while allowing 47 hits, striking out 69, and posting an ERA of 2.63. Clemens was shut down for the year after suffering a slight muscle tear in his pitching forearm on August 31.*

JULY 31

The Red Sox wallop the White Sox 14–4 in Chicago.

AUGUST 7

The Red Sox tie a major league record with two grand slams during a 12–7 win over the Tigers in the first game of a doubleheader at Fenway Park. Bill Buckner hit a grand slam in the first inning, and Tony Armas went deep in the second. Both were struck off Jack Morris.

AUGUST 9

Making his major league debut, Red Sox pitcher Charlie Mitchell allows a home run on the first batter he faces during a 7–3 loss to the Rangers in Arlington. Mitchell allowed the homer to Pete O'Brien.

AUGUST 21

Roger Clemens strikes out 15 batters without issuing a walk to defeat the Royals 11–1 at Fenway Park.

AUGUST 25

The Red Sox score eight runs in the fourth inning and level the Indians 11–6 at Fenway Park.

From July 3 through the end of the season, the Red Sox had a record of 50–34. The finish didn't do much to stir New England baseball fans, however. Attendance fell to 1,661,618, the lowest figure since 1974 (not counting the strike-shortened 1981 season) and a significant drop from the 2,353,114 the club drew in 1979.

AUGUST 29

Oil Can Boyd pitches a two-hitter to defeat the Twins 2–0 at the Metrodome. The only Minnesota hits were singles by Kirby Puckett in the fourth inning and Tim Teufel in the sixth.

Dennis (Oil Can) Boyd acquired his nickname in his college days at Jackson State in Mississippi where beer was called oil. Boyd was talented but emotionally troubled and alienated teammates and opponents alike. He was well-known for flamboyantly pumping his fists after a strikeout, which won him few friends in the league. Despite his frail six-foot-one-inch, 155-pound frame, Boyd was a 15-game winner in 1985 and had 11 wins by the All-Star break in 1986. He seemed to come unhinged after being left off the All-Star team, however, and checked himself into a hospital (see July 10, 1986). He won only five games in the second half of the season and was bothered by blood clot problems in his right shoulder for the remainder of his major league career, which ended in 1991.

AUGUST 31

The Red Sox score four runs in the ninth inning to defeat the Indians 8–7 in Cleveland. The four-run rally climaxed with a three-run homer form Dwight Evans, who also hit a two-run homer in the first inning.

SEPTEMBER 3

Jim Rice collects the 300th homer of his major league career during the fifth inning of an 8–5 win over the Brewers in Milwaukee. The victim of the milestone home run was Jaime Coconower.

SEPTEMBER 9   Wade Boggs collects four hits, including two doubles, in five at-bats during a 10–1 rout of the Yankees in New York. It was Boggs's second consecutive four-hit game. He had four hits the previous day in a 12–6 loss to the Yankees. In four games from September 5 through 9, Boggs had 13 hits in 18 at-bats.

SEPTEMBER 19   Dwight Evans hits a pair of three-run homers during a 10–4 thumping of the Blue Jays in Toronto. Both were hit off Jim Clancy in the third and fifth innings.

SEPTEMBER 21   Bill Buckner collects five hits in five at-bats during an 8–0 win over the Orioles in Baltimore.

SEPTEMBER 25   The Red Sox crush the Blue Jays 14–6 at Fenway Park.

Prior to the game, Ralph Houk announced that he was retiring. He had a record of 312–282 in four seasons as manager of the Red Sox.

OCTOBER 17   Wade Boggs puts out a cookbook called *Fowl Tips*. The book contained all of his favorite chicken recipes.

OCTOBER 18   Two weeks before Ronald Reagan wins a second term as president in an election against Walter Mondale, the Red Sox name fifty-one-year-old John McNamara as manager to succeed Ralph Houk. McNamara and Haywood Sullivan had been friends for 20 years, becoming acquainted when both were in the Athletics organization during the 1960s.

McNamara never reached the majors as a player, but his leadership skills were recognized as a minor league catcher. His first job as a manager was in 1959 when he was only twenty-six and he led Lewiston, Idaho, to the Northwest League Championship. McNamara managed in the majors with the Athletics (1968–69), Padres (1974–77), Reds (1979–82), and Angels (1983–84) before arriving in Boston. He managed the Red Sox for three full seasons and part of a fourth before he was fired in July 1988. The low-key McNamara put the Red Sox in the World Series in 1986 and within one out of a World Championship.

1985   B

Season in a Sentence

Expected to contend as an improving young team, the Red Sox need a strong September to reach the .500 mark.

Finish • Won • Lost • Pct • GB

Fifth   81   81   .500   16.5

Manager

John McNamara

Stats   Red Sox • AL • Rank

Batting Avg:	.282	.261	1
On-Base Pct:	.350	.330	1
Slugging Pct:	.429	.406	2
Home Runs:	162		4
Stolen Bases:	66		14
ERA:	4.06	4.15	6
Fielding Pct:	.977	.979	10
Runs Scored:	800		3
Runs Allowed:	720		6 (tie)

Starting Lineup

Rich Gedman, c
Bill Buckner, 1b
Marty Barrett, 2b
Wade Boggs, 3b
Jackie Gutierrez, ss
Jim Rice, lf
Steve Lyons, cf
Dwight Evans, rf
Mike Easler, dh
Tony Armas, cf
Glenn Hoffman, ss

Pitchers

Oil Can Boyd, sp
Bruce Hurst, sp
Al Nipper, sp
Bobby Ojeda, sp-rp
Roger Clemens, sp
Steve Crawford, rp
Bob Stanley, rp
Mark Clear, rp

Attendance

1,786,633 (seventh in AL)

Club Leaders

Batting Avg:	Boggs	.368
On-Base Pct:	Boggs	.450
Slugging Pct:	Rice	.487
Home Runs:	Evans	29
RBI:	Buckner	110
Runs:	Evans	110
Stolen Bases:	Buckner	18
Wins:	Boyd	15
Strikeouts:	Hurst	189
ERA:	Boyd	3.70
Saves:	Crawford	12

JANUARY 14   The Red Sox sign Bruce Kison, most recently with the Angels, as a free agent.

APRIL 8   The Red Sox open the season with a 9–2 win over the Yankees before 34,282 at Fenway Park. Oil Can Boyd was the winning pitcher. The starting outfield of Jim Rice, Tony Armas, and Dwight Evans hit home runs.

The following day, Boyd missed a mandatory workout, claiming the horde of media around his locker following his Opening Day victory blocked his view of the blackboard where the workout announcement was posted. Boyd was fined frequently by the Sox for being late for games, meetings, workouts, and buses.

APRIL 10   The Red Sox score seven runs in the second inning and defeat the Yankees 14–5 at Fenway Park.

The Sox started the season with a record of 4–0.

APRIL 18   Jim Rice hits a homer in the fourteenth inning to defeat the Royals 4–3 at Fenway Park.

Rice batted .281 with 27 homers and 103 RBIs in 1985.

APRIL 20   Marty Barrett hits a grand slam in the ninth inning off Bob James that breaks an 8–8 tie and lifts the Red Sox to a 12–8 win over the White Sox in Chicago.

APRIL 28   Oil Can Boyd strikes out 12 batters, but the Red Sox lose 5–2 to the Royals at Fenway Park.

MAY 3   The Red Sox score seven runs in the fifth inning and clobber the Athletics 10–0 in Oakland. Oil Can Boyd pitched the shutout and struck out 12 batters for the second consecutive start.

              Boyd was 11–7 with a 3.15 ERA and 11 complete games by midseason, but he didn't make the All-Star team. Unable to get the snub out of his mind, he became depressed, lost his confidence, and went from July 14 to September 5 without winning a game. During the drought, Boyd was involved in a scuffle with Jim Rice after complaining about a lack of offensive support. Boyd ended the season with a 15–13 record and a 3.70 earned run average.

MAY 15   The Red Sox' only hit off Mark Langston is a fifth-inning home run by Marc Sullivan, the first homer of his career.

              Sullivan was the son of Red Sox owner Haywood Sullivan. Marc played five years in the majors as a catcher, all with the Red Sox, but played in only 137 games and batted .186, which led to charges that nepotism was the only thing keeping him on a major league roster.

MAY 27   In his first major league start, Steve Lyons hits two homers and drives in four runs in a 9–2 win over the Twins at Fenway Park. Lyons played center field for the injured Tony Armas.

              Lyons played in the majors until 1993 and never had another multi-home-run game. He appeared in 853 major league games and struck 19 homers.

JUNE 1   Rich Gedman hits a grand slam off Frank Tanana in the sixth inning of a 6–0 win over the Rangers at Fenway Park.

              The Red Sox expected Roger Clemens to win 20 games in 1985 after his promising rookie season. Clemens was 6–4 at the end of May when he began to have shoulder problems. He made only five more starts and eventually underwent season-ending arthroscopic surgery in August.

JUNE 3   In the first round of the amateur draft, the Red Sox select pitcher Dan Gabriele from Western High School in Walled Lake, Michigan.

              Gabriele never made it past Class AA. The only future major leaguers drafted and signed by the Red Sox in June 1985 were Todd Pratt (sixth round) and Brady Anderson (10th). Anderson became a star, but the Red Sox traded him to the Orioles after his rookie season. The Sox drafted Tino Martinez out of high school in the third round, but he opted to attend the University of Tampa instead. Martinez was selected in the first round by the Mariners in 1988.

JUNE 9   The Red Sox score seven runs in the ninth inning to cap a 12–0 win over the Orioles in Baltimore.

JUNE 10   A three-run, walk-off homer by Jim Rice gives the Red Sox a 4–2 win over the Brewers at Fenway Park. It was the Sox' eighth win in a row.

JUNE 17   Dwight Evans hits a two-run homer in the ninth inning to defeat the Tigers 3–2 in Detroit.

              The win was the high point of the 1985 season. The club had won 17 of their last 19 games and had a 35–26 record, just 2½ games behind the first-place Blue Jays. The Sox were 52–44 on July 26, then lost 24 of their next 32 games. A 19–9 record in September allowed the Red Sox to reach the .500 mark by the end of the season.

JUNE 23   A bench-clearing brawl erupts in the fourth inning of an 8–1 loss to the Blue Jays in Toronto. George Bell was hit by a Bruce Kison pitch, then charged the mound and kicked Kison in the groin area. After nine minutes of pushing and shoving during which Blue Jays coach John Mitchell wrestled Kison to the ground, Bell was ejected.

JULY 5   Rick Miller fights with fans during a 13–4 loss to the Angels in Anaheim. Unruly fans began to fight with a friend of Miller, prompting the outfielder to jump into the stands to enter the fracas. After leaping over the railing and catching one of the fans in a choke hold, Miller evacuated his wife and son, who were sitting nearby, through the clubhouse.

JULY 11   Al Nipper (5⅓ innings) and Steve Crawford (3⅔ innings) combine on a one-hitter to down the Mariners 7–1 at the Kingdome. The only Seattle hit was a single by Ivan Calderon in the sixth inning off Nipper.

              Nipper missed the early part of the season because of anemia caused by a stomach ulcer.

JULY 18   The Red Sox score eight runs in the eighth inning of a 10–1 win over the Angels at Fenway Park.

JULY 25   Wade Boggs extends his hitting streak to 28 games during a 5–3 win over the Mariners at Fenway Park.

              Boggs reached base in 57 consecutive games in June and July, the ninth-longest streak in major league history. He won his second career batting title in 1985 by hitting .368 with 240 hits, 107 runs, 42 doubles, and 96 walks and led the AL in on-base percentage with a mark of .450. The 240 hits broke a club record, previously held by Tris Speaker, who had 222 in 1912. It was also the most hits by a major leaguer since Bill Terry of the Giants collected 254 in 1930. From May 27 through October 1, Boggs hit .404 in 114 games.

AUGUST 6   The game between the Red Sox and White Sox is canceled by a strike of the major league players. The August 7 game was also called off before the strike was settled on August 8. The two missed games were made up with doubleheaders.

AUGUST 14   Bill Buckner hits a grand slam off Joe Beckwith during a 16–3 thrashing of the Royals at Fenway Park. The Sox had 21 hits in the contest.

Buckner hit .299 with 16 home runs and 110 RBIs in 1985.

AUGUST 29   The Red Sox score seven runs in the eighth inning to cap the scoring in a 17–2 rout of the Indians in Cleveland.

AUGUST 31   Mike Easler hits a grand slam off Bert Blyleven in the sixth inning, but the Red Sox lose 6–5 to the Twins in the first game of a doubleheader at the Metrodome. Minnesota also won the second game, 5–4.

SEPTEMBER 2   Mike Easler hits his second grand slam in three days, helping the Sox to an 11–2 win over the Rangers in Texas. The slam came in the third inning off Chris Welsh.

SEPTEMBER 5   Dwight Evans and Wade Boggs lead off the first inning with homers off Neil Heaton of the Indians to spark the Red Sox to a 13–6 victory at Fenway Park.

SEPTEMBER 7   A three-run homer by Rich Gedman in the eighth inning defeats the Indians 11–9 at Fenway Park.

Gedman hit .295 with 18 homers in 1985.

SEPTEMBER 14   Dwight Evans hits a two-run homer in the eleventh inning to defeat the Brewers 10–8 in Milwaukee.

Evans hit .263 with 29 homers, 110 runs, and a league-leading 114 walks in 1985.

SEPTEMBER 18   Rich Gedman hits for the cycle and drives in seven runs during a 13–1 win over the

Steve Babineau

Originally seen by Sox management as a pinch hitter, at best, Wade Boggs became of the best-hitting third basemen of all time, finishing his career with 3,010 hits and a .328 batting average.

Blue Jays at Fenway Park. He hit a solo homer in the third inning, a three-run triple in the fourth, an RBI single in the fifth, and a two-run double in the seventh. Gedman got his hits off of Jim Clancy, Dennis Lamp, John Cerutti, and Tom Filer.

SEPTEMBER 25   Rookie outfielder Mike Greenwell hits a two-run homer in the thirteenth inning to beat the Blue Jays 4–2 in Toronto. It was also Greenwell's first major league hit.

Each of Greenwell's first four major league hits were home runs.

NOVEMBER 13   The Red Sox trade Bobby Ojeda, Tom McCarthy, John Mitchell, and Chris Bayer to the Mets for Calvin Schiraldi, Wes Gardner, John Christenson, and LaSchelle Tarver.

Ojeda was nearly twenty-eight and had a 44–39 record and a 4.21 ERA with the Red Sox. Club management had all but given up on the notion that Ojeda would develop into a consistent starter, and a stint in the bullpen was a failure. With starters like Roger Clemens, Oil Can Boyd, Bruce Hurst, and Al Nipper on the staff, the Sox believed that Ojeda was expendable. Ojeda was 18–5 with a 2.57 ERA for the Mets in 1986, however, and as fate would have it, met the Red Sox in the World Series and was the winning pitcher in Game Three. Schiraldi pitched effectively out of the bullpen for Boston in 1986, but the World Series wasn't among his finer moments. He was the losing pitcher in both the sixth and seventh games.

DECEMBER 10   The Red Sox trade Mark Clear to the Brewers for Ed Romero.

DECEMBER 17   The Sox trade Jackie Gutierrez to the Orioles for Sammy Stewart.

DECEMBER 20   Coach Tommy Harper receives a letter from the Red Sox notifying him that he had been fired. After playing for the club from 1973 through 1976, Harper had been a coach with the Red Sox from 1980 through 1984 and a minor league instructor in 1985. The previous spring, he had exposed the fact that the Red Sox had allowed white players to receive passes to an openly segregated Elks Lodge in the club's spring-training home of Winter Haven, Florida. Harper's revelations were reported in the *Boston Globe* and embarrassed the team. The club severed ties with the group, which had been inviting players to the lodge since 1966 when the club began training in Winter Haven. Sox management allowed players and other employees to frequent the establishment for 20 years, even though the lodge made it clear that African Americans weren't permitted.

The Sox claimed that Harper was fired for performance-related reasons. Harper believed it was retribution for speaking out. He went to work at a body shop in Boston. On July 1, 1986, the United States Equal Employment Opportunity Commission agreed with Harper's claim and went a step further, claiming the Red Sox fostered a climate of antipathy toward minority employees. The Sox disputed the findings of the commission but eventually settled out of court on December 5, 1986. Harper later served as a coach for the Expos from 1990 through 1999 and again with the Red Sox under Jimy Williams from 2000 through 2002.

1986

B

Season in a Sentence

The Red Sox surprise most everyone by defying the odds to win a division title, perform a miracle to overtake the Angels in the ALCS, and are one strike from a World Championship in Game Six of the World Series, only to suffer a haunting loss to the Mets.

Finish • Won • Lost • Pct • GB

First   95   66   .590   5.5

AL Championship Series

The Red Sox defeated the California Angels four games to three.

World Series

The Red Sox lost to the New York Mets four games to three.

Manager

John McNamara

Stats

Stats	Red Sox	AL	Rank
Batting Avg:	.271	.262	3
On-Base Pct:	.349	.333	2
Slugging Pct:	.415	.408	7
Home Runs:	144		11
Stolen Bases:	41		14
ERA:	3.93	4.18	4
Fielding Pct:	.979	.979	9
Runs Scored:	794		5
Runs Allowed:	696		3

Starting Lineup

Rich Gedman, c
Bill Buckner, 1b
Marty Barrett, 2b
Wade Boggs, 3b
Ed Romero, ss
Jim Rice, lf
Tony Armas, cf
Dwight Evans, rf
Don Baylor, dh
Rey Quinones, ss

Pitchers

Roger Clemens, sp
Oil Can Boyd, sp
Bruce Hurst, sp
Al Nipper, sp
Tom Seaver, sp
Jeff Sellars, sp
Bob Stanley, rp
Joe Sambito, rp

Attendance

2,147,641 (fifth in AL)

Club Leaders

Batting Avg:	Boggs	.357
On-Base Pct:	Boggs	.453
Slugging Pct:	Rice	.490
Home Runs:	Baylor	31
RBI:	Rice	110
Runs:	Boggs	107
Stolen Bases:	Barrett	15
Wins:	Clemens	24
Strikeouts:	Clemens	238
ERA:	Clemens	2.46
Saves:	Stanley	16

MARCH 28   Two months after the space shuttle Challenger explodes, killing six astronauts and teacher Christa McAuliffe, and two months after the Patriots lose to the Bears in the Super Bowl, the Red Sox swap Mike Easler to the Yankees for Don Baylor. Easler, an ordained minister, was traded by the Red Sox on Good Friday.

Baylor was thirty-six years old and had previous postseason experience with the Orioles and Angels. The Yankees were convinced that Baylor could no longer play every day, but he appeared in 160 games for the Red Sox in 1986. He hit only .238, but struck 31 homers, drove in 94 runs, and provided some much-needed clubhouse leadership. Baylor also set an American League record during the season when he was hit by 35 pitches. Overall, the trade of the two designated hitters was a wash. Easler batted .302 with 14 homers for the Yankees in 1986.

APRIL 7   Facing Jack Morris of the Tigers in Detroit, Dwight Evans hits the first pitch of the game for a homer, but the Red Sox lose, 6–5. In his first game with the Sox, Don Baylor collected three hits, including a homer, in four at-bats. Jim Rice and Rich Gedman also homered.

Evans's homer on the first pitch occurred in the 1986 major league season. There were five big league games on the opening day of the campaign, and with a 1:30 PM start at Tiger Stadium, the Boston-Detroit clash was the first of the day.

APRIL 13   The Red Sox rout the White Sox 12–2 in Chicago.

APRIL 14   In the home opener, the Red Sox lose 8–2 to the Royals before 34,764 at Fenway Park. Kansas City broke a 2–2 tie with six runs in the eighth inning off Oil Can Boyd and Bob Stanley.

New Red Sox pitcher Joe Sambito said of Fenway Park, "The toughest thing about the park is getting here. I could see the stadium, I just couldn't reach it." For almost 100 years, countless players and fans have told similar tales about traveling to the park for the first time on the oddly angled Boston streets.

APRIL 17   The day after the United States bombs Libya in response to terrorist attacks, Don Baylor breaks a 2–2 tie in the eighth inning with a grand slam off Steve Farr to put down the Royals 6–2 at Fenway Park.

APRIL 23   Rich Gedman hits into three double plays during a 3–1 loss to the Tigers at Fenway Park.

APRIL 29   Roger Clemens breaks a major league record with 20 strikeouts during a 3–1 win over the Mariners at Fenway Park. Dwight Evans provided the Boston scoring with a three-run homer in the seventh inning over the center field wall off Mike Moore. Clemens had 14 strikeouts in the first six innings, including an American League–record-tying eight in a row. Clemens tied the previous record for strikeouts in a nine-inning game of 19 shared by Tom Seaver, Nolan Ryan, and Steve Carlton by fanning Spike Owen to start the ninth. Clemens then struck out Phil Bradley for the record before inducing Ken Phelps to ground out to end the game. He recorded the 20 strikeouts without walking a single batter. He allowed three hits, one of them a homer by Gorman Thomas in the seventh, and threw 138 pitches, 97 of them strikes. Only 10 balls were put into play, and just two of those were pulled. Of the 30 batters Clemens faced, only on five did he fail to get two strikes. Prior to Clemens, the Red Sox record for strikeouts was 17 by Bill Monbouquette in 1961. The Fenway Park record was 15 by Jack Harshman of the White Sox in 1954.

APRIL 30   Three Red Sox pitchers combine for 16 strikeouts in a 9–4 win over the Mariners at Fenway Park. Bruce Hurst struck out eight batters in 5⅔ innings, Sammy Stewart six in 2⅔, and Bob Stanley in two-thirds of an inning. In the process, the Sox set a major league record for most strikeouts by a pitching staff in consecutive nine-inning games. Combined with the 20 Roger Clemens fanned the previous evening, Sox hurlers struck out 36 Seattle hitters in the two contests.

MAY 1   The Red Sox clobber the Mariners 12–2 at Fenway Park.

Glenn Hoffman began the season as the Red Sox starting shortstop but was on the disabled list from May 17 through September 8 with a mild cardiac condition.

20 K's

When the 1986 season began, Roger Clemens was little known outside of Boston. He was twenty-three years old and had a 16–9 career record and a 3.88 ERA in two seasons cut short by arm injuries. Clemens had yet to pitch a game in the month of September. The Sox believed that Clemens had the talent, ability, and confidence to become one of the best pitchers in the history of the franchise, but many such hopes had been dashed in the past by pitchers who suffered the types of injuries that Clemens experienced in 1984 and 1985. He began the season as Boston's number four starter behind Bruce Hurst, Oil Can Boyd, and Al Nipper.

That all changed on April 29, 1986, when Clemens struck out 20 Seattle Mariners for a 3–1 win before a crowd of 13,414 at Fenway Park. He was the first pitcher in major league history to fan 20 batters in a nine-inning game. At the end of the third inning, Clemens had six strikeouts. From the fourth through the sixth, he fanned eight batters in a row to tie an American League record and raise his total to 14. Clemens struck two batters in the seventh and two more in the eighth to give him 18 and break the club record of 17 set by Bill Monbouquette in 1961. Clemens was one shy of the major league mark. Steve Carlton struck out 19 in 1969, Tom Seaver matched it in 1970, and Nolan Ryan accomplished the feat in 1974, facing the Red Sox.

Clemens was unaware that he was close to a record until Nipper told him at the end of the eighth. Clemens opened the ninth with his 19th strikeout, victimizing Spike Owen, his teammate at the University of Texas. Phil Bradley, who had struck out in his previous three plate appearances of the night, was called out on a 2–2 pitch to break the record. Clemens closed the game on his 138th pitch by inducing Ken Phelps to ground out.

By midseason, anyone with any interest in baseball knew the name of Roger Clemens. He won his first 14 decisions. Clemens gained a national stage in the All-Star Game when he pitched three shutout innings in his hometown of Houston. By the end of the year, he had a 24–4 record, appeared in the World Series, and won both the Cy Young and Most Valuable Player awards.

THE 20 STRIKEOUTS

First inning (three): Spike Owen, Phil Bradley, and Ken Phelps each struck out on 3-and-2 counts.

Second inning (two): With one out, Jim Presley struck out on 0-and-2. Ivan Calderon was called out on 0-and-2.

Third inning (one): With one out, Dave Henderson was called out on 0-and-2.

Fourth inning (three): Owen led off the inning with a single, Seattle's first hit. Bradley struck out on 2-and-2. Phelps struck out on 2-and-2. Don Baylor, making a rare appearance as a first baseman because Bill Buckner was injured, dropped Gorman Thomas's pop foul for an error. Thomas was called out on 3-and-2.

Fifth inning (three): Presley was called out on 2-and-2. Calderon was called out on 2-and-2. Danny Tartabull was called out on 2-and-2.

Sixth inning (two): Henderson struck out on 2-and-2. Steve Yeager was called out on 2-and-2 for Clemens's eighth consecutive strikeout. Owen ended the strikeout streak by lining out to deep center.

Seventh inning (two): Bradley struck out on 1-and-2. Phelps struck out on 2-and-2. Thomas hit a two-out homer to give the Mariners a 1-0 lead. In the Boston half of the inning, Dwight Evans hit a three-run homer off Mike Moore to put the Red Sox ahead, 3-1.

Eighth inning (two): Calderon struck out on 2-and-2. After a single by Tartabull, Henderson struck out on 2-and-2, which gave Clemens 18 strikeouts to break the Red Sox club record. With two out, Al Cowens pinch hit for Yeager and flied to right.

Ninth inning (two): Owen struck out on 1-and-2, and Clemens had tied the major league record of 19 strikeouts. Bradley was called out on 2-and-2 to make Clemens the first pitcher to strike out 20 batters in a nine-inning game. Ken Phelps, who struck out his first three times up, ended the game by grounding to shortstop Ed Romero on a 2-and-1 pitch.

Clemens wasn't just the first pitcher to strike out 20 batters in a nine-inning game, but the second as well. He fanned 20 in defeating the Tigers 4–0 in Detroit on September 18, 1996, in what would be his last victory in a Red Sox uniform. As he did in his first 20-strikeout game, Clemens didn't walk a batter.

Since 1996, only one other pitcher has struck out 20 in a nine-inning game. Kerry Wood of the Cubs became the first National Leaguer to accomplish the feat on May 6, 1998, against the Astros, winning 2–0. While pitching for the Dia-mondbacks, Randy Johnson struck out 20 batters in nine innings against the Reds on May 8, 2001. He left the contest with the score tied 1–1. Arizona won the game 4–3 in 11 innings. Wood and Johnson also accumulated their 20 strikeouts without walking a batter.

The all-time record for strikeouts in a game remains 21 by Tom Cheney of the Senators against the Orioles on September 12, 1962. But Cheney worked 16 innings that night to record his 21 punchouts.

MAY 7   A fight highlights an 11–5 win over the Mariners in Kingdome. It started when Al Nipper knocked down Seattle's Phil Bradley, who rushed the mound. The right-handed Nipper dropped his glove and hit Bradley with a left jab.

MAY 10   Don Baylor hits a two-run homer in the tenth inning to beat the Athletics 4–2 in Oakland.

MAY 14   The Red Sox move into a first-place tie with the Yankees by defeating the Angels 8–5 in Anaheim. The Sox trailed 4–1 after six innings and broke a 5–5 tie with three runs in the ninth.

             The Sox took sole possession of first place on May 15 when the Yankees lost 8–1 to the White Sox in New York. Boston held onto the top spot in the AL East for the remainder of the season.

MAY 16   Bruce Hurst strikes out 14 batters, but the Red Sox lose 4–1 to the Rangers at Fenway Park.

MAY 17   In his major league debut, Red Sox shortstop Rey Quinones hits a pair of RBI doubles off the left field wall during an 8–2 win over the Rangers at Fenway Park.

MAY 18   Steve Lyons has a bad day at Fenway Park. During a 5–4 win in 10 innings over the
          Rangers, Lyons made an error that cost a run, overthrew a cutoff man, messed up
          a sacrifice bunt, got picked off, and ran to the wrong base. Strangely, his base-
          running error led to the Sox victory. Lyons was on second base in the tenth with the
          Sox trailing 4–3 and one out. Marty Barrett blooped a double down the right field
          line that eluded Texas outfielder George Wright, who dove for the ball and held it
          momentarily before it popped loose. As Lyons approached third, he looked back
          and thought the ball had been caught. He headed back to second and arrived at the
          same time as Barrett. Not believing what he saw, Wright began running the ball
          toward the infield as Lyons took off for third again. Wright threw to the bag, but
          the toss was wide. Pitcher Greg Harris backed up the play, but the ball went threw
          his legs and into the dugout. The two-base error allowed both Lyons and Barrett to
          score to give the Sox a 5–4 victory.

MAY 19   With his club leading 8–7 in the ninth at Fenway Park, Twins pitcher Ron Davis
          walks Jim Rice with the bases loaded, then hits Marc Sullivan to give the Sox a
          9–8 win.

MAY 20   Wade Boggs had five hits, including a double, in six at-bats, to highlight a 20-hit
          attack that batters the Twins 17–7 at Fenway Park.

          *Boggs won his third career batting title in 1986 by hitting .357. He also scored
          107 runs, collected 207 hits, smacked 47 doubles, and led the AL in walks with
          105 and in on-base percentage with a mark of .453.*

MAY 25   Roger Clemens is within four outs of a no-hitter against the Rangers in Arlington
          when Oddibe McDowell singles with two outs in the eighth. Clemens settled for a
          two-hitter and a 7–1 victory. The second Texas hit was a homer by Darrell Porter in
          the ninth. Wade Boggs hit a grand slam off Mike Mason in the second inning.

MAY 27   The game between the Red Sox and Indians in Cleveland is called by fog blowing in
          off Lake Erie with two outs in the bottom of the sixth inning with the Sox leading,
          2–0. The umpires instructed Cleveland coach Bobby Bonds to hit a few test fungoes,
          which were lost in the pea soup, after Tony Armas made a remarkable catch to save
          the game. With two Cleveland runners on base, Mel Hall hit a shot into the fog.
          Armas saw it off the bat, guessed where it was going to land, ran back to the fence,
          and caught it out of the sight of almost everyone in the ballpark, perhaps even the
          umpires. After the game, Oil Can Boyd noted, "That's what you get when you build
          a ballpark by the ocean."

MAY 28   The Red Sox crush the Indians 13–7 in Cleveland.

MAY 31   Wade Boggs collects five hits, including a double, in five at-bats during a 7–2 win
          over the Twins in Minneapolis.

          *In a span of 165 games from May 27, 1985, through May 31, 1986, Boggs hit
          .398 with 263 hits in 660 at-bats.*

JUNE 2   In the first round of the amateur draft, the Red Sox select outfielder Greg
          McMurtry from Brockton High in Brockton, Massachusetts.

McMurtry failed to sign a contract with the Sox, opting instead to accept a football scholarship at the University of Michigan, where he was a wide receiver. McMurtry was drafted by the Patriots in the third round of the NFL draft in 1990. He played four seasons with the Patriots and one with the Chicago Bears and caught 128 career passes, five of them for touchdowns. The only player drafted and signed by the Sox in the June 1986 draft who reached the majors was Scott Cooper, who was selected in the third round. The Red Sox drafted Curt Schilling in the second round of the regular phase of the January 1986 draft but traded him to the Orioles in 1988 before he reached the majors.

JUNE 4   The Red Sox defeat the Indians 6–4 at Fenway Park. The victory gave the Sox a record of 36–15 on the season.

JUNE 9   The day after the Celtics win their 16th NBA title by defeating the Houston Rockets in a six-game series, Wade Boggs loses his balance and suffers a cracked rib while removing his cowboy boots in a Toronto hotel room. Boggs smacked his side against the arm of the couch. He was the first of two Red Sox players injured in a hotel in 1986. In July in Oakland, Bob Stanley was hurt while getting a bucket of ice. The top of the ice machine fell on his arm, injuring his wrist.

JUNE 17   Wade Boggs's mother, Sue, is killed in a traffic accident. The vehicle driven by Mrs. Boggs was struck broadside when a cement truck ran a red light. Boggs missed six games because of the tragedy.

JUNE 18   A three-run double by Don Baylor in the ninth inning breaks a 2–2 tie and lifts the Red Sox to a 5–2 win over the Yankees in New York.

Tim Lollar had a winning percentage of 1.000 (in two decisions), a batting average of 1.000 (with a single in his lone at-bat), and a 1.000 fielding percentage (in 11 chances) in 1986, but he was hardly effective with a 6.91 ERA in 43 innings.

JUNE 26   The Red Sox trade Steve Lyons to the White Sox for Tom Seaver.

The swap was made to accommodate Seaver's request to be dealt to a team near his Connecticut home. Seaver was forty-one years old and had a career record of 306–198 when acquired by the Red Sox. In Boston he pitched 104 1/3 innings in 16 starts and had a record of 5–7 with an ERA of 3.80.

JUNE 27   Roger Clemens runs his season record to 14–0 with a 5–3 decision over the Orioles in Baltimore.

JULY 2   Roger Clemens loses his first game of the 1986 season with a 4–2 defeat at the hands of the Blue Jays at Fenway Park. Clemens had a 2–1 lead when Toronto scored three runs in the eighth inning.

During Clemens's 14-game winning streak, he pitched 123 2/3 innings in 15 starts (one a no-decision) and allowed 82 hits with 125 strikeouts and a 2.18 ERA. It's the longest winning streak by a Red Sox pitcher at the start of a season, breaking the previous record of 11 by Roger Moret in 1973, and it's the second longest overall in franchise history behind the 16 consecutive victories by Smoky Joe Wood in 1912. Ellis Kinder, with 13 in a row in 1949, has the third-longest winning streak in Sox history. Cy Young in 1901, Dutch Leonard in 1914, and Boo Ferriss in 1946 have each won 12 in succession.

JULY 10   In a thrilling rally, the Red Sox score four runs in the bottom of the twelfth inning to defeat the Angels 8–7 at Fenway Park. In the top of the tenth with the score 4–4, Ed Romero made a game-saving catch in center field. It was the only time in his 12-year major league career that Romero played the position. California scored three times in the top of the twelfth to take a 7–4 advantage. It was still 7–4 with two outs in the Sox' half of the twelfth when Jim Rice hit a two-run homer to pull Boston within a run. Don Baylor reached base on an error by third baseman Rick Burleson, and Dwight Evans walked before Rich Gedman singled to score Baylor after fouling off five 1–2 pitches. Evans reached third on the Gedman hit, which tied the game, 7–7. Angels manager Gene Mauch brought in reliever Todd Fischer. Before delivering a pitch, Fischer committed a balk by taking his hand out of his glove while standing on the rubber. Evans scored on the balk to give the Sox the 8–7 win.

Oil Can Boyd wasn't on hand for the rally, having walked out on the club earlier in the day. Boyd's troubles began in spring training. Severe weight loss (he was down to 138 pounds) and liver trouble that was diagnosed as a non-contagious form of hepatitis sent him to the hospital for a brief period. Later he was tardy for several workouts and exhibition games, resulting in a fine. On July 10, he went into an emotional tirade in the Red Sox clubhouse upon learning that he had not been selected for the All-Star team. At the time, he had a record of 11–6. Boyd was having financial troubles, and his contract called for a $25,000 bonus if he was an All-Star. He was also snubbed in the All-Star selections in 1985 when he was 11–7 at the break. After ripping off his uniform, Boyd littered the locker room with clothing, verbally assaulted John McNamara and many of his teammates, and threw a cup of soda at Kevin Romine before leaving Fenway Park. When he failed to report the next evening, the Red Sox suspended him and announced he would have to apologize to his teammates before being reinstated.

Boyd did apologize on July 13, but on the night of the All-Star Game on July 15, he had a run-in with police while driving near his suburban Chelsea home. On a tip from informants that Boyd had been involved in a drug deal, Boyd was stopped and searched by two narcotics officers. Boyd began swearing at the officers and threatened to shoot them, although no gun was found on his person or in the vehicle. Following the altercation with police, the pitcher was suspended indefinitely by the club. Boyd subsequently checked himself into the University of Massachusetts Medical Center in Worcester on July 17 for what team officials said was "a comprehensive evaluation including testing for drugs." While he reportedly tested negative for drugs, he was placed in a counseling and support system. Upon leaving the hospital on July 24, Boyd was a passenger when his wife was stopped for speeding. He was arrested again on an outstanding warrant stemming from his own speeding ticket three years earlier, for which he failed to appear in court. The Red Sox finally reinstated Boyd on August 1. He finished the season with a record of 16–10 and a 3.78 ERA.

JULY 15   Roger Clemens is the starting American League pitcher in the All-Star Game and thrills the crowd at the Astrodome and the national television audience with three perfect innings. It was also a homecoming for Clemens, who grew up in the Houston suburb of Katy. The NL came into the game with 26 wins in the previous 29 Midsummer Classics. Clemens was baseball's fastest-rising star, with a 14–0 start to the 1986 season and a 20-strikeout performance in April. He came into the All-Star Game with a 15–2 record. In setting down nine National Leaguers in a row, Clemens struck out Ryne Sandberg and Darryl Strawberry. He was also the winning pitcher in a 3–2 AL victory.

Clemens started the All-Star Game in Houston again in 2004 as a member of the Astros at Minute Maid Park. He began the 2004 season, his first in the National League, with a 9–0 record and was 10–3 at the All-Star break. Clemens's second All-Star start in Houston didn't work out nearly as well as the first, as he gave up five runs in an inning.

Steve Babineau

Roger Clemens exploded into national fame with a spectacular season in 1986, winning 24 games. He would win 20 games five more times in his career, twice more for the Sox.

JULY 20   Don Baylor collects his 300th career home run during a 9–5 loss to the Mariners in Seattle.

               During the 1986 season, Bill Buckner played in 153 games and hit .267 with 18 homers and 102 RBIs despite a pair of aching ankles. He had to ice down his ankles two hours before a game, for an hour or so afterward, and even at home in his spare time. He was always assigned a hotel room near the ice machine on the road.

JULY 25   Roger Clemens pitches a two-hitter to beat the Angels 8–1 in Anaheim. The only hits off Clemens were doubles by Reggie Jackson in the fifth inning and Jerry Narron in the seventh.

JULY 30   Roger Clemens is ejected from a 7–2 loss to the White Sox in Chicago. In the fifth inning with the score 2–2 and a runner on third with two out, Clemens caught a throw from first baseman Bill Buckner and, according to umpire Greg Kosc, missed the bag, which allowed the go-ahead run to score. Angry over the call, Clemens leaped into the air and fell into Kosc. After he learned that he had been ejected, Clemens turned his cap around and went jaw to jaw with the ump before being carried away, horizontally, by Don Baylor and Jim Rice. Clemens was suspended for two days by the American League for bumping the umpire.

AUGUST 2   With the score 2–0 in the favor of the Red Sox at Fenway Park, the Royals explode for 11 runs in the seventh inning off Tom Seaver, Bob Stanley, and Tim Lollar. Kansas City went on to win the contest, 13–2.

AUGUST 10   Trailing 6–4, the Red Sox score five runs in the eighth inning and defeat the Tigers 9–6 in Detroit. Rich Gedman climaxed the rally with a pinch-hit grand slam off Willie Hernandez.

AUGUST 19   The Red Sox trade Rey Quinones, Mike Brown, Mike Trujillo, and John Christensen to the Mariners for Dave Henderson and Spike Owen.

               Henderson and Owen were acquired for the 1986 stretch run in exchange for four youngsters who never developed into valuable major leaguers. Henderson didn't provide much help to the Sox in the pennant race but was the hero in the ALCS against the Angels when he put the Red Sox ahead twice in Game Five with his dramatic homer in the ninth inning and sacrifice fly in the eleventh, and he would have been remembered as a World Series hero for another game-winning homer if Game Six had resulted in a Red Sox victory. Owen was acquired to fill a hole at shortstop that existed all year, but he hit only .183 for the Sox in 42 games in 1986. Spike was not a nickname but Owen's real first name. His full name was Spike Dee Owen.

AUGUST 20   Roger Clemens pitches a two-hitter to defeat the Twins 9–1 at the Metrodome. The only Minnesota hits were singles by Randy Bush and Gary Gaetti in the fourth inning.

AUGUST 21   The Red Sox smash the Indians 24–5 in Cleveland. The Sox scored 12 runs in the sixth inning, 11 of them with two outs, on six hits and five walks, to take an 18–1 lead. Boston batters collected 24 hits. The first six runs were given up by Cleveland starter Greg Swindell, who was making his major league debut. In only his third game as a member of the Red Sox, Spike Owen tied a modern major league record by scoring six runs after reaching base on a homer, three singles, and two walks. Tony Armas drove in six runs, including a grand slam off Jose Roman. Bill Buckner had five singles in six at-bats. Oddly, Wade Boggs was hitless in the contest.

Owen is one of only three players in AL history to score six runs in a game. One of the other two was also a Red Sox shortstop. Johnny Pesky scored six times on May 8, 1946. The third was Joe Randa of the Royals in 2004.

AUGUST 29   Joe Carter of the Indians hits three homers and two singles to lead his club to a 7–3 win over the Red Sox at Fenway Park.

The loss closed the gap between the first-place Red Sox and the second-place Blue Jays to 3 1/2 games. The Sox had led by as many as eight games in early July. From August 30 through September 10, the Red Sox won 11 in a row to all but wrap up the AL East pennant.

AUGUST 30   Roger Clemens earns his 20th victory of the season with a 7–3 win over the Indians at Fenway Park.

SEPTEMBER 5   Jim Rice hits a grand slam off Frank Viola in the third inning of a 12–2 win over the Twins at Fenway Park.

Rice hit .324 in 1986 with 20 homers, 110 RBIs, 39 doubles, and 200 hits in 1986. He never had another good season, however, as his career suffered a precipitous drop. From 1987 through his last season in 1989, Rice hit .263 with 31 homers in 1,098 at-bats.

SEPTEMBER 6   Red Sox first baseman Pat Dodson's first major league hit is a single that starts a ninth-inning rally and downs the Twins 3–2 at Fenway Park.

SEPTEMBER 7   Jim Rice hits his second grand slam in three days. It was struck off Neal Heaton in the third inning of a 9–0 win over the Twins at Fenway Park. The victory was the Red Sox' eighth in a row.

SEPTEMBER 8   The Red Sox erupt for six runs in the eleventh inning to defeat the Orioles 9–3 in Baltimore. It was Boston's ninth consecutive victory.

SEPTEMBER 10   The Red Sox win their 11th game in a row with a 9–4 decision over the Orioles in Baltimore. It was the 22nd win of the season for Roger Clemens.

Earlier in the day, Clemens visited the White House, where he was congratulated by President Ronald Reagan for his 20-strikeout performance in April. Clemens was joined by teammates Don Baylor, Joe Sambito, Al Nipper, and Mike Greenwell, plus broadcasters Ken Coleman and Joe Castiglione and traveling secretary Jack Rogers.

SEPTEMBER 13   Jim Rice goes into the stands at Yankee Stadium after a fan who steals Rice's cap and shouts racist obscenities during an 11–6 loss to the Yankees. The cap was stolen in the bottom of the eighth inning after Rice and Spike Owen collided chasing a foul ball near the left field stands. The fan stuffed Rice's cap into his trousers and took off. Red Sox players, led by John McNamara, followed Rice into the stands. He got his cap back, and the fan was arrested.

SEPTEMBER 18   Wade Boggs extends his hitting streak to 20 games with a 7–1 win over the Brewers at Fenway Park.

SEPTEMBER 19   Tom Seaver injures his knee during a 6–4 loss to the Blue Jays in Toronto.

The game proved to be the last of Seaver's major league career. The injury prevented him from playing in the 1986 postseason, including a possible World Series confrontation against the Mets. Seaver pitched for the Mets for 12 seasons, including World Series appearances in 1969 and 1973. The Red Sox decided not to exercise a contract option on Seaver for the 1987 season. He tried a brief comeback in June 1987 with the Mets but gave up on the notion of pitching again in the majors after a couple of weeks.

SEPTEMBER 21   Roger Clemens wins his 24th game of the season with a 3–2 decision over the Blue Jays in Toronto.

Clemens finished the regular season with a 24–4 record. He led the AL in victories, winning percentage (.857), and earned run average (2.48) and was second in strikeouts (238 in 254 innings). He won both the Cy Young and Most Valuable Player awards. Clemens would eventually win six more Cy Young Awards with the Sox (1987 and 1991), Blue Jays (1997 and 1998), Yankees (2001), and Astros (2004).

SEPTEMBER 28   The Red Sox clinch the AL East pennant with a 12–3 win over the Blue Jays at Fenway Park.

When the Sox clinched the pennant in 1967, thousands of fans swarmed the field, damaging the turf. To prevent a repeat in 1986, eight policemen on horseback entered through the large garage door in center field at the end of the sixth inning and took positions on the exits ramps near the playing field. In the eighth, officers wearing black leather jackets and carrying billy clubs emerged from the dugouts and ringed the field. After the final out, Roger Clemens mounted a police horse and rode behind an officer for a few strides.

The Sox met the California Angels in the American League Championship Series. Managed by Gene Mauch, the Angels had a record of 92–70 in 1986. Mauch was sixty years old and was in his 25th season as a major league manager, and he had yet to lead a club into the World Series. He came tantalizingly close twice. Mauch managed the 1964 Phillies when the club blew a six-game lead in the final two weeks of the season. His Angels in 1982 led the Brewers two games to none in the best-of-five ALCS but lost three games in a row. The Angels were in their 26th season and had yet to reach the World Series.

OCTOBER 7   In the first game of the ALCS, the Angels easily handle the Red Sox 8–1 before 32,993 at Fenway Park behind Mike Witt's complete-game five-hitter. Witt retired the first 16 batters he faced. Roger Clemens, in his first postseason start, was charged with the loss, allowing eight runs, seven of them earned, in 7⅓ innings. The Angels broke the game open with four runs in the second inning.

OCTOBER 8   The Red Sox even the ALCS with a 9–2 win in Game Two before 32,786 at Fenway Park. Bruce Hurst went all the way, surrendering 11 hits. Three California errors opened the door for three runs in the seventh, which put the Sox ahead, 6–2. Marty Barrett collected three hits, including a double, and Jim Rice hit a home run.

Barrett had one of the best postseasons of any batter in major league history. In the ALCS, he collected 11 hits in 30 at-bats. In the World Series, he had 13 hits in 30 at-bats. Four of Barrett's 24 postseason hits were doubles. The 13 World Series hits tied an all-time record. The first two players with 13 hits in a single Fall Classic were Bobby Richardson of the Yankees in 1964 and Lou Brock with the Cardinals in 1968. Strangely, all three players with 13 hits played on the losing side. Barrett's success didn't carry over to his other two postseason appearances, in which he had only one hit in 15 at-bats in the 1988 and 1990 ALCS.

OCTOBER 10   In Game Three, the Angels down the Red Sox 5–3 in Anaheim. Red Sox starter Oil Can Boyd had a 1–0 lead before he gave up a run in the sixth inning and three in the seventh.

OCTOBER 11   The Red Sox are one game from elimination in the ALCS after losing Game Four 4–3 in 11 innings in Anaheim. The Sox took a 3–0 lead into the ninth with Roger Clemens on the mound. Clemens gave up a homer to Doug DeCinces and two singles before John McNamara brought in Calvin Schiraldi with one out. Schiraldi gave up a double to Gary Pettis that Jim Rice lost in the lights. He then offered an intentional walk and hit a batter to score two more California runs and tie the game, 3–3. Schiraldi was still on the mound in the eleventh when Bobby Grich drove in the winning run with a single.

OCTOBER 12   On the brink of elimination, the Red Sox win a breathtaking 6–5 win over the Angels in 11 innings in Anaheim. Rich Gedman hit a two-run homer in the second inning to give the Sox a 2–0 lead, but the Angels score once in the third inning, twice in the sixth, and twice more in the seventh off Bruce Hurst and Bob Stanley to lead, 5–2. The two sixth-inning runs scored on a homer by Bobby Grich that glanced off center fielder Dave Henderson's glove after he lost sight of the ball in the sun. Henderson had just come into the game as a replacement for Tony Armas, who sprained an ankle.

Bill Buckner led off the ninth with a single off Bobby Witt. One out later, Don Baylor hit a two-run homer to cut the California lead to 5–4. Dwight Evans popped up for the second out. Police encircled the field to protect it from the impending celebration. Gene Mauch brought in Gary Lucas to face Gedman, who called time to ask the umpires to have a sign removed from his line of vision in center field. The sign read, "Another Boston Choke." Lucas hit Gedman with his first pitch. It was the first time that Lucas had hit a batter with a pitch in four years. Lucas was replaced by Donnie Moore to face Dave Henderson, who appeared to be the goat of the game for knocking Grich's fly ball over the fence. Moore had a 1–2 count on Henderson, putting the Angels one strike away from the World Series. After a ball on a low pitch, Henderson fouled off two Moore deliveries. On Moore's third 2–2 pitch, Henderson lined a homer into the left field seats for a 6–5 Boston lead.

The Angels tied the game in the ninth, however, on a single, a sacrifice, and another single off Bob Stanley and Joe Sambito. The bases were loaded when Steve Crawford entered the game and worked out of the jam by retiring two hitters.

Moore was still pitching in the eleventh when the Sox scored the winning run. The Sox loaded the bases when Don Baylor was hit by a pitch and Dwight Evans and Gedman singled. Henderson stepped to the plate again and hit a sacrifice fly into center field. Calvin Schiraldi pitched a perfect inning with two strikeouts to earn the save. Crawford earned the victory after posting an 0–2 record in 40 games during the regular season. Crawford also picked up a victory in the World Series.

Three years after serving the home-run pitch to Henderson, Moore took his own life by shooting himself in the head. Moore's agent, David Pinter, said, "Ever since Henderson's home run, he was extremely depressed. He blamed himself for the Angels not going to the World Series."

OCTOBER 14   The Red Sox defeat the Angels in Game Six to even the ALCS at three games apiece with a 10–4 victory before 32,998 at Fenway Park. Both teams scored twice in the first inning before the Sox erupted with five tallies in the third. Spike Owen had four hits, including a triple, in four at-bats. Oil Can Boyd was the winning pitcher.

OCTOBER 15   The Red Sox carry their momentum into Game Seven and win the American League pennant with an 8–1 decision over the Angels before 32,788 at Fenway Park. The Sox took a 7–0 lead with three runs in the second inning and four in the fourth. Roger Clemens went seven innings and allowed a run and four hits. Jim Rice and Dwight Evans hit home runs.

The Red Sox faced the New York Mets in the World Series. Managed by Dave Johnson, the Mets had a regular-season record of 108–54 in 1986, easily winning the NL East, then polished off the Astros in six games in the NLCS. Only two National League clubs since 1909 have won more than 106 games in a season, and the Red Sox faced both of them in the World Series. The other one was the 1975 Reds, who were also 108–54. The Mets were heavy favorites to defeat the Sox.

OCTOBER 18   The Red Sox win Game One of the 1986 World Series by defeating the Mets 1–0 at Shea Stadium when New York second baseman Tim Teufel botches Rich Gedman's routine grounder in the seventh inning, allowing Jim Rice to score the game's only run. Rice reached on a walk and moved to second on a wild pitch from Ron Darling before Gedman's grounder skipped through Teufel's legs. Bruce Hurst (eight innings) and Calvin Schiraldi (one inning) combined on a four-hitter for the Sox.

OCTOBER 19   The Red Sox take a two-games-to-none lead over the Mets with a 9–3 victory at Shea Stadium. The much-anticipated matchup of Roger Clemens and Dwight Gooden proved to be a disappointment, as neither pitcher had his best stuff. The Sox collected 18 hits off Dwight Gooden and four relievers. Dave Henderson and Dwight Evans each hit homers. Clemens lasted only $4\frac{1}{3}$ innings, allowing three runs and exiting with the Sox leading, 6–3. Steve Crawford ($1\frac{2}{3}$ innings) and Bob Stanley (three innings) pitched shutout ball for the remainder of the game. Crawford picked up the win.

OCTOBER 21   Len Dykstra leads off Game Three with a homer on a 1–1 pitch from Oil Can Boyd. The Mets went on to score four runs in the first inning and cruised to a 7–1 win over the Red Sox before 33,595 at Fenway Park. Ex-Red Sox pitcher Bobby Ojeda went seven innings for the victory.

OCTOBER 22   Gary Carter hits two home runs to lead the Mets to a 6–2 win before 33,920 at
              Fenway Park to even the Series at 2–2. The road team won each of the first four
              games. Ron Darling, who grew up as a Red Sox fan in Worcester, Massachusetts,
              was the winning pitcher. John McNamara gambled by starting Al Nipper, who
              hadn't pitched in 18 days and had a 5.38 ERA during the regular season. Nipper
              gave up three runs in six innings. McNamara went with Nipper because he wanted
              Roger Clemens, Bruce Hurst, and Oil Can Boyd available for Games Five, Six,
              and Seven on four days' rest.

OCTOBER 23   The Red Sox move to within one game of a World Championship by defeating
              the Mets 4–2 before 34,010 at Fenway Park. Bruce Hurst scattered 10 hits for the
              complete-game victory.

OCTOBER 25   The Red Sox take a two-run lead into the bottom of the tenth inning and are twice
              within a strike of a World Championship only to suffer a crushing 6–5 loss to the
              Mets at Shea Stadium. The Red Sox touched Bobby Ojeda for a run in the first
              inning and another in the second to take a 2–0 lead. Roger Clemens struck out six
              of the first nine batters he faced and pitched perfect baseball over the first four
              innings before allowing the Mets to score two runs in the fifth to tie the score, 2–2.
              The Sox took a 3–2 lead in the seventh off reliever Roger McDowell. Clemens was
              forced to leave the game at the end of the seventh after breaking a blister on the
              middle finger of his pitching hand. The Mets tied the score at 3–3 with a run in the
              eighth against Calvin Schiraldi, and the game went into extra innings.
                  Dave Henderson, whose heroics had given the Red Sox the storybook come-
              from-behind victory in Game Five of the ALCS, smacked a Rick Aguilera delivery
              over the left field wall to give the Sox a 4–3 lead. With two outs, Wade Boggs
              lined a double to left-center and scored on a single by Marty Barrett. Schiraldi
              retired the first two batters in the tenth. The first World Championship in Boston
              since 1918 seemed to be a certainty. The scoreboard operator prematurely flashed
              a message reading "Congratulations Red Sox." In the press box, Bruce Hurst was
              announced as the MVP of the Series. In the Red Sox clubhouse, NBC-TV crews
              went to work setting up staging to televise the victory celebration. Cameras were
              wheeled in, and plastic was taped to the front of the lockers to protect clothing
              from champagne stains. Twenty cases of Great Western were wheeled into the
              clubhouse. In New England, where it was past midnight, parents were waking
              their children so they could watch the Sox win a World Championship that had
              eluded the region for 68 years.
                  But one of the most bizarre turnarounds in World Series history was about to
              take place. Gary Carter started the string of improbable events by lining a single to
              left. Pinch hitter Kevin Mitchell, who was already in the clubhouse changing into
              his street clothes when called by Mets manager Dave Johnson, singled to center.
              Schiraldi got two strikes on Ray Knight to put the Sox one strike away from the
              title. But Knight looped an 0–2 pitch to center, scoring Carter and sending Mitchell
              to third. Bob Stanley entered the game, replacing Schiraldi. The Sox were again one
              strike away from the championship when Stanley bounced a 2–2 pitch to Mookie
              Wilson to the screen. Mitchell scored to tie the game 5–5, and Knight went to sec-
              ond. On the next pitch, Wilson then bounced a routine grounder to first baseman
              Bill Buckner, but Buckner let the ball get under his glove and through his legs, and
              Knight crossed the plate with the winning run. The Red Sox dejectedly trudged off
              the field as stadium workers hustled to remove all the champagne and television
              cameras from the Boston clubhouse.

McNamara was criticized for leaving Buckner in the game. In each of the previous six postseason victories, Dave Stapleton had replaced Buckner for defensive purposes because of Buckner's painfully sore ankles. The manager also drew heat for removing Clemens too early and leaving Schiraldi in the game to start his third inning of relief. Buckner received a standing ovation from Mets fans before Game Seven and was heckled by mean-spirited Red Sox fans for the rest of his career. Although he played in the majors for 22 seasons and collected 2,715 hits, he will always be remembered for one ground ball he failed to catch. New England's pain and anger over his misplay was so intense that Buckner sold his home in Boston and moved his family to Idaho.

In one of the most horrifying moments in team history, Mookie Wilson of the Mets hits a grounder off Bob Stanley to first baseman Bill Buckner, who will misplay the ball. Ray Knight (22) will score from second base with the winning run, giving the victory in Game Six, and ultimately the '86 Series, to the Mets.

OCTOBER 26   Game Seven between the Red Sox and Mets is rained out. John McNamara had planned on having Oil Can Boyd pitch the seventh game but decided on Bruce Hurst instead with the extra day of rest.

OCTOBER 27   The Red Sox take a 3–0 lead into the bottom of the sixth inning but lose 8–5 to the Mets in Game Seven at Shea Stadium. The Sox scored three times in the second. Dwight Evans and Rich Gedman hit back-to-back homers off Ron Darling, and another run scored on an RBI single by Wade Boggs. Hurst allowed only one base runner through the first five innings but tired in the sixth. Darryl Strawberry hit a bases-loaded single for the first two runs. The tying run scored when Evans, in right field, tried for a diving catch on Gary Carter's blooper but couldn't control the ball.

Calvin Schiraldi replaced Hurst in the seventh, and Ray Knight greeted him with a homer to put the Mets ahead, 4–3. The Mets added two more runs in the inning off Al Nipper to go ahead, 6–3. The Red Sox added two runs in the eighth on a double by Evans, but the Mets countered with two in their half to take an 8–5 advantage. In the ninth, Jesse Orosco retired the Sox in order. Marty Barrett struck out to end the game.

The 1986 Red Sox are the only team in history to be one strike away from a World Championship and come up empty.

1987   B

Season in a Sentence

The Red Sox hope to redeem themselves following the crushing World Series loss, but nearly everything goes wrong in a losing season.

Finish • Won • Lost • Pct • GB

Fifth   78   84   .481 20.0

Manager

John McNamara

Stats

Stats	Red Sox	AL	Rank
Batting Avg:	.278	.265	1
On-Base Pct:	.355	.336	1
Slugging Pct:	.430	.425	4
Home Runs:	174		9
Stolen Bases:	77		13
ERA:	4.77	4.46	12
Fielding Pct:	.982	.980	5
Runs Scored:	842		4
Runs Allowed:	825		11

Starting Lineup

John Marzano, c
Bill Buckner, 1b
Marty Barrett, 2b
Wade Boggs, 3b
Spike Owen, ss
Jim Rice, lf
Ellis Burks, cf
Dwight Evans, rf-1b
Don Baylor, dh
Mike Greenwell, lf
Ed Romero, 2b-3b-ss
Todd Benzinger, rf
Dave Henderson, rf-cf
Sam Horn, dh

Pitchers

Roger Clemens, sp
Bruce Hurst, sp
Al Nipper, sp
Jeff Sellars, sp
Bob Stanley, sp-rp
Wes Gardner, rp
Calvin Schiraldi, rp
Joe Sambito, rp

Attendance

2,231,551 (fifth in AL)

Club Leaders

Batting Avg:	Boggs	.363
On-Base Pct:	Boggs	.461
Slugging Pct:	Boggs	.588
Home Runs:	Evans	34
RBI:	Evans	123
Runs:	Evans	109
Stolen Bases:	Burks	27
Wins:	Clemens	20
Strikeouts:	Clemens	256
ERA:	Clemens	2.97
Saves:	Gardner	10

MARCH 5 — Oil Can Boyd screams obscenities at a Lakeland, Florida, reporter who questions him about money he owed to a store for videotapes he rented but failed to return during spring training in 1986. The Red Sox paid the store $367.20 to settle the dispute.

Boyd was embarrassed when the titles of the tapes were published in the newspaper. The movies included Nudes in Limbo *and* Sexcetera. *The sampling was dubbed "The Can's Film Festival." He spent much of the season on the disabled list with a blood clot in his shoulder and had a 1–3 record and a 5.89 ERA in seven starts.*

MARCH 14 — Both benches empty during an exhibition game against the Mets when Al Nipper hits Darryl Strawberry with a pitch. Nipper was still seething at Strawberry's slow trot around the bases after his home run in Game Seven of the previous fall's World Series. The Red Sox won the game 7–2 in St. Petersburg. Among those in attendance were baseball commissioner Peter Ueberroth and National League president Bart Giamatti.

APRIL 4 — Two days before the season opener, Roger Clemens rejoins the team after walking out on the Red Sox for 29 days in a contract dispute.

APRIL 6 — The Red Sox lose the opener 5–1 to the Brewers in Milwaukee. Bob Stanley was the starter and loser.

APRIL 10 — In the first game of the season at Fenway Park, Bruce Hurst pitches a two-hitter to defeat the Blue Jays 3–0 before 33,679. Jim Rice and Marc Sullivan hit homers. The only Toronto hits were singles by Garth Iorg in the third inning and Tony Fernandez in the sixth.

Fans were unable to get out-of-town scores during the first homestand in 1987 because the nameplates of the other teams on the manually operated scoreboard were stolen. A multicolored videoboard replaced the electronic message board, which had been installed behind the bleachers in 1976.

APRIL 15 — With the Red Sox trailing 4–1 in the sixth inning, Dwight Evans hits a grand slam off Dale Mohorcic to beat the Rangers 5–4 at Fenway Park.

APRIL 20 — The Red Sox celebrate the 75th anniversary of the opening of Fenway Park with festivities prior to a 10–2 loss to the Royals. The club honored the late Tom Yawkey and 11 players. The players saluted were Babe Ruth, Smoky Joe Wood, Jimmie Foxx, Joe Cronin, Ted Williams, Carl Yastrzemski, Jim Lonborg, Carlton Fisk, Luis Tiant, Jim Rice, and Roger Clemens.

APRIL 22 — An RBI single by Dwight Evans in the fourth inning accounts for the only run in a 1–0 victory over the Royals at Fenway Park. Bob Stanley pitched the shutout. It was his first shutout since 1980 and the last of seven he pitched during his career.

APRIL 27 — Don Baylor collects his 2,000th career hit during a 5–2 loss to the Athletics in Oakland. The milestone hit was a single off Curt Young.

MAY 2 — Rich Gedman returns to the Red Sox.

Gedman declared himself a free agent at the end of the 1986 season, unaware that major league owners had entered into an illegal agreement not to sign each other's free agents. Although he was considered to be one of the top catchers in baseball, Gedman received no offers from other clubs and was forced to return to the Red Sox. The rules of free agency stipulated that he could not negotiate a contract with his old club until May 1. Gedman was never again the same player and went into a mysterious and spectacular decline. He had a helicopter swing, where he took one hand off the bat with a distinctive follow-through, but the unique and once-potent batting style betrayed him sometime during the 1986–87 offseason. Gedman had only one hit in his first 31 at-bats in 1987 and finished the season with a .205 average and one home run. He struggled with similar batting averages until the Sox traded him to the Astros in 1990.

MAY 5   Bruce Hurst strikes out 14 batters in a 6–0 win over the Athletics at Fenway Park.

MAY 7   In a charity exhibition game against the Mets at Shea Stadium to benefit Boston's Jimmy Fund and New York's Sandlot Baseball Federation, Bill Buckner receives a standing ovation from the crowd of 32,247 when he bats in the second inning. The Mets won, 2–0.

MAY 17   The Red Sox score seven runs in the seventh inning to take an 8–6 lead but allow the Twins to score two runs in the ninth and two in the tenth to defeat the Sox 10–8 in Minneapolis. The game ended on a home run by Kent Hrbek off Calvin Schiraldi.

MAY 19   Bill Buckner collects his 2,500th career hit during a 4–1 loss to the Royals in Kansas City. The milestone was achieved with a single off Bret Saberhagen.

MAY 25   Ellis Burks hits a grand slam off Mark Huismann to snap a 6–6 tie in the fifth inning, boosting the Red Sox to a 10–6 win over the Indians at Fenway Park.

As a twenty-two-year-old rookie center fielder, Burks hit 20 homers and stole 27 bases in 1987. He was only the third Red Sox player with at least 20 homers and 20 steals in the same season. The first two were Jackie Jensen in 1954 and 1959 and Carl Yastrzemski in 1970. Since 1987, the feat has been accomplished by John Valentin in 1995 and Nomar Garciaparra in 1997.

MAY 27   Roger Clemens outduels Phil Niekro to beat the Indians 1–0 at Fenway Park. Bill Buckner drove in the lone run of the game with a sacrifice fly in the fifth inning.

MAY 28   Dwight Evans drives in six runs on a homer and two singles during a 12–8 win over the Indians at Fenway Park. Joe Carter hit three home runs for Cleveland.

Carter also hit three home runs in a game at Fenway on August 29, 1986. He was the first player in the history with two three-home run games at the ballpark. The only Red Sox batters who have accomplished the feat are Mo Vaughn in 1996 and 1997 and Nomar Garciaparra in 1999 and 2002.

MAY 29   Wade Boggs trades places with Playboy photographer David Mecey. Boggs took nude photos of Playboy Playmate Sandy Greenberg during a shoot with Mecey standing alongside him giving advice. Boggs was the subject of the interview in the July 1987 issue of the magazine. Mecey fulfilled his fantasy by taking batting practice with the Red Sox' third baseman before a game against the White Sox at Comiskey Park. During the contest, Boggs hit a homer into the center field bullpen, breaking the windshield of a car used by the White Sox in promotions. The Red Sox lost, 8–6.

> *Boggs won his third straight batting title in 1987 and his fourth in five years by batting .363. He also topped the league in on-base percentage with .461 and added power to his repertoire. Boggs hit 24 homers. The only other season in his career in which he reached double digits in home runs was 11 with the Yankees in 1994. In addition to the batting title, Boggs collected 200 hits, 40 doubles, 108 runs, and 105 walks.*

MAY 31   A two-run, two-out, pinch-double by Mike Greenwell in the ninth inning beats the White Sox 10–9 in Chicago. The Red Sox trailed 9–2 before scoring two runs in the third inning, one in the fifth, and three in the sixth prior to the ninth-inning rally.

JUNE 1   Dwight Evans collects his 300th career homer during a 9–5 loss to the Twins in Minneapolis. The milestone homer came off Frank Viola.

JUNE 2   A two-out, two-run, walk-off single by Bill Buckner beats the Twins 6–5 at Fenway Park.

> *On the same day, the Red Sox selected pitcher Reggie Harris from Waynesboro High School in Waynesboro, Virginia, in the first round of the amateur draft. Harris was a bust, with an 0–1 record, no saves, and a 4.91 ERA in 121 innings and 86 games in the majors between 1990 and 1999. It was a bad draft year for the Sox. The only other future major leaguer drafted and signed by the club was Phil Plantier in the 11th round.*

JUNE 3   The Red Sox score two runs in the ninth and one in the tenth to defeat the Twins 7–6 at Fenway Park. A walk-off single by Wade Boggs drove in the winning run.

JUNE 10   The Red Sox tie a major league record with two grand slams during a 15–4 win over the Orioles in Baltimore. Ellis Burks hit two homers in the game, including a slam off Eric Bell in the fourth inning. Marty Barrett cleared the bases with a homer off Jack O'Connor in the seventh.

JUNE 17   Roger Clemens strikes out 12 batters during a 4–0 win over the Indians in Cleveland. Mike Greenwell drove in all four runs with a groundout in the second inning and a three-run homer in the eighth.

> *The 29 days that Clemens missed during spring training because of his holdout hampered his effectiveness at the start of the 1987 season. After a 24–4 season in 1986, Clemens headed into his June 17 start with a 4–6 record and a 3.51 ERA in 100 innings. From June 17 through the end of the 1987 season, Clemens was 16–3 and finished the year with a 20–9 record, a 2.97 earned run average in $281^{2}/_{3}$ innings, and his second Cy Young Award. He topped the AL in wins, complete games (18), and shutouts (seven) and was second in strikeouts (256).*

JUNE 24   Wade Boggs runs his hitting streak to 25 games during an 8–7 win over the Brewers at Fenway Park. Boggs hit .485 in 101 at-bats in the month of June.

JUNE 26   The Red Sox blow a nine-run lead and lose 12–11 to the Yankees in 10 innings in New York. The Sox led 9–0 before the Yankees scored 11 runs in the third inning off Roger Clemens and Steve Crawford. The Sox then tied the game 11–11 with two runs in the fourth. There was no more scoring until the Yankees won the contest in the tenth. Jim Rice hit a grand slam in the second off Rich Bordi.

With Bill Buckner still trying to function on gimpy ankles and outfielder Mike Greenwell playing well enough to earn a spot in the starting lineup, the Red Sox moved Dwight Evans from right field to first base in June. Evans hadn't played the position since 1971, when he appeared in four games there at Winston-Salem. He appeared in 79 of his 154 games at first base during the 1987 season and finished with 109 runs scored and a league-leading 106 walks. At the age of thirty-five, he established career highs in batting average (.305), home runs (34), and RBIs (123). Evans hit 13 homers in August to tie a club record for homers in a month set by Jimmie Foxx in 1940.

JUNE 29   Wade Boggs drives in seven runs during a 14–3 win over the Orioles at Fenway Park. Boggs had an RBI single in the first inning, a two-run double in the fourth, and a grand slam off Scott McGregor in the sixth.

JUNE 30   Down 9–4, the Red Sox score four runs in the fifth inning, three in the six, one in the seventh, and one in the eighth to beat the Orioles 13–9 at Fenway Park.

JULY 14   John McNamara manages the American League to a 13-inning, 2–0 loss in the All-Star Game, played in Oakland.

JULY 18   Dave Henderson strikes a walk-off homer in the tenth inning to beat the Athletics 5–3 at Fenway Park. Jim Rice tied the contest 3–3 with a homer in the ninth.

JULY 21   Roger Clemens pitches a complete-game shutout without striking out a batter in a 3–0 victory over the Angels at Fenway Park.

JULY 23   The Red Sox release Bill Buckner.

Buckner signed with the Angels on July 28. He would return to the Red Sox in 1990.

JULY 25   In his first major league game, Red Sox designated hitter Sam Horn hits a home run. The blow, which came in Horn's third at-bat, broke a 5–5 tie in the fifth inning and sparked the Sox to an 11–5 win over the Mariners at Fenway Park. The night didn't start well. He struck out in the first inning and hit into a double play in the third.

JULY 26   Sam Horn hits his second major league homer in his second game during an 11–1 victory over the Mariners at Fenway Park. In Roger Clemens's first start since pitching a complete-game shutout without a strikeout on July 21, he fanned 14 batters.

Horn is the only player in Red Sox history with homers in each of his first two games. The only other batter with two homers after two big-league games was Dave Stapleton in 1980, who hit a pair in his second game. Horn was only twenty-three and looked like an upcoming star after hitting nine homers with a .346 batting average in his first 81 big-league at-bats and 14 homers and a .278 average in 158 at-bats during the 1987 season. He hit 30 homers at Pawtucket before his promotion. The Red Sox gave up on Horn and released him, however, after he hit .148 with two homers in 115 at-bats in 1988 and 1989.

AUGUST 2   Kevin Seitzer of the Royals collects six hits, including two homers and a double, in six at-bats and drives in seven runs during a 13–5 win over the Red Sox in Kansas City.

The Red Sox were 50–30 at home in 1978 but 28–54 on the road.

AUGUST 3   John Marzano's first major league hit is a three-run homer during an 11–2 win over the Rangers in Texas.

AUGUST 10   Sam Horn hits a grand slam off Jose Nunez in the eighth inning of a 9–1 win over the Blue Jays at Fenway Park.

AUGUST 16   The Red Sox wallop the Rangers 12–2 at Fenway Park.

AUGUST 18   The Red Sox collect 20 hits and defeat the White Sox 14–8 in Chicago.

AUGUST 22   Todd Benzinger is injured in an auto accident while driving home from a game. His car was hit by a truck and flipped over three times. Benzinger missed four games with leg and back injuries.

AUGUST 23   Don Baylor hits a grand slam off Steve Carlton in the sixth inning of a 6–4 win over the Twins at Fenway Park.

AUGUST 31   The Red Sox trade Don Baylor to the Twins for Enrique Rios.

Baylor is the only player in major league history to play in the World Series three consecutive years for three different teams. He played in the Fall Classic for the Red Sox in 1986, the Twins in 1987, and the Athletics in 1988.

SEPTEMBER 1   The Red Sox trade Dave Henderson to the Giants for Randy Kutcher.

Henderson was in the last year of his contract, and with a stable full of outfielders, the Red Sox had little interest in signing him. It was a mistake. Henderson signed with the Athletics and was Oakland's starting center fielder, playing between Rickey Henderson (no relation) in left and Jose Canseco in right in the World Series in 1988, 1989, and 1990.

SEPTEMBER 3   In his first start since 1985, Calvin Schiraldi strikes out 11 batters in seven shutout innings, but the Red Sox lose 2–1 to the Twins in 10 innings in Minnesota. Wes Gardner allowed a run in the ninth on Kirby Puckett's two-out homer and another in the tenth on a bases-loaded walk. The Sox infield didn't have a single assist in the game.

Schiraldi appeared in 87 games for the Red Sox in 1986 and 1987, and this was his lone start with the club.

SEPTEMBER 9   Roger Clemens strikes out 12 batters in a 5–3 win over the Yankees at Fenway Park.

SEPTEMBER 15   Todd Benzinger collects seven RBIs on a grand slam and two singles, but the Red Sox lose 9–8 to the Tigers in Detroit. The slam was struck in the first inning off Frank Tanana.

SEPTEMBER 28   The Red Sox blow a 7–0, sixth-inning lead and lose 9–7 to the Yankees in New York. The Sox still led 7–3 heading into the ninth before the Yanks scored six runs. The game ended on a walk-off homer by Mike Easler off Calvin Schiraldi.

SEPTEMBER 30   Roger Clemens strikes out 13 batters in a 7–0 win over the Yankees in New York.

OCTOBER 2   A walk-off homer by Spike Owen in the twelfth inning beats the Brewers, 3–2. It was only the second homer of the year for Owen.

OCTOBER 4   On the final day of the season, Roger Clemens pitches a two-hitter and strikes out 12 batters to notch his 20th win of the season with a 4–0 win over the Brewers at Fenway Park. The only Milwaukee hits were doubles by Mike Felder in the third inning and Dale Sveum in the eighth.

DECEMBER 8   Three weeks after the end of the six-month congressional hearings investigating the Iran-Contra hearings, the Red Sox trade Al Nipper and Calvin Schiraldi to the Cubs for Lee Smith.

The holder of the all-time record for saves in a career with 478, Smith had 180 saves to his credit when the Red Sox acquired him. In Boston, he had 58 saves, a 12–7 record, and a 3.04 ERA over three seasons. Neither Nipper nor Schiraldi were missed in Boston.

1988   B

Season in a Sentence

Trailing by nine games at the All-Star break, the Sox win 19 of 20 in July and August immediately after replacing John McNamara with Joe Morgan, and they win a division title before being swept by the Athletics in the ALCS.

Finish • Won • Lost • Pct • GB

First   89   73   .549   +1.0

AL Championship Series—

The Red Sox lost to the Oakland Athletics four games to none.

Managers

John McNamara (43–42)
Joe Morgan (46–31)

Stats

Stats	Red Sox	AL	Rank
Batting Avg:	.283	.259	1
On-Base Pct:	.360	.327	1
Slugging Pct:	.420	.391	2
Home Runs:	124		10 (tie)
Stolen Bases:	65		14
ERA:	3.97	3.97	7
Fielding Pct:	.984	.981	2
Runs Scored:	813		1
Runs Allowed:	689		7

Starting Lineup

Rich Gedman, c
Todd Benzinger, 1b-rf
Marty Barrett, 2b
Wade Boggs, 3b
Jody Reed, ss
Mike Greenwell, lf
Ellis Burks, cf
Dwight Evans, rf-1b
Jim Rice, dh
Rick Cerone, c
Spike Owen, ss

Pitchers

Roger Clemens, sp
Bruce Hurst, sp
Wes Gardner, sp-rp
Oil Can Boyd, sp
Mike Smithson, sp-rp
Mike Boddicker, sp
Jeff Sellars, sp-rp
Lee Smith, rp
Bob Stanley, rp
Dennis Lamp, rp

Attendance

2,464,851 (fourth in AL)

Club Leaders

Batting Avg:	Boggs	.366
On-Base Pct:	Boggs	.476
Slugging Pct:	Greenwell	.531
Home Runs:	Greenwell	22
RBI:	Greenwell	119
Runs:	Boggs	128
Stolen Bases:	Burks	25
Wins:	Clemens	18
	Hurst	18
Strikeouts:	Clemens	291
ERA:	Clemens	2.93
Saves:	Smith	29

JANUARY 11   The Red Sox sign Dennis Lamp following his release by the Athletics.

Bob Stanley was injured in January, damaging tendons and nerves in the middle and ring fingers of his pitching hand when he slipped on some ice and fell on broken glass at his home. He didn't pitch in a game until May 15.

APRIL 4   On Opening Day, the Red Sox lose 5–3 in 10 innings to the Tigers before 34,781 at Fenway Park. The winning runs were scored on a two-out, two-run homer by Alan Trammell off Lee Smith, who was making his Red Sox debut. Rogers Clemens pitched nine innings and struck out 11. Brady Anderson made his major league debut and collected three hits in five at-bats while batting leadoff and playing center field.

The Red Sox had two television teams beginning in 1988. On WSKB-TV, Sean McDonough and Bob Montgomery were the announcers. The cable telecasts over NESN were handled by Ned Martin and Jerry Remy. Previously, Martin and Montgomery performed on both the over-the-air and cable broadcasts. McDonough and Remy were new to the Sox announcing team. Ken Coleman and Joe Castiglione were still on the radio.

APRIL 8   Marty Barrett and Rangers pitcher Mitch Williams exchange words, then shoves, after Barrett crosses the plate in the ninth inning of a 4–0 win in Arlington. The disagreement developed when Williams threw several high and inside pitches near the heads of Boston hitters.

APRIL 14   Roger Clemens strikes out 13 batters in a complete-game shutout, defeating the Brewers 1–0 at Fenway Park.

On the same day, the Red Sox signed Rick Cerone following his release by the Yankees.

APRIL 17   Mike Greenwell drives in six runs on a three-run homer and two singles during a 15–2 win over the Rangers at Fenway Park. The Red Sox collected 20 hits in the contest.

The Red Sox were 14–6 in April, but that was followed by an 11–16 May. On June 7, the Red Sox were 26–27 and in fifth place, nine games out of first.

MAY 5   The Red Sox swamp the White Sox 16–3 at Fenway Park.

MAY 9   Roger Clemens strikes out 16 batters in a complete-game shutout, winning 2–0 against the Royals in Kansas City. Clemens retired 24 consecutive batters from the first inning through the ninth. The streak was broken by an infield single by Willie Wilson. Clemens allowed a total of three hits in the contest.

Clemens had an 18–12 record and a 2.93 ERA in 264 innings in 1988. He led the AL in strikeouts (291), complete games (14), and shutouts (eight). The 291 strikeouts are an all-time Red Sox record for a season, and the eight shutouts are the most of any Sox pitcher since 1920. Clemens was 15–5 at the end of July, however, before losing all five of his decision in August.

MAY 13   The Red Sox overpower the Mariners 14–6 at Fenway Park.

MAY 21   The Red Sox retired uniform number 1 in honor of Bobby Doerr prior to an 8–4 win over the Angels at Fenway Park.

Doerr wore number 1 from 1939 through 1951. He was number 9 in 1937 and 1938 before yielding it to Ted Williams. While Doerr was in the service in 1945, his number 1 adorned the uniforms of Ty LaForest and Ben Steiner. From 1952 through 1988, number 1 was worn by several players and managers including Fred Hatfield, George Kell, Grady Hatton, Bill Consolo, Jim Mahoney, Herb Plews, Don Buddin, Ed Bressoud, Joe Foy, Joe Azcue, Luis Alvarado, Phil Gagliano, Bernie Carbo, Jim Dwyer, Chico Walker, and John McNamara. After Doerr's number 1 was put in mothballs, McNamara switched to number 2 for the 1988 season.

MAY 27   Dwight Evans collects his 2,000th career hit during the 3–2 loss to the Athletics in
              Oakland. The milestone hit was a single off Curt Young.

              Evans hit .293 with 21 homers and 111 RBIs in 1988.

MAY 30   Roger Clemens pitches while his wife, Debbie, is in labor with the couple's second
              child, and he is the winning pitcher in a 5–2 decision over the Angels in Anaheim.
              Clemens flew to Houston in time for the birth of his second son, named Kory Allen.

JUNE 1   In the first round of the amateur draft, the Red Sox select pitcher Tom Fischer of
              the University of Wisconsin.

              *Fischer was the nephew of Red Sox pitching coach Bill Fischer. He never
              reached the majors, however, peaking at Class AAA. The players drafted and
              signed by the Red Sox in 1988 who reached the majors were John Valentin
              (fifth round), Tim Naehring (third round), and John Flaherty (25th round).*

JUNE 3   Wade Boggs is sued by Margo Adams for twelve million dollars.

              *Adams was a thirty-two-year-old woman from Costa Mesa, California, who filed
              the suit in Orange County Superior Court claiming Boggs broke promises that he
              would support her during a four-year relationship. The suit charged Boggs with
              fraud and breach of oral contract. Boggs's attorney, Jennifer King, called Adams
              "a groupie who feels somewhat rejected and in her obsession has tried to black-
              mail Mr. Boggs." Adams claimed she sacrificed her career to travel the country
              with the Sox' third baseman during an affair that began in 1984 when she met
              him in a bar in Anaheim. The suit sought $500,000 in wages Adams said she lost
              in income and commissions as a mortgage broker while she accompanied the
              married Boggs on 65 road trips in four years. Boggs later admitted that Adams
              was his companion on road trips, but denied there was an oral agreement on an
              amount that she would be paid for compensation. The twelve-million-dollar
              amount was arrived at by Adams by claiming $500,000 in lost income and $11.5
              million for emotional distress. In February 1989, a judge threw out the emotional
              distress petition, reducing the suit to $500,000 (see June 19, 1988).*

JUNE 15   Ellis Burks collects four hits, including a grand slam, in five at-bats to lead the Red
              Sox to an 8–3 win over the Yankees at Fenway Park. The slam was hit off Al Leiter
              in the second inning.

              Burks hit .294 with 18 homers in 1988.

JUNE 19   The Red Sox collect 23 hits and bombard the Orioles 15–7 in Baltimore.

              *Following the Sunday-afternoon game in Baltimore, the Red Sox flew to Cleve-
              land for a series against the Indians. Once in Cleveland, several Red Sox players,
              including Dwight Evans, Wade Boggs, and Rick Cerone, engaged in a shouting
              match that started on the bus from the airport and escalated into a fight at the
              team's hotel. Evans and Cerone fought in the elevator of the Hollendale House
              in front of guests, and the two had to be physically restrained. The verbal joust-
              ing was an outgrowth of the suit filed against Boggs by Margo Adams, who
              claimed she was involved in a four-year affair with Boggs. Adams's attorney*

sought depositions from eight Red Sox players, two wives, and the team trainer in an attempt to prove Adams often traveled with Boggs and should be compensated for giving up her job to travel with him (see July 12, 1988).

JUNE 20   The Red Sox collect 20 hits and whip the Indians 14–7 in Cleveland.

JUNE 21   The Red Sox reach double digits in runs for the third game in a row, defeating the Indians 10–6 in Cleveland.

JUNE 25   The Red Sox break a 3–3 tie with seven runs in the eighth inning to defeat the Orioles 10–3 at Fenway Park.

From June 18 through June 28, Mike Greenwell drove in 22 runs and scored 12 in a span of 10 games. He had 21 hits, including six homers, a triple, and two doubles, in 43 at-bats. Greenwell was only twenty-four when the 1988 season began and hit .325 with 192 hits, 22 homers, and 119 RBIs. He was the runner-up to Jose Canseco in the MVP balloting. Greenwell never reached those numbers again, but he was a solid contributor on Boston teams until his retirement in 1996. During his 12-year career, all of which was spent in Boston, Greenwell appeared in 1,269 games and had 657 runs, 1,400 hits, 275 doubles, 130 homers, 726 RBIs, and a .303 batting average.

JULY 8   Trailing 5–3, the Red Sox score seven runs in the fifth inning to beat the White Sox 10–7 in the second game of a doubleheader in Chicago. The Sox collected nine straight hits in the big inning. The feat was accomplished by Jody Reed, Marty Barrett, Wade Boggs, Mike Greenwell, Ellis Burks, Jim Rice, Todd Benzinger, Rich Gedman, and Kevin Romine.

JULY 9   Playing a doubleheader at Comiskey Park for the second day in a row, the Red Sox explode for six runs in the tenth inning to beat the White Sox 8–2 in the second game. Roger Clemens pitched eight innings and struck out 15 batters. The White Sox won the first game, 8–7. In the fourth inning, Wes Gardner gave up consecutive homers to Dan Pasqua, Greg Walker, and Daryl Boston.

JULY 12   Margo Adams tells her side of her affair with Wade Boggs on Phil Donahue's talk show.

During her appearance on Donahue, *Adams alleged that Boggs devised a scheme called "Delta Force," in which he broke into the rooms of Red Sox teammates and took "compromising" photographs to use as leverage against them. She said she still had the negatives and some of Boggs's photos but did not intend to make them public and would not identify any of the players.*

JULY 14   The Red Sox fire John McNamara as manager and hire Joe Morgan four hours before a scheduled game against the Royals at Fenway Park that was rained out.

In the spring, Red Sox president John Harrington said that if the team wasn't in the pennant race on Memorial Day, McNamara would be fired. That deadline passed with the Sox out of contention, but McNamara wasn't dismissed until just after the All-Star break, with the Red Sox posting a record of 43–42 and in fourth place, nine games out of first. The firing was directed by Harrington and

Jean Yawkey, two of the three members of the club's ownership team. Haywood Sullivan, the third member of the group, objected to the decision. McNamara later managed the Indians (1990–91) and Angels (1996).

Morgan was fifty-seven years old and the Red Sox' third base coach, a job he had held since 1985. A native of Walpole, Massachusetts, in suburban Boston and a graduate of Boston College, he had an 88-game playing career as an infielder from 1959 through 1964 with four big-league clubs. Morgan managed for 16 years in the minors with a record of 1,140–1,102. He was the first native of Greater Boston to manage the Sox since Shano Collins in 1931–1932. To supplement his income during the offseason, Morgan drove a snow plow on the Massachusetts Turnpike, served as a census taker, a toll taker, a substitute teacher, a truck driver, and a debt collector. Morgan was a man who received little respect prior to his hiring as manager. He regularly received autograph requests from fans wanting the signature of Hall of Fame second baseman Joe Morgan. The 1988 Red Sox media guide had Morgan's biography accompanied by a photo of fellow coach Rac Slider. At first, Morgan was named interim manager, but the designation was made permanent after the Sox made an immediate turnaround under their new manager, a phenomenon that was dubbed "Morgan Magic." The club won their first 12 games and 19 of their first 20 under Morgan's direction and overcame the nine-game deficit to win the AL East. The 12-game winning streak was Boston's longest in 40 years. The Sox also won their first 19 home games under Morgan as part of an American League–record 24-game winning streak at Fenway Park.

JULY 15   In Joe Morgan's first game as a manager, Roger Clemens strikes out 16 batters to beat the Royals 3–1 in the first game of a doubleheader at Fenway Park. Clemens fanned 31 batters in consecutive starts, combining with the 15 he posted against the White Sox on July 9. The Red Sox completed the sweep with a 7–4 victory in the nightcap.

On the same day, the Red Sox signed Larry Parrish following his release by the Rangers.

JULY 16   Kevin Romine hits a walk-off homer to beat the Royals 7–6 at Fenway Park. The Sox were down 6–0 before scoring four runs in the sixth inning. Dwight Evans tied the game 6–6 with a two-run homer in the eighth.

The homer was Romine's first as a major leaguer. He played with the Sox from 1985 through 1991 as a spare outfielder and pinch hitter and hit five homers in 630 at-bats over 331 games.

JULY 19   Mike Smithson pitches no-hit ball for 6⅓ innings before giving up two hits and beating the Twins 5–0 at Fenway Park.

JULY 20   Joe Morgan becomes involved in a shoving match with Jim Rice. With the Sox leading 5–4 in the eighth inning, Morgan replaced Rice with pinch hitter Spike Owen, who sacrificed Ellis Burks to second base. Rice stormed back to the dugout and slammed his batting helmet and bat to the ground. Rice made a remark to Morgan, and the two began shoving each other. The Sox went on to win the game in dramatic fashion. Minnesota scored twice in the top of the tenth inning to take a 7–5 lead, but Boston rallied for four runs in their half to win, 9–7. Todd Benzinger ended the contest with a three-run homer.

Rice was suspended for three days by the Red Sox for his shoving match with Morgan.

JULY 21   Oil Can Boyd retires the first 19 batters he faces and allows only one hit over seven innings, leading the Red Sox to their eighth win without a loss under Joe Morgan by a 6–1 score over the White Sox at Fenway Park. It was also the Red Sox' 13th consecutive win at home.

During the game, a Red Sox fan jumped from the stands, ran to second base, and mooned the crowd in a misguided salute to Jim Rice, who was suspended a day earlier. On one of his buttocks was the word "Jim." On the other was "Rice."

JULY 23   Mike Smithson pitches 6 $\frac{1}{3}$ innings of one-hit, shutout relief during an 11–5 win over the White Sox at Fenway Park. The Sox collected 20 hits in the contest. It was Boston's 10th win in a row.

JULY 25   The Red Sox run their record under Joe Morgan to 12–0 by defeating the Rangers 2–0 in Arlington. Roger Clemens struck out 14 batters in the complete-game shutout.

JULY 26   The Red Sox lose for the first time under Joe Morgan, dropping a 9–8 decision to the Rangers in Arlington.

JULY 27   Ellis Burks hits a grand slam off Jeff Russell in the sixth inning with the Red Sox trailing 3–1, sparking a 10–7 win over the Rangers in Arlington.

JULY 29   Jody Reed collects seven hits, including two doubles, in nine at-bats in a 6–4 and 5–3 doubleheader sweep of the Brewers at Fenway Park. The wins ran the Sox streak of wins at home to 18.

Bernstein Associates/Getty Images

Ellis Burks became a star for the Sox in his early 20s, but the team traded him when he was only 27. Fans were pleased by his return in 2004, though at 39 his playing time was limited during the World Championship season.

On the same day, the Red Sox traded prospects Curt Schilling and Brady Anderson to the Orioles for Mike Boddicker. Anderson opened the 1988 season as the Sox' starting center fielder but was sent to Pawtucket in May. Schilling was at Class AA New Britain and had yet to appear in a big-league game. In the short term, this was an excellent trade. If the Sox hadn't completed the swap, it's unlikely that the club would have reached the postseason in either 1988 or 1990. Neither Anderson nor Schilling was ready for the majors by that time, and Boddicker provided a necessary veteran presence to the pitching staff. Over the remainder of the 1988 season, Boddicker was 7–3 with an ERA of 2.68. He followed it up with records of 15–11 in 1989 and 17–8 in 1990.

In the long haul, the deal was a disaster. It took awhile for Anderson to develop into a valuable major leaguer, but from 1992 through 1999, he was among the best outfielders in the American League. In 1996, Anderson hit 50 homers for the Orioles. Schilling too, spent some difficult early years in the majors. Heading into the 1992 season, he had a career record of 4–11 with the Phillies and Astros. From 1992 through 2003, Schilling was 159–106 for the Phillies and Diamondbacks and returned to the Red Sox organization in a trade in November 2003. He became a New England folk hero with a 21–6 record in the regular season in 2004 and three postseason wins while battling a severe ankle injury.

JULY 30   Roger Clemens strikes out 13 batters in a 3–2 win over the Brewers at Fenway Park. The winning run scored on a walk-off single by Marty Barrett in the ninth inning. It was the Red Sox' 19th win in a row at home.

JULY 31   In his first start with the Red Sox, Mike Boddicker pitches 7⅓ innings of shutout ball, leading the club to a 5–0 win over the Brewers at Fenway Park. It was the Sox' 20th win in a row at home.

AUGUST 2   Mike Greenwell hits a grand slam off Jeff Russell in the first inning of a 7–2 win over the Rangers. It was the second grand slam allowed by Russell to a Boston batter in six days. It was also the Red Sox' 21st consecutive win at home, tying the club record set by the 1949 Sox.

AUGUST 3   The Red Sox win a club-record 22nd game in a row at Fenway Park with a 5–4 win over the Rangers at Fenway Park. It was also the Sox' 19th win in 20 games under Joe Morgan and pulled the club into a first-place tie with the Tigers.

AUGUST 7   The Red Sox score three runs in the tenth inning to beat the Tigers 3–0 in Detroit. Bruce Hurst pitched the complete-game shutout.

Hurst had the best season of his career in 1988 with an 18–6 record and a 3.66 ERA. He was 13–2 at Fenway Park.

AUGUST 12 The Red Sox set an American League record by winning their 23rd consecutive game at home with a 9–4 triumph over the Tigers at Fenway Park. The previous record was held by the 1931 Philadelphia Athletics. Jim Rice played in his 2,000th career game and celebrated the occasion by hitting a two-run homer.

AUGUST 13 The Red Sox win their 24th consecutive game at Fenway Park with a 16–4 pounding of the Tigers at Fenway Park. Dwight Evans drove in seven runs with a two-run homer in the first inning, a two-run homer in the sixth, and a bases-loaded triple in the eighth. The Sox scored seven runs in the eighth.

AUGUST 14   The Red Sox' American League–record 24-game home winning streak comes to end when the Tigers thump the Sox, 18–6. Roger Clemens allowed eight runs in $1\frac{1}{3}$ innings. The Tigers led 13–0 in the third inning. It was the Sox' first loss at Fenway since June 24.

The 24 wins were accomplished by two managers. The first five victories were under the direction of John McNamara. The winning streak came at the expense of the Orioles (two games), Indians (three), Royals (four), Twins (three), White Sox (four), Brewers (four), Rangers (two), and Tigers (two). The Sox outscored the opposition 167–77 during the 24 contests. The Red Sox had a record of 53–28 at Fenway in 1988.

SEPTEMBER 4   Larry Parrish leads off the tenth inning with a homer, beating the Angels 6–5 in Anaheim.

SEPTEMBER 5   The Red Sox win 4–1 against the Orioles in Baltimore to take sole possession of first place from the Tigers.

SEPTEMBER 10   Roger Clemens pitches a one-hitter to defeat the Indians 6–0 at Fenway Park. The only Cleveland hit was a single by Dave Clark in the seventh inning.

SEPTEMBER 13   Jim Rice hits a grand slam off Pete Harnisch in the third inning of a 6–4 win over the Orioles at Fenway Park.

SEPTEMBER 14   Mike Greenwell hits for the cycle with a homer in the second inning, a double in the fourth, a triple in the sixth, and a single in the eighth during a 4–3 win over the Orioles in Baltimore. The first three hits were off Jose Bautista and the fourth against Tom Niedenfuer.

SEPTEMBER 18   The Red Sox take a six-game lead over the Tigers with a 9–4 win over the Yankees at Fenway Park.

The Red Sox drew 2,464,851 fans in 1988, breaking the previous record of 2,353,114 set in 1979.

SEPTEMBER 20   Ellis Burks is forced to leave a 13–2 win after his bat breaks and a piece of wood strikes him in the right eye. Burks suffered blurred vision but was back in the lineup the next day.

Wade Boggs got his 200th hit of the season during the game. It was his sixth consecutive season with at least 200 hits, a post-1900 major league record. Those with five straight 200-hit campaigns are Al Simmons (1929–33), Chuck Klein (1929–33), and Charlie Gehringer (1933–37). Boggs's streak reached seven with an even 200 hits in 1989. The all-time record is held by Willie Keeler, who had eight 200-hit seasons in a row from 1894 through 1901. Refusing to be distracted by the Margo Adams scandal, Boggs had one of his best seasons in 1988. Boggs won his fifth batting title, and fourth in a row, by hitting .366. He also led the AL in runs (128), doubles (45), walks (125), and on-base percentage (.476) in addition to collecting 214 hits.

SEPTEMBER 21   The Red Sox play at Exhibition Stadium in Toronto for the last time and lose 1–0 to the Blue Jays.

The Blue Jays opened Skydome in 1989.

SEPTEMBER 23   Down 9–5, the Red Sox score one run in the seventh inning, one in the eighth, and three in the ninth to defeat the Yankees 10–9 in New York. A two-run single by Spike Owen drove in the tying and winning runs.

SEPTEMBER 29   The Red Sox clinch at least a tie for the AL East pennant with a 12–0 win over the Indians in Cleveland. The Sox scored seven runs in the seventh inning.

SEPTEMBER 30   The Red Sox lose 4–2 to the Indians in Cleveland but clinch the AL East pennant when the Yankees and Brewers both lose.

The Red Sox had a six-game lead on September 18 but won the pennant by only one game after losing nine of their last 13 games.

OCTOBER 1   Jeff Sellars takes a no-hitter into the eighth inning before giving up a homer to Luis Medina with one out, which results in a 1–0 loss to the Indians in Cleveland. It was Sellars's first start since June 21, when he was struck on the hand with a line drive. He never pitched another game for the Sox.

The Red Sox met the Athletics in the ALCS. Managed by Tony La Russa, the A's were 104–58 in 1988 and had 13 more wins than any other American League club. It was Oakland's first postseason appearance since losing the ALCS to the Red Sox in 1975.

OCTOBER 5   The Athletics win the opener of the ALCS 2–1 over the Red Sox before 34,104 at Fenway Park. Dave Henderson, Boston's hero in the 1986 ALCS, broke a 1–1 tie with an RBI single in the eighth inning. The hit made a loser of Bruce Hurst, who pitched a complete game and allowed only six hits. Jose Canseco gave the A's a 1–0 lead with a homer in the fourth. The Sox tied the contest in the seventh on a sacrifice fly by Wade Boggs.

OCTOBER 6   Walt Weiss drives in the winning run with a single in the ninth inning off Lee Smith to give the Athletics a 4–3 victory over the Red Sox before 34,605 at Fenway Park. The Sox led 2–0 before the A's scored three runs in the seventh off Roger Clemens, the first two on a homer by Jose Canseco. Rich Gedman homered for the Sox.

During the two games at Fenway Park, Sox fans taunted Canseco by chanting "Ster-roids! Ster-roids!" After the game, Canseco said, "They're chanting rumors," denying the allegation that he used steroids.

OCTOBER 8   The Athletics crack four homers and defeat the Red Sox 10–6 in Oakland to take a three-games-to-none lead in the ALCS. The Sox led 5–0 after scoring three runs in the first inning and two in the second before the A's mounted the comeback. Boston lost at least one run in the sixth when Rich Gedman slid hard into second baseman Mike Gallego in an attempt to break up a double play. Umpire Ken Kaiser called Gedman out for interference. Mike Greenwell homered for the Sox.

OCTOBER 9   The Athletics defeat the Red Sox 4–1 in Oakland to complete the four-game sweep of the ALCS. Ex–Red Sox pitcher Dennis Eckersley saved all four games for the A's, yielding only one hit in six shutout innings. He was named series MVP. The A's lost to the Dodgers in the World Series in five games.

The flight back to Boston turned into a drunken round of recrimination. Bruce Hurst, a devout Mormon, left the plane during a layover when he felt his teammates got out of hand. Hurst never pitched for the Red Sox again, leaving the club for the Padres via free agency for less money than offered by the Sox.

DECEMBER 8   A month after George Bush defeats Massachusetts governor Michael Dukakis in the presidential election, the Red Sox trade Spike Owen and Dan Gakeler to the Expos for John Dopson and Luis Rivera. On the same day, Bruce Hurst signed a free-agent contract with the Padres.

Hurst was coming off of an 18–6 season, and his loss put a hole in the Sox starting rotation that was difficult to fill. Over the next four seasons with San Diego, Hurst had a record of 55–37.

DECEMBER 13   The Red Sox trade Todd Benzinger, Jeff Sellars, and Luis Vasquez to the Reds for Nick Esasky and Rob Murphy.

DECEMBER 28   Wade Boggs is cut in the neck by two assailants in Gainesville, Florida.

Boggs was cut in the neck and threatened by a man at knifepoint. The inch-long cut was not serious enough to warrant medical attention. Police charged George Young Jr., twenty-three, with armed burglary and two counts of aggravated robbery. Edward Benjamin Cox, thirty-one, was charged with aggravated assault and carrying a concealed weapon. Boggs said he was in his Jeep outside a Gainesville bar showing a handgun to two friends when two men blocked them with their vehicle. Young got out of the car carrying a knife and Cox waved a revolver at Boggs and his friends. Young jumped into the back seat of the Jeep and held a knife to Boggs's throat. In an interview with the press, Boggs said that he used transcendental meditation to will himself invisible. Young was sentenced to 25 years in prison in July 1989.

1989   B

Season in a Sentence

"Morgan Magic" runs its course, and the Sox finish in third place.

Finish • Won • Lost • Pct • GB

Third   83   79   .512   6.0

Manager

Joe Morgan

Stats   Red Sox • AL • Rank

	Red Sox	AL	Rank
Batting Avg:	.277	.261	1
On-Base Pct:	.355	.329	1
Slugging Pct:	.403	.384	1
Home Runs:	108		12
Stolen Bases:	56		14
ERA:	4.01	3.88	10
Fielding Pct:	.980	.980	8
Runs Scored:	774		1
Runs Allowed:	735		10

Starting Lineup

Rick Cerone, c
Nick Esasky, 1b
Marty Barrett, 2b
Wade Boggs, 3b
Jody Reed, ss
Mike Greenwell, lf
Ellis Burks, cf
Danny Heep, rf
Dwight Evans, dh-rf
Luis Rivera, ss
Kevin Romine, cf-rf
Rich Gedman, c
Jim Rice, dh

Pitchers

Roger Clemens, sp
Mike Boddicker, sp
John Dopson, sp
Wes Gardner, sp
Lee Smith, rp
Rob Murphy, rp
Bob Stanley, rp
Dennis Lamp, rp
Mike Smithson, rp

Attendance

2,510,012 (fifth in AL)

Club Leaders

Batting Avg:	Boggs	.330
On-Base Pct:	Boggs	.430
Slugging Pct:	Esasky	.500
Home Runs:	Esasky	30
RBI:	Esasky	106
Runs:	Boggs	113
Stolen Bases:	Burks	21
Wins:	Clemens	17
Strikeouts:	Clemens	230
ERA:	Clemens	3.13
Saves:	Smith	25

JANUARY 9   Carl Yastrzemski is elected to the Hall of Fame on the first ballot. Formal induction ceremonies were held at Cooperstown on July 23.

FEBRUARY 13   Bucky Dent's "Little Fenway" opens in Delray Beach, Florida.

Built to almost identical scale as the real Fenway (without the 35,000 seats), Dent's mini-Fenway is the centerpiece of his baseball school. The numbers on the Little Fenway scoreboard represent those on October 2, 1978, just prior to Dent's home run, which defeated the Red Sox and contributed to one of the worst days ever for the Red Sox Nation. Mike Torrez, who surrendered Dent's 1978 homer, gleefully participated in the grand opening of Little Fenway, going so far as to pitch to Dent again to christen the park. Dent hit Torrez's fifth pitch onto the screen in left center.

MARCH 17   Joe Morgan creates controversy by missing an exhibition game against the Phillies to fly back to Massachusetts, where he was the grand marshall of the St. Patrick's Day parade in his hometown of Walpole. A few weeks earlier, he left the Red Sox camp in Winter Haven to attend a Communion breakfast at Boston College, his alma mater.

MARCH 24   With the suit filed by Margo Adams still pending in court, Wade Boggs tells his side of the affair to Barbara Walters on the ABC-TV program 20-20. Boggs was joined by his wife, Debbie, for part of the interview.

Boggs opened himself up to further ridicule by stating that he was addicted to sex. Boggs said that he came to the realization while watching Geraldo Rivera's program about oversexed people. Meanwhile, Adams countered by posing nude and granting a two-part interview in the April and May issues of Penthouse magazine. In the interviews, Adams related many negative comments attributed to Boggs about his Red Sox teammates. There were several clubhouse meetings during spring training to clear the air between Boggs and peeved teammates (see December 8, 1989).

APRIL 3   In the season opener, the Red Sox lose 5–4 to the Orioles in 11 innings in Baltimore. Roger Clemens blew a lead, and Lee Smith pulled a groin muscle warming up. In the eleventh, Morgan employed a five-man infield by bringing Mike Greenwell in from left field to a position between the second baseman and shortstop with one out and Orioles runners on first and third. Craig Worthington foiled the strategy by blooping a single into left-center field for the winning run. Greenwell homered earlier in the game. Newly elected President George Bush threw out the ceremonial first pitch. He wore the first baseman's mitt he used while playing for Yale University in 1947 and 1948 on two clubs that were runners-up in the College World Series.

Greenwell hit a homer in each of the first three games of the 1989 season. He finished the season with 14 homers, 95 RBIs, and a .308 batting average.

APRIL 9   Down 4–0 after three innings and 5–2 after six, the Red Sox rally to win 8–6 against the Royals in Kansas City. It was the Red Sox' first win of 1989 after opening the season with four straight losses.

APRIL 10   The Red Sox win their season opener by defeating the Indians 5–2 before 32,909 at Fenway Park. In his first game with the Red Sox in Boston, Nick Esasky hit a home run.

In pregame ceremonies, Wade Boggs was given a standing ovation despite his admission of an extramarital affair. Roger Clemens was booed heavily for alienating fans because of his offseason remarks stating that he was unhappy in Boston. Clemens said that the area didn't provide the family atmosphere he desired and that he believed the team didn't do enough to protect his family from rowdy fans. Clemens also complained that he had to carry his own luggage. In addition, Clemens said that if reporters didn't stop writing about his family, "Somebody's going to get hurt."

APRIL 25   The Red Sox pummel the White Sox 11–0 at Fenway Park.

In 1989, the old press box was gutted to make room for the 600 Club behind home plate, and a new press box was built on top of the 600 Club, giving sportswriters a perch 100 feet above the batter's box. The 600 Club consisted of luxury boxes to give the Sox more revenue and has been often criticized for altering the unique character of Fenway Park. The 600 Club was renamed the .406 Club in honor of Ted Williams (for his batting average in 1941) in 2004.

APRIL 28   Nick Esasky hits a grand slam off Kevin Brown in the first inning to put the Red Sox up 5–0 against the Rangers in Arlington, but the Texas club rallies to tie the game 6–6 before it's called by curfew at the end of the tenth inning at 1:21 AM. Rain held up play for over two hours. The contest was completed the following evening and resulted in a 7–6 Boston loss in 12 innings. The Sox won the regularly scheduled game, 8–5.

MAY 1   The Red Sox score seven runs in the first inning to beat the Twins 13–6 in Minneapolis.

MAY 12   Roger Clemens pitches a two-hitter to defeat the Mariners 2–0 at the Kingdome. The only Seattle hits were a single by Harold Reynolds in the first inning and a double by Jim Presley in the eighth.

MAY 19   Dwight Evans hits a grand slam off Dennis Eckersley in the tenth inning to lift the Red Sox to a 7–4 win over the Athletics in Oakland.

            At the age of thirty-seven, Evans hit .285 with 20 homers and 100 RBIs in 1989.

MAY 25   The Red Sox take sole possession of first place with a 10–0 win over the Mariners at Fenway Park.

            The Sox took first with a less-than-overwhelming record of 22–21. The stay at the top of the AL East ended the next day. By June 28, the Sox dropped to 34–39.

JUNE 4   The Red Sox blow a 10-run lead and lose 13–11 in 12 innings to the Blue Jays at Fenway Park. It was the biggest blown lead in the history of the franchise. The Sox took a 10–0 advantage with two runs in the sixth inning, but Toronto scored two in the seventh, four in the eighth, and five in the ninth to move ahead 11–10. The Sox sent the game into extra innings with a tally in the ninth, but the Jays scored two in the twelfth on a homer by Junior Felix for the win. The pitchers who surrendered the lead were Mark Smithson, Bob Stanley, Rob Murphy, Lee Smith, and Dennis Lamp.

            A superstitious sort, Murphy refused to pitch unless he was wearing black underwear. His grandfather, Frank Ashley, was a track announcer at Churchill Downs, Arlington Park, and Oaklawn Park. Murphy became nationally known in horse-racing circles for setting up a computer program used to cross-check the lineage of racehorses, and he served as a bloodstock agent for clients interested in purchasing thoroughbreds. He often handicapped horses while sitting in the Red Sox bullpen.

JUNE 5   In the first round of the amateur draft, the Red Sox select outfielder Greg Blosser from Sarasota High School in Sarasota, Florida.

            Blosser proved to be a waste of a first-round pick by playing two seasons in the majors in which he appeared in 22 games and hit .077 in 39 at-bats. Fortunately, the Sox had two first-round choices in 1989 and used the second one to obtain Seton Hall University first baseman Mo Vaughn, who hailed from Norwalk, Connecticut. It was an excellent draft year for the Sox. Other future major leaguers drafted and signed by the club included Eric Wedge (third round), Jeff Bagwell (fourth round), Paul Quantrill (sixth round), and Greg Hansell (tenth round). Bagwell proved to be the best of the bunch, but the Red Sox traded him before he reached the majors (see August 31, 1990).

JUNE 10 — The Red Sox rock the Yankees 14–8 in New York.

JUNE 13 — Joe Dopson sets a club record and ties an American League mark by committing four balks, but the Red Sox recover to win 8–7 against the Tigers at Fenway Park.

JUNE 16 — Roger Clemens pitches a two-hitter and strikes out 12 batters to defeat the White Sox 2–0 at Comiskey Park. Both Boston runs scored in the ninth inning. The only White Sox hits were singles by Steve Lyons in the fourth inning and Ozzie Guillen in the seventh.

> *Clemens had a 17–11 record, compiled a 3.13 ERA, and struck out 230 batters in 253 $\frac{1}{3}$ innings in 1989.*

JUNE 17 — Dwight Evans hits a grand slam off Melido Perez in the third inning of a 6–1 win over the White Sox in Chicago.

JUNE 22 — In the fourth inning of a 9–1 loss to the Rangers at Fenway Park, Mike Smithson hits Rafael Palmeiro with a pitch. Palmeiro took a couple of steps toward the mound and was intercepted by Sox catcher Rick Cerone. The entire Rangers team poured out of the dugout, but only a handful of Red Sox left the bench. After the contest, Mike Greenwell called his teammates "wimps and fairies."

JUNE 30 — The Red Sox play at Skydome in Toronto for the first time and beat the Blue Jays, 3–1.

JULY 2 — Danny Heep hits a three-run, pinch-hit homer in the eleventh inning that defeats the Blue Jays 4–1 in Toronto. Kevin Romine collected five hits, including two doubles, in five at-bats and started the rally in the eleventh inning with a single.

JULY 11 — Bo Jackson and Wade Boggs lead off the first inning of the All-Star Game with homers off Rick Reuschel. At the time, former president Ronald Reagan was the guest announcer on television. The two blows tied the score 2–2, and the AL went on to win 5–3 at Anaheim Stadium.

> *Boggs collected 205 hits in 1989. It was his seventh consecutive season with at least 200 hits, which extended his major league record. Boggs led the league in runs (113), doubles (51), and on-base percentage (.430). He hit .330 and drew 107 walks. It was the fourth consecutive season in which Boggs had at least 200 hits and 100 walks to break a record set by Lou Gehrig, who accomplished the feat three seasons in a row from 1930 through 1932.*

JULY 24 — The Red Sox' scheduled exhibition game against the Reds in Cooperstown is canceled when the Reds are unable to arrive in time because their plane was grounded in Montreal with hydraulic problems. The Sox played a seven-inning intrasquad game instead.

JULY 25 — Wade Boggs ties a club record with four extra-base hits during a 10–0 win over the Royals at Fenway Park. Boggs collected three doubles and a triple.

JULY 29 — Mike Smithson (eight innings) and Rob Murphy (one inning) team up on a two-hitter to defeat the Indians 5–0 at Municipal Stadium. The only Cleveland hits were singles by Pete O'Brien in the fourth inning and Jerry Browne in the fifth.

AUGUST 1   The Red Sox win a doubleheader from the Orioles 5–3 and 6–2 at Fenway Park to pull within one game of first place. Boston had a record of 52–51.

                The Sox reduced Baltimore's nine-game lead of July 19 to just one, but Boston could get no closer to the AL East lead.

AUGUST 2   With a chance to take first place with a victory, the Red Sox hold a 6–0 lead over the Orioles at the end of the fifth inning, but the Sox wind up losing 9–8 at Fenway Park.

AUGUST 5   The Red Sox score seven runs in the seventh inning to defeat the Indians 10–2 at Fenway Park.

AUGUST 6   Carl Yastrzemski's number 8 is officially retired in ceremonies before a 6–2 win against the Indians at Fenway Park.

                Yastrzemski's number 8 had been unofficially retired since he played his last game in 1983. He joined three others whose numbers had been previously retired. They were Ted Williams (9), Joe Cronin (4), and Bobby Doerr (1). The numbers were posted on the facing of the right field roof in 9-4-1-8 order until someone pointed out that the date 9-4-18 was the day prior to the first game of the 1918 World Series, the last time the Sox claimed the world title. Between the 1997 and 1998 seasons, the Red Sox took down the numbers and ordered them numerically.

AUGUST 7   The Red Sox purchase Greg Harris from the Phillies.

                The Sox were Harris's sixth team in a career that started in 1981. Often confused with another Greg Harris who pitched in the big leagues from 1988 through 1995, he played for the Red Sox until 1994 as both a reliever and a starter. In 1993, Harris set the club record for games pitched in a season with 80. Although a right-handed pitcher, he was ambidextrous. In his final major league appearance with the Expos in 1995, Harris pitched both right-handed and left-handed using a specially made six-fingered glove.

AUGUST 19   The Red Sox defeat the Brewers 3–1 in 14 innings in Milwaukee. A bases-loaded single by Ellis Burks provided the winning runs.

AUGUST 20   Mike Greenwell extends his hitting streak to 21 games during a 6–3 loss to the Brewers in Milwaukee.

AUGUST 27   Ellis Burks hits a grand slam off Brian DuBois in the fifth inning of a 7–1 win over the Tigers at Fenway Park. Wes Gardner had to leave the game in the fifth when he was hit in the face by a line drive, resulting in a fractured cheekbone. Gardner was out of action for the remainder of the year.

                The Red Sox topped the 2.5 million mark in attendance for the first time, drawing a final figure of 2,510,012.

AUGUST 29   The Red Sox sweep the Angels 8–4 and 13–5 at Fenway Park to extend their winning streak to nine games. The Sox scored nine runs in the fourth inning of the second game.

The winning streak gave Boston a 67–65 record. The club was four games out of first. An eight-game losing streak from September 5 through 13 dispelled any notions of a division title, however.

AUGUST 31   Roger Clemens strikes out 13 batters in a 5–2 win over the Angels at Fenway Park.

SEPTEMBER 10   Pitcher Joe Price is suspended for four days after cursing Joe Morgan following a 14-inning, 2–1 loss to the Angels in Anaheim.

SEPTEMBER 19   Mike Greenwell suffers thigh and facial injuries when struck by a grounds-crew cart at Skydome in Toronto. Greenwell missed one game.

SEPTEMBER 26   The Red Sox score eight runs in the first inning and defeat the Yankees 9–5 in New York.

Near the end of the season, the Red Sox announced that they wouldn't pick up the option on Jim Rice's contract for the 1990 season. In 1989, Rice didn't play after August 3 because of a bad elbow. He hit .234 with three homers in 209 at-bats. Rice hoped to hook up with another club, but no one called. The relationship between Rice and the Sox was cool for several years, but he was later hired by the club as a hitting instructor and served as a coach at the major league level from 1994 through 2000. Bob Stanley also played in his last big-league game in 1989 and announced his retirement.

NOVEMBER 7   Three weeks after the San Francisco earthquake interrupts the World Series, Nick Esasky signs a free-agent contract with the Braves.

It appeared as though the Red Sox had found the right-handed, power-hitting first baseman they desired when Esasky hit 30 homers, drove in 108 runs, and batted .277 in his first season with the club. Esasky's stay in Boston lasted only one year. He was from suburban Atlanta and turned down a long-term deal in order to play for the Braves. Esasky played only nine big-league games after 1989, however, after developing problems with vertigo caused by an ear infection.

NOVEMBER 27   The Red Sox sign Tony Peña, most recently with the Cardinals, as a free agent.

Peña was the Red Sox' starting catcher from 1990 through 1993. Peña's signature move was stretching out one leg and setting up a target as low as possible. It helped him win four Gold Gloves, one of them with the Red Sox.

DECEMBER 6   The Red Sox sign Jeff Reardon, most recently with the Twins, as a free agent.

A native of Dalton, Massachusetts, Reardon spent three seasons with the Red Sox and saved 88 games.

DECEMBER 7   Oil Can Boyd signs a free-agent contract with the Expos.

DECEMBER 8   Wade Boggs settles his palimony case with Margo Adams out of court for an undisclosed amount.

BOSTON RED SOX
THE 1990s

THE STATE OF THE RED SOX

The Red Sox were 814–741 during the 1990s for a winning percentage of .523, fourth best in the league behind the Yankees (851–702), Indians (823–728), and White Sox (816–735). Boston reached the postseason as AL East champs in 1990 and 1995 and was the wild card in both 1998 and 1999. The Sox played in the American League Championship Series in 1990 and 1999 and lost on both occasions. AL champs during the 1990s were the Athletics (1990), Twins (1991), Blue Jays (1992 and 1993), Indians (1995 and 1997), and Yankees (1996, 1998, and 1999). AL East title holders, besides the Sox, were the Blue Jays (1991, 1992, and 1993), Yankees (1996, 1998, and 1999), and Orioles (1997). There were no champions in 1994 because of the player's strike.

THE BEST TEAM

In terms of winning percentage, the best club was the 1995 club, which had a record of 86–58 (.597) in the strike-delayed season before losing the Division Series in a sweep against the Indians. The 1999 club was 94–68 and made it to the ALCS before losing to the Yankees in five games.

THE WORST TEAM

The 1992 Red Sox were 73–89 under first-year manager Butch Hobson and finished seventh in the seven-team AL East.

THE BEST MOMENT

In one of his final games as a member of the Red Sox, Roger Clemens struck out 20 batters for the second time in his career, defeating the Tigers 4–2 in Detroit on September 17, 1996.

THE WORST MOMENT

The Red Sox lost the 1999 ALCS to the hated Yankees in part because the umpires blew two crucial calls, which they later admitted to.

THE ALL–DECADE TEAM · YEARS WITH BRS

Tony Peña, c	1990–93
Mo Vaughn, 1b	1991–98
Jody Reed, 2b	1987–92
Wade Boggs, 3b	1982–92
Nomar Garciaparra, ss	1996–2004
Mike Greenwell, lf	1985–96
Ellis Burks, cf	1987–92
Tom Brunansky, rf	1990–92, 1994
Reggie Jefferson, dh	1995–99
Roger Clemens, p	1984–96
Pedro Martinez, p	1998–2004
Tim Wakefield, p	1995–2005
Tom Gordon, p	1996–99

Boggs is in the Hall of Fame, and Clemens is a first-ballot lock. Both Martinez and Garciaparra are well on their way to eventual enshrinement at Cooperstown. Clemens and Boggs were also on the 1980s All-Decade team. Shortstop–third baseman John Valentin (1992–2001), outfielder Troy O'Leary (1995–2001), and third baseman Tim Naehring (1991–97) played significant roles for the Red Sox during the decade. Center field, right field, and designated hitter were trouble spots for the Sox throughout most of the decade.

THE DECADE LEADERS

Batting Avg:	Garciaparra	.322
On-Base Pct:	Vaughn	.394
Slugging Pct:	Vaughn	.542
Home Runs:	Vaughn	230
RBI:	Vaughn	752
Runs:	Vaughn	628
Stolen Bases:	Garciaparra	53
Wins:	Clemens	97
Strikeouts:	Clemens	1,375
ERA:	Clemens	3.05
Saves:	Reardon	88

THE HOME FIELD

The Orioles opened Camden Yards in 1992, which caused a revolution in baseball. The "retro" ballpark was an immediate hit, and most clubs in baseball wanted something similar. The Red Sox were no exception. Even though the Sox had a genuinely "retro" ballpark, club owner John Harrington believed that the club would have to move from Fenway Park to meet escalating payroll costs and remain competitive, and he began petitioning state and city legislators for the funds to build a "new Fenway" in 1994. A financing strategy and design plans for a new ballpark, to be built south of Fenway Park, were unveiled in 1999. As with such movements in the past, the old Fenway won out.

THE GAME YOU WISH YOU HAD SEEN

The All-Star Game in 1999 with an emotion-packed pregame ceremony that featured 41 legends of the past, including Ted Williams.

THE WAY THE GAME WAS PLAYED

Baseball experienced one of its pivotal transitions during the 1990s, as offensive numbers soared to new heights. Fueled by expansion to 30 teams and newer ballparks with fences closer to home plate, the average number of home runs in the AL increased from 123 per team in 1989 to 188 per team in 1999, with a peak of 196 in 1996. The average number of runs per game leaped from 8.6 in 1989 to 10.4 in 1999, with a high of 10.8 in 1996. The trend of the 1970s and 1980s toward artificial turf ended as every new ballpark that opened or was on the drawing board had a grass field. The new ballparks, beginning with Camden Yards in Baltimore in 1992, had "retro" features that tried to emulate the older, classic venues like Fenway Park. Four new teams were added: in Miami, Denver, St. Petersburg, and Phoenix. Beginning in 1994, there were three divisions in each league, adding a new tier of playoffs.

THE MANAGEMENT

The decade began with the three-headed ownership team of Jean Yawkey, Haywood Sullivan, and John Harrington. The three often had trouble agreeing on the time of day, much less the direction of the team. Yawkey died in 1992, and Sullivan agreed to a buyout in 1993, leaving Harrington in control of the club. General managers were Lou Gorman (1984–94) and Dan Duquette (1994–2002).

Directing the club from the dugout were Joe Morgan (1988–91), Butch Hobson (1992–94), Kevin Kennedy (1995–96), and Jimy Williams (1997–2001).

THE BEST PLAYER MOVE

The best move was the selection of Nomar Garciaparra in the first round of the 1994 amateur draft. The best trade brought Pedro Martinez from the Expos for Carl Pavano and Tony Armas Jr. in December 1997.

THE WORST PLAYER MOVE

The worst player move was sending Jeff Bagwell to the Astros in August 1990 for Larry Anderson. Losing Wade Boggs to the Yankees (1992) and Roger Clemens to the Blue Jays (1996) in free agency was also less than inspired.

1990 B

Season in a Sentence

The Red Sox win a division title with a patchwork team that finishes 12th in the AL in home runs and last in the majors in stolen bases.

Finish • Won • Lost • Pct • GB

First   88   74   .543   +2.0

AL Championship Series—

The Red Sox lost to the Oakland Athletics four games to none.

Manager

Joe Morgan

Stats   Red Sox • AL • Rank

	Red Sox	AL	Rank
Batting Avg:	.272	.259	1
On-Base Pct:	.344	.327	1
Slugging Pct:	.395	.388	4
Home Runs:	106		12
Stolen Bases:	53		14
ERA:	3.72	3.91	4
Fielding Pct:	.980	.981	5
Runs Scored:	699		7
Runs Allowed:	664		4

Starting Lineup

Tony Peña, c
Carlos Quintana, 1b
Jody Reed, 2b
Wade Boggs, 3b
Luis Rivera, ss
Mike Greenwell, lf
Ellis Burks, cf
Tom Brunansky, rf
Dwight Evans, dh
Marty Barrett, 2b

Pitchers

Roger Clemens, sp
Mike Boddicker, sp
Greg Harris, sp
Dana Kiecker, sp
Tom Bolton, sp
Jeff Reardon, rp
Rob Murphy, rp
Dennis Lamp, rp
Jeff Gray, rp

Attendance

2,528,986 (fourth in AL)

Club Leaders

Batting Avg:	Boggs	.302
On-Base Pct:	Boggs	.386
Slugging Pct:	Burks	.486
Home Runs:	Burks	21
RBI:	Burks	89
Runs:	Burks	89
	Boggs	89
Stolen Bases:	Burks	9
Wins:	Clemens	21
Strikeouts:	Clemens	209
ERA:	Clemens	1.93
Saves:	Reardon	21

JANUARY 24   Tony Conigliaro dies of kidney failure at the age of forty-five. He had spent the previous eight years with round-the-clock nursing care following a massive heart attack.

The Red Sox wore black arm bands during the 1990 season in honor of Conigliaro.

FEBRUARY 15   The owners lock the players out of spring training because of a lack of progress during negotiations for a new basic agreement.

MARCH 18   The dispute between the players and owners is resolved.

Spring training camps opened on March 20. The season, scheduled to open April 2, was delayed a week with the games made up on open dates, with doubleheaders, and by extending the close of the campaign by three days. The Red Sox were supposed to play the White Sox on April 6, 7, and 8 at Fenway Park, and those games were moved back to October 1, 2, and 3. This proved significant when the Red Sox–White Sox series settled the AL East pennant.

APRIL 9   The Red Sox open the season with a 5–2 win over the Tigers before 35,199 at Fenway Park. Wade Boggs collected three hits, including a double, in four at-bats. Roger Clemens held the Tigers hitless until Tony Phillips singled to start the sixth inning. Clemens went 6⅔ innings and allowed two runs and three hits. A three-run double by Dwight Evans started the scoring.

Bill Buckner returned to the Red Sox in 1990 and was given a standing ovation by fans in pregame introductions. He hit .186 in 43 at-bats and was released on June 5, ending his 22-year major league career.

APRIL 10   Wade Boggs ties an American League record for most intentional walks in a nine-inning game with three during a 4–2 win over the Tigers at Fenway Park.

Boggs failed to extend his record of collecting 200 or more hits in a season seven years in a row, but still picked up 187 hits and batted .302.

APRIL 16   On Patriots' Day, the Brewers wallop the Red Sox 18–0 at Fenway Park.

Bob Starr replaced Ken Coleman on the Red Sox radio broadcasts in 1990. Starr previously announced games for the Angels. He remained in Boston for three seasons, then returned to the Angels.

APRIL 22   John Dopson (1⅓ innings), Dennis Lamp (4⅔ innings), Jeff Reardon (two innings), and Lee Smith (three innings) combine on a two-hitter over 11 innings to defeat the Brewers 4–2 at County Stadium. Milwaukee scored two runs in the first inning on three walks by Dopson and on an error. The only Brewers hits were singles by Greg Vaughn in the fifth inning (off Lamp) and Robin Yount in the ninth (off Smith). Jody Reed drove in the winning runs with a two-out, two-run single.

APRIL 26   Jody Reed hits a walk-off homer in the ninth inning to beat the Angels 5–4 at Fenway Park.

Reed hit .289 with five homers and led the league in doubles with 45 in 1990.

APRIL 27   The Red Sox score three runs in the ninth inning to beat the Athletics 7–6 at Fenway Park. The rally was capped by a two-out, two-run, walk-off single by Ellis Burks.

Burks batted .296 with 21 homers in 1990.

APRIL 30   The Red Sox bash the Mariners 11–0 at Fenway Park.

During the contest, two mallards landed on the outfield grass and stayed around to watch a couple of innings.

MAY 4   The Red Sox trade Lee Smith to the Cardinals for Tom Brunansky.

MAY 5   Rickey Henderson hits Mike Boddicker's first pitch for a homer, but the Athletics score no more runs and the Red Sox win 5–1 in Oakland.

The Red Sox' road uniforms had names on the back for the first time in 1990. There was also a change on the front. The word "Boston," which had been in plain navy-blue block letters from 1979 through 1989, was replaced by the city name in Old English scarlet lettering with navy blue trim. Piping was added on both sides of the buttons in the center of the shirt.

MAY 7   Rob Murphy shaves in the middle of a three-inning relief stint against the Mariners in Seattle. Murphy came into the game in the seventh with the Red Sox holding a 5–2 lead, then gave up two runs in the eighth that narrowed the gap to one run. When he finally secured the last out of the eighth, Murphy stormed into the visitors' clubhouse, grabbed a razor, and dry shaved his four-day beard. When he went out for the ninth inning, he had a different look and got the last three outs to preserve the 5–4 victory.

MAY 19   Tom Brunansky collects five hits, including two homers and a double, in five at-bats and drives in seven runs in a 13–1 trouncing of the Twins at Fenway Park. It was only Brunansky's second game at Fenway as a member of the Red Sox. Boston batters totaled 20 hits in the contest.

MAY 25   The Twins smash the Red Sox 16–0 in Minneapolis. Outfielder Danny Heep pitched the eighth inning and allowed a run and four hits.

JUNE 3   Roger Clemens sparks a first-inning fight in Cleveland by hitting Indians leadoff hitter Stan Jefferson on the right elbow on his second pitch. It was retaliation for a brushback by Cleveland's Doug Jones of Tony Peña in the ninth inning the night before. In the brawl prompted by Clemens's pitch, Peña and Chris James of the Indians were ejected. After the game, Joe Morgan said, "I loved it. We got even, didn't we? We voted as a team, 34–0, that it would be such." AL president Bobby Brown took exception to the inflammatory remarks and suspended Morgan for three games.

JUNE 4   With their first pick in the amateur draft, the Red Sox select pitcher Frank Rodriguez from Howard Junior College in Texas.

             Rodriguez was drafted in the second round. The Sox had no first-round pick in 1990. Rodriguez was enough of an athlete that there was an argument in the Sox' front office over whether he should be a shortstop or a pitcher. He started as a shortstop but switched to pitching in 1992. Rodriguez pitched only nine games for the Sox before being traded to the Twins in 1995. He lasted seven seasons in the majors and had a 29–39 record with a 5.53 ERA. It wasn't a good year for the Sox' scouting department. The only other future major leaguers drafted and signed by the Red Sox in 1990 were Walt McKeel (third round) and Gar Finnvold (sixth), two players who combined to play in only 19 big-league games.

JUNE 6   Mike Boddicker pitches a two-hitter to beat the Yankees 8–1 at Fenway Park, spoiling the managerial debut of Stump Merrill, who replaced Bucky Dent as skipper of the Yanks. The only New York hits were singles by Roberto Kelly and Matt Nokes in the second inning.

             The Red Sox were 7–0 against the Yankees at Fenway in 1990, outscoring them 50–17.

JUNE 7

Greg Harris (seven innings) and Jeff Reardon (one inning) combine on a one-hitter to defeat the Yankees 3–0 at Fenway Park. The lone New York hit was a single by Jesse Barfield in the fifth inning. The Yanks collected only three hits in consecutive games off Sox pitching.

The Red Sox traded Rich Gedman to the Astros for Louie Meadows.

JUNE 9

Ellis Burks drives in six runs on a homer, double, and single during an 11–6 victory over the Indians at Fenway Park. It was Dana Kiecker's first major league win. Kiecker was a twenty-nine-year-old rookie from the town of Sleepy Eye, Minnesota.

Kiecker was 8–9 with a 3.96 ERA as a rookie but faded to 2–3 with an earned run average of 7.36 in 1991, his last season in the majors.

JUNE 23

After the Orioles take a 3–2 lead in the top of the tenth, the Red Sox come back in their half of the inning to win 4–3 on a two-run, walk-off homer by Dwight Evans with two outs. Earlier, Evans homered in the eighth to tie the score, 2–2.

JUNE 24

Dwight Evans stars again, driving in both runs in a 2–0 win over the Orioles at Fenway Park with a home run in the seventh inning and a sacrifice fly in the eighth. Greg Harris (eight innings) and Jeff Gray (one inning) combined on the shutout.

JUNE 25

The Red Sox take first place from the Blue Jays by defeating them 10–8 at Fenway Park. The victory ended Toronto's 15-game winning streak at Fenway Park, dating back to 1987.

The Red Sox swept the four-game series from the Blue Jays to take a 3 1/2-game lead in the AL East.

JULY 1

The Red Sox score eight runs in the second inning to take a 9–4 lead in a 15–4 rout of the Rangers at Fenway Park.

JULY 2

Kevin Romine hits a walk-off homer in the ninth inning off Kenny Rogers to beat the Rangers 3–2 at Fenway Park. Mike Boddicker was the winning pitcher, earning his 10th victory in a row.

The July 2 win gave Boddicker an 11–3 record on the 1990 season. He finished the year at 17–8 with a 3.36 ERA.

JULY 4

Dwight Evans hits a two-out, three-run homer in the ninth inning in a 4–3 win over the Twins in Minneapolis.

JULY 14

Ellis Burks hits a three-run, pinch-hit homer in the eighth inning that caps a five-run rally to beat the Royals 8–7 in the second game of a doubleheader at Fenway Park. Kansas City won the first game, 2–1.

JULY 17

The Red Sox become the only major league team in history to hit into two triple plays in one game. The Sox overcame the miscues to win 1–0 over the Twins at Fenway Park. Tom Bolton (eight innings) and Jeff Reardon (one inning) combined on the shutout. Tom Naehring drove in the lone run of the game with a single in the fifth inning.

The July 17 contest is also the only one in major league history in which two triple plays have been recorded. Both triple plays were started by third baseman Gary Gaetti, who fielded a bases-loaded smash by Tom Brunansky in the fourth inning and Jody Reed's sharp grounder in the eighth, each with runners on first and second. On both plays, Gaetti stepped on third and threw to Al Newman at second, who relayed to Kent Hrbek at first. The Boston base runners retired were Reed and Carlos Quintana in the fourth and Tim Naehring and Wade Boggs in the eighth.

JULY 18   A day after hitting into two triple plays, the Red Sox hit into six double plays, including five in the first five innings, but win again 6–4 against the Twins at Fenway Park. The Sox helped themselves with four double plays of their own. The two clubs set another big-league mark for the most double plays in a contest with 10.

Nine different batters hit into the record-setting 10 double plays. The five Red Sox were Jody Reed (first inning), Kevin Romine (second and fourth), Carlos Quintana (third), Mike Greenwell (fifth), and Tim Naehring (eighth). The four Twins were Kent Hrbek (first), Shane Mack (third), Gary Gaetti (fifth), and John Moses (ninth).

JULY 20   After giving up three runs in two-thirds of an inning during a 5–0 loss to the Royals in Kansas City, Rob Murphy tears up the clubhouse, smashing candy bowls with a baseball bat.

Later in the same series, Murphy threw his glove into the outfield after being taken out of the game by Joe Morgan. Sox fans shuddered every time Murphy entered a game as he suffered through a horrible year in 1990, posting an 0–6 record and an ERA of 6.32 in 57 innings over 68 relief appearances.

JULY 24   After scoring a total of six runs in five road defeats from July 19 through 23, the Red Sox try a little voodoo to drive the evil spirits from their bats. In a scene inspired by the hit movie *Major League*, Mike Greenwell, Wade Boggs, and Tony Peña built an altar in the Milwaukee clubhouse. Above it they hung a number 13 jersey with a rope tied around the neck and a stuffed rooster pinned to the tail. A Buddha statue, vigil candles, and rubber spiders and snakes were placed on a table. The club's bats were then put around the table and left until game time. The Sox scored five runs but lost 6–5 to the Brewers in 10 innings.

JULY 27   The Red Sox defeat the Tigers 1–0 in Detroit. Tom Bolton (7⅔ innings), Dana Kiecker (one-third of an inning), and Rob Murphy (one inning) combined on the shutout. Carlos Quintana drove in the only run of the game with a sacrifice fly in the fourth inning.

JULY 29   The Red Sox collect an American League–record 12 doubles in a 13–3 win over the Tigers in Detroit. Wade Boggs led the way with three doubles. Ellis Burks, Jody Reed, and Tim Naehring each hit a pair of two-baggers. Mike Greenwell, Carlos Quintana, and Randy Kutcher added one apiece.

The major league record for doubles by a team in a game is 13, set by the Cardinals in the second game of a doubleheader against the Cubs in St. Louis on July 12, 1931. On that day, thousands of fans were standing on the field near

the outfield wall after all of the seats had been sold. Any ball hit into the over-
flow was a ground-rule double.

JULY 31   The Red Sox sign Joe Hesketh following his release by the Braves.

Hesketh was a pleasant surprise. He posted a 12–4 record for the Red Sox in 1991.

AUGUST 3   The day after Iraq's invasion of Kuwait and four days before Operation Desert Storm troops leave for Saudi Arabia, the Red Sox score seven runs in the first inning of a 14–5 rout of the Tigers at Fenway Park.

AUGUST 9   The Red Sox rout the Angels 14–3 in Anaheim.

AUGUST 11   Dwight Evans hits a two-run homer in the fourteenth inning to defeat the Mariners 4–2 in Seattle. Both teams scored in the eleventh.

AUGUST 12   Five Red Sox runs in the ninth inning break a 2–2 tie and ensure a 7–2 win over the Mariners in Seattle.

AUGUST 22   The Red Sox wallop the Orioles 13–2 at Fenway Park.

AUGUST 24   The Red Sox score two runs in the ninth inning to defeat the Blue Jays 2–0 in Toronto. Dana Kiecker (eight innings) and Jeff Gray (one inning) combined on the shutout.

AUGUST 25   Dwight Evans hits a homer in the seventh inning off David Wells to defeat the Blue Jays 1–0 in Toronto. Roger Clemens pitched the shutout.

AUGUST 26   The Red Sox win 1–0 for the second day in a row and pick up their third consecutive shutout against the Blue Jays in Toronto. Greg Harris ($7\frac{2}{3}$ innings) and Jeff Gray ($1\frac{1}{3}$ innings) combined for the shutout. Jody Reed drove in the lone run of the game with a two-out single in the eighth.

The Red Sox won three in row despite scoring only four runs. The August 26 win gave Boston a four-game lead over Toronto.

AUGUST 27   Ellis Burks hits two homers during the Red Sox' eight-run fourth inning to lead Boston to a 12–4 win over the Indians in Cleveland. Burks was the first Red Sox player with two homers in an inning since Bill Regan in 1928. Burks led off the fourth with a homer off Tom Candiotti and added a three-run blast against Colby Ward. Mike Boddicker pitched shutout ball over the first six innings to extend the streak of scoreless innings by Boston pitchers to 33.

AUGUST 28   The Red Sox score three runs in the ninth inning, the last two on Mike Greenwell's triple, to beat the Indians 6–5 in Cleveland.

AUGUST 30   Roger Clemens earns his 20th win of the season with a 9–2 decision over the Indians in Cleveland.

The win gave Clemens a record of 20–5, but he was sidelined for nearly four weeks in September due to shoulder tendonitis. He finished the season with a

21–6 record and led the league in ERA (1.93) and shutouts (four). Clemens struck out 209 batters in 228 1/3 innings.

AUGUST 31   Luis Rivers hits a grand slam off Jeff Robinson in the eighth inning of a 7–3 win over the Yankees at Fenway Park. It was Boston's eighth win in a row.

On the same day, the Red Sox traded minor league prospect Jeff Bagwell to the Astros for Larry Andersen. Andersen was acquired to shore up a shaky bullpen for the pennant drive. He did just that, pitching 22 innings in 15 games with an ERA of 1.23. Andersen went to the Padres as a free agent after the season was over, however. Meanwhile, Bagwell reached the majors with the Astros in 1991 and immediately became a star, winning the Rookie of the Year Award with a .294 average and 15 homers. That was only the beginning. Within two years, Bagwell was one of the best players in baseball and maintained the position for more than a decade. A New Englander through and through, he was born in Boston, and went to high school in Middletown, Connecticut, and college at the University of Hartford. Bagwell's family was filled with lifelong Red Sox fans who were thrilled when he was drafted by the club in the fifth round of the 1989 draft. Bagwell played at Class AA New Britain in the Eastern League in 1990 as a twenty-two-year-old third baseman and hit .333, but he had only four homers in 481 at-bats and just two homers in 229 at-bats at the Rookie and Class A level in 1989.

The Sox were concerned about Bagwell's potential as a power hitter, and the only positions he could play adequately on defense were third and first. In 1990, the club had the best third baseman in baseball in Wade Boggs, and Mo Vaughn put together a tremendous season as a first baseman in 1990 at Class AAA Pawtucket. The Red Sox also believed that Scott Cooper, who played third at Pawtucket in 1990, was going to be a star. Bagwell looked expendable, but it was a monumental miscalculation. With remarkable foresight, Bill James wrote during the 1990–91 offseason, "It could be one of those deals, like Lou Brock for Ernie Broglio, Nolan Ryan for Jim Fregosi and Frank Robinson for Milt Pappas, that haunts the man who made it." The Bagwell deal has continued to haunt Lou Gorman and the Sox, and is the second-worst deal ever made by the club behind the sale of Babe Ruth. In 2001, James rated Bagwell as the fourth-best first baseman of all time behind Lou Gehrig, Jimmie Foxx, and Mark McGwire. Bagwell entered the 2005 season with 446 career homers. If he had played his entire career at Fenway Park, instead of most of it at the Astrodome, he would have had many more homers.

SEPTEMBER 1   The Red Sox score seven runs in the fifth inning and win their ninth game in a row with a 15–1 decision over the Yankees at Fenway Park. Mike Greenwell hit an inside-the-park grand slam in the fifth inning off Greg Cadaret.

Greenwell hit two inside-the-park homers during his big-league career, and both were against Cadaret. The other one was in 1989.

SEPTEMBER 2   The Red Sox win their 10th game in succession with a 7–1 decision over the Yankees at Fenway Park. The game was televised nationally on ESPN and was the first time that the Red Sox played a scheduled game on a Sunday night in Boston.

The 10-game winning streak gave the Red Sox a 76–57 record and a 6 1/2-game lead over the second-place Blue Jays. Without Roger Clemens in the starting rotation, the Sox stumbled, however, and lost 15 of their next 21 games to drop out of first place (see September 19, 1990).

SEPTEMBER 3   Bob Stanley is honored for his 13-year Red Sox career prior to a 9–5 loss to the Athletics at Fenway Park.

The Sox planned a similar night for Jim Rice, but Rice, still angry over his release the previous September, declined to participate.

SEPTEMBER 4   During a 6–2 loss to the Athletics at Fenway Park, Red Sox fan Ron Vachon misses two fouls balls from Rickey Henderson. The balls ricocheted off a luxury box right next to Vachon within 30 seconds of each other, but he fumbled both attempts.

SEPTEMBER 7   Carlos Quintana ties the score with a sacrifice fly in the ninth inning and drives in the winning run in the eleventh with a single to beat the Mariners 5–4 at Fenway Park.

SEPTEMBER 16   The Red Sox play at old Comiskey Park for the last time and lose 4–2 to the White Sox.

The White Sox' new Comiskey Park, now known as U.S. Cellular Field, opened in 1991.

SEPTEMBER 19   The Red Sox drop one game behind the Blue Jays in the AL East race after losing 8–4 to the Orioles in Baltimore.

SEPTEMBER 21   The Red Sox move into a first-place tie with the Blue Jays after a 3–0 win over the Yankees in New York.

SEPTEMBER 25   The Red Sox fall 1 ½ games back of the Blue Jays with a 5–2 loss to the Indians in Cleveland. There were eight games left on the schedule.

SEPTEMBER 27   The Red Sox edge the Tigers 3–2 to tie the Blue Jays for first place. Both Boston and Toronto had 84–72 records and were scheduled to meet each other over the next three days at Fenway Park.

SEPTEMBER 28   The Red Sox take a one-game lead in the AL East by scoring two runs in the ninth inning for a thrilling 7–6 victory over the Blue Jays at Fenway Park. Toronto scored two runs in the top of the ninth to take a 6–5 lead. The Red Sox wrapped up the win in an unlikely manner. Boston loaded the bases on a Jody Reed walk, Carlos Quintana sacrifice, Wade Boggs walk, and an Ellis Burks single. Jeff Stone stepped to the plate for the first time all season. He had been recalled by the Sox in early September after spending most of the season at Pawtucket in the International League. Stone put a Hollywood ending on the Friday evening by delivering a two-run single to win the game.

Stone played two seasons with the Red Sox at the end of an eight-year big-league career that began in 1983. As a member of the Red Sox, he played in 28 games and collected only four hits in 17 at-bats. Stone's game-winning single on September 28, 1990, was his last major league base hit.

SEPTEMBER 29   Tom Brunansky clubs three homers in consecutive at-bats, and Roger Clemens pitches for the first time since September 4 and hurls six shutout innings to give the Red Sox a 7–5 win over the Blue Jays at Fenway Park. All five Toronto runs were scored in the ninth with two outs. Brunansky hit his homers off Todd Stottlemyre in the fifth, Duane Ward in the sixth, and Rick Luecken in the eighth. All three homers went into the net above the left field wall. The victory gave the Red Sox a two-game lead in the AL East with four contests left on the schedule.

Brunansky hit five homers in the crucial three-game, final-week series against the Blue Jays.

SEPTEMBER 30   The Red Sox lose 10–5 to the Blue Jays at Fenway Park, which closes the gap to one game.

OCTOBER 1   The Red Sox defeat the White Sox at Fenway Park to clinch at least a tie for the AL East pennant. A single by Dwight Evans in the eighth inning broke a 3–3 tie.

OCTOBER 2   The Red Sox lose 3–2 in 11 innings to the White Sox at Fenway Park, while the Blue Jays win 2–1 against the Orioles in Baltimore. The Red Sox had a one-game lead heading into the final day of the season.

OCTOBER 3   The Red Sox win the pennant on the last day of the season with a 3–1 win over the White Sox at Fenway Park. In the ninth inning, Chicago had runners on first and second with two outs when Tom Brunansky made a spectacular sliding catch of a drive by Ozzie Guillen in the right field corner to end the game. The catch was made inches above the ground in a spot at Fenway Park that is out of the sight line of most of the fans in the ballpark. The contest was nationally televised on ESPN, and none of the network's cameras was able to catch Brunansky's grab because of the blind spot in that corner. Fortunately, first-base umpire Tim McClellan saw the play. His out call was delayed, however, because he was struck by a frenzied fan that leaped onto the field in celebration.

The Red Sox faced the Oakland Athletics in the American League Championship Series. The A's were gunning for their third straight AL pennant and were defending World Champions. Oakland swept the Sox in the 1988 ALCS. The 1990 A's were managed by Tony La Russa and had a record of 103–59.

OCTOBER 6   In the first game of the ALCS, Roger Clemens pitches six shutout innings, but the Athletics rally for one run in the seventh, one in the eighth, and seven in the ninth to win 9–1 before 35,192 at Fenway Park. Wade Boggs gave the Red Sox a 1–0 lead with a homer in the fourth off Dave Stewart.

OCTOBER 7   Harold Baines drives in three runs to lead the Athletics to a 4–1 win over the Red Sox in Game Two of the ALCS before 35,070 at Fenway Park.

OCTOBER 9   The Red Sox fail to hold a 1–0 lead for the third straight game as the Athletics open a commanding three-games-to-none lead in the ALCS with a 4–1 win at Oakland.

OCTOBER 10   After Roger Clemens is ejected in the second inning for cursing at home-plate umpire Terry Cooney, the Athletics defeat the Red Sox 3–1 in Oakland to complete a four-game sweep of the ALCS. The Red Sox scored only four runs in the four games.

After Clemens was thrown out of the game, Joe Morgan rushed from the dugout and Marty Barrett threw a tub of Gatorade. Coach Dick Berardino tried to restrain Barrett and got shoved down the dugout steps. Both Morgan and Barrett were also ejected. Clemens was fined $10,000 and suspended for the first five games of the 1991 season for the incident. The Athletics were swept by the Reds in the 1990 World Series.

OCTOBER 29   The Red Sox release Dwight Evans, ending his association with the club that began in 1972 when he made his major league debut.

Evans signed a contract with the Orioles on December 6 and played one more big-league season before retiring.

NOVEMBER 19   The Red Sox trade Greg Hansell, Ed Peruzo, and Paul Williams to the Mets for Mike Marshall.

NOVEMBER 21   Mike Boddicker signs a free-agent contract with the Royals.

DECEMBER 4   The Red Sox sign Matt Young, most recently with the Mariners, as a free agent.

Young was signed to be the number-two starter behind Roger Clemens but was an extreme disappointment. In two seasons in Boston, he was 3–11 with a 4.91 ERA. After a 1–6 season with the Indians in 1993, Young finished his career with a record of 55–95.

DECEMBER 14   The Red Sox release Marty Barrett.

Barrett ended his Red Sox career with 906 games at second base, third all-time at the position to Bobby Doerr (1,852) and Hobe Ferris (983).

DECEMBER 15   The Red Sox sign Jack Clark, most recently with the Padres, as a free agent.

Clark signed for three years at $8.5 million, but gave the Sox only one productive season before slumping in 1992, hitting only .210 with five homers. He ended up a villain in Boston, booed by the fans and ripped by the media. Clark could be his own worst enemy. He would get depressed over a slump, then say something stupid or outrageous. Just after the All-Star break in 1992, Clark declared bankruptcy because he was $6.7 million in debt. He had sponsored a drag racing enterprise, which lost one million dollars a year, built a multimillion-dollar mansion that he was forced to sell, operated a restaurant that was losing money, and owned 18 automobiles. When the season ended, the Red Sox released Clark and he never played in the big leagues again.

DECEMBER 19   The Red Sox sign Danny Darwin, most recently with the Astros, as a free agent.

Like Young and Clark, Darwin came with a high price and was a complete waste of money. Darwin spent four seasons in Boston but was an above-average pitcher in only one of them.

DECEMBER 21   Larry Andersen signs a free-agent contract with the Padres.

1991

B

Season in a Sentence

The Red Sox win 31 of 41 in August and September to pull within half a game of first place, but they collapse during the final two weeks, costing Joe Morgan his job.

Finish • Won • Lost • Pct • GB

Second   84   78   .519   7.0

Manager

Joe Morgan

Stats

Stats	Red Sox	AL	Rank
Batting Avg:	.269	.260	4
On-Base Pct:	.340	.329	3
Slugging Pct:	.401	.395	4
Home Runs:	126		9 (tie)
Stolen Bases:	59		13
ERA:	4.01	4.10	7
Fielding Pct:	.981	.981	8
Runs Scored:	731		7
Runs Allowed:	712		6

Starting Lineup

Tony Peña, c
Carlos Quintana, 1b
Jody Reed, 2b
Wade Boggs, 3b
Luis Rivera, ss
Mike Greenwell, lf
Ellis Burks, cf
Tom Brunansky, rf
Jack Clark, dh
Mo Vaughn, 1b
Steve Lyons, cf
Phil Plantier, rf-lf

Pitchers

Roger Clemens, sp
Mike Gardiner, sp
Tom Bolton, sp
Matt Young, sp
Kevin Morton, sp
Jeff Reardon, rp
Greg Harris, rp-sp
Joe Hesketh, rp-sp
Dennis Lamp, rp
Jeff Gray, rp

Attendance

2,562,435 (fourth in AL)

Club Leaders

Batting Avg:	Boggs	.332
On-Base Pct:	Boggs	.421
Slugging Pct:	Clark	.466
Home Runs:	Clark	28
RBI:	Clark	87
Runs:	Boggs	93
Stolen Bases:	Greenwell	15
Wins:	Clemens	18
Strikeouts:	Clemens	241
ERA:	Clemens	2.62
Saves:	Reardon	40

JANUARY 19   Two days after the United States and its allies launch an air attack on Iraq to start the Persian Gulf War, Roger Clemens and his brother Randy are arrested at Bayou Mama's Swamp Bar in Houston. Coming three months after his ejection in the 1990 ALCS, the incident added to Clemens's increasing reputation for erratic behavior. According to police, the Red Sox pitcher was arrested after he jumped on the back of Houston policeman Louis Olvedo and choked him as the officer tried to arrest Randy during a disturbance at the bar. Clemens was charged with aggravated assault on a police office and spent 11 hours in jail before making bail. The charges were dropped on January 9, 1992, but the officer filed a civil suit against Clemens because of injuries he claimed he suffered in the altercation.

This wasn't the only off-the-field incident to make news during the early months of 1991. During spring training, Wade Boggs fell out of a moving pickup truck driven by his wife. "I'm just lucky to be alive," he said. "The back tire just missed running over my head." Boggs walked away with a few cuts and bruises.

APRIL 1   A month after George Bush orders a cease fire to end the Persian Gulf War, the Red Sox trade Rob Murphy to the Mariners for Mike Gardiner.

APRIL 8   In the season opener, the Red Sox defeat the Blue Jays 6–2 in Toronto. In his Red Sox debut, Jack Clark hit a grand slam in the third inning off Dave Stieb. Roger Clemens was the winning pitcher, allowing one run in eight innings.

Clemens was pitching while his five-game suspension for arguing with umpire Terry Cooney in the 1990 ALCS was being appealed. The appeal was denied by Commissioner Fay Vincent, and Clemens served it from April 28 through May 2.

APRIL 11   In the first game of the season at Fenway Park, the Red Sox lose 6–4 to the Indians before 34,134. In his Red Sox debut, Danny Darwin allowed six runs in $1\frac{2}{3}$ innings.

At the start of the season, Ellis Burks was the only African American on the roster, adding to the racist reputation of the Red Sox front office. The only other minorities on the roster were Latin players: Tony Peña (Dominican Republic), Carlos Quintana (Venezuela), Tony Fossas (Cuba), and Luis Rivera (Puerto Rico).

APRIL 15   Matt Young allows only two hits in nine shutout innings, but the Red Sox lose 1–0 in 13 innings against the Indians at Fenway Park. Cleveland won the game on a homer by Brook Jacoby off Dennis Lamp.

APRIL 18   Roger Clemens (eight innings), Tony Fossas (one-third of an inning), and Jeff Reardon (two-thirds of an inning) combine to shut out the Royals 1–0 at Fenway Park.

Fossas's family escaped from Cuba when he was ten. He grew up in the Jamaica Plain section of Boston, less than two miles from Fenway Park, playing his youth ball on Daisy Field. Fossas was thirty years old when he made his big-league debut with the Rangers in 1988, but had an 11-year big-league career, four years of which was spent with the Red Sox.

APRIL 21   The Red Sox charter flight has a terrifying return from Cleveland. Coming in to land at Hanscom Field in Bedford, Massachusetts, the aircraft dropped 200 to 500 feet in foggy conditions. Kevin Romine, whose father was a professional pilot, laughed off the incident and gave a play-by-play of the encounter, but Tom Brunansky and Mike Greenwell were unamused and threatened him with physical harm.

APRIL 26   In Kansas City, Jack Clark does one thousand dollars in damage to the visitors' clubhouse when he smashes a toilet with a bat after going hitless in four at-bats during a 5–3 loss to the Royals.

MAY 3   The Red Sox play at new Comiskey Park in Chicago for the first time and defeat the White Sox, 7–2. Roger Clemens pitched a complete game in his first game following his five-game suspension for arguing with umpire Terry Cooney in the 1990 ALCS. Ironically, Cooney was the home plate umpire in the May 3 game against the White Sox, but the game passed without incident. Clemens came into the game with a streak of 30 consecutive scoreless innings that ended when the White Sox scored twice in the first, but Clemens held the opposition without a run the rest of the way.

Clemens started the 1991 season with a 6–0 record and an ERA of 0.73 in 49 innings. He finished the year with an 18–10 record and his third career Cy Young Award. Clemens led the AL in ERA (2.62), strikeouts (241), innings pitched ($271\frac{1}{3}$) and shutouts (four).

MAY 5   Kevin Romine hits a grand slam off Alex Fernandez in the second inning of a 9–1 win over the White Sox in Chicago.

             The Red Sox had an 18–9 record and a two-game lead in the AL East on May 10.

MAY 12   Ted Williams and Joe DiMaggio are honored prior to a 12–5 Red Sox loss to the Rangers at Fenway Park. The ceremonies were held on the 50th anniversary of the 1941 season in which both played starring roles. Williams batted .406 to become baseball's last .400 hitter, and DiMaggio had a record 56-game hitting streak.

MAY 15   The Red Sox spot the White Sox a 5–0 lead, then rally to win 9–6 at Fenway Park. In the sixth, Chicago catcher Carlton Fisk allowed a passed ball on a two-out, two-strike pitch that would have ended the inning. A run scored from third on the play that tied the game, 6–6. Mike Greenwell followed with a two-run double. The contest took four hours and 11 minutes to complete.

MAY 20   Jeff Reardon picks up his 300th career save by closing out a 3–0 win over the Brewers at Fenway Park.

             Reardon had 40 saves and a 3.03 ERA in 1991.

MAY 21   The Red Sox overcome a 5–0 deficit with a six-run third inning and defeat the Brewers 10–6 at Fenway Park.

MAY 27   While stretching in the outfield during batting practice prior to a 6–5 loss to the Yankees in New York, Dennis Lamp is struck in the jaw by a drive off the bat of John Marzano. Lamp needed 10 stitches.

JUNE 3   With the first of three picks in the first round of the amateur draft, the Red Sox select pitcher Aaron Sele from Washington State University. Later in the first round, the Sox chose Scott Hatteberg, who was Sele's catcher at Washington State.

             Sele pitched five seasons for the Red Sox and had a 38–33 record. His best seasons came after leaving Boston. He entered the 2005 season with a career record of 131–92. Hatteberg played seven seasons for Boston as a catcher before moving on to the Athletics, where he became Oakland's starting first baseman. Other future major leaguers drafted and signed by the Red Sox in 1991 were Luis Ortiz (eighth round), Tony Rodriguez (10th), Cory Bailey (15th), Tim Van Egmond (17th), Ron Mahay (18th), and Joel Bennett (21st).

JUNE 6   In his first start at Oakland-Alameda County Coliseum since his ejection from Game Four of the 1990 ALCS, Roger Clemens allows the Athletics only one run and two hits in eight innings. Dennis Lamp pitched a perfect ninth for an 8–1 win. The only Oakland hits were a home run by Dave Henderson in the second inning and a double by Ernest Riles in the fourth.

JUNE 14   Trailing 4–2, the Red Sox score seven runs in the seventh inning to defeat the Angels 9–4 at Fenway Park.

JUNE 15   The Red Sox score seven runs in the first inning and beat the Angels 13–3 at Fenway Park.

JUNE 27	Mo Vaughn makes his major league debut and is hitless in two at-bats during an 8–0 loss to the Yankees at Fenway Park.

Mo Vaughn was the Red Sox' starting first baseman from 1991 through 1998. He was one of the most popular players in Red Sox history as much for what he did off the field as on. His mother did charity work for Jackie Robinson's wife, Rachel, and Vaughn wore number 42 in honor of Robinson. Vaughn was involved with a number of local charities and often visited hospitals and clinics to cheer up young people. He promised, and delivered, a home run for eleven-year-old leukemia patient Jason Leader in 1993. Vaughn remained in contact with the boy for the last 15 months of his life. He was a pallbearer and delivered a touching eulogy at Leader's funeral. He also started the Mo Vaughn Youth Development Program and was active in the day-to-day operation of the facility in the Boston neighborhood of Dorchester. Even after he missed two games in the middle of the 1995 pennant race because of injuries suffered after defending his girlfriend in a barroom scuffle, Vaughn received a standing ovation from Boston fans when he stepped to the plate in his first game back. That season, "M. V." stood for "Most Valuable" as he won the AL MVP Award. In eight seasons with the Red Sox, Vaughn played in 1,046 games and scored 628 runs, hit 230 homers, drove in 752 runs, batted .304, and had a slugging percentage of .542.

JULY 2	The Red Sox collect 22 hits and bury the Brewers 14–4 in Milwaukee.
JULY 5	Jack Clark drives in seven runs in a 10–1 rout of the Tigers at Fenway Park. Clark drove in a run on a fielder's choice in the first, singled home two runs in the second, smacked a three-run homer in the sixth, and hit a sacrifice fly in the eighth.
JULY 6	A brawl breaks out during a 7–4 win over the Tigers at Fenway Park. In the second inning, Roger Clemens gave up back-to-back homers to Pete Incaviglia and Rob Deer to fall behind 4–2, then hit John Shelby with a pitch. Shelby charged the mound with his bat in his hand, sparking a bench-clearing fight. Clemens wound up at the bottom of the pile on the mound. Shelby was ejected. Clemens allowed no more runs before he was relieved after the eighth.
JULY 21	Steve Lyons pitches the ninth inning of a 14–1 loss to the Twins at Fenway Park. Lyons allowed no runs and two hits and struck out Chuck Knoblauch.
JULY 24	Joe Hesketh ($6\frac{2}{3}$ innings), Jeff Gray ($1\frac{1}{3}$ innings), and Jeff Reardon (one inning) combine on a two-hitter to defeat the Rangers 2–1 in Arlington. The only Texas hits were a single by Rafael Palmeiro in the first inning and a homer by Brian Downing in the fourth.
JULY 28	Jeff Gray suffers a slight stroke before a 5–2 loss to the White Sox at Fenway Park.

Gray was sitting in front of his locker preparing to go out on the field for his daily routine. He was speaking to Jeff Reardon and Joe Hesketh when he slumped to the floor. Gray's speech was slurred and his right side was paralyzed. After an examination, it was determined that he suffered a slight stroke caused by an enlarged blood vessel in his brain. Only twenty-eight when stricken, Gray never played another major league game.

JULY 30 — Carlos Quintana ties an American League record by driving in six runs in an inning during an 11–6 win over the Rangers at Fenway Park. In the third inning, Quintana hit a grand slam off Oil Can Boyd and a two-run double against Wayne Rosenthal. The Sox scored 10 runs in the inning to take an 11–2 lead. The win ended the Sox' nine-game losing streak at Fenway, the club's longest since 1927. Quintana is one of two Red Sox to drive in six runs in an inning. The other was Tom McBride on August 4, 1945.

JULY 31 — Jack Clark hits three homers, the last one a walk-off blast in the fourteenth off Steve Chitren, to beat the Athletics 11–10 at Fenway Park. Earlier, Clark hit a grand slam in the third against Dave Stewart and a solo shot facing Gene Nelson in the eighth. The Sox trailed 10–6 before scoring three runs in the eighth and one in the ninth. Wade Boggs reached base six times in eight plate appearances on three doubles, two singles, and a walk.

AUGUST 7 — The Red Sox lose 2–0 to the Royals at Kansas City to fall 11 ½ games behind the Blue Jays.

> *The Red Sox were 50–57 and in third place. Beginning with a four-game sweep of the Blue Jays from August 9 through 12, the Sox won 31 of their next 41 games to overcome the 11½-game deficit and pull within one-half game of first place (see September 21, 1991).*

AUGUST 9 — The Red Sox tally 21 hits and defeat the Blue Jays 12–7 in Toronto.

AUGUST 16 — The Red Sox trade Mickey Peña to the Braves for Dan Petry.

AUGUST 21 — The Red Sox sweep the Indians 13–5 and 5–4 at Fenway Park. The second game ended with a two-run homer by Wade Boggs in the ninth inning.

> *Boggs hit .332 with 42 doubles and eight homers in 1991. It was his seventh consecutive season with at least 40 or more doubles to tie a record set by Joe Medwick from 1933 through 1939.*

AUGUST 24 — Mike Greenwell and Mo Vaughn scuffle around the batting cage prior to a 1–0 loss to the Angels in Anaheim.

> *In June, Greenwell fought Luis Rivera after an argument over who should have caught a fly ball.*

AUGUST 26 — Jack Clark tears a calf muscle on his home-run swing during a 3–0 win over the Athletics on Oakland. Clark limped around the bases before being taken out of the game.

SEPTEMBER 1 — The Red Sox score four runs in the first inning and six in the second to take a 10–0 lead and move on to down the Mariners 13–2 in Seattle.

SEPTEMBER 7 — Mike Greenwell drives in six runs on a homer and two doubles during an 11–10 win over the Mariners at Fenway Park.

SEPTEMBER 8 — Jody Reed hits two doubles during a seven-run third inning as the Red Sox wallop the Mariners 17–6 at Fenway Park.

SEPTEMBER 10   Roger Clemens pitches a two-hitter to beat the Tigers 4–0 in Detroit. Clemens retired the first 19 batters before Lou Whitaker walked with one out in the seventh. Alan Trammell broke up the no-hitter later in the inning with a single. Milt Cuyler added another single in the ninth.

SEPTEMBER 15   Roger Clemens survives an odd brushback battle to beat the Yankees 5–4 in New York. In the sixth inning, Matt Nokes was hit beneath the right shoulder with a fastball from Clemens. Nokes caught the ball under his armpit and, with a grimace, snapped the ball back at the Red Sox ace. Clemens caught the ball easily, and the two players began exchanging words. Players in both dugouts and bullpens poured onto the field, but there were no punches thrown as umpires kept the teams apart.

Steve Babineau

Roger Clemens supplied another outstanding year for an otherwise weak staff in 1991, winning his third Cy Young Award.

SEPTEMBER 21   The Red Sox rout the Yankees 12–1 at Fenway Park to charge within one-half game of the Blue Jays with a record of 81–67. The Sox scored in every inning but the fourth.

SEPTEMBER 22   The Red Sox suffer a devastating 10-inning, 7–5 loss to the Yankees at Fenway Park. The Sox led 5–4 with two outs in the ninth inning and two strikes on Roberto Kelly when Kelly struck a home run off Jeff Reardon to tie the score. In the tenth, Matt Young gave up two runs for the loss.

The Sox never recovered from the defeat and lost 11 of their last 14 games. At the end of the season, Boston was seven games behind Toronto.

SEPTEMBER 26   The Red Sox play at Memorial Stadium in Baltimore for the last time and split a doubleheader with the Orioles. The Sox won the first game 2–1 and lost the second, 6–5. The second-game loss was crushing to the Sox' dwindling pennant hopes. Boston led 5–4 in the ninth when Greg Harris loaded the bases, then threw eight straight balls to allow two runs. The Red Sox ended the day 2½ games behind the Blue Jays with 10 games left.

The Orioles opened Camden Yards in 1992.

OCTOBER 1   Rookie outfielder Phil Plantier strikes out five times in five plate appearances during an 8–5 loss to the Tigers at Fenway Park.

Despite the October 1 performance, Plantier looked like a future All-Star. Hitting out of a squat position that Joe Morgan called "the toilet seat stance," Plantier hit .331 with 11 homers in 148 at-bats in 1992 at the age of twenty-two. He never developed, however, and finished his big-league career in 1997 with a .243 batting average after playing for five clubs.

OCTOBER 8   In a surprise move, the Red Sox fire Joe Morgan and hire forty-year-old former player Butch Hobson.

Hobson had been the manager of the Red Sox' top farm club in Pawtucket. General manager Lou Gorman said the move had less to do with any failure on Morgan's part than with the fear that someone else would hire Hobson, who was seen as a rising managerial talent by the Sox even though he had received no offers from any other big-league club. The front office loved Hobson's perceived toughness, which drew comparisons to Dick Williams. Hobson played for the Sox from 1975 through 1980, when he was one of Don Zimmer's favorite players. Hobson's first move as manager was to hire Zimmer as his third-base coach. Hobson was overmatched as a manager, however. In 1992, the Sox were 73–89, their worst season since 1966. After two more losing campaigns in 1993 and 1994, Hobson was let go. Morgan never managed another big-league team. He had some revenge by doing commercials for Suffolk Downs in which he made unfavorable comparisons between Red Sox players and race horses.

DECEMBER 20   The Red Sox sign Frank Viola, most recently with the Mets, as a free agent.

Viola was a Cy Young Award–winner with the Twins in 1987 when he was 24–7, and had a 20–12 mark for the Mets in 1990. With the Sox, Viola posted respectable records of 13–12 in 1992 and 11–8 in 1993.

1992

B

Season in a Sentence

In their first season under new manager Butch Hobson, the Red Sox finish second in the AL in ERA but thud into last place with one of the worst offenses in baseball.

Finish • Won • Lost • Pct • GB

Seventh 73 89 .451 23.0

Manager

Butch Hobson

Stats	Red Sox	AL	Rank
Batting Avg:	.246	.259	13
On-Base Pct:	.330	.337	9
Slugging Pct:	.347	.385	13
Home Runs:	84		12
Stolen Bases:	44		14
ERA:	3.63	3.95	2
Fielding Pct:	.978	.981	12
Runs Scored:	599		13
Runs Allowed:	669		5

Starting Lineup

Tony Peña, c
Mo Vaughn, 1b
Jody Reed, 2b
Wade Boggs, 3b
Luis Rivera, ss
Billy Hatcher, lf
Bob Zupcic, cf-lf
Tom Brunansky, rf
Jack Clark, dh
Scott Cooper, 1b-3b
Phil Plantier, rf
Ellis Burks, cf
Herm Winningham, lf-cf
Tim Naehring, ss-2b
John Valentin, ss
Mike Greenwell, lf

Pitchers

Roger Clemens, sp
Frank Viola, sp
Joe Hesketh, sp
John Dopson, sp
Mike Gardiner, sp
Jeff Reardon, rp
Greg Harris, rp
Tony Fossas, rp
Danny Darwin, rp

Attendance

2,468,574 (sixth in AL)

Club Leaders

Batting Avg:	Brunansky	.266
On-Base Pct:	Brunansky	.354
Slugging Pct:	Brunansky	.445
Home Runs:	Brunansky	15
RBI:	Brunansky	74
Runs:	Reed	64
Stolen Bases:	Reed	7
Wins:	Clemens	18
Strikeouts:	Clemens	208
ERA:	Clemens	2.41
Saves:	Reardon	27

FEBRUARY 26   Jean Yawkey dies at the age of eighty-three, six days after suffering a stroke. The club ownership passed to a trust, managed by John Harrington, who continued as club president.

APRIL 7   The Red Sox open the 1992 season with a 4–3 loss to the Yankees in New York. Mo Vaughn and Phil Plantier homered for the Sox. Roger Clemens pitched a complete game.

APRIL 11   The Red Sox win a 19-inning marathon by a 7–5 score over the Indians at Municipal Stadium. A two-run homer by Tim Naehring was the winner, which gave Butch Hobson his first win as manager. Attendance was 65,813 in the Cleveland home opener. The Sox led 5–0 in the fourth before allowing the Indians to tie the score 5–5 in the seventh. There was no scoring from the eighth through the eighteenth.

APRIL 12   Matt Young pitches an eight-inning complete game without allowing a hit, but loses 2–1 to the Indians in the first game of a doubleheader in Cleveland. The Indians scored a run in the first inning when Kenny Lofton walked, stole second and third, and scored on an error by shortstop Luis Rivera. In the third, Cleveland added its second run on two walks, a force play, and a fielder's choice. Young walked seven and struck out five. He doesn't get credit for a no-hitter in the official record books, however, because he failed to pitch nine innings. As the home team with a lead, the Indians didn't bat in the ninth. Cleveland won without a hit just one game after collecting 20 hits in a 19-inning loss. Roger Clemens added another terrific pitching performance in the second game of the twin bill, hurling a two-hitter to win, 3–0. The only Cleveland hits were singles by Carlos Baerga in the first inning and Glenallen Hill in the third. The two hits by Cleveland in the two tilts are the fewest in major league history by a club in a doubleheader.

> *Clemens wasn't scheduled to start. He was left behind in Boston to prepare for a start against the Orioles at Fenway Park on April 13. But the 19-inning game on April 11 depleted the pitching staff, and in the seventeenth inning of the contest, Clemens called Butch Hobson in the dugout and volunteered to pitch in the second game of the April 12 doubleheader. After Hobson said yes, Clemens hopped a plane to Cleveland. Young had little success after his truncated no-hitter. Over the remainder of his career, Young was 1–9, with the lone win coming as a member of the Indians in 1993.*

APRIL 13   In the first game of the season at Fenway Park, the Red Sox lose 8–6 to the Orioles before 34,472. The Sox scored three runs in the seventh inning to tie the game 6–6, but Baltimore tallied once in the eighth and once in the ninth.

APRIL 17   Roger Clemens (seven innings), Greg Harris (one inning), Tony Fossas (one-third of an inning), and Jeff Reardon (two-thirds of an inning) combine to defeat the Blue Jays 1–0 at Fenway Park. The lone run of the contest was driven in by Mike Greenwell with a single in the fourth. Two rain delays held up the game for three hours and 10 minutes.

> *Clemens was 18–11 in 1992 with a league ERA of 2.41. It was the third straight year he led the league in earned run average and the fourth overall. Clemens also topped the AL in shutouts with five, and fanned 208 batters in 246 2/3 innings.*

APRIL 19   The Red Sox score four runs in the ninth inning to stun the Blue Jays 5–4 at Fenway Park. The winning runs scored on a two-run, walk-off single by Scott Cooper which struck the pitching rubber.

MAY 1   Two days after the start of rioting in the South Central section of Los Angeles, resulting in the deaths of 52 people, a two-run, walk-off single by Mo Vaughn in the ninth inning beats the Royals 6–5 at Fenway Park.

MAY 10   Jack Clark drives in six runs on two homers and a single during a 10–6 win over the Royals at Fenway Park.

MAY 17   Wade Boggs collects his 2,000th career hit during a 3–1 loss to the Angels at Fenway Park.

MAY 20   Ellis Burks hits a grand slam in the eighth inning off Mickey Schooler during a 6–4 win over the Mariners at Fenway Park. Burks's homer broke a 2–2 tie.

JUNE 1   The Red Sox fail to select any viable players in the amateur draft. The Sox had no first-round pick as a result of compensation to other clubs for signing their free agents. The only future major leaguers drafted and signed by Boston in 1992 were Steve Rodriguez (fifth round), Bill Selby (13th), and Joe Hudson (27th), none of whom ever had to worry about being besieged by autograph seekers.

JUNE 8   The Red Sox play at Camden Yards in Baltimore for the first time and lose 5–2 to the Orioles.

JUNE 12   Wade Boggs hits a grand slam off Dave Stieb in the fifth inning of a 5–0 win over the Blue Jays in Toronto.

JUNE 15   John Dopson (eight innings) and Jeff Reardon (one inning) combine to shut out the Yankees 1–0 at Fenway Park. Phil Plantier drove in the lone run of the game with a homer in the fifth inning off Scott Sanderson. The save was the 342nd of Reardon's career, which broke the all-time record set by Rollie Fingers. Reardon was carried on the shoulders of several players to the stands behind home plate, where he kissed his wife. Then she joined him on the field.

              Reardon held the record for less than a year. He was passed by Lee Smith early in 1993. Reardon finished his career with 367 saves.

JUNE 27   The Red Sox blow a seven-run lead, but bounce back to beat the Brewers 8–7 in 13 innings at Fenway Park. The Sox led after 7–0 after seven innings, but Roger Clemens gave up three runs in the eighth, and Greg Harris and Jeff Reardon surrendered four in the ninth. The Sox won the contest on a bases-loaded, walk-off single by Herm Winningham.

JUNE 30   Bob Zupcic's walk-off grand slam off Mike Henneman in the ninth inning beats the Tigers 8–5 at Fenway Park. The Sox trailed 5–0 before scoring three runs in the second and one in the eighth to set up the rally in the ninth.

JULY 9   The Red Sox trade Tom Bolton to the Reds for Billy Hatcher.

JULY 10   Bob Zupcic hits a grand slam off Bobby Thigpen in the eighth inning of a 6–5 win over the White Sox at Fenway Park. The slam put the Sox ahead 5–2, but Chicago scored three times in the ninth. Boston won in their half of the ninth on a walk-off single by Billy Hatcher, playing in his second game as a Red Sox.

JULY 11   Tom Brunansky hits a grand slam off Donn Pall in the sixth inning of an 11–2 win over the White Sox at Fenway Park.

JULY 18   Roger Clemens pitches a two-hitter to defeat the Twins 1–0 at the Metrodome. The lone run of the game was driven in on a single by Wade Boggs in the first inning. The only Minnesota hits were singles by Shane Mack and Gene Larkin.

              After the game, Clemens threw a fit when he spotted a newspaper columnist whom he felt had blamed him for the death of a young man. Clemens refused to talk to the media until George Kimball of the Boston Herald *left the group of about 20 reporters who gathered around his locker. "You are a low life,"* Clemens *shouted at Kimball. "Get out of here." Clemens then picked up two hamburger buns and threw them at Kimball. Finally, Kimball went to another part of the locker room and Clemens addressed the rest of the media. Kimball wrote in a column several weeks earlier that he had received a letter from an elderly woman who said she was refused an autograph by Clemens for her grandson, who was suffering from Down Syndrome. The young man subsequently died. Clemens said he didn't remember the incident and defended his relationship with the public. Kimball said that Clemens had several earlier chances to confront him but "instead waited to collect an audience."*

JULY 27   Tom Brunansky hits a grand slam off Kevin Brown in the first inning of a 7–5 win over the Rangers at Fenway Park.

AUGUST 4   Actor Charlie Sheen, who starred in the baseball movies *Major League* and *Eight Men Out*, shells out $85,000 for the ball that rolled through the legs of Bill Buckner in the 1986 World Series. Sheen bought the ball at a Manhattan auction.

AUGUST 9   The Red Sox and Yankees tie a major league record for the fewest assists by two clubs in a nine-inning game with five. The Yankees had only one assist, defeating the Sox 6–0 in New York. Yankee hurler Sam Militello made his major league debut and allowed only one hit, a second-inning single by Tony Peña, in seven innings.

AUGUST 22   John Valentin hits a grand slam off Mickey Schooler in the sixth inning of a 10–8 win over the Mariners at Fenway Park. It was Valentin's first major league homer and the second grand slam allowed by Schooler at Fenway in 1992.

                   Valentin and Mo Vaughn were roommates at Seton Hall University.

AUGUST 30   The Red Sox trade Jeff Reardon to the Braves for Stan Ross and Nate Minchey.

                   Reardon pitched in the 1992 World Series for Atlanta, where he allowed ninth-inning runs in two games that led to losses against the Blue Jays.

SEPTEMBER 7   In a matchup of two of the greatest pitchers of all time, Roger Clemens bests Nolan Ryan and the Rangers 3–0 in Arlington. The two icons pitched seven scoreless innings before the Sox scored twice in the eighth. Clemens struck out seven batters in a row from the fourth through the sixth innings.

SEPTEMBER 16   A squeeze bunt by Bob Zupcic in the fifteenth inning scores Jody Reed from third base and beats the Brewers 2–1 at Fenway Park.

SEPTEMBER 20   The Red Sox score four runs in the fourteenth inning to beat the Orioles 7–3 in Baltimore. Bob Zupcic's double broke the 3–3 tie.

SEPTEMBER 30   Frank Viola takes a no-hitter into the ninth inning against the Blue Jays in Toronto before allowing a single to Devon White. Viola settled for a one-hitter and a 1–0 victory. The lone run scored on a fourth-inning homer by John Valentin off David Cone.

                   The Red Sox scored only 599 runs and hit only 84 homers in 1992. The 3.7 runs per game were the fewest by the Red Sox club since 1943. The home runs were the least by a Fenway Park crew since 1945. The anemic offense wasted a solid performance by a pitching staff that finished second in the AL with an earned run average of 3.63. It was the first time that a Red Sox club finished as high as second in ERA since 1936. (No Red Sox team led the AL in ERA between 1914 and 1999.) Injuries, unexpected slumps, and old age led to the offensive collapse. Carlos Quintana was injured in a traffic accident in Venezuela in February and missed the entire season with a broken left arm, broken right foot, and nerve damage to his wrist and fingers. Mike Greenwell, Ellis Burks, and Jody Reed missed most of the campaign with injuries. Wade Boggs hit under .300 for the first time in his career, with his batting dropping to an alarming .259. Advancing age caught hold of players like Jack Clark and Tony Peña and slowed their offensive contributions to virtually nothing.

NOVEMBER 17   Two weeks after Bill Clinton defeats George Bush in the presidential election, the Red Sox lose Jody Reed and Eric Wedge to the Rockies in the expansion draft.

DECEMBER 1   The Red Sox sign Scott Fletcher, most recently with the Brewers, as a free agent.

DECEMBER 8   The Red Sox trade Mike Gardiner and Terry Powers to the Expos for Ivan Calderon.

DECEMBER 9   The Red Sox sign Andre Dawson, most recently with the Cubs, as a free agent.

Dawson was thirty-eight and had 399 home runs, eight All-Star appearances, and an MVP award on his resume when the Red Sox signed him to a two-year contract. He battled injuries during his two years in Boston and hit .260 with 29 homers in 196 games.

DECEMBER 15   Wade Boggs signs a free-agent contract with the Yankees.

Boggs had the worst season of his career in 1992, batting only .259. He was thirty-four, and many in the Red Sox organization believed that he was finished. But Boggs hit over .300 in each of the next four seasons and played for the Yankees' 1996 World Championship club. He collected his 3,000th career hit as a Devil Ray in 1999.

DECEMBER 18   The Red Sox fail to offer Ellis Burks a contract for the 1993 season.

Burks signed with the White Sox on January 4. Hailed as a future MVP, Burks never came close to reaching those heights with the Sox. There was always the feeling that his shy, laconic personality was holding back a tremendous talent. After playing for the White Sox, Rockies, Giants, and Indians, Burks returned to the Sox in 2004 for one season.

1993 · B

Season in a Sentence

The Red Sox win 33 of 44 in a midseason tear and hold first place for three days in July but collapse down the stretch.

Finish · Won · Lost · Pct · GB

Fifth   80   82   .494   15.0

Manager

Butch Hobson

Stats   Red Sox · AL · Rank

	Red Sox	AL	Rank
Batting Avg:	.264	.267	9
On-Base Pct:	.330	.337	10
Slugging Pct:	.395	.408	10
Home Runs:	114		13 (tie)
Stolen Bases:	73		12
ERA:	3.77	4.32	2
Fielding Pct:	.980	.981	10
Runs Scored:	686		12
Runs Allowed:	698		3

Starting Lineup

Tony Peña, c
Mo Vaughn, 1b
Scott Fletcher, 2b
Scott Cooper, 3b
John Valentin, ss
Mike Greenwell, lf
Billy Hatcher, of
Bob Zupcic, of
Andre Dawson, dh
Carlos Quintana, 1b-of
Ivan Calderon, of
Bob Melvin, c

Pitchers

Danny Darwin, sp
Roger Clemens, sp
Frank Viola, sp
John Dopson, sp
Aaron Sele, sp
Jeff Russell, rp
Greg Harris, rp
Tony Fossas, rp
Paul Quantrill, rp
Ken Ryan, rp

Attendance

2,422,021 (fourth in AL)

Club Leaders

Batting Avg:	Greenwell	.315
On-Base Pct:	Vaughn	.390
Slugging Pct:	Vaughn	.525
Home Runs:	Vaughn	29
RBI:	Vaughn	101
Runs:	Vaughn	86
Stolen Bases:	Fletcher	16
Wins:	Darwin	15
Strikeouts:	Clemens	160
ERA:	Viola	3.14
Saves:	Russell	33

JANUARY 28   Tom Brunansky signs a free-agent contract with the Brewers.

FEBRUARY 18   The Red Sox sign Jeff Russell, most recently with the Athletics, as a free agent.

FEBRUARY 26   On the day that a terrorist bomb in the garage of the World Trade Center in New York kills six people, the Red Sox release Jack Clark.

The Red Sox trained at Fort Myers for the first time in 1993.

MARCH 26   Roger Clemens receives a contract extension with the Red Sox through 1996.

After signing the deal, Clemens said that he would remain with the Sox through the end of his career. The 1993 season was a struggle, however, as Clemens battled a groin pull and spent four weeks on the disabled list. He finished the season with an 11–14 record and a 4.46 ERA.

APRIL 2   Frank Viola (seven innings) and Cory Bailey (two innings) combine on a spring training no-hitter to defeat the Phillies 10–0 in Clearwater, Florida.

APRIL 5

The Red Sox win the season opener 3–1 against the Royals in Kansas City. Mike Greenwell drove in all three runs with a bases-loaded triple in the fifth inning. Roger Clemens went eight innings for the win.

The Red Sox broadcasters in 1993 were Joe Castiglione and Jerry Trupiano on radio, Sean McDonough and Bob Montgomery on WSBK-TV, and Bob Kurtz and Jerry Remy on NESN. Trupiano replaced Bob Starr, and Kurtz replaced Ned Martin.

APRIL 13

In the first game of the season at Fenway Park, the Red Sox win 6–2 over the Indians before 29,606. Playing for the Red Sox in Boston for the first time, Scott Fletcher hit a two-run homer.

The Red Sox lost reliever Jose Melendez for six weeks in April and May as a result of a bizarre injury. He was walking past Ivan Calderon's locker as Calderon was gesturing to another player when he swung his hand and caught Melendez's thumb.

APRIL 15

After the Indians score in the top of the thirteenth inning, the Red Sox rally for two runs in their half to win 4–3 at Fenway Park. Utility infielder Jeff Richardson doubled home the winning run. In the first inning, Andre Dawson collected his 400th career homer. The milestone homer was struck off Jose Mesa.

Richardson played only 15 games with the Red Sox and drove in only two runs, which were his first major league RBIs since 1989 and the last two of his career.

APRIL 20

The day after the raid on the Branch Davidian compound in Waco, Texas, the Red Sox defeat the Mariners 5–2 at Seattle. The win gave the Sox an 11–3 record and a 2½-game lead in the AL East.

The Sox lost their next six games to drop out of first. The club finished the year with an 80–82 record in a roller-coaster season. After the 11–3 start, the Sox lost 35 of the next 54 games to drop to 30–38 on June 20. Boston was 13 games out of first. From June 21 through August 10, the Red Sox won 33 of 44. Bouncing back from the 13-game deficit, the Sox were in first place for three days in late July and were one game out of first on August 10. Then the Sox went into a slide again, losing 33 of their last 50 games to finish in fifth place 15 games behind the pennant-winning Blue Jays.

APRIL 22

Chris Bosio of the Mariners pitches a no-hitter to beat the Red Sox, 7–0. Bosio started the first inning by walking Ernest Riles and Carlos Quintana, then pitched perfect ball the rest of the way. The game ended on a grounder by Riles to shortstop Omar Vizquel, who caught the ball barehanded and threw out Riles by two steps.

MAY 7

Danny Darwin (eight innings) and Jeff Russell (one inning) combine to beat the Brewers 1–0 in Milwaukee. The lone run of the game scored on a sacrifice fly by Ivan Calderon in the second inning.

MAY 11

Roger Clemens strikes out 13 batters in a 4–0 win over the Orioles in Baltimore.

MAY 12   Danny Darwin (7⅔ innings), Greg Harris (one-third of an inning), and Jeff Russell (one inning) combine on a two-hitter to defeat the Orioles 2–0 at Camden Yards. Darwin retired 21 of the first 22 batters he faced. David Segui collected both Baltimore hits with a single in the third inning and a double in the eighth, both off Darwin.

MAY 18   The Red Sox score four runs in the first inning and six in the second to take a 10–0 lead and defeat the Blue Jays 10–5 at Fenway Park.

MAY 19   On the night before the airing of the last episode of *Cheers*, John Ratzenberger throws out the ceremonial first pitch before a 10–5 win over the Blue Jays. Ratzenberger played know-it-all postal employee Cliff Clavin on the series. The actor threw the ball over the head of Tony Peña. Later, Ratzenberger helped the grounds crew rake the infield.

MAY 20   The Sox start a night game against the Blue Jays at 6:05 PM, 90 minutes earlier than usual, so that it will not interfere with the airing of the final episode of *Cheers*, scheduled to begin at 9:20 PM. Toronto won, 4–3.

MAY 21   In his first game as a visiting player at Fenway Park, Wade Boggs collects four hits in four at-bats in a 7–2 Red Sox win over the Yankees.

Boggs received a standing ovation when he batted in the first inning and paused to remove his helmet. Raising it in one hand, Boggs acknowledged the cheers by gesturing to every corner of the ballpark.

MAY 28   Roger Clemens (eight innings) and Jeff Russell (one inning) combine on a two-hitter to defeat the Rangers 4–1 at Fenway Park. The only two Texas hits were a single by Rafael Palmeiro in the third inning and a triple by Ivan Rodriguez in the seventh.

MAY 29   The Red Sox rout the Rangers 15–1 at Fenway Park. Jose Canseco pitched the eighth inning for Texas and allowed three runs. He tore a ligament in his elbow and missed the rest of the season.

MAY 30   The Red Sox rally to tie the Rangers at Fenway Park with runs in the ninth and tenth innings, then win 6–5 in the twelfth. John Valentin's double drove in the winning run.

JUNE 3   In the first round of the amateur draft, the Red Sox draft outfielder Trot Nixon from New Hanover High School in Wilmington, North Carolina.

Nixon passed up a chance to play quarterback at North Carolina State to sign with the Red Sox. He reached the majors in 1996 and has been one of the best first-round picks in club history. Other future major leaguers drafted and signed by the Red Six in 1993 were Jeff Suppan (second round), Ryan McGuire (third), Pete Munro (sixth), Lou Merloni (10th), and Shayne Bennett (25th).

JUNE 4   Danny Darwin (seven innings), Tony Fossas (one-third of an inning), Greg Harris (two-thirds of an inning), and Jeff Russell (one inning) combine to defeat the White Sox 1–0 in Chicago. Bob Melvin drove in the lone run of the game with a single in the ninth inning. Melvin entered the game as a catcher after Tony Peña was lifted for a pinch hitter.

The one-third-of-an-inning appearance was typical for Fossas, a southpaw who specialized in retiring left-handed batters. In 1992 and 1993, Fossas pitched in 111 games for the Red Sox, but accumulated only 69 $^2/_3$ innings.

JUNE 26   The Red Sox wallop the Tigers 13–4 at Fenway Park.

JUNE 28   A two-run, bases-loaded, walk-off single with one out in the ninth by Scott Cooper on a 3–2 pitch beats the Brewers 4–3 at Fenway Park.

JUNE 30   The Red Sox rout the Brewers 12–2 at Fenway Park. The Sox scored three runs in four consecutive innings from the fifth through the eighth.

JULY 4   Paul Quantrill pitches a two-hitter to beat the Mariners 6–0 at the Kingdome. The only Seattle hits were a single by Jay Buhner and a double by Mackey Sasser, both in the second inning. Chris Bosio, who no-hit the Red Sox on April 22, was the Seattle starting pitcher. Bosio held batters hitless until the seventh inning, when Mike Greenwell singled. Before the inning was over, Mo Vaughn hit a three-run homer.

Steve Babineau

Vaughn and Greenwell were the top Boston hitters in 1993. Vaughn was somewhat of a disappointment in his first two seasons in Boston. In 1991 and 1992, he had a .244 batting average and 17 homers in 574 at-bats. With the help of new hitting coach Mike Easler, whom Vaughn credited with saving his career, he hit .297 with 29 homers and 101 RBIs in 1993. Greenwell batted .315 with 13 homers.

Following his breakout year in 1993, Mo Vaughn supplied plenty of power for the Sox for five years, until being traded after the 1998 season. Fans were displeased, but the Sox let Vaughn go at the right time.

JULY 8   Mo Vaughn hits a grand slam off Todd Van Poppel in the first inning of an 11–9 win over the Athletics in Oakland.

JULY 18   Trailing 6–1, the Red Sox score three runs in the seventh inning and three in the eighth to beat the Mariners 7–6 at Fenway Park.

JULY 23   The Red Sox move into first place by winning their eighth game in a row with a 10-inning, 6–5 decision over the Athletics at Fenway Park. The Sox trailed 5–2 before scoring three runs in the eighth inning, two of them on a Mike Greenwell homer off Dennis Eckersley, and another in the tenth. The winning run was driven in on a double by Bob Zupcic high off the left field wall.

JULY 25   The Red Sox win their 10th game in a row with an 8–1 decision over the Athletics at Fenway Park. Mo Vaughn hit a grand slam in the fifth inning off Rick Honeycutt.

               The Red Sox were 25–5 from June 21 through July 25. Four of the five losses were by one run, with the other by two runs.

AUGUST 1   Roger Clemens is bitten by a dog on a Baltimore highway.

               Clemens was driving at 6:30 AM when he noticed that a dog had apparently been hit by a car. He went to move the dog to the side of the road and was bitten on the right thumb. Clemens went to Johns Hopkins Hospital for treatment and a tetanus shot. The dog was put to sleep.

AUGUST 4   Rookie pitcher Aaron Sele runs his career record to 6–0 with a 5–4 victory over the Twins in Minneapolis.

               The six wins at the start of a career was the second best in Red Sox history, trailing only the 8–0 mark established by Boo Ferriss in 1945. Sele finished the 1993 season with a record of 7–2 with an ERA of 2.74.

AUGUST 18   Danny Darwin pitches a one-hitter to beat the White Sox 5–0 at Fenway Park. Darwin was five outs from a no-hitter when Dan Pasqua tripled with one out in the eighth inning. Pasqua's drive hit the center field wall inches above the glove of five-foot-ten-inch Billy Hatcher.

AUGUST 21   The Red Sox purchase Rob Deer from the Tigers.

AUGUST 22   In his first at-bat with the Red Sox, Rob Deer hits a home run. Deer later added two singles and a diving catch in right field, but the Sox lost 3–2 in 11 innings to the Indians at Fenway Park.

               Deer hit seven homers in 143 at-bats for the Red Sox, but struck out 49 times and batted only .196.

AUGUST 26   The Red Sox play at Arlington Stadium for the last time and beat the Rangers, 3–1.

               The Rangers opened The Ballpark in Arlington in 1994.

SEPTEMBER 4   The Red Sox hand out emblems to the surviving family members of the 1918 World Championship club in ceremonies prior to a 4–2 loss to the Royals at Fenway Park. The emblems were withheld from the players following the Fall Classic that season because they threatened to go on strike prior to Game Five (see September 10, 1918).

SEPTEMBER 6   A bench-clearing brawl highlights a 3–1 win over the White Sox in Chicago. George Bell charged the mound in the second inning after he was hit by an Aaron Sele pitch, causing both benches to empty. Rob Deer scored all three runs on two homers and a double.

SEPTEMBER 12   The Red Sox crush the Indians 11–1 in Cleveland. It was the last game that the Sox played at Municipal Stadium.

The Indians opened Jacobs Field in 1994.

SEPTEMBER 14   Major League Baseball announces its three-division alignment, plus an extra round of playoff games, including a wild-card team, to be put into effect for the 1994 season. The Red Sox were placed in the Eastern Division with the Yankees, Orioles, Blue Jays, and Tigers. In 1998, the Tigers moved to the Central Division, and the expansion Devil Rays were placed in the AL East.

Red Sox president John Harrington was one of the chief proponents of the three-division plan. No team has benefited more from the format than the Red Sox. In the first 10 seasons of the new playoff format (which actually began in 1995 because of the 1994 strike), the Red Sox reached the playoffs five times from 1995 through 2004, once as division champs and four times as a wild card, one of which resulted in the 2004 World Championship. Under the old two-division setup, it's unlikely that the Sox would have made the postseason in any of those years. The wild card didn't exist, and in the season that the Sox won the AL East (1995), the club had 14 fewer wins than former division-rival Cleveland.

SEPTEMBER 18   The Yankees beat the Red Sox 4–3 in New York on an "extra out" in the ninth inning. With two outs in the bottom of the ninth, the Sox leading 3–1, Greg Harris on the mound, and a Yankee runner on first base, Mike Stanley flied out to Mike Greenwell in left field to apparently end the game. But third-base umpire Tim Welke waved off the play because a fan jumped the box seat railing and ran onto the field. Given another chance, Stanley singled. Wade Boggs followed with a single to score a run. After Dion James walked, Don Mattingly drove in two runs with another single, and the Yankees won, 4–3. The Red Sox protested the game but the American League disallowed it.

According to many of the Red Sox, the pitch by Harris to Stanley was on the way to the plate before Welke called time. The fan who ran onto the field was a fifteen-year-old from Pleasantville, New York, who was attending the game with a church group. It wasn't the only bizarre play of the day. In the first inning, Mo Vaughn threw his bat away and trotted to first base believing he had received ball four from Jimmy Key. It was ball three. On the next pitch, Vaughn hit a home run.

SEPTEMBER 22   Rob Deer hits a two-run homer in the tenth inning that beats the Blue Jays 7–5 in Toronto.

NOVEMBER 23   Haywood Sullivan agrees to a buyout and sells his 12-percent share of the Red Sox. John Harrington became the club's virtual owner as the head of the trust that owned the club.

Harrington first joined the team as comptroller in 1973 and made an improbable rise to club president by 1987. He grew up in the Boston neighborhood of

Jamaica Plain and attended Boston College. Harrington became one of base-ball's more powerful owners, working closely with Commissioner Bud Selig.

DECEMBER 7   The Red Sox sign Otis Nixon, most recently with the Braves, as a free agent.

Nixon brought some speed to a slow-moving Red Sox club. He stole 42 bases in 103 games in the strike-shortened 1994 season, his only season in Boston. Nixon hit .274 that year, but had no homers and a slugging percentage of only .317. During his 17-year big-league career with nine clubs, Nixon hit only 11 homers but stole 620 bases in 1,709 games.

DECEMBER 30   The Red Sox sign Dave Valle, most recently with the Mariners, as a free agent.

1994   B

Season in a Sentence

After a 20–7 start, the Red Sox finish with a losing record for the third year in a row when the player's strike brings an end to the season in August.

Finish • Won • Lost • Pct • GB

Fifth   54   61   .470   17.0

Manager

Butch Hobson

Stats   Red Sox • AL • Rank

Batting Avg:	.263	.273	12
On-Base Pct:	.334	.345	13
Slugging Pct:	.421	.434	10
Home Runs:	120		9 (tie)
Stolen Bases:	81		6
ERA:	4.93	4.80	9
Fielding Pct:	.981	.981	6
Runs Scored:	552		11
Runs Allowed:	621		10

Starting Lineup

Damon Berryhill, c
Mo Vaughn, 1b
Tim Naehring, 2b
Scott Cooper, 3b
John Valentin, ss
Mike Greenwell, lf
Otis Nixon, cf
Tom Brunansky, rf
Andre Dawson, dh
Scott Fletcher, 2b
Lee Tinsley, lf-cf
Carlos Rodriguez, ss
Billy Hatcher, rf
Wes Chamberlain, rf
Rich Rowland, c

Pitchers

Roger Clemens, sp
Mike Gardiner, sp
Tom Bolton, sp
Matt Young, sp
Kevin Morton, sp
Jeff Reardon, rp
Greg Harris, rp-sp
Joe Hesketh, rp-sp
Dennis Lamp, rp
Jeff Gray, rp

Attendance

1,775,818 (fifth in AL)

Club Leaders

Batting Avg:	Valentin	.316
On-Base Pct:	Vaughn	.408
Slugging Pct:	Vaughn	.576
Home Runs:	Vaughn	26
RBI:	Vaughn	82
Runs:	Vaughn	65
Stolen Bases:	Nixon	42
Wins:	Clemens	9
Strikeouts:	Clemens	168
ERA:	Clemens	2.85
Saves:	Ryan	13

JANUARY 26   Three weeks after Nancy Kerrigan is attacked by assailants connected to rival skater Tonya Harding, the Red Sox hire thirty-five-year-old Dan Duquette as general manager to replace Lou Gorman.

Duquette was a lifelong Red Sox fan and a native of Dalton, Massachusetts, where he caught Jeff Reardon in Little League. Duquette played football and baseball at Amherst College, then joined the Brewers in scouting and player development, where he earned a reputation as a savvy judge of talent. He then moved to the Expos in 1991, where he became the youngest general manager in baseball and built one of the best farm systems in the game with limited resources. Duquette was a new breed of baseball executive with his use of computer analysis and performance analysis by using a new generation of statistics pioneered by Bill James. He took over a deteriorating Red Sox club that had losing records in both 1992 and 1993. It was the first time that the Sox lost more than they won in consecutive seasons since 1965–66.

JANUARY 27   Sherm Feller, who had been the public-address announcer since 1967, dies of a heart attack. Feller was also a songwriter and composer whose works included the 1958 hit "Summertime, Summertime." In April, the Red Sox hired Leslie Sterling to replace Feller. Sterling became the second woman to handle public address announcements for a major league club. She was the ballpark announcer for three seasons before being replaced by Ed Brickley.

FEBRUARY 8   The Indians sign Tony Peña to a free-agent contract.

APRIL 1   The Red Sox trade John Flaherty to the Tigers for Rich Rowland.

APRIL 4   In the season opener, the Red Sox defeat the Tigers 9–8 at Fenway Park before a crowd of 34,023. The Sox overcame an 8–6 deficit with three runs in the eighth inning. Otis Nixon, in his Red Sox debut, scored the winning run on a passed ball.

APRIL 8   The Red Sox run their season record to 4–0, winning 8–6 over the White Sox in Chicago.

APRIL 12   The Red Sox blast the Royals 22–11 in Kansas City. The Sox scored six runs in the first inning and added eight more in the fifth. Scott Cooper hit for the cycle, including two doubles, in six at-bats, and drove in five runs. He homered in the third inning off Kevin Appier and completed the cycle with a single in the ninth off utility infielder David Howard, who pitched for the Royals when the contest was hopelessly lost. Cooper's four extra-base hits tied a Red Sox record.

APRIL 18   On Patriots' Day, Tim Raines hits three homers against the Red Sox in a 12–1 White Sox victory at Fenway Park.

APRIL 19   The Red Sox pummel the Athletics 13–5 with six homers at Fenway Park. Mo Vaughn and Tim Naehring hit back-to-back homers twice, first off Bob Welch in the second inning and again in the eighth against Carlos Reyes. Scott Cooper hit a grand slam off Welch in the third. Mike Greenwell also homered.

APRIL 20   Roger Clemens pitches a two-hitter to defeat the Athletics 2–0 at Fenway Park. The only Oakland hits were singles by Stan Javier in the fourth inning and Mike Brumley in the fifth.

APRIL 27   Frank Viola (six innings), Scott Bankhead (two innings), and Jeff Russell (one inning) combine on a two-hitter to defeat the Athletics 1–0 in Oakland. The only two Athletics hits were a double by Troy Neel in the fourth inning and a single by Junior Noboa in the fifth. Billy Hatcher drove in the lone run of the game with a single off Ron Darling in the third inning.

              It was the first time that Viola and Darling had met each other since a classic NCAA tournament game on May 22, 1981. In that matchup, Darling pitched 11 no-hit innings for Yale but dropped a 1–0 decision to Viola and St. John's in 12 innings.

MAY 1   The Red Sox score seven runs in the third inning and defeat the Angels 10–1 in Anaheim.

MAY 3   The Red Sox lose two pitchers to injury in the third inning of a 7–6 win over the Mariners at Fenway Park. Frank Viola left with an injured elbow, which popped while he was pitching to Eric Anthony. Paul Quantrill relieved Viola and threw a high-and-tight pitch to Anthony. After Anthony walked, he went halfway to first, then charged the mound, causing both benches to empty. In the ensuing brawl, Quantrill ended up at the bottom of the pile-up and had to leave the game with an injured finger.

              Viola had to undergo Tommy John transplant surgery and never pitched another game with the Sox.

MAY 4   The Red Sox defeat the Mariners 4–2 at Fenway Park to run their season record to 20–7. It was the Sox' best 27-game start since 1946, when they were 23–4.

              The fast start gave the Red Sox a 2½-game lead in the AL East. The Sox lost their next five games, however, to drop out of first in a slide that remained unabated until the strike ended the season. From May 5 through the strike, the Sox were 34–54.

MAY 5   The Red Sox sell Bob Zupcic to the White Sox.

MAY 20   The Twins drub the Red Sox 21–2 at the Metrodome. Minnesota scored all 21 of their runs in the first five innings, including an 11-run fifth off Todd Frowirth and Greg Harris. Outfielder Andy Tomberlain pitched the eighth and ninth and allowed one hit with a walk and a strikeout.

              Frowirth pitched 22 games and 26⅔ innings for the Red Sox and had an ERA of 10.80.

MAY 26   The Red Sox score eight runs in the second inning and defeat the Indians 13–5 at Fenway Park.

MAY 27   The Red Sox play at The Ballpark in Arlington for the first time and lose 4–3 to the Rangers.

MAY 31   The Red Sox trade Billy Hatcher and Paul Quantrill to the Phillies for Wes Chamberlain and Mike Sullivan.

JUNE 2   In the first round of the amateur draft, the Red Sox select shortstop Nomar Garcia-parra from Georgia Tech University.

Garciaparra made his major league debut on August 31, 1996, and was an immediate star. Other future major leaguers drafted and signed by the Sox in 1994 included Brian Rose (third round), Brian Barkley (fifth), Donnie Sadler (11th), Carl Pavano (13th), and Michael Coleman (18th).

JUNE 7   Roger Clemens strikes out 12 batters in a 5–1 win over the Tigers in Detroit.

JUNE 16   The Red Sox play at Jacobs Field in Cleveland for the first time and lose 7–6 to the Indians.

The Red Sox trade Dave Valle to the Brewers for Tom Brunansky.

JUNE 19   Two days after ninety-five million Americans tune in to the eight-hour police chase of O. J. Simpson, the Red Sox lose their 11th game in a row, the club's longest since 1932, by dropping a 6–5 decision to the Indians in Cleveland.

JUNE 20   The Red Sox break the 11-game losing streak with a 4–1 victory over the Blue Jays at Skydome.

Andre Dawson was hit twice by Toronto pitcher Todd Stottlemyre during the game. Dawson was plunked in the shoulder in the sixth inning and threw the ball over the pitcher's head into center field. In the eighth, Dawson was struck on the elbow and took a few steps toward the pitcher's mound as both benches emptied. Stottlemyre was ejected but didn't go quietly. He heaved water coolers and a large Gatorade bucket out of the dugout on his way to the clubhouse.

JUNE 21   The Red Sox explode for 10 runs in the first inning on six hits and seven walks to cruise to a 13–1 win over the Blue Jays at Fenway Park. The inning took 41 minutes to complete.

JUNE 24   Damon Berryhill hits a two-out, two-run single in the ninth inning that beats the Brewers 4–3 at County Stadium. Berryhill got his chance for heroics after Tom Brunansky, eight days after being reacquired by the Sox from Milwaukee, reached second base safely after being caught in a two-out rundown.

JUNE 26   A two-run homer by Mo Vaughn in the twelfth inning beats the Brewers 10–8 in Milwaukee.

Vaughn batted .310 with 26 homers in 1994.

JUNE 28   Butch Hobson is ejected after Red Sox pitcher Sergio Valdez is issued a warning after throwing a pitch behind the head of Mike Gallego of the Yankees during a 10–4 loss at Fenway Park. Hobson bumped umpire Larry Barnett several times trying to get at home plate arbiter Greg Kosc. Hobson was suspended for five days because of the incident.

JUNE 30   The Red Sox defeat the Yankees 6–5 at Fenway Park, ending a 12-game losing streak at Fenway, the club's longest since 1926.

On the same day, the Red Sox trade Jeff Russell to the Indians for Steve Farr and Chris Nabholtz.

JULY 2   Tom Brunansky hits a grand slam off Billy Taylor in the fifth inning of a 10–2 win over the Athletics at Fenway Park.

JULY 8   Playing shortstop, John Valentin turns an unassisted triple play before hitting a three-run homer in the sixth inning of a 4–3 win over the Mariners at Fenway Park. With Seattle runners moving from first and second in the top of the sixth, Valentin went to one knee to catch a line drive by Marc Newfield. Valentin then stepped on second to double Mike Blowers and trotted a few steps to tag Keith Mitchell. The Red Sox were trailing 2–0 at the time. In the bottom of the sixth, the Sox scored four times, three of them on Valentin's homer. The game ended when right fielder Wes Chamberlain went over the bullpen wall to take a game-tying homer away from Reggie Jefferson. The contest was also notable because it was the major league debut of Alex Rodriguez, who was only eighteen years old and played short for the Mariners.

              The Mariners returned to Fenway for a series from July 22 through 24. The games were originally scheduled for Seattle but were moved to Boston because of falling ceiling tiles at the Kingdome.

JULY 12   Scott Cooper drives in a run with a double in the All-Star Game, but the American League loses 8–7 in 10 innings at Three Rivers Stadium in Pittsburgh.

JULY 14   Roger Clemens pitches a two-hitter to defeat the Athletics 2–1 in Oakland. Clemens had a no-hitter until Ruben Sierra led off the seventh with a single. Troy Neel added a one-out homer in the ninth.

JULY 15   The Red Sox score four runs in the ninth, the last three on a homer by Tom Brunansky off Dennis Eckersley, to defeat the Athletics 4–1 in Oakland.

JULY 16   Red Sox pitcher Jose Melendez comes into a 9–0 loss against the Athletics in Oakland and is ejected after his first pitch hits Rickey Henderson. Melendez had just been recalled from the minors and was making his first big-league appearance since June 26, 1993.

JULY 28   Tom Brunansky hits a homer off Scott Kamieniecki for a 1–0 win over the Yankees in the second game of a doubleheader at Yankee Stadium. Joe Hesketh (7⅔ innings), Tony Fossas (two-thirds of an inning), and Ken Ryan (two-thirds of an inning) combined on the shutout. New York won the first game, 4–3.

AUGUST 2   Wes Chamberlain hits a grand slam off Dave Stewart in the fourth inning of an 8–7 loss to the Blue Jays at Fenway Park.

AUGUST 6   John Valentin collects five hits, including two doubles, and drives in five runs in an 8–4 win over the Indians in the first game of a doubleheader at Fenway Park. Cleveland won the second game, 5–0.

              Valentin hit .316 with nine homers in 1994.

AUGUST 7   Second baseman Carlos Rodriguez collects three hits, including three doubles, in a 4–1 win over the Indians in the first game of a doubleheader at Fenway Park. Cleveland won the second game, 15–10.

Rodriguez finished his three-year career in 1995 with only 67 hits, although with a respectable batting average of .278.

AUGUST 10   In the last game before the strike, the Red Sox lose 17–7 to the Twins in Minneapolis.

Although the season ended after 115 games, the Red Sox had already used 46 different players in 1994 as Dan Duquette ran players off and on the roster all season.

AUGUST 12   With about 70 percent of the season completed, the major league players go on strike.

The strike, baseball's eighth interruption since 1972, had been anticipated all season. The owners wanted to put a lid on escalating payrolls by capping salaries and revising, if not eliminating, the arbitration process. The players, who were obviously not interested in these reforms, had only one weapon once talks broke down—a strike.

SEPTEMBER 14   The owners of the 28 major league clubs vote 26–2 to cancel the remainder of the 1994 season, including the playoffs and the World Series.

SEPTEMBER 20   The Red Sox fire Butch Hobson as manager.

Hobson never managed another big-league club. In 1996, while coaching for the Scranton/Wilkes-Barre Red Barons in the Phillies' minor league system, Hobson was arrested for receiving a package of cocaine at his hotel room in Pawtucket, Rhode Island. At first, he said that he was bewildered by the receipt of the package and maintained his innocence. Later, he admitted that he used the drug and avoided jail time by entering a program for first-time criminal offenders.

OCTOBER 18   The Red Sox hire forty-year-old Kevin Kennedy as manager. Kennedy had been fired by the Rangers at the end of the 1994 season after two years on the job and a record of 138–138. The Rangers were leading the AL West with a record of 52–62 when the strike ended the 1994 season. Kennedy never played in the majors, although he was a high school teammate of Robin Yount in Woodland Hills, California.

NOVEMBER 4   Damon Berryhill signs a free-agent contract with the Reds.

DECEMBER 7   The Red Sox trade Nate Minchey and Jeff McNeely to the Cardinals for Luis Alicea.

DECEMBER 9   The Red Sox trade Otis Nixon and Luis Ortiz to the Rangers for Jose Canseco.

Although the end of the strike was nowhere in sight, the acquisition of Canseco made headlines in Boston. Canseco played for Kevin Kennedy in Texas, and the two were close. Canseco played two injury-plagued seasons with the Sox and hit .298 with 52 homers in 198 games.

DECEMBER 13   The Red Sox trade a player to be named later to the Royals for Terry Shumpert.

1995   B

Season in a Sentence

With the club coming off a stretch of three straight losing seasons, Kevin Kennedy and Dan Duquette look like geniuses when the Red Sox spend most of the season in first place with their best winning percentage since 1978.

Finish • Won • Lost • Pct • GB

First   86   58   .597   +7.0

AL Division Series—The Red Sox lost three games to none to the Cleveland Indians.

Manager

Kevin Kennedy

Stats

Stats	Red Sox	AL	Rank
Batting Avg:	.280	.270	3
On-Base Pct:	.357	.344	2
Slugging Pct:	.455	.427	2
Home Runs:	175		4
Stolen Bases:	99		8
ERA:	4.39	4.71	3
Fielding Pct:	.978	.982	14
Runs Scored:	791		4
Runs Allowed:	698		6

Starting Lineup

Mike Macfarlane, c
Mo Vaughn, 1b
Luis Alicea, 2b
Tim Naehring, 3b
John Valentin, ss
Mike Greenwell, lf
Lee Tinsley, cf
Troy O'Leary, rf
Jose Canseco, dh
Willie McGee, rf-cf
Bill Haselman, c

Pitchers

Tim Wakefield, sp
Erik Hanson, sp
Roger Clemens, sp
Zane Smith, sp
Vaughn Eshelman, sp-rp
Stan Belinda, rp
Rheal Cormier, rp-sp

Attendance

2,164,410 (fourth in AL)

Club Leaders

Batting Avg:	Naehring	.307
On-Base Pct:	Naehring	.415
Slugging Pct:	Vaughn	.575
Home Runs:	Vaughn	39
RBI:	Vaughn	126
Runs:	Valentin	108
Stolen Bases:	Valentin	20
Wins:	Wakefield	16
Strikeouts:	Hanson	139
ERA:	Wakefield	2.95
Saves:	Aguilera	20

JANUARY 13   Major league owners vote to use replacement players during the 1995 season if the strike is not settled.

APRIL 2   The 234-day strike of Major League Baseball players comes to an end.

The season was scheduled to begin on April 26, with each team playing 144 games. The replacement players were either released or sent to minor league teams.

APRIL 8   Mike Macfarlane, most recently with the Royals, signs a free-agent contract with the Red Sox. The Red Sox also signed free agents Stan Belinda and Reggie Jefferson. In addition, the Red Sox traded Scott Cooper and Cory Bailey to the Cardinals for Mark Whiten and Rheal Cormier, and Andre Dawson signed a free-agent contract with the Marlins.

Macfarlane spent a year as the Red Sox starting catcher, then went back to the Royals after the end of the 1995 season.

APRIL 9   The Red Sox sign free agent Stan Belinda.

APRIL 10   Danny Darwin signs a free-agent contract with the Blue Jays. On the same day, the Red Sox also signed Alejandro Peña.

APRIL 11   The Red Sox sign free agent Erik Hanson.

Hanson gave the Red Sox one good season, posting a 15–5 record in 1995.

APRIL 14   The Red Sox purchase Troy O'Leary from the Brewers.

Picked up on waivers, O'Leary played 962 games for the Red Sox over seven seasons as a corner outfielder.

APRIL 18   The Red Sox sign Zane Smith, most recently with the Pirates, as a free agent.

APRIL 26   In the strike-delayed season opener, the Red Sox defeat the Twins 9–0 before 32,980 at Fenway Park. Five pitchers combined on a two-hitter for the Sox. Aaron Sele hurled five innings, and Frankie Rodriguez, Alejandro Peña, Jeff Pierce, and Ken Ryan added one each. The only Minnesota hits were singles by Kevin Maas in the fifth inning (off Sele) and Scott Leius in the eighth (off Pierce). Mike Greenwell collected four hits, including a double, in four at-bats. Mo Vaughn drove in three runs.

The distance from home plate to the left field wall had been listed at 315 feet since the ballpark was remodeled in 1934. Many believed it was shorter than 315 feet, but the Red Sox wouldn't allow anyone to measure it. During the first homestand in 1995, Boston Globe *columnist Dan Shaughnessy measured the distance with a 100-foot Stanley Steelmaster Long Tape. The distance, according to Shaughnessy's calculations, was 309 feet, three inches. In mid-May of that season, after Shaughnessy's story appeared in the* Globe, *the Sox put up a new sign reading 310 feet. "That's about what it is," admitted groundskeeper Joe Mooney. "We rounded it off. It came out in that story, so why hide it?"*

APRIL 27   The Red Sox sign free agent Tim Wakefield following his release by the Pirates.

Wakefield was on baseball's scrap heap when acquired by the Red Sox. After a fine rookie season with the Pirates in 1992, Wakefield had a horrible sophomore season in 1993, with a 6–11 record and a 5.61 ERA. He spent the entire 1994 campaign in the minors, where he posted a 5–15 record with an earned run average of 5.84 for Buffalo. During spring training in 1995, Wakefield worked with Phil and Joe Niekro to perfect his trademark knuckleball, and the results were astonishing. After starting the season at Pawtucket, Wakefield was called up on May 20 and was an immediate sensation. In his first 17 starts with the Sox, Wakefield was 14–1, including a 10-game winning streak, with an ERA of 1.65. He cooled off but finished the season at 16–8 with an earned run average of 2.95. Since 1995, Wakefield has filled in wherever he has been needed on the Red Sox pitching staff, performing as a starter, long reliever, and closer.

MAY 2   Two Red Sox grand slams account for all of the runs in an 8–0 win over the Yankees in New York. John Valentin hit a slam off Sterling Hitchcock in the third inning, and Mo Vaughn followed with one in the fourth facing Brian Boehringer.

Vaughn won the Most Valuable Player Award in 1995 with 39 homers, 126 RBIs, and a batting average of .300.

MAY 7   The Red Sox score seven runs in the sixth inning and defeat the Tigers 12–1 in Detroit.

MAY 9   A pinch-hit, walk-off homer by Wes Chamberlain in the ninth inning beats the Orioles 4–3 at Fenway Park.

MAY 13   The Red Sox take first place with a 6–4 win over the Yankees at Fenway Park. The victory gave the Sox a record of 10–5 on the season. Rookie pitcher Vaughn Eshelman started the game and held the Yankees hitless for $5\frac{2}{3}$ innings before Jim Leyritz homered.

Eshelman started his major league career with $18\frac{1}{3}$ scoreless innings, the second best in Red Sox history. Boo Ferriss began his career with 22 scoreless innings in 1945. Eshelman had little more success after his early run, however. He finished his big-league career in 1997 with a 15–9 record, but his ERA was 6.07 in 212 innings.

MAY 14   After the Yankees score two runs in the ninth to tie the score 2–2, Mike Macfarlane hits a walk-off homer in the bottom of the inning to lift the Red Sox to a 3–2 win at Fenway Park. The ball landed 10 rows into the center field bleachers above the 420-foot sign.

In May, the Red Sox announced plans for the Red Sox Hall of Fame, to be housed in the nearby New England Sports Museum. The initial inductees were Jimmy Collins, Eddie Collins, Joe Cronin, Bobby Doerr, Rick Ferrell, Jimmie Foxx, Lefty Grove, Harry Hooper, Babe Ruth, Tris Speaker, Ted Williams, Carl Yastrzemski, Tom Yawkey, and Cy Young.

MAY 26   Reggie Jefferson hits a grand slam off Mike Butcher in the sixth inning of an 8–1 win over the Angels in Anaheim.

MAY 27   The Red Sox bury the Angels 12–1 in Anaheim.

MAY 30   Tim Wakefield ($7\frac{2}{3}$ innings), Stan Belinda (one-third of an inning), Rheal Cormier (one-third of an inning), and Ken Ryan (one inning) combine on a shutout to defeat the Athletics 1–0 in Oakland. Tom Naehring drove in the lone run of the game with a sacrifice fly in the fifth inning.

In the offseason, Cormier worked as a lumberjack in a remote section of the Canadian province of New Brunswick.

JUNE 1   In their first choice in the amateur draft, the Red Sox select pitcher Andy Yount from Kingwood High School in Kingwood, Texas.

Yount failed to reach the majors. The only future major leaguers drafted and signed by the Sox in 1995 have been Steve Lomasney (fifth round), Matt Kinney (sixth), Cole Liniak (seventh), and Paxton Crawford (ninth), none of whom became regulars.

JUNE 2

John Valentin hits three homers, a double, and a single during a 10-inning, 6–5 win over the Mariners at Fenway Park. He homered off Chris Bosio in the first and third innings and against Ron Villone in the eighth. Valentin's double started the game-winning tenth-inning rally. His 15 total bases are the second highest single-game total in Red Sox history, trailing only the 16 by Fred Lynn in 1975.

Valentin scored 108 runs, drove in 102, clubbed 27 homers, and batted .298 in 1995.

JUNE 4

After the Mariners score in the top of the tenth at Fenway Park, Troy O'Leary hits a two-run, walk-off homer in the bottom half to lift the Red Sox to a 4–3 victory.

JUNE 6

The Red Sox sign Willie McGee to a contract.

JUNE 9

Tim Wakefield holds the Athletics hitless for the first 7 ⅓ innings before settling for a three-hitter and a 4–1 win at Fenway Park. The first Oakland hit was a single by Stan Javier.

JUNE 11

Mark McGwire hits his fifth homer in a span of two days at Fenway Park. On June 10, McGwire homered twice in an 8–5 Athletics victory. On June 11, McGwire hit three more in Oakland's 8–1 win. All five homers went over the left field wall.

JUNE 23

During a 7–5 loss to the Orioles in Baltimore, a fan wearing a Red Sox T-shirt throws a souvenir batting helmet at Mike Greenwell and strikes the Sox outfielder above the right eye, raising a welt.

JUNE 27

Bill Haselman hits a walk-off homer in the eleventh inning to beat the Blue Jays 6–5 at Fenway Park. Haselman entered the game as a catcher in the ninth inning after Mike Macfarlane was lifted for a pinch runner.

At UCLA, Haselman was a backup quarterback to Troy Aikman.

JULY 2

Lee Tinsley's walk-off, bases-loaded single in the ninth inning beats the Tigers 12–11 at Fenway Park. The Red Sox trailed 5–0 before erupting for eight runs in the third. The Sox stretched their lead to 11–5 before allowing the Tigers to score one run in the eighth and five in the ninth to tie the contest. Mo Vaughn hit two homers in the game.

JULY 3

Mo Vaughn hits two homers for the second day in a row, along with a triple, to account for six RBIs during a 12–5 victory over the Royals in Kansas City.

JULY 6

The Red Sox trade Frank Rodriguez and Jermaine Johnson to the Twins for Rick Aguilera.

Aguilera pitched only 30 games for the Red Sox, but the trade proved to be beneficial because he saved 20 games during the 1995 pennant drive while posting an ERA of 2.67. Aguilera went back to Minnesota via free agency at the end of the 1995 season, but the Red Sox gave up little talent to "borrow" him from the Twins for three months.

JULY 7   A day after being acquired by the Red Sox, Rick Aguilera faces his former Twins teammates in Minneapolis and earns a save by striking out Kirby Puckett to end a 5–4 victory.

JULY 9   Tim Wakefield takes a no-hitter into the eighth inning before giving up a leadoff single to Jeff Reboulet of the Twins in Minneapolis. Wakefield finished with a four-hitter and a 7–0 win.

JULY 14   Mo Vaughn is assaulted in a Boston nightclub.

              At the Roxy, an upscale dance club, Vaughn was confronted by a notorious gang member, his girlfriend's former boyfriend. The two fought, and Vaughn was knocked to the ground and then kicked by his opponent's entourage. Vaughn sustained a bruised left eye and missed two games. Vaughn was given a standing ovation in his first game back and remained as popular as ever with the fans, but the front office took a dim view of the nightclub fracas. The relationship between Vaughn and John Harrington and Dan Duquette cooled considerably.

JULY 17   In his major league debut, Jeff Suppan gives up a homer to Keith Lockhart, the first batter he faces. Suppan wound up as the losing pitcher in a 4–3 decision to the Royals at Fenway Park.

JULY 21   Mo Vaughn hits a grand slam off Scott Klingenbeck in the fifth inning of a 13–5 win over the Twins at Fenway Park. Troy O'Leary and John Valentin led off the first inning with back-to-back homers off Mike Trombley.

JULY 25   The Red Sox trade Mark Whiten to the Phillies for Dave Hollins.

JULY 28   Luis Alicea homers from both sides of the plate during a 6–2 win over the Rangers in Arlington. Alicea homered off right-hander Scott Taylor and lefty Terry Burrows.

JULY 29   Bill Haselman hits a grand slam off Kevin Gross in the sixth inning of a 7–1 win over the Rangers in Arlington.

JULY 31   The Red Sox trade Marc Lewis and Michael Jacobs to the Braves for Mike Stanton.

AUGUST 1   John Valentin drives in six runs on a homer and two singles during a 13–3 win over the Tigers in Detroit.

AUGUST 3   Mo Vaughn hits a grand slam off Joe Boever in the ninth inning of a 10–2 win over the Tigers in Detroit.

AUGUST 11   The Red Sox win their ninth game in a row with an 11–1 decision over the Orioles at Fenway Park.

AUGUST 13   Tim Wakefield carries a no-hitter into the seventh inning for the third time in 1995 before beating the Orioles 3–2 with a two-hitter at Fenway Park. Rafael Palmeiro broke up the no-hitter with a homer with one out in the seventh. Brady Anderson added a triple in the ninth. After Anderson's triple, Stan Belinda relieved Wakefield and got the last two Baltimore outs. A three-run homer by Jose Canseco in the first accounted for all three Boston runs. It was the Sox' 11th win in a row.

AUGUST 14   The Red Sox win their 12th game a row with a 9–3 decision over the Yankees at Fenway Park.

From August 3 through August 24, the Red Sox won 20 of 22.

AUGUST 24   The Red Sox score seven runs in the third inning to take a 13–3 lead and cruise to a 13–6 win over the Athletics in Oakland. The victory gave the Sox a 15½-game lead.

AUGUST 26   Mike Macfarlane hits a grand slam off Todd Stottlemyre in the fourth inning against the Athletics in Oakland, but the Red Sox lose, 11–4.

AUGUST 30   Down 5–0, the Red Sox score two runs in the fourth inning and five in the seventh to defeat the Mariners 7–6 at Fenway Park.

SEPTEMBER 5   Jose Canseco hits a two-out, three-run, walk-off homer in the fourteenth inning to beat the Athletics 7–4 at Fenway Park.

SEPTEMBER 8   The Red Sox tie a major league record with four consecutive pinch hits during the eighth inning of an 8–4 loss to the Yankees in New York. The pinch hits were strung together by Scott Hatteberg (his first major league hit), Lee Tinsley, Carlos Rodriguez, and Chris Donnels.

The Red Sox used 53 players in 1995.

SEPTEMBER 13   Tim Wakefield (8⅓ innings) and Stan Belinda (two-thirds of an inning) combine on a two-hitter to defeat the Orioles 2–0 at Camden Yards. The only two Baltimore hits were singles by Bret Barbarie in the third inning and Bobby Bonilla in the seventh.

SEPTEMBER 20   The Red Sox clinch the AL East pennant with a 3–2 win over the Brewers at Fenway Park.

Several players took celebratory rides on the horses of mounted policemen who rode onto the field after the victory.

SEPTEMBER 28   Two days after the Bruins play the last hockey game at Boston Garden, the Red Sox smack five homers during an 11–6 win over the Brewers in Milwaukee. The homers were struck by Reggie Jefferson, Dwayne Hosey, John Valentin, Tim Naehring, and Mike Macfarlane.

Naehring had an eight-year career as an infielder with the Red Sox but spent almost as much time on the disabled list as he did on the active roster. In 1995, he played in a career-high 126 games and hit .307 with 10 homers.

SEPTEMBER 29   The Red Sox edge the Brewers 11–9 in Milwaukee.

The Red Sox met the Cleveland Indians in the American League Division Series (ALDS). The Indians were managed by Mike Hargrove and posted a 100–44 record in 1995 and won the AL Central by 30 games. The Red Sox, at 86–58, had the second-best record in the AL.

OCTOBER 3   On the day O. J. Simpson is found not guilty of double murder, the Red Sox lose the first game of the Division Series 5–4 to the Indians in 13 innings at Jacobs Field. John Valentin started the scoring with a two-run homer in the third. After the Indians scored three times off Roger Clemens in the sixth, Luis Alicea tied the game 3–3 with a homer in the eighth. The Sox took a 4–3 lead in the eleventh on Tim Naehring's homer, but Albert Belle countered with a homer in the Cleveland half of the inning. In the thirteenth, ex–Red Sox catcher Tony Peña, who had only 12 homers over the previous four seasons, delivered a two-out, game-winning smash off Zane Smith.

With five hours and one minute of playing time, plus two rain delays, the contest ended at 2:10 AM, eastern time. After Belle's homer, the Red Sox asked the umpires to confiscate his bat because of suspicions that it might be corked. x-rays taken on the bat proved to be negative.

OCTOBER 4   In the second game of the best-of-five Division Series, the Indians shut out the Red Sox 4–0 behind the pitching of Orel Hershiser, who yields only three hits in 7⅓ innings.

Mo Vaughn (0 for 14 with seven strikeouts) and Jose Canseco (0 for 13) combined for 27 hitless at-bats in the series against the Indians.

OCTOBER 6   The day before the Bruins play the first hockey game at the Fleet Center, the Indians complete their sweep of the Red Sox with an 8–2 win before 34,211 at Fenway Park.

The loss was the 13th in a row for the Red Sox in the postseason. The Sox lost the last two games of the 1986 World Series, were swept four straight by the Athletics in both 1988 and 1990, and lost in three contests by the Indians in 1995.

DECEMBER 11   Rick Aguilera signs a free-agent contract with the Twins.

DECEMBER 14   The Red Sox sign Mike Stanley, most recently with the Yankees, as a free agent.

In his first season with the Red Sox, Stanley hit .270 with 24 homers.

DECEMBER 17   Mike Macfarlane signs a free-agent contract with the Royals.

DECEMBER 21   The Red Sox sign Tom Gordon, most recently with the Royals, as a free agent.

DECEMBER 22   Erik Hanson signs a free-agent contract with the Blue Jays.

DECEMBER 25   Dave Hollins signs a free-agent contract with the Twins.

1996 B

Season in a Sentence

After losing 19 of their first 25 games and dropping 14 games below .500 in July, the Red Sox start winning and make a bid for the wild-card berth in September.

Finish • Won • Lost • Pct • GB

Third   85   77   .525   7.0

In the wild-card race, the Red Sox finished tied for third place, three games behind.

Manager

Kevin Kennedy

Stats	Red Sox	AL	Rank
Batting Avg:	.283	.277	6
On-Base Pct:	.359	.350	5
Slugging Pct:	.457	.445	5
Home Runs:	209		6
Stolen Bases:	91		8
ERA:	4.98	4.99	7
Fielding Pct:	.978	.982	13
Runs Scored:	928		5
Runs Allowed:	921		12

Starting Lineup

Mike Stanley, c
Mo Vaughn, 1b
Jeff Frye, 2b
Tim Naehring, 3b
John Valentin, ss
Mike Greenwell, lf
Lee Tinsley, cf
Troy O'Leary, rf
Reggie Jefferson, dh-lf
Jose Canseco, dh
Bill Haselman, c
Darren Bragg, cf-rf
Wil Cordero, 2b

Pitchers

Tim Wakefield, sp
Tom Gordon, sp
Roger Clemens, sp
Aaron Sele, sp
Heathcliff Slocumb, rp
Mike Stanton, rp
Vaughn Eshelman, rp-sp
Jamie Moyer, rp-sp

Attendance

2,315,231 (sixth in AL)

Club Leaders

Batting Avg:	Vaughn	.326
On-Base Pct:	Vaughn	.420
Slugging Pct:	Vaughn	.583
Home Runs:	Vaughn	44
RBI:	Vaughn	143
Runs:	Vaughn	118
Stolen Bases:	Frye	18
Wins:	Wakefield	14
Strikeouts:	Clemens	257
ERA:	Clemens	3.63
Saves:	Slocumb	31

JANUARY 2   The Red Sox sign Jamie Moyer, most recently with the Orioles, as a free agent.

JANUARY 10   The Red Sox trade Rheal Cormier, Ryan McGuire, and Shayne Bennett to the Expos for Wil Cordero and Bryan Eversgerd.

JANUARY 29   The Red Sox trade Lee Tinsley, Glenn Murray, and Ken Ryan to the Phillies for Heathcliff Slocumb and Larry Wimberly.

MARCH 8   The Red Sox sign Kevin Mitchell as a free agent.

APRIL 1   The Red Sox lose the season opener 5–3 to the Rangers in Arlington. Roger Clemens took the loss. Tim Naehring homered and Mo Vaughn collected three hits.

APRIL 7   Four days after "Unabomber" Theodore Kaczynski was arrested in Montana, the Red Sox win their first game of the season following an 0–5 start, by defeating the Royals 3–1 in Kansas City on Easter Sunday.

By April 17, the Red Sox were 2–12, the worst 14-game start in franchise history, and were already 9 1/2 games out of first. The Sox were 6–19 on April 29. As late as August 1, the Sox had a record of 47–59 and were 17 games behind the Yankees in the AL East and 11 back of the White Sox in the wild-card chase. But the Sox were 38–18 the rest of the way to make things interesting for a while. On August 28, Boston was six behind the Yankees and 1 1/2 games out in the wild-card race, but could draw no closer.

APRIL 8   The Red Sox' scheduled season opener against the Twins is postponed by snow.

APRIL 9   The Red Sox open their home schedule with a 9–1 win over the Twins before 30,843 frozen fans at Fenway Park. The game-time temperature was just forty-four degrees.

APRIL 24   The Rangers score seven runs in the second inning at Fenway Park to take a 7–0 lead, but the Red Sox rally to win 11–9. Reggie Jefferson's third double of the game broke a 7–7 tie in the seventh.

APRIL 30   The Red Sox wallop the Tigers 13–4 at Fenway Park.

MAY 1   Roger Clemens strikes out 13 batters to beat the Tigers 5–1 at Fenway Park.

MAY 9   The Brewers pound the Red Sox 17–2 in Milwaukee.

MAY 10   After John Valentin ties the score 5–5 with a homer in the ninth, Troy O'Leary beats the Blue Jays 6–5 with a home run in the eleventh in Toronto.

                 The Red Sox played three extra-inning games in a three-game set at Skydome. The Sox lost 9–8 in 11 innings on May 11, and 8–7 in 10 frames on May 12.

MAY 14   The Red Sox play their fourth consecutive extra-inning game, beating the Angels 4–3 in 12 innings at Fenway Park.

MAY 15   The Red Sox score in each of the first seven innings and clobber the Angels 17–6 at Fenway Park.

MAY 17   A two-run, walk-off homer by Wil Cordero in the eleventh inning beats the Athletics 5–3 at Fenway Park.

MAY 19   The Red Sox rout the Athletics 12–2 at Fenway Park.

MAY 20   The Red Sox score seven runs in the third inning and collects 21 hits for a 16–4 victory over the Athletics at Fenway Park.

                 In a stretch of 12 games from May 5 through May 20, Mo Vaughn hit nine homers.

MAY 23   Roger Clemens pitches a shutout and collects his first major league hit with a single in his first regular-season at-bat in the majors during an 11–5 win over the Mariners at Fenway Park. Clemens was forced into the batting order after designated hitter Jose Canseco went to left field in the eighth inning.

MAY 30 — Outfielder Milt Cuyler hits two homers in a 10–1 win over the Mariners in Seattle.

The homers were the only ones that Cuyler hit in the majors between 1994 and 1998. They were also the only two that he hit with the Red Sox in 110 at-bats.

JUNE 4 — The Red Sox select pitcher Josh Garrett from South Spencer High School in Richland, Indiana in the first round of the amateur draft.

With their second pick of the first round, the Sox selected Chris Reitsma, but traded him to the Reds before he reached the majors. Other future major leaguers drafted and signed by the Sox in 1996 included Dernell Stenson (third round), Rob Ramsay (seventh), Justin Duchscherer (eighth), and Shea Hillenbrand (10th).

JUNE 5 — Mo Vaughn collects five hits, including a double, in six at-bats, but the Red Sox lose 8–6 in 12 innings at Fenway Park.

JUNE 6 — John Valentin hits for the cycle in a 7–4 win over the White Sox at Fenway Park. Valentin had a homer in the first inning, a triple in the third, a single in the fourth, and a double in the sixth. All four hits were off Joe Magrane. The Sox won despite hitting into a triple play in the first inning. It was the first time that a major league game featured both a cycle and a triple play since a Cubs-Phillies clash in 1931.

On the same day, the Red Sox signed Jeff Frye following his release by the Rangers. Frye was twenty-nine years old and spent the first two months of the 1996 season in the minors before drawing his release from the Rangers organization. Given new life in Boston, Frye filled the hole at second base and at the top of the batting order, hitting .285 with 74 runs in 105 games.

JUNE 7 — Down 7–1, the Red Sox score three runs in the fifth inning, two in the seventh, and four in the eighth to beat the Brewers 10–7 at Fenway Park. The four eighth-inning runs came on homers by Jose Canseco (his second of the game) and Reggie Jefferson.

JUNE 9 — Tim Naehring hits a grand slam off Ricky Bones in the first inning, but the Red Sox lose 11–8 in 10 innings to the Brewers at Fenway Park.

The Red Sox traded Scott Bakkum to the Phillies for Lee Tinsley. The deal came less than five months after the Sox traded Tinsley to Philadelphia.

JUNE 11 — The Red Sox score seven runs in the seventh inning and beat the White Sox 9–2 in Chicago.

JUNE 13 — Red Sox rookie Alex Delgado singles home the winning run with his second major league hit to cap a thrilling 10-inning, 8–7 win over the Rangers at Fenway Park. The Red Sox trailed 6–4 before scoring twice in the ninth to send the game into extra innings. After Texas scored a run in the top of the tenth, the Sox came back with two in their half.

This was the only RBI in the big-league career of Alex Delgado. He had five hits in 20 at-bats in 26 games in the majors. Despite his short stay, the versatile Delgado played six different positions, appearing in 14 contests as a catcher, one at first base, one at second, four at third, five in left field, and two in right.

JUNE 16   Reggie Jefferson's three-run, walk-off homer in the ninth inning beats the Rangers 10–9 at Fenway Park. The Red Sox trailed 9–3 before scoring four times in the seventh.

JUNE 26   Tim Naehring hits a two-run, walk-off homer in the fifteenth inning that beats the Indians 6–4 at Fenway Park. The win ended Boston's 14-game losing streak against Cleveland, which included the three-game sweep in the 1995 playoffs.

JUNE 29   The Red Sox trounce the Tigers 13–6 at Fenway Park.

JULY 7   Seven days after a bomb explodes in an Atlanta park filled with people attending the Olympics, Mo Vaughn hits a three-run homer with two out in the ninth that beats the Orioles 7–5 in Baltimore. It was Vaughn's second homer of the game.

               Vaughn put up better numbers in 1996 than he had in his MVP seasons of 1995. He hit .326 with 44 homers, 143 RBIs, and 207 hits.

JULY 11   The Red Sox down the Tigers 11–4 in Detroit.

JULY 12   Mo Vaughn hits a grand slam off Omar Olivares in the second inning of an 11–3 win over the Tigers in Detroit.

JULY 13   Tim Naehring scores five runs during a 10–5 win over the Tigers in Detroit. Naehring reached base on a homer, a single, two walks, and an error in five plate appearances. It was the third game in a row that the Red Sox reached double digits in runs against the Tigers.

JULY 17   The Red Sox score three runs in the ninth inning to beat the Yankees 12–11 at Fenway Park. The Sox led 9–2 after six innings, but the Yanks scored three runs in the seventh inning, two in the eighth, and four in the ninth to take an 11–9 lead.

JULY 19   The Red Sox thrash the Orioles 13–2 at Fenway Park.

JULY 24   The Red Sox overwhelm the Royals 12–2 at Fenway Park.

JULY 27   Red Sox rookie second baseman Arquimedez Pozo, making his first major league start, breaks a 5–5 tie with a bases-loaded triple and scores on John Valentin's single to defeat the Twins 9–5 in Minneapolis.

               The triple was the only one of Pozo's major league career.

JULY 28   In his second major league start, Arquimedez Pozo clears the bases in the ninth inning for the second game in row, this time with a grand slam off Eddie Guardado, although the Red Sox come up short 9–8 against the Twins in Minneapolis.

               The homer was the only one of Pozo's brief big-league career. As a major leaguer, he played in 26 games, 25 of them with the Red Sox, and hit .189 in 74 at-bats.

JULY 30   The Red Sox trade Jamie Moyer to the Mariners for Darren Bragg. On the same day, the Sox dealt Kevin Mitchell and Brad Tweedlie to the Reds for Roberto Mejia.

The Moyer trade has turned out horribly for the Red Sox. From 1996 through 2003, he had a record of 119–55 for the Mariners. Bragg became somewhat of a cult hero in Boston because of his fearless, kamikaze playing style, especially on defense where he made many highlight reel catches. Bragg hit 264 with 20 homers in 340 games over three seasons with the Sox.

JULY 31   The Red Sox trade Mike Stanton to the Rangers for Mark Brandenburg and Kerry Lacy.

The Red Sox dealt Moyer and Stanton for prospects because they believed they had no chance of getting back in the pennant race. Like the Moyer trade made only a day earlier, the swap with the Yankees worked out badly. Stanton was a reliable reliever in New York from 1997 through 2002. He has pitched in a total of six World Series for the Braves and Yankees. Neither Lacy nor Brandenburg were anything more than staff fillers at the big-league level.

AUGUST 2   The Red Sox rally for four runs in the ninth inning to defeat the Twins 11–10 at Fenway Park, the final two on a two-out, walk-off triple by Troy O'Leary that glanced off the glove of center fielder Rich Becker.

AUGUST 4   The Red Sox score seven runs in the second inning of a 13–6 win over the Twins at Fenway Park.

AUGUST 22   Troy O'Leary's walk-off homer off the right field foul pole in the ninth inning beats the Athletics 2–1 at Fenway Park. Roger Clemens pitched eight shutout innings to run his scoreless streak to 28 innings before allowing a run in the ninth.

AUGUST 24   Darren Bragg hits a grand slam off Randy Johnson in the sixth inning of a 9–5 win over the Mariners at Fenway Park. It was the first home run by a left-handed batter off Johnson in four years.

AUGUST 31   Nomar Garciaparra makes his major league debut during an 8–0 loss to the Athletics in Oakland. Garciaparra entered the game as a substitute second baseman in place of Jeff Frye. Garciaparra was hitless in his lone at-bat.

To date, this is Garciaparra's only game at second base during his professional baseball career.

SEPTEMBER 1   In his first major league start, Nomar Garciaparra hits a home run off John Wasdin during an 8–3 win over the Athletics in Oakland.

SEPTEMBER 2   Mike Greenwell drives in all nine of the Red Sox runs in a 10-inning, 9–8 win over the Mariners in Seattle. Greenwell set a major league record for most RBIs while driving in all of a team's runs in a game. The previous record was eight, set by George Kelly of the Giants in 1924 and Bob Johnson of the Athletics in 1938. The Red Sox were behind 5–0 when Greenwell hit a two-run homer in the fifth inning off Bob Wolcott. Greenwell put the Sox ahead 6–5 with a grand slam in the sixth facing Bobby Ayala. The Mariners took an 8–6 lead with three runs in the seventh, however. Greenwell tied it 8–8 with a two-run double in the eighth against Norm Charlton. Mike drove in the winning run in the tenth with a single off Rafael Carmona. Greenwell also had four of the Red Sox' seven hits.

After his big nine-RBI night, Greenwell drove in only 10 more runs during his big-league career. He retired at the end of the 1996 season.

SEPTEMBER 15   Frank Thomas hits three homers for the White Sox, but the Red Sox win 9–8 at Fenway Park. The winning run scored on a walk-off single by Troy O'Leary in the ninth inning.

Outfielder Rudy Pemberton was called up from Pawtucket in September and collected 21 hits in 41 at-bats for an average of .512. It is the best batting average in major league history for anyone with at least 40 at-bats in a season. Previously, he played for the Tigers in 1995 and hit .300 in 30 at-bats. Pemberton played only one more season after 1996 and batted .238 in 27 games. He finished his American major league career with 134 at-bats and a .338 batting average. In 1998, Pemberton went to play in Japan.

SEPTEMBER 18   Roger Clemens strikes out 20 batters to tie his own major league record for most strikeouts in a nine-inning game, defeating the Tigers 4–0 in Detroit. Clemens threw 151 pitches, 101 of them for strikes, and allowed four hits. Of the 20 strikeouts, 15 were on swinging strikes. Clemens struck out the side in the second, fifth, and sixth innings. He fanned every player in the Tigers starting lineup at least once and didn't walk a batter. Clemens entered the ninth with 19 strikeouts, but Alan Trammell popped out, Ruben Sierra singled, and Tony Clark flied out. Travis Fryman, who struck out in his three previous plate appearances, was next. Clemens went to a 2–1 count on Fryman before striking him out to tie the record.

Clemens also tied two long-standing Red Sox career records with the victory. He tied Cy Young for most wins in Red Sox history with 192. He also tied Young for most shutouts with the club with 38. It proved to be Clemens's last victory as a member of the Red Sox.

SEPTEMBER 20   The Red Sox defeat the Yankees 4–2 in New York to stay in the chase for a wild card berth.

After the win, the Sox were three games back of the Orioles for the wild-card slot with 10 contests left on the schedule, but could pull no closer.

SEPTEMBER 24   Mo Vaughn hits three homers in a 13–8 win over the Orioles at Fenway Park. Vaughn had a solo homer in the first inning, a two-run bomb in the third, and a solo shot in the sixth, all three off David Wells. Vaughn also contributed an RBI single in the eighth.

SEPTEMBER 30   The Red Sox fire Kevin Kennedy as manager.

Kennedy was fired despite a 171–135 record, including a division title, in two seasons as Red Sox manager. His player-friendly style angered management. Dan Duquette said that Kennedy didn't have the players prepared for Opening Day, resulting in the slow start in 1996, failed to work well with prospects and pitchers, and could not, or would not, stifle clubhouse criticism of the front office. Kennedy went on to work on television with ESPN and never managed another big-league club.

NOVEMBER 19   Two weeks after Bill Clinton wins re-election as president in a race against Bob Dole, the Red Sox hire Jimy Williams as manager.

During a seven-week search for a new manager, the Red Sox courted Jim Leyland, Whitey Herzog, and Felipe Alou, among others, before settling on Williams. He previously managed the Blue Jays from the start of the 1986 season through May 1989. Williams was a third-base coach under Bobby Cox with the Braves from 1990 through 1996.

NOVEMBER 25   The Red Sox sell Lee Tinsley to the Mariners.

DECEMBER 9   The Red Sox sign Bret Saberhagen following his release by the Rockies.

Saberhagen didn't pitch in either 1995 or 1996 because of arm miseries, and was limited to six ineffective games in 1997. But he gave the Red Sox two good seasons with a 15–8 record in 1998 and 10–6 in 1999.

DECEMBER 13   Roger Clemens signs with the Blue Jays as a free agent. On the same day, the Red Sox signed Shane Mack, most recently with the Yomiyuri Giants of the Japanese Central League.

The headlines in the Boston papers the following day did not herald the acquisition of Shane Mack. The Red Sox lost one of the best pitchers in baseball history. Clemens wanted a four-year contract and publicly stated that he hoped to end his career in Boston. The Red Sox were in a tough position in determining whether Clemens was worth a mega-million, four-year deal that would keep him among the highest-paid players in baseball. He was thirty-four years old. Over the previous four years, he had gone 40–39 with a 3.77 ERA while battling groin and shoulder problems. In 1996 he pitched much better than his won-lost record indicated, however. Clemens was 10–13 with an earned run average of 3.63 that year. His ERA was well below the league average of 4.99, and he led the AL in strikeouts with 257 in 242⅔ innings, his best strikeout per inning rate since 1988. In his last 10 starts of 1996, Clemens was 6–2 with an ERA of 2.09, including a 20-strikeout game. In the end, Dan Duquette believed that Clemens was "in the twilight of his career" and not worth a long-term deal. The Blue Jays and several other clubs involved in the bidding war for Clemens didn't share Duquette's reservations. To the Red Sox' everlasting regret, Clemens signed with the Blue Jays for three years and $24.75 million, the most money ever paid to a pitcher up to that point. Clemens returned to his former glory with a 21–7 record and a 2.05 ERA for Toronto in 1997. From 1997 through 2004, Clemens won four Cy Young Awards with three different clubs. His record in those eight seasons was 136–53.

DECEMBER 20   The Reds sign Stan Belinda as a free agent.

1997   B

Season in a Sentence

The Red Sox get off to a wretched start and suffer a losing season under new manager Jimy Williams.

Finish • Won • Lost • Pct • GB

Fourth   78   84   .481   20.0

In the wild-card race, the Red Sox were in sixth place, 18 games behind.

Manager

Jimy Williams

Stats

Stats	Red Sox	AL	Rank
Batting Avg:	.291	.271	1
On-Base Pct:	.352	.340	4
Slugging Pct:	.463	.428	3
Home Runs:	185		6
Stolen Bases:	68		13
ERA:	4.85	4.57	12
Fielding Pct:	.978	.982	14
Runs Scored:	851		4
Runs Allowed:	857		12

Starting Lineup

Scott Hatteberg, c
Mo Vaughn, 1b
Jeff Frye, 2b
John Valentin, 3b-2b
Nomar Garciaparra, ss
Wil Cordero, lf
Darren Bragg, cf
Troy O'Leary, rf
Reggie Jefferson, dh
Tim Naehring, 3b
Mike Stanley, dh-1b
Bill Haselman, c

Pitchers

Tim Wakefield, sp
Aaron Sele, sp
Tom Gordon, sp-rp
Jeff Suppan, rp
Heathcliff Slocumb, rp
Butch Henry, rp
Jim Corsi, rp
John Wasdin, rp

Attendance

2,216,136 (seventh in AL)

Club Leaders

Batting Avg:	Vaughn	.315
On-Base Pct:	Vaughn	.420
Slugging Pct:	Vaughn	.560
Home Runs:	Vaughn	35
RBI:	Garciaparra	98
Runs:	Garciaparra	122
Stolen Bases:	Garciaparra	22
Wins:	Sele	13
Strikeouts:	Gordon	159
ERA:	Gordon	3.74
Saves:	Slocumb	17

JANUARY 5   Tim Wakefield suffers a broken leg when struck by a car while jogging near his home in Melbourne, Florida. Wakefield recovered in time for the start of the season.

JANUARY 10   Steve Avery, most recently with the Braves, signs with the Red Sox as a free agent.

Avery proved to be a waste of money. He was 16–14 in two seasons with the Red Sox, but with a horrendous ERA of 5.64.

JANUARY 27   The day after the Patriots lose the Super Bowl 35–21 to the Packers, the Red Sox trade Jose Canseco to the Athletics for John Wasdin.

Canseco was critical of the Red Sox' firing of his friend Kevin Kennedy and demanded a trade. Over the next three seasons, Canseco hit 103 homers for the Athletics, Blue Jays, and Devil Rays, but with a batting average of only .249. Wasdin was little more than an average arm out of the bullpen in four seasons with the Sox.

APRIL 2   The Red Sox open the 1997 season with a thrilling four-run rally in the ninth inning to defeat the Angels 6–5 in Anaheim. All four runs were scored after two were out and no one was on base. Anaheim closer Troy Percival began the ninth by striking out Darren Bragg and Nomar Garciaparra. John Valentin started the rally with a double. Then Mo Vaughn walked on a 3–2 pitch. Reggie Jefferson loaded the bases with an infield single with two strikes on him. Tim Naehring and Wil Cordero both walked on 3–2 pitches to make the score 5–4. Rudy Pemberton was hit by a pitch to tie the score. Percival was replaced by Pep Harris, who gave up a go-ahead single to pinch hitter Troy O'Leary. Earlier in the game, Tim Naehring hit a homer off Mark Langston.

APRIL 8   The Red Sox score seven runs in the seventh inning of a 13–7 victory over the Athletics in Oakland. Darren Bragg hit a grand slam in the big inning off Reggie Lewis.

APRIL 11   In the first game of the season at Fenway Park, the Red Sox lose 5–3 to the Mariners before 34,210. John Valentin hit two homers, both off Randy Johnson.

           Valentin walked out of spring training camp for two days because he was angry over a move from shortstop to second base to make room for Nomar Garciaparra. Valentin hit .306 with 18 homers in 1997.

APRIL 13   Tim Naehring hits a grand slam off Steve Sanders in the third inning that breaks a 1–1 tie against the Mariners and sparks the Red Sox to a 7–1 win at Fenway Park. Wil Cordero homered off the three 25-foot-tall Coke bottles installed on the top of the left field wall just prior to the start of the season.

           The Red Sox had three different cap designs in 1997. In addition to the navy blue one worn by the club for decades, the Sox brought back the red cap with the blue "B" and blue bill used from 1975 through 1978. There was also a white cap with a blue bill and a red "B" outlined in blue.

APRIL 16   Mo Vaughn drives in six runs with a pair of three-run homers to lead the Red Sox to an 11–6 win over the Indians at Fenway Park.

APRIL 24   Nomar Garciaparra hits a homer in the twelfth inning to beat the Orioles 2–1 in Baltimore.

APRIL 26   Roberto Alomar hits three homers for the Orioles in a 14–5 win over the Red Sox in Baltimore.

APRIL 27   Bill Haselman ties a Red Sox record for most extra-base hits in a game with a homer and three doubles in a 13–7 win over the Orioles in Baltimore. Mo Vaughn, Tim Naehring, Troy O'Leary, and Wil Cordero also homered for the Sox.

           On the same day, University of Massachusetts pitcher Scott Barnsby pitched a no-hitter to defeat Northeastern in the semifinals of the Beanpot Tournament at Fenway Park. Since 1990, the Red Sox have hosted the four-college Beanpot Tournament each April. Boston College, Harvard, Northeastern, and Boston University competed the first six years. After BU dropped out, UMass replaced the school.

MAY 7 — Scott Hatteberg hits the first and second homers of his major league career during an 11–3 win over the Twins at Fenway Park.

MAY 8 — Rudy Pemberton hits a grand slam off Rich Robertson in the second inning that puts the Red Sox ahead 4–1, but the Twins rally to win 10–7 at Fenway Park.

MAY 22 — Wil Cordero collects five hits, including a double, in six at-bats during an 8–2 win over the Yankees in New York.

MAY 26 — A two-run, walk-off double by Tim Naehring beats the Brewers 3–2 at Fenway Park.

MAY 30 — Mo Vaughn hits three homers, along with a single and a walk, in five plate appearances during a 10–4 victory over the Yankees at Fenway Park. Vaughn hit solo shots off Ramiro Mendoza in the third inning, Danny Rios in the fourth, and Graeme Lloyd in the eighth. Troy O'Leary, Scott Hatteberg, and Wil Cordero also homered for the Red Sox.

> *Major League Baseball retired uniform number 42 in honor of Jackie Robinson in 1997. Mo Vaughn had worn number 42, but he was allowed to keep it for the remainder of his career.*

JUNE 3 — In the first round of the amateur draft, the Red Sox select pitcher John Curtice from Great Bridge High School in Chesapeake, Virginia.

> *Curtice failed to reach the majors. The only players drafted and signed by the Red Sox in 1997 who have played in the majors are Travis Harper (third round), Justin Wayne (ninth round), and David Eckstein (19th round). Eckstein is the only one to become a regular, but the Sox traded him before he reached the big leagues.*

JUNE 8 — The Indians build a 5–0 lead before the Red Sox explode for nine runs in the fourth inning and cruise to a 12–6 win at Fenway Park.

> *The Red Sox had a record of 24–37 on June 10. The club nosed above the .500 mark in August at 64–63 before finishing the year with a losing record of 78-84.*

JUNE 11 — Wil Cordero is arrested for assaulting his wife, Ana, in their Cambridge apartment.

> *According to the police report, Cordero slapped his wife, hit her with a phone when she attempted to call for help, and threatened to kill her. Ana emerged with a bloody nose and bruises. Some in the Red Sox front office supported Cordero, while others wanted to hang him from the nearest lamppost, leading to indecisiveness and inaction. The Sox reluctantly bowed to community pressure and suspended Cordero for two weeks, brought him back, then benched him again when his wife made more allegations. Later, he shrugged off the incident during an ESPN interview in which he denied he had a problem. Cordero finished the season with the Sox under a cloud and a torrent of boos whenever he stepped to the plate. He was released in September. Cordero received a suspended sentence when he pleaded guilty to a lesser crime to avoid jail time.*

JUNE 13 | The Red Sox play a regular-season game against a National League team for the first time and gain a measure of revenge for the 1986 World Series by defeating the Mets 8–4 at Shea Stadium.

JUNE 16 | In the first interleague game at Fenway Park, the Red Sox beat the Phillies 5–4 with two runs in the ninth inning and one in the tenth.

JUNE 21 | Infielder Mike Benjamin pitches the eighth inning of a 15–4 loss to the Tigers in Detroit. Performing much better than the real pitchers, Benjamin retired the Tigers 1–2–3.

JUNE 25 | The Red Sox outlast the Blue Jays 13–12 in Toronto. Nomar Garciaparra hit the first pitch of the game for a homer off Pat Hentgen. It was the first of five Boston homers. Mike Stanley, Reggie Jefferson, Troy O'Leary, and Darren Bragg hit the others.

JUNE 30 | The Red Sox play the Marlins for the first time in the regular season and lose 8–5 at Fenway Park.

JULY 12 | Taking the mound to a mixture of cheers and boos, Roger Clemens makes a triumphant return to Fenway Park by striking out 16 batters in eight innings in leading the Blue Jays to a 3–1 win over the Red Sox.

JULY 14 | The Red Sox collect 21 hits and bash the Tigers 18–4 at Fenway Park.

JULY 17 | The Red Sox again bash 21 hits and defeat the Orioles 12–9 in Baltimore. Ron Mahay, an outfielder turned pitcher, made his major league debut and earned the victory in relief.

JULY 26 | A three-run, walk-off homer by Mo Vaughn beats the Angels 7–6 at Fenway Park.

Vaughn was sensational again in 1997, with a .315 batting average and 35 homers.

JULY 27 | A three-run rally in the ninth beats the Angels for the second game in a row, this time by a 6–5 score. The winning run scored on Wil Cordero's bases-loaded single.

JULY 30 | The Red Sox continue their late-inning magic and overcome a 7–2 deficit by scoring two runs in the eighth inning, three in the ninth, and one in the tenth to beat the Mariners 8–7 at Fenway Park. The winning run scored on a bases-loaded single by Nomar Garciaparra.

JULY 31 | The Red Sox trade Heathcliff Slocumb to the Mariners for Derek Lowe and Jason Varitek.

The Red Sox swindled the Mariners by sending a washed-up Slocumb for two players who were around long enough to be key contributors to the 2004 World Championship team.

AUGUST 5 | The Red Sox score eight runs in the third inning and collect 24 hits in a 17–1 battering of the Rangers in Arlington.

AUGUST 8   Reggie Jefferson runs his hitting streak to 22 games during an 8–2 win over the Royals at Fenway Park.

AUGUST 13   The Red Sox trade Mike Stanley and Randy Brown to the Yankees for Tony Armas Jr. and Jim Mecir.

AUGUST 20   The Red Sox score seven runs in the fifth inning to provide all of the runs necessary to defeat the Athletics 7–5 in the first game of a doubleheader in Oakland. The Sox also won the nightcap 5–4 in 13 innings after scoring two runs in the ninth to tie the score.

AUGUST 29   The Braves return to their original hometown and beat the Red Sox 9–1 at Fenway Park. The Braves played in Boston from 1871 until 1953. Despite the loss, Nomar Garciaparra extended his hitting streak to 30 games.

Garciaparra had one of the greatest rookie seasons in Boston history, winning the Rookie of the Year Award by a unanimous vote. He hit .306 with 209 hits, 44 doubles, 11 triples, 30 homers, 98 RBIs, and 122 runs scored. Garciaparra's 30-game hitting streak was the longest ever by an American League rookie. He set the major league rookie record for most homers by a shortstop. Garciaparra also set a major league record for most RBIs by a lead-off hitter, breaking the old mark of 85 set by Harvey Kuenn in 1956. In addition, Garciaparra became the first Red Sox batter to reach double figures in doubles, triples, and homers since Jackie Jensen in 1956.

Nomar Garciaparra's outstanding rookie season heralded a new star in Fenway. Rather than suffer a sophomore jinx, he increased his numbers in nearly every offensive category the following year.

Brian Babineau

AUGUST 30   Wearing replica 1908 uniforms, the Red Sox lose 15–2 to the Braves at Fenway Park.

SEPTEMBER 1   The day after Princess Diana dies following a car accident in Paris, the Red Sox play in Montreal during the regular season for the first time and lose 4–2 to the Expos.

SEPTEMBER 3   Aaron Sele pitches seven innings and allows only one hit, but the hit is a homer by Mike Lansing that beats the Red Sox 1–0 in Montreal. The Sox collected only two hits off Carlos Perez.

SEPTEMBER 7   Troy O'Leary hits a grand slam in the third inning off Jeff D'Amico during an 11–2 win over the Brewers at Fenway Park. There were six Boston homers in all. John Valentin hit two homers, and Bill Haselman, Jeff Frye, and Wil Cordero added one each.

SEPTEMBER 18   A two-run, walk-off single by Jeff Frye defeats the Blue Jays 3–2 at Fenway Park.

Counting designated hitter, Frye played eight positions in 1997, appearing in a game everywhere but as a pitcher and a catcher. He played 80 games as a second baseman, 18 at third, five in left field, five in center, three in right, three at shortstop, one at first base, and 11 as a designated hitter.

SEPTEMBER 19   Curtis Pride and Scott Hatteberg both hit pinch-homers in the ninth inning to tie the score, but the Red Sox lose 5–4 in 10 innings to the White Sox at Fenway Park.

The homer came in Pride's first at-bat as a member of the Red Sox and was the only one that he hit with the club.

SEPTEMBER 28   The Red Sox release Wil Cordero just hours after the last game of the season as a result of his June arrest for spousal abuse.

Cordero signed with the White Sox during the 1998 season, and through the 2005 season drifted from club to club, playing for the Indians, Pirates, Indians, Expos, Marlins, and Nationals.

NOVEMBER 6   The Red Sox trade Aaron Sele and Mark Brandenburg to the Rangers for Jim Leyritz and Damon Buford.

The Red Sox didn't believe that Sele was tough enough to be a consistent winner at the big-league level, but he proved them wrong. In his first four seasons after leaving Boston, Sele had a record of 69–35 with the Rangers and Mariners.

NOVEMBER 18   The Red Sox trade Carl Pavano and Tony Armas Jr. to the Expos for Pedro Martinez. On the same day, the Red Sox lost Jeff Suppan to the Diamondbacks and Jim Mecir to the Devil Rays in the expansion draft.

The Expos could no longer afford to keep Martinez and had to put him on the market. Dan Duquette, who had worked as a general manager in Montreal, had the inside track and took advantage of the situation by swapping two top pitching prospects for Martinez. At the time of the trade, Martinez was twenty-six years old and signed only through 1998, but the Red Sox locked him up for six years *and $75 million. It was a huge gamble. Prior to 1997, Martinez was a solid but unspectacular pitcher with a 48–31 career record and a 3.39 ERA. In 1997, he broke loose and was 17–8 with a league-leading earned run average of 1.90 and 305 strikeouts in 241 $\frac{1}{3}$ innings in winning the Cy Young Award. Martinez proved to be worth the huge investment, as he had only scratched the surface of his potential in Montreal. In seven seasons with the Red Sox, he had a record of 117–37 and an ERA of 2.52 along with 1,649 strikeouts in 1,383 $\frac{2}{3}$ innings. His winning percentage of .760 during his seven seasons with the Sox has been exceeded by only one other major league pitcher over seven consecutive seasons (with a minimum of 75 decisions). The only hurler to post a better mark was Lefty Grove, whose winning percentage was .776 (160–49) from 1928 through 1934. Among Red Sox pitchers over a career, Martinez ranks first in winning percentage, fifth in wins, second in strikeouts and sixth in ERA (minimum 1,000 innings). All five of the pitchers ranked ahead of Martinez in earned run average pitched for the Red Sox before 1920. He led the league in earned run average four times and strikeouts three seasons and won two Cy Young Awards.*

DECEMBER 9   The Red Sox sign Dennis Eckersley, most recently with the Cardinals, as a free agent.

Eckersley returned to Boston for his major league swan song after pitching for the Red Sox from 1978 through 1984. In 1998, his final big-league season, Eckersley was 4–1 with a 4.76 ERA in 50 relief appearances. He was elected to the Hall of Fame on the first ballot in 2004.

DECEMBER 22   Shane Mack signs as a free agent with the Athletics.

DECEMBER 23   The Red Sox sign Darren Lewis, most recently with the Dodgers, as a free agent.

The Red Sox dubious history of race relations took another hit during the 1997–98 offseason. Thomas Sneed, the club's former African-American manager of the 600 Club, revealed that his white girlfriend's photograph on his desk had been defaced and that he had been the victim of racially motivated threats. He had tried to resolve the issue through proper channels, but he felt the Red Sox failed to address the problem, and Sneed filed a complaint with the Massachusetts Commission Against Discrimination. He agreed to an out-of-court settlement in 1999.

1998 B

Season in a Sentence

The Red Sox post the second-best record in the American League but are a distant 22 games behind the Yankees, who won 114 games, before succumbing to the Indians in the first round of the playoffs.

Finish • Won • Lost • Pct • GB

Second   92   70   .568 22.0

In the wild-card race, the Red Sox finished in first place, four games ahead of the Toronto Blue Jays.

AL Division Series—The Red Sox lost to the Cleveland Indians three games to one.

Manager

Jimy Williams

Stats

Stats	Red Sox	AL	Rank
Batting Avg:	.280	.271	2
On-Base Pct:	.348	.340	2
Slugging Pct:	.463	.432	2
Home Runs:	205		5
Stolen Bases:	72		14
ERA:	4.18	4.65	2
Fielding Pct:	.983	.981	4
Runs Scored:	876		3
Runs Allowed:	729		2

Starting Lineup

Scott Hatteberg, c
Mo Vaughn, 1b
Mike Benjamin, 2b
John Valentin, 3b
Nomar Garciaparra, ss
Troy O'Leary, lf
Darren Lewis, cf-rf
Darren Bragg, rf
Reggie Jefferson, dh
Jason Varitek, c
Damon Buford, cf
Mike Stanley, dh

Pitchers

Pedro Martinez, sp
Tim Wakefield, sp
Bret Saberhagen, sp
Steve Avery, sp
Tom Gordon, rp
Derek Lowe, rp
John Wasdin, rp
Dennis Eckersley, rp
Jim Corsi, rp

Attendance

2,343,947 (eighth in AL)

Club Leaders

Batting Avg:	Vaughn	.337
On-Base Pct:	Vaughn	.402
Slugging Pct:	Vaughn	.591
Home Runs:	Vaughn	40
RBI:	Garciaparra	122
Runs:	Valentin	113
Stolen Bases:	Lewis	29
Wins:	Martinez	19
Strikeouts:	Martinez	251
ERA:	Martinez	2.89
Saves:	Gordon	46

MARCH 26   Two months after the Bill Clinton–Monica Lewinsky sex scandal is exposed, the Red Sox sign Mark Lemke, most recently with the Braves, as a free agent.

Lemke was signed to play second base after Jeff Frye suffered a knee injury during a rundown drill in spring training that put him out for the season. Lemke then suffered a concussion during a base-path collision in May, however, and his season was over after 31 games.

APRIL 1   Pedro Martinez makes his debut and strikes out 11 and allows only three hits in seven shutout innings. Martinez retired the first 11 batters. Dennis Eckersley (two-thirds of an inning in his first game with the Sox since 1984) and Tom Gordon (1 ⅓ innings) completed the shutout to give the Sox a 2–0 win over the Athletics in Oakland.

Darren Lewis was the Red Sox' seventh different starting center fielder on Opening Day in a seven-year span. The other six were Ellis Burks (1992), Bill Hatcher (1993), Otis Nixon (1994), Lee Tinsley (1995), Dwayne Hosey (1996), and Shane Mack (1997).

APRIL 10   In the home opener, the Red Sox stage an incredible seven-run rally in the ninth inning, capped by Mo Vaughn's walk-off homer off Paul Spoljaric, to defeat the Mariners 9–7 before 32,805 at Fenway Park. Through eight innings, Randy Johnson allowed only two hits and struck out 15 batters, but he was removed after throwing 131 pitches. The Red Sox scored their seven final inning runs off four relievers without a batter being retired on three hits, two walks, a hit batsman, and Vaughn's homer.

Because the opener fell on Good Friday, there was no beer sold at Fenway Park for the first time since Prohibition.

APRIL 12   Pedro Martinez strikes out 12 batters and throws a two-hitter to beat the Mariners 5–0 at Fenway Park. The only Seattle hits were singles by Joey Cora in the fourth inning and Alex Rodriguez in the sixth.

In his first season with the Red Sox, Martinez was 19–7 with a 2.89 ERA and 251 strikeouts in 233 2/3 innings.

APRIL 17   The Red Sox score two runs in the ninth inning and one in the tenth to defeat the Indians 3–2 at Fenway Park. A bases-loaded single by Darren Bragg drove in the winning run. Jimy Williams was down to his last position player by the end of the game and used outfielder Damon Buford at third base against left-handed batters and at second against right-handers, alternating with John Valentin.

APRIL 22   The Red Sox score four runs in the ninth inning, three of them on a home run by reserve outfielder Midre Cummings, to beat the Tigers 8–5 in Detroit.

After three wins and five losses on a three-city trip to the West Coast to open the season, the Red Sox won 14 of 15 with a pair of seven-game winning streaks. By May 10, Boston had a record of 24–11 and was two games out of first place. The Yankees made history in 1998, however, by posting a record of 114–48. The Red Sox finished at 92–70, a distant 22 games behind New York but good enough for the second-best record in the American League and a wild-card berth.

MAY 8   The Red Sox collect 20 hits and rout the Royals 14–3 in Kansas City.

MAY 10   Tim Wakefield holds the Royals hitless for 6 2/3 innings in Kansas City before Shane Mack singles. Wakefield wound up allowing two hits in 8 2/3 innings for a 3–1 win. Tom Gordon earned the save by nailing down the final out. Johnny Damon collected the second Royals hit with a single in the ninth.

Gordon set a Red Sox single-season record for saves in 1998 with 46. He had a 7–4 record and a 2.72 ERA.

MAY 15   Lou Merloni, who grew up in suburban Framingham, Massachusetts, homers in his first Fenway Park at-bat to spark the Red Sox to a 5–2 win over the Royals.

The homer was the only one that Merloni hit in 1998. He didn't hit another home run at Fenway until 2002.

MAY 31   The Red Sox score 11 runs in the third inning and defeat the Yankees 13–7 in New York. The Sox sent 16 batters to the plate, making the most of nine hits, three walks, and poor Yankee fielding for the 11 tallies.

JUNE 2   In the first round of the amateur draft, the Red Sox select shortstop Adam Everett from the University of South Carolina.

The Sox traded Adam Everett to the Astros for Carl Everett in 1999. Other future major leaguers drafted and signed by the Red Sox in 1998 included Mike Maroth (third round), Josh Hancock (fifth), and Lenny DiNardo (10th). Mark Teixeira was drafted out of high school in the ninth round but chose to attend Georgia Tech. He was drafted and signed by the Rangers in 2001.

JUNE 5   The Mets play a regular-season game at Fenway Park for the first time and clobber the Red Sox, 9–2.

JUNE 6   Tim Wakefield pitches one-hit ball over eight innings but loses 1–0 to the Mets at Fenway Park on a disputed balk call in the sixth inning. The only hit off Wakefield was a single by Edgardo Alfonso in the second inning.

JUNE 8   The Red Sox play a regular-season game in Atlanta for the first time and lose a stunning 7–6 decision when the Braves score six runs in the ninth inning off Tom Gordon and John Wasdin at Turner Field.

JUNE 12   The Red Sox play the Tampa Bay Devil Rays for the first time and win 5–1 at Fenway Park.

JUNE 18   The Red Sox play the Devil Rays in St. Petersburg for the first time and win 7–5 in 10 innings.

JUNE 21   Pedro Martinez allows only one hit in eight innings of pitching in leading the Red Sox to a 3–1 win over the Devil Rays in St. Petersburg. The only hit off Martinez was a triple by Miguel Cairo in the fifth inning.

On the same day, the Red Sox traded Jim Leyritz to the Padres for Carlos Reyes, Mandy Romero, and Dario Veras.

JUNE 24   The Red Sox play the Phillies in Philadelphia for the first time during the regular season and lose 11–8 at Veterans Stadium.

JUNE 26   The Red Sox play in Miami for the first time during the regular season and win 6–1 over the Marlins.

JUNE 30   The Expos play at Fenway Park for the first time and lose 7–4 to the Red Sox.

JULY 2   The Red Sox collect 20 hits and trounce the Expos 15–0 at Fenway Park.

JULY 3   Nomar Garciaparra extends his hitting streak to 24 games in a 15–2 thrashing of the White Sox at Fenway Park. The Red Sox scored in each of the first seven innings. Billy Ashley hit a grand slam in the fifth inning off Jason Bere.

Garciaparra hit .323 with 35 homers, 122 RBIs, and 111 runs scored in 1998. He was runner-up to Juan Gonzalez in the MVP balloting. John Valentin, Garciaparra's cohort over at third base, batted only .247 but had 113 runs, 44 doubles, and 23 homers.

JULY 4   After scoring 15 runs in consecutive games, the Red Sox are shut out 3–0 by the White Sox at Fenway Park.

JULY 5   The Red Sox score exactly 15 runs for the third time in four games, this time edging the White Sox 15–14 at Fenway Park. The Red Sox led 11–3 after five innings but allowed Chicago to tie the contest 11–11 with eight runs in the sixth. The Red Sox broke the deadlock with four runs in the seventh before surviving a three-run uprising by the opposition in the eighth. Boston batters collected 20 hits in the contest.

JULY 15   Midre Cummings hits a homer in the fifth inning off Bartolo Colon to defeat the Indians 1–0 at Fenway Park. Pedro Martinez pitched the shutout.

JULY 16   With the Red Sox trailing 4–1, Troy O'Leary hits a grand slam off Dwight Gooden in the fifth inning to spark Boston to a 15–5 belting of the Indians at Fenway Park. A seven-run rally in the eighth put the game away. Angry over the failure of Cleveland manager Mike Hargrove to select him for the All-Star Game, Nomar Garciaparra got four hits in four at-bats, including a homer and two doubles, and drove in five runs.

JULY 18   The Red Sox score seven runs on four homers hit after two were out in the fourth inning during a 9–4 win over the Tigers in Detroit. With Frank Castillo pitching, Donnie Sadler started the scoring with a three-run homer that struck the left field foul pole. It was his first homer in the majors. Darren Lewis followed with another home run. After Midre Cummings reached base on a walk, Dean Crow replaced Castillo. Nomar Garciaparra hit Crow's first pitch for a homer. Mo Vaughn came up next and struck Boston's fourth homer of the inning to tie a club record.

JULY 23   Down 6–1, the Red Sox score four runs in the eighth inning, two in the ninth, and one in the tenth to beat the Blue Jays 7–6 at Fenway Park. Damon Buford's grand slam off Dan Plesac accounted for the four eighth-inning runs.

JULY 30   The Red Sox trade Peter Munro and Jay Yennaco to the Yankees for Mike Stanley.

JULY 31   The Red Sox trade Matt Kinney, Joe Thomas, and Joe Barnes to the Twins for Greg Swindell and Orlando Merced.

AUGUST 4 Steve Avery (six innings), Derek Lowe (two innings), and Tom Gordon (one inning) combine on a two-hitter to defeat the Mariners 2–1 at the Kingdome. The only Seattle hits were a single by Ken Griffey Jr. in the fourth inning and a homer by Jay Buhner in the fifth.

          This was the last time that the Red Sox played at the Kingdome. The Mariners opened Safeco Field in 1999.

AUGUST 7 Pedro Martinez strikes out 13 batters in 6⅔ innings but loses 4–3 at the hands of the Rangers in Arlington.

AUGUST 8   The Red Sox score in every inning but the fourth and defeat the Rangers 11–1 in Arlington. Darren Bragg collected four hits, including two homers, in six at-bats.

AUGUST 9   The Red Sox clobber the Rangers 14–8 in Arlington. Both teams scored six times in the fifth inning.

AUGUST 11   A three-run, walk-off homer by Nomar Garciaparra in the tenth inning beats the Royals 7–4 at Fenway Park. It was his second homer of the game.

AUGUST 14   The Red Sox outslug the Twins 13–12 at Fenway Park. Minnesota took a 6–0 lead with four runs in the third inning before the Sox tied the score with six tallies in their half. The contest was still deadlocked 11–11 when Boston scored twice in the seventh.

AUGUST 19   Mike Stanley drives in six runs with two homers and a single during an 11–1 win over the Royals in Kansas City.

SEPTEMBER 2   Nomar Garciaparra hits a walk-off homer off Bobby Ayala in the ninth inning that beats the Mariners 7–3 at Fenway Park.

                The win gave the Red Sox an eight-game lead in the wild-card race. The club appeared to be a lock for the playoffs but gave its fans plenty of anxious moments by losing 12 of the next 17 contests to cut the advantage to three games before clinching a spot in the postseason.

SEPTEMBER 9   Scott Hatteberg hits a grand slam off Orlando Hernandez in the fourth inning, but the Red Sox lose 7–5 to the Yankees at Fenway Park.

SEPTEMBER 17   Dennis Eckersley becomes the oldest Red Sox pitcher in history to earn a victory with the decision in a 10-inning, 3–2 victory over the Orioles in Baltimore.

SEPTEMBER 24   The Red Sox clinch a wild-card berth with a 9–6 win over the Orioles at Fenway Park.

SEPTEMBER 26   During a 5–2 loss to the Orioles in Baltimore, Dennis Eckersley makes his 1,071th appearance on the mound to break the all-time major league record for games as a pitcher. Hoyt Wilhelm held the previous record. This would be Eckersley's last big-league game. He retired after the season. Since 1998, Eckersley has dropped to third on the games-pitched list behind Jesse Orosco and John Franco.

                The Red Sox met the Cleveland Indians in the best-of-five Division Series. Managed by Mike Hargrove, the defending American League champion Indians were 89–73 during the regular season.

SEPTEMBER 29   In the first game of the Division Series, the Red Sox maul the Indians 11–3 in Cleveland behind the pitching of Pedro Martinez and seven RBIs from Mo Vaughn, who had two homers and a double. Three batters and 15 pitches into the game, the Sox had a 3–0 lead on singles by Darren Lewis and John Valentin and a homer by Vaughn. It was Vaughn's first postseason hit. He was 0 for 14 against the Indians in 1995. Nomar Garciaparra also hit a homer and drove in the other four Boston runs.

The victory was the Red Sox' first in postseason play after 13 consecutive defeats dating back to the 1986 World Series.

SEPTEMBER 30   At Jacobs Field, the Indians parlay a five-run second inning into a 9–5 win in Game Two of the Division Series. Tim Wakefield took the loss.

OCTOBER 2   The Indians take a two-games-to-one lead in the Division Series by winning 4–3 at Fenway Park. Cleveland's Manny Ramirez hit a homer in the ninth inning off Dennis Eckersley to put the Indians up 4–1 and allowed them to withstand a two-run blast by Nomar Garciaparra in the bottom of the inning. It was Ramirez's second homer of the game. Four of Cleveland's five hits were home runs, three of them off Bret Saberhagen. Kenny Lofton and Jim Thome accounted for the other two.

                Playing in his first postseason, Garciaparra hit three homers and drove in 11 runs in the four games against the Indians.

OCTOBER 3   The Indians wrap up the Division Series by defeating the Red Sox 2–1 at Fenway Park. A homer by Nomar Garciaparra in the fourth inning put the Sox ahead, 1–0. The Indians scored two in the eighth on David Justice's double off Tom Gordon. It was Gordon's first blown save since April 14. He had converted 43 in a row.

                Manager Jimy Williams created a controversy over his choice of a starting pitcher. Rather than bring Pedro Martinez back on three days' rest, Williams started journeyman Pete Schourek, who was 1–3 with a 4.30 ERA since being acquired from the Astros in August. Fortunately for the Sox—and Williams— Schourek pitched 5 1/3 scoreless innings.

NOVEMBER 11   Greg Swindell signs as a free agent with the Diamondbacks.

NOVEMBER 13   The Red Sox sign Jose Offerman, most recently with the Royals, as a free agent.

                Offerman signed a four-year deal. He gave the Red Sox one good season, hitting .294 with eight homers in 1999 before becoming an overpriced drag on the budget during his last three years in Boston.

NOVEMBER 25   Mo Vaughn signs as a free agent with the Angels.

                Negotiations between Vaughn and the Red Sox had dominated the headlines for two years, as the two sides swiped at each other in an ongoing soap opera with ugly accusations and innuendo. The war of words led to a bitter divorce. Vaughn was heavily involved in charity work, and the fans wanted him back. "Sign Mo Now" chants were commonplace at Fenway Park in 1998. But the Red Sox front office was concerned about a fight involving Vaughn in a night club in 1995, another fight in the parking lot of a strip club in 1997, and a drunk-driving arrest in 1998 in which he flipped his pickup truck after striking another vehicle. There were also questions about his knee and increasing weight. Still, there was no sign of a decline in productivity, as Vaughn had a terrific season in 1997 with a .337 batting average, 40 homers, 115 RBIs, 107 runs scored, and 205 hits. The Sox offered Vaughn a reported five years at $63 million, but he accepted an offer from the Angels for six years at $80 million, which at the time made him the highest-paid player in baseball. In the end, the

Sox were lucky that Vaughn turned down their offer. Almost immediately after inking the deal, his career declined rapidly. During the life of his six-year contract, in which he played for the Mets in addition to the Angels, Vaughn missed two entire seasons with injuries and played in only 27 games of another.

DECEMBER 9   The Red Sox sign Mark Portugal, most recently with the Phillies, as a free agent.

DECEMBER 11   Steve Avery signs as a free agent with the Reds.

1999   B

Season in a Sentence

Led by incredible seasons from Pedro Martinez and Nomar Garciaparra and a deep pitching staff, the Red Sox reach the American League Championship Series for the first time since 1990.

Finish • Won • Lost • Pct • GB

Second   94   68   .580   4.0

In the wild-card race, the Red Sox finished in first place, seven games ahead of the Oakland Athletics.

AL Division Series—The Red Sox defeated the Cleveland Indians three games to two.

AL Championship Series—The Red Sox lost to the New York Yankees four games to one.

Manager

Jimy Williams

Stats   Red Sox • AL • Rank

	Red Sox	AL	Rank
Batting Avg:	.278	.275	6
On-Base Pct:	.350	.347	7
Slugging Pct:	.448	.439	6
Home Runs:	176		9
Stolen Bases:	67		14
ERA:	4.00	4.86	1
Fielding Pct:	.979	.981	12
Runs Scored:	836		9
Runs Allowed:	718		1

Starting Lineup

Jason Varitek, c
Mike Stanley, 1b
Jose Offerman, 2b
John Valentin, 3b
Nomar Garciaparra, ss
Troy O'Leary, lf
Darren Lewis, cf-rf
Trot Nixon, rf
Brian Daubach, dh-1b
Damon Buford, cf
Reggie Jefferson, dh

Pitchers

Pedro Martinez, sp
Bret Saberhagen, sp
Mark Portugal, sp
Pat Rapp, sp
Brian Rose, sp
Derek Lowe, rp
Tim Wakefield, rp-sp
Rheal Cormier, rp
Mark Guthrie, rp

Attendance

2,446,162 (sixth in AL)

Club Leaders

Batting Avg:	Garciaparra	.357
On-Base Pct:	Garciaparra	.418
Slugging Pct:	Garciaparra	.603
Home Runs:	O'Leary	28
RBI:	Garciaparra	104
Runs:	Offerman	107
Stolen Bases:	Offerman	18
Wins:	Martinez	23
Strikeouts:	Martinez	313
ERA:	Martinez	2.07
Saves:	Lowe	15
	Wakefield	15

JANUARY 11   The Red Sox sign Pat Rapp, most recently with the Giants, as a free agent.

Stephen King, a diehard Red Sox fan, had a new book in 1999 titled The Girl Who Loved Tom Gordon. *The plot centered on a nine-year-old who was lost in the Maine woods but was able to tune into Red Sox radio broadcasts. Sox closer Tom Gordon became her make-believe friend.*

MARCH 11   A month after Bill Clinton is acquitted following his impeachment trial in the House of Representatives, the Red Sox sign Pedro Martinez's older brother Ramon as a free agent.

APRIL 5   The Red Sox defeat the Royals 5–3 in Kansas City in the season opener. In his first game with the Red Sox, Jose Offerman collected four hits, including a triple and a double, in five at-bats against his former Kansas City teammates. John Valentin hit a homer.

From 1988 through 1999, the Red Sox had 12 different players start in right field on Opening Day. They were Mike Greenwell (1988), Dwight Evans (1989), Kevin Romine (1990), Tom Brunansky (1991), Phil Plantier (1992), Andre Dawson (1993), Billy Hatcher (1994), Mark Whiten (1995), Troy O'Leary (1996), Rudy Pemberton (1997), Darren Bragg (1998), and Trot Nixon (1999).

APRIL 10   The Red Sox run their season record to 5–0 with a 5–3 win over the Devil Rays in St. Petersburg. It left the Sox one short of the club record for most consecutive wins at the start of a season, which was six in 1918.

After the 5–0 start, the Red Sox fell to 12–14 by May 5 before rebounding to win 20 of their next 25 games for a 32–19 record on June 1.

APRIL 13   In the home opener, the Red Sox defeat the White Sox 6–0 before 31,874 at Fenway Park. Bret Saberhagen (6⅔ innings), Derek Lowe (1⅓ innings,) and Mark Guthrie (one inning) combined on the shutout. Troy O'Leary hit a home run.

April 20   On the day that 15 die in a shooting at Columbine High School in Littleton, Colorado, Troy O'Leary homers off Jeff Weaver of the Tigers in the fourth inning to lift the Red Sox to a 1–0 win in Detroit. Pedro Martinez (7⅔ innings), Rheal Cormier (two-thirds of an inning), and Derek Lowe (two-thirds of an inning) combined on the shutout.

O'Leary hit .280 with 28 homers in 1999.

APRIL 23   Two brawls highlight a 7–6 loss to the Indians at Fenway Park. In the fifth inning, Darren Lewis took exception to a Jaret Wright pitch thrown near his head and charged the mound, causing both dugouts to empty. Wright had beaned Lewis in the 1998 playoffs. In the sixth, Rheal Cormier hit Jim Thome with a pitch, leading to a second bench-clearing melee. Cormier was suspended for three days for the incident.

APRIL 28   Trot Nixon has an unusual stat line at the end of a 9–4 win over the Twins in Minneapolis. Nixon scored four runs despite only one hit in one official at-bat. He homered and crossed the plate three times after drawing walks.

MAY 1   Pedro Martinez strikes out 13 batters in seven innings during a 7–2 win over the Athletics in Oakland.

Martinez had one of the greatest seasons ever by a Red Sox pitcher in 1999, posting a 23–4 record. He won the Cy Young Award by a unanimous vote and was a close second to Ivan Rodriguez in the MVP balloting. Martinez's ERA of 2.07 not only led the league, it was also far ahead of second-place finisher David Cone's earned run average of 3.44. He posted the 2.07 ERA in a season in which the league average was 4.86. He also led the AL in victories, winning percentage (.852), and strikeouts (313 in 213 1/3 innings). The strikeout mark was an all-time Red Sox single-season record, breaking Roger Clemens's record of 291 from 1988. Martinez struck out 13.2 batters per nine innings. The only starting pitcher in baseball history with a better ratio is Randy Johnson, who fanned 13.4 batters per nine innings with the Diamondbacks in 2001. Martinez helped the Sox lead the AL in team earned run average for the first time since 1914.

MAY 3   The first major league hit of Red Sox rookie catcher Creighton Gubanich is a grand slam off Jimmy Haynes in the first inning of a 10-inning, 12–11 loss to the Athletics in Oakland. The Sox had a 7–0 lead after two innings and were still ahead 11–6 at the end of the seventh before frittering away the advantage.

This proved to be Gubanich's only big-league homer. He had 47 at-bats in 18 games in the majors.

MAY 7   Mo Vaughn plays at Fenway Park for the first time as a visiting player, but Pedro Martinez steals the show with 15 strikeouts and no walks for a 6–0 win over the Angels. Vaughn received a standing ovation when he came to bat in the first. He was hitless in four at-bats with two strikeouts.

MAY 8   In his major league debut, twenty-one-year-old Juan Peña pitches six innings and allows only one run during a 6–1 win over the Angels at Fenway Park.

In Peña's second start, six days later, he hurled the first seven innings of a 5–0 win over the Blue Jays in Toronto. He suffered a shoulder injury in 1999 and tore a ligament in his elbow in 2000, however, and never pitched another big-league game after May 14, 1999. Peña closed his career with a 2–0 record and a 0.69 ERA with 15 strikeouts in 13 innings.

MAY 10   Nomar Garciaparra hits three homers, including two grand slams, and racks up 10 RBIs to lead the Red Sox to a 12–4 win over the Mariners at Fenway Park. Garciaparra hit a grand slam off Brett Hinchliffe in the first inning. Garciaparra then sliced a two-run shot in the third off Hinchliffe that curved fair around the right field foul pole. After fouling out in the fourth and walking in the sixth, he hit his second grand slam in the eighth while facing Eric Weaver. The 10 RBIs tied a club record with Rudy York (June 27, 1946), Norm Zauchin (May 27, 1955), and Fred Lynn (June 18, 1975).

Garciaparra won the batting title in 1999 with a .357 average. He also had 103 runs, 42 doubles, 27 homers, and 104 RBIs.

MAY 12   Pedro Martinez strikes out 15 batters in his second consecutive start while pitching eight innings during a 9–2 win over the Mariners at Fenway Park.

MAY 17   The Red Sox defeat the Blue Jays 8–7 in Toronto. Trailing 4–3, the Red Sox scored five runs in the ninth inning before the Blue Jays answered with three in their half. Brian Daubach broke the 4–4 tie with a three-run homer. It was his first home run as a major leaguer.

MAY 15   The Red Sox announce plans for a 44,000-seat stadium to be built on a parcel of land some 600 feet south of Fenway Park. The team hoped to play in the new park in 2003, but the proposal was still subject to financing, including assistance from the city and state. The $550 million plan included $350 million for stadium construction. The new ballpark would have all the desired modern amenities, such as luxury boxes, preferred seating, and expanded concessions. In an attempt to appease preservationists, it would have retained much of the famed Green Monster in a park area and part of the original tapestry wall along the current Yawkey Way as part of a grand entranceway. The plans for the playing field echoed the current ball yard: a 37-foot left field wall with a manual scoreboard, a short poke in right, bullpens in front of the right field bleachers, and a center field triangle. The park also would have included a cantilevered upper deck with thousands of new seats far more remote than any in old Fenway and the virtual banishment of outside vendors. "Building a new ballpark is not an optional choice for the Red Sox or any other ball club, but a necessity," general manager Dan Duquette said.

            The new Fenway Park never got off the ground. In March 2005, the Red Sox announced that they were no longer pursuing a new facility and would remain at Fenway Park for the foreseeable future.

MAY 19   Jason Varitek collects four hits, including two homers, in four at-bats during a 6–0 win over the Yankees at Fenway Park.

            The win put the Red Sox in first place, a position the club held until June 8.

MAY 22   John Valentin collects four hits, including a grand slam in the third inning off Chris Carpenter, to lead the Red Sox to a 6–4 win over the Blue Jays at Fenway Park.

MAY 25   The Red Sox take a 2½-game lead in the AL East with a 5–2 win over the Yankees in New York.

MAY 28   The Red Sox hit five homers in a 12–5 pounding of the Indians in Cleveland. Nomar Garciaparra hit two homers and Mike Stanley, Jason Varitek, and Brian Daubach added one each. Trying to catch Tim Wakefield's knuckleball, Varitek had five passed balls in the game to set the Red Sox club record and was one short of the modern major league mark. Three of the passed balls were in the first inning.

JUNE 2   In their first pick in the first round of the amateur draft, the Red Sox select outfielder Rick Asadoorian from Northbridge High School in Whitinsville, Massachusetts, a small town about halfway between Worcester and Providence.

            Asadoorian has never gotten close to playing in the major leagues. The only player drafted and signed by the Red Sox in 1999 who has reached the majors thus far is Casey Fossum (the Sox' third pick in the first round).

JUNE 4   Pedro Martinez strikes out 16 batters in a three-hit complete game, defeating the Braves 5–1 at Fenway Park. It was his 10th win in a row.

JUNE 5   Tom Gordon's streak of 54 consecutive regular-season saves comes to an end when the Braves string together three two-out hits for two runs and a 6–6 win over the Red Sox at Fenway Park. The 54 consecutive saves was a major league record until it was broken by Eric Gagne, who saved 85 in a row from 2002 through 2004.

Gordon blew a second straight save opportunity on June 11, then went on the disabled list for more than three months with a tender elbow. Gordon missed the entire 2000 season with the injury, then signed a free-agent deal with the Cubs.

JUNE 14   Down 3–2 with one out in the ninth, the Sox' Darren Lewis and Jeff Frye hit back-to-back homers to beat the Twins 4–3 at Fenway Park.

The home runs were hit by two of the least likely Red Sox batters to drive a ball out of the park. It was the only homer that Frye hit all season. Lewis hit only two in 1999.

JUNE 25   Pedro Martinez is "tied up" during a 6–1 win over the White Sox at Fenway Park. In the ninth inning, Martinez found himself bound and gagged in the Red Sox dugout, tied mummy-style to a pole with tape. Martinez had been enjoying a running commentary with the White Sox dugout, in particular manager Jerry Manuel. "The White Sox called us and asked if we could shut him up, somehow, so we obliged," Nomar Garciaparra said.

JUNE 26   The Red Sox score 11 runs in the first inning and cruise to a 17–1 thrashing of the White Sox at Fenway Park. There were five homers in the game. Nomar Garciaparra hit two, and Mike Stanley, Jason Varitek, and Brian Daubach each added one.

JUNE 28   Jose Offerman drives in six runs on a grand slam and a two-run homer during a 14–1 romp over the White Sox at Fenway Park. The slam came in the seventh inning off Bryan Ward. The Red Sox collected 21 hits in the game.

JULY 2   In the Red Sox' 79th game of the season, Pedro Martinez remains on a pace to win 30 games by picking up his 15th victory in a 6–1 win over the White Sox in Chicago.

Martinez didn't win another game until August 8 because of soreness in his pitching shoulder. He was on the disabled list from July 19 through August 3.

JULY 13   Pitching before his hometown fans, Pedro Martinez is named the MVP for his work in a 4–1 American League win in the All-Star Game, played before 34,187 at Fenway Park. Martinez was the starting pitcher and hurled two innings, fanning five batters, including the first four of the game. Pedro set down Barry Larkin, Larry Walker, Sammy Sosa, Mark McGwire, and Jeff Bagwell. The only hitter to reach base off Martinez was on an error. The AL took a 2–0 lead in the first inning, and after the NL plated a run in the third, the American Leaguers added two in the fourth. No one hit a home run. The only two extra-base hits were doubles.

It was the third All-Star Game played at Fenway. The other two were in 1946 and 1961. The highlight of the evening was not the game but the emotion-packed pregame ceremonies, which included 41 baseball legends walking in from the outfield, similar to the scene from Field of Dreams. *Eighty-year-old Ted Williams shook hands and shared hugs with many past and current players before throwing out the first pitch. Among those who played in the All-Star Game in 1999 were Roberto Alomar, Jeff Bagwell, Jay Bell, David Cone, Nomar Garciaparra, Luis Gonzalez, Ken Griffey Jr., Derek Jeter, Randy Johnson, Jeff Kent, Barry Larkin, Pedro Martinez, Mark McGwire, Rafael Palmeiro, Mike Piazza, Manny Ramirez, Cal Ripken Jr., Ivan Rodriguez, Garry Sheffield, Curt Schilling, Sammy Sosa, Jim Thome, and Larry Walker.*

JULY 18   Two days after John F. Kennedy Jr. and his wife die in a plane crash, the Red Sox outlast the Marlins 11–9 at Fenway Park.

JULY 24   Trot Nixon hits three of Boston's seven homers during an 11–4 victory over the Tigers in Detroit. The three Nixon homers were hit in the second inning with two on against Jeff Weaver, a solo shot off Weaver in the fourth, and a solo homer off Willie Blair in the eighth. Nomar Garciaparra hit two homers, and Brian Daubach and Troy O'Leary each added one.

JULY 25   The Red Sox play at Tiger Stadium for the last time and lose, 9–1.

               The Tigers opened Comerica Park in 2000.

JULY 27   The Red Sox outslug the Blue Jays 11–9 in Toronto. The Sox trailed 7–3 before scoring six runs in the fifth inning to take the lead.

JULY 28   In only his second game with the Red Sox after being acquired from the Mariners, Butch Huskey hits a grand slam and a solo homer during an 8–0 win over the Blue Jays at Skydome. The slam came in the sixth inning off Joey Hamilton. Pat Rapp (eight innings) and Tim Wakefield (one inning) combined on a two-hitter. The only Toronto hits were singles by Terry Steinbach in the seventh inning and Chad Allen in the eighth.

AUGUST 7   The Red Sox smack the Angels 14–3 in Anaheim.

AUGUST 10   Against the Royals in Kansas City, Tim Wakefield strikes out four batters in the ninth inning but blows the save when he surrenders a two-run homer to Carlos Febles that ties the score, 5–5. Jason Varitek allowed a passed ball on what should have been the game-ending third strike to Johnny Damon. The Red Sox won the game 9–6 with four runs in the tenth before the Royals came back with one in their half.

AUGUST 13   Darren Lewis scores five runs during an 11–6 win over the Mariners at Fenway Park.

AUGUST 14   Brian Daubach drives in six runs on a five for five day to lead the Red Sox to a 13–2 win over the Mariners at Fenway Park. Daubach had four singles and a homer.

               Pedro Martinez was scheduled to start the game but was scratched when he showed up 15 minutes late. Bryce Florie started in his place. Martinez pitched the final four innings of the contest, however, and earned his 17th win of the season. It was his first relief appearance since 1994 (see August 19, 1999).

AUGUST 16   A two-out, three-run, walk-off homer by Brian Daubach beats the Athletics 6–5 at Fenway Park. Daubach fouled off five pitches on a full count before hitting the ball over the Green Monster.

> *During August, Daubach hit six homers in a seven-game stretch and drove in 20 runs over nine games. One of the great stories of the 1999 season, Daubach was a twenty-seven-year-old rookie who won the starting first base job after spending nine years in the minors. The Red Sox signed Daubach after he was released by the Marlins in 1998. During his years in the majors, he was the target of many a beanball from pitchers with long memories who were angry because Daubach was a replacement player with the Mets during spring training in 1995 when major leaguers were on strike.*

AUGUST 19   Pedro Martinez loses 6–2 to the Athletics at Fenway Park after launching an obscenity-laced pregame tirade at Dan Duquette in the clubhouse. Martinez was also angry at the camera people and the media for invading his privacy and at manager Jimy Williams for scratching his start against the Mariners five days earlier.

AUGUST 24   Pedro Martinez strikes out 15 batters in the eighth inning to defeat the Twins 7–1 in Minneapolis.

> *On the same day, the Red Sox traded Mike Matthews and David Benham to the Cardinals for Kent Mercker.*

AUGUST 31   The Red Sox trade Mark Guthrie and Cole Liniak to the Cubs for Rod Beck.

SEPTEMBER 1   In his debut with the Red Sox, Rod Beck earns the save with a perfect ninth inning to defeat the Royals 4–3 at Fenway Park. Beck arrived at the ballpark only 25 minutes before the start of the game.

SEPTEMBER 3   The Red Sox play at Safeco Field in Seattle for the first time and lose 2–1 to the Mariners.

SEPTEMBER 4   Pedro Martinez earns his 20th save of the season with a 15-strikeout performance, leading the Red Sox to a 4–0 win over the Mariners in Seattle. Martinez allowed only two hits in eight innings.

SEPTEMBER 10   Pedro Martinez strikes out 17 batters while allowing only one hit during a 3–1 complete-game victory over the Yankees in New York. There were only two Yankee base runners. Chuck Knoblauch was hit by a pitch leading off the first inning, and Chili Davis homered in the second. Martinez retired the last 22 batters to face him, the final five on strikeouts.

SEPTEMBER 11   The Red Sox use five homers to beat the Yankees 11–10 in New York. Nomar Garciaparra hit two home runs, and Butch Huskey, Troy O'Leary, and Trot Nixon each added one.

SEPTEMBER 12   The Red Sox complete a three-game sweep of the Yankees at Yankee Stadium with a 4–1 win. The victory cut New York's lead in the AL East to 3½ games. The Sox were 8½ games out on August 30. Boston had a three-game lead in the wild-card race over the Athletics.

SEPTEMBER 15   Jason Varitek and Trot Nixon homer in the thirteenth inning to defeat the Indians
6–4 in Cleveland. Pedro Martinez fanned 14 batters in seven innings. Boston pitchers struck out 20 during the game. Rheal Cormier struck out one, Rod Beck two,
and John Wasdin three.

SEPTEMBER 17   The Red Sox wallop the Tigers 14–3 at Fenway Park.

SEPTEMBER 21   Pedro Martinez strikes out 12 batters to give him 300 for the season, breaking
Roger Clemens's single-season club record of 291 in 1988. The Sox won 3–0
against the Blue Jays at Fenway Park. Martinez tied the record by fanning Tony
Batista in the second inning. Declining to save the ball for posterity, Martinez
used the same ball to strike out Willis Otanez for the record breaker. He then sent
the ball into the dugout for safekeeping.

One of the team's great acquisitions of the 1990s, Pedro Martinez posted a 23–4 record in 1999 on
his way to his second Cy Young Award.

SEPTEMBER 24   The Red Sox release Mark Portugal. Although Portugal was 7–12 with an ERA of
5.51, he was second on the team in games started and innings pitched. With the
team set to go to the playoffs, it was an unusual move to say the least, and angered
players and fans alike.

SEPTEMBER 26   Tom Gordon is nearly brought into an 8–5 loss to the Orioles at Fenway Park illegally. Gordon was about to make his first appearance in a game since being placed on the disabled list on June 11. After he tossed a few warm-up pitches, general manager Dan Duquette spotted him and realized that the pitcher had not been activated off the disabled list. Had Gordon thrown a pitch, the Red Sox would have forfeited the game. Duquette made a hurried call to Williams in the dugout and had Gordon yanked.

SEPTEMBER 27   Pedro Martinez strikes out 12 batters in eight innings and earns his 23rd victory of the season with a 5–3 decision over the Orioles at Fenway park.

SEPTEMBER 29   The Red Sox clinch the wild-card berth with a 6–2 win over the White Sox in the first game of a doubleheader at Comiskey Park. Chicago won the second game, 4–2.

OCTOBER 2   Damon Buford hits a grand slam off Gabe Molina in the ninth inning of an 8–0 win over the Orioles in Baltimore.

OCTOBER 3   In the last regular-season game, the Red Sox defeat the Orioles 1–0 in 10 innings in Baltimore. Jeff Frye drove in the winning run with a single. Eight different pitchers combined on the shutout as Jimy Williams strived to keep his staff fresh for the playoffs. The Red Sox set a major league record for most pitchers used in a shutout. The eight pitchers were Pat Rapp (two innings), Rheal Cormier (one inning), Rich Garces (one inning), Derek Lowe (one inning), Tom Gordon (one inning), Rod Beck (one inning), Brian Rose (two innings), and Tim Wakefield (one inning).

OCTOBER 6   In the first game of the Division Series, the Indians beat the Red Sox 3–2 in Cleveland. Jim Thome hit a two-run homer for the Indians in the sixth inning off Derek Lowe to tie the score 2–2 following an error by John Valentin, and Travis Fryman's single in the ninth drove in the winning run. Nomar Garciaparra drove in both Boston runs with a homer in the second inning and a double in the fourth. Mike Stanley collected three hits. Pedro Martinez started and pitched four shutout innings, but a sore back forced him out of the game.

The Red Sox were meeting the Indians in the playoffs for the third time in five years. The Sox lost to Cleveland in both 1995 and 1998. Managed by Mike Hargrove, the Indians were 97–65 in 1999.

OCTOBER 7   The Indians take a 2–0 lead in the ALDS with an 11–1 trouncing of the Red Sox at Jacobs Field. Cleveland scored six runs in the third inning and five in the fourth. Jim Thome hit a grand slam in the fourth off John Wasdin.

The loss gave the Red Sox a 1–18 record in the postseason beginning with Game Six of the 1986 World Series.

OCTOBER 9   The Red Sox stay in the series by breaking a 3–3 tie with a six-run seventh inning leading to a 9–3 victory over the Indians before 33,539 at Fenway Park. John Valentin and Brian Daubach each homered and drove in three runs for the Sox.

OCTOBER 10   Records fall as the Red Sox collect 24 hits and maul the Indians 23–7 before 33,898 at Fenway Park to even the series. The Red Sox broke postseason marks for most runs and most hits in a game. The 16-run victory margin was also a record. John Valentin had two homers, a double, and a single and drove in seven runs.

Jose Offerman and Jason Varitek also homered for the Sox. Varitek set a postseason record with five runs scored. He also drove in three runs and had two doubles and a single in addition to his homer. Offerman drove in five runs and scored three. Mike Stanley got five hits, including a triple, in six at-bats. Trot Nixon drove five runs and scored three, and Darren Lewis crossed the plate three times. The Sox scored two runs in the first inning, five in the second, three in the third, five in the fourth, three in the fifth, three in the seventh, and two in the eighth.

OCTOBER 11   Coming back from a two-games-to-none deficit, the Red Sox win the Division Series by defeating the Indians 12–8 in Cleveland. Troy O'Leary drove in seven runs. The Red Sox trailed 5–2 after two innings before scoring five runs in the third, four of them on O'Leary's grand slam off Charles Nagy. The slam followed an intentional walk to Nomar Garciaparra. The score was 8–8 in the seventh with a runner on base when Indians manager Mike Hargrove ordered another intentional pass to Garciaparra. O'Leary responded with a three-run blast off Paul Shuey. In a spectacular performance, Pedro Martinez hurled the final six innings as a reliever and pitched hitless ball while striking out eight batters. Garciaparra drove in three runs and scored three. Brian Daubach contributed two doubles and a single.

> The seven RBIs by O'Leary tied a postseason record for a single game. Only three other players have managed seven RBIs in a playoff game. They are Edgar Martinez of the Mariners in 1995, Mo Vaughn in 1998, and John Valentin the day before O'Leary's feat. Valentin drove in 12 runs in the five Division Series games to tie a record for a postseason series. Bobby Richardson of the Yankees drove in 12 runs in a seven-game World Series in 1960.
>
> The Sox moved forward to meet their longtime rivals the Yankees in the American League Championship Series. It was the first time that the Yankees and Red Sox met in a postseason series. Managed by Joe Torre, the Yankees were the defending World Champions and had a record of 98–64 in 1999.

OCTOBER 13   In Game One of the ALCS, Bernie Williams homers leading off the bottom of the tenth on Rod Beck's second pitch to give the Yankees a 4–3 win over the Red Sox in New York. The Red Sox jumped to a 2–0 lead in the first and added one run in the second to take a 3–0 lead, but the Yankees scored two in their half on a home run by Scott Brosius off Kent Mercker and tied the game with a run in the seventh. Jose Offerman had three singles for the Sox and was involved in a controversial play in the top of the tenth. Umpire Rick Reed ruled that Yankee second baseman Chuck Knoblauch held on to a throw from third baseman Scott Brosius long enough to record a force-out, but replays showed that Knoblauch never had full control and that Offerman should have been ruled safe. Reed admitted that he blew the call. There would be another controversial call involving Knoblauch and Offerman in Game Four.

OCTOBER 14   The Yankees make it two in a row by downing the Red Sox 3–2 in New York. The Sox took a 2–1 lead in the fifth inning on a homer by Nomar Garciaparra, but the Yanks scored twice in the seventh for the win. Ramon Martinez, Pedro's older brother, took the loss. Garciaparra and Troy O'Leary each had three hits.

OCTOBER 16   The Red Sox win Game Three 13–1 over the Yankees before 33,190 at Fenway Park. The game began with fans eagerly anticipating the storied matchup of Pedro Martinez and Roger Clemens. Martinez was brilliant, striking out 12 batters in seven innings while allowing only two hits. Clemens lasted only two innings and got shelled for five runs and six hits. Boston rapped out 21 hits, including homers from Nomar Garciaparra, Brian Daubach, and John Valentin. Valentin also had two singles and drove in five runs. In addition to his homer, Garciaparra had a double and two singles and drove in three runs. Jose Offerman hit a triple and two singles, and Trot Nixon collected two doubles and a single.

OCTOBER 17   The Yankees win a controversial game 9–2 over the Red Sox before 33,586 at Fenway Park. With the Yankees ahead 3–2 in the bottom of the eighth, Chuck Knoblauch fumbled a hard hit grounder and tried to tag Jose Offerman running from first base to second. Knoblauch missed the tag and threw wide of second in an attempt to force the runner, but umpire Tim Tschida called Offerman out. Tschida later admitted he made the wrong call. The Red Sox failed to recover. The Yanks scored six runs in the top of the ninth, four of them on a Ricky Ledee grand slam, to seal the victory. Jimy Williams was ejected for arguing a call in the ninth. First-base ump Dale Scott called Nomar Garciaparra out, but replays showed he was safe. Fans threw debris onto the field, delaying the game for eight minutes and causing the players to be removed from the Yankees bullpen. A forfeit was threatened over the loudspeakers.

Carlton Fisk threw out the ceremonial first pitch.

OCTOBER 18   The Yankees close out the ALCS with a 6–1 Game Five victory over the Red Sox before 33,589 at Fenway Park. Jason Varitek's homer in the eighth when the Yanks were leading 4–0 accounted for the only Boston run.

Babe Ruth's daughter, Julia Ruth Stevens, threw out the first pitch.

DECEMBER 15   The Red Sox trade Adam Everett and Greg Miller to the Astros for Carl Everett.

DECEMBER 22   The Red Sox sign Jeff Fassero, most recently with the Rangers, as a free agent.

BOSTON RED SOX
THE 2000s

THE STATE OF THE RED SOX

Through 2005, the Red Sox have a record of 548–423 in the twenty-first century (a .564 winning percentage), third best in the AL behind the Yankees and Athletics. The Sox reached the postseason as a wild card in 2003, 2004, and 2005, made the ALCS in 2003 and 2004, and won the World Series in 2004. The Yankees won each of the first six AL East titles during the 2000s. American League representatives in the World Series, besides the Red Sox, have been the Yankees (2000, 2001, and 2003), Angels (2002), and White Sox (2005).

THE BEST TEAM

Is there any question? The 2004 edition will remain in the hearts of Red Sox fans forever as the team that removed the curse by winning the World Championship after falling behind three games to none in the American League Championship Series against the Yankees.

THE WORST TEAM

The 2001 Red Sox were 82–79 and finished 13 ½ games behind the Yankees.

THE BEST MOMENT

The best moment was the final out of the 2004 World Series.

THE WORST MOMENT

The Red Sox blew a 5–2, eighth-inning lead in the seventh game of the 2003 ALCS against the Yankees and lost 6–5 on Aaron Boone's walk-off homer in the eleventh.

THE ALL–DECADE TEAM • YEARS WITH BRS

Jason Varitek, c	1997–2005
Brian Daubach, 1b	1999–2002, 2004
Jose Offerman, 2b	1999–2002
Bill Mueller, 3b	2003–05
Nomar Garciaparra, ss	1996–2004
Manny Ramirez, lf	2001–05
Johnny Damon, cf	2002–05
Trot Nixon, rf	1996, 1998–2005
David Ortiz, dh	2003–05
Pedro Martinez, p	1998–2004
Derek Lowe, p	1997–2004
Tim Wakefield, p	1995–2005
Curt Schilling, p	2004–05

First base has been a particular problem in Boston since Mo Vaughn left via free agency at the end of the 1999 season. The Sox have also had trouble finding a year-in, year-out second baseman for more than 10 years. The last player to appear at least 100 games at second base in consecutive seasons was Jody Reed in 1991–92.

THE DECADE LEADERS

Batting Avg:	Ramirez	.315
On-Base Pct:	Ramirez	.412
Slugging Pct:	Ramirez	.608
Home Runs:	Ramirez	199
RBI:	Ramirez	611
Runs:	Ramirez	512
Stolen Bases:	Damon	98
Wins:	Martinez	75
Strikeouts:	Martinez	1,119
ERA:	Martinez	2.52
Saves:	Lowe	66

THE HOME FIELD

When the decade began, the Red Sox were actively seeking a new ballpark to be built just south of Fenway Park. The club wanted help from state and/or local governments to construct the facility, however, and the funds were not forthcoming. A group headed by John Henry bought the Red Sox in 2002 and began a series of projects designed to improve the club's cash flow by increasing capacity and the number of advertisements inside the ballpark. The most innovative idea was the construction of seats atop the Green Monster in 2003. Red Sox management announced in 2005 that the team had abandoned plans to build a new ballpark and would remain at Fenway Park for the foreseeable future.

THE GAME YOU WISH YOU HAD SEEN

Game Four of the American League Championship Series against the Yankees. Down three games to none, the Red Sox trailed 4–3 in the ninth with Mariano Rivera on the mound. Coming back to win 6–4 in 12 innings, the Sox won the next three contests to take the AL pennant, then won four in a row in the World Series.

THE WAY THE GAME WAS PLAYED

The offensive explosion baseball experienced during the late 1990s continued into the 2000s (Manny Ramirez and David Ortiz combined to hit 244 home runs from 2003 through 2005), as did the trend toward baseball-only ballparks with grass fields.

THE MANAGEMENT

The Jean R. Yawkey Trust sold the Red Sox in 2002 to a group headed by John Henry. With the sale, the club presidency passed from John Harrington to Larry Lucchino. General mangers were Dan Duquette (1994–2002), Mike Port (2002), Theo Epstein (2002–2005), and Jed Hoyer and Ben Cherrington (2006–). Field managers were Jimy Williams (1997–2001), Joe Kerrigan (2001), Grady Little (2002–03), and Terry Francona (2004–present).

THE BEST PLAYER MOVE

The signing of Manny Ramirez following the 2000 season has been the best move thus far, but it came at a steep price—$160 million over eight years. In terms of money spent, the best move was the acquisition of David Ortiz in 2003 after the Twins released him. The best trade with another club was the Red Sox' November 2003 deal in which they sent four players to the Diamondbacks for Curt Schilling.

THE WORST PLAYER MOVE

The worst trade to date sent Shea Hillenbrand to Arizona for Byung-Hyun Kim in May 2003.

2 0 0 0   B

Season in a Sentence

Backed by another Cy Young year from Pedro Martinez, the Red Sox top the league in ERA, but an inadequate offense keeps the club out of the postseason despite Nomar Garciaparra's herculean efforts.

Finish • Won • Lost • Pct • GB

Second   85   77   .525   2.5

In the wild-card race, the Red Sox finished in third place, six games back.

Manager

Jimy Williams

Stats

Stats	Red Sox	AL	Rank
Batting Avg:	.267	.276	13
On-Base Pct:	.341	.349	11
Slugging Pct:	.423	.443	12
Home Runs:	167		11
Stolen Bases:	43		13
ERA:	4.23	4.91	1
Fielding Pct:	.982	.982	7
Runs Scored:	792		12
Runs Allowed:	745		1

Starting Lineup

Jason Varitek, c
Brian Daubach, 1b
Jose Offerman, 2b
Manny Alexander, 3b
Nomar Garciaparra, ss
Troy O'Leary, lf
Carl Everett, cf
Trot Nixon, rf
Dante Bichette, dh
Darren Lewis, of
Scott Hatteberg, c-dh
Jeff Frye, 2b
Mike Stanley, 1b-dh
Wilton Veras, 3b

Pitchers

Pedro Martinez, sp
Ramon Martinez, sp
Jeff Fassero, sp
Pete Schourek, sp
Derek Lowe, rp
Rich Garces, rp
Rheal Cormier, rp
Tim Wakefield, rp-sp

Attendance

2,586,032 (sixth place in AL)

Club Leaders

Batting Avg:	Garciaparra	.372
On-Base Pct:	Garciaparra	.434
Slugging Pct:	Garciaparra	.599
Home Runs:	Everett	34
RBI:	Everett	108
Runs:	Garciaparra	104
Stolen Bases:	Everett	11
Wins:	P. Martinez	18
Strikeouts:	P. Martinez	284
ERA:	P. Martinez	1.74
Saves:	Lowe	42

JANUARY 11   Ten days after the dawn of the new millennium and the end of worries about the Y2K problem, Carlton Fisk is elected to the Hall of Fame.

> *Three days later, Fisk announced that the cap on his plaque at Cooperstown would bear the Red Sox' Old English "B" instead of the White Sox insignia. Fisk played 13 seasons with Chicago and 11 in Boston. The Red Sox retired Fisk's number 27 in ceremonies on September 4. It was the fifth number the Red Sox retired, joining numbers 1 (Bobby Doerr), 4 (Joe Cronin), 8 (Carl Yastrzemski), and 9 (Ted Williams). In addition, number 42 is retired throughout Major League Baseball in honor of Jackie Robinson. Six other Red Sox numbers are in "suspended animation" and weren't issued to anyone in 2005: 5 (Nomar Garciaparra), 6 (Johnny Pesky), 14 (Jim Rice), 21 (Roger Clemens), 26 (Wade Boggs), and 45 (Pedro Martinez).*

JANUARY 19   The Red Sox sign Marty Cordova, most recently with the Twins, as a free agent.

APRIL 4   The Red Sox win the season opener 2–0 over the Mariners in Seattle behind the dominant pitching of Pedro Martinez, who went seven innings while allowing only two hits and striking out 11. Derek Lowe added two perfect innings. The only Seattle hits were singles by Carlos Guillen in the third inning and John Olerud in the fourth.

APRIL 9   Pedro Martinez strikes out 12 batters in 7⅓ innings to defeat the Angels 5–2 in Anaheim.

Martinez won the Cy Young Award for the second season in a row. He had an 18–6 record and a league-leading 284 strikeouts in 217 innings. Martinez walked only 32 batters. His 1.74 ERA led the AL by a wide margin. Roger Clemens was second in the category with a 3.70 ERA. The league ERA was 4.91. AL players batting against Martinez in 2000 had only a .167 average, .213 on-base percentage, and .259 slugging percentage.

APRIL 11   The Red Sox overpower the Twins 13–4 in the first home game of the season before 33,114. The Sox took charge with two runs in the first inning and eight in the second to take a 10–1 lead. In his first game with the club at Fenway Park, switch-hitting Carl Everett homered from both sides of the plate off left-hander Mike Redman and right-hander Joe Mays.

In his first season with the Red Sox, Everett batted .300 with 34 homers and 108 RBIs, but his erratic personality made him a constant nuisance. During his two years with the club, Everett had numerous run-ins with the front office, his managers, his teammates, the umpires, the fans, and the media.

APRIL 15   The Red Sox trounce the Athletics 14–2 at Fenway Park.

APRIL 16   Carl Everett's walk-off homer leading off the ninth inning lifts the Red Sox to a 5–4 win over the Athletics at Fenway Park.

APRIL 18   The Red Sox play at Comerica Park in Detroit for the first time and win 7–0 over the Tigers.

APRIL 19   The Red Sox clout five home runs, including a Trot Nixon grand slam in the sixth inning off Jim Poole, during a 10–0 win over the Tigers in Detroit. Nomar Garciaparra, Mike Stanley, Troy O'Leary, and Jose Offerman hit the others.

Garciaparra was batting .400 on July 17 with 108 hits in his first 270 at-bats. He finished the season leading the American League in batting average with a .372 mark. It was the fourth highest average in Sox history, trailing only Ted Williams's .406 in 1941 and .388 in 1957 and Tris Speaker's .383 in 1912. Garciaparra also hit 51 doubles and 21 homers in 2000.

APRIL 26   The Red Sox collect 21 hits and rout the Rangers 14–4 in Arlington.

APRIL 30   Pedro Martinez is ejected from a 2–1 win over the Indians in Cleveland for throwing at Roberto Alomar. Earlier in the game, Charles Nagy hit Jose Offerman with a pitch, and Offerman charged the mound.

Martinez was suspended for five days for the incident.

MAY 6	Pedro Martinez strikes out 17 batters but loses 1–0 to the Devil Rays at Fenway Park. Steve Trachsel pitched the shutout for Tampa Bay. The loss ended his 13-game winning streak over two seasons. He struck out 12 batters in the first five innings. Greg Vaughn singled in Dave Martinez in the eighth inning after Martinez singled and stole second.
MAY 12	Pedro Martinez strikes out 15 batters and pitches a two-hit shutout to win 9–0 over the Orioles in Baltimore. He retired the first 12 batters of the game and the last 14. In between, Albert Belle and Jeff Conine singled in the fifth inning. The 15 strike-outs tied an American League record for most strikeouts in consecutive games: 32.
MAY 14	The Red Sox pass the Yankees for first place by defeating the Orioles 10–1 in Baltimore.
MAY 24	Brian Daubach's three-run, walk-off homer in the eleventh inning beats the Blue Jays 6–3 at Fenway Park.
MAY 30	Pedro Martinez outduels Roger Clemens for a 2–0 win over the Yankees in New York. The two Sox runs scored in the ninth inning. With two outs, Jeff Frye hit a ball up the middle that glanced off Clemens, and Frye was able to beat it out for an infield single.

The victory gave the Red Sox a 29–18 record and a 1 1/2-game lead in the AL East.

JUNE 1	Carl Everett hits a grand slam off Chris Fussell in the third inning, but the Red Sox lose 13–11 to the Royals at Fenway Park. The Sox led 8–2 before Kansas City scored nine runs in the sixth inning.
JUNE 5	In the first round of the amateur draft, the Red Sox select pitcher Phil Dumatrait from Bakersfield Junior College in California.

The Sox traded Dumatrait to the Reds in 2003. His arrival in the majors is still on hold. The first product of the 2000 draft to reach the majors was 11th-rounder Freddy Sanchez. The second was second-rounder Manny Delcarmen.

JUNE 8	Pedro Martinez allows only one hit in eight innings to beat the Indians 3–0 at Fenway Park. Russell Bryan got the only Cleveland hit off Martinez, a double in the fifth inning.
JUNE 19	The Yankees humiliate the Red Sox 22–1 at Fenway Park. The Yankees scored nine runs in the eighth inning off Rob Stanifer and seven in the ninth off Tim Wakefield.
JUNE 23	The Red Sox drop out of first place with a 5–4 loss to the Blue Jays at Fenway Park.

The Sox never regained first place in 2000, but they remained within striking distance of the top spot until the first week of September.

JUNE 29	Brian Daubach drives in six runs during a 12–4 win over the Orioles at Fenway Park.
JUNE 30	The Red Sox trade Dennis Tankersley and Cesar Seba to the Pirates for Ed Sprague Jr.

On the same day, Manny Alexander was arrested. He lent his car to twenty-year-old Carlos Cowart, the team's batboy, who was wanted by the police on a previous warrant for driving without a license and failing to stop for police. A state trooper spotted the car, checked the license plate, and learned the car was registered to Alexander. Fearing it was stolen, the trooper arrested Cowart on the outstanding warrant and had the car impounded. An envelope of steroids, addressed to Alexander, was found in the glove compartment, and Alexander was arrested. The charges were later dismissed. After the 2000 season, Alexander didn't play in another game until 2004 with the Padres.

JULY 1   Rookie Israel Alcantara earns infamy for an awful performance in a 7–2 loss to the White Sox in Chicago. He committed two errors: loafed on a ball that allowed the opposing catcher to score from first and failed to run out a grounder. This led to a three-week battle of wills between Dan Duquette and Jimy Williams in which Duquette refused to send Alcantara to the minors and Williams refused to play him.

JULY 3   The Red Sox hit four home runs in a nine-run fourth inning during an 11–8 win over the Twins in Minneapolis. The Sox headed into the inning trailing 3–1. Carl Everett and Troy O'Leary started the fireworks with consecutive homers off Mike Lincoln. Two batters later, Jason Varitek added a homer off Jay Ryan. Ryan gave up the fourth Boston homer of the inning to Morgan Burkhart. Carl Everett and Troy O'Leary also doubled in the inning.

              The homer was Burkhart's first as a major leaguer. He was a twenty-eight-year-old rookie first baseman-designated hitter in 2000 who played for four seasons in the independent Frontier League from 1995 through 1998.

JULY 4   The Red Sox rout the Twins 14–4 in Minneapolis. Bernard Gilkey played in his first game with the Red Sox following his release from the Diamondbacks, and he had a home run, double, single, and four RBIs in four at-bats.

JULY 13   A two-out, two-run, walk-off homer by Brian Daubach on a 2–2 pitch beats the Mets 4–3 at Fenway Park.

JULY 15   Carl Everett head-butts umpire Ron Kulpa, shoves him twice during a heated argument, and gets ejected during the second inning of a 6–4 win over the Mets at Fenway Park. Brian Daubach, Everett's replacement, hit a three-run homer to key the victory. Everett became enraged after Kulpa told him that he was standing outside the batter's box. He was suspended for 10 days.

JULY 16   Pedro Martinez strikes out 12 batters in a 3–1 win over the Expos at Fenway Park.

JULY 23   Pedro Martinez strikes out 15 batters and walks none in a 1–0 victory over the White Sox at Fenway Park. Jason Varitek drove in the Red Sox' run with a single in the fourth inning.

JULY 27   The Red Sox trade Jeff Frye, John Wasdin, Brian Rose, and Jeff Taglienti to the Rockies for Mike Lansing, Rolando Arrojo, and Rich Croushore.

JULY 31   The Red Sox release Mike Stanley.

AUGUST 1   The Red Sox lose 5–4 to the Mariners in a 19-inning marathon in Seattle. The teams combined for 12 consecutive scoreless innings before Mike Cameron ended the game with a homer off Jeff Fassero leading off the nineteenth. The contest ended at 3:39 AM Boston time.

AUGUST 3   The Red Sox purchase Rico Brogna from the Phillies.

AUGUST 14   Rico Brogna hits a walk-off grand slam in the ninth inning that defeats the Devil Rays 7–3 at Fenway Park. After Darren Lewis reached third base with one out, Tampa Bay intentionally walked Carl Everett and Nomar Garciaparra to load the bases and set the stage for Brogna's heroics.

AUGUST 17   The Red Sox score three runs in the ninth inning to defeat the Rangers 8–7 at Fenway Park. The Rangers led 6–1 in the seventh inning before Mike Lansing keyed a Boston comeback. Entering the game as a pinch hitter in the eighth, Lansing doubled home two runs. In the ninth, he hit a two-run, walk-off double that knocked in the tying and winning runs.

AUGUST 21   Brian Daubach stars in a 7–6 win over the Angels at Fenway Park. Daubach tied the score 5–5 with a two-run homer in the ninth. After the Angels scored in the top of the eleventh, Daubach hit a two-run, walk-off single in the bottom half to win the game.

AUGUST 24   Down 6–1 after two innings, the Red Sox rally to defeat the Royals 9–7 in 10 innings at Fenway Park.

AUGUST 28   The Red Sox drop out of first place in the wild-card race following a 5–2 loss to the Devil Rays in St. Petersburg.

AUGUST 29   Pedro Martinez strikes out 13 batters and comes within three outs of a no-hitter, and Carl Everett drives in six runs by hitting homers from both sides of the plate during a brawl-filled 8–0 win over the Devil Rays in St. Petersburg. After hitting leadoff man Gerald Williams in the first inning in just his fourth pitch of the night, Martinez retired 24 batters in a row before John Flaherty hit a lead-off single to right-center on a 2–2 pitch in the ninth. Martinez then retired the next three batters to finish with a one-hitter. Umpires ejected eight Devil Rays, including five players, in the first seven innings of the game, which featured five confrontations. Tampa Bay manager Larry Rothschild and Williams were ejected in the first inning. Williams charged the mound after Martinez hit him and set off a bench-clearing brawl. The game was delayed 12 minutes. Dugouts emptied four more times during the evening. Two Devil Ray coaches, serving as acting managers, were ejected after pitchers threw at Red Sox batters in the third and seventh innings.

AUGUST 31   The Red Sox trade Chris Reitsma and John Curtice to the Reds for Dante Bichette.

SEPTEMBER 4   The Red Sox retire Carlton Fisk's number 27 in ceremonies prior to a 5–1 win over the Mariners at Fenway Park.

              Between the time Fisk left the Red Sox in 1981 and 2000, when number 27 was retired, several players wore it, including Mike Brown, Pat Dodson, Greg Harris, Mark Whiten, Dave Hollins, Butch Henry, and Kip Gross.

SEPTEMBER 5   The Red Sox score seven runs in the first inning, four of them on a grand slam by Manny Alexander off Kevin Appier, sparking a 10–3 win over the Athletics at Fenway Park.

The Red Sox led the AL in ERA in 2000. It was the first time that the Sox led the league in earned run average in consecutive seasons since they did it three in a row from 1902 through 1904.

SEPTEMBER 8   Red Sox pitcher Bryce Florie suffers one of the more horrific injuries in Red Sox history when the Yankees' Ryan Thompson's drive hits him in the face in the ninth inning. Florie suffered three fractures of the orbital socket around the eye and damage to the retina. The Red Sox lost the home game, 4–0.

Florie was never the same after the injury. He returned in 2001 but pitched in only seven games and posted an 11.42 ERA.

SEPTEMBER 10   The Red Sox lose for the third day in a row to the Yankees at Fenway Park. The 6–2 defeat dropped the Sox nine games back of the Yankees in the AL East and all but eliminated any hope for a division title.

SEPTEMBER 20   The Red Sox lose a day-night doubleheader to the Indians 2–1 and 5–4 at Fenway Park. The defeats dropped the Sox into fourth place in the wild-card race, four games out, to virtually eliminate any chance of a postseason series in Boston.

SEPTEMBER 21   Playing a day-night doubleheader against the Indians at Fenway Park for the second day in a row, Cleveland scores seven runs in the first inning, but the Red Sox counter with two in their half and six more in third, leading to a 9–7 win. The Indians won the second tilt, 8–5.

SEPTEMBER 29   Nomar Garciaparra extends his hitting streak to 20 games, but the Red Sox lose 8–6 to the Devil Rays in St. Petersburg.

DECEMBER 7   With the result of the November 7 presidential election between George Bush and Al Gore still in doubt, the Red Sox sign Frank Castillo, most recently with the Blue Jays, as a free agent. On the same day, Ed Sprague Jr. signed as a free agent with the Padres.

DECEMBER 8   Jeff Fassero signs with the Cubs as a free agent.

DECEMBER 13   The day after the Supreme Court declares George Bush the winner in the disputed election against Al Gore, the Red Sox sign Manny Ramirez, most recently with the Indians, as a free agent.

The Red Sox paid Ramirez a staggering $160 million over eight seasons. In five seasons with the Red Sox through 2005, Ramirez has 199 homers, 611 RBIs, 512 runs, a .315 batting average, and a .608 slugging percentage. Among players with at least 2000 at-bats with the Red Sox, Ramirez is second to Ted Williams in slugging percentage.

DECEMBER 14   Rico Brogna signs with the Braves as a free agent.

DECEMBER 15   The Red Sox sign Hideo Nomo, most recently with the Tigers, as a free agent.

Nomo quickly inserted himself into Red Sox lore by pitching a no-hitter in his first game with the club (see April 4, 2001). He added a one-hitter in May and had an 11–4 record in August, but he was frustratingly inconsistent, finishing the year at 13–10 with a 4.50 ERA. Nomo struck out 220 batters in 196 innings. At the end of the 2001 season, he signed as a free agent with the Dodgers.

2001   B

Season in a Sentence

The Red Sox are in first place in late July, but injuries to stars Pedro Martinez and Nomar Garciaparra doom the club.

Finish • Won • Lost • Pct • GB

Second   82   79   .509   13.5

In the wild-card race, the Red Sox finished in fourth place, 19.5 games back.

Managers

Jimy Williams (65–53)
Joe Kerrigan (17–26)

Stats

Stats	Red Sox	AL	Rank
Batting Avg:	.266	.267	7
On-Base Pct:	.334	.334	7
Slugging Pct:	.439	.428	5
Home Runs:	198		5
Stolen Bases:	46		14
ERA:	4.15	4.47	4
Fielding Pct:	.981	.981	7
Runs Scored:	772		6
Runs Allowed:	745		4

Starting Lineup

Scott Hatteberg, c
Brian Daubach, 1b
Jose Offerman, 2b
Shea Hillenbrand, 3b
Mike Lansing, ss
Troy O'Leary, lf-rf
Carl Everett, cf
Trot Nixon, rf
Manny Ramirez, lf-dh
Chris Stynes, 3b-2b
Jason Varitek, c
Darren Lewis, rf-lf-cf

Pitchers

Hideo Nomo, sp
Frank Castillo, sp
David Cone, sp
Pedro Martinez, sp
Derek Lowe, rp
Rod Beck, rp
Rich Garces, rp
Rolando Arrojo, rp
Tim Wakefield, rp-sp

Attendance

2,625,333 (sixth in AL)

Club Leaders

Batting Avg:	Ramirez	.306
On-Base Pct:	Ramirez	.405
Slugging Pct:	Ramirez	.609
Home Runs:	Ramirez	41
RBI:	Ramirez	125
Runs:	Nixon	100
Stolen Bases:	Nixon	9
Wins:	Nomo	13
Strikeouts:	Nomo	220
ERA:	Wakefield	3.90
Saves:	Lowe	24

JANUARY 5   Bernard Gilkey signs with the Cardinals as a free agent.

JANUARY 11   The Red Sox sign David Cone, most recently with the Yankees, as a free agent.

Cone was thirty-eight when he arrived in Boston and had a decent season in 2001—a 9–7 record and a 4.31 ERA.

APRIL 2   In the season opener, the Red Sox lose 2–1 in 11 innings to the Orioles in Baltimore. Brady Anderson drove in the winning run with a single off Derek Lowe. The Sox run scored on a homer by Trot Nixon in the fourth inning.

On the day of the opener, Nomar Garciaparra underwent surgery to repair a split tendon in his right wrist. The injury limited the shortstop to just 21 games in 2001. Garciaparra returned to the lineup on July 29, but his wrist wasn't up to the demands of playing regularly, and he was shut down again.

APRIL 4   In his first game with the Red Sox, Hideo Nomo pitches a no-hitter for a 3–0 win over the Orioles in Baltimore. He threw 110 pitches, walked three, and struck out 11. Second baseman Mike Lansing saved the no-hitter when he made a backhanded, tumbling catch of Mike Bordick's soft looper to center field for the second out of the ninth inning. Two pitches later, Delino DeShields hit a routine fly ball to Troy O'Leary in right field.

It was the second no-hitter of Nomo's career. His first was with the Dodgers on September 17, 1996, against the Rockies at Coors Field. It was also the first nine-inning no-hitter by a Red Sox pitcher since Dave Morehead on September 16, 1965. In addition, Nomo's no-hitter marked the first regular-season game behind the microphone for NESN announcer Dan Orsillo.

APRIL 6   In the home opener, before 33,989, Manny Ramirez lines a three-run homer on the first pitch thrown to him at Fenway Park as a member of the Red Sox, leading to an 11–4 win over the Devil Rays. Mike Lansing and Carl Everett also hit homers.

In his first Red Sox season, Ramirez batted .306 with 41 homers and 125 RBIs.

APRIL 8   Pedro Martinez strikes out 16 batters in eight innings of a 3–0 win over the Devil Rays at Fenway Park. The contest was played in forty-two-degree weather and intermittent rain.

Shea Hillenbrand made his debut in 2001 and hit safely in his first nine games to set a Red Sox record for the longest hitting streak at the start of a career. The previous mark was seven by Ted Williams in 1939 and Ben Steiner in 1945.

APRIL 13   After the Yankees score a run in the top of the tenth inning, the Red Sox come back with a rally capped by a two-run, walk-off single by Manny Ramirez off Mariano Rivera to win, 3–2.

APRIL 17   The Red Sox cruise past the Devil Rays 10–0 in St. Petersburg.

APRIL 18   Trailing 1–0, the Red Sox explode for nine runs in the eighth inning to beat the Devil Rays 9–1 in St. Petersburg. It was Hal McRae's first game as Tampa Bay manager after replacing Larry Rothschild.

APRIL 19   Pedro Martinez strikes out 13 batters in six innings to beat the Devil Rays 8–3 in St. Petersburg.

APRIL 24   Carl Everett hits a grand slam off Mark Redman in the second inning of a 9–4 win over the Twins at Fenway Park.

APRIL 26   Hideo Nomo (seven innings) and Derek Lowe (two innings) combine on a two-hitter to defeat the Twins 2–0 at Fenway Park. The only hit off Nomo was questionable. In the seventh inning, Torii Hunter hit a drive that glanced off Darren Lewis's glove in right field. Official scorer Bob Ellis ruled it a single. Ellis was working his first game as official scorer at Fenway Park, substituting for regular Charles Scroggins. Doug Mientkiewicz had the other Tampa Bay hit, a single in the ninth.

The game was played on the 100th anniversary of the first game in Red Sox history, a 10–6 loss to the Orioles on April 26, 1901, in Baltimore.

APRIL 27   Carl Everett hits his second grand slam in three days, helping the Red Sox to a 9–2 win over the Royals at Fenway Park. The homer came off Jose Santiago in the sixth inning.

The Red Sox stole a major league–low 46 bases in 2001 and allowed a major league–high 223.

MAY 1   Pedro Martinez strikes out 12 batters in eight innings during a 2–0 win over the Mariners in Seattle.

MAY 12   Pedro Martinez fans seven batters in seven innings of a 9–3 triumph over the Athletics at Fenway Park.

MAY 13   Jason Varitek's walk-off homer in the eleventh inning beats the Athletics 5–4 at Fenway Park.

MAY 15   A power surge in downtown Minneapolis causes a bank of lights to go out in the Metrodome with the Red Sox leading 3–0 in the fifth inning. After an 18-minute delay, the Sox went on to win, 5–2.

MAY 18   Pedro Martinez strikes out 12 batters over eight shutout innings to pace the Red Sox to a 6–3 win over the Royals in Kansas City.

MAY 20   Jason Varitek drives in seven runs on three homers and a single in four at-bats to power the Red Sox to a 10–3 win over the Royals in Kansas City. Varitek hit a solo homer off Brian Meadows in the second inning, a three-run shot off Meadows in the third, and a two-run drive in the eighth facing Mac Suzuki.

MAY 23   Red Sox fan Paul Giorgio goes to great lengths to reverse the curse of the Bambino.

On the advice of a Tibetan Buddhist holy man, Giorgio, thirty-seven, placed a Sox cap next to the chorten, a stone altar at the base of Mount Everest where each climbing team burns juniper branches as an offering to the gods. Then he carried the cap to the summit and placed it at 29,028 feet, along with an American flag, to reverse the curse. When he returned to the base camp, Giorgio, as directed by the lama, burned a Yankees cap.

MAY 25

Hideo Nomo strikes out 14 batters and gives up no walks in a one-hitter against the Devil Rays at Fenway Park. The Sox won, 4–0. Nomo faced only 28 batters. The only Tampa Bay base runner was Shannon Stewart, who doubled in the fourth inning.

In his next start, on May 31, Nomo retired the first 13 batters he faced and defeated the Blue Jays 11–5 in Toronto.

MAY 30

Pedro Martinez strikes out 13 batters in eight innings of a 3–0 win over the Yankees at Fenway Park.

The victory gave Martinez a 7–1 record and a 1.44 ERA with 121 strikeouts in 81 innings. It was his last victory of the season. Afterward he was 0–2 with a 4.54 ERA in 35 2/3 innings before being placed on the disabled list with a small tear in his rotator cuff.

JUNE 2

Carl Everett hits a towering homer off the Windows Restaurant at SkyDome to break a 1–1 tie in the ninth inning and lift the Red Sox to a 2–1 win over the Blue Jays. In the fifth inning, Manny Ramirez hit a homer into the fifth deck, a drive estimated at 491 feet.

JUNE 5

Shea Hillenbrand hits a homer in the eighteenth inning to end a 4–3 marathon against the Tigers at Fenway Park. Neither team scored from the eighth inning through the seventeenth. The contest lasted five hours and 52 minutes and ended at 12:58 AM. Manny Ramirez drew four intentional walks to tie an American League record.

On the same day, the Red Sox selected catcher Kelly Shoppach of Baylor University with their first pick in the amateur draft. Shoppach was chosen in the second round; the Red Sox lost their first round pick because of free-agent compensation. Shoppach reached the majors in 2005. By the end of the 2005 season, the only other Red Sox drafted and signed in 2001 to play at the big-league level was eighth-rounder Kevin Youkilis.

JUNE 7

Jason Varitek suffers a season-ending injury during an 8–1 win over the Tigers at Fenway Park. Varitek broke his elbow on the hard rubber on-deck circle diving for a ball.

JUNE 14

With the Red Sox trailing 3–0, Brian Daubach hits a grand slam off Chuck Smith in the fourth inning to key a 6–4 win over the Marlins at Fenway Park.

JUNE 19

Tim Wakefield carries a no-hitter into the ninth inning, but the Red Sox barely escape with a 5–4 win over the Devil Rays at Tropicana Field. The Sox led 5–0 heading into the ninth before Randy Winn singled for the first Tampa Bay hit. By the time the inning ended, the Devil Rays had scored four times off Wakefield and Derek Lowe.

JUNE 20

The Red Sox score four runs in the ninth inning with two outs, the last three on a double by Manny Ramirez, to beat the Devil Rays 7–4 in St. Petersburg.

The win gave the Red Sox a 43–27 record and a four-game lead in the AL East.

JUNE 25   Dante Bichette hits a grand slam off Ryan Rupe in the third inning to put the Red Sox up 6–4, leading to a 12–8 win over the Devil Rays at Fenway Park.

JUNE 26   Trot Nixon hits a grand slam off Travis Phelps in the seventh inning to tie the score 5–5, sparking a 7–6 win over the Devil Rays at Fenway Park.

JULY 2   Rolando Arrojo (seven innings), Rod Beck (one inning), and Derek Lowe (one inning) combine on a two-hitter to defeat the Blue Jays 4–0 in Toronto. Arrojo had a no-hitter until Alex Gonzalez singled in the seventh inning. Shannon Stewart added another single off Lowe in the ninth.

JULY 3   The Red Sox trounce the Blue Jays 16–4 in Toronto. The Sox scored five runs in the first inning and six in the third to take an 11–0 lead.

JULY 4   The Red Sox clobber the Indians 13–4 in Cleveland.

JULY 5   Jose Offerman hits a two-out, two-run single in the ninth inning off John Rocker to defeat the Indians 5–4 in Cleveland. Heading into the seventh, the Sox were hitless off Bartolo Colon and trailed, 4–0. Boston scored a run in the seventh inning and two in the eighth to set up the ninth-inning rally.

JULY 22   The Red Sox lose 13–8 to the White Sox to drop out of first place.

            The Sox never regained the top spot in the division, but they remained in the playoff hunt until late August.

JULY 27   The Red Sox score seven runs in the first inning to beat the White Sox 9–5 at Fenway Park. Bret Saberhagen made his first appearance on the mound since pitching Game Four of the ALCS on October 17, 1999, a span of 648 days. Saberhagen pitched six innings and allowed only one run and three hits. At one point, he retired 14 batters in a row.

            Saberhagen's comeback was short lived. He pitched in only two more games, in which he gave up nine earned runs in nine innings, before retiring.

JULY 29   In his first game back from wrist surgery, Nomar Garciaparra hits a homer and a single during a 4–3 win over the White Sox at Fenway Park.

            Garciaparra played only 21 games before going back onto the disabled list on August 27.

JULY 31   The Red Sox trade Tomokazu Ohka and Richard Rundles to the Expos for Ugueth Urbina.

            Ugueth Urtain Urbina is the only player in major league history whose initials are U.U.U.

AUGUST 4   The Red Sox smack eight homers in 10–4 and 6–2 wins over the Rangers at Fenway Park. In the first game, Trot Nixon and Troy O'Leary each hit two homers, and Carl Everett and Brian Daubach added one apiece. In the second game, Mike Lansing launched a pair of home runs.

AUGUST 6   Scott Hatteberg becomes the first player in major league history to hit into a triple play and hit a grand slam in the same game during a 10–7 win over the Rangers at Fenway Park. It happened in consecutive at-bats. In the fourth inning, Hatteberg lined to shortstop Alex Rodriguez with the runners on first and second moving with the pitch. Hatteberg hit the grand slam in the sixth off Juan Moreno.

AUGUST 12   The Red Sox score six runs in the first inning and outlast the Orioles 12–10 in Baltimore.

AUGUST 16   In his fifth season as manager of the Red Sox, Jimy Williams is fired after the club loses for the sixth time in seven games. His replacement was pitching coach Joe Kerrigan.

There were years of friction between Williams and Dan Duquette during which the two constantly sniped at each other in the press, but there was no indication that a firing was imminent. The club had a record of 65–53 and was five games behind the Yankees. Williams was 414–352 as a manager in Boston. Kerrigan was forty-six years old. He had been the Red Sox pitching coach since 1997 and never been a manager at any level. Kerrigan was given a two-year contract but lasted only 43 games in a meltdown that saw the club go 17–26. After a change in club ownership, Kerrigan was fired during spring training in 2002. Williams managed the Astros from 2002 through 2004.

AUGUST 19   Manny Ramirez hits a grand slam off Calvin Maduro in the second inning that gives the Red Sox a 5–0 lead, but the Orioles rally to beat the Red Sox 13–7 at Fenway Park.

AUGUST 21   The Red Sox score all eight of their runs in the third inning for an 8–5 victory over the Angels in Anaheim. Doug Mirabelli hit a grand slam off Scott Schoeneweis.

AUGUST 24   Trot Nixon's grand slam off Dan Kolb in the eighth inning breaks a 3–3 tie and leads to a 7–4 win over the Rangers in Arlington.

AUGUST 25   The Red Sox lose 8–7 to the Rangers in an 18-inning marathon in Arlington. The contest was scoreless from the ninth inning throughout the seventeenth and lasted six hours and 35 minutes. Derek Lowe gave up the winning run.

The loss sent the Red Sox into a tailspin. Entering the game, the Sox had a record of 71–56 and were three games behind the Yankees in the AL East and one game back of the Athletics in the wild-card chase. Without the services of Pedro Martinez, Nomar Garciaparra, and Jason Varitek, the club completely fell apart. From August 25 through October 2, the Red Sox lost 23 of 29 games interrupted by the September 11 attacks and their aftermath.

SEPTEMBER 11 Two hijacked commercial airliners strike and destroy the twin towers of the World Trade Center in New York City in the worst-ever terrorist attack on American soil. A third hijacked plane destroyed a portion of the Pentagon, and a fourth crashed in Pennsylvania. Some 3,000 were killed including about 2,800 at the World Trade Center. Many from Greater Boston died in the disaster because the two flights that struck the Trade Center took off from Logan Airport. Red Sox pitcher David Cone, who earlier pitched for the Yankees and Mets, lost many friends and acquaintances who were working in the buildings.

Almost immediately, Bud Selig canceled games scheduled for that day, including the Red Sox–Devil Rays contest in St. Petersburg. Later in the week, he announced that all games through Sunday, September 16 would be postponed. They were made up by extending the regular season by a week. When play resumed, an air of heightened security and patriotism imbued every game. "God Bless America" replaced "Take Me Out to the Ball Game" as the song of choice during the seventh-inning stretch. Because of the nationwide sympathy toward New York City in a time of extreme tragedy, many Red Sox fans publicly declared their allegiance to the rival Yankees during the 2001 postseason.

SEPTEMBER 13   With plane travel restricted in the wake of the September 11 terrorist attacks, the Red Sox begin a journey from Florida to Boston that requires 27 hours. The Sox took a bus from Tampa to Sanford, Florida, traveled by Amtrak from Sanford to Lorton, Virginia, boarded another bus to Baltimore, flew from Baltimore to Providence, and then rode a third bus to Boston.

SEPTEMBER 16   Carl Everett is suspended for four days after a heated, profanity-filled tirade directed at manager Joe Kerrigan during a workout at Fenway Park. Everett had been fined for showing up late. He had been a time bomb for two seasons and was fined countless times during the season for habitual lateness to workouts, games, medical treatments, and team buses. During spring training the team suspended him for one day and fined him $100,000 because of persistent tardiness.

SEPTEMBER 18   In the first game following the terrorist attacks, the Red Sox defeat the Devil Rays 7–2 at Fenway Park.

SEPTEMBER 20   In his first start with the Red Sox, first baseman Calvin Pickering hits a homer in the second inning and starts the go-ahead rally in the eighth with a single to give the Sox a 2–1 win over the Devil Rays at Fenway Park.

OCTOBER 4   Trot Nixon's two-run homer in the eleventh inning beats the Orioles 7–5 in the second game of a doubleheader in Baltimore. The Sox also won the first game, 5–0.

NOVEMBER 20   The Red Sox purchase Tony Clark from the Tigers.

DECEMBER 12   The Red Sox trade Carl Everett to the Rangers for Darren Oliver.

The Sox reached the breaking point with the talented but volatile Everett and tired of his indifference to the most basic team rules. Oliver lasted fewer than two months with Boston. He was released in July with a 4–5 record.

DECEMBER 15   The Red Sox trade Luis Garcia, Rick Asadoorian, and Dustin Brisson to the Expos for Dustin Hermanson.

Expected to fill a spot in the Red Sox rotation, Hermanson pitched only 22 innings for the club and had a 7.77 ERA. In his first game with the Sox, he slipped on a wet Fenway Park mound in a contest that was eventually rained out. Hermanson suffered a strained groin muscle and later developed a staph infection in his elbow.

DECEMBER 18   The Red Sox trade Scott Hatteberg to the Rockies for Pokey Reese.

This was one of the strangest trades in Red Sox history. Three days later, both players became free agents when their new clubs failed to offer them contracts. Hatteberg signed with the Athletics and Reese with the Pirates. Reese later played for the Red Sox in 2003 and 2004.

DECEMBER 19   The Red Sox sign John Burkett, most recently with the Braves, as a free agent.

Burkett won his first seven decisions in a Red Sox uniform. He was 13–8 with Boston in 2002 and 12–9 in 2003.

DECEMBER 20   The Jean R. Yawkey Trust sells the Red Sox to a group headed by Marlins owner John Henry, former Padres owner Tom Werner, and former Orioles and Padres executive Larry Lucchino.

The sale ended a Red Sox connection with the Yawkey family that began when Tom Yawkey bought the club in 1933. The sale price was $660 million, plus an assumption of debts totaling forty million dollars. The price included Fenway Park and 80 percent of the New England Sports Network (NESN). Henry sold his stake in the Marlins to Jeffrey Loria, who owned the Expos. The Expos were subsequently operated by the other 29 clubs in major league baseball, a situation that still existed at the start of the 2005 season after the Expos moved to Washington as the Nationals. Major League Baseball formally recognized the transfer of the Red Sox to new ownership on January 16, 2002. The Henry group took control of the Red Sox on February 27 (see February 28, 2002). Before the sale was completed, Massachusetts Attorney General Thomas Reilly intervened. Reilly claimed that the Red Sox had rejected a larger offer, said to be $750 million from a group headed by Miles Prentice. Reilly's responsibility was ensuring that the charities and charitable trusts standing to gain from liquidation of the Yawkey Trust's interests would receive maximum benefit from the sale. After a couple of weeks of negotiation, Reilly announced that the Henry group had agreed to donate an additional twenty million dollars over 10 years to youth and educational organizations and that the Red Sox' limited partners would add ten million dollars to the Yawkey Trust's share.

DECEMBER 21   The Red Sox sign Johnny Damon, most recently with the Athletics, as a free agent.

Damon proved to be a tremendous addition. With his long hair and beard, he became the face, quite literally, of the self-proclaimed "idiots" that won the World Championship in 2004.

2002   B

Season in a Sentence

Under completely new management, the Red Sox win 27 of their first 36 games and 93 games in all, but they finish second to the Yankees and miss the postseason.

Finish • Won • Lost • Pct • GB

Second   93   69   .574   10.5

In the wild-card race, the Red Sox tied for second place, six games back.

Manager

Grady Little

Stats   Red Sox • AL • Rank

Stats	Red Sox	AL	Rank
Batting Avg:	.277	.264	2
On-Base Pct:	.345	.331	3
Slugging Pct:	.444	.424	3
Home Runs:	177		7
Stolen Bases:	80		7
ERA:	3.75	4.46	3
Fielding Pct:	.983	.982	8
Runs Scored:	859		2
Runs Allowed:	665		3

Starting Lineup

Jason Varitek, c
Tony Clark, 1b
Rey Sanchez, 2b
Shea Hillenbrand, 3b
Nomar Garciaparra, ss
Manny Ramirez, lf-dh
Johnny Damon, cf
Trot Nixon, rf
Carlos Baerga, dh
Brian Daubach, 1b-lf-dh
Jose Offerman, 1b-dh
Lou Merloni, 2b
Rickey Henderson, lf
Cliff Floyd, lf-dh

Pitchers

Derek Lowe, sp
Pedro Martinez, sp
John Burkett, sp
Frank Castillo, sp
Tim Wakefield, rp-sp
Casey Fossum, rp-sp
Ugueth Urbina, rp

Attendance

2,650,063 (fourth in AL)

Club Leaders

Batting Avg:	Ramirez	.349
On-Base Pct:	Ramirez	.450
Slugging Pct:	Ramirez	.647
Home Runs:	Ramirez	33
RBI:	Garciaparra	120
Runs:	Ramirez	118
Stolen Bases:	Damon	31
Wins:	Lowe	21
Strikeouts:	Martinez	239
ERA:	Martinez	2.26
Saves:	Urbina	40

JANUARY 10   The Red Sox sign Carlos Baerga as a free agent.

JANUARY 14   Darren Lewis signs with the Cubs as a free agent.

JANUARY 29   Troy O'Leary signs with the Devil Rays as a free agent.

JANUARY 30   John Valentin signs with the Mets as a free agent.

FEBRUARY 13   Ten days after the Patriots defeat the Rams 20–17 in the Super Bowl, the Red Sox sign Rickey Henderson, most recently with the Padres, as a free agent.

Henderson was forty-three years old and in the second-to-last year of his major league career. When he arrived in Boston, Henderson had accumulated 3,000 hits and was the all-time career leader in stolen bases, runs, and walks. (Barry Bonds has since passed him in walks.) Henderson played in 72 games with the Red Sox and hit .223 with five homers.

FEBRUARY 27   The Red Sox signed Rey Sanchez, most recently with the Braves, as a free agent.

FEBRUARY 28   Less than a day after taking over control of the Red Sox, team president Larry Lucchino fires Dan Duquette as general manager. Mike Port, who was the Sox' vice president of baseball operations, assumed Duquette's duties on an interim basis until a permanent replacement could be found. Previously, Port was the general manager of the Angels from 1984 through 1991 (see November 25, 2002).

Duquette was Boston's general manager for eight seasons. He took over the losing club before the 1994 season and put the Sox in the postseason in 1995, 1998, and 1999. Duquette was known for acquiring Pedro Martinez, Derek Lowe, and Jason Varitek in trades and Manny Ramirez in free agency. But his impersonal management style and bitter clashes with players, most notably Roger Clemens and Mo Vaughn, and with former manager Jimy Williams, proved to be Duquette's undoing.

MARCH 5   The new owners continue to remake the Red Sox by firing Joe Kerrigan as manager.

The firing of a manager during spring training was an unusual move, especially when the club had no permanent replacement ready to take over. Third base coach Mike Cubbage took the title of interim manager.

Though overshadowed by the likes of Roger Clemens, Pedro Martinez, and Curt Shilling, knuckleballer Tim Wakefield has baffled hitters since 1995, enjoying consistent success in hitter-friendly Fenway.

Steve Babineau

MARCH 11   Grady Little is hired as manager of the Red Sox.

Little was fifty-two years old and had never reached the majors as a player. He was a coach with the Padres in 1996, the Red Sox from 1997 through 1999, and the Indians in 2001 and 2002.

APRIL 1   The Red Sox lose the season opener 12–11 to the Blue Jays before 33,820 at Fenway Park. Pedro Martinez struggled through one of the worst starts of his career, giving up eight runs in three innings. The Sox trailed 8–3 before taking an 11–8 lead with three runs in the third and five in the fourth. Toronto tied the score 11–11 with a three-run fifth and won the contest with a tally in the ninth in Darrin Fletcher's sacrifice fly off Ugueth Urbina. In his first game with the Red Sox, Tony Clark hit a home run, double, and a single.

Martinez went into the season as a major question mark after missing most of the second half of 2001 with a small tear in his rotator cuff. He recovered from the Opening Day debacle to post a 20–4 record in 2002. He led the league in winning percentage (.833), ERA (2.26), strikeouts (239 in 199 1/3 innings), lowest opponent batting average (.198), and lowest opponent on-base percentage (.254).

APRIL 5   Derek Lowe comes six outs from a no-hitter in his first start of 2002 and defeats the Orioles 3–0 in Baltimore. Grady Little took Lowe out of the game after he allowed a walk and a single to start the eighth inning. The only hit off Lowe was a dribbler down the third-base line by Tony Batista. Shea Hillenbrand fielded the ball but threw too late to first to nail Batista. Rich Garces pitched the rest of the eighth, and Ugueth Urbina picked up the save in the ninth. The Orioles collected a second hit on a double by Chris Singleton in the ninth.

Heading into the 2002 season, Lowe was twenty-eight years old and had appeared in 298 big-league games, but only 22 as a starter. In a bold experiment, Lowe was converted to a full-time starter in 2002. He responded with a 21–8 record and a 2.58 ERA. Lowe pitched a no-hitter on April 27.

APRIL 16   The Red Sox trounce the Blue Jays 14–3 in Toronto.

APRIL 19   Pedro Martinez allows only one hit over eight innings and defeats the Royals 4–0 in Kansas City with ninth-inning relief help from Rich Garces. The Royals collected a second hit in the ninth on a two-out single by Neifi Perez. Martinez also recorded his 2,000th career strikeout when he fanned Michael Tucker in the fourth inning.

APRIL 21   Johnny Damon hits a grand slam off Bryan Rekar in the third inning of an 8–7 win over the Royals in the second game of a doubleheader in Kansas City. The Red Sox also won the first game, 12–2.

APRIL 25   Pedro Martinez (seven innings), Sunny Kim (one inning), and Willie Banks (one inning) combine on a two-hitter to defeat the Orioles 7–0 at Camden Yards. Martinez held Baltimore hitless until Gary Matthews Jr. singled with two outs in the sixth. Brook Fordyce added a single in the eighth.

APRIL 27   Derek Lowe pitches a no-hitter to defeat the Devil Rays 10–0 at Fenway Park. It was the first no-hitter in Boston since 1965. The only base runner was Brent Abernathy, who walked leading off the third inning. In the ninth, Lowe retired Russ Johnson on a soft liner to second baseman Rey Sanchez, Felix Escalona on a fly ball to Rickey Henderson in center field, and Jason Tyner on a grounder to Sanchez. Lowe's catcher was Jason Varitek. The two came to Boston together in 1997 in a trade with the Mariners. Lowe struck out six and threw 96 pitches.

The Red Sox added 400 seats in 2000 by converting standing room with permanent chairs. The number of concession areas selling food and beverages increased from 57 to 78. The number of turnstiles increased from 18 to 30. To create more space, the club removed cumbersome, intrusive, and unfriendly wire fences inside Gates B and C. Two rows of "dugout seats" (on the infield side of both dugouts to the backstop) were also added. The improvements continued over the next several years: More room was added inside the gates, on the concourses, and on Yawkey Way, and new menu items were added in the concession areas. In keeping with National Park Service *standards, the brick masonry of the building was restored to its early 1900s look, along with the addition of historic arched windows, light fixtures, and awnings.*

MAY 1   The Red Sox rout the Orioles 15–3 at Fenway Park.

MAY 4   The Red Sox score five runs in the ninth inning to beat the Devil Rays 7–5 in St. Petersburg. Shea Hillenbrand capped the rally with a grand slam off Victor Zambrano.

MAY 8   The Red Sox score seven runs in the third inning to take a 10–2 lead and cruise to a 12–6 victory over the Athletics in Oakland. It was Boston's eighth win in a row.

MAY 9   The Red Sox win their ninth game in a row with a 5–1 decision over the Athletics in Oakland.

The win gave the Red Sox a 24–7 record and a five-game lead in the AL East.

MAY 12   Pedro Martinez strikes out 12 batters in eight innings during a 10–4 win over the Mariners in Seattle.

MAY 18   After the game against the Mariners at Fenway Park is delayed for more than two hours by rain, Pedro Martinez strikes out the side in the first inning on the minimum nine pitches. He fanned Ichiro Suzuki, Mark McLemore, and Ruben Sierra, then stymied the rest of the Seattle lineup to win, 4–1.

JUNE 4   With their first selection in the amateur draft, the Red Sox choose pitcher Jon Lester from Bellarmine Prep in Puyallup, Washington. Lester went in the second round. The Sox forfeited their first-round pick due to free-agent compensation.

JUNE 5   The Red Sox rout the Tigers 11–0 on a cold and rainy night in Detroit.

The Red Sox were road warriors in 2002 with a 51–30 away record, but they were 42–39 at Fenway Park. The Sox also struggled in one-run games, going 13–23.

JUNE 7   The Red Sox play the Diamondbacks for the first time and lose 7–5 at Fenway Park.

JUNE 10   The Red Sox play the Rockies for the first time and win 7–3 at Fenway Park.

JUNE 16	While the Red Sox are in Atlanta, fans are invited into Fenway Park on Father's Day. Approximately 20,000 fans spent part of their afternoon playing catch on the Fenway Park outfield grass.
JUNE 18	The Red Sox play the Padres for the first time and win 4–2 in San Diego.
JUNE 20	Pedro Martinez (eight innings) and Chris Haney (one inning) combine on a two-hitter to beat the Padres 5–0 in San Diego. The only Padres hits were singles by D'Angelo Jiminez in the second and Mark Kotsay in the third.
JUNE 21	The Red Sox play the Dodgers for the first time during the regular season and lose 3–2 in Los Angeles.

The Red Sox were 5–13 against National League clubs in 2002.

JUNE 28	The Red Sox are knocked out of first place in the AL East with a 4–2 loss to the Braves in Atlanta.

The Sox never regained the top spot in 2002. The club was out of contention in both the division and wild-card races by the end of August.

JULY 1	Pedro Martinez strikes out 14 batters and gives up no walks in eight innings of a 4–0 win over the Blue Jays in Toronto.
JULY 5	Ted Williams dies at age eighty-three in Inverness, Florida, after suffering cardiac arrest. Williams battled an array of ailments during the last years of his life. That evening, the Red Sox wore black arm bands in his honor during a 9–5 win over the Tigers at Fenway Park. Williams's number 9 was cut into the grass in left field, where he played from 1939 through 1960. The center field flag was lowered to half-mast. The team set aside nine minutes for a moment of silence, a trumpeter playing taps, and a two-minute video of Williams. Number 9 appeared on players' sleeves for the rest of the 2002 season, and the team permanently renamed the 600 Club the .406 Club in honor of Williams's .406 batting average in 1941, the last time a player hit over .400 for a season.

Williams's death led to a bizarre legal battle between his two children. His son, John Henry, had his father's severed head cryogenically frozen at the Alcor Life Extension Foundation in Scottsdale, Arizona, to sell his DNA. Barbara Joyce, Ted's daughter from his first marriage and John Henry's half-sister, fought the decision in court for a proper burial. Eventually, John Henry won the case, in large part because Barbara ran out of funds to continue litigation. John Henry died of an illness in 2004.

JULY 6	Pedro Martinez (five innings), Wayne Gomes (two innings), Chris Haney (one inning), and Willie Banks (one inning) combine on a two-hitter to defeat the Tigers 8–0 at Fenway Park. The only two Detroit hits were singles by Ramon Santiago in the third inning and Shane Halter in the sixth.

In July 2002, advertising signs were added again to the Green Monster for the first time since 1946.

JULY 16   Manny Ramirez collects five hits in six at-bats during a 9–4 win over the Tigers in Detroit. Ramirez hit a two-run homer during a three-run eighth that knotted the game, 4–4. In the ninth the Sox scored five runs to break the 4–4 tie, thanks to Ramirez's RBI double and Trot Nixon's grand slam, both off Jose Paniagua.

JULY 17   Derek Lowe (eight innings) and Rich Garces (one inning) combine on a two-hitter to beat the Devil Rays 6–1 in St. Petersburg. The only Tampa Bay hits were doubles by Randy Winn and Aubrey Huff in the fourth inning.

Garces had a 23–8 record in 269 games, all in relief, with the Red Sox from 1996 through 2002. Listed at six feet and 250 pounds, Garces became a favorite of Red Sox fans with his rotund body, which earned him the nickname "El Guapo."

JULY 22   Nomar Garciaparra hits two homers, but the Red Sox lose 9–8 in New York when the Yankees score two runs in the ninth inning.

JULY 23   On his 29th birthday, Nomar Garciaparra hits three homers, two of them in one inning, and drives in eight runs during the Red Sox' trouncing of the Devil Rays 22–4 at Fenway Park. The Devil Rays led 4–0 before the Sox exploded for 10 runs in the third inning. Garciaparra set a major league record for most homers in consecutive innings with three, tied a major league record for most homers in an inning, and tied another record for most homers in consecutive games with five. Garciaparra homered off Tanyon Sturtze and Brandon Backe in the third. An inning later, he clubbed a grand slam off of Backe. There were seven Red Sox homers in all. Manny Ramirez hit two, and Trot Nixon and Johnny Damon each added one.

After wrist surgery wiped out most of his 2001 season, Garciaparra hit .310 in 2002 with 24 homers, 120 RBIs, 197 hits, and a league-leading 56 doubles.

JULY 28   Derek Lowe hits Gary Mathews Jr. of the Orioles with a pitch in the fourth inning and causes a bench-clearing brawl at Fenway Park. The Red Sox won, 12–3.

JULY 30   Pedro Martinez (eight innings) and Ugueth Urbina (one inning) combine on a two-hitter to defeat the Angels 6–0 in Anaheim. Brad Fullmer and Darin Erstad got the only Angels hits, Fullmer in the second and Erstad in the fourth, both singles.

On the same day, the Red Sox traded Seung Jun Song and Sunny Kim to the Expos for Cliff Floyd.

AUGUST 2   The Red Sox score seven runs in the eighth inning and wallop the Rangers 13–0 in Arlington. One night earlier, the Sox lost 19–7 to the Rangers.

AUGUST 8   The Red Sox sell Jose Offerman to the Mariners.

AUGUST 14   The Red Sox score seven runs in the sixth inning and defeat the Mariners 12–5 in Seattle.

AUGUST 22   Manny Ramirez drives in six runs on two homers, a double, and a single during a 12–3 win over the Rangers at Fenway Park. He drove in all the runs in the first three innings as the Sox built an 11–0 lead.

From August 21 through 24, Ramirez reached base in 14 consecutive plate appearances on nine hits and five walks. Ted Williams holds the all-time major league record with 16 in 1957. Ramirez won the American League batting title in 2002 with a .349 average. He also hit 33 homers and drove in 107 runs.

AUGUST 26   Johnny Damon hits a walk-off homer just inside the right field foul pole in the tenth inning to beat the Angels 10–9 at Fenway Park. The Red Sox scored four runs in the ninth inning to send the game into extra innings. Manny Ramirez was the star of the stunning comeback with five hits, including two homers, in five at-bats.

AUGUST 30   The Red Sox score 11 runs in the first three innings and clobber the Indians 15–5 in Cleveland.

When the day dawned, the MLB Players Association and owners were in negotiation over a new Basic Agreement. The players planned to go on strike if an agreement wasn't reached by noon. With the game in Cleveland that evening in doubt, the Red Sox gathered at Fenway Park at 7:30 AM. When they learned that the issue had been settled, the Sox left for the airport and took off at 1:00 PM, just six hours before the scheduled start of the game in Cleveland. The club got to the hotel at 3:30 PM and went straight to Jacobs Field but didn't take batting practice. The final score would indicate that a workout wasn't necessary.

SEPTEMBER 5   The Red Sox open the Yawkey Way concourse, an expansion of the park onto the neighboring street. The move added 25,000 square feet, doubled the fans' space on the third-base side, and cleared away more metal clutter inside Gate A.

SEPTEMBER 10   The Red Sox rout the Devil Rays 12–1 in St. Petersburg.

SEPTEMBER 11   Manny Ramirez hits a grand slam in the fifth inning off Paul Wilson during a 6–3 win over the Devil Rays in St. Petersburg.

The contest was stopped at 9:11 PM for a moment of silence in honor of the victims of the September 11, 2001, terrorist attacks.

SEPTEMBER 14   Derek Lowe wins his 20th game of the season with a 6–4 decision over the Orioles at Fenway Park.

Lowe became the first pitcher in major league history to save at least 40 games in a season and then win 20 or more games in another. Dennis Eckersley and John Smoltz did it the other way around.

SEPTEMBER 21   John Burkett (eight innings) and Ugueth Urbina (one inning) combined on a two-hitter to defeat the Orioles 3–0 at Camden Yards. Jay Gibbons and Luis Lopez claimed the two hits. Gibbons singled in the second inning, and Lopez doubled in the sixth.

SEPTEMBER 22   Pedro Martinez picks up his 20th win of the season with a 13–2 decision over the Orioles in Baltimore. Trot Nixon hit a grand slam off Steve Bechler in the ninth inning.

Martinez and Lowe were the first pair of Red Sox pitchers to win 20 or games in a season since Mel Parnell (25–7) and Ellis Kinder (23–6) accomplished the feat in 1949.

SEPTEMBER 23   The Red Sox defeat the Orioles 5–4 in 15 innings in Baltimore. Johnny Damon scored the winning run on a wild pitch. Both teams scored in the fourteenth.

NOVEMBER 25   The Red Sox hire Theo Epstein as general manager, replacing Dan Duquette, who was fired the previous February. Interim general manager Mike Port went back to his former position as the Sox' vice president of baseball operations. Epstein was not the team's first choice. The club tried and failed to hire Billy Beane away from the Athletics and J. P. Ricciardi from the Blue Jays.

At twenty-eight, Epstein became the youngest general manager in major league history. Epstein had been director of baseball operations with the Padres from 2000 through 2002, and the Red Sox hired him in March 2002 as assistant general manager. Epstein grew up in Brookline, about a mile from Fenway Park as a diehard Red Sox fan. "He brings a lifetime fan's understanding of Red Sox gestalt," said Red Sox president and CEO Larry Lucchino. Epstein was a twelve-year-old in the family room on October 25, 1986, during Game Six against the Mets when the Sox were on the brink of winning the World Series for the first time since 1918. "I was watching the game with my brother," he said. "We wanted to be off the ground, if possible in midair, when the ball went into the glove for the last out, so we got on top of the couch to jump. We were standing on top of the couch for about a half an hour. It was painful." The hiring of someone so young was a leap of faith for Red Sox owners, but with Epstein's help, Red Sox fans reveled in a World Championship in 2004. He resigned suddenly in October 2005 after nearly three years on the job.

DECEMBER 12   The Red Sox trade Tony Blanco and Josh Thigpen to the Reds for Todd Walker.

DECEMBER 20   Cliff Floyd signs with the Mets as a free agent.

DECEMBER 22   Ugueth Urbina signs with the Rangers as a free agent.

DECEMBER 24   The Red Sox sign Mike Timlin, most recently with the Phillies, as a free agent.

DECEMBER 27   Rey Sanchez signs with the Mets as a free agent.

2 0 0 3   B

Season in a Sentence

Five outs from reaching the World Series with a three-run lead over the Yankees in Game Seven of the American League Championship Series, the Red Sox suffer another crushing defeat.

Finish • Won • Lost • Pct • GB

Second   95   67   .586   6.0

In the wild-card race, the Red Sox finished in first place by two games.

AL Division Series—The Red Sox defeated the Oakland Athletics three games to two.

AL Championship Series—The Red Sox lost to the New York Yankees four games to three.

Manager

Grady Little

Stats   Red Sox • AL • Rank

	Red Sox	AL	Rank
Batting Avg:	.289	.267	1
On-Base Pct:	.360	.333	1
Slugging Pct:	.491	.428	1
Home Runs:	238		2
Stolen Bases:	88		9
ERA:	4.48	4.52	8
Fielding Pct:	.982	.983	10
Runs Scored:	961		1
Runs Allowed:	809		8

Starting Lineup

Jason Varitek, c
Kevin Millar, 1b
Todd Walker, 2b
Bill Mueller, 3b
Nomar Garciaparra, ss
Manny Ramirez, lf
Johnny Damon, cf
Trot Nixon, rf
David Ortiz, dh-1b
Shea Hillenbrand, 3b-1b

Pitchers

Derek Lowe, sp
Pedro Martinez, sp
Tim Wakefield, sp
John Burkett, sp
Byung-Hyun Kim, rp
Mike Timlin, rp
Alan Embree, rp
Brandon Lyon, rp

Attendance

2,724,165 (fourth in AL)

Club Leaders

Batting Avg:	Mueller	.326
On-Base Pct:	Ramirez	.427
Slugging Pct:	Ramirez	.587
Home Runs:	Ramirez	37
RBI:	Garciaparra	105
Runs:	Garciaparra	120
Stolen Bases:	Damon	30
Wins:	Lowe	17
Strikeouts:	Martinez	206
ERA:	Martinez	2.22
Saves:	Kim	16

JANUARY 14   The Red Sox purchase Kevin Millar from the Marlins.

It took some effort to get Millar into a Red Sox uniform. The Marlins sold his contract to the Chunchi Dragons in Japan, but the Red Sox blocked it with a waiver claim. After six weeks of international haggling, the two parties struck a deal that brought Millar to Boston and satisfied all the parties involved. He also became a clubhouse favorite and something of a cult hero in Red Sox Nation for his "cowboy up" rallying cry and a scoreboard clip of his karaoke routine videotaped as a teenager while he was singing and dancing to Bruce Springsteen's "Born in the U.S.A."

JANUARY 21   Carlos Baerga signs with the Diamondbacks as a free agent.

JANUARY 22   The Red Sox sign David Ortiz following his release by the Twins.

The signing of Ortiz has thus far been one of the best moves in club history. He immediately became a fan favorite. Ortiz was fifth in AL MVP voting in 2003, fourth in 2004 (before his numerous clutch hits in the postseason), and second in 2005. In his first three seasons in Boston, 2003–2005, Ortiz hit .297 with 119 homers and 388 RBIs. The last Red Sox player to drive that many runs over a three-year period was Vern Stephens, who had 440 from 1948 through 1950.

JANUARY 28   The Red Sox announce the creation of a new section of seats on top of the left field wall.

The seats, actually 280 bar stools, were built in 10 sections on top of the 37-foot-high, 231-foot-long Green Monster and sold for fifty dollars each. The idea was to add revenue, but there was another motive. "I also think there's the feeling that these seats could be very cool," Red Sox president Larry Lucchino said. "There's something very special about seeing a game at Fenway from that perspective." The seats also eliminated the unsightly netting on top of the wall that had been in place since 1936. "Nobody likes watching a ball go into a net," Sox chairman Tom Werner said. "The thrill of not only accommodating a few hundred people with a great seat but actually having a ball go into a crowd is a much more exciting experience." Above the wall were three rows of countertops with bar stools behind them, another row of standing room, concession stands, and a short back screen to prevent fans from falling.

FEBRUARY 4   The Red Sox purchase Bronson Arroyo from the Pirates.

FEBRUARY 20   Tony Clark signs with the Mets as a free agent.

FEBRUARY 25   The Reds purchase Dernell Stenson from the Red Sox.

Stenson played in 37 games for the Reds in 2003 before he was murdered on November 5 in Chandler, Arizona, while playing in the Arizona Fall League.

MARCH 31   Twelve days after a U.S.-led military offensive aimed at ousting Saddam Hussein gets under way in Iraq, the Red Sox open the season with a stunning 6–4 loss when the Devil Rays score five runs in the ninth inning in St. Petersburg. Carl Crawford ended the contest with a three-run homer off Chad Fox, who was making his Red Sox debut. Pedro Martinez had an excellent start, allowing an unearned run and three hits in seven innings. It was the Red Sox' first ever regular-season game in the month of March.

Martinez had a 14–4 record and a league-leading 2.22 ERA in 2003.

APRIL 1   In his second game as a member of the Red Sox, Kevin Millar hits a home run in the sixteenth inning to defeat the Devil Rays in St. Petersburg. Millar entered the game as a pinch-hitter in the fourteenth inning.

APRIL 3   The Red Sox blast the Devil Rays 14–5 in St. Petersburg.

APRIL 6   The Red Sox clobber the Orioles 12–2 in Baltimore. Shea Hillenbrand drove in six runs on a homer, a double, and a single. Nomar Garciaparra hit a home run, a triple, and a double.

APRIL 11   The scheduled home opener against the Orioles is rained out.

APRIL 12   The Red Sox open the home schedule with a 13–6 loss to the Orioles before
               32,029. Pedro Martinez had one of the worst starts of his career by allowing 10
               runs, all earned, in 4⅓ innings.

               *The Red Sox added National League scores to the manually operated score-
               board on the left field wall at Fenway Park. The NL scores had been absent
               since 1975 when the scoreboard and wall were redesigned. The opening behind
               the wall did not extend far enough to change the NL scores from behind, how-
               ever. The scores were changed between innings from the front by one or more
               individuals carrying a ladder.*

APRIL 20   Nomar Garciaparra hits a walk-off homer in the ninth inning that beats the Blue
               Jays 6–5 at Fenway Park. The Sox trailed 5–0 before scoring two runs in the
               sixth inning and three in the seventh. Garciaparra tied the score 5–5 with a two-
               run double.

               *Garciaparra hit .301 with 28 homers, 105 RBIs, 120 runs, 198 hits, 37 dou-
               bles, and 13 triples in 2003.*

APRIL 27   David Ortiz and Jason Varitek hit back-to-back homers in the fourteenth inning of
               a 6–4 win over the Angels in Anaheim.

               *In his first season with the Red Sox, Ortiz was a stunning surprise. He hit with
               31 homers, drove in 101 runs, and had a .288 batting average. He was also a
               uniting force in a clubhouse full of diverse personalities.*

APRIL 30   The Red Sox score three runs in the ninth inning to beat the Royals 5–4 at Fen-
               way Park. Kansas City pitchers hit three batters in the inning to tie a major
               league record. Hector Carrasco plunked Johnny Damon and Mike McDougal hit
               Shea Hillenbrand and Nomar Garciaparra. A wild pitch and two errors in the
               inning also contributed to the three Boston runs.

MAY 3   Pedro Martinez strikes out 12 batters in a 9–1 win over the Twins at Fenway Park.
               The Red Sox scored seven runs in the sixth inning.

MAY 7   The Red Sox come from behind to win 9–6 against the Royals at Kauffman Stadi-
               um. Kansas City scored six runs in the sixth inning to take a 6–1 lead before the
               Red Sox scored four runs in the seventh inning and four more in the eighth.

MAY 26   Nomar Garciaparra extends his hitting streak to 26 games during an 8–4 win over
               the Yankees in New York. The victory gave the Red Sox a 31–19 record and a 2½-
               game lead in the AL East.

               *Roger Clemens entered the game with 299 career wins but was tagged for
               eight runs and 10 hits in 5⅔ innings. The game was delayed for one hour
               and 42 minutes by rain. Clemens's routine was further disrupted after his
               first-inning warm-up. Red Sox manager Grady Little walked out to question
               Clemens's glove. He was wearing a brand-new glove with a shiny new "300"
               logo on the back of it. Plate umpire Bill Miller agreed with Little and made
               Clemens change it.*

MAY 29

The Red Sox trade Shea Hillenbrand to the Diamondbacks for Byung-Hyun Kim.

Kim had a rocky two seasons with the Red Sox before he was traded to the Rockies during spring training in 2005. Kim made an obscene gesture at Sox fans during the 2003 postseason. In 2004, he landed on the disabled list and made a trip to his native Korea to fix a "leg imbalance."

JUNE 3

In the first round of the amateur draft, the Red Sox select outfielder David Murphy from Baylor University.

The first 2003 draftee to play for the Red Sox was second rounder Abe Alvarez. He was followed by fourth-rounder Jon Papelbon.

JUNE 4

The Red Sox play the Pirates for the first time in the regular season and win 11–4 and 8–3 in a doubleheader at PNC Park in Pittsburgh.

The June 4 games were the first meaningful meetings between the Red Sox and Pirates since the 1903 World Series, 100 years earlier. The Pittsburgh portion of the 1903 Series was played at Exposition Park, which was on almost the same spot where PNC Park stands today.

JUNE 5

Todd Walker extends his hitting streak to 20 games in a 5–4 loss to the Pirates in Pittsburgh.

JUNE 6

The Red Sox play at Miller Park in Milwaukee for the first time and lose 9–3 to the Brewers. It was also the first that the Sox had played the Brewers since the club's move to the National League in 1998.

JUNE 7

Consecutive home runs by Trot Nixon and Jason Varitek in the ninth inning beat the Brewers 11–10 in Milwaukee. The Sox trailed 10–4 after five innings before coming back with one run in the sixth inning and four in the seventh to set the stage for the dramatics in the ninth. The four seventh-inning runs scored on Kevin Millar's grand slam off Jayson Durocher.

Nixon batted .306 with 28 homers in 2003.

JUNE 10

The Red Sox play the Cardinals for the first time during the regular season and lose 9–7 at Fenway Park.

JUNE 11

The Red Sox score seven runs in the second inning and wallop the Cardinals 13–1 at Fenway Park.

JUNE 12

The Red Sox are knocked out of first place with a tough 13-inning, 8–7 loss to the Cardinals at Fenway Park. The Sox scored three runs in the ninth to tie the score 3–3 and two more in the tenth to deadlock the game 5–5. After the Cards scored three times in the thirteenth on Jim Edmonds's homer, Boston scored two in a futile rally.

The Sox never regained first place in 2003, but they remained in contention for the AL East pennant into September.

JUNE 13   The Red Sox play the Astros during the regular season for the first time and win 4–3 at Fenway Park.

JUNE 15   The Red Sox outlast the Astros 3–2 in 14 innings at Fenway Park. Nomar Garciaparra tied a team record for extra-base hits in a game with three doubles and a triple. His first sacrifice bunt since 1997 set the stage for the game-winning single by Manny Ramirez.

> *Ramirez batted .325 with 37 homers, 104 RBIs, and 117 runs in 2003. He led the league in on-base percentage with a .427 mark. Ramirez's season wasn't without controversy, however. He missed a crucial series against the Yankees in late August with a throat ailment, amid published reports that he was seen in a hotel bar one night and that he failed to show up at the park the next day. The following day, Ramirez begged off a pinch-hitting assignment and then was benched for a game. After the season, the Red Sox put him on waivers, but no team was willing to take on his contract.*

Fan favorite Johnny Damon brought a new level of hustle and grit to the Sox in 2002 and was a key part of the World Championship team in 2004.

Steve Babineau

JUNE 19   After scoring three runs on one hit in the first inning, the Red Sox go hitless for eight consecutive innings before winning the game 4–3 in the tenth against the White Sox in Chicago. Johnny Damon's single drove in the winning run.

JUNE 21   Nomar Garciaparra reaches base seven times in seven plate appearances with six singles and a walk, but the Red Sox blow three late leads and lose 6–5 in 13 innings to the Phillies in Philadelphia. The Sox led 2–1 in the sixth, 3–2 in the twelfth, and 5–3 in the thirteenth but the bullpen was unable to hold the advantages.

                 Garciaparra was the fourth Red Sox player to collect six hits in a game. The others were Jimmy Piersall (1952), Pete Runnels (1960), and Jerry Remy (1981).

JUNE 24   Three days after his six-hit game, Nomar Garciaparra collects five singles in five at-bats before being lifted for a pinch hitter in a 10–1 win over the Tigers at Fenway Park.

JUNE 25   The Red Sox score nine runs in the eighth inning to beat the Tigers 11–2 at Fenway Park.

JUNE 27   The Red Sox clobber the Marlins in a record-setting 25–8 win at Fenway Park. The Sox set a major league record by scoring 10 runs in the first inning before a batter was retired, tied an American League record for most runs in the first inning of a game with 14, and tied a club record with 28 hits. Johnny Damon tied a major league record for most hits in an inning, three, on a triple, a double, and a single, and finished the day with five hits in seven at-bats. Since 1883, the only other player in the majors to get three hits in an inning has been Gene Stephens of the Red Sox, on June 18, 1953. The half-inning took 50 minutes and 91 pitches to complete and included seven singles, four doubles, a triple, a homer (by Manny Ramirez), and four walks. The Sox collected 13 hits in 14 at-bats in the big inning. Nomar Garciaparra, the 12th batter, made the first out on a foul pop to Ivan Rodriguez. The other two outs were on Kevin Millar's sacrifice fly and Bill Mueller's scoring attempt, when left fielder Miguel Cabrera threw him out at the plate. Mueller led Red Sox batters with six RBIs. The 25 runs represented the second largest single-game run total in Red Sox history, trailing only the 29–4 victory over the St. Louis Browns on June 8, 1950.

                 The game also included a frightening injury and a near brawl. In the seventh, Todd Walker's line drive hit Marlins pitcher Kevin Olsen behind the right ear. Olsen was on the ground for nine minutes before being taken off on a stretcher. He didn't pitch in a major league game for the rest of the season. In the ninth, tempers flared after an exchange of bean balls. Players from both sides walked slowly toward each other, but there was no contact.

JUNE 28   At Fenway Park, the Red Sox score seven runs in the sixth inning to take a 9–2 lead, but they lose 10–9 when the Marlins score four runs in the eighth inning and four more in the ninth. In his first game with the Red Sox, Gabe Kapler collected four hits, including two doubles, in four at-bats and drove in three runs.

JUNE 29   In his second game with the Red Sox, Gabe Kapler hits two homers and drives in four runs in an 11–7 victory over the Marlins at Fenway Park.

Kapler had 13 hits in his first 27 at-bats with the Red Sox. His good looks made him a favorite of female fans and earned him the nickname "Gabe the Babe."

JULY 2   The Red Sox sign Todd Jones following his release by the Rockies.

JULY 4   The Red Sox play their own version of the Boston Pops by launching seven homers on the Fourth of July, walloping the Yankees 10–3 in New York. Bill Mueller homered from both sides of the plate, off lefty David Wells and right-hander Dan Miceli. Jason Varitek and David Ortiz also hit two homers, and Manny Ramirez added one. Ramirez's homer reached the distant third deck of Yankee Stadium.

              In his first season with the Red Sox, Mueller won the batting title with an average of .326. He also hit 19 homers.

JULY 21   The Red Sox score five runs in the second inning and seven in the third to take a 12–0 lead and cruise to a 14–5 win over the Tigers at Fenway Park.

JULY 22   The Red Sox trade Brandon Lyon and Anastacio Martinez to the Pirates for Scott Sauerbeck and Mike Gonzalez.

              Lyon, Martinez, and Gonzalez were involved in another Boston-Pittsburgh trade nine days later. Lyon was returned to the Red Sox because of concerns over his elbow.

JULY 23   Trot Nixon homers twice, including a grand slam in the seventh inning off Al Levine, during a 10–4 win over the Devil Rays at Fenway Park. The Sox scored seven times in the seventh.

JULY 29   Bill Mueller becomes the first player in major league history to hit grand slams from both sides of the plate during a 14–7 win over the Rangers in Arlington. Mueller had three homers overall and drove in nine runs. Batting left-handed, Mueller hit a solo homer in the third inning off R. A. Dickey. Batting right-handed in the seventh, he hit a grand slam against Aaron Fultz. An inning later, he connected again for his second grand slam of the game, this one as a lefty facing Jay Powell.

              On the same day, the Red Sox trade Phil Dumatrait and Tyler Pelland to the Reds for Scott Williamson.

JULY 31   The Red Sox send Freddy Sanchez, Mike Gonzalez, and cash to the Pirates for Jeff Suppan, Brandon Lyon, and Anastacio Martinez.

AUGUST 3   David Ortiz hits two of the Red Sox' six homers during a 7–5 win over the Orioles in Baltimore. Doug Mirabelli, Johnny Damon, Trot Nixon, and Bill Mueller hit the other four.

AUGUST 5   Trailing the Angels 5–0 at Fenway Park, the Red Sox score seven runs in the third inning, break a 7–7 tie with two runs in the fifth inning, and score one in the seventh to snap a 9–9 deadlock. They won the game, 10–9.

              During the second half of the 2003 season, Red Sox players urged each other to "cowboy up." It was the title of a Ryan Reynolds song. Reynolds is the son of

Archie Reynolds, who pitched for the Angels during the 1970s. The song typi-fied the clubhouse spirit with the lines "Cowboy up, dust yourself off, get back in the saddle, give it one more try. Sweat and blood, give it all you got. The road to heaven is a hell of a ride. The tough get going when the going gets tough so come on and cowboy up."

AUGUST 20   Six days after a power failure affects fifty million people in Ohio, Michigan, Ontario, and the northeastern United States, the Red Sox fall 7 1/2 games behind the Yankees in the AL East race following an 8–6 loss to the Athletics at Fenway Park.

AUGUST 21   The Red Sox overwhelm the Athletics 14–5 at Fenway Park.

The Red Sox in 2003 set major league records for most extra-base hits in a season (649), most total bases in a season (2,832), and highest slugging percentage (.491).

SEPTEMBER 1   The Red Sox score six runs in the ninth inning to beat the Phillies 13–9 in Philadel-phia in a makeup of a game postponed in June. Trot Nixon broke the 9–9 tie with a grand slam off Turk Wendell. Nixon drove in six runs in the contest.

SEPTEMBER 3   David Ortiz hits homers in back-to-back plate appearances, including the game-winner in the tenth inning, to defeat the White Sox 5–4 in Chicago. The victory moved the Red Sox into a first-place tie with the Mariners in the wild-card race.

SEPTEMBER 6   The Red Sox breeze to an 11–0 win over the Yankees to cut New York's lead in the AL East race to 1 1/2 games.

On September 6 and 7, Bruce Springsteen and the E Street Band performed in the first ever rock concerts at Fenway Park.

SEPTEMBER 7   With a chance to cut the Yankees' lead to one-half game, the Red Sox lose 3–1 in New York. The Sox maintained their 1 1/2-game advantage over the Mariners in the wild-card chase, however.

The Red Sox failed to come any closer to the Yankees in the Eastern Division but never lost their lead in the wild-card race before clinching a postseason spot on September 25.

SEPTEMBER 12   Johnny Damon walks twice with the bases loaded in a 7–4 win over the White Sox at Fenway Park.

SEPTEMBER 25   The Red Sox clinch the wild-card berth with a 14–3 win over the Orioles at Fenway Park. The Sox led 12–0 after four innings.

SEPTEMBER 28   On the final day of the season, Bill Mueller wins the batting title with a .326 aver-age in one of the closest races in history. Mueller was 0 for 1 as a pinch hitter in a 3–1 loss to the Devil Rays in St. Petersburg. Manny Ramirez, who sat out the final contest, just missed winning his second straight batting title, finishing the year at .325. Derek Jeter was 0 for 3 on the final day to end the season with a .324 aver-age. Nomar Garciaparra receives club permission to travel to Columbus, Ohio, and watch fiancée Mia Hamm play for the U.S. team in the World Cup soccer match against North Korea.

The Red Sox met the AL West–champion Oakland Athletics in the Division Series. Managed by Ken Macha, the A's were 96–66 in 2003.

OCTOBER 1   In the first game of the Division Series, the Red Sox lose 5–4 to the Athletics in 12 innings in Oakland. The Sox scored first on a solo homer by Todd Walker in the first inning, but the A's countered with three in the third off Pedro Martinez. Jason Varitek narrowed the gap to 3–2 with a homer in the fifth, and Boston took a 4–3 advantage with two in the seventh on a two-out single by Nomar Garciaparra and another Walker homer. Oakland tied the game in the ninth with a run off Byung-Hyun Kim and another in the twelfth against Derek Lowe, who was making his first relief appearance of the season, on three walks and Ramon Hernandez's bunt single.

OCTOBER 2   The Athletics take a two-games-to-none lead in the best-of-five series with a 5–1 win over the Red Sox in Oakland. The A's scored all five of their runs in the second inning off Tim Wakefield.

OCTOBER 4   Pinch hitting for Gabe Kapler, Trot Nixon hits a one-out, two-run, walk-off homer in the eleventh to beat the Athletics 3–1 in Game Three of the Division Series before 35,460 at Fenway Park. Nixon's homer followed a single by Doug Mirabelli. The Red Sox scored their first run in the second inning, and the Athletics tied the score in the sixth. Derek Lowe went seven innings and allowed only one run, unearned. Mike Timlin pitched three innings of perfect relief, and Scott Williamson retired Oakland in order in the eleventh.

During the 2004 postseason, Williamson was 2–0 with three saves. He allowed one run and three hits in eight innings while striking out 14 batters.

OCTOBER 5   The Red Sox even the series with a come-from-behind 5–4 win over the Athletics before 35,048 at Fenway Park. Oakland took a 4–2 lead in the sixth with three runs off John Burkett before Todd Walker homered on a full count leading off the Red Sox' half. Boston was still trailing 4–3 with one out and no one on base in the eighth, just five outs from elimination. Nomar Garciaparra started the game-winning rally with a double. After Walker lined out to center, Manny Ramirez singled Garciaparra to third. David Ortiz followed with a two-run double to put the Sox ahead, 5–4. Scott Williamson pitched a perfect eighth and ninth and struck out three.

Byung-Hyun Kim was booed during pregame introductions and flipped off the crowd. He didn't pitch again for the rest of the playoffs.

OCTOBER 6   After losing the first two games of the series, the Red Sox win their third in a row and advance to the American League Championship Series with a 4–3 win over the Athletics in Oakland. The Sox trailed 1–0 before a four-run rally in the sixth. Jason Varitek led off the inning with a homer. After Johnny Damon walked and Todd Walker was hit by a pitch, Manny Ramirez hit a three-run homer off Barry Zito. The A's scored a run in their half of the sixth and another in the eighth off Pedro Martinez before a succession of four relievers nailed down the victory. Derek Lowe struck out the final two batters, both looking, with the tying run on third. There was a scary moment in the seventh inning when Johnny Damon and second baseman Damian Jackson collided head-to-head while chasing Jermaine's Dye's fly ball.

Jackson shook it off but Damon was knocked unconscious with a concussion and left the field in an ambulance. He missed the first two games of the ALCS.

The Red Sox met the Yankees in the ALCS. Managed by Joe Torre in his eighth season with the club, the Yankees were 101–61 in 2003 and finished the season six games ahead of the Sox in the AL East. The Sox were the overwhelming favorites of neutral fans around the country, as were the Cubs, who were facing the Marlins in the NLCS. The possibility of a World Series between the star-crossed franchises heightened anticipation nationwide.

OCTOBER 8   The Red Sox draw first blood in the ALCS with a 5–2 victory over the Yankees in Game One in New York. David Ortiz started the scoring with a two-run homer in the fourth off Mike Mussina. In the fifth, Todd Walker and Manny Ramirez added solo home runs. Walker's homer struck the foul pole. Right field umpire Angel Hernandez ruled it foul, but home plate ump Tim McClelland overruled him. The Sox added another run in the seventh before the Yankees scored two in their half. Ramirez had three singles in addition to his homer and scored three runs. Tim Wakefield (six innings) and relievers Alan Embree, Mike Timlin, and Scott Williamson (one inning each) limited the Yankees to three hits.

OCTOBER 9   The Yankees even the series with a 6–2 win over the Red Sox at Yankee Stadium. The Sox held a brief 1–0 lead in the second, but the Yankees scored two in their half off Derek Lowe and never trailed again. Jason Varitek hit a homer and a double and scored both Boston runs.

OCTOBER 11   In a matchup of Pedro Martinez and Roger Clemens, the Yankees take a two-games-to-one lead in the ALCS with a 4–3 win over the Red Sox before 34,209 at Fenway Park. A two-run single by Manny Ramirez in the first inning put the Sox up, 2–0. The Yankees countered with a run in the second, one in the third, and two in the fourth against Martinez. The Sox added a tally in the seventh but couldn't close the gap.

Game Three will be long remembered for the altercation between thirty-one-year-old Pedro Martinez and seventy-two-year-old Don Zimmer and a scuffle in the bullpen between a groundskeeper and two Yankees, a bizarre chapter in baseball's most bitter rivalry. The fight began after Martinez threw behind Karim Garcia's head in the fourth inning and Roger Clemens threw a high pitch at Manny Ramirez. The Red Sox outfielder veered toward the mound, and both benches cleared. Zimmer lunged at Martinez, who sidestepped him, grabbed him by the head, and tossed him to the ground. Zimmer landed face down and rolled on his back. Yankees trainer Gene Monahan treated the coach and former Red Sox manager for a cut on his head. In the ninth there was a fight between Fenway Park groundskeeper Paul Williams and Yankee players Karim Garcia and Jeff Nelson. Williams contended that Garcia and Nelson attacked him. According to Nelson, Williams was waving a rally flag in the Yankee bullpen. When asked to leave, Williams jumped in Nelson's face and tried to attack him. Garcia, playing right field, jumped over the fence to join the fray. He hurt his hand and had to leave the game. Williams acknowledged pumping his fist twice while holding a white towel after the Red Sox turned a double play in the ninth. Later, Boston police charged Williams, Garcia, and Nelson with assault and battery.

OCTOBER 12   Game Four is postponed for a day by rain.

OCTOBER 13   The Red Sox even the series with 3–2 triumph over the Yankees before 34,599 at Fenway Park. Todd Walker put the Sox ahead with a homer off Mike Mussina leading off the fourth. After the Yankees tied the contest with a run in the fifth, Trot Nixon hit a home run in the Boston half. The Sox never relinquished the lead, scoring one in the seventh before the Yanks plated a run in the ninth. Tim Wakefield pitched seven innings and allowed just one run on five hits for the victory.

OCTOBER 14   The Red Sox are one game from elimination after losing Game Five 4–2 to the Yankees before 34,619 at Fenway Park. The Yankees took a 3–0 lead in the second inning and never looked back.

OCTOBER 15   The Red Sox force a seventh game with a 9–6 win over the Yankees at Yankee Stadium. The Sox took a 4–1 lead in the third with four runs. Jason Varitek led off the inning with a homer off Andy Pettitte. Three more runs scored on three singles, a walk, and a fielder's choice. The Yankees took a 6–4 advantage with four runs in the fourth and another in the fifth. Three runs in the seventh put the Sox ahead, 7–6. Nomar Garciaparra led off with a triple and scored on an error. Manny Ramirez doubled and crossed the plate on a single by David Ortiz to tie the score, 6–6. A Bill Mueller single, a wild pitch, an intentional walk to Jason Varitek, and an unintentional walk to Johnny Damon created the go-ahead run. The Sox added two insurance runs in the ninth on Trot Nixon's homer. Garciaparra had four hits in the game, and Mueller collected three, including two doubles.

OCTOBER 16   The Red Sox suffer an agonizing 6–5 Game Seven loss to the Yankees at Yankee Stadium, costing Boston a shot at the World Series. The starting pitchers were Pedro Martinez and Roger Clemens. The Sox took a 3–0 lead in the second inning. Trot Nixon hit a two-run homer, followed by a double from Jason Varitek, who scored on an error. Kevin Millar homered on the first pitch of the fourth inning to make it 4–0. Jason Giambi homered for the Yanks in the fifth and the seventh to close the gap to 4–2. A David Ortiz home run in the eighth off David Wells gave the Red Sox a little breathing room with a 5–2 advantage. Martinez was still on the mound when the Yankees came to bat in the eighth. Grady Little's decision to leave Martinez in the game will remain a source of controversy for decades. He had shown some signs of weakening, giving up a homer and a single in the seventh. Up to that point, the bullpen had been brilliant, allowing only two runs in 31 innings in the playoffs. Nick Johnson led off the eighth by popping out to Nomar Garciaparra. But Martinez quickly allowed four straight hits: Derek Jeter doubled, Bernie Williams singled, Jorge Posada doubled, and Hideki Matsui singled to tie the score at 5–5. Finally, Grady Little pulled Martinez and brought in Alan Embree, who got the second out. Mike Timlin followed Embree and walked two batters to load the bases before Alfonso Soriano grounded out to end the inning. It was still 5–5 when Aaron Boone homered on the first pitch of the eleventh inning from Tim Wakefield and crushed the hopes of Red Sox Nation once more.

               The Yankees moved on to the World Series against the Marlins and lost in six games.

OCTOBER 27   The Red Sox fire Grady Little as manager.

Little brought the Red Sox to the brink of the World Series in 2003, but his decision not to lift Pedro Martinez with a late-inning lead in Game Seven of the ALCS caused widespread second-guessing and had much to do with his dismissal.

NOVEMBER 28   The Red Sox trade Casey Fossum, Brandon Lyon, Jorge DeRosa, and Michael Goss to the Diamondbacks for Curt Schilling.

Schilling returned to the Red Sox organization after a 15-year absence. The Sox drafted him in 1986 but traded him to the Orioles two years later before he reached the majors. In exchange for four marginal prospects, Schilling gave the Red Sox a 21–6 record in 2004, leading the AL in wins and winning percentage and posting a 3.26 ERA. Schilling was also an inspiration in the postseason by overcoming a severe ankle injury to win three games.

DECEMBER 4   The Red Sox hire Terry Francona as manager.

Red Sox fans didn't greet the announcement warmly. Francona had previously managed the Phillies to a 285–353 record, a less-than-stellar .440 winning percentage, from 1997 through 2000. He was a coach with the Rangers in 2002 and the Athletics in 2003. From 1981 through 1990 he was a light-hitting first baseman with the Expos, Reds, Indians, and Brewers. His father, Tito, played in the majors with nine clubs between 1956 and 1970.

DECEMBER 13   On the day that Saddam Hussein is captured, the Red Sox sign Keith Foulke, most recently with the Athletics, as a free agent.

An unstable bullpen contributed to the Red Sox' failure to reach the World Series in 2003. Foulke helped stabilize the relief situation in 2004 with a 5–3 record, 32 saves, and a 2.17 ERA.

DECEMBER 16   The Red Sox acquire Mark Bellhorn from the Rockies.

DECEMBER 23   Todd Walker signs with the Cubs as a free agent.

2 0 0 4   B

Season in a Sentence

The Sox reverse the curse with an improbable ALCS win over the Yankees, after falling behind three games to none, and a sweep of the Cardinals in the World Series.

Finish • Won • Lost • Pct • GB

Second   98   64   .605   3.0

In the wild-card race, the Red Sox finished in first place by two games.

AL Division Series—The Red Sox defeated the Anaheim Angels three games to one.

AL Championship Series— The Red Sox defeated the New York Yankees four games to three.

World Series—The Red Sox defeated the St. Louis Cardinals in four games.

Manager

Terry Francona

Stats   Red Sox • AL • Rank

	Red Sox	AL	Rank
Batting Avg:	.282	.270	1
On-Base Pct:	.360	.338	1
Slugging Pct:	.472	.433	1
Home Runs:	222		4
Stolen Bases:	68		11
ERA:	4.18	4.63	3
Fielding Pct:	.981	.982	10
Runs Scored:	949		1
Runs Allowed:	768		4

Starting Lineup

Jason Varitek, c
Kevin Millar, 1b
Mark Bellhorn, 2b
Bill Mueller, 3b
Orlando Cabrera, ss
Manny Ramirez, lf
Johnny Damon, cf
Gabe Kapler, rf
David Ortiz, dh
Pokey Reese, ss
Kevin Youkilis, 3b
Doug Mirabelli, c
Trot Nixon, rf
Nomar Garciaparra, ss

Pitchers

Curt Schilling, sp
Pedro Martinez, sp
Derek Lowe, sp
Tim Wakefield, sp
Branson Arroyo, sp
Keith Foulke, rp
Mike Timlin, rp
Alan Embree, rp

Attendance

2,837,304 (fourth in AL)

Club Leaders

Batting Avg:	Ramirez	.308
On-Base Pct:	Ramirez	.397
Slugging Pct:	Ramirez	.613
Home Runs:	Ramirez	43
RBI:	Ramirez	130
Runs:	Damon	123
Stolen Bases:	Damon	19
Wins:	Schilling	21
Strikeouts:	Martinez	227
ERA:	Schilling	3.26
Saves:	Foulke	32

JANUARY 12   Todd Jones signs with the Devil Rays as a free agent.

JANUARY 22   The Red Sox sign Tony Womack, most recently with the Cubs, as a free agent.

FEBRUARY 5   Four days after the Patriots defeat the Panthers 32–29 in a Super Bowl highlighted by Janet Jackson's "wardrobe malfunction," the Red Sox sign Ellis Burks, most recently with the Indians, as a free agent.

> *Burks was returning to Boston, where he played for the Red Sox from his rookie season in 1987 through 1992.*

FEBRUARY 16   The Yankees trade Alfonso Soriano to the Rangers for Alex Rodriguez and cash.

> *The acquisition of Rodriguez by the "Evil Empire" was a smack in the face to Red Sox fans. The Sox had a deal in place the previous December to send*

Manny Ramirez to the Rangers for Rodriguez. If the Red Sox had obtained Rodriguez, Nomar Garciaparra would have been traded to another club, most likely the White Sox. The trade with the Rangers was contingent on restructuring A-Rod's contract, however, and the players union refused to sign off on the deal because the restructuring would reduce the value of the contract. The Red Sox were one of many teams interested in trading for Rodriguez, who expressed a desire to leave Texas. The Yankees had no interest because they were set in the infield. That changed in late January when third baseman Aaron Boone tore up his knee playing basketball. The Yankees then entered the race to obtain A-Rod's services. Ironically, it was Boone whose home run defeated the Red Sox in Game Seven of the 2003 ALCS.

MARCH 21   The Red Sox trade Tony Womack to the Cardinals for Matt Duff.

APRIL 4   The Red Sox play the season opener on Sunday night in a game televised nationally on ESPN and lose 7–2 to the Orioles in forty-three-degree weather in Baltimore.

APRIL 6   Curt Schilling makes his Red Sox debut and allows only one run on six hits in six innings of a 4–1 win over the Orioles in Baltimore.

APRIL 7   The Red Sox score seven runs in the second inning of a 10–3 win over the Orioles in Baltimore. Johnny Damon collected five hits, including a double, in five at-bats. He also took a three-run homer away from David Segui by leaping above the fence.

              Damon had a new look in 2004: a beard and long hair.

APRIL 9   In the home opener, the Red Sox lose 10–5 to the Blue Jays before 34,337 at Fenway Park. Jason Varitek hit a home run. First baseman David McCarty pitched two-thirds of an inning.

              McCarty made three pitching appearances in 2004 when Terry Francona wanted to rest his staff. McCarty pitched 3 2/3 innings and allowed one run, two hits, and one walk while striking out four.

APRIL 11   David Ortiz hits a two-run, walk-off homer in the twelfth inning that beats the Blue Jays 6–4 at Fenway Park. After trailing 4–2, the Red Sox scored in the eighth and ninth to send the game into extra innings.

              Ortiz hit .301 in 2004 with 41 homers and 139 RBIs.

APRIL 16   Prior to a 6–2 win over the Yankees, the Red Sox unveil a statue of Ted Williams outside Gate B on Van Ness Avenue.

              New seating atop the right field stands debuted in 2004.

APRIL 19   The Red Sox defeat the Yankees 5–4 on Patriots' Day at Fenway Park and take three of the four games in the series.

APRIL 25   The Red Sox complete a three-game sweep of the Yankees at Yankee Stadium with a 2–0 victory. Both runs scored on Manny Ramirez's home run in the fourth inning off Javier Vasquez.

With the win, the Red Sox won six of their first seven meetings with the Yankees, the first time that had happened since 1913. After the three-game sweep in New York, the Sox were 12–6, 1½ games ahead of the Orioles and 4½ up on the Yankees.

APRIL 28   Curt Schilling (7⅓ innings), Alan Embree (two-thirds of an inning), and Lenny DiNardo (one inning) combine to shut out the Devil Rays 6–0 at Fenway Park.

APRIL 29   Red Sox pitchers record their third straight shutout in the afternoon set of a day-night doubleheader at Fenway Park. Byung-Hyun Kim (five innings), Tim Wakefield (two innings), Mike Timlin (1⅔ innings), and Alan Embree (one-third of an inning) combined to defeat the Devil Rays, 4–0. In the night game, the Sox scored seven runs in the first inning, enough for a 7–3 triumph.

The Red Sox closed April with a 15–6 record and a three-game lead in the AL East.

MAY 7   Trailing 6–2 in the eighth inning, the Red Sox rally to beat the Royals 7–6 in 10 innings at Fenway Park. Mark Bellhorn tied the score with a two-run homer in the ninth, and pinch hitter Jason Varitek doubled home the winning run.

Varitek batted .296 with 18 homers in 2004.

MAY 8   Pokey Reese hits two homers, one of them inside the park in the fifth inning and another over the wall in the sixth, during a 9–1 win over the Royals at Fenway Park.

Reese hadn't hit a homer in a major league game since April 3, 2003. He hit only one more during the 2004 season.

MAY 10   Manny Ramirez misses a 10–6 loss to the Indians at Fenway Park to travel to Miami to become a U.S. citizen.

In his first game back, Ramirez trotted out to his position in left field carrying an American flag. He batted .308 with 43 homers, 130 RBIs, and 108 runs scored in 2004.

MAY 15   In his major league debut, Red Sox third baseman Kevin Youkilis hits a home run during a 4–0 win over the Blue Jays at Fenway Park. It was also his first major league hit, and it came in his second at-bat.

MAY 21   Johnny Damon shaves off his beard for charity to benefit the literacy program at the Boston Public Library. Gillette sponsored the event to kick off its new line of razors. A crowd gathered on the plaza by the Prudential Center to watch models lather him up, and Damon sat while they took the blades to his face.

MAY 25   The Red Sox wallop the Athletics 12–2 at Fenway Park.

MAY 28   David Ortiz hits a grand slam off Joel Pineiro in the fifth inning of an 8–4 win over the Mariners at Fenway Park. The Sox were trailing 4–2 when Ortiz cleared the bases.

MAY 30   David McCarty hits a two-run, walk-off homer in the twelfth inning that beats the Mariners 9–7 at Fenway Park. Curt Schilling retired the first 17 batters he faced before the Mariners began knocking his pitches all over the lot. The Mariners took a 7–5 lead with six runs in the eighth inning. The Sox tied the game with two in their half.

MAY 31   The Red Sox drop out of first place with a 13–4 loss to the Orioles at Fenway Park.

The Sox never regained the top spot in the AL East in 2004. By August, Boston trailed the Yankees by 10½ games.

JUNE 2   Vladimir Guerrero drives in nine runs for the Angels in a 10–7 win over the Red Sox in Anaheim.

On the same day, with their first selection in the amateur draft, the Red Sox selected shortstop Dustin Pedroia from Arizona State University. Pedroia was chosen in the second round. The Sox had no first-round pick due to free-agent compensation. The first 2004 draftee to reach the majors was sixth-rounder Clay Meredith.

JUNE 8   Pedro Martinez (eight innings) and Kevin Foulke (one inning) combine on a two-hitter to defeat the Padres 1–0 at Fenway Park. It was the first time that the Padres played a game at Fenway Park. The only two San Diego hits were a single by Mark Loretta in the first inning and a double by Terrence Long in the fifth.

JUNE 10   Nomar Garciaparra plays in his first game of 2004, a 9–3 win over the Padres at Fenway Park.

Garciaparra missed the first 57 games with Achilles' tendinitis.

JUNE 11   David Ortiz hits a homer in the seventh inning and a walk-off single in the ninth to beat the Dodgers 2–1 at Fenway Park. It was the first time that the Dodgers played a regular-season game in Boston.

JUNE 15   The Red Sox play the Colorado Rockies in Denver for first time and lose, 6–3.

JUNE 17   The Red Sox wallop the Rockies 11–0 in Denver.

JUNE 18   The Red Sox play the Giants for the first time during the regular season and defeat them 14–9 in San Francisco. The Sox scored seven runs in the fifth inning.

JUNE 22   Nomar Garciaparra hits a grand slam off Joe Roa in the seventh inning of a 9–2 win over the Twins at Fenway Park.

On the same day, the Red Sox signed Curtis Leskanic, released by the Royals.

JUNE 25   The Red Sox beat the Phillies 12–1 at Fenway Park in a contest called after eight innings by rain. Pedro Martinez (seven innings) and Curtis Leskanic (one inning) combined on a two-hitter. Placido Polanco singled in the fourth inning, and Jim Thome homered in the seventh for the only two Philadelphia hits.

Martinez was 16–9 in 2004 with an ERA of 3.90.

JULY 3   Doug Mirabelli hits a grand slam in the sixth inning off John Thomson during a 6–1 win over the Braves in Atlanta.

JULY 6   Johnny Damon collects five hits in six at-bats during an 11–0 win over the Athletics in Oakland.

JULY 9   Johnny Damon hits two homers, a double, and a single in a 7–0 win over the Rangers at Fenway Park.

JULY 10   Manny Ramirez hits two of the Red Sox' five homers during a 14–6 win over the Rangers at Fenway Park. Nomar Garciaparra, Mark Bellhorn, and Jason Varitek also homered for Boston. The Sox collected 21 hits.

JULY 13   In the All-Star Game, Manny Ramirez and David Ortiz homer in the American League's 9–4 win at Minute Maid Park in Houston. Ramirez homered in the first inning against Roger Clemens with a runner on. Ortiz went deep off Carl Pavano with a runner on in the sixth.

JULY 16   David Ortiz draws a five-game suspension for a bat-throwing incident during a 4–2 win over the Angels in Anaheim. Ortiz was ejected after objecting to home-plate umpire Matt Hollowell's called third strike in the seventh inning. When he reached the dugout, Ortiz flung two bats toward home plate and nearly struck two other umpires standing on the first-base line.

JULY 19   Bronson Arroyo strikes out 12 batters in seven innings, but the bullpen blows a lead and the Red Sox lose 8–4 in 11 innings to the Mariners in Seattle. The game ended on a grand slam by Bret Boone off Curtis Leskanic.

JULY 20   The Red Sox score eight runs in the fourth inning and hang on to defeat the Mariners 9–7 in Seattle.

JULY 23   Kevin Millar hits three homers, but the Red Sox lose 8–7 to the Yankees at Fenway Park to fall 9 ½ games behind in the AL East race. Millar hit solo homers off Jon Lieber in the fourth inning, Paul Quantrill in the sixth, and Tom Gordon in the eighth. Millar's third homer tied the score, 7–7.

JULY 24   The Red Sox score three runs in the ninth off Mariano Rivera to defeat the Yankees 11–10 in a fight-filled game at Fenway Park. In the ninth, Nomar Garciaparra doubled and scored on Kevin Millar's single before Bill Mueller hit a two-run, walk-off homer. The Sox trailed 9–4 in the sixth before coming back.

            Alex Rodriguez, Kenny Lofton, Jason Varitek, and Gabe Kapler all were ejected during a third-inning brawl that started when Bronson Arroyo hit Rodriguez with a pitch. Rodriguez jawed at Arroyo while walking slowly to first. Varitek followed A-Rod and planted his gloved hand and bare hand in A-Rod's face. Both benches emptied, and fights erupted all over the field. Several players were treated for bruises and bloody scratches.

JULY 25   After presidential candidate John Kerry throws out the ceremonial first pitch in a nationally televised Sunday-night contest at Fenway Park, the Red Sox beat the Yankees, 9–6.

JULY 31   In a blockbuster four-team deal, the Red Sox send Nomar Garciaparra, Matt Murton, and cash to the Cubs and receive Orlando Cabrera from the Expos and Doug Mientkiewicz from the Twins. In another trade, the Sox sent Henri Stanley to the Dodgers for Dave Roberts.

Garciaparra was in the last year of his contract, and the Sox had doubts they could sign him. He had turned down the Sox' offer of sixty million dollars over four years the previous offseason. The Red Sox also were worried that with Garciaparra's injury history, signing him to a long-term deal was a risk.

AUGUST 1   In his first at-bat with the Red Sox, Orlando Cabrera hits a home run, but the Sox lose 4–3 to the Twins in Minneapolis.

AUGUST 6   The Red Sox reach the low point of the 2004 season with an 8–6 loss to the Tigers in Detroit.

Following the defeat, the Sox had a record of 58–49 and had gone 43–43 since the end of April. They were 10$\frac{1}{2}$ games behind the Yankees and two games back of the Rangers in the wild-card race. From August 7 through the end of the regular season, the Sox had a 40–15 record before going 11–4 in the postseason.

AUGUST 8   Tim Wakefield ties a modern major league record by allowing six home runs but winds up with the victory as the Red Sox outslug the Tigers 11–9 in Detroit. Wakefield allowed two homers to Ivan Rodriguez and one each to Eric Munson, Craig Monroe, Carlos Peña, and Dmitri Young. Wakefield left after five innings with a 10–7 lead. Later, Munson hit the seventh Tiger homer of the game against Mike Timlin.

Wakefield is one of only six pitchers since 1900 to allow six homers in a game and the only one since 1940.

AUGUST 11   The Red Sox lead 13–1 after three innings and cruise to a 14–4 win over the Devil Rays at Fenway Park.

AUGUST 20   Manny Ramirez hits a grand slam off Mark Buehrle in the second inning of a 10–1 win over the White Sox in Chicago.

AUGUST 31   Sixteen-year-old Lee Gavin is hit in the face by a Manny Ramirez foul ball during a 10–7 win over the Angels at Fenway Park. Gavin lost two teeth in the accident.

Gavin lived at 558 Dutton Road in suburban Sudbury, Massachusetts, in the very house where Babe Ruth resided from 1916 through 1926. The Red Sox hoped that the connection was an indication that the curse of the Bambino had been lifted. Stranger still, on the very same night, the Yankees lost 22–0 to the Indians to tie the record for the most lopsided shutout in modern major league history.

SEPTEMBER 3   The Red Sox extend their winning streak to 10 games with a 2–0 win over the Rangers at Fenway Park. It was also the Sox' 16th win in the last 17 games and their 22nd in the last 26.

The September 3 victory cut the Yankees' lead in the AL East to 2$\frac{1}{2}$ games and extended the Red Sox' advantage in the wild-card race to 4$\frac{1}{2}$ games.

SEPTEMBER 4   Mark Bellhorn hits a grand slam in the seventh inning off Ron Mahay, but the 10-game winning streak ends with an 8–6 loss to the Rangers at Fenway Park.

> *Novelist Stephen King threw out the ceremonial first pitch. It was filmed and used in the movie* Fever Pitch, *which starred Drew Barrymore and Jimmy Fallon and was released in April 2005. King himself wrote a book about the 2004 season with Stewart O'Nan called* Faithful: Two Diehard Boston Red Sox Fans Chronicle the Historic 2004 Season. *The cover used a photo of Jason Varitek shoving Alex Rodriguez in the face during a July game against the Yankees (see July 24, 2004). Published shortly after the World Series, it became, like most of King's books, a bestseller.*

SEPTEMBER 10   Manny Ramirez hits a grand slam off Aaron Taylor in the seventh inning of a 13–2 win over the Mariners in Seattle.

SEPTEMBER 16   Curt Schilling earns his 20th win of the season with an 11–4 decision over the Devil Rays at Fenway Park.

SEPTEMBER 17   The Red Sox score two runs in the ninth inning off Mariano Rivera on RBI singles by Orlando Cabrera and Johnny Damon to beat the Yankees 3–2 in New York. The win cut the Yankees' lead to 2 ½ games in the division with 16 contests left on the schedule. The Sox were ahead by 5 ½ games in the wild-card chase.

SEPTEMBER 18   The Yankees rout the Red Sox 14–4 in New York.

SEPTEMBER 19   The Red Sox' hopes of winning the AL East receive another jolt with an 11–1 loss to the Yankees in New York. The Sox were 4 ½ games behind the Yankees with 14 left to play, but they were 5 ½ games ahead in the wild-card race, which virtually ensured a place in the postseason.

SEPTEMBER 21   After the Orioles score two runs in the ninth to take a 2–1 lead, the Red Sox come roaring back with two in their half to win 3–2 at Fenway Park. Mark Bellhorn's two-run single ended the game. Curt Schilling struck out 14 batters in eight innings of shutout ball.

SEPTEMBER 22   Orlando Cabrera's walk-off homer leading off the twelfth inning beats the Orioles 7–6 at Fenway Park.

SEPTEMBER 24   The Yankees take a 5 ½-game lead in the AL East by defeating Pedro Martinez and the Red Sox 6–4 at Fenway Park.

> *After the game, Martinez lamented his inability to beat the Yankees. "What can I say?" Martinez said. "Just tip my hat and call the Yankees my daddy."*

SEPTEMBER 25   The Red Sox score seven runs in the eighth inning to break a 5–5 tie and beat the Yankees 12–5 at Fenway Park.

SEPTEMBER 27   The Red Sox clinch the wild-card berth with a 7–3 win over the Devil Rays in St. Petersburg. Benches emptied briefly in the fourth inning when Tampa Bay pitcher Scott Kazmir hit Manny Ramirez and Kevin Millar in a span of four pitches.

The contest was very nearly postponed because Hurricane Jeannie knocked out power in the Tampa Bay area.

OCTOBER 2   A pair of 7–5 wins against the Orioles in a doubleheader in Baltimore gives the Red Sox 98 wins for the first time since 1978. During the day, Ellis Burks played in his 2,000th, and final, major league game.

At 98–64, the Red Sox had the second-best record in the American League in 2004. Boston's opponent in the Division Series was the Anaheim Angels. Managed by Mike Scioscia, the AL West–champion Angels were 92–70.

OCTOBER 5   The Red Sox open the American League Division Series with a 9–3 win over the Angels in Anaheim. The Sox broke the game open with a seven-run fourth inning that gave the club an 8–0 lead. Kevin Millar hit a two-run homer, and Manny Ramirez connected for a three-run shot. Curt Schilling went 6⅔ innings for the win but aggravated his right ankle fielding a slow roller.

Schilling sustained a dislocated tendon. Surgery was necessary to permanently heal the tendon, but an operation would put Schilling out for the rest of the season. As a temporary measure, the Red Sox' medical staff sutured the tendon together before each of Schilling's remaining postseason starts. He also wore a specially made shoe that was a half size larger and contained extra foam padding.

OCTOBER 6   The Red Sox take a two-game lead in the Division Series with an 8–3 victory in Anaheim. The Sox trailed 3–1 before scoring two runs in the sixth inning, one in the seventh, and four in the eighth. In the sixth, Kevin Millar hit a two-out single, and Jason Varitek followed with a homer. A sacrifice fly by Manny Ramirez in the seventh put Boston ahead. Orlando Cabrera hit a three-run double in the ninth. Pedro Martinez went seven innings for the win.

OCTOBER 8   David Ortiz hits a two-run, walk-off homer in the tenth inning to give the Red Sox an 8–6 win and a sweep of the Angels before 35,547 at Fenway Park. Ortiz finished the day with two doubles and a single, in addition to the game-winning homer, in six at-bats. The Sox seemed to have the contest put away with a 6–1 lead before the Angels tied the game with a five-run seventh, four of them on Vladimir Guerrero's grand slam off Mike Timlin. In the game-winning tenth, Johnny Damon led off with a single off Felix Rodriguez. Mark Bellhorn grounded into a fielder's choice, and Manny Ramirez struck out. Mike Scioscia brought in southpaw Jarrod Washburn to face left-handed-hitting Ortiz, who responded with an opposite-field homer over the Green Monster on Washburn's first pitch.

The Red Sox moved on to the American League Championship Series against the Yankees. Managed by Joe Torre, the Yankees were the defending AL champs and posted a 101–61 record in 2004 while winning the AL East.

OCTOBER 12   The ALCS opens with a 10–7 Yankee win over the Red Sox in New York. Mike Mussina retired the first 19 batters to face him and had an 8–0 lead before the Sox showed incredible resiliency by erupting for five runs in the seventh and two in the eighth to close the gap to 8–7. The seventh-inning rally started with Mark Bellhorn's double. Curt Schilling, pitching with a dislocated tendon in his right ankle, lasted only three innings.

OCTOBER 13   The Red Sox drop Game Two to the Yankees 3–1 at Yankee Stadium. The lone Boston run scored in the eighth after the Yanks had built a 3–0 lead. Pedro Martinez was the losing pitcher. It was his third loss to the Yankees in a span of 25 days.

OCTOBER 15   Game Three of the American League Championship Series is postponed by rain.

OCTOBER 16   With a 19–8 pounding at the hands of the Yankees before 35,126 at Fenway Park, the Red Sox fall behind three games to none in the ALCS. The game was tied 6–6 at the end of three innings when the Yankees scored five in the fourth, two in the fifth, and four in the seventh to take a 17–6 lead. The Yankees had 22 hits in the game. Trot Nixon and Jason Varitek hit homers for the Sox. Orlando Cabrera had three hits, including two doubles. David Ortiz collected three singles.

> *The odds against the Red Sox seemed insurmountable. Previously, 26 major league teams had lost the first three games of a postseason series. None came back to win the series. In fact, none of the 26 even forced a seventh game. In addition, 74 NBA teams had trailed 0–3 in the postseason, and none won the series. There had been 142 NHL clubs down three games to none in the Stanley Cup playoffs, and just two came back to win four straight.*

October 15   The Red Sox stay alive with a thrilling 12-inning, 6–4 win over the Yankees before 35,120 at Fenway Park. The Sox trailed 2–0 before scoring three times in the fifth. David Ortiz put Boston ahead with a two-out, two-run single. The Yankees quickly got the lead back with a pair in the sixth. It was still 4–3 Yankees heading into the ninth with Mariano Rivera on the mound. Rivera entered the game with a 0.69 ERA in 104⅓ postseason innings. Kevin Millar led off the inning with a walk. Dave Roberts pinch-ran for Millar and stole second. Bill Mueller singled to score Roberts and tie the score. The Sox loaded the bases, but Ortiz popped out to end the inning. Ortiz made amends in the twelfth, however, by hitting a two-run, walk-off homer off Paul Quantrill on a 2–1 pitch with no outs. Manny Ramirez led off the inning with a single.

OCTOBER 18   David Ortiz provides a walk-off hit for the second night in a row, and the third in the 2004 postseason, to beat the Yankees 5–4 in 14 innings before 35,120 at Fenway Park. The Sox took a 2–0 lead in the first off Mike Mussina on an RBI single by Ortiz and a bases-loaded walk to Jason Varitek, but the Yankees took a 4–2 advantage with a run in the second and three in the sixth. It was still 4–2 heading into the eighth, and the Red Sox were six outs from elimination. Ortiz led off the inning with a homer off Tom Gordon. A walk to Kevin Millar, a single by Trot Nixon, and a sacrifice fly by Jason Varitek tied the score, 4–4. The game remained 4–4 until the fourteenth inning. Johnny Damon walked with one out, and Manny Ramirez drew a pass on a full count with two down. Ortiz followed with his game-winning hit. The game lasted a postseason-record five hours and 49 minutes.

October 19   The Red Sox even the series at three games apiece by defeating the Yankees 4–2 at Yankee Stadium. The game was scoreless when the Red Sox crossed the plate four times in the fourth. Jason Varitek singled in the first run, and Mark Bellhorn closed out the scoring with a three-run homer. Left field umpire Jim Joyce originally ruled Bellhorn's homer "in play." The ruling was overturned after Joyce conferred with the other five umpires, who saw the ball hit a spectator just beyond the outfield wall. A Yankee rally was cut short in the eighth when Alex Rodriguez was called out for interference by swatting the ball out of Bronson Arroyo's glove on a tag play on the first-base line. In a performance of true grit by pitching with his injured ankle, Curt Schilling went seven innings and allowed only one run on four hits.

OCTOBER 20   The Red Sox complete their incredible comeback over the Yankees and advance to the World Series by winning Game Seven 10–3 at Yankee Stadium. The Sox put the game away early. David Ortiz hit a two-run homer in the first off Kevin Brown, and Johnny Damon clouted a grand slam against Javier Vasquez in the second to put Boston ahead, 6–0. Damon also hit a two-run homer in the fourth facing Vasquez, and Mark Bellhorn homered in the eighth. Pitching on two days' rest, Derek Lowe allowed only one run and one hit in six innings.

The Red Sox played the St. Louis Cardinals in the World Series. Managed by Tony La Russa, the Cards were 105–57 in 2004.

OCTOBER 23   In Game One of the World Series, the Red Sox outslug the Cardinals 11–9 before 35,035 at Fenway Park. The Sox jumped out to a 4–0 lead in the first on David Ortiz's three-run homer and Bill Mueller's RBI single. After three innings, Boston led 7–2, but the Cards bounced back with three in the fourth and two in the sixth to tie the game, 7–7. The Sox went back on top in the seventh on RBI singles by Manny Ramirez and Ortiz. The Cards again tied the game with two in the eighth, with the help of two errors by Manny Ramirez, but Mark Bellhorn hit a two-run homer off the right field foul pole in the bottom of the inning for an 11–9 advantage, which held up when Kevin Foulke closed out the ninth.

Tim Wakefield became the first knuckleballer to start a World Series game since 1948, when rookie Gene Bearden helped the Cleveland Indians win the championship.

OCTOBER 24   The Red Sox win Game Two 6–2 over the Cardinals in front of a crowd of 35,001 at Fenway Park. The Sox scored two in the first on Jason Varitek's two-out triple and never trailed. Curt Schilling, who earlier in the day had all but ruled himself out of the start because of pain from the sutured tendon in his right ankle, decided to pitch just hours before the game and went on to allow just one unearned run in six innings. Alan Embree pitched the seventh and struck out the only three batters he faced.

The Red Sox won despite making four errors in each of the first two games.

OCTOBER 26   The Red Sox move within one game of a World Championship with a 4–1 victory over the Cardinals in St. Louis. Manny Ramirez homered in the first inning to put the Sox ahead, 1–0. The lone Cardinal run scored in the ninth. Pedro Martinez went seven innings and allowed no runs and only three hits. Two defensive plays keyed the win. In the first, Ramirez ended a bases-loaded, one-out jam by throwing out Larry Walker, who was trying to score after tagging up from third on Jim Edmonds's fly-ball out. In the third inning, with Cardinal pitcher Jeff Suppan on third and Edgar Renteria on second, Walker grounded to Mark Bellhorn, who threw to David Ortiz at first for the out. Suppan was caught between third and home on the play, and Ortiz threw a strike to Bill Mueller at third to get the pitcher as he dived back to the bag.

In terms of regular-season winning percentage, the Red Sox have played the best
NL teams of the 1960s (1967 Cardinals), 1970s (1975 Reds), 1980s (1986 Mets),
and 2000s (2004 Cardinals) in the World Series.

Steve Babineau

Since coming to the Red Sox from Cleveland in 2001, Manny Ramirez has anchored the offense
with both power and run production, making him one of the most feared hitters in team history.

OCTOBER 27   The Red Sox shut out the Cardinals 3–0 in St. Louis for their first World Championship since 1918. Johnny Damon led off the first with a homer. It was the fourth
game in a row that the Sox scored in the first. Trot Nixon provided a two-run double
on a 3–0 pitch in the third. The pitchers were Derek Lowe (seven innings), Bronson
Arroyo ((one-third of an inning), Alan Embree (two-thirds of an inning), and Kevin
Foulke (one inning). Lowe was the winning pitcher in the final game of all three 2004
postseason series. The final out came when Edgar Renteria hit a comebacker to
Foulke, who flipped to Doug Mientkiewicz at first base. The Red Sox were only the
fourth team to complete a World Series sweep without trailing in any of the four
games, joining the 1963 Dodgers, 1966 Orioles, and 1989 Athletics.

OCTOBER 30   The city of Boston celebrates its first World Championship baseball title since 1918 with
a huge parade. The Red Sox boarded the eclectic, brightly colored, amphibious World
War II–era vehicles known in Boston as "duck boats" and passed a cheering throng estimated at 3.2 million that jammed the rain-soaked streets and the banks of the Charles
River. On the final leg of the seven-mile parade, the duck boats slid into the water.

DECEMBER 14   Six weeks after Massachusetts Senator John Kerry loses the presidential election to
George Bush, the Red Sox sign David Wells, most recently with the Padres, as a
free agent.

Obsessed with Babe Ruth, Wells asked for and was given uniform number 3, which Ruth wore during his years with the Yankees. (Ruth wore no uniform number while with the Red Sox from 1914 through 1919. Numbers did not become a permanent part of major league uniforms until 1929.) Wells traded his number 3 to Edgar Renteria in late May 2005, however, and took number 16.

DECEMBER 16   Pedro Martinez signs as a free agent with the Mets.

DECEMBER 17   The Red Sox sign Edgar Renteria, most recently with the Cardinals, as a free agent.

DECEMBER 20   The Red Sox send Dave Roberts to the Padres for Jay Payton, Ramon Vasquez, David Pauley, and cash. On the same day, Orlando Cabrera signed with the Angels as a free agent.

DECEMBER 22   The Red Sox sign Matt Clement, most recently with the Cubs, as a free agent.

2 0 0 5   B

Season in a Sentence

Entering a season as defending champions for the first time in 86 years, the Red Sox spend most of the season in first place before entering the postseason as a wild card and losing in the first round.

Finish • Won • Lost • Pct • GB

First (tie)   95   67   .586   0

The Yankees and Red Sox had the same regular-season record, but the Yanks were declared AL East champions because New York had the better record (10–9) in head-to-head matchups. The Red Sox won the wild card by two games over the Indians.

AL Division Series—The Red Sox lost three games to none to the Chicago White Sox.

Manager

Terry Francona

Stats

Stats	Red Sox	AL	Rank
Batting Avg:	.281	.268	1
On-Base Pct:	.357	.330	1
Slugging Pct:	.454	.424	2
Home Runs:	199		5
Stolen Bases:	45		13
ERA:	4.74	4.35	11
Fielding Pct:	.982	.983	12
Runs Scored:	910		1
Runs Allowed:	805		11

Starting Lineup

Jason Varitek, c
Kevin Millar, 1b
Mark Bellhorn, 2b
Bill Mueller, 3b
Edgar Renteria, ss
Manny Ramirez, lf
Johnny Damon, cf
Trot Nixon, rf
Tony Graffanino, 2b
John Olerud, 1b

Pitchers

Tim Wakefield, sp
Bronson Arroyo, sp
David Wells, sp
Matt Clement, sp
Wade Miller, sp
Keith Foulke, rp
Mike Timlin, rp
Mike Myers, rp
Alan Embree, rp

Attendance

2,847,888 (third in AL)

Club Leaders

Batting Avg:	Damon	.316
On-Base Pct:	Ortiz	.397
Slugging Pct:	Ortiz	.604
Home Runs:	Ortiz	47
RBI:	Ortiz	148
Runs:	Damon	117
Stolen Bases:	Damon	18
Wins:	Wakefield	16
Strikeouts:	Wakefield	151
ERA:	Wakefield	4.15
Saves:	Foulke	15

JANUARY 11   Derek Lowe signs with the Dodgers as a free agent.

JANUARY 26   The Red Sox trade Doug Mientkiewicz to the Mets for Ian Bladergroen.

> *Mientkiewicz was traded amid a controversy over the ownership of the final
> ball used in the Game Four 2004 World Series victory. Mientkiewicz caught the
> final out and kept the ball. After he was dealt to the Mets, Mientkiewicz final-
> ized an agreement with the Red Sox to lend the club the baseball for one year.
> The ball joined the World Series trophy on a tour throughout New England.*

MARCH 2   A month after the Patriots win their third Super Bowl, the Red Sox visit the White
                  House to be honored by George Bush for their first World Series victory in 86 years.
                  A former owner of the Texas Rangers, Bush summed up the feelings of Red Sox
                  Nation by turning to the team and asking with a grin, "So, like, what took you so
                  long?" The audience of political dignitaries included Boston mayor Tom Menino and
                  Bush's 2004 presidential rival, John Kerry. To win the World Series, "it took a lot of
                  guts, and it took a lot of hair," Bush joked as Johnny Damon flipped his trademark
                  shaggy hair. Curt Schilling presented Bush with a Red Sox jersey that bore his name
                  and the number 43, signifying his status as the nation's 43rd president.

MARCH 23   The Red Sox announce that they will stay at Fenway Park for the foreseeable
                  future. The club had been petitioning city, county, and state legislators for a new
                  Fenway to be built just south of the old one since 1999. The decision came without
                  any conditions, though the club would like to see improvements made to the sur-
                  rounding neighborhood. "This is a no-strings-attached commitment," team presi-
                  dent Larry Lucchino said. Since buying the Red Sox in February 2002, the team's
                  owners made several upgrades and seat additions to Fenway. The Sox front office
                  said that it would still like to see improved streets and sidewalks around the ball-
                  park, one or more parking garages, and a new train station at Yawkey Way.

MARCH 30   The Red Sox trade Byung-Hyun Kim to the Rockies for Charles Johnson and Chris
                  Narveson. Johnson was promptly released.

APRIL 3   The defending World Champion Red Sox open the season on a Sunday night on a
                  game televised nationally on EPSN, and they lose to the Yankees 9–2 in New York.
                  David Wells had a rough debut with the Sox, allowing four runs in $4\frac{2}{3}$ innings.
                  The game-time temperature was a brisk forty-three degrees.

APRIL 8   Johnny Damon suffers a freak injury during a 6–5 win over the Blue Jays at the
                  Rogers Centre (formerly SkyDome) in Toronto. Damon gashed his left elbow on a
                  protruding screw on the LCD display on the outfield wall. He required six stitches
                  to close the wound and missed one game.

APRIL 11   The Red Sox open their home schedule with an 8–1 win over the Yankees before a
                  crowd of 33,702, Boston's 146th straight sellout. The Sox led 7–1 by the end of the
                  seventh inning. Tim Wakefield pitched seven innings for the win. Doug Mirabelli hit
                  a home run.

> *Before the game, the Red Sox raised their first World Championship pennant
> at Fenway Park since 1918. Helping to raise the flag were former Red Sox
> Dom DiMaggio, Johnny Pesky, Bobby Doerr, Frank Malzone, Ted Lepcio,*

Rico Petrocelli, Jim Lonborg, Luis Tiant, Bob Montgomery, Jerry Moses, Joe Morgan, Tommy Harper, Rick Miller, Rich Gale, Ken Ryan, Butch Hobson, Jim Corsi, Jim Rice, Sam Horn, Bruce Hurst, Rich Gedman, Bill Lee, Oil Can Boyd, Dennis Eckersley, Fred Lynn, Dwight Evans, and Carl Yastrzemski. The pregame ceremony started with the Boston Symphony Orchestra and Boston Pops in white dinner jackets behind second base playing Strauss' "Also Sprach Zarathustra," as championship banners from 1903, 1912, 1915, 1916, and 1918 dropped from the Green Monster. Wearing special gold-trimmed jerseys, the 2004 Red Sox players walked out one by one from the dugout to first base on a red carpet to receive their World Series rings. Veterans of the war in Iraq, some of them in wheelchairs, brought out the rings. First-pitch honors went to four other championship athletes from Boston: Bill Russell of the Celtics, Bobby Orr of the Bruins, and Richard Seymour and Tedy Bruschi of the Patriots.

APRIL 14 — Yankee right fielder Gary Sheffield has a run-in with a fan during an 8–5 Red Sox win at Fenway Park. In the eighth inning, Sheffield fielded a ball along the right field fence when a fan swung his arm in Sheffield's direction. Sheffield picked up the ball, then shoved the fan before throwing the ball back to the infield. He whirled around with a cocked fist but restrained himself. A security official quickly jumped over the three-foot fence and into the stands to separate the two. The fan, identified as Christopher House of Dorchester, Massachusetts, was ejected but not arrested. House had his season tickets revoked by the Red Sox four days later.

APRIL 15 — The Red Sox score seven runs in the second inning and thrash the Devil Rays 10–0 at Fenway Park. David Ortiz hit a grand slam in the big inning off Hideo Nomo.

Because of the Gary Sheffield incident the previous night, the Red Sox installed signs in the first rows around the ballpark reading: "Fans who attempt to interfere with balls in play will be ejected."

APRIL 16 — Manny Ramirez drives in all six Red Sox runs in a 6–1 victory over the Devil Rays at Fenway Park. Ramirez struck a two-run homer in the third inning and a grand slam in the fourth, both off Dewon Brazelton.

An addition to Fenway Park in 2005 was the display of the AL East standings on the left field wall.

APRIL 21 — Matt Clement (eight innings) and Keith Foulke (one inning) combine on a shutout to defeat the Orioles 1–0 in Baltimore.

APRIL 24 — Jay Payton hits a grand slam off Rob Bell in the eighth inning of a bean ball–filled 11–3 victory over the Devil Rays in St. Petersburg. There were six ejections, three from each team (including both managers), following a sequence of inside pitches and two bench-clearing scuffles. Manny Ramirez hit a homer in the seventh one pitch after ducking a high-and-inside ball from Lance Carter.

As a result of the brawl, the American League handed down suspensions to Terry Francona (three games), Bronson Arroyo (six games), and Trot Nixon (two games).

MAY 3 — Doug Mirabelli hits a grand slam off Mike Maroth in the fifth inning of a 5–3 win over the Tigers in Detroit.

MAY 5 — Bronson Arroyo carries a no-hitter into the seventh inning and defeats the Tigers 2–1 in Detroit. Overall, Arroyo allowed three hits in eight innings.

MAY 9 — The Red Sox score seven runs in the seventh inning of a 13–5 victory over the Athletics at Fenway Park.

MAY 10 — Kevin Millar hits a two-run, walk-off homer in the ninth off Octavio Dotel to defeat the Athletics 3–2 at Fenway Park. Millar atoned for two earlier errors that led to both Oakland runs.

MAY 11 — Jason Varitek hits a two-run, walk-off homer in the ninth off Octavio Dotel to defeat the Athletics 7–6 at Fenway Park. The Athletics took a 6–5 lead in the top of the inning on a two-run homer by Eric Byrnes off Kevin Foulke. It was the second day in a row that Dotel gave up a walk-off homer to the Sox. Both came with one out after walking a batter.

Varitek hit .281 with 22 homers in 2005.

MAY 14 — Trot Nixon hits a grand slam off J. J. Putz in the seventh inning of a 6–3 win over the Mariners in Seattle.

MAY 28 — The Red Sox collect 27 hits and crush the Yankees 17–1 in New York. The Sox scored seven runs in the fifth inning, in which Edgar Renteria hit a grand slam off Paul Quantrill. In his first game with the Red Sox, John Olerud picked up three hits.

JUNE 2 — David Ortiz hits a two-out, three-run, walk-off homer on a 3–2 pitch to defeat the Orioles 6–4 at Fenway Park.

Steve Babineau

Designated hitter David Ortiz's offense in 2005 propelled him to a close second-place finish behind A-Rod in MVP voting.

Ortiz batted .300 with 47 homers, 148 RBIs, and 119 runs scored in 2005. The 47 homers were the second most in Red Sox history, topped only by Jimmie Foxx's 50 in 1938. Ortiz's 148 RBIs were the most of any Boston batter since Ted Williams and Vern Stephens both had 159 in 1949. Manny Ramirez hit 45 homers in 2005, a figure that only Foxx, Ortiz, and Jim Rice have bested among Red Sox players. Rice hit 46 homers in 1978. Ramirez also batted .292 and had 144 RBIs and 112 runs scored in 2005.

JUNE 7
In a rematch of 2004 World Series opponents, the Red Sox lose 7–1 to the Cardinals in St. Louis. It was the first time that the Red Sox had played the Cardinals in St. Louis during the regular season. On the same day, in the first round of the amateur draft, the Red Sox select pitcher Craig Hansen from St. John's University in New York. Hansen pitched four games for the Sox during a late-season promotion to the majors.

JUNE 10
In a matchup of two of baseball's most storied and cursed franchises, the Red Sox play the Cubs for the first time during the regular season and lose 14–6 at Wrigley Field.

JUNE 12
Johnny Damon collects a homer, a triple, and a double during an 8–1 win over the Cubs in Chicago.

JUNE 13
The Reds Sox play the Reds for the first time during the regular season and win 10–3 at Fenway Park.

JUNE 14
David Wells (seven innings), Mike Timlin (one inning), and Kevin Foulke (one inning) combine on a one-hitter to defeat the Reds 7–0 at Fenway Park. Ryan Freel had the only Cincinnati hit, a single in the sixth inning.

JUNE 17
The Red Sox play the Pirates for the first time at Fenway Park and win 6–5 on a walk-off single by Johnny Damon in the ninth inning.

JUNE 24
The Red Sox pass the Orioles to take first place with an 8–0 win over the Phillies in Philadelphia. It was the first time that the Sox had played a game at Citizens Bank Park.

JUNE 26
Manny Ramirez hits a grand slam off Brett Myers in the fourth inning of a 12–8 win over the Phillies in Philadelphia. The slam gave the Sox a 7–0 lead, which they managed to fritter away. The Phils tied the score 8–8 with three runs in the seventh before Boston scored four times in the eighth.

JULY 2
David Wells is ejected by second-base umpire Chris Guccione during the seventh inning of a 6–4 win over the Blue Jays at Fenway Park. Wells turned his back to home plate and waved his glove in apparent disgust after allowing a single to Shea Hillenbrand. After being thrown out, Wells walked toward Guccione and the pair screamed at each other brim to brim. Wells was suspended for six days for making contact with Guccione and with umpire Angel Hernandez, who came over to settle things down.

JULY 5
Manny Ramirez hits a grand slam off Chris Young in the third inning of a 7–4 win over the rangers in Arlington.

Ramirez's slam was the 20th of his career, good enough for second on the career list behind Lou Gehrig's 23.

July 10   Three Red Sox fans win a raffle for the same jewelry-encrusted World Series rings that Sox players earned for the team's first championship in 86 years. The ten-dollar raffle tickets raised nearly two million dollars for the charitable Red Sox Foundation. The 18-karat white-gold rings were valued at fifteen thousand dollars.

July 12   Terry Francona manages the American League to a 7–5 win in the All-Star Game at Comerica Park in Detroit. David Ortiz collected two singles in three at-bats and drove in a run.

July 13   The Red Sox trade Jay Payton to the Athletics for Chad Bradford. The deal was made a week after Payton had a verbal confrontation with Terry Francona in the dugout during a game. Payton had been griping about a lack of playing time all season.

July 15   Playing at Fenway Park, the Red Sox defeat the Yankees 17–1 for the second time in 2005, duplicating their May 28 feat. David Ortiz hit a grand slam off Buddy Groom in the fifth inning.

July 17   Second baseman Mark Bellhorn injures his left thumb on a line drive by Jason Giambi in a 5–3 loss to the Yankees at Fenway Park. The injury put Bellhorn on the DL, and he hadn't played another game when the Red Sox designated him for assignment barely a month later (see August 19, 2005).

July 18   The Red Sox are knocked out of first place with a 3–1 loss to the Devil Rays at Fenway Park. Johnny Damon's 29-game hitting streak came to end when he went hitless in five at-bats.

July 19   In his new role as closer, Curt Schilling earns his first save since 1992 with a scoreless ninth inning during a 5–2 win over the Devil Rays at Fenway Park. The win put the Red Sox back into first place.

July 20   The Red Sox win 6–5 over the White Sox in Chicago on a tie-breaking home run by Manny Ramirez in the ninth inning. On the previous pitch, third baseman Joe Crede had dropped Ramirez's pop foul.

            The Red Sox picked up second baseman Tony Graffanino from Kansas City for Juan Cedeño and Chip Ambres.

July 26   The Red Sox score two runs in the ninth inning and two in the tenth to take a 10–8 lead as they defeat the Devil Rays 10–9 in St. Petersburg. Johnny Damon homered in the tenth.

            Matt Clement survived a scare in the third inning when he was hit behind the right ear by a line drive from Carl Crawford. Clement was placed in a neck brace and taken off the field on a stretcher. Fortunately, he was back on the mound nine days later.

July 29   John Olerud hits a grand slam off J. C. Romero in the eighth inning of an 8–3 win over the Twins at Fenway Park.

| JULY 31 | Manny Ramirez delivers a pinch-single in the eighth inning for the deciding run in a 4–3 win over the Twins at Fenway Park. |

Ramirez wasn't in the starting lineup for either the July 30 or 31 contests after demanding to be traded earlier in the week. He went to Red Sox officials on the morning of July 31 and said that he wanted to stay in Boston. His game-winning hit came 54 minutes after the trade deadline.

| AUGUST 4 | Down 5–1, the Red Sox score eight times in the fourth inning and defeat the Royals 11–9 at Fenway Park. The eight runs scored on only two hits, one of them Jason Varitek's grand slam. |

| AUGUST 9 | The Red Sox send Olivo Astacio and cash to the Cubs for Mike Remlinger. |

| AUGUST 10 | The Red Sox explode for nine runs in the eighth inning and wallop the Rangers 16–5 at Fenway Park. |

| AUGUST 11 | David Ortiz hits two homers, a double, and a single, drives in six runs, and scores three during a 9–8 win over the White Sox at Fenway Park. He put the Red Sox ahead for good by breaking a 5–5 tie with a solo homer in the seventh. |

| AUGUST 16 | The Red Sox erupt for seven runs in the tenth inning and withstand a grand slam by Craig Monroe of the Tigers in the bottom half to win 10–7 in Detroit. David Ortiz and Jason Varitek each homered twice in the contest. Varitek homered from both sides of the plate. He hit home runs off left-hander Nate Robertson in the second inning and right-hander Franklyn German in the tenth. |

| AUGUST 19 | The Red Sox designate Mark Bellhorn for assignment. The move came with Bellhorn in a deep slump, batting .116 in July with 23 strikeouts in 13 games, before he injured his left thumb in a July 17 game against the Yankees. The oft-whiffing second baseman signed with the Yankees on August 30, joining former teammate Alan Embree. Bellhorn had 109 strikeouts in 85 games with the Red Sox in 2005. |

| AUGUST 26 | The Red Sox' game against the Tigers at Fenway Park is delayed 65 minutes because of a Rolling Stones concert held at the ballpark five days earlier. The grounds crew needed time to replace 40,000 square feet of sod destroyed by the concert stage. The Sox won, 9–8. |

| AUGUST 30 | The day after Hurricane Katrina devastates New Orleans and the Gulf Coast, the Red Sox rally to beat the Devil Rays 7–6 at Fenway Park after trailing, 5–0. Trot Nixon broke the 6–6 tie by stroking a walk-off single with two outs in the ninth inning. |

| SEPTEMBER 1 | John Olerud homers twice and drives in six runs during a 7–4 win over the Devil Rays at Fenway Park. |

| SEPTEMBER 6 | A walk-off homer by David Ortiz in the ninth inning beats the Angels 3–2 at Fenway Park. |

| SEPTEMBER 16 | In the tenth inning, Manny Ramirez gets hit by a pitch with the bases loaded, which beats the Athletics 3–2 at Fenway Park. |

On the same day, six police officers involved in a fatal pellet-gun shooting on October 21, 2004, were suspended, demoted, or reprimanded. On that day, during a celebration of the Red Sox' ALCS win over the Yankees outside Fenway Park, an officer killed twenty-one-year-old Victoria Snelgrove by firing a pepper-spray pellet gun at a reveler who was throwing objects at police. He missed his intended target and hit Snelgrove in the eye socket instead. The city settled with the Snelgrove family for $5.1 million in May 2005.

SEPTEMBER 20   The Red Sox collect 21 hits and hammer the Devil Rays 15–2 in St. Petersburg. David Ortiz, Manny Ramirez, Trot Nixon, and Jason Varitek each had four hits to tie a major league record for most players with four or more hits in a game. Ortiz and Ramirez also had two homers each, and Nixon hit one.

SEPTEMBER 28   The Red Sox lose 7–2 to the Blue Jays at Fenway Park to fall one game behind the Yankees in the AL East race. The Sox were tied with the Indians in the wild-card race. Each team had four games left on the schedule.

SEPTEMBER 29   The Red Sox keep their playoff hopes alive with a come-from-behind 5–4 win over the Blue Jays at Fenway Park. The Sox trailed 4–1 before Manny Ramirez hit a two-run homer in the sixth inning. David Ortiz drove in the tying run with a homer in the eighth and the winning run with a walk-off single in the ninth.

SEPTEMBER 30   The Red Sox move into a first-place tie in the AL East with a 5–3 victory over the Yankees at Fenway Park. Both teams had 94–66 records. The Indians lost to the White Sox 3–2 in 13 innings in Cleveland to fall one game behind both clubs in the wild-card chase.

OCTOBER 1   The Yankees clinch the AL East title with an 8–4 win over the Red Sox at Fenway Park. Although the Red Sox still had a chance to tie the Yankees for the best record in the division with a win on October 2, the final day of the regular season, the Yankees were declared champions based on their better record in head-to-head matchups. The Yankees won 10 of the 19 meetings. Heading into the final day, the Red Sox led the Indians by one game in the wild-card race.

OCTOBER 2   The Red Sox clinch the wild-card berth in the playoffs with a 10–1 triumph over the Yankees at Fenway Park. Both the Yankees and Red Sox finished the season 95–67.

The Red Sox met the White Sox in the American League Division Series. Managed by Ozzie Guillen, the White Sox were 99–63 in 2005 and beat out the Indians by six games in the AL Central race.

OCTOBER 4   The White Sox rout the Red Sox 14–2 at U. S. Cellular Field in Chicago in Game One of the Division Series. The White Sox got things rolling in a hurry with five runs in the first inning off Matt Clement.

OCTOBER 5   The Red Sox blow a 4–0 lead and lose 5–4 to the White Sox to lose Game Two of the Division Series in Chicago. Boston scored two runs in the first inning and two more in the third, but the White Sox rallied with five in the fifth off David Wells. With the score 4–2 and one out in the fifth, Red Sox second baseman Tony Graffanino let a potential double-play grounder roll through his legs for an error.

One out later, Tadahito Iguchi hit a three-run homer to give Chicago the lead and eventually the win.

OCTOBER 7   The White Sox complete a three-game sweep of the Red Sox with a 5–3 win before 35,496 at Fenway Park. David Ortiz and Manny Ramirez hit back-to-back homers off Freddy Garcia in the fourth to tie the score, 2–2. Chicago broke the deadlock with two runs in the top of the sixth. In the bottom half, Ramirez homered again to make the score 4–3, and later in the inning, the Red Sox had the bases loaded with no outs but failed to score.

On the same day, former Red Sox player Nomar Garciaparra and his uncle Victor Garciaparra rescued two women who had fallen into Boston Harbor. Garciaparra was in his Charleston condominium with his uncle when they heard a scream and a splash. The two swam toward the women, one of whom appeared to be unconscious, and brought them to shore.

OCTOBER 31   Theo Epstein shocks the Red Sox by resigning as general manager. Epstein was twenty-eight, at the time the youngest general manager in baseball history, when the Red Sox hired him in March 2002. His crowning achievement was putting together the club that won the 2004 World Series.

NOVEMBER 14   The Baseball Writers Association of America announces the results for 2005 MVP voting, and David Ortiz finishes a close second to Yankee star Alex Rodriguez, who also won the award in 2003. Rodriguez cited his play at third base: "Defense—for the most part, being a balanced player and saving a lot of runs on the defensive side—was a major factor," he said. Red Sox president and CEO Larry Lucchino had a different perspective: "I cannot imagine a player having a bigger impact on a team than David Ortiz had on ours in 2005," he said. "I think that is, or should be, the definition of the MVP."

NOVEMBER 23   The Red Sox trade Hanley Ramirez, Anibal Sanchez, Jesus Delgado, and Harvey Garcia to the Marlins for Josh Beckett, Mike Lowell, and Guillermo Mota.

DECEMBER 5   The Red Sox sign Deivi Cruz, most recently with the Nationals, as a free agent.

DECEMBER 7   The Red Sox trade Doug Mirabelli to the Padres for Mark Loretta.

DECEMBER 8   The Red Sox trade Edgar Renteria and cash to the Braves for Andy Marte.

DECEMBER 12   The Red Sox name Ben Cherington and Jed Hoyer as co-general managers, replacing Theo Epstein, who resigned on October 31, 2005. Cherington had been the farm director and Hoyer the assistant general manager.

DECEMBER 20   Johnny Damon agrees to a four-year, $52 million contract with the Yankees.

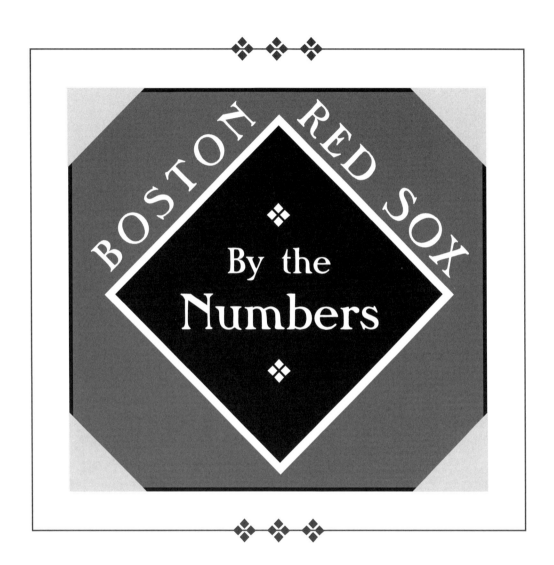

BOSTON RED SOX

By the
Numbers

Red Sox All-Time Offensive Leaders 1901–2005

Games

1	Carl Yastrzemski	3,308
2	Dwight Evans	2,505
3	Ted Williams	2,292
4	Jim Rice	2,089
5	Bobby Doerr	1,865
6	Harry Hooper	1,646
7	Wade Boggs	1,625
8	Rico Petrocelli	1,553
9	Dom DiMaggio	1,399
10	Frank Malzone	1,359
11	Mike Greenwell	1,269
12	George Scott	1,192
13	Duffy Lewis	1,184
14	Billy Goodman	1,177
15	Joe Cronin	1,134
16	Larry Gardner	1,122
17	Rick Miller	1,101
18	Everett Scott	1,096
19	Carlton Fisk	1,078
20	Tris Speaker	1,065

Runs

1	Carl Yastrzemski	1,816
2	Ted Williams	1,798
3	Dwight Evans	1,435
4	Jim Rice	1,249
5	Bobby Doerr	1,094
6	Wade Boggs	1,067
7	Dom DiMaggio	1,046
8	Harry Hooper	988
9	Johnny Pesky	776
10	Jimmie Foxx	721
11	Nomar Garciaparra	711
12	Tris Speaker	704
13	Billy Goodman	688
14	Mike Greenwell	657
15	Rico Petrocelli	653
16	Joe Cronin	646
17	Frank Malzone	641
18	Mo Vaughn	628
19	Carlton Fisk	627
20	Jackie Jensen	592

At-Bats

1	Carl Yastrzemski	11,988
2	Dwight Evans	8,726
3	Jim Rice	8,225
4	Ted Williams	7,706
5	Bobby Doerr	7,093
6	Harry Hooper	6,270
7	Wade Boggs	6,213
8	Dom DiMaggio	5,640
9	Rico Petrocelli	5,390
10	Frank Malzone	5,273
11	Mike Greenwell	4,623
12	Billy Goodman	4,399
13	Duffy Lewis	4,325
14	George Scott	4,234
15	Johnny Pesky	4,085
16	Rick Burleson	4,084
17	Nomar Garciaparra	3,968
18	Tris Speaker	3,935
19	Larry Gardner	3,915
20	Joe Cronin	3,882

Ted Williams

Courtesy of Transcendental Graphics/theruckerarchive.com

Hits

1	Carl Yastrzemski	3,416
2	Ted Williams	2,654
3	Jim Rice	2,452
4	Dwight Evans	2,373
5	Wade Boggs	2,098
6	Bobby Doerr	2,042
7	Harry Hooper	1,707
8	Dom DiMaggio	1,680
9	Frank Malzone	1,454
10	Mike Greenwell	1,400
11	Rico Petrocelli	1,352
12	Billy Goodman	1,344
13	Tris Speaker	1,327
14	Nomar Garciaparra	1,281
15	Johnny Pesky	1,277
16	Duffy Lewis	1,248
17	Joe Cronin	1,168
18	Mo Vaughn	1,165
19	Rick Burleson	1,114
20	Larry Gardner	1,106

Triples

1	Harry Hooper	130
2	Tris Speaker	106
3	Buck Freeman	90
4	Bobby Doerr	89
5	Larry Gardner	87
6	Jim Rice	79
7	Hobe Ferris	77
8	Dwight Evans	72
9	Ted Williams	71
10	Jimmy Collins	65
11	Freddy Parent	63
12	Chick Stahl	62
	Duffy Lewis	62
14	Carl Yastrzemski	59
15	Dom DiMaggio	57
16	Phil Todt	56
17	Jake Stahl	50
	Nomar Garciaparra	50
19	Heinie Wagner	47
	Wade Boggs	47

Doubles

1	Carl Yastrzemski	646
2	Ted Williams	525
3	Dwight Evans	474
4	Wade Boggs	422
5	Bobby Doerr	381
6	Jim Rice	373
7	Dom DiMaggio	308
8	Nomar Garciaparra	279
9	Mike Greenwell	275
10	Joe Cronin	270
11	John Valentin	266
12	Duffy Lewis	254
13	Billy Goodman	248
14	Harry Hooper	246
15	Tris Speaker	241
16	Rico Petrocelli	237
17	Frank Malzone	234
18	Fred Lynn	217
19	Jason Varitek	212
20	Carlton Fisk	207

Home Runs

1	Ted Williams	521
2	Carl Yastrzemski	452
3	Jim Rice	382
4	Dwight Evans	379
5	Mo Vaughn	230
6	Bobby Doerr	223
7	Jimmie Foxx	222
8	Rico Petrocelli	210
9	Manny Ramirez	199
10	Nomar Garciaparra	178
11	Jackie Jensen	170
12	Tony Conigliaro	162
	Carlton Fisk	162
14	George Scott	154
15	Reggie Smith	149
16	Frank Malzone	131
17	Mike Greenwell	130
18	Trot Nixon	125
19	Fred Lynn	124
20	Vern Stephens	122

RBIs

1	Carl Yastrzemski	1,844
2	Ted Williams	1,839
3	Jim Rice	1,451
4	Dwight Evans	1,346
5	Bobby Doerr	1,247
6	Jimmie Foxx	778
7	Rico Petrocelli	773
8	Mo Vaughn	752
9	Joe Cronin	737
10	Jackie Jensen	733
11	Mike Greenwell	726
12	Frank Malzone	716
13	Nomar Garciaparra	690
14	Wade Boggs	687
15	Duffy Lewis	629
16	Dom DiMaggio	618
17	Manny Ramirez	610
18	Carlton Fisk	568
19	Vern Stephens	562
	George Scott	562

Strikeouts

1	Dwight Evans	1,643
2	Carl Yastrzemski	1,423
3	Dwight Evans	1,393
4	Mo Vaughn	954
5	Rico Petrocelli	926
6	George Scott	850
7	Ted Williams	709
8	Jason Varitek	693
9	Bobby Doerr	608
10	Carlton Fisk	588
11	Tony Conigliaro	577
12	Dom DiMaggio	571
13	Manny Ramirez	570
14	Jimmie Foxx	568
15	Trot Nixon	565
16	Reggie Smith	498
17	Butch Hobson	495
18	John Valentin	487
19	Wade Boggs	470
20	Ellis Burks	458

Walks

1	Ted Williams	2,019
2	Carl Yastrzemski	1,845
3	Dwight Evans	1,337
4	Wade Boggs	1,004
5	Harry Hooper	826
6	Bobby Doerr	809
7	Dom DiMaggio	750
8	Jim Rice	670
9	Rico Petrocelli	661
10	Jimmie Foxx	624
11	Joe Cronin	585
	Jackie Jensen	585
13	Johnny Pesky	581
14	Billy Goodman	561
15	Mo Vaughn	519
16	Mike Greenwell	460
17	Tris Speaker	459
18	John Valentin	441
19	Reggie Smith	425
20	George Scott	418

Stolen Bases

1	Harry Hooper	300
2	Tris Speaker	267
3	Carl Yastrzemski	168
4	Heinie Wagner	141
5	Larry Gardner	134
6	Freddy Parent	129
7	Bill Werber	107
	Tommy Harper	107
9	Chick Stahl	105
10	Jimmy Collins	102
	Chick Stahl	102
12	Dom DiMaggio	100
13	Jerry Remy	98
	Johnny Damon	98
15	Jackie Jensen	95
	Ellis Burks	95
17	Reggie Smith	84
	Nomar Garciaparra	84
19	Clyde Engle	80
	Mike Greenwell	80

Batting Average

(minimum 2,000 plate appearances)

1	Ted Williams	.344
2	Wade Boggs	.338
3	Tris Speaker	.337
4	Nomar Garciaparra	.323
5	Pete Runnels	.320
6	Jimmie Foxx	.320
7	Manny Ramirez	.315
8	Roy Johnson	.313
9	Johnny Pesky	.313
10	Fred Lynn	.308
11	Billy Goodman	.306
12	Mo Vaughn	.304
13	Mike Greenwell	.303
14	Doc Cramer	.302
15	Rick Ferrell	.302
16	Lou Finney	.301
17	Joe Cronin	.300
18	Jim Rice	.298
19	Dom DiMaggio	.298
20	Jimmy Collins	.296

Slugging Percentage

(minimum 2,000 plate appearances)

1	Ted Williams	.634
2	Manny Ramirez	.608
3	Jimmie Foxx	.605
4	Nomar Garciaparra	.553
5	Mo Vaughn	.542
6	Fred Lynn	.520
7	Jim Rice	.502
8	Vern Stephens	.492
9	Trot Nixon	.489
10	Tony Conigliaro	.488
11	Joe Cronin	.484
12	Tris Speaker	.482
13	Carlton Fisk	.481
14	Tony Armas	.480
15	Jackie Jensen	.478
16	Dwight Evans	.473
17	Reggie Smith	.471
18	Mike Greenwell	.463
19	Wade Boggs	.462
20	Carl Yastrzemski	.462

On-Base Percentage

(minimum 2,000 plate appearances)

1	Ted Williams	.482
2	Jimmie Foxx	.429
3	Wade Boggs	.428
4	Tris Speaker	.414
5	Manny Ramirez	.413
6	Pete Runnels	.408
7	Johnny Pesky	.401
8	Joe Cronin	.394
9	Rick Ferrell	.394
10	Mo Vaughn	.394
11	Roy Johnson	.387
12	Billy Goodman	.386
13	Dom DiMaggio	.383
14	Fred Lynn	.383
15	Carl Yastrzemski	.379
16	Jackie Jensen	.374
17	Ira Flagstead	.374
18	Nomar Garciaparra	.370
19	Dwight Evans	.369
20	Mike Greenwell	.368

Red Sox All-Time Pitching Leaders 1901–2005

Wins

1	Cy Young	192
	Roger Clemens	192
3	Tim Wakefield	130
4	Mel Parnell	123
5	Luis Tiant	122
6	Pedro Martinez	117
7	Smoky Joe Wood	116
8	Bob Stanley	115
9	Joe Dobson	106
10	Lefty Grove	105
11	Tex Hughson	96
	Bill Monbouquette	96
13	Bill Lee	94
14	Tom Brewer	91
15	Dutch Leonard	90
	Frank Sullivan	90
17	Babe Ruth	89
18	Bruce Hurst	88
	Dennis Eckersley	88
20	Ellis Kinder	86

Winning Percentage

(minimum 100 decisions)

1	Pedro Martinez	.760
2	Smoky Joe Wood	.674
3	Babe Ruth	.659
4	Tex Hughson	.640
5	Roger Clemens	.634
6	Cy Young	.632
7	Lefty Grove	.629
8	Ellis Kinder	.623
9	Mel Parnell	.621
10	Jesse Tannehill	.620
11	Wes Ferrell	.608
12	Luis Tiant	.601
13	Joe Dobson	.596
14	Dutch Leonard	.588
15	Carl Mays	.585
16	Bill Lee	.580
17	Ray Collins	.575
18	Derek Lowe	.560
19	Dennis Eckersley	.553
20	Ray Culp	.550

Losses

1	Tim Wakefield	113
2	Cy Young	112
3	Roger Clemens	111
4	George Winter	97
5	Bob Stanley	97
6	Red Ruffing	96
7	Jack Russell	94
8	Bill Monbouquette	91
9	Bill Dinneen	85
10	Tom Brewer	82
11	Luis Tiant	81
12	Frank Sullivan	80
13	Danny MacFayden	78
14	Mel Parnell	75
15	Bruce Hurst	73
16	Joe Dobson	72
	Willard Nixon	72
	Ike Delock	72
19	Dennis Eckersley	71
20	Bill Lee	68

Games

1	Bob Stanley	637
2	Tim Wakefield	420
3	Derek Lowe	384
4	Roger Clemens	383
5	Ellis Kinder	365
6	Cy Young	327
7	Ike Delock	322
8	Bill Lee	321
9	Mel Parnell	289
10	Greg Harris	287
11	Mike Fornieles	286
	Dick Radatz	286
13	Luis Tiant	274
14	Rich Garces	261
15	Sparky Lyle	260
16	Joe Dobson	259
17	Jack Wilson	258
18	Bill Monbouquette	254
19	Frank Sullivan	252
20	Jack Russell	242

Games Started

1	Roger Clemens	382
2	Cy Young	297
3	Tim Wakefield	283
4	Luis Tiant	238
5	Mel Parnell	232
6	Bill Monbouquette	228
7	Tom Brewer	217
	Bruce Hurst	217
9	Joe Dobson	202
10	Frank Sullivan	201
	Pedro Martinez	201
12	Dennis Eckersley	191
13	Lefty Grove	190
14	Willard Nixon	177
15	George Winter	176
16	Bill Dinneen	174
17	Bill Lee	167
18	Jim Lonborg	163
19	Dutch Leonard	160
20	Smoky Joe Wood	157
	Mike Torrez	157

Shutouts

1	Cy Young	38
	Roger Clemens	38
3	Smoky Joe Wood	28
4	Luis Tiant	26
5	Dutch Leonard	25
6	Mel Parnell	20
7	Ray Collins	19
	Tex Hughson	19
9	Sad Sam Jones	18
10	Babe Ruth	17
	Joe Dobson	17
12	Bill Dinneen	16
	Bill Monbouquette	16
14	Rube Foster	15
	Lefty Grove	15
16	Jesse Tannehill	14
	Carl Mays	14
	Frank Sullivan	14
19	Four tied at	13

Complete Games

1	Cy Young	275
2	Bill Dinneen	156
3	George Winter	141
4	Smoky Joe Wood	121
5	Lefty Grove	119
6	Mel Parnell	113
	Luis Tiant	113
8	Babe Ruth	105
9	Roger Clemens	100
10	Tex Hughson	99
11	Dutch Leonard	95
12	Ray Collins	90
	Joe Dobson	90
14	Carl Mays	87
15	Jesse Tannehill	85
16	Howard Ehmke	83
17	Sad Sam Jones	82
18	Wes Ferrell	81
19	Tom Brewer	75
20	Red Ruffing	73

Courtesy of Transcendental Graphics/theruckerarchive.com

Cy Young

Innings Pitched

1	Roger Clemens	2,776.0
2	Cy Young	2,728.1
3	Tim Wakefield	2,071.2
4	Luis Tiant	1,774.2
5	Mel Parnell	1,752.2
6	Bob Stanley	1,707.0
7	Bill Monbouquette	1,622.0
8	George Winter	1,599.2
9	Joe Dobson	1,544.0
10	Lefty Grove	1,539.2
11	Tom Brewer	1,509.1
12	Frank Sullivan	1,505.1
13	Bill Lee	1,503.1
14	Bill Dinneen	1,501.0
15	Bruce Hurst	1,459.0
16	Smoky Joe Wood	1,418.0
17	Pedro Martinez	1,383.2
18	Tex Hughson	1,375.2
19	Dennis Eckersley	1,371.2
20	Dutch Leonard	1,361.1

Strikeouts

1	Roger Clemens	2,590
2	Pedro Martinez	1,683
3	Tim Wakefield	1,480
4	Cy Young	1,341
5	Luis Tiant	1,075
6	Bruce Hurst	1,043
7	Smoky Joe Wood	986
8	Bill Monbouquette	969
9	Frank Sullivan	821
10	Ray Culp	794
11	Jim Lonborg	784
12	Dutch Leonard	771
	Dennis Eckersley	771
14	Lefty Grove	742
15	Tom Brewer	733
16	Mel Parnell	732
17	Earl Wilson	714
18	Tex Hughson	693
	Bob Stanley	693
20	Joe Dobson	690

Walks

1	Roger Clemens	856
2	Tim Wakefield	787
3	Mel Parnell	758
4	Tom Brewer	669
5	Joe Dobson	604
6	Jack Wilson	564
7	Willard Nixon	530
8	Ike Delock	514
9	Mickey McDermott	504
10	Luis Tiant	501
11	Fritz Ostermueller	491
12	Earl Wilson	481
13	Bruce Hurst	479
14	Frank Sullivan	475
15	Bob Stanley	471
16	Red Ruffing	459
17	Bill Lee	448
18	Lefty Grove	447
19	Danny MacFayden	430
20	Babe Ruth	425

Strikeouts/9 Innings

(minimum 1,000 innings pitched)

1	Pedro Martinez	10.95
2	Roger Clemens	8.40
3	Ray Culp	6.54
4	Bruce Hurst	6.43
5	Tim Wakefield	6.43
6	Jim Lonborg	6.42
7	Earl Wilson	6.27
8	Smoky Joe Wood	6.26
9	Derek Lowe	5.86
10	Luis Tiant	5.45
11	Bill Monbouquette	5.38
12	Dutch Leonard	5.10
13	Dennis Eckersley	5.06
14	Oil Can Boyd	5.05
15	Ike Delock	4.93
16	Frank Sullivan	4.91
17	Jack Wilson	4.75
18	Tex Hughson	4.53
19	Willard Nixon	4.49
20	Cy Young	4.42

ERA			Saves	
(minimum 1,000 innings pitched)			1 Bob Stanley	132
1 Smoky Joe Wood	1.99		2 Dick Radatz	104
2 Cy Young	2.00		3 Ellis Kinder	91
3 Dutch Leonard	2.14		4 Jeff Reardon	88
4 Babe Ruth	2.19		5 Derek Lowe	85
5 Carl Mays	2.21		6 Sparky Lyle	69
6 Pedro Martinez	2.52		7 Tom Gordon	68
7 Ray Collins	2.53		8 Lee Smith	58
8 Bill Dinneen	2.81		9 Bill Campbell	51
9 George Winter	2.91		10 Ugueth Urbina	49
10 Tex Hughson	2.94		11 Mike Fornieles	48
11 Roger Clemens	3.06		Heathcliff Slocumb	48
12 Ellis Kinder	3.28		13 Keith Foulke	47
13 Lefty Grove	3.34		14 Jeff Russell	45
14 Luis Tiant	3.36		15 Dick Drago	41
15 Sad Sam Jones	3.39		16 Tom Burgmeier	40
16 Frank Sullivan	3.47		17 Mark Clear	38
17 Ray Culp	3.50		18 Ike Delock	31
18 Mel Parnell	3.50		19 Leo Kiely	28
19 Joe Dobson	3.57		John Wyatt	28
20 Bob Stanley	3.64		Bobby Bolin	28

Red Sox All-Time Roster 1901–2005

A		B	
Aase, Don	1977	Bader, Loren	1917–18
Abad, Andy	2003	Baerga, Carlos	2002
Adair, Jerry	1967–68	Bagby, Jim, Jr.	1938–40, 1946
Adams, Bob	1925	Bailey, Bob	1977–78
Adams, Terry	2004	Bailey, Cory	1993–94
Adkins, Doc	1902	Bailey, Gene	1920
Agbayani, Benny	2002	Baker, Al	1938
Agganis, Harry	1954–55	Baker, Floyd	1953–54
Agnew, Sam	1916–18	Baker, Jack	1976–77
Aguilera, Rick	1995	Baker, Tracy	1911
Alcantara, Israel	2000–01	Ball, Neal	1912–13
Alexander, Dale	1932–33	Bankhead, Scott	1993–94
Alexander, Manny	2000	Banks, Willie	2001–02
Alicea, Luis	1995	Barbare, Walter	1918
Allenson, Gary	1979–84	Barberich, Frank	1910
Almada, Mal	1933–37	Bark, Brian	1995
Almonte, Hector	2003	Barkley, Brian	1998
Altrock, Nick	1902–03	Barrett, Bob	1929
Alvarado, Luis	1968–70	Barrett, Frank	1944–45
Alvarez, Abe	2004–05	Barrett, Jimmy	1907–08
Anderson, Larry	1990	Barrett, Marty	1982–90
Anderson, Brady	1988	Barrett, Tommy	1992
Anderson, Fred	1909, 1913	Barry, Ed	1905–07
Anderson, Jimmy	2004	Barry, Jack	1915–17, 1919
Andres, Ernie	1946	Batts, Matt	1947–51
Andrew, Kim	1975	Baumann, Frank	1955–59
Andrews, Ivy	1932–33	Baylor, Don	1986–87
Andrews, Mike	1966–70	Bayne, Bill	1929–30
Andrews, Shane	2002	Beck, Rod	1999–2001
Aparicio, Luis	1971–73	Bedient, Hugh	1912–14
Aponte, Luis	1980–83	Belinda, Stan	1995–96
Arellanes, Frank	1908–10	Bell, Gary	1967–68
Armas, Tony	1983–86	Bell, Juan	1995
Armbruster, Charley	1905–07	Bellhorn, Mark	2004–05
Arrojo, Rolando	2000–02	Beltre, Esteban	1995
Arroyo, Bronson	2003–05	Beniquez, Juan	1971–72, 1974–75
Asbjornson, Asby	1928–29	Benjamin, Mike	1997–98
Ashley, Billy	1998	Bennett, Dennis	1965–67
Aspromonte, Ken	1957–58	Bennett, Frank	1927–28
Astacio, Pedro	2004	Benton, Al	1952
Atkins, Jim	1950, 1952	Benzinger, Todd	1987–88
Auker, Elden	1939	Berberet, Lou	1958
Aulds, Doyle	1947	Berg, Moe	1935–39
Avery, Steve	1997–98	Berger, Boze	1939
Avila, Bobby	1959	Berry, Charley	1928–32
Aviles, Ramon	1977	Berry, Sean	2000
Azcue, Joe	1969	Berryhill, Damon	1994

Bevan, Hal	1952	Bowsfield, Ted	1958–60
Beville, Ben	1901	Boyd, Dennis	1982–89
Bichette, Dante	2000–01	Bradford, Chad	2005
Bigelow, Elliott	1929	Bradley, Herb	1927–29
Billingham, Jack	1980	Bradley, Hugh	1910–12
Bird, Doug	1983	Brady, Cliff	1920
Bischoff, John	1925–26	Brady, King	1908
Bishop, Max	1934–35	Bragg, Darren	1996–98
Black, Dave	1923	Brandenburg, Mark	1996–97
Blackwell, Tim	1974–75	Brandon, Darrell	1966–68
Blethen, Clarence	1923	Bratchi, Fred	1926–27
Blosser, Greg	1993–94	Bressoud, Eddie	1962–65
Bluhm, Red	1918	Brett, Ken	1967, 1969–71
Boddicker, Mike	1988–90	Brewer, Tom	1954–61
Boerner, Larry	1932	Brickner, Ralph	1952
Boggs, Wade	1982–92	Brillheart, Jim	1931
Bolin, Bob	1970–73	Brodowski, Dick	1952, 1955
Bolling, Milt	1952–57	Brogna, Rico	2000
Bolton, Tom	1987–92	Brohamer, Jack	1978–80
Boone, Ike	1923–25	Brown, Adrian	2000
Boone, Ray	1960	Brown, Hal	1953–55
Borland, Toby	1997	Brown, Jamie	2004
Boudreau, Lou	1951–52	Brown, Kevin	2002
Bowen, Sam	1977–78, 1980	Brown, Lloyd	1933
Bowers, Stew	1935–37	Brown, Mace	1942–43, 1946
Bowman, Joe	1944–45	Brown, Mike	1982–86

Courtesy of Transcendental Graphics/theruckerarchive.com

1918 World Series Champion Red Sox

Brumley, Mike	1991–92	Cepeda, Orlando	1973–74
Brunansky, Tom	1990–92, 1994	Cerone, Rick	1988–89
Bucher, Jim	1944–45	Chadbourne, Chet	1906–07
Buckner, Bill	1984–87, 1990	Chakales, Bob	1957
Buddin, Don	1956, 1958–61	Chamberlain, Wes	1994–95
Buford, Damon	1998–99	Chaney, Esty	1913
Bullinger, Kirk	1999	Chaplin, Ed	1920–22
Burchell, Fred	1907–09	Chapman, Ben	1937–38
Burda, Bob	1972	Charton, Pete	1964
Burgmeier, Tom	1978–82	Chase, Ken	1942–43
Burkett, Jesse	1905	Chech, Charley	1909
Burkett, John	2002–03	Checo, Robinson	1997–98
Burkhart, Morgan	2000–01	Chen, Bruce	2003
Burks, Ellis	1987–92, 2004	Chesbro, Jack	1909
Burleson, Rick	1974–80	Chittum, Nels	1959–60
Burns, George	1922–23	Cho, Jin Ho	1998–99
Burton, Jim	1975, 1977	Christopher, Joe	1966
Busby, Jim	1959–60	Christopher, Lloyd	1945
Bush, Joe	1918–21	Cicero, Joe	1929–30
Bushelman, Jack	1911–12	Cicotte, Ed	1908–12
Bushey, Frank	1927, 1930	Cisco, Galen	1961–62, 1967
Butland, Bill	1940–42, 1946–47	Cissell, Bill	1934
Byerly, Bill	1958	Clark, Danny	1924
Byrd, Jim	1998	Clark, Jack	1991–92
		Clark, Otey	1945
C		Clark, Phil	1996
Cabrera, Orlando	2004	Clark, Tony	2002
Cady, Hick	1912–17	Clear, Mark	1981–85
Caldwell, Earl	1948	Clemens, Roger	1984–96
Caldwell, Ray	1919	Clement, Matt	2005
Calderon, Ivan	1993	Clemons, Lance	1974
Camilli, Dolf	1945	Cleveland, Reggie	1974–78
Campbell, Bill	1977–81	Clevenger, Tex	1954
Campbell, Paul	1941–42, 1946	Clinton, Lu	1960–64
Canseco, Jose	1995–96	Clowers, Bill	1926
Carbo, Bernie	1974–78	Cochran, George	1918
Carey, Tom	1939–42, 1946	Cole, Jr., Alex	1996
Carlisle, Walter	1908	Coleman, Dave	1977
Carlstrom, Swede	1911	Coleman, Michael	1997, 1999
Carlyle, Cleo	1927	Collier, Lou	2003
Carlyle, Roy	1925–26	Collins, Jimmy	1901–07
Carrasco, Hector	2000	Collins, Ray	1909–15
Carrigan, Bill	1906, 1908–16	Collins, Rip	1922
Carroll, Ed	1929	Collins, Shano	1921–25
Casale, Jerry	1958–60	Combs, Merrill	1947, 1949–50
Cascarella, Joe	1935–36	Comstock, Ralph	1915
Cassidy, Scott	2005	Cone, David	2001
Castillo, Carlos	2001	Congalton, Bunk	1907
Castillo, Frank	2001–02, 2004	Conigliaro, Billy	1969–71
Cater, Danny	1972–74	Conigliaro, Tony	1964–67, 1969–70, 1975
Cecil, Rex	1944–45	Conley, Gene	1961–63

Connolly, Sr., Ed	1929–32	Deininger, Pep	1902
Connolly, Jr., Ed	1964	Delcarmen, Manny	2005
Connolly, Joe	1924	Delgado, Alex	1996
Conroy, Bill	1942–44	Delock, Ike	1952–53, 1955–63
Consolo, Billy	1953–59	Demeter, Don	1966–67
Cooke, Dusty	1933–36	Denman, Brian	1982
Cooney, Jimmy	1917	Dente, Sam	1947
Cooper, Cecil	1971–76	Derrick, Mike	1970
Cooper, Guy	1914–15	Desautels, Gene	1937–40
Cooper, Scott	1990–94	Deutsch, Mel	1946
Cora, Alex	2005	Devine, Mickey	1920
Cordero, Wil	1996–97	Deviney, Hal	1920
Cormier, Rheal	1995, 1999–2000	De Vormer, Al	1923
Correll, Vic	1972	Diaz, Bo	1977
Corsi, Jim	1997–99	Diaz, Juan	2002
Coughtry, Marlan	1960	Dickey, George	1935–36
Coumbe, Fritz	1914	Dickman, Emerson	1936, 1938–41
Cox, Ted	1977	Didier, Bob	1974
Cramer, Doc	1936–40	Dillard, Steve	1975–77
Cravath, Gavvy	1908	DiMaggio, Dom	1940–42, 1946–53
Crawford, Paxton	2001–01	DiNardo, Lenny	2004–05
Crawford, Steve	1980–82, 1982–87	Dinneen, Bill	1902–07
Creeden, Pat	1931	DiPietro, Bob	1951
Cremins, Bob	1927	Dobens, Ray	1929
Crespo, Cesar	2004	Dobson, Joe	1941–43, 1946–50, 1954
Criger, Lou	1901–08	Dodge, Sam	1921–22
Cronin, Joe	1935–45	Doerr, Bobby	1937–44, 1946–51
Crouch, Zach	1988	Doherty, John	1996
Croushore, Rick	2000	Dominique, Andy	2004
Cruz, Jr., Jose	2005	Donahue, John	1923
Culberson, Leon	1943–47	Donahue, Pat	1908–10
Culp, Ray	1968–73	Donnels, Chris	1995
Cummings, Midre	1998, 2000	Donohue, Pete	1932
Cuppy, Nig	1901	Dopson, John	1989–93
Curry, Steve	1988	Doran, Tom	1904–06
Curtis, John	1970–73	Dorish, Harry	1947–49, 1956
Cuyler, Milt	1996	Dorsey, Jim	1984–85
		Dougherty, Patsy	1902–04

D

		Dowd, Tommy	1901
Dahlgren, Babe	1935–36	Doyle, Danny	1943
Daley, Pete	1955–59	Doyle, Denny	1975–77
Dallesandro, Dom	1937	Dreiseward, Clem	1944–46
Damon, Johnny	2002–05	Dropo, Walt	1949–52
Danzig, Babe	1909	Dubuc, Jean	1918
Darwin, Bobby	1976–77	Duffy, Frank	1978–79
Darwin, Danny	1991–94	Dugan, Joe	1922
Daubach, Brian	1999–2002, 2004	Duliba, Bob	1965
Daughters, Bob	1937	Dumont, George	1919
Dawson, Andre	1993–94	Durham, Ed	1929–32
Deal, Cot	1947–48	Durst, Cedric	1930
Deer, Rob	1993	Dwyer, Jim	1979–80

E

Earley, Arnold	1960–65
Easler, Mike	1984–85
Eckersley, Dennis	1978–84, 1996
Eggert, Elmer	1927
Ehmke, Howard	1922–26
Eibel, Hack	1920
Ellsworth, Dick	1968–69
Ellsworth, Steve	1988
Embree, Alan	2002–05
Engle, Clyde	1910–14
Erdos, Todd	2001
Esasky, Nick	1989
Eshelman, Vaughn	1995–97
Evans, Al	1951
Evans, Bill	1951
Evans, Dwight	1972–90
Everett, Carl	2000–01
Evers, Hoot	1952–54
Ezzell, Homer	1924–25

F

Fanzone, Carmen	1970
Farr, Steve	1994
Farrell, Doc	1935
Farrell, Duke	1903–05
Fassero, Jeff	2000
Ferguson, Alex	1922–25
Ferrell, Rick	1933–37
Ferrell, Wes	1934–37
Ferris, Hobe	1901–07
Ferriss, Boo	1945–50
Fewster, Chick	1922–23
Finch, Joel	1979
Fine, Tom	1947
Finney, Lou	1939–42, 1944–45
Finnvold, Gar	1994
Fiore, Mike	1970–71
Fischer, Hank	1965–67
Fisk, Carlton	1969, 1971–80
Fitzgerald, Howie	1926
Flagstead, Ira	1923–29
Flaherty, John	1992–93
Flair, Al	1941
Fleming, Bill	1940–41
Fletcher, Scott	1993–94
Florie, Bryce	1999–2001
Flowers, Ben	1951, 1953
Floyd, Cliff	2002
Fonville, Chad	1999

Foreman, Frank	1901
Foreman, Happy	1926
Fornieles, Mike	1957–63
Fortune, Gary	1920
Fossas, Tony	1991–94
Fossum, Casey	2001–03
Foster, Eddie	1920–22
Foster, Rube	1913–17
Fothergill, Fats	1933
Foukle, Keith	2004–05
Fowler, Boob	1926
Fox, Chad	2003
Fox, Pete	1941–45
Foxx, Jimmie	1936–42
Foy, Joe	1966–68
Francis, Ray	1925
Freeman, Buck	1901–07
Freeman, Hersh	1952–53, 1955
Freeman, John	1927
French, Charley	1909–10
Friberg, Barney	1933
Friend, Owen	1955
Frohwirth, Todd	1994
Frye, Jeff	1996–97, 1999–2000
Fuhr, Oscar	1924–25
Fuller, Frank	1923
Fullerton, Curt	1921–25, 1933

Jimmie Foxx

G

Gaetti, Gary	2000
Gaffke, Fabian	1936–39
Gagliano, Phil	1971–72
Gainer, Del	1914–17, 1919
Gale, Rich	1984
Galehouse, Denny	1939–40, 1947–49
Gallagher, Bob	1972
Gallagher, Ed	1932
Galvin, Jim	1930
Garbark, Bob	1945
Garces, Rich	1996–2002
Garciaparra, Nomar	1996–2004
Gardiner, Mike	1991–92
Gardner, Billy	1962–63
Gardner, Larry	1908–17
Gardner, Wes	1986–90
Garman, Mike	1969, 1971–72
Garrison, Cliff	1928
Garrison, Ford	1942–43
Gaston, Alex	1926, 1929
Gaston, Milt	1929–31
Gedman, Rich	1980–90
Geiger, Gary	1959–65
Gelbert, Charley	1940
Gessler, Doc	1908–09
Geygan, Chappie	1924–26
Giambi, Jeremy	2003
Giannani, Joe	1911
Gibson, Norwood	1903–06
Gibson, Russ	1967–69
Gilbert, Andy	1942, 1946
Gile, Don	1959–62
Gilhooley, Frank	1919
Gilkey, Bernard	2000
Gillespie, Bob	1950
Gillis, Grant	1929
Ginsberg, Joe	1961
Glaze, Ralph	1906–08
Gleason, Harry	1901–03
Glenn, Joe	1940
Godwin, John	1905–06
Goggin, Chuck	1974
Gomes, Wayne	2002
Gonzales, Eusebio	1918
Gonzales, Joe	1937
Gonzalez, Jeremi	2005
Gooch, Johnny	1933
Goodman, Billy	1947–57
Gordon, Tom	1996–99
Gosger, Jim	1963, 1965–66

Graffanino, Tony	2005
Graham, Charley	1906
Graham, Lee	1983
Graham, Skinny	1934–35
Gray, Dave	1964
Gray, Jeff	1990–91
Grebeck, Craig	2001
Green, Lenny	1965–66
Green, Pumpsie	1959–62
Greenwell, Mike	1985–96
Gregg, Vean	1914–16
Griffin, Doug	1971–77
Griffin, Marty	1928
Grillo, Guido	1966
Grimes, Ray	1920
Grimshaw, Moose	1905–07
Grissom, Marv	1953
Gross, Kip	1999
Gross, Turkey	1925
Grove, Lefty	1934–41

Courtesy of Transcendental Graphics/theruckerarchive.com

Lefty Grove

Grundt, Ken	1996–97
Gubanich, Creighton	1999
Guerra, Mike	1951
Guerrero, Mario	1973–74
Guindon, Bob	1964
Gumpert, Randy	1952
Gunderson, Eric	1995–96
Gunning, Hy	1911
Guthrie, Mark	1999
Gutierrez, Jackie	1983–85
Gutierrez, Ricky	2004
Gutteridge, Don	1946–47

H

Hageman, Casey	1911–12
Halama, John	2005
Hale, Odell	1941
Haley, Ray	1915–16
Hall, Sea Lion	1909–13
Hammond, Chris	1997
Hancock, Garry	1978, 1980–82
Hancock, Josh	2002
Haney, Chris	2002
Hansen, Craig	2005
Hanson, Erik	1995
Hardy, Carroll	1960–62
Harikkala, Tim	1999
Harper, Harry	1920
Harper, Tommy	1972–74
Harrell, Billy	1961
Harrelson, Ken	1967–69
Harris, Bill	1938
Harris, Greg	1989–94
Harris, Joe	1905–07
Harris, Joe	1922–25
Harris, Mickey	1940–41, 1946–49
Harris, Reggie	1996
Harriss, Slim	1926–28
Harshman, Jack	1959
Hartenstein, Chuck	1970
Hartley, Grover	1927
Hartley, Mike	1995
Hartman, Charley	1908
Harville, Chad	2005
Haselman, Bill	1995–97, 2003
Hash, Herb	1940–41
Hassler, Andy	1978–79
Hatcher, Billy	1992–94
Hatfield, Fred	1950–52
Hatteberg, Scott	1995–2001
Hatton, Grady	1954–56

Hausmann, Clem	1944–45
Hayden, John	1906
Hayes, Frankie	1947
Hearn, Ed	1910
Heep, Danny	1989–90
Heffner, Bob	1963–65
Heflin, Randy	1945–46
Heimach, Fred	1926
Heise, Bob	1975–76
Helms, Tommy	1977
Hemphill, Charley	1901
Henderson, Dave	1986–87
Henderson, Rickey	2002
Hendryx, Tim	1920–21
Henriksen, Olaf	1911–17
Henry, Bill	1952–55
Henry, Butch	1997–98
Henry, Jim	1936–37
Hermanson, Dustin	2002
Hernandez, Ramon	1977
Herrera, Mike	1925–26
Herrin, Tom	1954
Hesketh, Joe	1990–94
Hetzel, Eric	1989–90
Heving, Joe	1938–40
Heving, Johnnie	1924–25, 1928–30
Hickman, Piano Legs	1902
Higgins, Pinky	1937–38, 1946
Hillenbrand, Shea	2001–03
Hiller, Hob	1920–21
Hillman, Dave	1960–61
Hinkle, Gordie	1934
Hinrichs, Paul	1951
Hinson, Paul	1928
Hisner, Harley	1951
Hitchcock, Billy	1948–49
Hoblitzel, Dick	1914–18
Hobson, Butch	1975–80
Hockette, George	1934–35
Hodapp, Johnny	1933
Hoderlein, Mel	1951
Hoeft, Billy	1959
Hoey, John	1906–08
Hoffman, Glenn	1980–87
Hofmann, Fred	1927–28
Holcombe, Ken	1953
Hollins, Dave	1995
Holm, Billy	1945
Hooper, Harry	1909–20
Horn, Sam	1987–89
Horton, Tony	1964–67

Hosey, Dwayne	1995–96
House, Tom	1976–77
House, Wayne	1991
Howard, Chris	1994
Howard, Elston	1967–68
Howard, Paul	1909
Howe, Les	1923–24
Howry, Bobby	2002–03
Hoy, Peter	1992
Hoyt, Waite	1919–20
Hudson, Joe	1995–97
Hudson, Sid	1952–54
Hughes, Long Tom	1902–03
Hughes, Terry	1974
Hughson, Tex	1941–44, 1946–49
Humphrey, Bill	1938
Hunt, Ben	1910
Hunter, Buddy	1971, 1973, 1975
Hunter, Herb	1920
Hurd, Tom	1954–56
Hurst, Bruce	1980–88
Huskey, Butch	1999
Husting, Bert	2002
Hyzdu, Adam	2004–05

I

Irvine, Daryl	1990–92

J

Jablonowski, Pete	1932
Jackson, Damian	2003
Jackson, Ron	1960
Jacobson, Baby Doll	1926–27
Jacobson, Benny	1907
Jamerson, Charley	1924
James, Bill	1919
James, Chris	1995
Janvrin, Hal	1911, 1913–17
Jarvis, Ray	1969–70
Jefferson, Reggie	1995–99
Jenkins, Ferguson	1976–77
Jenkins, Tom	1925–26
Jensen, Jackie	1954–59, 1961
Jensen, Marcus	2001
Johns, Keith	1998
Johnson, Bob	1944–45
Johnson, Deron	1974–76
Johnson, Earl	1940–41, 1946–50
Johnson, Hank	1933–35
Johnson, John Henry	1983–84
Johnson, Rankin	1914

Johnson, Roy	1932–35
Johnson, Vic	1944–45
Johnston, Joel	1995
Jolley, Smead	1932–33
Jones, Bobby	2004
Jones, Charley	1901
Jones, Dalton	1964–69
Jones, Jake	1947–48
Jones, Rick	1976
Jones, Sad Sam	1916–21
Jones, Todd	2003
Joost, Eddie	1955
Josephson, Duane	1971–72
Judd, Oscar	1941–45
Judge, Joe	1933–34
Jurak, Ed	1982–85

K

Kallio, Randy	1925
Kapler, Gabe	2003–05
Karger, Ed	1909–11
Karl, Andy	1941
Karow, Marty	1927
Karr, Benn	1920–22
Kasko, Eddie	1966
Kell, George	1952–54
Kellett, Red	1934
Kellum, Win	1901
Kelly, Ed	1914
Keltner, Ken	1950
Kemmerer, Russ	1954–55, 1957
Kendall, Fred	1978
Kennedy, Bill	1953
Kennedy, John	1970–73
Keough, Marty	1956–60
Kiecker, Dana	1990–91
Kiefer, Joe	1925–26
Kiely, Leo	1951, 1954–56, 1958–59
Killilay, Jack	1911
Kim, Byung–Hyun	2003–04
Kim, Sun–Woo	2001–02
Kinder, Ellis	1948–55
Kinney, Walt	1918
Kison, Bruce	1985
Klaus, Billy	1955–58
Kleinow, Red	1910–11
Kline, Bob	1930–33
Kline, Ron	1969
Klinger, Bob	1946–47
Knackert, Brent	1996
Knight, John	1907

Kolstad, Hal	1962–63
Koonce, Cal	1970–71
Kosco, Andy	1972
Kramer, Jack	1948–49
Krausse, Lew	1972
Krueger, Rick	1975–77
Kroh, Rube	1906–07
Kroner, John	1935–36
Krug, Marty	1912
Kutcher, Randy	1988–90
LaChance, Candy	1902–05
Lacy, Kerry	1996–97
LaForest, Ty	1945
LaFrancois, Roger	1982

L

Lhoud, Joe	1968–71
Lake, Eddie	1943–45
Lamabe, Jack	1963–65
Lamar, Bill	1919
Lamp, Dennis	1988–91
Lancellotti, Rick	1990
Landis, Bill	1967–69
Landis, Jim	1967
Langford, Sam	1926
Lansford, Carney	1981–82
Lansing, Mike	2000–01
LaPorte, Frank	1908
LaRose, John	1978
Lary, Lyn	1934
Lazor, Johnny	1943–46
Lee, Bill	1969–78
Lee, Dud	1924–26
Lee, Sang–Hoon	2000
LeFebvre, Lefty	1938–39
Legett, Lou	1933–35
Leheny, Regis	1932
Lehner, Paul	1952
Leibold, Nemo	1921–23
Leister, John	1987, 1990
Lemke, Mark	1998
Lenhardt, Don	1952, 1954
Leonard, Dutch	1913–18
Lepcio, Ted	1952–59
Lerchen, Don	1910
LeRoy, Louis	1910
Leskanic, Curtis	2004
Lewis, Darren	1998–2001
Lewis, Duffy	1910–17
Lewis, John	1911
Lewis, Ted	1901

Leyritz, Jim	1998
Lickert, John	1981
Liliquist, Derek	1998
Lipon, Johnny	1952–53
Lisenbee, Hod	1929–32
Littlefield, Dick	1950
Litton, Greg	1994
Lock, Don	1969
Lockwood, Skip	1980
Loepp, George	1928
Lofton, James	2001
Lollar, Tim	1985–86
Lomansey, Steve	1999
Lonborg, Jim	1965–71
Lonergan, Walt	1911
Looney, Brian	1995
Lord, Harry	1907–10
Lowe, Derek	1997–2004
Lucas, Johnny	1931–32
Lucey, Joe	1925
Lucier, Lou	1943–44
Lundgren, Del	1926–27
Lupien, Tony	1940, 1942–43
Lyle, Sparky	1967–71
Lynch, Walt	1922
Lynn, Fred	1974–79
Lyon, Brandon	2003
Lyons, Steve	1985–86, 1991–93

M

Macfarlane, Mike	1995
MacFayden, Danny	1926–32
Machado, Alejandro	2005
Mack, Shane	1997
MacLeod, Bill	1962
MacWhorter, Kevin	1980
Madden, Tom	1909–11
Maddux, Mike	1995–96
Magrini, Pete	1966
Mahay, Ron	1995, 1997–98
Mahomes, Pat	1996–97
Mahoney, Chris	1910
Mahoney, Jim	1959
Malaska, Mark	2004
Malave, Jose	1996–97
Mallett, Jerry	1959
Maloy, Paul	1913
Malzone, Frank	1955–65
Mantei, Mike	2005
Mantilla, Felix	1963–65
Manto, Jeff	1996

Manush, Heinie	1936	McNair, Eric	1936–38
Manzanillo, Josias	1991	McNally, Mike	1915–17, 1919–20
Marchildon, Phil	1950	McNaughton, Gordon	1932
Marcum, Johnny	1936–38	McNeely, Jeff	1993
Marichal, Juan	1974	McNeil, Norm	1919
Marquardt, Ollie	1931	McWilliams, Bill	1931
Marshall, Bill	1931	Mejias, Roman	1963–64
Marshall, Jim	1990–91	Mele, Sam	1947–49, 1954–55
Martin, Babe	1948–49	Melendez, Jose	1993–94
Martinez, Anastacio	2004	Melillo, Oscar	1935–37
Martinez, Pedro	1998–2004	Melvin, Bob	1993
Martinez, Ramon	1999–2000	Mendoza, Ramiro	2003–04
Martinez, Sandy	2004	Menosky, Mike	1920–23
Marzano, John	1987–92	Meola, Mike	1933, 1936
Masterson, Walt	1949–52	Merced, Orlando	1998
Matchick, Tommy	1970	Mercker, Kent	1999
Mathews, Bill	1909	Merchant, Andy	1975–76
Mauch, Gene	1956–57	Meredith, Cla	2005
Maxwell, Charley	1950–52, 1954	Merena, Spike	1934
Mayer, Wally	1917–18	Merloni, Lou	1998–2003
Maynard, Chick	1922	Merson, Jack	1953
Mays, Carl	1915–19	Metkovich, Catfish	1943–46
McAuliffe, Dick	1974–75	Meyer, Russ	1957
McBride, Tom	1943–47	Michaels, John	1932
McCall, Windy	1948–49	Midkiff, Dick	1938
McCann, Emmett	1926	Mientkiewicz, Doug	2004
McCarthy, Tom	1985	Miles, Dee	1943
McCarty, David	2003–05	Millar, Kevin	2003–05
McCarver, Tim	1974–75	Miller, Bing	1935–36
McConnell, Amby	1908–10	Miller, Elmer	1922
McDermott, Mickey	1948–53	Miller, Hack	1918
McDill, Allen	2001	Miller, Otto	1930–32
McDonald, Jim	1950	Miller, Rick	1971–77, 1981–85
McFarland, Ed	1908	Miller, Wade	2005
McGah, Ed	1946–47	Mills, Buster	1937
McGee, Willie	1995	Mills, Dick	1970
McGlothlen, Lynn	1972–73	Minarcin, Rudy	1956–57
McGovern, Art	1905	Minchey, Nate	1993–94, 1996
McGraw, Bob	1919	Mirabelli, Doug	2001–05
McGuire, Deacon	1907–08	Mitchell, Charlie	1984–85
McHale, Jim	1908	Mitchell, Fred	1901–02
McHale, Marty	1910–11, 1916	Mitchell, Johnny	1922–23
McInnis, Stuffy	1918–21	Mitchell, Keith	1998
McKain, Archie	1937–38	Mitchell, Kevin	1996
McKeel, Walt	1996–97	Moford, Herb	1959
McLaughlin, Jud	1931–33	Molyneaux, Vince	1918
McLean, Larry	1901	Monbouquette, Bill	1958–65
McMahon, Doc	1908	Moncewicz, Freddie	1928
McMahon, Don	1066–67	Montgomery, Bob	1970–79
McManus, Marty	1931–33	Moore, Bill	1926–27
McMillan, Norm	1923	Moore, Wilcy	1931–32

Morehead, Dave	1963–68	Newson, Bobo	1937
Moret, Roger	1970–75	Newsome, Dick	1940–42
Morgan, Cy	1907–09	Newsome, Skeeter	1941–45
Morgan, Eddie	1934	Niarhos, Gus	1952–53
Morgan, Red	1906	Nichols, Chet	1960–63
Morris, Ed	1928–31	Nichols, Reid	1980–85
Morrissey, Deacon	1901	Niemiec, Al	1934
Morton, Guy	1954	Niles, Harry	1908–10
Morton, Kevin	1991	Nipper, Al	1983–87
Moseley, Earl	1913	Nippert, Merlin	1962
Moser, Walter	1911	Nixon, Otis	1994
Moses, Jerry	1965, 1968–70	Nixon, Russ	1960–65, 1968
Moses, Wally	1946–48	Nixon, Trot	1996, 1998–2005
Moskiman, Doc	1910	Nixon, Willard	1950–58
Moss, Les	1951	Nomo, Hideo	2001
Moyer, Jamie	1996	Nonnenkamp, Leo	1938–40
Mueller, Bill	2003–05	Nourse, Chet	1909
Mueller, Gordy	1950	Nunamaker, Les	1911–14
Muffett, Billy	1960–62	Nunnally, Jon	1999
Mulleavy, Greg	1933		
Muller, Freddie	1933–34	**O**	
Mulligan, Joe	1934	Oberlin, Frank	1906–07
Mulroney, Frank	1930	O'Berry, Mike	1979
Mundy, Bull	1913	O'Brian, Buck	1911–13
Murphy, Johnny	1947	O'Brien, Jack	1903
Murphy, Rob	1989–90	O'Brien, Syd	1969
Murphy, Tom	1976–77	O'Brien, Tom	1949–50
Murphy, Walter	1931	O'Doul, Lefty	1923
Murray, George	1923–24	Offerman, Jose	1999–2002
Murray, Matt	1995	Oglivie, Ben	1971–73
Muser, Tony	1969	Ohka, Tomokazu	1999–2001
Musser, Paul	1919	Ojeda, Bobby	1980–85
Mustaikis, Alex	1940	Okrie, Len	1952
Myer, Buddy	1927–28	O'Leary, Troy	1995–2001
Myers, Elmer	1920–22	Olerud, John	2005
Myers, Hap	1910–11	Oliver, Darren	2002
Myers, Mike	2004–05	Oliver, Gene	1968
		Oliver, Joe	2001
N		Oliver, Tom	1930–33
Nabholz, Chris	1994	Olmstead, Hank	1905
Naehring, Tim	1990–97	Olson, Karl	1951, 1953–55
Nagle, Judge	1911	Olson, Marv	1931–33
Nagy, Mike	1969–72	Olson, Ted	1936–38
Narleski, Bill	1929–30	O'Neill, Bill	1904
Neal, Blaine	2005	O'Neill, Emmett	1943–45
Neitzke, Ernie	1921	O'Neill, Steve	1924
Nelson, Bryant	2002	Ontiveros, Steve	2000
Nelson, Joe	2004	Orme, George	1920
Neubauer, Hal	1925	O'Rourke, Frank	1922
Newhauser, Don	1972–74	Ortiz, David	2003–05
Newman, Jeff	1983–84	Ortiz, Luis	1993–94

Osinski, Dan	1966–67	Patterson, Hank	1932
Ostdiek, Harry	1908	Pattin, Marty	1972–73
Ostermueller, Fritz	1934–40	Pavletich, Don	1970–71
Ostrowski, John	1948	Paxton, Mike	1977
Owen, Marv	1940	Payton, Jay	2005
Owen, Mickey	1954	Peacock, Johnny	1937–44
Owen, Spike	1986–88	Pellagrini, Eddie	1946–47
Owens, Frank	1905	Pemberton, Rudy	1996–97
		Pena, Alejandro	1995
P		Pena, Jesus	2000
Pagliaroni, Jim	1955, 1960–62	Pena, Juan	1999
Palm, Mike	1948	Pena, Tony	1990–93
Pankovits, Jim	1990	Pennington, Brad	1996
Papai, Al	1950	Pennock, Herb	1915–17, 1919–22, 1934
Pape, Larry	1909, 1911–12	Perez, Tony	1980–82
Papelbon, Jonathan	2005	Perisho, Matt	2005
Papi, Stan	1979–80	Perrin, Jack	1921
Parent, Freddy	1901–07	Person, Robert	2003
Parnell, Mel	1947–56	Petagine, Roberto	2005
Parrish, Larry	1988	Pertica, Bill	1918
Partee, Roy	1943–44, 1946–47	Pesky, Johnny	1942, 1946–52
Partenheimer, Stan	1944	Peters, Gary	1970–72
Paschal, Ben	1920	Peterson, Bob	1906–07
Patten, Casey	1908	Petrocelli, Rico	1963, 1965–76

Courtesy of Transcendental Graphics/theruckerarchive.com

Bobby Doerr and Johnny Pesky
turn a double play

Petry, Dan	1991	Ramirez, Manny	2001–05
Philley, Dave	1962	Rapp, Pat	1999
Phillips, Ed	1970	Reardon, Jeff	1990–92
Pichardo, Hipolito	2000–01	Reder, Johnny	1932
Pickering, Calvin	2001	Reed, Jerry	1990
Picinich, Val	1923–25	Reed, Jody	1987–92
Pickering, Urbane	1931–32	Reese, Pokey	2004
Pierce, Jeff	1995	Regan, Bill	1926–30
Piercy, Bill	1922–24	Rehg, Wally	1913–15
Piersall, Jimmy	1950, 1952–58	Reichle, Dick	1922–23
Pipgras, George	1933–35	Remlinger, Mike	2005
Pirkl, Greg	1996	Remmerswaal, Win	1979–80
Pittenger, Pinky	1921–23	Remy, Jerry	1978–84
Pizarro, Juan	1968–69	Renko, Steve	1979–80
Plantier, Phil	1990–92	Renna, Bill	1958–59
Plews, Herb	1959	Renteria, Edgar	2005
Plympton, Jeff	1991	Repulski, Rip	1960–61
Poindexter, Jennings	1936	Reyes, Carlos	1998
Pole, Dick	1973–76	Reynolds, Carl	1934–35
Polly, Nick	1945	Rhodes, Gordon	1932–35
Pond, Ralph	1910	Rhodes, Tuffy	1995
Poquette, Tom	1979, 1981	Rhyne, Hal	1929–32
Porter, Dick	1934	Rice, Jim	1974–89
Porterfield, Bob	1956–58	Rich, Woody	1939–41
Portugal, Mark	1999	Richardson, Jeff	1993
Potter, Nelson	1941	Richter, Al	1951, 1953
Poulsen, Ken	1967	Riggert, Joe	1911
Pozo, Arquimedez	1996–97	Rigney, Topper	1926–27
Pratt, Del	1921–22	Riles, Ernest	1993
Pratt, Larry	1934	Ripley, Allen	1978–79
Prentiss, George	1901–02	Ripley, Walt	1935
Price, Joe	1989	Rising, Pop	1905
Pride, Curtis	1997, 2000	Ritchie, Jay	1964–65
Prothro, Doc	1925	Rivera, Luis	1989–93
Pruett, Tex	1907–08	Roberts, Dave	2004
Pulsipher, Bill	2001	Robidoux, Billy Jo	1990
Purtell, Billy	1910–11	Robinson, Aaron	1951
Pytlak, Frankie	1941, 1945–46	Robinson, Floyd	1968
		Robinson, Jack	1949
Q		Rochford, Mike	1988–90
Quantrill, Paul	1992–94	Rodgers, Bill	1915
Quinn, Frank	1949–50	Rodriguez, Carlos	1994–95
Quinn, Jack	1922–25	Rodriguez, Frankie	1995
Quinones, Ray	1986	Rodriguez, Steve	1995
Quintana, Carlos	1988–91, 1993	Rodriguez, Tony	1996
		Rogell, Billy	1925, 1927–28
R		Rogers, Lee	1938
Radatz, Dick	1962–66	Roggenburk, Garry	1966, 1968–69
Rader, Dave	1980	Rohr, Billy	1967
Rainey, Chuck	1979–82	Rollings, Red	1927–28
Ramirez, Hanley	2005	Romero, Ed	1986–89

Romero, Mandy	1998
Romine, Kevin	1985–91
Romo, Vicente	1969–70
Rosar, Buddy	1950–51
Rose, Brian	1997–2000
Rosenthal, Si	1925–26
Ross, Buster	1924–26
Roth, Braggo	1919
Rothrock, Jack	1925–32
Rowland, Rich	1994–95
Royer, Stan	1994
Rudi, Joe	1981
Ruel, Muddy	1921–22, 1931
Ruffing, Red	1924–30
Runnels, Pete	1958–62
Rupe, Ryan	2003
Russell, Allen	1919–22
Russell, Jack	1926–32, 1936
Russell, Jeff	1993–94
Russell, Rip	1946–47
Ruth, Babe	1914–19
Ryan, Jack	1909
Ryan, Jack	1929
Ryan, Ken	1992–95
Ryan, Mike	1964–67
Ryan, Mike	1941–46
Rye, Gene	1931

S

Saberhagen, Bret	1997–2001
Sadler, Donnie	1998–2000
Sadowski, Bob	1966
Sadowski, Ed	1960
Sambito, Joe	1986–87
Sanchez, Freddy	2002–03
Sanchez, Rey	2002
Sanders, Ken	1966
Santiago, Jose	1966–70
Santana, Marino	1999
Santos, Angel	2001
Satriano, Tom	1969–70
Sauerbeck, Scott	2003
Sax, Dave	1985–87
Sayles, Bill	1939
Scarborough, Ray	1951–52
Scarritt, Russ	1929–31
Schang, Wally	1918–20
Schanz, Charley	1950
Scherbarth, Bob	1950
Schilling, Chuck	1961–65
Schilling, Curt	2004–05

Courtesy of Transcendental Graphics/theruckerarchive.com

Babe Ruth

Schiraldi, Calvin	1986–87	Skok, Craig	1973
Schlesinger, Rudy	1965	Slattery, Jack	1901
Schlitzer, Biff	1909	Slayton, Steve	1928
Schmees, George	1952	Slocumb, Heathcliff	1996–97
Schmidt, Dave	1981	Small, Charley	1930
Schmidt, Johnny	1956	Smith, Al	1964
Schofield, Dick	1969–70	Smith, Bob	1955
Schourek, Pete	1998, 2000–01	Smith, Brodaway Aleck	1903
Schreckengost, Ossee	1901	Smith, Charley	1909–11
Schroll, Al	1958–59	Smith, Dan	2000
Schwall, Don	1961–62	Smith, Doug	1912
Scott, Everett	1914–21	Smith, Eddie	1947
Scott, George	1966–71, 1977–79	Smith, Elmer	1922
Seanez, Rudy	2003	Smith, Frank	1910–11
Seaver, Tom	1986	Smith, George	1930
Seeds, Bob	1933–34	Smith, George	1966
Segui, Diego	1974–75	Smith, John	1931
Seibel, Phil	2004	Smith, Lee	1988–90
Selbach, Kip	1904–06	Smith, Paddy	1920
Selby, Bill	1996	Smith, Pete	1962–63
Sele, Aaron	1993–97	Smith, Reggie	1966–73
Sellers, Jeff	1985–88	Smith, Riverboat	1958
Settlemire, Merle	1928	Smith, Zane	1995
Shaner, Wally	1926–27	Smithson, Mike	1988–89
Shanks, Howard	1923–24	Snell, Wally	1913
Shannon, Red	1919	Snopek, Chris	1998
Shaw, Al	1907	Snyder, Earl	2004
Shea, John	1928	Solters, Moose	1934–35
Shea, Merv	1933	Sommers, Rudy	1926–27
Sheaffer, Danny	1987	Sothoron, Allen	1921
Shean, Dave	1918–19	Spanswick, Bill	1964
Sheets, Andy	2000	Sparks, Tully	1902
Sheldon, Rollie	1966	Speaker, Tris	1907–15
Shepherd, Keith	1995	Spence, Stan	1940–41, 1948–49
Sheridan, Neill	1948	Spencer, Tubby	1909
Shields, Ben	1930	Spognardi, Andy	1932
Shiell, Jason	2003	Sprague, Jr., Ed	2000
Shofner, Strick	1947	Spring, Jack	1957
Shoppach, Kelly	2005	Sprowl, Bobby	1978
Shore, Ernie	1914–17	Stahl, Chick	1901–06
Short, Bill	1966	Stahl, Jake	1903, 1908–10, 1912–13
Shorten, Chick	1915–17	Stairs, Matt	1995
Shouse, Brian	1999	Stallard, Tracy	1960–62
Shumpert, Terry	1995	Standaert, Jerry	1929
Siebern, Norm	1967–68	Stange, Lee	1966–70
Siebert, Sonny	1969–72	Stanifer, Rob	2000
Simmons, Al	1943	Stanley, Bob	1977–89
Simmons, Pat	1928–29	Stanley, Mike	1996–2000
Sisler, Dave	1956–59	Stansbury, John	1918
Sizemore, Ted	1979–80	Stanton, Mike	1995–96, 2005
Skinner, Camp	1923	Stapleton, Dave	1980–86

Statz, Jigger	1920
Steele, Elmer	1907–09
Steiner, Ben	1945–46
Steiner, Red	1945
Stenhouse, Mike	1986
Stephens, Gene	1952–53, 1955–60
Stephens, Vern	1948–52
Stephenson, Jerry	1963, 1965–68
Stern, Adam	2005
Stewart, Sammy	1986
Stigman, Dick	1966
Stimson, Carl	1923
Stobbs, Chuck	1947–51
Stokes, Al	1925–26
Stone, Dean	1957
Stone, George	1902
Stone, Jeff	1989–90
Stone, Howie	1931–32
Stringer, Lou	1948–50
Strunk, Amos	1918–19
Stuart, Dick	1963–64

Stumpf, George	1931–33
Sturdivant, Tom	1960
Stynes, Chris	2001
Suchecki, Jim	1950
Sullivan, Denny	1907–08
Sullivan, Frank	1953–60
Sullivan, Haywood	1955, 1957, 1959–60
Sullivan, Marc	1982, 1984–87
Sumner, Carl	1928
Suppan, Jeff	1995–97, 2003
Susce, George	1955–58
Swanson, Bill	1914
Sweeney, Bill	1930–31
Swindell, Greg	1998
Swormstedt, Len	1906

T

Tabor, Jim	1938–44
Taitt, Doug	1928–29
Tanana, Frank	1981
Tannehill, Jesse	1904–08

Courtesy of Transcendental Graphics/theruckerarchive.com

Tris Speaker

Tarbert, Arlie	1927–28	Valdez, Julio	1980–83
Tartabull, Jose	1966–68	Valdez, Sergio	1994
Tarver, LaSchelle	1986	Valentin, John	1992–2001
Tasby, Willie	1960	Valle, Dave	1994
Tate, Bernie	1932	Van Camp, Al	1931–32
Tatum, Jim	1996	Vandenburg, Hy	1935
Tatum, Ken	1971–73	Van Dyke, Ben	1912
Tavares, Jesus	1997	VanEgmond, Tim	1994–95
Taylor, Harry	1950–52	Varitek, Jason	1997–2005
Taylor, Scott	1992–93	Vasquez, Ramon	2005
Tebbetts, Birdie	1947–50	Vaughn, Mo	1991–98
Terry, Yank	1940, 1942–45	Veach, Bobby	1924–25
Thielman, Jake	1908	Veale, Bob	1972–74
Thomas, Blaine	1911	Veras, Dario	1998
Thomas, Fred	1918	Veras, Wilton	1999–2000
Thomas, George	1966–71	Vernon, Mickey	1956–57
Thomas, Lee	1964–65	Vick, Sammy	1921
Thomas, Pinch	1912–17	Viola, Frank	1992–94
Thomas, Tommy	1937	Vitt, Oscar	1919–21
Thomson, Bobby	1960	Vollmer, Clyde	1950–53
Thoney, Jack	1908–09, 1911	Volz, Jake	1901
Thormahlen, Hank	1921	Vosmik, Joe	1938–39
Throneberry, Faye	1952, 1955–57		
Tiant, Luis	1971–78	**W**	
Tillman, Bob	1962–67	Wade, Jake	1939
Timlin, Mike	2003–05	Wagner, Charlie	1938–42, 1946
Tinsley, Lee	1994–96	Wagner, Gary	1969–70
Tobin, Jack	1926–27	Wagner, Hal	1944, 1946–47
Tobin, Jackie	1945	Wagner, Heinie	1906–13, 1915–16, 1918
Todt, Phil	1924–30	Wakefield, Tim	1995–2005
Tolar, Kevin	2003	Walberg, Rube	1934–37
Tomberlin, Andy	1994	Walker, Chico	1980–81, 1983–84
Tonneman, Tony	1911	Walker, Tilly	1916–17
Torrez, Mike	1978–82	Walker, Todd	2003
Trautwein, John	1988	Wall, Murray	1957–59
Trimble, Joe	1955	Walsh, Jimmy	1916–17
Trlicek, Ricky	1994, 1997	Walters, Bucky	1933–34
Trout, Dizzy	1952	Walters, Fred	1945
Truesdale, Frank	1918	Walters, Roxy	1919–23
Trujillo, Mike	1985–88	Wambsganss, Bill	1924–25
Tudor, John	1979–83	Wanninger, Pee Wee	1927
Turley, Bob	1963	Warner, John	1902
		Warstler, Rabbit	1930–33
U		Wasdin, John	1997–2000
Umphlett, Tom	1953	Waslewski, Gary	1967–68
Unglaub, Bob	1904–05, 1907–08	Watson, Bob	1979
Urbina, Ugueth	2001–02	Watwood, Johnny	1932–33
		Weaver, Monte	1939
V		Webb, Earl	1930–32
Vache, Tex	1925	Webster, Lenny	1999
Valdez, Carlos	1998	Wabster, Ray	1960

Wedge, Eric	1991–92, 1994	Williams, Denny	1924–25, 1928
Weiland, Bob	1932–34	Williams, Dib	1935
Welch, Frank	1927	Williams, Dick	1963–64
Welch, Herb	1925	Williams, Ken	1928–29
Welch, Johnny	1932–36	Williams, Rip	1911
Wells, David	2005	Williams, Stan	1972
Welzer, Tony	1926–27	Williams, Ted	1939–42, 1946–60
Wenz, Fred	1968–69	Williamson, Scott	2003–04
Werber, Bill	1933–36	Willoughby, Jim	1975–77
Werle, Bill	1953–54	Wills, Ted	1959–62
Wertz, Vic	1959–61	Wilson, Archie	1952
West, David	1998	Wilson, Duane	1958
White, Matt	2003	Wilson, Earl	1959–60, 1962–66
White, Sammy	1951–59	Wilson, Gary	1902
Whiteman, George	1907, 1918	Wilson, Jack	1935–41
Whiten, Mark	1995	Wilson, Jim	1945–46
Whitt, Ernie	1976	Wilson, John	1927–28
Widmar, Al	1947	Wilson, Les	1911
Wight, Bill	1951–53	Wilson, Squanto	1914
Wilber, Del	1952–54	Wiltse, Hal	1926–28
Wilhoit, Joe	1919	Wingfield, Ted	1924–27
Williams, Dana	1989	Winn, George	1919
Williams, Dave	1902	Winningham, Herb	1992

Courtesy of Transcendental Graphics/theruckerarchive.com

Brothers Joe DiMaggio (left) and Dom DiMaggio (right)
Ted Williams (center)

Winsett, Tom	1930–31, 1933
Winter, George	1901–08
Winters, Clarence	1924
Wise, Rick	1974–77
Wittig, Johnny	1949
Wolcott, Bob	1999
Wolfe, Larry	1979–80
Wolter, Harry	1909
Wood, Joe	1944
Wood, Ken	1952
Wood, Smoky Joe	1908–15
Wood, Wilbur	1961–64
Woodard, Steve	2003
Woods, John	1924
Woods, Pinky	1943–45
Woodward, Rob	1985–88
Wooten, Shawn	2005
Workman, Hoge	1924
Worthington, Al	1960
Wright, Jim	1978–79
Wright, Tom	1948–51
Wyatt, John	1966–68
Wyckoff, John	1916–18

Y

Yastrzemski, Carl	1961–83
Yerkes, Steve	1909, 1911–14
York, Rudy	1946–47
Youkilis, Kevin	2004–05
Young, Cy	1901–08
Young, Matt	1991–92
Young, Tim	2000

Z

Zahniser, Paul	1925–26
Zarilla, Al	1949–50, 1952–53
Zauchin, Norm	1951, 1955–57
Zeiser, Matt	1914
Zuber, Bill	1946–47
Zupcic, Bob	1991–94

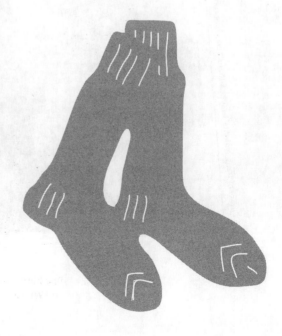

Managers

Baker, Del	1960
Barrow, Ed	1918–21
Barry, Jack	1917
Boudreau, Lou	1952–54
Carrigan, Bill	1913–16, 1927–29
Chance, Frank	1923
Collins, Jimmy	1901–06
Collins, Shano	1931–32
Cronin, Joe	1935–47
Donovan, Patsy	1910–11
Fohl, Lee	1924–26
Francona, Terry	2004–05
Harris, Bucky	1934
Herman, Billy	1964–66
Higgins, Pinky	1955–59, 1960–62
Hobson, Butch	1992–94
Houk, Ralph	1981–84
Huff, George	1907
Johnson, Darrell	1974–76
Jurges, Billy	1959–60
Kasko, Eddie	1970–73
Kennedy, Kevin	1995–96
Kerrigan, Joe	2001
Lake, Fred	1908–09
Little, Grady	2002–03
McCarthy, Joe	1948–50
McGuire, Deacon	1907–08
McManus, Marty	1932–33
McNamara, John	1985–88
Morgan, Joe	1988–91
O'Neill, Steve	1950–51
Pesky, Johnny	1963–64, 1980
Popowski, Eddie	1969, 1973
Runnels, Pete	1966
Stahl, Chick	1906
Stahl, Jake	1912–13
Unglaub, Bob	1907
Wagner, Heinie	1930
Williams, Dick	1967–69
Williams, Jimy	1997–2001
York, Rudy	1959
Young, Cy	1907
Zimmer, Don	1976–80

Coaches

Allenson, Gary	1992–94
Bailey, Buddy	2000
Baker, Del	1945–46, 1953–60
Berardino, Dick	1989–91
Berg, Moe	1939–41
Brown, Mace	1965
Bryant, Don	1974–76
Bumbry, Al	1988–93
Burke, Jimmy	1921–23
Burleson, Rick	1992–93
Burns, Jack	1955–59
Camilli, Doug	1970–73
Carey, Tom	1946–47
Carlucci, Dave	1996
Cloninger, Tony	2002–03
Coleman, Bob	1928
Combs, Earl	1948–52
Cubbage, Mike	2002–03
Cumberland, John	1995, 1999–2001
Cuyler, Kiki	1949
Daly, Tom	1933–46
Doerr, Bobby	1967–69
Dorish, Harry	1963
Down, Rick	2001
Duffy, Hugh	1931, 1939
Easler, Mike	1993–94
Ellis, Sammy	1996
Evans, Dwight	2002
Falk, Bibb	1934
Ferriss, Boo	1955–59
Fischer, Bill	1985–91
Gale, Rich	1992–93
Gardner, Billy	1965–66
Gregson, Goose	2003
Haddix, Harvey	1971
Harper, Tommy	1980–84, 2000–02
Haselman, Bill	2005
Hebner, Richie	1989–91
Herman, Billy	1960–64
Hriniak, Walt	1977–78
Hulswitt, Randy	1931–33
Jackson, Al	1977–79
Jackson, Ron	2003–05
Jauss, Dave	1997–99, 2001
Johnson, Darrell	1968–69
Johnson, Tim	1995–96
Jones, Lynn	2004–05
Kerrigan, Joe	1997–2001
Kim, Wendell	1997–2000
Kipper, Bob	2002

Lachemann, Rene	1985–86		Wallace, Dave	2003–05
Lakeman, Al	1963–64, 1967–69		White, Frank	1994–95
Lamont, Gene	2001		Williams, Dallas	2003
Leifield, Lefty	1924–26		Williams, Stan	1975–76
Lenhardt, Don	1970–71		Woodall, Larry	1942–48
Little, Grady	1997–99		York, Rudy	1959–62
Maglie, Sal	1960–62, 1966–67		Yost, Eddie	1977–84
Malmberg, Harry	1963–64		Zimmer, Don	1974–76, 1992
Mayo, Eddie	1951			
McCallister, Jack	1930			
McKechnie, Bill	1952–53			
McLaren, John	1991			
McNertney, Jerry	1988			
Melillo, Oscar	1952–53			
Miller, Bing	1937			
Miller, Brad	2004–05			
Miller, Buster	1954			
Morgan, Joe	1985–88			
Narron, Jerry	2003			
Nipper, Al	1995–96			
Norman, Nelson	2001			
Okrie, Len	1961–62, 1965–66			
Oliver, Dave	1995–96			
O'Neill, Steve	1950			
Onslow, Dave	1934			
Owen, Mickey	1955–56			
Pennock, Herb	1936–39			
Pesky, Johnny	1975–84			
Podres, Johnny	1980			
Pole, Dick	1998			
Popowski, Eddie	1967–74, 1976			
Rice, Jim	1995–2000			
Roarke, Mike	1994			
Rojas, Euclides	2003–04			
Runnels, Pete	1965–66			
Ryan, John	1923–27			
Schacht, Al	1935–36			
Schreiber, Paul	1947–58			
Schulte, John	1949–50			
Shellenbeck, Frank	1940–44			
Slider, Rac	1987–90			
Stange, Lee	1972–74, 1981–84			
Stanley, Mike	2002			
Starrette, Herm	1995–97			
Susce, George	1950–54			
Sveum, Dave	2004–05			
Thomas, George	1970			
Torchia, Tony	1985			
Treuel, Ralph	2001			
Turley, Bib	1964			
Wagner, Charlie	1970			

2004 World Series trophy

Books of Interest

Each book in the **Baseball Behind the Seams** series focuses on a single position, exploring it with the kind of depth serious fans crave. Through extensive research, including interviews with hundreds of players past and present, the authors have brought together the most original and informative series ever published on the game.

Each book in the series covers
- The physical and mental qualities of the position
- The position's history
- The plays, and how to make them
- Profiles of the position's top all-time players
- The best defenders of the position
- A day in the life of one player, from arriving at the ball park to the final out
- Lists of Gold Glovers, MVPs, and Rookies of the Year
- Fun and quirky facts about the position

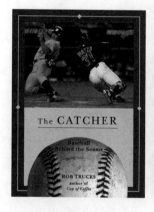

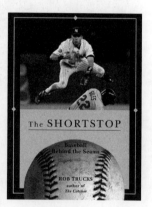

Books of Interest

Red Legs and Black Sox
Edd Roush and the Untold Story of the 1919 World Series

By Susan Dellinger
Paperback $16.95
ISBN: 1-57860-229-7

"This is a book that should have been published a long time ago. The author gives a fresh look at the 1919 World Series through the eyes of the city of Cincinnati and the star of the Reds."
—Bob Feller, Cleveland Indians Pitcher, Member of the Baseball Hall of Fame

"What a terrific saga."
—William A. Cook, Author of *The 1919 World Series: What Really Happened*

"I couldn't put it down! Susan Dellinger has expanded our knowledge of the events of 1919 and what actually went down on the diamond."
—Robert H. Schaefer, 3-Time Winner of the McFarland-SABR Best Baseball Research Award

All self-respecting baseball fans are familiar with the 1919 World Series between the Cincinnati Reds and the Chicago White Sox, in which eight members of the White Sox were banned from baseball for intentionally losing several games in that series. But there is another side to the story, revealed for the first time in *Red Legs and Black Sox*.
The star of the 1919 Reds was center fielder Edd Roush, who was later elected to the Baseball Hall of Fame. Roush's granddaughter, author Susan Dellinger, presents the Cincinnati Reds' perspective on this infamous event through research, historical documents, and most importantly, Roush's own words on the subject. This is a story that is far more complicated than previous movies and books have alluded to, involving fixes on both teams—and corruption right down to the leagues themselves.

Available at local and online booksellers or at www.emmisbooks.com.
Emmis Books, 1700 Madison Road, Cincinnati, Ohio 45206

Books of Interest

Our Red Sox
A Story of Family, Friends, and Fenway

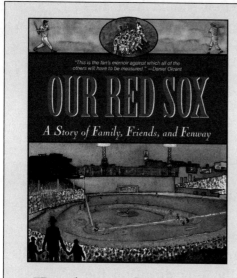

By Robert Sullivan
With a foreword by Peter Gammons
Hardcover $18.95
ISBN: 1-57860-234-3

"How can any Bosox fan resist reliving the heartaches Sullivan details in such glorious despair?"
> —Frank Deford, *Sports Illustrated* Senior Contributing Writer and NPR commentator

"Reading Robert Sullivan is like sitting by the fire with a lively and scholarly seanchie, as satisfying as a pint of Guinness or a Connemara sunset."
> —Frank McCourt, author of *Angela's Ashes*

"This is not just another memoir about a fan's relationship to the game he loves and the team he loves—this is the fan's memoir against which all others will have to be measured."
> —Daniel Okrent, author of *Nine Innings* and *Great Fortune: The Epic of Rockefeller Center*

Robert Sullivan cannot remember a day when he was not a Red Sox fan. It seems he was born a Sox fan; he certainly was raised to be one. From Ted to Yaz, this to-the-death pledge was a rite of passage for anyone growing up in Massachusetts in the 1950s and '60s.

Sullivan has stuck by the Sox through thick and (long periods of) thin, and his reports from Fenway on time.com gained him a wide audience and served as catalyst for *Our Red Sox*.

Sullivan explains, the "our" in the title refers to "me and my family and friends, and the larger 'our,' too: you, them, all of us. It's a universe with the pitcher's mound at Fenway Park as its heart, the sun around which everything revolves, at distances near and far."

The Red Sox World Series victory broke the long-standing "curse of the Bambino" and transcended the sport, the players, even the team. *Sports Illustrated* referred to it as a victory about a people (New Englanders), a loyalty, a family, a nation. *Our Red Sox* is a funny, gentle, and moving memoir from deep inside the strange land called Red Sox Nation.

Available at local and online booksellers or at www.emmisbooks.com.
Emmis Books, 1700 Madison Road, Cincinnati, Ohio 45206